DRAMAS *from the*
AMERICAN THEATRE
1762-1909

THE FIRST VOLUME OF THE

NEW WORLD LITERATURE SERIES

PUBLISHED UNDER THE GENERAL EDITORSHIP OF

EDWIN H. CADY, INDIANA UNIVERSITY

DRAMAS *from the* AMERICAN THEATRE 1762-1909

Edited with Introductory Essays

By RICHARD MOODY

INDIANA UNIVERSITY

THE WORLD PUBLISHING COMPANY

CLEVELAND AND NEW YORK

Published by The World Publishing Company, 2231 West 110th Street, Cleveland, Ohio 44102

Published simultaneously in Canada by Nelson, Foster & Scott Ltd.

FIRST PRINTING 1966

Copyright © 1966 by Richard Moody

Library of Congress Catalog Card Number: 66-13958

Printed in the United States of America

For CAROL

CONTENTS

LIST OF ILLUSTRATIONS

INTRODUCTION

FROM the early days of colonization the pioneers of the new American world found excitement, pleasure, and education in the theatre. "Pleasure the means; the end virtue" read the legend on the proscenium-arch scroll of the first theatre in Providence, Rhode Island. The agonies of the fight for survival in the colonies, in the new republic, and on the expanding frontier were relieved by the make-believe escapades of light hearts and playful tempers. The sobriety and solemnity necessary to achieving their manifest destiny did not preclude an indulgence in a variety of theatricalisms both in the playhouse and in real life. The theatre-in-life play spirit in American society was persistently demonstrated, whether in "husking bees" and "building bees," plain joshing and tall-tale telling, in spectacular and ingenious punishments for witchcraft, in "Yankee trading," in dealing with the savages, in a Boston Tea Party for the British, or in a regular play on the rough boards of an improvised stage.

Americans began early to project themselves onto the public platform and stage, first in simple dialogues and then in standard dramatic pieces. Plays echoed, illustrated, and epitomized American notions about society, politics, and the prevailing virtues and vices in human conduct. All facets of the American scene were explored: the birth and growth of the new republic, the rise of the democratic society, the native goodness and simplicity of the common man, the struggles and glories of the wars, the romantic exploits of the noble red man. Nor were these dramas bare polemics; they were enriched with a lusty and robust theatre life employing all the multifarious stage arts. Few lay claim to literary distinction.

American dramas of the eighteenth and nineteenth centuries were designed for the playhouse and not for the library, although many patrons later purchased playbooks in order to relive the playhouse scenes. These plays demanded stage accouterments – actors and stage settings – and more often than not they required special actors and startling and ingenious stage scenes. To study only the literary pretenders among nineteenth-century American dramas is to miss the vital, exciting, and real story of the American theatre. But at the same time to contend that American dramatic literature of the past century was inferior in its literary qualities to that of England is a misrepresentation of fact. These two misconceptions have frequently been propounded. As dramatic literature the American plays of the period cannot compare with

Elizabethan or Restoration drama or with the best examples of the eighteenth-century British drama, but they do hold their honors, as literature and as stage art, against the best the mother country could offer during the same period.

The American theatregoer loved the theatre. He loved the high-blown, full-flowered sentiments, the glorious patriotic flag-waving, the sympathetic exploration of America's political and social adventures; he loved the theatrical trappings of the stage and the playhouse; the gaudy, glamorous, and often shabby scenery; the shoutings and posturings of the unrestrained romantic actors. Demands, if any, for realistic illusion were supplied by the spectator's own imagination. On the stage he asked only for dialogues, stories, scenes, and actors that were fully and unequivocally theatrical. When he entered the playhouse, he expected and delighted in the grandeur and ecstasy of another world, a theatrical world. He demanded and got new and ingenious experiments with theatrical manners and forms. And at least one form, one of his favorites, the Negro minstrel show, sprang from his own land.

The dramas and playscripts in this volume were chosen to illustrate the theatregoers' story of the American theatre in the eighteenth and nineteenth centuries and to center attention on the distinctly American qualities in the dramas, both in theme and technique. Literary merit may be almost totally absent from many of the selections, but they all have significance in our social and theatrical history. Not all of them belong to the formal playhouse; not all of them were "hit" shows, though many of them were; but each in its way reflects a current fashion, either in manner or in theme, or illustrates a public exploration into some aspect of our social or political history. They range from the college commencement dialogues, the exposition and glorification of our early history, the newsreel-like projections of the American scene, the theatricalized spectacles and burlesques, the stories of the wars, the comments on prohibition, slavery, fashionable society, and finally to the early-twentieth-century forerunners of the modern drama.

The nineteenth-century American theatregoer demanded variety, "well cooked and well served." Present-day snobbish separation and categorizing of the "legitimate" play, the musical, vaudeville, and the revue was unknown in the last century. Mixtures of variety show, burlesque, melodrama, and serious tragedy on the same evening's program and frequently within the same play were willingly and delightedly accepted. These selections illustrate this prevailing theatrical taste.

The introductory essays tell the story *about* the play, leaving the story and meaning *of* the play to unfold undulled and unprejudiced. The pertinent biographical and theatrical details set the scene; they provide the stage environment so necessary to the fullest understanding and appreciation of any drama, and more particularly the non-literary drama.

No single collection of plays can thoroughly tell the whole story of the

American theatre or satisfy the tastes of all readers. I have tried to get a fairly even distribution over the whole period and to illustrate most facets of the American social and theatrical scene. A few "classics," notably *The Contrast*, *Fashion* and *Francesca da Rimini* have previously been anthologized, but the larger share of the items are here available for the first time in a collected edition. Many of them have had no previous twentieth-century printing.

For the happiest understanding of these plays, let the reader release his God-given genius for make-believe and follow his theatrical imagination to the John Street Theatre, to the Park Theatre; let him paint the stage scene for a *Glory of Columbia* or a *Trip to Niagara,* hear and see the commanding presence of an Edwin Forrest or a John Brougham, and mingle with the cheering crowds at a performance of *Shenandoah* or *The Great Divide.* Let the symbols on the page be vitalized with their original color and excitement.

Americans have loved the theatre and found in it a wide range of pleasure and stimulation. The following pieces demonstrate this range of theatrical experience, the colorful story of the American theatre.

DRAMAS *from the*
AMERICAN THEATRE
1762-1909

A DIALOGUE AND ODE

FRANCIS HOPKINSON

A DIALOGUE BETWEEN
AN ENGLISHMAN AND AN INDIAN

A LITTLE TEATABLE CHITCHAT

JOHN SMITH

COLLEGE DIALOGUES

WHEN Lord Loudoun arrived in Philadelphia in January, 1757, to consult with the Colonial governors on means and manners of dealing with the Indians, he was honored with a special performance of *The Masque of Alfred* by students of the College of Philadelphia. Written originally by Thomson, revised by Mallet, and further added to by William Smith, first Provost of the College, it had been first played by the students during the previous Christmas holiday.

The collegiate thespians of the eighteenth century had none of the play-production apparatus of our present academic theatres, nor did they restrict their presentations to what we would now regard as regular plays. Frequently their dramatic pieces were in the form of dialogues and disputations designed as exercises in speaking. Their teachers held to the medieval monastic concept of a play as a rhetorical document that could exercise the oratorical talents of their young scholars and thus make them more effective preachers, lawyers, and public servants. Provost Smith certainly regarded this 1757 performance in this light. In reporting on their endeavor, he wrote in the *Pennsylvania Gazette*, "Ever since the foundation of the College and Academy in this city, the improvement of the youth in oratory and correct speaking, has always been considered an essential branch of their education."

Probably the first school drama performed in this country was the "pastoral colloquy" given by students at William and Mary College in 1702. In 1736 the young gentlemen of the same college played *Cato* and *The Drummer* in Wil-

I

liamsburg. On September 24, 1754, Reverend Ezra Stiles noted in his diary, "Waited on President Burr and that evening two young gentlemen of the college [College of New Jersey, later Princeton] acted *Tamerlane* and *Bajazet*." In January, 1756, a memorandum from the Yale faculty judgments carried the following charge: "Whereas it appears that a play was acted at the house of William Lyon on the evenings after the 2nd, 4th, 7th, and 8th, days of January instant, and that all the students (excepting some few) were present at one or other of those times, and many of them continued there until after nine of the clock, and had a large quantity of wine, and sundry people of the town were also present, . . . And whereas this practice is of a very pernicious nature, tending to corrupt the morals of the seminary of religion and learning, and of mankind in general, and to the mispence of precious time and money. . . ." The Yale faculty did not extend Christian charity to the offenders. Student spectators were fined eightpence and the actors three shillings.

In 1761 Francis Hopkinson, later one of the signers of the Declaration of Independence and designer of the American flag, wrote "An Exercise: Containing a Dialogue [by Provost Smith] and Ode, Sacred to the Memory of his Late Gracious Majesty George II. Performed at the Public Commencement in the College of Philadelphia." The following year he wrote the ode which is reprinted here. (The dialogue section is attributed to Jacob Duché, a Philadelphia clergyman.) That same year, 1762, the students of the College of New Jersey (Princeton) recited a dialogue on "The Military Glory of Great Britain" at their commencement exercises. On at least one occasion Francis Hopkinson was involved with the professional theatre. The Douglass Company gave a benefit performance of *George Barnwell* on the final night of their Philadelphia engagement, December 27, 1759, to help purchase an organ for the College Hall. A special Prologue, "In Praise of Music," by Hopkinson was spoken by the leading actor, Lewis Hallam.

Aside from Hopkinson, Hugh Brackenridge and Philip Freneau were the only conspicuous literary figures of the century whose names were associated with the school drama. They collaborated on a patriotic dialogue, "The Rising Glory of America," which was recited at the College of New Jersey in 1771.

Dartmouth apparently took up the practice as early as 1774. In that year Jeremy Belknap, the New Hampshire historian, reported on the Dartmouth commencement proceedings in his diary: "McGregore and Swetland, two bachelors, spoke a dialogue of Lord Lyttleton's between Apicius and Darteneuf upon good eating and drinking. The Mercury (who comes in at the close of the piece) performed his part but clumsily; but the two epicures did well, and the President laughed as heartily as the rest."

The first of the following dialogues is notable for its expression of strong loyalist sympathies. Remarkable indeed that a signer of the Declaration of Independence could have held such unqualified devotion to the Crown in 1762.

The two Dartmouth Dialogues, written by John Smith (1752–1809), a professor of learned languages at Dartmouth, were performed sometime during the Revolutionary War period. They not only illustrate this eighteenth-century form of school drama, they also provide authentic and pointed comment on contemporary social problems. When reading the passages in which the Indian demonstrates his social and intellectual superiority over the Englishman, for example, it is well to recall not only the prevailing enmity for the British but also the status of the Indian in the college life of the time. Dartmouth, like most of the colleges, was open to Indian students, and a sizable number of them had demonstrated scholarly abilities. Certainly this is apparent in the first disputation. The Indian's case for Christian and humane benevolence toward his race is sincere, well conceived, and well argued. And as such dialogues were intended to demonstrate the powers of rhetorical persuasion, the Englishman obligingly recognizes the validity and justice of the Indian's claims. Dartmouth and John Smith were unmistakably aligned in the cause of Christian tolerance; for even though Smith pleads eloquently and successfully the cause of the Indian, no touch of bitterness or vindictiveness is evident in the treatment of the Englishman.

The second dialogue is a farcical satire on inflation and its attendant evils. The tolerant spirit of the Indian dialogue seems less surprising when compared with the light-hearted and almost flippant comments on the ministry in this second recitation. The public performance must have been rendered with unmistakable gaiety; for religious subjects were not regarded lightly by Dartmouth students, as is indicated in the prefatory letter Smith addressed to Doctor Phillips. The *Teatable Chitchat* does not possess the directness and force of the Indian dialogue, nor does it ever really reach any resolution or concluding statement; yet its playful spirit and its social comment indicate that not all commencement dialogues were serious oratorical disputations.

After the war the colleges expanded their dramatic activities, depending more on standard plays for their speaking exercise. In November, 1782, Peter Elmendorf, a student at the College of New Jersey, reported to his parents that "our minds have been a little relaxed from the laborious task by acting of a tragedy [John Home's *Douglas*]. Never were people better pleased than with our performance, our dress was silk and elegant and every circumstance to render it noble was strictly adhered to, it was so affecting that it caused tears to flow from many." Zadoc Squier wrote from Nassau Hall on February 22, 1783: "It is now all hurry with us here in college. Next Thursday evening is appointed for our public exhibitions, and besides delivering orations we shall act a play called *The Rival Queens*, and a farce called *The Mock Doctor*." By 1787 the College of New Jersey had apparently accepted these performances as an integral part of the college program. Dr. Manasseh Cutler reported in his journal: "I was very much pleased with the hall and the stage erected in it for exhibitions. It is well formed for plays, which are permitted here, and dialogue speaking principally cultivated."

Although the extensive theatrical programs of present-day academic institutions are a twentieth-century phenomenon, college dramatics had an early and firm beginning.

AN EXERCISE CONTAINING
A DIALOGUE AND ODE

On the Accession of His present gracious Majesty George III

FRANCIS HOPKINSON

Performed at the public Commencement in the College of
Philadelphia, May 18th, 1762

CHARACTERS
LORENZO   EUGENIO   AMYNTOR

LORENZO: Enough, ye Sons of Science! Honours meet
At your maternal Shrine have now been paid.
From the fair Fount of Helicon divine
Pure living streams enraptur'd have ye drawn
Of Classic Lore, and bade them copious flow
To grace the Prospects of this festive Day.
Meanwhile each Patriot Eye with Transport gaz'd;
Each Friend of Worth, of Science and of Man
With chearing Smiles their silent Plaudit gave.
Say then, my Friends, have ye no Chaplets weav'd,
No jocund Song prepar'd, of sprightliest Strain,
To crown the Labours of the learned Tribe,
And sooth with Warblings sweet the parting Ear?
EUGENIO: Yes, my Lorenzo! grateful will we pay
All seemly Tribute to this glad Occasion:
Nor Chaplets gay, nor Song of Sprightliest Strain
Will we refuse. See good Amyntor's Eye
Sparkles with Joy, and speaks some rapt'rous Theme.
AMYNTOR: What Theme more joyous, or can better suit
The glad Return of this auspicious Day,
Than that which occupies my present Thought
And which the faithful Index of my Heart
Pointed to thy Discerning. Know, Eugenio,
The Joy, that sports in thy Amyntor's Breast
And o'er his Visage spreads this placid Smile,
Springs from no other Source than the loud Fame

Of his young Monarch's Worth. Be this our Theme.
EUGENIO: And is it thus, Amyntor? Ah! how soon
To Sounds of Grief succeeds the Voice of Joy,
And gilded Trappings to the Garb of Woe!
Far other Scenes thy lab'ring Breast disclos'd,
When last I met Thee at these annual Rites,
With Visage wan, with dark and downward Brow;
When royal Dust receiv'd the duteous Tear.
When trembled with the Dirge this stately Dome,
And gloom'd these hallow'd Walls with Wreaths funereal.
AMYNTOR: O name it not, my Friend! all custom'd Dues
To Majesty entomb'd were then discharg'd.
To dwell desponding on the mournful Theme,
Or hang like Statues o'er the kingly Urn
Pale, motionless as Marble, this were impious,
A Censure weak and rash of Heaven's Decree.
Shout then, ye favour'd Race, ye Sons of Freedom!
Bound every Heart with Joy, and every Breast
Pour the warm Tribute of a grateful Praise!
For o'er the Realms of Britain reigns supreme,
The Darling of his People, George the Good.
Bright-clustring round his Throne the Virtues stand
In meet Array, obsequious, at his Call,
To fly, triumphant, thro' his wide Domain,
And deal their salutary Influence round.

LORENZO: Thrice happy Monarch! skill'd in every
  Art
To win a Nation's smile and fix their Love.
Thy youthful Blossoms are the Earnests sure
Of future Glories to thy native Land.
Hence, in the mighty Rolls of British Fame,
Thy Reign shall shine distinguish'd from the
  Rest
By Deeds of Valour, Piety and Love.
AMYNTOR: Nor only in the Sphere of Royalty,
The wise Exertions of his kingly Power,
Doth George illustrious move: each milder Vir-
  tue,
Each soft endearing Scene of private Life
His tender Soul embraces; modest Worth,
Grace unaffected, true Simplicity
With Dignity combin'd, each nameless Joy
That Hymen twines around his silken Bands,
He meets with Transport in his Charlotte's
  Arms,
The pleasing Partner of his Heart and Throne.
But let us not in fond and growing Parley
Thus waste the Day. – Begin, ye Choral Band,
For whom the festive Song hath been prepar'd,
And with loud Paeans rend the vaulted Roof.

ODE

Bright ascending in the Skies
See Britannia's Glory rise!
Cease your Sorrows, cease your Fears!
Night recedes and Day appears!
Another George majestic fills the Throne,
And glad Britannia calls him all her own.

Chorus
Let the tuneful Chorus join
And high their Voices raise,
To celebrate in Notes divine
The youthful Monarch's Praise.

II

Rejoicing Science, with each polish'd Art,
Beneath his Reign shall with Success conspire
To form the Manners, humanize the Heart,
And virtuous Thoughts, and virtuous Deeds
inspire.
The Sweets of Liberty shall care beguile,
And Justice still her happy Influence spread,
Religion chear him with a sacred Smile,
And bid the Crown sit gently on his Head.

Chorus
Let the tuneful Chorus join
And high their Voices raise,
To celebrate in Notes divine
The pious Monarch's Praise.

III

See resplendent at his Side
Sits his modest blooming Bride!
Glowing Youth and Beauty join
To make the Fair conspicuous shine:
Every Virtue warms her Breast –
How is Britain's Monarch blest!
Unsullied Bliss shall crown the royal Pair,
The Good and Great are Heaven's peculiar
  Care.

Chorus
Let the tuneful Chorus join,
And high their Voices raise,
To celebrate in Notes divine
The happy Monarch's Praise.

IV

Rough War shall humbly at his Feet
Her bloody Laurels lay;
Him gentle Peace shall kindly greet
And smile beneath his Sway.
Then Britain! hail these golden Days!
Illustrious shalt thou shine:
For George shall gain immortal Praise;
And, Britain! George is thine.
To distant Times he shall extend thy Name,
And give thy Glories to a deathless Fame.

Chorus
Let the tuneful Chorus join,
And high their Voices raise,
To celebrate in Notes divine
The British Monarch's Praise.

Finis

DARTMOUTH DIALOGUES

DARTMOUTH COLLEGE
24 March 1782

Honored Sir,

Permit me to present you with two dialogues: *The Englishman and Indian* and *The Teatable Chitchat*. As you have been pleased, heretofore, to grant me your attention to productions of this kind, I rely on your candor, even without an apology.

The first mentioned dialogue was acted pretty naturally, as a real Aboriginal defended the part of the Indian. The other incurred no censure; and passed for a humor.

I suppose, Honored Sir, you have been minutely informed of the happy religious attention, that has obtained, and yet continues, amongst us. The work appears to be very genuine. Mr. Ticknor, who will have the honor to deliver this letter, will be able to give you a particular, and I believe, a very pleasing account of this important affair. He is a Junior Sophister, – a young gentleman of modesty, and, indeed, a worthy member of this Seminary.

Mrs. Smith joins in presenting the greatest respects to you and Madame Phillips, with,

Honored Sir,

> your very obedient and obliged
> humble servant
> JOHN SMITH

Honorable Doctor Phillips

A DIALOGUE BETWEEN
AN ENGLISHMAN AND AN INDIAN

JOHN SMITH

CHARACTERS

ENGLISHMAN   INDIAN

ENGLISHMAN: [*Walking in the road overtakes Indian*] Who is this? have I not seen you before?

INDIAN: I'm Joseph Yannhoontough. You once saw me at Onaida.

ENGLISHMAN: You appear serious. What's the matter, Joseph?

INDIAN: As I was walking alone today, I have been pondering on the opinion the English entertain of us poor Indians!

ENGLISHMAN: Do you think they entertain an opinion of you worse than you deserve? Are you not sensible, you are a savage, cruel race?

INDIAN: I know we are an uncultivated and un-polished people; but I am inclined to think there are some among the Europeans, and their descendants, as bad as we are, on many accounts.

ENGLISHMAN: You are a vile, barbarous race! Your tenderest mercies are *cruel!* You delight in devastation and massacre! With what hellish pleasure do you murder defenseless women and children! You delight in every impious act, that men are capable of perpetrating. I wish you were all destroyed, and sent to the . . .

INDIAN: Sir, I acknowledge the Indians have been very cruel; but I am indeed very sorry to find you thus disposed! You discover a temper,

7

in yourself, not much better than that, you so severely censure, in the Indians.

ENGLISHMAN: What? do you defend the conduct, – the barbarous conduct of savages? – I have heard something lately, that makes me so angry, I can hardly refrain . . .

INDIAN: May I ask what that is, Sir?

ENGLISHMAN: Why I have been informed, that Doctor W——k keeps a number of Indian boys yet; and has been lately soliciting contributions to support them, at his college. I am surprised to think any one can imagine, that Indians will ever learn any thing, but to serve Satan. Rather than expend money on Indians in such a way, and for such a purpose, I would throw it into the ocean. I would chearfully contribute powder and bullets, to kill you all.

INDIAN: It is happy not only for us Indians; but indeed, Sir, for society in general, that there are some men in the world, who are possessed of generous souls, and actuated by principles of virtue and religion. But, I fear, you are blackened with a character sadly contrasted to theirs. Because the Indians are uncivilized, you want to kill them all! Does this temper quadrate with christianity? or indeed with humanity? Upon your principle, ought not the most of the Europeans to have been extirpated a thousand years ago, when they were in a state similar to that of the Indians? Indeed, Sir, I suspect, that if you had sufficient power, you would be as fierce a destroyer of mankind, as cruel a tyrant, as ever existed.

ENGLISHMAN: You seem to talk very *learnedly*, and with fluency. Have you been one of Doctor W——k's scholars?

INDIAN: Sir, I have been one; – and my soul blesses that generous man. – But if you will be pleased to attend, and keep yourself from being carried away with a torrent of rage, I will endeavor to demonstrate, that you are mistaken in your opinion, that the American Indians surpass all other people, in cruelty.

ENGLISHMAN: If you have any thing to say, on this subject, I will hear you; although I'm persuaded, you can never make *that* appear.

INDIAN: Did not the Spaniards exercise such acts of cruelty towards the Indians of Mexico and Florida, and South-America, as must make every humane mind, that attends to their horrid massacres and devastations, shudder? –

They wantonly butchered near twenty millions of these natives, and plundered their countries of almost infinite wealth. Without provocation, they would cut off the noses and ears of the Indians, and give them to their dogs. Yes, they hunted them with their hounds, and boasted of the number they had killed in a day! Were the Indians ever guilty of barbarity superior to this?

ENGLISHMAN: I know nothing about the Spaniards; but suppose, they are pretty much like the *Indians*.

INDIAN: I would, by no means, defend the cruelty, and bad conduct of my brethren, the Indians; but are the English always more merciful than they? Did not Major R——rs promiscuously kill men, women and children, at St. Francois?

ENGLISHMAN: Come, come, because you have got a little learning, you mean to dispute me; do you? I wish you, and all the rest of Doctor Whee——ks Indians were sent to Guinea, or had your throats cut.

INDIAN: Sir, you use me very ill, – if I am an Indian. Do you discover the temper of a christian, when you wish destruction to whole nations? Have you one spark of that *generous benevolence* to mankind, which stamps a *dignity* on the human soul, when you regret, that endeavors should be used to civilize and christianize an unpolished and savage people; yet *capable* of improvement, and of being made *good members* of society? Ought you not to have *Malevolence* branded on your forehead, when you curse pious men, for using endeavors for this purpose? In case it is decreed, by Divine Providence, that the Indians must be extirpated, ought not those, who have opportunity and ability, to use vigorous efforts, to save them? When you shall be calm; and moderation shall succeed in the place of rage, I trust, you will be fully sensible of your impious disposition. I hope you will yet exhibit a meek, merciful and benevolent temper of mind. Surely, I wish you no hurt; although I am grieved you should thus discover a mind replenished with the malice of Satan!

ENGLISHMAN: S'blood! Joseph, I hardly know what to say. You seem to talk fluently. – Perhaps I have been too much prejudiced against the Indians. [*Curtains fall*]

March 2, 1779.

A LITTLE TEATABLE CHITCHAT, *alamode;*
or an ancient discovery reduced to modern practice;
– Being a Dialogue, and a dish of Tea

JOHN SMITH

Parturiunt montes, nascetur ridiculusmus. Horace

CHARACTERS

MR. SHARP	MISS TOAST
MR. SHARP'S LADY	MISS TWATTLE
MR. PENDULUM	

June, 1781

Mr. Sharp and his Lady alone.

MR. SHARP: Good wife, who are to come to our house, this afternoon?

MRS. SHARP: Why, husband, I expect Miss Toast, and Miss Twattle.

MR. SHARP: This will never answer, old woman; this will never answer, to give 60 dollars for a pound of tea, and give it away again. Where, and how, wife, can I get money, at this rate?

MRS. SHARP: O never mind it. I don't think tea is a *despot* deal dearer, than it was in silver-money times. Why you can get 60 dollars for a bushel of wheat.

MR. SHARP: Well; – I don't know – I hope we shall all live our appointed time. – But, I tell you, old woman, you must patch, and mend, and fly round like a top, – like a whirligig.

[*Enter Miss Toast and her Uncle Pendulum*]

MISS TOAST: Mr. Sharp, this is my uncle Pendulum. [*Mr. Sharp and Mr. Pendulum shake hands, and pass the usual ceremonies*]

MR. PENDULUM: I came into town last night, and am fatigued, but my cousin Toast would insist upon my coming here with her, to see you. If her eloquence in courting, is equal to what she has employed upon me, she can do wonders that way, I know. [*All laugh*]

MR. SHARP: Well, I'm glad to see you. I hope for better acquaintance. How goes paper money with you, now?

MR. PENDULUM: O about 60 for 1, they say. – And silver is going to pot too. I believe in my soul, it is depreciated one third. We see strange times, Mr. Sharp, don't we?

MR. SHARP: Why, yes we do. But farmers make out well enough, for all. I never made out so well, since I was born, as I have, since the war began. I have really made a *grand* interest. In the year 1775, I ow'd 1200£. You know money soon began to depreciate. Well I soon pay'd it up, as the law obliged my creditors to take the nominal sum, or nothing. Since I have pay'd up my debts, I have been getting money like smoke and fog. Why I can pay my rates now, with more ease, than I ever could. And I can buy cloth, and rum, and salt and pins of the merchants cheaper than ever. And I will tell you something; only do you keep it secret. I would not have it known *for the world*, for the people about would break my neck, and draw me in quarters if they knew it.

MR. PENDULUM: O, Sir, I will not expose a friend, upon my honor.

MR. SHARP: Why, Sir, ever since these new times came along, I have been a member of our assembly. It was some time ago proposed, that old debts should be made good; pay'd 8 for 1. – I knew I was in debt myself, and that it would not answer. So I opposed the motion, – and gained the point. – And poor creditors have been obliged to take the nominal sum. – I will tell you something more; we have pay'd our own debts, and others owe us: And now we determine money pay'd in paper shall be made equal to silver and gold.

MR. PENDULUM: That's right. – And I have, that way, saved six hundred pounds. O how clever it is, that these gentlemen, and merchants, and ministers should lie at our mercy. [*All laugh*]

MR. SHARP: There is another affair of more importance yet, I will communicate, in confidence.

MR. PENDULUM: Sir, you will greatly oblige me, upon honor.

MR. SHARP: We are now preparing a bill for the purpose of abolishing christianity. And we shall make matters work well too. It takes with all our gentlemen of importance.

MR. PENDULUM: That's the thing. I have been *wishing* for it. We shall not be obliged to maintain ministers, shall we?

MR. SHARP: Why no. You may do what you will, then. You may kill half the town, and yourself into the bargain, and nobody will care. [*Tea ready. Mrs. Sharp invites her guests to sit at the table*]

MISS TOAST: This is despot good tea. [*Sips with great formality*] 'Tis better than mother's. [*Oversets her cup into her lap*]

MISS TWATTLE: This is good bacon. I love bacon and tea much.

MR. PENDULUM: This is plaguy good bread. Mr. Sharp what makes your wife so much fatter than you are? [*All laugh*]

MISS TWATTLE: I hear Mr. Tim Tago has stolen a horse; – and that Betty Fly-catcher is with child. [*Pendulum laughs*]

MRS. SHARP: Mr. Pendulum do drink another dish.

MR. PENDULUM: No, my belly is as full as a tick. Twas plaguy good.

MRS. SHARP: Do, Sir, take another; you may in welcome. Do eat, till you split; I wish you would.

MR. PENDULUM: No; I've got enough. And enough is as good as a feast. [*Curtains fall*]

THE CANDIDATES

OR

THE HUMOURS OF A VIRGINIA ELECTION

COLONEL   ROBERT   MUNFORD

COLONEL ROBERT MUNFORD'S *The Candidates* represents the transitional step from commencement dialogues to a more conventional play form. Written in 1770 and published in 1798, it has no recorded performance. By strict dramaturgical standards, it probably cannot be considered a good play; yet it is more nearly a play than the dialogues, and certainly many of the scenes, particularly the farce sequences, would be highly effective on the stage. It is principally distinguished for its accurate and vivid picture of electioneering in Virginia in the latter part of the eighteenth century.

Munford wrote from first-hand knowledge and from honest sympathy for the aristocratic politician. He was born in Prince George County, Virginia, about 1730; and although his father's death in 1743 left the family destitute, his uncle, William Beverley, provided for his education at the Wakefield School in Leeds, England. After returning to Virginia, he rapidly established himself as an honest politician and a substantial Virginia gentleman. He held offices as county lieutenant, sheriff, and representative in the House of Burgesses from 1765 to 1775 and in the General Assembly in 1779 and 1780. Although he was never a revolutionist by temper, he spoke and voted for Patrick Henry's Stamp Act Resolution in 1765 and served as a major in the Continental Army. He was first and foremost a large-scale Virginia planter – "Richland," his estate in Mecklenburg County, could boast of ninety-one slaves in 1782. Politics came second and writing third.

Like most of the refined gentlemen of his society, Munford had the advantage of a well-stocked private library; and like his fellow Virginians, he sought pleasure and culture at the public theatres. Virginia, unlike the other colonies, had never placed any restraining bans or limitations on plays or players, and fondness for theatrical presentations had been demonstrated by the early establishment of theatres at Williamsburg, Norfolk, Petersburg, Hobb's Hole, Fredericksburg, and Dumfries.

In addition to *The Candidates*, Munford wrote numerous poems and another play, *The Patriots. The Patriots* was written just at the time of the outbreak of hostilities and represented Munford's plea for a middle-of-the-road political course. He felt that the genuine, true, tolerant, and gentlemanly believer in the cause of independence was usually put down as a Tory and that one did not normally achieve the appellation of Whig unless one was loud-mouthed, self-conscious, noisy, and blustering. The gist of the play, and Munford's sympathy, is expressed in the following speech of Meanwell: "Never may I signalize my attachment to liberty by persecuting innocent men, only because they differ in opinion from me." As in the earlier play, *The Candidates*, the leading figure in *The Patriots* was drawn after Munford's own image: a citizen of the world, an honest public servant filled with an unselfish sense of public responsibility.

Although this exalted picture of the public servant seems somewhat foreign to twentieth-century politics, when one follows the electioneering procedures in *The Candidates* and observes the electorate's whole-hearted support of Worthy it appears less surprising that statesmen of the Washington and Jefferson type were elected to high political office. The Virginia voter made his choice on the basis of the personal qualifications of the candidates. He recognized the intellectual superiority of the aristocrat, and fortunately, the aristocrat accepted office with a sense of duty and with no thought of financial gain. Nor did these political leaders have any fear of mob rule or coercion once they were elected. Their constituents respected them and trusted their judgments.

Current dramatic classifiers might label *The Candidates* a kind of documentary play, an eighteenth-century "Living Newspaper." With a few minor alterations it might even pass for a twentieth-century commentary. Many of the electioneering practices certainly have a contemporary ring: the whispering campaign, the fantastic political promises, the hand-shaker who knows everyone's name, the barbecue picnic – even the offer of whiskey for votes is not too remote. All the inner workings of the procedure are minutely described, from "hats in the ring" to the "landslide swing" in favor of the aristocrat Worthy.

Although principally marked as a political satire, *The Candidates* commands attention on other counts: Ralpho is the first Negro character in the American drama, and, although a servant and slave, he is not servile and humble; neither is his master, Wouldbe, condescending and patronizing. They regard each other with mutual respect. The rough-and-tumble and sometimes mildly bawdy farce scenes between Sir John, Guzzle, and Mrs. Guzzle are worthy predecessors to *The Contrast* as native American comedy. They are genuinely amusing and would appear so on the stage today.

THE CANDIDATES

OR

THE HUMOURS OF A VIRGINIA ELECTION

COLONEL ROBERT MUNFORD

CHARACTERS

SIR JOHN TODDY ⎫ *Candidates for*
MR. WOU'DBE ⎪ *the office of*
MR. STRUTABOUT ⎬ *delegates to the*
MR. SMALLHOPES ⎭ *general assembly*

MR. JULIP ⎫ *Gentlemen*
CAPT. PAUNCH ⎬ *Justices*

GUZZLE ⎫
TWIST ⎪
STERN ⎬ *Freeholders*
PRIZE ⎭

MRS. GUZZLE ⎫
LUCY TWIST ⎪ *Freeholders'*
CATHARINE STERN ⎬ *Wives*
SARAH PRIZE ⎭

RALPHO, *Wou'dbe's servant*
JACK, *a tool to Mr. Strutabout*
NED, *the same to Mr. Smallhopes*

MR. WORTHY, *formerly a delegate,*
but now declines
FREEHOLDERS, COUNTRY GIRLS, *etc.*

PROLOGUE
By a Friend

Ladies and gentlemen, to-night you'll see
A bard delighting in satiric glee;
In merry scenes his biting tale unfold,
And high to Folly's eye the mirror hold:
Here eager candidates shall call for votes,
And bawling voters louder stretch their throats:
Here may you view, in groups diverting, join'd
The poor and wealthy rabble of mankind;
All who deserve the lash, the lash will find.
Here characters, whose names are now unknown,
Shall shine again, as in their spheres they shone;
While some may make malicious explanation,
And know them all still living in the nation.
If any present, say, fie, shameless bard!
Hast thou for decency no more regard
Than at thy betters, thus to make a stand,
And boldly point out meanness, contraband,
Depreciating the wisdom of the land?
Tho' such, the wond'rous sympathy of wits,
That every fool will wear the cap that fits,
I boldly answer, how could he mean you,
Who, when he wrote, about you nothing
knew?
The state of things was such, in former times,

'Ere wicked kings were punish'd for their
crimes:
When strove the candidates to gain their seats
Most heartily, with drinking bouts, and treats;
The meanest vices all the people stain'd,
And drunkenness, and monarchy both reign'd,
With such strong cause his anger to engage,
How could our Bard restrain satiric rage?
But, God forbid, its edge shou'd now apply,
Or on our race-field, when you cast an eye
You there a home-election – should espy.
Science and virtue, now are wider spread,
And crown with dignity, fair Freedom's head.
We only pray this satire ne'er be just,
Save when apply'd to other times, and trust
Its keenness only, a rememb'rancer,
And guard from future evils, may appear.
If, after this, objections should remain,
The motive's envy, consciousness disdain,
Or any thing, except the poet's want
Of sense, which no true publisher will grant.
Yet virtue is not in our story lost,
E'en then, Virginians could much virtue boast.
With plaudits, therefore, and free laughter own
Virginia's first and only comic son;
Ah! could the bard, rejoicing, raise his head
To hear his praise! – Alas! the bard is dead.

ACT I. Scene 1

Mr. Wou'dbe's house. Enter Wou'dbe with a news-paper in his hand.

WOU'DBE: I am very sorry our good old governor Botetourt has left us. He well deserved our friendship, when alive, and that we should for years to come, with gratitude, remember his mild and affable deportment. Well, our little world will soon be up, and very busy towards our next election. Must I again be subject to the humours of a fickle crowd? Must I again resign my reason, and be nought but what each voter pleases? Must I cajole, fawn, and wheedle, for a place that brings so little profit?

Enter Ralpho

RALPHO: Sir John Toddy is below, and if your honour is at leisure, would beg to speak to you.

WOU'DBE: My compliments to Sir John, and tell him, I shall be glad of his company. So – Sir John, some time ago, heard me say I was willing to resign my seat in the house to an abler person, and he comes modestly to accept of it.

Enter Sir John Toddy

SIR JOHN TODDY: Mr. Wou'dbe, your most obedient servant, sir; I am proud to find you well. I hope you are in good health, sir?

WOU'DBE: Very well, I am obliged to you, Sir John. Why, Sir John, you surely are practising the grimace and compliments you intend to make use of among the freeholders in the next election, and have introduced yourself to me with the self-same common-place expressions that we candidates adopt when we intend to wheedle a fellow out of his vote – I hope you have no scheme upon me, Sir John?

SIR JOHN TODDY: No, sir, upon my honour, sir, it was punctually to know how your lady and family did, sir, 'pon honour, sir, it was.

WOU'DBE: You had better be more sparing of your honour at present, Sir John; for, if you are a candidate, whenever you make promises to the people that you can't comply with, you must say upon honour, otherwise they won't believe you.

SIR JOHN TODDY: Upon honour, sir, I have no thought to set up for a candidate, unless you say the word.

WOU'DBE: Such condescension from you, Sir John, I have no reason to expect: you have my hearty consent to do as you please, and if the people choose you their Representative, I must accept of you as a colleague.

SIR JOHN TODDY: As a colleague, Mr. Wou'dbe! I was thinking you did not intend to stand a poll, and my business, sir, was to get the favour of you to speak a good word for me among the people.

WOU'DBE: I hope you have no occasion for a trumpeter, Sir John? If you have, I'll speak a good word to you, and advise you to decline.

SIR JOHN TODDY: Why, Mr. Wou'dbe, after you declin'd, I thought I was the next *fittenest* man in the county, and Mr. Wou'dbe, if you would be ungenerous, tho' you are a laughing man, you would tell me so.

WOU'DBE: It would be ungenerous indeed, Sir John, to tell you what the people could never be induced to believe. But I'll be ingenuous enough to tell you, Sir John, if you expect any assistance from me, you'll be disappointed, for I can't think you the *fittenest* man I know.

SIR JOHN TODDY: Pray, sir, who do you know besides? Perhaps I may be thought as fit as your honour. But, sir, if you are for that, the hardest fend off: damn me, if I care a farthing for you; and so, your servant, sir. [*Exit Sir John Toddy*]

WOU'DBE: So, I have got the old knight, and his friend Guzzle, I suppose, against me, by speaking so freely; but their interest, I believe, has not weight enough among the people, for me to lose any thing, by making them my enemies. Indeed, the being intimate with such a fool as Sir John, might tend more to my discredit with them, for the people of Virginia have too much sense not to perceive how weak the head must be that is always filled with liquor. Ralpho! –

Enter Ralpho

RALPHO: Sir, what does your honour desire?

WOU'DBE: I'm going into my library, and if any gentleman calls, you may introduce him to me there.

RALPHO: Yes, sir. But, master, as election-times are coming, I wish you would remember a poor servant, a little.

WOU'DBE: What do you want?

RALPHO: Why, the last suit of clothes your honour gave me is quite worn out. Look here, [*Showing his elbows*] the insigns, (as I have heard your honour say, in one of your fine speeches) the insigns of faithful service. Now, methinks, as they that set up for burgesses, cut a dash, and have rare sport, why might not their servants have a little decreation?

WOU'DBE: I understand you, Ralpho, you wish to amuse yourself, and make a figure among the girls this Election, and since such a desire is natural to the young, and innocent if not carried to excess, I am willing to satisfy you; you may therefore, have the suit I pulled off yesterday, and accept this present as an evidence that I am pleased with your diligence and fidelity, and am ever ready to reward it. [*Exit Wou'dbe*]

RALPHO: God bless your honour! what a good master! who would not do every thing to give such a one pleasure? But e'gad, it's time to think of my new clothes: I'll go and try them on. Gadso! this figure of mine is not reconsiderable in its delurements, and when I'm dressed out like a gentleman, the girls, I'm a thinking, will find me desistible. [*Exit*]

Scene 2

A porch of a tavern: a Court-house on one side, and an high road behind. Captain Paunch, Ned, and several Freeholders discovered.

NED: Well, gentlemen, I suppose we are all going to the barbecue together.

CAPTAIN PAUNCH: Indeed, sir, I can assure you, I have no such intention.

NED: Not go to your friend Wou'dbe's treat! He's such a pretty fellow, and you like him so well, I wonder you won't go to drink his liquor.

CAPTAIN PAUNCH: Aye, aye, very strange: but your friends Strutabout and Smallhopes, I like so little as never to take a glass from them, because I shall never pay the price which is always expected for it, by voting against my conscience: I therefore don't go, to avoid being asked for what I won't give.

NED: A very disteress [*sic*] motive, truly, but for the matter of that, you've not so much to boast of your friend Wou'dbe, if what I have been told of him is true; for I have heard say, he and the fine beast of a gentleman, Sir John Toddy, have joined interests. Mr. Wou'dbe, I was creditly 'formed, was known for to say, he wouldn't serve for a burgess, unless Sir John was elected with him.

1ST FREEHOLDER: What's that you say, neighbour? has Mr. Wou'dbe and Sir John joined interest?

NED: Yes, they have; and ant there a clever fellow for ye? a rare burgess you will have, when a fellow gets in, who will go drunk, and be a sleeping in the house! I wish people wouldn't pretend for to hold up their heads so high, who have such friends and associates. There's poor Mr. Smallhopes, who isn't as much attended to, is a very proper gentleman, and is no drunkard, and has no drunken companions.

1ST FREEHOLDER: I don't believe it. Mr. Wou'dbe's a cleverer man than that, and people ought to be ashamed to vent such slanders.

2ND FREEHOLDER: So I say: and as we are of one mind, let's go strait, and let Mr. Wou'dbe know it. [*Exeunt two Freeholders*]

3RD FREEHOLDER: If Mr. Wou'dbe did say it, I won't vote for him, that's sartain.

4TH FREEHOLDER: Are you sure of it, neighbour? [*To Ned*]

NED: Yes, I am sure of it: d'ye think I'd speak such a thing without having good authority?

4TH FREEHOLDER: I'm sorry for't; come neighbour, [*to the 3rd Freeholder*] this is the worst news that I've heard for a long time. [*Exeunt 3rd and 4th Freeholder*]

5TH FREEHOLDER: I'm glad to hear it. Sir John Toddy is a clever openhearted gentleman as I ever knew, one that wont turn his back upon a poor man, but will take a chearful cup with one as well as another, and it does honour to Mr. Wou'dbe to prefer such a one, to any of your whifflers who han't the heart to be generous, and yet despise poor folks. Huzza! for Mr. Wou'dbe and for Sir John Toddy.

6TH FREEHOLDER: I think so too, neighbour. Mr. Wou'dbe, I always thought, was a man of sense, and had larning, as they call it, but he did not love diversion enough, I like him the better for't. Huzza for Mr. Wou'dbe and Sir John Toddy.

BOTH: Huzza for Mr. Wou'dbe and Sir John Toddy. Wou'dbe and Toddy, for ever, boys! [*Exeunt*]

CAPTAIN PAUNCH: The man that heard it is mistaken, for Mr. Wou'dbe never said it.

NED: I'll lay you a bowl he did.

CAPTAIN PAUNCH: Done.

NED: Done, sir, Oh! Jack Sly, Jack Sly.

JACK: [*Without*] Halloa.

Enter Jack, saying, who call'd me? what's your business?

NED: [*Winking to Jack*] I have laid a bowl with the Captain here, that Mr. Wou'dbe did say, that he would not serve as a burgess, unless Sir John Toddy was elected with him.

JACK: I have heard as much, and more that's little to his credit. He has hurt us more than he'll do us good for one while. It's his doings our levies are so high.

CAPTAIN PAUNCH: Out upon you, if that's your proof, fetch the bowl. Why gentlemen, if I had a mind, I could say as much and more of the other candidates. But, gentlemen, 'tis not fair play: don't abuse our friend, and we'll let your's alone. Mr. Wou'dbe is a clever gentleman, and perhaps so are the rest: let every man vote as he pleases, and let's raise no stories to the prejudice of either.

NED: Damn me, if I don't speak my mind. Wou'dbe shan't go if I can help it, by God, for I boldly say, Mr. Wou'dbe has done us more harm, than he will ever do us good. [*Raising his voice very high. Exeunt into the house*]

JACK: So say I. [*Exit after him*]

CAPTAIN PAUNCH: Go along: bawl your hearts out: nobody will mind you, I hope. Well, rejoice that Mr. Wou'dbe is determined still to serve us. If he does us no good, he will do us no harm. Mr. Strutabout would do very well if he was not such a coxcomb. As for Smallhopes, I'd as soon send to New-Market, for a burgess, as send him, and old Sir John loves tipple too well: egad, I'll give Wou'dbe my vote, and throw away the other. [*Exit*]

Scene 3

Wou'dbe's house. Enter Wou'dbe, looking at a letter.

WOU'DBE: This note gives me information, that the people are much displeased with me for declaring in favour of Sir John Toddy. Who could propagate this report, I know not, but was not this abroad, something else would be reported, as prejudicial to my interest; I must take an opportunity of justifying myself in public.

Enter Ralpho

RALPHO: Mr. Strutabout waits upon your honour.

WOU'DBE: Desire him to walk in.

Enter Mr. Strutabout

STRUTABOUT: Mr. Wou'dbe, your servant. Considering the business now in hand, I think you confine yourself too much at home. There are several little reports circulating to your disadvantage, and as a friend, I would advise you to shew yourself to the people, and endeavour to confute them.

WOU'DBE: I believe, sir, I am indebted to my brother candidates, for most of the reports that are propagated to my disadvantage, but I hope, Mr. Strutabout is a man of too much honour, to say anything in my absence, that he cannot make appear.

STRUTABOUT: That you may depend on, sir. But there are some who are so intent upon taking your place, that they will stick at nothing to obtain their ends.

WOU'DBE: Are you in the secret, sir?

STRUTABOUT: So far, sir, that I have had overtures from Mr. Smallhopes and his friends, to join my interest with their's, against you. This, I rejected with disdain, being conscious that you were the properest person to serve the county; but when Smallhopes told me, he intended to prejudice your interest by scattering a few stories among the people to your disadvantage, it raised my blood to such a pitch, that had he not promised me to be silent, I believe I should have chastised him for you myself.

WOU'DBE: If, sir, you were so far my friend, I am obliged to you: though whatever report he is the author of, will, I am certain, gain little credit with the people.

STRUTABOUT: I believe so; and therefore, if you are willing, we'll join our interests together, and soon convince the fellow, that by attacking you he has injured himself.

WOU'DBE: So far from joining with you, or any body else, or endeavouring to procure a vote for you, I am determined never to ask a vote for myself, or receive one that is unduly obtained.

Enter Ralpho

RALPHO: Master, rare news, here's our neighbour Guzzle, as drunk as ever Chief Justice Cornelius was upon the bench.

WOU'DBE: That's no news, Ralpho: but do you call it rare news, that a creature in the shape of man, and endued with the faculties of reason, should so far debase the workmanship of heaven, by making his carcase a receptacle for such pollution?

RALPHO: Master, you are hard upon neighbour Guzzle: our Justices gets drunk, and why not poor Guzzle? But sir, he wants to see you.

WOU'DBE: Tell him to come in. [*Exit Ralpho*] All must be made welcome now.

Re-enter Ralpho and Guzzle, with an empty bottle

GUZZLE: Ha! Mr. Wou'dbe, how is it?

WOU'DBE: I'm something more in my senses than you, John, tho' not so sensible as you would have me, I suppose.

GUZZLE: If I can make you sensible how much I want my bottle filled, and how much I shall love the contents, it's all the senses I desire you to have.

RALPHO: If I may be allowed to speak, neighbour Guzzle, you are wrong; his honour sits up for a burgess, and should have five senses at least.

GUZZLE: Five senses! how, what five?

RALPHO: Why, neighbour, you know, eating, drinking, and sleeping are three; t'other two are best known to myself.

WOU'DBE: I'm sorry Mr. Guzzle, you are so ignorant of the necessary qualifications of a member of the house of burgesses.

GUZZLE: Why, you old dog, I knew before Ralpho told me. To convince you, eating, drinking, and sleeping, are three; fighting and lying are t'others.

WOU'DBE: Why fighting and lying?

GUZZLE: Why, because you are not fit for a burgess, unless you'll fight; suppose a man that values himself upon boxing, should stand in the lobby, ready cock'd and prim'd, and knock you down, and bung up both your eyes for a fortnight, you'd be ashamed to shew your face in the house, and be living at our expence all the time.

WOU'DBE: Why lying?

GUZZLE: Because, when you have been at Williamsburg, for six or seven weeks, under pretence of serving your county, and come back, says I to you, what news? none at all, says you; what have you been about? says I, – says you – and so you must tell some damned lie, sooner than say you have been doing nothing.

WOU'DBE: No, Guzzle, I'll make it a point of duty to dispatch the business, and my study to promote the good of my county.

GUZZLE: Yes, damn it, you all promise mighty fair, but the devil a bit do you perform; there's Strutabout, now, he'll promise to move mountains. He'll make the rivers navigable, and bring the tide over the tops of the hills, for a vote.

STRUTABOUT: You may depend, Mr. Guzzle, I'll perform whatever I promise.

GUZZLE: I don't believe it, damn me if I like you. [*Looking angry*]

WOU'DBE: Don't be angry, John, let our actions hereafter be the test of our inclinations to serve you. [*Exit Strutabout*]

GUZZLE: Agreed, Mr. Wou'dbe, but that fellow that slunk off just now, I've no opinion of.

WOU'DBE: [*Looking about*] What, is Mr. Strutabout gone? Why, surely, Guzzle, you did not put him to flight?

GUZZLE: I suppose I did, but no matter, [*Holding up his bottle, and looking at it*] my bottle never was so long a filling in this house, before; surely, there's a leak in the bottom. [*Looks at it again*]

WOU'DBE: What have you got in your bottle, John, a lizard?

GUZZLE: Yes, a very uncommon one, and I want a little rum put to it, to preserve it.

WOU'DBE: Hav'n't you one in your belly, John?

GUZZLE: A dozen, I believe, by their twisting, when I mentioned the rum.

WOU'DBE: Would you have rum to preserve them, too?

GUZZLE: Yes, yes, Mr. Wou'dbe, by all means; but, why so much talk about it, if you intend to do it, do it at once, man, for I am in a damnable hurry.

WOU'DBE: Do what? Who are to be burgesses, John?

GUZZLE: Who are to be what? [*Looking angry*]

WOU'DBE: Burgesses, who are you for?

GUZZLE: For the first man that fills my bottle: so Mr. Wou'dbe, your servant. [*Exit Guzzle*]

WOU'DBE: Ralpho, go after him, and fill his bottle.

RALPHO: Master, we ought to be careful of the rum, else 'twill not hold out, [*Aside*] it's always a feast or a famine with us; master has just got a little Jamaica for his own use, and now he must spill it, and spare it till there's not a drop left.

WOU'DBE: [*Pulling out his watch*] 'Tis now the time a friend of mine has appointed for me to meet the freeholders at a barbecue; well, I find, in order to secure a seat in our august senate, 'tis necessary a man should either be a slave or a fool; a slave to the people, for the privilege of serving them, and a fool himself, for thus begging a troublesome and expensive employment.

To sigh, while toddy-toping sots rejoice,
To see you paying for their empty voice,
From morn to night your humble head decline,
To gain an honour that is justly thine,
Intreat a fool, who's your's at this day's treat,
And next another's, if another's meat,
Is all the bliss a candidate acquires,
In all his wishes, or his vain desires.

[*Exit*]

End of the First Act

ACT II. Scene I

A race-field, a bullock, and several hogs barbecued. Twist, Stern, Prize, Lucy, Catharine, and Sarah, sitting on four fence rails.

TWIST: Well, gentlemen, what do you think of Mr. Strutabout and Mr. Smallhopes? it seems one of the old ones declines, and t'other, I believe, might as well, if what neighbour Sly says, is true.

STERN: Pray, gentlemen, what plausible objection have you against Mr. Wou'dbe? he's a clever civil gentleman as any, and as far as my poor weak capacity can go, he's a man of as good learning, and knows the punctilios of behaving himself, with the best of them.

PRIZE: Wou'dbe, for sartin, is a civil gentleman, but he can't speak his mind so boldly as Mr. Strutabout, and commend me to a man that will speak his mind freely; – I say.

LUCY: Well, commend me to Mr. Wou'dbe, I say, – I nately like the man; he's mighty good to all his poor neighbours, and when he comes into a poor body's house, he's so free and so funny, isn't he, old man? [*Speaking to Twist*]

TWIST: A little too free sometimes, faith; he was funny when he wanted to see the colour of your garters; wa'nt he?

LUCY: Oh! for shame, husband. Mr. Wou'dbe has no more harm about him, than a sucking babe; at least, if he has, I never saw it.

TWIST: Nor felt it, I hope; but wife, you and I, you know, could never agree about burgesses.

LUCY: If the wives were to vote, I believe they would make a better choice than their husbands.

TWIST: You'd be for the funniest – wou'dn't you?

LUCY: Yes, faith; and the wittiest, and prettiest, and the wisest, and the best too; you are all for ugly except when you chose me.

CATHARINE: Well done, Lucy, you are right, girl. If we were all to speak to our old men as freely as you do, there would be better doings.

STERN: Perhaps not, Kate.

CATHARINE: I am sure there would; for if a clever gentleman, now-a-days, only gives a body a gingercake in a civil way, you are sullen for a week about it. Remember when Mr. Wou'dbe promised Molly a riband, and a pair of buckles, you would not let the poor girl have 'em: but you take toddy from him; – yes, and you'll drink a little too much, you know, Richard.

STERN: Well, it's none of our costs, if I do.

CATHARINE: Husband, you know Mr. Wou'dbe is a clever gentleman; he has been a good friend to us.

STERN: I agree to it, and can vote for him without your clash.

SARAH: I'll be bound when it comes to the pinch, they'll all vote for him: won't you old man? he stood for our George, when our neighbour refused us.

PRIZE: Mr. Wou'dbe's a man well enough in his neighbourhood, and he may have learning, as they say he has, but he don't shew it like Mr. Strutabout.

Enter Guzzle, and several Freeholders

GUZZLE: Your servant, gentlemen, [*Shakes hands all round*] we have got fine weather, thank God: how are crops with you? we are very dry in our parts.

TWIST: We are very dry here; Mr. Guzzle, where's your friend Sir John, and Mr. Wou'dbe? they are to treat to-day, I hear.

GUZZLE: I wish I could see it, but there are more treats besides their's; where's your friend Mr. Strutabout? I heard we were to have a treat from Smallhopes and him to-day.

TWIST: Fine times, boys. Some of them had better keep their money; I'll vote for no man but to my liking.

GUZZLE: If I may be so bold, pray, which way is your liking?

TWIST: Not as your's is, I believe; but nobody shall know my mind till the day.

GUZZLE: Very good, Mr. Twist; nobody, I hope, will put themselves to the trouble to ask.

TWIST: You have taken the trouble already.

GUZZLE: No harm, I hope, sir.

TWIST: None at all, sir: Yonder comes Sir John, and quite sober, as I live.

Enter Sir John Toddy

SIR JOHN TODDY: Gentlemen and ladies, your servant, hah! my old friend Prize, how goes it? how does your wife and children do?

SARAH: At your service, sir. [*Making a low courtsey*]

PRIZE: How the devil come he to know me so well, and never spoke to me before in his life? [*Aside*]

GUZZLE: [*Whispering Sir John*] Dick Stern.

SIR JOHN TODDY: Hah! Mr. Stern, I'm proud to see you; I hope your family are well; how many children? does the good woman keep to the old stroke?

CATHARINE: Yes, an't please your honour, I hope my lady's well, with your honour.

SIR JOHN TODDY: At your service, madam.

GUZZLE: [*Whispering Sir John*] Roger Twist.

SIR JOHN TODDY: Hah! Mr. Roger Twist! your servant, sir. I hope your wife and children are well.

TWIST: There's my wife. I have no children, at your service.

SIR JOHN TODDY: A pretty girl: why, Roger, if you don't do better, you must call an old fellow to your assistance.

TWIST: I have enough to assist me, without applying to you, sir.

SIR JOHN TODDY: No offence, I hope, sir; excuse my freedom.

TWIST: None at all, sir; Mr. Wou'dbe is ready to befriend me in that way at any time.

SIR JOHN TODDY: Not in earnest, I hope, sir; tho' he's a damn'd fellow, I believe.

LUCY: Why, Roger, if you talk at this rate, people will think you are jealous; for shame of yourself.

TWIST: For shame of yourself, you mean.

GUZZLE: A truce, a truce – here comes Mr. Wou'dbe.

Enter Mr. Wou'dbe

WOU'DBE: Gentlemen, your servant. Why, Sir John, you have entered the list, it seems; and are determined to whip over the ground, if you are treated with a distance.

SIR JOHN TODDY: I'm not to be distanc'd by you, or a dozen such.

WOU'DBE: There's nothing like courage upon these occasions; but you were out when you chose me to ride for you, Sir John.

SIR JOHN TODDY: Let's have no more of your algebra, nor proverbs, here.

GUZZLE: Come, gentlemen, you are both friends, I hope.

WOU'DBE: While Sir John confined himself to his bottle and dogs, and moved only in his little circle of pot-companions, I could be with him; but since his folly has induced him to offer himself a candidate for a place, for which he is not fit, I must say, I despise him. The people are of opinion, that I favour this undertaking of his; but I now declare, he is not the man I wish the people to elect.

GUZZLE: Pray, sir, who gave you a right to choose for us?

WOU'DBE: I have no right to choose for you; but I have a right to give my opinion: especially when I am the supposed author of Sir John's folly.

GUZZLE: Perhaps he's no greater fool than some others.

WOU'DBE: It would be ungrateful in you, Mr. Guzzle, not to speak in favour of Sir John; for you have stored away many gallons of his liquor in that belly of you's.

GUZZLE: And he's the cleverer gentleman for it; is not he, neighbours?

1ST FREEHOLDER: For sartin; it's no disparagement to drink with a poor fellow.

2ND FREEHOLDER: No more it is, tho' some of the quality are mighty proud that way.

3RD FREEHOLDER: Mr. Wou'dbe shou'dn't speak so freely against that.

TWIST: Mr. Wou'dbe.

WOU'DBE: Sir.

TWIST: We have heard a sartin report, that you and Sir John have joined interest.

WOU'DBE: Well; do you believe it?

TWIST: Why, it don't look much like it now, Mr. Wou'dbe; but, mayhap, it's only a copy of your countenance.

WOU'DBE: You may put what construction you please upon my behaviour, gentlemen; but I assure you, it never was my intention to join with Sir John, or any one else.

TWIST: Moreover, I've heard a 'sponsible man

say, he could prove you were the cause of these new taxes.

WOU'DBE: Do you believe that too? or can you believe that it's in the power of any individual member to make a law himself? If a law is enacted that is displeasing to the people, it has the concurrence of the whole legislative body, and my vote for, or against it, is of little consequence.

GUZZLE: And what the devil good do you do then?

WOU'DBE: As much as I have abilities to do.

GUZZLE: Suppose, Mr. Wou'dbe, we were to want you to get the price of rum lower'd – wou'd you do it?

WOU'DBE: I cou'd not.

GUZZLE: Huzza for Sir John! he has promised to do it, huzza for Sir John!

TWIST: Suppose, Mr. Wou'dbe, we should want this tax taken off – cou'd you do it?

WOU'DBE: I could not.

TWIST: Huzza for Mr. Strutabout! he's damn'd, if he don't. Huzza for Mr. Strutabout!

STERN: Suppose, Mr. Wou'dbe, we that live over the river, should want to come to church on this side, is it not very hard we should pay ferryage; when we pay as much to the church as you do?

WOU'DBE: Very hard.

STERN: Suppose we were to petition the assembly could you get us clear of that expence?

WOU'DBE: I believe it to be just; and make no doubt but it would pass into a law.

STERN: Will you do it?

WOU'DBE: I will endeavour to do it.

STERN: Huzza for Mr. Wou'dbe! Wou'dbe forever!

PRIZE: Why don't you burgesses, do something with the damn'd pickers? If we have a hogshead of tobacco refused, away it goes to them; and after they have twisted up the best of it for their own use, and taken as much as will pay them for their trouble, the poor planter has little for his share.

WOU'DBE: There are great complaints against them; and I believe the assembly will take them under consideration.

PRIZE: Will you vote against them?

WOU'DBE: I will, if they deserve it.

PRIZE: Huzza for Mr. Wou'dbe! you shall go, old fellow; don't be afraid; I'll warrant it.

Exeunt severally; some huzzaing for Mr. *Wou'dbe – some for Sir John – some for Mr. Strutabout*

Scene 2

Another part of the field. Mr. Strutabout, Mr. Smallhopes, and a number of Freeholders round them.

1ST FREEHOLDER: Huzza for Mr. Strutabout!

2ND FREEHOLDER: Huzza for Mr. Smallhopes!

3RD FREEHOLDER: Huzza for Mr. Smallhopes and Mr. Strutabout!

4TH FREEHOLDER: Huzza for Mr. Strutabout and Mr. Smallhopes!

Exeunt, huzzaing. Enter Guzzle, drunk

GUZZLE: Huzza for Sir John Toddy, the cleverest gentleman – the finest gentleman that ever was. [*Hickuping*]

Enter Mrs. Guzzle, drunk

MRS. GUZZLE: Where's my drunken beast of a husband? [*Hickups*] Oh John Guzzle, Oh John Guzzle.

GUZZLE: What the devil do you want?

MRS. GUZZLE: Why don't you go home, you drunken beast? Lord bless me, how the gingerbread has given me the hickup.

GUZZLE: Why, Joan, you have made too – free with the bottle – I believe.

MRS. GUZZLE: I make free with the bottle – you drunken sot! – Well, well, the gingerbread has made me quite giddy.

GUZZLE: Hold up, Joan, don't fall – [*Mrs. Guzzle falls*] The devil, you will? Joan! Why woman, what's the matter? are you drunk?

MRS. GUZZLE: Drunk! you beast! No, quite sober; but very sick with eating gingerbread.

GUZZLE: For shame, Joan get up – [*Offers to help her up, and falls upon her*]

MRS. GUZZLE: Oh Lord! John! you've almost killed me.

GUZZLE: Not I – I'll get clear of you as fast as I can.

MRS. GUZZLE: Oh John, I shall die, I shall die.

GUZZLE: Very well, you'll die a pleasant death, then.

MRS. GUZZLE: Oh Lord! how sick! how sick!

GUZZLE: Oh Joan Guzzle! Oh Joan Guz-zle! – Why don't you go home, you drunken beast. Lord bless me, how the gingerbread has given me the hickup.

MRS. GUZZLE: Pray, my dear John, help me up.

GUZZLE: Pray, my dear Joan, get sober first.

MRS. GUZZLE: Pray John, help me up.

GUZZLE: Pray, Joan, go to sleep; and when I am as drunk as you, I'll come and take your place. Farewell, Joan. Huzza for Sir John Toddy! [*Exit huzzaing*]

Scene changes to another part of the field. Strutabout, Smallhopes and Freeholders

STRUTABOUT: Gentlemen – I'm much obliged to you for your good intentions; I make no doubt but (with the assistance of my friend Mr. Smallhopes) I shall be able to do every thing you have requested. Your grievances shall be redress'd; and all your petitions heard.

FREEHOLDERS: Huzza for Mr. Strutabout and Mr. Smallhopes!

Enter Mr. Wou'dbe

WOU'DBE: Gentlemen, your servant; you seem happy in a circle of your friends, I hope my company is not disagreeable.

STRUTABOUT: It can't be very agreeable to those you have treated so ill.

SMALLHOPES: You have used me ill, and all this company, by God –

WOU'DBE: If I have, Gentlemen, I am sorry for it; but it never was my intention to treat any person ungenteelly.

SMALLHOPES: You be damn'd; you're a turn-coat, by God.

WOU'DBE: Your abuse will never have any weight with me: neither do I regard your oaths or imprecations. In order to support a weak cause, you swear to what requires better proof than your assertions.

SMALLHOPES: Where's your friend, Sir John Toddy? he's a pretty fellow, an't he, and be damn'd to you; you recommend him to the people, don't you?

WOU'DBE: No, sir; I should be as blamable to recommend Sir John, as you, and your friend there [*Pointing to Strutabout*] in recommending one another.

STRUTABOUT: Sir, I am as capable of serving the people as yourself; and let me tell you, sir, my sole intention in offering myself is, that I may redress the many and heavy grievances you have imposed upon this poor county.

WOU'DBE: Poor, indeed, when you are believed, or when coxcombs and jockies can impose themselves upon it for men of learning.

1ST FREEHOLDER: Well, its no use; Mr. Wou'dbe is too hard for them both.

2ND FREEHOLDER: I think so too: why Strutabout! speak up, old fellow, or you'll lose ground.

STRUTABOUT: I'll lay you fifty pounds I'm elected before you.

WOU'DBE: Betting will not determine it; and therefore I shall not lay.

STRUTABOUT: I can lick you, Wou'dbe. [*Beginning to strip*]

WOU'DBE: You need not strip to do it; for you intend to do it with your tongue, I suppose.

SMALLHOPES: [*Clapping Strutabout upon the back*] Well done Strutabout, – you can do it, by God. Don't be afraid, you shan't be hurt; damn me if you shall. [*Strips*]

WOU'DBE: What! Gentlemen, do they who aspire to the first posts in our county, and who have ambition to become legislators, and to take upon themselves part of the guidance of the state, submit their naked bodies to public view, as if they were malefactors; or, for some crimes, condemned to the whipping-post?

SMALLHOPES: Come on, damn ye; and don't preach your damn'd proverbs here.

WOU'DBE: Are the candidates to fight for their seats in the house of burgesses? If so, perhaps I may stand as good a chance to succeed, as you.

SMALLHOPES: I can lick you, by God. Come on, if you dare – [*Capering about*]

1ST FREEHOLDER: Up to him – I'll stand by you. [*To Wou'dbe*]

2ND FREEHOLDER: They are not worth your notice, Mr. Wou'dbe; but if you have a mind to try yourself, I'll see fair play.

WOU'DBE: When I think they have sufficiently exposed themselves, I'll explain the opinion I have of them, with the end of my cane.

SMALLHOPES: Up to him, damn ye. [*Pushing Strutabout*]

STRUTABOUT: You need not push me, I can fight without being pushed to it; fight yourself, if you are so fond of it. [*Putting on his clothes*]

SMALLHOPES: Nay, if you are for that, and determined to be a coward, Mr. Strutabout, I can't help it; but damn me if I ever hack. [*Putting on his clothes*]

WOU'DBE: So you are both scared, gentlemen, without a blow, or an angry look! ha, ha, ha! Well, gentlemen, you have escaped a good caning, and though you are not fit for burgesses, you'll make good soldiers; for you are excellent at a retreat.

1ST FREEHOLDER: Huzza for Mr. Wou'dbe!

2ND FREEHOLDER: Huzza for Mr. Wou'dbe!

Enter Guzzle

GUZZLE: Huzza for Sir John Toddy! Toddy [*Hickups*] forever, boys!

Enter Sir John, drunk

GUZZLE: Here he comes – as fine [a] gentleman, tho' I say it, as the best of them.

SIR JOHN TODDY: So I am, John, as clever a fellow [*Hickups*] as the famous Mr. Wou'dbe, tho' I [*Hickups*] say it.

STRUTABOUT: There's a pretty fellow to be a burgess, gentlemen: lord, what a drunken beast it is.

SIR JOHN TODDY: What beast, pray? am I a beast?

STRUTABOUT: Yes, Sir John, you are a beast, and you may take the name of what beast you please; so your servant, my dear. [*Exeunt Strutabout and Smallhopes*]

WOU'DBE: Except an ass, Sir John, for that he's entitled to.

SIR JOHN TODDY: Thank you, sir.

WOU'DBE: A friend in need, Sir John, as the proverb says, is a friend indeed.

SIR JOHN TODDY: I thank you, I know you are my friend [*Hickups*] Mr. Wou'dbe, if you'd speak your mind – I know you are.

WOU'DBE: How do you know it, Sir John?

SIR JOHN TODDY: Did not you take my part just now, Mr. Wou'dbe? [*Hickups*] I know it.

WOU'DBE: I shall always take your part, Sir John, when you are imposed upon by a greater scoundrel than yourself, and when you pretend to what you are not fit for, I shall always oppose you.

SIR JOHN TODDY: Well, Mr. Wou'dbe, an't I as *fitten* a [*Hickups*] man as either of those?

WOU'DBE: More so, Sir John, for they are knaves, and you, Sir John, are an honest blockhead.

SIR JOHN TODDY: Is that in my favour, or not, John? [*To Guzzle*]

GUZZLE: In your favour, by all means; for [*Hickups*] he says you are honest. Huzza for Mr. Wou'dbe and the honest [*Hickups*] Sir John Blockhead.

Enter Ralpho – gives a letter to Wou'dbe

WOU'DBE: [*Reads*] – this is good news indeed.

1ST FREEHOLDER: Huzza for Mr. Wou'dbe!

2ND FREEHOLDER: Huzza for Mr. Wou'dbe!

GUZZLE: Huzza for the honest Sir John Block –

[*Hickups*] head.

WOU'DBE: Silence, gentlemen, and I'll read a letter to you, that (I don't doubt) will give you great pleasure. [*He reads*] *Sir, I have been informed that the scoundrels who opposed us last election (not content with my resignation) are endeavouring to undermine you in the good opinion of the people: It has warmed my blood, and again call'd my thoughts from retirement; speak this to the people, and let them know I intend to stand a poll, etc. Your's affectionately.*

WORTHY.

FREEHOLDERS: Huzza for Mr. Wou'dbe and Mr. Worthy!

SIR JOHN TODDY: Huzza for Mr. Worthy and Mr. Wou'dbe! [*Hickups*] I'm not so fitten as they, and therefore gentlemen I recline. [*Hickups*] Yes, gentlemen [*Staggering about*] I will; for I am not [*Hickups*] so fitten as they. [*Falls*]

GUZZLE: Huzza for the drunken Sir John Toddy. [*Hickups*]

SIR JOHN TODDY: Help me up John – do, John, help.

GUZZLE: No, Sir John, stay, and I'll fetch my wife, Joan, and lay – her along side of you. [*Exit*]

WOU'DBE: Ralpho.

RALPHO: Sir.

WOU'DBE: Take care of Sir John, least any accident should befall him.

RALPHO: Yes, sir. [*Exeunt Wou'dbe and Freeholders, huzzaing for Wou'dbe and Worthy*]

Enter Guzzle, with his wife in his arms

GUZZLE: Here, Sir John, here's my wife fast asleep, to keep you company, and as drunk as a sow. [*Throws her upon Sir John, and returns to one side*]

SIR JOHN TODDY: Oh Lord! You've broke my bones.

JOAN: [*Waking*] John! John! [*Punching Sir John*] get up; [*Looking round, sees Sir John*] what have we here? Lord, what would our John give to know this? He would have reason to be jealous of me, then!

Enter Guzzle

GUZZLE: Well, Joan, are you sober?

JOAN: [*Getting up*] How came that man to be lying with me? Its some of your doings, I'm sure; that you may have an excuse to be jealous of me.

GUZZLE: I want no excuse for that, child.

JOAN: What brought him there?

GUZZLE: The same that brought you, child; rum, sugar, and water.

JOAN: Well, well, as I live, I thought it was you, and that we were in our own clean sweet bed. Lord! how I tremble for fear he should have done what you do, sometimes, John.

GUZZLE: I never do any thing when I am drunk. Sir John and you have done more than that, I believe.

JOAN: Don't be jealous, John; it will ruin us both.

GUZZLE: I am very jealous of that.

JOAN: If you are, I'll beat the cruel beast that is the cause of it, 'till he satisfies you I am innocent.

GUZZLE: Don't, Joan, it will make me more jealous.

JOAN: I will, I tell you I will. [*Beats Sir John, who all the time cries murder, help, help!*]

RALPHO: Stop, madam, this gentleman is in my care; and you must not abuse him.

MRS. GUZZLE: I will, and you too, you rascal. [*Beats him first, and then Sir John*]

RALPHO: Peace, stop, madam, peace, peace.

SIR JOHN TODDY: Oh lord! help, John, for God's sake, help.

RALPHO: Do as you please, madam, do as you please. [*Runs off*]

JOAN: [*Beating Sir John*] I'll learn you to cuckold a man without letting his wife know it.

SIR JOHN TODDY: Help, murder! help.

GUZZLE: [*Taking hold of Joan*] Stop, Joan, I'm satisfied – quite satisfied.

JOAN: What fellow is it?

GUZZLE: Sir John Toddy, our good friend; Oh, Joan, you should not have beat poor Sir John, he is as drunk as you and I were, Joan. Oh! poor Sir John. [*Cries*]

JOAN: Good lack, why didn't you tell me? I would have struck you as soon as him, John. Don't be angry, good Sir John, I did not know you.

SIR JOHN TODDY: It's well enough: help me out of the mire, neighbours, and I'll forget and forgive.

GUZZLE: Yes, Sir John, and so we will. [*They help him up*] Come, Sir John, let's go home, this is no place for us: come Joan. [*Exeunt Guzzle and Joan, supporting Sir John*]

Scene 3

Another part of the field. Enter Wou'dbe and Ralpho.

WOU'DBE: Where's Sir John?

RALPHO: In the hands of a woman, sir, and as I left him in such good hands, I thought there was no farther occasion for my attendance.

WOU'DBE: Are you sure he'll be taken care of?

RALPHO: Yes, the lady, an't please your honour, seemed devilish kind to him.

WOU'DBE: See that you have all ready; its high time we thought of going home, if we intend there to-night.

RALPHO: All shall be ready, sir. [*Exit Ralpho*]

WOU'DBE: Well, I've felt the pulse of all the leading men, and find they beat still for Worthy, and myself. Strutabout and Smallhopes fawn and cringe in so abject a manner, for the few votes they get, that I'm in hopes they'll be soon heartily despised.

The prudent candidate who hopes to rise,
Ne'er deigns to hide it, in a mean disguise.
Will, to his place, with moderation slide,
And win his way, or not resist the tide.
The fool, aspiring to bright honour's post,
In noise, in shouts, and tumults oft, is lost.

[*Exit*]

End of the Second Act

ACT III. Scene 1

Wou'dbe's house. Enter Wou'dbe and Worthy.

WOU'DBE: Nothing could have afforded me more pleasure than your letter; I read it to the people, and can with pleasure assure you, it gave them infinite satisfaction.

WORTHY: My sole motive in declaring myself was to serve you, and if I am the means of your gaining your election with honour, I shall be satisfied.

WOU'DBE: You have always been extremely kind, sir, but I could not enjoy the success I promised myself, without your participation.

WORTHY: I have little inclination to the service; you know my aversion to public life, Wou'dbe, and how little I have ever courted the people for the troublesome office they have hitherto imposed upon me.

WOU'DBE: I believe you enjoy as much domestic happiness as any person, and that your aversion to a public life proceeds from the pleasure you find at home. But, sir, it surely is the duty of every man who has abilities to serve his country, to take up the burden, and bear it with patience.

WORTHY: I know it is needless to argue with you upon this head: you are determined I shall serve with you, I find.

WOU'DBE: I am; and therefore let's take the properest methods to insure success.

WORTHY: What would you propose?

WOU'DBE: Nothing more than for you to shew yourself to the people.

WORTHY: I'll attend you where ever you please.

WOU'DBE: To-morrow being the day of election, I have invited most of the principal freeholders to breakfast with me, in their way to the court-house, I hope you'll favour us with your company.

WORTHY: I will; till then, adieu. [*Exit Worthy*]

WOU'DBE: I shall expect you. It would give me great pleasure if Worthy would be more anxious than he appears to be upon this occasion; conscious of his abilities and worth, he scorns to ask a vote for any person but me; well, I must turn the tables on him, and solicit as strongly in his favour.

'Tis said self-interest is the secret aim,
Of those uniting under Friendship's name.
How true this maxim is, let others prove –
Myself I'd punish for the man I love.

[*Exit Wou'dbe*]

Scene 2

Mr. Julip's house. Enter Captain Paunch and Mr. Julip.

CAPTAIN PAUNCH: Well, neighbour, I have come to see you on purpose to know how votes went at the treat yesterday.

JULIP: I was not there; but I've seen neighbour Guzzle this morning, and he says, Sir John gives the matter up to Mr. Worthy and Mr. Wou'dbe.

CAPTAIN PAUNCH: Mr. Worthy! does he declare, huzza, my boys! well, I'm proud our county may choose two without being obliged to have one of those jackanapes at the head of it, faith: Who are you for now, neighbour?

JULIP: I believe I shall vote for the two old ones, and tho' I said I was for Sir John, it was be-

cause I lik'd neither of the others; but since Mr. Worthy will serve us, why, to be sartin its our duty to send Wou'dbe and him.

CAPTAIN PAUNCH: Hah, faith, now you speak like a man; you are a man after my own heart: give me your hand.

JULIP: Here it is, Wou'dbe and Worthy, I say.

CAPTAIN PAUNCH: Done, but who comes yonder? surely, it's not Mr. Worthy! 'Tis, I declare.

Enter Mr. Worthy

WORTHY: Gentlemen, your servant, I hope your families are well.

CAPTAIN PAUNCH: At your service, sir.

WORTHY: I need not, I suppose, gentlemen, inform you that I have entered the list with my old competitors, and have determined to stand a poll at the next election. If you were in the crowd yesterday, my friend Wou'dbe, I doubt not, made a declaration of my intentions to the people.

CAPTAIN PAUNCH: We know it, thank heaven, Mr. Worthy, tho' neither of us were there: as I did not like some of the candidates I did not choose to be persecuted for a vote that I was resolved never to bestow upon them.

JULIP: My rule is never to taste of a man's liquor unless I'm his friend, and therefore, I stay'd at home.

WORTHY: Well, my honest friend, I am proud to find that you still preserve your usual independence. Is it possible Captain, that the people can be so misled, as to reject Wou'dbe, and elect Strutabout in his room?

CAPTAIN PAUNCH: You know, Mr. Worthy, how it is, as long as the liquor is running, so long they'll be Mr. Strutabout's friends, but when the day comes, I'm thinking it will be another case.

WORTHY: I'm sorry, my countymen, for the sake of a little toddy, can be induced to behave in a manner so contradictory to the candour and integrity which always should prevail among mankind.

CAPTAIN PAUNCH: It's so, sir, you may depend upon it.

JULIP: I'm thinking it is.

WORTHY: Well, gentlemen, will you give me leave to ask you, how far you think my declaring will be of service to Mr. Wou'dbe?

CAPTAIN PAUNCH: Your declaring has already silenced Sir John Toddy; and I doubt not, but

Strutabout and Smallhopes will lose many votes by it.

WORTHY: Has Sir John declined? poor Sir John is a weak man, but he has more virtues to recommend him than either of the others.

JULIP: So I think, Mr. Worthy, and I'll be so bold as to tell you that, had you not set up, Mr. Wou'dbe and Sir John should have had my vote.

WORTHY: Was I a constituent, instead of a candidate, I should do the same.

JULIP: Well, captain, you see I was not so much to blame.

CAPTAIN PAUNCH: Sir John may be honest, but he is no fitter for that place than myself.

JULIP: Suppose he was not, if he was the best that offered to serve us, should not we choose him?

WORTHY: Yes, surely: Well, my friends, I'm now on my way, to breakfast at Mr. Wou'dbe's, but I hope to meet you at the court-house today.

BOTH: Aye, aye, depend upon us. [*Exit Worthy*]

CAPTAIN PAUNCH: Well, neighbour, I hope things now go on better; I like the present appearance.

JULIP: So do I.

CAPTAIN PAUNCH: Do all you can, old fellow.

JULIP: I will.

CAPTAIN PAUNCH: I hope you will, neighbour. I wish you well.

JULIP: You the same. [*Shake hands, and exeunt*]

Scene 3

Wou'dbe's house, a long breakfast table set out. Wou'dbe, Worthy, Captain Paunch, Mr. Julip, Twist, Stern, Prize and other Freeholders; several negroes go backwards and forwards, bringing in the breakfast.

1ST FREEHOLDER: Give us your hand, neighbour Worthy, I'm extremely glad to see thee with all my heart: So my heart of oak, you are willing to give your time and trouble once more to the service of your country.

WORTHY: Your kindness does me honour, and if my labours be productive of good to my country, I shall deem myself fortunate.

2ND FREEHOLDER: Still the same sensible man I always thought him. Damn it, now if every county cou'd but send such a burgess, what a noble house we should have?

3RD FREEHOLDER: We shall have no polling now, but all will be for the same, I believe. Here's neighbour Twist, who was resolute for Strutabout, I don't doubt, will vote for Mr. Worthy and Mr. Wou'dbe.

TWIST: Yes, that I will: what could I do better?

ALL: Aye, so will we all.

WOU'DBE: Gentlemen, for your forwardness in favour of my good friend Worthy, my sincere thanks are but a poor expression in the pleasure I feel. For my part, your esteem I shall always attribute more to his than my own desert. But come, let us sit down to breakfast, all is ready I believe; and you're heartily welcome to batchelors quarters. [*They all sit down to the table, he asks each of the company which they prefer, coffee, tea, or chocolate, and each chooses to his liking; he pours out, and the servants carry it around*]

WORTHY: Gentlemen, will any of you have a part of this fine salt shad? [*They answer, yes, if you please; and he helps them*]

CAPTAIN PAUNCH: This warm toast and butter is very fine, and the shad gives it an excellent flavour.

MR. JULIP: Boy, give me the spirit. This chocolate, me thinks, wants a little lacing to make it admirable. [*The servants bring it*]

PRIZE: Mr. Wou'dbe, do your fishing places succeed well this year?

WOU'DBE: Better than they've been known for some seasons.

STERN: I'm very glad of it: for then I can get my supply from you.

MR. JULIP: Neighbour Stalk, how do crops stand with you?

1ST FREEHOLDER: Indifferently well, I thank you; how are you?

MR. JULIP: Oh, very well! we crop it gloriously.

WOU'DBE: You have not breakfasted yet, neighbour, give me leave to help you to another dish.

2ND FREEHOLDER: Thank ye, sir, but enough's as good as a feast.

CAPTAIN PAUNCH: [*Looking at his watch*] I'm afraid we shall be late, they ought to have begun before now.

WOU'DBE: Our horses are at the gate, and we have not far to go.

FREEHOLDERS ALL: Very well, we've all breakfasted. [*They rise from table and the servants take away*]

IST FREEHOLDER: Come along, my friends, I long to see your triumph. Huzza for Wou'dbe and Worthy! [*Exit huzzaing*]

Scene 4

The Court-house yard. The door open, and a number of Freeholders seen crowding within.

IST FREEHOLDER: [*To a Freeholder coming out of the house*] How do votes go, neighbour? for Wou'dbe and Worthy?

2ND FREEHOLDER: Aye, aye, they're just come, and sit upon the bench, and yet all the votes are for them. 'Tis quite a hollow thing. The poll will be soon over. The People crowd so much, and vote so fast, you can hardly turn around.

IST FREEHOLDER: How do Strutabout and Smallhopes look? very doleful, I reckon.

2ND FREEHOLDER: Like a thief under the gallows.

3RD FREEHOLDER: There you must be mistaken, neighbour; for two can't be like one.

IST & 2ND FREEHOLDERS: Ha, ha, ha, – a good joke, a good joke.

3RD FREEHOLDER: Not so good neither, when the subject made it so easy.

IST & 2ND FREEHOLDERS: Better and better, ha, ha, ha. Huzza for Worthy and Wou'dbe! and confusion to Strutabout and Smallhopes.

Enter Guzzle

GUZZLE: Huzza for Wou'dbe and Worthy! and huzza for Sir John Toddy! tho' he reclines.

IST FREEHOLDER: So Guzzle, your friend Sir John reclines, does he? I think he does right.

GUZZLE: You think he does right! pray sir, what right have you to think about it? nobody but a fool would kick a fallen man lower.

IST FREEHOLDER: Sir, I won't be called a fool by any man, I'll have you to know, sir.

GUZZLE: Then you oughtn't to be one; but here's at ye, adrat ye, if ye're for a quarrel. Sir John Toddy would have stood a good chance, and I'll maintain it, come on, damn ye.

IST FREEHOLDER: Oh! as for fighting, there I'm your servant; a drunkard is as bad to fight as a madman. [*Runs off*]

GUZZLE: Houroa, houroa, you see no body so good at a battle as a staunch toper. The milk-

sops are afraid of them to a man.

3RD FREEHOLDER: You knew he was a coward before you thought proper to attack him; if you think yourself so brave, try your hand upon me, and you'll find you're mistaken.

GUZZLE: For the matter of that, I'm the best judge myself; good day, my dear, good day. Huzza, for Sir John Toddy. [*Exit*]

3RD FREEHOLDER: How weak must Sir John be to be governed by such a wretch as Guzzle!

The Sheriff comes to the door, and says, Gentlemen freeholders, come into court, and give your votes, or the poll will be closed.

FREEHOLDERS: We've all voted.

SHERIFF: The poll's closed. Mr. Wou'dbe and Mr. Worthy are elected.

FREEHOLDERS *without and within.* Huzza – huzza! Wou'dbe and Worthy for ever, boys, bring 'em on, bring 'em on, Wou'dbe and Worthy for ever!

Enter Wou'dbe and Worthy, in two chairs, raised aloft by the Freeholders

FREEHOLDERS ALL: – Huzza, for Wou'dbe and Worthy – Huzza for Wou'dbe and Worthy – huzza, for Wou'dbe and Worthy! – [*They traverse the stage, and then set them down*]

WORTHY: Gentlemen, I'm much obliged to you for the signal proof you have given me to-day of your regard. You may depend upon it, that I shall endeavour faithfully to discharge the trust you have reposed in me.

WOU'DBE: I have not only, gentlemen, to return you my hearty thanks for the favours you have conferred upon me, but I beg leave also to thank you for shewing such regard to the merit of my friend. You have in that, shewn your judgment, and a spirit of independence becoming Virginians.

CAPTAIN PAUNCH: So we have Mr. Wou'dbe, we have done as we ought, we have elected the ablest, according to the writ.

Henceforth, let those who pray for wholesome laws,
And all well-wishers to their country's cause,
Like us refuse a coxcomb – choose a man –
Then let our senate blunder if it can.

[*Exit omnes*]

End of THE CANDIDATES

THE CONTRAST

ROYALL TYLER

With *The Contrast* "we arrive at the commencement of the American drama as united with the American theatre." Although in strict fact this appraisal by William Dunlap in his *History of the American Theatre* may be questionable, in spirit it is essentially true. As to fact, certainly *The Contrast* was the first wholly successful American play performed by professional actors. And the judgment, if not the language, of the *Independent Journal* after the third performance on May 5, 1787, coincides with twentieth-century opinion: "When the disadvantage under which I hear this piece has been produced is considered, candour must allow its being an extraordinary effort of genius . . . and it must give sincere satisfaction to every lover of his country, to find that this, the most difficult of all the works of human genius, has been attempted with such success."

Like so many of the later American dramatists, Tyler was not a professional playwright or even a professional writer but, like Colonel Munford and many succeeding playwrights, a distinguished citizen and a respected and accomplished professional man. In 1803, at the peak of his legal career, he was appointed Chief Justice of the Supreme Court of the State of Vermont.

Royall Tyler was born in Boston, in the vicinity of Faneuil Hall, in July, 1757. His father was a prosperous merchant and a member of the King's Council in Boston. When young Tyler graduated from Harvard in 1776 as valedictorian of his class, Yale perceived a future worthy son and also gave him a degree. After college Tyler studied law with John Adams in Braintree (later Quincy), Massachusetts, and in 1779 he began his practice in Falmouth, Maine. In 1782 he was back in Braintree and more intimately involved with the Adams family, courting their seventeen-year-old daughter, Abigail, or "Nabby," as she was commonly known. Mrs. Adams alerted her husband in France to the prospects of this developing romance. Although she spoke of Tyler's "attainments in literature," she also alluded to his "dissipation of too much of his fortune." John Adams replied immediately, "I don't like the subject at all. My child is too young for such thoughts. I am not looking out for a Poet, not a Professor of belle letters." In spite of the family's objections, Tyler continued his pursuit; apparently his affection did not waver during the spring of 1783, when Abigail was sent off to Boston. He was diligent in his profession and by December was able to purchase one of the finest houses in Braintree. Finally, John Adams reluctantly consented to an engagement, but with the proviso that Mrs. Adams and Abigail should join him in Europe in June of 1784. His scheme was successful. Although the young couple continued to correspond during the first few months, the romance finally disintegrated and in June, 1786, Abigail was married to Colonel William Smith, secretary of the American Legation in London.

Tyler saw active military service in the Revolution and in the suppression of Shays' Rebellion as aide-de-camp to General Benjamin Lincoln. After several years of successful practice as a trial lawyer, he became Vermont state's attorney in 1796, judge of the Supreme Court in 1801, and finally chief justice in 1803. After eight years on the bench, he retired. For a year he was professor of law at the University of Vermont, and in 1812 he resumed private practice in Brattleboro. When he was thirty-five, he had married Mary Palmer, a cousin of the Adamses. One wonders how they managed with their eleven children on the nine hundred dollars (one thousand as chief justice) he received while he was on the bench. Part of the explanation may be found in Tyler's sense of humor and friendly spirit. Twice every year Tyler journeyed over the entire state of Vermont holding court. These were happy journeys. He was respected and liked by all who knew him, and practically everybody knew him. As Pliny H. White said, "He had a good presence, a copious flow of words, and a voice as clear and musical as a flute, wit that never failed him and sometimes accomplished what law, evidence, and logic could not do." His rich personal endowments were of little consequence during the last years of his life. He was afflicted with cancer of the face and died from this disease on August 16, 1826.

Because they were often published anonymously, Tyler's literary efforts were not widely known during his lifetime. His small bits of witticism and social comment, particularly, were widely circulated. On the subject of slavery, for example, he suggested that the only justification he was willing to accept was "a quitclaim deed of ownership from the Almighty." In one of his pamphlet columns he projected a comic grammar in which "a lady crowned her favored lover's virtuous wishes in the passive voice, and dismissed an unsuccessful admirer in the imperative mood."

Tyler never regarded himself as a professional writer even though he was a regular contributor to a variety of newspapers and periodicals. As part of the literary "firm" of Colon and Spondee – "wholesale dealers in verse, prose and music" – his verses, songs, epigrams, and essays, on all subjects, flowed spontaneously and regularly to the pages of the *Farmers' Museum* (Walpole, New Hampshire), the *Portfolio* (Philadelphia), and many other journals. Nor were these his only literary efforts; a month after the opening of *The Contrast*, his comic opera *May Day in Town, or New York in an Uproar* was performed for Thomas Wignell's benefit at the John Street Theatre (May 19, 1787). Although generally regarded as an insignificant piece, it did provoke appreciative comment from Congressman Grayson. He wrote to James Madison:

Dear Sir, We have lately had a new farce, wrote by Poet Tyler called *May Day*. It has plot and incident and is as good as several of the English farces. It has, however, not succeeded well, owing I believe to the author's making his principal character a scold. New York ladies were alarmed for fear strangers should look upon Mrs. Sanders (the shrew of the piece) as the model of the gentlewomen of the place.

His only other acted play, *The Georgia Spec., or Land in the Moon*, a satire on land speculation, was produced by his brother Colonel John Tyler, manager of the Boston Theatre. *The Columbian Centinel* of October 28, 1797, praised it for containing "a rich diversity of national character and native humor."

Other plays by Tyler were *The Female Duellists*, a farce; *The Doctor in Spite of Himself*, an adaptation of Molière; *The Island of Barrataria*, a farce; *The Origin of the Feast of Purim*, a sacred drama in three acts taken principally from the Book of Esther; *Joseph and His Brethren*, a sacred drama; and *The Judgement of Solomon*, a sacred drama. The last four appear in Volume XV of *America's Lost Plays*.

Excepting *The Contrast*, Tyler's principal claim to literary fame rests with the anonymously published *The Algerine Captive, or The Life and Adventures of Dr. Updike Underhill*, the first American novel to be republished in England. Initially printed in this country in 1797, it was brought out in England in 1802, and in 1804 ran serially in the British periodical *The Lady's Magazine*. Although it began as a fictitious memoir of Yankee life, it developed into an exciting account of adventure among the Algerine pirates. The simple force of the diction, not unlike the style of Defoe, gave it the quality of factual narrative rather than fiction. Tyler's talent as a humorist reached its mature expression in a series of fictitious letters called *The Yankey in London* (1809). One story from these letters will illustrate the quality: An Englishman found our clear American air unbearable. To relieve his distress he went into a blacksmith shop, closed all the doors and the aperture of the chimney, built a fire of damp earth coal, and then boasted that "he had recruited his spirits by a very excellent imitation of the London atmosphere."

One-hundred-per-cent Americanism combined with an ever-ready ear for the humorous episode or expression characterized most of Tyler's writing. The program for *The Contrast* at the Charleston Theatre, on February 25, 1793, carried the subtitle *The American Son of Liberty* and the author credit "written by Major Tyler, a citizen of the United States." After the first performance of the play in New York on April 16, 1787, a newspaper critic wrote, "The sentiments of the play are the effusions of an honest patriot heart. . . . The repeated bursts of applause gave the most unequivocal proof of its possessing the true requisites of comedy in a very great degree. Merit with novelty forces applause." John Lauber, a present-day critic, has suggested that in endowing Manly with an American simplicity of manner and moral innocence, Tyler went at least halfway toward the creation of an "American Adam" (R. W. B. Lewis's phrase), "a figure of heroic innocence and vast potentialities, poised at the start of a new history."

Only a few of the circumstantial facts attending the writing of *The Contrast* are known. In March, 1787, Tyler made his first trip to New York and attended a performance of *The School for Scandal* at the John Street Theatre. Although this was his first time at a regular theatre, he had undoubtedly read a number of eighteenth-century English plays. Without stretching the internal evidence unduly, various critics have discovered echoes of *The Rivals, The Conscious Lovers, The Poor Soldier, False Delicacy*, and half a dozen other eighteenth-century plays. Tyler may not have had an opportunity to see the drama vitalized in the theatre, but he was certainly not unfamiliar with it in the library.

Within a month after his visit to New York, he delivered the finished copy of *The Contrast* to the John Street manager, Thomas Wignell, and on April 16 the play had its first performance. Two days before the opening, a skeptical critic wrote: "I wait with impatience for the new comedy, for I believe it will supply a great deal of game." Tyler may have shared the critic's doubts. He did not allow the family name to be connected with this risky theatrical experiment. It was billed simply as by a "citizen of the United States."

Tyler's hesitancy was unwarranted. The play had five successive performances that spring at the John Street Theatre, followed by productions in Philadelphia, Baltimore, Boston, Alexandria, and Charleston. In Boston it was announced as a "moral lecture." A record of twenty performances from April 16, 1787, in New York to June 27, 1796, in Philadelphia was a distinguished run for the last decade of the eighteenth century. There are hints of a number of other performances and some intimations that theatrical jealousies among the players may have reduced the number of performances in Baltimore and Philadelphia. Lewis Hallam as Dimple and John Henry as Manly apparently felt that Thomas Wignell as Jonathan, the first "stage Yankee," commanded too much attention. When the company played in Baltimore, Henry refused to appear as Manly; and in Philadelphia, Wignell explained the indisposition of his actors with the theatrical euphemism that the "production was impracticable." Unable to give a regular performance and conscious of his own success in the play, Wignell gave a public reading at the City Tavern in Philadelphia on December 10, 1787.

After the initial performance in New York, Tyler had assigned the copyright to Wignell, who thereupon announced in various newspaper advertisements that "he solicits the patronage and assistance that are necessary to enable him to print and embellish this work in a form suitable to its intrinsic merit." When the play was printed in 1790, with the drawing by William Dunlap as frontispiece, the list of 658 subscribers was headed by President Washington, followed by Henry Knox, Secretary of War, and Edmund Randolph, Attorney General. Almost half the copies were distributed in Maryland and the remainder in New York, Virginia, South Carolina, Massachusetts, Jamaica (twenty copies), and London (five copies). There would seem to be little justification for Dunlap's comment that "it was coldly received in the closet."

Critical opinion at the time of the first performances was extremely favorable. The *Pennsylvania Journal* said, "He deserves the warmest approbation of his country, and particularly the applauses of the fair, for exhibiting in such true colors the pernicious maxims of the Chesterfieldian system, of all others the most dangerous to the peace of society." The *Daily Advertiser* (New York) praised it as "certainly the production of a man of genius. . . . The characters are drawn with spirit, particularly Charlotte's; the dialogue is easy, sprightly, and often witty. . . ." and the *Pennsylvania Herald*, "These blossoms of the comic muse wear every mark of vigor and are an additional specimen in proof that these new climes are particularly favorable to the cultivation of arts and sciences." Even Dunlap, after mentioning the deficiencies of plot and dialogue, found in the character of Jonathan, as "played by Wignell, a degree of humour and knowledge of what is termed Yankee dialect, which, in the hands of a favourite performer, was relished by an audience gratified by the appearance of home manufacture."

Present-day evaluation focuses on many of the same qualities, if with somewhat different emphasis. Even though many of the heroic speeches may now seem grandiloquent and the indebtedness to *The School for Scandal* may appear too pronounced (Odell feels that "Sheridan is at least twenty miles away"), one is still impressed by the force and conviction of the honest, common-sense praise of native American quality and sentiment expressed by a distinguished American citizen. The caricature of the would-be Lord Chesterfield plainly indicates the attitude of Tyler and his fellow Americans toward England and English society. And the sympathetic portrayal of Jonathan, with his solid native integrity and common sense, reflects an honest belief in the social product of "home manufacture." Jonathan was further distinguished as the first of a long line of "stage Yankees" (see *The Forest Rose*), and his description of his unwitting visit to the theatre provides as clear a picture of the late-eighteenth-century American playhouse as exists in our theatre annals. It is not unreasonable to assume that Tyler attended the John Street Theatre on March 21, 1787, when both *The School for Scandal* and *The*

Poor Soldier were performed, and that Jonathan's report is essentially an autobiographical account of Tyler's initiation to the theatre.

Here is the first comedy of American manners with an authentic rendering of current tastes, sentiments, dress, and morals, combined with a heroic espousal of national unity and the native and unequivocal worth of American culture.

THE CONTRAST

R O Y A L L   T Y L E R

CHARACTERS

COLONEL MANLY	CHARLOTTE
DIMPLE	MARIA
VAN ROUGH	LETITIA
JESSAMY	JENNY
JONATHAN	SERVANTS

PROLOGUE
*Written by a young gentleman of New York,
and spoken by Mr. Wignell*

Exult, each patriot heart! – this night is shewn
A piece, which we may fairly call our own;
Where the proud titles of "My Lord! Your
　Grace!"
To humble *Mr.* and plain *Sir* give place.
Our Author pictures not from foreign climes
The fashions or the follies of the times;
But has confin'd the subject of his work
To the gay scenes – the circles of New-York.
On native themes his Muse displays her pow'rs;
If ours the faults, the virtues too are ours.
Why should our thoughts to distant countries
　roam,
When each refinement may be found at home?
Who travels now to ape the rich or great,
To deck an equipage and roll in state;
To court the graces, or to dance with ease,
Or by hypocrisy to strive to please?
Our free-born ancestors such arts despis'd;
Genuine sincerity alone they priz'd;
Their minds, with honest emulation fir'd;
To solid good – not ornament – aspir'd;
Or, if ambition rous'd a bolder flame,
Stern virtue throve, where indolence was
　shame.

But modern youths, with imitative sense,
Deem taste in dress the proof of excellence;
And spurn the meanness of your homespun
　arts,
Since homespun habits would obscure their
　parts;
Whilst all, which aims at splendour and pa-
　rade,
Must come from Europe, *and be ready made.*
Strange! we should thus our native worth dis-
　claim,
And check the progress of our rising fame.
Yet *one*, whilst imitation bears the sway,
Aspires to nobler heights, and points the way.
Be rous'd, my friends! his bold example view;
Let your own Bards be proud to copy *you!*
Should rigid critics reprobate our play,
At least the patriotic heart will say,
"Glorious our fall, since in a noble cause.
"The bold *attempt alone* demands applause."
Still may the wisdom of the Comic Muse
Exalt your merits, or your faults accuse.
But think not, 'tis her aim to be severe: –
We all are mortals, and as mortals err.
If candour pleases, we are truly blest;
Vice trembles, when compell'd to stand con-
　fess'd.
Let not light Censure on your faults offend,
Which aims not to expose them, but amend.
Thus does our Author to your candour trust;
Conscious, the *free* are generous, as just.

ACT I

*Scene, New York. An apartment at Charlotte's.
Charlotte and Letitia discovered.*

LETITIA: And so, Charlotte, you really think the
pockethoop unbecoming.

CHARLOTTE: No, I don't say so. It may be very
becoming to saunter round the house of a rainy
day; to visit my grandmamma, or to go to
Quakers' meeting; but to swim in a minuet,
with the eyes of fifty well-dressed beaux upon

me, to trip it in the Mall, or walk on the battery, give me the luxurious, jaunty, flowing, bellhoop. It would have delighted you to have seen me the last evening, my charming girl! I was dangling o'er the battery with Billy Dimple; a knot of young fellows were upon the platform; as I passed them I faultered with one of the most bewitching false steps you ever saw, and then recovered myself with such a pretty confusion, flirting my hoop to discover a jet black shoe and brilliant buckle. Gad! how my little heart thrilled to hear the confused raptures of – *"Demme, Jack, what a delicate foot!" "Ha! General, what a well-turned——"*

LETITIA: Fie! fie! Charlotte [*Stopping her mouth*], I protest you are quite a libertine.

CHARLOTTE: Why, my dear little prude, are we not all such libertines? Do you think, when I sat tortured two hours under the hands of my friseur, and an hour more at my toilet, that I had any thoughts of my aunt Susan, or my cousin Betsey? though they are both allowed to be critical judges of dress.

LETITIA: Why, who should we dress to please, but those who are judges of its merit?

CHARLOTTE: Why, a creature who does not know *Buffon* from *Souflee* – Man! – my Letitia – Man! for whom we dress, walk, dance, talk, lisp, languish, and smile. Does not the grave Spectator assure us that even our much be-praised diffidence, modesty, and blushes are all directed to make ourselves good wives and mothers as fast as we can? Why, I'll undertake with one flirt of this hoop to bring more beaux to my feet in one week than the grave Maria, and her sentimental circle, can do, by sighing sentiment till their hairs are grey.

LETITIA: Well, I won't argue with you; you always outtalk me; let us change the subject. I hear that Mr. Dimple and Maria are soon to be married.

CHARLOTTE: You hear true. I was consulted in the choice of the wedding clothes. She is to be married in a delicate white sattin, and has a monstrous pretty brocaded lute string for the second day. It would have done you good to have seen with what an affected indifference the dear sentimentalist turned over a thousand pretty things, just as if her heart did not palpitate with her approaching happiness, and at last made her choice and arranged her dress with such apathy as if she did not know that plain white sattin and a simple blond lace

would shew her clear skin and dark hair to the greatest advantage.

LETITIA: But they say her indifference to dress, and even to the gentleman himself, is not entirely affected.

CHARLOTTE: How?

LETITIA: It is whispered that if Maria gives her hand to Mr. Dimple, it will be without her heart.

CHARLOTTE: Though the giving the heart is one of the last of all laughable considerations in the marriage of a girl of spirit, yet I should like to hear what antiquated notions the dear little piece of old-fashioned prudery has got in her head.

LETITIA: Why, you know that old Mr. John-Richard-Robert-Jacob-Isaac-Abraham-Cornelius Van Dumpling, Billy Dimple's father (for he has thought fit to soften his name, as well as manners, during his English tour), was the most intimate friend of Maria's father. The old folks, about a year before Mr. Van Dumpling's death, proposed this match: the young folks were accordingly introduced, and told they must love one another. Billy was then a good-natured, decent-dressing young fellow, with a little dash of the coxcomb, such as our young fellows of fortune usually have. At this time, I really believe she thought she loved him; and had they then been married, I doubt not they might have jogged on, to the end of the chapter, a good kind of a sing-song lack-a-daysaical life, as other honest married folks do.

CHARLOTTE: Why did they not then marry?

LETITIA: Upon the death of his father, Billy went to England to see the world and rub off a little of the patroon rust. During his absence, Maria, like a good girl, to keep herself constant to her *nown true-love*, avoided company, and betook herself, for her amusement, to her books, and her dear Billy's letters. But, alas! how many ways has the mischievous demon of inconstancy of stealing into a woman's heart! Her love was destroyed by the very means she took to support it.

CHARLOTTE: How? – Oh! I have it – some likely young beau found the way to her study.

LETITIA: Be patient, Charlotte; your head so runs upon beaux. Why, she read Sir Charles Grandison, Clarissa Harlow, Shenstone, and the Sentimental Journey; and between whiles, as I said, Billy's letters. But, as her taste improved, her love declined. The contrast was so striking betwixt the good sense of her books and the flimsiness of her love-letters, that she discovered she had unthinkingly engaged her hand without her heart; and then the whole transaction, managed by the old folks, now appeared so unsentimental, and looked so like bargaining for a bale of goods, that she found she ought to have rejected, according to every rule of romance, even the man of her choice, if imposed upon her in that manner. Clary Harlow would have scorned such a match.

CHARLOTTE: Well, how was it on Mr. Dimple's return? Did he meet a more favourable reception than his letters?

LETITIA: Much the same. She spoke of him with respect abroad, and with contempt in her closet. She watched his conduct and conversation, and found that he had by travelling acquired the wickedness of Lovelace without his wit, and the politeness of Sir Charles Grandison without his generosity. The ruddy youth, who washed his face at the cistern every morning, and swore and looked eternal love and constancy, was now metamorphosed into a flippant, palid, polite beau, who devotes the morning to his toilet, reads a few pages of Chesterfield's letters, and then minces out, to put the infamous principles in practice upon every woman he meets.

CHARLOTTE: But, if she is so apt at conjuring up these sentimental bugbears, why does she not discard him at once?

LETITIA: Why, she thinks her word too sacred to be trifled with. Besides, her father, who has a great respect for the memory of his deceased friend, is ever telling her how he shall renew his years in their union, and repeating the dying injunctions of old Van Dumpling.

CHARLOTTE: A mighty pretty story! And so you would make me believe that the sensible Maria would give up Dumpling manor, and the all-accomplished Dimple as a husband, for the absurd, ridiculous reason, forsooth, because she despises and abhors him. Just as if a lady could not be privileged to spend a man's fortune, ride in his carriage, be called after his name, and call him her *nown dear lovee* when she wants money, without loving and respecting the great he-creature. Oh! my dear girl, you are a monstrous prude.

LETITIA: I don't say what I would do; I only intimate how I suppose she wishes to act.

CHARLOTTE: No, no, no! A fig for sentiment.

If she breaks, or wishes to break, with Mr. Dimple, depend upon it, she has some other man in her eye. A woman rarely discards one lover until she is sure of another. Letitia little thinks what a clue I have to Dimple's conduct. The generous man submits to render himself disgusting to Maria, in order that she may leave him at liberty to address me. I must change the subject. [*Aside, and rings a bell*]

Enter Servant

Frank, order the horses to ———. Talking of marriage, did you hear that Sally Bloomsbury is going to be married next week to Mr. Indigo, the rich Carolinian?

LETITIA: Sally Bloomsbury married! – why, she is not yet in her teens.

CHARLOTTE: I do not know how that is, but you may depend upon it, 'tis a done affair. I have it from the best authority. There is my aunt Wyerly's Hannah. You know Hannah; though a black, she is a wench that was never caught in a lie in her life. Now, Hannah has a brother who courts Sarah, Mrs. Catgut the milliner's girl, and she told Hannah's brother, and Hannah, who, as I said before, is a girl of undoubted veracity, told it directly to me, that Mrs. Catgut was making a new cap for Miss Bloomsbury, which, as it was very dressy, it is very probable is designed for a wedding cap. Now, as she is to be married, who can it be to but to Mr. Indigo? Why, there is no other gentleman that visits at her papa's.

LETITIA: Say not a word more, Charlotte. Your intelligence is so direct and well grounded, it is almost a pity that it is not a piece of scandal.

CHARLOTTE: Oh! I am the pink of prudence. Though I cannot charge myself with ever having discredited a tea-party by my silence, yet I take care never to report any thing of my acquaintance, especially if it is to their credit, – *discredit*, I mean, – until I have searched to the bottom of it. It is true, there is infinite pleasure in this charitable pursuit. Oh! how delicious to go and condole with the friends of some backsliding sister, or to retire with some old dowager or maiden aunt of the family, who love scandal so well that they cannot forbear gratifying their appetite at the expense of the reputation of their nearest relations! And then to return full fraught with a rich collection of circumstances, to retail to the next circle of our acquaintance under the strongest injunctions of secrecy, – ha, ha, ha! – interlarding the melancholy tale with so many doleful shakes of the head, and more doleful "Ah! who would have thought it! so amiable, so prudent a young lady, as we all thought her, what a monstrous pity! well, I have nothing to charge myself with; I acted the part of a friend, I warned her of the principles of that rake, I told her what would be the consequence; I told her so, I told her so." – Ha, ha, ha!

LETITIA: Ha, ha, ha! Well, but, Charlotte, you don't tell me what you think of Miss Bloomsbury's match.

CHARLOTTE: Think! why I think it is probable she cried for a plaything, and they have given her a husband. Well, well, well, the puling chit shall not be deprived of her plaything: 'tis only exchanging London dolls for American babies. – Apropos, of babies, have you heard what Mrs. Affable's high-flying notions of delicacy have come to?

LETITIA: Who, she that was Miss Lovely?

CHARLOTTE: The same; she married Bob Affable of Schenectady. Don't you remember?

Enter Servant

SERVANT: Madam, the carriage is ready.

LETITIA: Shall we go to the stores first, or visiting?

CHARLOTTE: I should think it rather too early to visit, especially Mrs. Prim; you know she is so particular.

LETITIA: Well, but what of Mrs. Affable?

CHARLOTTE: Oh, I'll tell you as we go; come, come, let us hasten. I hear Mrs. Catgut has some of the prettiest caps arrived you ever saw. I shall die if I have not the first sight of them. [*Exeunt*]

Scene 2

A Room in Van Rough's House. Maria sitting disconsolate at a Table, with Books, Etc.

Song

I

The sun sets in night, and the stars shun the day;
But glory remains when their lights fade away!
Begin, ye tormentors! your threats are in vain,
For the son of Alknomook shall never complain.

II

Remember the arrows he shot from his bow;
Remember your chiefs by his hatchet laid low:
Why so slow? – do you wait till I shrink from the pain?
No – the son of Alknomook will never complain.

III

Remember the wood where in ambush we lay,
And the scalps which we bore from your nation away:
Now the flame rises fast, you exult in my pain;
But the son of Alknomook can never complain.

IV

I go to the land where my father is gone;
His ghost shall rejoice in the fame of his son:
Death comes like a friend, he relieves me from pain;
And thy son, Oh Alknomook! has scorn'd to complain.

MARIA: There is something in this song which ever calls forth my affections. The manly virtue of courage, that fortitude which steels the heart against the keenest misfortunes, which interweaves the laurel of glory amidst the instruments of torture and death, displays something so noble, so exalted, that in despite of the prejudices of education I cannot but admire it, even in a savage. The prepossession which our sex is supposed to entertain for the character of a soldier is, I know, a standing piece of raillery among the wits. A cockade, a lapell'd coat, and a feather, they will tell you, are irresistible by a female heart. Let it be so. Who is it that considers the helpless situation of our sex, that does not see that we each moment stand in need of a protector, and that a brave one too? Formed of the more delicate materials of nature, endowed only with the softer passions, incapable, from our ignorance of the world, to guard against the wiles of mankind, our security for happiness often depends upon their generosity and courage. Alas! how little of the former do we find! How inconsistent! that man should be leagued to destroy that honour upon which solely rests his respect and esteem. Ten thousand temptations allure us, ten thousand passions betray us; yet the smallest deviation from the path of rectitude is followed by the contempt and insult of man, and the more remorseless pity of woman; years of penitence and tears cannot wash away the stain, nor a life of virtue obliterate its remembrance. Reputation is the life of woman; yet courage to protect it is masculine and disgusting; and the only safe asylum a woman of delicacy can find is in the arms of a man of honour. How naturally, then, should we love the brave and the generous; how gratefully should we bless the arm raised for our protection, when nerv'd by virtue and directed by honour! Heaven grant that the man with whom I may be connected – may be connected! Whither has my imagination transported me – whither does it now lead me? Am I not indissolubly engaged, "by every obligation of honour which my own consent and my father's approbation can give," to a man who can never share my affections, and whom a few days hence it will be criminal for me to disapprove – to disapprove! would to heaven that were all – to despise. For, can the most frivolous manners, actuated by the most depraved heart, meet, or merit, any thing but contempt from every woman of delicacy and sentiment?

VAN ROUGH: [*Without*] Mary!

MARIA: Ha! my father's voice – Sir! –

Enter Van Rough

VAN ROUGH: What, Mary, always singing doleful ditties, and moping over these plaguy books.

MARIA: I hope, Sir, that it is not criminal to improve my mind with books, or to divert my melancholy with singing, at my leisure hours.

VAN ROUGH: Why, I don't know that, child; I don't know that. They us'd to say, when I was a young man, that if a woman knew how to make a pudding, and to keep herself out of fire and water, she knew enough for a wife. Now, what good have these books done you? have they not made you melancholy? as you call it. Pray, what right has a girl of your age to be in the dumps? haven't you everything your heart can wish; an't you going to be married to a young man of great fortune; an't you going to have the quit-rent of twenty miles square?

MARIA: One-hundredth part of the land, and a lease for life of the heart of a man I could love, would satisfy me.

VAN ROUGH: Pho, pho, pho! child; nonsense, downright nonsense, child. This comes of your reading your storybooks; your Charles Grandisons, your Sentimental Journals, and your Robinson Crusoes, and such other trumpery. No, no, no! child; it is money makes the mare go; keep your eye upon the main chance, Mary.

MARIA: Marriage, Sir, is, indeed, a very serious affair.

VAN ROUGH: You are right, child; you are right. I am sure I found it so, to my cost.

MARIA: I mean, Sir, that as marriage is a portion for life, and so intimately involves our happiness, we cannot be too considerate in the choice of our companion.

VAN ROUGH: Right, child; very right. A young woman should be very sober when she is making her choice, but when she has once made it, as you have done, I don't see why she should not be as merry as a grig; I am sure she has reason enough to be so. Solomon says that "there is a time to laugh, and a time to weep." Now, a time for a young woman to laugh is when she has made sure of a good rich husband. Now, a time to cry, according to you, Mary, is when she is making choice of him; but I should think that a young woman's time to cry was when she despaired of *getting* one. Why, there was your mother, now: to be sure, when I popp'd the question to her she did look a little silly; but when she had once looked down on her apron-strings, as all modest young women us'd to do, and drawled out ye-s, she was as brisk and as merry as a bee.

MARIA: My honoured mother, Sir, had no motive to melancholy; she married the man of her choice.

VAN ROUGH: The man of her choice! And pray, Mary, an't you going to marry the man of your choice – what trumpery notion is this? It is these vile books [*Throwing them away*]. I'd have you to know, Mary, if you won't make young Van Dumpling the man of *your* choice, you shall marry him as the man of *my* choice.

MARIA: You terrify me, Sir. Indeed, Sir, I am all submission. My will is yours.

VAN ROUGH: Why, that is the way your mother us'd to talk. "My will is yours, my dear Mr. Van Rough, my will is yours"; but she took special care to have her own way, though, for all that.

MARIA: Do not reflect upon my mother's memory, Sir –

VAN ROUGH: Why not, Mary, why not? She kept me from speaking my mind all her *life*, and do you think she shall henpeck me now she is *dead* too? Come, come; don't go to sniveling; be a good girl, and mind the main chance. I'll see you well settled in the world.

MARIA: I do not doubt your love, Sir, and it is my duty to obey you. I will endeavour to make my duty and inclination go hand in hand.

VAN ROUGH: Well, well, Mary; do you be a good girl, mind the main chance, and never mind inclination. Why, do you know that I have been down in the cellar this very morning to examine a pipe of Madeira which I purchased the week you were born, and mean to tap on your wedding day? – That pipe cost me fifty pounds sterling. It was well worth sixty pounds; but I overreach'd Ben Bulkhead, the supercargo. I'll tell you the whole story. You must know that –

Enter Servant

SERVANT: Sir, Mr. Transfer, the broker, is below. [*Exit*]

VAN ROUGH: Well, Mary, I must go. Remember, and be a good girl, and mind the main chance. [*Exit*]

MARIA: [*Alone*] How deplorable is my situation! How distressing for a daughter to find her heart militating with her filial duty! I know my father loves me tenderly; why then do I reluctantly obey him? Heaven knows! with what reluctance I should oppose the will of a parent, or set an example of filial disobedience; at a parent's command, I could wed awkwardness and deformity. Were the heart of my husband good, I would so magnify his good qualities with the eye of conjugal affection, that the defects of his person and manners should be lost in the emanation of his virtues. At a father's command, I could embrace poverty. Were the poor man my husband, I would learn resignation to my lot; I would enliven our frugal meal with good humour, and chase away misfortune from our cottage with a smile. At a father's command, I could almost submit to what every female heart knows to be the most mortifying, to marry a weak man, and blush at my husband's folly in every company I visited. But to marry a depraved wretch, whose only virtue is 'a polished exterior; who is actuated by the unmanly ambition of conquering the defenceless; whose heart, insensible to the emotions of pa-

triotism, dilates at the plaudits of every unthinking girl; whose laurels are the sighs and tears of the miserable victims of his specious behaviour, – can he, who has no regard for the peace and happiness of other families, ever have a due regard for the peace and happiness of his own? Would to heaven that my father were not so hasty in his temper? Surely, if I were to state my reasons for declining this match, he would not compel me to marry a man, whom, though my lips may solemnly promise to honour, I find my heart must ever despise. [*Exit*]

End of the First Act

ACT II. Scene 1

Enter Charlotte and Letitia.

CHARLOTTE: [*At entering*] Betty, take those things out of the carriage and carry them to my chamber; see that you don't tumble them. My dear, I protest, I think it was the homeliest of the whole. I declare I was almost tempted to return and change it.

LETITIA: Why would you take it?

CHARLOTTE: Didn't Mrs. Catgut say it was the most fashionable?

LETITIA: But, my dear, it will never fit becomingly on you.

CHARLOTTE: I know that; but did not you hear Mrs. Catgut say it was fashionable?

LETITIA: Did you see that sweet airy cap with the white sprig?

CHARLOTTE: Yes, and I longed to take it; but, my dear, what could I do? Did not Mrs. Catgut say it was the most fashionable; and if I had not taken it, was not that awkward gawky, Sally Slender, ready to purchase it immediately?

LETITIA: Did you observe how she tumbled over the things at the next shop, and then went off without purchasing anything, nor even thanking the poor man for his trouble? But, of all the awkward creatures, did you see Miss Blouze endeavouring to thrust her unmerciful arm into those small kid gloves?

CHARLOTTE: Ha, ha, ha, ha!

LETITIA: Then did you take notice with what an affected warmth of friendship she and Miss Wasp met? when all their acquaintance know how much pleasure they take in abusing each other in every company.

CHARLOTTE: Lud! Letitia, is that so extraordinary? Why, my dear, I hope you are not going to turn sentimentalist. Scandal, you know, is but amusing ourselves with the faults, foibles, follies, and reputations of our friends; indeed, I don't know why we should have friends, if we are not at liberty to make use of them. But no person is so ignorant of the world as to suppose, because I amuse myself with a lady's faults, that I am obliged to quarrel with her person every time we meet: believe me, my dear, we should have very few acquaintance at that rate.

Servant enters and delivers a letter to Charlotte, and – Exit

CHARLOTTE: You'll excuse me, my dear. [*Opens and reads to herself*]

LETITIA: Oh, quite excusable.

CHARLOTTE: As I hope to be married, my brother Henry is in the city.

LETITIA: What, your brother, Colonel Manly?

CHARLOTTE: Yes, my dear; the only brother I have in the world.

LETITIA: Was he never in this city?

CHARLOTTE: Never nearer than Harlem Heights, where he lay with his regiment.

LETITIA: What sort of a being is this brother of yours? If he is as chatty, as pretty, as sprightly as you, half the belles in the city will be pulling caps for him.

CHARLOTTE: My brother is the very counterpart and reverse of me: I am gay, he is grave; I am airy, he is solid; I am ever selecting the most pleasing objects for my laughter, he has a tear for every pitiful one. And thus, whilst he is plucking the briars and thorns from the path of the unfortunate, I am strewing my own path with roses.

LETITIA: My sweet friend, not quite so poetical, and a little more particular.

CHARLOTTE: Hands off, Letitia. I feel the rage of simile upon me; I can't talk to you in any other way. My brother has a heart replete with the noblest sentiments, but then, it is like – it is like – Oh! you provoking girl, you have deranged all my ideas – it is like – Oh! I have it – his heart is like an old maiden lady's bandbox; it contains many costly things, arranged with the most scrupulous nicety, yet the misfortune is that they are too delicate, costly, and antiquated for common use.

LETITIA: By what I can pick out of your flowery description, your brother is no beau.

CHARLOTTE: No, indeed; he makes no pretension to the character. He'd ride, or rather fly, an hundred miles to relieve a distressed object, or to do a gallant act in the service of his country; but should you drop your fan or bouquet in his presence, it is ten to one that some beau at the farther end of the room would have the honour of presenting it to you before he had observed that it fell. I'll tell you one of his antiquated, anti-gallant notions. He said once in my presence, in a room full of company, – would you believe it? – in a large circle of ladies, that the best evidence a gentleman could give a young lady of his respect and affection was to endeavour in a friendly manner to rectify her foibles. I protest I was crimson to the eyes, upon reflecting that I was known as his sister.

LETITIA: Insupportable creature! tell a lady of her faults! if he is so grave, I fear I have no chance of captivating him.

CHARLOTTE: His conversation is like a rich, old-fashioned brocade, – it will stand alone; every sentence is a sentiment. Now you may judge what a time I had with him, in my twelve months' visit to my father. He read me such lectures, out of pure brotherly affection, against the extremes of fashion, dress, flirting, and coquetry, and all the other dear things which he knows I doat upon, that I protest his conversation made me as melancholy as if I had been at church; and heaven knows, though I never prayed to go there but on one occasion, yet I would have exchanged his conversation for a psalm and a sermon. Church is rather melancholy, to be sure; but then I can ogle the beaux, and be regaled with "here endeth the first lesson," but his brotherly *here*, you would think had no end. You captivate him! Why, my dear, he would as soon fall in love with a box of Italian flowers. There is Maria, now, if she were not engaged, she might do something. Oh! how I should like to see that pair of pensorosos together, looking as grave as two sailors' wives of a stormy night, with a flow of sentiment meandering through their conversation like purling streams in modern poetry.

LETITIA: Oh! my dear fanciful –

CHARLOTTE: Hush! I hear some person coming through the entry.

Enter Servant

SERVANT: Madam, there's a gentleman below who calls himself Colonel Manly; do you chuse to be at home?

CHARLOTTE: Shew him in. [*Exit Servant*] Now for a sober face.

Enter Colonel Manly

MANLY: My dear Charlotte, I am happy that I once more enfold you within the arms of fraternal affection. I know you are going to ask (amiable impatience!) how our parents do, – the venerable pair transmit you their blessing by me. They totter on the verge of a well-spent life, and wish only to see their children settled in the world, to depart in peace.

CHARLOTTE: I am very happy to hear that they are well. [*Coolly*] Brother, will you give me leave to introduce you to our uncle's ward, one of my most intimate friends?

MANLY: [*Saluting Letitia*] I ought to regard your friends as my own.

CHARLOTTE: Come, Letitia, do give us a little dash of your vivacity; my brother is so sentimental and so grave, that I protest he'll give us the vapours.

MANLY: Though sentiment and gravity, I know, are banished the polite world, yet I hoped they might find some countenance in the meeting of such near connections as brother and sister.

CHARLOTTE: Positively, brother, if you go one step further in this strain, you will set me crying, and that, you know, would spoil my eyes; and then I should never get the husband which our good papa and mamma have so kindly wished me – never be established in the world.

MANLY: Forgive me, my sister, – I am no enemy to mirth; I love your sprightliness; and I hope it will one day enliven the hours of some worthy man; but when I mention the respectable authors of my existence, – the cherishers and protectors of my helpless infancy, whose hearts glow with such fondness and attachment that they would willingly lay down their lives for my welfare, – you will excuse me if I am so unfashionable as to speak of them with some degree of respect and reverence.

CHARLOTTE: Well, well, brother; if you won't be gay, we'll not differ; I will be as grave as you wish. [*Affects gravity*] And so, brother, you have come to the city to exchange some of your commutation notes for a little pleasure?

MANLY: Indeed you are mistaken; my errand is not of amusement, but business; and as I neither drink nor game, my expenses will be so trivial, I shall have no occasion to sell my notes.

CHARLOTTE: Then you won't have occasion to do a very good thing. Why, here was the Vermont General – he came down some time since, sold all his musty notes at one stroke, and then laid the cash out in trinkets for his dear Fanny. I want a dozen pretty things myself; have you got the notes with you?

MANLY: I shall be ever willing to contribute, as far as it is in my power, to adorn or in any way to please my sister; yet I hope I shall never be obliged for this to sell my notes. I may be romantic, but I preserve them as a sacred deposit. Their full amount is justly due to me, but as embarrassments, the natural consequences of a long war, disable my country from supporting its credit, I shall wait with patience until it is rich enough to discharge them. If that is not in my day, they shall be transmitted as an honourable certificate to posterity, that I have humbly imitated our illustrious WASHINGTON, in having exposed my health and life in the service of my country, without reaping any other reward than the glory of conquering in so arduous a contest.

CHARLOTTE: Well said heroics. Why, my dear Henry, you have such a lofty way of saying things, that I protest I almost tremble at the thought of introducing you to the polite circles in the city. The belles would think you were a player run mad, with your head filled with old scraps of tragedy; and as to the beaux, they might admire, because they would not understand you. But, however, I must, I believe, introduce you to two or three ladies of my acquaintance.

LETITIA: And that will make him acquainted with thirty or forty beaux.

CHARLOTTE: Oh! brother, you don't know what a fund of happiness you have in store.

MANLY: I fear, sister, I have not refinement sufficient to enjoy it.

CHARLOTTE: Oh! you cannot fail being pleased.

LETITIA: Our ladies are so delicate and dressy.

CHARLOTTE: And our beaux so dressy and delicate.

LETITIA: Our ladies chat and flirt so agreeably.

CHARLOTTE: And our beaux simper and bow so gracefully.

LETITIA: With their hair so trim and neat.

CHARLOTTE: And their faces so soft and sleek.

LETITIA: Their buckles so tonish and bright.

CHARLOTTE: And their hands so slender and white.

LETITIA: I vow, Charlotte, we are quite poetical.

CHARLOTTE: And then, brother, the faces of the beaux are of such a lily-white hue! None of that horrid robustness of constitution, that vulgar corn-fed glow of health, which can only serve to alarm an unmarried lady with apprehension, and prove a melancholy memento to a married one, that she can never hope for the happiness of being a widow. I will say this to the credit of our city beaux, that such is the delicacy of their complexion, dress, and address, that, even had I no reliance upon the honour of the dear Adonises, I would trust myself in any possible situation with them, without the least apprehensions of rudeness.

MANLY: Sister Charlotte!

CHARLOTTE: Now, now, now, brother [*Interrupting him*], now don't go to spoil my mirth with a dash of your gravity; I am so glad to see you, I am in tiptop spirits. Oh! that you could be with us at a little snug party. There is Billy Simper, Jack Chaffé, and Colonel Van Titter, Miss Promonade, and the two Miss Tambours, sometimes make a party, with some other ladies, in a side-box at the play. Every thing is conducted with such decorum. First we bow round to the company in general, then to each one in particular, then we have so many inquiries after each other's health, and we are so happy to meet each other, and it is so many ages since we last had that pleasure, and if a married lady is in company, we have such a sweet dissertation upon her son Bobby's chincough; then the curtain rises, then our sensibility is all awake, and then, by the mere force of apprehension, we torture some harmless expression into a double meaning, which the poor author never dreamt of, and then we have recourse to our fans, and then we blush, and then the gentlemen jog one another, peep under the fan, and make the prettiest remarks; and then we giggle and they simper, and they giggle and we simper, and then the curtain drops, and then for nuts and oranges, and then we bow, and it's pray, Ma'am, take it, and pray, Sir, keep it, and oh! not for the world, Sir; and then the curtain rises again, and then we blush and giggle and simper and bow all over again. Oh! the sentimental charms of a side-box conversation!

All laugh

MANLY: Well, sister, I join heartily with you in the laugh; for, in my opinion, it is as justifiable to laugh at folly as it is reprehensible to ridicule misfortune.

CHARLOTTE: Well, but, brother, positively I can't introduce you in these clothes: why, your coat looks as if it were calculated for the vulgar purpose of keeping yourself comfortable.

MANLY: This coat was my regimental coat in the late war. The public tumults of our state have induced me to buckle on the sword in support of that government which I once fought to establish. I can only say, sister, that there was a time when this coat was respectable, and some people even thought that those men who had endured so many winter campaigns in the service of their country, without bread, clothing, or pay, at least deserved that the poverty of their appearance should not be ridiculed.

CHARLOTTE: We agree in opinion entirely, brother, though it would not have done for me to have said it: it is the coat makes the man respectable. In the time of the war, when we were almost frightened to death, why, your coat was respectable, that is, fashionable; now another kind of coat is fashionable, that is, respectable. And pray direct the taylor to make yours the height of the fashion.

MANLY: Though it is of little consequence to me of what shape my coat is, yet, as to the height of the fashion, there you will please to excuse me, sister. You know my sentiments on that subject. I have often lamented the advantage which the French have over us in that particular. In Paris, the fashions have their dawnings, their routine, and declensions, and depend as much upon the caprice of the day as in other countries; but there every lady assumes a right to deviate from the general *ton* as far as will be of advantage to her own appearance. In America, the cry is, what is the fashion? and we follow it indiscriminately, because it is so.

CHARLOTTE: Therefore it is, that when large hoops are in fashion, we often see many a plump girl lost in the immensity of a hoop-petticoat, whose want of height and *en-bon-point* would never have been remarked in any other dress. When the high head-dress is the mode, how then do we see a lofty cushion, with a profusion of gauze, feathers, and ribband, supported by a face no bigger than an apple! whilst a broad full-faced lady, who really would have appeared tolerably handsome in a large head-dress, looks with her smart chapeau as masculine as a soldier.

MANLY: But remember, my dear sister, and I wish all my fair country-women would recollect, that the only excuse a young lady can have for going extravagantly into a fashion is because it makes her look extravagantly handsome. – Ladies, I must wish you a good morning.

CHARLOTTE: But, brother, you are going to make home with us.

MANLY: Indeed I cannot. I have seen my uncle and explained that matter.

CHARLOTTE: Come and dine with us, then. We have a family dinner about half-past four o'clock.

MANLY: I am engaged to dine with the Spanish ambassador. I was introduced to him by an old brother officer; and instead of freezing me with a cold card of compliment to dine with him ten days hence, he, with the true old Castilian frankness, in a friendly manner, asked me to dine with him to-day – an honour I could not refuse. Sister, adieu – Madam, your most obedient – . [*Exit*]

CHARLOTTE: I will wait upon you to the door, brother; I have something particular to say to you. [*Exit*]

LETITIA: [*Alone*] What a pair! – She the pink of flirtation, he the essence of everything that is *outré* and gloomy. – I think I have completely deceived Charlotte by my manner of speaking of Mr. Dimple; she's too much the friend of Maria to be confided in. He is certainly rendering himself disagreeable to Maria, in order to break with her and proffer his hand to me. This is what the delicate fellow hinted in our last conversation. [*Exit*]

Scene 2

The Mall. Enter Jessamy.

JESSAMY: Positively this Mall is a very pretty place. I hope the cits won't ruin it by repairs. To be sure, it won't do to speak of in the same day with Ranelagh or Vauxhall; however, it's a fine place for a young fellow to display his person to advantage. Indeed, nothing is lost here; the girls have taste, and I am very happy to find they have adopted the elegant London fashion of looking back, after a genteel fellow like me has passed them. – Ah! who comes here? This, by his awkwardness, must be the Yankee colonel's servant. I'll accost him.

JESSAMY: *Votre très-humble serviteur, Monsieur.* I understand Colonel Manly, the Yankee officer, has the honour of your services.

JONATHAN: Sir! –

JESSAMY: I say, Sir, I understand that Colonel Manly has the honour of having you for a servant.

JONATHAN: Servant! Sir, do you take me for a neger, – I am Colonel Manly's waiter.

JESSAMY: A true Yankee distinction, egad, without a difference. Why, Sir, do you not perform all the offices of a servant? do you not even blacken his boots?

JONATHAN: Yes; I do grease them a bit sometimes; but I am a true blue son of liberty, for all that. Father said I should come as Colonel Manly's waiter, to see the world, and all that; but no man shall master me. My father has as good a farm as the colonel.

JESSAMY: Well, Sir, we will not quarrel about terms upon the eve of an acquaintance from which I promise myself so much satisfaction; – therefore, *sans cérémonie* –

JONATHAN: What? –

JESSAMY: I say I am extremely happy to see Colonel Manly's waiter.

JONATHAN: Well, and I vow, too, I am pretty considerably glad to see you; but what the dogs need of all this outlandish lingo? Who may you be, Sir, if I may be so bold?

JESSAMY: I have the honour to be Mr. Dimple's servant, or, if you please, waiter. We lodge under the same roof, and should be glad of the honour of your acquaintance.

JONATHAN: You a waiter! by the living jingo, you look so topping, I took you for one of the agents to Congress.

JESSAMY: The brute has discernment, notwithstanding his appearance. – Give me leave to say I wonder then at your familiarity.

JONATHAN: Why, as to the matter of that, Mr. ——; pray, what's your name?

JESSAMY: Jessamy, at your service.

JONATHAN: Why, I swear we don't make any great matter of distinction in our state between quality and other folks.

JESSAMY: This is, indeed, a levelling principle. – I hope, Mr. Jonathan, you have not taken part with the insurgents.

JONATHAN: Why, since General Shays has sneaked off and given us the bag to hold, I don't care to give my opinion; but you'll promise not to tell – put your ear this way – you won't tell? – I vow I did think the sturgeons were right.

JESSAMY: I thought, Mr. Jonathan, you Massachusetts men always argued with a gun in your hand. Why didn't you join them?

JONATHAN: Why, the colonel is one of those folks called the Shin – Shin, dang it all, I can't speak them lignum vitae words – you know who I mean – there is a company of them – they wear a china goose at their button-hole – a kind of gilt thing. – Now the colonel told father and brother, – you must know there are, let me see – there is Elnathan, Silas, and Barnabas, Tabitha – no, no, she's a she – tarnation, now I have it – there's Elnathan, Silas, Barnabas, Jonathan, that's I – seven of us, six went into the wars, and I staid at home to take care of mother. Colonel said that it was a burning shame for the true blue Bunker Hill sons of liberty, who had fought Governor Hutchinson, Lord North, and the Devil, to have any hand in kicking up a cursed dust against a government which we had, every mother's son of us, a hand in making.

JESSAMY: Bravo! – Well, have you been abroad in the city since your arrival? What have you seen that is curious and entertaining?

JONATHAN: Oh! I have seen a power of fine sights. I went to see two marble-stone men and a leaden horse that stands out in doors in all weathers; and when I came where they was, one had got no head, and t'other wern't there. They said as how the leaden man was a damn'd tory, and that he took wit in his anger and rode off in the time of the troubles.

JESSAMY: But this was not the end of your excursion?

JONATHAN: Oh, no; I went to a place they call Holy Ground. Now I counted this was a place where folks go to meeting; so I put my hymn-book in my pocket, and walked softly and grave as a minister; and when I came there, the dogs a bit of a meeting-house could I see. At last I spied a young gentlewoman standing by one of the seats which they have here at the doors. I took her to be the deacon's daughter, and she looked so kind, and so obliging, that I thought I would go ask her the way to the lecture, and – would you think it? – she called me dear, and sweeting, and honey, just as if we were married: by the living jingo, I had a month's mind to buss her.

JESSAMY: Well, but how did it end?

JONATHAN: Why, as I was standing talking with her, a parcel of sailor men and boys got round me, the snarl-headed curs fell a-kicking and cursing of me at such a tarnal rate, that I vow I was glad to take to my heels and split home, right off, tail on end, like a stream of chalk.

JESSAMY: Why, my dear friend, you are not acquainted with the city; that girl you saw was a – [*Whispers*]

JONATHAN: Mercy on my soul! was that young woman a harlot! – Well! if this is New-York Holy Ground, what must the Holy-day Ground be!

JESSAMY: Well, you should not judge of the city too rashly. We have a number of elegant, fine girls here that make a man's leisure hours pass very agreeably. I would esteem it an honour to announce you to some of them. – Gad! that announce is a select word; I wonder where I picked it up.

JONATHAN: I don't want to know them.

JESSAMY: Come, come, my dear friend, I see that I must assume the honour of being the director of your amusements. Nature has given us passions, and youth and opportunity stimulate to gratify them. It is no shame, my dear Blueskin, for a man to amuse himself with a little gallantry.

JONATHAN: Girl huntry! I don't altogether understand. I never played at that game. I know how to play hunt the squirrel, but I can't play anything with the girls; I am as good as married.

JESSAMY: Vulgar, horrid brute! Married, and above a hundred miles from his wife, and thinks that an objection to his making love to every woman he meets! He never can have read, no, he never can have been in a room with a volume of the divine Chesterfield. – So you are married?

JONATHAN: No, I don't say so; I said I was as good as married, a kind of promise.

JESSAMY: As good as married! –

JONATHAN: Why, yes; there's Tabitha Wymen, the deacon's daughter, at home; she and I have been courting a great while, and folks say as how we are to be married; and so I broke a piece of money with her when we parted, and she promised not to spark it with Solomon Dyer while I am gone. You wou'dn't have me false to my true-love, would you?

JESSAMY: May be you have another reason for constancy; possibly the young lady has a fortune? Ha! Mr. Jonathan, the solid charms: the chains of love are never so binding as when the links are made of gold.

JONATHAN: Why, as to fortune, I must needs say her father is pretty dumb rich; he went representative for our town last year. He will give her – let me see – four times seven is – seven times four – nought and carry one, – he will give her twenty acres of land – somewhat rocky though – a Bible, and a cow.

JESSAMY: Twenty acres of rock, a Bible, and a cow! Why, my dear Mr. Jonathan, we have servant-maids, or, as you would more elegantly express it, waitresses, in this city, who collect more in one year from their mistresses' cast clothes.

JONATHAN: You don't say so! –

JESSAMY: Yes, and I'll introduce you to one of them. There is a little lump of flesh and delicacy that lives at next door, waitress to Miss Maria; we often see her on the stoop.

JONATHAN: But are you sure she would be courted by me?

JESSAMY: Never doubt it; remember a faint heart never – blisters on my tongue – I was going to be guilty of a vile proverb; flat against the authority of Chesterfield. I say there can be no doubt that the brilliancy of your merit will secure you a favourable reception.

JONATHAN: Well, but what must I say to her?

JESSAMY: Say to her! why, my dear friend, though I admire your profound knowledge on every other subject, yet, you will pardon my saying that your want of opportunity has made the female heart escape the poignancy of your penetration. Say to her! Why, when a man goes a-courting, and hopes for success, he must begin with doing, and not saying.

JONATHAN: Well, what must I do?

JESSAMY: Why, when you are introduced you must make five or six elegant bows.

JONATHAN: Six elegant bows! I understand that; six, you say? Well –

JESSAMY: Then you must press and kiss her hand; then press and kiss, and so on to her lips and cheeks; then talk as much as you can about hearts, darts, flames, nectar, and ambrosia – the more incoherent the better.

JONATHAN: Well, but suppose she should be angry with I?

JESSAMY: Why, if she should pretend – please to observe, Mr. Jonathan – if she should pretend to be offended, you must – But I'll tell you how my master acted in such a case: He was seated by a young lady of eighteen upon a sofa, plucking with a wanton hand the blooming sweets of youth and beauty. When the lady thought it necessary to check his ardour, she called up a frown upon her lovely face, so irresistibly alluring, that it would have warmed the frozen bosom of age; remember, said she, putting her delicate arm upon his, remember your character and my honour. My master instantly dropped upon his knees, with eyes swimming with love, cheeks glowing with desire, and in the gentlest modulation of voice he said: My dear Caroline, in a few months our hands will be indissolubly united at the altar; our hearts I feel are already so; the favours you now grant as evidence of your affection are favours indeed; yet, when the ceremony is once past, what will now be received with rapture will then be attributed to duty.

JONATHAN: Well, and what was the consequence?

JESSAMY: The consequence! – Ah! forgive me, my dear friend, but you New England gentlemen have such a laudable curiosity of seeing the bottom of everything; – why, to be honest, I confess I saw the blooming cherub of a consequence smiling in its angelic mother's arms, about ten months afterwards.

JONATHAN: Well, if I follow all your plans, make them six bows, and all that, shall I have such little cherubim consequences?

JESSAMY: Undoubtedly. – What are you musing upon?

JONATHAN: You say you'll certainly make me acquainted? – Why, I was thinking then how I should contrive to pass this broken piece of silver – won't it buy a sugar-dram?

JESSAMY: What is that, the love-token from the deacon's daughter? – You come on bravely. But I must hasten to my master. Adieu, my dear friend.

JONATHAN: Stay, Mr. Jessamy – must I buss her when I am introduced to her?

JESSAMY: I told you, you must kiss her.

JONATHAN: Well, but must I buss her?

JESSAMY: Why kiss and buss, and buss and kiss, is all one.

JONATHAN: Oh! my dear friend, though you have a profound knowledge of all, a pugnency of tribulation, you don't know everything. [*Exit*]

JESSAMY: [*Alone*] Well, certainly I improve; my master could not have insinuated himself with more address into the heart of a man he despised. Now will this blundering dog sicken Jenny with his nauseous pawings, until she flies into my arms for very ease. How sweet will the contrast be between the blundering Jonathan and the courtly and accomplished Jessamy!

End of the Second Act

ACT III. Scene 1

Dimple's room.

DIMPLE: [*Discovered at a toilet, reading*] "Women have in general but one object, which is their beauty." Very true, my lord; positively very true. "Nature has hardly formed a woman ugly enough to be insensible to flattery upon her person." Extremely just, my lord; every day's delightful experience confirms this. "If her face is so shocking that she must, in some degree, be conscious of it, her figure and air, she thinks, make ample amends for it." The sallow Miss Wan is a proof of this. Upon my telling the distasteful wretch, the other day, that her countenance spoke the pensive language of sentiment, and that Lady Wortley Montague declared that if the ladies were arrayed in the garb of innocence, the face would be the last part which would be admired, as Monsieur Milton expresses it, she grinn'd horribly a ghastly smile. "If her figure is deformed, she thinks her face counterbalances it."

Enter Jessamy with letters

DIMPLE: Where got you these, Jessamy?

JESSAMY: Sir, the English packet is arrived.

DIMPLE: [*Opens and reads a letter enclosing notes*]

"SIR,

"I have drawn bills on you in favour of Messrs. Van Cash and Co. as per margin. I have taken up your note to Col. Piquet, and discharged your debts to my Lord Lurcher and Sir Harry Rook. I herewith enclose you copies of the bills, which I have no doubt will be immediately honoured. On failure, I shall empower some lawyer in your country to recover the amounts.

"I am, Sir,
"Your most humble Servant,
"JOHN HAZARD"

Now, did not my lord expressly say that it was unbecoming a well-bred man to be in a passion, I confess I should be ruffled. [*Reads*] "There is no accident so unfortunate, which a wise man may not turn to his advantage; nor any accident so fortunate, which a fool will not turn to his disadvantage." True, my lord; but how advantage can be derived from this I can't see. Chesterfield himself, who made, however, the worst practice of the most excellent precepts, was never in so embarrassing a situation. I love the person of Charlotte, and it is necessary I should command the fortune of Letitia. As to Maria! – I doubt not by my *sang-froid* behaviour I shall compel her to decline the match; but the blame must not fall upon me. A prudent man, as my lord says, should take all the credit of a good action to himself, and throw the discredit of a bad one upon others. I must break with Maria, marry Letitia, and as for Charlotte – why, Charlotte must be a companion to my wife. – Here, Jessamy!

Enter Jessamy. Dimple folds and seals two letters

DIMPLE: Here, Jessamy, take this letter to my love. [*Gives one*]

JESSAMY: To which of your honour's loves? – Oh! [*Reading*] to Miss Letitia, your honour's rich love.

DIMPLE: And this [*Delivers another*] to Miss Charlotte Manly. See that you deliver them privately.

JESSAMY: Yes, your honour. [*Going*]

DIMPLE: Jessamy, who are these strange lodgers that came to the house last night?

JESSAMY: Why, the master is a Yankee colonel; I have not seen much of him; but the man is the most unpolished animal your honour ever disgraced your eyes by looking upon. I have had one of the most *outré* conversations with him! – He really has a most prodigious effect upon my risibility.

DIMPLE: I ought, according to every rule of Chesterfield, to wait on him and insinuate myself into his good graces. – Jessamy, wait on the colonel with my compliments, and if he is disengaged I will do myself the honour of paying him my respects. – Some ignorant, unpolished boor –

Jessamy goes off and returns

JESSAMY: Sir, the colonel is gone out, and Jonathan his servant says that he is gone to stretch his legs upon the Mall. – Stretch his legs! what an indelicacy of diction!

DIMPLE: Very well. Reach me my hat and sword. I'll accost him there, in my way to Letitia's, as by accident; pretend to be struck by his person and address, and endeavour to steal into his confidence. Jessamy, I have no business for you at present. [*Exit*]

JESSAMY: [*Taking up the book*] My master and I obtain our knowledge from the same source; – though, gad! I think myself much the prettier fellow of the two. [*Surveying himself in the glass*] That was a brilliant thought, to insinuate that I folded my master's letters for him; the folding is so neat, that it does honour to the operator. I once intended to have insinuated that I wrote his letters too; but that was before I saw them; it won't do now; no honour there, positively. – "Nothing looks more vulgar, [*Reading affectedly*] ordinary, and illiberal than ugly, uneven, and ragged nails; the ends of which should be kept even and clean, not tipped with black, and cut in small segments of circles." – Segments of circles! surely my lord did not consider that he wrote for the beaux. Segments of circles; what a crabbed term! Now I dare answer that my master, with all his learning, does not know that this means, according to the present mode, let the nails grow long, and then cut them off even at top. [*Laughing without*] Ha! that's Jenny's titter. I protest I despair of ever teaching that girl to laugh; she has something so execrably natural in her laugh, that I declare it absolutely discomposes my nerves. How came she into our house! [*Calls*] Jenny!

Enter Jenny

JESSAMY: Prythee, Jenny, don't spoil your fine face with laughing.

JENNY: Why, mustn't I laugh, Mr. Jessamy?

JESSAMY: You may smile; but, as my lord says, nothing can authorise a laugh.

JENNY: Well, but I can't help laughing. – Have you seen him, Mr. Jessamy? ha, ha, ha!

JESSAMY: Seen whom?

JENNY: Why, Jonathan, the New England colonel's servant. Do you know he was at the play last night, and the stupid creature don't know where he has been. He would not go to a play for the world; he thinks it was a show, as he calls it.

JESSAMY: As ignorant and unpolished as he is, do you know, Miss Jenny, that I propose to introduce him to the honour of your acquaintance?

JENNY: Introduce him to me! for what?

JESSAMY: Why, my lovely girl, that you may take him under your protection, as Madame Rambouillet did young Stanhope; that you may, by your plastic hand, mould this uncouth cub into a gentleman. He is to make love to you.

JENNY: Make love to me! –

JESSAMY: Yes, Mistress Jenny, make love to you; and, I doubt not, when he shall become *domesticated* in your kitchen, that this boor, under your auspices, will soon become *un amiable petit Jonathan*.

JENNY: I must say, Mr. Jessamy, if he copies after me, he will be vastly, monstrously polite.

JESSAMY: Stay here one moment, and I will call him. – Jonathan! – Mr. Jonathan – [*Calls*]

JONATHAN: [*Within*] Holla! there. – [*Enters*] You promise to stand by me – six bows you say. [*Bows*]

JESSAMY: Mrs. Jenny, I have the honour of presenting Mr. Jonathan, Colonel Manly's waiter, to you. I am extremely happy that I have it in my power to make two worthy people acquainted with each other's merits.

JENNY: So, Mr. Jonathan, I hear you were at the play last night.

JONATHAN: At the play! why, did you think I went to the devil's drawing-room?

JENNY: The devil's drawing-room!

JONATHAN: Yes; why an't cards and dice the devil's device, and the play-house the shop where the devil hangs out the vanities of the world upon the tenter-hooks of temptation? I believe you have not heard how they were acting the old boy one night, and the wicked one came among them sure enough, and went right off in a storm, and carried one quarter of the play-house with him. Oh! no, no, no! you won't catch me at a play-house, I warrant you.

JENNY: Well, Mr. Jonathan, though I don't scruple your veracity, I have some reasons for believing you were there: pray, where were you about six o'clock?

JONATHAN: Why, I went to see one Mr. Morrison, the *hocus pocus* man; they said as how he could eat a case knife.

JENNY: Well, and how did you find the place?

JONATHAN: As I was going about here and there, to and again, to find it, I saw a great crowd of folks going into a long entry that had lantherns over the door; so I asked a man whether that was not the place where they played *hocus pocus?* He was a very civil, kind man, though he did speak like the Hessians; he lifted up his eyes and said, "They play *hocus pocus* tricks enough there, Got knows, mine friend."

JENNY: Well –

JONATHAN: So I went right in, and they shewed me away, clean up to the garret, just like meeting-house gallery. And so I saw a power of topping folks, all sitting round in little cabbins, "just like father's corn-cribs"; and then there was such a squeaking with the fiddles, and such a tarnal blaze with the lights, my head was near turned. At last the people that sat near me set up such a hissing – hiss – like so many mad cats; and then they went thump, thump, thump, just like our Peleg threshing wheat, and stampt away, just like the nation; and called out for one Mr. Langolee, – I suppose he helps act the tricks.

JENNY: Well, and what did you do all this time?

JONATHAN: Gor, I – I liked the fun, and so I thumpt away, and hiss'd as lustily as the best of 'em. One sailor-looking man that sat by me, seeing me stamp, and knowing I was a cute fellow, because I could make a roaring noise, clapt me on the shoulder and said, "You are a d——d hearty cock, smite my timbers!" I told him so I was, but I thought he need not swear so, and make use of such naughty words.

JESSAMY: The savage! – Well, and did you see the man with his tricks?

JONATHAN: Why, I vow, as I was looking out for him, they lifted up a great green cloth and let us look right into the next neighbour's house. Have you a good many houses in New-York made so in that 'ere way?

JENNY: Not many; but did you see the family?

JONATHAN: Yes, swamp it; I see'd the family.

JENNY: Well, and how did you like them?

JONATHAN: Why, I vow they were pretty much like other families; – there was a poor, good-natured, curse of a husband, and a sad ranti-pole of a wife.

JENNY: But did you see no other folks?

JONATHAN: Yes. There was one youngster; they called Mr. Joseph; he talked as sober and as pious as a minister; but, like some ministers that I know, he was a sly tike in his heart for all that. He was going to ask a young woman to spark it with him, and – the Lord have mercy on my soul! – she was another man's wife.

JESSAMY: The Wabash!

JENNY: And did you see any more folks?

JONATHAN: Why, they came on as thick as mustard. For my part, I thought the house was haunted. There was a soldier fellow, who talked about his row de dow, dow, and courted a young woman; but, of all the cute folk I saw, I liked one little fellow –

JENNY: Aye! who was he?

JONATHAN: Why, he had red hair, and a little round plump face like mine, only not altogether so handsome. His name was – Darby; – that was his baptizing name; his other name I forgot. Oh! it was Wig – Wag – Wag-all, Darby Wag-all, – pray, do you know him? – I should like to take a sling with him, or a drap of cyder with a pepper-pod in it, to make it warm and comfortable.

JENNY: I can't say I have that pleasure.

JONATHAN: I wish you did; he is a cute fellow. But there was one thing I didn't like in that Mr. Darby; and that was, he was afraid of some of them 'ere shooting irons, such as your troopers wear on training days. Now, I'm a true born Yankee American son of liberty, and I never was afraid of a gun yet in all my life.

JENNY: Well, Mr. Jonathan, you were certainly at the play-house.

JONATHAN: I at the play-house! – Why didn't I see the play then?

JENNY: Why, the people you saw were players.

JONATHAN: Mercy on my soul! did I see the wicked players? – Mayhap that 'ere Darby that I liked so was the old serpent himself, and had his cloven foot in his pocket. Why, I vow, now I come to think on't, the candles seemed to burn blue, and I am sure where I sat it smelt tarnally of brimstone.

JESSAMY: Well, Mr. Jonathan, from your account, which I confess is very accurate, you must have been at the play-house.

JONATHAN: Why, I vow, I began to smell a rat. When I came away, I went to the man for my money again; you want your money? says he; yes, says I; for what? says he; why, says I, no man shall jocky me out of my money; I paid my money to see sights, and the dogs a bit of a sight have I seen, unless you call listening to people's private business a sight. Why, says he, it is the School for Scandalization. – The School for Scandalization! – Oh! ho! no wonder you New-York folks are so cute at it, when you go to school to learn it; so I jogged off.

JESSAMY: My dear Jenny, my master's business drags me from you; would to heaven I knew no other servitude than to your charms.

JONATHAN: Well, but don't go; you won't leave me so –

JESSAMY: Excuse me. – Remember the cash. [*Aside to him, and – Exit*]

JENNY: Mr. Jonathan, won't you please to sit down? Mr. Jessamy tells me you wanted to have some conversation with me. [*Having brought forward two chairs, they sit*]

JONATHAN: Ma'am! –

JENNY: Sir! –

JONATHAN: Ma'am! –

JENNY: Pray, how do you like the city, Sir?

JONATHAN: Ma'am! –

JENNY: I say, Sir, how do you like New-York?

JONATHAN: Ma'am! –

JENNY: The stupid creature! but I must pass some little time with him, if it is only to endeavour to learn whether it was his master that made such an abrupt entrance into our house, and my young mistress's heart, this morning. [*Aside*] As you don't seem to like to talk, Mr. Jonathan – do you sing?

JONATHAN: Gor, I – I am glad she asked that, for I forgot what Mr. Jessamy bid me say, and I dare as well be hanged as act what he bid me do, I'm so ashamed. [*Aside*] Yes, Ma'am, I can sing – I can sing Mear, Old Hundred, and Bangor.

JENNY: Oh! I don't mean psalm tunes. Have you no little song to please the ladies, such as Roslin Castle, or the Maid of the Mill?

JONATHAN: Why, all my tunes go to meeting tunes, save one, and I count you won't altogether like that 'ere.

JENNY: What is it called?

JONATHAN: I am sure you have heard folks talk about it; it is called Yankee Doodle.

JENNY: Oh! it is the tune I am fond of; and if I know anything of my mistress, she would be glad to dance to it. Pray, sing!

JONATHAN: [*Sings*]

Father and I went up to camp,
Along with Captain Goodwin;
And there we saw the men and boys,
As thick as hasty-pudding.
Yankee doodle do, etc.

And there we saw a swamping gun,
Big as log of maple,
On a little deuced cart,
A load for father's cattle.
Yankee doodle do, etc.

And every time they fired it off
It took a horn of powder,
It made a noise – like father's gun,
Only a nation louder.
Yankee doodle do, etc.

There was a man in our town,
His name was—

No, no, that won't do. Now, if I was with Tabitha Wymen and Jemima Cawley down at father Chase's, I shouldn't mind singing this all out before them – you would be affronted if I was to sing that, though that's a lucky thought; if you should be affronted, I have something dang'd cute, which Jessamy told me to say to you.

JENNY: Is that all! I assure you I like it of all things.

JONATHAN: No, no; I can sing more; some other time, when you and I are better acquainted, I'll sing the whole of it – no, no – that's a fib – I can't sing but a hundred and ninety verses; our Tabitha at home can sing it all. – [*Sings*]

Marblehead's a rocky place,
And Cape-Cod is sandy;
Charlestown is burnt down,
Boston is the dandy.
Yankee doodle, doodle do, etc.

I vow, my own town song has put me into such topping spirits that I believe I'll begin to do a little, as Jessamy says we must when we go a-courting. – [*Runs and kisses her*] Burning rivers! cooling flames! red-hot roses! pig-nuts!

hasty-pudding and ambrosia!

JENNY: What means this freedom? you insulting wretch. [*Strikes him*]

JONATHAN: Are you affronted?

JENNY: Affronted! with what looks shall I express my anger?

JONATHAN: Looks! why as to the matter of looks, you look as cross as a witch.

JENNY: Have you no feeling for the delicacy of my sex?

JONATHAN: Feeling! Gor, I – I feel the delicacy of your sex pretty smartly, [*Rubbing his cheek*] though, I vow, I thought when you city ladies courted and married, and all that, you put feeling out of the question. But I want to know whether you are really affronted, or only pretend to be so? 'Cause, if you are certainly right down affronted, I am at the end of my tether; Jessamy didn't tell me what to say to you.

JENNY: Pretend to be affronted!

JONATHAN: Aye, aye, if you only pretend, you shall hear how I'll go to work to make cherubim consequences. [*Runs up to her*]

JENNY: Begone, you brute!

JONATHAN: That looks like mad; but I won't lose my speech. My dearest Jenny – your name is Jenny, I think? – My dearest Jenny, though I have the highest esteem for the sweet favours you have just now granted me – Gor, that's a fib, though; but Jessamy says it is not wicked to tell lies to the women. [*Aside*] I say, though I have the highest esteem for the favours you have just now granted me, yet you will consider that, as soon as the dissolvable knot is tied, they will no longer be favours, but only matters of duty and matters of course.

JENNY: Marry you! you audacious monster! get out of my sight, or, rather, let me fly from you. [*Exit hastily*]

JONATHAN: Gor! she's gone off in a swinging passion, before I had time to think of consequences. If this is the way with your city ladies, give me the twenty acres of rock, the Bible, the cow, and Tabitha, and a little peaceable bundling.

Scene 2

The Mall. Enter Manly.

MANLY: It must be so, Montague! and it is not all the tribe of Mandevilles that shall convince me that a nation, to become great, must first become dissipated. Luxury is surely the bane of a nation: Luxury! which enervates both soul and body, by opening a thousand new sources of enjoyment, opens, also, a thousand new sources of contention and want: Luxury! which renders a people weak at home, and accessible to bribery, corruption, and force from abroad. When the Grecian states knew no other tools than the axe and the saw, the Grecians were a great, a free, and a happy people. The kings of Greece devoted their lives to the service of their country, and her senators knew no other superiority over their fellow-citizens than a glorious pre-eminence in danger and virtue. They exhibited to the world a noble spectacle, – a number of independent states united by a similarity of language, sentiment, manners, common interest, and common consent, in one grand mutual league of protection. And, thus united, long might they have continued the cherishers of arts and sciences, the protectors of the oppressed, the scourge of tyrants, and the safe asylum of liberty. But when foreign gold, and still more pernicious foreign luxury, had crept among them, they sapped the vitals of their virtue. The virtues of their ancestors were only found in their writings. Envy and suspicion, the vices of little minds, possessed them. The various states engendered jealousies of each other; and, more unfortunately, growing jealous of their great federal council, the Amphictyons, they forgot that their common safety had existed, and would exist, in giving them an honourable extensive prerogative. The common good was lost in the pursuit of private interest; and that people who, by uniting, might have stood against the world in arms, by dividing, crumbled into ruin; – their name is now only known in the page of the historian, and what they once were is all we have left to admire. Oh! that America! Oh! that my country, would, in this her day, learn the things which belong to her peace!

Enter Dimple

DIMPLE: You are Colonel Manly, I presume?

MANLY: At your service, Sir.

DIMPLE: My name is Dimple, Sir. I have the honour to be a lodger in the same house with you, and, hearing you were in the Mall, came hither to take the liberty of joining you.

MANLY: You are very obliging, Sir.

DIMPLE: As I understand you are a stranger here, Sir, I have taken the liberty to introduce myself to your acquaintance, as possibly I may have it in my power to point out some things in this city worthy your notice.

MANLY: An attention to strangers is worthy a liberal mind, and must ever be gratefully received. But to a soldier, who has no fixed abode, such attentions are particularly pleasing.

DIMPLE: Sir, there is no character so respectable as that of a soldier. And, indeed, when we reflect how much we owe to those brave men who have suffered so much in the service of their country, and secured to us those inestimable blessings that we now enjoy, our liberty and independence, they demand every attention which gratitude can pay. For my own part, I never meet an officer, but I embrace him as my friend, nor a private in distress, but I insensibly extend my charity to him. – I have hit the Bumkin off very tolerably. [*Aside*]

MANLY: Give me your hand, Sir! I do not proffer this hand to everybody; but you steal into my heart. I hope I am as insensible to flattery as most men; but I declare (it may be my weak side) that I never hear the name of soldier mentioned with respect, but I experience a thrill of pleasure which I never feel on any other occasion.

DIMPLE: Will you give me leave, my dear Colonel, to confer an obligation on myself, by shewing you some civilities during your stay here, and giving a similar opportunity to some of my friends?

MANLY: Sir, I thank you; but I believe my stay in this city will be very short.

DIMPLE: I can introduce you to some men of excellent sense, in whose company you will esteem yourself happy; and, by way of amusement, to some fine girls, who will listen to your soft things with pleasure.

MANLY: Sir, I should be proud of the honour of being acquainted with those gentlemen; – but, as for the ladies, I don't understand you.

DIMPLE: Why, Sir, I need not tell you, that when a young gentleman is alone with a young lady he must say some soft things to her fair cheek – indeed, the lady will expect it. To be sure, there is not much pleasure when a man of the world and a finished coquette meet, who perfectly know each other; but how delicious is it to excite the emotions of joy, hope, expecta-

tion, and delight in the bosom of a lovely girl who believes every tittle of what you say to be serious!

MANLY: Serious, Sir! In my opinion, the man who, under pretensions of marriage, can plant thorns in the bosom of an innocent, unsuspecting girl is more detestable than a common robber, in the same proportion as private violence is more despicable than open force, and money of less value than happiness.

DIMPLE: How he awes me by the superiority of his sentiments. [*Aside*] As you say, Sir, a gentleman should be cautious how he mentions marriage.

MANLY: Cautious, Sir! No person more approves of an intercourse between the sexes than I do. Female conversation softens our manners, whilst our discourse, from the superiority of our literary advantages, improves their minds. But, in our young country, where there is no such thing as gallantry, when a gentleman speaks of love to a lady, whether he mentions marriage or not, she ought to conclude either that he meant to insult her or that his intentions are the most serious and honourable. How mean, how cruel, is it, by a thousand tender assiduities, to win the affections of an amiable girl, and, though you leave her virtue unspotted, to betray her into the appearance of so many tender partialities, that every man of delicacy would suppress his inclination towards her, by supposing her heart engaged! Can any man, for the trivial gratification of his leisure hours, affect the happiness of a whole life! His not having spoken of marriage may add to his perfidy, but can be no excuse for his conduct.

DIMPLE: Sir, I admire your sentiments; – they are mine. The light observations that fell from me were only a principle of the tongue; they came not from the heart; my practice has ever disapproved these principles.

MANLY: I believe you, Sir. I should with reluctance suppose that those pernicious sentiments could find admittance into the heart of a gentleman.

DIMPLE: I am now, Sir, going to visit a family, where, if you please, I will have the honour of introducing you. Mr. Manly's ward, Miss Letitia, is a young lady of immense fortune; and his niece, Miss Charlotte Manly, is a young lady of great sprightliness and beauty.

MANLY: That gentleman, Sir, is my uncle, and Miss Manly my sister.

DIMPLE: The devil she is! [*Aside*] Miss Manly your sister, Sir? I rejoice to hear it, and feel a double pleasure in being known to you. – Plague on him! I wish he was at Boston again, with all my soul. [*Aside*]

MANLY: Come, Sir, will you go?

DIMPLE: I will follow you in a moment, Sir. [*Exit Manly*] Plague on it! this is unlucky. A fighting brother is a cursed appendage to a fine girl. Egad! I just stopped in time; had he not discovered himself, in two minutes more I should have told him how well I was with his sister. Indeed, I cannot see the satisfaction of an intrigue, if one can't have the pleasure of communicating it to our friends. [*Exit*]

End of the Third Act

ACT IV. Scene i

Charlotte's apartment. Charlotte leading in Maria.

CHARLOTTE: This is so kind, my sweet friend, to come to see me at this moment. I declare, if I were going to be married in a few days, as you are, I should scarce have found time to visit my friends.

MARIA: Do you think, then, that there is an impropriety in it? – How should you dispose of your time?

CHARLOTTE: Why, I should be shut up in my chamber; and my head would so run upon – upon – upon the solemn ceremony that I was to pass through! – I declare, it would take me above two hours merely to learn that little monosyllable – *Yes*. Ah! my dear, your sentimental imagination does not conceive what that little tiny word implies.

MARIA: Spare me your raillery, my sweet friend; I should love your agreeable vivacity at any other time.

CHARLOTTE: Why, this is the very time to amuse you. You grieve me to see you look so unhappy.

MARIA: Have I not reason to look so?

CHARLOTTE: What new grief distresses you?

MARIA: Oh! how sweet it is, when the heart is borne down with misfortune, to recline and repose on the bosom of friendship! Heaven knows that, although it is improper for a young lady to praise a gentleman, yet I have ever concealed Mr. Dimple's foibles, and spoke of him as of one whose reputation I expected would be linked with mine; but his late conduct towards me has turned my coolness into contempt. He behaves as if he meant to insult and disgust me; whilst my father, in the last conversation on the subject of our marriage, spoke of it as a matter which lay near his heart, and in which he would not bear contradiction.

CHARLOTTE: This works well; oh! the generous Dimple. I'll endeavour to excite her to discharge him. [*Aside*] But, my dear friend, your happiness depends on yourself. Why don't you discard him? Though the match has been of long standing, I would not be forced to make myself miserable: no parent in the world should oblige me to marry the man I did not like.

MARIA: Oh! my dear, you never lived with your parents, and do not know what influence a father's frowns have upon a daughter's heart. Besides, what have I to alledge against Mr. Dimple, to justify myself to the world? He carries himself so smoothly, that every one would impute the blame to me, and call me capricious.

CHARLOTTE: And call her capricious! Did ever such an objection start into the heart of woman? For my part, I wish I had fifty lovers to discard, for no other reason than because I did not fancy them. My dear Maria, you will forgive me; I know your candour and confidence in me; but I have at times, I confess, been led to suppose that some other gentleman was the cause of your aversion to Mr. Dimple.

MARIA: No, my sweet friend, you may be assured, that though I have seen many gentlemen I could prefer to Mr. Dimple, yet I never saw one that I thought I could give my hand to, until this morning.

CHARLOTTE: This morning!

MARIA: Yes; one of the strangest accidents in the world. The odious Dimple, after disgusting me with his conversation, had just left me, when a gentleman, who, it seems, boards in the same house with him, saw him coming out of our door, and, the houses looking very much alike, he came into our house instead of his lodgings; nor did he discover his mistake until he got into the parlour, where I was; he then bowed so gracefully, made such a genteel apology, and looked so manly and noble! –

CHARLOTTE: I see some folks, though it is so

great an impropriety, can praise a gentleman, when he happens to be the man of their fancy. [*Aside*]

MARIA: I don't know how it was, – I hope he did not think me indelicate, – but I asked him, I believe, to sit down, or pointed to a chair. He sat down, and, instead of having recourse to observations upon the weather, or hackneyed criticisms upon the theatre, he entered readily into a conversation worthy a man of sense to speak, and a lady of delicacy and sentiment to hear. He was not strictly handsome, but he spoke the language of sentiment, and his eyes looked tenderness and honour.

CHARLOTTE: Oh! [*Eagerly*] you sentimental, grave girls, when your hearts are once touched, beat us rattles a bar's length. And so you are quite in love with this he-angel?

MARIA: In love with him! How can you rattle so, Charlotte? am I not going to be miserable? [*Sighs*] In love with a gentleman I never saw but one hour in my life, and don't know his name! No; I only wished that the man I shall marry may look, and talk, and act, just like him. Besides, my dear, he is a married man.

CHARLOTTE: Why, that was good-natured – he told you so, I suppose, in mere charity, to prevent you falling in love with him?

MARIA: He didn't tell me so; [*Peevishly*] he looked as if he was married.

CHARLOTTE: How, my dear; did he look sheepish?

MARIA: I am sure he has a susceptible heart, and the ladies of his acquaintance must be very stupid not to –

CHARLOTTE: Hush! I hear some person coming.

Enter Letitia

LETITIA: My dear Maria, I am happy to see you. Lud! what a pity it is that you have purchased your wedding clothes.

MARIA: I think so. [*Sighing*]

LETITIA: Why, my dear, there is the sweetest parcel of silks come over you ever saw! Nancy Brilliant has a full suit come; she sent over her measure, and it fits her to a hair; it is immensely dressy, and made for a court-hoop. I thought they said the large hoops were going out of fashion.

CHARLOTTE: Did you see the hat? Is it a fact that the deep laces round the border is still the fashion?

DIMPLE: [*Within*] Upon my honour, Sir.

MARIA: Ha! Dimple's voice! My dear, I must take leave of you. There are some things necessary to be done at our house. Can't I go through the other room?

Enter Dimple and Manly

DIMPLE: Ladies, your most obedient.

CHARLOTTE: Miss Van Rough, shall I present my brother Henry to you? Colonel Manly, Maria, – Miss Van Rough, brother.

MARIA: Her brother! [*Turns and sees Manly*] Oh! my heart! the very gentleman I have been praising.

MANLY: The same amiable girl I saw this morning!

CHARLOTTE: Why, you look as if you were acquainted.

MANLY: I unintentionally intruded into this lady's presence this morning, for which she was so good as to promise me her forgiveness.

CHARLOTTE: Oh! ho! is that the case! Have these two penserosos been together? Were they Henry's eyes that looked so tenderly? [*Aside*] And so you promised to pardon him? and could you be so good-natured? have you really forgiven him? I beg you would do it for my sake. [*Whispering loud to Maria*] But, my dear, as you are in such haste, it would be cruel to detain you; I can show you the way through the other room.

MARIA: Spare me, my sprightly friend.

MANLY: The lady does not, I hope, intend to deprive us of the pleasure of her company so soon.

CHARLOTTE: She has only a mantua-maker who waits for her at home. But, as I am to give my opinion of the dress, I think she cannot go yet. We were talking of the fashions when you came in, but I suppose the subject must be changed to something of more importance now. Mr. Dimple, will you favour us with an account of the public entertainments?

DIMPLE: Why, really, Miss Manly, you could not have asked me a question more *mal-apropos*. For my part, I must confess that, to a man who has travelled, there is nothing that is worthy the name of amusement to be found in this city.

CHARLOTTE: Except visiting the ladies.

DIMPLE: Pardon me, Madam; that is the avocation of a man of taste. But for amusement, I positively know of nothing that can be called so, unless you dignify with that title the hopping once a fortnight to the sound of two or three squeaking fiddles, and the clattering of the old tavern windows, or sitting to see the miserable mummers, whom you call actors, murder comedy and make a farce of tragedy.

MANLY: Do you never attend the theatre, Sir?

DIMPLE: I was tortured there once.

CHARLOTTE: Pray, Mr. Dimple, was it a tragedy or a comedy?

DIMPLE: Faith, Madam, I cannot tell; for I sat with my back to the stage all the time, admiring a much better actress than any there – a lady who played the fine woman to perfection; though, by the laugh of the horrid creatures round me, I suppose it was comedy. Yet, on second thoughts, it might be some hero in a tragedy, dying so comically as to set the whole house in an uproar. Colonel, I presume you have been in Europe?

MANLY: Indeed, Sir, I was never ten leagues from the continent.

DIMPLE: Believe me, Colonel, you have an immense pleasure to come; and when you shall have seen the brilliant exhibitions of Europe, you will learn to despise the amusements of this country as much as I do.

MANLY: Therefore I do not wish to see them; for I can never esteem that knowledge valuable which tends to give me a distaste for my native country.

DIMPLE: Well, Colonel, though you have not travelled, you have read.

MANLY: I have, a little; and by it have discovered that there is a laudable partiality which ignorant, untravelled men entertain for everything that belongs to their native country. I call it laudable; it injures no one; adds to their own happiness; and, when extended, becomes the noble principle of patriotism. Travelled gentlemen rise superior, in their own opinion, to this; but if the contempt which they contract for their country is the most valuable acquisition of their travels, I am far from thinking that their time and money are well spent.

MARIA: What noble sentiments!

CHARLOTTE: Let my brother set out where he will in the fields of conversation, he is sure to end his tour in the temple of gravity.

MANLY: Forgive me, my sister. I love my country; it has its foibles undoubtedly; – some foreigners will with pleasure remark them – but such remarks fall very ungracefully from the lips of her citizens.

DIMPLE: You are perfectly in the right, Colonel – America has her faults.

MANLY: Yes, Sir; and we, her children, should blush for them in private, and endeavour, as individuals, to reform them. But, if our country has its errors in common with other countries, I am proud to say America – I mean the United States – has displayed virtues and achievements which modern nations may admire, but of which they have seldom set us the example.

CHARLOTTE: But, brother, we must introduce you to some of our gay folks, and let you see the city, such as it is. Mr. Dimple is known to almost every family in town; he will doubtless take a pleasure in introducing you.

DIMPLE: I shall esteem every service I can render your brother an honour.

MANLY: I fear the business I am upon will take up all my time, and my family will be anxious to hear from me.

MARIA: His family! but what is it to me that he is married! [*Aside*] Pray, how did you leave your lady, Sir?

CHARLOTTE: My brother is not married; [*Observing her anxiety*] it is only an odd way he has of expressing himself. Pray, brother, is this business, which you make your continual excuse, a secret?

MANLY: No, sister; I came hither to solicit the honourable Congress, that a number of my brave old soldiers may be put upon the pension-list, who were, at first, not judged to be so materially wounded as to need the public assistance. My sister says true: [*To Maria*] I call my late soldiers my family. Those who were not in the field in the late glorious contest, and those who were, have their respective merits; but, I confess, my old brother-soldiers are dearer to me than the former description. Friendships made in adversity are lasting; our countrymen may forget us, but that is no reason why we should forget one another. But I must leave you; my time of engagement approaches.

CHARLOTTE: Well, but, brother, if you will go, will you please to conduct my fair friend home? You live in the same street – I was to have gone with her myself. – [*Aside*] A lucky thought.

MARIA: I am obliged to your sister, Sir, and was just intending to go. [*Going*]

MANLY: I shall attend her with pleasure. [*Exit

with Maria, followed by Dimple and Charlotte]

MARIA: Now, pray, don't betray me to your brother.

CHARLOTTE: *[Just as she sees him make a motion to take his leave]* One word with you, brother, if you please. *[Follows them out]*

Manent, Dimple and Letitia

DIMPLE: You received the billet I sent you, I presume?

LETITIA: Hush! – Yes.

DIMPLE: When shall I pay my respects to you?

LETITIA: At eight I shall be unengaged.

Reenter Charlotte

DIMPLE: Did my lovely angel receive my billet? *[To Charlotte]*

CHARLOTTE: Yes.

DIMPLE: What hour shall I expect with impatience?

CHARLOTTE: At eight I shall be at home unengaged.

DIMPLE: Unfortunate! I have a horrid engagement of business at that hour. Can't you finish your visit earlier and let six be the happy hour?

CHARLOTTE: You know your influence over me. *[Exeunt severally]*

Scene 2

Van Rough's house.

VAN ROUGH: *[Alone]* It cannot possibly be true! The son of my old friend can't have acted so unadvisedly. Seventeen thousand pounds! in bills! Mr. Transfer must have been mistaken. He always appeared so prudent, and talked so well upon money matters, and even assured me that he intended to change his dress for a suit of clothes which would not cost so much, and look more substantial, as soon as he married. No, no, no! it can't be; it cannot be. But, however, I must look out sharp. I did not care what his principles or his actions were, so long as he minded the main chance. Seventeen thousand pounds! If he had lost it in trade, why the best men may have ill-luck; but to game it away, as Transfer says – why, at this rate, his whole estate may go in one night, and, what is ten times worse, mine into the bargain. No, no; Mary is right. Leave women to look out in these matters; for all they look as if they didn't know a journal from a ledger, when their interest is concerned they know what's what; they mind the main chance as well as the best of us. I wonder Mary did not tell me she knew of his spending his money so foolishly. Seventeen thousand pounds! Why, if my daughter was standing up to be married, I would forbid the banns, if I found it was to a man who did not mind the main chance. – Hush! I hear somebody coming. 'Tis Mary's voice; a man with her too! I shouldn't be surprised if this should be the other string to her bow. Aye, aye, let them alone; women understand the main chance. – Though i' faith, I'll listen a little. *[Retires into the closet]*

Manly leading in Maria

MANLY: I hope you will excuse my speaking upon so important a subject so abruptly; but, the moment I entered your room, you struck me as the lady whom I had long loved in imagination, and never hoped to see.

MARIA: Indeed, Sir, I have been led to hear more upon this subject than I ought.

MANLY: Do you, then, disapprove my suit, Madam, or the abruptness of my introducing it? If the latter, my peculiar situation, being obliged to leave the city in a few days, will, I hope, be my excuse; if the former, I will retire, for I am sure I would not give a moment's inquietude to her whom I could devote my life to please. I am not so indelicate as to seek your immediate approbation; permit me only to be near you, and by a thousand tender assiduities to endeavour to excite a grateful return.

MARIA: I have a father, whom I would die to make happy; he will disapprove –

MANLY: Do you think me so ungenerous as to seek a place in your esteem without his consent? You must – you ever ought to consider that man as unworthy of you who seeks an interest in your heart contrary to a father's approbation. A young lady should reflect that the loss of a lover may be supplied, but nothing can compensate for the loss of a parent's affection. Yet, why do you suppose your father would disapprove? In our country, the affections are not sacrificed to riches or family aggrandizement: should you approve, my family is decent, and my rank honourable.

MARIA: You distress me, Sir.

MANLY: Then I will sincerely beg your excuse

for obtruding so disagreeable a subject, and retire. [*Going*]

MARIA: Stay, Sir! your generosity and good opinion of me deserve a return; but why must I declare what, for these few hours, I have scarce suffered myself to think? – I am –

MANLY: What?

MARIA: Engaged, Sir; and, in a few days, to be married to the gentleman you saw at your sister's.

MANLY: Engaged to be married! And have I been basely invading the rights of another? Why have you permitted this? Is this the return for the partiality I declared for you?

MARIA: You distress me, Sir. What would you have me say? You are too generous to wish the truth. Ought I to say that I dared not suffer myself to think of my engagement, and that I am going to give my hand without my heart? Would you have me confess a partiality for you? If so, your triumph is compleat, and can be only more so when days of misery with the man I cannot love will make me think of him whom I could prefer.

MANLY: [*After a pause*] We are both unhappy; but it is your duty to obey your parent – mine to obey my honour. Let us, therefore, both follow the path of rectitude; and of this we may be assured, that if we are not happy, we shall, at least, deserve to be so. Adieu! I dare not trust myself longer with you. [*Exeunt severally*]

End of the Fourth Act

ACT V. Scene 1

Dimple's lodgings.

JESSAMY: [*Meeting Jonathan*] Well, Mr. Jonathan, what success with the fair?

JONATHAN: Why, such a tarnal cross tike you never saw! You would have counted she had lived upon crab-apples and vinegar for a fortnight. But what the rattle makes you look so tarnation glum?

JESSAMY: I was thinking, Mr. Jonathan, what could be the reason of her carrying herself so coolly to you.

JONATHAN: Coolly, do you call it? Why, I vow, she was fire-hot angry: may be it was because I buss'd her.

JESSAMY: No, no, Mr. Jonathan; there must be some other cause; I never yet knew a lady angry at being kissed.

JONATHAN: Well, if it is not the young woman's bashfulness, I vow I can't conceive why she shouldn't like me.

JESSAMY: May be it is because you have not the Graces, Mr. Jonathan.

JONATHAN: Grace! Why, does the young woman expect I must be converted before I court her?

JESSAMY: I mean graces of person: for instance, my lord tells us that we must cut off our nails even at top, in small segments of circles – though you won't understand that; in the next place, you must regulate your laugh.

JONATHAN: Maple-log seize it! don't I laugh natural?

JESSAMY: That's the very fault, Mr. Jonathan. Besides, you absolutely misplace it. I was told by a friend of mine that you laughed outright at the play the other night, when you ought only to have tittered.

JONATHAN: Gor! I – what does one go to see fun for if they can't laugh?

JESSAMY: You may laugh; but you must laugh by rule.

JONATHAN: Swamp it – laugh by rule! Well, I should like that tarnally.

JESSAMY: Why, you know, Mr. Jonathan, that to dance, a lady to play with her fan, or a gentleman with his cane, and all other natural motions, are regulated by art. My master has composed an immensely pretty gamut, by which any lady or gentleman, with a few years' close application, may learn to laugh as gracefully as if they were born and bred to it.

JONATHAN: Mercy on my soul! A gamut for laughing – just like fa, la, sol?

JESSAMY: Yes. It comprises every possible display of jocularity, from an *affettuoso* smile to a *piano* titter, or full chorus *fortissimo* ha, ha, ha! My master employs his leisure hours in marking out the plays, like a cathedral chanting-book, that the ignorant may know where to laugh; and that pit, box, and gallery may keep time together, and not have a snigger in one part of the house, a broad grin in the other, and a d——d grum look in the third. How delightful to see the audience all smile together, then look on their books, then twist their mouths into an agreeable simper, then altogether shake the house with a general ha, ha, ha! loud as a full chorus of Handel's at an Abbey commemoration.

JONATHAN: Ha, ha, ha! that's dang'd cute, I swear.

JESSAMY: The gentlemen, you see, will laugh the tenor; the ladies will play the counter-tenor; the beaux will squeak the treble; and our jolly friends in the gallery a thorough base, ho, ho, ho!

JONATHAN: Well, can't you let me see that gamut?

JESSAMY: Oh! yes, Mr. Jonathan; here it is. [*Takes out a book*] Oh! no, this is only a titter with its variations. Ah, here it is. [*Takes out another*] Now, you must know, Mr. Jonathan, this is a piece written by Ben Jonson, which I have set to my master's gamut. The places where you must smile, look grave, or laugh outright, are marked below the line. Now look over me. "There was a certain man" – now you must smile.

JONATHAN: Well, read it again; I warrant I'll mind my eye.

JESSAMY: "There was a certain man, who had a sad scolding wife," – now you must laugh.

JONATHAN: Tarnation! That's no laughing matter though.

JESSAMY: "And she lay sick a-dying"; – now you must titter.

JONATHAN: What, snigger when the good woman's a-dying! Gor, I –

JESSAMY: Yes, the notes say you must – "and she asked her husband leave to make a will," – now you must begin to look grave; – "and her husband said" –

JONATHAN: Ay, what did her husband say? Something dang'd cute, I reckon.

JESSAMY: "And her husband said, you have had your will all your life-time, and would you have it after you are dead, too?"

JONATHAN: Ho, ho, ho! There the old man was even with her; he was up to the notch – ha, ha, ha!

JESSAMY: But, Mr. Jonathan, you must not laugh so. Why you ought to have tittered *piano*, and you have laughed *fortissimo*. Look here; you see these marks, A, B, C, and so on; these are the references to the other part of the book. Let us turn to it, and you will see the directions how to manage the muscles. This [*Turns over*] was note D you blundered at. – You must purse the mouth into a smile, then

titter, discovering the lower part of the three front upper teeth.

JONATHAN: How? read it again.

JESSAMY: "There was a certain man" – very well! – "who had a sad scolding wife," – why don't you laugh?

JONATHAN: Now, that scolding wife sticks in my gizzard so pluckily that I can't laugh for the blood and nowns of me. Let me look grave here, and I'll laugh your belly full, where the old creature's a-dying.

JESSAMY: "And she asked her husband" – [*Bell rings*] My master's bell! he's returned, I fear. – Here, Mr. Jonathan, take this gamut; and I make no doubt but with a few years' close application, you may be able to smile gracefully. [*Exeunt severally*]

Scene 2

Charlotte's apartment. Enter Manly.

MANLY: What, no one at home? How unfortunate to meet the only lady my heart was ever moved by, to find her engaged to another, and confessing her partiality for me! Yet engaged to a man who, by her intimation, and his libertine conversation with me, I fear, does not merit her. Aye! there's the sting; for, were I assured that Maria was happy, my heart is not so selfish but that it would dilate in knowing it, even though it were with another. But to know she is unhappy! – I must drive these thoughts from me. Charlotte has some books; and this is what I believe she calls her little library. [*Enters a closet*]

Enter Dimple leading Letitia

LETITIA: And will you pretend to say now, Mr. Dimple, that you propose to break with Maria? Are not the banns published? Are not the clothes purchased? Are not the friends invited? In short, is it not a done affair?

DIMPLE: Believe me, my dear Letitia, I would not marry her.

LETITIA: Why have you not broke with her before this, as you all along deluded me by saying you would?

DIMPLE: Because I was in hopes she would, ere this, have broke with me.

LETITIA: You could not expect it.

DIMPLE: Nay, but be calm a moment; 'twas

from my regard to you that I did not discard her.

LETITIA: Regard to me!

DIMPLE: Yes; I have done everything in my power to break with her, but the foolish girl is so fond of me that nothing can accomplish it. Besides, how can I offer her my hand when my heart is indissolubly engaged to you?

LETITIA: There may be reason in this; but why so attentive to Miss Manly?

DIMPLE: Attentive to Miss Manly! For heaven's sake, if you have no better opinion of my constancy, pay not so ill a compliment to my taste.

LETITIA: Did I not see you whisper her to-day?

DIMPLE: Possibly I might – but something of so very trifling a nature that I have already forgot what it was.

LETITIA: I believe she has not forgot it.

DIMPLE: My dear creature, how can you for a moment suppose I should have any serious thoughts of that trifling, gay, flighty coquette, that disagreeable –

Enter Charlotte

DIMPLE: My dear Miss Manly, I rejoice to see you; there is a charm in your conversation that always marks your entrance into company as fortunate.

LETITIA: Where have you been, my dear?

CHARLOTTE: Why, I have been about to twenty shops, turning over pretty things, and so have left twenty visits unpaid. I wish you would step into the carriage and whisk round, make my apology, and leave my cards where our friends are not at home; that, you know, will serve as a visit. Come, do go.

LETITIA: So anxious to get me out! but I'll watch you. [*Aside*] Oh! yes, I'll go; I want a little exercise. Positively, [*Dimple offering to accompany her*] Mr. Dimple, you shall not go; why, half my visits are cake and caudle visits; it won't do, you know, for you to go. [*Exit, but returns to the door in the back scene and listens*]

DIMPLE: This attachment of your brother to Maria is fortunate.

CHARLOTTE: How did you come to the knowledge of it?

DIMPLE: I read it in their eyes.

CHARLOTTE: And I had it from her mouth. It would have amused you to have seen her! She, that thought it so great an impropriety to praise

a gentleman that she could not bring out one word in your favour, found a redundancy to praise him.

DIMPLE: I have done everything in my power to assist his passion there: your delicacy, my dearest girl, would be shocked at half the instances of neglect and misbehaviour.

CHARLOTTE: I don't know how I should bear neglect; but Mr. Dimple must misbehave himself indeed, to forfeit my good opinion.

DIMPLE: Your good opinion, my angel, is the pride and pleasure of my heart; and if the most respectful tenderness for you, and an utter indifference for all your sex besides, can make me worthy of your esteem, I shall richly merit it.

CHARLOTTE: All my sex besides, Mr. Dimple! – you forgot your *tête-à-tête* with Letitia.

DIMPLE: How can you, my lovely angel, cast a thought on that insipid, wry-mouthed, ugly creature!

CHARLOTTE: But her fortune may have charms?

DIMPLE: Not to a heart like mine. The man, who has been blessed with the good opinion of my Charlotte, must despise the allurements of fortune.

CHARLOTTE: I am satisfied.

DIMPLE: Let us think no more on the odious subject, but devote the present hour to happiness.

CHARLOTTE: Can I be happy when I see the man I prefer going to be married to another?

DIMPLE: Have I not already satisfied my charming angel, that I can never think of marrying the puling Maria? But, even if it were so, could that be any bar to our happiness? for, as the poet sings,

"Love, free as air, at sight of human ties,
Spreads his light wings, and in a moment flies."

Come, then, my charming angel! why delay our bliss? The present moment is ours; the next is in the hand of fate. [*Kissing her*]

CHARLOTTE: Begone, Sir! By your delusions you had almost lulled my honour asleep.

DIMPLE: Let me lull the demon to sleep again with kisses. [*He struggles with her; she screams*]

Enter Manly

MANLY: Turn, villain! and defend yourself. – [*Draws*]

Van Rough enters and beats down their swords

VAN ROUGH: Is the devil in you? are you going

to murder one another? [*Holding Dimple*]

DIMPLE: Hold him, hold him, – I can command my passion.

Enter Jonathan

JONATHAN: What the rattle ails you? Is the old one in you? Let the colonel alone, can't you? I feel chock-full of fight, – do you want to kill the colonel? –

MANLY: Be still, Jonathan; the gentleman does not want to hurt me.

JONATHAN: Gor! I – I wish he did; I'd shew him Yankee boys play, pretty quick. – Don't you see you have frightened the young woman into the *hystrikes*?

VAN ROUGH: Pray, some of you explain this; what has been the occasion of all this racket?

MANLY: That gentleman can explain it to you; it will be a very diverting story for an intended father-in-law to hear.

VAN ROUGH: How was this matter, Mr. Van Dumpling?

DIMPLE: Sir, – upon my honour, – all I know is, that I was talking to this young lady, and this gentleman broke in on us in a very extraordinary manner.

VAN ROUGH: Why, all this is nothing to the purpose; can you explain it, Miss? [*To Charlotte*]

Enter Letitia through the back scene

LETITIA: I can explain it to that gentleman's confusion. Though long betrothed to your daughter, [*To Van Rough*] yet, allured by my fortune, it seems (with shame do I speak it) he has privately paid his addresses to me. I was drawn in to listen to him by his assuring me that the match was made by his father without his consent, and that he proposed to break with Maria, whether he married me or not. But, whatever were his intentions respecting your daughter, Sir, even to me he was false; for he has repeated the same story, with some cruel reflections upon my person, to Miss Manly.

JONATHAN: What a tarnal curse!

LETITIA: Nor is this all, Miss Manly. When he was with me this very morning, he made the same ungenerous reflections upon the weakness of your mind as he has so recently done upon the defects of my person.

JONATHAN: What a tarnal curse and damn, too!

DIMPLE: Ha! since I have lost Letitia, I believe I

had as good make it up with Maria. Mr. Van Rough, at present I cannot enter into particulars; but, I believe, I can explain everything to your satisfaction in private.

VAN ROUGH: There is another matter, Mr. Van Dumpling, which I would have you explain. Pray, Sir, have Messrs. Van Cash & Co. presented you those bills for acceptance?

DIMPLE: The deuce! Has he heard of those bills! Nay, then, all's up with Maria, too; but an affair of this sort can never prejudice me among the ladies; they will rather long to know what the dear creature possesses to make him so agreeable. [*Aside*] Sir, You'll hear from me. [*To Manly*]

MANLY: And you from me, Sir –

DIMPLE: Sir, you wear a sword –

MANLY: Yes, Sir. This sword was presented to me by that brave Gallic hero, the Marquis De la Fayette. I have drawn it in the service of my country, and in private life, on the only occasion where a man is justified in drawing his sword, in defence of a lady's honour. I have fought too many battles in the service of my country to dread the imputation of cowardice. Death from a man of honour would be a glory you do not merit; you shall live to bear the insult of man and the contempt of that sex whose general smiles afforded you all your happiness.

DIMPLE: You won't meet me, Sir? Then I'll post you for a coward.

MANLY: I'll venture that, Sir. The reputation of my life does not depend upon the breath of a Mr. Dimple. I would have you to know, however, Sir, that I have a cane to chastise the insolence of a scoundrel, and a sword and the good laws of my country to protect me from the attempts of an assassin –

DIMPLE: Mighty well! Very fine, indeed! Ladies and gentlemen, I take my leave; and you will please to observe in the case of my deportment the contrast between a gentleman who has read Chesterfield and received the polish of Europe and an unpolished, untravelled American. [*Exit*]

Enter Maria

MARIA: Is he indeed gone? –

LETITIA: I hope, never to return.

VAN ROUGH: I am glad I heard of those bills; though it's plaguy unlucky; I hoped to see Mary married before I died.

MANLY: Will you permit a gentleman, Sir, to offer himself as a suitor to your daughter? Though a stranger to you, he is not altogether so to her, or unknown in this city. You may find a son-in-law of more fortune, but you can never meet with one who is richer in love for her, or respect for you.

VAN ROUGH: Why, Mary, you have not let this gentleman make love to you without my leave?

MANLY: I did not say, Sir –

MARIA: Say, Sir! – I – the gentleman, to be sure, met me accidentally.

VAN ROUGH: Ha, ha, ha! Mark me, Mary; young folks think old folks to be fools; but old folks know young folks to be fools. Why, I knew all about this affair. This was only a cunning way I had to bring it about. Hark ye! I was in the closet when you and he were at our house. [*Turns to the company*] I heard that little baggage say she loved her old father, and would die to make him happy! Oh! how I loved the little baggage! And you talked very prudently, young man. I have inquired into your character, and find you to be a man of punctuality and mind the main chance. And so, as you love Mary and Mary loves you, you shall have my consent immediately to be married. I'll settle my fortune on you, and go and live with you the remainder of my life.

MANLY: Sir, I hope –

VAN ROUGH: Come, come, no fine speeches; mind the main chance, young man, and you and I shall always agree.

LETITIA: I sincerely wish you joy; [*Advancing to Maria*] and hope your pardon for my conduct.

MARIA: I thank you for your congratulations, and hope we shall at once forget the wretch who has given us so much disquiet, and the trouble that he has occasioned.

CHARLOTTE: And I, my dear Maria, – how shall I look up to you for forgiveness? I, who, in the practice of the meanest arts, have violated the most sacred rights of friendship? I can never forgive myself, or hope charity from the world; but, I confess, I have much to hope from such a brother; and I am happy that I may soon say, such a sister.

MARIA: My dear, you distress me; you have all my love.

MANLY: And mine.

CHARLOTTE: If repentance can entitle me to forgiveness, I have already much merit; for I despise the littleness of my past conduct. I now find that the heart of any worthy man cannot be gained by invidious attacks upon the rights and characters of others; – by countenancing the addresses of a thousand; – or that the finest assemblage of features, the greatest taste in dress, the genteelest address, or the most brilliant wit, cannot eventually secure a coquette from contempt and ridicule.

MANLY: And I have learned that probity, virtue, honour, though they should not have received the polish of Europe, will secure to an honest American the good graces of his fair countrywomen, and, I hope, the applause of THE PUBLIC.

The End

BUNKER-HILL

OR

THE DEATH OF GENERAL WARREN

JOHN DALY BURK

JOHN DALY BURK, a distant kin of the British statesman Edmund Burke, came to America from Ireland in 1796. He had been expelled from Trinity College, Dublin, on charges of deism and republicanism. In this enforced flight from Dublin a Miss Daly had lent him the female apparel in which he escaped from the British authorities, and out of gratitude to her he added her name to his own. Shortly after his arrival in Boston, a report circulated that a reward for his arrest had been posted by the British government; but the Boston newspaper *Columbian Centinel* insisted that he had fled "not from prosecution, but from persecution. . . . He is a gentleman of talents and modesty, and his principles of government are rational and republican."

He began his American literary activity in October, 1796, as editor of a Boston newspaper, *Polar Star and Boston Daily Advertiser*. Unfortunately, this journal ceased publication on February 2, 1797. After this failure and after the success of his *Bunker-Hill* (Haymarket Theatre, Boston, February 17, 1797) Burk moved to New York to edit another newspaper. Again his tenure was short. *Time-Piece* suspended operation when Burk was arrested on charges of "publishing a libel contrary to the provisions of the sedition law of 1798." Sometime around the turn of the century he moved to Petersburg, Virginia, to devote himself to law and literature. Here his "hot head" and "loose tongue" provoked an argument of more serious consequence. He had the bad grace to tell a Monsieur Coquebert that he deplored the unfriendly attitude of Napoleonic France toward the American Republic. Burk may have been right, but the Frenchman was a superior duelist. Burk was killed on April 11, 1808.

The principal product of his Virginia literary days was a *History of Virginia* in three volumes. He paid tribute to his native land with a *History of the Late War in Ireland, with an Account of the United Irish Association, from the First Meeting in Belfast, to the Landing of the French at Kilala*, published in 1799 in Philadelphia. A posthumous publication demonstrated a similar predilection: *An Historical Essay on the Character and Antiquity of Irish Songs*, printed in the *Richmond Enquirer* in May, 1808.

Of his seven dramatic pieces, three are known only by name: *The Fortunes of Nigel, The Innkeeper of Abbeville*, and *Which Do You Like Best, the Poor Man or the Lord?* Of the others, *Bunker-Hill* (1797) is his first and best. Like *Bunker-Hill*, his other three were derived from historical events: *Female Patriotism, or The Death of Joan of Arc*, played at the Park Theatre, New York, April, 1798; *The Death of General Montgomery in Storming the City of Quebec;* and *Bethlem Gabor, Lord of Transylvania, or The Man-Hating Palatine*, an historical drama in three acts based on the struggle of the Protestants in Transylvania in the seventeenth century, published in Petersburg, Virginia, in 1807. This last play was acted by the "author and fellow-amateurs" and, on at least one occasion, by the Richmond Theatre company. The spirit of a revolutionary rebel was evident in all of the plays. Even in his *Joan of Arc*, the characters and their sentiments clearly belonged to Burk's eighteenth-century America rather than to Joan's medieval France. Burk had been obsessed with his libertarian notions long before he landed in Boston; in fact, he wrote *Bunker-Hill*, his first American testament to his faith, during the voyage.

Bunker-Hill, or The Death of General Warren: An Historic Tragedy had a remarkable stage history in spite of the early criticism directed against it. William Dunlap, who had found Burk's *History of Virginia* "exhibiting talent and learning" labeled *Bunker-Hill* a "deplorable play." After its initial performance at the Haymarket Theatre, Boston, on February 17, 1797, John B. Williamson, manager of the rival Federal Street Theatre, called it "the most execrable of the Grub Street kind." He attributed its unwarranted success to "its locality in title, the burning of Charlestown and peppering of the British." The *Centinel*, a newspaper whose favorable regard for Burk has already been indicated, found it "not less unrivalled as a play than it has been unequalled in the history of military glory." The audiences apparently subscribed to the *Centinel's* view. The initial Boston run included ten performances between February 17 and May 10, 1797, a fact duly noted on the title page of its first printing in 1797: "As performed at the Theatres in America, for Fourteen Nights, with Unbounded Applause." The editor might well have reset this statement in boldface above the title if he had counted up the thirty performances recorded before the second-printing date, 1817; and this thirty does not include the unspecified number of performances in the towns around Boston that Clapp alludes to in his *Record of the Boston Stage*. Another mark of the play's acceptance, equally uncommon in our early theatre, was the two-thousand-dollar profit Burk realized from his endeavor.

Quite naturally after his Boston success, Burk sought a production of the play in New York. Sometime in March, 1797, he wrote to John Hodgkinson, who was then one of the triumvirate managing the John Street Theatre. (The others were Dunlap and Hallam.) This letter, here quoted in its entirety, is an important document in our early theatre history. It provides an elaborate and precisely drawn account of a stage spectacle of the period with exact instructions for any manager charged with preparing the play for the stage. Such descriptions of stage mounting are rare. Even in a period when spectacular effects were greatly admired, few pictures and documents describe them in such detail.

Dear Sir,

From a wish that you should be possessed of my play as early as possible I have preferred sending on the original copy rather than wait to have a fair one transcribed – where it was incomplete I have written and made it good, interspersing occasionally such remarks as, from seeing the effect in representation, appeared to me serviceable in getting it up. It was played seven nights successively, and on the last night was received with the same enthusiasm as on the first – it revived old scenes, and united all parts of the house. Mr. Powell intends it for a stock play, and it will be represented on all festivals – such as 4th July, 19th June, etc. It will be played here in a few nights again, immediately after Columbus. The lines marked by inverted commas are those spoken. The hill is raised gradually by boards extended from the stage to a bench. Three men should walk abreast on it, and the side where the English march up, should for the most part be turned towards the wings; on our hill there was room for eighteen or twenty men, and they were concealed by a board painted mud colour, and having two cannon painted on it – which board was three feet and a half high. The English marched in two divisions from one extremity of the stage, where they ranged, after coming from the wing near the hill – firing commences – they are again beaten back – windows on the stage should be open to let out the smoak [sic]. All the English make the attack and mount the hill. After a brisk fire, the Americans leave works and meet them. Here is room for effect, if the scuffle be nicely managed. Sometimes the English falling back, sometimes the Americans – two or three Englishmen rolling down the hill. A square piece about nine feet high and five wide, having some houses and a meeting-house painted on fire, with flame and smoak issuing from it, should be raised two feet distance from the horizon scene at the back of your stage, the windows and doors cut out for transparencies – in a word, it should have the appearance of a town on fire. We had painted smoak suspended – it is raised at the back wing, and is intended to represent Charlestown, and is on a line with the hill, and where it is lowest. The fire should be played skilfully behind this burning town, and the smoak to evaporate. When the curtain rises in the fifth, the appearance of the whole is good – Charlestown on fire, the breast-work of wood, the Americans appearing over the works and the muzzles of their guns, the English and the American music, the attack of the hill, the falling of the English troops, Warren's half descending the hill and animating the Americans, the smoak and confusion, all together produce an effect scarce credible. We had a scene of State street – if you had one it would not be amiss – we used it instead of the scene of Boston Neck – it appears to me you need not be particular, but the hill and Charlestown on fire. We had English uniforms for men and officers. You can procure the coats of some company at New York which dresses in red. Small cannon should be fired during the battle, which continued with us for twelve or fifteen minutes. I am thus prolix that you may find the less difficulty in getting it up – it is not expensive, and will always be a valuable stock piece. I should not wonder if every person in New York, and some miles round it, should go to see it represented. There will no doubt be some who will call in question your prudence in getting up this piece, as being not in favour of England. Those are blockheads, and know not the public opinion in America. Boston is as much divided as New York – party was forgotten in the representation of it. Others there are who will endeavour to prejudice you against its merit; of them I shall say nothing. You have the play and can judge for yourself – my reason for mentioning the latter description of men is, that a man from Boston, who pretends to criticise without knowing how to spell, has been industrious in depreciating the value of my piece in Boston, and I conceived it not improbable that he would act in the same manner in New York. When he found it had succeeded, he ascribed its success alone to its locality. This man took a letter to you from Mr. Barrett. I send you the prologue and elegy.

After consulting Mr. Barrett, who was delicate in advising, lest he should be thought partial to one interest or the other, I have concluded to charge you one hundred guineas for the copy, seventy of which I request you will send to Mr. Barrett immediately on receipt of the piece, the remaining thirty on the fourth night of representation. Mr. Barrett thinks it will run ten nights in succession at New York. I think not of printing it for one year, when I do I shall dedicate it to the president. Mr. Bates has sent on to me for a copy. I am in treaty with Mr. Wignell. The terms shall not be lower than with you. I shall send you on from time to time such pantomimes and entertainments as I shall arrange, on reasonable terms. I have three at present, which I shall send on when you please, as cheap as you can get a pirated copy of a farce. My new tragedy, entitled Joan of Arc, or the Maid of Orleans, is ready for representation. Excuse this wretched scrawl, it has been written too hastily.

JOHN BURK

We had our hill on the left side of the stage – the painting of Charlestown on fire should not be seen till the fifth set. If there is any thing you would wish to be informed on further, by directing a line to me, you shall receive the speediest answer. As I look on this only as the basis of a future negotiation, I shall not be adverse to abate something of my demand, if you think it high, though I am tolerably certain you will clear four thousand dollars in its run only.

Whether prejudiced by an earlier letter about the play from John B. Williamson, or perhaps on the advice of Dunlap, who found the scenic effects an abomination, Hodgkinson returned the manuscript to Burk. Burk sent it back immediately offering it "on the usual terms given by you [Hodgkinson] for new pieces." Again Hodgkinson refused.

In the fall of 1797, the John Street Theatre was leased by Hodgkinson and Dunlap to John Solee, former manager of the Charleston, South Carolina, theatre. Under his guidance New York got its first look at *Bunker-Hill*, brought out with what Dunlap called "all the smoke, noise, and nonsense belonging to Mr. John Burk's muse." Undoubtedly it was not presented on the recommendation of the theatre owners. In fact, a letter from Dunlap to Hodgkinson indicates that Burk was in New York at the time claiming that the play was being presented without his permission. His claim seems plausible. Solee scheduled this opening New York performance for September 8, the same night that Wignell and Reinagle at the Greenwich Street Theatre had announced a performance of *The Revenge*, with the eminent tragedian James Fennell in his first New York appearance, for the "relief of the unfortunate sufferers by the late dreadful fire at Albany." Solee's unfeeling disregard for his competitor's charitable endeavor paid off for him. Dunlap reported receipts of five hundred dollars for the first night of *Bunker-Hill* and two hundred for the second. (Solee had taken in only two hundred for the entire previous week.) Still Dunlap insisted that "the piece is, as it ought to be, execrated." Perhaps Dunlap's later failure as a theatre manager resulted from such fanciful disregard for the box office.

Although the following account of the New York opening in the *Gazette* might sound manager-inspired, it does give some insight into the delight the audience found in such patriotic spectacles:

Mr. Barrett's General Warren is a most finished piece of acting; and, had we not been well assured he was from the city of Dublin, we must, for his apparent feelings in the above character, have pronounced him a staunch true born American. . . . Mrs. Barrett pleaded the cause of the fair American in so elegant a style, that no hearer could do otherwise than pity her sufferings, and applaud the actress. . . . The scenery was most beautifully striking – the view of State street in Boston – American Camp – with Charlestown burning, and the encampment on Bunker Hill, was far superior to any thing ever brought forward on this stage. No doubt but the manager will reap a profitable harvest from his labours. . . . We never recollect greater bursts of applause than when Warren addressed the Americans on the Hill. . . . Which was, from the feeling of the audience, echoed from all parts of the theatre.

The play was repeated during September and October, and sometime after October 17, 1797, a sixth New York showing was given for President John Adams. In his letter to Hodgkinson, Burk had said that he intended to dedicate the play to Adams. However, the dedication that finally appeared in print is addressed to Aaron Burr. When Adams saw the play on this occasion, he is reported to have told Barrett, who had performed General Warren, "My friend, General Warren, was a scholar and a gentleman but your author has made him a bully and a blackguard." For one of Burk's rebellious nature, here was cause enough for a change in the dedication.

After its initial series of performances in Boston and New York, the play was done in Alexandria and Charleston. By the end of the 1798–99 season, some thirty performances had been recorded. Thereafter it settled into the American theatre repertoire as a patriotic piece to be brought out on the Fourth of July or on November 25 (Evacuation Day). Dunlap continued to wail and cheer over its success. As manager of the Park, he offered it on July 5, 1802 (the 4th had been on Sunday), and reported, ". . . the house overflowed to that vile trash . . . the receipts were the greatest ever known at that time, $1245." Before that, on November 25, 1800, not only had Dunlap staged the play at the Park but Hodgkinson had played the part of Warren. No matter what they might have thought in 1797, audiences had clearly over-ruled them. It was probably the continuing success of this piece that prompted Dunlap to devise his own patriotic spectacle, *The Glory of Columbia* (1803).

The reception of the play in other cities was similar to that in New York. In Albany it "met with great applause, although utterly without merit." In Providence it was "well received . . . it survived many dramas superior to it in every respect." In Charleston the reporter registered his sentiments with a quotation from the prologue:

> A nobler theme than this to grace the stage
> Where can we find in all the historic page?
> Of Rome and Cato's fall the world has rung
> Why not Columbia's rising fame be sung?

The patriotic effusions of *Bunker-Hill* were close to the minds and hearts of the theatre patrons of the day. The play reflected the prevailing thoughts of the populace in these early days of the Republic; thus when the early-nineteenth-century theatre manager needed a patriotic piece, he turned invariably to *Bunker-Hill*. During the dark days of the War of 1812, it was played frequently. On August 29, 1814, the Anthony Street Theatre announced its performance with a line from the play: "Let the Rallying Word be Liberty or Death." (On this same date Dunlap's *Glory of Columbia* was given at the Park.)

Burk's *Bunker-Hill* was not the first play based on a Revolutionary War theme or the first employing this incident. In 1776 Hugh Brackenridge had published his *The Battle of Bunkers Hill*. His play was also devoted to glorifying the cause of freedom and the noble fight of the colonists against their tyrannical adversaries. Just before the battle Warren addressed his soldiers:

> Three thousand, 'gainst seven hundred, rang'd this day
> Shall give the world, an ample specimen,
> What strength, and noble confidence, the sound
> Of Liberty inspires.

Its inadequacies as a theatrical piece were at least partly explained in Brackenridge's dedication: The play was "first drawn up for an Exercise in Oratory, to a number of young Gentlemen in a Southern Academy." There is no authenticated record of a production of the play, but it seems likely that it was performed at the Somerset Academy in Maryland, where Brackenridge was teaching.

Even before 1776 a number of plays had exploited various aspects of the struggle for independence. In *A Dialogue Between a Southern Delegate and His Spouse on His Return from the Grand Continental Congress*, an anonymous work published in 1774, a wife with Tory sympathies chastised her patriot husband, insisting that the future of the country would have been more secure if she had held his delegate's seat in the Congress. Another anonymous Tory document, *Americans Roused in a Cure for the Spleen*, was printed in Boston in 1775. The *dramatis personae* of this "conversation of the times over a friendly Tankard and Pipe" clearly indicated the sympathies of the author. The Tory cause was represented by Sharp, Bumper, and Trim, while the colonial views rested with Puff and Fillpot.

Of the many satires of the British that were printed immediately preceding the Declaration of Independence, those of Mrs. Mercy Otis Warren, sister of the patriot statesman James Otis, were the most incisive. Her first satire, *The Adulateur* (1773), was directed chiefly against Thomas Hutchinson, and her second, *The Group* (1775), attacked the men involved with the abrogation of the charter of Massachusetts. To anyone familiar with the historical personages, the identification of her *dramatis personae* was immediately apparent. These two plays were not intended for performance and might be more properly called dialogues than dramas. *The Blockheads, or The Affrighted Officers*, an anonymous prose farce published in 1776, recording imaginary conversations between British officers and Tory refugees lamenting their starvation in Boston, has been mistakenly attributed to Mrs. Warren. Certainly the bawdy language of this play could not have come from the pen of the genteel Mrs. Warren. As the text clearly indicates, *The Blockheads* was devised as an answer to General Burgoyne's *The Blockade*, which had been performed at Faneuil Hall in Boston in January, 1775. Burgoyne's farce had ridiculed the patriot army, representing Washington as an uncouth figure wearing an oversized wig and a rusty sword.

Most of the dramatic activity during the war years was carried on by the British soldiers. In 1774 the Continental Congress recommended suspension of all public amusements, and four years later it issued a more stringent decree prohibiting play-acting in any form. Thus, from 1775 to 1784 the American stage was almost fully controlled by the British military. It should be noted, however, that American officers and soldiers attempted some theatricals in spite of the prohibition. Following the bitter winter at Valley Forge (1777–78), Colonel William Bradford wrote to his sister: "The theatre is opened.

Last Monday *Cato* was performed before a very numerous and splendid audience. His excellency [Washington] and Lady; Lord Sterling, the Countess and Lady Kitty, and Mr. Green were part of the Assembly. The scenery was in taste and the performance admirable." Not too surprising to find Washington in attendance, even under the circumstances. He had been an avid theatregoer since the time he had seen his first play in Barbados in 1751. When he became President he held a box at the John Street Theatre, and after the capital was moved to Philadelphia he was a regular patron at the Southwark and the Chestnut Street theatres.

While the British held Boston, New York, and Philadelphia, they quite naturally made use of the available theatrical facilities. As already noted, General Burgoyne wrote a play which was performed in Boston; Major André painted scenery for General Howe's thespians at the Southwark Theatre in Philadelphia; and in New York the John Street Theatre, renamed the Theatre Royal, had two notable openings: *The Rivals* on April 21, 1777, and *The School for Scandal* on April 15, 1782.

The native drama of the war years, as might be expected, exploited both loyalist and rebel sentiments. One of the lustiest Tory farces, *The Battle of Brooklyn*, possibly from the pen of a British soldier, was published in New York in 1776 by J. Rivington, a known Tory. Most of the play was devoted to a satirical representation of the Continental Army, but it concluded with a Tory plea for allegiance to the Crown that resembled the Whig pleas for revolution:

O almighty . . . open the eyes of my deluded fellow subjects, in this once, happy country; encourage them to a free exercise of that reason, which is the portion of every individual, that each may judge for himself: then peace and order will smile triumphant; over the rugged face of war and horror; the same hand that sows shall reap the field; and our vines and vineyards shall be our own.

In 1777, a year after his *Bunkers Hill*, Brackenridge wrote another play devoted to patriotic purpose and to an historical event, *The Death of General Montgomery*. *The Fall of British Tyranny*, published in Philadelphia in 1776 and somewhat uncertainly attributed to John Leacock, was broader in scope than either of the Brackenridge plays. A grand, sweeping chronicle satire in which the action shifted back and forth between England and the Colonies, it incorporated the military actions at Lexington, Bunker Hill, and Quebec, introduced General Washington as one of the characters, and represented the struggles within the English parliament – certainly an unmanageable panorama for a single play.

The Motley Assembly, like *The Blockheads*, has often been attributed to Mrs. Warren, but without substantial evidence. Printed in Boston in 1779, it was devoted to ridiculing that Boston group who were unsympathetic to the

Revolution because they thought the rebels not socially acceptable. A bit of Tory propaganda that seems to have had some measure of success was contained in an anonymous two-act opera called *The Blockheads, or Fortunate Contractor*. This was performed first in New York, was reprinted in London in 1782, and dealt with the conflicting opinions in America as to whether a closer alliance with France or with England was to be preferred after the War.

Immediately following the conflict there appear to have been no plays celebrating the final victory in the fight for independence or glorying in the newly established democracy. Burk's play was the first to celebrate the valiant achievement.

Bunker-Hill claims little attention as first-rank dramatic literature. The stage representation of the famous battle itself provides most of the drama: the poor, ill-equipped, but high-spirited minutemen battling against the well-trained, self-assured, and pompous redcoats. Burk's invented scenes, the ill-fated sentimental romance between the British officer Abercrombie and the American girl Elvira, are on the whole pretty feeble. However, as a spectacle extolling and demonstrating in action the gallant stand of our warriors, and of General Warren in particular, on the now-hallowed ground of Bunker Hill and as a highly approved and applauded theatrical diatribe on the glories of "freedom," "sacred rights," "pure republic," "proud democracy," "equal laws," and the evils of "tyrants," "despotism," "thrones," "bondage," and "lawless power," Burk's play occupies a landmark position in our early theatre.

BUNKER-HILL

OR

THE DEATH OF GENERAL WARREN

JOHN DALY BURK

DEDICATION

SIR,

Tho' averse from pride as well as principle, to personal dedications, in which an Author, in search of a patron, generally sacrifices his love of truth and independence; and though in obedience to this opinion, I have permitted many Compositions to go undedicated, and unpatronized on the world; for once, to indulge a sentiment of private gratitude and esteem, I depart from my system and present to you my Tragedy of *Bunker-Hill*. I shall find few difficulties in justifying to myself this individualism, when I reflect with what courage and patriotism you stepped forward to fight the battles of your country, to one of which I am indebted for the sub-ject of my drama: but I fear I shall not so easily justify myself to you and the public, from the imputation of presumption in intruding on the importance of your time, and the lustre of your talents and erudition, a trifle so every way unworthy of you. To the latter I only can say, it is my best offering; and had it been better, it should have the same direction. With earnest wishes for the success of the piece and its patron, praying a length of years and increase of honors for both,

I am, With esteem and respect,

Yours J. BURK

Aaron Burr, Esq.

CHARACTERS

GENERAL WARREN	SIR WILLIAM HOWE
LORD PERCY	AMERICAN GRENADIER
GENERAL PRESCOTT	ABERCROMBIE
GENERAL PUTNAM	ANNA
GOVERNOR GAGE	ELVIRA
AMERICAN OFFICERS, SOLDIERS, and ATTENDANTS	

PROLOGUE

When o'er Columbia's fields in fearful hour,
Glared the red Comet of Britannia's power,
From horrid hair shook flakes of burning
   wrath,
And war and desolation mark'd its path:
Rous'd by the fury of her ruthless foes,
The angry Genius of Columbia rose:
Then, with a voice more loud, more deep than
   fate,
Was rent the fabric of Monarchic State,

And instantaneous, soothing as the lyre,
Which wakes the soul and kindles soft desire,
She called the *great Republic* into day,
And to a world, restored its legal sway:
Behold; her patriot band the low lands fills
Like to the torrents of a thousand hills,
Which thund'ring to the plain their waters roll,
Unite, condense, and form a mighty whole;
Columbia's Sons down Alleghany's sides,
Their fiery cohorts pour in rapid tides:
Whilst o'er the glassy surface of the flood,

Light'd by the Sun, a gallant vessel rode;
The Ark which bears the charter of the land,
It sails directed by the Almighty hand:
'Till safe at length from tempest and from
flood,
Secure on freedom's Ararat it stood.
Thus did this great, this glorious Empire rise,
Which lifts its patriot honors to the skies;
Spite of the bloody lash, the tyrant's frown,
The shock of armies and a fleet's renown.
A nobler theme than this, to grace the stage,
Where can we find in all th' historic page?
Of Rome's and Cato's fall, the World has
rung:
Why not Columbia's rising fame be sung?
If Rome her Brutus and her Cato boast;
Her Washington and Warren, each a host,
Columbia owns; with thousand names beside,
The least of which would swell the Roman
pride:
And midst these themes sublime, these subjects
grand
Which tempt the poet's fancy in this land,
Where is there one more potent to inspire
Conceptions vast, and wake Parnassian fire,
Than when on Bunker's top a glorious band
Pour'd out their sacred blood to save the land?
And ere they fell, such fierce destruction
hurl'd,
As when Volcanoes burn and tear the world.
Such is our Bard's excuse that he this night
Renews the horrors of fam'd Bunker's fight,
And, bending suppliant at your awful shrine,
His Child to your protection doth consign:
Assur'd of Justice, he has dar'd to trace,
Columbia's Glories to *Columbia's* race.

ACT I

*A view of Boston from Roxbury Neck. A party
of English fly across the stage as if pursued.
Lord Percy faint, and leaning on his sword is
addressed by Governor Gage.*
GOVERNOR GAGE: How's this my Lord!
What means this shameful rout among the
troops!
But lately from these gates they issued
In all the proud array of glorious war,
Looking as if they were invincible:
Now pale dismay affrights them; they appear
Worn down by heat, and want of sustenance;
Afflicted, sprightless, desiring rest

More than renown! Speak, I guess the truth!
But yet it cannot be, that senseless rebels,
Brave only in a mob when pillage calls
And loud sedition gathers them together,
Should cope with discipline, or knee to knee
The sun burnt veteran combat.
LORD PERCY: Your Excellency shall be satisfied
In each particular of this toilsome day,
So fatal to our Warriors; but first,
Let the drums beat to arms, man all the
works,
For if I do mistake not, ere the night
Shall o'er the town her dusky mantle draw,
A furious foe will thunder at our posts.
GOVERNOR GAGE: It shall be done: but yet it can-
not be,
That all at once they will assume such bold-
ness,
And shew Rebellion's face without a mask:
However, they shall find here such reception,
As will, if they approach, their ardor damp,
And make them think their former chains a
blessing
When measured with the heavier punishment
Of bayonet and cannon.
Harman, ho: [*Calls to one of his aids*]

Enter Harman

Let all the guards be doubled;
Look to your guns and see them charg'd with
grape.
And more than usual vigilance command
To all the sentinels. [*Officer bows and exit*]
[*Turns to Lord Percy*] Now my Lord,
I wait impatiently for thy account
Of this strange business.
LORD PERCY: According to your Excellency's
orders,
With the detachment under my command,
I posted on to Lexington; with a view
To succor Smith, or take what other course
Requir'd by circumstances; judge my surprise,
When I beheld Smith's party in full rout,
With thousands and ten thousands at his heels,
All order fled, confusion through the ranks
Stalking with death and terror in his train:
In haste I form'd my forces to repel
The numbers which assail'd him: for a while
My cannon kept the foe at distance,
But soon their numbers so increased, and fury
Beyond all calculation; and beside
Their trim and movements seem'd so soldier
like,

That fearing for the safety of the troops
Committed to my charge, I thought it best
With all convenient speed to hasten back,
Lest these rebellious townsmen should attack
The quarters in our absence, and cut off
All intercourse between the troops and Boston:
But tho' the wisest measures were adopted
For this retreat, they hung upon our rear,
Rushing on with fury next to madness;
Till every inch of ground was bought with
blood.

GOVERNOR GAGE: I thought two thousand British
troops might march
Through all America! driving before them,
Like chaff, th' affrighted colonists. How in
England
Will sound this news; too distant to observe,
Our names will be the subject of reproach:
For they will ne'er believe a peasant rout,
Unexperienc'd to arms, unus'd to War,
Could stand before a British soldiery,
Unless by some misconduct in their chiefs.
Beside, 'twill have another bad effect:
The spirits of those rebels will be rais'd,
Before too high: like rivers swell'd by rain,
Which spurn the narrow limits of their banks;
Their hearts will swell with arrogance and
pride;
Our discipline and order will be slighted;
Our military character contemn'd,
Which oftener gains the battle than the sword:
But did you well observe their countenance;
Did it but seem the flash of short liv'd anger,
Which pushed them on; or the determin'd
frown
Which marks the settled purpose of the mind.

LORD PERCY: Imagine to yourself the Roman le-
gion,
Or Grecian phalanx rang'd in battalia;
The furious aspect of the ancient Gaul,
Or painted Briton our brave ancestor:
Think all their terrors center'd in the foe,
With whom we wrestled: 'twill be near the
truth:
Whilst on our march a thousand fierce attacks
Rag'd on our rear; when we fac'd about,
Like the incursive Parthians they were gone:
Again we march'd, again the battle rag'd.

GOVERNOR GAGE: This business is unlucky;
Our project was to keep the shew of friend-
ship,
And seem as if we would concede, till troops
Arriv'd from England; but this affair

Has disconcerted all our best laid schemes.
Now all America will rise in arms,
And thus a war, which in its infancy
Might have been crush'd with ease, will yet re-
main
An heritage to our posterity –
Or, leave these rebels masters of this land.

LORD PERCY: Your Excellency has not yet inquired
What loss our troops sustained at Lexington.

GOVERNOR GAGE: Ay very true; my mind was so
engaged
With doubts and apprehensions I forgot it.
Have you yet muster'd them?

LORD PERCY: I have my lord:
And I am griev'd to tell you, that one half
Of Colonel Smith's detachment is cut off.

GOVERNOR GAGE: By heaven this business is
alarming!
Now fame will bear the tidings of this loss
Thro' all this continent; exaggerating all,
Destroying ten for every one that died:
And those Americans will so exult,
As when, of old, the Mexicans they bore
The head of a slain Spaniard, through the
land;
To shew the people that the foe was mortal:
The weak and timid now will lose their fears
Of our experience and our discipline;
And those who trembled at a soldier's cap
Will henceforth dash defiance in our teeth.

Enter an Officer in haste

OFFICER: May it please your Excellency –

GOVERNOR GAGE: What tidings do you bear?

OFFICER: As on the isthmus we patrol'd the lines
To see that all the passes were secur'd,
According to your Excellency's orders,
A cloud of dust approaching to the town
Darken'd the air – instant we sent scouts,
Who, breathless with affright and haste, re-
turn'd
With information, that the foe was near
And hither bent their course.

LORD PERCY: I told your Excellency it would be
so.

GOVERNOR GAGE: This seems to speak the foe in
earnest:
But let them come; they spare us the fatigue
Of following them: blow winds from England,
And waft the British navy to these shores:
We then shall pay these Mutineers with inter-
est:

Their Chiefs and Senators shall grace the gibbet,
Whilst on the vulgar herd we'll heap subjec-
tion,
'Till that their bones do ache.

Exeunt. Abercrombie comes on as they go off
ABERCROMBIE: [*Solus*] Such are the men who
  sow this world with broils:
Incendiaries, who blow the coals of war,
And civil strife and havoc loose abroad:
Unhappy England! how art thou abus'd?
Alas my Country, I forsee thy fate:
A prey to hungry courtiers, thou wilt fall
Like ancient Rome when she had lost her
  rights.
A cursed junto, like Prometheus' vulture,
Lives on thy vitals; but more voracious:
'Tis not enough for them to drink thy blood,
But they must turn their carrion stained beaks,
To tear the bowels of these guiltless shores:
Such is the British government, and such,
Must ever be the government of kings:
I know that in the world's opinion,
I shall be deem'd a man of little wisdom
For reasoning thus; what care I for the world?
Love has resign'd my soul,
And stript it of those merciless resolves,
Those sanguinary politics, inspir'd
By regal pride; no more I look on man
As born my enemy, because we live
On different sides of rivers, or of lakes;
I love the race of man in every clime:
Elvira, peerless maid, hath wrought this
  change;
O might I pass with her, remote from war,
In some sequester'd dale my span of life:
The pageantry of camps should be resigned.
But ah vain wish! like to the galley slave,
Chain'd down by honor, to the cannon's
  breech,
I have no choice, no agency of will.

Enter Elvira and Anna, she beckons Anna
Elvira! what busy thoughts have call'd thy gen-
tle limbs,
At such an hour as this, from calm repose?
Scarce has the Nightingale withdrawn his
  song,
And left the field's dominion to the lark:
'Tis yet but grey-ey'd morn, and the air
Keen edg'd with east wind's coldness would
  offend

A coarser form than thine; how then, sweet
  maid,
Dost thou in cold's defiance venture here.
ELVIRA: Oppress'd by care, I pass'd a sleepless
  night;
Griev'd by the thought of what my parents
  feel,
Uncertain of my fate, and fill'd with fears
Of the rude elements and ruder war;
Bold fancy conjur'd up a thousand forms,
And frightful images of black despair,
To haunt my slumbers; at length, fatigu'd
With tossing to and fro, I left my chamber,
And hasted here to taste the essenc'd breeze,
Which on the dewy pinions of the morn
Is borne from off the sea; beside I wish'd
From yonder eminence, to view the hosts
Which gird this city round, if by some chance
The face of friend or kinsman I might see
Amongst the shining squadrons.
ABERCROMBIE: Lovely Elivira, may I without
  offence thy promise claim
To tell thy story; oft have I observed
Thy lovely face o'ercast with melancholy;
Oft have I mark'd the sigh escape thy breast,
Seen the tear start in my Elvira's eye;
Hide not thy griefs from me, not thy own soul
Can feel them with more poignance.
ELVIRA: My friend I know it;
And should but make a poor return, indeed;
Was I to answer thee with cold denial.
My father in the Carolinas lives,
A wealthy man and high in reputation
Acquired in our continental wars,
What time the warlike French their inroads
  made,
To spoil the borders of your provinces;
Me, his sole daughter, he to England sent,
At earnest wish of his beloved sister,
Who rich and childless begg'd me for her own:
With her, three years I liv'd, 'till cruel death
Depriv'd me of her care; my father then
His brother sent in one of his own ships,
To lead me back again to Carolina:
From him I learnt the tyranny of England,
The near approach of war, and that my fa-
ther,
Fir'd with the love of freedom, had resolv'd,
To join his country: when we reach'd this coast
An English cruiser seiz'd upon our bark,
And brought us into Boston; what follow'd
then
Thou best can tell, who with a brother's care

Reliev'dst me from the worst of ills, dishonor.

ABERCROMBIE: Alas! I see the ruin of my hopes
In this short story; I am an English soldier,
Sent here, to rob thy country of its rights:
As such, thy father must reject my suit;
He must detest me as the sworn foe
Of all that he holds dear.

ELVIRA: Thou know'st him not:
He is a grateful, wise, and generous man.

ABERCROMBIE: There lie my fears;
Had he been one, amongst the vulgar herd,
Devoid of sense, unprincipled;
Who, like the present race of warlike men,
For wretched hire would fight on any side,
It might be easy to succeed with him;
But as he is, the soldier of his country,
The champion of her rights, he will detest me
For fighting in the cause of despotism.

ELVIRA: I'll tell him that thou hat'st the present
measures,
And mean'st to leave the service.

ABERCROMBIE: Not for the world:
Much as I love thee, I love honor more;
How would my friends in England feel to hear
That in the teeth of danger I resign'd,
And on the eve of battle left the camp?
They could not, would not comprehend my
scruples,
And to ignobler motives may ascribe
What flow'd from justice and conviction.

ELVIRA: It cannot be dishonor to resign
When murder takes the place of generous war!
When frantic tyrants, arm'd with savage rage,
Direct their baneful march through peaceful
fields,
Wasting with fire and sword the peasants' toil!
No Abercrombie, honor calls the soul
From scenes of blood to taste the purer joys
Which spring from social life.

ABERCROMBIE: Thus will thy father argue, thus
declaim;
Thus will he reason on the crimes of kings;
And thus alas will he destroy my hopes:
My soul approves of all that thou hast said:
And was I sure my conduct would be judg'd
By such as thee, so prudent and so pure,
Long since decision would have crown'd thy
wish;
But as it is, when flimsy fashion rules,
And guides the helm where honor should pre-
side,
'Twere madness so to risk my reputation.

ELVIRA: And can'st thou then, to humor paltry
fashion,
Go cooly forth to shed thy brother's blood?
How differently did Cato think of honor!
Its semblance he despis'd, but to itself
He clung with all the constancy of Cato.

ABERCROMBIE: Surely Elvira doth not wish to see
Her friend dishonor'd!

ELVIRA: Heaven is my witness;
Thy honor is not dearer to thyself.

ABERCROMBIE: Sweet maid, I crave thy pardon; I
know it;
I am unworthy of such matchless worth:
What shall I do? O counsel me Elvira;
Be my good angel and direct my cause.

ELVIRA: Alas! what can I do that I will not;
But when before,
I counsel'd thee in love's and reason's voice,
And spoke the artless language of the soul,
My suit thou didst reject; O now again
Let me my former admonition urge;
Forsake the hateful standard of oppression;
And with Elvira and her father live,
Bless'd with the gifts of fortune and of love.

ABERCROMBIE: Dearest Elvira.
How good art thou, and how unworthy I;
This day at three o'clock I'll meet thee here,
For now my hour it is t' relieve the guard,
Which watches on the neck – till then fare-
well.

ELVIRA: Farewell.
Let not the gorgeous pomp of laurell'd war
Seduce thy mind from me.
[*Go off at different sides*]

End of the First Act

ACT II. Scene 1

*A chamber. General Warren seated at a table,
holds a letter in his hand announcing the defeat
of the British at Lexington.*

GENERAL WARREN: At length the sun of freedom
'gins to rise
Upon the world; a glorious dawn of day,
Breaking in lucid streaks of every hue,
Shedding its incens'd breathing on the mind:
And the deep night, where tyrants sat en-
thron'd,
Shrouding their horrid forms from the world,
Now passes on, like mists before the sun.

The day is come for which through every age
Sages have sighed: which like a magic spell,
Shall dash down tyrants and their thrones to-
    gether,
And make their blood-stain'd idols fall before
    it;
Too long the world has groan'd beneath the
    yoke
Of frantic despotism; war followed war,
And horrid rage deform'd the works of heaven.
Now a new era rises on the world;
The spirit of old Rome inspires the land;
Fir'd with a glorious ardor, young and old
Fly to the field, determin'd to assert
Those sacred rights, which nature hath de-
    sign'd
Alike, for all the children of this earth.
And shall I then, inglorious, stay behind,
While my brave countrymen are braving death
To purchase glory; I too am fond of glory,
And such a cause will make ambition, virtue.
But I can do good service otherwise;
By writing, I can help the public cause,
And heal my brethren wounded in the fight.
'Tis cowardice that reasons: *all* is best.
I never heard that Brutus was content,
That he had done just so much, and no more;
No – Liberty will ne'er be woo'd by halves,
But like the jealous female, must have all
The lover's heart or none: but then again –
I am not young, and feel beside, the ties
Of family endearments; what of that?
Was Cato young, or had he no connections,
When thro' Numidia's burning sands he led
His little Senate in pursuit of freedom;
Preferring pain and every ill to bondage?
Was Cincinnatus young, when from the
    plough,
Call'd by his country's voice, he flew to battle?
The patriot should o'erleap all obstacles
Which stand between him and his darling
    country;
Not age, not sex, nor scarcely pain itself,
Should be exempt from this important duty,
But ALL before the sacred voice of country,
When to her children she doth cry for succor,
Should fly to her relief, and guard from insult,
The soil, which holds the bones of their fore-
    fathers;
This sentiment is heavenly and doth bind
The wandering Tartar to the little spot,
Whére the dead bodies of his tribe are laid:
How then can the remainder of my life,

Be better spent, than in my country's service?
A thousand bright examples point the way,
Trodden by heroes: shall I then keep back,
When such a glorious harvest may be won?
No – from this hour, my resolution's fixt:
Here in the face of heaven, I devote [*Kneels*]
Myself, my services, my life to Freedom:
    [*Rises*]
And I can think of nothing but of souls,
Who in contempt of death their country sav'd;
Of Curtius, of Scoevola and of Brutus,
Of Cato, Cassius, Decii and Camilli;
And if to these, sweet heaven, I could add
The name of Warren, and hand them together
Down in succession to posterity,
By heaven I'd gladly meet their hardest fate
And think my life well lost to merit it. [*A
knock at the door*]
Come in –

Enter a Servant

SERVANT: A stranger waits below to see you sir,
    On business, as he says, of consequence.
GENERAL WARREN: Shew him up stairs.

*Servant bows and exits and shortly after enters
with an Officer*
OFFICER: Just from the camp arriv'd, I bear to
    thee
    A message from the soldiers and their chiefs;
    With one consent, they have deputed me
    To call thee to command.
GENERAL WARREN: Yes, I will go;
    And share with them the hardships of the war:
    Whether as private, or as leader rang'd;
    My post is honor and my country's good.
    But was all quiet; did the troops retain
    The spirit which prevail'd at Lexington?
OFFICER: The army grows in spirit every hour:
    Scarce can the chiefs restrain their burning ar-
    dor;
    So strong is their resentment of their wrongs,
    That loudly they demand to be led out,
    Promising if this be done, they will expel
    The British troops from Boston.
GENERAL WARREN: Supreme disposer of events! I
    thank thee:
    Now Britain do thy worst, we fear thee not:
    Now let thy sultan issue his vain threats,
    His windy proclamations to these shores;
    They will not scare a baby; knit by love,
    Columbia's gallant sons will scorn his rage;
    Whilst o'er the ruins of his lawless power,

That pride of human policy, shall rise
A Pure Republic; whose glory shall eclipse
The Roman and the Grecian commonwealths
Much as the sun outshines the dimmed star.
Then Revolutions *"will be so in use,"*
That kings, when they behold the morning
  break,
Will bless their stars for living one day more.
But while we speak, the battle may be won,
And we have lost our portion of the glory:
Tell the army, my sense of the high favor
Confer'd by them, calls forth my gratitude,
And never, till the mighty debt be paid
To them, and to my country, will I know
Rest or repose, that if no way be found,
But death, to prove my title to their favor,
Why then I die! and swell the glorious list
Of Patriots, who have died for suffering vir-
  tue.
OFFICER: These sentiments are noble;
  Worthy the glorious cause which we maintain;
  I shall repeat them faithfully, and now
  I take my leave, hoping your success
  And safe return when the fight is done.
GENERAL WARREN: Farewell; and I shall follow
  close behind thee;
But ere this hand shall grasp the vengeful steel
For one short hour I must put off the soldier,
And on the necks of my bewailing kindred,
Falter a sad farewell; 'tis nature's call:
I feel the father's, and the brother's fears:
Yes, I shall weep 'till the stern frown of war
Is drown'd in tears.
  [*Exeunt*]

Scene 2

Generals Putnam, Prescott.
GENERAL PRESCOTT: Well Putnam;
  What think you of our troops' appearance?
GENERAL PUTNAM: It doth outrun my warmest
  expectations:
Thro' the whole line I rode along to Mystick,
And not one coward face could I observe;
One soul appear'd to animate them all;
They look'd at once like Patriots and like
  brothers.
GENERAL PRESCOTT: Such were my observations;
  Is it yet known if Warren joins the army?
GENERAL PUTNAM: This day he is expected at the
  camp.
GENERAL PRESCOTT: I'm glad on it;

Our circumstances call for men of talent,
Whose genius may direct us in the ways
Of untry'd war; but is it not a question,
If he be not more wanted in the cab'net?
His choice alone this question must decide.
GENERAL PUTNAM: Then he hath made his
  choice; and that is war.
His active soul disdains to court repose,
To lie down in the lap of ease and pleasure,
When foreign usurpation frights the land.
GENERAL PRESCOTT: So Cato, the great Roman,
  us'd to act:
When freedom wak'd him from the sleep of
  peace,
Over his senatorial robe, he threw
The mail of Mars; and stalk'd along to battle,
Terrible to view, as when he fill'd the senate,
And rail'd and thunder'd at the nation's vices.
GENERAL PUTNAM: Methinks he does resemble
  that great Roman:
Exalted by his virtues to the place
Of President of our provincial congress;
It seem'd a'tho' fortune had no more to give,
To raise him higher; yet is he not content,
But must have share in every kind of glory.
  [*A shout*]
What shout is that I hear, perhaps he's come,
And thus it is the Soldiers welcome him.
GENERAL PRESCOTT: Most surely it is he:
And yonder comes the great, the honest man,
Bending this way; behold what dignity!
I will suppose that heaven hath sent him here,
To light us in the twilight of the war. [*Enter
  General Warren*]
Welcome, good sir;
It joys me to behold you here amongst us.
GENERAL PUTNAM: And me.
GENERAL WARREN: I thank you my brave coun-
  trymen,
My brothers and companions of the war:
This single day has made me full amends
For all the tedious hours of painful life,
Which I have dragg'd along this wretched
  land:
I've seen this day, what once not e'en my zeal
Did dare to hope; my country a vast camp,
Glowing with ardor and enthusiasm:
'Tis good; most good; let me but live to see
The English power in these states dissolv'd
I've liv'd then long enough.
GENERAL PRESCOTT: That day is not far distant I
  expect.

GENERAL PUTNAM: With such a cause as ours
'twere wrong to doubt.

GENERAL WARREN: I have no doubts;
While in our host appear such names as Mercer,
As Prescott, Thomas, Ward, and Washington,
Himself a host; Gates, Hancock and Adams,
Wooster and Putnam, Franklin and Montgomery,
And thousand other names of high repute,
Which forward press to save the sinking state:
Let us leave doubt and terror to our foes:
It better doth become us to salute
Our revolution's dawn, with choral hymns
And songs of gratulation.

GENERAL PRESCOTT: There is a name, which in
thy list of patriots
Thou hast not mention'd; tho' of equal value
With all the rest.

GENERAL WARREN: Many there are, thank heaven, leagued with us,
Whose virtues merit an eulogium:
But none in my opinion
Deserve such high pre-eminence of praise.

GENERAL PRESCOTT: Had any but thyself, made
out the list
The name of Warren had stood foremost on it.

GENERAL WARREN: It might be so, if partial
friendship spake:
But yours, and yours and mine and all our stations
Are undetermin'd yet; this war will fix them,
And candid history fearless will decide,
Who best has serv'd his country; then my
friends
Let all of us so act that 'twill perplex
Posterity to name the worthiest man:
So that at length, unable to decide,
It leaves the affair in doubt.

GENERAL PUTNAM: With what a noble modesty
he waives
The praise, which only truth has drawn from
us. [*Aside*]
The counsel sir is good:
But have we yet a plan of operations
Whereon to act;
The English chief but waits a reinforcement,
Which may with every favoring gale arrive
To take the field; methinks this is the time
To strike a blow, while the king's troops are
weak
And ours are hot in blood since Lexington.

GENERAL WARREN: Thou'rt right my friend;
The foe should have no time to gather
strength,
We must alarm him by some rapid movement,
Seize some important post, threaten the town,
Burn the ships, and keep on the alert
To guard against his sallies; this will make
Boston of small advantage; and force him
To quit his holds, and meet us in the field
Or fly back in his ships to Britain.

GENERAL PUTNAM: The sufferings of this town
afflict my soul:
Fame says that Gage discharges his command
With savage fury; loading the inhabitants
With taunts and injuries: e'en the house of
prayer
Is now become a stable; and their horses
When smoaking from the carnage they retire
Their hoofs red with freedom's dearest blood,
Are litter'd there, and by their echoed neighs
Supply the place of worship.

GENERAL WARREN: Let him rage on;
Let him exhaust his fury to invent
New modes of torture, for the brave and free;
His hour of fell dominion soon expires,
And execrations then will follow him:
While Boston, glorious town, shall long survive
The fall of monarchies, the sack of states:
And live with Rome and Athens in the page
Of History; great parent of our rights!
How largely hast thou sacrific'd to freedom,
How greatly hast thou dar'd the tyrant's rage,
How gloriously withstood seduction,
How patiently supported stern misfortune;
By heaven I would not change my station
As citizen of these illustrious states,
To sway the British sceptre.

GENERAL PRESCOTT: It is a glorious town.

GENERAL PUTNAM: Can nothing be devised for
its relief?

GENERAL WARREN: Yes, thanks to heaven, this
moment I conceive
A plan, which shall afford the wish'd relief:
The post of Bunker Hill commands the town,
The isthmus, with a spacious range beside
Of sea and ships; this will we take by night,
And fortify with all convenient speed
So that our cannon by the morning's dawn,
May play upon the foe.

GENERAL PUTNAM: The project is most excellent,
And suits exactly with our circumstances.

GENERAL PRESCOTT: One thing alone is wanting
  to ensure
  Success to it?
GENERAL WARREN: What is that?
GENERAL PRESCOTT: That General Warren should
  command the troops
  Sent on this service.
GENERAL WARREN: If that be it, there is no want
  at all:
Warren will ne'er refuse the post of danger:
We have no time to lose, let us propose
The matter in full council; so that night
May hide our motions from the wily foe:
Beside the choicest spirits we must choose
From all the troops; souls, who look down on
  death
And value freedom more than life itself.
[*Exeunt*]

End of the Second Act

ACT III. Scene 1

ABERCROMBIE: [*Solus*] Unhappy Abercrombie!
Dost thou still hold this passion in thy breast?
I am the veriest slave of empty honor,
And yet the truest votary of love;
Heavens can it be, that madness should be-
  reave
A man so of his senses, as to doubt
Which of the two to choose:
This moment, both shall come to settlement;
And I will strike the balance: first for love.
I love Elvira, loveliest of her sex;
And she, sweet maid, above the little arts
Of her light sex; has own'd a mutual flame;
And tries to win me by a thousand arts
Of sweet endearment, to retire with her,
And leave the noisy paths of guilty life.
O extacy! this savors of a tale,
Of lovers, living in the golden age,
Walking o'er flowery fields of fairy joy,
And arm in arm, beguiling lazy time,
By soft carresses:
Next honor comes, and lays before my view,
My great forefathers, who acquir'd great
  names,
For fighting for their country; and who seem
To frown on me, for tarnishing their fame,
A censuring world putting their soil'd fingers
On my fair name, and coupling it with cow-
  ard;

It is too much, there's madness in the thought:
Yes, tyrant fashion! thou shalt be obey'd,
Thou shalt be glutted with my life's dear
  blood.
But yonder comes the lovely maid herself,
The source of all my hopes, and all my fears;
I must not trust my weak resolves with her,
One look and honor dies.

Is retiring. Enter Elvira

ELVIRA: Stop Abercrombie!
Am I then grown so odious in thy sight,
That thou wilt fly me.
ABERCROMBIE: Dearest Elvira,
Do not afflict my soul with such reproaches;
By heaven, the light's not dearer to these eyes,
Than is to me thy presence; that alone
Is sunshine to me; that, when I shall lose,
All will be black as night; this world a vault,
Where pleasure lies entomb'd:
Alas I breathe, I live but in thy sight;
But I was willing to conceal my griefs,
Not wound thy tender heart.
ELVIRA: My dearest friend;
How long wilt thou indulge this gloom of
  mind;
My father's on his way from Carolina;
So speaks this letter, and will soon arrive;
To thee in liveliest terms, he describes
His gratitude; he calls thee his protector,
Defender of the honor of his house,
And longs t'embrace thee, and to call thee
  friend.
ABERCROMBIE: I must not see him.
ELVIRA: Not see him! you surprise me.
ABERCROMBIE: The scales, which hold my honor
  and my love,
Are nicely balanc'd; neither side inclines,
But if thy father's powerful reasoning
Be put 'gainst honor, in the scale with love;
I fear 'twill break the balance.
ELVIRA: Thou mean'st false honor.
ABERCROMBIE: I mean the tie, which binds me to
  my oath;
Know'st thou not, Elvira, I have sworn
Allegiance to the king?
ELVIRA: My friend I know it;
But the first oath, a solemn binding one,
Enjoin'd by heaven itself; was due from thee,
To nature and thy country; that, my friend,
No after stipulation can expunge;
Surely, if Britain's king commanded thee
To drag thy aged parents from their house,

And murder them, thou art not bound t'obey him.

ABERCROMBIE: Most certainly I should be disobedient
To such commands!

ELVIRA: No more, art thou oblig'd to hear his voice,
If drunk with frantic wrath, he order thee
To bear the sword and torch of civil war,
Against thy peaceful, unoffending countrymen.

ABERCROMBIE: I cannot, must not reason:
Persuasion lurks in every word of thine:
Reject me, hate, despise me, cast me off,
Nor let the sunshine of thy patriot virtues
Be darken'd by uniting with a slave.

ELVIRA: Hold, my friend;
Thou shalt not so calumniate thyself.
Immortal Brutus scorn'd not fetters more!
But oh! if e'er thy soul did virtue know,
If e'er true honor did obtain from thee
A hearing on thy breast; pluck from thine eye,
The allusive beam, which so discolors objects,
That twixt true honor and its opposite
Thou fairly may'st distinguish.

ABERCROMBIE: Angelic goodness! soul of innocence,
Pure as the sacred fire, which us'd to burn
In Vesta's temple; tell me what to do,
That by the execution of thy counsel,
I may deserve thy love.

ELVIRA: Forsake the hateful standard of oppression!
Elvira then will mourn her lack of virtues,
And pray for more, to make her worthy of thee.

ABERCROMBIE: Of all things, thou has mention'd what alone
I must not do:
Bid me ascend grim Niagara's top,
And on its torrent sail the horrid steep,
Stunn'd by the thunder of its falling flood;
It shall be done: command me to describe
A nautic circle round the various globe;
As Cook of deathless fame and Anson did,
All, all but honor will I yield to thee.

ELVIRA: Do I now hear thy final resolution?

ABERCROMBIE: Yes, much as the sacrifice costs me I resign thee;
How dearly thou art lov'd, witness those tears,
Those agonizing drops which wring the soul;
And here, great heaven! bear witness to my vow;

If to these wretched arms I e'er admit
One of the race of woman, save Elvira,
May barrenness, and care, and want attend
The monstrous union.

ELVIRA: [*Kneels*] And I, here in the presence of the sun,
Do also vow; be witness for me Heaven:
And mark the breach of it by all your vengeance.
If e'er Elvira doth her hand bestow
On any man but thee, may angry heaven,
Even in the bridal hour, its wrath inflict,
And take away her reason. – Farewell, forever.

Is going

ABERCROMBIE: Ah, cruel maid! Why dost thou say forever?
The word *farewell*, without it, is enough
To tear my heart; one kiss – one sad embrace –
And then we part.

ELVIRA: O! cruel fate.
Why did we meet, or why now having met?
Is heaven averse, and frowns upon our love?
O Abercrombie leave this wicked war;
Blest in each other we can bear the taunts,
The idle censures of a worthless world.

ABERCROMBIE: O thou bewitching goodness, how thou temptest me,
To lay my captive honor at thy feet;
But I must break from thee, I must not stay.
England and honor, everything forbid it:
Farewell sweet maid, farewell, I fear, forever. [*Exit*]

ELVIRA: [*Sola*] Ha! then he's gone, and gone, mayhap, forever;
And yet I speak, and think, and hold my reason!
Rare flintiness of heart! perhaps this day
He may be sent to battle; this very hour,
E'en while I speak, the order may have come,
And he, O wayward fortune! may have march'd
And may have died: Why did I not detain him;
Why on my· knees did I not pray to him
To stay with me; mayhap I had prevailed;
Won by my tears and sighs, his tender soul
Had been subdued, and we had both been happy. [*Pauses*]
But ah Elvira! hast thou not a father,
Whose patriot soul impels him to the fight;
And fear'st thou not for him? lest in the shock,

Pierc'd by a thousand wounds his body lie:
Lest wash'd in blood his hoar locks trail the
dust.
Unnatural child – O cruel Pelican –
Is the soft call of nature silenc'd in thee?
Or does the furious spirit of a pard
Thy soul inhabit? 'tis cursed treason:
When like the torrents of a thousand hills,
Glittering in steel, my country moves to battle,
Bearing on its cheek, the flush of independence,
For me to mourn the soldier of a king;
But then how brave, how good the royalist is,
How soft, how pure, how tender, and beside
The savior of my honor; hateful war –
Thou reeking monster, dear to kings alone,
Thou red destroyer – what a host of ills
Doth follow in thy train. Falls her brave lover,
Or, her patriot sire, Elvira will not live.
[*Exit*]

Scene 2

*American camp. Enter General Warren, at one
wing, at the other Harman, a British officer,
preceded by a trumpet and flag of truce.*
GENERAL WARREN: You say you wish to speak
  with General Warren.
HARMAN: With that intent, have I been here
  dispatch'd
By General Gage; who values your endow-
  ments,
And thinks too highly of you, not to grieve,
To see you an accomplice in rebellion,
In cursed treason, 'gainst your sovereign:
He has commission'd me, to tell you
That in respect of your unspotted fame,
Your life, and matchless qualities, he sends
Remission of all past offences;
With this condition, that you come to Boston,
And leave the rebel camp.
GENERAL WARREN: Take back this answer to your
  master:
Tell him the *rebel* Warren, thinks too low
Of his endowments, both of head and heart;
Not to despise his pity and his powers;
How comes he by the right to pardon me,
Insolent man – if heaven hath wrought a
  change
In his black heart; and soften'd it to pity,
He has the amplest field to shew his mercy;
Boston, town of heroes, calls on him

To sheath the sword, which frights her guiltless
  sons,
To muzzle up the fury of his slaves,
His abject, murderous, mercenary slaves,
Which shed the townsmen's blood.
HARMAN: I must not surely take this answer
  back;
At least his goodness calls for better language.
GENERAL WARREN: Goodness! weak man! you
  know not what you say;
Is't goodness to seduce the soldier's worth,
To rob him of that loftiness of soul,
That pride, which makes him spurn dishonor
  from him;
To make him a vile traitor, a base slave:
Is this what now in England is called good-
  ness?
Rather sweet heaven! than be that abject thing
Your bashaw's goodness wishes me to be,
I'd sink into the meanest drudge at once,
And eat the scanty pittance of hard labor.
HARMAN: Surely – there's no dishonor in obedi-
  ence,
No crime in taking you from foul rebellion;
Your passions make you take this matter
  wrong.
GENERAL WARREN: 'Tis thou, good sir, who tak-
  est this matter wrong;
When nations lose their rights, words of best
  sense
Are tortur'd to mean what the rulers please;
And the infection has laid hold on you.
Instance *obedience*, which in earliest sense,
Design'd submission to the wisest laws,
Is made to mean a base, unmanly, fawning,
An abject acquiescence under wrongs;
And thus *rebellion*, which of old was us'd
To mark the conduct of a *Catiline*,
Is made to represent the glorious act
Of a *whole people*, bursting from their chains.
HARMAN: Our English laws are fam'd thro'out
  the world
For their impartial justice and their mildness,
'Tis therefore rank rebellion, to resist them.
GENERAL WARREN: What are your boasted Eng-
  lish laws to us,
Or any laws, which sanctify injustice?
Is it an English law, to rob the weak,
To wring his pittance from the shiv'ring poor,
To levy taxes like a Russian czar,
To stop the course of justice, and let fly
The fiery banners of destructive war,
Of martial law o'er the devoted heads

Of guiltless cities; know you not, good sir,
All laws and usages are made to bend
Before the *magic* influence of an act,
And ordinance of your parliament.

HARMAN: O then thou'rt angry, that our parliament
Encroaches too much on the king's prerogative;
It has, you think, too great a share of power.

GENERAL WARREN: It matters not to us, what
power it has
In *England*, whether too little, or too much:
That is *your* care; *look* to it if you're wise:
Your parliament is not ours, nor shall be ours,
Why then presume to legislate for us?
Why dare to levy taxes? that's the question:
'Tis childish to dispute on points of policy,
In which *you* are determin'd, *I* convinc'd.

HARMAN: O then I see how 'tis, a king displeases you;
You want a commonwealth.

GENERAL WARREN: If once the British government's dissolv'd,
We should not choose a monarchy, tho' sway'd
By Trajan or an Antonine; what are kings?
Kings form a horrid junto of conspiracy,
A *Catilinian* compact, 'gainst the lives,
The rights, the peace, the freedom of the
world:
They are the Manichean demons, who undo
The good which heaven has done:
They waste with fire
The purple vintage, and the waving grain:
Their butcher hordes they send out to destroy
Themselves, like vultures screaming o'er the
field,
Snuff up the blood of armies; horrid sights!
As they appear, young spring her face conceals,
And vegetation shrinks at their approach;
They live by blood, and tears, and sweat, and
groans,
They exercise oppression, lust and piracy:
Famine and war, their iron-hearted ministers,
Before them go; while prostrate at their feet
Science and freedom, downward to the dust,
Point their dishonor'd faces.

HARMAN: If these are your opinions, I have
done;
Tho' if I might presume to give advice,
You should not slight his excellency's offer;
He will commend you to the royal favor,
And fame and honors will pour fast upon
you.

GENERAL WARREN: What! then you'd have me be
an abject slave,
A sycophant, to follow in his train,
And when he's out of humor – talk to him:
Amuse him with the account of slaughter'd rebels,
Recount his own achievements in the field,
And close with history of my own apostacy:
'Till at the horrid tale, his furious eyes
Run o'er with brutal joy; young man 'tis well:
Good nature may have prompted you to this.
Now *once for all* my final answer take:
The man you speak to, holds himself as good,
Of as much value as the *man you serve*,
Ay: and of more, while he defends his country,
Than any *pamper'd monarch* on the globe:
All riches and rewards my soul detests,
Which are not earn'd by virtue: I prefer
One hour of life, spent in my country's services,
To ages wasted midst a servile herd
Of *lazy, abject, fawning, cringing* courtiers.
All future business 'twixt your lord and me,
Must be determin'd in the field.
[*Exeunt*]

ACT IV. Scene I

A chamber.

ELVIRA: [*Sola*] Be still my heart, nor aggravate
thy woes:
Mayhap, my letter, wet with new fall'n tears
Back'd by the entreaties of my faithful Anna,
May shake his purpose; shou'd it not, sweet
Heaven –
What will become of me: O wretched state!
Bounded by love and duty, who keep watch,
And every ray of hope, that wou'd beam in,
To cheer the joyless prospect of the waste,
Keen as the dragon of th' Hesperides,
They intercept; and leave my soul a night,
So thick and black, that thought doth lose its
way.
Anna comes –
Now gracious heaven, support my fainting
soul,
And give me strength to hear.

Enter Anna

Anna; this face of woe portends no good:
O did you see him?

ANNA: I did my lady.

ELVIRA: And into his own hands my letter give?
What said he, did he read it, will he come,
Where did you find him, tell, O tell me all.

ANNA: Alas my lady, I will tell thee all;
But not one breath of comfort can I give:
Alarm fills the town, and the hoarse note
Of warlike preparation, peals around;
The British troops are sent to storm the post
Of Bunker Hill; I saw them all embark'd,
And steer towards it.

ELVIRA: O misery! finish, free me from suspense:
Tell me you saw him proudly tread the deck,
Anticipating triumphs o'er this land;
Tell me you saw him tear my foolish note,
And fling it to the winds: while cutting smiles
Of insolent contempt, play'd on his face:
Say that he curs'd me, call'd me doating fool:
Fear not, say all, my soul doth joy to dwell
On kindred horrors.

ANNA: Ah no –
Cold and distressing as my tidings are,
They do not reach to this; when from the ship,
The gallant youth espy'd me on the shore,
Holding with anxious zeal, thy note aloft:
In agony he clasp'd his hands, and spoke,
I'm sure his lips did move, as if he spoke,
But the big thunder of a hundred guns
Which play'd upon the hill, did drown all sounds,
Save those of its own roaring.

ELVIRA: Come near me Anna;
My tottering limbs refuse to bear me up:
O thought! O recollection cease forever.

Exeunt. Elvira leaning on Anna

Scene 2

A view of Bunker Hill.
GENERAL WARREN: [*A view of Sea and Ships*]
Here am I:
Fix'd on the utmost verge of angry fate,
Which frowning round the summit of this hill,
With threatening gestures, seems to chide my stay.
Yes, Bunker Hill: I view thee as the line,
Which bounds my earthly prospects; as the field,
Which shall enroll me with the mighty dead.
How came I here? not by the stern command

Of any higher power; not dispatch'd,
As forlorn hope, devoted sacrifice,
To take the edge of fury off the foe,
And by my death, to seal an army's safety;
But freely, and of mine own accord,
Have I solicited this arduous post,
To teach my countrymen contempt of death,
To kindle great ideas in their minds:
So Leonidas (I'm vain of the example)
With proud disdain his mighty soul resign'd,
To stem the torrent of invading foes,
Which roar'd upon his country; Godlike man!
And with his little band repress'd the foe;
'Till the proud Persian learnt by thousands slain,
That little Greece, contending for her rights,
Was more than equal to a world in arms.
This hill shall be America's *Thermopylae;*
Here shall her little band of patriot sons,
Oppose those modern Persians; while the flames
Of smoking harvests, fir'd at Lexington,
Hairs pluck'd from off the heads of hoary age
By fierce Janizaries, in brutal mirth;
The shrieks of ravish'd matrons, and the cries
Of infants, toss'd upon the ruthless pike;
Shall fill our souls with tenfold fury,
And put a keener edge upon our swords.
[*Two cannon*]
Roar on, you hollow ministers of fate –
Fit emblems of the furies, who preside
O'er Britain's councils; we regard you not –
Our cannon shall observe the deepest silence;
But such a silence 'twill be, as exists
In AEtna or Vesuvius; ere they roll
Their scalding lava o'er the works of men:
By and *by* our answer shall arrive in death,
Borne on the wings of thunder. [*Two cannon*]
Double your peals,
Until you burst your throats; you do but use
Our new rais'd soldiers to your surly sounds.

Enter General Prescott

GENERAL PRESCOTT: A soldier comes from Gridly, t'inform us,
That thro' his glass, he can see the foe
Embark, and hither bend their rapid course:
He wants to know, if he shall fire on them
Before they land, or let them disembark,
And unmolested march towards the works.

GENERAL WARREN: By all means, let them land:
We wish not to engage at children's play:

When once we meet, the combat shall be mor-
tal,
Let not a gleam or flash inform the foe,
That we await them; keep in dreadful quiet;
Grim as hush'd whirlwinds, or wild beasts in
ambush,
That all at once our fire
May bolt upon them, like the wrath of heaven.
GENERAL PRESCOTT: I'll take these orders back.
GENERAL WARREN: Do not fail
To fan the flame of freedom in the troops:
Tell them their suffering country depends,
Their wives, their children and their aged
sires,
On this day's issue; and let the rallying word,
Thro' all the day, be, *Liberty or Death*. [*Gen-
eral Prescott exits. General Warren kneels*]
Now liberty array thee for the fight:
Now from thy proper armory, draw out
The furious weapons of destructive war,
As thou wast wont, when to Thermopylae,
Or Salamis, thou led'st thy Grecians out:
Enrobe thyself in *Thunder;* to thy eyes
Add *Lightning*, to thy visage *wrath:*
Assume the gate of *war*, the whoop of *battle*
Which hoarsely sounding thro' the burning files
Doth sadden *armies:* then hither fly;
And, with Columbia's new born sons, advance
To raise thy self a temple more superb
Than Rome's proud capitol. [*Trumpet sounds*]
This signal summons me away to battle:
Mildness farewell – adieu now soft ey'd pity –
[*Draws his sword*]
Now savage strife and fury fill my soul –
And when my nature yields to soft compassion
Let Boston's injuries rise before my view
And steel my heart to pity. [*Exit*]

Scene 3

*A view of water. The English are seen passing
in boats, to the sound of British music – they
disembark at the foot of Bunker Hill, and
form. Lord Percy, Sir William Howe, Abercrombie.*

LORD PERCY: 'Tis strange, these rebels suffer'd us
to land
Without attempting to oppose us.
ABERCROMBIE: A little time will clear this matter
up;
You'll find they've meaning in it.

SIR WILLIAM HOWE: Perhaps they have repented
of their treason.
ABERCROMBIE: That, I will last believe.
SIR WILLIAM HOWE: Have you discover'd who
the leader is,
They have entrusted with this enterprize.
LORD PERCY: A straggler whom we seiz'd with-
out the works,
Declares his name is Warren.
ABERCROMBIE: That is a name, in high repute
among them,
And such a one, these works bespeak the foe,
Rais'd as it were by magic, in a night.
SIR WILLIAM HOWE: They're truly formidable.
I've reconnoitr'd them, on every side,
And found them so well lin'd with men and
cannon,
That to us it appears expedient,
To send to Boston for a reinforcement.
LORD PERCY: Had we not better see if the supply
Is on its way: what say you Abercrombie?
Why so dejected man? does the fair captive
Refuse to be propitious to thy wish?
ABERCROMBIE: Hold Percy:
At naming her, my wounds will bleed afresh,
Leave me behind, look you out the supply.
SIR WILLIAM HOWE: Look close, toward the foe,
lest ere supplies arrive,
They meditate a sally.

*Exeunt Lord Percy and Sir William Howe.
Manet Abercrombie*

ABERCROMBIE: Farewell Elvira;
Thy lover bids adieu to thy dear image.
Perhaps the various fortunes of this day
May shut these eyes forever on thy sight;
Grieve not for me,
If fame should bear the tidings of my fall:
Tho' angry fate forbids us to unite,
Here on the earth; yet in the realms above,
Where threat'ning tyrants and their ministers
Forever are shut out; we'll meet again.
Curse on the authors of all war and strife:
They are, who fill the world with wretched-
ness;
Who tread on honor and humanity:
Who rend all ties, which knit the soul togeth-
er:
E'en love, the solace of the human race,
Their phrenzy spares not.

End of the Fourth Act

ACT V. Scene 1

Bunker Hill fortified – Distant view of sea and ships. English reinforced, march towards the Hill. The cannon play at intervals to make breaches in the works. English bands strike up Yankee Doodle in contempt of the Americans. A dead silence reigns among the Americans. They are seen just appearing above the works, waiting the attack. Three times the English make the assault, and three times they are beat back. After the third repulse General Warren half descends the Hill, and addresses his Soldiers.

GENERAL WARREN: *Courage, Americans!*
  The spirits of those heroes, who expir'd
  Massacred at Boston and at Lexington,
  Are this day witnesses of your renown;
  Suspended o'er this hill; let them behold
  Vengeance inflicted on their murderers:
  Let's give them in their names another fire,
  And in their ears shout, LIBERTY OR DEATH.

Americans shout. English again advance, and are again beat back. General Warren descends the Hill with his Soldiers

GENERAL WARREN: Heroes retire; this day you've
  done your part:
  To-morrow we will take another post,
  And inch by inch contest it with the foe.
  If every trifling hill be so ennobled,
  In our vast Continent's Geography;
  Columbia may with Rome hold up her head,
  And move along with empires – Retreat
  Brothers, in danger as in victory;
  This glorious spot myself the last will leave;
  Prescott bring off the troops.
GENERAL PRESCOTT: You must not stay behind.
GENERAL WARREN: I will not stir till every soul be
  safe,
  Who fought with me this day.

Here a shot comes from the opposite wing, which mortally wounds General Warren. He falls into the arms of a Grenadier. The English advance. The battle is renewed by the efforts of the Americans to carry off their general. Americans retire – field of battle

Scene 2

Sir William Howe, Lord Percy.

SIR WILLIAM HOWE: This is a melancholy scene
  of triumph;
Our bravest troops and soldiers strew the plain.
LORD PERCY: I'm grieved to know it;
  We have a melancholy list to send to England
  With kill'd and wounded fill'd:
  There's Abercrombie dead, and valiant Pit-
  cairn,
  With hundred other souls of generous stamp,
  Exclusive of those mountain heaps of slain,
  Which baffle calculation.
SIR WILLIAM HOWE: How many of the foe, in
  your opinion,
  Have we dispatched?
LORD PERCY: They've left but thirty of their dead
  behind.
SIR WILLIAM HOWE: We've lost our bravest
  troops; and in return,
  Have gained a paltry hill – This is defeat;
  And will be construed so in England:
  Who would have thought the rebels would
  have dar'd
  To fire on us?
LORD PERCY: I knew they would.
  Since the first settling of the northern states,
  The revolution principles are held
  In high esteem; and with the parent state
  The Colonists oft wag'd rebellious fight.
  What females these? Elvira and her maid!
  [*Elvira is seen coming in preceded, by Anna; her hair loose; her bosom disordered; her eyes wild and haggard*]
  The news of Abercrombie's death has reach'd
  her ears,
  And she is come to seek his mangled corpse.
ANNA: O sirs, my lady is beside herself;
  Her lover's death, soon as it reach'd her ears
  Depriv'd her of her senses. See her air.
  Listen, hear her raving.
ELVIRA: They stuck him round with arrows,
  And flung his lovely corpse upon the shore.
ANNA: God's mercy on her.
ELVIRA: Wolves, do not tear him thus.
ANNA: O heaven, have pity on her.
ELVIRA: I do not aim at him, my countrymen;
  'Twas all my fault.
SIR WILLIAM HOWE: Sweet lady, let us lead thee
  from this place.
ELVIRA: O Abercrombie, love, sweet love, dear
  love.
LORD PERCY: Sweet lady, be prevail'd on to re-
  tire.
ELVIRA: Who are you? did *you* kill all these
  Poor soldiers? look in my face – ha! there's
  Guilt in those eyes – if you kill me, do

Not expose my body with those wretched
Carcases – are you sure they are dead! [*Treads
softly*]
Hard hearted men, will
You let them die, without assistance!
Soldiers of kings, O spare my gentle father;
Here on my knees, O grant me his sweet life.

SIR WILLIAM HOWE: Sweet lady, do not fear, we
will not hurt thee.

ELVIRA: Are you not English soldiers?

LORD PERCY: We are men of honor, lady.

ELVIRA: Ah, it may be; Abercrombie was an
Englishman.
My harden'd heart will burst, I cannot weep –
O Abercrombie, love, sweet love, dear love.

Falls faint, on the body of Abercrombie

SIR WILLIAM HOWE: She faints:
And tired nature gives the struggle up.
Let us convey her from this horrid scene;
Lest when the light revisit her sad eyes,
This scene of slaughter and her lover's blood
May root her Phrenzy so, that it will live,
As long as life.

They bear her off

Scene 3

Scene changes to another part of the hill. General Warren, mortally wounded, is borne in by a Grenadier.

GENERAL WARREN: Here lay me down:
That I may take one sad, one farewell look
Of this beloved land; [*Soldier lays him down*]
My short career of glory soon is run;
But I have fall'n according to my wish:
Fighting amidst my countrymen in arms.
'Tis true, the foe are masters of the field:
But 'tis a slaughter house, fill'd with their
dead;
A spectacle, to wring their flinty hearts,
And make them cautious, how they rouse the
brave.
This day, has been a proud one for the land:
My countrymen have fought with Spartan
valor,
Like hungry lions, bathing them in blood,
And like the Romans, in their first encounter
With Epire's king; have but resign'd the field,
A wretched solace to the mourning foe,
Who in such triumphs sees his strength decay.

My soul now flutters on the wing, to leave
Its earthly mansion, and aspires to live
With Brutus, and the virtuous souls immortal!
I had but *one poor life*, to give my country:
Had I ten thousand, it should have them all.
[*Pauses through weakness*]
O might I look into the womb of time
And see my country's future destiny:
Cou'd I but see her proud democracy,
Founded on equal laws, and stript entire,
Of those unnatural titles, and those names
Of *King*, of *Count*, of *Stadtholder*, and *Duke*,
Which, with *degrading awe*, possess the world:
My cheered soul, would gather life anew,
And parting from my body, as the dove
Sails from her nest, would singing soar to
heaven.
[*To the Soldier*] I see that thou art mov'd,
good friend;
Heaven will reward thee, for thy pious care,
In bearing from the carnage of this day,
Thy wounded General; consult thy safety:
Nor vainly strive to save a dying man –
The foe's at hand.

Drums beat

SOLDIER: I'm not afraid of death sir;
I will defend your person to the last:
Where can I hope to die more gloriously
Than in defence of my belov'd commander?

GENERAL WARREN: Thy general orders thee to fly
from hence:
Would'st thou deprive thy country of thy serv-
ice,
When she doth so much need it? go my friend,
And lend thy aid, to crush the savage foe.
Tell the world, 'tis all I ask of thee,
The patriot Warren died without a groan:
That, smiling, midst the agonies of death,
His darling country occupied his thoughts:
That he enjoin'd his sorrowing kindred
To render thanks to the great God of freedom,
That Warren did his duty: – leave me now.
America – my country! bless thee heaven,
O God protect this land – I faint – I die.
Live the Republic. Live; O live, forever.

Scene 4

Scene changes to the American camp. American army moves slowly to the sound of solemn music. Second. The troops out of uniform, who fought on the hill. *Third. Children bearing flowers. Fourth. The Bier is brought in, on one side General Prescott, on the other General Putnam, at proper intervals, the standards decorated with republican emblems, and popular devices.*

 First standard, THE RIGHTS OF MAN
 Second, LIBERTY AND EQUALITY
 Third, HE DIED FOR HIS COUNTRY
 Fourth, BOSTON, PARENT OF THE REVOLUTION
 Fifth, HATRED TO ROYALTY
 Sixth, A FEDERAL CONSTITUTION

The Bier is laid down. Two virgins advance to it, and leaning over it, sing – tune, Roslin Castle

 He dy'd for his country – rain our tears,
 His death has banish'd all our fears;
 You daughters of Columbia mourn,
 With tresses loose, and hearts forlorn:
 Amidst the heaps of British slain,

Thy Warren's body strews the plain;
His precious blood was shed for you,
O let us shed our tears in lieu.

When Britain's tyrant, o'er the waves,
Had sent his *slaves*, to make you *slaves*,
Thy gallant Warren, fearless stood,
And dar'd the angry torrent's flood.
Pale with affright, the foe retires,
Swift as he hurls Columbia's fires:
But now he's gone, his spirit flies
From earth, and seeks its kindred skies.

You sons and daughters of the land,
From all *his* virtues tears demand,
You soldiers and you farmers, hear
Your hero's glories with a tear.
And you of Boston, who have seen
Oft in your streets his warlike mien,
Join in the general song of grief,
Which freedom gives to freedom's chief.

[Curtain drops slowly. Solemn Dirge]

THE GLORY OF COLUMBIA: HER YEOMANRY!

WILLIAM DUNLAP

WHEN William Dunlap saw a performance of *The Contrast* at the John Street Theatre in 1788 and became aware of its phenomenal success, he determined to try his hand at dramatic composition; and although his initial effort, *The Modest Soldier, or Love in New York*, was never produced, it marked the beginning of the remarkable theatrical career of the "father of American drama." Dunlap was in and out of the theatre all his life, as manager and as playwright. He was the first American to devote himself to the profession of playwriting, the first to write and manage his own plays, the first to champion the cause of native subject matter and the native dramatist – this in spite of the fact that he was also the first to prepare and present a long list of translations and adaptations from the French and German and the first to write a history of the American theatre.

Dunlap was born on February 19, 1766, in Perth Amboy, New Jersey. His Irish father, Samuel Dunlap, had served with General Wolfe at the Battle of Quebec and maintained an active association with his military cronies in Perth Amboy. When the family moved to New York in 1777 and lived among the Loyalists, Dunlap was obliged to repress the strong patriotic spirit which had been nurtured by his father and the veterans of Quebec. The only pleasant memory Dunlap had of these years between 1777 and 1783 was of his first visit to the theatre, where he saw a performance of *The Beaux' Stratagem* given by British soldiers. When the family returned to New Jersey, Dunlap had an immediate opportunity to reaffirm his natural patriotism. In his *History of the American Theatre* he recorded his memory of the occasion when he first caught a glimpse of Washington: "They passed, and I gazed after them. It was a precious moment. I had seen Washington." Shortly after this incident, he met Washington and painted a full-length portrait of him. Dunlap had demonstrated his talent with paint and brush even before the move to New York. In fact, he had begun painting portraits when he was sixteen, and this now seemed the path he should follow.

On May 4, 1784, he sailed for London to further his artistic career under the tutelage of Benjamin West. After three years of little painting and much theatregoing – he saw such plays as *The School for Scandal* and *The Critic* with the original casts – his father summoned him home. On February 16, 1789, he married Nabby Woolsey, and then began his lifelong predilection for shifting from one occupation to another: portraitist, playwright, poet, and partner with his father in the cut-glass business. In the spring of 1796, he added to his repertoire the position of theatrical manager. He bought half of Hodgkinson's half interest in the John Street Theatre. The other half was owned by Hallam. Hodgkinson and Hallam had not been on good terms, and Dunlap was commissioned to effect a rapport that might prove profitable to all. Unfortunately, Dunlap's theatrical fortunes seemed always to push toward the red side of the accounting ledger. When, in January, 1798, the American Company moved into the new and still unfinished Park Theatre, the opening-night attendance gave promise of a change in Dunlap's fortunes. It was a mistaken omen. Succeeding nights enlarged the previous losses. In spite of the unprofitable operation, his partners had faith in Dunlap; they made him sole director and manager in April, 1798. When the next season began amidst the recurring scourge of a yellow-fever epidemic, Dunlap was prepared for the worst; yet the seasons of 1798–99 and 1799–1800 proved to be the most profitable of his career. During the succeeding years, difficulties with Hodgkinson, poor receipts, plus shoddiness in Dunlap's stage direction led to almost complete disaster. In 1803 he was obliged to mortgage his farm to meet the operating expenses of the theatre. The theatre finally closed down on February 22, 1805, and Dunlap lost everything except his mother's house at Perth Amboy.

His spirits, if not his fortunes, were rapidly restored. After a year of trying to recoup his losses by painting miniatures, he was back as manager of the Park in the fall of 1806. This time he had no stock in the enterprise. He was hired by the actor T. A. Cooper simply to perform the managerial duties. His colleagues seem always to have retained their faith in Dunlap's abilities. This return interval of management lasted until the close of the 1810–11 season; and although not spectacularly successful, it was not disastrous.

Several factors contributed to Dunlap's lack of significant success as a manager. In addition to repeated periods of ill health, the eternal bickerings of his partners, and the yellow-fever epidemics (see the comments of Dennis Dougherty in *A Trip to Niagara*), he had not been expertly schooled in theatrical affairs, and he was unwilling to allow business judgments to interfere with his good-natured trust in his associates. In an over-all appraisal, however, Dunlap must be credited with such managerial advances as the encouragement of scene painting and scenic display and the introduction of new American plays and plays from Germany and France. Previous managements had devoted themselves almost exclusively to an English repertoire. Certainly he was filled with a remarkable supply of vital energy. During his entire period of theatrical management he had been writing, and in 1806 he published the first volume of his dramatic works.

From 1814 to 1816 Dunlap was employed by the state as assistant paymaster general of the militia. He enjoyed the traveling demanded by this position. It enabled him to get back to painting; on one occasion he managed forty days of sketching at Niagara Falls.

The next years were mainly devoted to painting and writing. Instead of plays he wrote biographies of the actor Cooke (1813) and of his close friend Charles Brockden Brown (1815). Instead of miniatures he painted panorama-sized religious canvases: in 1822, "Christ Rejected" (twelve by eighteen feet); in 1823, "The Bearing of the Cross"; and in 1825, "Death on the Pale Horse." Most of these paintings were exhibited in special showings in Boston, Norfolk, and Philadelphia, and the "Christ Rejected" was shown as far west as Urbana, Ohio. Dunlap had now become a substantial and respected figure in the art world. In 1817 he became a director of the American Academy of Fine Arts, in 1826 one of the founders of the National Academy of Design; from 1830 to 1839 he was a professor of historical painting at the National Academy.

Even though the final period of his life was one of great productivity – *History of the American Theatre* (1832), *History of the Arts of Design* (1834), *Thirty Years Ago, or Memoirs of a Water Drinker* (1836), and *History of New York for Schools* (1837) – Dunlap seems never to have got far above a perpetually distressing economic state. He died at his home in Greenwich Lane on September 28, 1839.

This recital of biographical items alone would testify to a full and lively existence; but more important to the present concern, Dunlap was distinguished as the most prolific American playwright of his time and for the next half century. Not until John Brougham did anyone devise as many plays as Dunlap, and only half a dozen playwrights in the entire history of American drama have equaled his output. A good many of his plays, to be sure, were translations and adaptations. Of the fifty-six plays attributed to Dunlap, twenty-seven were originals, thirteen translations from Kotzebue, ten translations from the French, four translations from other Germans, and two of doubtful originality. Dunlap's ever-precarious financial condition did not deter him from writing. More correctly, it must have prompted him to write. Certainly the multitude of Kotzebue adaptations were prepared in the hope of improving the health of the box office. But in spite of the popularity of some of Dunlap's plays, particularly *Pizarro* and *The Glory of Columbia*, they provided meager monetary reward for him.

The Glory of Columbia was not Dunlap's only patriotic play. *Darby's Return*, an interlude performed in 1789, was distinguished for its glowing references to Washington; and Dunlap's account of the President's reactions when he attended a performance is one of the few first-hand accounts we have of Washington at the theatre:

His countenance showed embarrassment from the expectation of one of those eulogiums which he had been obliged to hear on many public occasions, and which doubtless must have been a severe trial to his feelings, but Darby's answer that he had not seen him (Washington) because he had mistaken a man "all lace and glitter, botherum and shine" for him until all the show had passed, relieved the hero from apprehension of further personality, and he indulged in that which was with him extremely rare, a hearty laugh.

Yankee Chronology, another patriotic interlude prepared for Fourth of July performances during the War of 1812, was composed originally as a song. Still another Fourth of July piece, *The Battle of New Orleans*, was based on the last battle of the war (January 8, 1815); and, of course, there was *André*, the play from which *The Glory of Columbia* was derived.

Dunlap had worked long and carefully at *André*, and its opening performance on March 30, 1798, with the benefits of new scenery and costumes, drew an eight-hundred-dollar house; but the second night brought in only $271, and the third (the author's benefit) $329. It was not played again. *André's* failure has sometimes been attributed to Cooper's shoddy performance – he had to be prompted – and to the audience's protest against Bland's unpatriotic stage business of tearing the cockade from his hat; but the absence of simple and direct theatrical "flag-waving" undoubtedly contributed markedly to the public lethargy. It was largely the introduction of such unadulterated patriotic spectacle that brought receipts of $1,287 to the Park management on the opening night of *The Glory of Columbia*, July 4, 1803, and kept the play in the American theatre repertory for the next fifty years, with some fifty recorded performances. A large share of these fifty repetitions came either on the Fourth of July or on November 25 (Evacuation Day).

The combination of Dunlap's exciting scenic conceptions with Ciceri's ingenious and splendid renderings stimulated sure-fire applause and wonderment:

Yorktown – at a distance is seen the town, with the British lines and the lines of the besiegers – nearer are the advanced batteries, one more distant from the audience than the other – cannonading commences from the besiegers on the town – explosion of a powder magazine – the French troops advance towards the most distant of the advanced batteries – the battery begins to cannonade – the troops advance and carry it at bayonet's point – while this is yet doing, the nearest battery begins to cannonade, and the American infantry attack and carry it with fixed bayonets, striking the English colors – shouts of victory.

and:

A transparency descends, and an eagle is seen suspending a crown of laurel over the commander in chief, with this motto – "IMMORTALITY TO WASHINGTON."

With this, it is surprising that the management thought it necessary to supplement the opening performance with Signor Manfredi walking on the tight rope from the stage to the upper part of the gallery over the heads of the audience.

Not only the regular holidays but also many other special occasions of a patriotic nature called out *The Glory of Columbia*. On May 12, 1804, Dunlap repeated it at the Park "to celebrate the cessation of Louisiana to the United States." On July 1, 1812, the year of the outbreak of war with England, it was performed with the subtitle "What we have done, we can do." When David Williams, then the only surviving captor of Major André and a character in Dunlap's play, visited the Park on December 3, and the Bowery on December 4, 1830, the play was performed especially for him. When Mr. Hamblin, an Englishman, changed the name of the Bowery Theatre to "American Theatre, Bowery," *The Glory of Columbia* was selected as the appropriate opening attraction.

Patriotic spectacles were not introduced into the American theatre by *The Glory of Columbia*. Charles Willson Peale had created a heavily emblazoned triumphal arch at Philadelphia for the ratification of the treaty of peace on January 22, 1784, and had later constructed an extensive series of transparencies of Washington and other national heroes and national triumphs. On December 28, 1799, fourteen days after the death of Washington, the Chestnut Street Theatre in Philadelphia exhibited the following solemn scene:

The curtain slowly rising, discovered a tomb in the centre of the stage, in the Grecian style of architecture. In the centre of it was a portrait of the General, encircled by a wreath of oaken leaves; under the portrait, a sword, shield, and helmet, and the colors of the United States. The top was in the form of a pyramid, in the front of which appeared the American Eagle, weeping tears of blood for the loss of her General, and holding in her beak a scroll on which was inscribed: "A Nation's Tears." The sides of the stage were decorated with black banners, containing the names of the several States of the Union.

Franklin had been celebrated as a national hero in a kind of masque entitled *Americana and Elutheria, or A New Tale of Genii* in which Franklin appeared in a stormy black cloud amidst lightning, with lightning rod in hand. Nor were such spectacles devoted exclusively to the new republic's heroes. On May 3, 1797, the Park Theatre presented an interlude entitled *Naval Gratitude, or The Generous Tar*, which concluded with a "view of Frigates United States, Constellation, and Constitution," fitted completely for sea, each firing three broadsides. Many other similar patriotic spectacles and "contemporaneous dramas" were shown in theatres throughout the country. For example, in Providence "two or three of these novelties were presented to the public" each season.

With the elaborate use of scenic display in *The Glory of Columbia*, it is interesting to note the real-life Major André's accomplishments as a scenic artist. He had painted a backdrop for the Southwark Theatre in Philadelphia in 1778, described by Durang as follows:

It presented a distant champagne country and a winding rivulet extending from the front of the picture to the extreme distance. In the foreground and centre was a gentle cascade – the water exquisitely executed – overshadowed by a group of majestic forest trees. The perspective was excellently preserved, the foliage, verdure and general coloring artistically toned and glazed. . . .

Certainly the more extensive use of scenic effect was one of the major changes in Dunlap's doctoring of his *André* play; but it was not the only alteration. Patriotic songs were added. The "salt-of-the-earth" freedom-loving rustics and their female counterpart, Sally, were new creations, as was the Irish comic, O'Bogg. This latter character served no function in the dramatic action and was undoubtedly added simply to provide the stock Irish actor with a part. Arnold was also included in the *dramatis personae;* he did not appear in *André*. Here he is on the stage for a brief moment near the beginning. In the early play André is already incarcerated when the play begins. Here his capture by the rustics is an essential episode in the dramatic action. In fact, the first scene of *André* became the first scene of the third act in *The Glory of Columbia*. There are numerous verbatim borrowings from the early play. In the 1817 edition of *The Glory of Columbia*, the five scenes of Act III are from *André*, as are scenes two, three, and four from the fourth act. However, the acting text reprinted here omitted several passages from these scenes, particularly some of the long soliloquies. The throwing-down-of-the-cockade business, which had proved offensive to the *André* audience, was also omitted. On the whole, the deletions and reworkings demonstrate an improved dramaturgy and certainly provide a more direct and forceful patriotic play. In *André* the theme was placed within the framework and restrictions of a well-unified neoclassic form. The patriotic sentiments were spoken with elevated and, on the whole, restrained tones. In *The Glory of Columbia* the outpourings are sentimental, simple, and unequivocal, and the dramatic action is revealed in a direct and straightforward pattern.

In 1833 the New York *Mirror* appraised Dunlap's contributions to American drama:

As a dramatist, Mr. Dunlap has never received his due praise. If we consider the number of his works, he will be found, we believe, to have been by far the most prolific writer for the American stage. If he be judged by the criterion of success, it will be discovered that as large a proportion of his pieces keep possession of the boards, as of the average of dramatic writers, who are numbered among the permanent classics of the theatre. His numerous pieces were almost invariably performed with applause; and, free as they are from false taste and extravagance, show the power of fixing attention and exciting interest by legitimate means – of touching the true springs of mirth and pity and terror. The diction of his blank verse is natural and spirited, and sometimes rises into beauty. In all his work he has been careful to keep in view the true and nobler uses of the drama, and to direct it to results favorable to virtue.

Although a later-day appraisal might wish to temper some of this exuberance, Dunlap unquestionably deserves the title "father of American drama." He established playwriting as a respectable, if not a profitable, profession.

THE GLORY OF COLUMBIA

Her Yeomanry!

WILLIAM DUNLAP, ESQ.

CHARACTERS

GENERAL WASHINGTON	PAULDING	AMERICAN OFFICER
ARNOLD	VAN VERT	1ST ENGLISH SOLDIER
ANDRE	DENNIS O'BOGG	2ND ENGLISH SOLDIER
BLAND	MRS. BLAND	3RD ENGLISH SOLDIER
MELVILLE	HONORA	1ST AMERICAN SOLDIER
WILLIAMS	SALLY WILLIAMS	TWO CHILDREN
	BRITISH OFFICER	

ACT I. Scene 1

A wild landscape near West Point, with a distant view of the Hudson – a british ship lying at anchor – moon light. Enter General Arnold.

ARNOLD: What is the conflict of contending hosts, the din of battle, or the smart of wounds, to this internal war? this raging contest of opposing thoughts, discordant interests, tumultuous passions striving to o'erpower the voice of struggling conscience. Avaunt tormenting phantoms! I must fly from real evil. The pressing creditor whose clamors will not cease at sight of scars received in honor's field – the prison where forgotten lies the soldier whose valor made the coward free who holds him as a slave. Gold! I must have thee! idol of mankind! I must have gold – else will my well earned name and gallant service nought avail me. Perish the public good! my private welfare henceforth be my aim! [*A boat is seen putting off from the ship and landing, afterwards, returning*] see where the tempter comes! I am resolved – Andre, you shall not come in vain.

Enter David Williams

WILLIAMS: A packet sir; the captain of the guard is waiting at your quarters and with him the messenger who brought those letters.

ARNOLD: [*Reads*] From the commander in chief!

WILLIAMS: I may as well break my mind to him by moonshine, as sunshine; as my mother used to say "of all the four-and-twenty hours *now* is the best hour for business."

ARNOLD: So soon! why then we must be quick. Fate urges me on. In two days Washington arrives, I am superceded in command, and the power of doing this stupendous good, or ill, is wrested from me. Tis well, Andre will soon be here.

WILLIAMS: General! I have been sometime back wanting to break my mind to you.

ARNOLD: Speak freely, honest Williams.

WILLIAMS: Why I always does that, you know, because I take it, it's what a man has a right to do, always saving respect to one's officers. And so, I'm not satisfied.

ARNOLD: Are you dissatisfied with the service?

WILLIAMS: Yes, if you please, sir, I am.

ARNOLD: And why – what does this fellow mean? what do you wish?

WILLIAMS: To quit. To change again.

ARNOLD: Would you go home?

WILLIAMS: No.

ARNOLD: Are you tired of being a soldier?

WILLIAMS: No, sir, it's not that.

ARNOLD: Why sure you would not – [*Pause*] change! would you join the enemy?

WILLIAMS: Me! *me* join the enemy? an't my

94

name David Williams? an't I a Jersey man? an't I an American?

ARNOLD: What would the fellow say?

WILLIAMS: The man who would give up one inch of this soil to any invader, much more join against his countrymen, must have such a heart as I would never button under my jacket! what a traitor? I?

ARNOLD: Did you not say you were dissatisfied with the service?

WILLIAMS: My *present* service. I dont like any longer being a waiter, sir; I want to go in the ranks again that's all. I hope I shall never desert my country's service come what will o' th' wind, I guess I shall never be a slinker or a turncoat.

ARNOLD: What do you wish, fellow?

WILLIAMS: I hope no offence, your honor.

ARNOLD: Offence! what is it to me? [*Agitated*]

WILLIAMS: All that I meant is, I dont relish being a waiter, for though it may be a kind of left-handed promotion to tend a general, some how or other I'd rather handle my musket in the ranks and feel more like a – like a man.

ARNOLD: You entered my service willingly.

WILLIAMS: Yes! I saw you fight bravely; I saw you wounded; I would have died for you; I wanted to help and nurse you: but now, now, I – you can do without me, and I had rather stand among my comrades again.

ARNOLD: You shall have your wish. Leave me.

WILLIAMS: Yes, your honor. [*Aside*] Yes, it's time to leave you; you dont look like the man that fought by the side of Montgomery and Gates; it's time to leave you. [*Exit*]

ARNOLD: Curse on the honest clown, he gave me a foretaste of the time when every thing of upright heart will shun me! torture! – no matter – hell do thy work! now to the rendezvous, and seal with Britain the downfal of my country. [*Exit*]

Scene 2

The camp – Morning. Enter Williams.

WILLIAMS: So I be free from brushing coats and blacking boots! dang it, pretty employment for a soldier! I be nation glad to part from the general; for certain he is changed dreadfully since I took him to serve him. Now 'fore I turn into the ranks again, I'll go and see how old father do, and Sal, and the pigs, and the cow; and then back again and shoulder my gun till no color is seen this side the water but blue.

Enter Sally, with a basket of fruit

SALLY: Young man can you tell a body, if one David Williams is in camp?

WILLIAMS: Why Sal! sister Sally, is it you?

SALLY: David! o, David, I'm glad to see you.

WILLIAMS: [*Kisses her*] So am I to see you, but not here: I was just a coming home to see father and all – how does he?

SALLY: Pure well! see I have brought you a basket of fruit. Why didn't you write, David, to tell us all about it?

WILLIAMS: Why dang it some how or other I'm no dab at a pen: my fist be made for a gun or a pitch fork, I believe. But what brought you here?

SALLY: Why first, David, I wanted to see you, and then I wanted to see the paradings, and soldiers, and officers and such – for you know, David –

WILLIAMS: Yes! I know better nor you know and so –

SALLY: But come now let's go see camp a bit, brother.

WILLIAMS: Stop a bit, sister.

SALLY: What's the matter?

WILLIAMS: You're too pretty by half. While I have any interest in a petticoat I'll keep it out of a camp.

SALLY: But Lord, brother, this is our own camp, you know. All friends –

WILLIAMS: And nation friendly fellows you'll find 'em. No, no, all camps are alike for that. If I had twenty brothers I should wish them all here under arms; but for a sister, a cow yard is better than a camp, and a milk-pail easier borne than an ill name. Petticoats at home, say I.

SALLY: Well, well, David, you know best; being a soldier yourself, you know the tricks of them. You'll go home with me, won't you?

WILLIAMS: I will. Let me just run to yon tent and fetch my side arms, for you know what with foraging parties and thieving parties, I may happen to have use for them, and I think a few shouldn't take you from me. [*Exit*]

SALLY: Well, brother must have his own way, but I have a dreadful mind to see the officers, and soldiers, and guns, and fortifications; and yet what has a woman to do with them? I dont know. I believe we have a natural propensity to be meddling with what dont belong to us.

Song and Duet

SALLY:
When a woman hears the sound
  Of the drum and fife
How her little heart will bound
  With a double life.
Rub a dub, rub a dub,
And a too, too, too,
Are the merry, merry sounds that will
  women woo.

Re-enter Williams, with belt and sword on

WILLIAMS:
When a man shall hear the sound
  Of the drum and fife
How his swelling heart will bound
  For the coming strife.
Rub a dub, rub a dub,
And a too, too, too,
Are the spirit-stirring sounds that the foe shall
  rue.

BOTH:
When the sound of the drum
  And the fife shall cease
And the blessing shall come
  Of a glorious peace,
Rub a dub, rub a dub,
And a too, too, too,
They shall still keep in mind what to
  valor is due. [*Exeunt*]

Scene 3

As at first, only by daylight, and the ship under sail, moving off and quickly disappearing – enter Arnold and Andre, the latter dressed as a british officer but having a surtout over his regimentals.

ARNOLD: The sum here specified [*Holding a paper*] shall be immediately paid: equal rank, command, and emolument, to that which now I hold, firmly assured me.

ANDRE: Such is the agreement I have signed; and in so doing I have in nothing over-stepped the power delegated to me. Now, sir, I must depart, point out the way by which I shall regain the ship.

ARNOLD: From this eminence we can see her place of anchorage – ha! she is gone –

ANDRE: Confusion!

ARNOLD: She has probably dropp'd further down the Hudson, and awaits you. You must remain conceal'd till night, then by my passport you may unquestion'd deceive our outposts.

ANDRE: Why wait till night? why passports? am I not on neutral ground? am I within your lines?

ARNOLD: Most certainly you are.

ANDRE: How! betrayed!

ARNOLD: Betrayed? there is no traitor, sir – [*Pauses*] hell – shame!

ANDRE: Waste not the time in words.

ARNOLD: I will not – you have now no road but by our posts; no means of escaping but by disguise and my passports – remain with me till night; leave your uniform with me and assume a peasant's dress; the rest be my care.

ANDRE: What doff the badge of my profession? has it come to this? assume disguise within an enemy's lines? assume perhaps another name?

ARNOLD: Tis necessary – the name of the adjutant general of the british army, would not lull suspicion if inserted in the passport –

ANDRE: And has my zeal to serve my country led me to the necessity of deceit? tis well! your pardon, sir, I attend you.

ARNOLD: We will return to my quarters and make the necessary preparations. The papers for sir Henry Clinton are ready, and if no mishap attends the coming night – our meditated blow will fall in sure destruction on their unwary heads.

ANDRE: I follow, sir.

ARNOLD: You must be cautious, sir; upon your circumspection hangs the enterprise, perhaps our lives.

ANDRE: Lead on – disguise! the adjutant general of the british army teaching his tongue a feigned tale – o fallen indeed! [*Exeunt*]

Scene 4

A wood. Enter three English Soldiers with muskets.

1ST SOLDIER: Do you know this part of the country?

2ND SOLDIER: Yes! we're not far from Tapan.

1ST SOLDIER: Then our comrades must have gone more to the right I take it.

2ND SOLDIER: I wish we had not straggled from them.

3RD SOLDIER: Why what do you fear, white-liver? have we not shared double booty by it?

1ST SOLDIER: Hush! soldiers!

2ND SOLDIER: Where? we are lost!

3RD SOLDIER: Pshaw! soldiers in petticoats.

2ND SOLDIER: One man!

3RD SOLDIER: And a girl. He has no fire arms – retire – let's make sure of them.

2ND SOLDIER: I'll shoot the rebel scoundrel. [*They retire*]

Enter Williams and Sally

SALLY: Lud – lud – how tired I am.

WILLIAMS: You needn't be tired yet, for you've got some long miles to trudge before you reach father's.

SALLY: The thought of that dont make me less weary.

WILLIAMS: Hang weariness! why I'm not tired.

SALLY: You have not walked half so much as I – if you had but let me rest myself at camp, I could have set off fresh again.

WILLIAMS: Yes! you would awalk'd about all day gaping at the soldiers by way of resting yourself. Come let us try t'other tug. Take my arm – [*Going*] if you tire down I'll take you on my back, a pretty girl is not the worst baggage in the world. [*A gun is fired – they start, Sally runs to the opposite side, Williams draws*] Whiz! I like to hear a ball whistle; it's a sign it did'nt hit me. That came from some rascally renegado refugee, an english soldier wouldn't a done it.

Enter 3rd Soldier and levels his piece at Williams

3RD SOLDIER: Surrender.

WILLIAMS: I won't.

3RD SOLDIER: I'll fire.

WILLIAMS: Fire and be hang'd.

1ST SOLDIER: [*Without*] Shoot him down.

SALLY: O dont, dont, dont.

3RD SOLDIER: Surrender! I dont want to murder you.

WILLIAMS: Fire away! [*Rushing on him wrests his musket which falls in the scuffle, the Soldier draws and retreats fighting off – during this the 1st and 2nd Soldiers level at Williams, but Sally seizes the fallen musket, levels it, fires, and then sinks on the stage – the Soldiers fly*]

Enter John Paulding and Issac Van Vert, habited as countrymen, but with arms and cockades

PAULDING: The firing was this way.

VAN VERT: What! a woman?

PAULDING: Sally Williams!

SALLY: Run and help brother David. That way! that way!

PAULDING: What's the matter? who?

SALLY: Go and see; while you're talking they'll kill him.

Enter Williams

WILLIAMS: Huzza! huzza! yankee doodle for ever, boys. Are you hurt, Sal?

SALLY: Are you wounded, brother?

WILLIAMS: Not a bit. Give us a kiss, my girl; you winged one of 'em. Pick up your musket – no, I'll take it. [*Does so*]

PAULDING: David Williams!

WILLIAMS: John Paulding! Isaac Van Vert! glad to see you, lads.

PAULDING: What's been doing here.

WILLIAMS: Sal and I ha' been skirmishing with the red coats a little. She can pull a trigger with the best o' us. We were going as far as father's to pay *um* a visit. Come let us be jogging, Sal, we've no time to lose.

SALLY: I'm dreadful tired –

PAULDING: I'll show you a short cut to Tarrytown; there you may rest, get something to eat and drink and then we will go part of the way with you.

SALLY: Ay do, brother.

WILLIAMS: Done. I do feel as if I could take a tolerable mess of saupawn and milk or molasses; or a nice hunch of pork and rye bread. Come, Sal, cheer up, girl, let's sing a stave and then go to dinner.

Chorus

To your arms, boys! to your arms, boys!
  Hark! the drum beats to arms, and the enemy's nigh;
To your ranks, boys! to your ranks, boys!
  For Washington leads us to conquer or die!

VAN VERT: [*Alone*]
For his country bravely fighting
  Conscience nerves the soldier's arm;
Victory beckons, all inviting!
  Heaven shields his breast from every harm.

Chorus
  To your arms, boys, etc.

SALLY WILLIAMS: [*Alone*]
From the glorious fight returning,
Proudly glad the victors move;
Every heart with rapture burning,
Greets the brave with peace and love.

Chorus
To your arms, boys, etc. [*Exeunt*]

End of the First Act

ACT II. Scene 1

Another wood – night. Enter Andre, disguised as a countryman.
ANDRE: The last out-post is past! thank heaven my danger's o'er. Once more on neutral ground, there lies no obstacle between me and New-York. I fly to receive the congratulations of my friends, and ensure the overthrow of my country's foes! [*Going*]

Enter Paulding and Van Vert
PAULDING: [*Comes down*] Stand!
VAN VERT: [*Comes down*] Stand! who goes there?
ANDRE: Friend!
PAULDING: Which way, friend: which way at this time o'night?
ANDRE: Tow'rds Tarrytown.
PAULDING: You are wrong. We're going to Tarrytown and will show you the way. Have you seen any rebels outside the lines?
ANDRE: Rebels! [*Hesitating*] why are not you –
PAULDING: [*With emphasis*] *We* are *not* rebels.
ANDRE: Ha! refugees then? british scouts! I'm glad to meet you. I'm on my way to the english lines and will reward you for your guidance and company.
PAULDING: You mistake, sir, we are neither rebels, or britons, but freemen; independent farmers; armed to defend the property and the rights we have inherited from our fathers.
VAN VERT: [*Placing himself on the opposite side*] You are our prisoner!
ANDRE: Ha! confusion? betrayed? – lost – lost!
PAULDING: Betrayed! there is no traitor here, – unless you know of one. If you are a briton, we are your open undisguised enemies. My name, John Paulding, his name, Isaac Van Vert; – such as we seem we are: our names and persons known and not afraid to be known.

ANDRE: Known? disguise? am I then? confusion! how am I sunk! how does the plain honesty of these men confound and lower me in my own esteem!
VAN VERT: You seem confused. Dont be down hearted man – tho' you are a prisoner, americans know what is due to humanity.

Enter David Williams
WILLIAMS: Who goes there?
PAULDING: Stand!
WILLIAMS: So I do, ha! Paulding and Van Vert! I've seen Sal safe home – who have you got here?
VAN VERT: A prisoner!
WILLIAMS: Oho! then let's back to camp.
ANDRE: Tis true I am your prisoner; yet my friends I hope when you consider the woes attendant on a state of captivity, and the little consequence of which a simple individual like me can be, for or against your cause, you will not detain me.
WILLIAMS: You dont seem so nation simple either.
ANDRE: By detaining me, you will involve my affairs in ruin, distress my family and relations; and what will be the gain?
PAULDING: We shall have done our duty.
ANDRE: Even that is doubtful. You see I am unarm'd. I could not have come here with any intent of violence.
WILLIAMS: Yes! but you might have come for mischief for all that.
ANDRE: Let me pass on. My money is freely yours. [*Takes out his purse, and offers it to Van Vert, who shakes his head and draws back – he then offers it to Paulding*] Take it!
PAULDING: No, no, we are soldiers, not robbers!
ANDRE: Tis gold, you're welcome to it. [*To Williams*]
WILLIAMS: No thank'ee, keep it yourself.
ANDRE: Take too my watch, [*Offers it*] tis likewise gold and of great value – take all but let me pass.
WILLIAMS: Why I tell you what, mister, very likely there is more in that there purse, than father's farm's worth stock and all: but somehow or other there is a sort of something here [*Pointing to his breast*] that we yankees dont choose to truck for money.
PAULDING: To be plain, sir, your words so little suited to your dress, but the more determines

us. What say you, comrades? what's to be done?

VAN VERT: Our duty!

ANDRE: Why this is noble! pardon me, countrymen, I did but try you, I am of your part and am entrusted with business of great consequence to the cause, which any longer detention might altogether frustrate, as a proof see general Arnold's passport. [*Produces it*]

PAULDING: How's this. [*Reads it*] This is our general's pass. What think you? he is called, John Anderson.

WILLIAMS: Why I think it may be so, and it may not be so.

ANDRE: Why do you doubt?

WILLIAMS: Why I dont know how it is, but I am apt to think, when a man gives two accounts of himself, he may as well give a third. So as we are but common soldiers, we will carry you to somebody else more 'cute at these here kind o'things, and let him hear the third story.

VAN VERT: You are right David Williams; – at any rate let us carry him to the nearest post.

PAULDING: It must be so, there are too many circumstances not to create suspicion – besides, sir, if all is right you will soon be dismissed you know, so the sooner we go on the better.

ANDRE: I see it is in vain, I will fully confess to you who I am.

WILLIAMS: So here comes the third story.

ANDRE: Curse on deceit! for ever shun'd by man the arts of falsehood. My name is Andre, my employment is confidential and near the person of the british commander in chief – my rank adjutant general of the british forces in North America.

PAULDING: The adjutant general of the british troops in disguise.

ANDRE: My motive for being thus and here, it is not my intention to speak of. I have the power, once within the british lines, to gratify the utmost wish you ever formed for riches; render me this service, and I will do it. Why are you silent? come with me to New-York, giving me by your company liberty and safety, and your desires shall not suggest a sum, for each too great for your reward.

VAN VERT: We are soldiers, but not mercenaries.

PAULDING: We have firesides to defend.

WILLIAMS: We be but poorish lads, your honor, but we have such things among us as fathers, and mothers, and brothers and sisters, and sweethearts, and wives and children, and friends and our good names; now tho' all these things mayhap be only trifles, yet – what sum do you think a man ought to sell *um* for?

ANDRE: Curse on the clowns! their honesty o'erwhelms me! resolve, my friends, one hour places you on the pinnacle of fortune: an hour which ne'er can come again.

VAN VERT: We have answered, we are soldiers!

ANDRE: So shall ye still be – nay officers – and wear with high promotion my royal master's livery.

WILLIAMS: Thank you kindly for myself, sir, but I dont want a master, or a livery. An american soldier *wears an uniform*, to show that *he serves his country*, and never will *wear a livery* or *serve a master*.

PAULDING: It is useless to waste time or multiply words: we mean no offence, sir, but we *will* do our duty. You *must* go with us.

ANDRE: Tis well: you have taught me to reverence an american farmer. You have given me a convincing proof, that it is not high attainments, or distinguished rank, which ensure virtue, but rather early habits, and moderate desires. You have not only captured – you have *conquered* me.

WILLIAMS: Though we wouldn't take your coin, we'll take your compliments, sir, and thank you heartily.

ANDRE: Whatever may be my fate, you have forced from me my esteem. Lead on [*To Williams*] I am your prisoner. While I live I shall always pronounce the names of Williams, Paulding and Van Vert, with that tribute of praise which virtue forces from every heart, that cherishes her image. [*Exeunt*]

Scene 2

The encampment – day-light. Enter General Washington, Melville, and Officers.

WASHINGTON: Tis well. Each sentinel upon his post
Stands firm, and meets me at the bayonet's point.
While in his tent the wearied soldier lies,
The sweet reward of wholesome toil enjoying.

MELVILLE: They know to whom they owe their present safety.

WASHINGTON: I hope they know that to themselves they owe it:

To that good discipline which they observe,
The discipline of men to order train'd
Who know its value, and in whom tis virtue;
To that prompt hardihood with which they
  meet,
Or toil or danger, poverty or death.
Virtue alone can save thee, o my country!
And while she hovers o'er these western shores,
No power on earth shall crush thee.

MELVILLE: At what hour does your excellency review the troops?

WASHINGTON: At ten. Have we any message yet from General Arnold?

MELVILLE: None, sir!

Enter officer, with papers, written on the back of each

OFFICER: General Arnold is not at his quarters, nor to be found.

WASHINGTON: Not at his quarters!

OFFICER: A prisoner has been brought by three soldiers to the camp, on whom these papers were found.

WASHINGTON: [*Looking over them*] A pass to John Anderson, signed Benedict Arnold: artillery orders Sept. 5th 1780, estimate of men at West-point.

MELVILLE: How's this! treachery!

WASHINGTON: Return of ordnance – remarks on the works – treachery indeed! and Arnold missing! give orders for pursuit. [*Exit officer*] Come let's away my friends, and spare no labor to find out the worst and guard against the evil. Treachery among us! oh that cuts deep and makes the heart weep blood. [*Exeunt*]

Scene 3

The camp. Enter Sally Williams, in boy's clothes.

SALLY: So adod, I've got into the camp in spite of David's preachifications, for when once a girl is got a thing into her head, it never lets her brain rest, while there is any novelty in it. I wonder whether David would know me in this dress? I think I make quite a tightish little lad – adod I'm a good mind to list for a soldier: no that wont do – I remember yesterday I was more inclined to cry out than to fight. I hope

no one will ever put on the american uniform, till well assured they will never disgrace it.

Song

1

He who his country's livery wears,
His country's honor proudly bears;
  Inglorious fear
  Must ne'er come near
The heart that battle's danger dares.

2

He firmly stands his country's trust,
In action brave in council just;
  By victory crown'd
  He lives renown'd,
Or sinks with glory to the dust.
[*Retires up*]

Enter Paulding, Van Vert and Williams

VAN VERT: Now comrades, we have received the only reward a soldier ought to look for; and though the general has assured us of reward from our country, yet all a soldier should wish is the thanks of his commander.

PAULDING: The thanks of his commander, and the approbation of his own conscience.

WILLIAMS: Dang it, what a nice warm feel. a man has here about the upper part of his waistcoat, when he knows he's been doing what he ought to do. I dont think I ever felt so proud as I did just now, when our great commander, our own glorious Washington, took me by the hand and said, "thank you," ay he said, "well done my lad, thank you."

PAULDING: We must always remember the moment as the most glorious of our lives. The approbation of our country is at all times precious, but when that approbation is made known by such a man, so glorious and so dignified, it becomes inestimable.

VAN VERT: What a noble soldierly mien!

PAULDING: What benevolence in his smiles.

WILLIAMS: O bless his face, say I! to a lad who has not seen any thing but continental bills for a twelvemonth, the sight of a white faced Carolus, or a yellow George Rex, moughtent be as bad as a wet Sunday; yet dang me, if I hadn't rather see a Washington's head, on a deal board, than all the gold heads in the bank of England.

SALLY: [*Coming forward*] I'll try if they'll know

me. I dont believe they will. [*To Paulding*]
Pray, sir, can you tell me – [*Laughs*]

PAULDING: What do you want, my lad?

SALLY: I want – I want – [*Laughs*]

PAULDING: [*Turns away*] To be whipt and sent
home.

SALLY: [*To Williams*] Can you tell me, sir.

WILLIAMS: Oh yes! I can tell you.

SALLY: Where captain – captain what's his name
lives?

WILLIAMS: Oh yes! – captain – what's his name?

SALLY: Yes, sir!

WILLIAMS: [*Aside*] Sure it is – it is the 'tarnal
baggage as sure as a gun. Comrades [*To
Paulding and Van Vert*] do you see yon fellow?

VAN VERT: What the little fellow?

WILLIAMS: As great a rogue as ever lived
[*Aside*] it's sister Sal – a spy in the camp
[*Aside*] I want to scare her out of these tricks.
Shall we take him prisoner and hang him, or
cut him to pieces on the spot?

SALLY: What wou'd the fellow be at?

WILLIAMS: [*Drawing his sword*] Dang it, I'll
whip off his head in the first place! you are discovered, you little pop-gun you!

SALLY: Dont you know me?

WILLIAMS: I know you! down on your marrow-
bones – say your prayers and die!

SALLY: Why, David, dont you know your own
sister?

WILLIAMS: You! no, I forbad my sister coming
to camp, I told her the danger.

SALLY: Yes! you told me it was dangerous for a
petticoat, so you see I left them at home. –
"Petticoats at home" ha, brother.

PAULDING: Ha, ha – fairly answered – you must
forgive her, David.

SALLY: You must forgive me, David.

WILLIAMS: I suppose so.

SALLY: And let me see the review, and then I'll
go home and never plague you any more.

WILLIAMS: Well take care and stick close to me
though – the general reviews the troops this
morning – it wont be long before we shall
march I suppose to some other part o'the continent – when I'm gone be a good girl Sal, take
care of father and the cows; and the children
and the pigs and the rest of the live stock –
come I'll take you where you shall see the
troops pass, and have your hearts delight, if
you are a true woman, noise, bustle and show,
till your head aches. [*Exeunt*]

Scene 4

*Distant view of the camp in perspective – distant
music heard. Enter Paulding, Van Vert, Williams and Sally – peasants, men and women –
half way up the stage each side a sentinel – soldiers enter and relieve the sentinels in due form.*

Chorus

*See they come – the heroes come!
Hark! the hollow sounding drum!
Gives distant notes of coming war,
And bids th' invaders keep afar,
Or for the battle's brunt prepare.
See the stately horse come prancing,
There the musketeers advancing,
While the cannoneers prepare their thund'ring
war.*

*See the standards float
Hark the trumpets note,
While every breath with conscious might,
Swells ardent for the coming flight.*

2
*But now to crown the glorious war,
See Washington! the battle's soul!
His worth binds envy in her cave,
In council sage, in battle brave!
Great Washington, a world can save!*
See the stately, etc.

End of the Second Act

ACT III. Scene 1

*A wood – star light – an encampment at a dis-
tance appearing between the trees. Enter Melville.*

MELVILLE: Methinks I hear the tread of feet this
way. [*Draws*]
My meditating mood may work my wo,
Stand whosoe'er thou art – answer, who's
there!

Enter Bland

BLAND: A friend.

MELVILLE: Advance and give the countersign.

BLAND: Hudson.

MELVILLE: What, Bland!

BLAND: Melville, my friend you here.

MELVILLE: And *well* my brave young friend; but why do you .
At this dead hour of night, approach the camp,
On foot and thus alone?
BLAND: I have but now dismounted;
My servant and my horses, spent with toil,
Wait till the morn.
MELVILLE: Why waited not yourself?
BLAND: Anxious to know the truth of those reports
Which, from the many mouths of busy fame,
Still as I pass'd, struck varying on my ear,
Each making th' other void, nor does delay
The color of my hasteful business suit.
I bring despatches for our great commander:
And hasted hither with design to wait,
His rising, or awake him with the sun.
MELVILLE: You will not need the last, for the blest sun
Ne'er rises on his slumbers; by the dawn
We see him mounted, gaily in the field,
Or find him wrapt in meditation deep,
Planning the welfare of our war-worn band.
BLAND: Prosper him heaven and recompense his cares.
MELVILLE: You're from the south if I presume a right?
BLAND: I am, and Melville, I am fraught with news,
The south teems with events, convulsing:
The briton there, plays at no mimic war:
With gallant face he moves, and gallantly is met.
MELVILLE: Justice is ours, what shall prevail against her?
BLAND: But as I past along, many strange tales,
And monstrous rumors, have my ears assail'd:
That Arnold had proved false; but he was ta'en,
And hang'd, or to be hang'd – I know not what.
Another told, that all our army, with their
Much !oved chief, sold and betray'd, were captured.
But, as I nearer drew, at vonder cot,
Twas said, that Arnold, traitor like, had fled;
And that a briton tried and proved a spy,
Was on this day, as such, to suffer death.
MELVILLE: As you drew near plain truth advanced to meet you,
Tis even as you heard, my brave young friend.
He offer'd bribes to tempt the band that seized him;

But the rough farmer, for his country arm'd,
That soil defending which his ploughshare turn'd,
Those laws, his father chose, and he approved,
Yet not a heart but pities and would save him;
For all confirm that he is brave and virtuous:
Known but till now the darling child of honor.
BLAND: [*Contemptuously*] And how is call'd this honorable spy.
MELVILLE: Andre's his name.
BLAND: [*Much agitated*] Andre!
O no, my friend, you're sure deceived.
MELVILLE: How might I be deceived?
BLAND: Pardon me, Melville; oh, that well known name,
So link'd with circumstances infamous!
My friend must pardon me. Thou will not blame
When I shall tell what cause I have to love him;
What cause to think him nothing less the pupil
Of honor stern, than sweet humanity.
Thus, thus to meet him on the brink of death, [*Kneels*]
A death so infamous! heav'n grant my prayers
That I may see him. O inspire my heart
With thoughts, my tongue with words that move to pity! [*Rises*]
Quick Melville, show me where my Andre lies.
MELVILLE: Good wishes go with you!
BLAND: I'll save my friend! [*Exeunt*]

Scene 2

A prison – Andre discover'd in a pensive posture sitting at a table – a book by him and candles – his dress neglected, his hair dishevelled – he rises and comes forward.

ANDRE: Kind heav'n be thank'd for that I stand alone
In this sad hour of life's brief pilgrimage!
Single in misery; no one else involving,
In grief, in shame, in ruin. Tis my comfort,
Thou my thrice honor'd sire, in peace went'st down
Unto the tomb, nor knew to blush, nor knew
A pang for me! and thou revered matron,
Could'st bless thy child, and yield thy breath in peace!
No wife shall weep, no child lament my loss.
Thus may I consolation find in what
Was once my wo. I little thought to joy

In not possessing, as I erst possessed,
Thy love, Honora! Andre's death perhaps,
May cause a cloud pass o'er thy lovely face;
The pearly tear may steal from either eye;
For thou may'st feel a transient pang, nor
  wrong
A husband's right: more than a transient
  pang,
O may'st thou never feel! the morn draws nigh
To light me to my shame; frail nature shrinks –
And *is* death then so fearful? I have braved
Him, fearless in the field, and steel'd my
  breast
Against his thousand horrors; but his cool,
His sure approach requires a fortitude
Which nought but conscious rectitude can give.
[*Retires and sits leaning*]

Enter Bland, unperceived by Andre

BLAND: And is that Andre! O how changed!
  alas!
Where is that martial fire, that generous
  warmth;
Which glowed his manly countenance through-
  out,
And gave to every look, to every act,
The tone of high chivalrous animation?
Andre my friend: look up.
ANDRE: Who call'd me friend?
BLAND: Young Arthur Bland!
ANDRE: [*Rising*] That name sounds like a
  friend's. [*With emotion*]
I have inquired for thee – wish'd much to see
  thee,
I prythee take no note of these fools tears –
My heart was full – and seeing thee –
BLAND: [*Embracing him*] O Andre!
I have but now arrived from the south –
Nor heard – till now – of this – I cannot speak –
Is this a place? o thou, my friend.
ANDRE: Still dost thou call me, friend? I, who
  dared act
Against my reason – my declared opinion;
Oft in the generous heat of glowing youth,
Oft have I said how fully I despised
All bribery base – all treacherous tricks in war;
Rather my blood should bathe these hostile
  shores,
And have it said "he died a gallant soldier,"
Than with my country's gold encourage trea-
  son,
And thereby purchase gratitude and fame.
Still is my heart the same. But there has past

A day, an hour, which ne'er can be recall'd!
BLAND: Not ev'ry record cancell'd – oh there are
  hearts,
Where virtue's image, when tis once engraved,
Can never know erasure.
ANDRE: Generous Bland! [*Takes his hand*]
The hour draws nigh which ends my life's sad
  story,
I should be firm.
BLAND: By heaven thou shalt not die. Betray'd
  perhaps,
I surely shall prevail.
ANDRE: It is in vain;
All has been tried, each friendly argument.
BLAND: All has not yet been tried. The powerful
  voice
Of friendship in thy cause, has not been
  heard.
My general favors me, and loves my father –
My gallant father! would that he were here!
But he, perhaps, now wants an Andre's care,
To cheer his hours: perhaps now languishes
Amidst those horrors whence thou sav'd'st his
  son –
The present moment claims my thought –
  Andre
I fly to save thee –
ANDRE: Bland, it is in vain –
But hold – there is a service thou may'st do me.
BLAND: Speak it!
ANDRE: Oh think, and as a soldier think,
How I must die – the *manner* of my death –
Like the base ruffian, or the midnight thief,
Ta'en in the act of stealing from the poor,
To be turn'd off the felon's – murderer's cart,
A mid-air spectacle to gaping clowns:
To run a short and envied course of glory,
And end it on a gibbet.
BLAND: Damnation!
ANDRE: Such is my doom, o! have the manner
  changed,
And of mere death I'll think not.
Perhaps thou canst gain that? –
BLAND: [*Almost in a phrenzy*] Thou shalt not
  die!
ANDRE: Let me, o let me die a soldier's death,
While friendly clouds of smoke shroud from all
  eyes,
My last convulsive pangs, and I'm content.
BLAND: [*With increasing emotion*] Thou shalt
  not die!
Curse on the laws of war!
If worth like thine must thus be sacrificed,

103

To policy so cruel and unjust,
I will forswear my country, and her service,
I will hie me to the briton, and with fire
And sword, and ev'ry instrument of death
Or devastation, join in the work of war!
What, shall worth weigh for nought? I will
  avenge thee!

ANDRE: Hold – hold my friend, thy country's
  woes are full.
What would'st thou make me cause another
  traitor?
No more of this; and if I die, believe me,
Thy country for my death incurs no blame.
Restrain thy ardor, but ceaselessly intreat,
That Andre, may at least die, as he lived,
A soldier!

BLAND: By heaven thou shalt not die –

*Bland rushes off – Andre, looks after him with
an expression of love and gratitude – then retires
up the stage*

Scene 3

*The general's quarters. Enter General, with pa-
pers in his hand, and Bland.*

GENERAL: Captain, you are noted here with hon-
  orable
Praises. Depend upon that countenance
From me, which you have proved yourself so
  richly
Meriting. Both from your father's virtues
And your own: your country owes you honor –
The sole return the poor can make for service.

BLAND: If from my country ought I've merited,
Or gain'd the approbation of her champion,
At any other time, I should not dare,
Presumptuously to shew my sense of it;
But now my tongue, all shameless, dares to
  name
The boon, the precious recompense I wish,
Which granted, pays all service, past or fu-
  ture,
O'erpays the utmost I can e'er achieve.

GENERAL: Brief, my young friend, briefly your
  purpose.

BLAND: If I have done my duty as a soldier;
If I have braved all dangers for my country;
If my brave father has deserved ought;
Call to mind – and cancel all – but grant
Me my request – mine and humanity's.

GENERAL: Be less profuse of words, and name
  your wish;

If fit, its fitness is the best assurance
That not in vain you sue; but, if unjust,
Thy merits, nor the merits of thy race,
Cannot its nature alter, nor my mind,
From its determined opposition change.

BLAND: You hold the fate of my most loved of
  friends!
As gallant soldier, as e'er faced a foe,
Blest with each polish'd gift of social life,
And every virtue of humanity.
To me a saviour from the pit of death,
To me and many more my countrymen.
If Andre lives, the prisoner finds a friend;
Else helpless and forlorn –
All men will bless the act, and bless thee for
  it.

GENERAL: Think'st thou thy country would not
  curse the man,
Who, by a clemency ill-timed, ill-judged,
Encouraged treason? that *pride* encouraged,
Which by denying us the rights of nations,
Hath caused those ills which thou hast now
  portray'd?
Our soldiers, brave and generous peasantry,
As rebels have been treated, not as men.
Tis mine, brave yeomen, to assert your rights;
Tis mine to teach the foe, that though array'd
In rude simplicity, ye, yet are men,
And rank among the foremost –

BLAND: O there are englishmen as brave, as
  good,
As ever land on earth might call its own;
And gallant Andre is among the best.

GENERAL: Since they have hurl'd war on us, we
  must shew,
That by the laws of war we will abide,
And have the power to bring their acts for trial
To that tribunal, eminent 'mongst men,
Erected by the policy of nations,
To stem the flood of ills, which else fell war,
Would pour uncheck'd, upon the sickening
  world,
Sweeping away all trace of civil life.

BLAND: To pardon him would not encourage ill,
His case is singular – his station high –
His qualities admired – his virtues loved.

GENERAL: No more, my good young friend; it is
  in vain.
The men entrusted with thy country's rights
Have weighed, attentive, every circumstance.
An individual's virtues, is by them,
As highly prized as it can be by thee.
I know the virtues of this man, and love them;

But the destiny of millions, millions
Yet unborn, depends upon the rigor
Of this moment. The haughty briton, laughs
To scorn our armies and our councils. Mercy,
Humanity, call loudly, that we make
Our now despised power, be felt vindictive.
Millions demand the death of this young man –
My injured country, he his forfeit life
Must yield, to shield the lacerated breast
From torture. [*To Bland*] Thy merits are not
overlook'd.
Promotion shall immediately attend thee.
[*Exit*]
BLAND: [*After a pause*] And is it even so! o
Andre,
How shall I dare to see thy face again,
Without one ray of comfort? [*Exit*]

Scene 4

*A village – at a distance some tents – in front,
muskets, drums, and other indications of sol-
dier's quarters. Enter Mrs. Bland, and Chil-
dren, attended by Melville.*
MELVILLE: The general's doors to you are ever
open.
But why, my worthy friend, this agitation?
Our colonel, your husband –
MRS. BLAND: [*In tears gives him the letter*] Read
Melville!
MELVILLE: [*Returning the letter*] Fear nothing,
madam, tis an empty threat.
A trick of policy – they dare not do it.
MRS. BLAND: Alas! alas! what dares not power to
do?
What art of reasoning, or what magic words,
Can still the storm of fears these lines have
raised?
The wife's – the mother's fears? poor inno-
cents,
Unconscious on the brink of what a perilous
Precipice you stand, unknowing that to-day
You are cast down the gulf, poor babe you
weep
From sympathy. Children of sorrow, nurst,
Nurtured, midst camps and arms, unknowing
man,
But as man's fell destroyer; must you now,
To crown your piteous fate, be fatherless?
O lead me, lead me to him! let me kneel,
Let these, my children, kneel till Andre par-
don'd

Ensures to me a husband, them a father.
MELVILLE: Madam, duty forbids further attend-
ance,
I am on guard to-day: but see your son,
To him I leave your guidance. Good wishes
Prosper you. [*Exit Melville*]

Enter Bland

MRS. BLAND: My Arthur! oh my Arthur!
BLAND: My mother! [*Embracing her*]
MRS. BLAND: My son, I have been wishing
For you. [*Bursts into tears, unable to proceed*]
BLAND: But whence this grief, these tears, my
mother?
Why are these little cheeks bedew'd with
sorrow?
[*He kisses the children, who exclaim*] – Broth-
er! brother!
Have *I* done ought to cause a mother's sadness?
MRS. BLAND: No, my brave boy! I oft have fear'd,
but never
Sorrow'd for thee.
BLAND: High praise! then bless me, madam;
For I have pass'd through many a bustling
scene
Since I have seen a father or a mother.
MRS. BLAND: Bless thee, my boy! oh bless him,
bless him heaven!
Render him worthy to support these babes!
So soon, perhaps all fatherless – dependant –
BLAND: What mean'st thou, madam, why these
tears?
MRS. BLAND: Thy father –
BLAND: A prisoner of war – I long have known
it –
But made so without blemish to his honor,
And soon exchanged, returns unto his friends,
To guard these little ones, and point and lead
To virtue and to glory.
MRS. BLAND: Never! never!
His life a sacrifice, to Andre's manes,
Must soon be offered. Even now endungeon'd,
Like a vile felon – on the earth he lies,
His death expecting. Andre's execution
Gives signal for the murder of thy father –
Andre now dies.
BLAND: My father! and thy friend! [*Despairing-
ly*]
MRS. BLAND: There is but one on earth can save
my husband –
But one can pardon, Andre –
BLAND: Haste my mother!
Thou wilt prevail – take with thee in each hand

An unoffending child of him thou weepest.
Save – save them both! this way – haste – lean
on me. [*Exeunt*]

Scene 5

The general's quarters. Enter general with a letter, followed by Melville.

GENERAL: Here have I intimation from the foe,
That still they deem the spy we have condemn'd,
Merely a captive, by the laws of arms
From death protected; and retaliation,
As they term it, threaten, if we our purpose
hold.
Bland is the victim they have singled out;
Hoping his threatened death, will Andre save.
MELVILLE: If I were Bland, I boldly might advise
My general how to act. Free and in safety,
I will now suppose my counsel needless.

Enter an american officer

OFFICER: Another flag hath from the foe arrived,
And craves admittance.
GENERAL: Conduct it hither. [*Exit officer*]
Let us, unwearied hear, unbiass'd judge,
Whate'er against our martial court's decision,
Our enemies can bring.

Enter british officer, conducted by the american officer, american officer exit

GENERAL: You are welcome, sir;
What further says sir Henry?
BRITISH OFFICER: This from him:
He calls on you to think what weighty woes
You now are busy bringing on your country.
He bids me say, that, if your sentence reach
The prisoner's life, prisoner of arms he deems
him,
And no spy, on him alone it falls not.
He bids me loud proclaim it, and declare,
If this brave officer, by cruel mockery
Of war's stern law, and justice feign'd pretence,
Be murder'd; the sequel of our strife, bloody,
Unsparing, and remorseless you will make.
Think of the many captives in our power.
When Andre's death unparallel'd in war
The signal gives, then colonel Bland must die.
GENERAL: Tis well, sir, bear this message in return.

Sir Henry Clinton knows the laws of arms,
He is a soldier, and I think a brave one.
The prisoner he retains, he must account for,
Perhaps the reckoning's near. I likewise am
A soldier; entrusted by my country,
What I shall judge most for that country's
good,
That shall I do. When doubtful, I consult
My country's friends, never her enemies.
In Andre's case there is no doubt: tis clear:
Sir Henry Clinton knows it.
BRITISH OFFICER: Weigh consequences!
GENERAL: In strict regard to consequence I act;
And much should doubt to call that action
right,
However specious, whose apparent end
Was misery to man. That brave officer
Whose death you threaten, for himself drew
not
The sword – his country's wrongs aroused his
mind,
Her good alone his aim, and if his fall
Can further fire that country to resistance,
He will, with smiles, yield up his glorious
life,
And count his death a gain; and though Columbians
Will lament his fall, they will lament in blood.
[*The general walks up the stage*]
MELVILLE: Hear this! hear this mankind!
BRITISH OFFICER: Thus am I answered?

Enter a sergeant with a letter

SERGEANT: Express from colonel Bland. [*Delivers it to general and exit*]
GENERAL: With your permission. [*Opens it*]
BRITISH OFFICER: Your pleasure, sir. It may my
mission further – .
GENERAL: Tis short, I will put form aside and
read it. [*Reads*] "Excuse me, my commander, for having a moment doubted your virtue;
but you love me – if you waver let this confirm
you – my wife and children, to you and my
country – do your duty!" Report this to your
General.
BRITISH OFFICER: I shall, sir! [*Bows and exit
with american officer*]
GENERAL: Oh Bland! my countryman! [*Exit
with emotion, followed by Melville*]

End of the Third Act

ACT IV. Scene 1

A wood. Enter Dennis O'Bogg, with arms and accoutrements as a british soldier – knapsack at his back – sings without.

Song – from the Picture of Paris

1

There was an Irish lad,
Who loved a cloister'd nun;
And it made him very sad,
For what was to be done:
He thought it was a big shame, a most con-
founded sin,
That she could not get out at all and he could
not get in;
Yet he went ev'ry day, he could do nothing
more,
Yet he went ev'ry day to the convent door,
And he sung sweetly Smalilou.
Gramachre! and Paddy Whack.

2

To catch a glimpse at her,
He play'd a thousand tricks,
The bolts he tried to stir,
And he gave the wall some kicks:
He stamp'd, and raved, and sigh'd, and pray'd,
and many times he swore,
The devil burn the iron bolts – the devil take
the door,
Yet he went ev'ry day, he made it a rule,
He went ev'ry day and look'd like a fool,
And he very sweetly sung Smalilou, etc.

3

One morn she left her bed,
Because she could not sleep,
And to the window sped,
To take a little peep;
And what did she do then? I'm sure you'll
think it right,
She bade the honest lad good day, she bade the
nuns good night:
Tenderly she listen'd to all he had to say,
Then jump'd into his arms, and so they ran
away.
And they sung sweetly Smalilou, etc.

O'BOGG: Devil burn the fashion, but this trotting with a full knapsack on an empty stomach is apt to make a man's back ache with hunger. [*Takes off the knapsack*] So, I have supported you long enough – let's see what you can do to support me. [*Sits, opens his pack and takes out some cold boil'd potatoes*] What, have I nothing left but wall fruit? not a delicate piece of ration beef? or a savory rind of bacon? well, they say hunger makes sauce to a man's meat. I wonder couldn't it make meat to his sauce. [*Eats*]

Enter Paulding, Van Vert and Williams

WILLIAMS: Who the nation have we got there? a fish out of water!

O'BOGG: And he sweetly sung smalilou, etc., etc.

WILLIAMS: No, dang it, he's a humming bird.

PAULDING: You seize his arms. [*Williams takes possession of Dennis' musket*]

VAN VERT: I'm afraid we shall spoil his singing. [*Paulding and Van Vert advance one on each side with bayonets presented towards Dennis' breast*]

O'BOGG: "One morn she left her bed, because she couldn't sleep." [*Singing*]

PAULDING: You're a prisoner!

O'BOGG: [*After looking round with great indifference*] You may put up your knives and forks, gentlemen, [*Pointing to the bayonets*] the devil of any carving is there to do.

VAN VERT: You are our prisoner!

O'BOGG: Will you ate a potatoe?

WILLIAMS: Civil enough! have you nothing better for dinner?

O'BOGG: [*Rises*] You may say that; for I ate all the best part of my dinner for breakfast. It's a trick my daddy learnt me. "Dennis," says he, for my name's, Dennis O'Bogg, at your sarvice: "Dennis," says he – I had just then began to nibble at the tail of a salt herring, "Dennis," says he——

WILLIAMS: Your daddy was very fond of your name: what else did he say?

O'BOGG: Always ate the best *first*, my boy, and you'll ate the best last.

VAN VERT: Soldier, are you alone?

O'BOGG: I should be sorry to say so much in *your* presence. But before the company came to dinner, the devil a christian soul was there here but I and the potatoes.

WILLIAMS: Dang my buttons, this fellow has fun in him – how the nation came you here all alone like a cat in a strange garret? are you a deserter?

O'BOGG: You may say that – saving any imputation on my honor. The short and the long of the story is, I never could be settled in any one place, but what with whiskey and love it grew too hot for me. So finding how your general Arnold is treated by sir Henry Clinton, at York, with honor and command, I thought I might as well get rid of my *little inconveniences*, for they will be springing up round an irishman, like mushrooms round a dunghill.

PAULDING: What do you mean by little inconveniences?

O'BOGG: O, debts, and children, and wives, and such like articles. So I thought I would come and take a little fresh air in the country here, join your army a bit and claim equal rank.

WILLIAMS: Rank! ha – ha – ha! – what rank? – what the deuce had you to do with rank.

O'BOGG: Rank! ay to be sure! rank and file too!

VAN.VERT: We shall be glad of a strong and well equip'd soldier; but before we take you into our mess, we should be glad to hear you give good reasons for quitting New-York?

O'BOGG: Oh, then you shall have more than one. – First, by mere accident I found I had two wives in the garrison.

WILLIAMS: Two wives! You *needn't* say *no more*.

PAULDING: How did that happen?

O'BOGG: Without the least intention on my part – I had but just got married, t'other day, when my widow came from Letterkenny to seek me.

VAN VERT: Your widow! how your widow?

O'BOGG: Fait, hadn't she lost her husband? and doesn't that make a widow any time?

WILLIAMS: Now give us your second reason for running away.

O'BOGG: Becase, general sir Henry Clinton gives good encouragement for it.

PAULDING: He encourages our soldiers to go and join him, but certainly he doesn't encourage desertion among his own troops.

O'BOGG: And a'n't that now the same thing? if it's as broad as tis long, won't it be square? if he invites your folks to come to him, doesn't he invite his own folks to go to you? isn't that plain now?

PAULDING: Not plain enough for my eyes.

O'BOGG: Arrah then put on your spectacles. Talking of spectacles puts me in mind of my mammy.

WILLIAMS: She wore spectacles, I guess.

O'BOGG: No, she couldn't; she had no nose.

VAN VERT: How did spectacles remind you of her then?

O'BOGG: Be azy and I'll tell you. When my brother Teddy was hanging up in a hempen necklace, "oh, what a spectacle!" says my mammy. "Dont blubber and howl so, mammy," says I, "see they're just stringing brother Phelim, and then you'll have a pair of spectacles, and all of your own making."

WILLIAMS: And how the dickens comes it they didn't hang you too?

O'BOGG: Becase, when my two twin brothers broke into the church, I was so drunk I couldn't go with them.

VAN VERT: You're a precious fellow.

O'BOGG: You may say that.

WILLIAMS: What did your brothers go into the church for, Dennis?

O'BOGG: And you may ax that. If they had kept in the way of their parents, as all good and dutiful children ought to do, and only have gone to the ale house, they might have been as pretty boys at this present spaking as your humble servant, Dennis O'Bogg.

VAN VERT: Dennis, are you most knave or fool?

O'BOGG: I believe I'm *between* both. But if I was to speak the honest truth, to-day –

VAN VERT: What would you say?

O'BOGG: Something I might be asham'd of to-morrow.

WILLIAMS: Come, let's move on to the camp. We'll carry your arms for you, though.

O'BOGG: Fait and I'd thank you if you'd carry my legs too.

PAULDING: If your good qualities on examination should sufficiently recommend you, you may perhaps be received as the comrade of an american soldier.

O'BOGG: So you list men for their good qualities – now in my country they pick them up for their bad.

WILLIAMS: So, so! then your army are all *pick'd* men.

O'BOGG: How is it with yours?

WILLIAMS: All *chosen* men! "chosen," as our chaplain told us last Sunday, "to establish an empire of freemen, as an example to the world, and a blessing to our latest posterity.

O'BOGG: What, I see you go to church.

WILLIAMS: Yes! to *steer clear* of the ale-house and the gallows. My family are not fond of spectacles. Shall I tell you what a true yankee boy is?

O'BOGG: Fait, you shall.

WILLIAMS: Listen and learn.

Song

1

A yankee boy is trim and tall,
And never over fat, sir,
At dance or frolic, hop and ball,
He's nimble as a gnat, sir.
Yankee doodle, etc.

2

He's always out on training day,
Commencement or election!
At truck and trade he knows the way,
Of thriving to perfection.
Yankee doodle, etc.

3

His door is always open found,
His cider of the best, sir,
His board with pumpkin pye is crown'd
And welcome every guest, sir.
Yankee doodle, etc.

4

Though rough and little is his farm,
That little is his own, sir;
His hand is strong, his heart is warm,
Tis truth and honor's throne, sir.
Yankee doodle, etc.

5

His country is his pride and boast,
He'll ever prove true blue, sir,
When call'd upon to give his toast,
Tis "yankee doodle do," sir.
Yankee doodle! fire away!
What yankee boy's afraid, sir?
Yankee doodle was the tune
At Lexington was play'd, sir!
[Exeunt]

Scene 2

A prison. Enter Andre and Bland.

ANDRE: Welcome, my Bland! cheerly, a welcome hither!
I feel assurance that my last request
Will not be slighted. Safely thy father
Shall return to thee. [*Holding out a paper*] See what employment
For a dying man. Take thou these verses;
And after my decease, send them to her
Whose name is woven in them; whose image
Hath control'd my destiny.
A gallant knight, erewhile
Of Coeur de Lion's day, would, dying, send
His heart home to its mistress; degenerate
Soldier, I send but some blotted paper.
BLAND: If't would not damp thy present cheerfulness
I would require the meaning of thy words.
I ne'er till now did hear of Andre's mistress.
ANDRE: Mine is a story of that common kind,
So often told, with scanty variation,
That the pall'd ear loaths the repeated tale!
Each young romancer chooses for his theme
The woes of youthful hearts, by the cold hand
Of frosty age, arm'd with parental power,
Asunder torn. But I long since have ceased
To mourn, well satisfied that she I love,
Happy in holy union with another,
Shares not my wayward fortunes, nor would I
Now these tokens send, remembrance to awaken,
But that I know her happy: and the happy
Can think on misery and share it not.
BLAND: [*Agitated*] Some one approaches.
ANDRE: Why, tis near the time.
But tell me, Bland, say – is the manner chang'd?
BLAND: I hope it; but I yet have no assurance.
ANDRE: Well, well.

Honora speaks without

HONORA: I must see him.
ANDRE: Who's voice was that?
My senses? do I dream? [*Leans on Bland*]

Enter Honora

HONORA: Where is he?
ANDRE: Tis she! [*Starts from Bland, and advances towards Honora – she rushes into his arms*]
HONORA: It is enough! he lives, and I shall save him. [*She faints in Andre's arms*]
ANDRE: She sinks! assist me, Bland! o save her! save her! [*Places her in a chair and looks tenderly on her*] How pale she looks! how worn that tender frame! She has known sorrow! who would injure her?
BLAND: She revives, Andre.

Andre kneels and supports her

HONORA: Andre!
ANDRE: Lov'd excellence!
HONORA: Yes! it is Andre. [*Rises and looks at him*] By him supported. [*Leans on him*]

ANDRE: Why is this?
Thou dost look pale, Honora, – sick and wan.
HONORA: All will be well:
But was it kind to leave me as thou didst?
So rashly to desert thy vow-link'd wife!
ANDRE: When made another's both by vows and laws.
HONORA: [*Quitting his support*] What mean'st thou?
ANDRE: Didst thou not marry him?
HONORA: Marry!
ANDRE: Didst thou not give thy hand away
From me?
HONORA: Oh never! never!
ANDRE: Not married!
HONORA: To none but thee, and but in will to thee.
ANDRE: O blind, blind wretch! thy father told me –
HONORA: Thou wast deceived: they hurried me away,
Spreading false rumors to remove thy love –
[*Tenderly*] Thou didst too soon believe them.
ANDRE: Thy father!
How could I but believe Honora's father?
I have destroy'd myself and thee! alas!
Ill-fated maid! why didst thou not forget me?
Has thou rude seas and hostile shores explored
For this? to see my death? witness my shame?
HONORA: I come to bless thee, Andre; and shall do it.
I bear such offers from thy kind commander,
As must prevail to save thee. Thus the daughter
May repair the ills the cruel sire inflicted.
My father, dying, gave me cause to think
That arts were used to drive thee from thy home:
But what those arts I knew not. An heiress left
Of years mature, with power and liberty,
I straight resolved to seek thee o'er the seas.
A long-known friend, who came to join her lord,
Yielded protection and lov'd fellowship.
Indeed, when I did hear of thy estate
It almost kill'd me: I was weak before –
ANDRE: Tis I have murder'd thee!
HONORA: All shall be well.
Thy general heard of me, and instant form'd
The plan of this my visit. I am strong
Compar'd with what I was. Hope strengthens me

Nay, even solicitude supports me now:
And when thou shalt be safe, *thou* wilt support me.
ANDRE: Support thee! o heaven! what! and *must* I die? –
Die! and leave her *thus* – suffering – unprotected!

Enter Melville, and guard

MELVILLE: I am sorry that my duty should require
Service, at which my heart revolts; but, sir,
Our soldiers wait in arms, all is prepared.
HONORA: To death! impossible! has my delay
Then murder'd him? a momentary respite.
MELVILLE: Lady, I have no power.
BLAND: Melville, my friend, [*To Melville*]
This lady bears despatches of high import,
Touching this business: should they arrive too late –
HONORA: For pity's sake, and heaven's, conduct me to him;
And wait the issue of our conference.
O twould be murder of the blackest dye,
Sin, execrable not to break thy orders –
Inhuman thou art not.
MELVILLE: Lady, thou sayest true;
For rather would I lose my rank in arms,
And stand cashiered for lack of discipline,
Than gain 'mongst military men all praise,
Wanting the touch of sweet humanity.
HONORA: Thou grantest my request?
MELVILLE: Lady, I do.
Retire! [*To the soldiers, who go off*]
BLAND: I know not what excuse, to martial men,
Thou canst advance for this; but to thy heart
Thou wilt need none, good Melville.
ANDRE: Oh, Honora!
HONORA: Cheer up, I feel assured. Hope wings my flight
To bring thee tidings of much joy to come.
[*Exit with Bland and Melville*]
ANDRE: Eternal blessings on thee, matchless woman!
If death now comes, he finds the veriest coward
That e'er he dealt withal. I cannot think
Of dying. Void of fortitude, each thought
Clings to the world – the world that holds
Honora! – [*Exit*]

Scene 3

The general's quarters. Enter General and Melville.

GENERAL: Ask her, my friend, to send by thee
her packets.
[*Exit Melville*] O, what keen struggles must I
undergo!
Unbless'd estate! to have the power to pardon;
The court's stern sentence to remit; give life;
Feel the strong wish to use such blessed power;
Yet know that circumstances strong as fate
Forbid to obey the impulse. O, I feel
That man should never shed the blood of man.

Re-enter Melville

MELVILLE: Nought can the lovely suitor satisfy,
But conference with thee; and much I fear
Refusal would cause madness.
GENERAL: Yet to admit,
To hear, be tortur'd, and refuse at last.
MELVILLE: Sure never man such spectacle of
sorrow
Saw before. Motionless the rough hewn soldiers
Silent view her, or walk aside and weep.
GENERAL: [*After a pause*] Admit her! [*Exit
Melville*] o, for the art, the precious art,
To reconcile the sufferer to his sorrows!

*Honora rushes in, and throws herself wildly on
her knees before him – he endeavors to raise
her*

HONORA: Nay, nay, here is my place, or here,
or lower,
Unless thou grant'st his life. All forms away!
Thus will I clasp thy knees, thus cling to thee.
I am his wife – tis I have ruin'd him –
Oh save him – give him to me! let us cross
The mighty seas, far, far – ne'er to offend
again.

*The general turns away and hides his eyes with
his hands. Re-enter Melville, and an officer*

GENERAL: Melville, support her, my heart is
torn in twain.

*Honora as if exhausted, suffers herself to be
raised and rests on Melville*

AMERICAN OFFICER: This moment, sir, a messenger arrived
With well confirm'd and mournful information,

That gallant Hastings, by the lawless scouts
Of Britain taken, after cruel mockery
With show of trial and of condemnation,
On the next tree was hung.
HONORA: [*Wildly*] Oh, it is false!
GENERAL: Why, why did I hesitate! [*Exit*]

Honora sinks, faints, and is borne off by Melville and Officer

Scene 4

The prison. Enter Andre, meeting Bland.

ANDRE: How speeds Honora? [*Pause*] art thou
silent, Bland?
Why, then I know thy task. The mind of
man,
If not by vice debased, debilitated,
Or by disease of body quite unton'd,
Hath o'er its thoughts a power – energy divine!
Of fortitude the source, and every virtue
A godlike power, which e'en o'er circumstance
Its sov'reignty exerts; now, from my thoughts,
Honora! yet she is left alone exposed –
BLAND: O Andre, spurn me, strike me to the
earth;
For what a wretch am I, in Andre's mind,
That he can think he leaves his love alone,
And I retaining life!
ANDRE: Forgive me, Bland!
My thoughts glanced not on thee. Imagination
Pictured only, then, her orphan state, helpless;
Her weak and grief exhausted frame. Alas!
This blow will kill her.
BLAND: [*Kneeling*] Here do I myself
Devote, my fortune consecrate to thee,
To thy remembrance, and Honora's service!
ANDRE: Enough; let me not see her more – nor
think of her.
Farewell! farewell, sweet image! now for
death –
BLAND: Yet that thou shouldst the felon's fate
fulfil,
Damnation, my blood boils. Indignation
Makes the current of my life course wildly
Through its round, and maddens each emotion.
ANDRE: Come, come, it matters not.
BLAND: I do remember,
When a boy at school, in our allotted tasks,

We by our puny acts strove to portray
The giant thoughts of Otway. I was Pierre.
O thou art Pierre's reality! a soldier,
On whose manly brow sits fortitude enamor'd!
A Mars' abhorring vice, yet doom'd to die
A death of infamy; thy corse exposed
To vulgar gaze – halter'd – distorted – oh!
[*Pauses – then adds in a low hollow voice*]
Pierre had a friend to save him from such shame –
And so hast thou.

ANDRE: No more, as thou dost love me.

BLAND: I have a sword that never fail'd me.

ANDRE: Bland, such an act would justly thee involve,
And leave that helpless one thou sworest to guard,
Expos'd to every ill. O! think not of it.

BLAND: If thou wilt not my aid – take it thyself. [*Draws and offers his sword*]

ANDRE: No: men will say that cowardice did urge me. –
In my mind's weakness, I did wish to shun
That mode of death which error represented
Infamous; now let me rise superior;
And with a fortitude too true to start
From mere appearances, show your country,
That she, in me, destroys a man, who might
Have lived in virtue.

BLAND: [*Sheathing his sword*] I will not think more of it; –
I was again the sport of erring passion.

ANDRE: Go thou and guide Honora from this spot.

Enter Honora

HONORA: Who shall oppose his wife? I will have way!
They cruel would have kept me, Andre, from thee.
Say, am I not thy wife? wilt thou deny me?
Indeed I am not drest in bridal trim,
But I have travell'd far; rough was the road
Rugged and rough – that must excuse my dress.
[*Seeing Andre's distress*]
Thou art not glad to see me.

ANDRE: Break, my heart!

HONORA: Indeed I feel not much in spirits. I wept but now.

Enter Melville, and guard

BLAND: [*To Melville*] Say nothing.

ANDRE: I am ready.

HONORA: [*Seeing the guard*] Are they here?
Here again! the same! but they shall not harm me –
I am with thee, my Andre, I am safe –
And thou art safe with me. Is it not so?
[*Clinging to him*]

Enter Mrs. Bland

MRS. BLAND: Where is the lovely victim?

BLAND: Thanks, my mother.

MRS. BLAND: My woes are past.
Thy father, by the foe released, already
Is in safety. This be forgotten now;
And every thought be turn'd to this sad scene.
Come, lady, home with me.

HONORA: Go home with thee?
Art thou my Andre's mother? we will home
And rest, for thou art weary – very weary.

Leans on Mrs. Bland – Andre retires to the guard, and goes off with them, looking on her to the last, and with an action of extreme tenderness takes leave of her – Melville and Bland accompany him
Now we will go. Come, love! where is he?
All gone – I do remember – I awake –
They have him – oh, murder! help! save him! save him! –

Honora attempts to follow, but falls – Mrs. Bland kneels to assist her – curtain drops

End of the Fourth Act

ACT V. Scene 1

A landscape. Enter General Washington, officers and soldiers.

GENERAL: Now, my brave countrymen, one glorious effort more, and we shall see the termination of our martial labors. From many a check and many a foul discomfiture we've gained the precious jewel, dear experience. Many of those who started with us in the race have fallen; our labors done, we'll find a time to weep them. One royal army yielded in the north and crowned our arms, and Gates, with endless glory. Here in the south, Morgan and Greene, Fayette and Wayne, have nobly done their duty – one effort more, a second royal army must submit! what for the third remains?

MELVILLE: Flight or submission! we are now very forward with our second parallel, and but for the two advanced redoubts, the enemy's works would be soon enfiladed in almost every part.

GENERAL: Those redoubts must be carried this day. By agreement with general Rochambeau, one shall be attacked by the troops under his command, while at the same moment the other must be carried by my americans. I say carried, for to doubt the event would be treason to my country. [*Exeunt*]

Enter, in uniform, Paulding, Van Vert, Williams, and soldiers

PAULDING: How do you know we shall beat 'em?

WILLIAMS: Beat 'em! to be sure we shall.

VAN VERT: We must beat them.

PAULDING: It is not for us to say so. We shall certainly try.

WILLIAMS: I say we must beat 'em. Dang it, an't we ordered to carry the fort?

VAN VERT: And what good soldier but obeys orders?

WILLIAMS: Ay, sure enough. Dont you remember, lads, at the battle of Monmouth; when we marched up and found our advanced corps retreating and the british pursuing, what were the general's orders?

VAN VERT: "Advance and check the enemy."

WILLIAMS: And we did it.

VAN VERT: Ay, that was a glorious day.

WILLIAMS: We obeyed our orders.

PAULDING: Advance!

WILLIAMS: And we did it!

PAULDING: Check them.

WILLIAMS: And we did it!

PAULDING: Beat them.

WILLIAMS: And we did it! they run!

ALL: Huzza! huzza! huzza!

PAULDING: It was a glorious day.

WILLIAMS: A nation hot one.

Enter Dennis O'Bogg, as an american soldier

O'BOGG: Och! that ever I should be born to see the face of this ugly looking day!

WILLIAMS: Why what's the matter, mister O'Bogg?

O'BOGG: And by my soul and it *is* matter. There is a black-guard countryman of mine that has deserted from York-town – divil burn him, why couldn't he stay where he was? by and by there will be so many irish deserters among us, that we shall be call'd the blue lobsters, and the grinning thieves will say, that a little boiling would turn us all red again.

PAULDING: But, Dennis, you shouldn't find fault with him for deserting.

WILLIAMS: I suppose he heard that you was here?

O'BOGG: That's it. I know the *tief*. Didn't I borrow five and two-pence of him the morning I ran away? and can't I tell what it is the spalpeen is come after? but I wouldn't mind that a pig's foot, *becase* I've got my pocket full of dollars that are good for nothing, but to pay old debts. [*Takes out some pieces of brown paper*] But then the news he brings – oh, that's the thing.

WILLIAMS: What news?

O'BOGG: Fait, he tells me my two wives are in York-town here.

WILLIAMS: Your two widows, you mean.

O'BOGG: So we shall fight and take the place: and what will Dennis O'Bogg get by it?

WILLIAMS: More than any of us, I'm sure. Two wives! an't that enough?

O'BOGG: Yes! I shall get out of the fire into the frying pan. A pretty day's work I shall make of it! we shall silence the redoubts, carry the lines, take the town, and then I shall have two batteries open'd upon poor Dennis alone, that the divil himself couldn't *silence*.

WILLIAMS: Take courage, man, you've a good chance of being kill'd in the action.

O'BOGG: Ah, sure enough, there's some comfort in that.

WILLIAMS: Besides it's ten to one but your widows are both married.

O'BOGG: No: that's impossible. After having had Dennis O'Bogg for a husband, they could never take up with anything else.

Song – from the Picture of Paris

I

The turban'd turk who scorns the world,
May strut about with his whiskers curl'd,
Keep a hundred wives under lock and key
For nobody else but himself to see;
Yet long may he pray with his alcoran,
Before he can love like an irishman.

2

The frenchman gay with his louis d'or,
The solemn don, and the soft signor,
The dutch mynheer, so full of pride,

The russian, prussian, swede beside;
They all may do whate'er they can
But they'll never love like an irishman.

WILLIAMS: Then your only chance is being shot; for if you're so wonderful lovely, you'll have no peace this side the grave. Huzza! to arms, boys!

SOLDIERS: Huzza! [*Drum rolls*]

1ST SOLDIER: When we carry the redoubts, let us remember New London.

WILLIAMS: Remember humanity.

1ST SOLDIER: We'll not spare them! New London!

WILLIAMS: Humanity! remember we are men, and they are our fellow men! what! when we shall have charg'd and carried their works — when we are in their redoubts, and they are at our mercy — when they kneel and cry for quarter, shall we murder them?

PAULDING: No, fellow soldiers!

VAN VERT: Never! never!

SOLDIERS: No, never, never!

WILLIAMS: Huzza! no, never! we will raise them up and show them what treatment americans deserve. [*Drum rolls*] To arms! on, lads! let the word be "victory and mercy." [*Exeunt*]

Scene 2

Draws and discovers York-town — at a distance is seen the town, with the british lines and the lines of the besiegers — nearer are the advanced batteries, one more distant from the audience than the other — cannonading commences from the besiegers on the town — explosion of a powder magazine — the french troops advance towards the most distant of the advanced batteries — the battery begins to cannonade — the troops advance and carry it at the bayonet's point — while this is yet doing, the nearest battery begins to cannonade, and the american infantry attack and carry it with fixed bayonets, striking the english colors — shouts of victory. Enter on one side, General Washington, Melville, Bland, officers, soldiers, drums and colors -- on the other, Williams, Paulding, Van Vert, Dennis O'Bogg, officers and soldiers.

GENERAL: Thanks, my brave countrymen! our toils are past. It now requires not the spirit of prophecy to see, we have gain'd our country's independence. May that spirit which has animated the sons of Columbia, in this glorious struggle, remain pure and unimpaired, for then long will she be free and happy.

Chorus
The fight is done!
The battle won!
Our praise is due to him alone,
Who from his bright eternal throne,
    The fates of battles and of men decides!
To him all praise be given,
    And under heaven,
To great Columbia's son.
    Blest Washington!
Who o'er the fight like fate presides!

A transparency descends, and an eagle is seen suspending a crown of laurel over the commander in chief, with this motto — "Immortality to Washington."

Chorus
All hail Columbia's son!
    Immortal Washington!
By fame renow'd
By victory crown'd
    Hail Washington!

The End of THE GLORY OF COLUMBIA

SHE WOULD BE A SOLDIER

OR

THE PLAINS OF CHIPPEWA

M. M. NOAH

MORDECAI M. NOAH sought his livelihood among editors and politicians and his pleasure among theatres and theatre folk. On July 11, 1832, he wrote to Dunlap:

From a boy, I was a regular attendant of the Chestnut Street Theatre, during the management of Wignell and Reinagle, and made great efforts to compass the purchase of a season ticket, which I obtained generally of the treasurer, George Davis, for $18. Our habits through life are frequently governed and directed by our early steps. I seldom missed a night; and always retired to bed, after witnessing a good play, gratified and improved: and thus, probably, escaped the haunts of taverns, and the pursuits of depraved pleasures, which too frequently allure and destroy our young men: hence I was always the firm friend of the drama, and had an undoubted right to oppose my example through life to the horror and hostility expressed by sectarians to plays and playhouses generally.

Although Noah was never an actor, a manager, or even, in his own view, a professional playwright, he was an inveterate playgoer and loyal friend to actors and managers. So strong was Noah's attachment for the theatre that Sol Smith, the frontier theatrical manager, was sure it would persist in the spirit world. After Noah's death, Smith wrote, "I shall try to hunt you up, wherever you may be. If there are any theatres there, there's where I shall look for you."

Noah was born in Philadelphia on July 19, 1785, the son of a Portuguese Jew. After an early and brief schooling, he plunged into the newspaper and political activities that were to engage his interest throughout his life. His first position was in the auditor's office in Philadelphia; his second, political reporter in Harrisburg. He then moved to Charleston, where he studied law and became editor of the Charleston *City Gazette*. Here his editorials championed the American cause in the quarrel with England that finally led to the War of 1812. In fact, his views were so vigorously expressed that he was obliged to defend them in a number of duels. At the time of the difficulties with Algerian piracy, he was sent by Monroe as consul to Tunis. (Earlier, President Madison had offered him a similar position at Riga, but he had refused.)

When he returned to New York, he resumed his dual career, in politics and in journalism. He advanced from sheriff to surveyor of the Port of New York, to judge of the Court of Sessions, and in 1841 to Supreme Court Commissioner. Undoubtedly his Tammany sympathies were instrumental in furthering his political fortunes. During this period of political enterprise, he was also variously associated with the New York *Enquirer, The Evening Star, The Commercial Advertiser, The Union*, and *The Times and Messenger*. One of Noah's notable extraprofessional projects was the establishment of the City of Ararat, a haven of Judaism, on Grand Island, near Buffalo. His Zionist activities, particularly the founding of this haven, formed the basis for Israel Zangwill's book *Noah's Ark*. Noah died in New York on March 22, 1851.

Like Tyler, Noah possessed the zeal for public service that distinguished the first-rank citizen of the early republic. That he was held in high esteem is evident from the following reminiscences of J. T. Trowbridge:

"Come with me," Mr. Noah said, putting on his hat; and we went out together, I with my roll of manuscript, he with his stout cane. Even if I had been unaware of the fact, I should very soon have discovered that I was in company with an important personage. Everybody observed him, and it seemed as if every third or fourth man we met gave him a respectful salute. He continued his friendly talk with me in a way that relieved me of all sense of my own insignificance in the shadow of his celebrity and august proportions.

The scope and coloring of Noah's interests in politics and the theatre are clearly expressed in two of his letters. The first of these, from which a passage has already been quoted, was written to Dunlap in 1832, and the second was addressed to Sol Smith on October 11, 1847. The entire letters may be found in Dunlap's *History of the American Theatre* and in Smith's *Theatrical Management*. Following are excerpts from the letter to Dunlap:

[I have] no claim to the character of a settled, regular, or domiciliated writer for the green-room – a sort of volunteer supernumerary – a dramatic writer by "particular desire, and for this night only," as they say in the bills of the play; my "line," as you well know, has been in the more rugged paths of politics, a line in which there is more fact than poetry, more feeling than fiction; in which, to be sure, there are "exits and entrances" – where the "prompter's whistle" is constantly heard in the voice of the people; but which, in our popular government, almost disqualifies us for the more soft and agreeable translation to the lofty conceptions of tragedy, the pure diction of genteel comedy, or the wit, gayety, and humour of broad farce.

. . . I ventured to attempt a little melo-drama, under the title *Fortress of Sorrento*, which, not having money enough to pay for printing, nor sufficient influence to have acted, I thrust the manuscript in my pocket, and having occasion to visit New York, I called in at David Longworth's Dramatic Repository one day, spoke of the little piece, and struck a bargain with him, by giving him the manuscript in return for a copy of every play he published, which at once furnished me with a tolerably large dramatic collection. I believe the play never was performed, and I was almost ashamed to own it; but it was my first regular attempt at dramatic composition.

. . . Miss Leesugg, afterwards Mrs. Hackett, was engaged at the Park as a singer, and Phillips, who was here about the same period fulfilling a most successful engagement, was decided and unqualified in his admiration of her talent. Every one took an interest in her success; she was gay, kind-hearted, and popular, always in excellent spirits, and always perfect. Anxious for her success, I ventured to write a play for her benefit, and in three days finished the patriotic piece of *She would be a Soldier, or the Battle* [*sic*] *of Chippewa*, which I was happy to find, produced her an excellent house.

. . . After this play, I became in a manner domiciliated in the green-room. My friends, Price and Simpson, who had always been exceedingly kind and liberal, allowed me to stray about the premises like one of the family, and always anxious for their success, I ventured upon another attempt for a holiday occasion, and produced *Marion, or the Hero of Lake George*. It was played on the 25th of November – Evacuation day, and I bustled about among my military friends, to raise a party in support of a military play, and what with generals, staff-officers, rank and file, the Park Theatre was so crammed that not a word of the play was heard, which was a very fortunate affair for the author. The managers presented me with a pair of handsome silver pitchers, which I still retain as a memento of their good will and friendly consideration. You must bear in mind that while I was thus employed in occasional attempts at play-writing, I was engaged in editing a daily journal, and in all the fierce contests of political strife; I had, therefore, but little time to devote to all that study and reflection so essential to the success of dramatic composition.

. . . My next piece, I believe, was written for the benefit of a relative and friend, who wanted something to bring a house; and as the struggle for liberty in Greece was at that period the prevailing excitement, I finished the melo-drama of *The Grecian Captive*, which was brought out with all the advantages of good scenery and music. As a "good house" was of more consequence to the actor than the fame of the author, it was resolved that the hero of the piece should make his appearance on an elephant, and the heroine on a camel, which were procured from a neighbouring menagerie, and the *tout ensemble* was sufficiently imposing, only it happened that the huge elephant, in shaking his skin, so rocked the castle on his back, that the Grecian general nearly lost his balance, and was in imminent danger of coming down from his "high estate," to the infinite merriment of the audience. On this occasion, to use another significant phrase, a "gag" was hit upon of a new character altogether. The play was printed, and each auditor was presented with a copy gratis, as he entered the house. Figure to yourself a thousand people in a theatre, each with a book of the play in hand – imagine the turning over a thousand leaves simultaneously, the buzz and fluttering it produced, and you will readily believe that the actors entirely forgot their parts, and even the equanimity of the elephant and camel were essentially disturbed.

. . . My last appearance as a dramatic writer was in another national piece, called *The Siege of Tripoli*, which the managers persuaded me to bring out for my own benefit, being my first attempt to derive any profit from dramatic efforts. The piece was elegantly got up – the house crowded with beauty and fashion – everything went off in the happiest manner; when a short time after the audience had retired, the Park Theatre was discovered to be on fire, and in a short time was a heap of ruins. May 24, 1820.[1] This conflagration burnt out all my dramatic fire and energy, since which I have been, as you well know, peaceably employed in settling the affairs of the nation, and mildly engaged in the political differences and disagreements which are so fruitful in our great state.

. . . I still, however, retain a warm interest for the success of the drama, and all who are entitled to success engaged in sustaining it, and to none greater than yourself, who has done more, in actual labour and successful efforts, than any man in America. That you may realize all you have promised yourself, and all that you are richly entitled to, is the sincere wish of

Dear sir,
Your friend and servant,
M. M. Noah

Sol Smith prefaced his letter from Noah with the following comment: "I here insert a letter from my old and valued friend, Major Noah, of New York, giving that worthy gentleman's views of theatrical affairs in general, and pretty women in particular."

Having some leisure on hand, I should be glad to correspond with a New Orleans paper of established reputation, furnishing all the foreign and local news, making a useful as well as agreeable correspondence, for which I have all the material on hand, and the experience in such matters. Should you learn that such an opening exists, have the kindness to drop me a line. Madame Augusta tells me she has written to you in relation to an engagement, but has not received an answer. I have known her since her first arrival in this country, and, although a prodigious favorite everywhere, the numerous adventurers from abroad, of less merit and beauty, ask more reasonable terms, and supersede her. In the aggregate, I doubt whether the economy is the best policy. Old Placide, the Charleston manager, once said to me, "Give me de prette vimin, and I vill fill my house," and he had a galaxy of beauty, and so I would have were I manager.

. . . We shall lose our election this fall in consequence of the division in the Democratic party, and I apprehend I shall be compelled once more to take the field with the Old Guard, and endeavor to recover the day. Whenever there is a fierce battle to be fought, I am called upon. The moment victory ensues, I am shelved. "Every puny whipster gets my sword." If Clay's name is not brought forward until next summer, and he writes no letters and keeps quiet, I think his chance is the best. I suppose you still adhere to old "Rough and Ready." It is impossible, in these trying times, when the political elements are all in confusion, to say who stands the best chance.

. . . Write to Augusta. I think her an excellent card for the South, and I am sure you will want her. Success attend you.

Sincerely yours,
M. M. Noah

[1]Noah insisted that his benefit receipts of two thousand dollars, which had happily been rescued from the fire, be distributed among the actors.

Few theatrical figures have revealed themselves so conveniently and concisely as Noah in these letters.

In addition to the plays Noah mentioned in his letter to Dunlap, he had written an early play, *Paul and Alexis*, which had been done in Charleston in 1812. This was adapted from a popular melodrama of Pixerécourt, *Le Pèlerin Blanc ou les Orphelins du Hameau.* Of those plays to which he referred, *The Fortress of Sorrento* (1808) was an unacted romantic drama derived from the French opera *Leonora; Marion, or The Hero of Lake George* (first acted at the Park on November 25, 1821), was a Revolutionary War play based on the Battle of Saratoga; *The Grecian Captive* (first performed at the Park on June 17, 1822) explored some of the adventures of the Greek Revolution; *The Siege of Tripoli* (first acted at the Park on May 15, 1820) was founded on the historical events of the Tripolitan difficulties with which Noah had had some first-hand acquaintance; and *The Siege of Yorktown* (first performed at the Park on September 8, 1824, with Lafayette as honored spectator) was based on that Revolutionary War episode.

The Siege of Tripoli and *The Grecian Captive* demand special attention. *The Siege of Tripoli* was one of the many plays that dealt with this exciting aspect of early American history. Immediately preceding and during the War of 1812, American naval vessels had been battling in the Mediterranean against the states of Algiers, Tripoli, Morocco, and Tunis in an effort to achieve free and unmolested shipping in that region. The romantic adventures of American and English sailors captured and put into slavery in this mysterious, far-away land of Algeria, were ready-made material for the dramatists. Susanna Haswell Rowson was the first to employ the subject, in *Slaves in Algiers, or A Struggle for Freedom*, performed at the Chestnut Street Theatre in Philadelphia on December 22, 1794. The exciting escape of the Americans from their Algerian captors by the use of disguise formed the principal incident of the play. Other plays dealing with the struggle were *The American Captive, or The Siege of Tripoli* (1812), by James Ellison; *The Siege of Algiers, or The Downfall of Hadgi-Ali-Bashaw* (1823), by J. S. Smith; *The Fall of Algeria* (1825), by John Howard Payne; and *The Bombardment of Algiers* (1829), by Richard Penn Smith.

Noah's *dramatis personae* for *The Grecian Captive* included principally Greeks and Turks. However, their patriotic utterances had a strong freedom-loving-American ring. As Noah indicated in his preface, he was not inhibited by historical fact: "If eventually the Greeks should not recover Athens, it will not be my fault, it was necessary to my play, and so I gave them possession of that interesting spot with a dash of my pen." The final scene of the play demonstrated how strongly the Americans felt about the Greek cause and how precisely they identified themselves with the Greeks' fight for independence.

Some passages will illustrate the vigor of American sympathy for this revolutionary struggle that stimulated the Greek Revival in America. The following is taken from the preface:

No citizens of a free country, can observe with indifference the present struggle for liberty in Greece. Though separated by a world of waters we are too familiar with the history of that country, with those illustrious events which mark the pages of her history, not to feel a deep interest in the success of that people, and the cause of freedom generally.

. . . In writing plays on Greece we must bear in mind the theatres of Aeschylus, Sophocles, Aristophanes, and Euripides. Despotism resulting from a frequent change of masters has impaired, if not destroyed, that great human energy, and those lovely blossoms springing from the cultivated mind, for which the Greeks were once distinguished, and celebrated. Still they are Greeks, and at this day we have the ruins of the magnificent Gymnasia, Odeum, Prytaneum, the Pnyx, and all the glory of Pericles, left to admire; and we feel a deep interest for the present, in consideration of the glories of the past.

In the second speech of the play, the Greek prince Ypsilanti, in disguise, looks out over the beauties of Athens and exclaims:

> O Greece! Greece! how lovely art thou even in captivity! how splendid are thy ruins! how soft and balsamic thy air! how rich and fruitful are thy valleys? – How long shall it be ere Liberty dwells in thy temples, and the song of Freedom is heard on thy mountains!

And in the next to the final scene is the following dialogue between Kiminski, a Greek, and Burrows, an American officer:

> KIMINSKI: Accept, sir, the thanks of an old Greek warrior. From England, may I ask?
> BURROWS: No sir, from America. My frigate is called the United States,[2] and I am proud of the opportunity to assist the cause of liberty in Greece.
> KIMINSKI: America? – the United States? – Let me embrace thee! Thou art from the country of a Washington, of the patriot and soldier, who gave freedom and glory to the Western world. Sacred be his name – illustrious his example.
> BURROWS: I thank you, sir, and may you establish in Greece a free and happy republic, founded upon the only true basis, virtue, law, and liberty.

Clearly, Noah's principal dramatic purpose was to represent the pride of the young American republic in its achievements and its natural sympathy for another nation that was embarked on the same course. A Greek theme, but a one-hundred-percent American play.

[2]She was at Athens in 1817.

When *She Would Be a Soldier, or The Plains of Chippewa* was first brought
out at the Anthony Street Theatre on June 21, 1819, as a benefit for Catherine
Leesugg, it was boldly announced as of American authorship and dealing with
American subject matter. As Noah reported in his letter to Dunlap, it was
written for Miss Leesugg; and although she seems to have achieved a personal
triumph in the role and considerable financial reward, she acted in the play
only once again, on July 5 of the same year. Edwin Forrest's association with
the play has more theatrical significance. As early as 1825, in Albany, Forrest
became identified with the part of the Indian. The critic for *The Advertiser*
(October 25, 1825) wrote of his performance, "Nature has been bountiful to
him. His face and figure are such as to prepossess an audience in his favor –
his voice (with the single exception of Mr. Cooper's) is, we think, superior to
any we have ever heard." When Forrest again appeared as the Indian at the
Bowery in New York on November 25, 1826, John Augustus Stone was a
member of the company and may well then have received his first inspiration
for *Metamora. She Would Be a Soldier* held the stage until 1868, with over
eighty positively identified performances. As with *The Glory of Columbia*,
almost half the performances were billed for the Fourth of July, Evacuation
Day, or Washington's Birthday. The play was extremely popular throughout
the country. For example, there were at least thirty-one performances in New
Orleans between 1825 and 1842.

Historical interest in the military events was certainly responsible for a great
part of the play's success. As a documentary report on the Battle of Chippewa
(July 5, 1814) in which General Jacob Brown's and General Winfield Scott's
army removed the sting of earlier defeats, it was essentially accurate. When
the play was performed at Barnum's Museum on July 2, 1866, it was called
The War of 1812, with *She Would Be a Soldier* as a subtitle, and the subtitle
The Plains of Chippewa that appears in the printed text was frequently elevated to the main title, presumably to draw larger audiences. Further evidence of the interest in the military nature of the play is found in the account
of a performance at Albany in 1825 in which "Captain Henrickson's company
of artillery appeared on the stage, attended by the band, and Miss Tilden went
through the manual with the troop, amid a perfect storm of applause."

Noah's play was not the first theatrical piece to take account of the War of
1812. On December 8, 1812, news reached Philadelphia of the capture of the
Macedonian by the *United States;* on December 11, the Chestnut Street
Theatre offered a patriotic sketch, *The Return from a Cruise*, commemorating
this event. The victory of the *Constitution* over the *Guerrière* on August 19,
1812, was commemorated in some additional verses and an introductory interlude added to Dunlap's *Yankee Chronology* for the performance on September 9. G. E. Grice's *The Battle of New Orleans*, performed at the Park on

July 4, 1816, celebrated the heroism of General Jackson. Another play devoted to the triumph of Jackson at New Orleans, *The Eighth of January*, by Richard Penn Smith, was performed at the Chestnut Street Theatre in Philadelphia on January 8, 1829, ten years after Noah's play. Smith wrote another War-of-1812 play using the setting of a northern battle ground, *The Triumph of Plattsburg*, which was seen at the Chestnut Street Theatre on January 8, 1830.

For its sincerity of tone, its brightness and charm, its democratic spirit, and its praise of the Indian, Noah's play ranks a full step above these other dramas dealing with similar historical events. Noah was a whole-hearted champion of native subject matter and of the native dramatist, but the views he expressed in the preface to *She Would Be a Soldier* are tempered with amazing common sense. The same temperate attitude is apparent throughout the play. Although the nationalistic sentiments are vividly expressed, there is none of the bitterness toward the enemy that is found in the Revolutionary War plays. Mercy and tolerance, in tune with the prevailing spirit of good will that followed the War of 1812, were the qualities that Noah cherished. His thrusts at the Englishman and his French manservant were aimed at their supercilious attributes and not at their nationality. And at the same time as Noah recognized that many true American patriots were foreigners by birth – Christine's father was a French citizen who had come to America with Lafayette – he was aware that American birth and name alone, Jerry Mayflower, for example, did not automatically make an admirable citizen. As Adela insisted, "Merit is the exclusive property of no country."

SHE WOULD BE A SOLDIER

OR

THE PLAINS OF CHIPPEWA

M . M . N O A H

PREFACE

The following dramatic *bagatelle* was written in a few days, and its reception, under every circumstance, far exceeded its merits. I had no idea of printing it, until urged to do so by some friends connected with theatres, who, probably, were desirous of using it without incurring the expense of transcribing from the original manuscript. Writing plays is not my "vocation;" and even if the mania was to seize me, I should have to contend with powerful obstacles, and very stubborn prejudices; to be sure, these, in time, might be removed, but I have no idea of being the first to descend into the arena, and become a gladiator for the American Drama. These prejudices against native productions, however they may be deplored as impugning native genius, are nevertheless very natural. An American audience, I have no doubt, would be highly pleased with an American play, if the performance afforded as much gratification as a good English one; but they pay their money to be pleased, and if we cannot afford pleasure, we have no prescriptive right to ask for approbation. In England, writing of plays is a profession, by which much money is made if the plays succeed; hence a dramatic author goes to work *secundum artem.* – He employs all his faculties, exhausts all his resources, devotes his whole time, capacity and ingenuity to the work in hand; the hope of reward stimulates him – the love of fame urges him on – the opposition of rivals animates his exertions – and the expectation of applause sweetens his labours – and yet, nine times out of ten, he fails. Mr. Dunlap, of this city, has written volumes of plays, and written well, "excellent well," but he made nothing; nay, he hardly obtained that civic wreath which he fairly earned. Barker, of Philadelphia, whose muse is the most delicate and enticing, has hung up his harp, which, I dare say, is covered with dust and cobwebs; and even Harby, of Charleston, whose talents are of the finest order, and who is a bold yet chaste poet, gained but little profit and applause from his labours. We must not expect, therefore, more encouragement for the American Drama than may be sufficient to urge us on. We will succeed in time, as well as the English, because we have the same language, and equal intellect; but there must be system and discipline in writing plays – a knowledge of stage effect – of sound, cadences, fitness of time and place, interest of plot, spirit of delineation, nature, poetry, and a hundred *et ceteras*, which are required, to constitute a good dramatic poet, who cannot, in this country, and while occupied in other pursuits, spring up over night like asparagus, or be watered and put in the sun, like a geranium in a flower pot.

I wrote this play in order to promote the benefit of a performer who possesses talent, and I have no objections to write another for any deserving object. New plays, in this country, are generally performed, for the first time, as anonymous productions: I did not withhold my name from this, because I knew that my friends would go and see it performed, with the hope of being pleased, and my opponents would go with other motives, so that between the two parties a good house would be the result. This was actually the case, and two performances produced nearly $2,400; I hope this may encourage Americans of more talent to attempt something.

National plays should be encouraged. They have done everything for the British nation, and can do much for us; they keep alive the recollection of important events, by representing them in a manner at once natural and alluring. We have a fine scope, and abundant materials to work with, and a noble country to justify the attempt. The "Battle of Chippewa" was selected, because it was the most neat and spirited battle fought during the late war, and I wish I was able to do it more justice.

N.

New York, July, 1819

CHARACTERS

GENERAL	1ST OFFICER
JASPER	SOLDIER
LENOX	WAITER
HON. CAPTAIN PENDRAGON	JAILOR
JERRY	CHRISTINE
LAROLE	ADELA
JENKINS	MAID
INDIAN CHIEF	SOLDIERS, PEASANTS, INDIANS, ETC.

ACT I. Scene 1

A Valley with a neat Cottage on the right, an Arbour on the left, and picturesque Mountains at a distance. Enter from the cottage, Jasper and Jenkins.

JENKINS: And so, neighbour, you are not then a native of this village?

JASPER: I am not, my friend; my story is short, and you shall hear it. It was my luck, call it bad or good, to be born in France, in the town of Castlenaudary, where my parents, good honest peasants, cultivated a small farm on the borders of the canal of Midi. I was useful, though young; we were well enough to live, and I received from the parish school a good education, was taught to love my country, my parents, and my friends; a happy temper, a common advantage in my country, made all things easy to me; I never looked for to-morrow to bring me more joy than I experienced to-day.

JENKINS: Pardon my curiosity, friend Jasper: how came you to leave your country, when neither want nor misfortune visited your humble dwelling?

JASPER: Novelty, a desire for change, an ardent disposition to visit foreign countries. Passing through the streets of Toulouse one bright morning in spring, the lively drum and fife broke on my ear, as I was counting my gains from a day's marketing. A company of soldiers neatly dressed, with white cockades, passed me with a brisk step; I followed them through instinct – the sergeant informed me that they were on their way to Bordeaux, from thence to embark for America, to aid the cause of liberty in the new world, and were commanded by the Marquis de la Fayette. That name was familiar to me; La Fayette was a patriot – I felt like a patriot, and joined the ranks immediately.

JENKINS: Well, you enlisted and left your country?

JASPER: I did. We had a boisterous passage to America, and endured many hardships during the revolution. I was wounded at Yorktown, which long disabled me, but what then? I served under great men, and for a great cause; I saw the independence of the thirteen states acknowledged, I was promoted to a sergeancy by the great Washington, and I sheathed my sword, with the honest pride of knowing, that I had aided in establishing a powerful and happy republic.

JENKINS: You did well, honest Jasper, you did well; and now you have the satisfaction of seeing your country still free and happy.

JASPER: I have, indeed. When the army was disbanded, I travelled on foot to explore the uncultivated territory which I had assisted in liberating, I purchased a piece of land near the great lakes, and with my axe levelled the mighty oaks, cleared my meadows, burnt out the wolves and bears, and then built that cottage there.

JENKINS: And thus became a settler and my neighbour; thanks to the drum and fife and the white cockade, that lured you from your home.

JASPER: In a short time, Jenkins, everything flourished; my cottage was neat, my cattle thriving, still I wanted something – it was a wife. I was tired of a solitary life, and married Kate, the miller's daughter; you knew her.

JENKINS: Ay, that I did; she was a pretty lass.

JASPER: She was a good wife – ever cheerful and industrious, and made me happy: poor Kate! I was without children for several years; at length my Christine was born, and I have endeavoured, in cultivating her mind, and advancing her happiness, to console myself for the loss of her mother.

JENKINS: Where is Christine? where is your daughter, neighbour Jasper?

JASPER: She left the cottage early this morning with Lenox, to climb the mountains and see the sun rise; it is time for them to return to breakfast.

JENKINS: Who is this Mr. Lenox?

JASPER: An honest lieutenant of infantry, with a gallant spirit and a warm heart. He was wounded at Niagara, and one stormy night, he presented himself at our cottage door, pale and haggard. His arm had been shattered by a ball, and he had received a flesh wound from a bayonet: we took him in – for an old soldier never closes his door on a wounded comrade – Christine nursed him, and he soon recovered. But I wish they were here – it is growing late: besides, this is a busy day, friend Jenkins.

JENKINS: Ah, how so?

JASPER: You know Jerry Mayflower, the wealthy farmer; he has offered to marry my Christine. Girls must not remain single if they can get husbands, and I have consented to the match, and he will be here to-day to claim her hand.

JENKINS: But will Christine marry Jerry? She has been too well educated for the honest farmer.

JASPER: Oh, she may make a few wry faces, as she does when swallowing magnesia, but the dose will go down. There is some credit due to a wife who improves the intellect of her husband; aye, and there is some pride in it also. Girls should marry. Matrimony is like an old oak; age gives durability to the trunk, skill trims the branches, and affection keeps the foliage ever green. But come, let us in. [*Jasper and Jenkins enter the cottage*]

Pastoral Music. – Lenox and Christine are seen winding down the mountains – his left arm is in a sling

CHRISTINE: At last we are at home. – O my breath is nearly gone. You soldiers are so accustomed to marching and counter-marching, that you drag me over hedge and briar, like an empty baggage-wagon. Look at my arm, young Mars, you've made it as red as pink, and as rough as – then my hand – don't attempt to kiss it, you – wild man of the woods.

LENOX: Nay, dear Christine, be not offended; if I have passed rapidly over rocks and mountains, it is because you were with me. My heart ever feels light and happy when I am permitted to walk with you; even the air seems newly perfumed, and the birds chaunt more melodiously; and see, I can take my arm out of confinement – your care has done this; your voice administered comfort, and your eyes affection. What do I not owe you?

CHRISTINE: Owe me? Nothing, only one of your best bows, and your prettiest compliments. But I do suspect, my serious cavalier, that your wounds were never as bad as you would have me think. Of late you have taken your recipes with so much grace, have swallowed so many bitter tinctures with a playful smile, that I believe you've been playing the invalid, and would make me your nurse for life – O sinner as you are, what have you to say for yourself?

LENOX: Why, I confess, dear Christine, that my time has passed with so much delight, that even the call of duty will find me reluctant to quit these scenes, so dear to memory, hospitality, and, let me add, to love. Be serious, then, dear Christine, and tell me what I have to hope; even now I expect orders from my commanding officer, requiring my immediate presence at the camp; we are on the eve of a battle – Speak!

CHRISTINE: Why, you soldiers are such fickle game, that if we once entangle you in the net, 'tis ten to one but the sight of a new face will be sufficiently tempting to break the mesh – you're just as true as the smoke of your cannon, and you fly off at the sight of novelty in petticoats, like one of your Congreve rockets – No, I won't love a soldier – that's certain.

LENOX: Nay, where is our reward then for deserving well of our country? Gratitude may wreath a chaplet of laurel, but trust me, Christine, it withers unless consecrated by beauty.

CHRISTINE: Well, that's a very pretty speech, and deserves one of my best courtesies. Now suppose I should marry you, my "dear ally Croaker," I shall expect to see myself placed on the summit of a baggage-wagon, with soldiers' wives and a few dear squalling brats, whose musical tones drown e'en the "squeaking of the wry-neck'd fife;" and if I should escape from the enemy at the close of a battle, I should be compelled to be ever ready, and "pack up my tatters and follow the drum." – No, no, I can't think of it.

LENOX: Prithee, be serious, dear Christine, your gaiety alarms me. Can you permit me to leave you without a sigh? Can I depart from that dear cottage and rush to battle without having the assurance that there is a heart within which beats in unison with mine? a heart which can participate in my glory, and sympathize in my misfortunes?

CHRISTINE: No – not so, Lenox; your glory is dear to me, your happiness my anxious wish. I have seen you bear pain like a soldier, and misfortune like a man. I am myself a soldier's daughter, and believe me, when I tell you, that under the appearance of gaiety, my spirits are deeply depressed at your approaching departure. I have been taught, by a brave father, to love glory when combined with virtue. There is my hand; – be constant, and I am ever your friend; be true, and you shall find me ever faithful.

LENOX: Thanks – a thousand thanks, beloved Christine; you have removed a mountain of doubts and anxious wishes from my heart: I did hope for this reward, though it was a daring one. Love and honour must now inspire me, and should we again be triumphant in battle, I shall return to claim the reward of constancy – a reward dearer than thrones – the heart of a lovely and virtuous woman.

CHRISTINE: Enough, dear Lenox; I shall never doubt your faith. But come, let us in to breakfast – stay – my knight of the rueful countenance, where is the portrait which you have been sketching of me? Let me look at your progress.

LENOX: 'Tis here. [*Gives a small drawing book*]

CHRISTINE: [*Opening it*] Heavens, how unlike! Why Lenox, you were dreaming of the *Venus de Medici* when you drew this – Oh, you flatterer!

LENOX: Nay, 'tis not finished; now stand there, while I sketch the drapery. – [*Places her at a distance, takes out a pencil, and works at the drawing*]

CHRISTINE: Why, what a statue you are making of me. Pray, why not make a picture of it at once? Place me in that bower, with a lute and a lap dog, sighing for your return; then draw a soldier disguised as a pilgrim, leaning on his staff, and his cowl thrown back; let that pilgrim resemble thee, and then let the little dog bark, and I fainting, and there's a subject for the pencil and pallet.

LENOX: Sing, dear Christine, while I finish the drawing – it may be the last time I shall ever hear you.

CHRISTINE: Oh, do not say so, my gloomy cavalier; a soldier, and despair?

THE KNIGHT ERRANT
Written by the late Queen of Holland

It was Dunois, the young and brave, was bound to Palestine,

But first he made his orisons before St. Mary's shrine:

And grant, immortal Queen of Heav'n, was still the soldier's prayer,

*That I may prove the bravest knight, and love
the fairest fair.*

*His oath of honour on the shrine he grav'd it
with his sword,
And follow'd to the Holy Land the banner of
his Lord;
Where, faithful to his noble vow, his war-cry
fill'd the air –
Be honour'd, aye, the bravest knight, beloved
the fairest fair.*

*They ow'd the conquest to his arm, and then
his liege lord said,
The heart that has for honour beat must be by
bliss repaid:
My daughter Isabel and thou shall be a wedded
pair,
For thou art bravest of the brave, she fairest of
the fair.*

*And then they bound the holy knot before St.
Mary's shrine,
Which makes a paradise on earth when hearts
and hands combine;
And every lord and lady bright that was in
chapel there,
Cry'd, Honour'd be the bravest knight, be-
lov'd the fairest fair.*

LENOX: There, 'tis finished – how do you like
it?

CHRISTINE: Why, so, so – if you wish something to remind you of me, it will do.

LENOX: No, not so; your image is too forcibly
impressed here to need so dull a monitor. But I
ask it to reciprocate – wear this for my sake,
[*Gives a miniature*] and think of him who,
even in the battle's rage, will not forget thee.
[*Bugle sounds at a distance*] Hark! 'tis a bugle
of our army. [*Enter a Soldier, who delivers a
letter to Lenox and retires – Lenox opens and
reads it*] "The enemy, in force, has thrown up
entrenchments near Chippewa; if your wounds
will permit, join your corps without delay – a
battle is unavoidable, and I wish you to share
the glory of a victory. You have been promoted
as an aid to the general for your gallantry in
the last affair. It gives me pleasure to be the
first who announces this grateful reward – lose
not a moment.

Your friend,
MANDEVILLE."

I must be gone immediately.

Enter Jasper and Jenkins from the cottage

JASPER: Ah! Lenox, my boy, good morning to
you. Why Christine, you have had a long ramble with the invalid.

CHRISTINE: Lenox leaves us immediately, dear
father; the army is on the march.

JASPER: Well, he goes in good time, and may
success attend him. Ods my life, when I was
young, the sound of the drum and fife was like
the music of the spheres, and the noise and
bustle of a battle was more cheering to me,
than "the hunter's horn in the morning." You
will not forget us, Lenox, will you?

LENOX: Forget ye? Never – I should be the
most ungrateful of men, could I forget that endearing attention which poured oil into my
wounds, and comforted the heart of a desponding and mutilated soldier. No, Jasper, no;
while life remains, yourself and daughter shall
never cease to live in my grateful remembrance.
[*Christine and Lenox enter the cottage*]

*Pastoral Music. – Peasants are seen winding
down the mountains, headed by Jerry, dressed
for a festive occasion, with white favours, nose-
gays, etc.*

JERRY: Here I am, farmer Jasper – come to
claim Miss Crissy as my wife, according to
your promise, and have brought all my neighbours. How do you do?

JASPER: Well – quite well – and these are all
your neighbours?

JERRY: Yes – there's Bob Short, the tanner;
Nick Anvil, the blacksmith; Patty, the weaver's daughter – and the rest of 'em; come
here, Patty, make a curtchey to the old soger
– [*Patty comes forward*] – a pretty girl! I
could have had her, but she wanted edication
– she wanted the airs and graces, as our schoolmaster says.

JASPER: Well, farmer, you are an honest man,
but I fear my Christine will not approve this
match, commenced without her advice, and
concluded without her consent. Then her education has been so different from –

JERRY: O, fiddle-de-dee, I don't mind how
larned she is, so much the better – she can
teach me to parlyvoo, and dance solos and
duets, and such elegant things, when I've done
ploughing.

JASPER: But I'm not sure that she will like you.

JERRY: Not like me? Come, that's a good one;
only look at my movements – why she can't

resist me. I'm the boy for a race, for an apple-paring or quilting frolic – fight a cock, hunt an opossum, or snare a partridge with any one. – Then I'm a squire, and a county judge, and a *brevet* ossifer in the militia besides; and a devil of a fellow at an election to boot. Not have me? damme, that's an insult. Besides, sergeant Jasper, I've been to the wars since I've seen ye – got experience, laurels and lilies, and all them there things.

JASPER: Indeed!

JERRY: Yes – sarved a campaign, and was at the battle of Queenstown. What do you think of that?

JASPER: And did you share in the glory of that spirited battle?

JERRY: O yes, I shared in all the glory – that is – I didn't fight. I'll tell you how it was: I marched at the head of my village sogers, straight as the peacock in my farm yard, and I had some of the finest lads in our county, with rifles – well, we march'd and camp'd, and camp'd and march'd, and were as merry as grigs until we arrived at the river: half the troops had cross'd and were fighting away like young devils: ods life, what a smoke! what a popping of small arms, and roaring of big ones! and what a power of red coats!

JASPER: Well, and you panted to be at them? clubb'd your rifles, and dashed over?

JERRY: Oh no, I didn't – I was afear'd that in such a crowd, nobody would see how I fought, so I didn't cross at all. Besides, some one said, it were contrary to law and the constitution, to go into the enemy's country, but if they com'd into our country, it were perfectly lawful to flog 'em.

JASPER: And you did not cross?

JERRY: Oh no, I stood still and look'd on; it were contrary to the constitution of my country, and my own constitution to boot – so I took my post out of good gun shot, and felt no more fear nor you do now.

JASPER: No doubt. Admirable sophistry, that can shield cowards and traitors, under a mistaken principle of civil government! I've heard of those scruples, which your division felt when in sight of the enemy. Was that a time to talk of constitutions – when part of our gallant army was engaged with unequal numbers? Could you calmly behold your fellow citizens falling on all sides, and not avenge their death? Could you, with arms in your hands, the enemy in view, with the roar of cannon thundering on your ear, and the flag of your country waving amidst fire and smoke – could you find a moment to think of constitutions? Was that a time to pause and suffer coward scruples to unnerve the arm of freemen?

JERRY: Bravo! bravo! sergeant Jasper; that's a very fine speech – I'll vote for you for our assemblyman; now just go that over again, that I may get it by heart for our next town meeting – blazing flags – fiery cannon – smoking constitutions –

JASPER: I pray you pardon me. I am an old soldier, and fought for the liberty which you enjoy, and, therefore, claim some privilege in expressing my opinion. But come, your friends are idle, let us have breakfast before our cottage door. – Ah, Jerry, my Crissy would make a fine soldier's wife: do you know that I have given her a military education?

JERRY: No, surely –

JASPER: Aye, she can crack a bottle at twelve paces with a pistol.

JERRY: Crack a bottle! Come, that's a good one; I can crack a bottle too, but not so far off.

JASPER: And then she can bring down a buck, at any distance.

JERRY: Bring down a buck? I don't like that – can't say as how I like my wife to meddle with bucks. Can she milk – knit garters – make apple butter and maple sugar – dance a reel after midnight, and ride behind her husband on a pony, to see the trainings of our sogers – that's the wife for my money. Oh, here she comes.

Enter Christine and Lenox from the cottage

JASPER: Christine, here is farmer Mayflower and his friends, who have come to visit our cottage, and you in particular.

CHRISTINE: They are all welcome. Good morning, Jerry – how is it with you?

JERRY: Purely, Miss Crissy, I'm stout and hearty, and you look as pretty and as rosy as a field of pinks on a sunshiny morning.

JASPER: Come here, farmer – give me your hand – Christine, yours – [*Joins them*] – there; may you live long and happy, and my blessings ever go with you.

CHRISTINE: [*Aside in amazement*] Heavens! what can this mean?

Lenox is agitated – pause – Jasper and group retire – Lenox remains at a distance

JERRY: Why, Miss Crissy, your father has consented that I shall marry you, and I've come with my neighbours to have a little frolic, and carry you home with me.

CHRISTINE: And am I of so little moment as not to be consulted? Am I thus to be given away by my father without one anxious question? [*With decision*] Farmer, pardon my frankness; on this ocassion, sincerity alone is required – I do not like you, I will not marry you – nay, do not look surprised. I am a stranger to falsehood and dissimulation, and thus end at once all hopes of ever becoming my husband.

JERRY: Why, now, Miss Crissy, that's very cruel of you – I always had a sneaking kindness for you, and when your father gave his consent, I didn't dream as how you could refuse me.

CHRISTINE: My father has ever found me dutiful and obedient, but when he bestows my hand, without knowing whether my heart or inclinations accompany it, I feel myself bound to consult my own happiness. I cannot marry you, farmer.

LENOX: [*Advancing*] All things are prepared, and I am now about to depart. Christine, farewell! Friends, good fortune await you! [*Aside*] Dear Christine, remember me. [*Exit hastily*]

JERRY: Lack-a-daisy! What a disappointment to me, when I had put my house in such nice order – painted my walls – got a new chest upon chest – two new bed quilts, and a pair of pumps, and had the pig-sty and dairy whitewashed. – Hang me, after all, I believe, she is only a little shy. Oh, I see it now, she only wants a little coaxing – a little sparking or so – I've a great mind to kiss her. I will, too. [*Approaches Christine, who stands at a distance, buried in deep thought*]

CHRISTINE: Begone – dare not touch me! Heavens, am I reserved for this humiliation? Could my father be so cruel?

JERRY: Now, Crissy, don't be so shy – you know you like me – you know you said t'other day, when I were out training, that I held up my head more like a soger than anybody in the ranks; come now, let's make up; you'll always find me a dutiful husband, and if I ever flog you, then my name's not Jerry.

Enter Jasper from the cottage, with a basket; Peasants following with fruit

JASPER: Come, let us have breakfast in the open air – help me to arrange the table.

JERRY: Breakfast! Oh, true, I've a powerful appetite. [*Assists*]

CHRISTINE: [*Aside*] What is to be done? I have not a moment to lose; my father is stern and unyielding – I know his temper too well, to hope that my entreaties will prevail with him – the farmer is rich, and gold is a powerful tempter. I must be gone – follow Lenox, and in disguise, to avoid this hateful match. I'll in, whilst unobserved. [*Enters the cottage*]

JASPER: Come, sit down, farmer and neighbours; and you, my pretty lads and lasses, let's have a dance. Ah, here is a foraging party. [*Enter Soldiers*]

Party dance – several pastoral and fancy dances – and as the whole company retires, Christine comes from the cottage with cautious steps – she is dressed in a frock coat, pantaloons and hat

CHRISTINE: They are gone – now to escape. Scenes of my infancy – of many a happy hour, farewell! Oh, farewell, forever! [*Exit*]

Jasper and Jerry return

JERRY: She refused me plumply.

JASPER: Impossible!

JERRY: No, it's quite possible. Farmer, said she, I will *not* marry you – and hang me if there's any joke in that.

JASPER: Refuse an honest man? A wealthy one, too? And one whom her father gives to her? Trifling girl! Insensible to her happiness and interest. What objections had she to you, farmer?

JERRY: Objections! Oh, none in the world, only she wouldn't marry me; she didn't seem struck at all with my person.

JASPER: Mere coyness – maiden bashfulness.

JERRY: So I thought, sergeant Jasper, and was going to give her a little kiss, when she gave me such a look, and such a push, as quite astounded me.

JASPER: I will seek and expostulate with the stubborn girl. Ah, Jerry, times have strangely altered, when young women choose husbands for themselves, with as much ease and indifference, as a ribbon for their bonnet. [*Enters the cottage*]

JERRY: So they do – the little independent creatures as they are – but what Miss Crissy could see in me to refuse, hang me if I can tell. I'm call'd as sprightly a fellow as any in our county, and up to everything – always ready for fun, and perfectly goodnatured. [*Enter Jasper from the cottage, agitated*]

JASPER: She is nowhere to be found – she has gone off and left her poor old father. In her room, I found these lines scrawled with a pencil: "You have driven your daughter from you, by urging a match that was hateful to her. Was her happiness not worth consulting?" What's to be done? Where has she gone? Ah, a light breaks in upon me – to the camp – to the camp!

JERRY: Oho! I smell a rat too – she's gone after Mr. Lenox, the infantry ossifer. Oh, the young jade! But come along, old soger – get your hat and cane, and we'll go arter her – I'm a magistrate, and will bring her back by a habes corpus. [*They enter the cottage*]

Scene 2

A Wood. Enter Christine in haste, looking back with fear.

CHRISTINE: On, on, or I shall be pursued and o'ertaken – I have lost my way. Ah, yonder is the camp – I see the flags and tents – a short time and I shall be with you, dear Lenox. [*Exit*]

Enter Jasper, Jerry and Peasants

JERRY: We're on the right track, farmer; I know all tracks – used to 'em when I hunt 'possums.

JASPER: Cruel girl! to desert her old father, who has ever been kind and affectionate.

JERRY: Cruel girl! to desert me, who intended to be so very affectionate, if she had given me a chance.

JASPER: We cannot be far from the outposts, let us continue our search. [*Exeunt*]

Scene 3

A Camp. A row of tents in the rear with camp flags at equal distances; on the right wing is a neat marquee, and directly opposite to it another. Sentinels on duty at each marquee. Enter from the marquee, Lenox and Adela.

LENOX: I never was more surprised! Just when I had brush'd up my arms, and prepared to meet the enemy, who should I find in camp but you, my old hoyden scholar. Why Adela, you have grown nearly as tall as a grenadier, and as pretty – zounds, I would kiss you, if I dare.

ADELA: I am delighted to see you, dear Lenox; you are still as gay and amiable as when you taught your little Adela to conjugate verbs, and murder French; I heard of your gallantry and wounds, and imagined I should see you limping on crutches, with a green patch over one eye, and a wreath of laurel around your head, a kind of limping, one-eyed cupid; but I find you recovered from your wounds, and ready for new ones, my soldier.

LENOX: Bravo! the little skipping girl, who was once so full of mischief, has grown a tall and beautiful woman. But what brings you to camp, Adela? What have you to do with "guns and drums? heaven save the mark!"

ADELA: Why, my father wrote for me, expecting that the campaign was drawing to a close; but scarcely had I arrived here, when intelligence reached us that the enemy, in force, had occupied a position near Chippewa; it was too late to return, so I remained to see a little skirmishing.

LENOX: And are you prepared to endure the privations of a camp?

ADELA: Oh, it is delightful! it is something out of the common order of things, something new – such echoing of bugles – glistening of firearms, and nodding of plumes – such marchings and countermarchings – and such pretty officers too, Lenox; but then a terrible accident happened to me the other day.

LENOX: Aye, what was it?

ADELA: Why you must know, that I accompanied my father, who with his suite, and a small detachment, went out on a reconnoitering project. – Just as we *debouched* from the wood, according to the military phrase, we came suddenly and unexpectedly on a foraging party of the enemy, who began to fight and retreat at the same time.

LENOX: Well?

ADELA: My horse happening to be an old trooper, the moment the bugles sounded, and he heard the prattle of the small arms, he dashed in amongst them, and there was I screaming in a most delightful style, which, by some, must have been mistaken for a war-whoop, and to mend the matter, a very polite and accomplished Indian took aim at me with his rifle, and actually shot away the plume from my hat, which, I dare say, was as valuable a prize to him as I should have been.

LENOX: And how did you escape from your perilous situation?

ADELA: Oh, I soon recovered my fright, and reined in my old horse; my father and a few soldiers cut in before me, and covered my retreat, so that in the conclusion of this little affair, I gained a feather in my cap, though the enemy carried off the plume; and I found myself at last on the field of battle, as cool as any hero in the army.

LENOX: And so, my lively Adela, you have been fairly introduced to Mars and Bellona: how do you like them?

ADELA: Prodigiously. I find, after all, that courage is something like a cold bath; take the first plunge, and all is over. Lord, Lenox, how delightful it would have been, had I been armed and fought gallantly in that affair; my name would have been immortalized like Joan of Arc's. Congress would have voted me a medal, I should have had a public dinner at Tammany-Hall, and his honour the mayor would have made me one of his prettiest speeches, in presenting me with the freedom of the great city in a gold box.

LENOX: And so, then, you admire a military life?

ADELA: Oh, I'm in raptures with it! I am a perfect female Quixote, and would relinquish a thousand dandy beaux for one brave fellow; and, therefore, Lenox, don't be surprised, if you should see me going about from tent to tent, chaunting the old songs of

"*Soldier, soldier, marry me,*
With your fife and drum."

Christine suddenly appears in the background and surveys the party with astonishment

CHRISTINE: Heavens! what do I see? Lenox, and with a female so affectionately?

LENOX: Your spirits charm me, dear Adela, and revive those feelings for you, that time has impaired, but not destroyed. But come, let us in and see your worthy father. [*Leads her into the tent to the left*]

CHRISTINE: Cruel, unkind, false Lenox! Are these your vows of constancy? are these your protestations of love? Scarcely are you free from our cottage, when your vows and pledges are but air. Wretched Christine! what will become of you? I have deserted my father's house to avoid a hateful match, and seek the protection of the man I love; he is false, and I am lost. What's to be done? Return home a penitent, and meet the frowns of my father, and be wedded to the man I hate? Never. Seek out Lenox, and upbraid him with his falsehood? No, pride and wounded honour will not permit me. Let him go – he is a wretch who trifles with the affections of a woman. I care not what becomes of me, despair is all that I have left. Ha! a thought strikes me with the lightning's force – the army – I will enlist – this disguise is favourable, and in the battle's rage, seek that death which quickly awaits me – 'tis resolved. [*Corporal passes over the stage*] Hist, corporal.

CORPORAL: Well, my lad, what would ye?

CHRISTINE: I would enlist, good corporal, and serve my country.

CORPORAL: Enlist! As a drummer or fifer, I suppose.

CHRISTINE: No; in the ranks – and though small, you will find me capable. Give me your musket. [*Christine takes the musket, shoulders, presents, and goes through a few motions*]

CORPORAL: Well done, my little fellow; you'll do, if it's only for a fugelman; come along to our sergeant, and receive the bounty. [*Exit*]

CHRISTINE: Now, Lenox, now am I fully revenged for your cruel desertion. [*Follows*]

End of the First Act

ACT II. Scene I

York, in Upper Canada; a Tavern meanly furnished. Enter LaRole, in pursuit of the chambermaid.

LAROLE: Come here, you littel demoiselle – you bootiful sauvage, vy you run vay from me – hay?

MAID: I wish you would let me alone, mounsure, you officers' gentlemen are very disagreeable things.

LAROLE: Disagreeable? ma foi! I am one joli garçon, one pretti batchelor; disagreeable? I vill tell you, ma belle grizette, I am maître de mode, I give de lecons for dance, to speake de English, and de Francaise aussi; I can fence, aha! or fight de duel, or de enemi, je suis un soldat.

MAID: Well, if you're a soldier, you have no business to be following me up and down the house like a pet lamb. Why don't you go to camp?

LAROLE: Camp? vat is de camp? Oho, le champ de bataille; I shall tell you, mademoiselle, I did fight at the bataille de Vittoria, com un diable, like littel devil. I did kill beaucoup d'Anglais. Mai my maître, le capitain, he did give me a dam tump on my head wis his rapier, and did knock me down from on top of my horse, and make a me von prisonier.

MAID: Poor fellow! And so, mounsure, you were made prisoner?

LAROLE: Oui, ven I could not run avay, begar I surrender like von brave homme, and now I am jentiman to capitain Pendragoon; I do brus his coat, poudre his hair, and pull his corset tight, and ven he was order to come to Amérique, and fight wis de Yankee Doodel, begar me come too. I arrive ici, I am here, to make a littel de love to you.

MAID: Well now, once for all, I tell you not to be following me; I don't like Frenchmen – I can't parlyvoo.

LAROLE: You no like de Frenchiman? O quell barbare! vy you ave von abominable goût, mademoiselle, von shockin taste. I shall tell you, mademoiselle, en my contree, en France, de ladies are ver fond of me. O beaucoup, I am so charmant – so aimable, and so jentee, I have three five sweetheart, ami de coeur, mai for all dat I do love you ver mush, par example.

MAID: Let me go! [*Bell rings*] There, your master calls you. [*Exit*]

LAROLE: Dam de littel bell, I vill not come; mon maître he always interrupt me ven I make de love to the pretti ladi, he be jealous, begar I vill not come. [*Exit opposite side*]

Enter Captain Pendragon, dressed in the British uniform, but in the extreme of fashion – throws himself into a chair

PENDRAGON: Oh, curse such roads! My bones are making their way out of their sockets – such vile, abominable, detestable – Waiter! – If my friends at Castle Joram only knew the excruciating fatigues which I am undergoing in this barbarous land – Why, waiter! – or if his highness the commander-in-chief was only sensible of my great sacrifices to – Why, waiter! where the devil are you?

Enter Waiter

WAITER: Here I be, sir.

PENDRAGON: Why didn't you come when I first called? Do you think I've got lungs like a hunter? I'm fatigued and hungry. Get me an anchovy, a toast, and a bottle of old port.

WAITER: A what, sir? an ancho——

PENDRAGON: Yes, sir, an anchovy – small ones – delicate.

WAITER: Why, sir, we don't know what these are in this country.

PENDRAGON: The devil you don't! Then pray, sir, what have you to eat in this damn'd house fit for a gentleman?

WAITER: Why, sir, not much – the army eats us out of house and home. We have some very excellent fresh bear meat, sir.

PENDRAGON: Bear meat! Why, what the devil, fellow, do you take me for a Chickasaw, or an Esquimau? Bear meat! the honourable captain Pendragon, who never ate anything more gross than a cutlet at Molly's chop-house, and who lived on pigeons' livers at Very's, in Paris, offered bear meat in North America! I'll put that down in my travels.

WAITER: Why, sir, it is considered here a great delicacy.

PENDRAGON: The devil it is! Then pray, sir, what are your ordinary fares, if bear's meat is considered a delicacy?

WAITER: Why, truly, sir, this is but a young country, and we have to live upon what we can catch. Pray, would you fancy some 'possum fat and hominy?

PENDRAGON: Oh, shocking! begone, fellow – you'll throw me into a fever with your vile bill of fare. Get me a cup of tea – mix it, hyson and souchong, with cream and muffins.

WAITER: We can't give you any of those things, sir. – However, you can have an excellent cup of sage tea, sweetened with honey.

PENDRAGON: Sage tea! Why, you rascal, do you intend to throw me into a perspiration by way of curing my hunger? or do you take me for a goose or a duck, that you intend stuffing me with sage? Begone, get out, you little deformed fellow! [*Exit Waiter*] I shall perish in this barbarous land – bear meat, 'possum fat, and sage tea! O dear St. James! I wish I was snug in my old quarters. LaRole! [*Enter La-Role*] Where the devil do you hide yourself in this damn'd house? Why, I shall starve – there's nothing to eat, fit for a gentleman.

LAROLE: Oui, monsieur, dis is von damn contree, I can find nosing to eat. I did look into all de pantri, mai parbleu, I find only a ver pretti demoiselle, mai, I could not eat her.

PENDRAGON: We must be off to the camp, La-Role, my quarters there will be infinitely more agreeable. I shall get the blue devils in this cursed place.

LAROLE: Vell, sair, I have all de devils ventre bleu, das you can imagine; dere is no politesse, no respect, nosing paid to me.

PENDRAGON: My fit of the blues is coming on me; sing me a song, LaRole.

LAROLE: A chanson? Vell, sair, I shall sing to frighten avay de littel blue devil; vill you I shall sing de English or de Française?

PENDRAGON: Oh, English, by all means – curse your foreign lingo.

LAROLE: Ahem! Ahem! you shall understand.

Vat is dis dull town to me,
Robin Hadair?
Vere is all de joys on earth, dat
Make dis town –
　　　　　[*A bugle sounds without*]

Ha! what is dat? who de devil intrup me in my chanson?

INDIAN CHIEF: [*Speaks without*] Have them all ready, with their rifles and tomahawks in order; [*Enters with another Indian*] and you, Coosewatchie, tell our priests to take their stand on yonder hill, and as my warriors pass them, examine whether they have fire in their eyes. [*Exit Indian*] How now, who have we here?

PENDRAGON: [*Examining him with his glass*] Where the devil did this character come from? he's one of the fancy, I suppose.

INDIAN: Who and what are you?

PENDRAGON: Who am I? Why, sir, I am the honourable captain Pendragon, of his majesty's guards, formerly of the buffs.

INDIAN: [*Aside*] The officer who is to be under my command. Well sir, you have lately arrived from across the great waters: How did you leave my father, the King of England?

PENDRAGON: How! call my most gracious sovereign your father? Why, sir, you are the most familiar – impertinent – s'death! I shall choke – What the devil do you mean?

INDIAN: [*Coolly*] What should I mean, young man, but to inquire after the health of my father, who commands my respect, who has honoured me with his favours, and in whose cause I am now fighting.

PENDRAGON: Well, sir, if you have the honour to hold a commission from his majesty, I desire that you will speak of him with proper awe, and not call him your father, but your gracious master.

INDIAN: Young man, the Indian warrior knows no master but the Great Spirit, whose voice is heard in thunder, and whose eye is seen in the lightning's flash; free as air, we bow the knee to no man; our forests are our home, our defence is our arms, our sustenance the deer and the elk, which we run down. White men encroach upon our borders, and drive us into war; we raise the tomahawk against your enemies, because your king has promised us protection and supplies. We fight for freedom, and in that cause, the great king and the poor Indian start upon equal terms.

PENDRAGON: A very clever spoken fellow, pon honour; I'll patronise him.

LAROLE: Parbleu, he is von very sensible sauvage; vill you take von pinch snuff?

INDIAN: Pshaw!

LAROLE: He say pshaw, I see he is born in de voods.

PENDRAGON: And are you prepared to fan these Yankees? We shall flog them without much fatigue, I understand.

INDIAN: Not so fast, young soldier; these pale-faced enemies of ours fight with obstinacy; accustomed to a hardy life, to liberty and laws, they are not willing to relinquish those blessings on easy terms; if we conquer them, it must be by no moderate exertions: it will demand force and cunning.

PENDRAGON: Oh, dry dogs, I suppose, not to be caught napping; well, I'm up to them, we'll fan them in high style; the ragged nabobs, I understand, are not far off, and our troops are in fine preservation.

INDIAN: True, preparation must be made to meet them. You are under my orders.

PENDRAGON: The devil I am!

INDIAN: Aye, sir; your general, at my request, has ordered you here to take command of a company of my warriors; but you must not appear in that dress: change it quickly, or they will not be commanded by you; they are men, and fight under the orders of men.

PENDRAGON: Change my dress! why what the devil do you mean, sir?

INDIAN: Mean? that you should appear in the ranks like a warrior, and not like a rabbit trussed for dressing – off with these garments, which give neither pleasure to the eye nor ease to the limbs – put on moccasins, wrap a blanket around you, put rings through your nose and ears, feathers in your head, and paint yourself like a soldier, with vermilion.

PENDRAGON: Why, this is the most impertinent and presuming savage in the wilds of North America. Harkee, sir, I'd have you to know, that I am a man of fashion, and one of the fancy – formerly of the buffs, nephew of a peer of the realm, and will be a member of parliament, in time; an officer of great merit and great services, Mr. – Red Jacket. Paint my face, and fight without clothes? I desire, sir, that you will please to take notice, that I fought at Badahoz with the immortal Wellington, and had the honour to be wounded, and promoted, and had a medal for my services in that affair, Mr. – Split-log. Put rings in my nose? a man of taste, and the *ne plus ultra* of Bond-street, the very mirror of fashion and elegance? Sir, I beg you to observe, that I am not to be treated in this manner – I shall resent this insult. Damme, I shall report you to the commander-in-chief at the Horse Guards, and have you courtmartialled for unfashionable deportment – Mr. – Walk-in-the-Water.

INDIAN: Come, come, sir, enough of this trifling; I do not understand it; you have heard my orders – obey them, or, after the battle, I'll roast you before a slow fire! [*Exit*]

LAROLE: O le barbare! O de dam sauvage! dis is de most impertinent dog in de vorld. Roast before de fire! Parbleu, mon maître, ve are not de littel pig.

PENDRAGON: I'm horrified! lost in amazement! but I'll resent it. Damme, I'll caricature him.

LAROLE: Oh, I vish I vas fight encore at Saragossa, vis mi lor Villainton; par example, I did get some hard tumps, mai I did get plenti to eat; but ici I ave nosing but de littel bear to mange.

PENDRAGON: Come along – courage, LaRole.

We'll fan the Yankee Doodles in our best style, and then get a furlough, and be off to White-Hall, and the rings in our noses will afford anecdotes for the bon-ton for a whole year. Allons. [*Exeunt*]

Scene 2

The American Camp at daybreak. The drum and fife plays the reveille. Sentinels on duty before the tents. Lenox enters from the tent on the right, General and Adela from the left.

LENOX: Good morning, general; you are "stirring with the lark" – and you also, Adela.

GENERAL: The times require the utmost vigilance, Lenox; the enemy cannot escape a battle now, and we must be prepared at all points to meet him. Decision and energy cannot fail to promote success.

ADELA: And what is to become of me, father, in the battle? Am I to ride the old trooper again, and run the risk of having the tip of my nose carried away by a musket ball, and left on the field of battle in all my glory?

GENERAL: You shall be taken care of, dear Adela; we will place you in the rear, among the baggage-wagons.

ADELA: And if they should be captured, I become also a prisoner, and probably a prize to some gallant Indian chief, who will make me his squaw, and teach me to kill deer. O delightful thought! [*Bugles sound*]

GENERAL: The troops are under arms, and approaching.

Quick march – the General, Lenox and Adela pass to the left, and stand near the tent; the troops advance; Christine is among them, dressed in uniform; they pass round the stage in regular order, then form the line two deep; Christine is in front on the right, and keeps her eye fixed anxiously on Lenox; drum beats the roll; the troops come to an order, and then proceed through the manual by the tap of drum, and finally to a present; the General, Lenox, and other officers advance, and pass through the line in review; the flags wave, and the band strikes up "Hail Columbia"

GENERAL: Well – everything is right. And now, soldiers, to your posts; remember, discipline, subordination, courage, and country, and victory will be ours.

General, Lenox, and Adela, enter the tent to the left. The troops march off. Christine and a Soldier, headed by a Corporal, return to relieve guard at each tent. Port arms and whisper the countersign. Christine is placed before the tent on the right, her comrade on the left. Corporal retires with the two relieved sentries. After a pause, she beckons to her comrade

CHRISTINE: Hist – comrade!

SOLDIER: Well, what is it?

CHRISTINE: Will you exchange places? There is no difference – and the sun will be too powerful for me presently. Look, here is a dollar.

SOLDIER: With all my heart. [*They cross quickly, the Soldier receives the money – Christine now paces before the tent into which Lenox, Adela and the General have retired*]

CHRISTINE: Could I but see the false, perfidious Lenox, and upbraid him with his cruelty! [*She is in great uneasiness, pauses occasionally, and looks into the tent – her comrade is watching her. Lenox sings within*]

Shall the pleasures of life unknown fade away,
In viewing those charms so lovely and gay?
Shall the heart which has breath'd forth rapturous flame,
Be hid from the world and unsought for by fame?

Thus spoke the fond Roscoe to Scylla the fair,
As he gaz'd on her charms, with a love-soothing care:
Hear now the last wish, that fondly I sigh,
I'll conquer in love, or in battle I'll die.

He girded his armour and flew to the field,
Determin'd while life flow'd never to yield;
The foe was subdued, but death's cruel dart
Was aim'd at the valiant and fond Roscoe's heart:

But the blow was defeated – he lived to enjoy
The sight of his Scylla, no longer so coy,
And his laurels fresh bloom'd, as she smil'd on the youth,
And gave her fair hand in reward for his truth.

CHRISTINE: Ha, that false voice! I can no longer bear it!

Throws down her gun, and is about entering the tent, when her comrade, who has been attentively regarding her movements, rushes over and seizes her

SOLDIER: Where are you going?

CHRISTINE: Unhand me this instant! [*Struggles*]

SOLDIER: Guards, there!

Enter an Officer with Soldiers, who attempts to seize Christine – she draws her sword and stands on the defensive, and after some resistance, escapes

OFFICER: Pursue him quickly! [*Soldiers pursue*]

SOLDIER: He crosses the bridge.

OFFICER: The sentinels will reach him with their guns. [*Muskets discharged*]

SOLDIER: They have him – he is not hurt.

General, Adela and Lenox rush from the tent

GENERAL: What means this confusion?

2ND OFFICER: The sentinel who was placed here on duty, attempted, for some desperate purpose, to enter your tent; but being discovered, he refused to surrender, drew his sword on me and the guard, and, after some resistance, has been disarmed and secured.

LENOX: Good heavens! What object could he have had?

2ND OFFICER: I know not – but he is a new recruit, probably a spy from the enemy.

GENERAL: It must be so – see that a court martial be called to try him, and bring the result to me without delay. If he is guilty, a dreadful example shall be made of him. Begone. [*Exeunt General, Soldiers, &C*]

Scene 3

Another Part of the Camp. Enter Jasper, Jerry and Peasants.

JASPER: Nowhere to be found. I have asked everybody in the camp in vain – she is lost to me. Unhappy, cruel girl! to quit her old and fond father thus.

JERRY: Unhappy girl! to leave me in such an ungenteel manner too, run away from me on my wedding day! but I'll find her out.

JASPER: Impossible! we must return, dejected and disappointed.

JERRY: I'll peep into every tent, bribe the sogers – I've got a little money left. [*Jasper and Peasants retire. Corporal crosses the stage*] Hist, corporal!

CORPORAL: Well, what would you?

JERRY: Why no, sure – it isn't – yes, it is – why Corporal Flash, how do you do? Don't you know me?

CORPORAL: Can't say I do, sir.

JERRY: Why, not know Jerry Mayflower? Don't you remember me at the battle of Queenstown, when you were in the boat and I on land, and you were crossing to fight Johnny Bull, and I didn't cross at all?

CORPORAL: Oh, I remember you now – I remember calling you a cowardly rascal at the time.

JERRY: So you did – how have you been? I am very glad to see you – you're not killed, I take it?

CORPORAL: No, not exactly killed – but I was wounded – an honour which you didn't seem to care much about.

JERRY: No, not much; I'm not very ambitious that way.

CORPORAL: What brings you to the camp, just when we are about having another brush with the enemy – do you want to run away again? Zounds! you deserve a round hundred at the halberts.

JERRY: Yes, I deserve many things that I don't get – but pray, corporal, mout you have seen a young woman in this here camp lately?

CORPORAL: Oh, plenty, among the suttlers.

JERRY: No, a kind of a pretty girl, a little lady-like, parlyvoos, and carries her head up straight.

CORPORAL: No – I've seen no such person.

JERRY: Well, Corporal Flash, I've a little cash, and what say you to a jug of whiskey punch? Brave men, you know, like you and I, should drink with one another. ·

CORPORAL: With all my heart; you're good for nothing else but to drink with.

JERRY: Then come along, my boy; we'll drown care, raise our spirits, and swallow the enemy in a bumper. [*Exeunt*]

Scene 4

A Prison. Enter two Officers, Guards and Christine. Officers seat themselves at a table, with pens and ink.

1ST OFFICER: Young man, come forward. You have been charged with an act of mutiny, and with an attempt, for some unknown cause, to force your way, with arms in your hand, into the tent of the commanding general. We are convened for your trial – we have examined the testimony; and as you are a stranger in our ranks, no feelings of prejudice could have given a false colouring to that testimony. What have you to say?

CHRISTINE: Nothing.

OFFICER: Nothing?

CHRISTINE: Nothing! [*With firmness*] I am guilty!

OFFICER: Have a care, pause before you make this avowal of your guilt.

CHRISTINE: [*With settled firmness*] I have considered it well, and am ready to meet the consequences. I am guilty. [*With a burst of anguish*] Oh, most guilty!

OFFICER: Unhappy young man, what could have tempted you to this act? Who set you on?

CHRISTINE: Seek not to know the cause, 'tis buried here. Do your duty – I am prepared for the result.

OFFICER: [*To the Board*] The charge is fully admitted, and the rules of war prescribe the punishment. The object he had in view must yet be discovered; 'tis plain, however, that he is a spy, and has no hope of pardon. Record the verdict and sentence, for the inspection and concurrence of the general. [*Officer writes. The company rise from the table, and one approaches Christine, who appears buried in thought*]

OFFICER: Young man, I deeply commiserate your unhappy situation, but the rules of war are rigid, and must be enforced. You must prepare to die!

CHRISTINE: [*Starts, but recovers herself quickly*] I am ready.

OFFICER: I would offer you hope, but acts of mutiny, and when covering such suspicious motives as yours, cannot be pardoned. You have but a day to live. I deeply regret it, for you appear to have qualities which, in time, would have made you a valuable citizen. You are cut off in youth, probably from the hopes of a fond parent.

CHRISTINE: [*In agony*] Oh, no more – no more!

OFFICER: All the sympathy and indulgence which can be offered you shall be yours! Farewell. [*Exit Officers, Guards, &C*]

CHRISTINE: At length 'tis concluded, and an ignominious death terminates my unmerited sufferings. Cruel father! and still more cruel Lenox! thus to have wounded the heart that loved you. Oh, what a situation is mine! separated from all I hold dear, sentenced to die, and in this disguise; to leave my poor father, and to know that death, alone, can tell my sad story. What's to be done? Discover all? No, no. Expose my weakness and folly – to see the false Lenox wedded to another, and I forced to accept the hand I loathe – to be pointed at for one who, lost to the delicacy of her sex, followed a perfidious lover in disguise, and, tortured by jealousy, enlisted, was mutinous, and sentenced to die; but who, to save a miserable life, avowed her situation, and recorded her disgrace at once? Never, never! let me die, and forever be forgotten – 'tis but a blow, and it will end the pangs which torment me here. [*Enter a Soldier, who beckons*] I am ready, lead the way. [*Exit*]

Scene 5

Another part of the Prison. Enter the Jailor, driving Jerry before him.

JAILOR: In, in, you mutinous dog! do you come here to breed a riot in our camp?

JERRY: Now, my dear good-natured jailor, only have pity on me, and I'll tell you all about it.

JAILOR: I won't hear you – didn't you breed a riot?

JERRY: Why no, it was not me. I am as innocent as a young lamb. I'll tell you how it was – come, sit down on this bench with me. [*They sit*] You must know that I'm a farmer, pretty well off, as a body mout say, and I wanted a wife; hard by our village, there lived an old soger with a pretty daughter, so I courted the old man for his daughter, and he consented to the match.

JAILOR: Well?

JERRY: And so I got together all my neighbours, and, with music, went to the old soger's to get my sweetheart, when, lo and behold! after all my trouble, she refused me plump.

JAILOR: No, did she?

JERRY: Ay, indeed; she didn't seem stricken with the proposal – and for fear her father would force her to marry me, egad, she run away.

JAILOR: And where did she go?

JERRY: I can't say, but her father and a whole *posse comitatus*, as we justices call 'em, went in search of her to the camp, and when I came here, I found some of my old comrades who

fought with me at Queenstown; and so having a little money, we went to take a comfortable pitcher of whiskey punch together, and so, while over our cups, they doubted my valour, and hinted that I run away before the battle.

JAILOR: Well, and what did you do?

JERRY: Why, I offered to fight 'em single-handed all round, and we got into a dispute, and so when my money was all gone, they tweaked my nose, boxed my ears, and kick'd me out of the tent. So I then kick'd up a row, and – that's all.

JAILOR: A very pretty story, indeed! You look like a mutinous dog – so come, get into the black hole.

JERRY: Now, my dear jailor, do let me escape, and I'll give you the prettiest little pig in my farmyard.

JAILOR: What! bribe an honest and humane jailor, and with a pig? In with you.

JERRY: Well, but I've nothing to eat – I shall be half starved.

JAILOR: Oh no, you shall have something to employ your grinders on. [*Goes out, and returns with a black loaf, and a pitcher of water*] There!

JERRY: O dear, nothing else but black bread and cold water? Can't you get me a pickle?

JAILOR: I think you're in a devil of a pickle already – come, get in! [*Removes a board from the scene, which discovers a small dark hole. Jerry supplicates*]

JERRY: How long am I to be here, Mr. Jailor, in company with myself?

JAILOR: That depends on your good behaviour. [*Cannon are heard*] There! the battle has commenced.

JERRY: [*Putting his head out of the hole*] O dear, what's that? The great guns are going off. Are you sure, my dear jailor, that this prison is bomb proof?

JAILOR: Take your head in, you great land turtle.

JERRY: Oh, what will become of me?

End of the Second Act

ACT III. Scene 1

Scene in front of a pavilion tent; trumpets and drums sounding. Enter General, Lenox, Soldiers, Officers, &C.

GENERAL: At length victory has crown'd our arms, and the result of this action will keep alive the spirits of our troops, and the hopes of our country. Hark! the bugles are sounding a retreat, and the enemy has abandoned the field and taken to his entrenchments. Lenox, your hand – your conduct this day has confirmed our hopes – allow me in the name of our country to thank you.

LENOX: Not a word, dear general, not a word; I have merely done my duty, and done no more than every soldier in our ranks.

GENERAL: What is the result of this day's action?

LENOX: The enemy has lost upwards of 500 in killed and wounded, and several principal officers have been taken prisoners.

GENERAL: In what position were they when the attack became general?

LENOX: The British commander, pressed by our artillery under Towson, issued in all his force from his entrenchments. It was a gallant sight, to see his solid columns and burnished arms advance on the margin of the river, and his cavalry, with lightning's force, dart on our flanks to turn and throw them into confusion; but they were met by the volunteers under the brave Porter, and gallantly repulsed.

GENERAL: Go on.

LENOX: The enemy then condensed his forces and crossed the bridge, and was encountered on the plains of Chippewa by Scott, with his brigade, when the action became severe and general. No ambuscade or masked batteries were held in reserve – the enemy was not a moment concealed from our view – no tangled thicket or umbrageous groves gave effect or facility to our rifles: the battle was fought on a plain – where man grappled man, force was opposed to force, skill to skill, and eye to eye, in regular, disciplined, and admirable order.

GENERAL: How near were you to the British general?

LENOX: In sight and hearing. Charge the Yankees! said a hoarse voice which I knew to be his. Charge away! said our ardent troops, as they advanced with fixed bayonets; the fire became dreadful, and our stars and stripes were seen waving in the blaze. Scott rode through the lines cheering the men, and gallantly leading them on; Jessup and his third battalion turned the right flank of the enemy after a dreadful conflict; Ketchum had kept up a cross and ruinous fire; and Towson, from his dread artillery, scattered grape like hail amongst them. On, on! cried Leavenworth, the day's our own, my boys! Just then a shot struck down my comrade, Harrison, and shattered his leg.

GENERAL: Well?

LENOX: He grasped his sword and fought on his stump, clinging to the spot like fire-eyed Mars; the enemy, pressed on all sides, gave way; our troops pursued, and the flight became general. At length we drove them to their entrenchments, and remained masters of the field. Our trumpets sounded their retreat; victory perched on our eagles, and our bands struck up the soul-inspiring air of "Hail, Columbia, happy land!"

GENERAL: Well done, my brave fellows! This action will teach the enemy to respect that valour which they cannot subdue. See that the wounded prisoners are taken care of: give them all succor: victory loses half its value, when it is not tempered with mercy. [*Exit General*]

LENOX: Now to my dear Christine, to receive from her the reward which I hope I have fairly earned, and seek with her the joys of tranquility and love.

Enter a Soldier

SOLDIER: Towards the conclusion of the battle we made two Indian warriors prisoners, who were fighting desperately; we have them with us.

LENOX: Bring them in; I will examine them, touching the number and force of their tribe. [*Exit Soldier, who returns with Pendragon and LaRole, with a file of men; both are painted and dressed as Indians; Pendragon preserves his opera-glass, and LaRole his snuff-box*]

PENDRAGON: What are we brought here for, fellow?

LENOX: Warriors, the fate of battle has placed you in our power; yet fear nothing, we shall treat you like men and soldiers. Deeply do we regret to see you take up arms against us, instigated by foreign influence, and bribed by foreign gold. How numerous is your tribe?

PENDRAGON: Why what the devil, sir, do you take us for Choctaws? Can't you tell a man of fashion in masquerade?

LENOX: Who and what are you?

PENDRAGON: I am the honourable Captain Pendragon, of his Majesty's Coldstream guards.

LENOX: The *honourable* Captain Pendragon, and taken prisoner fighting in the ranks with Indians, and in disguise? A man of rank and fashion, and a soldier, changing his complexion, his nature and his character – herding with savages – infuriating their horrid passions, and whetting their knives and tomahawks against their defenceless prisoners? Impossible! And who are you, sir? [*To LaRole*]

LAROLE: [*Taking snuff*] Begar, sair, I am von man of fashion aussi, I am valet de sham to capitain Pendragoon; ve are in de masquerade, sair.

PENDRAGON: It's very true, sir, 'pon honour – we are in masquerade, though you look as if you doubt it. War, sir, is a kind of a – a singular science, and if you are to be knock'd on the head, 'tis of very little consequence whether your nose is tipped with blue or red, damme. I am in your power, sir, and a man of fashion, 'pon honour.

LENOX: Well, sir, if your example is to govern men of honour or men of fashion, I hope I am ignorant of the attributes of the one, or the eccentricities of the other. However, mercy to prisoners, even when they have forfeited mercy, may teach your nation lessons of toleration and humanity. Your life is safe, sir.

PENDRAGON: Sir, you speak very like a gentleman, and I shall be happy to taste Burgundy with you at the Horse Guards.

LENOX: I thank you, sir.

LAROLE: Par example, dis Yankee Doodel is von very pretti spoken jeune gentiman, I will give him de encouragement. Sair, I vill be ver happy to serve you en my contree, to take un tasse de caffee at de Palais Royale en Paris wid you, to dress your hair, or pull your corset tight.

Enter General, Adela and Officer

GENERAL: Who have we here?

LENOX: Prisoners, sir, and in disguise.

ADELA: As I live, an Indian dandy!

PENDRAGON: A lady? [*With an air of fashion*] Ma'am, your most devoted slave – inexpressibly happy to find a beautiful creature in this damn'd wilderness. You see, ma'am, I am a kind of a prisoner, but always at home, always at my ease, *à-la-mode* St. James – extremely rejoiced to have the honour of your acquaintance. A fine girl, LaRole, split me!

LAROLE: Oh, oui, she is very fine, I like her ver mush.

ADELA: Pray, sir, may I ask how came you to fancy that disguise?

PENDRAGON: Oh, it's not my fancy, 'pon honour, though I am one of the fancy; a mere *russe de guerre*. We on the other side of the water, have a kind of floating idea that you North Americans are half savages, and we must fight you after your own fashion.

ADELA: And have you discovered that any difference exists in the last affair in which you have been engaged?

PENDRAGON: Why, 'pon my soul, ma'am, this Yankee kind of warfare is inexpressibly inelegant, without flattery – no order – no military arrangement – no *deploying* in solid columns – but a kind of helter-skelter warfare, like a reel or a country-dance at a village inn, while the house is on fire.

ADELA: Indeed?

PENDRAGON: All true, I assure you. Why, do you know, ma'am, that one of your common soldiers was amusing himself with shooting at me for several minutes, although he saw from my air, and my dodging, that I was a man of fashion? Monstrous assurance! wasn't it?

ADELA: Why ay, it was rather impertinent for a common soldier to attempt to bring down a man of fashion.

LAROLE: Oui – it is dam impertinent, mai par example, de littel bullet of von common soldat, he sometime kill von great general.

PENDRAGON: Pray, ma'am, will you permit me to ask, when you arrived from England, and what family has the honour to boast of so beautiful a representative?

ADELA: Sir, I am not of England, I stand on my native soil.

PENDRAGON: Oh.

ADELA: And much as I esteem English women for their many amiable qualities, I hope that worth and virtue are not wholly centered in that country.

PENDRAGON: Why, 'pon my soul, ma'am, though it is not fashionable this year to be prejudiced, yet were I to admit that I saw any beauty or elegance in America, my Bond-Street friends would cut me – split me!

ADELA: I cannot admire their candour. Merit is the exclusive property of no country, and to form a just estimate of our own advantages, we should be ever prepared to admit the advantages possessed by others.

Enter a Soldier

SOLDIER: We have surprised and made captive the celebrated Indian chief, who fought so desperately against us.

GENERAL: Bring him before us. [*Exit Soldier*] He has long been the terror of the neighbourhood, and the crafty foe of our country.

Enter Soldiers with the Indian Chief

INDIAN: Who among you is the chief of these pale-faced enemies of our race?

GENERAL: I am he.

INDIAN: 'Tis well, sir; behold in me your captive, who has fallen into your power after a resistance becoming a warrior. I am ready to meet that death which I know awaits me.

GENERAL: Chief, your fears are groundless; we intend you no harm, but by our example, teach you the blessings of valour and mercy united.

INDIAN: Wherefore show me mercy? I ask it not of you. – Think you that I cannot bear the flames? that a warrior shrinks from the uplifted tomahawk? Try me – try how a great soul can smile on death. Or do you hope that I will meanly beg a life, which fate and evil fortune has thrown into your hands?

GENERAL: We ask no concessions of you, warrior; we wish to see you sensible of the delusions into which foreign nations have plunged you. We wish to see you our friend.

INDIAN: Your friend? Call back the times which we passed in liberty and happiness, when in the tranquil enjoyment of unrestrained freedom we roved through our forests, and only knew the bears as our enemy; call back our council fires, our fathers and pious priests; call back our brothers, wives and children, which cruel white men have destroyed. – Your friend? You came with the silver smile of peace, and we received you into our cabins; we hunted for you, toiled for you; our wives and daughters cherished and protected you; but when your numbers increased, you rose like wolves upon us, fired our dwellings, drove off our cattle, sent us in tribes to the wilderness, to seek for shelter; and now you ask me, while naked and a prisoner, to be your friend!

GENERAL: We have not done this, deluded man; your pretended advocates, over the great waters, have told you this tale.

INDIAN: Alas! it is a true one; I feel it here; 'tis no fiction: I was the chief of a great and daring tribe, which smiled on death with indifference and contempt; my cabin was the seat of hospitality and of love; I was first in council, and first in the field; my prosperity increased, my prospects brightened; but the white man came, and all was blasted.

GENERAL: What has been done, was the result of war.

INDIAN: Wherefore wage war against us? Was not your territory sufficiently ample, but did you sigh for our possessions? Were you not satisfied with taking our land from us, but would you hunt the lords of the soil into the den of the otter? Why drive to desperation a free and liberal people? Think you I would be your enemy unless urged by powerful wrongs? No, white man, no! the Great Spirit whom we worship, is also the God whom you adore; for friends we cheerfully lay down our lives; but against foes, our lives are staked with desperation. Had I taken you prisoner, death should have been your portion; death in cruel torments. Then why spare me? why spare the man whose knife was whetted against your life?

GENERAL: To show, by contrast, the difference of our principles. You would strike down the captive who implores your protection: we tender life and liberty to the prisoner, who asks himself for death.

INDIAN: Is this your vengeance?

GENERAL: It is. The Great Spirit delights in mercy. Be thou our friend, warrior; bury thy tomahawk deep in earth; let not jealous foreigners excite thy vengeance against us; but living as we do in one territory, let us smoke the calumet of peace, you and all your tribe, and let concord hereafter reign amongst us. – Be this the token. [*Gives a belt of wampum*]

INDIAN: Brother, I accept the token; forgive my rage, and pardon my unjust anger. Protect our warriors and wives; guard their wigwams from destruction; soften their prejudices and remove their jealousies. Do this, and the red man is your friend. I have urged you far to end my life: you have tempered your passions with mercy, and we are no longer foes. Farewell! [*Exit*]

LAROLE: Parbleu, dis general is like von great

Roman. I vill speak von vord pour myself, I vill make de speech like de sauvage.

GENERAL: [*To LaRole*] And you, sir, it appears, are in disguise, unlike a civilized soldier; you have been taken in the ranks with Indians.

LAROLE: Sair, mon general, you sall here vat I am goin to say. I am von Frenchiman; in my contree every Frenchiman he is von soldat.

GENERAL: Well?

LAROLE: Begar, sair, I must fight vid somebody, because it is my bisness. In de Egypt I did fight 'gainst de Turc; in Europe I did fight de whole vorld vis de Grand Napoleon, and in Amérique I did fight against you vid myself. Mais, you take a me de prisonier, I can fight no more; I vill trow myself on de protection of dis contree; I vill no more fight contree de Yankee Doodel; I vill stay here and eat de ros beef vid you, and mon capitain là, he may go to de devil.

GENERAL: Admirably concluded. And you, sir, what can we do to lighten your captivity?

PENDRAGON: Why sir, if war was not my profession, I'd sell out; but it's always my maxim to obey orders, whatever they may be: therefore, shall be happy to have a brush with you in war, and equally happy to crack a bottle of Burgundy with you in peace; a flash in the pan in one way, or a puff from a segar in another; a bullet under the ribs in battle, or a country dance in a ballroom; all's one to me, if it's only fashionably conducted.

GENERAL: Well, let's into my tent and partake of some refreshment. We may not always meet as enemies.

PENDRAGON: [*To Adela*] Allow me the felicity of your little finger. [*Aside*] She's struck with my figure, split me! LaRole, take notice.

LAROLE: Oh, you are de littel devil among de ladies. [*Exeunt*]

Scene 2

A Prison. Christine seated on a bench; her appearance betrays grief and despair.

CHRISTINE: At length the weary night has passed away, and day dawns, but brings no joy or comfort to my aching heart. Alas! alas! Christine, where are all the bright visions thy fond fancy painted? where is that content and love which gleamed through the casement of our cottage, when my dear father smiled on his child, and entwined around her his protecting arms: when the false Lenox, too, with honeyed lips, and tones soft as zephyrs, vow'd eternal love? Let me not think of them, or I shall go mad. Oh, what a contrast! pent up in a vile prison, and in disguise! condemned to die, and perishing unknown and unprotected. On the one side, my grave yawns for me; and on the other, a false lover, and a cruel father, drive me to despair. My brain is on fire! [*Hurries about with rapid strides. Music loud and violent*] Ha! what is this? [*Tears the miniature from around her neck*] Lenox, these are thy features! thy mild looks beam hope and joy upon me. [*Kisses it*] Could such a face be false? Away with it! even now he weds another. [*Throws the miniature indignantly from her*] So, 'tis gone, and I am left alone in darkness and despair. [*She stands transfixed with grief – muffled drum rolls – she starts*] Ha! they come for me! Be firm, my heart!

Enter an Officer and a file of Soldiers

OFFICER: Young man, your hour has arrived: the detachment waits without to receive you.

CHRISTINE: [*Faintly*] I am ready.

OFFICER: Can I serve you in any manner? Is there no letter – no remembrance that you would wish sent to father or friend?

CHRISTINE: Oh, forbear!

SOLDIER: [*Picking up the miniature*] See, sir, here is a miniature.

OFFICER: [*Examining it*] By Heavens, they are the features of Captain Lenox! How came you by this? What! a thief too? 'Tis well your career is cut short.

CHRISTINE: Oh no, no! Give it me, I implore you; 'tis mine.

OFFICER: I shall restore it to the rightful owner. Come, we wait.

CHRISTINE: Lead on. A few fleeting moments, and all my troubles will be at an end. [*Exeunt*]

Scene 3

Before the Tent. Enter General, Soldiers, &C., with papers.

GENERAL: He has not confessed who set him on?

OFFICER: He has not, but admits the crime.

GENERAL: [*Returning papers*] 'Tis well – see him

executed according to the sentence. Hard and imperious duty, which, at once, shuts out hope and mercy! [*Exit General*]

OFFICER: Now to seek for Lenox, and restore to him his miniature. [*Exit*]

Scene 4

The Camp, as in Act I, Scene 3; the stage is thrown open, drums roll, and the procession enters for the execution of Christine; she is in the centre, between the two detachments; her coat is off, and the stock unloosened from her neck – her step is firm, until she reaches the tent of Lenox, when she clasps her hands and hangs down her head in despair. Procession makes the circuit of the stage with slow steps, and when opposite the tent she kneels; an Officer places the bandage over her eyes, and gives a sign to a detachment of four to advance; they step forward, and level their muskets at her; at the moment, Lenox rushes from the tent with the miniature in his hand and strikes up their guns.

LENOX: Hold! for your lives! [*Rushes down to Christine, and tears the bandage from her eyes*] 'Tis she! 'tis she! 'tis my own, my beloved Christine! [*Holds her in his arms; she faints*]

2ND OFFICER: What means this?

LENOX: Stand off, ye cruel executioners, would you destroy a woman?

OFFICER: A woman? Heavens! how did this happen?

Enter General, Adela, LaRole, Soldiers, &C

LENOX: Support her, Adela, support my dear Christine! [*Adela assists*]

CHRISTINE: [*Recovering*] Where am I? [*Sees Lenox and Adela*] Hide me, save me from that horrid sight!

LENOX: Do you not know me, dear Christine?

CHRISTINE: Traitor, begone! let me die at once! Is she not your bride?

LENOX: No, by Heavens, no! 'tis my early friend, my dear companion. Could you doubt my love?

CHRISTINE: Not married? not your betrothed? O Lenox, are you then faithful?

LENOX: Could Christine doubt my vows?

CHRISTINE: I see it all – I have been deceived. Pardon me, dear Lenox; but driven to despair by your supposed perfidy, I enlisted, and rushed on my fate – which in a moment (horrid thought!) would have terminated. But you are true, and I am happy. [*Embrace*]

LAROLE: Parbleu! it is a littel voman vidout de petticoat. Suppose she take a me von prisonier, O quell disgrâce!

Enter Jasper, Jerry and Peasants

JASPER: Where is she? where is my daughter?

CHRISTINE: My father? I dare not look upon him.

JASPER: Come to my arms, dear wanderer. Could you leave your poor old father thus? You've nearly broke my heart, Christine.

CHRISTINE: My sufferings have been equally severe; but do you pardon your child?

JASPER: I do – I do! and further prove my love, by making you happy. Take her, Lenox, she is yours; and never let father attempt to force his child into a marriage which her heart abhors.

JERRY: Well, I vow, Miss Crissy, you look very pretty in pantaloons, and make a fine soger; but after all, I'm glad to have escaped a wife who wears the breeches before marriage – so I consent that you shall have the infantry ossifer, because I can't help it; and so I'll marry Patty, the weaver's daughter, though she can't crack a bottle nor bring down a buck.

GENERAL: All things have terminated happily. Our arms have been triumphant, and our gallant soldiers rewarded with the approbation of their country. Love has intwined a wreath for your brows, Lenox, and domestic peace and happiness await you; and when old age draws on apace, may you remember the PLAINS OF CHIPPEWA, and feel toward Britain as freemen should feel towards all the world: *"Enemies in war – in peace, friends."*

Finis

THE FOREST ROSE

OR

AMERICAN FARMERS

SAMUEL WOODWORTH

LIKE many early-nineteenth-century literary figures, Samuel Woodworth made his lasting impression on the American scene with a popular song. "The Old Oaken Bucket" (originally "The Bucket") is probably as widely sung today as any tune from this period. Few, however, could identify its author. Although Woodworth wrote eight plays, a patriotic novel based on the War of 1812, and numerous odes, religious effusions, and sentimental ballads and edited a dozen or more periodicals and newspapers, he is remembered for "the moss covered bucket that hung by the well." A sad fate for a playwright whose *Forest Rose* provided the principal acting material for the "stage Yankee," certainly the most popular stage character in the first half of the nineteenth century, and for an editor who established the New York *Mirror*, for twenty years the leading literary newspaper in New York.

Samuel Woodworth was born in Scituate, Massachusetts, on January 13, 1785. He was a bright, strong, and observant youth who began early to write poetry on themes taken from his simple surroundings. Although his father, Benjamin Woodworth, a soldier in the Revolutionary War, approved of Samuel's scholarly inclinations, he did not have the means to foster them. At fourteen the young Woodworth was placed in the home of Reverend Nehemiah Thomas, and in a year he felt ready to tackle literary Boston. He apprenticed himself to Benjamin Russell, the editor of *The Columbian Centinel*, and thus began his peripatetic career as editor and writer. During this first assignment, one of his longest (1800–1806), he contributed poetry to various Boston publications under the *nom de plume* "Seline." In 1806 he became associated with John Howard Payne as editor of a juvenile paper called *The Fly*. Payne, like Woodworth, is not remembered for his acting or for his playwriting but for his "Home, Sweet Home." *The Fly* was a short-lived enterprise for Woodworth, as were most of those that followed. In 1807 he went to New Haven, where he published a weekly periodical, *Belles-Lettres Repository*. Then he went to Baltimore, and finally in 1809 to New York. After a year in the printing business in New York, he was sufficiently convinced of the stability of his fortunes to marry Lydia Reeder on September 24, 1810. The acquisition of family responsibilities, which finally included ten children, combined with his natural proclivity for unsteady employment, kept him and his family on the verge of poverty for the rest of his life. His publishing and editorial ventures, except for the New York *Mirror* (1823–1842), were all of short duration. Even with the *Mirror*, he remained as editor only for its first year. A catalogue of his enterprises will indicate the diversity as well as the unsteadiness of his occupations: 1812–1814, a weekly paper called *The War;* during the same period, *Halcyon Luminary*, a magazine devoted to the Swedenborgian faith; 1817, *Republican Chronicle*, a newspaper; 1819, *Ladies Literary Cabinet;* 1821, *Woodworth's Literary Casket*, a miniature magazine; 1823, the New York *Mirror;* 1823, *The New Jerusalem Missionary and Intellectual Repository*, another Swedenborgian journal; 1824, *The Literary Gazette;* 1827, *The Parthenon*. During this period he also produced quantities of poetry and a patriotic novel, *The Champions of Freedom, or The Mysterious Chief* (1816). This last was conventional history (War of 1812) mixed with conventional romance. His poetry was highly praised in its day. Some poems seem to have reached England and were compared and even confused with those of Wordsworth. Many of Woodworth's versifications were written for the theatre: epilogues, prologues, and readings.

Typical of these theatrical pieces was the address delivered at the reopening of the Park Theatre in September, 1821. The first Park had been destroyed by fire on May 25, 1820. For the fall reopening the management conducted a contest for a "prize address." From sixty entries, Charles Sprague of Boston had won first prize and thus had his poem spoken on the opening night, September 1, 1821, and Samuel Woodworth was judged second. His offering was spoken by Mrs. Barnes before the performance on September 3, 1821. The following short extract of two stanzas from the seven indicates the nature of his patriotic and theatrical interests:

> Ye generous freemen, who in danger stand
> The shield and bulwark of your happy land;
> Who, mid the sweeter luxuries of peace,
> Behold your greatness and your arts increase,
> Whose liberal minds throw lustre on the age,
> Oh! still protect and patronize the stage;
> That bright auxiliar in Refinement's cause,
> Which raised proud Greece to what at length she was;
> Invited forth and scattered unconfined
> The boundless treasures of a Shakespeare's mind,
> And taught the vulgar barbarous sons of strife
> The gentler courtesies that sweeten life.

Jon: Do you want to kill the Colonel?
I feel chock full of fight.

The Contrast

The Forest Rose

Columbians all! ye patriots and ye fair,
Still let the Drama claim your generous care;
Cherished by you, it will the champion prove
Of Freedom, virtue, and the Arts you love;
So shall this city, by refinement blest,
Become the pride and mistress of the West
So shall your Country rise to greater fame,
And endless glory gild Columbia's name!

Woodworth was a prolific composer of opening and closing addresses, whether for the Glorious Fourth, for the Fire Department Fund program, for a new play (*Oswali of Athens*, by his friend Payne), or for his own benefits. On February 19, 1822, he prepared a "Literary and Musical Entertainment" in which he "and four amateurs recited."

The popularity of his poetic effusions in and on the theatre quite naturally led him to attempt a play. His *The Deed of Gift* was produced on March 25, 1822, at the Boston Theatre and on January 21, 1823, at Mrs. Baldwin's City Theatre in New York. Woodworth's dedication to Mrs. M. Mumford referred to it as an "operatic production" and the title page called it a "comic opera." The play was a melodramatic hodge-podge of villainy, virtue, and dexterous disguisings, with virtue triumphant. The rural setting, the introduction of songs, and the glorification of the American spirit of liberty and the "independence of the American farmer" anticipated similar elements in *The Forest Rose*.

His second play, *LaFayette, or The Castle of Olmutz* was given at the Park Theatre on February 23, 1824, and again on September 9, 1824, in honor of the visit of Lafayette. The plot was derived directly from the historical incident of Lafayette's imprisonment in Germany in 1792 and the attempt of a young German physician and a young American to effect his escape from the Castle of Olmutz in Austria. There were no songs in this play, but there were abundant patriotic outpourings in the cause of liberty and the glory of Lafayette: "May the star of Freedom, which enlightens happy America, increase in brightness until every quarter of the world feels and confesses its benignant influence."

The Forest Rose was Woodworth's third play, and *The Widow's Son, or Which Is the Traitor?* his fourth. This melodrama of hairbreadth escapes and fast action was first produced at the Park Theatre on November 25, 1825, by Price and Simpson, with music by J. H. Swindells. Here again Woodworth was concerned with patriotism and liberty in a plot built around the domestic complications resulting from Whig and Tory sympathies during the Revolutionary War. The introduction of various demonstrations of the "black art" indicated an influence of the then-popular Gothic romance. Sentiments favoring liberty and the glory of fighting for one's country were introduced in several of the songs.

The Cannibals, or The Massacre Islands, a thriller, was produced at the Bowery Theatre on February 20, 1833. This was based on Captain Benjamin Morrell's *Narrative of Four Voyages*, which had been published in New York the year before. *Blue Laws, or Eighty Years Ago*, a farce, was given at the Bowery on March 15, 1833. *King's Bridge Cottage*, produced at the Richmond Hill Theatre on February 22, 1833, has been attributed to Woodworth, although the title page lists the author simply as a "gentleman of N. York." Internal evidence of similarity in language and sentiment to other known works of Woodworth prompts the listing among Woodworth's works. Inferior as it is in character and plot to the other plays, the patriotic sentiments, particularly his praise of Washington, are honest and robust:

. . . the cause which has roused such a spirit as Washington's, would succeed, though all the tyrants of Europe were combined against him. It is the cause of suffering thousands, who are determined to throw off the yoke of oppression and assert their freedom; and when led on by Washington, with heaven for his guide, what power on earth can resist them?

Woodworth's last play, *The Foundling of the Sea*, first performed on May 14, 1833, at the Park, was never published. It had been written in response to G. H. Hill's offer of four hundred dollars for the best play containing a Yankee character. Although the committee – composed of Irving, Verplanck, Webb, and King – found none of the plays submitted worthy of the prize, Hill paid Woodworth the money and used the play at least six times in New York and Philadelphia.

Although Woodworth's literary output reached respectable proportions and his plays were often performed, he too seems never to have been able to eke out an existence from his writing. Continuing royalties were unknown at this time. Even the benefits given in his behalf were not sufficient to relieve his "pecuniary misfortunes." Of the four known benefits for Woodworth – March 5, 1828, Lafayette Theatre; March 11, 1829, Park Theatre; October 31, 1837, Bowery Theatre; and November 21, 1837, Bowery Theatre – the first two and the last employed his most popular piece, *The Forest Rose*. (*Cato* was performed for the October 31 benefit.) Woodworth suffered the ironic economic humiliation visited upon so many dramatists. His *Forest Rose* provided a handsome living for many actors years after his death.

Woodworth gave up his literary endeavors in 1836 and went to work at the Navy Yard in Boston. In February, 1837, he suffered an apoplectic attack from which he never fully recovered. A partial paralysis and loss of sight compelled him to cease all his activities, and on December 9, 1842, he died in poverty.

The Forest Rose, the nineteenth-century *Oklahoma!*, is without question Woodworth's best play. Its distinct features – the patriotic glorification of American democracy; the praise of the native honesty of the American farmer; the contrast between the bungling, awkward shrewdness of the "Yankee" and the polished stupidity of the noble Englishman; and the sentimental songs – are all comparable to similar elements in the other plays, but they were rendered with greater skill.

On the basis of theatrical popularity, *The Forest Rose* stands out as the first "hit" show of the American theatre and as the first successful musical play. After its first performance, at the Chatham Garden Theatre on October 6, 1825, it was repeatedly played for the next forty years. Even in 1866, Ireland wrote that *The Forest Rose* still "retains possession of the stage." An incomplete canvass of performances indicates the following: New York, 49; Philadelphia, 55; New Orleans, 17; St. Louis, 4; Mobile, 1; Chicago, 1; California, 40; and London, 150 plus. No other play in the first half of the century matched this record. Certainly the English audience was here exposed to a reasonably accurate account of how the American regarded the Englishman and how the "Yankee" viewed himself and his recently acquired freedom.

Like so many other plays that retain their place in the repertoire season after season, *The Forest Rose* possessed that magic theatrical formula of sincere, honest character portrayal and significant social comment, combined with an acting part that permitted a star actor to introduce his own theatrical embellishments. Apparently the play was not regarded as an actor's vehicle when it was first introduced as an afterpiece to a dramatization of Scott's *Lady of the Lake*. Alec Simpson, a comparatively unknown actor from Albany, played the part of Jonathan. In October, 1825, no one believed the play or the part offered remarkable opportunities. At the time Simpson appeared in *The Forest Rose*, he was not regarded as a "Yankee" actor. Noah Ludlow, the peripatetic nineteenth-century theatrical manager of the Ohio and Mississippi river towns, reported that Alec Simpson made the part "simply a comic New Jersey boy, without any of the more eastern peculiarities." The "Down East" qualities were added and established for succeeding generations of actors by George Handel Hill.

Even though Hill is credited with molding the part into a "stage Yankee," he apparently perceived the possibilities from watching Simpson. When the play was first performed, Hill, then a youngster of fifteen or sixteen, was employed regularly in a jeweler's establishment near the Chatham Theatre and irregularly as a "super" at the theatre. He first attempted his Yankee characterizations in a sequence of readings and songs as part of an olio entertainment in Brooklyn in 1826. His early stage appearances seem to have been somewhat intermittent, but he must have regarded himself as an actor; for in 1828, when he married a Miss Cordelia Thompson, he was reported to have "retired from the stage" (at the insistence of her parents). For this brief period of retirement he worked as a storekeeper in LeRoy, New York. The following year, 1829, he went to Albany, ostensibly to find work as a paperhanger. Instead he found an audience for his Yankee songs and stories in a dark little lecture room called the Albany Museum. Henry Stone saw these impersonations and suggested to Duffy and Forrest, the Albany managers, that he be engaged to appear at the Pearl Street Theatre. This gave him the firm start he had been seeking. During the summer he was in New York at the Chatham Garden and the New York Museum reciting his famous Yankee story, "Jonathan's Visit to Buffalo and a Seneca Village." In the fall he moved to the Arch Street Theatre in Philadelphia as a regular member of the company. Here his Yankee talents were employed for the first time in a regular play: he did the Yankee impersonation in Dunlap's *Trip to Niagara*. After a brief engagement in Charleston during the spring, he returned to Philadelphia for the winter season of 1832. The managers invited him to choose a play to exhibit his peculiar Yankee qualities. He chose *The Forest Rose*. After the first performance, his course was set. The "stage Yankee" was established as a significant theatrical type and Hill, at the age of twenty-two, was declared the principal exponent. During the next fifteen years he played the part in Baltimore, Boston, Cincinnati, Louisville, New Orleans, Mobile, and Albany.

Hill was a Yankee by birth (Boston, October 9, 1809) and seems to have been well suited to the part. Stone, who certainly might be somewhat prejudiced as his discoverer, says that "his voice, with its natural nasal twang, peculiarly and admirably adapted him to the character. He was easy, quiet, and perfectly natural in his every impersonation, surpassing, beyond all doubt, Hackett, Dan Marble and others who assumed the Yankee role." The *Herald*, writing of his performance at the Chatham Theatre in 1840, praised him as "the funniest actor, and the cleverest fellow, in the Yankee signification of the word – in Christendom. No wonder every other house is deserted, except the Chatham." In May, 1838, the *Knickerbocker Magazine* had written of Hill's merits as an actor and as a man: "Touching the former, we but echo public opinion when we affirm, that in the exhibition of the quiet humor, peculiar to the Yankee, par excellence, he stands unrivalled." After his initial success in *The Forest Rose*, it was natural that he should seek other Yankee parts. These he found in, or injected into, such plays as *Seth Slope, The Yankee Pedlar, The Green Mountain Boy*, and *Jonathan in England*.

"Yankee" Hill's success was not limited to the United States (the "George Handel" was practically forgotten). In 1836 he appeared at the Drury Lane in London. The English audience took to him and his Yankee immediately. They found him not unlike their own "canny Yorkshire lads" and his dialect "not wholly unlike that of our own eastern counties." They enjoyed his sleek, plausible cunning, his great industry, and his scanty and pliant honesty. They delighted in his pitch for his peddler's wares: "Lookin' glasses that you can see a mile deep in; Boston clocks which go all the days except Sunday and razors so keen that if you only 'ile 'em well, and put them under your pillow at night, you'll get up in the morning clean shaved."

London had been introduced to the Yankee character even before Hill. Charles Mathews had given them a glimpse as early as 1824, and James Hackett had exposed the character somewhat more authentically in 1827. Mathews was an English actor who specialized in a hodge-podge entertainment, labeled "At Homes," which combined an assortment of stories and impersonations. After Mathews visited America during the season of 1822–23, he returned to England with a new entertainment called *Trip to America*. As might have been expected, Jonathan W. Doubikin, a "real" Yankee, became one of the most fascinating characters in his new gallery. In 1824 he formalized his new Jonathan character in a more proper drama, *Jonathan in England*. James Hackett, an American actor who had tried his talent at Yankee stories, became acquainted with Mathews during his visit to America. When Hackett went to England in 1827, to explore his powers over the audience at Covent Garden, he devised a Mathews-like entertainment called *Sylvester Daggerwood* in which a series of Yankee stories figured most prominently. The English stage had been set for Hill's arrival.

Hill was so stimulated by his success in London that he gave the American audiences only a single season of his Yankee characters before returning again to England. Unfortunately, after he returned to his native country again in the fall of 1839, he was unable to re-establish himself at the same level of popularity he had known before his departure. Part of his undoing was his own doing. He ventured into the risky area of theatrical management, and with disastrous results. During one brief period in 1841 he became so disenchanted with the theatre that he took up the study of medicine, apparently with some notion of seeking a medical degree at Harvard. Even though this new career never developed, his theatrical career never regained its former strength and he was never able to raise sufficient income at the box office to match his accumulated debts. He gave his final Yankee impersonation in Saratoga Springs in August, 1849, one month before his death.

Hill was not the only Yankee actor. A popular and profitable stage character is always adopted by as many actors as can reasonably fit themselves to the demands of the part. Joshua Silsbee and Danforth Marble devoted themselves even more completely than Hill to the "stage Yankee." And many other well-known comedians were identified with the "Jonathan" roles. (The Yankee character was almost invariably called Jonathan.) Among these were Alexander Simpson (the original), Henry Placide, George E. Locke, John Weaver, J. H. Hackett, Louis F. Mestayer (he played *The Forest Rose* some forty nights in California), and Joseph Jefferson.

Marble first appeared in *The Forest Rose* in New York at the Park on July 28, 1837. From then until his last appearance on the stage – again in *The Forest Rose*, at the Bowery on May 5, 1849 – he appeared throughout the country as Jonathan Ploughboy. After a performance at St. Louis on June 4, 1839, the local critic labeled him "a Yankee up to the hub" and "perfectly killing." Marble was, however, more closely identified with *Sam Patch* and with *The Vermont Wool Dealer*. When he performed *The Vermont Wool Dealer* in London in 1844, one reporter noted that the "Strand was filled nightly with merry folks, laughing until their sides were sore." Yankee acting was a more profitable enterprise for Marble than for Hill. At his death in 1849, he left his widow an estate of twenty-five thousand dollars.

Like his predecessors, Silsbee also invaded London. Of his performances at the Adelphi and the Haymarket in 1851, *Tallis's Dramatic Magazine* reported:

His style of acting differs considerably from theirs [Hill and Marble], and is indeed so far peculiar, that it may be said to form a new and original school. Faithfully as he portrays the Yankee character, still his performances are permeated with the natural humour of the man. His looks, gesture, and action – even the arch twinkle of his eye – impress the spectator with ludicrous emotions, and his inflexible countenance rigidly innocent of fun, while his audience are in roars of laughter, gives an additional zest to the humour of the language and the absurdity of the situations.

Although he was generally praised in London, one critic found "an occasional indistinctness of utterance, 'Yeou git eout . . .'Taint no euse o' your scroungin, 'taint,' though exceedingly humorous, and, no doubt, perfectly truthful, perhaps interfere with that clearness of articulation which we look for upon the stage." During this London engagement he played 123 consecutive nights of *The Forest Rose*.

Silsbee was born in Steuben County, New York, on December 1, 1813. His first stage appearance was as "general utility" in 1838, in Natchez, Mississippi. Like Hill, he made his first "Yankee" venture as a solo-act story-teller. This was in Cincinnati in 1840. During this same engagement, he made his initial appearance in *The Forest Rose*. In 1841 he was in Philadelphia, in 1842 at the Tremont in Boston, and in 1843 at the Chatham Garden in New York. After the deaths of Hill and Marble, he became the principal "Yankee" actor. His last recorded New York performance was at the Broadway Theatre on August 15, 1853, the opening of the 1853–54 season. In the spring of 1855, he performed his entire repertoire at the Metropolitan Theatre in San Francisco. The reviewer for the San Francisco *Pioneer* described Silsbee as "the best

Yankee we have had in California . . . not made up entirely of whittling a piece of pine, and uttering remarks with an extravagant twang." Silsbee died in 1855. These "Yankee" actors did not limit themselves to *The Forest Rose*, but certainly they owed a substantial debt to Woodworth.

Although the Davies music seems to have been omitted from most of the later presentations of *The Forest Rose*, a share of the play's distinction lies in its musical nature. There had been earlier attempts at this form – Mrs. Hatton's opera *Tammany* (1794), with music by James Hewitt; Dunlap's *The Wild Goose Chase* (1800), with music by Hewitt; Dunlap's *The Archers* (1796), with music by Benjamin Carr – but none of these compared in quality or popularity to *The Forest Rose*. Although there is insufficient evidence on which to judge the music – only such vague generalizations as "The music of the piece was a very pleasing style, and was long popular" (Ireland) – Woodworth clearly regarded it as integral to the play. The title page of the 1825 edition reads: "a Pastoral Opera, Music, By John Davies, Esq." This credit was set in boldface, and in the preface Woodworth elaborated on his indebtedness to John Davies.

The Forest Rose commands a high position among the early nineteenth-century American dramas, not because it contains startling innovations in plot structure, character, or language, but because Woodworth endowed familiar and homely situations and persons with charm and wit. The gay, lighthearted spirit that permeates the entire proceedings is unmatched by any drama in the first half of the century.

Woodworth was particularly skillful in his handling of the musical element. Songs and dances are introduced casually and appropriately. The initial melody, ringing with the glories of the early-morning rustic scene and the joys of country living, evolves as naturally as "Oh, What a Beautiful Morning" in *Oklahoma!* In the same way, Jonathan's comedy interpolations appear as reasonable and instinctive expressions of a fun-loving rustic character.

Except for the stupid, blundering Englishman Bellamy, the characters are all lighthearted and playful. The ladies, particularly, are filled with high spirits. They are delighted and delightful when they play cat-and-mouse games with their humble suitors. For example, Harriet addresses Jonathan, "I hope, sir, that you don't mean to impose upon my youth and inexperience, to win my virgin heart, then take advantage of my unsuspecting innocence. You do not mean to ruin me! Oh! (*Weeps*)." Commonly, in the nineteenth century, such a speech would signal a melodramatic heroine rather than a spirited, coquettish, play-acting young farm girl.

The Yankee character was, of course, not invented by Woodworth. "Jonathan" appeared earlier in *The Contrast*. Woodworth might also have been influenced by Henry Placide's playing of Zekiel Homespun in George Colman's *The Heir at Law* at the Park in 1823. Although *The Forest Rose* is set in New Jersey, Jonathan says he is from Massachusetts and certainly his speeches indicate that he is a true Yankee, or at least a true "stage Yankee": taciturn, obstructionist, awkward, honest, enterprising, and tricky. His first dialogue with Bland in Act I, Scene 3, typical of the evasive verbal technique that has become so closely identified with this character, is not unlike the specimen quoted by Mrs. Trollope. She reported hearing the following dialogue between two Yankees on an Erie Canal boat:

"Well, now, which way may you be traveling?"
"I expect this canal runs pretty nearly west."
"Are you going far with it?"
"Well, now, I don't rightly know how many miles it may be."
"I expect you'll be from New York."
"Sure enough I have been at New York, often and often."
"I calculate, then, 'tis not there as you stop?"
"Business must be minded, in stopping and in stirring."
"You may say that. Well, I look then you'll be making for the Springs?"
"Folks say as all the world is making for the Springs, and I expect a good sight of them is."
"Do you calculate upon stopping long when you get to your journey's end?"
" 'Tis my business must settle that, I expect."
"I guess that's true, too; but you'll be for making pleasure a business for once, I calculate?"
"My business don't often lie in that line."
"Then, may be, it is not the Springs as takes you this line?"
"The Springs is a right elegant place, I reckon."

The struggle between Jonathan's Yankee sense of honesty, of rendering service that has been bought and paid for, and the dreadful Yankee fear that he might have to surrender the purse that is already warming his palm becomes one of the liveliest comedy scenes of the play, particularly as Jonathan proposes to have the question argued out by his debating society.

Jonathan Ploughboy, compared with Yankee characters in later plays, seems neatly and even sparsely written. His peculiarities of speech and action are not excessive. When the final song and dance are concluded, the audience is not satiated with too much Yankee. This same wise dramaturgical attitude is evident in other parts of *The Forest Rose*: the gentle pokes at the Englishman and his family pride, the introduction of songs and dances, and the patriotic praise of the American farmer. Woodworth limited himself not only to what came reasonably to the character but to what, in quantity, would not surfeit his audience. And all is clearly integrated into the two short acts. Woodworth had a strong sense for integration and verisimilitude. Even in providing music for his songs and dances, he gave a jew's harp to Jonathan and a fiddle to Caesar to avoid the artificiality of a music-gallery accompaniment.

Woodworth was equally conscious of the possibilities and restrictions of theatrical effects – in the time sequence of scenes indicated by a clock on the village spire (it even strikes in one scene); in mistaken identities manipulated by veils and scarfs; in stage directions indicating dumb-show scenes; and in the use of such properties as Bellamy's glass. The non-literary character of his approach to the stage is evident also in the changes that were made for the acting version. In his address to the public, he labeled these "improvements," though for the most part he seems to have made the changes at the suggestion of others and against his better judgment. He found them "somewhat fastidious." The changes reflected a moral squeamishness not consistent with the tone of the play. Some of these alterations might have been directed at the "reading public." For example, substitution of the word "bosom" for "breast" in a stage direction. Other "improvements" he suggested were "big book" for "Bible"; "go call a justice of the peace" for "give me a Bible"; "villain" for "ravisher"; and the deletion of "and was rifling those virgin lips of their nectareous sweets." The final change, however, was certainly designed for theatrical effectiveness, giving Miller a rousing, flag-waving closing speech in praise of American farmers, "the lords of the luxuriant soil which feeds us." His prefatory address to the public concluded with the following comments:

Many of the foregoing alterations were suggested by friends whom I highly respect and esteem, but whose objections, I cannot help thinking, are somewhat *fastidious*. For how, I would ask, can the *character* of a *libertine* be successfully delineated, without putting some *libertine expressions* into his mouth? Unless the outlines of a vicious character be strongly defined, it is impossible to excite these sensations of disapprobation which constitute the *moral* of the drama. It will be observed, that no offensive *words* or *allusions* are uttered by any one of my virtuous characters, who all unite in condemning the sentiments of the unprincipled dandy.

I cannot, in justice, conclude this article, without acknowledging the immense obligations I am under to those ladies and gentlemen of Chatham Theatre, whose talents and exertions secured the favourable reception with which the *Forest Rose* was honoured; every one of them did for the piece all that could be done with such homely materials as the author had furnished.

Mrs. Burks (for whom the part was written) raised the character of the volatile Harriet, the rural coquettey, far above my hopes and anticipations; while the drooping Lydia, as portrayed by Mrs. Wallack, excited the sympathy and affection of all the audience. Mrs. LaCombe (formerly Mrs. Allen) rendered the frolick-some Sally a very efficient personage in the play; and even the black *Rose* received a real beauty and fragrance from the pretty Miss Eberle.

The part of Blandford, with the exception of his songs, is trifling in itself, but was rendered very interesting by the vocal powers of Mr. Howard, for whom the songs were expressly written and composed. Mr. Keene very generously consented to play the jealous William, a character far below his talents and just pretensions, but which was thus rendered very attractive. Mr. Thayer, as Bellamy, needs no praise, the unanimous voice of a very numerous and respectable audience pronounced it to be an excellent representation. Simpson's Jonathan was every way equal to my hopes and wishes; and the respectable old Jersey farmer, Squire Miller, as portrayed by Mr. Somerville, was eminently calculated to elevate the character of our "lords of the soil."

Once more I thank them all; and will only add, that I shall never forget that a large portion of the approbation which the piece received, is due to my friend Mr. Davies, who composed the music.

The Author.

New York, October 18, 1825.

Like most good playwrights, Woodworth had a high regard for the actor's talent and fully realized his dependence on the good graces and theatrical perfection of his performers. In the light of his own contributions as author, the humility of his praise for the actors may seem too self-effacing; or perhaps Woodworth was aware of the actor's proverbial response to flattery and his dependence upon their good will for future performances. He need not have worried. Actors and managers found profit and pleasure in *The Forest Rose* for many years.

THE FOREST ROSE

OR

AMERICAN FARMERS
A Pastoral Opera

SAMUEL WOODWORTH   Music by JOHN DAVIES

CHARACTERS

MILLER	CAESAR
BLANDFORD	1ST FARMER
BELLAMY	2ND FARMER
WILLIAM	LYDIA
JONATHAN	HARRIET
WAITER	SALLY
VILLAGERS, LABOURERS, MAIDENS	ROSE

NOTE: *Lydia and Harriet are dressed exactly alike, which occasions Bellamy's mistake, in the 4th scene of Act 1*

ACT I. Scene 1

(NOTE: *The overture expresses the various sounds which are heard at early dawn, in the country, commencing at that hour of silence when even the ticking of the village clock is supposed to be heard. It strikes four, and a gentle bustle succeeds, indicating the first movements of the villagers. A confused murmur gradually swells on the ear, in which can be distinguished the singing of birds, the shepherd's pipe, the hunter's horn, &c. &c. &c. until the united strength of the band represents the whole village engaged in their rustic employments.*)

Distant view of a village spire, on which the dial plate of a clock indicates the hour. The stage represents a farm-yard, separated from a field by a pale fence with a gate. On the right of the actor is a cottage, and on the opposite side a rustic arbour of grape-vine. William is discovered in the field, giving directions to the labourers. Lydia and Harriet enter from the cottage, the latter with a milk-pail; William joins them, and they sing the following

Trio
Here, in scenes of sweet seclusion,

Far from bustling towns we dwell,
While around, in rich profusion,
Autumn's yellow bounties swell.

There, the loaded fruit-trees, bending,
Strew with mellow gold the land;
Here, on high, from vines impending,
Purple clusters court the hand.

All the day, to recreate us,
Strains of music freight the breeze,
Healthful sports at eve await us –
What are city joys to these?

HARRIET: This may all sound very well in song, Lydia; but, for all that, I should like to have an opportunity of judging for myself.
LYDIA: So, you are sighing for a city life?
HARRIET: I will confess, Lydia, that I should like to see the city, and not remain altogether ignorant of the polite world.

William returns into the field, and disappears
LYDIA: Just so I once thought, and dearly have I paid for the experiment. Let my example be a

155

caution to you, my dear friend; for depend upon it that poet is correct, who says, "When ignorance is bliss, 'tis folly to be wise."

HARRIET: Why, surely it does not necessarily follow, because you placed your affections on an unworthy object, that every country girl who goes to town must do the same!

LYDIA: Nay, Harriet; that is unkind. I have yet to learn that Mr. Blandford *is* unworthy.

HARRIET: That man cannot be otherwise, who will first win the affections of an artless girl, and then doom her to wear the willow; singing every hour of the day – [*Sings*]

Though mourning like a mateless dove.

LYDIA: That was *his* favourite song. But you should recollect the circumstances of our separation. I could not consent to his wild scheme of a secret marriage; and so we parted: for mystery and concealment, in such cases, can never be productive of good. I dare not tell even Harriet, that I wear his miniature in my bosom – a keepsake with which I most solemnly promised never to part. [*Aside*]

HARRIET: Had you been a girl of spirit, like me, you would have taken him at his word; and might now, perhaps, have been rolling in your coach in the great city, instead of being secluded, like a nun, here in the country. I wish I could have such an offer.

LYDIA: And I might, on the other hand, have been an unpitied beggar, destitute of that consoling consciousness of duty which now supports me. Besides, could you be happy as the wife of a man whose haughty relatives affected to despise your plebeian blood?

Enter William

But I will not detain you from your morning task, and here comes, my gallant brother to attend you. Breakfast will be ready by the time you have finished milking. [*Exit into the cottage*]

HARRIET: Your sentiments are doubtless very correct, Miss Lydia; but still I should like to live in the city one whole year.

WILLIAM: A whole year, Harriet! How would you contrive to pass your time?

HARRIET: As other people do, to be sure, in seeing the fashions, and the Park, and the Battery, and Castle Garden, and the Museum, and the Theatres, and Chatham Garden, and the circuses, and the Gas-lights, and the Water-works, and the Fire-works and the Stepping-mill, and all other places of amusement. Then, when I came home again, all the girls would so envy me, and the young men would quarrel for me. O, it would be delightful. Hem! [*Affecting disdain*] – Please to keep your distance, Sir.

WILLIAM: Why, what the deuce is the matter with you, Harriet?

HARRIET: Please mend your manners, sir, and address me as Miss Miller.

WILLIAM: Ha, ha, ha! Miss Miller! Ha, ha, ha! I say Miss Mill—— Ha, ha, ha! You recollect the milkmaid in the spelling-book, who lost her fortune by a toss of her head?

HARRIET: I was only jesting, William. But seriously, I intend to see the city, that is poz.

WILLIAM: Indeed! When do you propose going?

HARRIET: As soon as I can find a beau with gallantry enough to take me there.

WILLIAM: Then, fare you well; for here comes a verification of the old proverb – the very thing you are speaking of – a scarecrow from the city. I say, Harriet, let us have a little sport with him.

HARRIET: A scarecrow! Why, he is a genteel, delightful looking fellow, neat as a starched tucker fresh from a bandbox. Why do you call him such names?

WILLIAM: Because he frightens the birds without killing any of them. Depend upon it, all the game he carries home will be brought down with silver shot, as it is said they shoot witches.

Enter Bellamy, with a double-barrelled gun and crosses the stage, disappearing behind the cottage

WILLIAM: I say, Harriet, he is as gaunt about the waist as your father's greyhound.

HARRIET: Or little Caesar's fiddle.

WILLIAM: Or Deacon Forest's hourglass. I hope he won't mistake the goslins for woodcocks, or the chickens for partridges.

HARRIET: I wonder he did not speak to me.

WILLIAM: Speak to *you!* Why, he did not see you.

HARRIET: Then he shall hear me. [*Song – Harriet*]

When bashful Lubin sought my hand,
My heart his suit approved,
But feigning not to understand,

I listened still unmoved.
For dim, I thought, must burn that flame,
Which such a check could smother,
And sprightly girls are not to blame
To spurn a bashful lover.

Enter Bellamy – listening

BELLAMY: Damn fine girl, 'pon honour. [*Eyeing her through his glass*]

Poor Lubin told a friend his case,
Who soon his fears allay'd,
And bade him wear a bolder face, –
He listen'd and obey'd.
Returning soon, with alter'd mien,
He might at once discover,
That sprightly girls, of gay sixteen,
Ne'er spurn a saucy lover.

BELLAMY: Tolerable voice, but damn'd little science. Wonder who she is. [*Aside, leaning over the fence*]

WILLIAM: He seems to like your singing, Harriet.

HARRIET: [*Singing louder*]

A sprightly girl of gay sixteen,
Ne'er spurns a saucy lover.

BELLAMY: [*Aside*] Then you will not spurn me, my charming little songstress; for bashfulness is not one of my failings. Who can the bumpkin be? [*Surveying William through his glass*] By his dress, I take him to be damn'd low.

Comes through the gate, and advances slowly down

HARRIET: I must pretend not to observe him. I say, William, tell me something more about the city. Did you say the houses all joined together? [*Affecting simplicity*]

WILLIAM: To be sure they do, Harriet, just like our corn-house and cart-shed. You may walk all the way from Whitehall to the Hospital, through a street that bends like the bow of an ox-yoke, without seeing an apple-tree or a turnip-patch.

BELLAMY: [*Aside*] A mere clodhopper, that fellow. I will astonish him directly.

HARRIET: Is it possible! How I should like to go there!

BELLAMY: [*Aside*] Sweet simpleton! How I should like to take you there. I must speak to her, and dash the native. Pardon me, miss; I thought I heard a nightingale; but I now perceive that it was a bird of paradise, 'pon honour.

HARRIET: Where, sir? Pray don't shoot it till I see it.

BELLAMY: So far from *my* harming the lovely songstress, miss, it has deeply wounded me, although it seems somewhat alarmed at my presence.

WILLIAM: I suspect, sir, that the birds in your walks, are generally more scared than hurt.

HARRIET: Wounded you, sir? You speak in riddles.

BELLAMY: Which your looking-glass will easily solve.

HARRIET: I do not understand you, sir. But, William, as you was saying – if the houses in New York are so close together, where do they keep their creatures? – the geese, the calves, and the pigs?

BELLAMY: Permit me to answer that question, if you please, miss; for though I have been but a short time in America, I am just from the city, and flatter myself that I know something about it. [*Aside*] What a charming little *Forest Rose* it is! I must take her under my protection.

HARRIET: Well, sir.

BELLAMY: The geese, you must know, are mostly seen, in term time, flocking round a marble house in the park, where they generally get confoundedly plucked before they are aware of it, in which particular, your little city much resembles my native London. The calves and donkies, are principally found in your Broadway, and in our Bond-Street. As for the other animals you mentioned, the pigs, I believe New York is the only place where they enjoy the freedom of the city.

HARRIET: You spoke of *donkies*, sir; does that mean the same thing as *dandies*?

BELLAMY: [*Aside*] Humph! Not quite so simple as I imagined. Perhaps *you*, sir can answer the lady's question.

WILLIAM: The two words, I believe, are derived from the same *root*. The real genuine dandy, however, is an *imported* animal; and the breed having been crossed in this country, the full-blooded bucks command but a low price in the market at the present time.

BELLAMY: [*Aside*] Ha, ha, ha! Tolerably fair, 'pon honour. Dem me, if the clodhopper hasn't astonish'd *me!*

HARRIET: Well, sir, how are the sheep provided for?

BELLAMY: The sheep! O the clergymen take care of their fleeces, I believe, in both countries, and leave the flock to pick up a living as they can. But, come, my dear, if you are so anxious to become acquainted with the city, place yourself under my protection, and you shall be there tomorrow. You shall, indeed, my dear, 'pon honour.

WILLIAM: [*Aside*] My dear! That's plaguy familiar, though.

HARRIET: [*Aside*] Poor William is getting jealous. Now I have a great mind to tease him a little.

BELLAMY: What say you, sweet girl, to my proposition?

HARRIET: If my father will give his consent.

WILLIAM: And if your father should consent, Harriet, would you go without *me?*

BELLAMY: [*Aside*] So, so! I shall have a rival to contend with, I perceive. I must observe this native.

HARRIET: Go without *you!* Is not one protector enough for any reasonable girl? [*Enter Miller*] O father! I am so glad you have come! I have such a favour to ask of you!

MILLER: You had better go and finish milking; it is time the cows were turned to pasture.

HARRIET: I will go in a moment, sir. But first hear my request. This gentleman, who is all the way from London, and, for aught I know, a prince or a nobleman, has kindly offered to take me to New York with him, free of all expense. Will you give your consent?

BELLAMY: [*Aside*] Her simplicity will ruin all, split me?

MILLER: Take you to New York! What does this mean, sir?

BELLAMY: [*Confused*] O nothing, sir; or merely this: Your daughter expressed a strong desire to see the city; as I happen to be a resident there, common courtesy, you know, would not allow me to do less than make a tender of my services. That is all sir, 'pon honour.

MILLER: [*Sarcastically*] You are very kind, sir.

BELLAMY: Not at all, sir. Pray don't name it. Such a compliment, in my country, is thought nothing of. But excuse me; it is now near breakfast time, and I shall be waited for at the tavern. I will see you again in the course of the day. Good morning. What a cursed bore! I must observe the old Hunks. [*Exit*]

MILLER: Your coquetry, Harriet, displeases me, and evidently distresses William. To be so familiar with a stranger! [*Bellamy returns and listens*]

HARRIET: But, then, you know, father, he is a sportsman, and a foreigner, and dresses so very genteely. [*Looking at William's dress*]

WILLIAM: I understand you, Harriet; and if you are so easily dazzled with outside show – why – consult your own happiness – that's all.

HARRIET: Now, William, you are jealous.

WILLIAM: You will never find a truer friend, however showy he may be.

MILLER: If I thought her in earnest, William, I should regret that you ever bestowed a thought on so worthless an object; for the girl who would reject the honest heart and hand of an American farmer, for a fopling of any country, is not worthy of affection or confidence.

HARRIET: When I thought I loved you, William, I had not seen this handsome Englishman.

BELLAMY: [*Aside*] 'Tis plain enough, the artless creature loves me, and will be mine upon my own terms. Blandford doubts my influence with the sex. I will not astonish him. [*Exit*]

WILLIAM: Very well, Miss Miller. Your father has been a kind guardian to poor Lydia and me ever since we lost our parents, for which I hope we are not ungrateful. I shall be of age next month, and if my farm be small –

MILLER: Spurn her coquetry, William, and not encourage it by such submissive tones. When you have more experience, you will know that it is the vice of her sex to torture those they love. But let me caution you, Harriet, against indulging this dangerous propensity. Learn to restrain it, or you may repent it when it is too late. [*Exit into the cottage*]

WILLIAM: I shall always rejoice to see you happy, Harriet, however much my own heart may ache.

HARRIET: And if ever I am happy, while your heart feels a pang, William, spurn me as a wretch unworthy of your regard.

WILLIAM: Are you in earnest! Now, you have made me so happy, Harriet! That for the English dandy, [*Snapping his fingers*] with his squinter. Ah! 'pon honour – [*Imitating*] But come, old Brindle is waiting to fill your pail, and I am waiting to bring it home for you. She is now making a hearty breakfast on fresh cornstalks.

HARRIET: You run and let down the bars, and I will be with you in a moment. [*Exit William*]

Song – Harriet

The morn awakes, in blushes dress'd,
  The lambs are all at play,
The blackbird quits his dewy nest,
  And carols on the spray;
The milkmaid hails the rosy dawn.
  The shepherd seeks his fleecy flock:
The woods resound to the hunter's horn,
  All roused by the village clock.
Tick! – tick! – tick! – tick! – tick! – tick!
  All roused by the village clock.

The milky herd their stores resign,
  And soon regain the mead,
Where cooling shades and streams combine,
  To cheer them while they feed.
When evening twilight veils the lawn,
  Again the milkmaid trips away,
While woods resound to the distant horn,
  At the closing hour of day.
Tick! tick! – tick! tick! – tick! tick!
  At the closing hour of day.

Scene 2

An apartment in Deacon Forest's house. A door in the centre of the flat. Enter Jonathan, hastily crossing the stage. Sally following him, calling.

SALLY: Jonathan! Jonathan! Stop a moment, till I say one word more.

JONATHAN: [*Returning*] I don't calculate, Sal, that you can say any thing to convince me that I didn't see Tom Clover kiss you last night, in the singing school.

SALLY: Tom Clover kiss *me!* A'nt you ashamed of yourself, Jonathan, to tell such a story?

JONATHAN: It is no story, because it is true. I saw him make believe whisper to you, and then I heard him smack you right on the cheek. There, deny it if you can.

SALLY: Can you swear to it?

JONATHAN: Yes, on the Bible.

SALLY: Then you would perjure yourself; for it was I that smacked him. Ha, ha, ha!

JONATHAN: So much the more shame for you. It is treating me like a brute. I wouldn't serve a negro so.

SALLY: La, Jonathan, what harm is there in a kiss?

JONATHAN: I tell you, there *is* harm in it. After keeping company with me, you hadn't ought to let another man touch you.

SALLY: Then, I am afraid, I should never be touched in my life; for you don't come within an arm's length of me, for fear I should bite you.

JONATHAN: 'Cause you are always playing tricks on me, if I offer any sich thing; but Tom may do what he pleases, and you like him the better for it.

SALLY: Now, Jonathan, didn't I sit on your knee last Sunday evening? Answer me that.

JONATHAN: And, 'cause I happened to get asleep, didn't you get up softly and put the big samp-mortar in your place; and did not your father find me hugging it, when he got up in the morning? Answer me that. I wouldn't serve a negro so.

SALLY: Ha, ha, ha! Now, Jonathan, what difference can it make to a man that is fast asleep, whether he is hugging a girl, or a samp-mortar? But, come, now, let us be friends once more, and I will never do any thing to vex you again.

Enter Rose at the door in the flat, unperceived by Jonathan. Sally directs her, in dumb show, not to advance

JONATHAN: I won't be friends with you, for I see plain enough what your drift is. Every body says you are only running after me 'cause I got a shop. But, I guess, you'll find yourself mistaken, for I know how the cat jumps, and will sooner burn my shop, pack up my duds, and go back to Taunton, to catch herrings for a living.

SALLY: O, Jonathan, now don't be so unforgiving. You know I don't care a fig for any other man. Come – give me a kiss.

JONATHAN: May I, though!

SALLY: Certainly you may. But stay; you are so apt to blush; let me cover your eyes with my shawl, for love, you know is blind as a bat. There, now, step a little this way, because the window is open. [*She places Rose between herself and Jonathan*] Now! I am ready. Give me a good hearty squeeze. [*Jonathan embraces and kisses Rose*]

JONATHAN: Now, that's a dear, sweet, kind, good girl! – Will you always love me so?

ROSE: Yes, Massa Jonathan, me lubber you berry bad.

SALLY: [*Taking the shawl from his eyes*]

There, Jonathan, is not that better than the samp-mortar? Ha, ha, ha!

JONATHAN: Darnation! If I have not been bussing Lid Rose! Now, Sal Forest, that is too bad! I would not serve a negro so. [*Exit Sally*]

ROSE: But you did serve poor negro so, and ax me to lubber you, and now you desert me. [*Exit*]

JONATHAN: Be off with you, garlic chops! Darn me, if ever I speak to Sal Forest again; but will take Granny Gossip's advice, and court Harriet Miller. Whew! how the wench smelt of onions. [*Exit*]

Scene 3

A Wood. Enter Blandford with his gun.

BLANDFORD: I can neither find my companion nor the road which leads to our lodging. No wonder. One subject alone occupies all my thoughts, and I struggle in vain to dissipate the mental abstraction. Cruel, cruel Lydia! to leave me without a single clew to discover her retreat. – Ignorant even of her guardian's name, and place of residence, I vainly wander about these rural scenes, making myself ridiculous by inquiries which none can answer. – O, could I but once more meet her, and find her still the same, these hours of misery should be repaid with years of joy. One smile from thee, my dearest Lydia, would cause this desponding heart to throb again with rapture.

Song – Blandford
A smile from thee would banish pain,
    And bid each doubt and sorrow flee,
I ask but this, once more to gain
        A smile from thee.

I've sought thee long, with fruitless sighs,
    And were my bright reward to be
A tender glance from those soft eyes,
        'Twere heaven to me.

But ah! if doomed no more to meet,
    Whate'er my future fate may be,
This faithful heart, will ever beat,
        With love for thee.

And when I close a life of pain,
    The gloomy hour of death will be,
An hour of bliss, if then I gain
        A tear from thee.

During the Song, enter Jonathan

JONATHAN: That's a darnation queer kind of a tune. I wonder if I could play it on my jew's-harp. Servant, sir. Guess it will rain to-day, don't you?

BLANDFORD: [*Aside*] It is a vain pursuit, and I will return to town.

JONATHAN: [*Aside*] Too darn'd proud to speak to a body in a homespun coat. This must be one of them city chaps that come over here a gunning. I say, mister! Servant, sir.

BLANDFORD: Tell me, my good fellow, how far am I from the Eagle Tavern?

JONATHAN: You don't belong to these parts, I calculate?

BLANDFORD: Of course, I do not. Will you answer my question?

JONATHAN: May be you are from New York? How does buckwheat sell?

BLANDFORD: Will you direct me to Major Butler's, who keeps the stage-house at the sign of the Spread Eagle?

JONATHAN: You an't acquainted with the major, are you? He trades at my shop. If I may be so bold, sir, what may I call your name?

BLANDFORD: Stupid – Pshaw! I will keep my temper.

JONATHAN: Stupid Shaw, 'Spose you an't any ways related to 'Squire Shaw of Taunton, are you? He that married the widow Lovett, mother of Ichabod Lovett, who was tried for horse-stealing?

BLANDFORD: [*Aside*] I must humour this fellow, or find the Eagle Tavern myself. No, sir, I have not the honour of an acquaintance with any member of the family you mention.

JONATHAN: Then, may be, you are related to the Shaws of Hacksensack, here in the Jarseys?

BLANDFORD: Perhaps so – our family is very numerous. But if I may be so bold, sir, what may I call your name? [*Imitating Jonathan's manner*]

JONATHAN: Jonathan Ploughboy, at your service, formerly of Taunton, in the state of Massachusetts.

BLANDFORD: Do you live hereabouts?

JONATHAN: I guess you'd think so, if you saw my name on the shop, down by the bridge.

BLANDFORD: So you are shop-keeper then?

JONATHAN: A little in the marchant way, and a piece of a farmer besides.

BLANDFORD: What do you sell?

JONATHAN: Every thing, whiskey, molasses,

calicoes, spelling-books, and patent gridirons.

BLANDFORD: With which you contrive to shave the natives?

JONATHAN: No sir; every body shaves themselves here. – There is no barber nearer than Paris.

BLANDFORD: You don't understand me. By shaving I mean making a *sharp* bargain; or what your parson or deacon might denominate cheating.

JONATHAN: I wouldn't serve a negro so. But as to the parson or deacon, folks say they are pretty cute that way themselves.

BLANDFORD: Are there any pretty girls in your neighbourhood?

JONATHAN: He, he, he! I guess you'd think so, if you saw Sally Forest, and Harriet Miller.

BLANDFORD: I dare say that your Sallies and your Harriets are very fine girls. But do you know of any one called Lydia?

JONATHAN: Lydia? O, yes; but in the country here we call her Lid. You can see her any time at Deacon Forest's.

BLANDFORD: Her other name?

JONATHAN: Think of the sweetest flower that blows. [*Aside*] Darnation take the garlic, I say.

BLANDFORD: Gracious Heavens! Should it be the same! What is her age, size, complexion? Has she black hair, dark eyes, pouting lips? Describe her person.

JONATHAN: I take her to be about eighteen or nineteen.

BLANDFORD: Just the age. Her size?

JONATHAN: Not very tall nor very slim.

BLANDFORD: It must be she! Her hair and eyes?

JONATHAN: Black, I reckon; but I am not sure.

BLANDFORD: I live again! Her teeth, breath, complexion? There is none like them on earth!

JONATHAN: I don't believe there is! and as for the pouting lips you mentioned, just see her mad once – that's all.

BLANDFORD: Mad!

JONATHAN: Was you ever in Wethersfield?

BLANDFORD: No. Why do you ask?

JONATHAN: Then you know nothing about her breath. – Have you ever seen the ace of spades? That's enough.

BLANDFORD: Of whom are you speaking?

JONATHAN: Lid Rose. Deacon Forest's negro wench. – They call her the black Rose.

BLANDFORD: Confound your stupidity, or shrewdness, I know not which to call it. The sweetest bud of hope has withered in a moment.

JONATHAN: Bud of hope! Darn me, if I don't think she's more like a clove of garlic. But, come, Mr. What-de-call-'em-Stupid Shaw – I will tell you what to do, and if you are wise, you will take a fool's advice. All the girls within half a mile will be at 'Squire Miller's this evening; perhaps your Lydia may be among them. Come along with me, and I will show you the place.

BLANDFORD: I thank you for the offer; but business calls me to my lodgings – the Eagle Tavern.

JONATHAN: Why, that's right on the road.

BLANDFORD: You will not direct me wrong!

JONATHAN: Me! I wouldn't serve a negro so. [*Exeunt*]

Scene 4

The farm yard – and cottage, as in Scene 1. The village clock now indicates 10 minutes before 12, and strikes during the scene. Enter Lydia, from the cottage.

LYDIA: Harriet is absent – all are engaged, and I can now enjoy one moment in contemplating features which are so deeply impressed on my heart. [*Takes a locket from her breast, which she presses to her lips, gazes on it a moment, and then conceals it*] Ah, Charles! Charles! Why did we ever meet! And yet I would not, if I could, forget the past, although I must look to the future without hope.

Song – Lydia
The heart sustained by Hope alone,
The pains of absence may endure,
But ah! when even Hope is flown,
Its sorrow has no cure.
'Tis then we sigh, where'er we roam,
For our maternal, peaceful home.

Though mourning like a mateless dove,
The languid heart be doomed to beat,
It cannot, will not, cease to love,
It finds the pain so sweet.
Yet heaves a sigh, where'er we roam,
For our maternal, peaceful home.
[Exit into the cottage]

Enter Bellamy

BELLAMY: I must have another interview, before I meet the moralizing Blandford. How shall I manage? Old Squaretoes must not suspect; and as for the bumpkin, her lover, he must take his walking-papers. As both are now in the harvest field, the coast must be clear, and this is my time.

Bellamy knocks at the cottage door, which is opened by Lydia. He seizes her in his arms. She screams and attempts to escape. In the struggle a locket falls from her bosom

BELLAMY: Listen to me a moment, sweet girl! I swear to Heaven I love you to distraction, and have no desire but to make you happy. The moment is propitious – fly with me to a scene where wealth and pleasure await you. [*She breaks from him, and enters the cottage*] This is strange! Can her coyness be real? Perhaps my visit is ill-timed. I will swear that she loves me, from what I overheard this morning. Ha! What the devil have we here? [*Takes up the locket*] I see it all, split me! To lull suspicion, she pretends to shun my advances, while she artfully drops a token of affection at my feet. This trophy will convince Blandford that my conquests are not all empty boasts. – Wait patiently till night, my dear, and you shall find I can take a hint. *Love in the dark*, shall be my motto.

Enter Harriet and Jonathan

HARRIET: Well, Jonathan, what is it you wish to tell me?

JONATHAN: Why, Miss Harriet, Granny Gossip and I had a long talk about it last night; and she said how –

HARRIET: She said how! Then what did you say?

JONATHAN: [*Confused*] I said how –

HARRIET: Well? You both said how! What next? Go on.

JONATHAN: Why, darn it! You won't let me tell.

HARRIET: You are so long about it. Don't you know that a smart girl, like me, wants every thing done quick?

JONATHAN: That's just what Granny Gossip said, by the hokey! She told me, says she –

HARRIET: Indeed! Then what did you tell her?

JONATHAN: I said, says I – No; Granny Gossip said, says she – Harriet Miller is the smartest girl in all the county, be the other who she may.

HARRIET: I am very much obliged to the old lady. Then, what did you say?

JONATHAN: I said, says I, so she is; for, says I, she can milk a cow, make a cheese, and boil a pudding, with any girl in the world, says I.

HARRIET: That was certainly very kind of you.

JONATHAN: Wan't it now? Then says she to me, says she, why don't you strike there, instead of running after the deacon's Sal, who don't care three skips of a flea for you, only for your money. Why don't you strike there? says Granny Gossip to me, says she.

HARRIET: Strike! Where?

JONATHAN: Here – you!

HARRIET: Strike me!

JONATHAN: No – no. She meant, why didn't I court you? He, he, he!

HARRIET: O, that alters the case. What reason did you give for not courting me!

JONATHAN: I told her I was afeard. But after talking a good while longer about it, I thought, thinks I to myself, there can be no great harm in axing the question; and if I get the sack, says I, to myself, I shan't be the first that's got it by hundreds.

HARRIET: That is true, Jonathan; and you won't be the last by thousands.

JONATHAN: And so, as you are to have a dance to-night, on account of the harvest, Granny Gossip said I had better come and ax you to be my partner.

HARRIET: The old lady is certainly a very considerate woman.

JONATHAN: Arn't she, now? She always has an eye to the main chance, as she calls it. So she says to me, says she, Harriet Miller has got something to make the pot boil, says she, and the deacon's Sal hasn't got a second *what-d'ye-call-it* to her back. So, if you have no objections, Miss Harriet, I will come to-night, and –

HARRIET: Stay a moment. May I depend upon your intentions being honourable? I hope, sir, that you don't mean to impose upon my youth and inexperience, to win my virgin heart, and then take advantage of my unsuspecting innocence. You do not mean to ruin me! Oh! [*Weeps*]

JONATHAN: Me! Ruin you! I wouldn't serve a negro so. Now, don't take it on so; pray don't.

HARRIET: Ha, ha, ha! Well, I believe I may

trust you. But do you know what to do next?

JONATHAN: No, I don't, but if you will tell me, I am a cute fellow to learn.

HARRIET: You must tell me all about my beautiful eyes, auburn hair, rosy cheeks, pouting lips, and ivory teeth.

JONATHAN: That's just what a fellow said to-day about the deacon's wench.

HARRIET: Then you must drop upon one knee, and swear that you love me better than all the world.

JONATHAN: I never swear, Miss Harriet, nor tell fibs neither, so don't insist upon my going on in that way.

HARRIET: Without swearing then, tell me exactly how much you do love me.

JONATHAN: I-I-I never can talk about love, Miss Harriet, I always stutter, when I try to speak about it.

HARRIET: Sing it, then.

Duett – Jonathan and Harriet

JONATHAN:

*I cannot tell the reason, but I really want a
    wife,*
*And every body tells me 'tis the sweetest thing
    in life;*
*But as for cheeks like roses, with pouting lips,
    and such,*
*I know no more about them, than Ponto does
    of Dutch.*

                    Tol de rol lol, &c.

HARRIET: [*Imitating*]

*If you expect to please me and win me for
    your bride,*
*You'll have to lie and flatter, and swear, my
    lad, beside –*
*So now begin to practice, and if you'd have me
    wed,*
*Declare you even love, sir, the ground on
    which I tread.*

                    Tol de rol lol, &c.

JONATHAN:

*I'll tell you that sincerely, nor think it any
    harm,*
*I love the ground you walk on, for 'tis your fa-
    ther's farm,*
*Could that be mine without you, I'd be a hap-
    py man,*
*But since you go together, I will love you if I
    can.*

                    Tol de rol lol, &c.

HARRIET:

*If I consent to have you, we must reside in
    town,*
*And sport a coach and horses, to travel up and
    down –*
*With footmen all in livery, to make a splendid
    show,*
*And when you don't attend me, I will get an-
    other beau.*

                    Tol de rol lol, &c.

JONATHAN:

If that's your calculation, we never can agree,
*For such a mode of living will never do for
    me –*
*And as for beaux and lovers, though you may
    like the fun,*
*I guess the deacon's Sally, will be content with
    one.*

                    Tol de rol lol, &c.

HARRIET:

        O, then, you do not love me!

JONATHAN:

            I never said I would!

HARRIET:

        Did you not swear this moment?

JONATHAN:

            To love you if I could.

HARRIET:

*Go take the deacon's Sally, in her linsey wool-
    sey gown.*

JONATHAN:

*I guess as how I'd better, for I will not live in
    town.*

                    Tol de rol lol, &c.

Clock strikes 12

HARRIET: Go, then, false-hearted man! and never speak to me again!

JONATHAN: Mayn't I come to the harvest bee to-night?

HARRIET: No – you shan't! So there!

JONATHAN: Then I'll have a little bit of a hop now, for here comes the stalk-cutters, and the apple-pickers, and the cider-grinders, and all the rest of them, to dinner.

*Enter Miller, William, farmers, lads, lasses &c.
then Lydia from the cottage*

MILLER: How soon will dinner be ready?

LYDIA: In a quarter of an hour, sir.

MILLER: In the mean time, we will rest ourselves in the shade of these venerable elms. Now the rest of you may amuse yourselves as you please.

1ST FARMER: I am for a song.

2ND FARMER: And I for a dance.

MILLER: Let us have both, then. Come, Harriet, you begin.

Finale, to Act I

Air – Harriet
Sweet the hour, when freed from labour,
    Lads and lasses thus convene,
To the merry pipe and tabor,
    Dancing gayly on the green.

Nymphs, with all their native graces,
    Swains with every charm to win,
Sprightly steps, and smiling faces,
    Tell of happy hearts within.

Chorus
Sweet the hour, when freed from labour, &c.

Air – William
Blest with plenty, here the farmer
    Toils for those he loves alone;
While some pretty smiling charmer,
    Like the land, is all his own.

Chorus
Sweet the hour, when freed from labour, &c.

Air – Lydia
Though a tear for prospects blighted,
    May, at times, unbidden flow,
Yet the heart will bound delighted,
    Where such kindred bosoms glow.

Chorus
Sweet the hour, when freed from labour, &c.

Air – Jonathan
What though, by my shilly shally,
    I have got the sack, you know,
Darn it, there's the deacon's Sally,
    Wouldn't serve a negro so.

Chorus
Sweet the hour, when freed from labour, &c.

JONATHAN: Now for the dance. Where's little Caesar with his fiddle? He's the boy for a jig.

Enter Caesar, from the cottage

That's you my little blackey. Come – tune up; and I will accompany you upon the jew's-harp.

Caesar plays, and a dance finishes the act

End of Act I

ACT II. Scene 1

An apartment in the Eagle Tavern. Enter Blandford and Waiter.

BLANDFORD: Has Mr. Bellamy returned?

WAITER: No, sir.

BLANDFORD: The moment he comes, tell him I wish to speak with him.

WAITER: Yes, sir. [*Exit Waiter*]

BLANDFORD: Where can he linger? [*Musing*] Yes, I will return to town, and once more try if business will not drive away the sad reflections which pleasure cannot dissipate. And yet I know the attempt will be vain; for there is but one charm that can ever restore peace to this harassed bosom, and that is the smile of affection from her I adore.

Song – Blandford
Is there a light whose effulgence can dry
    The tear of affliction, and rapture restore?
'Tis the bright sunny ray of a love-beaming eye,
    The smile of affection from one we adore.

I'd sigh not for grandeur, for fame, or for wealth,
    But thankful for little, would wish for no more;
If blest with contentment, with friendship and health,
    And the smile of affection from one I adore.

Enter Bellamy

BELLAMY: Still in the dumps, Charles! Cheer up, man, and "thread the thicket," as I do. There's plenty of game, my dear fellow, there is indeed. [*Playing with the locket, which is now suspended to his neck*]

BLANDFORD: You are in spirits, I perceive.

BELLAMY: To be sure I am, and I have reason to be; for [*Sings*]

    "There's nothing half so sweet in life,
    As Love's young dream."

BLANDFORD: Are you ready to return to town?

BELLAMY: To town! Are you mad, Charles? We are just beginning to enjoy ourselves. Don't think of returning this month.

BLANDFORD: I shall go immediately.

BELLAMY: I am very sorry that I can't have the pleasure of accompanying you; but I shall soon follow, with one of the sweetest little *Forest Roses* that ever graced a sportsman's bosom. True, 'pon honour.

BLANDFORD: A Forest Rose?

BELLAMY: Ay, man! Blushing like Innocence, and smiling like Venus. A woman, you sly one, or rather an angel in petticoats.

BLANDFORD: An acquaintance?

BELLAMY: Of a very short standing, for I saw her for the first time this morning, and then only for about ten minutes. – But she loves me, and in her artless simplicity confessed it. That is enough for my purpose, you know.

BLANDFORD: And has consented to accompany you to town?

BELLAMY: Begged me to take her. She did, indeed.

BLANDFORD: And how is she to be situated there? What arrangement have you made for the future?

BELLAMY: O, you must know, I seldom concern myself about the future; but let that take care of itself. Though I think, on the present occasion, that I can speak with safety, if I say, that, (provided I do not change my mind,) I shall keep her a month.

BLANDFORD: A month, Bellamy!

BELLAMY: Aye, a whole month; I shall, 'pon honour. So, after this, reproach me no more with fickleness and inconstancy. Why, in London, we change them once a fortnight; we do, indeed.

BLANDFORD: And how will you provide for her then?

BELLAMY: How provide for her? Set her up in a soda-water shop, or something of that kind. The thing is done every day, on both sides the Atlantic. It is, indeed.

BLANDFORD: And can you so calmly, so unfeelingly, and with so much self-complacency, meditate the ruin of an artless girl, and the consequent misery of every one to whom she is dear? I can pity the errors of a fashionable education; but I feel a different sentiment towards a wilful, deliberate act of perfidy.

BELLAMY: Moralizing again! I say, Charles, it is a devilish pity that you are not a parson; your preaching goes so directly to the heart. It does, indeed, my dear fellow.

BLANDFORD: Would to heaven it did. But, pshaw! This is another of your empty boasts; and I can forgive all your imaginary sins Edward, numerous as they are.

BELLAMY: You may judge for yourself, Charles, whether this be an empty boast, or an imaginary sin. When a lover wears a lady's favour in his bosom, it generally means something. Look at this, and convince yourself. [*Displays the locket*]

BLANDFORD: [*Aside*] Gracious Heaven! It is – it is the very trinket which she vowed to wear for ever for my sake! Where is she? lead me to her instantly!

BELLAMY: Excuse me, Charles; I shall not consider it friendly in you to interfere in this affair; and must, therefore, decline giving you an introduction.

BLANDFORD: Interfere! Grant me patience, heaven! Do you say – dare you swear – that – that – that – *she* consented? No – it is impossible!

BELLAMY: What the devil is the matter with you, Charles?

BLANDFORD: Matter! Can she – Oh, can she thus have fallen! She who was all modesty – diffidence – chastity! It cannot be. The sensitive plant would not shrink more instinctively from the touch, than she from the thought of such a proposition. The thing is impossible. That locket has been lost, and you found it, Bellamy.

BELLAMY: I say, Waiter! Go call a justice of the peace, and I will immediately swear that the lovely wearer of this trinket was in my arms today.

BLANDFORD: Then is she lost indeed!

BELLAMY: Do you know the fair Harriet?

BLANDFORD: Harriet! No, I know nothing of any Harriet. But I did know the angelic Lydia Roseville, who promised to preserve and wear this locket next her heart, for the sake of the giver. Look at it again.

BELLAMY: The initials C.B. and L.R. in your own hair, are sufficient evidence of its having been your property. But how came it in possession of this milkmaid?

BLANDFORD: That is what I am impatient to learn. Show me where she lives; it may lead to a discovery of the utmost importance to the happiness of your friend.

BELLAMY: Then this will be the pleasantest intrigue in which I was ever engaged, as I may at once restore to you a lost mistress, and provide myself with a new one. Come along, and I will soon show you my little Forest Rose. I will, indeed. [*Exeunt*]

Scene 2

The farm-yard and cottage as before. The Village clock now indicates a quarter past 4 o'clock in the afternoon. Enter William and Harriet from the cottage.

HARRIET: Where did you leave your sister?

WILLIAM: In the orchard, conversing with Dobson, who has just arrived from Goshen with all the documents respecting my father's estate, and is ready to put us in possession immediately. O, Harriet, you will be delighted with the situation.

HARRIET: How do you know that I will ever see it?

WILLIAM: Because it shall be yours, or I will never see it again.

HARRIET: Well, I will think of it, while you return to the orchard, and tell Lydia I wish to speak with her. Go – that's a good fellow.

WILLIAM: Will you remain here?

HARRIET: To be sure I will. Are you afraid that some magician will bear me off to his enchanted castle?

WILLIAM: No – but that English dandy is in the next field; and I thought you would not like to be left alone.

HARRIET: Go along, you jealous fellow! [*Exit William*] I wonder if the old saying be true, that love and jealousy always go together? I think I should be convinced, if I saw William very particular to another girl.

Song – Harriet
When infant Cupid ventured first
   To spread his purple wing,
It chanced he stopp'd, to slake his thirst,
   At the Pierian spring;
When, rising from the crystal stream,
   A monster caught his eye,
Poor Cupid started with a scream,
   But strove in vain to fly.

To slay the little winged boy,
   The daemon vainly strove,
His fangs could wound, but not destroy
   The son of peerless Jove.
He follows still – (they never part)
   But vainly vents his ire,
Though jealous tortures wring the heart,
   Yet ne'er can love expire.

Enter Blandford and Bellamy

BELLAMY: [*Apart*] That is she, Charles. Is she not an angel?

BLANDFORD: I shall think so, if she furnishes me with a clew to find Lydia.

BELLAMY: Stay, lovely girl, one moment, until I apologise for the alarm which my ill-timed proposal must have given you, when this locket came into my possession.

HARRIET: I do not understand you, sir.

BELLAMY: [*Apart to Blandford*] You see how it is, Charles; the sly thing won't confess before you. I say, my dear, say what you please before this gentleman. He is our mutual friend, I assure you. He is indeed, my love, and will assist us to deceive old Squaretoes.

HARRIET: I am still at fault, as you sportsmen would say; just as I was this morning respecting a bird of paradise.

BELLAMY: You see, Charles; she pretends to know nothing about me. You had better retire, and leave us alone. *You* had, indeed.

BLANDFORD: Pardon me, Miss Miller; (for that I understand, is your name,) – Pray inform me, if you have not, this morning, lost a trinket – a locket?

HARRIET: I have not, sir. I never owned one, or had one in my possession.

BELLAMY: [*Aside*] Never! – Split me! but she plays her part divinely. She does, indeed.

HARRIET: Never. Do you doubt my word?

BLANDFORD: Do not be offended Miss Miller. I am particularly interested in this inquiry.

BELLAMY: You need be under no restraint on this subject, as no one is present but ourselves. My friend is in my confidence, and may be trusted; he is acquainted with every circumstance. He is, indeed, my dear.

HARRIET: Then he has the advantage of me, sir; for I am totally ignorant of any circumstance connected with the subject of your inquiry.

BLANDFORD: Perhaps, Miss Miller, in the alarm which this gentleman's sudden appearance gave you – being alone.

HARRIET: You labour under a mistake, sir. His appearance was not sudden – neither was I alone; nor did I feel alarmed. Did I appear frightened, sir, when I was asking you about dandies, and donkeys, and calves? Ha, ha, ha!

BELLAMY: My friend alludes to our second interview. [*Aside*] No city belle could perform better.

HARRIET: This is our second interview; for I have not seen you since you took so hasty a leave of my father this morning.

BELLAMY: Not when you opened the door to see who knocked? I hope, however, that you will excuse that act of apparent rudeness, when you recollect that I am yet almost a stranger to the manners and customs of this country, being but recently imported.

HARRIET: Then I forgive you every thing, in consideration of the benefit you have done our revenue; for a heavy duty, I am told, is paid on all articles the principal ingredient of which is brass.

BELLAMY: She is only throwing dust in your eyes, Charles. She is indeed, 'pon honour.

Enter William and Jonathan

JONATHAN: Darn it, Bill! if there isn't the very fellow that ax'd me so many questions about Lid Rose.

WILLIAM: The other is the English dandy I was telling you about. See! He is honouring us with a squint through his quizzer.

HARRIET: Have you any more questions to ask, gentlemen.

BELLAMY: [*Apart to Blandford*] She is now throwing dust in the eyes of her rustic lover there.

BLANDFORD: To come to the point at once, Miss Miller, do you, or do you not, know the owner of this trinket?

HARRIET: I do not indeed, sir. I never saw it before.

BELLAMY: [*Aside*] Her assurance is truly astonishing. It is, indeed.

JONATHAN: Nor I neither, if I did darn me! There's a C. for cows; and B. for bulls; and L. for lambs; and R. for rams. What a curious thing it is!

BELLAMY: [*Surveying Jonathan*] Split me! but here's a clodhopper that knows his letters. Been to Sunday-school I suppose. A real abo-

riginal, 'pon honour. Wonder where he was caught.

BLANDFORD: Let me entreat you, madam, if a glow of compassion ever warmed your bosom, to tell me how this locket came into your possession?

HARRIET: Into my possession, sir! Have I not solemnly assured you that I never saw it before!

BLANDFORD: Nor this?

[*Presses a spring which opens the locket, and exhibits a miniature*]

HARRIET: No, sir. But I perceive that it is a very striking likeness of yourself.

BLANDFORD: Then, Bellamy, I *demand* an explanation of you.

BELLAMY: Upon my honour, Charles, I have told you all I know upon the subject. I found that trinket, this morning, in the manner I described, and if it did not fall from this lady's bosom, it must have dropped from the moon. It must, indeed.

JONATHAN: I would as soon believe the moon was made of green cheese.

WILLIAM: It is, certainly, very singular! How can you account for it, Harriet?

HARRIET: Indeed, I don't know.

BLANDFORD: She must be in this neighbourhood, and by heaven, I will find her, if I have to search every house in the county. I will neither taste of food, nor sleep until I call her mine, or ascertain that she has ceased to love me. [*Exit*]

BELLAMY: Stay, Charles, one moment.

JONATHAN: Poor fellow! He is a little crack'd I calculate. [*William and Harriet confer apart*]

BELLAMY: You *calculate*, do you, sir?

JONATHAN: I guess I do, a little, in the way of trade.

BELLAMY: And might one calculate on your assistance and fidelity, in an affair of importance?

JONATHAN: I take it he can, if he pays me well.

BELLAMY: In that respect you shall be fully satisfied. You shall, indeed. Step this way, and I will explain. [*They retire up the stage*]

Enter Lydia

HARRIET: O my dear, you know not what a treat you have lost, by being absent for the last quarter of an hour. But I suppose you have been chaunting your favourite ditty. [*Sings*]

Though mourning like a mateless dove.

LYDIA: Nay, Harriet, you know not what a treat I have enjoyed, by being absent; and you cannot know, until you have, like me, been for five years absent from your paternal home.

HARRIET: But I can guess. You have seen Dobson!

LYDIA: Yes – and have strayed with him, in imagination, through every corner of our little farm. Every thing, William, is pretty much as it used to be, when we lived at home, and were so happy. Even the old cider-mill, is in being yet, and the cool dairy-house, by the side of the well. You recollect them well, William?

WILLIAM: What is there about the old place, that I do not recollect Lydia? The mill-pond, the little waterfall, the meadow, the orchard, the well, and even the old bucket, out of which I so often drank.

Song – William

Believe me, if there's aught on earth,
That can each grief disarm,
'Tis the sweet spot which gave me birth,
When smiling Memory paints its worth,
It is my father's farm.
For every native rural charm
Adorns my father's farm.

Though Fancy's flight may mock the blast,
To seek some distant charm,
How soon her eyes are homeward cast,
She roves awhile, but lights, at last,
Upon my father's farm.
For every native rural charm
Adorns my father's farm.

During the song, Bellamy is seen conferring with Jonathan, and finally gives him a purse, which the latter accepts reluctantly. Bellamy then gazes a moment at Lydia, appears to ask Jonathan some questions respecting her, and on receiving his answer, retires precipitately. Jonathan examines the contents of the purse, puts it in his pocket, and advances, just as the song is concluded

WILLIAM: How now, Jonathan! What have you done with the dandy?

JONATHAN: Darn me, Bill, if that fellow an't a little crack'd too.

WILLIAM: Not about the middle I hope; or he will certainly break off.

HARRIET: [*In reply to Lydia*] Yes – and would insist upon it that I was the owner, as one of them said he found it here, by our door.

LYDIA: A locket! [*Feeling in her bosom*]

HARRIET: Yes; containing a miniature likeness of the other gentleman. [*Lydia shrieks, and rushes into the cottage*]

JONATHAN: I'll be darn'd if she an't a little crack'd too.

HARRIET: Lydia! Lydia! What is the matter? [*Runs after her*]

JONATHAN: She's crack'd too, by Hokey!

WILLIAM: Good day, Jonathan. [*Exit into the cottage*]

JONATHAN: That's very pretty manners, to be sure! Darn me if they an't all crack'd. I wouldn't serve a negro so. Now darn me if I tell him a word about what's going on 'twixt me and the dandy. He may cut him out in welcome, shut the door in my face! I wouldn't serve a negro so. [*Exit*]

Scene 3

A wood. Enter Blandford.

BLANDFORD: Involved in the mazes of this intricate forest, every step increases my perplexity, and adds to my fatigue. I must rest awhile upon this bank. [*Throws himself down*] Fool that I am, to engage in such a wild-goose chase. I shall never see her more. This trinket, however, will be dear to me, for she once wore it near her heart: it once rested on that pure bosom which I would rather press, than possess the Indies. [*Kisses the locket, and lays it down on the bank; then takes a miniature from his bosom*] But here is her own sweet countenance. Those lips appear to move. Those eyes! How could the artist do them justice, when their sweet gaze was fixed on him? [*He rises and comes forward*]

Song – Blandford

That tranquil brow, and pensive eye,
Those parted lips of ruby die;
Each grace that life and reason give,
Is kindling here, and seems to live!
A playful smile illumes the cheek!
Those rubies move! 'Twill speak! 'Twill speak!

'Twas fancy all! That senseless bone,
Could ne'er be taught her dulcet tone;
No art can teach that eye to move,
Those ruby lips are dead to love.

Illusive dream! – too soon it flies,
The vision fades! it dies! it dies!

[*Report of a gun*]

BLANDFORD: That must be Bellamy's piece. So, ho! ho! Halloo! Bellamy! Halloo! Halloo!

Exit, and is heard shouting behind the scenes

Enter Jonathan

JONATHAN: I don't calculate I feel exactly right about keeping this purse; and yet, I believe, I should feel still worse to give it back. Twenty-three dollars is a speculation that an't to be sneezed at, for it an't to be catch'd every day. But will it be right to keep the money, when I don't intend to do the job? Now if I was at home, in Taunton, I would put that question to our debating society; and I would support the affirmative side of the question. "Mr. Chairman! Hem! If A. gives B. a sum of money to do an unlawful act; and if A. – no, if B., instead of doing that wicked act, exposes A., then B. prevents a crime, and deserves a reward; while A., having intended, with malice aforethought, to do a wicked action, is justly punished; and that, Mr. Chairman, which punishes the aggressor, ought to reward the – the – the informer." No – stop, I don't like that word *informer*. "That, Mr. Chairman which punishes – [*Sees the locket on the bank*] – may I be darn'd now, if old Nick ha'nt baited another hook for my honesty. Here's the very thing that has made all the fuss. By the hokey! wouldn't Sal Forest cut a dash with this dangling at her neck. She may as well keep it till we find the owner, and get the reward. Now some folks would keep it, out and out. I wouldn't serve a negro so. [*Exit*]

Scene 4

An apartment in Deacon Forest's house. Enter Jonathan and Sally.

JONATHAN: Now, darn it, what's the use of plaguing a body so? Why cannot you say yes, at once?

SALLY: Because I don't mean to say "yes" at all. I won't dance with any fellow Jack-at-a-pinch. You couldn't get Harriet Miller, and I think myself as good as her, any day, if her father is a 'Squire. Besides, there is Tom Clover –

JONATHAN: Darn Tom Clover! So you won't go along with me, hey!

SALLY: No, I won't.

JONATHAN: Very well, Miss Sally. I calculate that I can find a girl that will go with me, and then we shall see which of the company will display the prettiest locket. [*Showing it*]

SALLY: O Jonathan! What is that? Let me see it! Whose is it?

JONATHAN: It is for my partner to wear at the dance, this evening.

SALLY: Is it, though? Well then, let's have it.

JONATHAN: Let *you* have it! Catch me that fellow. Just now I wan't good enough for you!

SALLY: Pshaw! You know, Jonathan, that I was only jesting. I never intended to dance with any one but you. Now, dear, good Jonathan, give me a sweet kiss, and let us be friends again.

JONATHAN: No – no. That cock won't fight, Sal. Remember the samp-mortar, and Lid Rose. I will take no girl Jack-at-a-pinch. Tom Clover won't have you, and I think myself as good as him, any day, though his father is a doctor.

SALLY: Go then, you cruel, unfeeling monster, and see if I don't make you smart for your falsehood and villainy! I will sue you for a breach of promise, so I will; for reputation; for keeping me in suspense; and see what will become of your shop, then, when I recover nine thousand dollars, which is the price every where. You know it is, you dear deceiver! Oh! Oh! [*Weeps*]

JONATHAN: Oh! Sally! now don't take on so, and I'll do any thing for you in the world.

SALLY: Ha, ha, ha! You will? Well, come now, what will you do?

JONATHAN: I'll marry you to-night, if you say so, and never speak to another girl again, only in the way of trade, when they come to the shop after molasses, and such like. Come Sally. Don't be cross, and here's something to buy you a wedding-dress. [*Shows the purse*]

SALLY: O what a beautiful purse that is! Where did you get it?

JONATHAN: If you like the outside so well, what do you think of the lining? – [*Puts the money into her hand*] – There's five guineas, and as many half dollars.

SALLY: Now you are a dear good Jonathan. Where upon earth did you get guineas, though?

JONATHAN: I will tell you, Sally, and then take your advice upon the subject. Sally, what do you think! I have promised to act like a damn'd scoundrel for that money.

SALLY: Then take it back, and restore it to the scoundrel who gave it you. Jonathan, you wouldn't keep such a promise as that, would you?

JONATHAN: Me! no! Sally, I wouldn't serve a negro so. But cannot you contrive some method by which I can keep the purse, instead of the promise?

SALLY: Who gave it to you?

JONATHAN: A white-gilled, baby-faced fellow from New York, who wants to cut out Bill Roseville, and take Harriet Miller off to the city.

SALLY: And what was you to do in such an affair?

JONATHAN: Only to decoy her into some private place, where two men were to wait for her, and conduct her to the sloop which is lying at the landing. He said Harriet was very anxious to go; but did not want to let her friends know any thing about it.

SALLY: What a scape-gallows wretch it must be! to tell you such a lie! I know Harriet Miller better, and will instantly run to put her on her guard.

JONATHAN: Then I must return the purse, you know. You are always ready enough to play tricks on me; now can't you contrive some method to quiz the dandy, and yet make him believe that I tried to do all I promised? Then you know, we can keep the purse with a good conscience.

SALLY: Let me see. We cannot deceive him with the samp-mortar instead of Harriet.

JONATHAN: Darn the samp-mortar!

SALLY: I have it. Ha, ha, ha! That will do.

JONATHAN: What is it?

SALLY: No matter. Go and tell your employer that Harriet has consented to accompany him on board the sloop, and that while the dances are going on this evening, she and you will slip away, and run to the willow-grove, where he must be in waiting for her. Tell him, also, that in order to prevent her being recognized by any one, she insists upon being closely veiled and perfectly silent, until she is safe on board the vessel, and beyond the danger of pursuit. Leave the rest to me.

JONATHAN: Why, what do you calculate to do, Sally?

SALLY: Perhaps I calculate to take Harriet's place and pay a visit to the city myself.

JONATHAN: What! with that fellow!

SALLY: Think what a chance there would be for you to immortalize yourself, Jonathan. Just as the ravisher had seized me in his arms, and was rifling these virgin lips of their nectareous sweets, a blow from my lover's hand lays him prostrate in the dust. O wouldn't that be delightful!

JONATHAN: So it would by the hokey. But would it be right to knock a man down who has given me thirty-five dollars?

SALLY: Not unless you value me at more than thirty-five dollars. But make haste, and do as I have told you. There is no time to be lost. Now you won't deceive me?

JONATHAN: Me! I wouldn't serve a negro so. [*Exeunt opposite*]

Scene 5

The farm-yard, cottage, and arbour of grape-vines. The village clock now indicates 20 minutes past seven in the evening. Enter Lydia and Harriet.

LYDIA: No, Harriet, it is better we should never meet again. Why does he seek me? And in company too, with that libertine wretch! He knows that I cannot be his; for I will never subject myself to the scorn and insults of his purse-proud family.

HARRIET: Do not make any rash promises. As to his family, some change may have taken place. At any rate, be composed, and prepared for the interview. I'll wage you a pair of gloves, now, that here comes a message from him, by the waiter of the Eagle tavern.

Enter Waiter

WAITER: I am directed, Miss Roseville, to deliver this into your own hand. The writer will come himself for an answer. [*Exit Waiter*]

HARRIET: There, didn't I tell you so? [*Lydia reads it*] I know by your looks that some happy change has taken place. Is it not so?

LYDIA: Read it yourself, my friend, and take no notice of these foolish tears.

HARRIET: [*Reads*] "My dearest, long-sought Lydia! After months of fruitless search, and heart-felt agony, accident has at length discovered to me your residence. I send this to prepare you for an interview, if you will have the goodness to grant one. There now exists no impediment to our public union, if your heart remains unaltered. My high-minded father now sleeps in the dust. He was an Englishman, you know, and that will account for his only foible, which was family pride. My mother and sister ardently desire to embrace you; and the aunt, whose affection you had some reason to doubt, is left dependent on my bounty. If Lydia is unchanged, happiness awaits us both. Your devoted   CHARLES."

HARRIET: Now is it better that you should never meet again?

LYDIA: I will confess, Harriet, that new and delicious hopes have arisen in my bosom. Let me retire awhile; and, when he comes, tell him –

HARRIET: That you are now ready to love, honour, and obey.

LYDIA: Nay, Harriet; do not trifle with my feelings. Tell him that –

HARRIET: There – go in and compose yourself. I know what to tell him. Be quick – change – presto, begone! for here he comes. [*Exit Lydia*]

Enter Blandford

BLANDFORD: Where is she? Where is –

HARRIET: Good evening, sir.

BLANDFORD: Pardon my want of courtesy, madam; but I am impatient to find –

HARRIET: Another owner of that unfortunate locket?

BLANDFORD: Rather, let me say, that *fortunate* locket. But O, in pity lead me to her.

HARRIET: To *her!* to whom? You must know, Sir, that I have thought better of it, and believe it is best to confess that I – I am – the owner of that trinket.

BLANDFORD: Nay, nay, Miss Miller. Where is your friend, Miss Roseville – my long sought, long adored Lydia – where is she?

HARRIET: Be patient, sir. She is, at present, invisible, and I alone possess the art of conjuring her before you.

BLANDFORD: Let me conjure, you, then, sweet magician, to exercise it quickly, or else teach me the charm.

HARRIET: Well, attend; and sing after me:

Though mourning like a mateless dove,

BLANDFORD:

The languid heart be doom'd to beat,

LYDIA [*In cottage*]:

It cannot, will not cease to love,
It finds the pain so sweet.

HARRIET: Open Sesame! There, enter the magic cavern, and possess the treasure. [*Exit Blandford into the cottage*]

Enter Sally

SALLY: O Miss Miller, I have prepared such a treat for you in the little willow grove! You must come and enjoy it.

HARRIET: What is it, Sally?

SALLY: I won't tell you, for that would spoil it all. But come, get your hat and veil, and go along with me, and see for yourself. It is something that will please you.

HARRIET: Well, I suppose that I must humour you. [*Goes into the cottage, and returns with a hat and veil*] I cannot be gone a moment, for it is now sundown, and the company will soon be here.

SALLY: My entertainment shall not detain you long. Come. [*Exeunt*]

Enter Miller, Blandford, William and Lydia

BLANDFORD: Believe me, sir, the transport of this moment is a rich recompense for the months of misery I have endured. Where is your friend, Harriet, my love?

LYDIA: We left her here but now.

MILLER: O she is not far off, I warrant you. William, here, will find her directly. He is never at fault in such a pursuit.

Enter upstage, youthful villagers, of both sexes, followed by Jonathan and Sally

JONATHAN: I'll be darn'd, now, if there ben't the very crack'd-brain'd fellow that lost the locket. What shall we do, Sally?

SALLY: We must make the best of it, Jonathan.

JONATHAN: Well, I guess I am 'cute enough to do that in the way of trade. I say, Mister, you han't lost nothing nowhere, have you?

BLANDFORD: Yes, the trinket you saw me have to-day. A locket.

JONATHAN: Not that curious thing with C. for cows; and B. for bulls; and L. for lambs; and R. for rams?

BLANDFORD: The same. Have you found it!

JONATHAN: What will you give the finder, and no questions ax'd?

BLANDFORD: A generous reward. Where is it?

JONATHAN: There, on Sal Forest's neck; and all the reward I ax is the privilege of her wearing it this evening.

BLANDFORD: What say you, Lydia? It is your property.

LYDIA: Let her wear it by all means; and to-morrow I will redeem it with what will purchase Sally a wedding-dress.

SALLY: Thank you, ma'am. Now, Jonathan, to the willow grove. [*Exeunt Jonathan and Sally*]

MILLER: And now, as there is not a sad countenance present, let the sports commence. Find Harriet, William, and let us have a dance. [*Exit William*]

The characters form a rural dance, which continues some time, when it is suddenly interrupted by a violent shriek from without. Sally rushes in and exclaims —

SALLY: Run! Fly! Save Harriet Miller! or she will be lost forever!

OMNES: Harriet Miller! Where is she?

SALLY: There! There! in the willow grove, yonder! Some wretches are attempting to carry her off by force!

MILLER: Follow me! [*Exit Miller, followed by the others*]

SALLY: [*Whispers to Lydia, who remains*]

Enter Jonathan

JONATHAN: Here they come with their prisoner — the very fellow that was here this morning.

Enter Miller and William, dragging in Bellamy, followed by Rose, closely veiled, Blandford, and all the rest

BLANDFORD: From this moment, Bellamy, our acquaintance terminates. I hope you are not alarmed, my love?

LYDIA: [*Whispers to Blandford*] Not in the least.

MILLER: What have you to say, sir, in palliation of so base an attempt! What blacker crime is there in the whole catalogue of human depravity, than to force an artless, innocent girl from the home of her infancy, and the arms of doting parents in order to initiate her into a life of vice and infamy?

WILLIAM: How can you answer this outrage to me, sir, knowing, as you did, in what relation I stood to the intended victim of your depravity?

SALLY: How can you answer it to me, sir? She is my particular friend?

JONATHAN: Or to me, sir? She is a customer to my shop, and I consider it a very *black* affair.

BELLAMY: Go on, ladies and gentlemen. Have you all done? Then I will condescend to explain. I have committed *no* outrage; but appeal to this sweet, trembling girl, if she did not voluntarily put herself under my protection. Speak, lovely creature, and do me justice. Did you not willingly consent to accompany me to New York? [*Rose bows her head in token of assent*]

MILLER: How! Harriet! Speak, and explain this mystery! Did you consent to abandon us all, and follow this foreign adventurer? — this libertine in principle and practice?

Rose nods assent

WILLIAM: And leave *me*, too, Harriet?

Rose nods assent

BELLAMY: This lady is doubtless her own mistress; and since she prefers me to you, sir, I cannot see by what right you seek to control her actions. Permit me to remove this veil, lovely girl, that they may all see on whom you look with the eye of affection.

ROSE: [*Throwing aside the veil*] On you, Massa Bellamy; cause you kissee me so sweet, in the grove, just now.

OMNES: Lid Rose! Ha! ha! ha!

BLANDFORD: This, then, is the Forest *Rose*, that was to grace a sportsman's bosom. Ha! ha! ha! Love in the *dark!* Hey Bellamy? Ha! ha! ha!

BELLAMY: [*Looking at Rose through his glass*] A damn black affair, sure enough. The bumpkin is right.

MILLER: Ha! ha! ha! But where is Harriet?

Enter Harriet, from arbour

HARRIET: Here she is, safe and sound. What, William, were you jealous again?

WILLIAM: Forgive me, Harriet.

MILLER: Let us all forgive and forget; and to prevent any further jealousies, William, there, take my daughter; and may you both be as happy as you deserve. As for you, Mr. Bellamy, let your present mortification teach you never again to endanger the happiness of an affectionate family for the gratification of a selfish passion.

BELLAMY: Old Squaretoes turned preacher, too, split me! I say, Charles, I give you joy of your rustic alliance. I shall return to town immediately, and quit the country of savages in the – packet which sails the – ; I shall, indeed; but I will not fail to notice you all when I publish my Three Months in America.

WILLIAM: And don't forget to notice the beauty and fragrance of our black roses! Ha! ha! ha!

BELLAMY: Fragrance, you creature! Strike me, exquisite, if all Roussell's perfume would annihilate the cloud of odours with which that caricature upon humanity has impregnated my glove. [*Exit*]

JONATHAN: How d'ye like onions?

MILLER: Now resume your amusements until the harvest-supper be served up, and remember that while we are lords of the luxuriant soil which feeds us, there is no lot on earth more enviable than that of AMERICAN FARMERS.

Finale

Any of the following Stanzas may be omitted, at the discretion of the Manager

MILLER:
And now relieved from day's turmoil,
  Let festive pleasures fill each breast,
And no intruding sorrows spoil,
  The song or mirthful jest.
For lords of the soil, and fed by our toil,
  American farmers are blest my boys,
  American farmers are blest.

CHORUS:
  For lords of the soil, &c.

LYDIA:
Ye fair, who seek a splendid lot,
  Behold content, a richer prize,
Within the humblest ploughman's cot,
  That rank and pride despise.
And palace or cot, whatever your lot,
  The farmer your table supplies, my dear
  The farmer your table supplies.

CHORUS:
  For lords of the soil, &c.

BLANDFORD:
Whate'er the charms of mead or grove,
  In nature's sweetest verdure drest,
Of all the flowers that bloom, I love
  The Forest Rose the best.
And husbandmen now, as they follow the plough,
  Will call it the pride of the west, my boys,
  Will call it the pride of the west.

CHORUS:
  For lords of the soil, &c.

HARRIET:
Ye, fair, who sigh for wedded life,
  No more your lovers' peace molest,
Nor sow the seeds of future strife,
  Within an honest breast;
Or, when you're a wife, I'll bet you my life,
  He'll make you repent of the jest, my dear,
  He'll make you repent of the jest.

CHORUS:
  For lords of the soil, &c.

WILLIAM:
If some gay rival gain a smile
  From her who holds your plighted vow,
Whatever pangs you feel the while,
  Let smiles adorn your brow;
For nought can annoy a husbandman's joy,
  If Heaven but prosper the plough, my boys,
  If Heaven but prosper the plough.

CHORUS:
  For lords of the soil, &c.

SALLY:
Ye lasses, of some rustic chap,
  A sheepish, awkward thing at best,
With wealth your tender heart entrap,
  And seek to be carest –
Just place on his knee, a big mortar you see,
  His fancy will furnish the rest, my dear
  His fancy will furnish the rest.

CHORUS:
  For lords of the soil, &c.

JONATHAN:
By girls we may be thus cajoled,
  But not by any dandy blade:
A Yankee's honour can't be sold,
  Whatever price be paid.

But tempters are told, as we pocket the gold,
  'Tis all in the way of trade, my boys,
  'Tis all in the way of trade.

CHORUS:
  For lords of the soil, &c.

ROSE:
Ye city beaux, accept a hint,
  If forest roses please you best,
Be sure there is no sable in't,
  Or you may rue the jest.
Our farmers all squint awhile at the tint,
  Before it is placed in their breast, my dear,
  Before it is placed in their breast.

CHORUS:
  For lords of the soil, &c.

BELLAMY:
Would you a maiden's heart assail,
  Be careful or you'll miss the mark,
For Hymen's torch with some prevail,
  While others choose a spark;
But modest or frail, peep under her veil,
  Before you make love in the dark, my boy
  Before you make love in the dark.

CHORUS:
  For lords of the soil, &c.

End of THE FOREST ROSE

A TRIP TO NIAGARA

OR

TRAVELLERS IN AMERICA

WILLIAM DUNLAP

DUNLAP had been away from the theatre some seventeen years when he wrote *A Trip to Niagara*. He may have prepared it "at the request of the management," as he says. Perhaps he wished to reassure himself that he could still turn out a popular theatrical piece. Or, with his interest in painting, he may simply have wanted to try his hand at a diorama spectacle. In all likelihood, each of these factors contributed. Dunlap had always been fascinated by the art of scene painting and in 1825 had even exhibited some of his large gallery canvases in much the same fashion that regular panorama paintings were being shown in public halls and theatres. On one occasion he wrote: "Panoramic exhibitions possess so much of the magic deceptions of the art as irresistibly to captivate all classes of spectators . . . for no study or cultivated taste is required fully to appreciate the merits of such representations."

When *A Trip to Niagara* was first produced at the Bowery Theatre on November 28, 1828, Dunlap could not have been unaware of two immediate sources of stimulation. The Erie Canal was in the news. It had been opened to traffic in 1825. Here was an opportunity to be the first to acquaint the theatre audience with this new American wonder. Also, late in the previous season (May 16, 1828) a diorama showing the trip from Calais to Dover, introduced into Moncrieff's *Paris and London, or A Trip to Both Cities*, had been enormously popular. Although panoramas had been presented in special showings for many years, integrating them with a play was a technique that seemed to offer new possibilities. In 1833, the production of *Mazeppa* at the Bowery boasted a "grand moving Panorama of the Banks of the Dneiper, the Confines of Tartary, Wolf's Hollow, a Mountain torrent and the Desert." And in 1853, J. B. Booth, Jr., offered San Francisco the *Grand Panoramic Play of New York and San Francisco*, showing "views of New York – Passage to the Pacific – City beside the Golden Gate."

In his preface Dunlap explained that *A Trip to Niagara* was only a kind of "running accompaniment to the more important product of the Scene-paint-

175

er," and certainly it was the diorama that attracted the audiences. After the initial exhibition on November 28, 1828, *A Trip to Niagara* was shown almost every night up to the closing of the theatre on January 14, 1829. After that there were only two definitely recorded showings: June 30, 1829, and December 25, 1829. On the latter date, the diorama by itself shared the program with *George Barnwell* and *The Lottery Ticket*. Painting evidently could hold its own without assistance from dialogue. That scenic spectacle was the chief attraction is clearly indicated on the original program copy. The credits for twenty-five thousand square feet of dioramic scenery read like those for a current Hollywood spectacle: painting by Jones, Gordon, and Reinagle, assisted by Haddock, White, and Leslie; the machinery by Danes, steamboats and other mechanical effects by Hudson.

Panoramas had first been exhibited in New York during the last decade of the eighteenth century. On January 28, 1790, from ten in the morning until ten at night, a panorama of Jerusalem was on view at Lawrence Hyer's Tavern in Chatham Street. Although this was followed by panoramas of "Westminster and London" (1795), "City of Charleston," two thousand square feet of canvas (1797), and "Battle of Alexandria in Egypt" (1804), it was not until 1808 that panoramic exhibits really took hold in New York. From the first showing of Stollenwerck's representation of a "commercial and manufacturing town, with surrounding water, with vessels entering and departing, carriages and people of all descriptions passing over the bridges, manufacturers at work at their different employments, etc.," on April 23, 1808, until the exhibition at Niblo's Garden in 1831 of twenty thousand square feet of canvas showing Waterloo, St. Helena, and the funeral of Napoleon, there was scarcely a year when New York did not witness some kind of panoramic show. Among the notable scene paintings were a circular view of the city of New York (1808), showing among other places the Narrows, Governor's Island, and Long Island; "City of Paris" (1812); "Scudder's Naval Panorama" (1813); "Naval and Land Engagements on Lake Champlain and at Plattsburgh" (1815); "Battle of Paris," at the Panoramic Rotunda (1818); "Panorama of Versailles" (1820); "Panorama of Athens," painted by Barker of London (1828); and the moving diorama of the Hudson River at the Bowery (1831), undoubtedly the moving scene from *A Trip to Niagara* brought out again.

And although they became somewhat less frequent after this date, scenic shows continued to delight. In 1834 New York saw a "Grand Picturesque and Mechanical Panoramic Exhibition of the Polish Revolution in Warsaw"; from June, 1838, to May, 1840, the Panorama Building at Prince and Mercer Streets exhibited "Jerusalem," "Niagara Falls," "Lima," and "The Bay Islands in New Zealand." A diorama "Battle of Bunker Hill" was at the Masonic Hall

Mr. E. Forrest as Metamora

Mr. E. Forrest as Spartacus, the Gladiator

in 1839, and Daguerre's "Panoramas from Paris" were at Lockwood's Room in 1840.

These spectacular displays did a flourishing business. Grand-scale paintings of battles, demolitions, "agitated rivers," and "raging storms" apparently satisfied a popular taste for these sublime phenomena. Certainly this was true of scenic depictions from *A Trip to Niagara* such as "The little falls of the Mohawk. A view of the stupendous rocks, through which the river flows. A part of the town. The canal and the aqueduct crossing the river." One is struck by the suggested strong similarity between these canvases and those of the Hudson River painters. Even the regular studio artists began to exhibit large canvases much after the fashion of the panoramists. For example, Guy's paintings were "lighted every evening" and shown with musical accompaniment; Trumbull's "Surrender of Cornwallis" was given a showing at Washington Hall on July 6, 1820; and, as already noted, Dunlap's paintings had special exhibitions.

Though common usage adopted *panorama* as the generic term to describe all these spectacles, the panoramic exhibition, strictly speaking, differed from the diorama. In the panorama hall the spectator stood on a stationary circular platform completely surrounded by the painting. The railing on the platform cut off the view of the bottom edge of the painting, and a canopy above, stretching out over the edge of the platform, masked the uppermost section of the canvas. Thus the spectator had the impression of viewing an unframed landscape. The diorama was a moving strip of canvas, unrolled from one large spool and onto another, lighted from in back, and usually shown with articulated cut-out figures and objects in front of it. The important distinction to be observed is that the diorama was a transparency showing views which changed while one looked; the panorama, lighted from in front, surrounded the spectator with a continuous but non-changing picture.

The dioramic exhibition, although the principal item in *A Trip to Niagara*, is not the only element of interest. The adventures of the Wentworths, an English brother and sister on their first visit to the wilds of America, may be inconsequential, but the visitors encounter a fascinating assortment of American stage types: a Negro; an Irishman; Leather-Stocking, "dress as described in J. F. Cooper's *Pioneers*"; a Frenchman and a Yankee, both impersonated by the same actor who played John Bull. Dunlap had not completely ignored the actors. As with Noah in *She Would Be a Soldier*, Dunlap also wished to speak to the cause of tolerance and understanding and to relieve some of the prejudice engendered by the "book making journalists." (Captain Basil Hall's *Travels in North America in the Years 1827 and 1828* had recently appeared.) At the same time as he provided a panoramic view of the natural beauties between New York and Niagara, he filled the landscape with a grand display of citizens and sights of the day in "this happy country."

A TRIP TO NIAGARA

OR

TRAVELLERS IN AMERICA

WILLIAM DUNLAP

PREFACE

The following Farce, for, be it remembered, it makes pretensions to no higher character, was written at the request of the Managers, and intended by them as a kind of running accompaniment to the more important product of the Scene-painter.

The Author has not hesitated to use any material, not already appropriated to the drama, which might answer the important purpose of keeping the audience, or spectators, in good humour while the scenery and machinery was in preparation; but the best jokes, he believes, were never book'd before. The plan of making the prejudiced traveller owe his cure to one of his own countrymen, prevents (or was so intended) any disagreeable nationalities, and serves the further purpose of giving the author an excuse for the imperfections of the French, or Yankee character, as the representative of both is an Englishman. As his Frenchman is no Frenchman, and his Yankee an Englishman, he gains this important advantage, that any mistake of idiom, will be characteristic.

CHARACTERS

MR. WENTWORTH	AMELIA WENTWORTH
MR. BULL	NANCY
DENNIS DOUGHERTY	STEAM ENGINEER
LEATHER-STOCKING	LANDLORD AT CATSKILL
JOB JERRYSON	WAITER AT CATSKILL
FIRST STEAM-BOAT RUNNER	WAITER AT BUFFALO
SECOND STEAM-BOAT RUNNER	PORTERS
TRAVELLERS	

ACT I. Scene 1

An Apartment in the City Hotel, New-York. Amelia Wentworth is discovered seated at a table, writing. Nancy, at some distance behind, sewing.

AMELIA: So! I have finished my description of Philadelphia, and given a sketch of our journey to New-York. Ninety miles, without fatigue, in nine hours. Superb steam-boats – good coaches – civil people. Landscapes presenting proofs of universal prosperity, and tables testifying overflowing abundance. And then the view on entering the bay of New-York; its islands, its rivers, its shipping, and its city! I think my sister will believe *me;* although my letters are so directly in opposition to the book-making journalists, who have prejudiced her mind against the land of civil and religious liberty. Nancy!

NANCY: Did you call, Ma'am?

AMELIA: I wish to see my brother before I seal my letters for England. Where is he?

NANCY: He has gone out, Ma'am.

AMELIA: It is no matter. I will not wait his return.

NANCY: O Miss Wentworth, I wish we were going to Lunnun again, instead of the letters you have been writing.

AMELIA: Why so? are you tired of travelling?

NANCY: No, Ma'am, but I don't like to be where the servants are neegurs. It makes a servant-body think one's self no better nor black almost.

AMELIA: You have only to look in the glass, to be convinced of the contrary.

NANCY: I'm sure, Ma'am, you can't like this country as well as ould England, if it is only because it isn't home.

AMELIA: Home is indeed dear to me, girl.

NANCY: Besides, Ma'am, here are no Princesses or Princes; no Dukes or Duchesses; no Lords or Ladies – why, Ma'am, I haven't seen one coach-and-six in the country!

AMELIA: That *is* terrible.

NANCY: And then, Ma'am, there is our Tummus, who came from home with us, a right good English serving-man – now – for all he as good as promised me – so he did – now, he says he wont go home and be a servant, but he will go into the woods, and buy wild lands, and be a Congress-man.

AMELIA: So! so! you fear you shall lose Thomas.

NANCY: No, indeed, Miss –

AMELIA: Well, well, go, and send Thomas to *me.*

NANCY: But you wont – Miss – mention –

AMELIA: Not a word – I will not betray you. [*Exit Nancy*] Poor Nancy! she has not seen one coach-and-six in the country! Is it not strange that those who are most debased by the splendid pageantry and inordinate wealth of the great, are the most ardent admirers, the most devoted adorers of that which destroys them. Like the worshippers of the Hindu Idol, they adore the tawdry image, whose chariot-throne crushes them under its wheels. [*Goes to the table, closes and seals her letters*]

Enter Mr. Wentworth

WENTWORTH: So, sister. Still scribbling.

AMELIA: I have finished my letters for the packet, and have given our sister some account of this interesting country. [*Comes forward*]

WENTWORTH: I wish I had never seen it. I should have taken warning from others, and not have commenced my travels in this fag-end of creation. I should have gone to Rome, and looked with delight on the ruins of greatness. But here every thing is new – no ivy crowned towers! no mouldering monuments – nothing worth a traveller's crossing a kennel to see – all fresh – all bright as a brummagem button.

AMELIA: Yes, all fresh, in youth, strength and beauty; and therefore most worthy of the attention of travellers from the Old World. I would rather, dear brother, see flourishing towns, with laughing inhabitants, than the ruins of barbaric Castles, or the tombs of their guilty and tyrannic Lords. I should prefer, any where, health to decrepitude. But here, I see society in all the vigour of early life, supported and protected by the wisdom and experience of past ages. If America takes warning by the errors of Europe, she will soon be the pride of the Universe!

WENTWORTH: Will be! Yes, you have the true Yankee cant. Every thing that is worth having is to come.

AMELIA: Better so than that the good should be past, and leave only ruins and tombs. Better the prospect of a glorious futurity, than the remains of past greatness.

WENTWORTH: Sister – I have no patience with you – you are a downright democrat! A radical in petticoats, and no Englishwoman.

AMELIA: Brother, you know better – I love dear old England, as every Englishwoman ought – but I can see and admire what is lovely in other lands. But you –

WENTWORTH: I am a true born Englishman – unprejudiced except in favour of my own country and countrymen, as I ought to be.

AMELIA: A truce! A truce! Have you secured our berths in the steam-boat for Albany?

WENTWORTH: They told me at the office that there were no berths in the boat.

AMELIA: You have made some mistake brother. The boat leaves the wharf at five o'clock this afternoon – arrives in Albany at six or seven to-morrow morning; and the passengers sleep, of course, during the night.

WENTWORTH: I was very particular in my inquiries, and was told that we should be in Brunswick before night.

AMELIA: Brunswick! Why this is as bad as going up the Delaware to Trenton, when you intended going to Baltimore. Where is your geography?

WENTWORTH: No man understands the geography of Europe better than I do.

AMELIA: But we are now in America – therefore, pray, brother, go and secure berths in the steam-boat for Albany – and do be particular as to where the boat is going; for one would not choose to be carried south when our destination is north – and do be civil to the people – do now – for my sake.

WENTWORTH: Well, well – I will – but they have no respect for a gentleman – talk to me as familiarly as if I was one of their own democratic herd, just broke loose from the sty. The more I endeavour to teach the brutes manners, the more they stiffen the bristles of their republican insolence.

AMELIA: But as we are travellers for our own pleasure, and not missionaries to teach manners, suppose we take things as we find them, and make the best of our bargain.

WENTWORTH: Well, well – it's a hard bargain, but I'll try. It's in vain to look for comfort out of old England. [*Exit*]

AMELIA: What would I not give that I could cure my good brother of his prejudices against America and Americans! It seems as if he had crossed the Atlantic for the sole purpose of confirming the notions he had previously gained from the misstatements of journalists and reviewers. He finds, or makes, all wrong – and turns the pleasures of life to torments.

Enter Mr. Bull

BULL: Miss Wentworth! Do I intrude?

AMELIA: Mr. Bull! You in America?

BULL: Yes, Amelia, John Bull in America. I heard, below, that your brother was here, or I should not have presumed –

AMELIA: Travelling has made you mighty ceremonious, Mr. Bull. To meet an old acquaintance abroad is not usually an unpleasant circumstance; but really you look as if you had met with a rattlesnake, instead of a country-woman and cousin. You are, I see, quite an altered man.

BULL: A little older, and I hope a little wiser than when I left England; but, at heart, still John Bull. I confess that I was surprised to hear of Mr. and Miss Wentworth being in New-York.

AMELIA: Surprised! Displeased, it would seem.

BULL: [*After a long pause*] Cousin Amelia Wentworth!

AMELIA: Well, Cousin John Bull!

BULL: You may, perhaps, remember, that I once on a time was silly enough to ask you to marry me.

AMELIA: Yes, by chance, I do remember it. And I told you, you may remember, that you were a very green young gentleman, and had best go abroad, grow older, and if possible wiser, and learn the value of your giddy home-made cousin, by comparison with women made of foreign materials.

BULL: You did. That is, you gave me a travelling ticket. I have since seen the women of France and Germany, Spain and Italy; – I have seen all their enchanting attractions combined in the sylph-like females of this Yankee-land – and, thank you for your sage advice, I find –

AMELIA: In comparison with those lovely and fascinating sylphs –

BULL: My home-made Cousin Amelia is the woman of my choice after all.

AMELIA: O, you most incorrigibly constant John Bull.

BULL: True; and if I had not heard of your arrival in New-York, I should have taken passage for England, to claim your implied promise.

AMELIA: My promise!

BULL: "Implied"; that if I did not change my mind, you would take –

AMELIA: Your case into serious consideration.

BULL: And, instead of waiting my return, here I find you three thousand miles from home, in the land of Yankee-doodles.

AMELIA: Poor Johnny Bull! And is the finding me a cause of complaint? How do you know but I came here to seek you. But, seriously, my brother promised to give you notice of our intention, by letter. He was seized violently with the rambling-fever, and I thought best to attend him, as his nurse, in the hope to cure his fault-finding propensities, or at least to protect him, Minerva like, from the evils which might result from them.

BULL: How does he like the country, now that he sees it.

AMELIA: He *will* not see it. He teazes me to death by his obstinate determination to see nothing but through the coloured glasses of the book-makers of our own dear country. Never was poor nurse more tired of the patient committed to her charge, than I am.

BULL: I think I could cure him, if I joined your party as a fellow-traveller.

AMELIA: You!

BULL: I have been several months in the United States. I have travelled from Maine to Louisiana. The objects of my pursuit were pleasure and instruction; and I found both. Good humour on my part was met by good humour on the part of the natives, whether consumers of codfish and switchel, or hoe-cake and bacon. I did not expect perfection in this country, any more than in my own; but I can say that my liking, both of the people and institutions, has increased every day since I landed among them. Now, with such a stock of experience, and a knowledge of the patient and disease, I will undertake to cure your brother – with the aid and co-operation of his nurse.

AMELIA: He is a desperate subject.

BULL: I can cure him – but I must be rewarded.

AMELIA: He *ought* to pay his physician.

BULL: *You*, must pay me.

AMELIA: Do you expect a fee beforehand.

BULL: No. No cure no pay. But if I succeed –

AMELIA: Well, well, I can be grateful –

BULL: And you will – [*Takes her hand*]

AMELIA: [*Withdrawing it*] No fee beforehand, you know.

BULL: It is enough – a bargain – one John Bull shall cure another. I will travel with you *incog.* Which way do you bend your course?

AMELIA: We are now bound for the Falls of Niagara.

BULL: When do you go?

AMELIA: This afternoon.

BULL: I have no time to lose then. You shall see me again before the time of embarkation. Adieu! Confide in the physician, Mrs. Nurse. [*Exit*]

Enter Nancy, followed by Job Jerryson

AMELIA: Where is Thomas?

NANCY: Tummus is gone, Ma'am. He tould master he was a free-MAN, and would have his wages, and set up for himself. So, Ma'am,

I have brought this black – gentleman – waiter – thinking he might do instead.

AMELIA: Give him the letters for England. [*To Job*] You will see them put in the letter-bag of the Liverpool packet. [*Exit*]

JOB: I shall do myself the honour, Madam.

NANCY: The black imp!

JOB: [*Taking snuff*] You – may – give me the letters – young woman.

NANCY: You may take them yourself. There they are.

JOB: O! – Ah! – [*Puts up his snuff-box*] Those are – [*Looks toward them through his eye glass*] But I – upon my honour had quite forgot – [*Looking at his watch*] I do not think I can be spared from the hotel at this time.

NANCY: Go and ask your Master.

JOB: "Master!" – I have no master. Master indeed! Demmee! That's well enough! I am my own master.

NANCY: I thought the keeper of the hotel was your master.

JOB: Not at all. He is keeper, and I am waiter. We have no masters here! You wait upon Miss Wentworth, but you would not call her mistress.

NANCY: But I would; and I do.

JOB: That may do for whites of the old country; but not for gentlemen and ladies of colour, in America. You will learn, Miss Nancy – Nancy, I think is your name?

NANCY: They call me Nancy for shortness, but my name is Ann.

JOB: Very well – Nancy, or Ann – you will learn Miss Ann, or Miss Nancy, after being a short time in this country, to set a proper value upon yourself. Now, if I might be permitted, I would propose for you –

NANCY: You! *You* propose for *me!*

JOB: If you would do me the honour, I would propose –

NANCY: I would have you know, fellow, that when I marry, I shall at least –

JOB: Marry! – 'pon honour, that is too good! – I do not marry I assure you – Miss – [*Takes snuff*] Nancy – I am not a marrying man. As the man of colour says, in the play – I would not my free condition put in confinement for seas of wealth. If you would like to see our theatre, I can give you an order. I am one of the managers. We rehearse every club night – the Shakespeare Club – and there is my friend

Tom Dickson, the young coloured gentleman next door, we rub up – I would say – we brighten our memories of a morning, as we rub up the brass knobs and knockers at the street doors.

NANCY: I think you had better rub up your memory now, and take my Mistress's letters.

JOB: [*Looking at the letters through his glass*] Ah, true! [*Takes snuff*] My honour is pledged for their safety. [*Takes letters from table*] – As I told Miss Diana Dingy, "The service of the fair sex is my delight." –Adieu – *mung share*. [*Exit*]

NANCY: O dear! O dear! Is not this too much for flesh and blood to bear! – Oh that I was in dear old England once more, and never might see a black face again. They may talk of well-favoured and ill-favoured – but of all favours, deliver me from a black favour!

Enter Dennis Dougherty

DENNIS: Faver! – Is it yellow faver you're spaking of, my dear.

NANCY: No – black.

DENNIS: Worse and worse. And didn't I meet a fine gentleman going out of the house, with a face as black as my shoe? Was it him you meant?

NANCY: Yes, I did mean him.

DENNIS: And does the yellow faver turn men black? To be alive, and turn black! Oh that's too bad! I am sure that the black-faced gentleman was alive; for he grinn'd when I ax't him for Mr. Wintwort, and told me to come up here.

NANCY: Do you wish to see Mr. Wentworth?

DENNIS: Fait, and I do. I want to see some person from the old country, to give me comfort and advice. His Britannic Majesty's Counsel is out of town, and the clerk told me that all the Irish who came to this country died of the faver in saisoning. So I ax't him to recommend me to some English gentleman for advice, and he sent me here to Mr. Wintwort – here's his name on the paper.

NANCY: [*Reading*] To Judy M'Graw.

DENNIS: That's not it. That's a letter I wrote aboard ship, to inform my friends of my safe arrival – but I think I shall carry it mysilf. That's the subscription for Mr. Wintwort. [*Offers another paper*]

NANCY: My Master has gone out, but I will inform my Mistress. [*Going, meets Mr. Bull*]

Enter Bull, as a Frenchman

BULL: Ah ha! Ma pretty leetle rogue a – vere is your Lady? Vere is Mam'selle Wentawort?

NANCY: I am going to call her to this gentleman. [*Exit*]

BULL: Ah ha! ver goot! [*Taking snuff*] Gentleman? Take a some snuff, Sair? I sink you are not of dis contree?

DENNIS: You may say that, Mounseer; and I wish you could as truly say I am not mysilf in this country.

BULL: Vye! – Vat is de mattare vid de contree? Ver goot contree.

DENNIS: Yes. If people could live in it.

BULL: Vye de peeps are lyve. Ha! You are not dead-man, Sair?

DENNIS: No, not yet. But I soon shall be, if I don't get off.

BULL: Get off? For vat you come here?

DENNIS: I came to settle, as they call it, because land is chape, and I have some money to buy with. But I had no desire to settle in the churchyard; or bagain for a plantation, six feet by two. Did not I see a shop full of coffins the first day I landed? O, what a divvil of a place is it where the coffins stand ready to catch a man the moment he stips ashore. I suppose my coffin was ready made for me before I left Ireland, without even the dacent ceremony of measuring the corpse. It's the faver, Mounseer, makes me want to be off – ready-made coffins and faver!

BULL: Ah! ha! ver goot! you ave got de fevare?

DENNIS: But have I tho'? – Do I begin to turn yellow or black?

BULL: Excuse-a-me. I voud say – ave a you got de fevare?

DENNIS: Not yet – I blave!

BULL: Ow long you ave been ere in Merreek?

DENNIS: In-*mer*-what?

BULL: In – a-merry-kee – ow long a ave you been in Amerrykee?

DENNIS: In a merry key! The divvil a bit of a merry key have I been in, since I saw the coffin shop. I have been chop-fallen ever since.

BULL: I say, ma frent, how long since you ave been in dis contree?

DENNIS: Just two weeks too long. I arrived a fortnight ago. And now, as there is no ship about sailing for Ireland, I want to go north, to his majesty's dominions.

BULL: And for what you go nord?

DENNIS: For what is it? That I may feel what it

is to be cool and comfortable once more, and safe under his majesty's flag.

Enter Amelia

BULL: [*Meeting her*] Ah, Mam'selle Wentawort, I ave de honour to pay ma respects to you.

AMELIA: Sir! My servant told me you were Irish.

BULL: No, Mam'selle, upon ma vord!

DENNIS: Oh! Who would ever mistake that mahogany faced gentleman for an Irishman. Sure it wasn't your *woman* made that *bull*.

BULL: Bull?

AMELIA: [*Between them*] Upon my word I am in a strange situation, with two persons upon whom I never before set eyes – and both pretty familiar.

DENNIS: For mysilf, my Lady, I thank you for the compliment. I was as pretty a lad, before I was sweated down, as ivver stept from the Green Isle to the Green Ocean. As to the other gentleman's beauty – it may spake for itsilf in black and yellow.

BULL: Mam'selle Wentawort, you no know a me?

AMELIA: Not I, Sir! Did you send for me?

DENNIS: That was mysilf.

BULL: Not know Monsieur Tonson!

AMELIA: Only on the stage.

BULL: Monsieur Tonson – Bee – you – double ell.

DENNIS: Bee – you – double ell!

AMELIA: Is it possible?

DENNIS: That's Bull, sure enough. If I thought you meant any national reflections, I'd ax you how you spell frog, Mounseer!

AMELIA: And this is for the purpose?

BULL: No cure no pay – Siss is de first part of a ma comedie. Ah, ha! Mam'selle, you acknowledge de acquaintance?

AMELIA: I do.

DENNIS: Now this would puzzle the almanac maker!

AMELIA: [*To Dennis*] Perhaps you, too, are an old acquaintance.

DENNIS: It may be so, my Lady – and the divvil an objection have I – but if it is so – it is so old, that I have quite forgot all about it.

AMELIA: Well – be that as it may – your business?

DENNIS: When I was at home, I was a farmer – but since I have been in New-York, I have

had no business but to wipe my forehead, and kill muskeetoes.

AMELIA: Ha, ha, ha! But your business with me? You sent word that you wanted to speak to my brother, or to me.

DENNIS: Oh – Ah – now that's it.

BULL: Siss very honnest a gentleman – tells a me zat he vould run avay nord to get avay from de ate, and find protection from de fevare under de flag of his Majesty Brittanique! Ha! zat is right, mon Ami?

AMELIA: Perhaps the gentleman can tell his story quite as intelligibly as you can, Monsieur Tonson! [*To Dennis*] You are discontented with this country, and would consult my brother as to the mode of getting home again.

DENNIS: That's *it*, my Lady – If I had bothered about it all day I could not have said it so well. Fait, I believe it's natural for a woman's tongue to make itself understood, any how, even if she don't spake at all. Long life to the dear cratures; it's musick and dancing too to hear them!

AMELIA: But what is your objection to staying in this country?

DENNIS: Hate, my Lady.

BULL: Hate! Vat, you hate de contree?

DENNIS: Not at all.

AMELIA: The heat, Monsieur – the heat.

DENNIS: Yes, my Lady, the *hate*. If I don't run away, I shall run away mysilf.

BULL: Dat is ver goot! – He runavay if he don't a run avay!

AMELIA: But if you *stay*, you will find it cold enough.

DENNIS: You may say that. It is cold enough under the sod in a churchyard. The first time I went to the Catedral, I took a bit of a walk in the burying ground, just to amuse mysilf wid reading the tombstones – but by my soul the place was planted with Irishmen thicker than potatoes in a well till'd patch, or crosses on a check shirt.

BULL: Sheck churt – ver goot!

DENNIS: I wonder where was the good? I thinks I to mysilf, Dennis, did you come here to be planted in a barbarous country, like these fine hearty fellows, that I see here under ground? Their ages were put on their tombstones; and, by my soul, not one that was over thirty.

AMELIA: How old are you?

DENNIS: Forty before I left Ireland.

AMELIA: Then you are safe.

DENNIS: And am I? Am I?

AMELIA: If no Irishman dies older than thirty. You are forty, and therefore safe.

DENNIS: And I may thank Ireland for that, and not this barbarous country.

BULL: Siss contree is ver fine contree.

DENNIS: What signifies *that*, if a man can't live in it?

AMELIA: Plenty to eat and drink.

DENNIS: Faver takes away a man's appetite.

BULL: For what you complain of favour, ha? I should a vish to ave de favour of dis contree ver mush, ma foi!

DENNIS: Every man to his liking, sure enough.

AMELIA: Our friend did not say favour, but fever.

DENNIS: Yes, my Lady – *faver* – that's it.

AMELIA: After a time you would be pleased with this New World.

BULL: Siss is de land of Liberty!

DENNIS: Liberty! O yes! Fait it is. If a man has no shoes and stockings he is at liberty to go barefoot! And then they tell me that in the winter, when the snow is up to a man's knees, he has the liberty to walk – if he can.

AMELIA: I see my brother coming – you and he will agree marvellously well! [*Bull and Dennis retire up*]

Enter Wentworth

WENTWORTH: All the berths for to-day were engaged – but as I was coming away, a pert forward Frenchman stept up and offered me his berth, then ran off, and in a minute secured two for you and your servant – I refused – but there is no getting rid of a Frenchman's civility and his snuff-box.

BULL: [*Offering his box*] Von pinch, if you please, Sair.

AMELIA: Monsieur Tonson.

WENTWORTH: Here he is again!

BULL: We are old acquaintance for som minutes. I ave been appy to accommodate Monsieur Wentawort wid a my birt in de boat!

AMELIA: It is to you, then, we owe –

BULL: Noting at all – I get a snug caban from de capitain upon deck – ver convenient.

WENTWORTH: So! – He gets a better place for himself by giving up some dirty hole to us – I thought so. That's French politeness!

BULL: [*Offering box*] Nodare leetle pinch, Sair.

WENTWORTH: [*Turns away*] Who have we here?

AMELIA: A stranger, like ourselves, come to visit America.

WENTWORTH: Another fool. [*Bull and Amelia retire laughing*]

DENNIS: You may say that. If ivver I get home again, I'll never complain of the hate, sure.

WENTWORTH: You don't like this country, it seems.

DENNIS: Is it the country? It's well enough, if one could get out of it alive.

WENTWORTH: You don't like the people?

DENNIS: I can't say much for their civility, any how. As I walk the streets of this town, when I meet a man, I give him the time of day, with a "good morning," says I, and "God bliss you." "Hay," says he – "Nan" – Now I nivver knew that "nan," and "hay," meant "thank you," and "God bliss you," before.

WENTWORTH: And you want to go home again.

DENNIS: Fait do I. It has cost me tree hundred dollars to larn what a hot day is.

AMELIA: But have you not consulted some friend, English or Irish, who has *resided* in this country?

DENNIS: That's *what* I did. I went to the office of his Britannic Majesty's Counsel, but he was not in town – there I found a clark, an Irishman from Dublin itsilf, and he told me to get home as fast as I could, for he had been twenty-nine years in the country, and all the Irish died as fast as they came over.

AMELIA: But he was alive!

DENNIS: As jolly and red in the gills as bafe and port wine could make him.

AMELIA: After twenty-nine years' residence?

BULL: Ma foi! He is vat you call touf – he take him twenty-nine years to die! And he lyvf and merry yet – ver goot!

DENNIS: Yes – but he is in the King's sarvice.

WENTWORTH: Come along with me my good fellow. I will do every thing in my power to get you out of this country. [*Exit, Dennis following him*]

AMELIA: Alive – I hope.

DENNIS: [*Turns about and bows*] Thank your Ladyship. [*Exit*]

AMELIA: My brother will be delighted with this loyal Hibernian. I must make preparation – you will be in time?

BULL: I will. My preparations are made – I have a snug cabin on deck, where I have deposited some disguises, borrowed from the Bowery Theatre – and doubt not a happy denouement to our Trip to Niagara. [*Exeunt Amelia and Bull*]

Scene 2

Steam-boat wharf, bottom of Courtlandt-street, New-York. Bell ringing. The usual bustle. Steam-boat runners inviting passengers. View of Jersey City. Ships in the stream, etc.

1ST RUNNER: This way, Sir! – This way.

Enter Gentlemen and Ladies

2ND RUNNER: Which boat, Sir?

GENTLEMAN: The New Philadelphia.

1ST RUNNER: The North America is the fastest, Sir!

2ND RUNNER: It's false! – This way, Sir! – This way, Sir! – This way, Ma'am!

1ST RUNNER: This way, Sir! – We beat them by twenty minutes last trip.

2ND RUNNER: We beat *them*, Sir!

GENTLEMAN: Stand out of the way.

1ST RUNNER: That's right, Sir – this way – [*Shows the Travellers on board, and returns*]

Enter Wentworth, followed by porters with baggage. Miss Wentworth. Nancy, with a small basket, and Dennis Dougherty

DENNIS: Let me be carrying that for you, my dear.

NANCY: No, thank you. It's my ridicule.

DENNIS: Your, what?

NANCY: My ridicule.

DENNIS: Your – that's enough.

2ND RUNNER: The New Philadelphia, Sir?

WENTWORTH: No. To Albany.

Enter Job Jerryson, showing Travellers to the boat

DENNIS: [*Looking at Job, and pulling Wentworth by the sleeve*] Sae him! – Sae him!

JOB: Permit me to have the honour of showing you the way. [*Goes with Travellers on board*]

WENTWORTH: Well – what then?

DENNIS: Don't go in the same boat with that gentleman – he has the black faver.

WENTWORTH: Black enough.

1ST RUNNER: The North America is the best boat, Sir.

AMELIA: We have taken our berths – in which boat, brother?

WENTWORTH: In the boat for Albany.

1ST RUNNER: They are all for Albany.

2ND RUNNER: Quick, Sir! This way.

DENNIS: How the craters are all running away from the faver!

2ND RUNNER: I remember, Sir, you engaged berths on board our boat – you, and a French gentleman.

WENTWORTH: Then take the baggage on board. No talking!

2ND RUNNER: That's not my business.

WENTWORTH: Yankee civility, again!

AMELIA: Nancy, show the porter – [*To 2nd Runner*] I'll thank you – Sir –

2ND RUNNER: I will see all safe on board, Ma'am – but one don't like to be snubb'd. [*Assists Nancy and Porter, and goes on board*]

1ST RUNNER: [*To Dennis*] North America?

Enter Job from the boat, and exit

DENNIS: Yes, as far north as his Majesty's dominions. Sae! There's the black faver again! By the powers he knows his place, and stays in New-York!

WENTWORTH: You go with us.

DENNIS: To be sure – but I've left my trunk –

WENTWORTH: Run –

DENNIS: Kape the boat! I'll run for dear life. [*Exit*]

Enter Bull from the boat as Jonathan, followed by the Engineer, in warm dispute

BULL: I say it is too short.

ENGINEER: Not at all.

BULL: But I know it is.

ENGINEER: You find as much fault with the machinery, as if you were an Englishman!

WENTWORTH: There! Amelia! You hear!

BULL: Why, you must admit, for sartin, that the piston is too short.

ENGINEER: No, I don't.

BULL: Goody gracious, you're so tied up to your own notions, that you won't see the nose on your face, for all it stands right between your eyes. I'll appeal to this here gentleman.

WENTWORTH: I know nothing about it. [*Turns away*]

BULL: I'll be darn'd but the piston is too short by abyout an inch and a quarter; and that there what d'you call it, is too long. If you would but have every thing to fit – slick – gracious me! you'd make your boat go like a streak o' chalk! so you would. Oh! I wish I had money enough to build a steam-boat – I wish I had!

ENGINEER: And what would *you* do, if you *had* the money?

BULL: Keep it. [*Bell rings*]

ENGINEER: [*Runs on board*] All on board.

BULL: Shall I help this Lady – Amelia!

AMELIA: [*Recognising him*] Is it possible!

WENTWORTH: Stand out of the way! Amelia, take my arm.

BULL: Well – when I want to learn politeness, I'll travel. [*All go on board*]

End of First Act

ACT II

The Bowery, with a view of the front of the Theatre. Enter Dennis, with a trunk and bundles, dropping one while he secures another.

DENNIS: I'm bother'd wid ye – so that's *that* – Sure I must be nare the stame-boat by this time – I've turn'd round 'till I don't know which turn will sarve my turn next. Och! there's the big church, and now I'm to turn to my lift hand – or my right – by my soul I forgot which – [*Enter two young men*] Good afternoon to you, and God bliss ye, and – [*They look at him, laugh, and exit*] Now there it is! That's all the information I get. [*Others pass in various directions, and pay no attention to him*] Good avening to ye, and Heaven bliss – So! They are gone too! [*Enter Job Jerryson, upper entrance, and comes down behind Dennis, and passes him, his back towards him*] Good avening to you, Sir, if you plase. [*Job turns*] Och! it's the black-faced gentleman! – No nearer, if you plase!

JOB: What is your wish, friend?

DENNIS: Kape off, if you plase. – Can you tell me the way – a little further off, if you plase.

JOB: As far off as you please, friend. I do not wish to be nearer, I assure you. I am black, Sir; so was "noble Othello." – How do I know but he was one of my forefathers?

DENNIS: Four fathers! You don't pretend you had four fathers!

JOB: Yes, Sir.

DENNIS: And how many mothers?

JOB: Contemptible!

DENNIS: But, before you go, tell me the way.

JOB: Which way would you go?

DENNIS: By stame.

JOB: Where?

DENNIS: To Albany – kape off, if you plase.

JOB: My good man, this is the road to Boston.

DENNIS: And where's the boat for Albany?

JOB: My good Sir, you are quite out of the way; you must go back again – that way – till you see a church on your right hand.

DENNIS: That's it.

JOB: That, Sir, is the Bowery Theatre, and no Church, upon my honour.

DENNIS: O thunder! A play house! Where shall I go?

JOB: Go directly back; and when you come to St. Paul's, ask any gentleman, and he will tell you or show you the way. – I must go this way – I am in haste – [*Looks at his watch*] – The ladies are waiting for me, 'pon honour. [*Exit*]

DENNIS: Back again – St. Paul's. – That's where the old gentleman stands night and day to keep watch over the door with a wooden sword – if he would show me the way to the river again, I'll get on board the first boat that goes by wind or stame – but may be Mr. Wintwort is waiting for me! O! let me get out of this divvil of a place, any how! [*Exit*]

Diorama, or Moving Scenery

The steam-boat is seen as passing up the river.

Scene 1. *Harbour of New-York. Governor's Island. Ships at anchor.*

Scene 2. *Frigate at anchor. Jersey City.*

Scene 3. *Hoboken.*

Scene 4. *Weehawk.*

Scene 5. *Palisades.*

Scene 6. *Approaching storm.*

Scene 7. *Storm.*

Scene 8. *Boats passing through a fog.*

Scene 9. *Clearing away and rainbow. Caldwell's landing. Boat stops.*

Scene 10. *Highlands.*

Scene 11. *Buttermilk Falls.*

Scene 12. *West Point. Sun setting.*

Scene 13. *Highlands continued.*

Scene 14. *Newburgh by moonlight.*

Scene 15. *Island near Newburgh.*

Scene 16. *Catskill Mountains in distance, and Mountain House.*

Scene 17. *Continuation of scenery.*

Scene 18. *Catskill landing.*

The boat stops, and the passengers are seen put-

ting off in a small boat, and landing at Catskill, at night

Bar-room of the Inn at Catskill-landing. Night. Candles

Enter Wentworth, followed by Landlord

WENTWORTH: So! Here we stay all night – the coach broke, and no other to be had.

LANDLORD: I am extremely sorry, Sir. But you may still be in time to see the sun rise from the front of the Mountain House. It is said to be the finest view in the world.

WENTWORTH: It may be very well for this country.

LANDLORD: I see this is a grumbler. [*Exit*]

WENTWORTH: What fools we are to leave home, and expose ourselves to dangers and insults! and for what purpose? Can you give us a decent supper? I suppose not though. Why don't you answer? I say, can we have——? Gone! That's free and easy! Familiar! Waiter! Waiter!

Enter Amelia and Nancy, attended by Landlord and Waiter, who assist with baggage, etc., etc.

AMELIA: Thank you, Sir.

LANDLORD: This way, Madam – Tom, show the Ladies into the parlour – carry the baggage up stairs!

AMELIA: Nancy, will you show which are our trunks, and have them taken care of.

LANDLORD: [*To Nancy*] This way, Miss! [*To Amelia*] I will see every thing attended to, Madam. [*Exeunt Landlord, Nancy and Waiter*]

WENTWORTH: So, sister, here we must stay, in this wretched dog-hole, to-night.

AMELIA: Dog-hole, brother? Every thing is very comfortable! And the people are very obliging.

WENTWORTH: Are they? I haven't found it out.

AMELIA: Perhaps you did not seek it by the right light. Civility begets civility. Nay, I find that civility is met by the most friendly attentions from the people of this country. But I *have seen* rudeness answered by the treatment it always merits. What a delightful journey we have had!

WENTWORTH: Have we?

AMELIA: Such weather! Such scenery!

WENTWORTH: I was reading newspapers in the cabin, glad to get rid of the boring of the passengers. There was that infernal Yankee – and that detestable Frenchman – I hate a Frenchman!

AMELIA: O brother! brother! You must look through the other end of the glass, or you look in vain for pleasure! [*Exit*]

WENTWORTH: I hope, by stopping here, I have got rid of my two tormentors, the Yankee and the Frenchman. That chattering Frenchman stuck to me like pitch. His civility and his snuff-box are eternally thrust into every man's face!

BULL: [*Without*] Malbrook s'en va – tang ta – Vaiter, my ver goot friend – good fellow – [*Enters, shaking hands with the Waiter*] Give a me some branty and vater – *vite*, queek!

WAITER: Yes, Sir! [*Runs off*]

WENTWORTH: Waiter! Here is my tormentor.

BULL: Sair! How you do, by dis time – aha – Von pinch snuff, Sair! You do not speak a to me. Dat is ver polite. Ven I meet a you, I say to you, "good morning, Sair" – You say, "homph" – I say, "take a pinch snuff, Sair" – "homph" – "very fine weddare, Sair" – "homph." Vat is dat "homph." Now I say "Sair" to you – "homph!" [*Turns off and sits*]

WENTWORTH: Contemptible! [*Seats himself*]

BULL: [*Waiter brings him brandy and water*] Dat is my goot fellow – John – you name John?

WAITER: Tom, Sir!

BULL: Ver pret name – Tom! goot fellow, Tom!

WENTWORTH: Waiter! Waiter, I say! Will no one attend to a gentleman! I suppose I can have no supper! Waiter! bring me a pair of slippers.

BULL: Vaiter! bring a me two pair slippares.

WENTWORTH: You infernal scoundrel, why don't you obey me? – I will go to bed.

BULL: I vill go to two beds.

WENTWORTH: [*Jumping up*] Bring me a candle, and show me to my room.

BULL: Bring a me two candles, and show me to two room.

WENTWORTH: There is nothing but vexation in the infernal country. I'll find the Landlord, and blow him to the devil. [*Exit*]

BULL: Ha! ha! ha! Vat you laugh at, Vaiter? Tom, for vat you laugh? you dam fellow – ha! – Tom, take a de candles, and show me to my suppare – marsh – Tom – aha! Malbrook sen va t'en guere. [*Exeunt. Waiter preceding him with candles*]

End of Second Act

ACT III

Scene – the Mountain, or Pine Orchard House. The stage represents the rock in front of the house – a view of the house and of the distant scenery. Sun rises during the scene. Enter Wentworth and Amelia.

AMELIA: This is indeed sublime.

WENTWORTH: Humph! Well enough for this country.

AMELIA: See how beautifully the majestic Hudson, diminished by distance to the size of a rivulet, meanders through fields, forests, and meadows, which are reduced in appearance to garden flower beds. You don't enjoy the prospect, brother.

WENTWORTH: I can think of nothing but that infernal Frenchman; he teazed me all day, insulted me in the evening, by calling, like an echo, for every thing I called for *doubled* – and in the middle of the night I heard him open his diabolical plan.

AMELIA: What? – His plan!

WENTWORTH: I heard him – but I discovered and defeated his plot – I discovered his intention.

AMELIA: Indeed – You have, then, discovered –

WENTWORTH: Yes – I have – I overheard him in the next room to mine, talking to himself – I got up and looked through the key-hole, and I discovered all. I heard enough to let me into the plot.

AMELIA: Well, it was an innocent attempt, for your good.

WENTWORTH: Innocent!

AMELIA: Yes, I am sure it was meant for your good, brother!

WENTWORTH: What? Murder me for my good!

AMELIA: Murder you?

WENTWORTH: Yes, Ma'am! I saw him sharpening a razor. I heard him say, "Aha! Mr. Bull, this will do your business, Mr. Bull."

AMELIA: Mr. Bull! Ah! now I understand. [*Aside*]

WENTWORTH: All these Frenchmen call us English, Mr. and Mrs. Bull, you know – "this will do your business, Mr. Bull" – There he stood by the table, the candle shining full upon the razor and his ugly black face, he stropping away and feeling the edge now and then, "aha!" says he, "this will do, this will take it off at one sweep." Meaning my head – no doubt.

AMELIA: Meaning his own beard, more likely. And was this all?

WENTWORTH: All! Sister! Sister! You are enough to provoke a saint! But I've got rid of the scoundrel – I took out my pistols –

AMELIA: You didn't murder him, I hope! Heavens!

WENTWORTH: If he had attempted to enter my chamber, I should have tried an English bullet on his French razor! But my taking out my pistols made such a noise, that he found I was prepared, and he gave up the attempt, and decamped, I suppose, for I see nothing of him this morning. Here's another torment.

Enter Leather-Stocking – dress as described in J. F. Cooper's Pioneers. On his head, a cap made of fox skin – hair gray – face sun burnt – check shirt – deer skin coat, with the hair on, tied with a belt of coloured worsted – buckskin breeches and leggins – a belt over his shoulder, suspending a horn for powder. A leather pouch before him for balls, etc. A long rifle

AMELIA: Is he an Indian? A wild and noble figure. An Indian?

WENTWORTH: I hope so – yes – yet he don't look like the wax Indian in the museum at New-York.

LEATHER-STOCKING: All changed! The beasts of the forest all gone! What is worth living for here, now! All spoilt! All spoilt!

WENTWORTH: He speaks English. Are you an Indian?

LEATHER-STOCKING: No – I am a white skin.

WENTWORTH: Not much of that.

LEATHER-STOCKING: Pure white, without a cross. But I have lived with the red skins most of my life, and that's not a short one.

AMELIA: Do you live here?

LEATHER-STOCKING: No! What's worth living for, here? I am going far west, with the deer and the Indians; and I thought I would look once more at the Catskills, for old acquaintance sake. But all is spoilt – the settlers spoil all!

AMELIA: All is lovely! What do you mean?

LEATHER-STOCKING: O! This was a Paradise once! The game was plenty – and none to meddle – only mayhap a party of Delaware's, now and then – or a scout of them thieves, the Iroquois.

WENTWORTH: Good shooting, and no French-men or Yankees! I like your taste.

LEATHER-STOCKING: There were two or three Frenchmen that squatted in the flats further west, and married squaws – but I had the mountains to myself.

AMELIA: It must have been a melancholy life. To roam over these hills, and look upon this beautiful stream below, without a soul to speak to.

LEATHER-STOCKING: Melancholy – no, young wo-man! It was cheerful. When the trees began to be kiver'd with leaves, and the ice was out of the river; when the birds came back from the south, and all nater lifted its song to its Maker – think you not that the hunter's thanksgiving went up to Heaven with the song of all around him?

AMELIA: Oh yes – but he was alone – but *now*, see the smoke rising from a thousand habita-tions, and the fields covered with grain and fruit, for a thousand happy families.

LEATHER-STOCKING: The smoke rises to heaven; but do the thanks of the people rise with it?

WENTWORTH: He's right – they are an un-thankful race! *You* are an Englishman?

LEATHER-STOCKING: By descent; but a *born* Yan-kee. As good as most men I meet with – always excepting the red skins. But I perceive, young woman, *you* look with pleasure on what you see from this hill.

AMELIA: I do, indeed.

LEATHER-STOCKING: So did I once! I was on that there hilltop when Vaughan burnt Sopus. The river was in sight under my feet for seventy miles, looking like a curled shaving, though it was eight long miles to its banks. I saw the Hampshire grants, the highlands, and all crea-tion beneath me. All that God had done, or man could undo, as far as eye could reach – and the red skins call *me, Hawks-eye.*

AMELIA: It was, and *is*, a glorious sight.

LEATHER-STOCKING: For them that likes to be a mile high in the air, and see men's farms and housen, *at your feet;* and rivers looking like ribands. But there's a place a short way back here, that I relish of late more than this; it's more kiver'd with trees, and the water falls from the hill like foam from heaven.

AMELIA: Where? Can you not guide us to it.

WENTWORTH: After breakfast – after breakfast.

LEATHER-STOCKING: I'll guide you, and help your delicate limbs over the rough and wet

places, although I am rough myself. On that spot I speak of, I once saved a beautiful wom-an, like you, from the spring of a painter.

AMELIA: A painter?

WENTWORTH: One of those foolish fellows, I suppose, who go about, to places like this, climbing precipices, at the risk of their necks, with port folios and three legged stools and pencils, to make sketches of what they call fine scenery. Ha! Wasn't it?

LEATHER-STOCKING: Anan?

WENTWORTH: What did you do with the paint-er?

LEATHER-STOCKING: I shot him.

AMELIA: Shot him!

LEATHER-STOCKING: I never miss my aim.

WENTWORTH: Poor devil – but it served him right. What do people thrust themselves into harm's way for, when they should be safe at home?

LEATHER-STOCKING: He was at home. It was the young woman who was abroad.

WENTWORTH: The painter was not an English-man, then?

LEATHER-STOCKING: Anan?

WENTWORTH: Was he a native?

LEATHER-STOCKING: No doubt – and the biggest I ever saw.

AMELIA: And you shot him?

LEATHER-STOCKING: Just as he was going to spring on the gal.

WENTWORTH: I always had a bad opinion of those vagabond sketching blades.

AMELIA: And you saved her?

LEATHER-STOCKING: She didn't see the creater, and he didn't see me – I leveld just over her shoulder, and hit him between the eyes. [*Chuckling*] He! he – He roll'd down the rock, harmless as a lamb – the gal was skeart – but I saved her! – I wore the creater's skin ever since.

AMELIA: Horrid! – His skin!

WENTWORTH: The painter's skin?

LEATHER-STOCKING: This coat is made of it.

AMELIA: O – a panther! Now I understand.

WENTWORTH: A panther – not a painter – a panther.

LEATHER-STOCKING: Anan? I don't know how the books call the animal, but his skin was the finest I ever saw of the kind.

AMELIA: And you saved a female from this terri-ble beast? The place is free from such now?

LEATHER-STOCKING: It is now only visited by men.

WENTWORTH: *Painters* of pictures, and fools who travel to see wonders.

AMELIA: And this happened near the beautiful cataract you mentioned.

LEATHER-STOCKING: It did. I had to drag the beast from the stream, that I might save his fur coat; for he fell where the water lights after it leaps from the rock.

AMELIA: To what river is the water you speak of tributary?

LEATHER-STOCKING: Anan?

AMELIA: Which way does it go?

LEATHER-STOCKING: It's a drop for old Hudson. I've sat on the shelving rock many a long hour, and watched the bubbles as they shot by me, and thought how long it would be before that very water would be under the bottom of a vessel and tossing in the salt sea.

AMELIA: And then raised to the clouds, and descending on the mountain top again. So turns the great wheel of nature! In one immutable round of mutation! One unchanging circle of incessant change!

LEATHER-STOCKING: Anan?

AMELIA: O! I am impatient to see the place you have so eloquently described.

WENTWORTH: After breakfast.

LEATHER-STOCKING: Well, when you wish to go, ask for Leather-Stocking, or Natty Bumpo; or if you ask of an Indian, call me Hawks-eye – I answer to all these names, and, he, he, he, [*Chuckling*] have one of my own, besides. [*Exit*]

WENTWORTH: Strange animal! Come Amelia.

Enter Bull, meeting them, as Jonathan, with a bell-shaped pumpkin tied to the bough of a pear tree

BULL: Good morning, Miss – and the same to you, Mister – I'm glad I've met you again, you're so tarnal agreeable, and take to my conversation *so* meazingly.

AMELIA: Good morning, Mr. Jonathan – what's your other name?

BULL: Doolittle – at your sarvice, Miss.

AMELIA: What have you got there?

BULL: It's a sample of our Yankee pears. I guess as how, Mister, you mightent ha got sich in your country.

AMELIA: Not as large.

WENTWORTH: Every bit as large.

AMELIA: Oh, brother!

WENTWORTH: Very nearly as large.

AMELIA: Oh, no!

WENTWORTH: Half as large, I'm sure.

AMELIA: No, no, brother.

WENTWORTH: I'm sure I've seen pears very nearly half as large.

AMELIA: Oh, no.

WENTWORTH: What! would you reduce English pears to the size of nutmegs.

BULL: I made a cargo of nutmegs once.

WENTWORTH: You make nutmegs. These Yankees will undertake to make any thing – they make nothing of saying they made it, whether they made it or no. You make nutmegs!

BULL: Yes, and made a pretty penny by 'em, too. I made 'em out of pine plank, and sold the whole cargo to a grocer in York. Uncle Ben said it was as slick a trick as ever was hatch'd east'ard. Did you ever hear of uncle Ben?

WENTWORTH: Damn your uncle Ben!

BULL: Oh no! don't darn uncle Ben. Darn me as much as you please – but uncle Ben's a deacon, and it's a kynd of blasphemy to darn a deacon. [*Bell rings*] Ha! I guess that's for breakfast, up at the house, there.

WENTWORTH: Come, Amelia – let's get rid of this fool – or knave. [*They are going*]

BULL: [*Following*] Won't you put the pear in your pocket?

WENTWORTH: Damn your pear!

BULL: I'll carry it in, and have it sarved up for sa'ace at the breakfast. [*Exeunt up the stage. Amelia looks back, and shakes her finger at Bull. He follows laughing*]

Scene 2

The waterfall and cave, or recess in the rock. Enter Amelia and Leather-Stocking, he assisting her. Wentworth following down the rocks – stops.

LEATHER-STOCKING: Now, you are safe, young woman.

AMELIA: Thank you. I felt safe all the time, under your care.

LEATHER-STOCKING: Any woman may do that.

WENTWORTH: You wild man, help me down this curst place! Oh, that I should ever leave home for this! Help!

LEATHER-STOCKING: [*Puts him in safety*] There! now look around you.

AMELIA: Sublime! How bold! How picturesque!

WENTWORTH: But I would rather sit at home and see it. Besides, I am tired of new plantations, and new towns. A traveller's delight is the remains of cities and temples, the proofs of Time's resistless power – as the poet says. – Give me broken pillars and obliterated inscriptions, bricks from Babel, and mummies from Egypt.

AMELIA: And give me present joy, in scenes of happiness spread around me, by the hand of my beneficent Creator. Oh, brother! I had rather, much rather, see the ruby lips, and sparkling glance of youth, than the ashen hue, and leaden eye of age.

WENTWORTH: Sister, have you lost your veneration for age?

AMELIA: For "age by itself age," as we used to say of the letters of the alphabet – yes. But for the wisdom which ought to accompany age, I entertain the deepest veneration.

LEATHER-STOCKING: You, young woman, see and feel the hand of your Creator in his mighty works. You, have a hunter's heart, a heart that is lifted to heaven, while you look on the wonders of the arth. You, enjoy, and are thankful.

AMELIA: You do me justice.

WENTWORTH: There is some sense in travelling with a man like you, that can help one at a pinch. I wish you were an Englishman.

LEATHER-STOCKING: What's the difference? Our fathers are the same. I have fought by the side of Englishmen in Wolfe's war, and helpt 'em cut up the French and Iroquois, in them there times; and many a tough fight, and wild skrimmage has Leather-Stocking shared with an Englishman at his side, though he is a Yankee.

WENTWORTH: You are no Yankee.

LEATHER-STOCKING: He, he, he! [*Chuckling*] But I am though, and I have proved it, at Saratoga, and at Tippacannoo, and Chippawa.

AMELIA: Have you been all your life a soldier?

LEATHER-STOCKING: No soger! I never carried smooth-bore or baggonet. I have been all my life a ranger, in peace and war. In peace this rifle never mist deer or duck; and in war, it has been as harmful to my country's invaders, as any smooth-bore or baggonet piece of 'em all. But times are alter'd, I am old, the game is driven west. This is no place for a ranger.

WENTWORTH: We are going north or west, too – I don't exactly know which – to Niagara.

LEATHER-STOCKING: That was once wild enough. Fit to look on – but it's spoilt now. What has housen and bridges to do among the wonders of heaven? They spoil all – they spoil all!

AMELIA: Go with us.

LEATHER-STOCKING: No. I go to the prairie and the wilderness. Men are not for me. I have performed my promise, and shown you a place worth looking at.

AMELIA: You have indeed.

LEATHER-STOCKING: Then good by! remember old Leather-Stocking, when you return to your country. The country of our fathers! Old England. [*Exit*]

AMELIA: Strange being! fit for scenes like this.

WENTWORTH: Come! I wish he had staid to help me back again. Come, Amelia – we must go farther, I suppose.

AMELIA: On, brother! on to Niagara. [*Exeunt*]

Scene 3

State-street, Albany. The Capitol at a distance. Enter Bull as Jonathan, and Amelia.

BULL: Could you have thought that prejudice would make any man believe that another man, merely because a native of another country, could design in cold blood to murder him, without cause or provocation? "This will do your business, Mr. Bull."

AMELIA: Prejudice will make men believe any thing. But I don't see how you are to cure my brother. You make him worse and worse.

BULL: The disease must be increased to make the cure radical. The crisis is nigh – . Here he comes. You are so tarnal good nater'd, Miss, that I could like to tell you stories all day long.

Enter Wentworth

WENTWORTH: I wonder you will suffer that clown to talk to you, sister.

AMELIA: You left me, brother, and I was glad to have a fellow-traveller near me. He is acquainted in Albany – knows everybody.

WENTWORTH: [*Takes out a snuff-box, and takes a pinch*] I have got a head-ach in that tiresome boat.

BULL: I see you English folk do like a pinch of snuff, now and then, as well as the French. That's very fine snuff, I guess.

WENTWORTH: Yes. I bought it in London for my own use. [*Puts the box in his pocket*]

BULL: For your own use! So it seems. Now darn it, that puts me in mind of Nathan's orange. [*Wentworth turns from him*] You must know, Miss, our Nathan went to town, and he brought home an orange; 'twas a meazing fine one, that's sartin. "Nathan," says I, "that's a beauty of an orange" – I thought the creetur would a gin me a bit. "Yes," says he, "Jonathan, it is a beauty. Look! You may look on it, Jonathan," says he, "and you may smell on it, but you mustn't taste on it – cause – *Mother* sets on it." Now, I guess, you *set on* your snuff, Mister, I reckon. [*Enter Porters and Nancy*]

WENTWORTH: Impertinent fool! I have forgot the name of the hotel or tavern they directed me to.

NANCY: Mr. Crooked Mans, Sir.

BULL: I guess as how you mean Cruttenden's – a little man, up on the top of the hill, yonder, by the Capitol.

WENTWORTH: Little! every thing is under size in this country.

AMELIA: You will except pears, brother.

NANCY: Do you know, Sir, they all said that *that* great pear was a pumpkin.

WENTWORTH: Go on, Miss Pert, with the baggage. All the servants are spoilt here. Who gave you leave to speak?

NANCY: Every body speaks, as likes, here.

AMELIA: Come Nancy – hush! [*Exeunt Amelia, Nancy and Porters with baggage*]

BULL: You find every thing under size in this country, Sir?

WENTWORTH: What if I do, Sir?

BULL: I'm of your opinion, Sir. I have been a gret traveller in this country, Sir. I have dicker'd tin-ware for old iron and brass, all the way from Maine to New-Orleans. And I've a notion that the Mississippi won't compare with the Thames, any more than the Falls of Niagara will stand by the side of the cascade in Vauxhall Garden. I know the people of this country brag, and for all I'm a native Yankee, you will find that I think them no better than they should be.

WENTWORTH: I see you are a man of more sense than I took you for. I like an unprejudiced man.

BULL: Like yourself, Sir. That's nateral. I'll show you the way to Cruttenden's, the little man on the hill, and I'll let you into the true notion of these Yankees – every mother's son of them.

WENTWORTH: Thank you. Come along.

BULL: I will. [*Takes Wentworth's arm, who shakes him off*] I'll open your eyes, Sir. [*Aside*] You shall know a pear from a pumpkin before we part. [*Exeunt. Bull following Wentworth*]

Scene 4

The little falls of the Mohawk. A view of the stupendous rocks, through which the river flows. A part of the town. The canal and the aqueduct crossing the river. Enter Wentworth, Amelia, and other travellers. Travellers pass over the stage, and go off.

AMELIA: This is delightful, brother.

WENTWORTH: Is it?

AMELIA: The opportunity we so frequently have, of stepping from the canal-boat, and thus walking on the bank, adds to the pleasure derived from the ever changing scenery that is presented to us.

WENTWORTH: Pleasure! To be dragged along upon a muddy ditch, hour after hour, in constant dread of lifting your head above your knees for fear of having it knock'd off your shoulders by a bridge!

AMELIA: But your head is safe, now, notwithstanding the Frenchman's razor, and the canal bridges, and you must admire this great patriotic work – this union of the inland seas with the Atlantic Ocean.

WENTWORTH: What is this, to the work of the Duke of Bridgewater.

AMELIA: Let praise be given, where praise is due. There are two names, which will live in the memories of Americans, as long as they can appreciate the blessings that flow in a rapid interchange of every good from one extreme of their republic to the other. Fulton and Clinton. And I hope that the gratitude of their countrymen, will not only be shown to their names and memories, but to their children, and their children's children.

WENTWORTH: Where's Doolittle? I begin to like that fellow. He sees things as I do.

AMELIA: We left him talking with a Dutchman. Here he comes.

Enter Bull as Jonathan

BULL: What do you think that tarnation Mohawk Dutchman says?

WENTWORTH: Praises the great canal, I suppose.

BULL: No. He says, "Effer since Glinton gut de pig canawl, de peef ant putter of de Sharman-flats ave falt fifty bur shent; ant dey pring all de tam dings to New-York, all de vay from Puffallo, ant de tuyvil knows vere."

AMELIA: Ha, ha, ha! Fault finding every where. Brother, I will walk on. [*Exit Amelia*]

WENTWORTH: I dare say he is right. But, Mr. Doolittle, when shall we get to the wilderness?

BULL: Ah, that's what every body says. But these curst creeturs have spoilt all that. What with their turnpike roads, and canals, they have gone, like tarnal fools as they are, and put towns and villages, gardens and orchards, churches and schools, and sich common things, where the woods and wild beasts and Indians and rattlesnakes ought to have ben. Shall I tell you what my uncle Ben said?

DENNIS: [*Without*] O, ho, ub bub bugh, hallo!

WENTWORTH: I see some one in that canal-boat, waving his hat to us. I think it is – yes – there! He jumps ashore and runs this way.

BULL: Who the nation is it?

WENTWORTH: I believe it's an Irish farmer that the boat left behind in New-York. It is!

DENNIS: [*Without*] Stop a bit Mr. Wintwort! Stop a bit.

BULL: He thinks the yellow fever is at his heels.

Enter Dennis

DENNIS: Ah! Sure enough it is you! I've cotch you at last! And now I may fale safe again, any how!

WENTWORTH: Safe! why, what has happened?

DENNIS: Why you know the *first* time I came with you, I came *last*, and I didn't come at all you know *before*, becase the boat left me *behind*.

BULL: So, you came *first* at *last, after all;* and you didn't come at all, because you were *behind, before*.

DENNIS: That's *it.* [*To Wentworth*] Who may this civil, *clare-spoken* gentleman be?

WENTWORTH: Mr. Doolittle. One of the natives of this country. A Yankee.

DENNIS: O! a Yankee. You nivver have the faver among yoursilves, you natives, but only kape it for us of the ould country.

BULL: Now, you, I wonder how we should keep it if we never have it? That would be cute – I guess.

DENNIS: I thought, once, I would be made a native, mysilf, that I might be safe.

WENTWORTH: But you were born in Ireland, you know.

DENNIS: What signifies *that?* And haven't I seen Irishmen all the way as I came along, and they told me they were made natives. But, now, how could you lave me, Mr. Wintwort?

WENTWORTH: I thought we had lost you, my friend.

DENNIS: Not at all; it was I lost my passage. But I wouldn't be left any more, any how, and so I went aboard of the nixt boat that wint off, thinking I would catch you, but she happend to go t'other way, and where do you think they took me to, of all places in the world?

WENTWORTH: That I can't tell.

DENNIS: How should you, if you don't know? Will then, they carried me to the place where they put all the yellow faver people at, I suppose to keep one another in countenance.

BULL: What? To the quarantine ground!

DENNIS: That's it. "What place is that?" says I. "It's the hospital for the faver," says he. "And sure you wouldn't put me there?" says I. "That's as you like," says he. "The divvil a bit of like, nor will I go ashore at all." And so I wouldn't till they brought me back again to York.

BULL: That was a Yankee trick. What them there sarpents call a joke.

WENTWORTH: So you went ashore at York?

DENNIS: I did. But not on the land. I went ashore on the river. I landed on a boat, for I took up my board and lodging in the stame-boat for Albany; and I made sure to get a bert in the *fore*-castle, that I mightn't be behind this time, any how.

WENTWORTH: And so followed me all this long way.

DENNIS: That I did. For I thought that would be the most likely way to overtake you. And I thought I would have your protection, sure I would, 'till I get safe into his Majesty's dominions. And I axt for you at Albany, and they said you had gone on up the canal.

WENTWORTH: They remembered me?

DENNIS: Yes. Says they, "the man that grumbles at every thing." "That's Mr. Wintwort," says I.

BULL: I told you what the Yankees were.

DENNIS: So, by the powers, I've been riding in a boat behind tree horses day and night to catch you – and here you are going a fut all the time.

WENTWORTH: Our boat is ahead.

DENNIS: Then you are behind this time.

BULL: See, Mister, what ignorant creeturs these Yankees are. [*Points to a sign by a hovel of a tavern*] T. R. O. F. for horses to drink out of.

DENNIS: Sure enough. And they might so azily spelt it right, by only putting another *ef* at the end.

BULL: True. I see you are a scholar.

DENNIS: I was once – when I was a little boy.

WENTWORTH: But, Dennis, my good fellow, you must want money by this time, after travelling so far.

DENNIS: O fait the stame-boat was chape enough, any how; and when I came to the canal, I work'd my passage.

WENTWORTH: Work'd your passage?

DENNIS: Yes. It was my own proposal. For I found my dollars grow light. "Work your passage, Pat," says a civil man, like that gentleman, [*Pointing to Bull*] laughing all the time. "You are the man I want," says he. "That's what they all say," says I. So I went on board, and when the boat started, they put me ashore to lade the horses.

BULL: Yankee, again, forever!

WENTWORTH: And you walk'd all the way before the horses?

DENNIS: I'll tell you. "Pat, how do you like sailing in the canal-boat?" says the civil grinning gentleman, like that [*Pointing to Bull*]. "Fait," says I, "if it was not for the name of the thing, I'm thinking I might as well be walking a fut."

BULL: Ha, ha, ha! and what said the Yankee?

DENNIS: "Stip aboard," says he, "and take some bafe and whiskey; you shall work the rest of your passage wid your tathe."

BULL: Well done, both Pat and Yankee! I see the boat is crossing the river on that unnatural

thingumbob they call an aqueduct; and if we don't hurry a bit, we shall be left.

DENNIS: Lift in this place! it would be horrible!

BULL: Wouldn't it. [*Exeunt – while the canal-boat is seen crossing the river on the aqueduct*]

Scene 5

Hotel at Buffalo. Chamber. Enter Bull as Jonathan, (a cart whip under his arm,) and Wentworth.

WENTWORTH: So, this is Buffalo! And I'm on the shores of Lake Erie! And what do I see after all. A town like other towns, water like other water, and people like other people – only made worse by democracy. I have not seen a well behaved man since I came into the country, only a wild half Indian.

BULL: You must a kept bad company, I guess. But you have such coaxing ways with you, you are so kind and accommodating, that it's a wonder every body doesn't try might and main to please you. But I must say, though I was misfortunate enough to be born in *this* country, that the Yankees are the most ungrateful creeturs upon arth. You are so civil to every body, and so agreeable to every thing – and yet I don't see any body cares a button for you.

WENTWORTH: What do you mean by that?

BULL: I've seen the waiters, blacks and all, laugh at you behind your back.

WENTWORTH: [*Aside*] I don't know what to make of this fellow.

Enter Dennis

DENNIS: Mr. Wintwort, Sir! Can you tell how all this great big sae came to be here on dry land, out of its place?

WENTWORTH: What do you mean?

DENNIS: They call it a lake, but it's a sae, for I saw the ships mysilf. But the people of this country would always be imposing upon furruners – as if I didn't know the Lake of Killarney – what's this to that?

BULL: I was just telling Squire Wentworth what a darn'd twistical country this is. Now *you* see the evil of the thing.

DENNIS: Fait and I see nothing else.

BULL: And nothing else will you see, among them sarpents, but one slippery trick or 'nother to get inside your head or your pocket. Did I ever tell you, Squire Wentworth, how my own brother Nathan serv'd me?

WENTWORTH: I don't want to hear.

BULL: Not about the orange, but another time.

DENNIS: Let's hare, if you plase.

BULL: Well – you must know, Nathan and I were out duck shooting on the Connecticut river in father's skiff. We had meazing fine sport. we had; but just as I was priming my gun, some how or 'nother I drops my powder horn, and the curst thing went right over, plump into the river, and pop down to the bottom. "There," says I, "only look o'that!" – "Nathan," says I, "lend me your powder horn to prime." And would you believe it? The stingy creetur wouldn't. "Well then," says I, "you're a good diver – Nathan – there it is – I see it – dive down and fetch it – and I'll give you some." Well – he did so. Down he went – and there he staid.

DENNIS: For what would he stay?

BULL: That puzzled me. But I look'd down – the water was meazing clear – and what do you think he was doing?

DENNIS: How should I know.

BULL: There I saw the tarnal creetur emptying my powder into his own powder horn.

WENTWORTH: At the bottom of the river? Do you think we believe such stuff?

DENNIS: I don't doubt it at all. And I shouldn't wonder if he had set fire to the river, and blow'd you and the boat to the divvil, and then he would have all the powder himsilf.

BULL: Did the tarnal creeturs ever feed you on tarrappin soup?

DENNIS: That's the very name of it sure enough! I was going to ate, but I saw something like little black fingers and toes in it.

BULL: O! you smok'd the thing. Tarrappin is the cant word for young nigger.

DENNIS: O, thunder!

WENTWORTH: How this Yankee is quizzing the Irishman.

BULL: They have another dish they like meazingly. Barbacued papoos. Papoos is the name they give the young Indians.

WENTWORTH: Pooh, pooh!

DENNIS: No. Not pooh, pooh – papoos.

BULL: Yes. Papoos.

DENNIS: And do they ate Indian?

BULL: Every day.

WENTWORTH: No, no! he's quizzing you. No such thing.

DENNIS: It's true! by the powers it's true! and *that* accounts for it. Didn't I mysilf, one day, in the skirts of New-York, just stip into a house, and ax an old woman, who had a big pot over the fire, to give me a drink of water. And what do you think she said? "As soon as I have put the Indian in the pot," says she. Och! I didn't know what it meant – at all – but that accounts for it. I don't wonder they have the faver! Ate Indian! It puts me in a faver to spake of it.

WENTWORTH: Nonsense, nonsense!

BULL: Nothing more common. They make Indian dumplings and Indian puddings, and the little white-headed Yankee children fatten upon Indian, as the English boys and girls do upon blood puddings.

WENTWORTH: This Irishman will believe any thing.

BULL: Do you see this here? [*The whip*] Now what do you think the people of this country do with sich.

DENNIS: Whip their horses, sure.

BULL: It's to whip niggers. They drive the black creeturs into the tobacco patches, and keep 'em working in the hot sun, 'till their wool blazes again.

DENNIS: O, the poor cratures! Fait, and I know what a hot sun is, and I paid for my larning.

WENTWORTH: Pooh, pooh! You must not believe such tales.

DENNIS: Now, Mister Wintwort, you naden't think to smooth it over wid blarney. I have sane enough mysilf to make me belave any thing of a country to which they saduce poor Irishmen only to bury them, and have their coffins ready made without even the dasent sirimony of measuring the corpse. And didn't I see the woman boil the Indian? Och! Let me once get safe to Canada, under the king's flag, and you will nivver catch Dennis Dougherty in the states again. [*Exit*]

WENTWORTH: Why would you encourage that poor fellow's prejudices, when you know that neither the people nor the country are as bad as you make them.

BULL: Ah, ha! do you begin to think so?

WENTWORTH: I begin to think that I have done both the people and country injustice.

BULL: I am glad of it, Mister, for your own sake. To tell you the truth, I have been quizzing *you* a little. Only for your own good. And though *you* do not believe that the Indian for the pot or the bake-pan is the same that wields the scalping-knife and the tomahawk, you have had prejudices almost as strong as Dennis Dougherty's. Prejudices which have made you a subject of ridicule to the people you have affected to despise.

WENTWORTH: This is very strange language – and yet – after all – there is a blunt sort of *John Bullism* about you – that I like – a little.

BULL: The more you know of me the better you will like me. And now, let me advise you, for your own comfort, to treat every body with civility, wherever you go – and you will find civility and kindness in return.

WENTWORTH: Well, well, well! I believe you are right. Here, Waiter! come here my good fellow!

BULL: That's right.

Enter Waiter

WAITER: Please to have, Sir?

WENTWORTH: Boot-jack and slippers, and a candle, if you please.

WAITER: Instantly, Sir! [*Running off*]

BULL: [*As Frenchman*] Vaitare! [*Waiter stops*] Von leetle piece candale, and *von* bed, after you ave a served my frent, Mistare Ventawort, if you please, Sair! [*Exit Waiter, Amelia appears*]

WENTWORTH: What, are you the Frenchman, too!

BULL: Neither Frenchman nor Yankee, but your old acquaintance, John Bull, of Westminster. [*Throws off disguise*] Give me your hand!

WENTWORTH: Is it possible.

Enter Amelia

AMELIA: Yes, brother, your English friend, and your English sister, have been in a plot – not to cut off your head, with a razor – but to cure you of a disease which made you unhappy, and caused that incivility from others of which you complained – *fault finding*.

WENTWORTH: You are right. Thank ye both. But I am glad my physicians were English! that's some consolation!

BULL: And I have been stimulated to play two parts in this travelling comedy, by the promise of your sister's hand, as my reward – if I cure you. No cure no pay.

WENTWORTH: I see it all. And you have been in the plot all this time. [*To Amelia*]

AMELIA: "An innocent plot, brother – I am sure it was meant for your good." – Ha, ha, ha!

WENTWORTH: Well, I will see things as they are. Take her hand.

BULL: With all my heart. That's the regular receiving speech, I believe, on such occasions. Remember the lesson, Wentworth, and John Bull will be as much respected and loved in America, as he is in every other part of the world. And now, huzza for the Falls of Niagara!

Scene 6

The Falls of Niagara, as seen from below, on the American side. Table-rock. Leather-Stocking is discovered sitting on a rock. He rises and comes forward.

LEATHER-STOCKING: This looks as it used to do, they can't spoil this – yet a while – Hawks-eye has taken his last look at the places he loved, and now away to the prairie, the woods, and the grave. [*He turns to go*]

Enter Amelia, Nancy, Wentworth, and Bull in his own dress

WENTWORTH: This is indeed a scene of wonders.

AMELIA: What? Our friend the hunter!

LEATHER-STOCKING: [*Comes forward*] Young woman – I thought I had taken leave of you – and all! But I am going.

WENTWORTH: Your hand. [*Grasps his hand*] Wherever you go, take the hearty salute of an Englishman.

LEATHER-STOCKING: It is not the first time this hand has grappled a Briton's – as friend and as foe.

WENTWORTH: Henceforth, forever friends!

LEATHER-STOCKING: Forever! [*Goes off slowly*]

Enter Dennis

DENNIS: [*Speaks as he enters*] Mr. Wintwort! Mr. Wintwort! And am I in Canada? Am I safe in his Majesty's dominions?

BULL: Not yet. But within sight of them.

DENNIS: And where is the blissed spot.

BULL: Do you see that rock?

DENNIS: Fait, I do.

BULL: That's it.

DENNIS: And is that Canada?

BULL: That's the famous Table-rock.

DENNIS: And sure if a man had his mate on that table, he would have enough water to mix with his whiskey, any how. And Mr. Wintwort, am I in the yellow faver states yet?

AMELIA: We are still in the United States. Still in the great and flourishing state of New-York.

DENNIS: O the divvil! New-York here!

WENTWORTH: We will cross over, good fellow, and take you with us to his Majesty's dominions.

DENNIS: And shall I then be safe under the King's flag?

BULL: As sure as you are an Irishman, travelling for improvement.

DENNIS: Why then that's sure enough.

BULL: You have learnt something.

DENNIS: And it isn't a little I've larnt. I've larnt what hate is; and that cost me something in flesh and money. I've sane the world, and it's cost me all I was wort in the world to see it. And I've sane liberty, of all shapes and colours; and now I'm at liberty to go home again – if I can get there.

WENTWORTH: You came to me for protection, and you shall find it. I will take you home – put you on a farm – and think myself happy to have so honest a friend and tenant.

DENNIS: Long life to your honour! I think I am a head of the faver this time, any how.

AMELIA: Well, brother, you are pleased, I hope.

WENTWORTH: I am amply repaid for all my dangers. When the film of prejudice is removed from the eye, man sees in his fellow man of every clime a brother. And in this happy country, the stranger has ever found a reception that calls for the warmest feelings of gratitude. Yes, sister, I *am* pleased; and if all present agree to be pleased, we shall have reason to bless our Trip to Niagara.

The End

METAMORA

OR

THE LAST OF THE WAMPANOAGS

JOHN AUGUSTUS STONE

IN the New York *Critic* for November 28, 1828, the American actor Edwin Forrest announced a playwriting competition: five hundred dollars plus a half-benefit for "the best tragedy, in five acts, of which the hero, or principal character, shall be an aboriginal of this country." John Augustus Stone read the announcement and, with the advantage over his competitors of having performed with the Bowery company when Forrest had played the Indian in *She Would Be a Soldier*, turned out a play that won the prize. His play became the "war-horse" piece for Forrest throughout his career, and after its first performance at the Park on December 15, 1829, it became firmly established as a smash hit with a record of over two hundred performances during the sixty years it held the stage.

Stone was born in Concord, Massachusetts, on December 15, 1800. When he was twenty, he made his first stage appearance at the Washington Garden Theatre in Boston as Old Norval in *Douglas*. Though twenty was an early age to start as a character actor, Stone's physical appearance and inclination apparently dictated the choice. He continued throughout his career to play either eccentric comics or "rough and bluff" old men. Although he never became a star or even a featured player, he was regarded as a favorite at the New York theatres from 1822 to 1831. After 1831 he acted at the Walnut Street and Chestnut Street theatres in Philadelphia. It is not surprising that such a theatre-wise actor-playwright should write so demanding and commanding a part as Metamora.

In 1821 he had married the actress Mrs. Legge (she later became the wife of the playwright H. N. Bannister) and had two sons, Christopher Lucius and Henry, both of whom became actors. During his brief years in Philadelphia, Stone suffered from ill health; he finally became despondent and committed suicide by jumping from the Spruce Street Wharf into the Schuykill River on May 29, 1834. His death was widely noted in the press. James Hunter, the editor of the Albany *Daily News*, wrote:

Within a few days past the public has been made acquainted with the melancholy fact that John Augustus Stone is no more! The tidings were received in this city with unfeigned regret, and the friends of the drama who knew him so well when living, at first intelligence of his departure from among us, retired, with melting hearts, to shed the bitter tears of sorrow. The news of his exit cast a solemnity and gloom over the countenances of a large circle of his acquaintances in our city, far surpassing any providential affliction of the kind that ever preceded it. The successful effort of Mr. Stone to elevate and establish permanently the dramatic character of our country, will ever be remembered. Under the patronage of Forrest, Mr. Stone has contributed more, both as author and performer, to raise the character of the stage, than any other native American.

In token of his respect and gratitude, Forrest placed a monument over Stone's grave in Machpelah Cemetery inscribed "To the Memory of John Augustus Stone, Author of Metamora, by His Friend Edwin Forrest."

Although Stone wrote other plays, none of them rivaled the success of *Metamora*. *Tancred, or The Siege of Antioch* (1827), the only play of Stone's to be published during his lifetime, was not acted. *Restoration, or The Diamond Cross* was performed at the Chatham Garden on November 4, 1824. *The Lion of the West*, a revision of James Kirke Paulding's play of the same name, was given at the Park on November 14, 1831. *The Demoniac, or The Prophet's Bride* was done at the Bowery on April 12, 1831; and *The Ancient Briton* at the Arch Street Theatre, Philadelphia, on March 27, 1833. *The Knight of the Golden Fleece, or The Yankee of Spain*, first performed at the Park on September 10, 1834, provided a successful role for the Yankee actor George H. Hill, who played the part of Sy Saco for fifteen years. Two other plays, of unestablished date, *Fauntleroy, or The Fatal Forgery* and *La Roque, the Regicide*, were performed in Charleston. One other play, *Touretoun* – only the title is known – has been attributed to Stone.

No previous first performance of a play had received the kind of pre-opening attention that was given to *Metamora*. The response to Forrest's contest was widely reported, and a committee of distinguished literary and theatrical gentlemen (William Cullen Bryant, Fitz-Greene Halleck, James Lawson, William Leggett, Prosper M. Wetmore, and J. G. Brooks) judged the fourteen plays submitted in this first American playwriting contest. Subsequently Forrest conducted other contests; they brought in some two hundred plays, of which nine received prizes. Of these later prize plays only Bird's *The Gladiator* and *The Broker of Bogota* and Conrad's *Jack Cade* were retained in Forrest's repertoire, and none of them approached the phenomenal success of *Metamora*. Forrest is said to have contributed some twenty thousand dollars to the encouragement of native dramatic literature. A shrewd investment, these plays along with those of Shakespeare constituted the bulk of Forrest's repertoire throughout his career.

Even after the preliminary attempts to create a favorable climate for the reception of a new American play, Forrest feared the skeptics. He commissioned Prosper M. Wetmore to write a prologue, and James Lawson an epilogue, to plead the cause of "native pens" and "native powers." Some lines from each will indicate the tone:

> Tonight we test the strength of native powers,
> Subject, and bard, and actor, all are yours –
> 'Tis yours to judge, if worthy of a name,
> And bid them live within the halls of fame!
> (from Wetmore's Prologue)

> A native bard – a native actor too,
> Have drawn a native picture to your view;
> Yet, not that they are native do I plead,
> 'Tis for their worth alone I ask your meed.
> (from Lawson's Epilogue)

If there were skeptics in the audience on opening night, December 15, 1829, their voice was not heard in the theatre or in the press reports that appeared the next day. "Forrest caught the very manner of their breathing," one reporter noted. "For sheer destructive energy," another observed, he had never heard anything so "tremendous in its sustained crescendo swell and crashing force of utterance. His voice surged and roared like the angry sea; as it reached its boiling, seething climax, in which the serpent hiss of hate was heard, at intervals amidst its louder, deeper, hoarser tones, it was like the falls of Niagara."

After its initial showing in New York, *Metamora* was performed throughout the country. In the next forty years, whenever Forrest played *Metamora*, the audiences crowded the theatres to capacity. In the twenty-five years from 1830 to 1855, Philadelphia had only two seasons without *Metamora*. When Sol Smith in St. Louis was at his wit's end to counter the drawing power of his competitor – Madame Caradori Allan "warbling Italian music" on the nights when Forrest played – he scheduled *Metamora* on May 10, 1839. The following morning Smith wrote to his partner, Noah Ludlow, "*Metamora* resulted in a house of $951! – Come, not so bad, my master. Stocks is riz." Previous receipts had been less than three hundred dollars per night. A later series of twelve performances in St. Louis brought in a record profit of $2,157. The story was the same in the other cities – in fact, wherever Forrest appeared. On April 9, 1830, *Metamora*'s first performance in Albany played "to the largest business of the engagement"; and at the same theatre in January, 1834, "the members of the orchestra had to leave their seats and retire behind the scenes, to accommodate the people, while hundreds were not able to enter the theatre." On January 5, 1842, the Bowery management announced: "In consequence of the number of persons unable to gain a sight of the stage on New Year's night, to witness the Indian play of *Metamora!* the manager has much pleasure in announcing Mr. Forrest in the above play one night more." In Mobile, during an engagement in March, 1844, *Othello* brought in $528, *Macbeth* $330, *King Lear* $324, and *Metamora* $656. At the Boston Theatre in November, 1846, two performances had receipts of $719 and $872. The other plays of Forrest's repertoire had only single performances, with a high mark of $694 for *Othello*. Again in Boston, at the National Theatre, during January, 1853, *Metamora*'s receipts for six performances totaled $3,928 and *The Gladiator*'s, second but well behind, $2,333 for four performances. Time and again *Metamora* was welcomed by managements in distress in spite of the fact that frequently half of the gross receipts went into Forrest's pocket.

Other actors attempted the role, but none with Forrest's success. After Forrest's death in 1872, Oliver Doud Byron, Edward Eddy, John McCullough, D. H. Harkins, and Edmund Collier tried the play, all for brief and undistinguished engagements.

The play was Forrest's and the part was Forrest's. As Ireland wrote, "Whatever faults this tragedy may possess as a literary or dramatic composition, its real merit keeps it living on the stage, and, in the character of its hero, no dissenting voice has qualified Mr. Forrest's claim to the highest excellence. It was created for, and entirely fitted all his peculiarities."

The brawny and tempestuous Forrest was marked as a star-caliber actor from the very beginning of his career. Mordecai Noah described his first view of Forrest at the Pearl Street Theatre in Albany in October, 1825:

Went to the theatre to see *Julius Caesar*. Forrest, a young man of nineteen or twenty, thick set, athletic, stiff and with coarse but powerful voice, played Mark Antony. Returning to Congress Hall, I found Gilfert [the manager of the theatre, who later produced *A Trip to Niagara* in New York] rapidly eating his lunch of corned beef and horse-radish. We commenced the following dialogue: "Gilfert, who is that young man who played Mark Antony," "His name is Forrest." "Where from," "Philadelphia, I believe." "What's his character?" "Good," "Is he sober – steady?" "Always perfect in his part?" "Always perfect." "How long have you engaged him?" "For a year or two." "What salary?" "Very small." We paused while Gilfert got through his supper, and after a glass of brandy and water, he looked at us across the table, over his specs, in his peculiar way and said, "Tell me, Noah, why you asked me those questions about that young man?" "Because," said I, "he has all the material of a great actor, and if his habits are good, we would advise you to make a long engagement with him, and by all means increase his salary."

The fan magazines of today would certainly describe Forrest's rise as "meteoric." When he announced his prize competition in 1828, his weekly salary had just jumped from forty dollars to four hundred dollars. He was the first American actor who could equal – some said "outplay" – the foreign giants Edmund Kean, Junius Brutus Booth, and William Macready. Forrest was an exciting, a high-luster performer on the stage and off. His stormy and scandalous divorce suit, even though it came at the height of his career, did not dim the ardor of his patriotic followers. The engagement that he began at the Broadway Theatre on February 9, 1852, was the most remarkable of his career. In fact, it was the longest run ever carried through by a tragedian up to that time. He played for sixty-nine nights, running through his entire repertoire.

Forrest was a fiery, untamed figure of a man who could be convincingly identified with Cooper's, and the audience's, conception of the "noble savage" – what Mark Twain later labeled "the extinct tribe which never existed."

The romantic conception of the Indian's character as the archetype of human nobility reflected the early-nineteenth-century notions of ethical excellence. The Indian was brave, chivalrous, kind, and gentle toward his squaw and his children. He respected the achievements of his forebears and honored their name. And he held an unfaltering belief and trust in the will of the Almighty Manitou. Even in his normal day-to-day conduct he epitomized the nineteenth-century concept of the virtuous man.

The first dramatist to perceive the dramatic possibilities in the Indian character had been Major Robert Rogers. His unproduced play *Ponteach* (1766) embodied most of the "noble savage" qualities that were to become the theatrical stereotype for the Indian. John Nelson Barker's *The Indian Princess, or La Belle Sauvage*, produced at the Chestnut Street Theatre in Philadelphia on April 6, 1808, followed the Pocahontas story almost literally as reported in Captain Smith's *General History of Virginia*. There were other predecessors of *Metamora*, notably *Oolaita* (1821), by Lewis Deffebach; *William Penn* (1829), by Richard Penn Smith; and George Washington Parke Custis's *The Indian Prophecy* (1827); however, the great surge of Indian dramas came after *Metamora*. Thirty-five plays, of varying dramatic value but with monotonous repetition of the "noble savage" theme, appeared during the next twenty years. Most notable among these were *Pocahontas* (1830), by Custis, and the burlesque *Po-ca-hon-tas*, by John Brougham, which is included in this collection. Brougham also wrote a similar treatment of *Metamora*, entitled *Metamora, or The Last of the Pollywogs* (1847). The burlesque was aimed more at Forrest's performance than at the play. For example, Metamora's magnificent bearing, so highly praised by Oceana in Stone's play, in Brougham's version was described as follows:

> His hair was glossy as the raven's wing;
> He looked and moved a sort of savage king;
> His speech was pointed, at the same time blunt –
> Something between a whisper and a grunt.

All told, there were some seventy-five Indian dramas written during the nineteenth century, but only *Metamora* achieved any marked success.

Although clearly Stone's play would not have achieved its phenomenal record in the hands of any other player, his is a mark above the other Indian dramas. His principal character was modeled on the famous New England sachem King Philip of Pokanoket, son of Massasoit. Metamora was a true child of nature, possessed of an infallible nobility of character and endowed with a remarkable facility for noble utterances. He valiantly resisted the encroachments of the white man, refusing "to forsake the home of his fathers and let the plough of strangers disturb the bones of his kindred." Yet he knew the battle was futile. With his mysterious prophetic gifts he foresaw the gloomy destiny of the Indians. "The power of dreams has been on me," he explained to his wife, "and the shadows of things that are to be have passed before me." Although the play was filled with thrilling actions and spectacular scenes, none of them matched the impact of the final pathetic scene, when, in his last futile stand, Metamora is forced to stab his wife as he embraces her. The basic ingredients of Stone's play were no different from those in the other Indian dramas. He simply managed to combine the beauty, the sublimity, the fierceness, the natural goodness of the "noble savage" and the drama of his struggle with the whites into a more thoroughly believable and satisfying theatrical document.

Until recently only incomplete texts of the play have been available. The copy in the Edwin Forrest Home in Philadelphia contains only Metamora's speeches and his cue lines. The fourth act is missing from the version in the University of Utah Library. In 1960, the present editor uncovered the fourth act among the Lord Chamberlain's plays in the British Museum.

METAMORA

OR

THE LAST OF THE WAMPANOAGS

JOHN AUGUSTUS STONE

CHARACTERS

INDIANS	
METAMORA, *chief of the Wampanoags*	SIR ARTHUR VAUGHAN
KANESHINE, *an Indian prophet*	MORDAUNT
ANNAWANDAH, *the traitor*	ERRINGTON, *chief of the council*
OTAH, *an Indian boy*	WALTER, *an orphan*
INDIAN BOY, *child of Metamora*	CAPTAIN CHURCH
NAHMEOKEE, *wife of Metamora'*	WOLFE
INDIANS, WARRIORS, ETC.	GOODENOUGH
	TRAMP
	OCEANA, *Mordaunt's daughter*

ENGLISH

LORD FITZARNOLD

SOLDIERS, SAILORS, PEASANTS, ETC.

PROLOGUE

Written by Mr. Prosper M. Wetmore.
Spoken by Mrs. Barrett, New Park Theater,
New York, December 15, 1829.

Not from the records of Imperial Rome,
Or classic Greece – the muses' chosen home –
From no rich legends of the olden day
Our bard hath drawn the story of his play;
Led by the guiding hand of genuis on,
He here hath painted Nature on her throne;
His eye hath pierced the forest's shadowy
  gloom,
And read strange lessons from a nation's tomb:
Brief are the annals of that blighted race –
These halls usurp a monarch's resting-place –
Traditions's mist-enshrouded page alone
Tells that an empire was – we know 'tis gone!
From foreign climes full oft the muse has
  brought
Her glorious treasures of gigantic thought;
And here, beneath the witchery of her power,
The eye hath poured its tributary shower:
When modern pens have sought th' historic
  page,

To picture forth the deeds of former age –
O'er soft Virginia's sorrows ye have sighed,
And dropt a tear when spotless beauty died;
When Brutus "cast his cloud aside"; to stand
The guardian of the tyrant-trampled land –
When patriot Tell his clime from thraldom
  freed,
And bade th' avenging arrow do its deed,
Your bosoms answered with responsive swell,
For freedom triumphed when th' oppressors
  fell!
These were the melodies of humbler lyres,
The lights of Genius, yet without his fires;
But when the master-spirit struck the chords,
And inspiration breathed her burning words –
When passion's self stalked living o'er the
  stage,
To plead with love, or rouse the soul to rage –
When Shakespeare led his bright creations
  forth,
And conjured up the mighty dead from earth –
Breathless – entranced – ye've listened to the
  line,
And felt the minstrel's power, all but divine!

While thus your plaudits cheer the stranger lay,
Shall native pens in vain the field essay?
To-night we test the strength of native powers,
Subject, and bard, and actor, all are ours –
'Tis yours to judge, if worthy of a name,
And bid them live within the halls of fame!

ACT I. Scene 1

Sunset. A wild, picturesque scene; high, craggy rocks in distance; dark pine trees, etc. Rocks cross stage, with platform cross behind. Steps, etc., at back. A rude tomb, flowers growing around it. Half dark. Mordaunt discovered leaning on tomb. Slow music.

MORDAUNT: The sun has sunk behind yon craggy rocks; and day's last beams are fading from the clouds that fleet in hurrying masses through the sky, like tattered banners of a flying host! England, my home! When will thy parent arms again enfold me? Oh! When for me will dawn a day of hope? Will not sincere repentance from my scathed brow efface the brand of regicide?

TRAMP: [*Outside*] What ho! Good Master Mordaunt! [*Cannon*]

MORDAUNT: Ha! What mean those sounds? Now, your news? [*Enter Tramp*]

TRAMP: A gallant bark, urged by the favoring breeze, makes for the crowded shore.

MORDAUNT: From England! Ha!

TRAMP: St. George's banner floats from her high mast, and her long signal pennon gleams with green and gold.

MORDAUNT: 'Tis he – he comes and with him hope arrives. Go, hasten, fellow; seek my daughter; say the Lord Fitzarnold comes to greet her. [*Tramp crosses to R. behind*] Marshal my followers in their best array – away to the beach and let loud music welcome him ashore. [*Exit Tramp*] What mingled feelings crowd about my heart, blended so strange and wild? Sunned by his sovereign's smile, Fitzarnold comes to woo and wed my daughter. Born on the heaving deep, the child of storms, and reared in savage wilds, her worth and beauty well may grace the courtly halls of England. And yet, to force her gentle will, whose every thought has been to soothe my sorrows and relieve my cares! Yet must she wed Fitzarnold. His alliance can with oblivion shroud the past, clear from my scutcheon every rebel stain, and give my franchised spirit liberty.

Exit. Slow music, four bars. Enter Oceana, looking around as if in search

OCEANA: Sure, 'twas my father's voice, and loud in converse. Father! Dear father! Not here? And yet I thought – [*Flute heard, distant*] Ha! whence that strain? So soft yet strange. Methinks some pious minstrel seeks the moonlight hour to breathe devotion forth in melody. [*Music changes*] Hark! It changes place and measure, too. Now deeper in the woods it warbles, now it seems aloft floating in plaintive tones through the air. This place – the hour – the day – heavens! 'tis my mother's birthday, and her grave undecked with flowers! O my mother, my dear mother! Perhaps her angel spirit hovers here o'er her lone daughter's steps, a guardian still. [*Kneels to tomb*] Ah, what flower is this? "Forgetmenot!" [*Music ceases*] My mother, look from thy seraph home upon thy child, and when for those thou lovest on earth thou breathest a prayer, oh, then forget me not. [*Places flower in bosom. Enter Walter*]

WALTER: Oceana!

OCEANA: Walter, was thine the strain but now I heard?

WALTER: 'Twas but an humble tribute to thy beauty, but could not match the sweetness of thy voice, whose every tone, attuned to dulcet sounds, can melt the soul to nature's harmony.

OCEANA: Walter, this from thee.

WALTER: Nay, blame me not; although dependent on Sir Arthur Vaughan, nameless and poor, yet do I not despair, for in my heart a sacred treasure lies I would not barter for my patron's gold.

OCEANA: What means't thou, Walter?

WALTER: Thine own sweet image, which naught on earth can banish or efface – a whispered hope I dare not speak aloud – a light thine own bright eyes have kindled up.

OCEANA: Nay, Walter, you ask not of the danger I escaped!

WALTER: Danger! What danger? When?

OCEANA: 'Twas yestere'en, when I was lingering on the eastern beach, all heedless of the coming night, a panther growling from the thicket rushed and marked me for his prey. Powerless I stood – my blood stood still – I shrieked as I strove to fly, when at the instant, from a ready hand, swift as the lightning's flash, an arrow came and felled the monster as he crouched to spring.

WALTER: Didst mark who sent it?

OCEANA: Full well I did. High on a craggy rock an Indian stood, with sinewy arm and eye that pierced the glen. His bowstring drawn to wing a second death, a robe of fur was o'er his shoulder thrown, and o'er his long, dark hair an eagle's plume waved in the breeze, a feathery diadem. Firmly he stood upon the jutting height, as if a sculptor's hand had carved him there. With awe I gazed as on the cliff he turned – the grandest model of a mighty man.

WALTER: 'Twas Haups great chieftain, Metamora called; our people love him not, nor is it strange; he stands between them and extended sway, ready alike with words of power to urge, or gleaming weapon force his princely dues.

METAMORA: [*Outside*] Hah! Ha!

OCEANA: [*Going up*] Behold his dread encounter with a wolf. His vanquished foe with mighty arm he hurls down the steep height where mortal never trod.

METAMORA: Hah! Hah! [*Enters on rock, passes across and off*]

WALTER: [*At Metamora's exit*] 'Tis Metamora, the noble sachem of a valiant race – the white man's dread, the Wampanoag's hope. [*Enter Metamora down R.*]

METAMORA: Ha, ha, ha! Turned on me – brave beast; he died like a red man.

OCEANA: Chief, you are hurt; this scarf will staunch the wound. [*Offers it*]

METAMORA: No! [*Rejects it*]

WALTER: 'Tis Oceana – she whose life you saved.

METAMORA: Metamora will take the white maiden's gift. [*Oceana ties his arm with scarf*]

OCEANA: But yestere'en thou savedst my life, great chief; how can I pay thee for the generous deed?

METAMORA: Hearken, daughter of the pale face; Metamora forgives not a wrong and forgets not a kindness. In the days of his age, Massasoit, my father, was in the white man's dwelling; while there, the spirit of the grave touched him and he laid down to die. A soft hand was stretched out to save him; it was the hand of thy mother. She that healed him sleeps in yonder tomb; but why should Metamora let his arrows sleep in the quiver when her daughter's

life was in danger and her limbs shook with fear? Metamora loves the mild-eyed and the kind, for such is Nahmeokee.

WALTER: Such words, and more than all, such deeds, should win you, chief, the love of all our people. Would you were more among us. Why never seek our homes? Sir Arthur Vaughan's doors will open to the Indian chief.

OCEANA: My sire will thank thee for his daughter's life.

METAMORA: The red man's heart is on the hills where his father's shafts have flown in the chase. Ha! I have been upon the high mountain top where the grey mists were beneath my feet, and the Great Spirit passed by me in his wrath. He spake in anger and the old rocks crumbled beneath the flash of his spear. Then I was proud and smiled, for I had slain the great bird whose wing never tires, and whose eye never shrinks; and his feathers would adorn the long black hair of Nahmeokee, daughter of Miantonemo, the great hunter. The war and the chase are the red man's brother and sister. The storm cloud in its fury frights him not. Wrapt in the spoils he has won, he lays him down and no one comes near to steal. The Great Spirit hears his evening prayer, and he sleeps amidst the roar of a mighty cataract.

WALTER: Were all thy nation mild and good like thee, how soon the fire of discord might be quenched.

METAMORA: Metamora has been the friend of the white man; yet if the flint be smitten too hard it will show that in its heart is fire. The Wampanoag will not wrong his white brother who comes from the land that is first touched by the rising sun; but he owns no master, save that One who holds the sun in his right hand, who rides on a dark storm, and who cannot die. [*Crosses to L.*]

WALTER: That lofty bearing – that majestic mien – the regal impress sits upon his brow, and earth seems conscious of her proudest son. [*Conch shell heard sounding, R.*]

METAMORA: Ha! My young men return from their evening toil, and their hands are filled with the sweet fish of the lake. Come to my wigwam; ye shall eat of fish that the Great Spirit of the waters sends, and your hearts shall be made glad. [*Going R. but returns and takes from his head an eagle plume*] Maiden, take this; it means speed and safety; when the startling whoop is heard and the war hatchet gleams in the red blaze, let it be found in thy braided hair. Despise not the red man's gift; it will bring more good to you than the yellow earth the white man worships as his god. Take it – no Wampanoag's hand will e'er be raised against the head or hand that bears the eagle plume. [*Crosses to Walter*] Young man, be thou like the oak in its spreading power and let thy tough branches shelter the tender flower that springs up under them. Look to the maiden of the eagle plume, and – come to my wigwam. [*Exit*]

OCEANA: Teach him, Walter; make him like to us.

WALTER: 'Twould cost him half his native virtues. Is justice goodly? Metamora's just. Is bravery virtue? Metamora's brave. If love of country, child and wife and home, be to deserve them all – he merits them.

OCEANA: Yet he is a heathen.

WALTER: True, Oceana, but his worship though untaught and rude flows from his heart, and Heaven alone must judge of it. [*Enter Tramp*]

TRAMP: Your father, lady, requires your presence.

OCEANA: Say I come. [*A distant drum*]

WALTER: What is that?

TRAMP: The drum that summons Lord Fitznold's escort. He comes a suitor for my lady's hand. [*Exit Tramp*]

WALTER: Deny it, Oceana – say 'tis false!

OCEANA: It is –

WALTER: Untrue?

OCEANA: Oh, most unwelcome.

WALTER: Heavens! You tremble – and your cheek is pale – my Lord Fitzarnold, that most courtly gentleman, and must my hopes –

OCEANA: Walter, dost thou mean –

WALTER: Obey thy sire. I cannot say farewell. But, oh, when highborn revelers carouse, and proud Fitzarnold lords it at the board, give one brief thought to me! That blessed thought shall soothe the fond complainings of my heart and hush them to repose. [*Exit Walter L. Oceana exit R.*]

Scene 2

Lights up. A room in Sir Arthur's house. Enter Sir Arthur and Walter.

WALTER: Yet hear me, sir.

SIR ARTHUR: Forebear; thou art too hot.

WALTER: 'Tis not the meanness of our state that galls us, but men's opinions. Poverty and toil and consciousness of lowly destiny sit lightly where no scorn is heaped upon them. But yesterday I was indeed content, for none despised, none had learned to scoff the son of charity, the wretched ship boy who could trace existence no further than the wreck from which you plucked him; but now 'tis changed, all suddenly begin to find me base.

SIR ARTHUR: Marry, go to! You wrong yourself and me. Have I not fostered you – like a father tutored you? In early life bereft of wife and child, wearied of discord and fierce civil strife, I left the haunts of wild and factious men, to woo contentment in this wilderness. My heart was vacant and received thee in. Do not by any rash, unworthy act forsake that heart. Who is it finds thee base?

WALTER: All, since Fitzarnold is expected here.

SIR ARTHUR: Fitzarnold! What a plague! There is naught talked of or thought of but Lord Fitzarnold! And yet this noble viscount, but for his coat and title were a man to look with scorn upon – a profligate and spendthrift as fame already has too truly shown him.

WALTER: And 'tis for such a man that Master Mordaunt sets me aside – for such a man his daughter must cast me off.

SIR ARTHUR: Tut! Master Mordaunt is too wise a man to give his daughter to this Lord Fitzarnold. Patience awhile, and watch the progress of this meteor. Patience, and trust to fortune. [*Exit*]

WALTER: This lordly suitor comes to wake me from my cherished dreams, and crush the hopes which lately looked so fair. And shall I yield the glorious prize I deemed was wholly mine? Yield, and without a struggle? No, by heaven! Look to thyself, Fitzarnold. Let Oceana be but true, I heed not all thy power, thy wealth, thy titles, backed though they be by Mordaunt's selfish views. [*Exit*]

Scene 3

The harbor. Ships anchored in the distance. Military music, Mordaunt, Errington, Goodenough, Church, Soldiers, Citizens (Male and female) discovered. A boat comes on from L., with Fitzarnold, Wolfe, and Sailors, who land. Shout.

MORDAUNT: Long live the king! Welcome Fitzarnold! Rest to the sea-worn! Joy to each and all!

FITZARNOLD: I thank thee, Mordaunt! But I did not think to see such faces in the wilderness! Thy woody shores are bright with sparkling eyes, like Argonaut's adventurous sailors. But where's the golden boon we look for, sir? Fair Oceana – Mordaunt, where is she? [*Walter enters, L., and stands against wing*]

MORDAUNT: So please you, my lord, at home, eager to pay your lordship's kindness back, and prove she can discern thy courtesy.

WALTER: [*Aside*] Indeed! Dost say so, worldling?

MORDAUNT: Pray thee, regard these gentlemen, my lord – our council's father, Errington – and this our army's leader; elders of the State.

Introducing them severally; Fitzarnold salutes them, and at last approaching Walter, extends his hand; Walter bows coldly but does not take it. Music eight bars

FITZARNOLD: How now, young sir? Mordaunt, who is this?

MORDAUNT: My noble lord, I pray thee, heed him not! A wayward youth, somewhat o'er worn with study. [*Crosses to Walter*] Rash boy! Be wise and tempt me not; I can destroy –

WALTER: Thy daughter's peace and wed her there. [*Mordaunt gives Walter a look of hate and turns from him*]

MORDAUNT: Forth to the hall – a strain of music there. [*Crosses to R.*]

FITZARNOLD: Young sir, I shall desire some further converse with you.

WALTER: At injury's prompting, deeds, not words, were best. My lord, you shall find me. [*Touches his sword*]

FITZARNOLD: Now for thy fair daughter, Mordaunt, come.

Music. Exeunt all but Walter and Wolfe. Peasants and Soldiers exeunt, R.

WOLFE: Thou goest not with them?

WALTER: No, nor before, nor follow after. But why dost thou ask?

WOLFE: Because I know thee.

WALTER: Then thou knowest one who will not take a lordling by the hand, because his fingers shine with hoops of gold – nor shun the beggar's grasp if it be honest. Thou knowest me?

WOLFE: Yes!

WALTER: To know oneself was thought task enough in olden time. What dost thou know?

WOLFE: That thou wert wrecked and saved.

WALTER: Aye, more's the pity! [*Aside*] Had I been drowned I had not lived to love and have no hope.

WOLFE: Thou art a good man's son.

WALTER: A pity then, again. Were I a rascal's offspring, I might thrive. What more?

WOLFE: Thou shalt possess thy mistress.

WALTER: Didst mark that lord?

WOLFE: He is my master.

WALTER: Then I am dumb. Be faithful to him, and now farewell. [*Crosses to L.*]

WOLFE: Yet in good time I will say that you will bestow a blessing for.

WALTER: Indeed! What mean you?

Enter Tramp, L., with packet

TRAMP: News from the Indians. [*Shows packet*] 'Tis for the council by a horseman left, who bade me see it with all haste delivered. The Indian tribes conspire from east to west and faithful Sasamond has found his grave! This packet must be borne to Mordaunt.

WALTER: Trust it with me.

TRAMP: That I will readily, so thou wilt bear it safely.

WALTER: Aye, and quickly, too. [*Takes packet, crosses to R.*] Let me remember Metamora's words – "Look to the maiden of the eagle plume."

Exit hastily, followed by Wolfe, and Tramp. Quick curtain

ACT II. Scene 1

Music. Interior of a wigwam; a skin rolled. Stage covered with skins, etc. Child on skin near R. entrance. Nahmeokee near it. Metamora at L., preparing for the chase.

NAHMEOKEE: Thou wilt soon be back from the chase.

METAMORA: Yes, before the otter has tasted his midday food on the bank of the stream, his skin shall make a garment for Nahmeokee when the snow whitens the hunting grounds and the cold wind whistles through the trees. Nahmeokee, take our little one from his rest; he sleeps too much.

NAHMEOKEE: Oh, no! But thou, Metamora, sleepst too little. In the still hour of midnight when Wekolis has sung his song, and the great light has gone down behind the hills, when Nahmeokee's arms like the growing vine were round thee – as if some danger lay waiting in the thick wood – thou didst bid me bring thy tomahawk and the spear that Massasoit had borne when the war cry of the Wampanoags was loudest in the place of blood! Why is thy rest like the green lake when the sudden blast passes across its bosom?

METAMORA: Nahmeokee, the power of dreams has been on me, and the shadows of things that are to be have passed before me. My heart is big with a great thought. When I sleep I think the knife is red in my hand, and the scalp of the white man is streaming.

NAHMEOKEE: Metamora, is not the white man our brother? And does not the Great Spirit look on him as he does on us? Do not go towards his home today because thy wrath is kindled and it spreads like the flames which the white man makes in the dark bosom of the forest. Let Nahmeokee clasp her arms around thee; rest thy head upon her bosom, for it is hot and thy eye is red with the thoughts that burn! Our old men counsel peace, and the aim of the white man will spare.

METAMORA: Yes, when our fires are no longer red, on the high places of our fathers; when the bones of our kindred make fruitful the fields of the stranger, which he has planted amidst the ashes of our wigwams; when we are hunted back like the wounded elk far toward the going down of the sun, our hatchets broken, our bows unstrung and war whoop hushed; then will the stranger spare, for we will be too small for his eye to see.

Trumpet. Enter Otah

OTAH: O son of Massasoit, the power of the white man approaches, and he looks not like one who seeks the Wampanoag's friendship! Look where the bright weapons flash through the clouds of his track.

METAMORA: Ha! Let the paleface come with the calumet or with the knife, Metamora does not fear their power. Where is Annawandah, skilled in talk? Let him approach me.

Exit Otah

NAHMEOKEE: Our child would not rest in the mid-hour of night for the hidden snake had bitten him as he lay stretched in the rays of the sun. I rose from my seat to get the dried leaves the Good Spirit has filled with power to heal; the moon was bright and a shadow passed me. It was Annawandah passed our wigwam; his step was like the course of the serpent and he paused and listened. My eye followed him to the seaside, and his light canoe shot like an arrow across the slumbering waters.

METAMORA: Humph! Was he alone?

NAHMEOKEE: Alone.

METAMORA: And he went with fear?

NAHMEOKEE: Like one who goes to steal.

Trumpet. Enter Otah

OTAH: Look! The white warrior comes.

Enter Church, Sir Arthur Vaughan, and Goodenough, with musqueteers [sic]

CHURCH: Although we come unbidden, chieftain, yet is our purpose friendly.

METAMORA: Why do you bring your fire weapons if you come to hold a talk of peace?

CHURCH: It is our custom.

METAMORA: Well, speak; my ears are open to hear.

SIR ARTHUR: Philip, our mission is –

METAMORA: Philip! I am the Wampanoag chief, Metamora.

SIR ARTHUR: We are directed by our council's head, for the times are filled with doubt, and to make *sure* our bond of peace and love to urge your presence at the council.

NAHMEOKEE: [*Aside*] Do not go.

METAMORA: Daughter of Miantinemo, peace! [*To them*] I will go.

CHURCH: Our troops shall form thy escort there.

METAMORA: I know the path.

SIR ARTHUR: We must not go without thee, chief.

METAMORA: I have breasted the cold winds of forty winters and to those that spoke kindly to me in the words of love I have been pliant – aye, very yielding like the willow that droops over the stream, but till with a single arm you can move the mighty rock that mocks the lightning and the storm seek not to stir Metamora when his heart says no. I will come! [*Crosses to R.*]

CHURCH: We shall expect thee, cnief.

METAMORA: Metamora cannot lie.

CHURCH: Stand to your arms.

Trumpet. Exit Church, Goodenough, Otah and Soldiers

SIR ARTHUR: Be thou not rash, but with thy tongue of manly truth dispel all charge that wrongs thy noble nature. Throw not the brand that kindles bloody war lest thou thyself should be the victim. [*Sir Arthur going L.*]

METAMORA: My father's deeds shall be my counsellors, and the Great Spirit will hear the words of my mouth. [*Exit Sir Arthur*] Now, Nahmeokee, I will talk to thee. Dost thou not love this little one, Nahmeokee?

NAHMEOKEE: Oh, yes!

METAMORA: When first his little eyes unclosed, thou saidst they were like mine; and my people rejoiced with a mighty joy, that the grandson of Massasoit, the white man's friend, should rule in the high places of his kindred; and hoped that his days would be long and full of glory. Nahmeokee, by the blood of his warlike race, he shall not be the white man's slave.

NAHMEOKEE: Thy talk is strange, and fear creeps over me. Thy heart is beating at thy side, as if thy bosom could not hold it.

METAMORA: Because 'tis full of thee – and thee, my little one. Humph! Bring me the knife thy brother wore in battle – my hatchet – the spear that was thy father's when Uncas slew him for the white man's favor. Humph! These things thou gavest me with thyself; thinkest thou this arm can wield them in the fight?

NAHMEOKEE: Ah! Thy bravery will lose thee to me.

METAMORA: Let not thy heart be troubled. If I require assistance from my people, I will lift up a flame on the lofty hill that shall gleam afar through the thick darkness.

NAHMEOKEE: I shall remember thy words.

METAMORA: Take in thy babe; I am going. [*Crosses to L.*]

NAHMEOKEE: Metamora, dost thou go alone?

METAMORA: No; Manito is with me.

Exit. Nahmeokee exit

Scene 2

A room in the house of Mordaunt. Enter Oceana.

OCEANA: Free from Fitzarnold's gaze, I feel myself again. Why came he here? His looks appalled [me] yet my father smiled – ah! he comes.

Enter Mordaunt

MORDAUNT: How now, my daughter; how is this? Why have you left his lordship thus?

OCEANA: I thought 'twas time.

MORDAUNT: It is not time to play the prude, when noble men confess thy charms and come fair suitors to thee. Fitzarnold loves thee and his alliance is so dear to me, I'll have no scruples of a timid girl to weigh against it. For long years I've nursed this fondness and I now command obedience.

OCEANA: That union must remain unblessed wherein the helpless hand is giving no heart to bear it company. O my father, how at the altar can I take that vow my heart now whispers never can be kept.

MORDAUNT: Hear me, rash girl, now that none o'erhear our converse. Learn thy father's destiny – the name I bear is not my own!

OCEANA: My father!

MORDAUNT: Thou didst not know my former life and deeds. Hardy adventure and the shock of arms, civil contention and a monarch's death make up the past, and poison all who come! 'Tis thou alone can clothe my future days with peace and shed one cheering ray o'er a dark scene of terror.

OCEANA: Art thou distraught?

MORDAUNT: Do not deny me, girl, and make me so! I am an outcast and a man forbid. Fitzarnold knows me and he asks my child – has power, and gaining thee preserves thy sire. Speak, Oceana! Thy resolve: what is it?

OCEANA: Thou canst not mean it, father! No, it cannot be!

MORDAUNT: Girl, it is as certain as our earthly doom. Decide, then, now between my honor and my instant death! For by thy mother's memory and by my soul, if my despair do find thee pitiless, my own right hand shall end a wretched life and leave thee nothing for a bridal dower but my curses and a blighted name. [*Crosses to R.*]

OCEANA: My throat is parched! I pray a moment's peace, a moment's pause.

Business. Mordaunt paces the stage in great agitation, at last falls on his knee to Oceana.

Walter enters, starts at seeing them and remains at back

MORDAUNT: Look at thy father, lowly begging life of thee. I will not swear, I will not rave, my child, but I'll implore thee! If thou hast ever loved me and dost so still, show that affection now! Let not thy father's name forever stand a mark for men to heap their curses on – relent, my child.

OCEANA: I can endure no more – rise, my father.

MORDAUNT: Dost thou promise?

OCEANA: All, all!

MORDAUNT: Swear, by truth! by honor! By the dead –

OCEANA: To wed Fitzarnold –

WALTER: [*Comes up*] Hold! Hold, rash girl, forebear! Thou art ensnared and wouldst pronounce thy doom.

MORDAUNT: Lightning consume thee, meddling fool! What bringst thou here?

WALTER: No pleasant duty, sir; a message which the council sends thee here. [*Gives packet to Mordaunt*] I am no spy, nor do I care to know secrets too dread for thine own heart to hold.

MORDAUNT: Beggar, begone!

Strikes him with packet and crosses to L. Walter draws sword. Oceana interposes

OCEANA: It is my father, Walter, mine.

WALTER: A blow.

OCEANA: Oh, thou wilt forgive him!

WALTER: Never! I will forth, and ere he shall enforce thee where thou hast no joy, will rend the mask he cheats us with. [*Crosses to L.*]

OCEANA: And if thou dost, by heaven I'll ne'er be thine.

WALTER: [*Sheathes sword*] Old man, an angel's bosom shelters thine. Instruct Fitzarnold in our quarrel's cause. No daughter bars my way to him.

Exit. Enter Fitzarnold

FITZARNOLD: How now, you tremble; what has chanced?

MORDAUNT: A moody beggar who abused my love and I chastised him for it – that's all.

OCEANA: My father –

MORDAUNT: Go to thy chamber.

OCEANA: Would it were my grave. [*Exit*]

MORDAUNT: My noble lord, that moody stripling whom you saw last night – whether set on by Vaughan, his patron, or by the vainness of his own conceits, resolves to break my daughter's marriage.

FITZARNOLD: And wilt thou suffer this? What is the villain's state?

MORDAUNT: Dependence on Sir Arthur Vaughan; his wealth a goodly person and the [law?] love of schools. [*sic*] [*Bell tolls*] Hark! I am summoned to the council. Wilt thou along?

Fitzarnold crosses to L.

FITZARNOLD: I trust he finds no favor with your daughter.

MORDAUNT: She shall be thine, my lord; thine with free will and full contentment. Now for the council.

Exeunt

Scene 3

Flourish. The council chamber. Errington, Sir Arthur and Church on raised platform. Mordaunt and Fitzarnold seated at table, L. Elders, etc. Goodenough and Soldiers, R. Villagers, etc. Walter and Tramp.

ERRINGTON: 'Tis news that asks from us most speedy action. Heaven has in sounds most audible and strange, in sights, too, that amazed the lookers-on, forewarned our people of their peril. 'Tis time to lift the arm so long supine, and with one blow cut off this heathen race, who spite of reason and the word revealed, continue hardened in their devious ways, and make the chosen tremble. Colleagues, your voices – speak – are you for peace or war?

SIR ARTHUR: What is your proof your Indian neighbors mean not as fairly towards our settlements as did King Philip's father, Massasoit?

ERRINGTON: Sir, we have full proof that Philip is our foe. Sasamond, the faithful servant of our cause, has been dispatched by Philip's men, set on to murder him. One of his tribe confessed the horrid truth – and will, when time shall call, give horrid proof on't. I say this chieftain is a man of blood, and Heaven will bless the valiant arm that slays him.

Metamora enters suddenly and remains at C. When Metamora enters, all start and grasp their swords. The soldiers prepare to fire. All are silent and confused

METAMORA: You sent for me and I am come. Humph! If you have nothing to say I will go back – if you fear to question, Metamora does not fear to answer.

ERRINGTON: Philip, 'tis thought you love us not, and all unmindful of our league of peace, plot with the Narragansetts, and contrive fatal disorder to our colony.

METAMORA: Do your fears counsel you? What is it makes your old men grave? And your young men grasp their fire weapons as if they awaited the onset of the foe? Brothers, what has Metamora done that doubt is in all your faces and your spirits seem troubled? The good man's heart is a stranger to fear, and his tongue is ready to speak the words of truth.

ERRINGTON: We are informed that thou gavest shelter to a banished man, whose deeds unchristian met our just reproof – one by our holy synod doomed – whom it is said you housed, and thereby hast incurred our church's censure – and given just cause to doubt thy honesty.

METAMORA: Why was that man sent away from the home of his joy? Because the Great Spirit did not speak to him as he had spoken to you? Did you not come across the great waters and leave the smoke of your fathers' hearth because the iron hand was held out against you, and your hearts were sorrowful in the high places of prayer. Why do you that have just plucked the red knife from your own wounded sides, strive to stab your brother?

ERRINGTON: Indian, this is no reply for us. Didst thou not know the sentence of the court on him whom thou didst shelter?

METAMORA: If my rarest enemy had crept unarmed into my wigwam and his heart was sore, I would not have driven him from my fire nor forbidden him to lie down upon my mat. Why then should the Wampanoag shut out the man of peace when he came with tears in his eyes and his limbs torn by the sharp thorns of the thicket? Your great book, you say, tells you to give good gifts to the stranger and deal kindly with him whose heart is sad; the Wampanoag needs no such counselor, for the Great Spirit has with his own fingers written it upon his heart.

MORDAUNT: Why dost thou put arms into thy people's hands, thereby engendering mischief towards us?

METAMORA: If my people do wrong, I am quick to punish. Do you not set a snare for them that they may fall, and make them mad with the fire water the Great Spirit gave you in his wrath? The red man sickens in the house of the palefaces, and the leaping stream of the mountains is made impure by the foul brooks that mingle with it.

SIR ARTHUR: Chieftain, since these things are so, sell us thy lands and seek another biding place.

METAMORA: And if I did, would you not stretch out your hand to seize that also? No! White man, no! Never will Metamora forsake the home of his fathers, and let the plough of the strangers disturb the bones of his kindred.

CHURCH: These are bold words, chief.

METAMORA: They are true ones.

ERRINGTON: They give no token of thy love of peace. We would deal fairly with thee – nay, be generous.

METAMORA: Then would you pay back that which fifty snows ago you received from the hands of my father, Massasoit. Ye had been tossed about like small things upon the face of the great waters, and there was no earth for your feet to rest on; your backs were turned upon the land of your fathers. The red man took you as a little child *and opened the door of his wigwam. The keen blast of the north howled in the leafless wood, but the Indian covered you with his broad right hand and put it back. Your little ones smiled when they heard the loud voice of the storm, for our fires were warm and the Indian was the white man's friend.*

ERRINGTON: Such words are needless now.

METAMORA: I will speak no more; I am going.

MORDAUNT: Hold! A moment, Philip; we have yet to tell of the death of Sasamond, who fell in secret and by treachery.

METAMORA: So should the treacherous man fall, by the keen knife in the darkness and not ascend from the strife of battle to the bright haven where the dead warrior dwells in glory.

ERRINGTON: Didst thou contrive his murder?

METAMORA: I will not answer.

ERRINGTON: We have those can prove thou didst.

METAMORA: I have spoken.

ERRINGTON: Bring in the witness. [*Exit Good-*

---

*Lines between asterisks are reprinted from the Forrest Home manuscript, because they are illegible in the University of Utah manuscript.

enough] We, too, long have stayed the arm of power from execution. Come, we parley with a serpent and his wiles are deep.

METAMORA: Injurious white man! Do not tread too hard upon the serpent's folds. His fangs are not taken out, nor has its venom lost the power to kill.

ERRINGTON: Approach!

Goodenough returns with Annawandah

METAMORA: Annawandah!

ERRINGTON: Behold, deceitful man, thy deeds are known.

METAMORA: Let me see his eye. Art thou he whom I snatched from the war club of the Mohigan [*sic*], when thou hadst sung thy death song, and the lips of the foe were thirsty for thy blood? Has Metamora cherished thee in his wigwam and hast thou put a knife into the white man's hand to slay him! The foul spirit hath entered thee, and the pure blood of the Wampanoag has left thy veins. Thy heart is a lie, and thine eye cannot rest upon the face of truth, when like the great light it shines on thee in unclouded glory. Elders, can he speak to you the words of truth, when he is false to his brother, his country and his god?

ERRINGTON: He was thy trusty agent, Philip, and conscience-smote revealed thy wickedness.

METAMORA: You believe his words?

ERRINGTON: We do, and will reward his honesty.

METAMORA: Wampanoag! No, I will not call thee so. Red man, say unto these people they have bought thy tongue, and thou hast uttered a lie!

ERRINGTON: He does not answer.

METAMORA: I am Metamora, thy father and thy king.

ERRINGTON: Philip o'erawes him – send the witness home.

METAMORA: I will do that! Slave of the white man, go follow Sasamond.

Stabs Annawandah, who staggers off, R. All stand up, general movement

ERRINGTON: Seize and bind him.

Soldiers make a forward movement

METAMORA: Come! My knife has drunk the blood of the false one, yet it is not satisfied! White man, beware! The mighty spirits of the Wampanoag race are hovering o'er your heads; they stretch out their shadowy arms to me and ask for vengeance; they shall have it. The wrath of the wronged Indian shall fall upon you like a cataract that dashes the uprooted oak down the mighty chasms. The war whoop shall start you from your dreams at night, and the red hatchet gleam in the blaze of your burning dwellings! From the east to the west, in the north and in the south shall cry of vengeance burst, till the lands you have stolen groan under your feet no more!

ERRINGTON: Secure him!

METAMORA: Thus do I smite your nation and defy your power.

ERRINGTON: Fire on him.

Business. Metamora hurls hatchet into stage, and rushes out, C. Soldiers fire after him. Mordaunt, who has moved forward, receives a shot and falls in chair. Tableau. Drums, trumpets, and general confusion. Quick curtain

ACT III. Scene 1

A chamber in Mordaunt's house. Enter Fitzarnold.

FITZARNOLD: Mordaunt wounded, and perhaps to death, struck by a shot that was leveled at the chief; and the fierce storm of war at distance heard, which soon may burst tremendous o'er our heads! This is no place for me. She must be mine tonight! Aye, this night, for fear his death may snatch his gold and daughter from me. Within there, Wolfe! [*Enter Wolfe*] Go get a surgeon for this Mordaunt's wounds, a scribe and priest for me – wilt be silent?

WOLFE: I will observe! Does my lord wed tomorrow?

FITZARNOLD: No, this night; and with tomorrow's sun I spread my sail for England.

WOLFE: Ha!

FITZARNOLD: How now! What meanest thou? Wouldst thou to' rival me?

WOLFE: My lord!

FITZARNOLD: Well, well; go see thy duty done. [*Exit*]

WOLFE: My lord, be sure on't. Now for young Walter. I will fulfill my duty but not to thee, my Lord Fitzarnold! Thou wilt not thank me for the priest I'll bring. [*Exit*]

Scene 2

An Indian village, deep wood, set wigwam, R. Lights half down. Conch shell heard. Nahmeokee enters from wigwam.

NAHMEOKEE: Sure 'twas the shell of Metamora, and spoke the strain it was wont when the old men were called to council, or when the scout returns from his long travel.

METAMORA: [*Outside*] Nahmeokee!

NAHMEOKEE: It is — it is Metamora.

Enter Metamora

METAMORA: Is our little one well, Nahmeokee?

NAHMEOKEE: He is. How didst thou leave the white man with whom thou hast been to hold a talk?

METAMORA: Like the great stream of the mountain when the spirit of the storm passes furiously over its bosom. Where are my people?

NAHMEOKEE: Here in the deep woods where Kaweshine,† the aged priest, tells them the mighty deeds of their people, and interprets to them the will of the Great Spirit.

METAMORA: Otah! [*Otah enters*] Summon my warriors; bid them with speed to council. [*Exit Otah*] I have escaped the swift flight of the white man's bullets but like the bounding elk when the hunters who follow close upon his heels. [*Reenter Otah with Kaweshine and all the Indians. Indian march, eight bars. Indians form at L.*] Warriors, I took a prisoner from the uplifted weapon of the Mohigan, when the victor's limbs were bloody and the scalps at his belt had no number. He lived in my wigwam; I made him my brother. When the spirit of sleep was upon me, he crept like a guilty thing away, and put into the white man's hand a brand of fire to consume me, and drive my people far away where there are no hunting grounds and where the Wampanoag has no protecting Spirit.

KAWESHINE: Annawandah?

METAMORA: Annawandah!

KAWESHINE: Where is he, chief of thy people, and where is the dog whose head the Great Spirit will smite with fire?

METAMORA: Where the ravenous bird of night may eat the flesh of his body. Here is the blood of the traitor's heart! [*Shows knife*] My peo-

† From this point on, the manuscript reads *Kaweshine* instead of the original reading, *Kaneshine*.

ple, shall I tell you the thoughts that fill me?

KAWESHINE: Speak, Metamora, speak!

METAMORA: When the strangers came from afar off, they were like a little tree; but now they are grown up and their spreading branches threaten to keep the light from you. They ate of your corn and drank of your cup, and now they lift up their arms against you. Oh my people, the race of the red man has fallen away like the trees of the forest before the axes of the palefaces. The fair places of his father's triumphs hear no more the sound of his footsteps. He moves in the region his proud fathers bequeathed him, not like a lord of the soil, but like a wretch who comes for plunder and for prey.

Distant thunder and lightning

KAWESHINE: The chief has spoken truly and the stranger is worthy to die! But the fire of our warriors is burnt out and their hatchets have no edge. O son of Massasoit, thy words are to me like the warm blood of the foe, and I will drink till I am full! Speak again!

METAMORA: "Chief of the people," said a voice from the deep as I lay by the seaside in the eyes of the moon — "Chief of the people, wake from thy dream of peace, and make sharp the point of thy spear, for the destroyer's arm is made bare to smite. O son of my old age, arise like the tiger in great wrath and snatch thy people from the devourer's jaws!" My father spoke no more; a mist passed before me, and from the mist the Spirit bent his eyes imploringly on me. I started to my feet and shouted the shrill battle cry of the Wampanoags. The high hills sent back the echo, and rock, hill and ocean, earth and air opened their giant throats and cried with me, "Red man, arouse! Freedom! Revenge or death!" [*Thunder and lightning. All quail but Metamora*] Hark, warriors! The Great Spirit hears me and pours forth his mighty voice with mine. Let your voice in battle be like his, and the flash from your fire weapons as quick to kill. Nahmeokee, take this knife, carry it to the Narragansett, to thy brother; tell him the hatchet is dug from the grave where the grass is grown old above it; thy tongue will move him more than the voice of all our tribe in the loud talk of war.

NAHMEOKEE: Nahmeokee will not fail in her

path; and her eyes will be quick to see where the stranger has set his snare.

METAMORA: Warriors! Your old and infirm must you send into the country of the Narragansett, that your hearts may not be made soft in the hour of battle.

NAHMEOKEE: Go you tonight, Metamora?

METAMORA: Tonight! I will not lay down in my wigwam till the foe has drawn himself together and comes in his height to destroy. Nahmeokee, I still will be the red man's father and his king, or the sacred rock whereon my father spoke so long the words of wisdom shall be made red with the blood of his race.

Hurried music. Metamora and Indians exeunt. Nahmeokee goes in wigwam

Scene 3

A chamber in Mordaunt's house. Clock strikes twelve as scene opens. Thunder distant. Enter Oceana in plain attire.

OCEANA: I know not how it is but every thunder peal seems to bear words portentous. The moaning blast has meaning in its sound and tells of distant horror – it is the hour when I bade Walter come! Can he have braved the tempest? Hark, I hear a step! [*Knock*] How my heart beats. [*Enter Fitzarnold*] It is – it is Fitzarnold!

FITZARNOLD: Fitzarnold, lady! Why this wonder? Is it fear? Can she whom thunder frights not shrink from me?

OCEANA: My lord, the hour is late; I feign would know who sent thee hither.

FITZARNOLD: Thy honored father.

OCEANA: Thy purpose?

FITZARNOLD: Read it there. [*Gives letter*]

OCEANA: Ha! Tonight! Be thine tonight?

FITZARNOLD: Aye, tonight. I have thy father's secret.

OCEANA: I know thou hast, and in that mean advantage wouldst mar his daughter's happiness forever – away! I blush that thus I parley words with thee – get thee gone. [*Crosses to L.*]

FITZARNOLD: Yes, when thou goest with me; not till then, lady. I will not waste the time that grows more precious every moment to me. [*Thunder*] What though the lightning flash and thunder roll – what though the tempest pours its fury down, Fitzarnold's soul does swell above the din! Nay more, dares brave the storm within thy breast, and shrinks not from the lightning of thine eye.

OCEANA: Would it could kill thee!

FITZARNOLD: It can do more – can conquer like the fiery serpent. It pierces, and as it pierces charms – Oceana!

OCEANA: Stand back! I will alarm my sire.

FITZARNOLD: And if thou dost, he will not aid thee. My treasures are embarked, aye, all but thee; thy father gives consent, the priest waits and ere morning, father, daughter, son, shall all be riding on the wave for England.

OCEANA: No, never!

FITZARNOLD: Convince thyself – [*Stamps his foot. Walter enters disguised as a priest*] Now, scornful lady, thy bridal hour has come; thy tauntings do but fan the flame that rages here.

OCEANA: Is there no refuge?

FITZARNOLD: None, but in these arms.

OCEANA: No hope – no rescue!

FITZARNOLD: None! None!

OCEANA: Walter, on thee I call – Walter, where art thou?

WALTER: [*Throws off disguise*] Walter is here.

FITZARNOLD: Villain! Thy life or mine!

Fitzarnold draws, Oceana throws herself between them

OCEANA: Forebear! No blood! [*To Walter*] Thou must come stainless to these arms.

WALTER: Sayest thou? Wilt thou take me to them?

OCEANA: I will – I do.

They embrace

FITZARNOLD: Thy father's blood be on thee; he is Fitzarnold's victim.

Exit, R. Bell rings. Enter Tramp, L.

TRAMP: The savages approach! The Wampanoag chieftain and his crew, at distance, peal their startling yell of war! Haste, sir, to meet them.

WALTER: Retire thee for a while, my Oceana – thou, sir, on the instant follow me – your sword! your sword!

Exit, R. with Oceana, Tramp follows

Scene 4

A view of Mordaunt's house on the beach, R.

Sea in distance, ship on fire. Garden and staircase leading down to the water. Lights down at opening of scene. Distant yells heard. Enter Fitzarnold hastily.

FITZARNOLD: Almighty powers! Hemmed in on every side! No hope. [*War whoop*] Hark to their savage yells! No means are left for flight, for on the waves my precious vessel burns – by the fell savage mastered! No retreat!

War whoops. Exit Fitzarnold hastily. Metamora and all the Indians enter up staircase entrances. Music hurried, forte till all are on

METAMORA: [*Pointing to Fitzarnold*] Follow him! [*To others*] Go into the white man's dwelling and drag him to me that my eye can look upon his torture and his scalp may tell Metamora's triumph to his tribe – go.

Otah and Kaweshine are about to enter the house when Oceana appears

OCEANA: Forebear, ye shall not enter.

METAMORA: Warriors, have I not spoken.

Throws her around to L., Indians go in

OCEANA: Great Chieftain! Dost thou not know me?

METAMORA: I am a Wampanoag in the home of mine enemy; I ride on my wrongs, and vengeance cries out for blood.

OCEANA: Wilt thou not hear me?

METAMORA: Talk to the rattling storm or melt the high rocks with tears; thou canst not move me. My foe! my foe! my foe!

OCEANA: Have mercy, Heaven!

The Indians return dragging in Mordaunt and down R.

METAMORA: Hah!

MORDAUNT: Mercy! Mercy!

OCEANA: My father! Spare my father! [*Rushes to Mordaunt*].

METAMORA: He must die! Drag him away to the fire of the sacrifice that my ear may drink the music of his dying groans.

OCEANA: Fiends and murderers!

METAMORA: The white man has made us such. Prepare.

Business

OCEANA: Then smite his heart through mine; our mangled breasts shall meet in death – one

grave shall hold us. Metamora, dost thou remember this? [*Shows eagle plume*]

METAMORA: Yes.

OCEANA: It was thy father's. Chieftain, thou gavest it to me.

METAMORA: Say on.

OCEANA: Thou saidst it would prove a guardian to me when the conflict raged. Were thy words true when with thy father's tongue thou saidst, whatever being wore the gift, no Indian of thy tribe should do that being harm.

METAMORA: The Wampanoag cannot lie.

OCEANA: Then do I place it here. [*Places it on Mordaunt's bosom*]

METAMORA: Hah!

OCEANA: The Wampanoag cannot lie, and I can die for him who gave existence to me.

MORDAUNT: My child! My child!

Red fire in house

METAMORA: Take them apart! [*Indians separate them*] Old man, I cannot let the tomahawk descend upon thy head, or bear thee to the place of sacrifice; but here is that shall appease the red man's wrath. [*Seizes Oceana; flames seen in house*] The fire is kindled in thy dwelling, and I will plunge her in the hot fury of the flames.

MORDAUNT: No, no, thou wilt not harm her.

OCEANA: Father, farewell! Thy nation, savage, will repent this act of thine.

METAMORA: If thou art just, it will not. Old man, take thy child. [*Throws her to him*] Metamora cannot forth with the maiden of the eagle plume; and he disdains a victim who has no color in his face nor fire in his eye.

Bugle sounds

MORDAUNT: Gracious heavens!

METAMORA: Hark! The power of the white man comes! Launch your canoes! We have drunk blood enough. Spirit of my father, be at rest! Thou art obeyed, thy people are avenged.

Exit hastily followed by the Indians. Drums and trumpet till curtain. Enter Walter, Goodenough, Church, Soldiers, Peasants, male and female, all from behind house. Soldiers are about to fire, when Walter throws himself before them and exclaims

WALTER: Forebear! Forebear!

Walter and Oceana embrace. Tableau. Curtain

ACT IV. Scene 1

Enter Errington – Lord Fitzarnold – Walter and Church L. H. A room in Sir Arthur's house.

SIR ARTHUR: Welcome my brother.

ERRINGTON: The strife is over: but the wail of those who mourn some captive friend still wounds the ear and fills our hearts with sadness.

FITZARNOLD: The follower of mine, surprised or else too venturous in the fight, was dragged away in bondage.

SIR ARTHUR: Old Wolfe.

FITZARNOLD: The same – a moody but a faithful man doomed no doubt to torture or to death.

WALTER: Faithful indeed. But not to him thou think'st. [*Aside*]

ERRINGTON: He will avenge the captives fall.

WALTER: But must they fall – is there no way to save them?

ERRINGTON: None young sir unless thy wisdom find it.

WALTER: They might be ransomed.

SIR ARTHUR: True they might. And from my wealth I'll pay whatever price the Indians power will yield them for.

ERRINGTON: But who so rash to bear such offer unto Philip in his present mood?

FITZARNOLD: [*Aside*] Could I but tempt this stripling to his death.

ERRINGTON: Say is there one so reckless and so brave will dare the peril to preserve his fellows?

FITZARNOLD: Grave sirs, I know of none more truly fit than young Walter to achieve the deed. How proud the name required by such an act. How vast the joy his daring heart must feel. Whose arm against such terror shall prevail. And rescue numbers from a lingering death.

WALTER: If my Lord so dearly holds the prize, Why not himself adventure to attain it? But I will go – for I have reasons for it Would move me, felt I not my Lords great pity for the captives woe.

SIR ARTHUR: Bravely said thou deserve'st our thanks, And if thou canst persuade the hostile chief To draw his arm'd bands away and save the blood, that else must flow so terribly.

ERRINGTON: Take swiftest horse young man and Heaven protect thee.

WALTER: No tongue so blest as that which heralds peace – No heart so mailed as that which beats, warm for his fellow man. Fare you well. [*Exit Walter*]

ERRINGTON: Now to our labours – those new levies made – We may exterminate, with one full blow This savage race, hated of man – unblessed of Heaven – Surely a land so fair was ne'er designed to feed the heartless infidel.

Cry L. H. "Indians! Indians!"

ERRINGTON: Hah! More massacre! Mercy Heaven!

Enter Oceana L. H.

OCEANA: Oh Sirs shew pity to a captive wretch whom heartless men abuse with taunts and blows. If ye are men oh let the helpless find in you kind pity – mercy and protection.

ERRINGTON: Maiden, Whom dost thou speak of?

OCEANA: An Indian woman And her infant child, by these made prisoners. Look there, they have ta'en her child from her.

Enter Nahmeokee with Officer, two Guards, as prisoner. Goodenough with the child. L. H.

ERRINGTON: How now, who hast thou there?

GOODENOUGH: An Indian woman, we captured in the glen. A spy, 'tis thought sent by the cursed foe.

ERRINGTON: Came she alone?

GOODENOUGH: No, a young and nimble man Was with her, but he 'scap'd pursuit. I am sure he is wounded, for I saw him fall.

ERRINGTON: Woman what art thou?

NAHMEOKEE: Give poor woman her child?

ERRINGTON: Dost thou hear my question?

NAHMEOKEE: Give poor Indian woman her child?

OCEANA: Do so.

GOODENOUGH: Why 'twas I that caught the creature – and –

OCEANA: Man didst thou hear me? [*Takes child from him*]

GOODENOUGH: Hard times indeed to lose so good a prize. [The brat is saleable] ‡ Tis mine.

‡Lined out in the original.

OCEANA: Measureless brute.

GOODENOUGH: For what? 'Tis only an Indian boy.

Oceana gives Nahmeokee her child, who touch'd with her kindness, takes her scarf to wipe Oceana's eyes. The latter recognises it to be the one bound round Metamora's arm in first scene

OCEANA: Nahmeokee!

NAHMEOKEE: Hush!

ERRINGTON: Who art thou woman?

NAHMEOKEE: I am the servant of the Great Spirit.

ERRINGTON: Who is thy husband?

NAHMEOKEE: One thou dost not love.

ERRINGTON: His name?

NAHMEOKEE: I will not tell thee.

ERRINGTON: We can enforce an answer.

NAHMEOKEE: Poor Indian woman cannot keep her limbs from pain; but she can keep silence.

ERRINGTON: Woman what is thy nation & thy race?

NAHMEOKEE: White man the Sun is my father and the Earth my mother – I will speak no more.

ERRINGTON: Captain take charge of this same stubborn wretch
Who neither will her name or nor purpose tell.
If she do prove as alleg'd a spy,
Nothing shall save her from a public death;
We must o'erawe our treacherous foe.
[And this obdurate & blasphemous witch
May in her death, keep death from many more.] ‡
Summon our Elders – my Lord Fitzarnold
Your counsel now may aid us.

FITZARNOLD: 'Tis thine, – & my poor service.

ERRINGTON: Take her away. [*Cross R.*] Justice is sometimes slow,
Yet is she sure.

NAHMEOKEE: Thy nation white man, yet may find it so.

Exeunt Errington R. H. Goodenough, Church, Nahmeokee and Soldiers L. H.

OCEANA: Fitzarnold of the Council – could I move
His sympathy? [*Approaching him tremblingly*] My lord.

FITZARNOLD: Well lady?

OCEANA: I have offended thee.

FITZARNOLD: I have forgotten it.

‡Lined out in the original.

OCEANA: I have a boon to ask.

FITZARNOLD: Sayst thou – of me?

OCEANA: It will not cost thee much.

FITZARNOLD: No price too great to purchase thy sweet smiles of thee.

OCEANA: Then be this female's advocate my lord.
Thou canst be eloquent and the heart of good,
But much misguided men may by thy speech
Be moved to pity and to pardon her.

FITZARNOLD: How so – a wandering wretch unknown?

OCEANA: Metamora has helpless prisoners.

FITZARNOLD: 'Tis true – and thou dost deeply feel for them.
Young Walter now seeks their enfranchisement.

OCEANA: I know it sir. [*Aside*] Be still my throbbing heart.
My lord what vengeance will her husband take.
Think you will aught appease dread Philip's wrath –
When he is told – chieftain thy wife's a slave?

FITZARNOLD: His wife – the Queen! Indeed! Dost say so?

OCEANA: Give not the secret unto mortal ear –
It might destroy all hopes of unity.
Preserve this captive from impending doom
And countless prayers shall pay thee for it.

FITZARNOLD: Thy kind approval is reward enough.

OCEANA: Shall she be saved?

FITZARNOLD: She shall be free – a word of mine can do it.

OCEANA: Thanks! Thanks! My Lord deceive me not.

FITZARNOLD: Fear not fair Lady. I have pledged my word.

Exit Oceana L. H.

FITZARNOLD: Thou thinks't me kind – ha! ha!
I will be so. Philip has
Captives – & young Walter's there.
The Council dare not take this woman's life
for that would doom their captive countrymen.
Imprisoned she is free from danger for the law
protects her. But turn her loose to the wild fury
of the senseless crowd *she dies* ere justice or the
Elder's arms can reach her. Ah! This way conducts me straight to the goal. I am resolved to
reach and seal at once my hated rivals doom.
[Oh! I will plead as Angels do in Heaven

For mortals when they err and mourn for it.] ‡
Her freedom is her death – the zealot crowd
Will rush upon her like the loosen'd winds
And prove as merciless – while the lion husband,
Madden'd with his loss, sheds blood to surfeiting.
Oh yes, dear pleader for the captive one
Thy boon is granted. She shall be free! [*Exit R. H.*]

Scene 2

One-half dark. An Indian Retreat. Wolfe bound to the Stake R. H. Metamora at a distance leaning on his rifle. Kaneshine§ & Warriors. Lights one-half down.

KANESHINE: Warriors, our enemies have been met, and the blood of the Stranger has sunk deep into the sand – yet the spirit of those who have fallen by the power of the foe are not yet appeas'd – prepare the captives for their hour of death. Come round the tree of sacrifice and lift up the flame, till it devour in its fiery rage, the abhor'd usurpers [*Gun L. H.*] of the red man's soil! Come my lips are dry for the captive's blood.

As they are about to fire the pile, a shot is heard. Enter Walter

METAMORA: Hold! Let the young man say why he comes into our country unbidden. Why does he tempt the ire of our warriors, when their weapons are red with the blood of the battle?

WALTER: That I come friendly let this emblem speak.
To check the dire advance of bloody war,
To urge the Wampanoags to disarm his band
And once again renew with us the bond
That made the white and red man brothers.

METAMORA: No, young man, the blood my warriors have tasted, has made their hearts glad and their hands are thrust out for more. Let the white man fear. The arrow he has shot into the mountain has turned back and pierced his own side. What are the Elders' words?

WALTER: Let Philip take our wampum and our coin
Restore his captives and remove his dead

‡Lined out in the original.
§The Lord Chamberlain's copy uses the original spelling.

And rest from causeless and destructive war,
Until such terms of lasting peace are made
As shall forever quell our angry feuds
And sink the hatchet to be raised no more.

METAMORA: *Humph!* And meanwhile he sharpens his long weapons in secret, and each day grows more numerous. When the great stream of the mountains first springs from the earth it is very weak, and I can stand up against its waters, but when the great rain descends, it is swift and swollen, death dwells in its white bosom and it will not spare.

WALTER: By Him who moves the stars and lights the Sun,
If thou dost shed the trembling captives blood,
A thousand warlike men will rush to arms
And terribly avenge their countryman.

METAMORA: Well, let them come! Our arms are as strong as the white man's. And the use of the fire-weapon he has taught us. My ears are shut against thee.

WALTER: [*To Wolfe*] Oh, my friend! I will achieve thy rescue if gold or prayers can move them.

WOLFE: I was prepared to die, and only mourned
For I am childless and a lonely man.
I had not told the secret of thy birth.
And shewn thy father to thee.

WALTER: My Father! Sayst thou?

WOLFE: Walter, listen to me.

OTAH: [*Speaks without*] Metamora!

METAMORA: Ha! [*Enter Otah*]

OTAH: Nahmeokee!

METAMORA: Dead!

OTAH: Our feet grew weary in the path, and we sate down to rest in the dark wood – the fire-weapons blazed in the thicket, and my arm was wounded, with the other I grasped the keen knife you gave Nahmeokee, but I sank down powerless and the white men bore off the queen a captive.

METAMORA: *Humph* – Nahmeokee is the white man's prisoner. Where is thy horse?

WALTER: Beneath yonder tree.

METAMORA: Unbind the captive! Young man! You must abide with the Wampanoag till Nahmeokee returns to her home. Woe unto you if the hard hand has been laid upon her. Take the white man to my wigwam.

WALTER: I thank thee Chieftain, this is kindness to me. Come good Wolfe tell me my father's name.

METAMORA: If one drop fall from Nahmeokee's eye, one hair from her head, the axe shall hew your quivering limbs asunder and the ashes of your bones be carried away on the rushing winds. Come old man.

Exeunt

Scene 3

Enter Fitzarnold.

FITZARNOLD: Nahmeokee now is free, and the fanatic herd all cry aloud, "Oh mad rulers! Mercy to her" – she comes – and witch, hag and Indian din her ears. They come this way – I must avoid their clamor. [*Enter Nahmeokee*]

NAHMEOKEE: Let them not kill the poor Indian women.

FITZARNOLD: Woman away.

NAHMEOKEE: They will murder my child.

FITZARNOLD: Hold off – I cannot help thee. [*Exit Fitzarnold*]

NAHMEOKEE: They come upon me from every side of the path. My limbs can bear me no farther. Mercy! Hah! They have missed my track and seek in the wood, and in the caves for my blood. Who is he that rides a swift horse there, through the narrow path way of the glen! The shade of the coming night is over him and he dimly appears a red man riding the swift cloud. [*Shouts*] Ha, they have traced me by the white garment, the brambles tore from me in my flight. They come. Cling to me my child. Cling to thy mother's bosom. [*Enter Goodenough and 4 Peasants*]

GOODENOUGH: Foul Indian witch thy race is run. Drag her to the lake. Take her child from her. [*Enter Metamora*]

METAMORA: Stand back! or the swift death shall take wing. Which of you has lived too long? Let him lift up his arm against her.

OFFICER: How is this? King Philip ventures here? What comest thou for?

METAMORA: Boy! Thou art a child, there is no mark of the war upon thee. Send me thy Elder, or thy Chief. I'll make my talk to him.

GOODENOUGH: Here comes Master Errington. [*Enter Errington & Soldiers*]

ERRINGTON: Philip a Prisoner!

METAMORA: No! He has arms in his hand and courage in his heart, he comes near you of his own will, and when he has done his work, he'll go back to his wigwam.

ERRINGTON: Indian, you answer boldly.

METAMORA: What is there I should fear?

ERRINGTON: Savage! The wrath of him who hates the Heathen and the man of blood.

METAMORA: Does he love mercy; and is he the white man's friend?

ERRINGTON: Yes.

METAMORA: How did Nahmeokee and her infant wrong you, that you hunted her through the thorny pathway of the glen, and scented her blood like the fierce red wolf in his hunger?

CHURCH: Why hold parley with him! Call our musqueteers and bear them both to trial and to doom. Heaven smiles on us – Philip in our power. His cursed followers would sue for peace.

METAMORA: Not till the blood of twenty English captives be poured out as a sacrifice. Elders beware, the knife is sharpened – the stake is fixed – and the captive's limbs tremble under the burning gaze of the prophet of wrath. Woe come to them when my people shall hear their chief has been slain by the pale faces or is bound in the dark place of doom.

NAHMEOKEE: Do not tempt them Metamora, they are many like the leaves of the forest and we are but as two lone trees standing in their midst.

METAMORA: Which can easier escape the hunter's spear? The tiger that turns on it in his wrath, or the lamb that sinks down and trembles? Thou has seen me look unmoved at a torturing death – shall mine eye be turned downward when the white man frowns?

ERRINGTON: Philip, the peace our young man offered thee. Didst thou regard his words?

METAMORA: Yes.

ERRINGTON: And wilt thou yield compliance?

METAMORA: I will. Nahmeokee shall bear the tidings to my people that the prisoners may return to their homes, and the war-whoop shall not go forth on the evening gale.

ERRINGTON: Let her set forth. Friends let me advise you,
Keep the Chieftain prisoner, let's muster men.
And in unlook'd for hour with one blow we will overwhelm
This accursed race. And furthermore – [*Converses apart*]

NAHMEOKEE: [*To Metamora*] I will remember thy words.

METAMORA: Grieve not that I linger in the dark place of the condemned, for the eye of the Great Spirit will be on me there.

ERRINGTON: We greet thee Philip and accept thy love. Nahmeokee may return.

METAMORA: 'Tis very good. The horse stands neath the brow of the hill – speak not – I read thy thought in thy eye. Go – go. Nahmeokee. I am ready to follow you.

ERRINGTON: Conduct him forth to prison. [*Soldiers attempt to take his gun*]

METAMORA: No! This shall be to me as my child and I will talk to it, until I go back to my people.

GOODENOUGH: Right well conceived, could it but talk.

METAMORA: It can – when the land of my great fore-fathers is trampled on by the foot of the foe – or when treachery lurks round the Wampanoag, while he bides in the white man's home.

End of Act Fourth

ACT V. Scene 1

Same as Act 1, Scene 1. Lights down. Oceana discovered leaning against tomb. Slow music, four bars.

OCEANA: Tomb of the silent dead, thou seemest my only refuge! O Walter, where art thou? Alas! the kindly promptings of thy noble heart have led thee to captivity, perhaps to death! Welcome the hour when these dark portals shall unfold again, and reunite parent and child in the long sleep of death. [*Enter Fitzarnold*] Ah! Fitzarnold here!

FITZARNOLD: I come with words of comfort to thee and feign would soothe thy sorrow.

OCEANA: I do not ask your sympathy, my lord.

FITZARNOLD: A sea of danger is around thee, lady, and I would be the skillful pilot to guide thy struggling bark to safety.

OCEANA: Nay, but let me rather perish in the waves than reach a haven to be shared with thee.

FITZARNOLD: Thou hast no choice; thy father willed thee mine, and with his latest breath bequeathed thee to me. Walter, my stripling rival in thy love, has left thee here defenseless and alone. I deem as nothing thy unnatural

hate, and only see thy fair and lovely form; and though thy flashing eyes were armed with lightning, thus would my arms enfold thee.

OCEANA: [*Clings to tomb*] Now, if thou darest, approach me – now whilst with my mother's spirit hovering o'er me – whilst thus with tearful eyes and breaking heart I call on Heaven to blast the bold audacious wretch, who seeks a daughter's ruin o'er her parents grave.

FITZARNOLD: Aye, despite of all.

METAMORA: [*In tomb*] Hold! Touch her not!

OCEANA: Hark to that voice! Kind Heaven has heard my prayers.

The door of the tomb opens, and Metamora appears. Oceana faints and falls

FITZARNOLD: Philip here!

METAMORA: He is the Great Spirit [who?] has sent me;|| the ghosts are waiting for thee in the dark place of doom! Now thou must go. Tremble, for the loud cry is terrible and the blaze of their eyes, like the red fire of war, gleams awfully in the night.

FITZARNOLD: I have not wronged thee.

METAMORA: Not? Didst thou not contrive the death of Nahmeokee, when the treacherous white man thirsted for her blood? Did she not with bended knees, her eyes streaming with woes of the heart, catch hold of thy shining broad garment thinking it covered man? Was not thy hand upraised against her, and thy heart, like thy hand, flint that wounds the weary one who rests upon it?

FITZARNOLD: No! no!

METAMORA: I saw thee when my quick step was on the hills, and the joy of Metamora's eyes felt thy blows. I feel them now! "Revenge!" cried the shadow of my father as he looked on with me. I, too, cried revenge and now I have it! The blood of my heart grows hotter as I look on him who smote the red cheek of Nahmeokee.

FITZARNOLD: As reparation I will give thee gold.

METAMORA: No! Give me back the happy days, the fair hunting ground, and the dominion my great forefathers bequeathed me.

FITZARNOLD: I have not robbed thee of them.

METAMORA: Thou art a white man, and thy veins hold the blood of a robber! Hark! The

||This is the actual reading of the manuscript. A more plausible reading would probably be: "He is. The Great Spirit has sent me."

spirits of the air howl for thee! Prepare – [*Throws him around to R.*]

FITZARNOLD: Thou shalt not conquer ere thou killest me. This sword a royal hand bestowed! This arm can wield it still.

Draws; Metamora disarms and kills him

METAMORA: Metamora's arm has saved thee from a common death; who dies by me dies nobly! [*Turns to Oceana*] For thee, Metamora's home shall screen thee from the spreading fury of his nation's wrath.

Hurry till change. Exit bearing Oceana

Scene 2

A chamber. Enter Sir Arthur, meeting Errington and Church.

SIR ARTHUR: I have news will startle you.

ERRINGTON: Is't of the chief?

SIR ARTHUR: It is; he has escaped our power!

ERRINGTON: Escaped! Confusion! How?

SIR ARTHUR: But now we sought his prison and found it tenantless.

ERRINGTON: But how escaped he? There was no egress thence, unless some treacherous hand unlocked the door.

SIR ARTHUR: And so we thought, at first; but on minute search we found some stones displaced, which showed a narrow opening into a subterranean passage, dark and deep, through which we crept until, to our surprise, we reached the tomb of Mordaunt.

ERRINGTON: The tomb of Mordaunt?

SIR ARTHUR: The ruined pile which now serves as our prison was, years since, when first he sought these shores, the residence of Mordaunt, and this secret passage, doubtless, was formed by him for concealment or escape in time of danger.

ERRINGTON: Indeed!

SIR ARTHUR: Yes, and he had cause to be so guarded, for once, unseen by him, I heard that wretched man commune with Heaven, and sue for pardon for the heinous sin of Hammond of Harrington!

ERRINGTON: Hammond! The outlawed regicide?

SIR ARTHUR: Even so; it was himself he prayed for, the guilty man who gave to death the king, his lord, the royal martyr Charles. As Mordaunt, he here sought refuge from the wrath of the rightful heir now seated on the throne.

ERRINGTON: Think you the chieftain knew this secret way?

SIR ARTHUR: 'Tis likely that he did, or else by chance discovered it and thus has won his freedom and his life.

CHURCH: We must summon our men. Double the guard and have their range extended.

Exeunt Church and Errington

WOLFE: [*Without*] Where is Sir Arthur Vaughan?

SIR ARTHUR: Who calls? [*Enter Wolfe*] Now, who art thou?

WOLFE: A suppliant for pardon.

SIR ARTHUR: Pardon – for what?

WOLFE: A grievous sin, I now would feign confess.

SIR ARTHUR: Indeed! Go on! Declare it then; I will forgive thee!

WOLFE: Long years have passed since then, but you must still remember when at Naples with your wife and child.

SIR ARTHUR: Ha! Dost thou mean –

WOLFE: The flames consumed thy dwelling and thou together with thy wife and boy, escaped almost by miracle.

SIR ARTHUR: Ha!

WOLFE: I there looked on midst the assembled throng, a stranger mariner. Urged by the fiend, and aided by the wild confusion of the scene, I snatched your boy and through the noisy throng I bore him to my anchored bark, thinking his waiting parents soon would claim with gold their darling. Next day came on a tempest and the furious winds far from the city drove us and thy child.

SIR ARTHUR: Heavens! Can this be true?

WOLFE: He grew up the sharer of my sea-born perils. One awful night our vessel stuck upon the rocks near these shores and the greedy ocean swelled over her shattered frame – thy son –

SIR ARTHUR: Go on – go on –

WOLFE: Was by mysterious power preserved and guided to his unconscious father. Walter is thy son.

SIR ARTHUR: Man! Why didst thou not tell me?

WOLFE: I feared thy just anger and the force of law. I became Fitzarnold's follower but to this hour has memory tortured me.

SIR ARTHUR: And Walter is a hostage to the savage foe; perchance they have murdered him!

WOLFE: No! Oceana's kindness to the Indian queen has purchased his freedom and my own.

SIR ARTHUR: Where is he?

WOLFE: Looking for her he loves, fair Oceana! Whom 'tis said, a party of the foe carried off.

SIR ARTHUR: Quick, let us arm and follow him. For thee, this act of justice pardons thee.

Exeunt

Scene 3

Indian village. Groups of Indians. Kaweshine and Otah discovered. Kaweshine has been addressing them. His looks are gloomy and bewildered.

METAMORA: [*Outside, at change of scene*] Where are my people?

KAWESHINE: Ha! 'Tis our chief – I know the sound of his voice, and some quick danger follows him.

Metamora enters, bearing Oceana. Nahmeokee enters from wigwam

METAMORA: Nahmeokee, take the white maiden in; I would speak to my people; go in and follow not the track of the warrior's band.

NAHMEOKEE: Come in, my mat is soft, and the juice of the sweet berry shall give joy to thy lips. Come in, thou art pale and yielding, like the lily, when it is borne down by the running waters.

She leads Oceana into wigwam

METAMORA: Warriors, I have escaped from the hands of the white man, when the fire was kindled to devour me. Prepare for the approaching hour if ye love the high places your fathers trod in majesty and strength. Snatch your keen weapons and follow me! If ye love the silent spots where the bones of your kindred repose, sing the dread song of war and follow me! If you love the bright lakes which the Great Spirit gave you when the sun first blazed with the fires of his touch, shout the war song of the Wampanoag race, and on to the battle follow me! Look at the bright glory that is wrapped like a mantle around the slain in battle! Call on the happy spirits of the warriors dead, and cry, "Our lands! Our nation's freedom! Or the grave!"

KAWESHINE: O chieftain, take my counsel and hold out to the palefaces the pipe of peace. Ayantic and the great Mohigan join with our foes against us, and the power of our brother, the Narragansett is no more! List, o chieftain, to the words that I tell of the time to come.

METAMORA: Ha! Dost thou prophesy?

KAWESHINE: In the deep wood, when the moon shone bright, my spirit was sad and I sought the ear of Manito in the sacred places; I heard the sound as of one in pain, and I beheld gasping under a hemlock, the lightning had sometime torn, a panther wounded and dying in his thick red gore. I thought of the tales of our forefathers who told us that such was an omen of coming evil. I spoke loudly the name of Metamora, and the monster's eyes closed instantly and he writhed no more. I turned and mourned, for I said, Manito loves no more the Wampanoag and our foes will prevail.

METAMORA: Didst thou tell my people this?

KAWESHINE: Chieftain, yes; my spirit was troubled.

METAMORA: Shame of the tribe, thou art no Wampanoag, thy blood is tainted – thou art half Mohigan, thy breath has sapped the courage of my warriors' hearts. Begone, old man, thy life is in danger.

KAWESHINE: I have spoken the words of truth, and the Great Manito has heard them.

METAMORA: Liar and coward! Let him preserve thee now!

About to stab him when Nahmeokee enters from wigwam and interposes

NAHMEOKEE: He is a poor old man – he healed the deep wound of our little one. [*Gets to L. of Metamora*]

METAMORA: Any breast but Nahmeokee's had felt the keen edge of my knife! Go, corrupted one, thy presence makes the air unwholesome round hope's high places. Begone!

KAWESHINE: Metamora drives me from the wigwam before the lightning descends to set it on fire. Chieftain, beware the omen. [*Exit*]

NAHMEOKEE: [*Aside*] Will he not become the white man's friend and show him the secret path of our warriors? Manito guard the Wampanoag!

METAMORA: Men of Po-hon-e-ket, the palefaces come towards your dwellings and no warrior's hatchet is raised for vengeance. The war whoop is hushed in the camp and we hear no more the triumph of battle. Manito hates you, for you have fallen from the high path of your fathers and Metamora must alone avenge the Wampanoag's wrongs.

OMNES: Battle! Battle!

METAMORA: Ha! The flame springs up afresh in your bosoms; a woman's breath has brought back the lost treasure of your souls. [*Distant march, drums and trumpet heard*] Ha! they come! Go, warriors, and meet them, and remember the eye of a thousand ages looks upon you. [*Warriors exeunt silently*] Nahmeokee, should the palefaces o'ercome our strength, go thou with our infant to the sacred place of safety. My followers slain, there will the last of the Wampanoags pour out his heart's blood on the giant rock, his father's throne.

NAHMEOKEE: O Metamora!

METAMORA: Come not near me or thou wilt make my heart soft, when I would have it hard like the iron and gifted with many lives. Go in, Nahmeokee. [*Distant trumpets. Nahmeokee goes in wigwam. Metamora kneels*] The knee that never bent to man I bend to thee, Manito. As the arm was broken that was put out against Nahmeokee, so break thou the strength of the oppressor's nation, and hurl them down from the high hill of their pride and power, with the loud thunder of thy voice. Confound them – smite them with the lightning of thine eye – while thus I bare my red war arm – while thus I wait the onset of the foe – [*Loud alarm*] They come! Death! Death, or my nation's freedom!

Rushes off. Loud shouts. Drums and trumpets till change

Scene 4

Rocky pass. Trumpet sounds retreat. Enter Errington and Church.

ERRINGTON: They fly! They fly – the field is ours! This blow destroys them. Victory cheaply bought at twice our loss; the red man's power is broken now forever. [*Enter Walter*] Is Oceana slain?

WALTER: No; the chieftain Metamora rescued her from the base passions of the Lord Fitzarnold whom Metamora slew to avenge the wrongs he offered to his wife, and Oceana by the chief was borne in safety to his lodge.

ERRINGTON: In safety?

WALTER: Yes; from the hands of Nahmeokee I received her, just as some Indians maddened by defeat, prepared to offer her a sacrifice.

ERRINGTON: Away then, Walter. [*Walter crosses to R.*] Sir Arthur now seeks thee out to claim thee as his own [son?]. [*Parenthetical word sic.*]

WALTER: My father! I fly to seek him. [*Exit*]

ERRINGTON: The victory is ours; yet while Philip lives we are in peril! Come, let us find this Indian prophet whom Metamora banished from his tribe. He may be bribed to show us the chieftain's place of safety.

Exeunt. Change

Scene 5

Metamora's stronghold. Rocks, bridge and waterfall. Nahmeokee discovered listening. The child lays under a tree, R., covered with furs. Slow music, four bars.

NAHMEOKEE: He comes not, yet the sound of the battle has died away like the last breath of a storm! Can he be slain? O cruel white man, this day will stain your name forever.

Slow music, sixteen bars. Metamora enters on bridge. Crosses and enters L.

METAMORA: Nahmeokee, I am weary of the strife of blood. Where is our little one? Let me take him to my burning heart and he may quell its mighty torrent.

NAHMEOKEE: [*With broken utterance*] He is here!

Lifts the furs and shows the child dead

METAMORA: Ha! Dead! Dead! Cold!

NAHMEOKEE: Nahmeokee could not cover him with her body, for the white men were around her and over her. I plunged into the stream and the unseen shafts of the fire weapons flew with a great noise over my head. One smote my babe and he sunk into the deep water; the foe shouted with a mighty shout, for he thought Nahmeokee and her babe had sunk to rise no more.

METAMORA: His little arms will never clasp thee more; his little lips will never press the pure bosom which nourished him so long! Well, is he not happy? Better to die by the stranger's hand than live his slave.

NAHMEOKEE: O Metamora! [*Falls on his neck*]

METAMORA: Nay, do not bow down thy head; let me kiss off the hot drops that are running down thy red cheeks. Thou wilt see him again in the peaceful land of spirits, and he will look smilingly as – as – as I do now, Nahmeokee.

NAHMEOKEE: Metamora, is our nation dead? Are we alone in the land of our fathers?

METAMORA: The palefaces are all around us, and they tread in blood. The blaze of our burning wigwams flashes awfully in the darkness of their path. We are destroyed – not vanquished; we are no more, yet we are forever – Nahmeokee.

NAHMEOKEE: What wouldst thou?

METAMORA: Dost thou not fear the power of the white man?

NAHMEOKEE: No.

METAMORA: He may come hither in his might and slay thee.

NAHMEOKEE: Thou art with me.

METAMORA: He may seize thee, and bear thee off to the far country, bind these arms that have so often clasped me in the dear embrace of love, scourge thy soft flesh in the hour of his wrath, and force thee to carry burdens like the beasts of the fields.

NAHMEOKEE: Thou wilt not let them.

METAMORA: We cannot fly, for the foe is all about us; we cannot fight, for this is the only weapon I have saved from the strife of blood.

NAHMEOKEE: It was my brother's – Coanchett's.

METAMORA: It has tasted the white man's blood, and reached the cold heart of the traitor; it has been our truest friend; it is our only treasure.

NAHMEOKEE: Thine eye tells me the thought of thy heart, and I rejoice at it. [*Sinks on his bosom*]

METAMORA: Nahmeokee, I look up through the long path of thin air, and I think I see our infant borne onward to the land of the happy, where the fair hunting grounds know no storms or snows, and where the immortal brave feast in the eyes of the giver of good. Look upwards, Nahmeokee, the spirit of thy murdered father beckons thee.

NAHMEOKEE: I will go to him.

METAMORA: Embrace me, Nahmeokee – 'twas like the first you gave me in the days of our strength and joy – they are gone. [*Places his ear to the ground*] Hark! In the distant wood I faintly hear the cautious tread of men! They are upon us, Nahmeokee – the home of the happy is made ready for thee. [*Stabs her, she dies*] She felt no white man's bondage – free as the air she lived – pure as the snow she died! In smiles she died! Let me taste it, ere her lips are cold as the ice.

Loud shouts. Roll of drums. Kaweshine leads Church and Soldiers on bridge, R.

CHURCH: He is found! Philip is our prisoner.

METAMORA: No! He lives – last of his race – but still your enemy – lives to defy you still. Though numbers overpower me and treachery surround me, though friends desert me, I defy you still! Come to me – come singly to me! And this true knife that has tasted the foul blood of your nation and now is red with the purest of mine, will feel a grasp as strong as when it flashed in the blaze of your burning dwellings, or was lifted terribly over the fallen in battle.

CHURCH: Fire upon him!

METAMORA: Do so, I am weary of the world for ye are dwellers in it; I would not turn upon my heel to save my life.

CHURCH: Your duty, soldiers.

They fire. Metamora falls. Enter Walter, Oceana, Wolfe, Sir Arthur, Errington, Goodenough, Tramp, and Peasants. Roll of drums and trumpet till all on

METAMORA: My curses on you, white men! May the Great Spirit curse you when he speaks in his war voice from the clouds! Murderers! The last of the Wampanoags' curse be on you! May your graves and the graves of your children be in the path the red man shall trace! And may the wolf and panther howl o'er your fleshless bones, fit banquet for the destroyers! Spirits of the grave, I come! But the curse of Metamora stays with the white man! I die! My wife! My Queen! My Nahmeokee!

Falls and dies; a tableau is formed. Drums and trumpet sound a retreat till curtain. Slow curtain

EPILOGUE

Written by Mr. James Lawson.
Spoken by Mrs. Hilson, New Park Theater,
New York, December 15, 1829.

Before this bar of beauty, taste, and wit,
This host of critics, too, who throng the pit,

A trembling bard has been this night arraigned;
And I am counsel in the cause retained.
Here come I, then, to plead with nature's art,
And speak, less to the law, than to the heart.

A native bard – a native actor too,
Have drawn a native picture to your view;
In fancy, this bade Indian wrongs arise,
While that embodied all before your eyes;
Inspired by genius, and by judgment led,
Again the Wampanoag fought and bled;
Rich plants are both of our own fruitful land,
Your smiles the sun that made their leaves expand;
Yet, not that they are native do I plead,
'Tis for their worth alone I ask your meed.
How shall I ask ye? Singly? Then I will –
But should I fail? Fail! I must try my skill.

Sir, I know you – I've often seen your face;
And always seated in that selfsame place;
Now, in my ear – what think you of our play?
That it has merit truly, he did say;
And that the hero, prop'd on genius' wing,
The Indian forest scoured, like Indian king!

See that fair maid, the tear still in her eye,
And hark! hear not you now that gentle sigh?
Ah! these speak more than language could relate,
The woe-fraught heart o'er Nahmeokee's fate;
She scans us not by rigid rules of art,
Her test is feeling, and her judge the heart.

What dost thou say, thou bushy-whiskered beau?
He nods approval – whiskers are the go.

Who is he sits the fourth bench from the stage?
There; in the pit! – why he looks wondrous sage!
He seems displeased, his lip denotes a sneer –
O! he's a critic that looks so severe!
Why, in his face I see the attic salt –
A critic's merit is to find a fault.
What fault find you, sir? eh! or you, sir?
None!
Then, if the critic's mute, my cause is won.
Yea, by that burst of loud heartfelt applause,
I feel that I have gained my client's cause.
Thanks, that our strong demerits you forgive,
And bid our bard and Metamora live.

THE GLADIATOR

ROBERT MONTGOMERY BIRD

JOHN AUGUSTUS STONE won the first of the Forrest playwriting contests with *Metamora*. Four of the winning entries in eight succeeding contests were from the pen of Dr. Robert Montgomery Bird of Philadelphia: *Pelopidas, or The Polemarchs; The Gladiator; Oralloossa, Son of the Incas;* and *The Broker of Bogota*. And one of these, *The Gladiator*, remained in Forrest's active repertoire throughout his lifetime, achieving a performance record almost equal to that of *Metamora*. Dr. Bird would not have attained his conspicuous position in our early theatre without Forrest's encouragement. He might well have contributed a more impressive list of dramas had Forrest been willing to share the financial rewards. His career as a dramatist was essentially limited to the four years between 1829 and 1833 and to these four plays.

Bird's biography is filled with radical turning points. He was perpetually at the crossroads. Adversity, misadventure, failing health, or simply new inclinations forced his path to change direction. At one time or another he was poet, musician, traveler, artist, doctor, dramatist, novelist, historian, scientist, inventor, mechanic, farmer, politician, teacher and journalist. On the surface, the life of a dilettante, but he pursued most of these activities so fervently that he might more properly be called a nineteenth-century "Renaissance man."

Robert Montgomery Bird was born on February 5, 1806 (just one month before Forrest), in New Castle, Delaware, to a pioneer family, his Irish great-grandfather having settled in Wilmington sometime around 1700. His father was a prosperous partner in the firm of Bird and Riddle, government navy agents. One of Bird's earliest scraps of writing, a three-stanza poem entitled "My Father – who died when I was 4 years old," recounts his first contact with adversity. When the family was forced to disband, his mother and brothers moved to Philadelphia and he was taken in by a rich uncle in New Castle, the Honorable Nicholas Van Dyke. His guardian enrolled him in the New Castle Academy and encouraged his developing musical aptitude with flute lessons.

Life at the Academy was not pleasant. In later years Bird recalled his brutal schoolmaster Mr. McGoggin: "He was six feet high, and limbed and shouldered like a Hercules . . . an illiterate, vulgar dolt." When Bird was fourteen, he rejoined his mother in Philadelphia and attended Germantown Academy and then the medical school at the University of Pennsylvania, from which he was graduated on April 6, 1827.

During his years in medical school, Bird kept up his flute-playing and began a notebook of quotations and comments on his extensive reading of Latin, American, and English literature, particularly the Elizabethan dramatists. He also wrote some short poems and in the summer of 1826 took the first of his excursions to explore and sketch the Delaware Water Gap. Clearly he had not developed an all-consuming passion for medicine. He wrote to his brother on May 20, 1827, "Gadzooks, I am tempted to cut my throat, but that I have an aversion to cold steel."

His disaffection toward medicine became clearer the following year, when he began practicing. Patients came. He cared for them, though without enthusiasm, and at the end of the year he discovered that his pathological aversion to charging for his services had left him poorer than when he began. Bird abandoned medicine and never practiced again.

Even during that trial year of doctoring, he had filled his notebooks with observations on the Elizabethan and Jacobean drama; had published some short poems in Dr. Snowden's *Philadelphia Monthly Magazine;* and had written two comedies, *'Twas All for the Best*, in the style of Congreve, and *News of the Night*, a farcical comedy set in Philadelphia but with comic action derived from Plautus, Terence, and Ben Jonson. He also began an active reading campaign in Spanish American history. After he had terminated his medical career, his literary output was enlarged. He finished *The City Looking Glass*, a comic exposure of low life in the big city. He wrote "Men of the Hills," a story inspired by the Delaware Water Gap, which later was expanded into a novel, *The Hawks of Hawk Hollow*. Then he took a quick fling at song-writing, with the intention of devising a volume to be called *Hymns of America;* this was never published, though one of the songs, "God Bless America," was printed in 1834 and later included in *The Gift Book of American Melodies* (1854). He also attempted two more serious dramatic offerings: *The Cowled Lover*, a Gothic adventure based on *Romeo and Juliet*, with a Byronic hero ("Earth's outcast, orphaned by the fates") and action laid on the shores of Lake Como; and *Caridorf*, also with a melancholy Gothic tone, with traces of *Othello* and *Macbeth*, and set in Vienna. The immediate effect of Bird's wide-ranging literary explorations is clearly apparent in these early plays. In addition to the unmistakable influence of the Elizabethans, there are clear evidences of his familiarity with Kotzebue, Schiller, Byron, and Brockden Brown. Bird apparently had no great hopes for these dramas. A proposed prologue read:

> 'Tis glorious sport, as all allow and say,
> To roast an author, and to damn a play;
> To wield the sword of satire, high and wild,
> And slay at once the father and the child.

Nor were these the only products of his apprenticeship. At twenty-two he mapped out his entire literary career. He proposed to devote himself first to poetry and drama, then to romances and novels, and finally, in his old age, to historical works. Bird was perpetually outlining work to be done, sketching a line of action for a play or novel, and even working through a portion of a manuscript and then laying it aside. Among his papers at the University of Pennsylvania, one list indicates titles for 112 poems, forty novels, nineteen comedies, and forty-three tragedies. Another, more conservative projection calls for seven comedies and twenty-four tragedies. In a small notebook labeled "Useful Works – if well prepared," Bird set his goal at nine biographies; thirty volumes of miscellaneous studies; three volumes of tales; some select novels of Boccaccio, to be revised and purified; the *Arabian Nights*, all purified; eleven tragedies; twelve comedies; thirty-three melodramas; and twenty-five novels. He left fragments of eight plays in various stages of development.

Bird did not approach his literary career casually; nor is it surprising that such a strenuous initial program had ill effects on his health. He spent the summer of 1829 in New Castle trying to recoup his strength with a regimen of long sleep and six to eight hours a day of tramping the woods and sketching. In the fall he extended his therapeutic exercise with the first of many trips to Kentucky. This western adventure gave him the basis for his best-known novel, *Nick of the Woods;* it also introduced him to Mammoth Cave, one of nature's inventions that held almost as much fascination for him as the Delaware Gap. On a later visit he wrote: "It is delightful and frightful, – glorious and horrible." Unfortunately, the journey did not nurse him back to health. Instead he was struck with an attack of "ague" that forced him to return to Philadelphia.

His turn toward home came at a propitious moment. He learned of Forrest's playwriting contest. Here was the catalyst he needed to give his dramatic composition a firm direction: an actor who apparently wished to encourage the native dramatists, and an actor whose vigorous and often violent stage manners were highly praised and whose passion for the libertarian cause was equally admired. Although his first entry in Forrest's competition, *Pelopidas, or The Fall of the Polemarchs*, won the prize in the third contest, it was never produced and not published until 1919, but it alerted Forrest to Bird's talent and gave the playwright a clearer grasp of what was required. *Pelopidas* had been based on Plutarch's account of the revolt of the Thebans against the Spartan tyrants and thus was filled with lofty libertarian sentiments; but, as Forrest instructed Bird, it lacked compelling incidents, many of the rhetorical passages were overextended, and it was deficient in stirring climaxes.

Bird was not depressed by the criticism. He set to work immediately on a drama that would fulfill both his and Forrest's demands. On May 1, 1831, he sent the manuscript of *The Gladiator* to Forrest with a letter explaining that it was "inordinately long" and that if he had had the whole summer he "could have discovered and annihilated some ten or a dozen pages. . . . But I galloped through the business. I am no horseman; I can't slash about me on a gallop . . . many useless lines still keep up the head and front of their offending, and will, till they are slashed by a more veteran hand." Forrest replied immediately:

My Dear Sir:

   The MS of *The Gladiator* came duly to hand with your letter of 1st instant. I think there can be no reasonable objections against producing your play in June, say, about the 20th. If you think otherwise I will be controlled entirely by your directions and order a postponement of the same until the fall season. In my mind *The Gladiator* must prove victorious winter or summer. To be sure he would not "groan and sweat" so much in cooler weather, but that will be his task not yours.

   I shall be in Philada. about the close of next week when we may discourse fully upon this subject.

Caius Marius[1] on Monday
Evening next   Yours sincerely,
N. York, 6th May, 1831   Edwin Forrest
Robert M. Bird, Esq.,
New Castle, Delaware

   Forrest was certain that he had struck a rich lode in this new prize winner, and when they met he was convinced that he had found a new friend. They both agreed that the play could be improved if they spent the summer at work. After a week of struggling with Spartacus in the Philadelphia heat, they sought a more favorable climate. In mid-June they headed for Niagara Falls, then swung up through New England and finally down the coast to the Natural Bridge in Virginia. Forrest was pleased to find a companion who delighted in the American natural wonders as he did. When they returned to Philadelphia in August, they were certain that they had an improved manuscript and a lasting friendship.

   As the production time drew near, however, Bird's confidence was not so strong as Forrest's. He confided his self-doubts to his "Secret Records"[2] on August 27, 1831:

. . . I wrote *The Gladiator* just on the Eve of my 25th year; but can have no satisfaction in noting its birth, till I can form some augury of the length of its life. To be sure, folks talk as agreeably as they can, particularly those who know the least about it. "Ah my dear Sir, I see you are coming out. Glad of it – am sure you'll have

---

[1] *Caius Marius*, by Richard Penn Smith, another Philadelphia playwright and a friend of Bird's, had won the prize in Forrest's second contest. Bird's notes indicate that Smith's play had some influence on *The Gladiator*.

[2] This "secret" journal contains only three entries: August 27, October 26, December 14, 1831. See R. M. Bird bibliography.

great success." And yet that ass hasn't seen a line of the play; and if he had, couldn't understand it. . . . I am disposed to be sanguine enough – that is my temperament.

And although he had tailored the play for the stage and for an actor, he wondered now if he had been wise to subject himself to their demands. In the same entry he wrote:

Our theatres are in a lamentable condition, and not at all fashionable. To write for, and be admired by the groundlings! villains, that will clap most, when you are most nonsensical, and applaud you most heartily when you are most vulgar! that will call you "a genius, by G——," when you can make the judicious grieve, and "a witty devil," when you can force a woman to blush! Fine, fine, fine, fine.

In spite of Bird's reservations, *The Gladiator* got off to a rousing start: first at the Park Theatre in New York on September 26, 1831; then at the Arch Street Theatre in Philadelphia on October 24; and the week of November 14 in Boston. The final judgments of the critics all carried the same high praise: "decidedly the best drama ever written in this century"; "the best native tragedy extant . . . bears the stamp of genius in every lineament"; "a genuine tragedy of native worth"; "replete with beautiful passages and noble sentiments"; "a keen perception of the emotions of the human heart, and poetic talent of a very superior grade." One critic thought it far superior to Payne's *Brutus* and Knowles's *Virginius*.

Although favorably regarded by critics and audience, the New York opening was not a happy experience for Bird. He reported in his "Secret Records" that "there fell such torrents of rains as had not visited New York for 15 to 20 years. Nevertheless the house was crammed." But, more disturbing, "The Park Company is the most wretched in the country. . . . There never was a play more miserably got up, old dresses, old scenes, many of them full of absurdities and to crown all, the performers with but two exceptions were horribly imperfect." The Philadelphia opening was more felicitous. On October 24, Bird reported to his "Records":

An American feeling was beginning to show itself in the theatrical matters. The managers of the Arch St. Theatre were Americans, all the chief performers were Americans and the play was written by an American. The play was very well got up. . . . It was played with a roar of applause and bravoed to the echo, all which was comfortable enough. Played 4 times to full houses. Forrest is undoubtedly the best man for Spartacus in Christendom; in which his figure and physique show to the best advantage and his voice and muscle hold out to the last.

Charles Durang reported that "the entire male portion of the audience rose to its feet and gave at least nine cheers. I never saw in my experience any theatrical applause so wildly and impulsively given."

Forrest had a strong addition to his repertoire, and Bird was marked as the promising new American playwright. By 1854 Forrest had given a thousand performances of Spartacus. According to one tabulator, *The Gladiator* was "the first play to be performed so often in the author's lifetime." After Forrest's death in 1872 it was frequently performed by John McCullough, and it was done as recently as 1893 by Robert Downing at the Grand Opera House in New York. Only in England did it fail to arouse the customary cheers. Although Forrest thought "they treated *The Gladiator* and Dr. Bird unfairly," when the audience's wishes were clear he quickly dropped it from his London repertoire. Bird's fellow dramatists in England were, however, quick to inform him that they did not share the audience's view. On October 26, 1836, Richard Brinsley Peake wrote: "I have the honor to inform you that at a general meeting of this society, you as the author of the play of *The Gladiator*, were unanimously elected an Honorary Member in token of respect for your Talent as a writer by the English Dramatic Authors [Society]. . . ." Bird had taken the London rebuff gracefully. He put it down simply to a "question of taste between the two people; and which is right and which is wrong, better judges than myself must determine."

Bird was firmly launched as a playwright, and with the enthusiastic blessings and support of America's leading actor. In the next contest he again won the prize, with *Oralloossa, Son of the Incas*. Bird had read widely in Spanish American history;[3] he was well aware of the popularity of Washington Irving's histories and sketches of Columbus and of the conquistadors; and, of course, the theatre audiences' enthusiasm for the Indian and Forrest's command of such a role had been clearly demonstrated with *Metamora*. Forrest and Bird were on easy, friendly terms during the preparation of the new manuscript. When Forrest remarked that he detected some slight "prettinesses of speech," Bird replied: "If you catch a 'prettiness of speech,' in any play of mine, geld me, – or take it for granted, I was drunk when I wrote it. I would sooner be guilty of breaking wind in company, than of clapping a prettiness of speech into a tragedy."

Oralloossa was given a magnificent production for its opening at the Arch Street Theatre in Philadelphia on October 10, 1832. Apparently Forrest's brother William, who was then manager of the theatre, invested the stage with new scenery, new costumes, and "new banners." There were "twelve splendid panoramic scenes with geographically accurate views of the Peruvian Andes." Only one unfortunate incident marred the opening performance. Forrest attacked F. C. Wemyss (the Don Christoval) so violently that he knocked out two of his front teeth. Again the critics gave their native son their full praise. The *United States Gazette* (October 12, 1832) reported that "it excels

---

[3]In his *History of the Conquest of Mexico* (1843), William H. Prescott praised Bird's historical accuracy.

every modern production that has been produced of late years." It was equally well spoken of when it played in Boston and New York later in the fall. The Boston *Evening Gazette* (November 4, 1832) said it was "the best tragedy ever produced by an American." And the New York *Mercantile Advertiser* (December 8, 1832) thought that "when the passion of the action rises it is poetical in a higher order than that of *The Gladiator*."

Despite its strong beginning, the play never achieved the popularity of *The. Gladiator*. Forrest played it only infrequently and in 1847 dropped it from his repertoire. After the initial enthusiasm had worn away, it became clear that it was not so strong a play as *The Gladiator*. The battle cry for freedom was not so thrilling, the rhetoric was less vigorous. The complexities of the struggle – not only Indian against Spaniard, but Indian against Indian and Spaniard against Spaniard – became confusing, and somehow Bird's sympathies were not so sharply defined. In championing the cause of the rebel patriot, he could never completely forget that the Indians were savages and the Spanish were Christians.

The following spring (1833) Forrest and Bird started on a trip that was to take them to New Orleans, then on to Mexico and Peru. In New Orleans they abandoned their South American plans. Perhaps the reported cholera epidemics persuaded them against the adventure, or, as Bird reported, he could not endure the prospect of "riding so far on stupid mules." They came back up the river to Memphis. Here they separated. Forrest continued by boat, while Bird took the stagecoach for Nashville, "thirteen days over the hills and swamps of West Tennessee – oh the horrors and purgatoriosities thereof," and then via Mammoth Cave to rejoin Forrest in Cincinnati. Then on to Detroit and Niagara Falls, and back to Philadelphia at the end of July.

During the journey they talked of Bird's new play and in the fall he completed the manuscript. In *The Broker of Bogota* he again turned to South America, though not to a remote time. In fact, though the action took place in Santa Fe de Bogotá in New Granada, essentially it belongs to no particular place nor time; unlike Bird's other dramas and Forrest's other prize plays, it is a domestic tragedy relating the pathetic story of Baptista Febro, a wealthy and honorable money lender who lavishes all his love on his children and is rewarded by having them turn against him. After a successful opening at the Bowery Theatre in New York on February 12, 1834, Forrest wrote to Bird, "I have just left the theatre – your tragedy was performed and crowned with entire success. *The Broker of Bogota* will live when our vile trunks are rotten. You have every reason to congratulate yourself." Forrest's prediction was not fulfilled. Though it was retained in his repertoire until 1862, it was performed infrequently. Bird always insisted that *The Broker* was his favorite play, largely because it depended less on bombast and "blood and thunder," theatrical necessities which he deplored. Even without the fiery ingredients required for a Forrest success, the play had a well-entangled plot and many effective scenes, and certainly the tragic action evolved reasonably and compellingly from the well-drawn characters of Febro and his son Ramon.

Even before Bird had completed *The Broker*, he had begun to turn away from the drama. He had been at work on a long poem, *The Vision*, on a review of James Montgomery's lectures on literature and poetry, and most particularly on his first novel, *Calavar*. And Bird had expressed his reservations about the theatre before he learned from bitter experience that it would prove unprofitable. He was not yet fully aware that he would not share in Forrest's success. On August 27, 1831, before the production of *The Gladiator*, he had confided to his "Secret Records": "What a fool I was to think of writing plays! To be sure, they are much wanted. But these novels are much easier sort of things, and immortalize one's pocket much sooner." He was well aware of the current vogue for Scott and Cooper.

Bird sailed for England in April, 1834, to seek a British publication of *Calavar* before it appeared in America, so as to forestall the inevitable pirating. He was not successful. However, the London scene made a strong impact upon him. Seemingly for the first time, he realized that there was contemporary truth in the doctrine he had been propounding in his plays. In one letter he wrote, "I am afraid if I stay here longer, I shall become a Jackson man! I begin to feel like a democrat, and for the first time in my life to think that God will lead the foot of the poor man to the neck of the rich, and that, in this, there will be justice. . . . I can't look about me here . . . without seeing an evidence of the corruption and misery that follow in the steps of privilege."

Calavar was an immediate success when it was published in October, 1834. Poe thought it was "beyond a doubt one of the best American novels," and the *Knickerbocker Magazine* reported that "we shall be exceedingly mistaken if the work does not place the author in the very highest rank among the writers of America." Bird began work immediately on a sequel, *The Infidel, or The Fall of Mexico*, which was ready for publication in the spring. He pursued his new career at his customary breakneck pace. His next novels appeared in quick order: *The Hawks of Hawk Hollow* (1835); *Sheppard Lee* (1836); *Nick of the Woods, or the Jibbenainosay* (1837); *The Adventures of Robin Day* (1839). His final novel, *A Belated Revenge*, was later finished by his son, Frederick M. Bird, and published in 1889. During this period he also published a two-volume collection of his shorter pieces under the title *Peter Pilgrim, or A Rambler's Recollections*. In the midst of this fervent period of novel writing he had rewritten Stone's *Metamora* for Forrest and on July 13, 1837, had married Mary Mayer.

The two events were not unconnected. His wife urged him to claim his professional rights in the plays out of which Forrest was making a fortune. In

November, 1837, Forrest called on Bird and requested repayment of the two-thousand-dollar loan he had advanced him when he began on *Metamora*. He had not used the revised version in England as he had anticipated. Bird refused, insisting that Forrest pay him the $6,000 which he rightfully owed him on the plays. "The state of affairs between us is simply this," Bird wrote later in summary, "I have received from him $1,000 on each of my plays, *The Gladiator, Oralloosa*, and *The Broker;* and $2,000 in loan, for which he had my note. But he owes me still (if there *was* a bargain between us, as I suppose there was), $2,000 on each of these plays, in all $6,000, minus the $2,000 loan; that is, $4,000. He owes me also $2,000 for *Metamora*, rewritten; for so much I think it worth." As both of them must have known before the quarrel began, Forrest did not pay. Three years later Bird had an opportunity to strike back: William Burton proposed to produce *Pelopidas* on the same nights as Forrest appeared in Conrad's *Jack Cade*. But at that moment Bird was apparently too weary to continue the struggle. In 1851 he contemplated bringing suit against Forrest, but his friend John Clayton advised him that his slim chances of collecting did not warrant the investment. Forrest's continuing prosperity was a perpetual annoyance. After Bird's death, Mrs. Bird estimated that Forrest must have made at least a hundred thousand dollars on *The Gladiator* alone. In 1869 Bird's son Frederick wrote to Forrest proposing to publish his father's plays. Forrest's reply was unequivocal: "The Heirs of the late Dr. R. M. Bird have neither right, title, nor any legal interest whatever in the plays. They are my exclusive property, by the right of purchase, and for many years by the law of copyright." After the rupture with Forrest, Bird did not attend the theatre more than half a dozen times during the remaining years of his life and never saw one of his own plays. In 1853, when he learned that George Boker was campaigning for a new copyright law, he volunteered his support, indicating that if such protection had been available a few years earlier he would never have deserted his career as a dramatist.

The five years from 1834 to 1839 had been filled with too much activity: six novels and part of a seventh, his marriage, the birth of his son in 1838, and his final bitter quarrel with Forrest. Bird determined that a new career as farmer might rejuvenate both mind and body. He bought 250 acres on the Eastern Shore of Maryland and in March, 1840, attacked his new enterprise with his usual passion: ". . . hammered doors and glazed windows, mended locks and fences, and played the general factotum from half past four in the morning till half past eight at night; and still the work grows upon my hands." He had planned to pursue agricultural projects during the day and at night write *A History of the United States*. It was a foolhardy wish. "If I wrote anything," he explained, "it must be a history of my own bothers." By the end of the year he was ready to quit. In addition to the hard labor for which he was not conditioned and the total absence of financial reward, rustic society had not fulfilled its promise. He wrote to a friend: "For all the poeticizing on the subject of the virtues of the tillers of the soil, it is quite certain that the wicked dwellers of town and cities make more agreeable companions and warmer friends."

Again he changed his occupation, this time reverting to his early calling. For two sessions, 1841–42 and 1842–43, he was Professor of the Institutes of Medicine and Materia Medica at the Pennsylvania Medical College in Philadelphia. During this period he met Senator John Clayton (later Zachary Taylor's Secretary of State), became interested in politics, was a delegate to the Whig Convention in Baltimore in 1844, and in 1848 wrote a campaign biography of General Zachary Taylor. Then, with financial support from Clayton, he bought a one-third interest in the Philadelphia *North American and United States Gazette*. He approached his final profession with his customary vigor – "my whole time from 8 A.M. to 1 next A.M. every day is laboriously occupied in my duties" – and under his guidance the *Gazette* became an influential Whig paper, widely known for its "well written and readable paragraphs."

When Bird became ill in the early winter of 1853, it was too late to seek a remedy in a change of occupation. He died on January 23, 1854, of "effusion of the brain."

With a writer so conscious of his literary task and so addicted to committing his workroom observations to his notebooks, it was natural that Bird would explore the manners and methods of dramatic composition. Certainly his plays achieved their effects because Bird understood precisely the demands of the drama and of the theatre. In his preface to *The Broker*, he explained that the dramatist must consider actors, audience, and critics as his enemies and "beware that he lays open no weakness to them." In the "Secret Records" he described the ideal dramatist as one possessed of "the sanguine and fiery ardour of an oriental, with the phlegmatic judgment of a German; he should be in himself capable of feeling, in the extremes, all the passions which elevate and debase, which subdue and torture the mind; and at the same time should mingle with them a coldblooded and restraining philosophy." Many of his observations are as pertinent now as they were for the dramatist in the 1830's:

The true secret of effect consists in having everything as well in details as in general structure epigrammatic or climacteric, the story rising to rapidity and closing with power; the chief characters increasing in passion and energy; the events growing in interest, the scenes and acts each accumulating power about their precursors; the strength of a speech augmenting at its close, and the important characters dismissed at each exit with some sort of point and emphasis.

The first part of the education of a dramatist is that which fits him to be a writer; the second makes him an actor; the third inducts him into the principles of criticism; and he has completed his studies when he can exercise the functions of the three not separately but together.

The great, perhaps the chief, secret of effect depends upon the style of language.

. . . The secret is simple: that writer stumbles upon dramatic effect whose characters speak like men; and he fails whose personages declaim like orators and poets. We sympathize in a theatre with nothing that is not natural; we even feel the homeliest expressions of passion, when they are like those of beings around us.

Certainly *The Gladiator*, in its preparation and its final realization in the theatre, illustrates the work of a diligent and conscious dramatic craftsman. Before he began the actual composition, Bird absorbed all the atmosphere and detail that was available in Plutarch, Livy, Florus, Eutropius, and Velleius Paterculus, in Hook's *Roman History* and in Ferguson's *History of the Roman Republic*. His reading furnished the background. His grasp of the spirit of his own time and the peculiar talents of Forrest set his goal. The patriotic hero struggling against despotism, against Old World tyranny, had been successfully exploited in such plays as Payne's *Brutus* (1818) and David P. Brown's *Sertorius, or The Roman Patriot* (1830) and in a way in Stone's *Metamora*. But the struggle against slavery, against privilege, was even more immediate. The cause of abolitionism was burning more brightly with the publication of William Lloyd Garrison's *The Liberator* (1831). Certainly Andrew Jackson's election just three years earlier had demonstrated a solid belief in the noble virtues of the freedom-loving common man. Ancient lineage and wealth were no longer the required insignia for a political leader. And Edwin Forrest's vibrant muscular frame, his distended neck, his swollen arteries and veins, his rigid jaws, "the orbs now rolling like the dilated and blazing eyes of a leopard, now white and wet like the ferocious deathly eyes of a bull, while smothered passion seemed to threaten an actual explosion of the whole frame," had become the popular stereotype of the elemental common man. His audiences knew that he was endowed with primitive virtues, with physical prowess, great courage, strong passions, and a heart filled with loving-kindness, that he was committed to a righteous struggle against the forces that would oppress and enslave. Spartacus may have been a Thracian in Rome. On the American stage, he was the symbol of every bound creature who had, through his own faith and power, broken the chains of an unnatural master.

In the heat of composing for the theatre Bird committed himself fully to what he had written. He deplored the selling of slaves, the parting of families, the unnatural belief that the Creator had destined one race to be inferior to another, that any religion – be it pagan or Christian – could sanction the practice of slavery. With his "phlegmatic judgment of the German," he also knew that if *The Gladiator* were produced in a slave state, "the managers, players, and perhaps myself in the bargain, would be rewarded with the Penitentiary!" He knew that he did not seriously advocate the re-enactment of his Thracian rebellion in America. He sadly feared that the Negro was little more than a murdering savage when he struck for freedom. At the time he was writing *The Gladiator*, Bird observed that some "six to eight hundred rebelling slaves under Nat Turner are murdering, ravishing, and burning in Virginia. . . . If they had a Spartacus among them to organize the half million of Virginia, the hundred of thousand of the other states, and lead them on in the Crusade of Massacre, what a blessed example might they not give to the world of the excellence of slavery!" Unhappily, Bird also recognized that the play boasted more "blood and thunder" than suited his personal tastes, that "as in most tragedies, the silliest and most ridiculous portions . . . draw the greatest applause."

Whatever Bird's qualifications, or those of later critics, *The Gladiator* exercised a remarkable power over theatre audiences during the middle forty years of the past century. When Spartacus called for the insurrection of the gladiators:

> Death to the Roman fiends . . .
> Ho, slaves, arise! it is your hour to kill!
> Kill and spare not – For wrath and liberty! –
> Freedom for bondmen – freedom and revenge!

there may have been "shouts and trumpets" on stage, but they were lost in the cheers and bravos from the other side of the lights.

THE GLADIATOR

ROBERT MONTGOMERY BIRD

CHARACTERS

MARCUS LICINIUS CRASSUS, *a Roman Praetor*	SPARTACUS, *a Thracian,*
LUCIUS GELLIUS, *a Consul*	PHASARIUS, *his brother,*
SCROPHA, *a Quaestor*	AENOMAIIS, *a Gaul,*
JOVIUS, *a Centurion*	CRIXUS, *a German,*
MUMMIUS, *lieutenant to* CRASSUS	*and others*
BATIATUS LENTULUS, *a Capuan Lanista, or*	*A boy, son of* SPARTACUS
master of gladiators	JULIA, *niece of* CRASSUS
BRACCHIUS, *a Roman Lanista*	SENONA, *wife of* SPARTACUS
FLORUS, *son of* B. LENTULUS	*Citizens, soldiers, etc.*

Gladiators

SCENE: *Rome, and parts of Italy.* TIME, B.C. 73

ACT I. Scene 1

Rome. The street before Bracchius's house.

Enter Phasarius, AEnomaiis, and other gladiators.

PHASARIUS: There never was a properer moment. I look around me on the Roman flocks, that are deserted by their watchdogs and shepherds, and my fingers itch to be at their throats. Rome has sent forth her generals to conquer the world, and left nothing but her name for the protection of her citizens. Where now is that warlike, arrogant, and envious coxcomb, Pompey? Quarrelling, – he and that old brawler, Metellus, – in Spain, with the rebel, Sertorius: Lucullus, the Spoiler? Chasing the braggart, Mithridates, over his Pontic mountains: and Marcus, his brother? Killing the rest of my countrymen, the furies speed him! That restless boy, young Caesar? Among the islands, crucifying the pirates. Marius dead, Sylla rotting. – There is not a man in Rome, that Rome could now look to for service.

AENOMAIIS: The praetor, Crassus.

PHASARIUS: The miserable rich man, the patrician monger, that, by traffic in human flesh, has turned a patrimony of an hundred talents into an hundred thousand! If there be any virtue in the love of wealth, then is the praetor a most virtuous man; for he loves it better than he loves the gods. And if he be great and magnanimous, who coins his gold from the sinews of his bondsmen, set me down Crassus as the beloved of all greatness. 'Sblood, brother sworder, what were such a counter of silver in the iron wars? Get me up a rebellion, and you shall see this great man brained by the least of his merchandise.

AENOMAIIS: Well, I should like to be at the killing of some dozen such tyrants.

PHASARIUS: Why should you not? Some thousands like ourselves,
Most scurvy fellows, that have been trained, like dogs,
To tear each other for their masters' pleasure,
Shed blood, cut throats, and do such mortal mischiefs
As men love best to work upon their foes, –
Of these there are some thousands in this realm,
Have the same wish with us, to turn their swords
Upon their masters. And, 'tis natural,

That wish, and reasonable, very reasonable.
I am tired of slaying bondmen like myself,
I am sick of it. That day the Roman knight,
To win the smile of the rich quaestor's daughter,
In the arena sprung, and volunteered
To kill a gladiator, and did find
His liver spitted, like a thing of naught,
Upon my weapon, – since that day I tasted
Of Roman blood, I have had no desire
To kill poor slaves – I've longed for naught but
Romans!

AENOMAIIS: Well, we can die, and kill some, ere
we die.

PHASARIUS: Ay, marry, some dozens;
And should those wretches be but moved to
join us,
We might, for dozens, count us glorious thousands.

AENOMAIIS: Well, we are all agreed to this.
We are thirty. But how
Shall we get weapons?

PHASARIUS: Set our dens afire,
And force the armory.

AENOMAIIS: Our master, Bracchius,
Has a sharp watch to that.

PHASARIUS: In half an hour,
We are at our morning's practice. Now, thou
knowest,
To keep me in good heart, he humors me
Most fulsomely. I have won him some great
wagers,
So I am worth his fooling. I will urge him,
For this day's play, instead of laths, to give us
True brands, for keener practice, that we may
Show nobler for him at the praetor's games.

AENOMAIIS: < He knows, indeed, 'tis needful we
have ready,
For these same games, the best of skill: >* I've
heard
That Lentulus the Capuan brings a troop
Of excellent swordsmen on that day.

PHASARIUS: What, excellent?
Did I not beat his boaster? – Excellent?

AENOMAIIS: 'Tis rumored so.

PHASARIUS: By Jove, we will put off
This thing a day! I have seen no excellence
In weapons for a month.

AENOMAIIS: Why need you see it?

PHASARIUS: Nay, if he have a man to meet a
man,

*Passages cut in the acting version.

I must be in the arena: No desertion,
When there's a peril to be dared and ended!
Faith, I will have a bout, if it but be
To make Rome talk. You shall see, AEnomaiis,
If he be matched with me in the Thracian combat,
How I will use that trick my brother taught
me,
When first I flashed a weapon.

AENOMAIIS: I doubt not,
You will maintain your reputation.

PHASARIUS: Faith,
I'll hear once more this Roman acclamation,
Ere it be changed to curses.

AENOMAIIS: See! Our master –

PHASARIUS: Well, get you gone.

AENOMAIIS: Forget not for the weapons.

PHASARIUS: Ay, ay – after the shows.

*Exit AEnomaiis and the Gladiators. Enter
Bracchius*

BRACCHIUS: How now, Phasarius; what did
these cutthroats here? Idling, sirrah?

PHASARIUS: No; they were moralizing over their
scars, and asking what they had got by 'em.

BRACCHIUS: Do the rogues think themselves soldiers, that their cuts should be worth anything
but showing?

PHASARIUS: No. But some of them hope to be
made freedmen one day, when they are no
longer fit for the arena.

BRACCHIUS: Fellow, thou knowest I love thee,
and will enfranchise thee.

PHASARIUS: Yes – when my eye is dimmed, my
arm stiffened, my heart chilled, my head gray:
I look for redemption no sooner. I am a lusty,
serviceable rogue yet: Why should you free me
now?

BRACCHIUS: Sirrah, are you insolent? I will
have the centupondium to your heels, and the
lash to your shoulders.

PHASARIUS: Which will make me fight the better
at the praetor's games, hah! Which of us is the
lunatic?

BRACCHIUS: What, you knave!

PHASARIUS: Thou art my master; but I know,
thou wouldst as soon set me free, as scourge
me. Both would destroy thy subsistence, and
one thy life; in either case, I would fight no
more. And if thou wert to touch me lawfully
with the thong, thou knowest, I would unlawfully murder thee.

BRACCHIUS: You shall be crucified!

PHASARIUS: Then shall the crows pick forty thousand crowns from my bones; for so much are these muscles worth.

BRACCHIUS: Out upon you, villain! It is my favor has made thee so insolent.

PHASARIUS: It is my knowledge of my own price, and not thy favor, which is more perilous than thine anger. Pr'ythee, threaten me no more; or I shall grow peaceable, and spoil thy fortune.

BRACCHIUS: You have sworn never to decline the combat.

PHASARIUS: Ay; so I have. But I have found no one regards a slave's oath; and why now should the slave? It is my humor, and not my oath, makes me a shedder of blood. But the humor may change.

BRACCHIUS: Well, thou art a most impudent talker; it is eternal Saturnalia with thee. But I forgive thee, and will do thee more kindness than I have done already.

PHASARIUS: Which is to say, you have some new jeopardy to put my neck in. You have some gladiator of fame you would have me fight, is it not?

BRACCHIUS: Ay, if rumor be worth the noting. Crassus has hired the gladiators from Capua; and, 'tis said, Lentulus will bring with them a man that will cut the coxcomb from thy pate, and utterly annihilate thee.

PHASARIUS: They say so? Annihilate me!

BRACCHIUS: Faith, 'tis so reckoned, and strong wagers are making against you.

PHASARIUS: Hah? Against me? Annihilate me! If he have a head of adamant and a breast of brass, he may do it; but if his scull be common bone, and his skin no thicker than bullhide – Mehercle! let me see this Cyclops.

BRACCHIUS: Now, by Jupiter, I love thy spirit.

PHASARIUS: Has he no name? No country? No voucher of triumphs? Marry, for a mushroom, a thing that was yesterday unknown, his credit is a jot too arrogant; and, as I am a Thracian, and feel the blood of the warlike god, the father of Thrace, still tingle in my fingers, I will make my iron acquainted with his ribs. – Out upon him, – Annihilate me!

BRACCHIUS: Come, thou art his better; but he is noted enough to make thy triumph the more glorious. Put thyself in the meanwhile to practice. But who comes here? What, Lentulus of Capua?

Enter Lentulus

By mine honesty, I am glad to see thee. Bringest thou any new cutthroats? What, man, here is my Mars of gladiators, my most unmatched and unmatchable, Phasarius the Thracian. Look how lusty the knave looks! Hast anything fit to be slashed by such a fellow?

LENTULUS: Nay, I know not. 'Tis a most gallant villain. < Slew he not six at the shows given by Gellius the consul?

BRACCHIUS: Yes, by Mars; and would have made eel's meat of the seventh, but that the people grew pitiful and pointed their thumbs. – I could have cuffed 'em, senators and all. – He had him on his hip, his body bent around him thus, his fist to his poll, his dagger to his throat. By Mars, 'twas the noblest sight I had seen for a month: and yet when he looked to them for the doom, the pitiful things cried *Nay*. – I could have cuffed 'em! >

LENTULUS: But is he thy best man?

BRACCHIUS: The best in Rome. I have a Gaul, too; but he is not his equal. I would thou hadst a match for either. Crassus will pay: the best gladiator in the land were no loss, if killed in his service.

LENTULUS: I have brought some indifferent good fellows: and one of them, I think, I would wager against your unmatchable.

BRACCHIUS: Hearest thou that, Phasarius? Get in and practice. [*Exit Phasarius*]

LENTULUS: But he will not take the gladiator's oaths.

BRACCHIUS: What, is he slave or felon?

LENTULUS: A slave that I bought of the quaestor just returned from the army of Thrace; a shepherd, I think, they told me, and leader of a horde of his savage countrymen. I bought him on the faith of the fame he brought with him, of being the most desperate, unconquerable, and, indeed, skilful barbarian in the province. < Thou hast not forgot Caius Clypeus, the centurion, that fought in the shows at the funeral of Sylla?

BRACCHIUS: He was accounted on that day the second swordsman in Rome.

LENTULUS: His bones, with those of two of his followers, are rotting on the banks of the Strymon. The three attacked the valiant savage, my bondman; and by Jupiter, without other help than fortune and extraordinary prowess, he slew them all.

BRACCHIUS: Hercules! he has magic weapons! > But how was he taken?

LENTULUS: Betrayed by his follower, while he slept; and yet he had vengeance on his betrayer, for he dashed his brains out upon a rock.

BRACCHIUS: Excellent! Dash his brains out! He is a Titan. I would have given a dozen common slaves to have seen him do that thing!

LENTULUS: But he will not swear.

BRACCHIUS: Come, thou knowest not the nature of these fellows. Didst thou speak him kindly?

LENTULUS: Ay: but I had better have talked softly to a hyena: he did but scowl at me. Faith, he will sit yon by the day, looking at his chains, or the wall; and if one has a word from him, it is commonly a question. How many leagues he is away from Thrace.

BRACCHIUS: Didst thou tell him of the honors of a gladiator?

LENTULUS: Ay; and he asked if cutting throats was the most honorable occupation in Rome?

BRACCHIUS: By Mars, thou shouldst have scourged him.

LENTULUS: I did.

BRACCHIUS: And how wrought it?

LENTULUS: I think the knave had killed me, when I struck him, – ay, even with his manacled fist, – but that he was felled by the staff of my freedman. I should have hanged him, but was loath to lose so bold a varlet. Wherefore I had him scourged again, and, faith, he took it as passively as a stone. But it will not make him swear.

BRACCHIUS: Didst thou vow to the gods to hang him up like a dog, if he were so obstinate?

LENTULUS: I had a halter put to his neck; but then he laughed, and thanked his barbarous gods for such indulgence.

BRACCHIUS: Nay, this is a madman.

LENTULUS: I had the fetters taken from his arm, and sent one to attack him with a weapon. But although I laid a sword by him, he would not use it; yet he struck the assailant with his fist, and felled him as one would a wall with a battering ram. But then he was angry. Another time, he sat still, and let the slave wound him, unresisting.

BRACCHIUS: Moody caitiff! Thou hadst better drown him. – Look thou – Mine eyes are dim – I have bought a troop of women and children

– Thracians too – and I think those be they coming yonder.

LENTULUS: Thou art mistaken. Those are mine own cutthroats, and the wild Thracian among them.

BRACCHIUS: Why didst thou bring him to Rome?

LENTULUS: In a last hope to urge him to the oath. Look, is he not a most warlike and promising fellow?

Enter Spartacus, chained, and Florus with the Capuan Gladiators

BRACCHIUS: A Hercules, a Mars! What, thou rogue, why dost thou droop thus? Why art thou so sullen and obstinate? No words? What, canst thou not speak? – Fetch me a scourge hither – I'll find thee a tongue.

LENTULUS: Come, sirrah, look up, speak, show thyself.

SPARTACUS: Is it a thousand leagues away to Thrace?

LENTULUS: What, thou fool, wilt thou always be harping on Thrace? 'Tis so far away, thou wilt never see it more.

SPARTACUS: Never.

LENTULUS: Why, I say, never. Why wilt thou be so mad as to think of it?

SPARTACUS: Have Romans fathers, and wives, and children?

BRACCHIUS: Truly! Thou art a Thracian; what is thy name?

SPARTACUS: Misery.

LENTULUS: Thou seest!

BRACCHIUS: Faith, thou hast scourged him too much; thou hast broke his heart. Come, sirrah, dost thou love thy country?

SPARTACUS: I have none, – I am a slave. I was bought; I say, I was bought. Do you doubt it? That man scourges me; *thou* didst threaten me with stripes; every Roman I look upon, speaks to me of scourging. Nay, they may: I was bought.

LENTULUS: Thou seest, Bracchius! This is the manner of his obstinacy.

BRACCHIUS: Nay, I see more than thou thinkest. I can move him yet. – Observe him. – He mutters to himself.

SPARTACUS: Is not this Rome? The great city?

BRACCHIUS: Ay; and thou shouldst thank the gods they have suffered thee to see it, before thou diest. –

SPARTACUS: I heard of it, when I was a boy

among the hills, piping to my father's flocks. They said, that spoke of it, it was the queen of cities, the metropolis of the world. My heart grew big within me, to hear of its greatness. I thought those men who could make it so, were greater than men; they were gods.

LENTULUS: And are they not, sirrah? –

SPARTACUS: How many palaces, that look like the habitations of divinities, are here about me! Here are marble mountains, that have been hewn down and shaped anew, for men to dwell among. Gold, and silver, and purple, and a million of men thronging the pillared hills!

BRACCHIUS: And what thinkest thou, now thou hast seen it?

SPARTACUS: That, – if Romans had not been fiends, Rome had never been great! Whence came this greatness, but from the miseries of subjugated nations? How many myriads of happy people – people that had not wronged Rome, for they knew not Rome – how many myriads of these were slain like the beasts of the field, that Rome might fatten upon their blood, and become *great*? Look ye, Roman, – there is not a palace upon these hills that cost not the lives of a thousand innocent men; there is no deed of greatness ye can boast, but it was achieved upon the ruin of a nation; there is no joy ye can feel, but its ingredients are blood and tears.

LENTULUS: Now marry, villain, thou wert bought not to prate, but to fight.

SPARTACUS: I will not fight. I will contend with mine enemy, when there is strife between us; and if that enemy be one of these same fiends, a Roman, I will give him advantage of weapon and place; he shall take a helmet and buckler; while I, with my head bare, my breast naked, and nothing in my hand but my shepherd's staff, will beat him to my feet and slay him. But I will not slay a man for the diversion of Romans.

BRACCHIUS: Thou canst boast, barbarian! If thou canst do this, what brought thee to Rome, a captive?

SPARTACUS: Treachery! I was friendless, sick, famished. My enemies came in numbers. They were like the rats of Egypt, that will not come near the crocodile while he is awake: they attacked me sleeping. Had they found me with a weapon in my hands, Gods! I had not now been a thing for Romans to scourge.

BRACCHIUS: Fellow, I love thee. What is thy name?

SPARTACUS: What matters it?

BRACCHIUS: Wilt thou be free?

SPARTACUS: Free!

BRACCHIUS: Take the oaths of a gladiator, and kill me a score of lusty fellows –

SPARTACUS: A score! kill a score of men? in cold blood? and for the diversion of Rome's rabble? I will not.

BRACCHIUS: By Mars, then you shall be sent to man young Caesar's galleys, and be whipped daily.

LENTULUS: Fight me half a score, and, by Jupiter, I will send thee back to thy wife.

SPARTACUS: My wife! – The last thing that mine eyes looked on,
When my steps turned from Thrace, it was my cottage,
A hideous ruin; the Roman fires had scorched it:
No wife sat sobbing by the wreck; no child
Wept on the sward; not even the watchdog howled:
There was no life there. – Well, why should I talk?
'Tis better they are perished.

LENTULUS: This is despair:
The slave is reckless. –

SPARTACUS: O ye heavens! that sight
Withered my heart; I was a man no more.
I had been happy, too! – Had ye spared them,
Then spoke of freedom, you should have had my blood,
For beastly ransome: All integrity
And pride of heart I would have sold for it.

BRACCHIUS: Sirrah, there are more wives in Thrace.

LENTULUS: Lo now!
He'll speak no more. – You, Bracchius, have more skill
To move these obstinates. You shall buy him of me.

BRACCHIUS: And hang him! Marry, not I. He is a madman.
I have some better merchandise here now,
Not warlike, but as gainful.

Enter Senona, with a child, and other slaves
                    Thou seest these creatures:
Here are some Thracians, too. – The moody villain!

He should be hanged. – The Thracian women
are
Most excellent spinners. Buy a brace of them
For your wife. I care not for so many.
LENTULUS: This woman
That weeps so, she with the brat, – is she a
Thracian?
BRACCHIUS: Hark ye, mistress, answer – are you
of Thrace?
One might swear it by her silence; for these
savages
Are always obstinate at the first. You like her?
Well, out of my friendship now, I'll almost
give her to you.
Three thousand drachmas –
LENTULUS: Three thousand furies!
BRACCHIUS: Ay, with the boy, too – 'Tis a lusty
imp.
LENTULUS: Three thousand sesterces; and that's
too much.
BRACCHIUS: Jove! talk of sesterces? This cub is
worth it!

Bracchius handling the child roughly
SENONA: Ah, hurt him not.
SPARTACUS: Hah!
LENTULUS: Three thousand sesterces. –
SPARTACUS: Did my ears mock me?
BRACCHIUS: Well, then, sesterces,
For the woman alone.
SENONA: You will not part us?
SPARTACUS: Hah!
Gods, pity me! does the grave give back the
dead?
Senona!
SENONA: Hah! Hah! My husband!
BRACCHIUS: What's the matter?
LENTULUS: A bargain –
BRACCHIUS: What, his wife? Six thousand
drachmas.
No more sesterces! – Caitiff, is this thy wife? –
[*To Spartacus*]
SPARTACUS: And my miserable boy, too,
Exposed in the street to sell!
BRACCHIUS: By Jove, I have you.
Six thousand drachmas.
SPARTACUS: Why didst thou not die? –
Villains, do you put them up for sale, like
beasts?
Look at them: they are human.
LENTULUS: Silence, rogue. –

SPARTACUS: I will not silence. I will ransome
them,
What way you will, with life or blood. –
BRACCHIUS: By Jove,
I will not sell her. Into the house, get in. –
Take her along.
SPARTACUS: You shall not – I will brain that man
That lays his hand upon her.
BRACCHIUS: Kill the villain. –
SPARTACUS: Man, master! – See, I am at your feet,
and call you,
Of mine own will, *My Master!* – I will serve
you
Better than slave e'er served; – grant me this
prayer,
And hire my blood out. Buy – yes, that's the
word;
It does not choke me – buy her, buy the boy;
Keep us together –
BRACCHIUS: Six thousand drachmas –
SPARTACUS: I will earn them,
Though they were doubled.
LENTULUS: Will you fight?
SPARTACUS: And die.
LENTULUS: Die! Then my gold is lost.
SPARTACUS: I will not die. –
Buy them, buy them.
LENTULUS: And you will swear?
SPARTACUS: I will, –
To be a cutthroat and a murderer, –
Whate'er you will, – so you will buy them.
LENTULUS: Unbind him.
BRACCHIUS: Six thousand –
LENTULUS: Three. Remember, Bracchius,
If you prevent his fighting, your own profit
Suffers as well as mine.
BRACCHIUS: Five thousand then.
LENTULUS: Nay, pr'ythee, four.
BRACCHIUS: Well, out of friendship,
It shall be four. – But, faith, my Gaul shall
kill him.
LENTULUS: We shall see. I'll wager even, and no
less
Than the purchase money. –
SPARTACUS: Come, dry your tears, Senona:
We are slaves: Why should slaves weep?
SENONA: O, dear my husband,
Though I ne'er thought to have the joy to
meet you
Again, in this dark world, I scarce feel joy –

I think, my heart is burst.
SPARTACUS: Come, be of better cheer: –
Art thou not now amid the gorgeous piles
Of the potential and the far-famed Rome?
SENONA: But oh, the hills of our own native
land!
The brooks and forests –
SPARTACUS: Ah! no more, no more:
Think of them not. –
SENONA: Where we fed sheep, and laughed
To think there could be sorrow in the world;
The bright, clear rivers, even that washed the
walls
Of our burned cottage –
SPARTACUS: No more, no more, no more.
Are there not hills and brooks in Italy,
Fairer than ours? Content you, girl.
SENONA: Alas,
This boy must be a Roman, and a slave.
SPARTACUS: By heaven, he shall not! Free as
rock-hatched eagles,
Thy boy was born, and so shall live and die! –
We wear our fetters only for a time –
Romans are not all like these men. We'll see
Our home yet. We are slaves but for a time. –
I need not ask thee for my mother, girl:
I know this thing has slain her. Her heart
cracked,
When they bore off my brother.
LENTULUS: With the Gaul then:
And if he beat him, as I think he will,
Then shall he battle with your best. – Now,
sirrah.
SPARTACUS: Hah!
SENONA: Husband!
SPARTACUS: Well, it is not chains alone
That make the slave. What will my master
have?
LENTULUS: I'll have thee exercise thine arm in
practice.
Thou wilt have brave men to contend with.
SPARTACUS: Well,
I will do so: but speak it not before my wife.
LENTULUS: Get thee along. Florus, conduct
them to
Their lodgings. See this Thracian exercised.

Exeunt

End of Act I

ACT II. Scene 1

A room in Crassus's house.

Enter Crassus, Jovius, an Artificer, and a Slave.
CRASSUS: To the full letter of the law. What, use
My excellent slave in thy most gainful craft,
And groan at the reckoning? By Jupiter,
Thou shalt his hire pay to the utmost sesterce,
Or have a quittance writ upon thy back.
Breed I then servants for the good of knaves?
Find me the money, or I'll have thee whipped.
Begone. [*Exit Artificer*] I built not up my for-
tunes thus,
By taking sighs for coin: had I done so,
Foul breath had ruined me. How should I
then
Have borne the hard expenses of these games,
The uproarious voters clamor for?
JOVIUS: What! true.
Wealth is the key to office, here in Rome, –
Or is the lock that best secures it.
CRASSUS: Sirrah,
Thou dost not mean, the officers bribe the
people?
JOVIUS: I had sooner lug old Cerberus by the
ears,
Than do aught to our citizens, but praise 'em.
But, in your gracious ears, – our sovereign Ro-
mans
Are something bauble-brained; and, like to
children,
Pass qualmish by their needful medicines,
To snatch at sugary playthings. What do they
In their elections? Faith, I have observed,
They ask not if their candidate have honor,
Or honesty, or proper qualities;
But, with an eager grin, *What is his wealth?*
If thus and thus – *Then he can give us shows
And feasts; and therefore is the proper man.*
An excellent mode of judging!
CRASSUS: Ancient comrade,
At me thou point'st now.
JOVIUS: Not irreverently:
I question of the people; and, I think,
They loved great Marius more for his rich
feasts,
Than his rich victories. Sooth, when angry
Sylla
Swept them, like dogs, out of his bloody path,

And made their hearts sore, they forgot their
fury,
When once they had looked upon his fighting
lions.
CRASSUS: Hence, thou inferrest, they have chose
me praetor,
Being rich enough to purchase them diversions!
But I have done them service in the wars,
And, out of gratitude – But no more of that. –
They shall be pleased: the games go bravely
on.
The Capuan hath brought me a new
sworder. –
Sirrah, go bid my niece here. [*Exit Slave*]
This Capuan hath
A son most insolent and troublesome.

Enter Florus

What, Sirrah, again? Hast thou not had thy
answer?
< Kill me these flies that being lean themselves,
Swarm after fatness. > Why art thou this fool,
To covet my rich niece?
FLORUS: I seek not riches.
CRASSUS: Pah! Will poor lovers sing eternally
The self-same song? They seek not riches!
Jove,
Why pass they then all poverty, where their
choice
Might find a wider compass?
FLORUS: Excellent praetor,
Give me the maid, and keep her lands thy-
self.
CRASSUS: Sirrah, thou know'st, the girl abhors
thee. Look,
She has the blood of nobles in her veins,
Distilling purely through a thousand years;
And thine comes grossly from a German
slave's,
That was thy grandsire.
FLORUS: Worth and deserving toil can raise me
up,
Even from my poverty, to wealth and honors.
And these shall do it.
CRASSUS: Get thee away, then,
To warring Pompey, and, with thy soiled
sword,
Carve out clean honors; not forgetting, whilst
Thy right hand grasps the enemy's throat, to
thrust
The left into his purse: For what is honor,
With empty pockets, in this thievish world?
Honor is men's consideration: men

Consider none, but those can profit them.
Therefore, if thou'lt be quick
In gaining honor, use thy right hand rather
For gathering gold than killing – or rather use
them both:
Make much, and thou shalt be most honor-
able.
JOVIUS: Thou hearest, Florus? This is the truer
wisdom.
I've fought for honor some good thirty years, –
< Courting her with such madman freaks, as
leaping,
First man, upon an arm'd wall in the storm;
Saving a comrade's life (some dozen of 'em,)
Out of the jaws of death; contesting singly
With scores, in divers places. > But being fool-
ish,
In my hot haste for slaughter, I forgot
To look for spoil; and lo, the consequence!
I bear the vine-branch,† and am only honored
As a gray-haired centurion.
CRASSUS: Get thee gone.
When thou art worthy, ask her, and no sooner.
[*Exit Florus*]
A most mad, insolent boy, and honest son
Of a breeder of cutthroats! Would some knave
would hang him.
He has the damsel's heart, too. See, she
comes. –
Is the litter ready?

Enter Julia

JULIA: It cannot be, dear uncle,
You will send me to the country?
CRASSUS: It cannot be!
What, chuff, it cannot be? In faith, it can be,
And instantly, it shall be: – Into the country,
To weep and meditate. I am ashamed
You have so poor a spirit as to love
This base-born Capuan, whose whole wealth
you might,
Piled up in coin, base on a puny drachma.
JULIA: Ah! When did love e'er think of drach-
mas, uncle?
< You would have me, when a lover moans,
demand him,
Could he coin gold, as easily as sighs;
Or when he wept, ask if his pockets had
As many talents as his eyes had tears.

†The MS contains the following note, written in
Bird's hand: "This (the vine-branch) was the badge
of a centurion's office, and he should carry it – at least
in camp and in his embassies."

Then should he change his manner, and where
  he might
Have wooed me with soft words, assault me
  with
A schedule of his properties; instead
Of flattering, boast me of his lands; his vows
Change into oaths of, lord, how rich he was.
How could I say him nay? >
CRASSUS: A milksop boy,
That has done nothing in the world but
  breathe, –
Has won no name or fortune. Why should
  such
A natural expletive, < a sack of breath, >
Aspire to wealth or woman? When he proves
  him
Worth his existence, then let him aspire.
Till then thou shalt be hid from his presump-
  tion,
Even in Campania.
JULIA: Oh, but not today.
Tomorrow, or the next day, when the games
  are done.
I must see them: 'twould kill me not to look
Once more upon the fighting gladiators.
CRASSUS: Pho!
Thou a green girl, and talk of gladiators!
My youth was pass'd in battles, and I am not
Unused to blood; but my flesh always creeps,
To see these cold-blood slaughters.
JULIA: So does mine.
Ugh! my heart stops with terror, and my eyes
Seem parting from their sockets; my brain
  reels,
While I look on; and while I look, each time,
I swear I ne'er will look again. But when
They battle boldly, and the people shout,
And the poor creatures look so fearless, – frown-
  ing,
Not groaning, when they are hurt: – Indeed
'tis noble!
< And though they fright me, always make
  me weep,
I love to see them. These are your own
  shows: >
Oh, I must see them.
JOVIUS: This is a brave maiden.
< You should look on a battle – two great ar-
  mies,
(Perhaps a hundred thousand men apiece:)
Fighting as staunchly as so many wolves,
Throttling and stabbing, dying in multitudes, –
A chaos of death: – Even such a one as that

(My own first fight) at Aqua Sextia,
Against the Ambrones, where a hundred thou-
  sand
Of the barbarians fell.
JULIA: An hundred thousand!
JOVIUS: Was it not glorious?
JULIA: Horrid!
JOVIUS: Horrid! Humph,
Still woman. – But these were barbarians.
JULIA: Were they not men?
JOVIUS: Why, yes, a sort of men.
They had legs and arms, noses and eyes like
  men,
They bled like men; but, being barbarians,
Of not much matter of account as men.
JULIA: That makes a difference. But an hundred
  thousand
Was many to kill, even of barbarians.
CRASSUS: Come, you're a goose, you know not
  what you say.
JULIA: O but these gladiators! My friend,
  Caloeia,
Told me that famous one, Phasarius,
Would fight today. He is a handsome rogue,
And kills a man the prettiest in the world. >
CRASSUS: You shall not see him.
JULIA: Dear my uncle.
CRASSUS: You came
Into this city, modest and obedient;
Now you have learnt to cog, cajole and cozen;
And, in the teeth of my authority,
Give private hopes to this low Capuan;
And, while mine eyes are tied upon the
  games,
Would – But I'll balk your hoped for inter-
  views.
The litter waits you at the door. Farewell.
This good old man, who once was my tried
  client,
Shall have you in charge. Now no more op-
  position.
Farewell. Be wise, and love none but the wor-
  thy. [*Exeunt*]

Scene 2

A court before Lentulus's house.

*Enter Florus with Spartacus, Crixus, and other
Gladiators.*
FLORUS: You have played well, and beaten Crix-
  us fairly.
Carry this skilfulness to the arena,

And you shall win great honor.

SPARTACUS: Great degradation.
No matter: I am sworn to be a caitiff.
Where have you placed my wife? It was condi-
tioned,
You should not part us.

FLORUS: She is lodged hard by:
After the combat, you shall see her. – Come,
Play me a bout here with Soturius.
I'll fetch you foils.

SPARTACUS: I'll play no more: I was not sworn to
that.

FLORUS: You cannot go too well prepared.

SPARTACUS: Even as I stand,
Awkward or skilful, doomed to die or kill,
So will I go. – I'll train no more for murder.

FLORUS: Well, as you will.

SPARTACUS: Will it not be enough,
If I disarm or worst my enemy?
May I not spare him?

FLORUS: Not unless the people
Grant you permission. < When you have him
at
Your mercy, look to the spectators then.
If they consent, they will their thumbs raise –
thus:
Then you shall spare. But if their hands be
clenched,
And the thumbs hid, then must you slay. >

SPARTACUS: Well, well;
I understand.

FLORUS: Breathe yourselves here awhile,
Then follow to the armory. [*Exit*]

SPARTACUS: Good brother,
Have you yet fought i' th' Amphitheatre?

CRIXUS: Ay.

SPARTACUS: And killed
Your adversary?

CRIXUS: Ay, Each one of us
Has won some reputation.

SPARTACUS: Reputation!
Call you this reputation?
This is the bulldog's reputation:
He and the gladiator only need
The voice o' the master, to set on to mischief. –
Love you your masters?

CRIXUS: No.

SPARTACUS: Or of your own wishes
Go ye to perish?

CRIXUS: No; but being slaves,
We care not much for life; and think it better
To die upon the arena, than the cross.

SPARTACUS: If ye care not for life, why die ye not
Rather like men, than dogs?

CRIXUS: What mean you?

SPARTACUS: Were it not better
To turn upon your masters, and so die,
Killing them that oppress you, rather than
fall,
Killing your brother wretches?

CRIXUS: True, it were.
Put arms into our hands, unlock our dun-
geons,
And set us out among the citizens;
Then ask this question.

SPARTACUS: Do you say this? By heaven,
This spirit joys me. – Fight ye all today?

CRIXUS: We are so ordered.

SPARTACUS: How many do you number?

CRIXUS: Fifty.

SPARTACUS: Fifty? How many hath this Roman,
This villain Bracchius?

CRIXUS: Some five and thirty.

SPARTACUS: And fight they all?

CRIXUS: Some forty pairs today.

SPARTACUS: O heaven, what, forty?

CRIXUS: And ere the shows are done,
Two hundred pairs.

SPARTACUS: Two hundred pairs! – Four hundred
Arm'd slaves, that hate their masters!

CRIXUS: On the third day,
All that survive, will fight in general battle.

SPARTACUS: In general battle! – If Senona now,
And the young infant were in Thrace. –
Alas,
To peril them. –

CRIXUS: What say'st thou, Thracian?

SPARTACUS: Nothing;
At least, not much. – Are there now troops in
Rome?

CRIXUS: Four legions of Praetorian Guards; and
now
Each legion counts five thousand.

SPARTACUS: 'Twill not do.

CRIXUS: What will not do?

SPARTACUS: I'll tell you by and by:
'Tis worth your ear. – But let us now go arm,
Then to the Arena, to begin the work
Of slavish murder. – We are gladiators.

Exeunt

Scene 3

*The Arena of an Amphitheatre, behind which
are many citizens. Crassus seated with his*

Lictors, Mummius, Lentulus, Bracchius, Florus,
and many officers, – AEdiles, Conquisitores, etc.
CRASSUS: Let our good friends, the citizens, be
  seated.
We purpose to delight their humors with
The bravest gladiators of this realm. –
What say'st thou, Capuan? Why, tell me,
  thou
Hast brought me some brave cutthroats, to be
  pitched,
Through the first hours, in single combat,
  with
The best slaves of our Bracchius.
LENTULUS: Even so,
Most noble praetor; and, with the consent
Of your appointed officers, we first
Will bring a lusty Thracian, who, although
Yet unadventured in the Arena, bears
A name of valor.
CRASSUS: Let him before us. [*Exit Florus*]
Had Thracians, by their firesides, fought as
  fiercely
As now they fight upon the Roman sand,
The cranes o' the Strymon still had been their
  sentries.

Reenter Florus, with Spartacus, as a gladiator
Is this the man? A very capital knave;
Yet, or I err, of but a little spirit.
Where is the fiery confidence, should flash
From his bold eyes? the keen and tameless spir-
  it,
Should brace his strong limbs to activity?
LENTULUS: Driveller, arouse thee! – Let not his
  gloom condemn him:
He is most wayward, but, in truth, right vali-
  ant.
What, sirrah, shake off these clouds, and do
  thy homage
To the most noble praetor. Bend thy knee.
SPARTACUS: Did I swear that? Kneel *thou*, whose
  servile soul
Was given for crouching. I am here to fight!
CRASSUS: This is some madman!
LENTULUS: A barbarian,
Bred in a savage roughness.
SPARTACUS: Well, I am here,
Among these beasts of Rome, a spectacle.
This is the temple, where they mock the Gods
With human butchery, – Most grand and glo-
  rious
Of structure and device! – It should have been
  a cave,

Some foul and midnight pit, or den of bones,
Where murder best might veil himself from
  sight. –
Women and children, too, to see men die,
And clap their hands at every stab! This is
The boastful excellence of Rome! I thank the
  Gods
There are Barbarians.
CRASSUS: Now, by Jupiter,
The rogue speaks well – But Romans must be
  pleased –
Sirrah, – [*Comes down center*]
SPARTACUS: Roman!
CRASSUS: Most impudently bold.
I did mistake him. Prepare thyself.
SPARTACUS: I am ready,
As ready to die, as thou to see me die.
Where is the opponent? Of what nation comes
The man that I must kill?
CRASSUS: What matters it?
SPARTACUS: Much, very much. Bring me some
  base ally
Of Roman rapine, or, if ye can, a Roman: –
I will not grieve to slay him.
CRASSUS: Faith, I like
This fearless taunting, and will sound it fur-
  ther.
Thy foe shall be a Spaniard.
SPARTACUS: Alas, I should
Bethink me of his country, as of mine,
Ruined and harried by our common foe;
His kinsmen slain, his wife and children sold,
And nothing left of all his country's greatness,
Save groans and curses on the conquerors.
CRASSUS: A Carthaginian.
SPARTACUS: What, a Carthaginian?
A relic of that noble tribe, that ne'er
Would call Rome friend, and perished rather
  than
Become Rome's vassal? I could not fight with
  him:
We should drop swords, and recollect together,
As brothers, how the Punic steel had smote,
Of yore, to Rome's chill'd heart; yea, how
  Rome quaked,
How shook her proud sons, when the African
Burst from the sea, like to its mightiest surge,
Swept your vain shores, and swallow'd up your
  armies!
How, when his weapons, gored with consular
  blood,
Waved o'er your towns, your bucklered boast-
  ers fled,

Or shook, like aguish boys, and wept and
prayed: –
Yea, feared to die, and wept and prayed.
LENTULUS: < Peace, villain. >
CRASSUS: Strike him not, Lentulus. The prattler
knows
There's scarce a man of the Punic stock left liv-
ing,
To boast of these mishaps. – Thy adversary
Is a brave Gaul.
SPARTACUS: Why, there again! The name
Speaks of Rome's shame. Name but a Gaul,
and I
Bethink me of the Tiber running blood,
His tributaries choked with knightly corses;
Of Rome in ashes, and of Brennus laughing
At the starved cravens in the Capitol.
CRASSUS: Sirrah, no more.
Be but thy sword as biting as thy tongue,
And I'll assure thee victory. – Bring in
The Gaul. Use thy best skill, if skill thou
hast,
Or I'll not lay an obolus on thy life. –

    A Gallic Gladiator is brought in
Clear the Arena. [*Ascends chair again*]
SPARTACUS: I will fight with him;
But give me to spare his life.
CRASSUS: That privilege
Rests with the people. Remember thy oath. –
Sound, trumpets. [*A flourish*]
SPARTACUS: Brother –
CRASSUS: No words; but do thy best. < He'll spit
thee. >

*They fight. The Gaul is disarmed, and thrown
on his knees. Spartacus looks to the people*
Thine oath! Strike, < villain! > Hah!

    Spartacus kills the Gaul
         Why, that was bravely done.
SPARTACUS: Well, I have done it. Let me go
hence.
CRASSUS: Not so. –
Most nobly fought!
SPARTACUS: Alas, alas, poor slave! –
CRASSUS: Bring me another.

    The body is taken away
SPARTACUS: I will fight no more.
CRASSUS: Sirrah!
SPARTACUS: I have heart enough to die, but not
to kill.

CRASSUS: Why, 'twas most capitally done! Re-
member
Thy oath.
SPARTACUS: I care not. I will fight no more.
CRASSUS: Thou shalt have freedom. Nay,
I'll ransome for thee,
Thy wife and boy.
SPARTACUS: Wilt thou?
CRASSUS: By Mars, I will.
Fight through these games; and thou and they
shall be
Sent back to Thrace.
SPARTACUS: Shall we see Thrace again? –
Let him come on; yes, though it sick my soul, –
Let him come on.
CRASSUS: Bring in the Thracian! [*Exit Brac-
chius*]
SPARTACUS: Thracian?
I will not fight a Thracian! 'Tis my country-
man.
CRASSUS: Nay, but thou shalt, and kill him too;
or thou
And they, are slaves eternally.
SPARTACUS: O heaven!
Bring me a Spaniard, German, Carthaginian,
Another Gaul, a Greek – any but Thracian.
CRASSUS: None
But this same Thracian is thy match; and
truly
If thou slay him, there will remain no other
Worthy of thee. Thou shalt be quickly free.
SPARTACUS: I will fight two – three – so they be
not Thracians.
CRASSUS: The Thracian, or eternal bondage;
bondage
For wife and child, too.
SPARTACUS: Wilt thou swear to free us?
Fight with a Thracian! – Wilt thou *swear* to
free us?
CRASSUS: Bring hither the *Vindicta*: With this
rod,
If thou escape this man, the praetor frees thee.

    Reenter Bracchius, with Phasarius
This is thy foe.
PHASARIUS: [*Aside*]: What, do I dream?
SPARTACUS: Alas,
Thou art a Thracian and my countryman,
And yet we meet as deadly foes. Forgive me.
PHASARIUS: [*Aside*]. This is no fantasy!
CRASSUS: Observe them, Bracchius:
Thy boaster hesitates.

PHASARIUS: Thou art a Thracian?

SPARTACUS: Would thou wert not.

PHASARIUS: Of the Ciconian tribe –
A son of blue-waved Hebrus?

SPARTACUS: Such I am.
And comest thou too of the same race? and set
Against thy brother?

PHASARIUS: Brother, indeed!
Thy name is Spartacus.

SPARTACUS: Where learnt you that?
Freemen have heard it, but not slaves.

PHASARIUS: How fares thy father?

SPARTACUS: Didst thou know him? – Dead –
I cannot fight thee.

PHASARIUS: Hadst thou not a brother?

CRASSUS: Why prate these cutthroats?
Come, prepare, prepare –

SPARTACUS: A young, brave heart, whose steps I taught to dare
The crags and chasms and roaring cataracts
Of his own native hills, till he was freer
Among them than the eagles. What art thou,
That seem'st to know him? I would be angry with thee:
These words make me look on thee as a friend.

PHASARIUS: Seem I not like Phasarius?

SPARTACUS: What, thou?
A mailed warrior like a singing boy?
The Romans slew him.

PHASARIUS: They enslaved him – Brother,
Changed as I am, and from a harmless boy,
Turned to a rough destroyer, still am I
The selfsame fool that once thou called'st brother.

SPARTACUS: Thou mock'st me. Thou!

PHASARIUS: My father, Menalon –

SPARTACUS: Thy father, Menalon?

PHASARIUS: My mother –

SPARTACUS: Ay, thy mother?

PHASARIUS: Laödice.

SPARTACUS: My brother!

CRASSUS: What mean these rogues, that they have dropped their swords,
And faln, like friends, about each other's necks?
What ho, ye slaves, give o'er this timeless juggling:
Take up your swords, and look ye to the signal.

SPARTACUS: I do believe the gods have given me o'er

To some new madness: First, I find in Rome,
Where naught I looked for but despair, my wife
And then my brother!

< CRASSUS: Villains!

SPARTACUS: But I am sorry
To find thee here, Phasarius. >

LENTULUS: < Whining miscreant, >
Why mark'st thou not the praetor?

CRASSUS: < Rogues, prepare. >
Let the trumpet sound.

SPARTACUS: Bring me my adversary.

CRASSUS: Thou hast him there.

SPARTACUS: What, he? This is my brother.
You would not have me fight with him!

CRASSUS: His brother?

PHASARIUS: 'Tis true, most excellent praetor.

CRASSUS: Now, by Hercules,
This is too strange for truth.

LENTULUS: Ye cogging rogues,
Think ye to balk us thus?

< BRACCHIUS: Conspiracy!
Shameful collusion! Out on you, Phasarius,
You're not afeard now? Out, ye cheating villain. >

PHASARIUS: Hear me, good praetor –

CRASSUS: < Rogues >, prepare yourselves.
This is a most evident knavery, to 'scape
From one another. – Brothers indeed! – Prepare;
Take up your arms.

SPARTACUS: Foul Roman –

CRASSUS: Bring me in
The guarding cohort: [*An Officer goes out*]
I'll have them cut to pieces,
If they refuse the battle. – Brothers indeed!

SPARTACUS: Thou hard, unnatural man –

PHASARIUS: Patience, brother –

SPARTACUS: Let them come in – We are armed. –

CRASSUS: Most strange and insolent contumacy!

PHASARIUS: [*Aside*]. 'Tis something sudden –
and in Rome! – Peace, brother. –

SPARTACUS: We will resist them, armed as we are.
Can we not die?

PHASARIUS: Most worthy praetor, pardon.
Grant us a word together, and we are ready.

CRASSUS: Fine knavery! I did almost suspect
Yon cutthroat for a coward – that 'twas skill alone
Gave him his courage, which he fear'd to try
With that more skilful savage. For the barbarian,

His soul is made of contrariety.

PHASARIUS: [*Apart to Spartacus*] I know them
all – This thing was hatch'd before. –
They wait without,
Circled by cohorts, but all arm'd for combat.
Let me but raise the cry of *Freedom* to them,
And each man strikes his Roman to the earth.

SPARTACUS: The slaves of Lentulus – they will
strike, too:
Let us but reach them, and they rise with us. –

PHASARIUS: One moment, princely praetor.

CRASSUS: Not an instant.
What, shall our shows wait on the time and
pleasure
Of our base bondmen? Sound the trumpets
there –
What, treachery, ho! Call in the soldiers! –

PHASARIUS: Freedom
For gladiators!

SPARTACUS: Death to all their masters! –

CRASSUS: Treachery! –

SPARTACUS: Death to the Roman fiends, that
make their mirth
Out of the groans of bleeding misery!
Ho, slaves, arise! it is your hour to kill!
Kill, and spare not – For wrath and liberty! –
Freedom for bondmen – freedom and revenge! –

*Shouts and trumpets – The guards and gladia-
tors rush and engage in combat, as the curtain
falls*

End of Act II

ACT III. Scene 1

A room in Crassus's house.‡

*Enter Crassus, Jovius, Lentulus, Bracchius,
Mummius.*

< CRASSUS: Incredible! What, fight a consular
army?
Or look one in the face?

JOVIUS: So says the courier.
'Tis sworn, that half the slaves of Italy
Are flocking to his banner.

CRASSUS: Fight a consul!
Fight Cneus Lentulus!

‡There is a query in Bird's handwriting "whether to
restore the beginning of this scene or some part of it?"
Dr. Bird submitted the MS. of *The Gladiator* to Edwin
Forrest for revision, who no doubt suggested many of
the cuts indicated.

JOVIUS: 'Tis not so much
To one who has already beat a proconsul.
You'll not doubt that? nor that these madman
slaves,
Led by this whirlwind slayer –

LENTULUS: My precious Thracian! –

JOVIUS: Have vanquished severally, and in
pitched battles,
Three praetors of the provinces.

CRASSUS: Shame upon them!
Sneers for their lives, contempt for epitaphs!
Beaten by slaves! – I warrant me, by mine –
Two thousand costly and ungrateful villains: –
I'll hang them, every man. – Beaten by slaves,
Gross, starving, unarmed slaves!

JOVIUS: Not now unarmed.
Each rogue has got a Roman harness on,
Filched from the carcass of a Roman veteran.
Not starving neither, whilst every day they
sack
Some camp or city – pouncing sudden down,
Like vultures, from their hills upon our
troops.

CRASSUS: Scandalous, scandalous! Slaves,
wretched slaves,
Led by a slave, too!

LENTULUS: Still my precious Thracian!

CRASSUS: A scurvy gladiator, with no brains;
An ignorant savage. –

JOVIUS: Come, give the rogue his due:
He has more brains than all our generals,
For he has beaten them; that's a soldier's
proof.
This Spartacus, so late a bondman, has
A soul for master; though a shepherd bred,
He has fought battles, ay, and led men, too, –
Some mountain malcontents in his own land, –
'Gainst Roman conquerors; and, by the faith
Of honesty, for honest I will be,
In courage, stratagem, resource, exploits,
He shows a good commander. He has formed,
Out of this slavish, ragged scum, an army;
Arms it and feeds it at his foeman's cost,
Recruits it in his foeman's territory;
Which foe is renowned Rome, resistless Rome,
Rome the great head and empress of the world!
Is he not then a general?

CRASSUS: I grant you,
The rogue is not a common one; but still
A slave. And much it shames me that the sen-
ate
Finds me no worthier enemy; whom to con-
quer,

Wins neither spoil nor honor.

JOVIUS: No spoil indeed,
Unless you count their arms and bodies such;
But honor enough to him that beats the van-
quisher
Of some half score commanders: There's your
honor.
Come, stir these centuries: My old bones are
aching
For one more battering, ere they fall to dust.
The reprobates must be put down, that's cer-
tain,
And by yourself, or Pompey. >

CRASSUS: Now the gods rest him!
Is there no trouble can befall the state,
But men must cry for Pompey? As if Rome
Had whelped no other fit to do her service.
< Still is it Pompey, great and valiant Pompey,
Must all our state thorns conjure into laurels. –
Well, Crassus is not Pompey, but may serve
For the besom.

JOVIUS: What, a besom?

CRASSUS: Ay, to sweep away
This filthy blush out of Rome's cheek. > –
These varlets,
These fooled *lanistæ*, that have trained slaves
up
To fight their masters, shall to camp with me,
And of the evils they have caused, partake.

LENTULUS: I am willing.
I'll kill my Thracian, though he be a general.

BRACCHIUS: It matters not how soon I am
knock'd o' the head.
I have not now a gladiator left. –
The rogues have ruined me.

CRASSUS: Where is thy son?
This knave shall march, too. Have you brought
the woman,
The wife o' the Thracian, here to Rome?

LENTULUS: I have sent for her.
My son has gone into Campania.

CRASSUS: What, to Campania? Now, by Jupiter,
This fool will set me mad.

LENTULUS: I know not that.
He went with the band of youthful volunteers,
To the camp of Gellius, the consul.

JOVIUS: Bravely done.
That was in memory of our counselling.
But now for action. < You remember, praetor,
This consul prays immediate succors, being
But ill provided, should the Gladiator,
In contest with his colleague, prove victorious,
As there is ground to fear; for Lentulus,

At the last word, was at extremities.
Being deprived, too, by the angry senate
Of their authority, their mutinous troops
But scurvily obey them. > Should the rebels
Come near your country-seat –

CRASSUS: No more of that:
The consul shall protect her. – Presently
Bring me six legions; which, being added to
The consular troops and the knights volun-
teers,
We'll have appointed to this service. Then
There shall be knocks enough, I promise you.
See that these people follow, and all men
Whose slaves have joined the rebels. It is rea-
son,
The rogues should kill no masters but their
own. [*Exeunt*]

Scene 2

*A plain in Campania, after the battle. Some
corses lying about. March of trumpets.*

*Enter sumptuously armed, Spartacus, Phasarius,
Crixus, AEnomaiis, and Attendants.*

SPARTACUS: So, we are victors, conquerors again.
The hotbrained boasters, that in mockery
thought
To ape the angry Scythian, and subdue us
With whips, instead of warlike instruments,
Lie hush'd and gory; and, despite the claim
Of their high honors and nobility,
There is no slave too base to tread upon them.
There he's a Consul. – I have known that word
Fright men more than the name of gorgeous
kings.
Say to barbaric States, *A Consul Comes,
A Roman Consul*, and their preparation
Of war or welcome, speaks a demigod.
And yet lies he on the opprobrious earth,
A palmy Consul, by a slave's hand slain,
No nobler than his horse – a thing to glut
The starved hyena's maw.§

PHASARIUS: Ay – and there's another
Must lie beside him.

SPARTACUS: Speak you of Gellius?

§The original reading, struck out in the MS., was, –
      " – a thing to rot
In a hyena's paunch."
The reading is written in a hand resembling Forrest's,
in pencil, and is probably his suggestion.

PHASARIUS: Ay, marry. I'll fight now nothing less
than consuls.
There is another of them, and I say,
Another battle and another victory.
CRIXUS: 'Tis but to will, and we have won it.
SPARTACUS: Ay;
But not today. Our medly bands have earned
Their armor, and are weary. – 'Tis full six
leagues
To Gellius' camp.
CRIXUS: My Germans will not fear it.
SPARTACUS: It cannot be, and must not.
CRIXUS: Must not, Spartacus?
SPARTACUS: Ay, man, I say so: this thing must
not be.
When ye were few, with one consent, ye chose
me
Your leader, with each man an oath to yield
To me sole guidance. This was little honor,
To be the chief of fourscore fugitives,
And none would have it, save myself. I took
it,
And ye have prospered. Under my authority,
In a few days your ranks have been swell'd up
To fearful thousands; and from a band of
slaves,
Skulking in caves, you have become an army
Can fight a Roman Consul. This is proof,
I have deserved obedience; and therefore,
I still command it.
CRIXUS: And my countrymen
Myself have made their leader; and they bid me
Lead them to Gellius.
SPARTACUS: We are but one army,
With but one object, howsoe'er our ranks
Are filled with various nations. We are slaves,
All of us slaves, contesting for our freedom;
And so far free, that we have arms and kill;
No further. We have yet to cut our way
Out of this tyrant empire; which to do,
We must destroy more armies, that are gather-
ing
To hem us in. We do not fight for conquest,
But conquer for our liberties; and they
Are lost by rashness. Let us rest our troops,
And think of Gellius on the morrow.
CRIXUS: Today, today,
Ere he have rallied this fight's fugitives.
SPARTACUS: The thousands that are crowding to
our lines
Will, by the dawn, have trebled all his gain.
CRIXUS: I will beat him with the Germans alone.
SPARTACUS: You shall not;

I am your general, and forbid you.
CRIXUS: Thracian,
I was a slave, but am not now.
PHASARIUS: Brother Crixus,
On second thoughts, 'tis better put this off,
According as the general commands.
CRIXUS: I am sole leader of my countrymen.
PHASARIUS: Sirrah, thou art a mutineer. –
SPARTACUS: Peace, brother. –
PHASARIUS: Defy the general! If one beggar's
rogue
Of all his Germans dare to leave the lines,
I'll have him spitted like a cur.
SPARTACUS: Peace, brother.
Contention will harm worse than this parti-
tion.
German, thou hast thy wish: depart in peace,
But without hope of succor, if the Roman
Prevail above thee.
PHASARIUS: Pray the gods he do!
< And thwack them till they are skinless, all.
Base rascals
And mutineers! >
SPARTACUS: Take all thy countrymen,
Or all that wish to follow thee. [*Exit Crixus*]
PHASARIUS: Rank mutiny!
Why did you let him go?
SPARTACUS: To teach him, brother,
Him and some others of our lieutenants,
(For we are growing mad upon success,)
An humbling lesson. A defeat were now
Better than victory; and, in his Germans,
We best can bear it.
PHASARIUS: Let them go, and hang;
They are all villainous hotheads, and presump-
tuous
Beyond all tolerance. And, to punish them,
They shall not share with us the fame and spoil
Of the sack'd city.
SPARTACUS: Brother, I think thou art
Almost as madbrained as the rest.
PHASARIUS: I have
A kind of ardor, that, for aught I know,
May be a lunacy. But this is clear:
Rome is a city; cities may be sack'd;
So Rome may be.
SPARTACUS: A city, that the world
Looks frighted at, even in her sleep of peace,
As gazers look at sleeping lions. I told
This German fool, we did not fight for con-
quest,
But for a passport to our several homes.
What care we then to waste our vigor on

The gates of fortressed cities?

PHASARIUS: But this city –

SPARTACUS: Is as impregnable as the storm-arm'd
sea.
Why should we talk of it? Great Mithridates,
Though populous Asia followed at his back,
Should, were his frothy hopes to point at it,
Be laughed at for a kingly maniac.
What should be said of us, the mushroom war-
riors
Of Roman dunghills, should our arrogance
Mad us so far? I think, we do not fight
To make the world talk?

PHASARIUS: I would have you do so;
Fight now for glory; let ambition raise you
Among the deathless, now while fate invites
you.
Rome has no greatness, but is now employed
In foreign climes: You have well tried yourself;
And consuls vanish, when your trumpet
sounds.
March on the city, and there swear to die,
Or live its master, and you are its master.
Think, brother, think what glorious fame
were ours,
As lasting as the eternal world, should we,
The upturned dregs of servitude, destroy,
As, by the inviting fates! We may destroy,
This lair of lions, this den of conquerors,
This womb of heroes, whose boastings fright
the earth,
And whose ambition (– look, Ambition!) –
chains it!

< SPARTACUS: This is a wild and most prepos-
terous hope.
Even the fierce Hannibal, with veteran troops,
And all the towns of Italy at his feet,
Save this alone, here paused his hopes.

PHASARIUS: Hope thou
T' excel the vaunted African, and dare
Beyond his daring. Hast thou not a heart
Bigger than his, that, with a herd of slaves,
Hast wrought as much as all his veterans?
Smiles heaven upon thee less, which, in an
hour,
Has, from a dungeon, raised thee to an army,
Still growing, still victorious? Do this deed,
And live for ever. >

SPARTACUS: Well, well, I'll think of it.
Perhaps Senona's there: – Ah, would to heav-
en, Phasarius,
I were with her now and my smiling boy,
In Thrace again, beside our mountain cot,

Or in those vales, where babbling Hebrus tum-
bles
Along his golden sands; and dreamt no more
Of sacks and battles.

PHASARIUS: Whilst this city stands,
This ne'er can be; for just so long our country
Remains a Roman province. Tear it down,
And you enfranchise Thrace, and half the
world.

SPARTACUS: We'll think of this again, when we
are stronger,
And when we have Senona sent to us.
Meanwhile we must the final effort make
To ransome her. < Did you secure a guide,
To lead us through the mountains? I have seen
The camp most strongly guarded, and fear not
To trust it with the trusty AEnomaiis.
When the tired troops have slept an hour, I'll
order
To bring them after us, to see indeed
How we may end, what Crixus may begin,
Disastrously for him, on Gellius,
In the confusion of the Consul's triumph. >
Pick me an hundred of our swiftest horses,
And have them presently in wait for me.
I shall fight better, when I know each blow
Strikes a protection for my family. [*Exeunt*]

Scene 3

A room in Crassus's Villa.

Enter Julia and Florus.

JULIA: I am glad to see thee. This terrific din
Of the near battle made a sparrow of me.
I was afeard to breathe, < lest I should swallow
Some of your horrid missiles; for I ran
Unto the housetop, to look on the fight.
But the moon was more coward than myself,
And hid her pale face in a cloud: so nothing
I saw. But I could hear the brazen trumps,
The conchs and cornets, the shouts and yells of
fury,
The clang of arms, and whistling in the air
Of stones and arrows. But, come tell me now,
My general, have you killed a foe tonight?

FLORUS: And won a civic crown, by saving a
friend.

JULIA: That's good; I am glad to hear it. >

FLORUS: But I am sorry
To find you here among these fears and perils.

I would you were in Rome.

JULIA: There is no peril.
Have you not beaten these wild gladiators?
A shepherd flying from his pastures, told me,
That Gellius had the victory, and had taken
Or killed the insurgent, bloody Spartacus.

FLORUS: I know not that. 'Tis true, that we have
beaten
A band of mad rogues, that assaulted us;
And 'tis believed, their general, Spartacus,
Is dead upon our trenches; for whose body
Search is now made. But one poor prisoner,
< I think, the only one whose life was
spared, >
Declared these troops to be but a small band
Of mutinous runagates, that had left their
leader,
Being thereto moved by their late victory
Over the consul Lentulus.

JULIA: What, Florus!
A victory over Lentulus?

FLORUS: 'Tis even so:
His army has been vanquished, himself slain
By the late bondman. And those, who give
faith
To the assurance of our prisoner,
Fear for *our* consul, should the Thracian
march,
After his mutineers, upon us now;
Our camp being all a confused festival
Of drunken triumph, – half our soldiers scat-
tered
In search of spoil and fugitives. –

SPARTACUS: [*Within*] Guard the doors:
Let none go out.

FLORUS: What voice is that? By heaven,
We are betrayed!

*Enter Spartacus, Phasarius, and others, AEno-
maiis*

SPARTACUS: < Sold, lost, and dead! > –
Look to the maiden.
< What, flourishing fool, > drop thy sword's
point, or die.

FLORUS: A thousand times, ere thou, malicious
rebel,
Touch this endangered lady.

SPARTACUS: Straw, I say!

He disarms Florus

Know I not this boy's face?||

FLORUS: I think thou should'st.
Spare thou the lady, rich will be her ransome.

And for myself, I know, thy deadly fury
Grants never quarter.

SPARTACUS: By the stripes not yet
Fled from mine outraged limbs, thou art the
son
Of Lentulus the scourger!

PHASARIUS: Ay, the same.
Let him atone his rascal father's sins:
Scourge him to death.

FLORUS: Give me a soldier's death:
Let me die by the sword. I never scourged
thee.

SPARTACUS: Thou! Miserable boy!

FLORUS: And well thou knowest,
Thou fierce and fiendish man, this tongue of
mine
Was oft thy intercessor.

SPARTACUS: I do know,
One of thy blood did give me to the scourge –
Me, a free son of a free sire, and imaged
After the semblance of the Only Master –
Gave me to thongs and whips, as a poor beast,
Till I became one. This I know; know thou,
From that shamed hour, when first my body
writhed
Under the merciless lash, I did devote
The scourger and his household to the furies,
To quick and murderous death. And thinkest
thou,
Thy whining kindness took away a pang?
Thou art the Roman's son, and thou shalt die.

FLORUS: Let it be so –

SPARTACUS: It shall be so. Thou seest,
Command and dignities have not wiped out
The memory of wrongs; and Roman blood,
Running in rivers ever at my feet,
Sates not the thirst for more! – Take him away;
Scourge him to death.

JULIA: [*To Spartacus*] Thou horrible monster,
spare him,
And name whate'er thou wilt for ransome.

SPARTACUS: Ransome!
Drachmas for stripes!

FLORUS: Beeseech him not, fair Julia.

||There are the following notes in Bird's hand, evi-
dently in answer to Forrest's suggested cuts.
"Think you had better keep these expressions particularly the *flourishing fool* and *straw*. They express,
in a very lofty and furious style, the contempt which
such a man as Spartacus would feel at finding himself
resisted by a younker."
"The term *boy's* was meant as a substitute for boyish;
not, as if asking the question of others, *the face of this
boy*."

Think of thyself, or let me think for thee.

JULIA: He never did thee hurt.

SPARTACUS: Let her be ta'en away.

FLORUS: Let her be ransomed, and for thine own wife.

SPARTACUS: Ay, so I will: 'twas e'en for that I took her.

FLORUS: Then may'st thou instantly exchange them. –

SPARTACUS: How!

FLORUS: Thy wife is in the consul's camp –

SPARTACUS: In the consul's camp?

FLORUS: There driven by the fright of her conductors.

And thou may'st instant ransome her. –

SPARTACUS: Ha, ha!

Now does Jove smile. What, ransome her?
Ay, ransome;

But with the steel. – I can almost forgive thee,
For this good news. – Praetor, I have thee now
In the same trap thou set'dst for me! – What, sirrah,
Ye have beaten my refractory lieutenant,
The German Crixus?

FLORUS: Ay, I thank the gods.

SPARTACUS: And so do I; it wins me victory,
And puts the second consul in my hands. –
Antistheus, see these captives safely guarded. –
Brother, the troops must now be nigh upon us. –
Take thou the Thracian cohorts, and in secret
Steal to the heights that overhang his rear,
Posting a strong guard on the river. Let none 'scape,
And let none live. Myself will force the camp,
And drive the rioting fools upon your swords. –
I say, spare none.

PHASARIUS: 'Twere much too troublesome
To imitate them, and build crucifixes
For the prisoners.

SPARTACUS: Let not a moment's rashness
Bring us a limping victory. Stand fast
Upon your post, and every rogue is dead. –
Roman, thou shalt see how I'll ransome her!
[*Exeunt*]

Scene 4

The Tent of Gellius, the Consul Gellius discovered, with Scorpha, Senona and her child, and attendants.

GELLIUS: There is no doubt, this foolish German lies.
'Twas the main body of the rebels surely.
No mere detachment would have impudence
To march upon a consul. Now this victory,
Which, on the morn, I'll follow up, will change
The tone o' the angry Senate, and restore me
To my full rank, and, what is better, send
The scheming Crassus empty-handed back.
This is a man should fight in the Velabrum,
Among the cheating mongers, and not bring
His brains of a broker to a glorious camp.
This woman here, the wife o' the Gladiator,
That cutthroat caitiff –

SENONA: Why dost thou slander him?
Has he not fought a consul?

GELLIUS: Pr'ythee, be silent.
He's a brave rebel, and will be renowned. –
Now, as I said, with this same woman here,
The Greek-brained Crassus did design some trick,
Some scurvy plot upon the Gladiator –
[*Alarums*]

SCROPHA: Hark!

GELLIUS: A device of the rejoicing drunkards. –
This thing meant Crassus, this –

SCROPHA: The clang increases!

A great shout is heard

GELLIUS: The knaves are noisy. –

Enter a Centurion, wounded

CENTURION: Fly for your lives! The camp is forced –

GELLIUS: What camp?

CENTURION: Your own. The Gladiators are upon us:
We are surprised, and all is lost. [*Exit*]

GELLIUS: My armor!
What ho, my armor! [*Exeunt all but Senona and child*]

Enter Spartacus, AEnomaiis, and Gladiators

SPARTACUS: # Victory! Ha! Ha!

#The reading probably suggested by Forrest. The original lines, crossed out in the MS., are:
"Victory! ha, ha.
Romans are sheep. – Search every tent – Ah, Jove!
I have found ye, wife, and in a noble hour.
When we met last, I was a slave; and now,
In a consul's camp, I stand a conqueror!
"(Drop.)"

259

Romans are sheep – search every tent – ah! Jove!
I have found ye wife, aye, and have ransomed ye.
What, did you think I had deserted you?
Look, I have found you in a noble hour:
When last we met I was a slave: and now
In a Consul's camp I stand a conqueror!

Curtain

End of Act III

ACT IV. Scene 1

*The Camp of Crassus.***

Enter Crassus, Mummius, Jovius, Lentulus, Bracchius, and Attendants.

CRASSUS: And Gellius beaten, too? both consuls beaten?
This is some demigod that hath ta'en man's shape,
To whip us for our sins. – Both consuls beaten?
I would I had those Macedonian legions.
JOVIUS: Have them thou shalt; ay, and the Spanish, too:
The senate, in their terror (for the victories
Of this great savage now add fright to shame),
Bid Pompey and Lucullus, with their troops,
Instant embark for Rome.
CRASSUS: Why should they send
For Pompey, too? – Perhaps it may be better. –
See that the fugitives from the consular camps
Be decimated, and so punished. The cowards should
Be slain by duplates rather than by tithes:
I'll make example of them. – Jovius,
Lay not this consul near my villa? I would not
My niece should come to harm; and it is horrid
To think her in the hands of the barbarians.
JOVIUS: I am sorry, praetor –
CRASSUS: What, man, is it so?
JOVIUS: A herdsman, fled that night from the estate,
Just on the eve of battle, saw the house
Beset by numerous slaves. –

**This scene is struck out in the MS. and, according to a note in Bird's handwriting, was "omitted in the representation."

CRASSUS: The gods be with her:
I loved her well. – Sirrah, where is that woman,
I bade thee bring me?
LENTULUS: Not yet reached the camp,
But on the road.
CRASSUS: Let her be hastened hither.
I did intend to use her as a check
On the uxorious chief. Now shall she ransome
My Julia from him. – Where lies the enemy?
JOVIUS: He is advancing on us.
CRASSUS: What, advancing?
JOVIUS: With countless multitudes at his heels. –
CRASSUS: What! come,
Intrench, intrench.
JOVIUS: Rather march out to meet him.
Shall it be said, that Crassus, the lieutenant
Of valiant Sylla, hid behind a trench,
When bondmen menaced him?
CRASSUS: Shall it be said,
Crassus, the praetor, like a hair-brained fool,
Helped these same bondmen to a victory?
Spear me these cowards; and intrench, I say. –
What, sirrah?

Enter a Messenger, who speaks with Jovius
JOVIUS: Happy tidings! Marcus Lucullus
Hath landed his army at Brundisium; –
CRASSUS: The gods be thank'd. –
JOVIUS: And legion'd Pompey, too,
At Ostia.
CRASSUS: Still thanks. Let messengers
Be sent o' the instant to both generals,
Praying them, as they love the gods and Rome,
Their march to hasten. [*Exit Messenger*]
                       Good centurion,
I will employ thee in a difficult office,
Wherein thou may'st the state and me do service.
JOVIUS: Let it be honest, then, and soldier-like.
CRASSUS: So it shall be. I'll have thee an ambassador
To this mad Thracian, to propose a ransome
For my unhappy niece, if niece I have;
Or to exchange for her his wife and brat,
Now in our hands. If she be living, have her
At any ransome; stick not at the sum. –
And hark ye, use your eyes and wisdom well.
Look me out, as a soldier, what 'twould profit
A soldier to have known; and if thou find'st
A man among his officers to be bribed

To any treason may advantage us,
Make him what gain thou wilt. – But see
thou bring
My Julia with thee. – If thou find'st a man,
That may be bought, at any price, to murder
The Thracian, buy him for that act.
JOVIUS: Not I:
No foul and dastard blows i' the back.
CRASSUS: Ay, none
For honest enemies; but felon foes
E'en crush feloniously. – Away: heaven speed
thee.
Kill we the chief, and I will end the war,
Ere Pompey comes to share with me the hon-
or. [*Exeunt*]

*In the acting version of the play, Act IV begins
at this point.*

Scene 1. The Camp of Spartacus.

Enter Senona, Julia, Florus, and AEnomaiis.
SENONA: Weep not, poor lady. –
JULIA: Why bid'st thou me not weep?
Hadst thou no tears, when thou didst find thy-
self
The slave of strangers? Yes, thou hadst, al-
though
In bond of the merciful, who were never used
To aught but gentleness with woman. Yet me,
The lily-cradled daughter of great nobles,
Brought to the slavish†† thrall of slaves, ex-
posed
To all their brutal cruelty, thou bid'st
To weep no more.
SENONA: It is thy fright, that conjures
These shapes of danger. Thou art here as safe
As woman may be in a troubled camp.
Thou art no slave; but, I am sure, art held
To timely ransome. Pray be comforted: –
I know, thou art safe.
JULIA: I have, I know, that safety
That may be found in den of wolves or
bears. –
Would I had died or e'er my fate had thrust me
Among these dreadful murderers.
SENONA: They are such
To none my husband favors.
JULIA: Is not he
As fierce and pitiless as the rest, who seeks
To venge his wrongs upon the innocent?

††There is a query in Bird's hand, – "Shall I substitute vile, odious, degrading, or some other word?"

He that has madly doomed that hapless captive
His father's crime in blood to expiate?
SENONA: He has not doomed him; nay, if he
said so,
It was in wrath; and he will pardon him.
The heart that throbs beneath his bloody mail,
Can melt to pity quickly as thine own.
I think, he'll free him; for thyself, I know,
Thou art protected.
JULIA: Am I from his brother,
The insolent Phasarius? – Heard I not
What claim that villain made to me? Alas,
Thou art a woman, and can pity me.
SENONA: Thine ears deceived thee; did they not,
AEnomaiis?
AENOMAIIS: I think so, lady.
SENONA: Did not this argument
Point to some claim of war?
AENOMAIIS: A bold proposal
Made by Phasarius, by the chief denied:
This was their argument.

Enter Spartacus

JULIA: Alas, behold
How frowns the angry fury on his face!
Bodes this no ill to Florus or to me?
SENONA: What is the matter, husband, that you
look
So sad and heavy?
SPARTACUS: Sad and heavy, am I? –
[*Aside*] And shall I, for this face of snow pro-
voke
A threatening ruin? Out of foolish pity
For one that loves me not, drive from my
heart,
The heart that loves me well?
SENONA: What say'st thou, Spartacus?
SPARTACUS: [*Aside*] To save her girlish body
from the shame,
Her baby bosom from the pang, – to rescue
From a short dream of sorrow, one young fool
Out of the million millions of the mourning,
Kill mine own coming glory and the hopes
Of a wrong'd world?
SENONA: I fear me, thou art angry.
SPARTACUS: Hark ye, my girl – that fool that
trembles yonder –
SENONA: I pity her.
SPARTACUS: Dost thou indeed? And art thou
Assured she is worth thy pity? Were the world
A jot the worse, were she removed from it?
SENONA: Alas, you will not harm her? She has
indeed

A kind and foolish heart.

SPARTACUS: Has she indeed?
Well, she shall to her father.

SENONA: She has none.

SPARTACUS: What, wife, an orphan? Now the
    incensed heaven
Smite my hard heart! A poor and feeble child
Left struggling fatherless in the world, and I
Consent to wrong her!

SENONA: What is't you say?

SPARTACUS: Not I,
Though forty thousand unjust brothers
    storm'd. –
One day mine own child will be fatherless. –
We'll ransome her.

SENONA: I'm glad to hear you say so.

SPARTACUS: [*To Julia*] What, foolish maid, why
    dost thou weep? Come, smile,
I'll send thee to the praetor – and the boy
    too. –
I think 'twould break her heart to kill him. –

Enter Phasarius

          Brother –
Brother, I hope thou hast forgot this folly.

PHASARIUS: I claim the captive.

SPARTACUS: Thou shalt have a thousand;
But not these twain.

PHASARIUS: I care not for the boy.
The girl is mine, – captured by mine own
    hands;
Therefore mine own.

FLORUS: Base caitiff!

SPARTACUS: Sirrah, begone. –

PHASARIUS: Deny me her, and, by the fates,
    thou art
No longer brother of mine. 'Twas I that
    helped thee
To this high station; and the troops thou rulest,
Are but my lending; for that hour I leave thee,
They leave thee, too.

SPARTACUS: Come, – look me in the face,
And let me see how bad desires have changed
    thee.

PHASARIUS: I claim the captive.

SPARTACUS: Set thine eye on *her:*
Lo you, she weeps, and she is fatherless.
Thou wouldst not harm an orphan? What, I
    say,
Art thou, whom I have carried in my arms
To mountain-tops, to worship the great God,
Art thou a man to plot a wrong and sorrow
(And thou a *man!*) against a feeble orphan?

Wilt thou now ask her?

PHASARIUS: Ay.

SPARTACUS: Thou art a changeling!
My father ne'er begot so base a heart. –
Brother, I do conjure thee, for I love thee,
Forget this thing.

PHASARIUS: Farewell.

SPARTACUS: Thou wilt not go?

PHASARIUS: Ay, by great Jove, I will. Play thou
    the tyrant
On those that follow thee.

SPARTACUS: My younger brother: –
Nay, I'll not call thee such, – but a hot fool
And heartless enemy. –

PHASARIUS: Call what thou wilt:
I am a man not to be mock'd and wrong'd,
Nor flouted in my counsels. I did ask you,
Now that you had the wind of the fooled prae-
    tor,
Now when rich Rome is emptied by her levies,
Now when the eager troops cry all, *for Rome,*
To march upon it, ere the joining armies
Of Pompey and Lucullus should prevent you.
This I did ask, and this you did deny,
Though, by a former promise, pledged there-
    to.

SPARTACUS: I promised not.

PHASARIUS: By heaven,
    you did – *when stronger.*
This you refuse; and when, forgiving this,
I ask my captive, you deny me her,
With many a sharp and contumelious word,
Such as is fitter for a dog than me.

SPARTACUS: Forgive me, if my anger used such
    shame;
I knew not what I said.

PHASARIUS: March then to Rome.

SPARTACUS: It cannot be. We should but set us
    down
Under her walls, where the three generals,
Ere we could force the gates, would hedge us
    in.
We cannot stand against them all even here;
But, when in Sicily, are invincible.

PHASARIUS: Rome, or the captive: no more Sicily.

SPARTACUS: To Sicily:
There, by the ocean fenced, rouse up and gath-
    er
The remnants of those tribes by Rome de-
    stroyed,
Invited to their vengeance. Then will come,
Arm'd with retributive and murderous hate,
The sons of fiery Afric, – Carthaginians

Out of their caves, Numidians from their
deserts;
The Gaul, the Spaniard, the Sardinian;
The hordes of Thessaly, Thrace, and Mace-
don,
And swarming Asia; – all at last assembled
In vengeful union 'gainst this hell of Rome.
Then may we crush, but now we crush our-
selves.
Let us to Sicily.

PHASARIUS: Those that will. Farewell.

SPARTACUS: Will you desert me?

PHASARIUS: I did think thee meant
For the most godlike enterprise of earth:
Thou fail'st. Farewell; protect thyself.

SPARTACUS: Mad boy,
Remember Crixus.

PHASARIUS: And his thousand Germans!
I go with Gauls and Thracians, and fifty
thousand. –
A Roman girl was worth this coil! – Farewell:
Learn to be juster. [*Exit*]

SPARTACUS: Gone! Alas, alas,
Am I unjust? I did not think my brother
Could e'er desert me.

AENOMAIIS: Spartacus –

SPARTACUS: AEnomaiis,
Dost thou remain? Why dost thou stay with
me?

AENOMAIIS: For that I know thee wiser than thy
brother.
I will stand, fight, or die with thee. But look;
If thou speak not, the army to a man,
Will follow this young madman.

SPARTACUS: Mad and ungrateful all! Will none
remain?

SENONA: Beseech you, speak with them, my
honored husband.

SPARTACUS: And he endanger'd thee, too! By the
heavens,
I'll ne'er forgive him. – Nay, go to your
couch.
I'll speak with them. They will not all desert
me. [*Exeunt*]

Scene 2

The Camp of Crassus.

Enter Crassus and Lentulus.

CRASSUS: Thy son was kill'd, then? I am sorry
for him.

I heard, he bore him soldier-like, and I,
Upon this promise, did intend him favor.

LENTULUS: I know not that he certainly was
killed;
But, I thank Jove, he did not fly his post.

Enter Bracchius

CRASSUS: What of the enemy? does he still approach?

BRACCHIUS: No, he is flying.

LENTULUS: Flying! thou art mad.

BRACCHIUS: That may be, for my slaves have
ruined me.
Why should brains stick where gold will not?

CRASSUS: Come, sirrah,
What didst thou mean by saying the foe fled?
< How flies he?

BRACCHIUS: As a hound, that having coursed
A stinking brock, upon a sudden turns,
To chase a noble stag. – Ourselves the badg-
er,
And Rome the worthier quarry.

CRASSUS: Tedious fool, >
What dost thou mean?

BRACCHIUS: That the fierce Gladiators
Instead of dinging us, as seemed designed,
Are now upon the highway to the city.

CRASSUS: To Rome?

BRACCHIUS: Yes, flying to Rome.

CRASSUS: Presumptuous fools!
< Now may we build a forest of crucifixes.
Bid the men cast away their picks, and arm. >
We'll after them.

BRACCHIUS: I think there's some division
Among the leaders; for the herds afoot,
March in disorder.

CRASSUS: Separated! Jove,
I thank thee for this boon. – Another Crixus!
To arms, I say. Send out the cavalry,
< To gain their flanks and front, letting them
get
Beyond the leader's camp. > – This is a
triumph. –
To arms, I say. [*Exeunt*]

Scene 3

The Camp of Spartacus.

Enter Spartacus and AEnomaiis.

SPARTACUS: Seven thousand true? A handful,
but enough,
Being staunch and prudent, for the enterprise. –

Desert me! Well, well, well. – Among the hills
Are many paths that may be safely trod;
Whereby we'll gain the sea, and so pass o'er
To safer Sicily. – Perhaps I spoke
Too roughly, – but no matter. – Did you send
To hire the shipping of those pirates? Well. –
And all prepared to march at nightfall? –
AEnomaiis,
Do you not think they'll beat him?

AENOMAIIS: I doubt it not;
Phasarius being a soldier, but no leader.

< SPARTACUS: An excellent leader, but that he is
rash.

AENOMAIIS: That is the misery. He will fight you
hotly
An army of lions; but a troop of foxes
May easily beat him. Now the praetor's brain
Is all o' the fox's color. >

SPARTACUS: Well, I care not:
We will to Rhegium. – Think you, AEnomaiis,
I might not, while the praetor steals upon
him,
Steal on the praetor, and so save the army?
What say'st thou?

AENOMAIIS: Hang them, no. This brings Lu-
cullus
On our seven thousand. Let the mutineers
Look to themselves.

SPARTACUS: Right, very right, right, AEnomaiis.
Let them look to themselves. He did desert
me;
My father's son deserted me, and left me
Circled by foes. I say, 'tis very right.
< He shall no help from me; not though they
beat him
An hundred times; no, no, no help from me. >

AENOMAIIS: Lo you, a messenger!

SPARTACUS: From Phasarius! –
Perhaps he is sorry. –

Enter Jovius

AENOMAIIS: Chief, an embassy
From Crassus.

SPARTACUS: And what would Crassus with the
Gladiator,
The poor base slave, and fugitive, Spartacus?
Speak, Roman: wherefore does thy master send
Thy gray hairs to the cutthroat's camp?

JOVIUS: Brave, rebel, –

SPARTACUS: Why, that's a better name than a
rogue or bondman;
But, in this camp, I am call'd general.

JOVIUS: Brave general; for, though a rogue and
bondman,
As you have said, I'll still allow you general,
As he that beats a consul surely is. –

SPARTACUS: Say, two, – two consuls; and to
that e'en add
A proconsul, three praetors, and some generals.

JOVIUS: Why, 'tis no more than true. – Are
you a Thracian?

SPARTACUS: Ay.

JOVIUS: There is something in the
air of Thrace
Breeds valor up as rank as grass. 'Tis pity
You are a barbarian.

SPARTACUS: Wherefore?

JOVIUS: Had you been born
A Roman, you had won by this a triumph.

SPARTACUS: I thank the gods I am barbarian;
For I can better teach the grace-begot
And heaven-supported masters of the earth,
How a mere dweller of a desert rock
Can bow their crown'd heads to his chariot
wheels.
Man is heaven's work, and beggar's brats may
'herit
A soul to mount them up the steeps of fortune,
With regal necks to be their stepping-blocks. –
But come, what is thy message?

JOVIUS: Julia, niece
O' the praetor, is thy captive.

SPARTACUS: Ay.

JOVIUS: For whom
Is offered in exchange thy wife, Senona,
And thy young boy.

SPARTACUS: Tell thou the praetor, Roman,
The Thracian's wife is ransomed.

JOVIUS: How is that?

SPARTACUS: What ho, Senona!

Senona appears with the child at a tent door
                              Lo, she stands before you,
Ransomed, and by the steel, from out the
camp
Of slaughtered Gellius. [*Exit Senona*]

JOVIUS: This is sorcery! –
But name a ransome for the general's niece.

SPARTACUS: Have I not now the praetor on the
hip?
He would, in his extremity, have made
My wife his buckler of defence; perhaps
Have doomed her to the scourge! But this is
Roman.

Now the barbarian is instructed. Look,
I hold the praetor by the heart; and he
Shall feel how tightly grip barbarian fingers.
JOVIUS: Men do not war on women. Name her
ransome.
SPARTACUS: Men do not war on women!
Look you:
One day I clomb upon the ridgy top
Of the cloud-piercing Haemus, where, among
The eagles and the thunders, from that height,
I look'd upon the world – or, far as where,
Wrestling with storms, the gloomy Euxine
chafed
On his recoiling shores; and where dim Adria
In her blue bosom quenched the fiery sphere.
Between those surges lay a land, might once
Have served for paradise, but Rome had made
it
A Tartarus. – In my green youth I look'd
From the same frosty peak, where now I
stood,
And then beheld the glory of those lands,
Where peace was tinkling on the shepherd's
bell
And singing with the reapers; < or beneath
The shade of thatch eaves, smiled with grey
old men,
And with their children laughed along the
green. >
Since that glad day, Rome's conquerors had
past
With withering armies there, and all was
changed:
Peace had departed; howling war was there,
Cheered on by Roman hunters: then, me-
thought,
Even as I looked upon the altered scene,
Groans echoed through the valleys, through
which ran
Rivers of blood, like smoking Phlegethons;
Fires flashed from burning villages, and fam-
ine
Shriek'd in the empty cornfields. Women and
children,
Robb'd of their sires and husbands, left to
starve –
These were the dwellers of the land! – Say'st
thou
Rome wars not then on women?
JOVIUS: This is not to the matter.
SPARTACUS: Now, by Jove,
It is. These things do Romans. But the earth
Is sick of conquerors. There is not a man,

Not Roman, but is Rome's extremest foe;
And such am I, sworn from that hour I saw
These sights of horror, while the gods support
me,
To wreak on Rome such havock as Rome
wreaks,
Carnage and devastation, wo and ruin.
Why should I ransome, when I swear to
slay? –
Begone: this is my answer!
< JOVIUS: With your leave
This prattling scares no Romans; and these
threats
Come weakly from a chief of mutineers.
SPARTACUS: Of mutineers?
JOVIUS: Ay, marry, 'tis well known,
Your cutthroats have deserted you. Content
you,
Crassus will punish the foul traitors.
SPARTACUS: Crassus!
JOVIUS: Ay, Crassus. – Hercules, how men
will talk!
Wreak wo on Rome! – I tell you, your lieuten-
ant
Will hang upon a cross before the morrow.
So name your ransome, while 'tis offered you.
SPARTACUS: Begone, I say. [*Exit Jovius*]
Alas, my AEnomaiis,
Should we not strike now? Now while we
might fall
Upon their rear, and take them by surprise?
AENOMAIIS: Let them be punished, castigated
well,
And they'll return to wisdom and obedience.
SPARTACUS: Right, right. Let them be punished,
hack'd to the bones:
This will speak better than my words. Prepare
For Rhegium. He'll return to us tomorrow.
[*Exeunt*] >

End of Act IV

ACT V. Scene I

*The Peninsula of Rhegium. The Camp of the
Gladiators.*

Enter Spartacus and AEnomaiis.
SPARTACUS: Routed and cut to pieces! – Said
I not?
Did I not tell them? – Utterly destroyed!

Scattered like chaff! – Now, by the eternal fates,
They did provoke high heaven, deserting me. –
How many slain?

AENOMAIIS: Indeed it is not known.

SPARTACUS: Many, I'm glad; I should be very glad:
Did I not lead them ever on to victory?
And did they not forsake me? Wretched fools,
This was my vengeance, yea, my best of vengeance,
To leave them to themselves, that Roman praetors
Might whip them for me. Art thou not rejoiced?
Art thou not, AEnomaiis, glad of this?
Glad, very glad?

< AENOMAIIS: I shall be, when I see
Half of them back again.

SPARTACUS: I'll decimate them:
Even as the Romans punish, so I'll punish. –
Ruin me all these grand and glorious hopes?
Nay, they were certainties. – An excellent army,
That might have fought with Pompey, broke and ruined
By their mad mutiny! An excellent army –

AENOMAIIS: Indeed, an excellent.

SPARTACUS: Foolish AEnomaiis,
Why did'st thou stay me, when I would have saved them?

AENOMAIIS: Had this been well? Had their ingratitude
Deserved it of thee?

SPARTACUS: Ay, ingratitude.
Did I oppress them? Did I tyrannise? >

AENOMAIIS: 'Tis rumored that Phasarius fell.

SPARTACUS: My brother,
My foolish brother – why did he part from me? –
Nay, I'll not mourn him.

AENOMAIIS: This evil news must now
Hasten our embarkation. The pirate ships
Already are launching from the shore.

SPARTACUS: Why, now
You are too fast. Bid them be beached again. –
< Alas, that foolish boy! We'll rest awhile,
And see what fugitives may come to us. >
Art sure Phasarius was slain? – the pride
Of his dead mother's heart; and, I do know,
Though prone to anger, of a loving spirit. –
We'll rest awhile here on this promontory.

AENOMAIIS: Each moment has a peril. For these pirates
They are most treacherous hounds, and may set sail
Without us; and the praetor, thou know'st well,
Is trenching us in on this peninsula.

SPARTACUS: What care I for the praetor and his trenches?
< This is a boy's trick, and a boy might meet it. >
Trenches to stop a Thracian! – Look you, now,
What drooping slave is that? By all the gods,
It is my brother! – But I'll not be glad.
Lo you, how humbled, spiritless he looks!
Where are his troops?

Enter Phasarius
          Sirrah, why comest thou here?
Did'st thou not part from me, and take mine army?
Did'st thou not teach my followers mutiny,
And lead them to destruction? Thou whipp'd fool,
Why comest thou here?

PHASARIUS: To ask thy pardon, and to die.

SPARTACUS: Couldst thou not die with those thou led'st to death,
That men, who after should have called thee madman,
Might not have called thee craven?

PHASARIUS: I am no craven;
A wretch, I grant you, but no craven.

SPARTACUS: Where are thy troops? that throng'd and valiant army
Thou stol'dst from me?

PHASARIUS: With Pluto. Why demand me?
I am alone of all.

SPARTACUS: Most wretched man,
Thou has murder'd fifty thousand men, destroyed
Thy brother and thy country, and all hope
Of the earth's disenthralment.

PHASARIUS: I have ruined
My brother, that's enough.

SPARTACUS: Ay, look, behold;
But yestermorn, I was a conqueror,
On the high verge and pinnacle of renown;
Today a skulking, trembling, despised man,
Thrust in a pit. Whose traitorous hand was it,
Pluck'd me from my high seat, and sunk so low?

Who did this thing, this foul, felonious thing?

PHASARIUS: Myself, that was thy brother.

SPARTACUS: Ay, that was!

PHASARIUS: Why shouldst thou stab me with thy
  words? O brother,
Strike me with thy sharp sword, but speak no
  more:
Give me to punishment, or drive me forth
To die by Romans; but upbraid no more.

SPARTACUS: Shall I forgive him? Look, he is
  penitent.

AENOMAIIS: But he has lost them all.

SPARTACUS: Ay, so he has. –
Ask'st thou for pardon, when thou hast slain
  all?
Away! thou did'st discard me from thy heart:
I banish thee from mine.

PHASARIUS: It is but just.
Why should I live, when I have ruined thee?
I should have died before. Farewell.

SPARTACUS: Come back:
I will forgive thee: nay, I have. – O brother,
Why did'st thou do this wrong? But I'll forget
  it. –
Let the ships now be launched, now, AEno-
  maiis;
Now cross to Sicily. [*Exit AEnomaiis*]
                    With these fifty thousand –
But I've forgot it. – What, were all de-
  stroyed?

PHASARIUS: All, all.

SPARTACUS: A disciplined army! –
But no matter. –
All slain upon the field?

PHASARIUS: Six thousand wretches
Yielded them prisoners to the praetor.

SPARTACUS: Well,
He took six thousand prisoners. These will
  now
Suffer a double wretchedness.

PHASARIUS: Never fear it:
They will not.

SPARTACUS: How is that, Phasarius?
Did not the praetor, in his proclamations,
Threat us with bondmen's deaths by cruci-
  fixion?

PHASARIUS: And he will keep his word – nay, he
  has kept it.

SPARTACUS: What!

PHASARIUS: Are men beasts, that life
  should count no more
Than a beast's sob?

SPARTACUS: Thou fill'st my soul with terror.

Are they condemned? All?

PHASARIUS: Executed.

SPARTACUS: Horror!
Six thousand men, and crucified!

PHASARIUS: Crucified.
I saw a sight last night, that turned my brain,
And set my comrade mad. The Roman high-
  way
Is, each side, lined with crosses, and on each
  cross
Is nailed a gladiator. – Well, 'twas night,
When, with a single follower, I did creep
Through the trenched army to that road, and
  saw
The executed multitude uplifted
Upon the horrid engines. Many lived:
Some moaned and writhed in stupid agony;
Some howled, and prayed for death, and
  cursed the gods;
Some turned to lunatics, and laughed at hor-
  ror;
And some with fierce and hellish strength, had
  torn
Their arms free from the beams, and so had
  died,
Grasping, headlong, at air. And, oh, the
  yells,
That rose upon the gusty sighs of night,
And babbled hideously along the skies,
As *they* were fill'd with murder!

SPARTACUS: Say no more:
This is too dreadful for man's ear. I swear
For this to make Rome howl. What, AEno-
  maiis.

Reenter AEnomaiis

Are the ships all afloat?

AENOMAIIS: And gone.

SPARTACUS: What, gone?

AENOMAIIS: These same perfidious pirates, with
  their hire,
Have set their sails, and fled.

SPARTACUS: The ocean god
Meet them with hurricanes, sink their ships,
  and feed
Sea-monsters with their corses!

AENOMAIIS: All is finished:
This is the fruit of mercy for deserters.

SPARTACUS: Be that forgot.

AENOMAIIS: What now remains for us,
But to sit down and die?

SPARTACUS: I'll tell thee, what:
To fight the praetor.

AENOMAIIS: Though his troops outnumber
Ten times our own!

SPARTACUS: Ay; our despair will make us
Each ten times stronger than his foe. Fill up
This schoolboy ditch with disregarded plun-
der,
And when the watchdogs sleep, like wolves,
steal on them
And take them by the throat. I have no fear,
But we shall find a pathway through their
camp.
Then to Tarentum; there we'll find us ships.
Or, if that fail, with a despairing fury,
Turn upon Rome, and perish there.

Enter Senona, with the child
                              What now?
Com'st thou to mourn o'er our mishaps, Seno-
na?
Be not dismayed: I'll find thee safety yet.

SENONA: Thou wouldst conceal these newer perils
from me;
But well I know, that every hour now brings
A menacing cloud about thee.

SPARTACUS: Clouds, ay, clouds:
A cloud is on my path, but my ambition
Sees glory in't: as travellers who stand
On mountains, view upon some neighboring
peak,
Among the mists, a figure of themselves,
Traced in sublimer characters; so I
Here see the vapory image of myself,
Distant and dim, but giantlike – I'll make
These perils glories.

SENONA: And the ships have left thee?

SPARTACUS: Thou art a soldier's wife, and wilt
not tremble
To share his danger. Look, through yonder
camp
Our path lies.

SENONA: I will walk it by thy side.

SPARTACUS: Not so; for though unharmed by
steel, the sight
Of the near fray would kill thee. I have discov-
ered
A path almost unguarded; where, whilst I
Assault the Roman in his sleep, thyself
And my war-cradled boy, with my Phasarius
To guard thee, shall in safety pass, and join
me
After the battle.

SENONA: Why not lead your army
By that unguarded path?

SPARTACUS: Trust me, dear wife,
I'll make it such for thee, but cannot have it
Safe for an army. The surprised distraction
Of the attack will call the guards away.
This is the safest.

SENONA: Let me go with thee.
I do not fear the horrors of the storm.

SPARTACUS: It cannot be. What, brother –

PHASARIUS: Let some one else
Be made her guard; while I, in fight, find ven-
geance,
And reparation of my faults.

SPARTACUS: Wilt thou
Refuse me this, Phasarius?

PHASARIUS: Am not I
A rash and witless fool? Trust not to me
What thou so valuest.

SENONA: I beseech you, hear him.
Let me not leave you, Spartacus: my heart
Is full of dismal and of ominous fear,
If I do leave you now, I leave for ever.
If I must die, let me die where thou art.

SPARTACUS: Why talk'st thou now of death?
I say, I'll make
This path most safe for thee. How could I
fight,
Or play the leader in a bloody storm,
With thy pale visage ever in my eye?

PHASARIUS: I do beseech you, make not me her
guard.

SPARTACUS: It must be so. And hear me now,
Phasarius;
I put into thy hands more than my soul:
See, my dear wife, and here my innocent
boy. –
These are the very jewels of my heart.
Protect them for me. Be not rash; steal softly,
With the small faithful troop I'll send with
thee,
Through glens and woods; and when the alarm
is sounded,
March fast but wisely. For thy life, and mine,
Avoid all contest, shouldst thou meet a foe;
Nay, though thou know'st thou hast advan-
tage, fight not.
Join me, with these in safety, and assure me
No man has drawn his sword. – And now
farewell.
Farewell, Senona: I pray you do not speak. –
Thou art very safe. Farewell.

Exeunt Senona, child, and Phasarius

AENOMAIIS: He is too rash.

268

SPARTACUS: Rash, had I given him a command in battle;
But will not be with them. – Rouse up the troops.
Fill up the ditch with baggage, as I told thee. –
< I'll see that all be schooled for this assault. >
[*Exeunt*]

Scene 2

Before the tent of Crassus.

Enter Crassus, Mummius, Jovius, Lentulus, and Bracchius.

CRASSUS: Now I lament me, on this overthrow
Of the chief army of the enemy,
I prayed for Pompey and Lucullus. If
I end not instant, by another blow,
The war I have so maimed, comes me a colleague
To chouse me of my triumphs.
JOVIUS: You must be quick then.
The dawn will show you Pompey by your side;
Or rather, dashing with a Roman scorn,
Amongst the ruffians you have trapp'd.
CRASSUS: I think,
Ourselves may do it. – And this hell-dog holds
The girl to doom?
JOVIUS: He says, he is instructed
By your fore-thought intentions with his spouse.
CRASSUS: But dost thou think he'll slay her?
JOVIUS: Not while he
May purchase mercy with her.
CRASSUS: Shall I take her
Out of his camp by force? or send thee back,
To offer mercy and receive submission?
JOVIUS: Propose him life and liberty, and make him
A Roman citizen.
CRASSUS: What, a rebel slave!
JOVIUS: In these rough, rotten times, we do not scruple
To raise our rogues to honor. Why, then, blush,
To anoint a slave, that's capable and honest?
The genius of this Thracian, had it been
In honorable trust display'd, had quell'd
A score of barbarous nations; and *may* yet,
Make but the man a Roman.

CRASSUS: We will make him
A captive first. – Were my poor Julia free! –

Loud Alarums

What is the matter?
JOVIUS: The rats are out! by Jove,
The slaves have pass'd the trenches, and assault us!
CRASSUS: Thou art mad! They dare not –
What, to arms, to arms!
Nay, if they will, let them into the camp,
But let not out. – To arms, to arms! [*Exeunt*]

Scene 3

Another part of the Roman Camp.

Enter Crassus, Jovius, Mummius, and Lentulus.

CRASSUS: Mischiefs and plagues, and slavish stripes disgrace
These shameless cowards! What, ope their ranks, and give
A path to these few madmen! Let them scape us!
JOVIUS: Nay, they are gone, that's certain, – but will drop
Into the jaws of Pompey.
CRASSUS: Bid the legions
Follow them.
JOVIUS: When the day breaks; but not now.
CRASSUS: Shall I let Pompey take them, and have Rome
Laugh at my shame? Have Pompey join the scorners,
And mock me, too? Hie thee away, good Jovius;
Follow the Thracian; offer pardon, freedom,
Whate'er thou wilt. Do but delay his march:
Let him not come near Pompey – Quick, away!
[*Exeunt*]

Scene 4

The Camp of Spartacus, among the hills.

Enter Spartacus and AEnomaiis.

SPARTACUS: Was not this well? When desperate men contend,
The brave will fly from them. To fight for life,
Fights surest for a victory. Fought we well?

I would not give these seven thousand poor rogues,
For a whole herd of angry Gauls. We'll win
The highway to Tarentum yet. – Lietuten-ant,
Should they not now be here?

AENOMAIIS: Who?

SPARTACUS: Who! Phasarius
And his care-chosen guard – my brother and my wife.

AENOMAIIS: They tread a rough and tangled path.

SPARTACUS: 'Tis true;
And finding there more guards than I had word of,
Their caution journeys them the slower. I
Am almost grieved, I brought them not with me. –
How fare the captives? Bring me to Taren-tum,
I'll send that girl unransomed to the praetor. –
Would they were here! – Bring in the prison-er,
And find how march the coming generals.

Bracchius is brought in, guarded

AENOMAIIS: This fellow was the master of thy brother.
Question him, and then hang him, for a bas-er,
More heartless master never yet struck slave.

SPARTACUS: I am sick of blood. – Is not the sun yet up?
If they be seen – but I'll not think of that. –
Be not afeard: hadst thou been worth a blow,
I had not spared thee. Speak, and truly speak,
Or thou shalt fat the kites: When looks the praetor
For Pompey and his Spanish troops?

BRACCHIUS: He looks
Not for, but at him.

SPARTACUS: Wretch!

BRACCHIUS: And so may'st thou,
Yonder among the heights upon thy left.

SPARTACUS: Wretch, if thou mock me, I will strike thee dead.
Know I not well the praetor's craft? These ea-gles
That spread their golden pinions on the hills,
Were wing'd by Crassus thither, to affright me.
Are they not Crassus's standards? Own me that,

Or look tonight to sup in Acheron.

BRACCHIUS: To sup on earth, then, I'll agree to this;
But I shall lie.

SPARTACUS: Rogue, answer me again:
Are those troops Pompey's?

BRACCHIUS: Ay.

SPARTACUS: The gods forbid!
They are in motion too! Now I begin
To feel my desolation, and despair.
What, AEnomaiis, send me out a scout
To view those hill-perched foes, and quick pre-pare
The army for the march. And my poor wife!
Why did I trust her with Phasarius?
< Send out a cunning guide to hunt the path. > [*Exit AEnomaiis*]
Roman, if thou speak false, I'll have thee slain. –
Where rests Lucullus?

BRACCHIUS: In no place he rests,
Save nightly on the highroad from Tarentum.

< SPARTACUS: Villain, thou liest! The gods have not so left me.
I say, thou speak'st not true.

BRACCHIUS: Well, I speak false;
But notwithstanding, he is on that road. –
These are the bloodiest cutthroats! – >

SPARTACUS: Now, out on me,
My heart is full of fear. The praetor on my rear,
Lucullus, Pompey on my front and left,
And naught but howling seas upon my right!
Seven thousand men against an hundred thou-sand!
If Crassus love the girl – He fears disgrace –
'Tis not infeasible – unless, alas,
My wife, perchance, be faln into his hands;
Then can the maiden buy me naught but her.

Reenter AEnomaiis, with Jovius

AENOMAIIS: The Roman praetor
Sends thee again an envoy.

SPARTACUS: Speak, centurion;
What word sends Crassus?

JOVIUS: For the Roman lady,
A princely ransome; for thyself, an offer
Of mercy, pardon, Roman denization,
And martial honor and command; provided –

SPARTACUS: Ay, provided!

JOVIUS: Thou instantly, ere Pompey leave the hills,
Surrender up these malefactious slaves

To whips and crosses. Therefore, most valiant Thracian,
Put by the frenzy, that would fight against
Three circling armies, and accept this boon
Generous and great.
SPARTACUS: I am unfortunate,
Thou know'st that well; but not being Roman yet,
I scorn the foul condition, that makes me
To my true friends a traitor. Give them freedom,
And they lay down their arms; but talk of crosses,
And they have yet the arms that cut a path
Through the proud praetor's camp.
JOVIUS: Why shouldst thou care,
Thou, who hast such a Roman soul, for these
Vile runagate rogues, who, at an opportunity,
Thee would betray as freely as their masters?
Let them be hanged, and be thou made a Roman.
Perhaps thy word may save the least offending;
But let the scum be punished.
SPARTACUS: They shall die,
Like soldiers, on the field, or live in freedom.
But hearken, Roman:
I know the praetor, that he loves his niece,
But honor more; I know, if Pompey strike
At me one blow, the honor all is his,
And nothing left for Crassus, but comparison
Betwixt what Pompey does, and what *he* could not.
He will not then have Pompey strike me, and
He would have back his niece. While I lie here
On this impregnable and forted hill,
Pompey approaches and sits down beside him.
Now he'll consent himself to lose the honor
O' the hunted gladiator's overthrow,
So Pompey wins it not.
JOVIUS: That may be true,
For Crassus loves not Pompey. But on that
What project found you?
SPARTACUS: This: Let him but wink,
While I steal darkly to Tarentum, there
T' embark my army.
JOVIUS: Hah!
SPARTACUS: I'll find a way
To cozen Pompey and pass by Lucullus,
Provided he not follow at my heels.
Gage me but this, and he shall have his niece
Unransomed back; deny me, and by Pluto,
Pompey alone shall gain the laurel.
JOVIUS: Jove!

This is a mad proposal. Help you fly!
Will you surrender, or be cut to pieces?
SPARTACUS: Bring forth the captives.

Julia and Florus are brought in
Lo, I'll march tonight:
If Crassus follow me, the girl shall die.
JOVIUS: Art thou a savage?
SPARTACUS: Ay; or if you will,
A beast, whose nature not being fierce, the hunters
Have toil'd and goaded into fury. Nature
Makes fewer rogues, than misery. But yesterday,
I had saved that maiden's blood, at cost of mine;
Now, with a cool ferocity, I doom her
To perish like a thing abhorred, whene'er
The praetor bids me.
JULIA: Out, alas, alas!
Didst thou not swear thou wouldst not harm my life?
Thou didst, unto thy wife.
SPARTACUS: Well, speak not of it. –
She is surely taken. – Roman, listen to me:
South of thy camp there liest a secret path,
Where, for a certain reason, I did send
A party, to escape the fears of conflict.
Have they been captured?
JOVIUS: I know not, but think so.
Who were they?
SPARTACUS: Well, they are not taken then?
JOVIUS: I'll not say that. A double guard was sent,
Under your one-time master, Lentulus,
Last night, to watch that path.
SPARTACUS: I have some prisoners,
I would exchange for them – Look, all but *her.*
JOVIUS: But who were these?
SPARTACUS: Some women and children. Yes,
Some helpless fools, not fit to look on battle. –
Not that I care for them; but I'll exchange them.
JOVIUS: Some women and children?
SPARTACUS: Sirrah, wilt thou have it?
Why, 'twas my wife then, and my child. If they
Be captured, I'll exchange them for my captives.
Crassus shall have his niece too. Nay, I'll send her,
Without the exchange, provided Crassus swear

To give them freedom, and send back to
Thrace.
Let him swear this: let them to Thrace, I
say, —
Let them be safe, and I can die. — [*Alarums*]
AENOMAIIS: Look, general!
We are attacked!
SPARTACUS: By heavens, a troop of horse
Rushing against our hill! Why, these are
madmen! —
Soft you, they chase some mounted fugitive;
Nay, he has cleared them — Look, man, look!
O gods,
Do I not know him? —
JOVIUS: For this proposed exchange —
SPARTACUS: Look, look! 'Tis he! They are lost!
AENOMAIIS: His horse has fallen:
He is bloody, too.
SPARTACUS: But where are they?

Enter Phasarius, wounded
                         What, brother, brother,
Speak, speak. — Where are they? Ah!
PHASARIUS: My brother!
SPARTACUS: Speak!
Dost thou not know me? By thy soul, I charge
thee,
Speak to me; tell me of my love, my boy!
Where hast thou left them?
PHASARIUS: Strike me to the heart:
I have robbed thee, brother, of much more
than life;
And all the blood these gaping wounds have
left,
Will not repay thee.
SPARTACUS: Art thou mad?
I ask thee of my wife, my boy, my loves!
And thou dost prate to me of wounds and
blood! —
Speak!
PHASARIUS: I can better speak than thou canst
hear. —
Why madest thou me their escort? Why, O
fool!
Thou should'st have known that I would
quickly lead them
Through the first perils that invited me;
And where a Roman throat was to be cut,
Would drag them to the hideous spectacle.
SPARTACUS: But thou did'st bear them off!
Come, say it, brother;
Thou wert imprudent, but still kind and true.

I'll not be angry — come, I know thou wert
worsted,
Thy troops cut off — but thou hast saved them,
brother!
PHASARIUS: I would have done it, let my
wounds speak for me.
SPARTACUS: They are captives, then? O
traitor! — my poor wife,
And my blithe boy!
PHASARIUS: The troops were cut to pieces;
The boy —
SPARTACUS: What of him?
PHASARIUS: Cried for mercy to
A Roman soldier —
SPARTACUS: Who spared him!
PHASARIUS: Struck him to the earth.
SPARTACUS: God! — And his mother?
PHASARIUS: She sprang upon the throat of the
black monster —
Ask me no more — I faint.
SPARTACUS: My wife! my wife!
Let furies lash thee into consciousness.
My wife, I say! She sprang upon his throat;
What then?
PHASARIUS: He slew her — but I clove him to
the nave.
I could not save, but with my best avenged.
[*Falls*]
SPARTACUS: There are no gods in heaven;
Pity has fled, and human rage reigns there. —
Wretch, doth the earth still hold thee? Murder-
er,
Most traitorous, foul, unnatural murderer,
If the warm blood of thy thrice-martyred vic-
tims
Reach not thy soul, and strike it dead within
thee,
My sword shall sacrifice thee to their fury. —
AENOMAIIS: Hold, hold! Thou wilt not strike
him? Look, he dies!

Phasarius dies
SPARTACUS: What, is he dead? All dead? and I
alone
Upon the flinty earth? No wife, no child,
(No brother) All slain by Romans? Yes, by
Romans. — Look,
I will have vengeance, fierce and bloody ven-
geance,
Upon the praetor's blood, upon the praetor's. —
Thou grey and hoary wretch, — for being Ro-
man,

A wretch thou art – I'll send back to the prae-
tor
His niece a corse, and thou shalt carry her. –
What ho, my Guards!

Enter Guards

JOVIUS: Savage fiend, forbear;
Shed not the blood o' the innocent.
SPARTACUS: < Foolish man, >
Was not Senona's innocent, and my child's?
Did they e'er harm a Roman? – Blood for
blood,
And life for life, and vengeance on the praetor!
FLORUS: Unhappy Spartacus, mar not thy glory
With this unnatural and unjust deed.
Let my head fall for hers.
SPARTACUS: Thy head *and* hers –
< Fools, ye are Romans, and shall die.
JOVIUS: Forbear – >
SPARTACUS: Take them away –
JULIA: Now may the heavens forgive thee.
SPARTACUS: Off, foolish girl; there is no pity left:
My heart now thirsts for blood, and blood will
have.
JULIA: I have your promise –
SPARTACUS: Breath, that I revoke.
JULIA: I have Senona's; pity me for her,
For she did love me; pity for your child,
Whom I have nestled in my arms, till it
Did love me, too, and thou, whilst looking
on,
Didst swear no harm should ever reach to me.
Yes, for thy babe and wife, thou didst swear
this;
And while thou think'st of them, thou canst
not kill me.
SPARTACUS: Well, thou art· saved.
JOVIUS: Wilt thou, unlucky chief,
Now claim the praetor's mercy? Let thy people
Return to bonds, and have their lives.
SPARTACUS: These twain
Shall go with you; the rest is for my ven-
geance.
To show thee that the Thracian still defies, –
Even in his hour of misery and despair, –
Still cries for vengeance, still derides the mercy
Of the accursed Roman, thou shalt see
I court his fury. – Hang this Roman cutthroat
Upon a cross, and set it where the Romans
May see him perish.

*Bracchius is taken out; and the body of Phasa-
rius*

JOVIUS: This will steel all hearts,
And change all pity into murderous hate.
SPARTACUS: It is for that I hang him to the tree:
There shall no life be spared in fight today.
Look – let the grooms there kill my horse. –
'Tis done:
There shall no flight be known; nothing but
death.
Begone, centurion and prisoners. Begone or
perish.
< FLORUS: I thought thee cruel, but I find thee
kind.
Spare that man, and accept the praetor's par-
don.
SPARTACUS: Begone, thou foolish boy, while yet
thou may'st.
JULIA: Shall I not thank thee, Thracian, for my
life?
SPARTACUS: Begone, or die, – and all the heart-
ed griefs,
That rack more bitterly than death, go with
you,
And reach your abhorred country: May the
gods,
Who have seen Rome fill the earth with wo and
death.
Bring worse than wo and death on Rome; light
up
The fires of civil war and anarchy,
Curse her with kings, imperial torturers;
And while these rend her bowels, bring the
hosts
Of Northern savages, to slay, and feed
Upon her festering fatness; till the earth,
Shall know, as it has known no land so great,
No land so curst as miserable Rome! –
Begone, or perish. > [*Exeunt Jovius, Julia,
and Florus*]
Let the troops array.
And all that would not die upon the cross,
Slaying their horses, to the plain descend,
And die in battle.
< AENOMAIIS: You will not fight today?
SPARTACUS: This day, this hour, this minute,
fight and die.
Why should we struggle longer, in this dream
Of life, which is a mocking lunacy,
With ever sunshine playing far ahead,
But thunderbolts about us? Fight, I say.
There is no Orcus blacker than the hell
That life breeds in the heart. >
AENOMAIIS: Alas, dear general,
You are not fit for battle.

SPARTACUS: Fit to make
The Roman mothers howl. – Spare not one
  life;
Shed blood, and laugh; and if ye meet a wom-
  an
Hiding her babe in her scared bosom, slay her,
Slay both. – O AEnomaiis, but to think
How lone I stand now on this pitiless earth! –
Had I not parted with them! – O ye heavens,
Could ye look on and see the merciless steel
Struck at their sinless hearts?
< AENOMAIIS: Alas, alas,
Give not this way to grief.
SPARTACUS: I will not, brother;
My grief is blackened into scowling ven-
  geance. >
AENOMAIIS: Pray you, come to your tent.
SPARTACUS: To tents no more;
I couch no more but on the corse-strown
  plain, –
Draw out the troops – I say, upon the
  ground,
Pillow'd on death; thus shall my slumbers be.
Come, battle, battle. [*Exeunt*]

Scene 5

The Camp of Crassus.

*Enter Crassus, Mummius, Jovius, Lentulus,
Florus, etc. Alarums.*
CRASSUS: Thus ends rebellious rage in lunacy;
Despair hath set the gladiator mad.
Look, how with wild and impotent wrath, he
  rushes
Upon our ready spearmen! – Lentulus,
I am sorry thou didst slay his family.
LENTULUS: Nay, 'twas not I. Perhaps, *I* am not
  sorry;
They were my slaves, punish'd as fugitives.
CRASSUS: Detach the third rank and the cavalry,
On all sides to surround them. Take them
  prisoners:
This soldier death befits them not. Ten thou-
  sand
Greek drachmae to the man that brings alive
The leader Spartacus. [*Exit Lentulus*]
< JOVIUS: That ne'er will be.
He slew his horse, and thus rejecting flight,
His life devoted to the infernal gods.
CRASSUS: A valiant madman! – Had he held my
  girl –

Nay, but I should have storm'd his mountain
  camp.
Look, moves not Pompey from the Hills?
  What, friends,
Shall we stand staring at this handful foes,
Till Pompey comes to help us? To the front,
Away, to the front! [*Exeunt*]

Scene 6

Another part of the same.

Enter Spartacus, AEnomaiis, and others.
SPARTACUS: Leave slaying in the ranks, and rush
  with me
Even to the forum and praetorium,
To strike the officers.
< AENOMAIIS: See, the troops of Pompey,
Are following on our rear!
SPARTACUS: What care I for the rear? I see alone
The inviting vengeance beck'ning to the front,
Where flows the blood that Rome may bitterest
  mourn.
Let me beside the praetor. Mark, no prisoners;
Kill, kill, kill all! There's nothing now but
  blood.
Can give me joy. Now can I tell how gore
Inspires the thirsty tiger, and gives strength
Unto the fainting wolf. – No prisoners!
On to the general! >

Enter Lentulus, with others
LENTULUS: Lo, the bloody chief!
Now yield thee, villain.
SPARTACUS: Murder-spotted fiend,
Thou led'st the band that slew my wife and
  boy!
Kill, kill, kill all! [*He kills Lentulus, and exits
with the rest fighting*]

Scene 7

The praetorium.

Enter Crassus, Jovius, Julia, etc.
CRASSUS: Get thee away; thou wilt be slain.
JULIA: I fear not;
Let me look on the battle, and perhaps
Return the gift of life to Spartacus.
CRASSUS: Pr'ythee, retire. This man has won
  more honor,

Than even the braggart Pompey; for all ages
Shall own there needed two united armies
To quell him, yea, two Roman armies.
What now? Why fliest thou?

Enter Florus

FLORUS: He has broken through
The second rank. Give me more troops, and fresh,
To venge my father's death.

CRASSUS: Nay, tarry here,
And mark, how like the timbers of a ship,
Crushed in the mighty seas, the sundered wrecks
Of this rebellion vanish from our eyes.

SPARTACUS: [*Within*] On to the general!

CRASSUS: What is that cry?
This is a victory, but Pompey shares it. –
What rout is this here at our tents? By heaven,
My guards are reeling in confusion! – Lo,
What man is this, unbuckler'd and unhelm'd,
Gored with a thousand deaths, that waves so wildly,
A broken weapon?

Enter Spartacus, wounded, etc.

SPARTACUS: All is lost; but cry

Victory! On: I'll reach the general.

CRASSUS: Smite him! 'tis Spartacus. [*Spartacus is wounded by several*]

SPARTACUS: Hah! Victory!
Crassus, thou diest! I know thee very well. –
Romans are straws. – No prisoners. – Naught but blood.
Why should there be night now? – [*He falls*]

JULIA: O dear uncle, strike not.
Let him be spared. – He gave me life. – Alas,
He dies, he dies!

SPARTACUS: Well – never heed the tempest –
There are green valleys in our mountains yet. –
Set forth the sails. – We'll be in Thrace anon. – [*Dies*]

CRASSUS: Thy bark is wreck'd, but nobly did she buffet
These waves of war, and grandly lies at last,
A stranded ruin on this fatal shore.
Let him have burial; not as a base bondman,
But as a chief enfranchised and ennobled.
If we denied him honor while he lived,
Justice shall carve it on his monument.

Dead March, etc. Curtain

The End

THE DRUNKARD

OR

THE FALLEN SAVED

W. H. SMITH

MANY twentieth-century theatregoers have booed, hissed, and cheered at college, community-theatre, or night-club burlesques of *The Drunkard, or The Fallen Saved*. In the early 1950's the play concluded a twenty-year stand in Los Angeles. Few realize that the play also held endurance records a century ago. The engagement that began at Barnum's Museum on July 8, 1850, and terminated on October 7 was the first uninterrupted run of one hundred performances in the American theatre. Even before this, it had reached the hundred-performance mark in Boston, although not in a consecutive run. Responding to the temperance agitation of the period and the drive to "clean up" Boston, the play had opened there on February 25, 1844. During the Temperance Week festivities in May, the Grand Total Abstinence Celebration on Boston Common was augmented with performances of *The Drunkard* at both the Tremont Temple and the Boston Museum. The play reached its hundredth performance a year later, during the Temperance Week anniversary. Those moral and immoral days of the "fabulous forties" gave the theatre manager profit in either direction. He could present mildly naughty *tableaux vivants* or he could exploit the craze for instruction in virtuous living.

W. H. Smith, the distinguished stage manager and actor of the Boston Museum, was particularly suited to preparing a theatricalized "moral lecture" for a temperance cause. An unidentified Boston journal supplied a portrait of this noble citizen:

. . . en route to his residence on Beach street, would come Harry Smith, the very embodiment of manly beauty. In the season he invariably wore a blue dress coat with bright buttons, buff trousers and a vest, silk hat, a gracefully knotted black silk handkerchief round his neck, over which there was a wide falling collar. He was the first man in Boston who regularly wore a boutonniere. What a sight it was to see him walk, with what firmness he would tread the ground beneath him; how "seemly" he would carry his body, and what a gracefully undulating swing there was in it. Oh! Those old actors knew the art of walking on and off the stage, an art which it is to be feared, is lost nowadays.

Smith was born in Montgomeryshire, North Wales, on December 4, 1806, the son of a British army officer. When he left home at the age of fourteen to join a group of strolling players, he substituted Smith for his paternal name of Sedley. In his first regular theatrical engagement he was employed as callboy and minor player at the theatre in Shrewsbury, England, and in 1822 he joined the Theatre Royal in Lancaster as "walking gentleman." In 1827 he received an offer from Edmund Simpson of the Walnut Street Theatre in Philadelphia. On May 16 he sailed and in June made his American debut in the part of Jeremy Diddler in *Raising the Wind*. From Philadelphia he moved to the Tremont Street Theatre, Boston, in 1828; subsequently he appeared at the National and Chatham Street Theatres in New York; then back to the Tremont in Boston. Finally he became stage manager and actor at the Boston Museum. His first appearance at the Museum was in the part of Meagrim in Colman's *The Hypochondriac* on September 4, 1843. From that date until 1860 his name appeared on most of the Museum programs. He played Mercutio in the first *Romeo and Juliet* to be done in Boston, on May 7, 1845, and alternated with Junius Brutus Booth in the parts of Othello and Iago. He was principally known, however, for his rendering of the Edward Middleton role in *The Drunkard* and for his remarkable career as a stage manager. Two testimonies indicate the extent and quality of his theatrical accomplishments. The Boston *Herald* for Sunday, June 11, 1893 wrote:

He was a gentleman and a scholar, generally well grounded in the whole range of English literature; he was a most accomplished actor, thoroughly at home in any branch of his profession; he was familiar with the business and traditions of all the standard dramas, tragedies, and comedies of his time: and he was withal the most thoroughly trained swordsman on the stage. He had all the qualifications which is the province of the stage manager to be, and not as is too often the case at the present day the mere holder of the book and the ringer-down of the curtain. With such a master, what other than the best results, were to be expected.

William Warren, the Boston actor, said of him:

He was the best stage manager, in every respect, I ever played under. He knew every in and out of his business, and his discipline was perfection. When he was directing a piece, we knew there was a head to the stage and a master over us. He was never exacting, but everyone knew as by instinct that he, and he only, was the ruling spirit.

Smith's expert stage management must have contributed markedly to the phenomenal popularity of the Boston Museum during these years.

No play before *The Drunkard* had so completely captured the public's fancy. Managements that were normally in vigorous competition and unwilling to recognize merit in each other's offerings were forced to bow before the unprecedented demand for *The Drunkard*. After the Chatham opened its New York engagement on June 14, 1850, the National took it up, then later in the same month P. T. Barnum at his Museum and on July 3 the Bowery Theatre; and finally, on July 8, Barnum's Museum reopened the play, with "a strengthened cast," to begin its sensational hundred-performance engagement. Barnum's amoral beasts, birds, and freaks gave way to the moral lesson of *The Drunkard*. For three weeks the Museum and the Bowery were in nightly competition with their respective renderings, but whether because of a better production at Barnum's or because of the superior playing of C. W. Clarke – he became known as "Drunkard Clarke" – the Bowery withdrew and left the field clear for Barnum. Prior to this New York summer devoted to the Demon Rum, the play had been performed in Brooklyn, Cincinnati, and Philadelphia. After 1850 it appeared regularly throughout the country: Cleveland, New Orleans, Davenport, San Francisco, Denver, Salt Lake City – in fact, everywhere there was a theatre. An incomplete tabulation records, in the thirty-four years from 1844 to 1878, some 450 performances of this greatest of the temperance plays.

The high moral tone of the performances drew spectators who had never before dared to expose themselves to the evils of the playhouse. For example, the Reverend John Pierpont, a prominent Boston clergyman and poet (grandfather of J. P. Morgan), took the risk in order to promote the temperance cause. The play was invariably billed as a "moral drama" or a "moral lecture." For one performance at the Bowery on Sunday, July 12, 1874, it was proclaimed as a "grand sacred concert with all the sacred music."

The customary manner of the performances probably approximated Dr. and Mrs. Robinson's rendering at the American Theatre in San Francisco in January, 1852. The San Francisco *Herald* described it as follows:

Robinson delineated most truly the downward career of the young husband and father, after the "first glass," until at the last moment, in the house of correction, rescued by the untiring devotion of his wife and restored to a life of sobriety and happiness. Mrs. Robinson was equally true to nature in the part of the wife, which she played better than any character in which we have yet seen her. At the climax the charming young Miss Coad sang "Home, Sweet Home." And then, at the end, the Doctor and Mrs. Robinson came out before the curtain, leading their small son between them, and the Doctor took this occasion to pay his helpmate "a feeling tribute to her devotion in sharing with him the arduous duties of the actor's life."

Although this appears to have been the normal pattern, some performances exhibited a morbid and burlesque interest, not unlike some of the current revivals. The Denver *Rocky Mountain News* (March 5, 1861) described the playing of E. W. Wynkoop, a former bartender:

His rendition of the Drunkard was given with most thrilling effect, and in the scenes of delirium – in the intensity and strength of his mania, – he exhibited more than ordinary histrionic ability. It has been our lot to witness, and our task to soothe, the terrible agonies of one who was wild with delirium tremens; and although the scenes will never fade from our memory, it was more vividly before us last night than we have seen it for some years. The audience gave Mr. Wynkoop the most hearty applause after the scene.

Occasionally this shattering episode was given as a solo exhibition. The program for Budworth's Minstrels at the Olympic Theatre, New York, in March 1859 listed Josh Hart in "the delirium scene." At a performance in Davenport, Iowa, on April 14, 1852, "the moral Domestic Temperance Drama" of *The Drunkard* was followed by "songs, duetts, instrumental solos, etc., concluding with a new laughable Temperance Farce." At the Academy of Music on November 20, 1856, Brougham announced that his *Drunkard* was to be bolstered with "one thousand children on the stage; a new quadrille by forty-eight lads and lasses, under ten years of age, and a Scotch Strathspey by eight young ladies, under the direction of Ben Yates." *The Drunkard* was not always simply a moral lesson.

In spite of these perversions, in its first and its later years the temperance message was the important element. The "cause" had an army of crusaders in the forties, as it did at various periods in our later history. For example, during the spring of 1844 Brooklyn heard Chief Peter Printup talk on "the Progress of Temperance among the red brethren" (March 19), saw a "series of temperance dramas" (April 22), and finally heard a temperance lecture by "Mr. Gough, of Boston" (May 14).

The Drunkard was the best example of the temperance drama. There had been previous plays of the kind, in fact with the same title. One had played in Nashville, Tennessee, in 1830 and another in St. Louis in 1838, but neither of these and none of the many later dramas – *Ten Nights in a Barroom, One Glass More, Fifteen Years of a Drunkard's Life, The Drunkard's Warning*, or even Taylor's "California Temperance Panorama, covering 3,000 feet of canvas, and representing all the horrors of the liquor traffic" – ever approached the record of W. H. Smith's *The Drunkard, or The Fallen Saved*.

Theatrical companies devoted exclusively to the temperance drama, or, perhaps more correctly, devoted to seeking profit from this new audience, began to appear in New England as early as January, 1843. For the next ten years these moralists blanketed the country. Dr. and Mrs. Robinson's troupe was typical. They had begun in New Hampshire in January, 1843; had played New York the following winter, then Rochester, Buffalo, Pittsburgh, and Cleveland; and in 1852 had reached San Francisco. Always aiming "to teach lessons the moderate and fashionable must heed if they would stand secure in the midst of temptation," Robinson boasted that of the two hundred thousand persons who had patronized them "more than 10,000 had taken the Abstinence Pledge, out of which number more than 12,000 [*sic*] were drunkards." A remarkable record!

The temperance movement was a noteworthy phenomenon in American social history that was well documented in the drama, particularly in this compelling temperance lesson by W. H. Smith.

THE DRUNKARD

OR

THE FALLEN SAVED

W. H. SMITH

CHARACTERS

EDWARD MIDDLETON	LANDLORD
LAWYER CRIBBS	BAR KEEPER
WILLIAM DOWTON	WATCHMAN
FARMER GATES	MARY WILSON
FARMER STEVENS	AGNES DOWTON, *a Maniac*
OLD JOHNSON	MRS. WILSON
SAM	PATIENCE
FIRST LOAFER	JULIA
SECOND LOAFER	MISS SPINDLE
MR. RENCELAW	VILLAGERS, LOAFERS,
	WATCHMEN, ETC.

ACT I. Scene 1

Interior of a pretty rural cottage – Mrs. Wilson discovered in arm-chair, R. – Mary seated by table, L.

MRS. WILSON: It was in that corner, Mary, where your poor father breathed his last – this chair is indeed dear to me for it was in this he sat the very day before he died. Oh, how he loved this calm retreat, and often in his last illness he rejoiced that the companion of his youth would close his eyes in these rural shades, and be laid in yon little nook beside him; but now –

MARY: Dear mother. It is true, this sweet cottage is most dear to us. But we are not the proprietors. Old Mr. Middleton never troubled us much. But as our late worthy landlord is no more, it is generally believed that our dear cottage will be sold. We cannot censure his son for that.

MRS. WILSON: No; the young must be provided for, and willingly would I bow with resignation to that great power that loveth while it chasteneth; but when I think that you, my beloved child, will be left exposed to the thou-

sand temptations of life, a penniless orphan. [*A knock, C.D.*] Hark! who knocks? Dry your tears, my darling. Come in.

Enter Lawyer Cribbs, C.D. – comes down C. Good morning, sir. Mary, my child, a chair.

CRIBBS: [*Sitting, L.C.*] Good morning, Mrs. Wilson; good morning, my dear young lady. A sad calamity has befallen the neighborhood, my good Mrs. Wilson.

MRS. WILSON: Many a poor person, I fear, will have reason to think so, sir.

CRIBBS: Yes, yes. You are right. Ah! he was a good man, that Mr. Middleton. I knew him well. He placed great confidence in my advice.

MARY: Was he not very rich once, Mr. Cribbs?

CRIBBS: Yes, yes; when the times were good, but bad speculations, unlucky investments, false friends – alas! alas! We have all our ups and downs, my dear madam!

MRS. WILSON: Ah! Mr. Cribbs, I perceive you are a man, who –

CRIBBS: Has a heart to feel for the unfortunate. True, madam, it is the character I have attained, though I am not the man to boast. Have you any prospect of – that is – have you provided –

MARY: It is true, then, too true, the cottage and garden will be sold?

CRIBBS: Why, what can the young man do, my dear? A gay young man like him. Fond of the world, given somewhat to excess, no doubt. But pardon me, my dear Miss Mary; I would not call up a blush on the cheek of modesty. But you know, the extravagance, that is, the folly –

MRS. WILSON: All, sir. I understand you – very much unlike his father, I would say.

CRIBBS: I place great confidence in your prudence, Mrs. Wilson. I wish the young man well, with all my heart. Heaven knows, I have cause to do so, for his honored father's sake. [*Puts a handkerchief to his eyes*]

MRS. WILSON: Come, come, Mr. Cribbs, he is better off. It is impiety to mourn a good man's death. His end was that of a Christian.

CRIBBS: Judge, then, of the interest which I take in the last remaining scion of that honored stock. But, madam, Edward Middleton. He is yet young, and –

MRS. WILSON: I think he is not more than twenty. I recollect him when a lad, a bright, blue-eyed boy, with flaxen hair, tall of his age.

CRIBBS: Twenty-three last July, madam; that is his age, precisely – he is giddy, wild, and reckless. As the good man says, "When I was a child, I thought as a child." [*A pause – Cribbs looks around the room*] Well, madam, business is business. I am a plain man, Mrs. Wilson, and sometimes called too blunt – and – and –

MARY: You mean to say that we must leave the cottage, sir.

CRIBBS: [*Pretending feeling*] No, not *yet*, my dear young lady – I would say it is best to be prepared, and as Edward is sudden in all his movements, and as my entreaties would never change him – why, if you could find a place before he moves in the matter, it might save you from much inconvenience, that's all.

MRS. WILSON: You impose upon us a severe task, my dear sir.

CRIBBS: Bear up, my dear madam, bear up. If I may be so officious, I would try Boston – at the Intelligence Offices there, any healthy young woman, like your daughter, can obtain a profitable situation – think of it, think of it,

my good madam. I will see you again soon, and now, heaven bless you. [*Exit, C.D., and off L. – Mrs. Wilson and Mary look for a moment at each other, and then embrace*]

MRS. WILSON: Well, comfort, my daughter, comfort. It is a good thing to have a friend in the hour of trouble. This Mr. Cribbs appears to be a very feeling man; but before taking his advice, we would do well to make our proposed trial of this young man, Edward Middleton. You have the money in your purse?

MARY: It is all here, mother. Thirty dollars – the sum we have saved to purchase fuel for the winter.

MRS. WILSON: That will partially pay the rent score. When this young man finds we are disposed to deal fairly with him, he may relent. You turn pale, Mary; what ails my child?

MARY: Dear mother, it is nothing; it will soon be over – it must be done. I fear this young man. He has been described so wild, so reckless. I feel a sad foreboding –

MRS. WILSON: Fear not, Mary; call him to the door. Refuse to enter the house – give him the money, and tell him your sad story. He must, from family and association at least, have the manners of a gentleman – and however wild a youth may be, when abroad among his associates, no gentleman ever insulted a friendless and unprotected woman.

MARY: You give me courage, dear mother. I should indeed be an unnatural child, if – [*Aside*] – yet I am agitated. Oh, why do I tremble thus? [*Puts on a village bonnet, &c.*]

MRS. WILSON: [*Kisses her*] Go forth, my child – go, as the dove flew from the ark of old, and if thou shouldst fail in finding the olive branch of peace, return, and seek comfort where thou shalt surely find it – in the bosom of thy fond and widowed mother. [*Exit, R.D., and Mary, C.D.*]

Scene 2

Front and cut woods in C.

Enter Lawyer Cribbs, L.

CRIBBS: Well, that interview of mock sympathy and charity is over, and I flatter myself pretty well acted too, ha! ha! Yes, the widow and her child must quit the cottage – I'm resolved. First for the wrongs I years ago endured from

old Wilson; and secondly, it suits my own interests; and in all cases, between myself and
others, I consider the last clause as a clincher.
Ha! here comes the girl – I must watch closely
here. [*Retires, L. 2 E.*]

Mary enters, fearful and hesitating, L.

MARY: I have now nearly reached the old mansion house. In a few moments I shall see the
young man, this dissipated collegian. Oh! my
poor mother must be deceived! Such a man can
have no pity for the children of poverty, misfortune's suppliants for shelter beneath the roof
of his cottage – oh! my poor mother, little do
you know the suffering that – ha! a gentleman
approaches. My fears tell me this is the man I
seek. Shall I ever have courage to speak to
him? I will pause till he has reached the house.
[*Retires, gathering flowers, R.*]

*Enter Edward Middleton, R. 2 E., and Cribbs,
L. 2 E., meeting*

CRIBBS: Good day, good day, son of my old
friend! I have been looking for you.

EDWARD: Mr. Cribbs, your most obedient; any
friends of my father are always welcome.

CRIBBS: Well said, nobly said. I see your father
before me, when I look on you.

EDWARD: You were enquiring for me, Mr.
Cribbs?

CRIBBS: I was. I wished to see you with regard
to the cottage and lands adjoining. I have an
opportunity of selling them. When last we
talked upon this subject –

EDWARD: I was then ignorant that a poor widow
– [*Mary at back, C., listening*] – and her
only daughter –

CRIBBS: Who are in arrears for rent –

EDWARD: Had lived there many years – that my
father highly esteemed them – to turn them
forth upon the world in the present condition
of the old lady –

CRIBBS: Which old lady has a claim upon the
Alms-House. [*Mary shudders*]

EDWARD: In short, Mr. Cribbs, I cannot think
of depriving them of a home, dear to them as
the apple of their eyes – to send them forth
from the flowers which they have reared, the
vines which they have trained in their course –
a place endeared to them by tender domestic
recollections, and past remembrances of purity
and religion.

CRIBBS: Oh! all that and more – the fences which

they have neglected; the garden gate off the
hinges; the limbs of the old birch tree broken
down for firewood; the back windows ornamented with an old hat –

EDWARD: Cease, Mr. Cribbs; all this has been
explained; my foster-brother, William, has
told me the whole story. The trees were broken down by idle school-boys, and with regard
to an old hat in the window, why, it was the
hat of a man; can as much be said of yours,
Mr. Cribbs?

CRIBBS: You are pleased to be pleasant, to-day, sir.
Good morning, sir; good morning. [*Exit L.
muttering*]

EDWARD: I'm sorry I offended the old man. After all, he was the friend of the family; though
it is strange, my poor father almost always
took his advice, and was invariably unfortunate when he did so.

Reenter Cribbs, L.

CRIBBS: Good morning again; beg pardon, sir. I
now understand you better. You are right; the
daughter – fine girl – eh! sparkling eyes, eh!
dimples, roguish glances! Ah, when I was
young, eh, ha? Well, never mind; you have
seen her, eh?

EDWARD: Never; explain yourself, Mr. Cribbs.

CRIBBS: If you have not seen her, you will, you
know, eh! I understand. Traps for wild fowl;
mother and daughter grateful; love-passion;
free access to the cottage at all hours.

EDWARD: Cribbs, do you know this girl has no
father?

CRIBBS: That's it; a very wild flower, growing
on the open heath.

EDWARD: Have you forgotten that this poor girl
has not a brother?

CRIBBS: A garden without a fence, not a stake
standing. You have nothing to do but to step
into it.

EDWARD: Old man! I respect your gray hairs. I
knew an old man once, peace to his ashes,
whose hair was as gray as yours; but beneath
that aged breast there beat a heart, pure as the
first throbs of childhood. He was as old as you
– he was more aged; his limbs tottered as
yours do not – I let you go in peace. But had
that old man heard you utter such foul sentences to his son; had he heard you tell me to
enter, like a wolf, this fold of innocence, and
tear from her mother's arms the hope of her
old age, he would have forgotten the winters

that had dried the pith within his aged limbs, seized you by the throat, and dashed you prostrate to the earth, as too foul a carcass to walk erect and mock the name of man. [*Crosses, L.*]

CRIBBS: But, Mr. Middleton, sir —

EDWARD: Leave me, old man; begone; your hot, lascivious breath cannot mingle with the sweet odor of these essenced wild flowers. Your raven voice will not harmonize with the warblings of these heavenly songsters, pouring forth their praises to that Almighty power, who looks with horror on your brutal crime. [*Crosses, R., Mary rushes forward, C., and kneels*]

MARY: The blessings of the widow and fatherless be upon thee; may they accompany thy voice to Heaven's tribunal, not to cry for vengeance, but plead for pardon on this wretched man.

CRIBBS: Ha! The widow's daughter! Mr. Middleton, you mistake me. I — I cannot endure a woman's tears. I — poor child! [*Aside*] I'll be terribly revenged for this. [*Exit Cribbs, L. 2 E.*]

EDWARD: This, then, is the widow's child, nurtured in the wilderness. She knows not the cold forms of the fashionable miscalled world. Cribbs, too, gone; a tale of scandal — I'll overtake the rascal, and at least give no color to his base fabrications. [*Crossing, and going, L.*]

MARY: [*R.*] Stay, sir, I pray you. I have an errand for you. This is part of the rent, which — [*Holding out money*]

EDWARD: Nay, then, you have not overheard my discourse with the old man, who has just left us. I have told him —

MARY: That we should still remain in the cottage. Oh sir! is that a reason we should withhold from you these dues? now paid with double pleasure, since we recognize a benefactor in our creditor — take this, I entreat, 'tis but a portion of the debt; but be assured, the remainder shall be paid as soon as busy, willing hands can earn it.

EDWARD: Nay, nay, dear girl; keep it as a portion of your dowry.

MARY: Sir!

EDWARD: If you have overheard the dialogue that I just held with that old man, you must know that I sometimes speak very plain.

MARY: [*Apprehensively*] Yes, sir.

EDWARD: I have spoken plainly to him: shall I now speak plainly to you?

MARY: Alas, sir! It is not our fault that the fences are broken down. When my poor father lived, it was not so. But since —

EDWARD: When that vile old man spoke to me of your charms, I heeded him not. There are plenty of pretty girls in this section of the country; but I have since discovered what I had before heard, something more than the ordinary beauty which he described. A charm that he is incapable of appreciating. The charm of mental excellence, noble sentiment, filial piety. These are the beauties that render you conspicuous above all the maidens I have seen. These are the charms which bind captive the hearts of men. I speak plainly, for I speak honestly, and when I ask you to keep that money as a portion of your dowry, need I say into whose hands I would like to have it fall at last.

MARY: [*Droops her head during the above*] To affect — to affect not to understand you, sir, would be an idle return for kindness such as yours, and yet —

EDWARD: I sometimes walk down in the vicinity of your cottage, and —

MARY: Should I see you go by without stopping — why, then —

EDWARD: Then what, dear Mary?

MARY: Then I should suppose you had forgotten where we lived.

EDWARD: Thanks! [*Kisses her hand*] Ah! little did I think when I thought of selling that dear old cottage, that it should be regarded as a casket, invaluable for the jewel it contained. [*Leads her off, L.U.E.*]

Scene 3

Interior of Miss Spindle's dwelling house. — Miss Spindle discovered at toilette table, R.

MISS SPINDLE: The attractions of the fair sex are *synonymous*. True, old *Bonus* is the destroyer of female charms; but as my beautiful poet, Natty P. says, in his sublime epistle to Lucinda Octavia Pauline, "Age cannot wither me, nor custom stale my infinite *vacuity*." But time is money, then money is time, and we bring back, by the aid of money, the times of youth. I value my beauty at fifty dollars a year, as that is about the sum it costs me for keeping it in repair year by year. Well, say that my beauty is repaired in this way, year by year; well, what then! I have heard a gentleman say that a pair of boots when repaired and foxed were better than they were when new. Why should it not be so with our charms? Certainly, they last longer in this way. We can have red cheeks at seventy, and, thanks to the dentist, good teeth at any time of life. Woman was made for love. They suppose that my heart is unsusceptible of the tender passion. But the heart can be regulated by money, too. I buy all the affecting novels, and all the terrible romances, and read them till my heart has become soft as maiden wax, to receive the impression of that cherished image I adore. Ah! as true as I live, there goes his foster-brother, William, by the window. Hem, William! [*Taps at window, C. – Williams sings without, L.*]

"When I was a young and roving boy,
Where fancy led me I did wander,
Sweet Caroline was all my joy,
But I missed the goose and hit the gander."

Enter William Dowton, L.

WILLIAM: Good day, Miss Spindle.

MISS SPINDLE: You heard my rap, William?

WILLIAM: As much as ever, Miss Spindle. Such fingers as yours don't make a noise like the fist of a butcher.

MISS SPINDLE: My hand is small, William, but I did not suppose that you had noticed it.

WILLIAM: I only noticed it by the lightness of your tap. So I supposed you must be very light fingered.

MISS SPINDLE: Pray, sit down, William; take a chair; don't be bashful; you're too modest.

WILLIAM: It's a failing I've got, Miss Spindle. I'm so modest I always go to bed without a candle. [*Both sit, C.*]

MISS SPINDLE: [*R.C.*] Shall I tell you what I have thought, William?

WILLIAM: [*L.C.*] Why that's just as you agree to with yourself. I don't care much about it, one way or t'other.

MISS SPINDLE: You were singing as you came in, William. I suppose you know I sometimes invoke the help of Polyhymnia.

WILLIAM: Why, I don't know as to the help of Polyhym-him-nina, but if you want a good *help*, you can't do better than hire Polly Striker, old Farmer Jones's wife's daughter, by her first husband.

MISS SPINDLE: You don't understand the Heathen mythology William.

WILLIAM: Why, I hear Parson Roundtext talk sometimes of the poor benighted heathen; but I am free to say, that I can't come anything in regard to their conchology, as you call it. Will you have some shell-barks, or chestnuts, Miss Spindle?

MISS SPINDLE: No, William. But this is what I have thought, William, there are two sorts of men.

WILLIAM: Oh, yes, Miss Spindle, long ones and short ones, like cigars. Sometimes the short ones are the best smoking, too.

MISS SPINDLE: You mistake my meaning, William. Some are warm and susceptible of the charms of women.

WILLIAM: Warm, oh, yes. Florida boys, and Carolina niggers, eh?

MISS SPINDLE: While others are *cold*, and apparently insensible to our beauties –

WILLIAM: Oh, yes. Newfoundlanders, Canada fellows, and Bluenoses.

MISS SPINDLE: Now, William, *dear* William, this is the confession I would confide in your generous secrecy. I have a trembling affection, and then, a warm, yet modest flame.

WILLIAM: Trembling affection, warm flame, why, the old girl's got the fever and ague.

MISS SPINDLE: And how to combat with this dear, yet relentless foe.

WILLIAM: Put your feet into warm water, and wood ashes, take two quarts of boiling hot arb tea. Cover yourself with four thick blankets, and six Canada comforters, take a good perspicacity, and you'll be well in the morning.

MISS SPINDLE: Sir!

WILLIAM: That's old Ma'am Brown's recipe for fever and ague, and I never yet found it fail.

MISS SPINDLE: Fever and ague! You mistake me, William, I have an ardent passion.

WILLIAM: Don't be in a passion, Miss Spindle, it's bad for your complaint.

MISS SPINDLE: You will not understand. I have a passion for one.

WILLIAM: For one! Well, it's very lucky it's only one.

MISS SPINDLE: Can you not fancy who that one is? He lives in your house.

WILLIAM: Well, I'm darned, Miss Spindle, it's either me or Mr. Middleton.

MISS SPINDLE: I never can bestow my hand without my heart, William –

WILLIAM: Why, I think myself they ought to be included in the same bill of sale.

MISS SPINDLE: Ah! William, have you ever read the "Children of the Abbey?"

WILLIAM: No, Miss Spindle, but I've read the "Babes of the Wood."

MISS SPINDLE: I have read all the Romantics of the day. I have just finished Mr. Cooper's Trapper.

WILLIAM: Oh! I dare say she understands trap, but she don't come the trapper over my foster-brother this year.

MISS SPINDLE: He understands little of the refinements of the civilized circular. I must try something else. How do you like my new green dress? How does it become me?

WILLIAM: Beautiful! It matches very well indeed, ma'rm.

MISS SPINDLE: Matches with what, William?

WILLIAM: With your eyes, ma'rm.

MISS SPINDLE: It becomes my complexion, William.

WILLIAM: It's a beautiful match – like a span of gray horses.

MISS SPINDLE: Does your master fancy green, William?

WILLIAM: Oh, yes, ma'rm. He loves it fine, I tell you.

MISS SPINDLE: But in what respect? How did you find it out?

WILLIAM: In respect of drinking, ma'rm.

MISS SPINDLE: Drinking!

WILLIAM: Yes. He always tells the cook to make green tea.

MISS SPINDLE: Well, William, how about the cottage? When are you going to turn out those Wilsons?

WILLIAM: The girl will be out of that place soon, depend on that ma'rm.

MISS SPINDLE: I'm glad to hear it. I never could endure those Wilsons, and it's a duty when one knows that respectable people like your master are injured, to speak out. I know they haven't paid their rent, and do you know, that girl was seen getting into a chaise with a young man, when she ought to have been at work, and she did not return till nine o'clock at night, William, for I took the pains to put on my hood and cloak and look for myself – though it was raining awful.

WILLIAM: That was the time you cotched the fever, the fever and ague, ma'rm. Well, good-bye.

MISS SPINDLE: Are you going, William?

WILLIAM: Yes, ma'rm. I shall be wanted to hum. You take care of your precious health, ma'rm. Keep your feet warm, and your head cool; your mouth shut, and your heart open, and you'll soon have good health, good conscience, and stand well on your pins, ma'rm. Good morning, ma'rm.

"To reap, to sow, to plough and mow,
And be a farmer's boy, and be a farmer's boy."

Exit William, L.

MISS SPINDLE: The vulgar creature! But what could I expect? He ought to know that American ladies ought never to have any pins. But I am certain for all this, Edward, dear Edward, is dying for me – as the poet, Dr. Lardner, says: "He lets concealment, like a worm in the bud, feed on the damask curtains of – his – cheek" – damask bud. I'm quite sure it's something about bud. Yes, I am convinced, my charms as yet are undecayed, and even when old age comes on, the charm of refined education will still remain – as the immortal Chelsea Beach Poet has it:

"You may break, you may ruin the vase, if
you will,
The scent of the roses will cling round it still."

Exit, affectedly, R.

Scene 4

Landscape view. Enter Patience Brayton, Sam Evans, Old Johnson, Male and Female Villagers, R.U.E. – Music.

PATIENCE: Come, there's young men enough, let's have a ring-play.

ALL: Yes, a ring-play. A ring-play! fall in here.

SAM: Come, darnation, who'll go inside?

PATIENCE: Go in yourself, Sam.

SAM: Well, I'm agreed. Go on. [*They form a circle and revolve round the young man, singing*]

"I am a rich widow, I live all alone,
I have but one son, and he is my own.
Go, son, go, son, go choose you one,
Go choose a good one, or else choose none."

Sam chooses one of the girls – She enters the

ring – He kisses her, and the ring goes round

"*Now, you are married you must obey*
What you have heard your parents say.
Now you are married you must prove true,
As you see others do, so do you."

The ring goes round – Patience, who is in the ring, chooses Old Johnson

PATIENCE:

"*Mercy on me, what have I done?*
I've married the father instead of the son.
His legs are crooked, and ill put on.
They are all laughing at my old man."

A general laugh

SAM: Come, girls, you forget 'tis almost time for Mary Wilson's wedding.

PATIENCE: [*R.C.*] Well, now, ain't we forgetting how proud she must be, going to marry a college-bred.

JOHNSON: [*L.C.*] She'll be none the better for that. Larning don't buy the child a new frock.

SAM: Well, let's have a dance, and be off at once.

ALL: Yes. Partners. A dance! a dance!

A village dance, and exit, L.

Enter Lawyer Cribbs, L.

CRIBBS: Thus ends my prudent endeavors to get rid of those Wilsons. But, young Middleton, there is yet some hope of him. He is at present annoyed at my well intended advice, but that shall not part us easily. I will do him some unexpected favor, worm myself into his good graces, invite him to the village barroom, and if he falls, then, ha! ha! I shall see them begging their bread yet. The wife on her bended knees to me, praying for a morsel of food for her starving children – it will be revenge! revenge! Here comes his foster-brother, William. I'll wheedle him – try the ground before I put my foot on it.

Enter William Dowton, whistling, L.

WILLIAM: Lawyer Cribbs, have you seen my poor, little, half-witted sister, Agnes, eh?

CRIBBS: No, William, my honest fellow, I have not. I want to speak to you a moment.

WILLIAM: [*Crossing, R.*] What does old Razor Chops want with me, I wonder. Well, lawyer, what is it?

CRIBBS: You seem to be in a hurry. They keep you moving, I see.

WILLIAM: These are pretty busy times, sir. Mr. Edward is going to be married – that's a dose. [*Aside*] Senna and salts.

CRIBBS: Yes, yes, ahem! Glad to hear it.

WILLIAM: Yes, I thought you seemed pleased. [*Aside*] Looks as sour as Sam Jones, when he swallowed vinegar for sweet cider.

CRIBBS: I am a friend to early marriages, although I never was married myself. Give my best respects to Mr. Edward.

WILLIAM: Sir?

CRIBBS: William, suppose I leave it to your ingenuity to get me an invitation to the wedding, eh? And here's a half-dollar to drink my health.

WILLIAM: No, I thank you, lawyer, I don't want your money.

CRIBBS: Oh, very well; no offence meant, you know. Let's step into the tavern, and take a horn to the happiness of the young couple.

WILLIAM: Lawyer Cribbs, or Squire, as they call you, it's my opinion, when your uncle Beelzebub wants to bribe an honest fellow to do a bad action, he'd better hire a pettifogging bad lawyer to tempt him, with a counterfeit dollar in one hand, and a bottle of rum in the other. [*Exit William, R.*]

CRIBBS: Ah, ah! You're a cunning scoundrel, but I'll fix you yet.

AGNES: [*Sings without, L.*]

"*Brake and fern and cypress dell,*
Where the slippery adder crawls."

CRIBBS: Here comes that crazy sister of his. She knows too much for my happiness. Will the creature never die! Her voice haunts me like the spectre of the youth that was engaged to her; for my own purposes, I ruined, I triumphed over him – he fell – died in a drunken fit, and she went crazy. Why don't the Alms-House keep such brats at home?

Enter Agnes, deranged, L.

AGNES:

"*Brake and fern and cypress dell,*
Where the slippery adder crawls.
Where the grassy waters well,
By the old moss-covered walls."

For the old man has his gray locks, and the young girl her fantasies.

"Upon the heather, when the weather
Is as mild as May,
So they prance, as they dance,
And we'll all be gay."

But they poured too much red water in his glass. The lawyer is a fine man, ha, ha! He lives in the brick house yonder. But the will. Ah, ha, ha! the will –

CRIBBS: [*Angrily*] Go home, Agnes, go home.

AGNES: Home! I saw a little wren yesterday. I had passed her nest often. I had counted the eggs, they were so pretty – beautiful, so beautiful – rough Robin of the mill came this morning and stole them. The little bird went to her nest, and looked in – they were gone. She chirruped mournfully and flew away. *She won't go home any more.*

CRIBBS: Agnes, who let you out? You distress the neighborhood with your muttering and singing. [*Threatening*] I'll have you taken care of.

AGNES: There's to be a wedding in the village. I saw a coffin carried in full of bridal cake.

"And the bride was red with weeping,
. *Cypress in her hair."*

Can you tell why they cry at weddings? Is it for joy? I used to weep when I was joyful. You never weep, old man. I should have been married, but my wedding dress was mildewed, so we put off the marriage till another day. They'll make a new dress for me. They say he won't come again to me, and then the will, ha, ha, old man, the will.

CRIBBS: Ha, confusion! Get you gone, or thus – [*Seizes her and raises cane – William enters rapidly, R., and throws him round to R. corner*]

WILLIAM: [*L.C.*] Why, you tarnation old black varmint! Strike my little, helpless, half-crazed sister! If it was not for your gray hairs, I'd break every bone in your black beetle body. If all I have heard be true, you'll have to account for –

CRIBBS: [*Rising, R.*] You'll rue this, young man, if there's any law in the land. A plain case of assault and battery. I'll put you in jail. Predicaments, premunires, fifa's and fieri fa-

cias. I'll put you between stone walls. [*Exit blustering, R.*]

WILLIAM: Put me between stone walls! If you'd have been put between two posts with a cross-beam long ago, you'd had your due, old land-shark. You stay here, darling Agnes, till I come back. Fiery faces, and predicaments! If I can get you near enough to a horse-pond, I'll cool your fiery face, I'll warrant. [*Exit, R.*]

AGNES: [*Scattering flowers and singing*]

"They lived down in the valley,
Their house was painted red,
And every day the robin came
To pick the crumbs of bread."

But the grass does not wither when they die. I will sit down till I hear the bells that are far off, for then, I think of his words. Who says he did not love me? It was a good character he wanted of the parson. A girl out of place is like an old man out of his grave. [*Bells chime piano*] They won't ask me to their merry-makings, now, though I washed my best calico in the brook.

"Walk up young man, there's a lady here,
With jewels in her hair."

[*Suddenly clasps her hands and screams*] Water, water! hear him, oh, hear him cry for water; quick! he'll turn cold again! his lips are blue; water, water! [*Exit frantically, L.*]

Scene 5

A village – Exterior of a beautiful cottage, L. Enter procession, R. U. E., of villagers – Edward, Mary, Mrs. Wilson – Clergyman, children with baskets of flowers – Bridesman and Bridesmaid, etc. etc. – Bells ringing – They enter, come down, R., to front, cross and up stage on L., singing chorus.

"Hail, hail! happy pair!
Bells are ringing, sweet birds singing,
All around now speaks of bliss;
Bright roses bringing – flowers flinging,
Peace, purity and happiness."

EDWARD: [*L.C.*] Dearest Mary, ah, now indeed, my own; words are too poor, too weak, to express the joy, the happiness that agitates my heart. Ah, dear, dear wife, may each propitious day that dawns upon thy future life, but add another flower to the rosy garland that now encircles thee.

MARY: [*L.*] Thanks, Edward, my own loved husband, thy benison is echoed from my inmost heart. Ah, neighbor Johnson, many thanks for your kind remembrance of your pupils. My dear friends, your children, too, are here.

JOHNSON: [*R.*] Yes, my dear Mary, your happiness sheds its genial rays around old and young. Young man, I was a witness at your father's wedding. May your life be like his – an existence marked by probity and honor, and your death as tranquil. Mrs. Wilson, I remember your sweet daughter, when but a child of nine years, and that seems only yesterday.

MARY: Dear Patience, I am glad to see you, too, and who is this, your brother? [*Points to Sam, L. corner*]

PATIENCE: [*L.*] No. An acquaintance, that –

SAM: Yes. An acquaintance that –

MARY: Oh, yes, I understand.

MRS. WILSON: My dearest children, the blessings of a bereaved heart, rest, like the dews of heaven, upon you. Come, neighbors, this is a festival of joy. Be happy, I entreat.

WILLIAM: Well, if there's any one here happier than Bill Dowton, I should like to know it, that's all. Come lads and lasses, sing, dance, and be merry. [*Dance – tableau*]

End of Act I

ACT II. Scene 1

A chamber in Miss Spindle's house. – Lawyer Cribbs and Miss Spindle discovered, seated, C.

CRIBBS: [*L.*] Be explicit, my dear madam; this is a most serious affair; breach of promise, marriage promise. How my heart bleeds for you, dear young lady, suffering virtue. But tell me the particulars.

MISS SPINDLE: [*R.*] Oh, sir, why will you cause me to harrow up my feelings; my bleeding heart, by the recital of my afflictions. I have "let concealment like a" caterpillar on a button-wood, feed on my cambric cheek – and – [*Aside*] I can't remember the rest of it.

CRIBBS: Alas, poor lady! pray go on.

MISS SPINDLE: The first of our acquaintance was down at a corn-husking. Not that I make a practice of attending such vulgar places, Squire, but –

CRIBBS: Oh, certainly not – certainly not.

MISS SPINDLE: Well, I was over-persuaded. I set up and stripped the dry coatings from the yellow corn – only two ears – I husked no more, Squire.

CRIBBS: Indeed, indeed! two ears – you are certain it was but two ears? It is best to be particular. We shall make out a prima facie case.

MISS SPINDLE: Well, I got hold of a red ear, it was the last I husked. I think it was a red ear; so I was obliged to be kissed. Oh, Squire, think of my mortification, when I was told that such was the invariable rule – the custom at a husking.

CRIBBS: [*With energy*] Your suffering must have been intolerable.

MISS SPINDLE: Oh, sir, you know how to feel for delicate timidity. A big, coarse, young man, called Bill Bullus, rose up to snatch the fragrance from my unwilling cheek –

CRIBBS: [*Groans*] Oh!

MISS SPINDLE: I put up my kerchief – it was a cambric, a fine cambric, Squire Cribbs, and said I had a choice in those things – looking at Edward, whom I took to be a gentleman, you know. He took the hint immediately. Bullus fell back, appalled at my manner, and Edward – oh, sir! spare my blushes.

CRIBBS: I understand – he – yes. I understand.

MISS SPINDLE: He did it, sir. I felt the pressure of his warm lip on –

CRIBBS: Your cheek, of course.

MISS SPINDLE: Oh, no, no, sir. It was said, by my friend, the Chelsea Beach Bard, that from my lips he stole ambrosial blisses.

CRIBBS: Enormous! but go on.

MISS SPINDLE: You may judge what was my confusion.

CRIBBS: Certainly, Miss Spindle.

MISS SPINDLE: The ear of corn was not more red than was my burnished cheek.

CRIBBS: I do not know, my dear young lady, but you might make out a case of assault and battery.

MISS SPINDLE: It was very rude for a college-bred. Well, after that he bowed to me as we were coming out of church.

CRIBBS: Aha! the evidence comes in. Have you got proof of that, most injured fair one?

MISS SPINDLE: Oh, sir, no proof would be required. I trust that a person of my respectability need bring no proof of what they know. Well, after that I was agoing down to Mr. Simmons', and lo, a cow stood in the road. I must pass within twenty feet of the ferocious animal if I continued my route; providentially, at the very instant, Edward came down the road that turns up by Wollcott's mill. He saw my strait. He saw that I stood trembling like some fragile flower tossed by the winds of heaven. Like Sir William Wallace flying to the rescue of the Greeks, he came panting on the wings of love. He rushed like an armed castle to the side of the cow, and she wheeled about like the great leviathan of the deep, and trotted down towards the school-house.

CRIBBS: I can imagine your feelings, Miss Spindle – a delicate young lady in imminent danger. But he did no more than any man would have done.

MISS SPINDLE: Well, sir, you may judge what were the feelings of my palpitating heart, tender as it always was –

CRIBBS: Have any letters passed between you?

MISS SPINDLE: Oh, yes, yes; five or six, sir.

CRIBBS: We've got him there, aha! If Miss Spindle would be so condescending as just to show me one of those letters.

MISS SPINDLE: He's got them all in his possession.

CRIBBS: Unfortunate! horrible! How did he obtain possession of those letters?

MISS SPINDLE: Oh! I sent them – sometimes by one person, sometimes by another.

CRIBBS: How, madam? *His* letters, I mean – how did he get –

MISS SPINDLE: Oh, sir, mark his ingratitude. I sent him half a dozen –

CRIBBS: [*Discouraged*] Oh! I understand. The correspondence was all on one side, then?

MISS SPINDLE: Not one letter did he write to me. Ah! sir, think of it; all my tenderness, all my devotion. Oh! my breaking heart.

CRIBBS: [*Aside*] Oh! humbug! Well, good day, Miss Spindle. I have a pressing engagement, and –

MISS SPINDLE: Well, but, lawyer Cribbs, what is your advice? How ought I to proceed?

CRIBBS: Get your friends to send you to the insane hospital, and place you among the incurable, as the most rusty, idiotic old maid that ever knit stockings. [*Exit hastily, R.*]

MISS SPINDLE: Spirit of Lucretia Borgia! Polish pattern of purity – was there ever such a Yankee hedgehog! [*Exit angrily, R.*]

Scene 2

A landscape. Enter William Dowton, R., Farmer Gates, and Farmer Stevens, meeting.

GATES: [*C.*] Good day, good day. Mr. Edward was not at church last Sabbath.

STEVENS: I heard tell where he was in the afternoon.

GATES: Aye, Stevens, you told me. Well, well, I'm right sorry. We used to consider Mr. Edward a promising young man, and when we seed him get married and settle among us, we thought to have a respectable man like his father for a neighbor, and that, like him, he'd go to the general court one of these days. I earnestly hope he hain't agoing to stick to these bad ways.

WILLIAM: [*R.*] I don't exactly know what you mean, Farmer Gates. Mr. Middleton is about the same free, kind-hearted fellow that he ever was, it appears to me. No longer ago than this blessed morning, he says to me, Bill, says he, your birth-day comes this day week, go to Ned Grogan's, the tailor, next the post-office, and get yourself measured for a new suit of clothes at my expense. Now if I, that lives with him, and sees everything he does, think well of him, I don't know as other folks need be so very perpendicular about it.

STEVENS: Well, well, I'll tell you what I have heard; you know Squire Cribbs?

WILLIAM: In course I does.

STEVENS: Well, he says that if your foster-brother doesn't attend a little more to his own interest –

WILLIAM: He'll do it for him, I suppose? Now, Mr. Stevens, I'll tell you what I think of that sly old fox, Squire Cribbs. He takes to wickedness just as natural as young ducks take to water. I think, really, if Mr. Edward's soul was put in a great box, that seven thousand such souls as that black beetle's wouldn't fill up the chinks – the spare room round the edges.

GATES: Give us your hand, Bill, my man. Lawyer Cribbs bears but a middling character hereabout. He has got a prodigious sight of larning, and 'tis not for the likes of me to pretend to decide between you; but I'll be darned if I don't like the man that stands up for him whose bread he eats; and so, Bill, any time you want a drink of cider, just call up our way, and you shall have what you can drink, if it's a gallon. [*Exit, R.*]

STEVENS: Well, well, William, after all neighbor Gates has said, I fear the young man's in a dangerous way – spending his Sabbaths going about the country from one tavern to another. I don't say that he does take too much liquor – but there's a great many that has begun that way. [*Exit, R.*]

WILLIAM: [*Rather serious*] Well, good bye to you, and thank ye. I don't think Mr. Edward drinks any too much – at least I hope not. For my part I wish he'd never seen anything stronger than milk or green tea. I wish I hadn't seen them two fellers, they've just made me feel as bad as ever, when I thought I was getting well over it, and beginning to see daylight again. What, dear Mr. Edward, with such a sweet lamb of a wife, and the prettiest little girl that ever drew breath – oh, no, it's nothing. I won't borrow trouble – he just took part of a bowl of punch with a friend at the Flying Horse – but that's no more than the parson himself might do, and there's Deacon Whiteleather, he never sits down to dinner without a stiff horn of something to wash it down. Well, now, I think it's better let alone altogether – for if a man doesn't put his hand in the fire, he runs a better chance of not burning his fingers. [*Exit, R.*]

Scene 3

A Country Bar-room – Stevens, the drover, seated at table – Several loafers – Landlord behind bar attending.

STEVENS: [*Seated, R.C.*] Well, I don't know, Mr. Landlord, them are 'counts we have about Queen Victory, amounts to just about as much as the frogs and mice.

LANDLORD: Oh, that's Pope; we've got the book in the house now – the battle of frogs and mice.

2ND LOAFER: Landlord, will you just score up another three-center – I feel deuced bad.

LANDLORD: No, thank'ye, Sam; rub off old scores, and then –

Enter Edward Middleton, dress rather shabby, from door, R. – All look at him; he walks up to the bar

EDWARD: Give me some brandy. [*Drinks*] How much, landlord?

LANDLORD: A six-pence, sir. This is something 'sperior; a bottle I keep for those who are willing to pay a little more – are you quite well, sir?

EDWARD: Well, well, quite well, I thank you – this is good, landlord, another glass.

Enter Cribbs, R.D.

CRIBBS: Ah! Mr. Middleton, you here! He! he! he! Well, come, that's a good one. First time I was ever here, except on business – dare say you can say the same. Well, this is fine. Now, my young friend, since we have met each other, we'll honor the house.

LANDLORD: Squire, how are you; glad to see you. [*Shakes hands across the bar*] What's it to be, gentlemen. The same, Mr. Middleton?

EDWARD: Oh! I must be excused; you know I have just drank.

CRIBBS: Well; well, I'll leave it to him. Landlord, how long is it since I've seen you?

LANDLORD: Why, Squire, it must be full ten years ago; you remember the day Si Morton had his raising? the day I saw you digging in the woods.

CRIBBS: [*Starts violently*] Go on, go on – nothing but the cramp. I'm subject to it.

LANDLORD: Well, Squire, I've never seed you since then.

CRIBBS: Well, come let's drink; come, Edward.

LANDLORD: Oh, take a little more, Mr. Middleton – the Squire wouldn't advise you to what wasn't right.

EDWARD: Well, I –

CRIBBS: Well, come, here's whiskey – good whiskey.

EDWARD: I believe I drank –

LANDLORD: Mr. Middleton drank brandy before.

CRIBBS: Not half so healthy as good whiskey.

EDWARD: Oh, whiskey be it. It can't be stronger than the other was. [*Stevens looks up and shakes his head*]

EDWARD: [*Drinks*] Well, this is pleasant, ha! ha! this goes to the right place, eh, Cribbs. Is this Irish whiskey?

LANDLORD: Yes, sir; pure Innishowen.

EDWARD: Well, the Irish are a noble people, ain't they, Cribbs? [*Slightly intoxicated*] Friend

Cribbs, I think I may call you. I never doubted it.

CRIBBS: Never!

EDWARD: Oh! I might have suspected; but "suspicion's but at best a coward's virtue;" the sober second thought –

CRIBBS: Oh, exactly. [*Shaking his hand earnestly*]

EDWARD: I have a heart, Cribbs – [*Getting tipsy*] I have a heart; landlord, more whiskey; come, gentlemen, come one, come all. Landlord!

LANDLORD: In one minute, sir.

EDWARD: Landlord, give them all anything they want. Come – a bumper – here's the health of my old tried friend, Cribbs. [*Drinks it off*]

CRIBBS: [*Throwing away his liquor unseen*] Well, here goes.

EDWARD: Landlord! landlord.

LANDLORD: Sir?

EDWARD: I have a heart, Cribbs. We know how to do the handsome thing, landlord. [*Cribbs slyly fills Edward's glass*]

LANDLORD: Don't we? It takes us, sir.

EDWARD: [*Drinks*] Well, I think, landlord, a little spirit hurts no man.

LANDLORD: Oh, no, sir; no – does him good.

EDWARD: I have a heart, Squibbs – a heart, my old boy. Come, let's have another horn. – [*1st loafer falls asleep on bench R. against partition*] – Come, boys, trot up, I'll pay.

2ND LOAFER: Well, I don't want to hurt the house.

3RD LOAFER: Oh, no – mustn't hurt the house. [*Walking up to bar*]

STEVENS: Come, don't you hear the news? [*Strikes 1st loafer with whip, and he falls on ground*]

1ST LOAFER: Hollo! what's that for?

EDWARD: Come, tread up, and drink.

1ST LOAFER: Well – [*Lazily*] – I don't want to hurt the house. [*Tumbles against wall*]

LANDLORD: You will hurt the house, if you butt off the plastering at that rate.

EDWARD: A bumper – well, in the absence of Burgundy, whiskey will do, eh, old Ribbs – [*Hitting Cribbs*] – Why don't you join us, old sulky. [*To Stevens*]

STEVENS: I drink when I'm dry, and what I drink I pay for.

EDWARD: You're saucy, old fellow.

STEVENS: Do you think I'm a sponge, to put my hands into another man's pocket? Go away, you make a fool of yourself.

EDWARD: A fool! Say that again, and I'll knock you down – a fool!

STEVENS: [*Rising*] I want nothing to say to you – be off – you're drunk.

EDWARD: [*Strikes him*] Death and fury! drunk?

STEVENS: Take that, then – [*Cribbs and others sneak off – struggle – Stevens hits him down with whip*] – Landlord, you see I was not to blame for this. [*Exit Stevens, R.D.*]

LANDLORD: Well, he's got it, anyhow – serve him right, quarrelsome young fool. House was quiet enough till he came in disturbing honest people. This is too bad. How to get this fellow home? He lives two miles from here, at least.

Enter William Dowton, R.D.

WILLIAM: Mr. Middleton – where is he? Lord ha'mercy, what is this? Speak! [*Seizes Landlord*] If you have done this, I'll tear out your cursed windpipe, old heathen.

LANDLORD: In my own house? Let go my throat.

WILLIAM: Who did this?

LANDLORD: Let go; it wasn't me, it was drover Stevens.

WILLIAM: [*Throws him off, kneels by Middleton*] Blood on his forehead – Mr. Edward, speak to me, oh, speak – his poor wife – poor, old, sick Mrs. Wilson, too.

EDWARD: [*Reviving*] What is this? What's been the matter here?

WILLIAM: Don't you know me, sir? It's William, sir, poor Bill, come to help you home. Sam Stanhope told me you were in a row at the tavern, sir.

EDWARD: Oh, yes, I remember; where are they all? Where's Cribbs? where's Cribbs?

WILLIAM: Cribbs! was he with him?

LANDLORD: Why, yes, I guess the Squire was here a short spell. Well, you can walk, sir, can't you?

EDWARD: Walk, yes, I can walk – what's the matter with my head? Blood? I must have fallen against the corner of the bench.

LANDLORD: Don't you remember Mr. Stevens?

EDWARD: I don't know what you mean by Stevens; what the devil have I been about?

LANDLORD: Why, Stevens said you were drunk, and you hit him, and he knocked you down with his whip-handle.

WILLIAM: And if I get hold of Mr. Stevens, I'll

make him smell something nastier than peaches, or my name's not Bill. Come, sir; come home.

EDWARD: Drunk! fighting! Oh, shame! shame!

WILLIAM: Lean on me, Mr. Edward. You go sand your sugar, and water your bad brandy, old corkscrew! His poor wife!

EDWARD: Hush, William, hush.

WILLIAM: Pray give me your pardon, sir; oh, I wish I had died before I had seen this.

EDWARD: Drunk, fighting – my wife, my children! Oh agony! agony! [*Exit leaning on William, L.D. – Landlord retires behind bar*]

Scene 4

Landscape view. Enter Cribbs, L.

CRIBBS: So far the scheme works admirably. I know his nature well. He has tasted, and will not stop now short of madness or oblivion. I mostly fear his wife, she will have great influence over him. Ah, who's this, Bill Dowton? Where, then, is Middleton. [*Retires, L.*]

Enter William Dowton, L.

WILLIAM: Well, I don't know but he's right; poor fellow, if he were to appear before his wife, without her being warned, it might frighten her to death, poor thing, and as he says, the walk alone may do him good, and sober him a bit. The old woman takes on most cruel, too, and she so very, very ill. Here he comes. I guess he'll follow me. I'll hasten on, for if he sees me, he'll be angry, and swear I'm watching him. That old sarpent Cribbs, he'd better keep out of my track. I'd think no more of wringing his old neck, than I would twisting a tough thanksgiving turkey. [*Exit threatening, R.*]

CRIBBS: [*Advancing cautiously*] I'm much obliged to you, most valiant Billy Dowton. I shall hold myself *non est inventus*, I promise you; here comes Edward. Caution, caution. [*Retires, L.*]

Enter Edward, L.

EDWARD: Is this to be the issue of my life? Oh, must I ever yield to the fell tempter, and bending like a weak bulrush to the blast, still bow my manhood lower than the brute? Why, surely I have eyes to see, hands to work with, feet to walk, and brain to think, yet the best gifts of Heaven I abuse, lay aside her bounties, and with my own hand, willingly put out the light of reason. I recollect my mother said, my dear, dying mother, they were the last words I ever heard her utter, – "Whoever lifts his fallen brother is greater far than the conqueror of the world." Oh, how my poor brain burns! my hand trembles! my knees shake beneath me! I cannot, will not appear before them thus; a little, a very little will revive and strengthen me. No one sees; William must be there ere this. Now, for my hiding place. Oh! the arch cunning of the drunkard! [*Goes to tree R., and from the hollow draws forth a bottle; looks round and drinks. Cribbs behind, exulting*] So, so, it relieves! it strengthens! oh, glorious liquor! Why did I rail against thee? Ha, ha! [*Drinks and draws bottle*] All gone! all! [*Throws the bottle away*] Of what use the casket when the jewel's gone? Ha, ha! I can face them now. [*Turns and meets Cribbs*] He here! Confusion!

CRIBBS: [*L.*] Why, Middleton! Edward, my dear friend, what means this?

EDWARD: [*R.*] Tempter! begone! Pretend not ignorance! Were you not there when that vile fray occurred? Did you not desert me?

CRIBBS: As I am a living man, I know not what you mean. Business called me out. I left you jovial and merry, with your friends.

EDWARD: Friends! Ha! ha! the drunkard's friends! Well, well, you may speak truth; – my brain wanders; – I'll go home! – Oh, misery! Would I were dead.

CRIBBS: Come, come, a young man like you should not think of dying. I am old enough to be your father, and I don't dream of such a thing.

EDWARD: You are a single man, Cribbs. You don't know what it is to see your little patrimony wasted away: – to feel that you are the cause of sufferings you would die to alleviate.

CRIBBS: Pooh, pooh! Suffering – your cottage is worth full five hundred dollars. It was but yesterday Farmer Amson was inquiring how much it could be bought for.

EDWARD: Bought for! Cribbs –

CRIBBS: Well, Edward, well.

EDWARD: You see yon smoke curling up among the trees?

CRIBBS: Yes, Edward. It rises from your own cottage.

EDWARD: You know who built that cottage, Cribbs?

CRIBBS: Your father built it. I recollect the day. It was –

EDWARD: It was the very day I was born that yon cottage was first inhabited. You know who lives there now?

CRIBBS: Yes. You do.

EDWARD: No one else, Cribbs?

CRIBBS: Your family, to be sure –

EDWARD: And you counsel me to sell it! – to take the warm nest from that mourning bird and her young, to strip them of all that remains of hope or comfort, to make them wanderers in the wide world, and for what? To put a little pelf into my leprous hands, and then squander it for rum. [*Crosses, R.*]

CRIBBS: You don't understand me, Edward. I am your sincere friend; believe me; come –

EDWARD: Leave me, leave me –

CRIBBS: Why, where would you go thus, Edward?

EDWARD: Home! Home! – to my sorrowing wife – her dying mother, and my poor, poor child. [*Crosses, L.*]

CRIBBS: But not thus, Edward, not thus. Come to my house, my people are all out. We'll go in the back way – no one will see you. Wash your face, and I'll give you a little – something to refresh you. I'll take care it shall not hurt you. Come, now, come.

EDWARD: Ought I – dare I? Oh, this deadly sickness. Is it indeed best?

CRIBBS: To be sure it is. If the neighbors see you thus – I'll take care of you. Come, come, a little brandy – good – good brandy.

EDWARD: Well, I – I –

CRIBBS: That's right – come. [*Aside*] He's lost. Come, my dear friend, come. [*Exeunt, L.*]

Scene 5

Interior of the cottage as in Act I. Enter Mary from set door, R. 2 E. – Her dress plain and patched, but put on with neatness and care. – She is weeping.

MARY: Oh, Heaven, have mercy on me! – aid me! – strengthen me! Weigh not thy poor creature down with woes beyond her strength to bear. Much I fear my suffering mother never can survive the night, and Edward comes not, and when he does arrive, how will it be? Alas, alas! my dear, lost husband! I think I could nerve myself against everything but – Oh, misery! this agony of suspense! it is too horrible.

Enter Julia from room, R. 2 E. – She is barefooted – Dress clean, but very poor

JULIA: Mother! dear mother, what makes you cry? I feel so sorry when you cry – don't cry any more, dear mother.

MARY: [*L.*] I cannot help it, dearest. Do not tell your poor father what has happened in his absence, Julia.

JULIA: No, dear mother, if you wish me not. Will it make him cry, mother? When I see you cry it makes me cry, too.

MARY: Hush, dear one, hush! Alas, he is unhappy enough already.

JULIA: Yes. Poor father! I cried last night when father came home, and was so sick. Oh, he looked so pale, and when I kissed him for good night, his face was as hot as fire. This morning he could not eat his breakfast, could he? What makes him sick so often, mother?

MARY: Hush, sweet one!

JULIA: Dear grandma so sick, too. Doctor and nurse both looked so sorry. Grandma won't die to-night, will she, mother?

MARY: Father of mercies! This is too much. [*Weeps*] Be very quiet, Julia, I am going in to see poor grandma. [*Crossing, R.*] Oh, *Religion!* sweet solace of the wretched heart! Support me! aid me, in this dreadful trial. [*Exit into room, R.2E.*]

JULIA: Poor, dear mother. When grandma dies, she'll go to live in Heaven, for she's good. Parson Heartall told me so, and he never tells fibs, for he is good, too.

Enter William, gently, D. in F.

WILLIAM: Julia, where is your mother, darling? [*Julia puts her finger on her lip, and points to door*]

WILLIAM: Ah, she comes.

Enter Mary, R.2E.

How is poor Mrs. Wilson now, madam?

MARY: Near the end of all earthly trouble, William. She lies in broken slumber. But where is my poor Edward? Have you not found him?

WILLIAM: Yes, ma'rm. I found him in the ta—— in the village – he had fallen, and slightly hurt his forehead; he bade me come before, so as you should not be frightened. He'll soon be here now.

MARY: Faithful friend. I wish you had not left him. Was he – Oh, what a question for a doating wife – was he sober, William?

WILLIAM: I must not lie, dear lady. He had been taking some liquor, but I think not much – all, I hope, will be well.

EDWARD: [Sings without] "Wine cures the gout," etc., Ha! ha!

MARY: Oh, great Heaven! [William rushes out, C.D., and off, L.U.E., and reenters with Edward drunk and noisy – William trying to soothe him, he staggers as he passes doorway]

EDWARD: I've had a glorious time, Bill. Old Cribbs –

MARY: [R.] Hush! dearest!

EDWARD: Why should I be silent? I am not a child, I –

MARY: My mother, Edward, my dear mother!

EDWARD: [Sinks in chair] Heaven's wrath on my hard heart. I – I – forgot. How is she? Poor woman; how is she?

MARY: Worse, Edward, worse. [Trying to hide her tears]

EDWARD: And I in part the cause. Oh, horrid vice! Bill, I remember my father's death-bed; it was a Christian's faith in his heart; hope in his calm, blue eye; a smile upon his lip; he had never seen his Edward drunk. Oh, had he seen it – had he seen it!

JULIA: [Crossing to her father from R. to C.] Father, dear father? [Striving to kiss him]

EDWARD: Leave me, child, leave me. I am hot enough already. [She weeps, he kisses her] Bless you, Julia dear, bless you. Bill, do you remember the young elm tree by the arbor in the garden?

WILLIAM: Yes, sir.

EDWARD: Well, I slipped and fell against it, as I passed the gate. My father planted it on the very day I saw the light. It has grown with my growth; I seized the axe and felled it to the earth. Why should it flourish when I am lost forever? [Hysterically] Why should it lift its head to smiling Heaven while I am prostrate? Ha, ha, ha! [A groan is heard, R.D. – Exit Mary – a pause – a shriek]

Enter Mary

MARY: Edward, my mother –

EDWARD: Mary! –

MARY: She is dead!

EDWARD: Horror! And I the cause? Death in the house, and I without doubt the means. I cannot bear this; let me fly –

MARY: [Springing forward and clasping his neck] Edward, dear Edward, do not leave me. I will work, I will slave, anything; we can live; but do not abandon me in misery; do not desert me, Edward, love! husband!

EDWARD: Call me not husband – curse me as your destroyer; loose your arms – leave me.

MARY: No, no! do not let him go. William, hold him.

WILLIAM: [Holding him] Edward, dear brother!

JULIA: [Clinging to him] Father! father!

MARY: You will be abused. No one near to aid you. Imprisoned, or something worse, Edward.

EDWARD: Loose me; leave me; why fasten me down on fire? Madness is my strength; my brain is liquid flame! [Breaks from her. – William is obliged to catch her] Ha! I am free. Farewell, forever. [Rushes off, C.D.]

MARY: Husband! Oh, Heaven! [Faints]

WILLIAM: [Bursting into tears] Edward! brother!

JULIA: Father, father! – [Runs to the door and falls on the threshold]

End of Act II

ACT III. Scene I

Broadway. Enter Lawyer Cribbs, R.

CRIBBS: I wonder where that drunken vagrant can have wandered? Ever since he came to New York, thanks to his ravenous appetite and my industrious agency, he has been going down hill rapidly. Could I but tempt him to some overt act, well managed, I could line my own pockets and ensure his ruin. Ha! here he comes, and two of his bright companions. He looks most wretchedly. Money gone, and no honest way to raise it. He'll be glad to speak to old Cribbs now. I must watch my time. [Retiring]

Enter Edward and two loafers

1ST LOAFER: Cheer up, Ned; there's more money where the last came from.

EDWARD: [Clothes torn and very shabby, hat the same] But I tell you my last cent is gone. I feel ill. I want more liquor.

1ST LOAFER: Well, well, you wait round here a spell. Joe and I will take a turn down to Cross street. [*Crosses L.*] We'll make a raise, I warrant you.

EDWARD: Well, be quick then; this burning thirst consumes me. [*Exit loafers, L.*]

CRIBBS: [*Advancing, L.*] Why! is that you, Mr. Middleton?

EDWARD: [*R.*] Yes, Cribbs; what there is left of me.

CRIBBS: Why, I don't see that you are much altered: though you might be the better for a stitch or two in your elbows –

EDWARD: Ah, Cribbs, I have no one to care for me. I am lost; a ruined, broken-hearted man.

CRIBBS: You won't be offended, Middleton, will you? Allow me to lend you a dollar. I am not very rich, you know, but you can always have a dollar or two when you want it; ask me – there! there! [*Offering it*] Before sundown he's a few yards nearer his grave. [*Aside*]

EDWARD: [*Slowly taking it, struggling with pride and necessity*] Thank you, Mr. Cribbs, thank'ye; you are from the village. I hardly dare ask you if you have seen *them*.

CRIBBS: Your wife and child? Oh, they are doing charmingly. Since you left, your wife has found plenty of sewing, the gentlefolks have become interested in her pretty face, and you know she has a good education. She is as merry as a cricket, and your little girl blooming as a rose, and brisk as a bee.

EDWARD: Then Mary is happy?

CRIBBS: Happy as a lark.

EDWARD: [*After a pause*] Well, I ought to be glad of it and since she thinks no more of me –

CRIBBS: O yes, she thinks of you *occasionally*.

EDWARD: Does she, indeed?

CRIBBS: Yes, she says she cannot but pity you. But that Heaven never sends affliction without the antidote, and that, but for your brutal – hem! – your strange conduct and drunkenness – hem! – misfortune, she should never have attracted the sympathy of those kind friends, who now regard her as the pride of their circle.

EDWARD: Did she really say all that?

CRIBBS: Yes, and she *pities* you. I am sure she thinks of you, and would be glad to see you – to see you become a respectable member of society.

EDWARD: [*Musing*] It is very kind of her – very – very kind! pities me! respectable! But, Cribbs, how can one become respectable, without out a cent in his pocket, or a whole garment on his wretched carcase?

CRIBBS: [*Pause*] There are more ways than one to remedy these casualties. If the world uses you ill, be revenged upon the world!

EDWARD: Revenged! But how, Cribbs, how?

CRIBBS: [*Cautiously*] Do you see this paper? 'Tis a check for five thousand dollars. You are a splendid penman. Write but the name of Arden Rencelaw, and you may laugh at poverty.

EDWARD: What! forgery? and on whom? The princely merchant! the noble philanthropist! the poor man's friend! the orphan's benefactor! Out and out on you for a villain, and coward! I must be sunk indeed, when you dare propose such a baseness to my father's son. Wretch as I am, by the world despised, shunned and neglected by those who should save and succor me, I would sooner perish on the first dunghill – than that my dear child should blush for her father's crimes. Take back your base bribe, miscalled charity; the maddening drink that I should purchase with it, would be redolent of sin, and rendered still more poisonous by your foul hypocrisy. [*Throws down the money*]

CRIBBS: [*Bursting with passion*] Ah, you are warm, I see. You'll think better when – when you find yourself starving. [*Exit, L.*]

EDWARD: Has it then come to this? – an object of pity to my once adored wife; no longer regarded with love – respect – but cold compassion, pity; other friends have fully made up my loss. She is flourishing, too, while I am literally starving – starving – this cold-blooded fiend, too; what's to become of me? Deserted, miserable, – but one resource. I must have liquor – ha! – my handkerchief, – 'twill gain me a drink or two, at all events. Brandy, aye, brandy, brandy! [*Rushes off, R.*]

Scene 2

A Street. – Stage half dark. Enter Cribbs, R.

CRIBBS: Plague take the fellow; who would have thought he would have been so foolishly conscientious? I will not abandon my scheme on the house of Rencelaw, though; the speculation is too good to be lost. Why! As I live here comes that old fool, Miss Spindle.

Enter Miss Spindle, L., her dress a ridiculous compound of by-gone days, and present fashions

MISS SPINDLE: Why! this New York is the most awful place to find one's way I was ever in; it's all ups and downs, ins and outs. I've been trying for two hours to find Trinity Church steeple – and I can't see it, though they tell me it's six hundred yards high.

CRIBBS: Why! angelic Miss Spindle, how *do* you do? How long have you been in the commercial emporium?

MISS SPINDLE: Oh, Squire Cribbs, how d'ye do? I don't know what you mean by the uproarium, but for certain it is the noisiest place I ever did see. But, Squire, what has become of the Middletons, can you tell?

CRIBBS: I've had my eye upon them; they're down, Miss Spindle, never to rise again; as for that vagrant, Edward –

MISS SPINDLE: Ah! Squire! what an escape I had! How fortunate that I was not ruined by the nefarious influence, the malignant coruscations of his illimitable seductions. How lucky that prim Miss Mary Wilson was subjected to his hideous arts, instead of my virgin immaculate innocence!

CRIBBS: Do you know why his wife left the village and came to New York?

MISS SPINDLE: Oh, she is low, degraded! She sank so far as to take in washing, to feed herself and child. She would sooner follow her drunken husband, and endeavor to preserve him as she said, than remain where she was.

CRIBBS: Well, well, they are down low enough now. Which way are you going, towards Broadway? Why, I'm going towards Broadway myself. Allow me the exquisite honor of beauing you – this way, perfection of your sex, and adoration of ours – your arm, lovely and immaculate Miss Spindle. [*Exit together, arm in arm, L.*]

Enter Edward and 1st and 2nd loafer, R.

1ST LOAFER: To be sure I did. I swore if he didn't let me have two or three dollars, I'd tell his old man of last night's scrape, and I soon got it to get rid of me.

2ND LOAFER: Hurrah for snakes! Who's afraid of fire. Come, Ned, two or three glasses will soon drive away the blue devils. Let's have some brandy.

EDWARD: With all my heart. Brandy be it. Since I am thus abandoned – deserted – the sooner I drown all remembrance of my wretchedness the better. Come! boys, brandy be it. Hurrah!

OMNES: [*Sing*] "Here's a health to all good lasses!" [*Exeunt, R.*]

Scene 3

Interior of the Arbor on Broadway – Two men playing at backgammon – Another reading paper and smoking – Others seated around, etc.

Enter Edward and loafers, R., singing, – "Here's a health," etc.

BAR-KEEPER: [*Behind bar*] The same noisy fellows that were here last night. What is it to be, gentlemen?

EDWARD: Oh, brandy, for me – brandy.

1ST LOAFER: Give me a gin-sling – that's what killed Goliath, ha, ha, ha!

2ND LOAFER: I'll have brandy. Come, old fellows, tread up, and wet your whistles. I'll stand, Sam, tread up. [*Edward and others after drinking, dance and sing, "Dan Tucker," "Boatman dance," etc.*]

BAR-KEEPER: I must civilly request, gentlemen, that you will not make so much noise; you disturb others – and we wish to keep the house quiet.

EDWARD: Steady, boys, steady; don't raise a row in a decent house. More brandy, young man, if you please. Come, Bill, try it again.

1ST LOAFER: With all my heart, hurrah!

EDWARD AND LOAFER: "Dance, Boatman, dance," etc. [*Laugh*] More brandy, hurrah!

BAR-KEEPER: I tell you once for all, I'll not have this noise. Stop that singing.

2ND LOAFER: I shan't; we'll sing as long as we please – give me some liquor.

EDWARD: Aye, more brandy – brandy.

BAR-KEEPER: Well, will you be still, then, if I give you another drink?

EDWARD: Oh, certainly, certainly.

1ST LOAFER: In course we will –

BAR-KEEPER: Well, help yourselves. [*Hands decanters*]

2ND LOAFER: What's yours, Ned?

EDWARD: Oh, brandy – here goes.

1ST LOAFER: Here goes for the last.

OMNES: [*Singing*] "We won't go home till morning," etc.

MAN: [*At table playing checkers*] Look here! that's my king.

2ND MAN: [*At table*] You're a liar. I have just jumped him.

1ST MAN: [*At table*] I tell you, you lie. [*Regular wrangle*]

EDWARD AND LOAFERS: Go it, you cripples. [*Singing and laughing*]

BAR-KEEPER: Stop that noise, I tell you. Come, get out. [*Pushing man from table – the two men fight*]

EDWARD AND LOAFERS: Go it, Charley. Hurrah, etc. [*Regular scene of confusion. – Bar-room fight, etc. – Scene changes*]

Scene 4

Exterior of a Bar-room on the Five Points – Noise inside – Cribbs enters and listens at door.

CRIBBS: So, a regular bar-room fight. Middleton must be secured – here's the watch. [*Enter 2nd watchman – Exit Cribbs, L.*]

Edward, Watchmen and loafers enter struggling, singing, shouting, etc., etc. – Exit fighting – Clubs are heard in all directions – First and second loafers enter clinching each other and fighting – several knockdowns; square off, recognize each other

1ST LOAFER: Why, Sam, is that you?

2ND LOAFER: Why, Ned, my dear fellow, is that you?

1ST LOAFER: [*Who has had his hat knocked entirely over his head, crown out*] To be sure it is; look here, you've completely caved in my best beaver.

2ND LOAFER: Well, I ask your pardon. [*Exeunt arm in arm, R.*]

Scene 5

A wretched garret – Old table and chair with lamp burning dimly – Mary in miserable apparel, sewing on slop-work; a wretched shawl thrown over her shoulders – Child sleeping on a straw bed on the floor, R., covered in part by a miserable ragged rug – Half a loaf of bread on the table. – The ensemble of the scene indicates want and poverty.

MARY: Alas, alas! It is very cold – faint with hunger – sick – heart weary with wretchedness, fatigue, and cold. [*Clock strikes one*] One o'clock, and my work not near finished. I – they must be done to-night. These shirts I have promised to hand in to-morrow by the hour of eight. A miserable quarter of a dollar will repay my industry, and then my poor, poor child, thou shalt have food.

JULIA: [*Awaking*] Oh, dear mother, I am so cold. [*Mary takes shawl from her shoulders and spreads it over the child*] No, mother, – keep the shawl. You are cold, too. I will wait till morning, and I can warm myself at Mrs. Brien's fire; little Dennis told me I should, for the gingerbread I gave him. [*Goes to sleep murmuring – Mary puts the shawl on herself, waits till the child slumbers, and then places it over Julia, and returns to work*]

MARY: Alas! where is he on this bitter night? In vain have I made every inquiry, and cannot gain any tidings of my poor wretched husband; no one knows him by name. Perhaps already the inmate of a prison. Ah, merciful Heaven, restore to me my Edward once again, and I will endure every ill, that can be heaped upon me. [*Looks toward child*] Poor Julia, she sleeps soundly, she was fortunate to-day, sweet lamb, while walking in the street in search of a few shavings, she became benumbed with cold. She sat down upon some steps, when a boy moved with compassion, took from his neck a handkerchief, and placed it upon hers; *the mother of that boy is blessed.* With the few cents he slipped into her hands, she purchased a loaf of bread, she ate a part of it. [*Taking bread from table*] And the rest is here. [*Looks eagerly at it*] I am hungry – horribly hungry. I shall have money in the morning. [*Pause*] No, no, my child will wake and find her treasure gone. I will not rob my darling. [*Replaces bread on table, sinks into chair, weeping*] That ever I should see his child thus! for myself, I could bear, could suffer all. [*Julia wakes noiselessly, perceiving shawl, rises and places it over her mother's shoulders*]

JULIA: Dear mother, you are cold. Ah, you tried to cheat your darling.

MARY: [*On her knees*] Now, Heaven be praised. I did not eat that bread.

JULIA: Why, mother, do you sit up so late? You cry so much, and look so white – mother, do not cry. Is it because father does not come to bring us bread? We shall find father bye and bye, shan't we, mother?

MARY: Yes, dearest – yes, with the kind aid of Him. [*Knock at the door, L.*] Who can that be? Ah, should it be Edward? [*Going to L.*]

Enter Cribbs – she gets C.

CRIBBS: [*L.*] Your pardon, Mrs. Middleton, for my intrusion at this untimely hour, but friends are welcome at all times and seasons, eh? So, so, you persist in remaining in these miserable quarters? When last I saw you, I advised a change.

MARY: Alas! sir, you too well know my wretched reasons for remaining. But why are you here at this strange hour; Oh, tell me, know you aught of him? Have you brought tidings of my poor Edward?

CRIBBS: [*Avoiding direct answer*] I must say your accommodations are none of the best, and must persist in it, you would do well to shift your quarters.

MARY: Heaven help me! where would you have me go? Return to the village, I will not. I must remain and find my husband.

CRIBBS: This is a strange infatuation, young woman; it is the more strange, as he has others to console him, whose soft attentions he prefers to yours.

MARY: What mean you, sir?

CRIBBS: I mean, that there are plenty of women, not of the most respectable class, who are always ready to receive presents from wild young men like him, and are not very particular in the liberties that may be taken in exchange.

MARY: Man, man, why dost thou degrade the form and sense the *Great One* has bestowed on thee by falsehood? Gaze on the sharp features of that child, where famine has already set her seal, look on the hollow eyes, and the care-worn form of the hapless being that brought her into life, then if you have the heart, further insult the helpless mother, and the wretched wife.

CRIBBS: These things I speak of, have been, and will be again, while there are wantons of one sex, and drunkards of the other.

MARY: Sir, you slander my husband. I know this cannot be. It is because he is poor, forsaken, reviled, and friendless, that thus I follow him, thus love him still.

CRIBBS: He would laugh in his drunken ribaldry, to hear you talk thus.

MARY: [*With proud disdain*] Most contemptible of earthborn creatures, it is false. The only fault of my poor husband, has been intemperance, terrible, I acknowledge, but still a weakness that has assailed and prostrated the finest intellects of men who would scorn a mean and unworthy action. [*Crosses, L.*]

CRIBBS: Tut, tut. You are very proud, considering – [*Looking round*] – all circumstances. But come, I forgive you. You are young and beautiful, your husband is a vagabond. I am rich, I have a true affection for you, and with me – [*Attempts to take her hand*]

MARY: Wretch! [*Throws him off*] Have you not now proved yourself a slanderer, and to effect your own vile purposes? But know, despicable wretch, that my poor husband, clothed in rags, covered with mire, and lying drunk at my feet, is a being whose shoes you are not worthy to unloose. [*Crosses, R.*]

CRIBBS: Nay, then, proud beauty, you shall know my power – 'tis late, you are unfriended, helpless, and thus – [*He seizes her, child screams*]

MARY: Help! mercy! [*She struggles, crosses, R. – Cribbs follows her – William enters hastily, L., seizes Cribbs and throws him round to L. – he falls*]

WILLIAM: Well, Squire, what's the lowest you'll take for your rotten carcase? Shall I turn auctioneer, and knock you down to the highest bidder? I don't know much of pronology, but I've a great notion of playing Yankee Doodle on your organ of rascality. Be off, you ugly varmint, or I'll come the steam ingine, and set your paddles going all-fired quick.

CRIBBS: I'll be revenged, if there's law or justice.

WILLIAM: Oh, get out! You're a bad case of villainy versus modesty and chastity, printed in black letters, and bound in calf; off with you, or I'll serve a writ of ejectment on you, a posteriori to you – I learnt that much from Mr. Middleton's law books.

CRIBBS: But I say, sir – I am a man –

WILLIAM: You a man? Nature made a blunder. She had a piece of refuse garbage, she intended to form into a *hog*, made a mistake, gave it your *shape*, and sent it into the world to be miscalled man. Get out. [*Pushes him off, L. – Noise of falling down stairs – Reenters*] I did not like to hit him before you, but he's gone down those stairs, quicker than he wanted to, I guess.

MARY: Kind, generous friend, how came you here so opportunely?

WILLIAM: Why, I was just going to bed, at a boardinghouse close by Chatham street, when I happened to mention to the landlord, a worthy man as ever broke bread, about you; he told me where you was. I thought you might be more comfortable there, and his good wife has made everything as nice and pleasant for you, as if you were her own sister. So come, Mrs. Middleton, come, Julia, dear.

MARY: But William, my poor husband. [*Clubs, R. and L.*]

WILLIAM: There's another row. Well, if this New York isn't the awfullest place for noise. Come, Mrs. Middleton, I'll find him if he's in New York, jail or no jail, watch-house or no watch-house.

MARY: Heaven preserve my poor, dear Edward. [*Exit, L.*]

Scene 6

The Five Points – Stage dark, clubs R. and L. – Enter Edward Middleton, in the custody of two watchmen – he is shouting – William Dowton enters hastily, knocks down watchmen, rescues Edward, and they exit, R. – Other rowdies enter, fight – Stage clear, shouts, etc., and off, R. – Enter Cribbs, with coat torn half off, and dancing, fighting about stage, from L.U.E.

CRIBBS: Oh, my! Oh, good gracious! How can I get out of this scrape? I came here with the best intentions. Oh, my! to see the law put in force! Oh, dear! somebody has torn my coat tail – good gracious! Lord have mercy! I've lost my hat – no, here it is. [*Picks up dreadful shabby hat and puts it on, runs from one side to another – Enter watchmen and mob, meeting him from R.*]

WILLIAM: [*Pointing out Cribbs to watchmen*] That's the chap, the worst among 'em. [*They seize Cribbs*]

CRIBBS: I'm a respectable man. [*They pick him up bodily and carry him off, R., shouting – he exclaims, "I'm a lawyer, I'm a respectable man," etc. – William follows laughing – General confusion*]

End of Act III

ACT IV. Scene 1

A wretched out-house or shed, supposed to be near a tavern, early morning – Stage dark –

Edward discovered lying on ground, without hat or coat, clothes torn, eyes sunk and haggard, appearance horrible, etc., etc.

EDWARD: [*Awakening*] Where am I? I wonder if people dream after they are dead? hideous! hideous! I should like to be dead, if I could not dream – parched! parched! 'tis morning, is it, or coming night, which? I wanted daylight, but now it has come, what shall I do in daylight? I was out of sight when it was dark – and seemed to be half-hidden from myself – early morning, the rosy hue of the coming sunshine, veiling from mortal sight the twinkling stars – what horrid dreams; will they return upon me, waking? Oh, for some brandy! rum! I am not so ashamed, so stricken with despair when I am drunk. Landlord, give me some brandy. What horrid place is this? Pain! dreadful pain! Heavens, how I tremble. Brandy! brandy! [*Sinks down in agony*]

Enter Landlord, with whip, R.

LANDLORD: Where in nature can my horse be gone? Is there nobody up in this place? Hollo!

EDWARD: Hollo! Landlord, I say.

LANDLORD: What's that? Oh! I say, have you seen my horse? What – as I live, that scapegallows, Middleton, how came he here? [*Aside*] I thought he was in Sing-Sing.

EDWARD: Oh! I know you, you needn't draw back – we have been acquainted before now, eh? Mr. –

LANDLORD: Zounds! he knows me – yes, yes, we were acquainted once, as you say, young man; but that was in other days.

EDWARD: You are the same being still – though I am changed – miserably changed – you still sell rum, don't you?

LANDLORD: I am called a respectable inn-keeper; few words are best, young fellow. Have you seen a horse saddled and bridled near here?

EDWARD: I've seen nothing – you are respectable, you say. You speak as if you were not the common poisoner of the whole village; am not I, too, respectable?

LANDLORD: [*Laughs rudely*] Not according to present appearances. You were respectable once, and so was Lucifer – like him you have fallen past rising. You cut a pretty figure, don't you? ha! ha! What has brought you in this beastly condition, young man?

EDWARD: [*Springing up*] You! Rum! Eternal curses on you! Had it not been for your infernal poison shop in our village, I had been still a man – the foul den, where you plunder the pockets of your fellow, where you deal forth death in tumblers, and from whence goes forth the blast of ruin over the land, to mildew the bright hope of youth, to fill the widow's heart with agony, to curse the orphan, to steal the glorious mind of man, to cast them from their high estate of honest pride, and make them – such as I. How looked I when first I entered your loathsome den, and how do I look now? Where are the friends of my happy youth? where is my wife? where is my child? They have cursed me; and forsaken me!

LANDLORD: Well, what brought you to my house? You had your senses then; I did not invite you, did I?

EDWARD: Doth hell send forth cards of invitation for its horrid orgies. Sick and faint – make me some amends, my brain is on fire. My limbs are trembling – give me some brandy – brandy. [*Seizes him*]

LANDLORD: How can I give you brandy? my house is far from here. Let me go, vagabond!

EDWARD: Nay, I beseech you – only a glass, a single glass of brandy, rum – anything – give me liquor, or I'll –

LANDLORD: Villain! let go your hold!

EDWARD: Brandy! I have a claim on you, a deadly claim! Brandy, brandy! or I'll throttle you. [*Choking him*]

LANDLORD: [*Struggling*] Help, murder! I am choking! help!

Enter William Dowton, R.

WILLIAM: Good lord! what is this? Edward, Edward!

Edward releases Landlord and falls, R.

LANDLORD: You shall pay for this – villain! you shall pay for this. [*Exit, hastily, L.*]

EDWARD: [*On ground in delirium*] Here, here, friend, take it off, will you – these snakes, how they coil round me. Oh! how strong they are – there, don't kill it, no, no, don't kill it, give it brandy, poison it with rum, that will be a judicious punishment, that would be justice, ha, ha! justice! ha, ha!

WILLIAM: He does not know me.

EDWARD: Hush! gently – gently, while she's asleep. I'll kiss her. She would reject me, did she know it, hush! there, heaven bless my Mary, bless her and her child – hush! if the globe turns round once more, we shall slide from its surface into eternity. Ha, ha! great idea. A boiling sea of wine, fired by the torch of fiends! ha! ha!

WILLIAM: He's quite helpless. Could I but gain assistance, he can not move to injure himself. I must venture.

Exit, rapidly and noiselessly, R.

EDWARD: So, so; again all's quiet – they think I cannot escape. I cheated them yesterday – 'tis a sin to steal liquor –

Enter Mr. Rencelaw, R.

But no crime to purloin sleep from a druggist's store – none – none. [*Produces phial*] Now for the universal antidote – the powerful conqueror of all earthly care – death. [*About to drink, Rencelaw seizes phial and casts it from him*] Ha! who are you, man? what would you?

RENCELAW: Nay, friend, take not your life, but mend it.

EDWARD: Friend, you know me not. I am a fiend, the ruin of those who loved me; leave me.

RENCELAW: I came not to upbraid, or to insult you. I am aware of all your danger, and come to save you. You have been drinking.

EDWARD: That you may well know. I am dying now for liquor – and – will you give me brandy. Who are you that takes interest in an unhappy vagabond – neither my father nor my brother?

RENCELAW: I am a friend to the unfortunate. You are a man, and if a man, a brother.

EDWARD: A brother! yes, but you trouble yourself without hope. I am lost, of what use can I be to you?

RENCELAW: Perhaps I can be of use to you. Are you indeed a fallen man? [*Edward looks at him, sighs and hangs his head*] There you have the greater claim upon my compassion, my attention, my utmost endeavors to raise you once more, to the station in society from which you have fallen, "for he that lifts a fallen fellow-creature from the dust, is greater than the hero who conquers a world."

EDWARD: [*Starts*] Merciful heaven! My mother's dying words! Who and what are you?

RENCELAW: I am one of those whose life and labors are passed in rescuing their fellow-men from the abyss into which you have fallen. I administer the pledge of sobriety to those who would once more become an ornament to society and a blessing to themselves and to those around them.

EDWARD: That picture is too bright, it cannot be.

RENCELAW: You see before you one who for twenty years was a prey to this dreadful folly.

EDWARD: Indeed! no, no; it is too late.

RENCELAW: You mistake; it is not too late. Come with me, we will restore you to society. Reject not my prayers; strength will be given you, the Father of purity smiles upon honest endeavors. Come, my brother, enroll your name among the free, the disenthralled, and be a man again. [*Takes his hand*]

EDWARD: Merciful heaven! grant the prayer of a poor wretch be heard. [*Exeunt, R.*]

Scene 2

Union Square – Lights up – Citizens passing during the scene – Children playing ball, hoop, etc.

Enter Lawyer Cribbs, R.

CRIBBS: Now, this is a lucky escape. It's fortunate that old Sykes, the miller, was in court, who knew me, or I might have found it difficult to get out of the infernal scrape. What a dreadful night I have passed, to be sure, – what with the horrid noise of the rats that I expected every moment would commence making a breakfast of my toes, the cold, and horrible language of my miserable and blackguard companions. I might as well have passed the crawling hours in purgatory, ugh! I'm glad it's over – catch me in such company again, that's all. Now for my design on Rencelaw & Co. I think there can be no detection, the signature is perfect. I'll get some well-dressed boy to deliver the check, receive the money, and I'm off to the far West or England, soon as possible. Would I were certain of the ruin of this drunken scoundrel, and the infamy of his tiger-like wife, I should be content.

Enter Boy, L.U.E., crossing to R.

Where are you going so quickly, my lad?

BOY: [*R.*] On an errand, sir.

Enter William Dowton, L.U.E.

CRIBBS: Do you want to earn half a dollar?

BOY: With pleasure, sir, honestly.

CRIBBS: Oh, of course, honestly.

WILLIAM: I doubt that, if he rows in your boat.

CRIBBS: I am obliged to meet a gentleman on business, precisely at this hour, by the Pearl St. House. Call at the Mechanics' Bank for me, deliver this check; the teller will give you the money, come back quickly, and I'll reward you with a silver dollar.

BOY: I'll be as quick as possible, sir, and thank you, too. [*Exit hastily, R.*]

WILLIAM: I knew the old skunk had money, but I was not aware that he banked in New York. Hallo! here's Miss Spindle a twigging the fashions; here'll be fun with the old rats. I told her half an hour ago, Cribbs was at a large party among the 'stocracy, last night.

CRIBBS: [*After putting up his wallet, sees Miss Spindle*] Confound it! here's that foolish old maid, at such a time, too. Ah! there's no avoiding.

Enter Miss Spindle, L.

MISS SPINDLE: Good gracious! Mr. Cribbs, how *do* you do? I declare, how well you do look – a little dissipation improves you.

CRIBBS: What?

WILLIAM: [*Aside*] She's beginning already. Hurrah! Go it, old gal.

MISS SPINDLE: I swow, now, I'm right glad to see you.

CRIBBS: You have all the pleasure to yourself.

WILLIAM: She'll find that out, bye and bye.

MISS SPINDLE: Now, don't be so snappish, Lawyer Cribbs; neighbors should be neighborly, you know. Who was it that had the pleasure to introduce you?

WILLIAM: [*Aside*] I rather guess I went that stick of candy. [*Cribbs stares at Miss Spindle*]

MISS SPINDLE: Now, don't look so cross about it. I think you ought to feel right slick, as I do. Now do tell what kind of music had you?

WILLIAM: [*Aside*] Plenty o' hollaring and clubs, with considerable running accompaniment.

MISS SPINDLE: Now don't look so angry, and scared. Who did play the fiddle? Was it Herr Noll, Young Burke, or Ole Bull. Don't keep my curiosity on the stretch.

CRIBBS: Beelzebub stretch your curiosity! What are you yelling about Herr Noll, Young Burke, and Ole Bull for?

WILLIAM: [*Aside*] I calculate Captain – [*Name

of captain of watch] – played first fiddle to the overture of "Lock and Key."

MISS SPINDLE: Well, I swow, I never seen such ill-temper. Why I know New York tip-tops always have somebody first chop among the fiddlers; for cousin Jemima told me when she was at the Tabernacle, her very hair stood on end when Herwig led the musicians with Heatoven's sympathy.

CRIBBS: [*Aside*] The old fool's perfectly crazy!

WILLIAM: [*Aside*] Well, if the old chap hadn't any music, it wasn't for want of bars and staves. I reckon he got out of his notes when they let him off.

MISS SPINDLE: Now, don't be angry, Lawyer Cribbs; you know I only ask for information. Do the 'stocracy go the hull temperance principle, and give their visitors nothing but ice water?

WILLIAM: [*Aside*] There was a big bucket and dippers, I reckon.

CRIBBS: Miss Spindle, will you only hear me?

MISS SPINDLE: Well, ain't I listening all the time, and you won't tell me nothin'. Were there are any real live lions there? Did Col. Johnson scalp a live Indian, to amuse the ladies? Did Dr. Dodds put everybody into a phospheric state, when they were all dancing, and the lights went out? Did Senator D—— dance a hornpipe to please the children, and make a bowl of punch at twelve o'clock? Did – [*Out of breath*]

WILLIAM: [*Aside*] She'll ask him directly if the elephants played at billiards.

CRIBBS: Madam! madam! will you listen? [*Shouts out*] In the name of confusion, what are you talking about?

MISS SPINDLE: Why, of the grand *sorrie* – the party, to be sure.

CRIBBS: I know nothing of any party; you're insane.

MISS SPINDLE: Oh, no, I ain't neither. I was told of it by one –

CRIBBS: Told by one? who?

WILLIAM: [*Coming forward, C.*] Me, I calculate. I watched you, I guess.

CRIBBS: Watched!

WILLIAM: Guess I did – so shut up.

CRIBBS: Confusion!

WILLIAM: I say, Squire, where did you buy your new coat?

CRIBBS: Go to the devil, both of you.

WILLIAM: Where's the tail of your old one? Ha! ha!

Exit Cribbs, R. – William follows laughing

MISS SPINDLE: Well, I swow, this is like Jedide's addle eggs. I can neither make ducks nor chickens on 'em. Well, I've got a good budget of news and scandal anyhow. So I'll be off back to the village, this very day; this vile city is no safe place for romantic sensibilities and virgin purity. [*Exit, L.*]

Scene 3

Broadway, with a view of Barnum's Museum. Enter Arden Rencelaw, L.; crosses to R. – Bank messenger enters after him, L.

MESSENGER: Mr. Rencelaw, Mr. Rencelaw! I beg pardon for hurriedly addressing you, but our cashier desires to know if this is your signature. [*Produces check*]

RENCELAW: My signature – good heavens, no! – five thousand dollars. Is it cashed?

MESSENGER: Not half an hour. The teller cashed it instantly.

RENCELAW: Who presented the check?

MESSENGER: A young boy, sir, whom I saw just now, recognized, and sent to the bank immediately; but the cashier, Mr. Armond, arriving directly afterwards, doubted it, and I was despatched to find you.

RENCELAW: Run to the bank directly; call for a police officer as you pass. I am rather infirm, but will soon follow; do not be flurried; our measures must be prompt and I fear not for the result. [*Exit Messenger, L.*]

Enter William Dowton, R.

Ah, honest William; I have been searching for you; Edward desired to see you.

WILLIAM: Thank and bless you, sir. How is he? – where?

RENCELAW: Comparatively well and happy, at my house. His wife and child will be here immediately; I have sent a carriage for them. Their home – their happy home – is prepared for them in the village, and I have obtained almost certain information of his grandfather's will.

WILLIAM: Thank heaven! But, sir, you appear alarmed, excited.

RENCELAW: A forgery has been committed, in

the name of our firm, upon the Mechanics' Bank.

WILLIAM: Bless me! the Mechanics' Bank? Who gave the check, sir?

RENCELAW: A boy, William.

WILLIAM: A boy? How long ago?

RENCELAW: Not half an hour! Why this eagerness?

WILLIAM: I – I'll tell you, sir. Mr. Middleton told me that Lawyer Cribbs, when the poor fellow was in poverty and drunkenness, urged him to commit a forgery. Not half an hour since, I saw Cribbs give a boy a check, and tell him to take it to the Mechanics' Bank, receive some money, and bring it to him somewhere near the Pearl Street House, where he would find him with a gentleman.

RENCELAW: So, so! I see it all. Come with me to the Tombs, and secure an officer. If you should meet Middleton, do not at present mention this – come. [*Exit, R.*]

WILLIAM: I'll follow you, sir, heart and hand. If I once get my grip on the old fox, he won't get easily loose, I guess. [*Exit hastily, R.*]

Scene 4

Room in Rencelaw's house, – very handsome table, chairs, handsome books, etc. Edward Middleton, C., discovered reading – dressed, and looking well, etc.

EDWARD: [*Side of table*] What gratitude do I not owe this generous, noble-hearted man, who, from the depths of wretchedness and horror, has restored me to the world, to myself, and to religion. Oh! what joy can equal the bright sensations of a thinking being, when redeemed from that degrading vice; his prisoned heart beats with rapture; his swelling veins bound with vigor; and with tremulous gratitude, he calls on the Supreme Being for blessings on his benefactor.

MARY: [*Outside, R.*] Where is my dear – my loved, redeemed one?

Mary enters with Julia, R.

Edward! my dear, dear husband. [*They embrace*]

EDWARD: Mary, my blessed one! My child, my darling. Bounteous heaven! accept my thanks.

JULIA: Father, dear father – you look as you did the bright sunshiny morning I first went to school. Your voice sounds as it used to when I sang the evening hymn and you kissed and blessed me. You cry, father. Do not cry; but your tears are not such tears as mother shed, when she had no bread to give me.

EDWARD: [*Kisses her*] No, my blessed child, they are not; they are tears of repentance, Julia, but of joy.

MARY: Oh! my beloved, my redeemed one, all my poor sufferings are as nothing weighed in a balance with my present joy.

Enter Rencelaw, R.

Respected sir, what words can express our gratification?

RENCELAW: Pay it where 'tis justly due, to heaven! I am but the humble instrument, and in your sweet content, I am rewarded.

JULIA: [*Going to Rencelaw, R.*] I shall not forget what mother last night taught me.

RENCELAW: What was that, sweet girl?

JULIA: In my prayers, when I have asked a blessing for my father and my mother, I pray to *Him* to bless *Arden Rencelaw*, too.

RENCELAW: Dear child. [*Kisses her*]

EDWARD: I will not wrong your generous nature, by fulsome outward gratitude, for your most noble conduct, but humbly hope, that He will give me strength to continue in the glorious path, adorned by your bright example. In the words of New England's favored poet:

"There came a change, the cloud rolled off,
A light fell on my brain,
And like the passing of a dream,
That cometh not again,
The darkness of my spirit fled,
I saw the gulf before;
And shuddered at the waste behind,
And am a man once more."

End of Act IV

ACT V. Scene 1

Village Landscape, as in Act I. – Side Cottage, L.U.E. Enter Farmer Stevens, R., and Farmer Gates, L., meeting.

STEVENS: Good afternoon, Mr. Gates. You've returned from Boston earlier than common today. Any news? – anything strange, eh?

GATES: Why, ye-es, I guess there is. Just by the

Post Office I met William Dowton; how are you, says I, and was driving slowly along, when he hailed me to stop, and – but I forgot to ask you, has Squire Cribbs been here to-day?

STEVENS: I have not seen the old knave – why do you ask so particular?

GATES: Well, William, you know, is as honest as the sun, and he told me there were dreadful suspicions that Cribbs had committed a heavy forgery on the firm of Rencelaw & Co., and as I was already in my wagon, and had a good horse, he wished I would drive out pretty quick, and if old Cribbs were here, manage to detain him till Mr. Rencelaw and William arrived with the police officers – that if the sly old fox were guilty, he might be caught before he absquatulated.

STEVENS: Well, I hope for the credit of the village, he is not guilty of this bad action, though I have long known his heart was blacker than his coat. Witness his conduct to the sweetheart of Will's poor sister, Agnes? Did you tell him the glad news that her senses were restored?

GATES: No, our hurry was so great; but his mind will be prepared for it, for good Dr. Woodworth always told him her malady was but temporary.

STEVENS: Well, the poor girl has got some secret, I'm sure, and she'll not tell it to any one but William. [*Exit, R.*]

GATES: Hark! that's his voice; yes, here's William, sure enough.

Enter William, L.

Well, William, everything is just as you directed, but no signs of the old one yet.

WILLIAM: The rascal's on his way be sure. Bill Parkins told me he saw him passing through Kings-bridge half an hour before we came through there. I guess he's taken the upper road, to lead all pursuit out of the track. Mr. Rencelaw and the police are at the cross-roads, and I rather guess we can take charge of the lower part of the village; so there's no fear of our missing him; mind, you're not to say anything to Edward Middleton. Mr. Rencelaw would not have him disturbed till all is secure.

GATES: Oh, I understand. How the whole village rejoiced when they saw him and his sweet wife return in peace and joy to the happy dwelling of their parents. Have you seen your sister, William?

WILLIAM: No, farmer, I haven't seen the poor girl yet. Nor do I wish it, till this business is all fixed.

GATES: Ay, but she wants to see you; she has got to tell you some secret.

WILLIAM: A secret! some of her wild fancies, I reckon, poor girl.

GATES: William, you are mistaken; your dear sister's mind is quite restored.

WILLIAM: What! how? Don't trifle with me, farmer, I could not stand it.

GATES: I tell you, William, she is sane, quite well, as Dr. Woodworth said she would be.

WILLIAM: What! will she know and call me by my name again? Shall I hear her sweet voice carolling to the sun at early morning – will she take her place among the singers at the old meeting-house again? Shall I once more at evening hear her murmur the prayers our poor old mother taught her? Thank heaven! thank heaven!

GATES: Come, William, come, rouse you, she's coming.

AGNES: [*Without, R.*]

"They called her blue-eyed Mary,
When friends and fortune smiled."

WILLIAM: Farmer, just stand back for a moment or two; all will be right in a few minutes. [*Exit Farmer, R.*]

Enter Agnes, plainly but neatly dressed, R. – sees her brother

AGNES: William! brother!

WILLIAM: My darling sister! [*Embrace*]

AGNES: I know, you, William; I can speak to you, and hear you, dear, dear brother.

WILLIAM: May He be praised for this.

AGNES: William, I have much to tell you, and 'tis important that you should know it instantly. I know Edward Middleton is here, and it concerns him most. When I recovered my clear senses, William, when I remembered the meeting-house, and the old homestead, and the little dun cow I used to milk, and poor old Neptune, and could call them by their names –

WILLIAM: Bless you!

AGNES: Strange fancies would still keep forming in my poor brain, and remembrances flit along my memory like half-forgotten dreams. But among them, clear and distinct, was that fearful day when old Cribbs would have abused me, and you, dear brother, saved me.

WILLIAM: Darn the old varmint!

AGNES: Hush, William, the memory of that precise spot would still intrude upon me, and a vague thought that when insane I had concealed myself, and seen something hidden. Searching round carefully one day, I saw a little raised artificial hillock close beneath the hedge. I went and got a hoe from Farmer Williams' barn, and after digging near a foot below, I found – what think you, William?

WILLIAM: What, girl – what?

AGNES: Concealed in an old tin case, the will of Edward's grandfather! Confirming to his dear son the full possession of all his property. The other deed under which Cribbs has acted was a forgery –

WILLIAM: Where is it now?

AGNES: In the house, safe locked up in mother's bureau till you returned.

Enter Rencelaw, Police Officers and Boy, hastily, L.

RENCELAW: Friend William, Cribbs is on the upper road, coming down the hill.

Enter Farmer Gates and Farmer Stevens, R.

WILLIAM: Farmer Gates, do you meet him here; answer any questions he may ask with seeming frankness. Sister, he is after that will, even now. Mr. Rencelaw, let us retire into the house and watch the old rascal. [*Exeunt into house, L. U. E., all except Gates*]

GATES: [*Alone*] Well, am I to lie now, if he asks any questions? It's a new thing to me, and I'm afeard I can't do it, even in a good cause. Well, if I mustn't tell truth exactly, I must do as the papers say the members do in Congress, and dodge the present question.

Enter Cribbs, L., hurriedly, evidently alarmed – Starts at seeing Farmer, then, familiarly

CRIBBS: Good day, farmer, good day; your folks all well?

GATES: All sound and hearty.

CRIBBS: Any news, eh?

GATES: Nothing particular; corn's riz a little; sauce is lower. Potatoes hold their own, and Wilkins' cow's got a calf.

CRIBBS: Been in New York, lately, eh?

GATES: Why, yes, I was in the city this morning.

CRIBBS: Did you see William Dowton, there, eh?

GATES: No, not in New York. [*Aside*] That's dodge number one.

CRIBBS: Fine afternoon, eh?

GATES: Yes, fine day, considering.

CRIBBS: Likely to rain, eh?

GATES: If it does we shall have a shower, I guess. Come, black-coat didn't make much out of me this time. [*Exit into house, L. U. E.*]

CRIBBS: He's gone. No one observes me. Now, then, for the will, and instant flight! If I take the lower road I shall escape all observation. Haste – haste! [*Exit, R.*]

Enter from house, William, Rencelaw, Agnes, Farmers, Police Officers, and Boy

WILLIAM: There he goes by the lower road. Boy, was that the man gave you the paper?

BOY: I'm sure of it, sir.

WILLIAM: Mr. Rencelaw, you know enough, sir, from what I have said, perfectly to understand our purpose?

RENCELAW: Perfectly, honest William.

WILLIAM: Now, Farmer Gates, he's gone round by the lower road, evidently to get clear of being seen if possible. Now, if we cut pretty quick across Farmer Williams' pasture we are there before him, and can keep ourselves concealed.

GATES: Certainly, William.

WILLIAM: Come along, then. Now, old Cribbs, I calculate you'll find a hornet's nest about your ears pretty almighty quick. [*Exeunt, R.*]

Scene 2

Front and Cut Wood. Enter William, Rencelaw, Agnes, Boy, Farmers, and Police Officers, R.

WILLIAM: All right; we're here first, now for ambuscade. All hide behind the trees. Hush! I hear a foot-step, he's coming round the barn. Close, close. [*All retire, L.*]

Enter Cribbs, cautious and fearful, L.

CRIBBS: All's safe – I'm certain no one has observed me.

WILLIAM: [*Aside*] What would you like to bet?

CRIBBS: Hark! 'tis nothing. Now for the will; from this fatal evidence I shall at least be secure. [*Advances to the mound R., and starts*] Powers of mischief! the earth is freshly turned. [*Searches*] The deed is gone!

Enter Agnes hastily, and down L. – In a tone of madness

The will is gone – the bird has flown.
The rightful heir has got his own – ha! ha!

CRIBBS: [*Paralyzed and recovering*] Ha! betrayed! ruined! Mad devil, you shall pay for this. [*Rushes towards her*]

William enters, catches his arm, and holds up the will – Police officer, who has got to R., seizes other arm, and points pistol to his head – Rencelaw holds up forged check, and points to it – Boy, R., pointing to Cribbs – Farmers, R. C. – Picture – Pause

WILLIAM: Trapped! All day with you, Squire.

RENCELAW: Hush! William, do not oppress a poor down-fallen fellow creature. Most unfortunate of men, sincerely do I pity you.

CRIBBS: [*Recovering – bold and obdurate*] Will your pity save me from the punishment of my misdeeds? No! when compassion is required, I'll beg it of the proud philanthropist, Arden Rencelaw.

RENCELAW: Unhappy wretch. What motives could you have? This world's goods were plenty with you – what tempted you into these double deeds of guilt?

CRIBBS: Revenge and avarice, the master-passions of my nature. With my heart's deepest, blackest feelings, I hated the father of Edward Middleton. In early life he detected me in an act of vile atrocity, that might have cost me my life. He would not betray, but pardoned, pitied, and despised me. From that hour I hated, with a feeling of intensity that has existed even beyond the grave, descending unimpaired to his noble son. By cunning means, which you would call hypocrisy, I wormed myself into the favor of the grandfather, who, in his dying hour, delivered into my hands his papers. I and an accomplice, whom I bribed, forged the false papers; the villain left the country. Fearful he should denounce me, should he return, I dared not destroy the real will; but yesterday the news reached me that he was dead. And now, one blow of evil fortune has destroyed me.

RENCELAW: Repentance may yet avail you?

CRIBBS: Nothing. I have lived a villain – a villain let me die. [*Exit with Officers and Farmers*]

RENCELAW: William, tell Middleton I shall see him in a day or two; I must follow that poor man to New York.

WILLIAM: Oh, Mr. Rencelaw, what blessings can repay you.

RENCELAW: The blessings of my own approving conscience. "The heart of the feeling man is like the noble tree, which, wounded itself, yet pours forth precious balm." When the just man quits this transitory world, the dark angel of death enshrouds him with heavenly joy, and bears his smiling spirit to the bright regions of eternal bliss. [*Exit Rencelaw, leading boy, R.*]

WILLIAM: Well, if there's a happier man in all the world than Bill Dowton, I should like to see him. My brother Edward again a man, – you, my dear sister, again restored to me – come, we'll go tell all the news; hurrah! hurrah! [*Singing*]

*"We'll dance all night by the bright moonlight,
And go home with the girls in the morning."*

Last Scene

Interior of Cottage as in Act 1st, Scene 1st. Everything denoting domestic peace and tranquil happiness – The sun is setting over the hills at back of landscape. – Edward discovered near music stand, R. – Julia seated on low stool on his L. – Mary sewing at handsome work table, L. – Elegant table, R. 2 E. with astral lamp not lighted – Bible and other books on it. – Two beautiful flower-stands, with roses, myrtles, etc., under window, L. and R. – Bird-cages on wings, R. and L. – Covers of tables, chairs, etc., all extremely neat, and in keeping.

Edward plays on flute. symphony to "Home, Sweet Home." – Julia sings first verse – Flute solo accompaniment – The burthen is then taken up by chorus of villagers behind – Orchestral accompaniments, etc. – Gradually crescendo, forte – Villagers enter from C. gradually, grouping L. and C. – Action of recognition and good wishes, etc., while the melody is progressing – The melody is repeated quicker, and all retire with the exception of Edward, Mary, Julia, William, and Agnes, singing, and becoming gradually diminuendo – Air repeated slowly – Julia kneels to Edward, who is at table, R., seated, in prayer – Edward's hand on Bible, and pointing up – Mary standing, leaning upon his chair – William and Agnes, L. C. – Music till curtain falls – Picture

The End

FASHION

ANNA CORA MOWATT

FASHION is another play from the past century that is frequently revived. One of the notable twentieth-century productions, which finally recorded 235 performances, was at the Provincetown Theatre in 1924 while the triumvirate of Kenneth Macgowan, Robert Edmond Jones, and Eugene O'Neill were directing the fortunes of that group. On that occasion, the critics, perhaps wishing to indicate their familiarity with the historical significance of the play, drew on Edgar Allen Poe for some of their comments. They selected such excerpts from Poe's two essays on *Fashion* (*Broadway Journal*, March 29 and April 5, 1845) as "total deficiency in verisimilitude," "there is not one particle of nature beyond green room nature," "no literary quality." The quotations were accurate but do not indicate that Poe liked the play. A longer passage represents him more correctly:

. . . there is much merit in *Fashion* and in many respects (and those of a *telling* character) it is superior to any American play. The entire getting-up was admirable. *Fashion*, upon the whole, was well received by a large, fashionable, and critical audience. Compared with the generality of modern dramas, it is a good play – compared with most American dramas it is a *very* good one.

What Poe did not like was the artificialities and absurdities, not of *Fashion*, but of the commonly accepted theatrical conventions: "the coming forward to the footlights when anything of interest is to be told, the reading of private letters in a loud rhetorical tone, the preposterous soliloquizing and even more preposterous asides." He felt that dramatic art had remained "stationary while all of its sisters have been making rapid progress. We need thought of our own, principles of dramatic action drawn not from the 'old dramatists' but from the fountain of a nature that can never grow old." Poe's most telling comment on *Fashion* appeared in his review of April 5, 1845: ". . . been to see it every night since its first production." It had then been playing for ten nights. Certainly this was not the attendance record of a disenchanted spectator.

Anna Cora Ogden Mowatt Ritchie, to use her full and final name, was born in Bordeaux, France, in 1819, the ninth of seventeen children of a genteel and substantially endowed family. Her father, S. G. Ogden, a prosperous New

York merchant, supplied the substance, and her mother, granddaughter of Francis Lewis, a signer of the Declaration of Independence, provided the gentility. The early life of Anna Cora was in reality not too sheltered. The family regularly got up theatricals in the parlor, and they had immediately available enough characters for a sizable *dramatis personae* without going outside the family. The first such performance that Anna Cora recalled was an *Othello* in French which the children prepared for their father's birthday. This was in 1825, when she was only six. In 1826 the family left their French chateau, La Castagne, and moved to New Rochelle, New York, where Anna entered boarding school with her sisters. The home theatricals continued in America. With some assistance with the costuming from their neighbor Edmund Simpson, the manager of the Park Theatre, the girls prepared a production of Voltaire's *Alzire*.

Ordinarily these performances were restricted to the domestic circle, but occasionally some intimate of the family was admitted. James Mowatt, a lawyer friend, was one of the select few. Anna was still at boarding school and just thirteen, but her immaturity did not prevent the blossoming of a love-at-first-sight romance with Mr. Mowatt. When Anna Cora turned fourteen, Mowatt proposed marriage; he had already been directing the reading and general education of his young love. The family did not disapprove of the match, but they insisted she wait until she had reached seventeen. Mowatt's entreaties were too strong. Anna Cora and one of her sisters pawned some jewels to buy a trousseau, and the young couple were married by a French clergyman on October 6, 1834, without the family's consent.

The fifteen-year-old bride and her husband settled in Flatbush, Long Island. Her family soon overcame their initial prejudice, and the Mowatts led a happy and playful life, marred only by Anna Cora's disposition to illness. In the first years of her marriage she suffered from the tuberculosis that was to plague her throughout her life. While restricted to bed she began to write, and at sixteen she published a long romantic poem (six cantos and 204 pages), *Pelayo, or The Cavern of Covadonga*, under the pseudonym "Isabel." The critics condemned the piece; though she herself later admitted it was "unmitigated stuff," she immediately prepared a protest to the critics, written in verse and called *Reviewers Reviewed*. When her health permitted, the Flatbush home was the scene of grand *fêtes*, concerts, *tableaux vivants;* Mrs. Mowatt's first original theatrical piece, an operetta called *The Gypsy Wanderer*, was performed for family and friends. Finally her health became so poor that the doctor recommended a sea voyage. Without her husband and with one of her father's sisters as a companion, she sailed for England in the spring of 1837. Mr. Mowatt joined her the following year.

After three years of traveling and theatregoing in England, Germany, and particularly France, where she saw Rachel, she returned to the happy amateur theatricals of Flatbush and the unpleasant discovery that her husband's stock speculations had left them penniless. A home production of the drama of *Gulzara, or The Persian Slave,* her first published play (in *The New World*), helped her spirits but not the family finances. To alleviate their pecuniary distress, she suppressed the prejudice against public theatrical performances which had been instilled in her by the sermons of the Reverend Manton Eastburn at Grace Church. She determined to try her talent at public reading for profit. Still not daring to risk an initial New York appearance, and with the written encouragement of such notables as Longfellow, she made her debut at the Masonic Temple in Boston reading as her principal selection "The Lay of the Last Minstrel." Her three Boston readings were warmly received, as was her appearance in Providence. However, when she appeared at the Stuyvesant Institute on November 18, 1841, many New Yorkers questioned the propriety of such an undertaking for a lady of quality. Some of her friends came to her defense. Mrs. Frances Osgood wrote a long poem praising her courage and daring; the first stanza read:

> Ne'er heed them, Cora, dear,
>   The carping few who say
> Thou leavest woman's holier sphere
>   For lights and vain display.

Having clearly seen her talents as a performer, the Park Theatre management offered her an acting engagement, but, even to Mrs. Mowatt, that step seemed a bit too adventurous.

Again her tuberculous condition restricted her activities. During her summer's rest at Lenox, Massachusetts, she was not, however, completely idle; she stage-managed a play for the girls in Miss Sedgwick's school. In the fall she was still not well enough to undertake further public readings. When normal medical treatment proved ineffective, Epes Sargent, the editor who had published her *Gulzara,* persuaded her to try the new science of mesmerism and introduced her to Dr. William Francis Channing, a mesmeric healer. Channing agreed to see whether she would be susceptible to his powers. The first hypnotic session was conducted in the Mowatts' parlor at the Astor House. Mrs. Mowatt proved to be a cooperative subject, and after coming out of the trance she reported that though she was slightly dizzy she definitely felt more rested than she had in weeks. Thereafter the mesmeric séances were adopted as regular therapy, and in this strange new world of dreams and fantasies Mrs. Mowatt apparently even developed a distinct trance personality, known as "the gypsy." While she was under the spell, "the gypsy" would converse with Channing, Sargent, or Mr. Mowatt. After she was brought back, Mrs. Mowatt had no knowledge of what "the gypsy" had said. She became enchanted with the new subworld and for the rest of her life submitted to mesmerism at the first signs of illness.

Even with the many hours spent in this other region, she continued her writing, producing a long list of periodical pieces, usually published under the pseudonym "Helen Berkley." She wrote stories and sketches for such publications as *The Columbian, The Democratic Review, Ladies' Companion, Godey's,* and *Graham's,* and wrote and edited "to order" such books and pamphlets as *Housekeeping Made Easy, Book of the Toilette,* and *Etiquette of Matrimony.*

Epes Sargent had followed her writing career as diligently as he had the mesmeric experiments. On one occasion he was reported to have told her that she had "more decided talent for the stage than for anything else": she should try her hand at a comedy for the theatre. Mrs. Mowatt tried; the result was *Fashion.* Mr. Simpson, the manager of the Park and Mrs. Mowatt's childhood neighbor, read it, approved, and immediately passed it on to Mr. Barry, his stage manager. Many a would-be playwright would envy the charmed fortune that seemed to direct all of Mrs. Mowatt's theatrical ventures. They invariably moved along with dispatch and success. *Fashion* opened at the Park on March 24, 1845.

With Mrs. Mowatt's name again in the public eye, the managers renewed their efforts to persuade her to act. Her new acquaintance with the stage and stage people had apparently melted all prejudice, and she made her debut as Pauline in *The Lady of Lyons* at the Park Theatre on June 13, 1845, after only three weeks of preparation. According to Mrs. Mowatt, the preparation consisted of exercise with dumbbells and four hours of voice drill per day. Anyone acquainted with present-day therapy for a tubercular will shudder at Mrs. Mowatt's activity. This was only the beginning. With her leading man, W. H. Crisp, she began a country-wide tour, starting at the Walnut Street Theatre in Philadelphia and ending in New York in May, 1846, after playing some two hundred nights in fourteen different roles in such cities as Richmond, Charleston, Savannah, New Orleans, and Mobile. The following season was equally demanding. With a new leading man, E. L. Davenport, in place of Crisp, she added Boston, Baltimore, Louisville, and Cincinnati to her itinerary.

In the summer of 1847, while Mr. Mowatt was in London arranging for her appearances there, she retired to her writing. Both enterprises were successful. Her new play, *Armand,* opened at the Park on September 27, 1847, and on December 7 she appeared at the Theatre Royal in Manchester. On January 5, 1848, she opened a six-week engagement at the Princess's Theatre in London. The following autumn Mr. Mowatt became ill. This was the beginning of a nightmarish four years of fulfilling engagements in London and the provinces between her illnesses and his. They had been inseparable in all their travels; it was now strange and frightening for Mrs. Mowatt to travel to new cities and new theatres without him. Mr. Mowatt died in January, 1851, while she was en route from Dublin to Newcastle. After a few months of idleness following her husband's death and another brief tour of the provinces, she returned to the United States and opened an engagement at Niblo's Garden Theatre. For the next two seasons she covered the country-wide theatrical circuit, even including such out-of-the-way stands as Terre Haute, Indiana, and Xenia, Ohio. This rigorous routine was beyond her capacity. Finally a severe cold and touch of New Orleans malaria brought on a complete collapse. In March, 1853, she was forced to cancel her Memphis engagement and return to her father's home in Astoria, Long Island. The following spring she was out again – this time for a farewell tour of the major cities, concluding with a benefit performance at Niblo's on June 3, 1854. It was reported that she received six thousand dollars for this single night. On June 6, 1854, she was married to William F. Ritchie, the editor of the Richmond *Enquirer*, whom she had first met two years earlier. It was not a happy marriage. In August, 1860, Mrs. Ritchie went abroad; she lived most of the rest of her life alone in England. She died at Twickenham on July 28, 1870.

During her lifetime Mrs. Mowatt was more widely known for her acting than for her writing; she received star billing and public adulation wherever she performed. After her debut, the New York *Herald* wrote:

When the curtain fell, the applause was tremendous. A gentleman in the pit called out "three cheers" and three loud cheers were given accordingly. Mrs. Mowatt soon appeared, led on by Mr. Crisp. The cheers – shouts – screams – plaudits burst forth afresh, whilst a whirlwind of pocket handkerchiefs swept over the boxes, and five or six hundred boots thundered in the galleries. Mrs. Mowatt courtesied, and a shower of bouquets fell at her feet.

But although her playing – Pauline in *The Lady of Lyons* and Juliet were her favorite roles – seems always to have enjoyed the full favor of the audience, the critics frequently modified their praise of her "force and refinement" with mild reproofs. *The Albion* wrote on September 25, 1847:

She reads her author delicately and with an evident appreciation of the beauties of language – and she declaims with energy – but it is but mere reading and declamation. We want to see Mrs. Mowatt throw herself into the real embodiment of her language. We look for that identification with her characters which alone constitutes great acting.

And the New York *Spirit of the Times* said on May 31, 1852:

Mrs. Mowatt possesses an extremely handsome figure, with a fine face, but she has in a degree acquired the unpleasant habit of raising up her shoulders then sinking them, for the purpose, it would appear, of giving intensity to her expressions of gesticulation, but when constantly resorted to becomes painful to the beholder; she has also acquired the habit of raising her voice to its highest compass, then suddenly dropping down to its lowest notes, producing most unmusical sounds – as her speaking organ is husky and inflexible in the extreme.

Mrs. Mowatt made two pertinent self-appraisals. Although she admired and somewhat envied the actors who exercised a cold-blooded control over their playing, she said, "No amount of study or discipline could have enabled me to belong to the grand and passionless school. I never succeeded in stirring the hearts of others unless I was deeply affected myself." And in her description of the young actress in "An Unknown Tragedian" (one of the narratives in *Mimic Life*) she was undoubtedly drawing a self-portrait.

The extreme polish of her delivery lent one great charm to her personations. Never was the Saxon tongue more musically syllabled than by her lips. Every word was cut fine and sharp and invested with a value and a meaning which betokened intellect, though unallied with ardor.

In the literary histories of the nineteenth century, Mrs. Mowatt is frequently described as a one-play (*Fashion*) author; but in addition to the three other plays already noted, the early poems, the magazine articles, and the compilations on domestic behavior, she wrote a series of romantic novels and narratives under such titles as *Evelyn, or A Heart Unmasked; The Twin Roses;* and *Italian Life and Legends;* two romantic tales of theatrical life of the period, under the title *Mimic Life, or Before and Behind the Curtain;* and a detailed account of her own experiences in *Autobiography of an Actress, or Eight Years on the Stage* – a striking list when one remembers that these were written largely between theatrical engagements and during her many illnesses.

The *Autobiography* provides a detailed documentation of the first performances of *Fashion*. Mrs. Mowatt echoed the sentiments of Poe, or rather was echoed by him, when she explained that this good-humored satire on "American parvenuism" was designed "wholly as an *acting* comedy; a *dramatic*, not a literary, success was what I desired to achieve. Caution suggested my not aiming at both at once." When she attended her first rehearsal, she reported that "it gave me an odd sensation to hear my own language uttered in all varieties of tones, and often conveying a meaning of which I did not suppose it to be susceptible." After the "unequivocally brilliant success" of the opening performance, the management, somewhat indulgently and distrustfully, invited her to attend the next day's rehearsal to institute cuts and changes. She reported on this rehearsal:

Mr. Barry arranged the cuts, requesting my approval in a manner which left me little alternative. [How many playwrights before and after have felt as Mrs. Mowatt did!] The principal actors were presented to me, and I made as many delicate hints concerning certain misrepresentations of the text as I dared venture upon. It was very evident that they singly and collectively entertained the opinion that an author never knew the true meaning of his own words. His suppositions to the contrary were mere hallucinations.

During the initial run of twenty nights in New York, which began on March 24, 1845, and which was described as a sumptuous, elaborate, and expertly acted production, *Fashion* was also performed at the Walnut Street Theatre in Philadelphia with equal style and success. Mrs. Mowatt was unable, or unwilling, to say which was the superior performance. The same year *Fashion* was repeated in theatres throughout the country: Charleston, Mobile, New Orleans, frequently with Mrs. Mowatt in the part of Gertrude. New York and Philadelphia saw it repeatedly during the summer of 1845. In January, 1850, it had its first performances in London with a two-week engagement at the Royal Olympic. On January 9, 1850, the London *Sun* reported:

America is worthily repaying the dramatic debt she owes us. The seeds of the dramatic art, which have been scattered by all our best dramatic artists broadcast on the American soil, have fructified, and are now bearing fruit. *Fashion* is worthy to take its place by the side of the English comedies.

Another London reviewer found it "little short of a great work" and urged Mrs. Mowatt to throw aside her timidity "and give us something of England and the English; we shall feel proud to claim her as one of us."

No other play of the nineteenth-century American theatre, except of course *Uncle Tom's Cabin*, has received so much attention from twentieth-century producing groups, particularly amateur and semiprofessional. The San Francisco Players Club Theatre performed it in 1924; the drama group of St. Bartholomew's Church, New York, in 1934; Hunter College, with the college president, George N. Shuster, as Tennyson Twinkle, in 1941; and the Honolulu Community Theatre in 1951. Notable among the hundred or more twentieth-century renderings was that of the Provincetown group in 1924. Undoubtedly some of these performances ridiculed the play as a relic of our dramatic past, but the wise ones played it straight as a delightful and witty family-album satire on New York society of the middle of the past century.

Many plays with similar intent appeared in the period immediately before and after *Fashion*, but none of them represented the times so vigorously, accurately, and gaily, or achieved comparable stage success. *Self*, by Mrs. Sidney F. Bateman, first performed at Burton's New Theatre on October 27, 1856, most nearly approached *Fashion* in theme and treatment. *Self* was more realistic in its representation of immediate local details, but it was decidedly inferior to *Fashion* in the quality of its characterizations and dialogue. The domestic social satires that appeared later in the century were, on the whole, superior: Howard's *The Henrietta*, Fitch's *The Climbers*, and Mitchell's *The New York Idea*. In a way *Fashion* was the forerunner, even of such twentieth-century society and family comedies as *Life With Father*.

Some of the particular social comment of *Fashion* – the rise of the "commercial emporium," the impending bankruptcy – belong to the midcentury; but the larger portion of Mrs. Mowatt's animated family album is timeless. The Mrs. Tiffanys, testing their society wings with amusing awkwardness; the Count Jolimaitres, with their foreign-dandy posturings; and the Adam Truemans, with their unabashed and outspoken disapproval of all frauds, are eternal characters in life and on the stage. Mrs. Mowatt wrote with an intimate knowledge of the society she portrayed, and, like all good playwrights, she sketched portraits that could be filled in by theatre-wise actors.

FASHION

ANNA CORA MOWATT

PREFACE

The Comedy of *Fashion* was intended as a good-natured satire upon some of the follies incident to a new country, where foreign dross sometimes passes for gold, while native gold is cast aside as dross; where the vanities rather than the virtues of other lands are too often imitated, and where the stamp of *Fashion* gives currency even to the coinage of vice.

The reception with which the Comedy was favoured proves that the picture represented was not a highly exaggerated one.

It was first produced at the Park Theatre, New York, in March, 1845.

The splendid manner in which the play was put upon the stage, and the combined efforts of an extremely talented company, ensured it a long continued success. It was afterwards received with the same indulgence in all the principal cities of the United States, for which the authoress is doubtless indebted to the proverbial gallantry of Americans to a countrywoman.

A.C.M.

London, January, 1850

CHARACTERS

ADAM TRUEMAN, *a Farmer from Catteraugus*
COUNT JOLIMAITRE, *a fashionable European Importation*
COLONEL HOWARD, *an Officer in the U. S. Army*
MR. TIFFANY, *a New York Merchant*
T. TENNYSON TWINKLE, *a Modern Poet*
AUGUSTUS FOGG, *a Drawing-Room Appendage*
SNOBSON, *a rare species of Confidential Clerk*

ZEKE, *a coloured Servant*
MRS. TIFFANY, *a Lady who imagines herself fashionable*
PRUDENCE, *a Maiden Lady of a certain age*
MILLINETTE, *a French Lady's Maid*
GERTRUDE, *a Governess*
SERAPHINA TIFFANY, *a Belle*

LADIES AND GENTLEMEN OF
THE BALL-ROOM

PROLOGUE
EPES SARGENT

Enter a Gentleman – Mr. Crisp – reading a newspaper
" *'Fashion, A Comedy.'* I'll go; but stay –
Now I read farther, 'tis a *native* play!
Bah! home-made calicoes are well enough,
But home-made dramas must be stupid stuff.

Had it the *London* stamp, 'twould do – but then,
For plays, we lack the manners and the men!"

Thus speaks *one* critic. Hear *another's* creed: –
" *'Fashion!'* – What's here? [*Reads*] It never can succeed!
What! from a *woman's* pen? It takes a *man*
To write a comedy – no woman can."

317

Well, sir, and what say *you?* And why that
frown?
His eyes uprolled, he lays the paper down: –
"Here! take," he says, "the unclean thing
away!
'Tis tainted with a notice of a *play!*"

But, sir! – but, gentlemen! – you, sir, who think
No comedy can flow from *native* ink, –
Are we such *perfect* monsters, or such *dull,*
That wit no traits for ridicule can cull?
Have we no follies here to be redressed?
No vices gibetted? no crimes confessed?

"But then, a female hand can't lay the lash
on!"
"How know you *that*, sir, when the theme is
'Fashion'?"

And now, come forth, thou man of sanctity!
How shall I venture a reply to thee?
The *Stage* – what is it, though beneath *thy*
ban,
But a *Daguerreotype* of life and man?
Arraign poor human nature, if you will,
But let the *Drama* have her mission still!
Let her, with honest purpose, still reflect
The faults which keen-eyed Satire may detect.
For there *be* men, who fear not an hereafter,
Yet tremble at the Hell of public laughter!

Friends, from these scoffers we appeal to you!
Condemn the *false*, but O! applaud the *true.*
Grant that *some* wit may grow on native soil,
And Art's fair fabric rise from woman's toil –
While we exhibit but to reprehend
The social vices, 'tis for *you* to mend!

ACT I

*A splendid Drawing-Room in the House of
Mrs. Tiffany. Open folding doors centre, discovering a Conservatory. On either side glass
windows down to the ground. Doors on right
and left. Mirror, couches, ottomans, a table
with albums, etc., beside it an arm-chair. Millinette dusting furniture, etc. Zeke in a dashing
livery, scarlet coat, etc.*

ZEKE: Dere's a coat to take de eyes ob all Broadway! Ah! Missy, it am de fixins dat make de
natural *born* gemman. A libery for ever!
Dere's a pair ob insuppressibles to 'stonish de
coloured population.
MILLINETTE: Oh, *oui.* Monsieur Zeke. [*Very*

politely] I not *comprend* one word he say!
[*Aside*]
ZEKE: I tell 'ee what, Missy, I'm 'stordinary
glad to find dis a bery 'spectabul like situation!
Now as you've made de acquaintance ob dis
here family, and dere you've had a supernumerary advantage ob me – seeing dat I only re-
ceibed my appointment dis morning. What I
wants to know is your publicated opinion, privately expressed, ob de domestic circle.
MILLINETTE: You mean vat *espèce*, vat kind of
personnes are Monsieur and Madame Tiffany?
Ah! Monsieur is not de same ting as
Madame, – not at all.
ZEKE: Well, I s'pose he ain't altogether.
MILLINETTE: Monsieur is man of business, –
Madame is lady of fashion. Monsieur make the
money, – Madame spend it. Monsieur nobody
at all, – Madame everybody altogether. Ah!
Monsieur Zeke, de money is all dat is *neces-
saire* in dis country to make one lady of fashion. Oh! it is quite anoder ting in *la belle
France!*
ZEKE: A bery lucifer explanation. Well, now
we've disposed ob de heads of de family, who
come next?
MILLINETTE: First, dere is Mademoiselle Seraphina Tiffany. Mademoiselle is not at all one
proper *personne.* Mademoiselle Seraphina is
one coquette. Dat is not de mode in *la belle
France;* de ladies, dere, never learn *la coque-
trie* until dey do get one husband.
ZEKE: I tell 'ee what, Missy, I disreprobate dat
proceeding altogeder!
MILLINETTE: Vait! I have not tell you all *la fam-
ille* yet. Dere is Ma'mselle Prudence – Madame's sister, one very *bizarre* personne. Den
dere is Ma'mselle Gertrude, but she is not anybody at all; she only teach Mademoiselle Seraphina *la musique.*
ZEKE: Well, now, Missy, what's your own spe-
cial defunctions?
MILLINETTE: I not understand, Monsieur Zeke.
ZEKE: Den I'll amplify. What's de nature ob
your exclusive services?
MILLINETTE: *Ah, oui! je comprend.* I am Mad-
ame's *femme de chambre* – her lady's maid,
Monsieur Zeke. I teach Madame *les modes de
Paris,* and Madame set de fashion for all New
York. You see, Monsieur Zeke, dat it is me,
moi-même, dat do lead de fashion for all de
American *beau monde!*
ZEKE: Yah! yah! yah! I hab de idea by de heel.

Well now, p'raps you can 'lustrify my officials?

MILLINETTE: Vat you will have to do? Oh! much tings, much tings. You vait on de table, – you tend de door, – you clean de boots, – you run de errands, – you drive de carriage, – you rub de horses, – you take care of de flowers, – you carry de water, – you help cook de dinner, – you wash de dishes, – and den you always remember to do everyting I tell you to!

ZEKE: Wheugh, am dat *all*?

MILLINETTE: All I can tink of now. To-day is Madame's day of reception, and all her grand friends do make her one *petite* visit. You mind run fast ven de bell do ring.

ZEKE: Run? If it wasn't for dese superfluminous trimmings, I tell 'ee what, Missy, I'd run –

MRS. TIFFANY: [*Outside*] Millinette!

MILLINETTE: Here comes Madame! You better go, Monsieur Zeke.

ZEKE: Look ahea, Massa Zeke, doesn't dis open rich! [*Aside*]

Exit Zeke

Enter Mrs. Tiffany right, dressed in the most extravagant height of fashion

MRS. TIFFANY: Is everything in order, Millinette? Ah! very elegant, very elegant indeed! There is a *jenny-says-quoi* look about this furniture, – an air of fashion and gentility perfectly bewitching. Is there not, Millinette?

MILLINETTE: Oh, *oui*, Madame!

MRS. TIFFANY: But where is Miss Seraphina? It is twelve o'clock; our visitors will be pouring in, and she has not made her appearance. But I hear that nothing is more fashionable than to keep people waiting. – None but vulgar persons pay any attention to punctuality. Is it not so, Millinette?

MILLINETTE: Quite *comme il faut*. – Great personnes always do make little personnes wait, Madame.

MRS. TIFFANY: This mode of receiving visitors only upon one specified day of the week is a most convenient custom! It saves the trouble of keeping the house continually in order and of being always dressed. I flatter myself that *I* was the first to introduce it amongst the New York *ee-light*. You are quite sure that it is strictly a Parisian mode, Millinette?

MILLINETTE: Oh, *oui*, Madame; entirely *mode de Paris*.

MRS. TIFFANY: This girl is worth her weight in gold. [*Aside*] Millinette, how do you say *arm-chair* in French?

MILLINETTE: *Fauteuil*, Madame.

MRS. TIFFANY: *Fo-tool!* That has a foreign – an out-of-the-wayish sound that is perfectly charming – and so genteel! There is something about our American words decidedly vulgar. *Fowtool!* how refined. *Fowtool! Arm-chair!* what a difference!

MILLINETTE: Madame have one charmante pronunciation. *Fowtool!* [*Mimicking aside*] Charmante, Madame!

MRS. TIFFANY: Do you think so, Millinette? Well, I believe I have. But a woman of refinement and of fashion can always accommodate herself to everything foreign! And a week's study of that invaluable work – *"French without a Master,"* has made me quite at home in the court language of Europe! But where is the new valet? I'm rather sorry that he is black, but to obtain a white American for a domestic is almost impossible; and they call this a free country! What did you say was the name of this new servant, Millinette?

MILLINETTE: He do say his name is Monsieur Zeke.

MRS. TIFFANY: Ezekiel, I suppose. Zeke! Dear me, such a vulgar name will compromise the dignity of the whole family. Can you not suggest something more aristocratic, Millinette? Something *French!*

MILLINETTE: Oh, *oui*, Madame; *Adolph* is one very fine name.

MRS. TIFFANY: A-dolph! Charming! Ring the bell, Millinette! [*Millinette rings the bell*] I will change his name immediately, besides giving him a few directions. [*Enter Zeke, left. Mrs. Tiffany addresses him with great dignity*] Your name, I hear, is *Ezekiel*. – I consider it too plebeian an appellation to be uttered in my presence. In future you are called A-dolph. Don't reply, – never interrupt me when I am speaking. A-dolph, as my guests arrive, I desire that you will inquire the name of every person, and then announce it in a loud, clear tone. *That* is the fashion in Paris.

Millinette retires up the stage

ZEKE: Consider de office discharged, Missus. [*Speaking very loudly*]

MRS. TIFFANY: Silence! Your business is to obey and not to talk.

ZEKE: I'm dumb, Missus!

MRS. TIFFANY: [*Pointing up stage*] A-dolph, place that *fowtool* behind me.

ZEKE: [*Looking about him*] I habn't got dat far in de dictionary yet. No matter, a genus gets his learning by nature.

Takes up the table and places it behind Mrs. Tiffany, then expresses in dumb show great satisfaction. Mrs. Tiffany, as she goes to sit, discovers the mistake

MRS. TIFFANY: You dolt! Where have you lived not to know that *fowtool* is the French for *arm-chair?* What ignorance! Leave the room this instant.

Mrs. Tiffany draws forward an arm-chair and sits. Millinette comes forward suppressing her merriment at Zeke's mistake and removes the table

ZEKE: Dem's de defects ob not having a libery education.

Exit left

Prudence peeps in, right

PRUDENCE: I wonder if any of the fine folks have come yet. Not a soul, – I knew they hadn't. There's Betsy all alone. [*Walks in*] Sister Betsy!

MRS. TIFFANY: Prudence! how many times have I desired you to call me *Elizabeth? Betsy* is the height of vulgarity.

PRUDENCE: Oh! I forgot. Dear me, how spruce we do look here, to be sure, – everything in first rate style now, Betsy. [*Mrs. Tiffany looks at her angrily*] Elizabeth, I mean. Who would have thought, when you and I were sitting behind that little mahogany-coloured counter, in Canal Street, making up flashy hats and caps –

MRS. TIFFANY: Prudence, what *do* you mean? Millinette, leave the room.

MILLINETTE: *Oui*, Madame.

Millinette pretends to arrange the books upon a side table, but lingers to listen

PRUDENCE: But I always predicted it, – I always told you so, Betsy – I always said you were destined to rise above your station!

MRS. TIFFANY: Prudence! Prudence! have I not told you that –

PRUDENCE: No, Betsy, it was *I* that told *you*, when we used to buy our silks and ribbons of

Mr. Antony Tiffany – *"talking Tony"* you know we used to call him, and when you always put on the finest bonnet in our shop to go to his, – and when you staid so long smiling and chattering with him, I always told you that *something* would grow out of it – and didn't it?

MRS. TIFFANY: Millinette, send Seraphina here instantly. Leave the room.

MILLINETTE: *Oui*, Madame. So dis Americaine ladi of fashion vas one *milliner?* Oh, vat a fine country for *les marchandes des modes!* I shall send for all my relation by de next packet! [*Aside*]

Exit Millinette

MRS. TIFFANY: Prudence! never let me hear you mention this subject again. Forget what we *have* been, it is enough to remember that we *are* of the *upper ten thousand!*

Prudence goes left and sits. Enter Seraphina, very extravagantly dressed

MRS. TIFFANY: How bewitchingly you look, my dear! Does Millinette say that that head-dress is strictly Parisian?

SERAPHINA: Oh yes, Mamma, all the rage! They call it a *lady's tarpaulin*, and it is the exact pattern of one worn by the Princess Clementina at the last court ball.

MRS. TIFFANY: Now, Seraphina, my dear, don't be too particular in your attentions to gentlemen not eligible. There is Count Jolimaitre, decidedly the most fashionable foreigner in town, – and so refined, – so much accustomed to associate with the first nobility in his own country that he can hardly tolerate the vulgarity of Americans in general. You may devote yourself to him. Mrs. Proudacre is dying to become acquainted with him. By the by, if she or her daughters should happen to drop in, be sure you don't introduce them to the Count. It is not the fashion in Paris to introduce – Millinette told me so.

Enter Zeke

ZEKE: [*In a very loud voice*] Mister T. Tennyson Twinkle!

MRS. TIFFANY: Show him up. [*Exit Zeke*]

PRUDENCE: I must be running away. [*Going*]

MRS. TIFFANY: Mr. T. Tennyson Twinkle – a very literary young man and a sweet poet! It is all the rage to patronize poets! Quick, Seraphina, hand me that magazine. – Mr. Twinkle writes for it.

Seraphina hands the magazine; Mrs. Tiffany seats herself in an arm-chair and opens the book

PRUDENCE: [*Returning*] There's Betsy trying to make out that reading without her spectacles. [*Takes a pair of spectacles out of her pocket and hands them to Mrs. Tiffany*] There, Betsy, I knew you were going to ask for them. Ah! they're a blessing when one is growing old!

MRS. TIFFANY: What do you mean, Prudence? A woman of fashion *never* grows old! Age is always out of fashion.

PRUDENCE: Oh, dear! what a delightful thing it is to be fashionable. [*Exit Prudence. Mrs. Tiffany resumes her seat*]

Enter Twinkle. He salutes Seraphina

TWINKLE: Fair Seraphina! The sun itself grows dim,
Unless you aid his light and shine on him!

SERAPHINA: Ah! Mr. Twinkle, there is no such thing as answering you.

TWINKLE: [*Looks around and perceives Mrs. Tiffany*] The "New Monthly Vernal Galaxy." Reading my verses, by all that's charming! Sensible woman! I won't interrupt her. [*Aside*]

MRS. TIFFANY: [*Rising and coming forward*] Ah! Mr. Twinkle, is that you? I was perfectly *abimé* at the perusal of your very *distingué* verses.

TWINKLE: I am overwhelmed, Madam. Permit me. [*Taking the magazine*] Yes, they do read tolerably. And you must take into consideration, ladies, the rapidity with which they were written. Four minutes and a half by the stop watch! The true test of a poet is the *velocity* with which he composes. Really, they do look very prettily, and they read tolerably – *quite* tolerably – *very* tolerably, – especially the first verse. [*Reads*] "To Seraphina T——."

SERAPHINA: Oh! Mr. Twinkle!

TWINKLE: [*Reads*] "Around my heart" –

MRS. TIFFANY: How touching! Really, Mr. Twinkle, quite tender!

TWINKLE: [*Recommencing*] "Around my heart" –

MRS. TIFFANY: Oh, I must tell you, Mr. Twinkle! I heard the other day that poets were the

aristocrats of literature. That's one reason I like them, for I do dote on all aristocracy!

TWINKLE: Oh, Madam, how flattering! Now pray lend me your ears! [*Reads*]
"Around my heart thou weavest" –

SERAPHINA: That is such a *sweet* commencement, Mr. Twinkle!

TWINKLE: [*Aside*] I wish she wouldn't interrupt me! [*Reads*]
"Around my heart thou weavest a spell" –

MRS. TIFFANY: Beautiful! But excuse me one moment, while I say a word to Seraphina! Don't be too affable, my dear! Poets are very ornamental appendages to the drawing-room, but they are always as poor as their own verses. They don't make eligible husbands! [*Aside to Seraphina*]

TWINKLE: [*Aside*] Confound their interruptions! My dear Madam, unless you pay the utmost attention you cannot catch the ideas. Are you ready? Well, now you shall hear it to the end! [*Reads*]
"Around my heart thou weavest a spell
"Whose" –

Enter Zeke

ZEKE: Mister Augustus Fogg! A bery misty lookin' young gemman? [*Aside*]

MRS. TIFFANY: Show him up, A-dolph! [*Exit Zeke*]

TWINKLE: This is too much!

SERAPHINA: Exquisite verses, Mr. Twinkle, – exquisite!

TWINKLE: Ah, lovely Seraphina! your smile of approval transports me to the summit of Olympus.

SERAPHINA: Then I must frown, for I would not send you so far away.

TWINKLE: Enchantress! It's all over with her. [*Aside*]

Retire up right and converse

MRS. TIFFANY: Mr. Fogg belongs to one of our oldest families, – to be sure he is the most difficult person in the world to entertain, for he never takes the trouble to talk, and never notices anything or anybody, – but then I hear that nothing is considered so vulgar as to betray any emotion, or to attempt to render oneself agreeable!

Enter Mr. Fogg, fashionably attired but in very dark clothes

FOGG: [*Bowing stiffly*] Mrs. Tiffany, your most obedient. Miss Seraphina, yours. How d'ye do, Twinkle?

MRS. TIFFANY: Mr. Fogg, how do you do? Fine weather, – delightful, isn't it?

FOGG: I am indifferent to weather, Madam.

MRS. TIFFANY: Been to the opera, Mr. Fogg? I hear that the *bow monde* make their *debutt* there every evening.

FOGG: I consider operas a bore, Madam.

SERAPHINA: [*Advancing*] You must hear Mr. Twinkle's verses, Mr. Fogg!

FOGG: I am indifferent to verses, Miss Seraphina.

SERAPHINA: But Mr. Twinkle's verses are addressed to me!

TWINKLE: Now pay attention, Fogg! [*Reads*] –
"Around my heart thou weavest a spell
"Whose magic I" –

Enter Zeke

ZEKE: Mister – No, he say he ain't no Mister –

TWINKLE: "Around my heart thou weavest a spell
"Whose magic I can never tell!"

MRS. TIFFANY: Speak in a loud, clear tone, A-dolph!

TWINKLE: This is terrible!

ZEKE: Mister Count Jolly-made-her!

MRS. TIFFANY: Count Jolimaitre! Good gracious! Zeke, Zeke, – A-dolph, I mean. – Dear me, what a mistake! [*Aside*] Set that chair out of the way, – put that table back. Seraphina, my dear, are you all in order? Dear me! dear me! Your dress is so tumbled! [*Arranges her dress*] What are you grinning at? [*To Zeke*] Beg the Count to *honour* us by walking up! [*Exit Zeke*] Seraphina, my dear [*Aside to her*] remember now what I told you about the Count. He is a man of the highest, – good gracious! I am so flurried; and nothing is so ungenteel as agitation! what will the Count think! Mr. Twinkle, pray stand out of the way! Seraphina, my dear, place yourself on my right! Mr. Fogg, the conservatory – beautiful flowers, – pray amuse yourself in the conservatory.

FOGG: I am indifferent to flowers, Madam.

MRS. TIFFANY: Dear me! the man stands right in the way, – just where the Count must make his *entray!* [*Aside*] Mr. Fogg, – pray –

Enter Count Jolimaitre, very dashingly dressed; he wears a moustache

MRS. TIFFANY: Oh, Count, this unexpected honour –

SERAPHINA: Count, this inexpressible pleasure –

COUNT: Beg you won't mention it, Madam! Miss Seraphina, your most devoted!

MRS. TIFFANY: What condescension! [*Aside*] Count, may I take the liberty to introduce – Good gracious! I forgot. [*Aside*] Count, I was about to remark that we never introduce in America. All our fashions are foreign, Count.

Twinkle, who has stepped foward to be introduced, shows great indignation

COUNT: Excuse me, Madam, our fashions have grown antediluvian before you Americans discover their existence. You are lamentably behind the age – lamentably! 'Pon my honour, a foreigner of refinement finds great difficulty in existing in this provincial atmosphere.

MRS. TIFFANY: How dreadful, Count! I am very much concerned. If there is anything which I can do, Count –

SERAPHINA: Or I, Count, to render your situation less deplorable –

COUNT: Ah! I find but one redeeming charm in America – the superlative loveliness of the feminine portion of creation, – and the wealth of their obliging papas. [*Aside*]

MRS. TIFFANY: How flattering! Ah! Count, I am afraid you will turn the head of my simple girl here. She is a perfect child of nature, Count.

COUNT: Very possibly, for though you American women are quite charming, yet, demme, there's a deal of native rust to rub off!

MRS. TIFFANY: *Rust?* Good gracious, Count! where do you find any rust? [*Looking about the room*]

COUNT: How very unsophisticated!

MRS. TIFFANY: Count, I am so much ashamed, – pray excuse me! Although a lady of large fortune, and one, Count, who can boast of the highest connections, I blush to confess that I have never travelled, – while you, Count, I presume are at home in all the courts of Europe.

COUNT: *Courts?* Eh? Oh, yes, Madam, very true. I believe I am pretty well known in some of the courts of Europe – [*Aside*] police courts. In a word, Madam, I had seen enough of civilized life – wanted to refresh myself by a sight of barbarous countries and customs – had my choice between the Sandwich Islands and New York – chose New York!

MRS. TIFFANY: How complimentary to our country! And, Count, I have no doubt you speak every conceivable language? You talk English like a native.

COUNT: Eh, what? Like a native? Oh, ah, demme, yes, I am something of an Englishman. Passed one year and eight months with the Duke of Wellington, six months with Lord Brougham, two and a half with Count d'Orsay – knew them all more intimately than their best friends – no heroes to me – hadn't a secret from me, I assure you, – *especially of the toilet.* [*Aside*]

MRS. TIFFANY: Think of that, my dear! Lord Wellington and Duke Broom! [*Aside to Seraphina*]

SERAPHINA: And only think of Count d'Orsay, Mamma! [*Aside to Mrs. Tiffany*] I am so wild to see Count d'Orsay!

COUNT: Oh! a mere man milliner. Very little refinement out of Paris! Why, at the very last dinner given at Lord – Lord Knowswho, would you believe it, Madam, there was an individual present who wore a *black* cravat and took *soup twice!*

MRS. TIFFANY: How shocking! the sight of him would have spoilt my appetite! Think what a great man he must be, my dear, to despise lords and counts in that way. [*Aside to Seraphina*] I must leave them together. [*Aside*] Mr. Twinkle, your arm. I have some really very *foreign exotics* to show you.

TWINKLE: I fly at your command. I wish all her exotics were blooming in their native soil! [*Aside, and glancing at the Count*]

MRS. TIFFANY: Mr. Fogg, will you accompany us? My conservatory is well worthy a visit. It cost an immense sum of money.

FOGG: I am indifferent to conservatories, Madam; flowers are such a bore!

MRS. TIFFANY: I shall take no refusal. Conservatories are all the rage, – I could not exist without mine! Let me show you, – let me show you.

Places her arm through Mr. Fogg's, without his consent. Exeunt Mrs. Tiffany, Fogg, and Twinkle into the conservatory, where they are seen walking about

SERAPHINA: America, then, has no charms for you, Count?

COUNT: Excuse me, – some exceptions. I find you, for instance, particularly charming! Can't

say I admire your country. Ah! if you had ever breathed the exhilarating air of Paris, ate creams at Tortoni's, dined at the Café Royale, or if you had lived in London – felt at home at St. James's, and every afternoon driven a couple of Lords and a Duchess through Hyde Park, you would find America – where you have no kings, queens, lords, nor ladies – insupportable!

SERAPHINA: Not while there was a Count in it!

Enter Zeke, very indignant

ZEKE: Where's de Missus?

Enter Mrs. Tiffany, Fogg, and Twinkle, from the conservatory

MRS. TIFFANY: Whom do you come to announce, A-dolph?

ZEKE: He said he wouldn't trust me – no, not eben wid so much as his name; so I wouldn't trust him up stairs; den he ups wid *his stick* and I *cuts mine.*

MRS. TIFFANY: Some of Mr. Tiffany's vulgar acquaintances. I shall die with shame. [*Aside*] A-dolph, inform him that I am *not at home.* [*Exit Zeke*] My nerves are so shattered, I am ready to sink. Mr. Twinkle, that *fowtool,* if you please!

TWINKLE: What? What do you wish, Madam?

MRS. TIFFANY: The ignorance of these Americans! [*Aside*] Count, may I trouble you? That *fowtool,* if you please!

COUNT: She's not talking English, nor French, but I suppose it's American. [*Aside*]

TRUEMAN: [*Outside*] Not at home!

ZEKE: No, Sar – Missus say she's not at home.

TRUEMAN: Out of the way, you grinning nigger!

Enter Adam Trueman, dressed as a farmer, a stout cane in his hand, his boots covered with dust. Zeke jumps out of his way as he enters. Exit Zeke

TRUEMAN: Where's this woman that's not *at home* in her own house? May I be shot! if I wonder at it! I shouldn't think she'd ever feel *at home* in such a show-box as this! [*Looking round*]

MRS. TIFFANY: What a plebeian looking old farmer! I wonder who he is? [*Aside*] Sir – [*Advancing very agitatedly*] What do you mean, sir, by this *ow*dacious conduct? How dare you intrude yourself into my parlor? Do you know who I am, sir? [*With great dignity*] You are in the presence of Mrs. Tiffany, sir!

TRUEMAN: Antony's wife, eh? Well now, I might have guessed that – ha! ha! ha! for I see you make it a point to carry half your husband's shop upon your back! No matter; that's being a good helpmate – for he carried the whole of it once in a pack on his own shoulders – now you bear a share!

MRS. TIFFANY: How dare you, you impertinent, *ow*dacious, ignorant old man! It's all an invention. You're talking of somebody else. What will the Count think! [*Aside*]

TRUEMAN: Why, I thought folks had better manners in the city! This is a civil welcome for your husband's old friend, and after my coming all the way from Catteraugus to see you and yours! First a grinning nigger tricked out in scarlet regimentals –

MRS. TIFFANY: Let me tell you, sir, that liveries are all the fashion!

TRUEMAN: The fashion, are they? To make men wear the *badge of servitude* in a free land, – that's the fashion, is it? Hurrah for republican simplicity! I will venture to say now, that you have your coat-of-arms too!

MRS. TIFFANY: Certainly, sir; you can see it on the panels of my *voyture*.

TRUEMAN: Oh! no need of that. I know what your escutcheon must be! A bandbox *rampant*, with a bonnet *couchant*, and a pedlar's pack *passant*! Ha! ha! ha! that shows both houses united!

MRS. TIFFANY: Sir! You are most profoundly ignorant, – what do you mean by this insolence, sir? How shall I get rid of him? [*Aside*]

TRUEMAN: [*Looking at Seraphina*] I hope that is not Gertrude! [*Aside*]

MRS. TIFFANY: Sir, I'd have you know that – Seraphina, my child, walk with the gentlemen into the conservatory. [*Exeunt Seraphina, Twinkle, Fogg into conservatory*] Count Jolimaitre, pray make due allowances for the errors of this rustic! I do assure you, Count – [*Whispers to him*]

TRUEMAN: Count! She calls that critter with a shoebrush over his mouth, Count! To look at him, I should have thought he was a tailor's walking advertisement! [*Aside*]

COUNT: [*Addressing Trueman, whom he has been inspecting through his eye-glass*] Where did you say you belonged, my friend? Dug out of the ruins of Pompeii, eh?

TRUEMAN: I belong to a land in which I rejoice to find that you are a foreigner.

COUNT: What a barbarian! He doesn't see the honour I'm doing his country! Pray, Madam, is it one of the aboriginal inhabitants of the soil? To what tribe of Indians does he belong – the Pawnee or Choctaw? Does he carry a tomahawk?

TRUEMAN: Something quite as useful, – do you see that?

Shaking his stick. Count runs to right, behind Mrs. Tiffany

MRS. TIFFANY: Oh, dear! I shall faint! Millinette! [*Approaching right*] Millinette!

Enter Millinette, without advancing into the room

MILLINETTE: *Oui*, Madame.

MRS. TIFFANY: A glass of water! [*Exit Millinette*] Sir, [*Crossing to Trueman*] I am shocked at your plebeian conduct! This is a gentleman of the highest standing, sir! He is a *Count*, sir!

Enter Millinette, bearing a salver with a glass of water. In advancing towards Mrs. Tiffany, she passes in front of the Count, starts and screams. The Count, after a start of surprise, regains his composure, plays with his eye-glass, and looks perfectly unconcerned

MRS. TIFFANY: What is the matter? What *is* the matter?

MILLINETTE: Noting, noting, – only – [*Looks at Count and turns away her eyes again*] only – noting at all!

TRUEMAN: Don't be afraid, girl! Why, did you never see a live Count before? He's tame, – I dare say your mistress there leads him about by the ears.

MRS. TIFFANY: This is too much! Millinette, send for Mr. Tiffany instantly! [*Crosses to Millinette, who is going*]

MILLINETTE: He just come in, Madame!

TRUEMAN: My old friend! Where is he? Take me to him – I long to have one more hearty shake of the hand!

MRS. TIFFANY: Shake of the fist, you mean. [*Crosses to him*] If I don't make him shake his in your face, you low, *ow*dacious – no matter, we'll see. Count, honour me by joining my daughter in the conservatory, I will return immediately.

Count bows and walks towards conservatory, Mrs. Tiffany following part of the way and then returning to Trueman

TRUEMAN: What a Jezebel! These women always play the very devil with a man, and yet I don't believe such a damaged bale of goods as *that* [*Looking at Mrs. Tiffany*] has smothered the heart of little Antony!

MRS. TIFFANY: This way, sir, sal vous plait. [*Exit, with great dignity*]

TRUEMAN: *Sal vous plait.* Ha, ha, ha! We'll see what Fashion has done for him. [*Exit*]

ACT II. Scene 1

Inner apartment of Mr. Tiffany's Counting-House. Mr. Tiffany seated at a desk looking over papers. Mr. Snobson on a high stool at another desk, with a pen behind his ear.

SNOBSON: [*Rising, advances to the front of the stage, regards Tiffany and shrugs his shoulders*] How the old boy frets and fumes over those papers, to be sure! He's working himself into a perfect fever – ex-actly, – therefore *bleeding's* the prescription! So here goes! [*Aside*] Mr. Tiffany, a word with you, if you please, sir?

TIFFANY: [*Sitting still*] Speak on, Mr. Snobson. I attend.

SNOBSON: What I have to say, sir, is a matter of the first importance to the credit of the concern – the *credit* of the concern, Mr. Tiffany!

TIFFANY: Proceed, Mr. Snobson.

SNOBSON: Sir, you've a handsome house – fine carriage – nigger in livery – feed on the fat of the land – everything first rate –

TIFFANY: Well, sir?

SNOBSON: My salary, Mr. Tiffany!

TIFFANY: It has been raised three times within the last year.

SNOBSON: Still it is insufficient for the necessities of an honest man, – mark me, an *honest* man, Mr. Tiffany.

TIFFANY: [*Crossing*] What a weapon he has made of that word! [*Aside*] Enough – another hundred shall be added. Does that content you?

SNOBSON: There is one other ·subject, which I have before mentioned, Mr. Tiffany, – your daughter, – what's the reason you can't let the folks at home know at once that I'm to be *the man*?

TIFFANY: Villain! And must the only seal upon this scoundrel's lips be placed there by the hand of my daughter? [*Aside*] Well, sir, it shall be as you desire.

SNOBSON: And Mrs. Tiffany shall be informed of your resolution?

TIFFANY: Yes.

SNOBSON: Enough said! That's the ticket! The CREDIT *of the concern's safe*, sir [*Returns to his seat*]

TIFFANY: How low have I bowed to this insolent rascal! To rise himself, he mounts upon my shoulders, and unless I can shake him off he must crush me! [*Aside*]

Enter Trueman

TRUEMAN: Here I am, Antony, man! I told you I'd pay you a visit in your money-making quarters. [*Looks around*] But it looks as dismal here as a cell in the State's prison!

TIFFANY: [*Forcing a laugh*] Ha, ha, ha! State's prison! You are so facetious! Ha, ha, ha!

TRUEMAN: Well, for the life of me I can't see anything so amusing in that! I should think the State's prison plaguy uncomfortable lodgings. And you laugh, man, as though you fancied yourself there already.

TIFFANY: Ha, ha, ha!

TRUEMAN: [*Imitating him*] Ha, ha, ha! What on earth do you mean by that ill-sounding laugh, that has nothing of a laugh about it! This *fashion*-worship has made heathens and hypocrites of you all! *Deception* is your household God! A man laughs as if he were crying, and cries as if he were laughing in his sleeve. Everything is something else from what it seems to be. I have lived in your house only three days, and I've heard more lies than were ever invented during a Presidential e.ection! First your fine lady of a wife sends me word that she's not at home – I walk up-stairs, and she takes good care that *I* shall not be *at home* – wants to turn me out of doors. Then *you* come in – take your old friend by the hand – whisper, the deuce knows what, in your wife's ear, and the tables are turned in a tangent! Madam curtsies – says she's enchanted to see me – and orders her grinning nigger to show me a room.

TIFFANY: We were exceedingly happy to welcome you as our guest.

TRUEMAN: Happy? *You* happy? Ah! Antony! Antony! that hatchet face of yours, and those criss-cross furrows tell quite another story! It's many a long day since you were *happy* at anything! You look as if you'd melted down your flesh into dollars, and mortgaged your soul in the bargain! Your warm heart has grown cold over your ledger – your light spirits heavy with calculation! You have traded away your youth – your hopes – your tastes for wealth! and now you *have* the wealth you coveted, what does it profit you? Pleasure it cannot buy; for you have lost your *capacity* for enjoyment. Ease it will not bring; for the love of gain is never satisfied! It has made your counting-house a penitentiary, and your home a fashionable *museum* where there is no niche for you! You have spent so much time *ciphering* in the one, that you find yourself at last a very *cipher* in the other! See me, man! Seventy-two last August! – strong as a hickory and every whit as sound!

TIFFANY: I take the greatest pleasure in remarking your superiority, sir.

TRUEMAN: Bah! no man takes pleasure in remarking the superiority of another! Why the deuce can't you speak the truth, man? But it's not the *fashion*, I suppose! I have not seen one frank, open face since – no, no, I can't say that either, though lying *is* catching! There's that girl, Gertrude, who is trying to teach your daughter music – but Gertrude was bred in the country!

TIFFANY: A good girl; my wife and daughter find her very useful.

TRUEMAN: Useful? Well, I must say you have queer notions of *use!* – But come, cheer up, man! I'd rather see one of your old smiles, than know you'd realized another thousand! I hear you are making money on the true, American high-pressure system – better go slow and sure – the more steam, the greater danger of the boiler's bursting! All sound, I hope? Nothing rotten at the core?

TIFFANY: Oh, sound – quite sound!

TRUEMAN: Well, that's pleasant – though I must say you don't look very pleasant about it!

TIFFANY: My good friend, although I am solvent, I may say, perfectly solvent – yet you – the fact is, you can be of some assistance to me!

TRUEMAN: That's the *fact*, is it? I'm glad we've hit upon one *fact* at last! Well –

Snobson, who during this conversation has been employed in writing, but stops occasionally to listen, now gives vent to a dry, chuckling laugh

TRUEMAN: Hey? What's that? Another of those deuced ill-sounding, city laughs! [*Sees Snobson*] Who's that perched up on the stool of repentance – eh, Antony?

SNOBSON: The old boy has missed his text there – *that's* the stool of repentance! [*Aside, and looking at Tiffany's seat*]

TIFFANY: One of my clerks – my confidential clerk!

TRUEMAN: Confidential? Why, he looks for all the world like a spy – the most inquisitorial, hang-dog face – ugh! the sight of it makes my blood run cold! Come, [*Crosses*] let us talk over matters where this critter can't give us the benefit of his opinion! Antony, the next time you choose a confidential clerk, take one that carries his credentials in his face – those in his pocket are not worth much without!

Exeunt Trueman and Tiffany

SNOBSON: [*Jumping from his stool and advancing*] The old prig has got the tin, or Tiff would never be so civil! All right – Tiff will work every shiner into the concern – all the better for me! Now I'll go and make love to Seraphina. The old woman needn't try to knock me down with any of her French lingo! Six months from to-day, if I ain't driving my two footmen tandem, down Broadway – and as fashionable as Mrs. Tiffany herself, then I ain't the trump I thought I was! that's all. [*Looks at his watch*] Bless me! eleven o'clock, and I haven't had my julep yet? Snobson, I'm ashamed of you! [*Exit*]

Scene 2

The interior of a beautiful conservatory; walk through the centre; stands of flower-pots in bloom; a couple of rustic seats. Gertrude, attired in white, with a white rose in her hair, watering the flowers. Colonel Howard, regarding her.

HOWARD: I am afraid you lead a sad life here, Miss Gertrude?

GERTRUDE: [*Turning round gaily*] What! amongst the flowers? [*Continues her occupation*]

HOWARD: No, amongst the thistles, with which Mrs. Tiffany surrounds you; the tempests, which her temper raises!

GERTRUDE: They never harm me. Flowers and herbs are excellent tutors. I learn prudence from the reed, and bend until the storm has swept over me!

HOWARD: Admirable philosophy! But still this frigid atmosphere of fashion must be uncongenial to you? Accustomed to the pleasant companionship of your kind friends in Geneva, surely you must regret this cold exchange?

GERTRUDE: Do you think so? Can you suppose that I could possibly prefer a ramble in the woods to a promenade in Broadway? A wreath of scented wild flowers to a bouquet of these sickly exotics? The odour of new-mown hay to the heated air of this crowded conservatory? Or can you imagine that I could enjoy the quiet conversation of my Geneva friends, more than the edifying chit-chat of a fashionable drawing-room? But I see you think me totally destitute of taste?

HOWARD: You have a merry spirit to jest thus at your grievances!

GERTRUDE: I have my *mania*, – as some wise person declares that all men have, – and mine is a love of independence! In Geneva, my wants were supplied by two kind old maiden ladies, upon whom I know not that I have any claim. I had abilities, and desired to use them. I came here at my own request; for here I am no longer *dependent! Voilà tout*, as Mrs. Tiffany would say.

HOWARD: Believe me, I appreciate the confidence you repose in me!

GERTRUDE: Confidence! Truly, Colonel Howard, the *confidence* is entirely on your part, in supposing that I confide that which I have no reason to conceal! I think I informed you that Mrs. Tiffany only received visitors on her reception day – she is therefore not prepared to see you. Zeke – Oh! I beg his pardon – Adolph made some mistake in admitting you.

HOWARD: Nay, Gertrude, it was not Mrs. Tiffany, nor Miss Tiffany, whom I came to see; it – it was –

GERTRUDE: The conservatory perhaps? I will leave you to examine the flowers at leisure! [*Crosses left*]

HOWARD: Gertrude – listen to me. If I only dared to give utterance to what is hovering upon my lips! [*Aside*] Gertrude!

GERTRUDE: Colonel Howard!

HOWARD: Gertrude, I must – must –

GERTRUDE: Yes, indeed you *must*, must leave me! I think I hear somebody coming – Mrs. Tiffany would not be well pleased to find you here – pray, pray leave me – that door will lead you into the street.

Hurries him out through door, takes up her watering-pot, and commences watering flowers, tying up branches, etc.

What a strange being is man! Why should he hesitate to say – nay, why should I prevent his saying, what I would most delight to hear? Truly, man *is* strange – but woman is quite as incomprehensible! [*Walks about gathering flowers*]

Enter Count Jolimaitre

COUNT: There she is – the bewitching little creature! Mrs. Tiffany and her daughter are out of ear-shot. I caught a glimpse of their feathers floating down Broadway, not ten minutes ago. Just the opportunity I have been looking for! Now for an engagement with this captivating little piece of prudery! 'Pon my honour, I am almost afraid she will not resist a *Count* long enough to give value to the conquest. [*Approaches her*] *Ma belle petite*, were you gathering roses for me?

GERTRUDE: [*Starts on first perceiving him, but instantly regains her self-possession*] The roses here, sir, are carefully guarded with thorns – if you have the right to gather, pluck for yourself!

COUNT: Sharp as ever, little Gertrude! But now that we are alone, throw off this frigidity, and be at your ease.

GERTRUDE: Permit me to *be alone*, sir, that I *may be* at my ease!

COUNT: Very good, *ma belle*, well said! [*Applauding her with his hands*] Never yield too soon, even to a *title!* But, as the old girl may find her way back before long, we may as well come to particulars at once. I love you; but that you know already. [*Rubbing his eye-glass unconcernedly with his handkerchief*] Before long I shall make Mademoiselle Seraphina my wife, and, of course, you shall remain in the family!

GERTRUDE: [*Indignantly*] Sir –

COUNT: 'Pon my honour you shall! In France we arrange these little matters without difficulty!

GERTRUDE: But I am an *American!* Your conduct proves that you are not one! [*Going*]

COUNT: [*Preventing her*] Don't run away, my immaculate *petite Americaine!* Demme, you've quite over-looked my condescension – the difference of our stations – you a species of upper servant – an orphan – no friends.

Enter Trueman unperceived

GERTRUDE: And therefore more entitled to the respect and protection of every *true gentleman!* Had you been one, you would not have insulted me!

COUNT: My charming little orator, patriotism and declamation become you particularly! [*Approaches her*] I feel quite tempted to taste –

TRUEMAN: [*Thrusting him aside*] An American hickory switch! [*Strikes him*] Well, how do you like it?

COUNT: Old matter-of-fact! [*Aside*] Sir, how dare you?

TRUEMAN: My stick has answered that question!

GERTRUDE: Oh! now I am quite safe!

TRUEMAN: Safe! not a bit safer than before! All women would be safe, if they knew how virtue became them! As for you, Mr. Count, what have you to say for yourself? Come, speak out!

COUNT: Sir, – aw – aw – you don't understand these matters!

TRUEMAN: That's a fact! Not having had *your* experience, I don't believe I *do* understand them!

COUNT: A piece of pleasantry – a mere joke –

TRUEMAN: A joke, was it? I'll show you a joke worth two of that! I'll teach you the way we natives joke with a puppy who don't respect an honest woman! [*Seizing him*]

COUNT: Oh! oh! demme – you old ruffian! let me go. What do you mean?

TRUEMAN: Oh! a piece of pleasantry – a mere joke – very pleasant, isn't it?

Attempts to strike him again; Count struggles with him. Enter Mrs. Tiffany hastily, in her bonnet and shawl

MRS. TIFFANY: What is the matter? I am perfectly *abimé* with terror. Mr. Trueman, what has happened?

TRUEMAN: Oh! we have been *joking!*

MRS. TIFFANY: [*To Count, who is re-arranging his dress*] My *dear* Count, I did not expect to find you here – how kind of you!

TRUEMAN: Your *dear* Count has been showing his *kindness* in a very *foreign* manner. Too *foreign*, I think, he found it to be relished by an *unfashionable native!* What do you think of a puppy, who insults an innocent girl all in the way of *kindness?* This Count of yours – this importation of –

COUNT: My dear Madam, demme, permit me to explain. It would be unbecoming – demme – particularly unbecoming of you – aw – aw – to pay any attention to this ignorant person. [*Crosses to Trueman*] Anything that he says concerning a man of my standing – aw – the truth is, Madam –

TRUEMAN: Let us have the truth, by all means, – if it is only for the novelty's sake!

COUNT: [*Turning his back to Trueman*] You see, Madam, hoping to obtain a few moments' private conversation with Miss Seraphina – with *Miss Seraphina*, I say – and – aw – and knowing her passion for flowers, I found my way to your very tasteful and *recherché* conservatory. [*Looks about him approvingly*] *Very* beautifully arranged – does you great credit, Madam! Here I encountered this young person. She was inclined to be talkative; and I indulged her with – with a – aw – demme – a few *commonplaces!* What passed between us was mere *harmless badinage* – on *my* part. You, Madam, you – so conversant with our European manners – you are aware that when a man of fashion – that is, when a woman – a man is bound – amongst noblemen, you know –

MRS. TIFFANY: I comprehend you perfectly – *perfittement*, my dear Count.

COUNT: 'Pon my honour, that's very obliging of her. [*Aside*]

MRS. TIFFANY: I am shocked at the plebeian forwardness of this conceited girl!

TRUEMAN: [*Walking up to Count*] Did you ever keep a reckoning of the lies you tell in an hour?

MRS. TIFFANY: Mr. Trueman, I blush for you! [*Crosses to Trueman*]

TRUEMAN: Don't do that – you have no blushes to spare!

MRS. TIFFANY: It is a man of rank whom you are addressing, sir!

TRUEMAN: A rank villain, Mrs. Antony Tiffany! A *rich* one he would be, had he as much *gold* as *brass!*

MRS. TIFFANY: Pray pardon him, Count; he knows nothing of *how ton!*

COUNT: Demme, he's beneath my notice. I tell you what, old fellow – [*Trueman raises his stick as Count approaches; the latter starts back*] the sight of him discomposes me – aw – I feel quite uncomfortable – aw – let us join your charming daughter? I can't do you the honour to shoot you, sir, – [*To Trueman*] you are beneath me – a nobleman can't fight a commoner! Good-bye, old Truepenny! I – aw – I'm insensible to your insolence!

Exeunt Count and Mrs. Tiffany

TRUEMAN: You won't be insensible to a cow-hide in spite of your nobility! The next time he practises any of his foreign fashions on you, Gertrude, you'll see how I'll wake up his sensibilities!

GERTRUDE: I do not know what I should have done without you, sir.

TRUEMAN: Yes, you do – you know that you would have done well enough! Never tell a lie, girl! not even for the sake of pleasing an old man! When you open your lips, let your heart speak. Never tell a lie! Let your face be the looking-glass of your soul – your heart its clock – while your tongue rings the hours! But the glass must be clear, the clock true, and then there's no fear but the tongue will do its duty in a woman's head!

GERTRUDE: You are very good, sir!

TRUEMAN: That's as it may be! – How my heart warms towards her! [*Aside*] Gertrude, I hear that you have no mother?

GERTRUDE: Ah! no, sir; I wish I had.

TRUEMAN: So do I! Heaven knows, so do I! [*Aside, and with emotion*] And you have no father, Gertrude?

GERTRUDE: No, sir – I often wish I had!

TRUEMAN: [*Hurriedly*] Don't do that, girl! don't do that! Wish you had a mother – but never wish that you had a father again! Perhaps the one you had did not deserve such a child!

Enter Prudence

PRUDENCE: Seraphina is looking for you, Gertrude.

GERTRUDE: I will go to her. [*Crosses*] Mr. Trueman, you will not permit me to thank you, but you cannot prevent my gratitude! [*Exit*]

TRUEMAN: [*Looking after her*] If falsehood harbours there, I'll give up searching after truth!

Retires up the stage musingly, and commences examining the flowers.

PRUDENCE: What a nice old man he is, to be sure! I wish he would say something! [*Aside. Walks after him, turning when he turns – after a pause*] Don't mind me, Mr. Trueman!

TRUEMAN: Mind you? Oh! no, don't be afraid [*Crosses*] – I wasn't minding you. Nobody seems to mind you much!

Continues walking and examining the flowers. – Prudence follows

PRUDENCE: Very pretty flowers, ain't they? Gertrude takes care of them.

TRUEMAN: Gertrude? So I hear – [*Advancing*] I suppose you can tell me now who this Gertrude –

PRUDENCE: Who she's in love with? I *knew* you were going to say that! I'll tell you all about it! Gertrude, she's in love with – Mr. Twinkle! and he's in love with her. And Seraphina, she's in love with Count Jolly – what-d'ye-call-it: but Count Jolly don't take to her at all – but Colonel Howard – he's the man – he's desperate about her!

TRUEMAN: Why, you feminine newspaper! Howard in love with that quintessence of affectation! Howard – the only frank, straightforward fellow that I've met since – I'll tell him my mind on the subject! And Gertrude hunting for happiness in a rhyming dictionary! The girl's a greater fool than I took her for! [*Crosses right*]

PRUDENCE: So she is – you see I know all about them!

TRUEMAN: I see you do! You've a wonderful knowledge – wonderful – of *other people's concerns!* It may do here, but take my word for it, in the county of Catteraugus you'd get the name of a great *busy-body*. But perhaps you know that, too?

PRUDENCE: Oh! I always know what's coming. I feel it beforehand all over me. I knew something was going to happen the day you came here – and what's more I can always tell a married man from a single – I felt right off that you were a bachelor!

TRUEMAN: Felt right off I was a bachelor, did you? you were sure of it – sure? – quite sure? [*Prudence assents delightedly*] Then you felt wrong! – a bachelor and a widower are not the same thing!

PRUDENCE: Oh! but it all comes to the same thing – a widower's as good as a bachelor any day! And besides, I knew that you were a farmer *right off*.

TRUEMAN: On the spot, eh? I suppose you saw cabbages and green peas growing out of my hat?

PRUDENCE: No, I didn't – but I knew all about you. And I knew – [*Looking down and fidgeting with her apron*] – I knew you were for getting married soon! For last night I dreamt I saw your funeral going along the streets, and the mourners all dressed in white. And a funeral is a sure sign of a wedding, you know! [*Nudging him with her elbow*]

TRUEMAN: [*Imitating her voice*] Well, I can't say that I *know* any such thing! you know! [*Nudging her back*]

PRUDENCE: Oh! it does, and there's no getting over it! For my part, I like farmers – and I know all about setting hens and turkeys, and feeding chickens, and laying eggs, and all that sort of thing!

TRUEMAN: May I be shot! if mistress newspaper is not putting in an advertisement for herself! This is your city mode of courting, I suppose, ha, ha, ha! [*Aside*]

PRUDENCE: I've been west, a little; but I never was in the county of Catteraugus, myself.

TRUEMAN: Oh, you were not? And you have taken a particular fancy to go there, eh?

PRUDENCE: Perhaps I shouldn't object –

TRUEMAN: Oh! – ah! – so I suppose. Now pay attention to what I am going to say, for it is a matter of great importance to yourself.

PRUDENCE: Now it's coming – I know what he's going to say! [*Aside*]

TRUEMAN: The next time you want to tie a man for life to your apron-strings, pick out one that don't come from the county of Catteraugus – for green-horns are scarce in those parts, and modest women plenty! [*Exit*]

PRUDENCE: Now, who'd have thought he was going to say that! But I won't give him up yet – I won't give him up. [*Exit*]

ACT III. Scene 1

Mrs. Tiffany's Parlor. Enter Mrs. Tiffany, followed by Mr. Tiffany.

TIFFANY: Your extravagance will ruin me, Mrs. Tiffany!

MRS. TIFFANY: And your stinginess will ruin me, Mr. Tiffany! It is totally and *toot a fate* impossible to convince you of the necessity of *keeping up appearances*. There is a certain display which every woman of fashion is forced to make!

TIFFANY: And pray who made *you* a woman of fashion?

MRS. TIFFANY: What a vulgar question! All women of fashion, Mr. Tiffany –

TIFFANY: In this land are *self-constituted*, like you, Madam – and *fashion* is the cloak for more sins than charity ever covered! It was for *fashion's* sake that you insisted upon my purchasing this expensive house – it was for *fashion's* sake that you ran me in debt at every exorbitant upholsterer's and extravagant furniture warehouse in the city – it was for *fashion's* sake that you built that ruinous conservatory – hired more servants than they have persons to wait upon – and dressed your footman like a harlequin!

MRS. TIFFANY: Mr. Tiffany, you are thoroughly plebeian, and insufferably *American*, in your grovelling ideas! And, pray, what was the occasion of these very *mal-ap-pro-pos* remarks? Merely because I requested a paltry fifty dollars to purchase a new style of head-dress – a *bijou* of an article just introduced in France.

TIFFANY: Time was, Mrs. Tiffany, when you manufactured your own French head-dresses – took off their first gloss at the public balls, and then sold them to your shortest-sighted customers. And all you knew about France, or French either, was what you spelt out at the bottom of your fashion-plates – but now you have grown so fashionable, forsooth, that you have forgotten how to speak your mother tongue!

MRS. TIFFANY: Mr. Tiffany, Mr. Tiffany! Nothing is more positively vulgarian – more *unaristocratic* than any allusion to the past!

TIFFANY: Why, I thought, my dear, that *aristocrats* lived principally upon the past – and traded in the market of fashion with the bones of their ancestors for capital!

MRS. TIFFANY: Mr. Tiffany, such vulgar remarks are only suitable to the counting-house; in my drawing-room you should –

TIFFANY: Vary my sentiments with my locality, as you change your *manners* with your *dress!*

MRS. TIFFANY: Mr. Tiffany, I desire that you will purchase Count d'Orsay's "Science of Etiquette," and learn how to conduct yourself – especially before you appear at the grand ball, which I shall give on Friday!

TIFFANY: Confound your balls, Madam; they make *footballs* of my money, while you dance away all that I am worth! A pretty time to give a ball when you know that I am on the very brink of bankruptcy!

MRS. TIFFANY: So much the greater reason that nobody should suspect your circumstances, or you would lose your credit at once. Just at this crisis a ball is absolutely *necessary* to save your reputation! There is Mrs. Adolphus Dashaway –she gave the most splendid fête of the season –and I hear on very good authority that her husband has not paid his baker's bill in three months. Then there was Mrs. Honeywood –

TIFFANY: Gave a ball the night before her husband shot himself – perhaps you wish to drive me to follow his example? [*Crosses right*]

MRS. TIFFANY: Good gracious! Mr. Tiffany, how you talk! I beg you won't mention anything of the kind. I consider black the most unbecoming color. I'm sure I've done all that I could to gratify you. There is that vulgar old torment, Trueman, who gives one the lie fifty times a day – haven't I been very civil to him?

TIFFANY: Civil to his *wealth*, Mrs. Tiffany! I told you that he was a rich old farmer – the early friend of my father – my own benefactor – and that I had reason to think he might assist me in my present embarrassments. Your civility was *bought* – and like most of your *own* purchases has yet to be *paid* for.

MRS. TIFFANY: And will be, no doubt! The condescension of a woman of fashion should command any price. Mr. Trueman is insupportably indecorous – he has insulted Count Jolimaitre in the most outrageous manner. If the Count was not so deeply interested – so *abimé* with Seraphina, I am sure he would never honour us by his visits again!

TIFFANY: So much the better – he shall never marry my daughter! – I am resolved on that. Why, Madam, I am told there is in Paris a regular matrimonial stock company, who fit out indigent dandies for this market. How do I know but this fellow is one of its creatures, and that he has come here to increase its dividends by marrying a fortune?

MRS. TIFFANY: Nonsense, Mr. Tiffany. The Count, the most fashionable young man in all New York – the intimate friend of all the dukes and lords in Europe – not marry my daughter? Not permit Seraphina to become a Countess? Mr. Tiffany, you are out of your senses!

TIFFANY: That would not be very wonderful, considering how many years I have been united to you, my dear. Modern physicians pronounce lunacy infectious!

MRS. TIFFANY: Mr. Tiffany, he is a man of fashion –

TIFFANY: Fashion makes fools, but cannot *feed* them. By the bye, I have a request, – since you are bent upon ruining me by this ball, and there is no help for it, – I desire that you will send an invitation to my confidential clerk, Mr. Snobson.

MRS. TIFFANY: Mr. Snobson! Was· there ever such an *you-nick* demand! Mr. Snobson would cut a pretty figure amongst my fashionable friends! I shall do no such thing, Mr. Tiffany.

TIFFANY: Then, Madam, the ball shall not take place. Have I not told you that I am in the power of this man? That there are circumstances which it is happy for you that you do not know – which you cannot comprehend, – but which render it essential that you should be civil to Mr. Snobson? Not you merely, but Seraphina also? He is a more appropriate match for her than your foreign favorite.

MRS. TIFFANY: A match for Seraphina, indeed! [*Crosses*] Mr. Tiffany, you are determined to make a *fow pas*.

TIFFANY: Mr. Snobson intends calling this morning. [*Crosses to left*]

MRS. TIFFANY: But, Mr. Tiffany, this is not reception day – my drawing-rooms are in the most terrible disorder –

TIFFANY: Mr. Snobson is not particular – he must be admitted.

Enter Zeke

ZEKE: Mr. Snobson.

Enter Snobson; exit Zeke

SNOBSON: How d'ye do, Marm? [*Crosses to centre*] How are you? Mr. Tiffany, your most! –

MRS. TIFFANY: [*Formally*] Bung jure. Comment vow porte vow, Monsur Snobson?

SNOBSON: Oh, to be sure – very good of you – fine day.

MRS. TIFFANY: [*Pointing to a chair with great dignity*] Sassoyez vow, Monsur Snobson.

SNOBSON: I wonder what she's driving at? I ain't up to the fashionable lingo yet! [*Aside*] Eh? what? Speak a little louder, Marm?

MRS. TIFFANY: What ignorance! [*Aside*]

TIFFANY: I presume Mrs. Tiffany means that you are to take a seat.

SNOBSON: Ex-actly – very obliging of her – so I will. [*Sits*] No ceremony amongst friends, you know – and likely to be nearer – you understand? O. K., all correct. How *is* Seraphina?

MRS. TIFFANY: Miss Tiffany is not visible this morning. [*Retires up*]

SNOBSON: Not visible? [*Jumping up, crosses*] I suppose that's the English for can't see her? Mr. Tiffany, sir – [*Walking up to him*] what am I to understand by this *de-fal-ca-tion*, sir? I expected your word to be as good as your bond – beg pardon, sir – I mean *better* – considerably *better* – no humbug about it, sir.

TIFFANY: Have patience, Mr. Snobson. [*Rings bell*]

Enter Zeke

Zeke, desire my daughter to come here.

MRS. TIFFANY: [*Coming down centre*] A-dolph – I say, A-dolph –

Zeke straightens himself and assumes foppish airs, as he turns to Mrs. Tiffany

TIFFANY: Zeke.

ZEKE: Don't know any such nigga, Boss.

TIFFANY: Do as I bid you instantly, or off with your livery and quit the house!

ZEKE: Wheugh! I'se all dismission. [*Exit*]

MRS. TIFFANY: A-dolph, A-dolph! [*Calling after him*]

SNOBSON: I brought the old boy to his bearings, didn't I though! Pull that string, and he is sure to work right. [*Aside*] Don't make any stranger of me, Marm – I'm quite at home. If you've got any odd jobs about the house to do, I sha'n't miss you. I'll amuse myself with Seraphina when she comes – we'll get along very cosily by ourselves.

MRS. TIFFANY: Permit me to inform you, Mr. Snobson, that a French mother never leaves her daughter alone with a young man – she knows your sex too well for that!

SNOBSON: Very *dis*-obliging of her – but as we're none French –

MRS. TIFFANY: You have yet to learn, Mr. Snobson, that the American *ee-light* – the aristocracy – the *how-ton* – as a matter of conscience, scrupulously follow the foreign fashions.

SNOBSON: Not when they are foreign to their interests, Marm – for instance – [*Enter Seraphina*] There you are at last, eh, Miss? How d'ye do? Ma said you weren't visible. Managed to get a peep at her, eh, Mr. Tiffany?

SERAPHINA: I heard you were here, Mr. Snobson, and came without even arranging my toilette; you will excuse my negligence?

SNOBSON: Of everything but *me*, Miss.

SERAPHINA: I shall never have to ask your pardon for *that*, Mr. Snobson.

MRS. TIFFANY: Seraphina – child – really –

As she is approaching Seraphina, Mr. Tiffany plants himself in front of his wife

TIFFANY: Walk this way, Madam, if you please. To see that she fancies the surly fellow takes a weight from my heart. [*Aside*]

MRS. TIFFANY: Mr. Tiffany, it is highly improper and not at all *distingué* to leave a young girl –

Enter Zeke

ZEKE: Mr. Count Jolly-made-her!

MRS. TIFFANY: Good gracious! The Count – Oh, dear! – Seraphina, run and change your dress, – no, there's not time! A-dolph, admit him. [*Exit Zeke*] Mr. Snobson, get out of the way, will you? Mr. Tiffany, what are you doing at home at this hour?

Enter Count Jolimaitre, ushered by Zeke

ZEKE: Dat's de genuine article ob a gemman. [*Aside*] [*Exit*]

MRS. TIFFANY: My dear Count, I am overjoyed at the very sight of you.

COUNT: Flattered myself you'd be glad to see me, Madam – knew it was not your *jour de reception*.

MRS. TIFFANY: But for you, Count, all days –

COUNT: I thought so. Ah, Miss Tiffany, on my honour, you're looking beautiful. [*Crosses right*]

SERAPHINA: Count, flattery from you –

SNOBSON: What? Eh? What's that you say?

SERAPHINA: Nothing but what etiquette requires. [*Aside to him*]

COUNT: [*Regarding Mr. Tiffany through his eye-glass*] Your worthy Papa, I believe? Sir, your most obedient.

Mr. Tiffany bows coldly; Count regards Snobson through his glass, shrugs his shoulders and turns away

SNOBSON: [*To Mrs. Tiffany*] Introduce me, will

you? I never knew a Count in all my life – what a strange-looking animal!

MRS. TIFFANY: Mr. Snobson, it is not the fashion to introduce in France!

SNOBSON: But, Marm, we're in America. [*Mrs. Tiffany crosses to Count*] The woman thinks she's somewhere else than where she is – she wants to make an *alibi*? [*Aside*]

MRS. TIFFANY: I hope that we shall have the pleasure of seeing you on Friday evening, Count?

COUNT: Really, Madam, my invitations – my engagements – so numerous – I can hardly answer for myself: and you Americans take offence so easily –

MRS. TIFFANY: But, Count, everybody expects you at our ball – you are the principal attraction –

SERAPHINA: Count, you *must* come!

COUNT: Since you insist – aw – aw – there's no resisting you, Miss Tiffany.

MRS. TIFFANY: I am so thankful. How can I repay your condescension. [*Count and Seraphina converse*] Mr. Snobson, will you walk this way? – I have *such* a cactus in full bloom – remarkable flower! Mr. Tiffany, pray come here – I have something particular to say.

TIFFANY: Then speak out, my dear – I thought it was highly improper just now to leave a girl with a young man? [*Aside to her*]

MRS. TIFFANY: Oh, but the Count, – that is different!

TIFFANY: I suppose you mean to say there's nothing of *the man* about him?

Enter Millinette with a scarf in her hand

MILLINETTE: A-dolph tell me he vas here. [*Aside*] Pardon, Madame, I bring dis scarf for Mademoiselle.

MRS. TIFFANY: Very well, Millinette; you know best what is proper for her to wear.

Mr. and Mrs. Tiffany and Snobson retire up; she engages the attention of both gentlemen

Millinette crosses towards Seraphina, gives the Count a threatening look, and commences arranging the scarf over Seraphina's shoulders

MILLINETTE: Mademoiselle, *permettez-moi. Perfide!* [*Aside to Count*] If Mademoiselle vil stand *tranquille* one *petit* moment. [*Turns Seraphina's back to the Count, and pretends to arrange the scarf*] I must speak vid you to-day,

or I tell all – you find me at de foot of de stair ven you go. *Prends garde!* [*Aside to Count*]

SERAPHINA: What is that you say, Millinette?

MILLINETTE: Dis scarf make you so very beautiful, Mademoiselle – *Je vous salue, mes dames.* [*Curtsies*] [*Exit*]

COUNT: Not a moment to lose! [*Aside*] Miss Tiffany, I have an unpleasant – a particularly unpleasant piece of intelligence – you see, I have just received a letter from my friend the – aw – the Earl of Airshire; the truth is, the Earl's daughter – beg you won't mention it – has distinguished me by a tender *penchant*.

SERAPHINA: I understand – and they wish you to return and marry the young lady; but surely you will not leave us, Count?

COUNT: If *you* bid me stay – I shouldn't have the conscience – I couldn't *afford* to tear myself away. I'm sure that's honest. [*Aside*]

SERAPHINA: Oh, Count!

COUNT: Say but one word – say that you shouldn't mind being made a Countess – and I'll break with the Earl to-morrow.

SERAPHINA: Count, this surprise – but don't think of leaving the country, Count – we could not pass the time without you! I – yes, yes, Count – I do consent!

COUNT: I thought she would! [*Aside, while he embraces her*] Enchanted, rapture, bliss, ecstasy, and all that sort of thing – words can't express it, but you understand. But it must be kept a secret – positively it *must*! If the rumour of our engagement were whispered abroad – the Earl's daughter – the delicacy of my situation, aw – you comprehend? It is even possible that our nuptials, my charming Miss Tiffany, *our nuptials* must take place in private!

SERAPHINA: Oh, that is quite impossible!

COUNT: It's the latest fashion abroad – the very latest! Ah, I knew that would determine you. Can I depend on your secrecy?

SERAPHINA: Oh, yes! Believe me.

SNOBSON: [*Coming forward in spite of Mrs. Tiffany's efforts to detain him*] Why, Seraphina, haven't you a word to throw to a dog?

TIFFANY: I shouldn't think she had after wasting so many upon a puppy. [*Aside*]

Enter Zeke, wearing a three-cornered hat

ZEKE: Missus, de bran new carriage am below.

MRS. TIFFANY: Show it up, – I mean, – very

well, A-dolph. [*Exit Zeke*] Count, my daughter and I are about to take an airing in our new *voyture*, – will you honour us with your company?

COUNT: Madam, I – I have a most *pressing* engagement. A letter to write to the *Earl of Airshire* – who is at present residing in the *Isle of Skye*. I must bid you good-morning.

MRS. TIFFANY: Good-morning, Count. [*Exit Count*]

SNOBSON: I'm quite at leisure, [*Crosses to Mrs. Tiffany*] Marm. Books balanced – ledger closed – nothing to do all the afternoon – I'm for you.

MRS. TIFFANY: [*Without noticing him*] Come, Seraphina, come!

As they are going, Snobson follows them

SNOBSON: But, Marm – I was saying, Marm, I am quite at leisure – not a thing to do; have I, Mr. Tiffany?

MRS. TIFFANY: Seraphina, child – your red shawl – remember – Mr. Snobson, *bon swear!* [*Exit, leading Seraphina*]

SNOBSON: Swear! Mr. Tiffany, sir, am I to be fobbed off with a *bon swear*? D——n it, I will swear!

TIFFANY: Have patience, Mr. Snobson, if you will accompany me to the counting-house –

SNOBSON: Don't count too much on me, sir. I'll make up no more accounts until these are settled! I'll run down and jump into the carriage in spite of her *bon swear*. [*Exit*]

TIFFANY: You'll jump into a hornet's nest, if you do! Mr. Snobson, Mr. Snobson! [*Exit after him*]

Scene 2

Housekeeper's Room. Enter Millinette.
MILLINETTE: I have set dat bête, Adolph, to vatch for him. He say he would come back so soon as Madame's voiture drive from de door. If he not come – but he vill – he vill – he *bien étourdi*, but he have *bon coeur*.

Enter Count
COUNT: Ah! Millinette, my dear, you see what a good-natured dog I am to fly at your bidding –
MILLINETTE: Fly? Ah! *trompeur!* Vat for you fly from Paris? Vat for you leave me – and I love you so much? Ven you sick – you almost die

– did I not stay by you – take care of you – and you have no else friend? Vat for you leave Paris?

COUNT: Never allude to disagreeable subjects, mon *enfant!* I was forced by uncontrollable circumstances to fly to the land of liberty –
MILLINETTE: Vat you do vid all de money I give you? The last sou I had – did I not give you?

COUNT: I dare say you did, ma petite – wish you'd been better supplied! [*Aside*] Don't ask any questions here – can't explain now – the next time we meet –

MILLINETTE: But, ah! ven shall ve meet – ven? You not deceive me, not any more.

COUNT: Deceive you! I'd rather deceive myself – I wish I could! I'd persuade myself you were once more washing linen in the Seine! [*Aside*]

MILLINETTE: I vil tell you ven ve shall meet – On Friday night Madame give one grand ball – you come *sans doute* – den ven de supper is served – de Americans tink of noting else ven de supper come – den you steal out of de room, and you find me here – and you give me one grand *explanation!*

Enter Gertrude, unperceived
COUNT: Friday night – while supper is serving – *parole d'honneur* I will be here – I will explain every thing – my sudden departure from Paris – my – demme, my countship – every thing! Now let me go – if any of the family should discover us –

GERTRUDE: [*Who during the last speech has gradually advanced*] They might discover more than you think it advisable for them to know!

COUNT: The devil!
MILLINETTE: *Mon Dieu!* Mademoiselle Gertrude!
COUNT: [*Recovering himself*] My dear Miss Gertrude, let me explain – aw – aw – nothing is more natural than the situation in which you find me –

GERTRUDE: I am inclined to believe that, sir.
COUNT: Now – 'pon my honour, that's not fair. Here is Millinette will bear witness to what I am about to say –

GERTRUDE: Oh, I have not the slightest doubt of that, sir.

COUNT: You see, Millinette happened to be lady's-maid in the family of – of – the Duchess Chateau D'Espagne – and I chanced to be a particular friend of the Duchess – *very particular* I assure you! Of course I saw Millinette, and she, demme, she saw me! Didn't you, Millinette?

MILLINETTE: Oh! *oui* – Mademoiselle, I knew him ver well.

COUNT: Well, it is a remarkable fact that – being in correspondence with this very Duchess – at this very time –

GERTRUDE: That is sufficient, sir – I am already so well acquainted with your extraordinary talents for improvisation, that I will not further tax your invention –

MILLINETTE: Ah! Mademoiselle Gertrude, do not betray us – have pity!

COUNT: [*Assuming an air of dignity*] Silence, Millinette! My word has been doubted – the word of a nobleman! I will inform my friend, Mrs. Tiffany, of this young person's audacity. [*Going*]

GERTRUDE: His own weapons alone can foil this villain! [*Aside*] Sir – sir – Count! [*At the last word the Count turns*] Perhaps, sir, the least said about this matter the better!

COUNT: [*Delightedly*] The least said? We won't say anything at all. She's coming round – couldn't resist me! [*Aside*] Charming Gertrude –

MILLINETTE: *Quoi?* Vat that you say?

COUNT: My sweet, adorable Millinette, hold your tongue, will you? [*Aside to her*]

MILLINETTE: [*Aloud*] No, I vill not! If you do look so from out your eyes at her again, I vill tell all!

COUNT: Oh, I never could manage two women at once, – jealousy makes the dear creatures so spiteful. The only valour is in flight. [*Aside*] Miss Gertrude, I wish you good-morning. Millinette, *mon enfant*, adieu. [*Exit*]

MILLINETTE: But I have one word more to say. Stop! Stop! [*Exit after him*]

GERTRUDE: [*Musingly*] Friday night, while supper is serving, he is to meet Millinette here and explain – what? This man is an impostor! His insulting me – his familiarity with Millinette – his whole conduct – prove it. If I tell Mrs. Tiffany this, she will disbelieve me, and one word may place this so-called Count on his guard. To convince Seraphina would be equally difficult, and her rashness and infatuation may render her miserable for life. No – she shall be saved! I must devise some plan for opening their eyes. Truly, if I *cannot* invent one, I shall be the first woman who was ever at

a loss for a stratagem – especially to punish a villain or to shield a friend. [*Exit*]

ACT IV. Scene 1

Ball-room splendidly illuminated. A curtain hung at the further end. Mr. and Mrs. Tiffany, Seraphina, Gertrude, Fogg, Twinkle, Count, Snobson, Colonel Howard, a number of guests – some seated, some standing. As the curtain rises, a cotillion is danced; Gertrude dancing with Howard, Seraphina with Count.

COUNT: [*Advancing with Seraphina to the front of the stage*] To-morrow then – to-morrow – I may salute you as my bride – demme, my Countess!

Enter Zeke with refreshments

SERAPHINA: Yes, to-morrow.

As the Count is about to reply, Snobson thrusts himself in front of Seraphina

SNOBSON: You said you'd dance with me, Miss – now take my fin, and we'll walk about and see what's going on.

Count raises his eye-glass, regards Snobson, and leads Seraphina away; Snobson follows, endeavouring to attract her attention, but encounters Zeke, bearing a waiter of refreshments; stops, helps himself, and puts some in his pockets Here's the treat! get my to-morrow's luncheon out of Tiff.

Enter Trueman, yawning and rubbing his eyes

TRUEMAN: What a nap I've had, to be sure! [*Looks at his watch*] Eleven o'clock, as I'm alive! Just the time when country folks are comfortably *turned in*, and here your grand *turn-out* has hardly begun yet! [*To Tiffany, who approaches*]

GERTRUDE: [*Advancing*] I was just coming to look for you, Mr. Trueman. I began to fancy that you were paying a visit to dream-land.

TRUEMAN: So I was child – so I was – and I saw a face – like yours – but brighter! – even brighter. [*To Tiffany*] There's a smile for you, man! It makes one feel that the world has something worth living for in it yet! Do you remember a smile like that, Antony? Ah! I see you don't – but I do – I do! [*Much moved*]

HOWARD: [*Advancing*] Good evening, Mr. Trueman. [*Offers his hand*]

TRUEMAN: That's right, man; give me your whole hand! When a man offers me the tips of his fingers, I know at once there's nothing in him worth seeking beyond his fingers' ends.

Trueman and Howard, Gertrude and Tiffany converse

MRS. TIFFANY: [*Advancing centre*] I'm in such a fidget lest that vulgar old fellow should disgrace us by some of his plebeian remarks! What it is to give a ball, when one is forced to invite vulgar people!

Mrs. Tiffany advances towards Trueman; Seraphina stands conversing flippantly with the gentlemen who surround her; amongst them is Twinkle, who, having taken a magazine from his pocket, is reading to her, much to the undisguised annoyance of Snobson

Dear me, Mr. Trueman, you are very late – quite in the fashion, I declare!

TRUEMAN: Fashion! And pray what is *fashion*, Madam? An agreement between certain persons to live without using their souls! to substitute etiquette for virtue – decorum for purity – manners for morals! to affect a shame for the works of their Creator! and expend all their rapture upon the works of their tailors and dressmakers!

MRS. TIFFANY: You have the most *ow-tray* ideas, Mr. Trueman – quite rustic, and deplorably *American*! But pray walk this way. [*Mrs. Tiffany and Trueman go up stage*]

COUNT: [*Advancing to Gertrude, who stands centre, Howard a short distance behind her*] Miss Gertrude – no opportunity of speaking to you before – in demand, you know!

GERTRUDE: I have no choice, I must be civil to him. [*Aside*] What were you remarking, sir?

COUNT: Miss Gertrude – charming Ger – aw – aw – I never found it so difficult to speak to a woman before. [*Aside*]

GERTRUDE: Yes, a very charming ball – many beautiful faces here.

COUNT: Only one! – aw – aw – one – the fact is – [*Talks to her in dumb show*]

HOWARD: What could old Trueman have meant by saying she fancied that puppy of a Count – that paste-jewel thrust upon the little finger of society.

COUNT: Miss Gertrude – aw – 'pon my honour –

you don't understand – really – aw – aw – will you dance the polka with me?

Gertrude bows and gives him her hand; he leads her to the set forming; Howard remains looking after them

HOWARD: Going to dance with him, too! A few days ago she would hardly bow to him civilly – could old Trueman have had reasons for what he said? [*Retires*]

Dance, the polka; Seraphina, after having distributed her bouquet, vinaigrette and fan amongst the gentlemen, dances with Snobson

PRUDENCE: [*Peeping in, as dance concludes*] I don't like dancing on Friday; something strange is always sure to happen! I'll be on the look out.

Remains peeping and concealing herself when any of the company approach

GERTRUDE: [*Advancing hastily to centre*] They are preparing the supper – now, if I can only dispose of Millinette while I unmask this insolent pretender! [*Exit*]

PRUDENCE: [*Peeping*] What's that she said? It's coming!

Reenter Gertrude, bearing a small basket filled with bouquets; approaches Mrs. Tiffany; they walk to the front of the stage

GERTRUDE: Excuse me, Madam – I believe this is just the hour at which you ordered supper?

MRS. TIFFANY: Well, what's that to you! So, you've been dancing with the Count – how dare you dance with a nobleman – *you*?

GERTRUDE: I will answer that question half an hour hence. At present I have something to propose, which I think will gratify you and please your guests. I have heard that at the most elegant balls in Paris, it is customary –

MRS. TIFFANY: What? what?

GERTRUDE: To station a servant at the door with a basket of flowers. A bouquet is then presented to every lady as she passes in – I prepared this basket a short time ago. As the company walk in to supper, might not the flowers be distributed to advantage?

MRS. TIFFANY: How *distingué!* You are a good creature, Gertrude – there, run and hand the *bokettes* to them yourself! You shall have the whole credit of the thing.

GERTRUDE: Caught in my own net! [*Aside*] But,

Madam, I know so little of fashions – Millinette, being French, herself will do it with so much more grace. I am sure Millinette –

MRS. TIFFANY: So am I. She will do it a thousand times better than you – there, go call her.

GERTRUDE: [*Giving basket*] But, Madam, pray order Millinette not to leave her station till supper is ended – as the company pass out of the supper room she may find that some of the ladies have been overlooked.

MRS. TIFFANY: That is true – very thoughtful of you, Gertrude. [*Exit Gertrude*] What a *recherché* idea!

Enter Millinette

Here, Millinette, take this basket. Place yourself there, [*Centre*] and distribute these *bokettes* as the company pass in to supper; but remember not to stir from the spot until supper is over. It is a French fashion, you know, Millinette. I am so delighted to be the first to introduce it – it will be all the rage in the *bowmonde!*

MILLINETTE: *Mon Dieu!* dis vill ruin all! [*Aside*] Madame, madame, let me tell you, Madame, dat in France, in Paris, it is de custom to present *les* bouquets ven everybody first come – long before de supper. Dis would be *outré! barbare!* not at all *la mode!* Ven dey do come in, dat is de fashion in Paris!

MRS. TIFFANY: Dear me! Millinette, what is the difference? besides, I'd have you to know that Americans always improve upon French fashions! here, take the basket, and let me see that you do it in the most *you-nick* and genteel manner.

Millinette poutingly takes the basket and retires up stage. A march. Curtain hung at the further end of the room is drawn back, and discloses a room, in the centre of which stands a supper-table, beautifully decorated and illuminated; the company promenade two by two into the supper room; Millinette presents bouquets as they pass; Count leads Mrs. Tiffany

TRUEMAN: [*Encountering Fogg, who is hurrying alone to the supper room*] Mr. Fogg, never mind the supper, man! Ha, ha, ha! Of course you are indifferent to suppers!

FOGG: Indifferent! suppers – oh, ah – no, sir – suppers? no – no – I'm not indifferent to suppers! [*Hurries away towards table*]

TRUEMAN: Ha, ha, ha! Here's a new discovery I've made in the fashionable world! Fashion don't permit the critters to have *heads* or *hearts*, but it allows them stomachs! [*To Tiffany, who advances*] So, it's not fashionable to *feel*, but it's fashionable to *feed*, eh, Antony? ha, ha, ha!

Trueman and Tiffany retire towards supper room

Enter Gertrude, followed by Zeke

GERTRUDE: Zeke, go to the supper room instantly, – whisper to Count Jolimaitre that all is ready, and that he must keep his appointment without delay, – then watch him, and as he passes out of the room, place yourself in front of Millinette in such a manner, that the Count cannot see her nor she him. Be sure that they do not see each other – everything depends upon that. [*Crosses to right*]

ZEKE: Missy, consider dat business brought to a scientific conclusion. [*Exit into supper room. Exit Gertrude*]

PRUDENCE: [*Who has been listening*] What can she want of the Count? I always suspected that Gertrude, because she is so merry and busy! Mr. Trueman thinks so much of her, too, – I'll tell him this! There's something wrong – but it all comes of giving a ball on a Friday! How astonished the dear old man will be when he finds out how much I know! [*Advances timidly towards the supper room*]

Scene 2

Housekeeper's room; dark stage; table, two chairs. Enter Gertrude, with a lighted candle in her hand.

GERTRUDE: So far the scheme prospers! and yet this imprudence – if I fail? Fail! to lack courage in a difficulty, or ingenuity in a dilemma, are not woman's failings!

Enter Zeke, with a napkin over his arm, and a bottle of champagne in his hand
Well, Zeke – Adolph!

ZEKE: Dat's right, Missy; I feels just now as if dat was my legitimate title; dis here's de stuff to make a nigger feel like a gemman!

GERTRUDE: But is he coming?

ZEKE: He's coming! [*Sound of a champagne*

cork heard] Do you hear dat, Missy? Don't it put you all in a froth, and make you feel as light as a cork? Dere's nothing like the *union brand*, to wake up de harmonies ob de heart. [*Drinks from bottle*]

GERTRUDE: Remember to keep watch upon the outside – do not stir from the spot; when I call you, come in quickly with a light – now, will you be gone!

ZEKE: I'm off, Missy, like a champagne cork wid de strings cut. [*Exit*]

GERTRUDE: I think I hear the Count's step. [*Crosses left; stage dark; she blows out candle*] Now, if I can but disguise my voice, and make the best of my French.

Enter Count

COUNT: Millinette, where are you? How am I to see you in the dark?

GERTRUDE: [*Imitating Millinette's voice in a whisper*] Hush! *parle bas.*

COUNT: Come here and give me a kiss.

GERTRUDE: Non – non – [*Retreating, alarmed; Count follows*] make haste, I must know all.

COUNT: You did not use to be so deuced particular.

ZEKE: [*Without*] No admission, gemman! Box office closed, tickets stopped!

TRUEMAN: [*Without*] Out of my way; do you want me to try if your head is as hard as my stick?

GERTRUDE: What shall I do? Ruined, ruined!

She stands with her hands clasped in speechless despair

COUNT: Halloa! they are coming here, Millinette! Millinette, why don't you speak? Where can I hide myself? [*Running about stage, feeling for a door*] Where are all your closets? If I could only get out – or get in somewhere; may I be smothered in a clothes' basket, if you ever catch me in such a scrape again! [*His hand accidentally touches the knob of a door opening into a closet*] Fortune's favorite yet! I'm safe!

Gets into closet, and closes door. Enter Prudence, Trueman, Mrs. Tiffany, and Colonel Howard, followed by Zeke, bearing a light

PRUDENCE: Here they are, the Count and Gertrude! I told you so! [*Stops in surprise on seeing only Gertrude*]

TRUEMAN: And you see what a lie you told!

MRS. TIFFANY: Prudence, how dare you create this disturbance in my house? To suspect the Count, too – a nobleman!

HOWARD: My sweet Gertrude, this foolish old woman would –

PRUDENCE: Oh! you needn't talk – I heard her make the appointment – I know he's here – or he's been here. I wonder if she hasn't hid him away! [*Runs peeping about the room*]

TRUEMAN: [*Following her angrily*] You're what I call a confounded – troublesome – meddling – old – prying – [*As he says the last word, Prudence opens closet where the Count is concealed*] Thunder and lightning!

PRUDENCE: I told you so!

They all stand aghast; Mrs. Tiffany, with her hands lifted in surprise and anger; Trueman, clutching his stick; Howard, looking with an expression of bewildered horror from the Count to Gertrude

MRS. TIFFANY: [*Shaking her fist at Gertrude*] You depraved little minx! this is the meaning of your dancing with the Count!

COUNT: [*Stepping from the closet and advancing*] I don't know what to make of it! Millinette not here! Miss Gertrude – Oh! I see – a disguise – the girl's desperate about me – the way with them all. [*Aside*]

TRUEMAN: I'm choking – I can't speak – Gertrude – no – no – it is some horrid mistake! [*Partly aside, changes his tone suddenly*] The villain! I'll hunt the truth out of him, if there's any in – [*Approaches Count threateningly*] Do you see this stick? You made its first acquaintance a few days ago; it is time you were better known to each other.

As Trueman attempts to seize him Count escapes, and shields himself behind Mrs. Tiffany, Trueman following

COUNT: You ruffian! would you strike a woman? – Madam – my dear Madam – keep off that barbarous old man, and I will explain! Madam, with – aw – your natural *bon gout* – aw – your fashionable refinement – aw – your – aw – your knowledge of *foreign customs* –

MRS. TIFFANY: Oh! Count, I hope it ain't a *foreign custom* for the nobility to shut themselves up in the dark with young women? We think such things *dreadful* in *America*.

COUNT: Demme – aw – hear what I have to say, Madam – I'll satisfy all sides – I am perfectly innocent in this affair – 'pon my honour I

338

am! That young lady shall inform you that I am so herself! – can't help it, sorry for her. Old matter-of-fact won't be convinced any other way, – that club of his is so particularly unpleasant! [*Aside*] Madam, I was summoned here *malgré moi*, and not knowing whom I was to meet – Miss Gertrude, favor this company by saying whether or not you directed – that – aw – aw – that coloured individual to conduct me here?

GERTRUDE: Sir, you well know –

COUNT: A simple yes or no will suffice.

MRS. TIFFANY: Answer the Count's question instantly, Miss.

GERTRUDE: I did – but –

COUNT: You hear, Madam –

TRUEMAN: I won't believe it – I can't! Here, you nigger, stop rolling up your eyes, and let us know whether she told you to bring that critter here?

ZEKE: I'se refuse to gib ebidence; dat's de device ob de skilfullest counsels ob de day! Can't answer, Boss – neber git a word out ob dis child – Yah! yah! [*Exit*]

GERTRUDE: Mrs. Tiffany, – Mr. Trueman, if you will but have patience –

TRUEMAN: Patience! Oh, Gertrude, you've taken from an old man something better and dearer than his patience – the one bright hope of nineteen years of self-denial – of nineteen years of –

Throws himself upon a chair, his head leaning on table

MRS. TIFFANY: Get out of my house, you *ow*dacious – you ruined – you *abimé* young woman! You will corrupt all my family. Good gracious! don't touch me, – don't come near me. Never let me see your face after to-morrow. Pack. [*Goes up stage*]

HOWARD: Gertrude, I have striven to find some excuse for you – to doubt – to disbelieve – but this is beyond all endurance! [*Exit*]

Enter Millinette in haste

MILLINETTE: I could not come before – [*Stops in surprise at seeing the persons assembled*] *Mon Dieu!* Vat does dis mean?

COUNT: Hold your tongue, fool! You will ruin everything. I will explain to-morrow. [*Aside to her*] Mrs. Tiffany – Madam – my dear Madam, let me conduct you back to the ball-room. [*She takes his arm*] You see I am quite innocent in this matter; a man of my standing, you know, –aw, aw – you comprehend the whole affair.

Exit Count leading Mrs. Tiffany

MILLINETTE: I vill say to him von vord, I vill! [*Exit*]

GERTRUDE: Mr. Trueman, I beseech you – I insist upon being heard, – I claim it as a right!

TRUEMAN: Right? How dare you have the face, girl, to talk of rights? [*Comes down stage*] You had more rights than you thought for, but you have forfeited them all! All right to love, respect, protection, and to not a little else that you don't dream of. Go, go! I'll start for Catteraugus to-morrow, – I've seen enough of what fashion can do! [*Exit*]

PRUDENCE: [*Wiping her eyes*] Dear old man, how he takes on! I'll go and console him! [*Exit*]

GERTRUDE: This is too much! How heavy a penalty has my imprudence cost me! – his esteem, and that of one dearer – my home – my – [*Burst of lively music from ball-room*] They are dancing, and I – I should be weeping, if pride had not sealed up my tears.

She sinks into a chair. Band plays the polka behind till Curtain falls

ACT V

Mrs. Tiffany's Drawing-room – same scene as Act I. Gertrude seated at a table, with her head leaning on her hand; in the other hand she holds a pen. A sheet of paper and an inkstand before her.

GERTRUDE: How shall I write to them? What shall I say? Prevaricate I cannot – [*Rises and comes forward*] and yet if I write the truth – simple souls! how can they comprehend the motives for my conduct? Nay – the truly pure see no imaginary evil in others! It is only vice, that reflecting its own image, suspects even the innocent. I have no time to lose – I must prepare them for my return. [*Resumes her seat and writes*] What a true pleasure there is in daring to be frank! [*After writing a few lines more, pauses*] Not so frank either, – there is one name that I cannot mention. Ah! that he should suspect – should despise me. [*Writes*]

Enter Trueman

TRUEMAN: There she is! If this girl's soul had only been as fair as her face, – yet she dared to speak the truth, – I'll not forget that! A woman who refuses to tell a lie has one spark of heaven in her still. [*Approaches her*] Gertrude, [*Gertrude starts and looks up*] what are you writing there? Plotting more mischief, eh, girl?

GERTRUDE: I was writing a few lines to some friends in Geneva.

TRUEMAN: The Wilsons, eh?

GERTRUDE: [*Surprised, rising*] Are you acquainted with them, sir?

TRUEMAN: I shouldn't wonder if I was. I suppose you have taken good care not to mention the dark room – that foreign puppy in the closet – the pleasant surprise – and all that sort of thing, eh?

GERTRUDE: I have no reason for concealment, sir! for I have done nothing of which I am ashamed!

TRUEMAN: Then I can't say much for your modesty.

GERTRUDE: I should not wish you to say more than I deserve.

TRUEMAN: There's a bold minx! [*Aside*]

GERTRUDE: Since my affairs seem to have excited your interest – I will not say *curiosity*, – perhaps you even feel a desire to inspect my correspondence? There, [*Handing the letter*] I pride myself upon my good nature, – you may like to take advantage of it?

TRUEMAN: With what an air she carries it off! [*Aside*] Take advantage of it? So I will. [*Reads*] What's this? "French chambermaid – Count – impostor – infatuation – Seraphina – Millinette – disguised myself – expose him." Thunder and lightning! I see it all! Come and kiss me, girl! [*Gertrude evinces surprise*] No, no – I forgot – it won't do to come to that yet! She's a rare girl! I'm out of my senses with joy! I don't know what to do with myself! Tol, de rol, de rol, de ra! [*Capers and sings*]

GERTRUDE: What a remarkable old man! [*Aside*] Then you do me justice, Mr. Trueman?

TRUEMAN: I say I don't! Justice? You're above all dependence upon justice! Hurrah! I've found one true woman at last! *True?* [*Pauses thoughtfully*] Humph! I didn't think of that flaw! Plotting and manoeuvering – not much truth in that? An honest girl should be above stratagems!

GERTRUDE: But my *motive*, sir, was good.

TRUEMAN: That's not enough – your *actions* must be *good* as well as your *motives*! Why could you not tell the silly girl that the man was an impostor?

GERTRUDE: I did inform her of my suspicions – she ridiculed them; the plan I chose was an imprudent one, but I could not devise –

TRUEMAN: I hate devising! Give me a woman with the *firmness* to be *frank*! But no matter – I had no right to look for an angel out of Paradise; and I am as happy – as happy as a lord! that is, ten times happier than any lord ever was! Tol, de rol, de rol! Oh! you – you – I'll thrash every fellow that says a word against you!

GERTRUDE: You will have plenty of employment then, sir, for I do not know of one just now who would speak in my favour!

TRUEMAN: Not *one*, eh? Why, where's your dear Mr. Twinkle? I know all about it – can't say that I admire your choice of a husband! But there's no accounting for a girl's taste.

GERTRUDE: Mr. Twinkle! Indeed you are quite mistaken!

TRUEMAN: No – really? Then you're not taken with him, eh?

GERTRUDE: Not even with his rhymes.

TRUEMAN: Hang that old mother meddle-much! What a fool she has made of me. And so you're quite free, and I may choose a husband for you myself? Heart-whole, eh?

GERTRUDE: I – I trust there is nothing *unsound* about my heart.

TRUEMAN: There it is again. Don't prevaricate, girl! I tell you an *evasion* is a *lie in contemplation*, and I hate lying! Out with the truth! Is your heart *free* or not?

GERTRUDE: Nay, sir, since you *demand* an answer, permit *me* to demand by what right you ask the question?

Enter Howard

Colonel Howard here!

TRUEMAN: I'm out again! What's the Colonel to her? [*Retires up stage*]

HOWARD: [*Crosses to her*] I have come, Gertrude, to bid you farewell. To-morrow I resign my commission and leave this city, perhaps for ever. You, Gertrude, it is you who have exiled me! After last evening –

TRUEMAN: [*Coming forward to Howard*] What

the plague have you got to say about last evening?

HOWARD: Mr. Trueman!

TRUEMAN: What have you got to say about last evening? and what have you to say to that little girl at all? It's Tiffany's precious daughter you're in love with.

HOWARD: Miss Tiffany? Never! I never had the slightest pretension –

TRUEMAN: That lying old woman! But I'm glad of it! Oh! Ah! Um! [*Looking significantly at Gertrude and then at Howard*] I see how it is. So you don't choose to marry Seraphina, eh? Well, now, whom do you choose to marry? [*Glancing at Gertrude*]

HOWARD: I shall not marry at all!

TRUEMAN: You won't? [*Looking at them both again*] Why, you don't mean to say that you don't like – [*Points with his thumb to Gertrude*]

GERTRUDE: Mr. Trueman, I may have been wrong to boast of my good nature, but do not presume too far upon it.

HOWARD: You like frankness, Mr. Trueman, therefore I will speak plainly. I have long cherished a dream from which I was last night rudely awakened.

TRUEMAN: And that's what you call speaking plainly? Well, I differ with you! But I can guess what you mean. Last night you suspected Gertrude there of – [*Angrily*] of what no man shall ever suspect her again while I'm above ground! You did her injustice, – it was a mistake! There, now that matter's settled. Go, and ask her to forgive you, – she's woman enough to do it! Go, go!

HOWARD: Mr. Trueman, you have forgotten to whom you dictate.

TRUEMAN: Then you won't do it? you won't ask her pardon?

HOWARD: Most undoubtedly I will not – not at any man's bidding. I must first know –

TRUEMAN: You won't do it? Then, if I don't give you a lesson in politeness –

HOWARD: It will be because you find me your *tutor* in the same science. I am not a man to brook an insult, Mr. Trueman! but we'll not quarrel in the presence of the lady. [*Crosses*]

TRUEMAN: Won't we? I don't know that –

GERTRUDE: Pray, Mr. Trueman – Colonel Howard, [*Crosses to centre*] pray desist, Mr. Trueman, for my sake! [*Taking hold of his arm to hold him back*] Colonel Howard, if you will

read this letter it will explain everything. [*Hands letter to Howard, who reads*]

TRUEMAN: He don't deserve an explanation! Didn't I tell him that it was a mistake? Refuse to beg your pardon! I'll teach him, I'll teach him!

HOWARD: [*After reading*] Gertrude, how I have wronged you!

TRUEMAN: Oh! you'll beg her pardon now? [*Between them*]

HOWARD: Hers, sir, and yours! Gertrude, I fear –

TRUEMAN: You needn't, – she'll forgive you. You don't know these women as well as I do, – they're always ready to pardon; it's their nature, and they can't help it. Come along, I left Antony and his wife in the dining-room; we'll go and find them. I've a story of my own to tell! As for you, Colonel, you may follow. Come along, come along! [*Leads out Gertrude, followed by Howard*]

Enter Mr. and Mrs. Tiffany. Mr. Tiffany with a bundle of bills in his hand

MRS. TIFFANY: I beg you won't mention the subject again, Mr. Tiffany. Nothing is more plebeian than a discussion upon economy – nothing more *ungenteel* than looking over and fretting over one's bills!

TIFFANY: Then I suppose, my dear, it is quite as ungenteel to *pay* one's bills?

MRS. TIFFANY: Certainly! I hear the *ee-light* never condescend to do anything of the kind. The honour of their invaluable patronage is sufficient for the persons they employ!

TIFFANY: *Patronage* then is a newly invented food upon which the working-classes fatten? What convenient appetites poor people must have! Now listen to what I am going to say. As soon as my daughter marries Mr. Snobson –

Enter Prudence, a three-cornered note in her hand

PRUDENCE: Oh, dear! oh, dear! what shall we do! Such a misfortune! Such a disaster! Oh, dear! oh, dear!

MRS. TIFFANY: Prudence, you are the most tiresome creature! What *is* the matter?

PRUDENCE: [*Pacing up and down the stage*] Such a disgrace to the whole family! But I always expected it. Oh, dear! oh, dear!

MRS. TIFFANY: [*Following her up and down the stage*] What are you talking about, Prudence?

Will you tell me what has happened?

PRUDENCE: [*Still pacing, Mrs. Tiffany following*] Oh! I can't, I can't! You'll feel so dreadfully! How could she do such a thing! But I expected nothing else! I never did, I never did!

MRS. TIFFANY: [*Still following*] Good gracious! what do you mean, Prudence? Tell me, will you tell me? I shall get into such a passion! What *is* the matter?

PRUDENCE: [*Still pacing*] Oh, Betsy, Betsy! That your daughter should have come to that! Dear me, dear me!

TIFFANY: Seraphina? Did you say Seraphina? What has happened to her? what has she done?

Following Prudence up and down the stage on the opposite side from Mrs. Tiffany

MRS. TIFFANY: [*Still following*] What *has* she done? What *has* she done?

PRUDENCE: Oh! something dreadful – dreadful – shocking!

TIFFANY: [*Still following*] Speak quickly and plainly – you torture me by this delay, – Prudence, be calm, and speak! What is it?

PRUDENCE: [*Stopping*] Zeke just told me – he carried her travelling trunk himself – she gave him a whole dollar! Oh, my!

TIFFANY: Her trunk? where? where?

PRUDENCE: Round the corner!

MRS. TIFFANY: What did she want with her trunk? You are the most vexatious creature, Prudence! There is no bearing your ridiculous conduct!

PRUDENCE: Oh, you will have worse to bear – worse! Seraphina's gone!

TIFFANY: Gone! where?

PRUDENCE: Off! – eloped – eloped with the Count! Dear me, dear me! I always told you she would!

TIFFANY: Then I am ruined! [*Stands with his face buried in his hands*]

MRS. TIFFANY: Oh, what a ridiculous girl! And she might have had such a splendid wedding! What could have possessed her?

TIFFANY: The devil himself possessed her, for she has ruined me past all redemption! Gone, Prudence, did you say gone? Are you *sure* they are gone?

PRUDENCE: Didn't I tell you so! Just look at this note – one might know by the very fold of it –

TIFFANY: [*Snatching the note*] Let me see it! [*Opens the note and reads*] "My dear Ma, – When you receive this I shall be a *countess*!

Isn't it a sweet title? The Count and I were forced to be married privately, for reasons which I will explain in my next. You must pacify Pa, and put him in a good humour before I come back, though now I'm to be a countess I suppose I shouldn't care!" Undutiful huzzy! "We are going to make a little excursion and will be back in a week. Your dutiful daughter – Seraphina." A man's curse is sure to spring up at his own hearth, – here is mine! The sole curb upon that villain gone, I am wholly in his power! Oh! the first downward step from honour – he who takes it cannot pause in his mad descent and is sure to be hurried on to ruin!

MRS. TIFFANY: Why, Mr. Tiffany, how you do take on! And I dare say to elope was the most fashionable way after all!

Enter Trueman, leading Gertrude, and followed by Howard

TRUEMAN: Where are all the folks? Here, Antony, you are the man I want. We've been hunting for you all over the house. Why – what's the matter? There's a face for a thriving city merchant! Ah! Antony, you never wore such a hang-dog look as that when you trotted about the country with your pack upon your back! Your shoulders are no broader now – but they've a heavier load to carry – that's plain!

MRS. TIFFANY: Mr. Trueman, such allusions are highly improper! What would my daughter, *the Countess*, say!

GERTRUDE: The Countess? Oh! Madam!

MRS. TIFFANY: Yes, the Countess! My daughter Seraphina, the Countess *dee* Jolimaitre! What have you to say to that? No wonder you are surprised after your *recherché, abimé* conduct! I have told you already, Miss Gertrude, that you were not a proper person to enjoy the inestimable advantages of my patronage. You are dismissed – do you understand? Discharged!

TRUEMAN: Have you done? Very well, it's my turn now. Antony, perhaps what I have to say don't concern you as much as some others – but I want you to listen to me. You remember, Antony, [*His tone becomes serious*] a blue-eyed, smiling girl –

TIFFANY: Your daughter, sir? I remember her well.

TRUEMAN: None ever saw her to forget her! Give me your hand, man. There – that will do! Now let me go on. I never coveted wealth –

yet twenty years ago I found myself the richest farmer in Catteraugus. This cursed money made my girl an object of speculation. Every idle fellow that wanted to feather his nest was sure to come courting Ruth. There was one – my heart misgave me the instant I laid eyes upon him – for he was a city chap, and not over-fond of the truth. But Ruth – ah! she was too pure herself to look for guile! His fine words and his fair looks – the old story – she was taken with him – I said, "no" – but the girl liked her own way better than her old father's – girls always do! and one morning – the rascal robbed me – not of my money, – he would have been welcome to that – but of the only treasure I cherished – my daughter!

TIFFANY: But you forgave her!

TRUEMAN: I did! I knew she would never forgive herself – that was punishment enough! The scoundrel thought he was marrying my gold with my daughter – he was mistaken! I took care that they should never want; but that was all. She loved him – what will not woman love? The villain broke her heart – mine was tougher, or it wouldn't have stood what it did. A year after they were married, he forsook her! She came back to her old home – her old father! It couldn't last long – she pined – and pined – and – then – she died! Don't think me an old fool – though I am one – for grieving won't bring her back. [*Bursts into tears*]

TIFFANY: It was a heavy loss.

TRUEMAN: So heavy that I should not have cared how soon I followed her, but for the child she left! As I pressed that child in my arms, I swore that my unlucky wealth should never curse it, as it had cursed its mother! It was all I had to love – but I sent it away – and the neighbors thought it was dead. The girl was brought up tenderly but humbly by my wife's relatives in Geneva. I had her taught true independence – she had hands – capacities – and should use them! Money should never buy her a husband! For I resolved not to claim her until she had made her choice, and found the man who was willing to take her for herself alone. She turned out a rare girl! and it's time her old grandfather claimed her. Here he is to do it! And there stands Ruth's child! Old Adam's heiress! Gertrude, Gertrude! – my child! [*Gertrude rushes into his arms*]

PRUDENCE: [*After a pause*] Do tell; I want to know! But I knew it! I always said Gertrude would turn out somebody, after all!

MRS. TIFFANY: Dear me! Gertrude an heiress! My dear Gertrude, I always thought you a very charming girl – quite YOU-NICK – an heiress! I must give her a ball! I'll introduce her into society myself – of course an heiress must make a sensation! [*Aside*]

HOWARD: I am too bewildered even to wish her joy. Ah! there will be plenty to do that now – but the gulf between us is wider than ever. [*Aside*]

TRUEMAN: Step forward, young man, and let us know what you are muttering about. I said I would never claim her until she had found the man who loved her for herself. I *have* claimed her – yet I never break my word – I think I *have* found that man! and here he is. [*Strikes Howard on the shoulder*] Gertrude's yours! There – never say a word, man – don't bore me with your thanks – you can cancel all obligations by making that child happy! There – take her! – Well, girl, and what do you say?

GERTRUDE: That I rejoice too much at having found a parent for my first act to be one of disobedience! [*Gives her hand to Howard*]

TRUEMAN: How very dutiful! and how disinterested!

Tiffany retires – and paces the stage, exhibiting great agitation

PRUDENCE: [*To Trueman*] All the *single folks* are getting married!

TRUEMAN: No they are not. You and I are single folks, and we're not likely to get married.

MRS. TIFFANY: My dear Mr. Trueman – my sweet Gertrude, when my daughter, the Countess, returns, she will be delighted to hear of this *deenooment!* I assure you that the Countess will be quite charmed!

GERTRUDE: The Countess? Pray, Madam, where *is* Seraphina?

MRS. TIFFANY: The Countess *dee* Jolimaitre, my dear, is at this moment on her way to – to Washington! Where, after visiting all the fashionable curiosities of the day – including the President – she will return to grace her native city!

GERTRUDE: I hope you are only jesting, Madam? Seraphina is not married?

MRS. TIFFANY: Excuse me, my dear, my daughter had this morning the honour of being united to the Count *dee* Jolimaitre!

GERTRUDE: Madame! He is an impostor!

MRS. TIFFANY: Good gracious! Gertrude, how can you talk in that disrespectful way of a man of rank? An heiress, my dear, should have better manners! The Count –

Enter Millinette, crying

MILLINETTE: Oh! Madame! I will tell everything – oh! dat monstre! He break my heart!

MRS. TIFFANY: Millinette, what is the matter?

MILLINETTE: Oh! he promise to marry me – I love him much – and now Zeke say he run away vid Mademoiselle Seraphina!

MRS. TIFFANY: What insolence! The girl is mad! Count Jolimaitre marry my *femmy de chamber*!

MILLINETTE: Oh! Madame, he is not one Count, not at all! Dat is only de title he go by in dis country. De foreigners always take de large title ven dey do come here. His name *à Paris* vas Gustave Tread-mill. But he not one Frenchman at all, but he do live one long time *à Paris*. First he live vid Monsieur Vermicelle – dere he vas de head cook! Den he live vid Monsieur Tire-nez, de barber! After dat he live vid Monsieur le Comte Frippon-fin – and dere he vas le Comte's valet. Dere, now I tell everyting, I feel one great deal better!

MRS. TIFFANY: Oh! good gracious! I shall faint! Not a Count! What will everybody say? It's no such thing! I say he *is* a Count! One can see the foreign *jenny says quoi* in his face! Don't you think I can tell a Count when I see one? I say he *is* a Count!

Enter Snobson, his hat on – his hands thrust in his pocket – evidently a little intoxicated

SNOBSON: I won't stand it! I say I won't!

TIFFANY: [*Rushing up to him*] Mr. Snobson, for heaven's sake – [*Aside*]

SNOBSON: Keep off. I'm a hard customer to get the better of! You'll see if I don't come out strong!

TRUEMAN: [*Quietly knocking off Snobson's hat with his stick*] Where are your manners, man?

SNOBSON: My business ain't with you, Catteraugus; you've waked up the wrong passenger! – Now the way I'll put it into Tiff will be a caution. I'll make him wince! That extra mint julep has put the true pluck in me. Now for it! [*Aside*] Mr. Tiffany, sir – you needn't think to come over me, sir – you'll have to get up a little earlier in the morning before you do *that*,

sir! I'd like to know, sir, how you came to assist your daughter in running away with that foreign loafer? It was a downright swindle, sir. After the conversation I and you had on that subject she wasn't your property, sir.

TRUEMAN: What, Antony, is that the way your city clerk bullies his boss?

SNOBSON: You're drunk, Catteraugus – don't expose yourself – you're drunk! Taken a little too much toddy, my old boy! Be quiet! I'll look after you, and they won't find it out. If you want to be busy, you may take care of my *hat* – I feel so deuced weak in the chest, I don't think I *could* pick it up myself. – Now to put the screws to Tiff. [*Aside*] Mr. Tiffany, sir – you have broken your word, as no virtuous individual – no honourable member – of – the – com-mu-mi-ty –

TIFFANY: Have some pity, Mr. Snobson, I beseech you! I had nothing to do with my daughter's elopement! I will agree to anything you desire – your salary shall be doubled – trebled – [*Aside to him*]

SNOBSON: [*Aloud*] No you don't. No bribery and corruption.

TIFFANY: I implore you to be silent. You shall become partner of the concern, if you please – only do not speak. You are not yourself at this moment. [*Aside to him*]

SNOBSON: Ain't I though. I feel *twice* myself. I feel like two Snobsons rolled into one, and I'm chock full of the spunk of a dozen! Now Mr. Tiffany, sir –

TIFFANY: I shall go distracted! Mr. Snobson, if you have one spark of manly feeling – [*Aside to him*]

TRUEMAN: Antony, why do you stand disputing with that drunken jackass? Where's your nigger? Let him kick the critter out, and be of use for once in his life.

SNOBSON: Better be quiet, Catteraugus. This ain't your hash, so keep your spoon out of the dish. Don't expose yourself, old boy.

TRUEMAN: Turn him out, Antony!

SNOBSON: He daren't do it! Ain't I up to him? Ain't he in my power? Can't I knock him into a cocked hat with a word? And now he's got my steam up – I *will* do it!

TIFFANY: [*Beseechingly*] Mr. Snobson – my friend –

SNOBSON: It's no go – steam's up – and I don't stand at anything!

TRUEMAN: You won't *stand* here long unless you

mend your manners – you're not the first man I've *upset* because he didn't know his place.

SNOBSON: I know where Tiff's place is, and that's in the *State's Prison!* It's bespoke already. He would have it! He wouldn't take pattern of me, and behave like a gentleman! He's a *forger*, sir!

Tiffany throws himself into a chair in an attitude of despair; the others stand transfixed with astonishment

He's been forging Dick Anderson's endorsements of his notes these ten months. He's got a couple in the bank that will send him to the wall anyhow – if he can't make a raise. I took them there myself! Now you know what he's worth. I said I'd expose him, and I have done it!

MRS. TIFFANY: Get out of the house! You ugly, little, drunken brute, get out! It's not true. Mr. Trueman, put him out; you have got a stick – put him out!

Enter Seraphina, in her bonnet and shawl – a parasol in her hand

SERAPHINA: I hope Zeke hasn't delivered my note. [*Stops in surprise at seeing the persons assembled*]

MRS. TIFFANY: Oh, here is the Countess! [*Advances to embrace her*]

TIFFANY: [*Starting from his seat, and seizing Seraphina violently by the arm*] Are – you – married?

SERAPHINA: Goodness, Pa, how you frighten me! No, I'm not married, *quite.*

TIFFANY: Thank heaven.

MRS. TIFFANY: [*Drawing Seraphina aside*] What's the matter? Why did you come back?

SERAPHINA: The clergyman wasn't at home – I came back for my jewels – the Count said nobility couldn't get on without them.

TIFFANY: I may be saved yet! Seraphina, my child, you will not see me disgraced – ruined! I have been a kind father to you – at least I have tried to be one – although your mother's extravagance made a *madman* of me! The Count is an impostor – you seemed to like him – [*Pointing to Snobson*] Heaven forgive me! [*Aside*] Marry *him* and save *me.* You, Mr. Trueman, you will be my friend in this hour of extreme need – you will advance the sum which I require – I pledge myself to return it. My wife – my child – who will support them were I – the thought makes me frantic! You will aid me? You had a child yourself.

TRUEMAN: But I did not *sell* her – it was her own doings. Shame on you, Antony! Put a price on your own flesh and blood! Shame on such foul traffic!

TIFFANY: Save me – I conjure you – for my father's sake.

TRUEMAN: For your *father's* SON's sake I will *not* aid you in becoming a greater villain than you are!

GERTRUDE: Mr. Trueman, – Father, I should say – save him – do not embitter our happiness by permitting this calamity to fall upon another –

TRUEMAN: Enough – I did not need your voice, child. I am going to settle this matter my own way.

Goes up to Snobson – who has seated himself and fallen asleep – tilts him out of the chair

SNOBSON: [*Waking up*] Eh? Where's the fire? Oh! it's you, Catteraugus.

TRUEMAN: If I comprehend aright, you have been for some time aware of your principal's forgeries?

As he says this, he beckons to Howard, who advances as witness

SNOBSON: You've hit the nail, Catteraugus! Old chap saw that I was up to him six months ago; left off throwing dust into my eyes –

TRUEMAN: Oh, he did!

SNOBSON: Made no bones of forging Anderson's name at my elbow.

TRUEMAN: Forged at your elbow? You saw him do it?

SNOBSON: I did.

TRUEMAN: Repeatedly?

SNOBSON: Re-pea-ted-ly.

TRUEMAN: Then you, Rattlesnake, if he goes to the State's Prison, you'll take up your quarters there too. You are an accomplice, an *accessory!*

Trueman walks away and seats himself. Howard rejoins Gertrude. Snobson stands for some time bewildered

SNOBSON: The deuce, so I am! I never thought of that! I must make myself scarce. I'll be off. Tiff, I say Tiff! [*Going up to him and speaking confidentially*] that drunken old rip has got us in his power. Let's give him the slip and be off. They want men of genius at the West, – we're sure to get on! You – you can set up for a writing-master, and teach copying *signatures;* and I – I'll give lectures on *temperance!* You won't come, eh? Then I'm off without you. Good-bye, Catteraugus! Which is the way to California? [*Steals off*]

TRUEMAN: There's one debt your city owes me. And now let us see what other nuisances we can abate. Antony, I'm not given to preaching, therefore I shall not say much about what you have done. Your face speaks for itself, – the crime has brought its punishment along with it.

TIFFANY: Indeed it has, sir! In *one year* I have lived a *century* of misery.

TRUEMAN: I believe you, and upon one condition I will assist you –

TIFFANY: My friend – my first, ever kind friend, – only name it!

TRUEMAN: You must sell your house and all these gew-gaws, and bundle your wife and daughter off to the country. There let them learn economy, true independence, and home virtues, instead of foreign follies. As for yourself, continue your business – but let moderation, in future, be your counsellor, and let *honesty* be your confidential clerk.

TIFFANY: Mr. Trueman, you have made existence once more precious to me! My wife and daughter shall quit the city to-morrow, and –

PRUDENCE: It's all coming right! It's all coming right! We'll go to the county of Catteraugus. [*Walking up to Trueman*]

TRUEMAN: No, you won't – I make that a stipulation, Antony; keep clear of Catteraugus. None of your fashionable examples there!

Jolimaitre appears in the Conservatory and peeps into the room unperceived

COUNT: What can detain Seraphina? We ought to be off!

MILLINETTE: [*Turns round, perceives him, runs and forces him into the room*] Here he is! Ah, Gustave, mon cher Gustave! I have you now and we never part no more. Don't frown, Gustave, don't frown –

TRUEMAN: Come forward, Mr. Count! and for the edification of fashionable society confess that you're an impostor.

COUNT: An impostor? Why, you abominable old –

TRUEMAN: Oh, your feminine friend has told us all about it, the cook – the valet – barber, and all that sort of thing. Come, confess, and something may be done for you.

COUNT: Well, then, I do confess I am no count; but really, ladies and gentlemen, I may recommend myself as the most capital cook.

MRS. TIFFANY: Oh, Seraphina!

SERAPHINA: Oh, Ma! [*They embrace and retire*]

TRUEMAN: Promise me to call upon the whole circle of your fashionable acquaintants with your own advertisements and in your cook's attire, and I will set you up in business to-morrow. Better turn stomachs than turn heads!

MILLINETTE: But you will marry me?

COUNT: Give us your hand, Millinette! Sir, command me for the most delicate *paté* – the daintiest *croquette à la royale* – the most transcendent *omelette soufflé* that ever issued from a French pastry-cook's oven. I hope you will pardon my conduct, but I heard that in America, where you pay homage to titles while you profess to scorn them – where *Fashion* makes the basest coin current – where you have no kings, no princes, no *nobility* –

TRUEMAN: Stop there! I object to your use of that word. When justice is found only among lawyers – health among physicians – and patriotism among politicians, *then* may you say that there is no *nobility* where there are no titles! But we *have* kings, princes, and nobles in abundance – of *Nature's stamp*, if not of *Fashion's* – we have honest men, warm-hearted and brave, and we have women – gentle, fair, and true, to whom no *title* could add *nobility*.

EPILOGUE

PRUDENCE: I told you so! And now you hear and see.

I told you *Fashion* would the fashion be!

TRUEMAN: Then both its point and moral I distrust.

COUNT: Sir, is that liberal?

HOWARD: Or is it just?

TRUEMAN: The guilty have escaped!

TIFFANY: Is, therefore, sin Made charming? Ah! there's punishment within!

Guilt ever carries his own scourge along.

GERTRUDE: Virtue her own reward!

TRUEMAN: You're right, I'm wrong.

MRS. TIFFANY: How we have been deceived!

PRUDENCE: I told you so.

SERAPHINA: To lose at once a title and a beau!

COUNT: A count no more, I'm no more of *account*.

TRUEMAN: But to a nobler title you may mount,
And be in time – who knows? – an honest man!

COUNT: Eh, Millinette?

MILLINETTE: Oh, *oui*, I know you can!

GERTRUDE: [*To audience*] But, ere we close the scene, a word with you, –
We charge you answer, – Is this picture true?
Some little mercy to our efforts show,
Then let the world your honest verdict know.
Here let it see portrayed its ruling passion,
And learn to prize at its just value – *Fashion*.

The End

UNCLE TOM'S CABIN

GEORGE L. AIKEN

In 1893, an itinerant "Tommer" with John Shea's troupe wrote to a friend back East: "Since we struck Illinois our business has been big. We now have the long green laid aside, whereas when we were at Cairo the silver was easily counted. Bessie and Lulu are doing splendid work in brass, and Mrs. Shea is becoming a good tuba player. Barney, the donkey, is the big attraction on parade; his bucking, kicking, and chasing Marks make the crowd shout every day. We close at Marshalltown, Iowa, October 15, making just one year, four months and nine days without closing the show, and having travelled eight thousand miles by wagon and boat without accident."

That same year an enterprising theatrical agent proposed that a national exchange for "Tom" actors be established in Chicago, undoubtedly anticipating a rush to his talent auction block from the diverse promoters who were pouring in for the Columbian Exposition. His public notice listed the following quotations:

> Uncle Toms, prime, $60; fair, $50; culls, $40.
> Little Evas, prime, $50; fair, $45; culls, $40.
> Legrees, prime, $50; fair, $40; culls, $35.
> Marks, prime, $45; fair, $40; culls, $35.

"Prime" were the extraordinarily able thespians who could double in brass and take care of the livestock; "fair," those who could double in brass; and "culls," mere actors.

The decade of the Nineties was the lush era for "Tomming." Some four to five hundred troupes were barnstorming across the country. Every season the resident companies in Philadelphia, Boston, Cincinnati, St. Louis – every town boasted a stock company in those days – dusted off their cakes of ice, called in the hounds, and painted up Uncle Tom's heavenly chariot. Eliza was sent skipping across the Ohio with the dogs in hot pursuit. Uncle Tom rode off majestically, if sometimes clumsily, to meet his beloved Eva in the celestial regions, upstage center.

Although the public's craze for *Uncle Tom's Cabin* reached its peak just before the turn of the century, this marked the mid-point in its colorful history. Just after Mrs. Stowe's novel appeared in the spring of 1852, Asa Hutchinson, a popular temperance singer, requested her permission to prepare a dramatization. Mrs. Stowe replied:

I have considered your application and asked advice of my different friends, and the general sentiment of those whom I have consulted so far agrees with my own, that it would not be advisable to make that use of the work which you propose. It is thought, with the present state of theatrical performances in this country, that any attempt on the part of Christians to identify themselves with them will be productive of danger to the individual character, and to the general cause. If the barrier which now keeps young people of Christian families from theatrical entertainments is once broken down by the introduction of respectable and moral plays, they will then be open to all the temptations of those who are not such, as there will be, as the world now is, five bad plays to one good. . . . The world is not good enough yet for it to succeed.

The multitude of later dramatizers never bothered to seek Mrs. Stowe's blessing, although they willingly admitted their dependence on her. In fact most were eager to advertise that theirs was the only "just, sensible, and faithful dramatic version of the original." Mrs. Stowe never associated herself with any of the dramatizations, nor did she ever receive a single cent from any stage version. The gold mine was wide open, and there were mighty few actors and managers in the United States during the last half of the century who did not scoop up a few nuggets. Mrs. Stowe's million-dollar theatrical property made millions, but not for her.

The first edition of Harriet Beecher Stowe's novel was published on March 20, 1852, although the final installment of its serialized version in the *National Era* did not appear until April. This Washington paper had printed the first segment of the story, "The Death of Uncle Tom," the previous summer. During the winter of 1851–52, the *National Era* was passed from hand to hand more eagerly with each new installment of the story. At the time the Boston publisher J. P. Jewett undertook the first book publication, the fervor was still building. Three thousand copies were sold the first day, ten thousand in the first week – the complete stock of the first edition. Jewett printed again immediately, and then again. Within the first year he had sold three hundred thousand copies. But this was less astonishing than the spectacular first-year history of the novel in England. Published in London in May, 1852, by the following May it had appeared in twenty-three different editions and sold well over a million copies. On September 3, 1852, the London *Times* wrote: "Mrs. Stowe has received $10,000 as her copyright premium on three months' sales of the work – we believe the largest sum of money ever received by any author, either American or European, from the sale of a single work in so short a period of time."

Uncle Tom's Cabin became one of the all-time sensations of book-publishing history. By 1878 the British Museum had shelved copies of the book in twenty different languages, including Bohemian, Modern Greek, Russian, Siamese, and Serbian. *Uncle Tom's Cabin* covered the globe. On December 17, 1852, George Sand wrote, "This book is in all hands and in all Journals. It has, and will have, editions in every form; people devour it, they cover it with tears." In 1856, Thomas Macaulay, having just returned from Italy, wrote to Mrs. Stowe, "There is no place where 'Uncle Tom' is not to be found."

Mrs. Stowe was besieged with laudatory letters and testimonials. On May 23, 1852, Jenny Lind wrote to her, "I have the feeling about *Uncle Tom's Cabin* that great changes will take place by and by from the impression people receive out of it." As a testament of their sympathies, "An Affectionate and Christian Address to the Women of America from the Women of England," signed by 562,448 Englishwomen, was sent to Mrs. Stowe. She was not prepared for the fervor with which the abolitionists took up her book. She had thought it too mild for them, and in a way had even hoped that it might help to unite the North and the South. When she met Lincoln after the war had begun, she was deeply grieved at his response to the introduction. He is reported to have said, "So you're the little woman who wrote the book that made this great war!"

That Mrs. Stowe did not want *Uncle Tom's Cabin* to be regarded as the emotional outburst of an abolitionist is apparent in her later, and less-known, *The Key to Uncle Tom's Cabin, Presenting the Original Facts and Documents upon which the Story is Founded, Together with Corroborative Statements Verifying the Truth of the Work*. Brought out in 1853, this document sought to dispel any mistaken notion that *Uncle Tom* was fictitious invention. As Mrs. Stowe said, "This work has been a collection and arrangement of real incidents, of actions really performed, of words and expressions really uttered, grouped together with reference to a general result." The *Key* documented the characters and incidents of *Uncle Tom's Cabin* with facts from life.

Mrs. Stowe's Christian object did not admit a transfer of her story to the stage. But with the enthusiasm of the reading public so abundantly clear, an early dramatization was inevitable. Theatre managers of the 1850's skimmed the cream from the best-seller list just as movie producers do today. The first stage version, *The Southern Uncle Tom*, was performed at the Baltimore Museum on January 5, 1852, almost three months before the serialization in the *National Era* was completed. After another performance or two at the Marshall Theatre in Richmond, Virginia, nothing more was heard of it. The second try was at Purdy's National Theatre in New York, with an hour-long "catch-house" adaptation by C. W. Taylor. All the St. Clare, Eva, and Topsy episodes were omitted and numerous songs and tableaux were added. Although it ran for eleven performances, from August 23 to September 4, 1852, and provoked a good deal of comment, it did not really catch on. The New

York *Herald* (September 3, 1852) called it "an exaggerated mockery of south-ern institutions calculated to poison the minds of our youth with the principles of abolitionism."

These two early productions provided the prelude. The phenomenal stage history of *Uncle Tom's Cabin* really began at the Troy Museum in Troy, New York, on September 27, 1852. G. C. Howard, manager of the Troy company, had commissioned his twenty-two-year-old cousin George L. Aiken to pre-pare a dramatization that would display the talents of Howard's four-year-old daughter, Cordelia. Although Aiken was regularly employed as resident playwright and juvenile of the company, Howard gave him a bonus of forty dollars and a gold watch for his week's work on *Uncle Tom*. To concoct a three-and-a-half-hour drama in one week, even though he lifted most of his dialogue directly from the novel, must have demanded considerable facility with the pen and entitled him to the extra reward.

The play opened on the twenty-seventh of September, but not without some difficulties. Green Germon, the leading man of the company, had rebelled at playing a "blacked-up" character. Even if he didn't carry a "tambo" or "bones," Germon insisted, audiences would expect a minstrel "breakdown" or a chorus or two of "Jim Crow." Howard finally convinced him that Uncle Tom was a new type of stage Negro. If the play caught on, Germon could advertise himself as the original Uncle Tom.

The fourth and final act of this first Aiken drama, subtitled *Life Among the Lowly*, concluded with the death of Eva. By the end of October – the play had been running continuously – the citizens of Troy clamored to see the remain-ing episodes of the novel. Aiken obliged with a sequel, *The Death of Uncle Tom, or the Religion of the Lowly*. On November 15, after the sequel had been playing for two weeks, Howard announced in the Troy newspapers:

Grand Combination of the two dramas (six acts) on the same evening. . . . The desire of the entire community being to see the work from beginning to end, and the manager wishing to gratify all patrons, is why this immense work is under-taken in one evening. Owing to the length of the drama, no other piece will be played. Change of time, doors open at 7, to commence at ¼ to 8.

The curtain was finally rung down on this sequence of Aiken dramatiza-tions on December 1, after the hundredth performance. No play in Troy has yet broken this record, and, as Howard explained, it was "equal to seven years run in New York, when the population of the cities is considered." The press repeatedly echoed the enthusiasm of the Troy citizenry: "The Museum is thronged nightly with the most respectable audiences. . . . This play has brought out our first citizens, many of whom have never before entered the Museum. . . . Its performances have been witnessed by over 25,000 people and the cry is still they come!" Troy then had a population of thirty thousand.

This was not the Howards' first encounter with a theatrical success. They, and the Germons also, had been in the original cast of *The Drunkard* at the Boston Museum in 1844. In fact, the Howards had met and married while playing in *The Drunkard;* but now, and for the rest of their theatrical days, they and their daughter Cordelia were firmly and faithfully joined to *Uncle Tom*. The Troy venture had really been a Howard family affair: little Cordelia's mother had played Topsy; her grandmother (Mrs. Fox), Aunt Ophelia; her father, St. Clare; her uncle (Charles Fox), Fletcher and Cute; and her father's cousin (Aiken), George Harris. For thirty-five years, until Howard's death in 1887, the Howard trio devoted themselves to "Tomming."

In 1854 Mrs. Stowe saw the Howards perform the play at the National Theatre in Boston. Francis R. Underwood, then managing editor of the *Atlantic Monthly*, who accompanied her, described the occasion for his readers: "I asked Mrs. Stowe to go with me to see the play. She had some natural reluctance, considering the position of her husband as a preacher; but she also had some curiosity as a woman and as an author to see in the flesh and blood the creations of her imagination. I think she told me she had never been in a theatre in her life. I procured the manager's box, and we entered privately, she being well muffled. She sat in the shade of the curtains of our box, and watched the play attentively. I never saw such delight upon a human face as she displayed when she first comprehended the full power of Mrs. Howard's 'Topsy.' She scarcely spoke during the evening; but her expression was eloquent – smiles and tears succeeding each other through the whole." Mrs. Stowe never recorded her reactions to this adventure, but surely she must have realized that nothing could stem the theatrical tide of *Uncle Tom's Cabin.*

Although the Howards had given a relatively straight rendering of the play in Troy, even they had introduced an orchestral accompaniment for Eliza's flight and crashing chord accents for Legree's whiplashes, and Mrs. Howard had performed a kind of Topsy "breakdown." But the all-out competition for more striking spectacular effects in acting, scenery, and music began with the New York opening the following season. Captain Purdy, the National Theatre manager who had sponsored the unsuccessful Taylor version the year before, engaged the Troy company – "six acts, eight tableaux, and thirty scenes, embracing the whole work" – for a grand opening on July 18, 1853. For the first time in a New York theatre, a single play constituted the entire evening's entertainment. Contrary to custom, there would be no curtain raiser, no afterpiece. This was Howard's idea. Strait-laced Puritans could be lured into the theatre if they were assured no unpalatable and sinful theatrical exhibitions would soil their souls.

By the end of July, Purdy was assured that his initial investment was secure. Against his better judgment he had been persuaded to pay the staggering sum of a hundred dollars per week to Mrs. Howard for the services of herself and little Cordelia. But when he was obliged to schedule anywhere from twelve to eighteen performances per week to meet the demand, Purdy freely admitted his "better judgment" had been wrong. He ripped out the orchestra boxes and replaced them with three hundred additional cushioned armchairs, for which he charged fifty cents; except for the price, not unlike the divans in some of the present-day Broadway theatres. On August 15 he advertised "a neat and comfortable parquette for colored persons" in his "Temple of the Moral Drama," as he now identified his National Theatre. He hung the lobby with Scriptural texts and commissioned a painter to portray him with a Bible in one hand and *Uncle Tom's Cabin* in the other. The play was on its way to a three-hundred-performance run at the National, the first leg of its long and gaudy career.

While Purdy's performances were still in progress, four other versions were brought out in New York: at the Bowery Theatre, at Barnum's American Museum, at the Franklin Museum, and finally in a burlesque concoction by Christy's Minstrels. Purdy sailed along untroubled by three of these invasions, but Barnum's offering worried him. Barnum was a showman to be feared, and his splashy advertising attracted customers.

The dramatization Barnum had acquired, by Henry J. Conway, was proclaimed as "the only just and sensible dramatic version of Mrs. Stowe's book." Furthermore: "It does not foolishly and unjustly elevate the Negro above the white man in intellect or morals. It exhibits a true picture of Negro life in the South, instead of absurdly representing the ignorant slave as possessed of all the polish of the drawing room, and the refinement of the educated white. And instead of turning away the audience in tears, the author has wisely consulted dramatic taste by having Virtue triumphant at last, and after all its unjust sufferings, miseries and deprivations, conducted to happiness by the hand of Him who watches over all." Barnum augmented his production with what he called "scenes in living pictures": a grand panorama of the Mississippi by moonlight, showing a steamer on the way to New Orleans with real rotating wheels, lights, and smoke puffs clearly visible to the audience.

Although Purdy publicly labeled this "tamed-down" atrocity the "humbug version," he was obliged to counteract its impact with some promotional ballyhoo of his own. Barnum's *Tom* had opened on November 7. Three days later Purdy's production reached its hundred-performance mark, an occasion not to be disregarded. Purdy proclaimed a "Grand Jubilee Festival." John Schiebel's National Brass Band, thirty musicians strong, blared out from the street balcony of the theatre commencing at 9 A.M. At 2 P.M., a special performance for ladies, families, and schools; at 6 P.M., "a grand display of fireworks under the direction of Isaac Edge of Jersey City," followed by an exhibition of

Professor Grant's Drummond Light on the rooftop of the theatre; and at the evening performance, the presentation by Captain Purdy of a gold-trimmed tea set to little Cordelia Howard.

Just after the Bowery Theatre entered the *Tom* running on January 16, 1854, featuring the popular minstrel performer T. D. "Daddy" Rice as Uncle Tom, Purdy prepared another distraction, a "Grand Uncle Tom Jubilee" to celebrate his two-hundredth performance on January 26. Koop's celebrated National Brass and Clarinet Band was on hand to supply the music, and Professor Grant and Isaac Edge repeated their respective lighting and pyrotechnic displays. In addition, Purdy spent two thousand dollars on redecorating the theatre and improving the scenery.

Just as the novel had found an immediate audience abroad, so did the play. In the fall of 1852, while the Howard company was still performing in Troy, there were two productions in London – at the Standard and at the Olympic. In October three more were added – at the Strand, the Surrey, and the Pavilion. In November *Slave Life, or Uncle Tom's Cabin* at the Adelphi and an "equestrian drama on the subject" showed at Astley's. On Boxing night (December 26) Drury Lane presented a pantomime version, with Henry Wallack playing Uncle Tom. For the next three years England was blanketed; there was probably not a single theatre in London or in the smallest provincial town that had not had at least one production of the *Tom* play. Even after this first great rage, Mrs. Stowe's slavery document did not disappear. In January, 1857, the Howard family appeared at the Marylebone. In 1878 Jarrett and Palmer's new dramatic version was on at the Royal Aquarium in the afternoons and at the Princess's at night. This production, which seems to have run for four hours, was augmented by hymns, choruses, breakdowns, a plantation festival, a mimic steamboat race, and rivers of floating ice. It featured a hundred real American freed slaves and Sarah Washington, "the celebrated camp leader and shouter." For the rest of the century, the play was a standard fixture of the London theatre.

Berlin first saw the play, called in German *Negersleben in Nord-Amerika*, in December, 1852. The French version, *La Case de l'Oncle Tom*, was brought out in Paris in January, 1853. A later French treatment, *L'Oncle Tom*, although claiming to adhere to Mrs. Stowe's original text, demonstrated a fanciful conception of American geography: the slaves escaped to Canada by sailing down the Ohio, in the course of which miraculous journey they performed the feat of "shooting the falls of Niagara."

The distinctive theatrical history of *Uncle Tom's Cabin*, however, belongs to America. Twelve different versions appeared in print before 1900, to say nothing of the numerous unpublished dramatizations. Colonel Robert E. J. Miles, manager of the Cincinnati Theatre, copied down an outline as he watched the performance of the Howards in New York, hurried back to Cincinnati, filled in the text from memory, and brought it out at the Melodeon Grand Concert Hall on December 5, 1853. Within two years after the Howards appeared in Troy, the play was performed by stock companies in Cleveland, Salt Lake City, San Francisco, Philadelphia, Detroit, and Chicago. When the Howards took to the road in 1854, playing Boston, Baltimore, Washington, and St. Louis, they invariably encountered competition from resident thespians.

If inhabitants of the small towns felt slighted in not getting a look at the new play, they hardly had time to register their complaints. As early as 1854, *Tom* shows under canvas were on the road. The first of these set out from Dayton, Ohio, under the banner of the pioneer barnstormer "Yankee" Robinson. For no accountable reason, other than that there were actors everywhere, home bases for *Tom* troupes sprang up in Carbondale, Pennsylvania; Kalamazoo, Michigan; Oneida, New York; and Williamsport, Ohio, to mention only a few. No play, before or since, swept across America in such prairie-fire fashion.

Up to the Civil War years, *Uncle Tom's Cabin* was a fixture in theatrical repertoires everywhere. Early in the conflict four New York managers, misjudging the temper of the time, prepared four new productions. Even though one of these included the Howards and another was billed as "the Equestrian Moral Drama" – bringing on the horses ordinarily meant sure-fire success–they all collapsed. The stage drama was eclipsed by the drama of real life.

Not until the seventies did "Tomming" begin again in earnest, but it was then more earnest than ever. In 1879 the New York *Dramatic Mirror* recorded the routes of forty-nine *Tom* companies. Twenty years later such a timetable would have had to list some five hundred. These companies were of all shapes, sizes, and descriptions. Some were family affairs. It was not at all uncommon for an actor to spend his entire life as a "Tommer," never playing in, or even seeing, any other play. Many troupes were ridiculously limited in their acting resources. An actor often played two or three different parts. One group, in 1885, is reported to have performed the entire text with only three players. There was, however, no hint of these inadequacies in the broadsides and streamers which announced "The McFadden Famous Original Boston Ideal Uncle Tom's Cabin Company," or the "Chicago Ideal Uncle Tom Cabin Combination," or "Hyers Sisters' Ideal Uncle Tom's Cabin Company." Some local critics were not taken in by this "ideal" ballyhoo, as the following poison-pen comments demonstrate:

Griffin, Georgia: The audience last week pelted the performers in *Uncle Tom's Cabin* with a lot of debased eggs. This is about the only way to get the drama off the stage, and the example of the Griffin people should be religiously followed by other communities.

Lancaster, Pennsylvania: Minnie Foster's Uncle Tom Cabin Company to fair house, 17th. This is about the tenth Uncle Tom company that has visited us this season, and no more wanted.

Shamokin, Pennsylvania: A party of barnstorming amateurs, three "dorgs" and a donkey meandering about the country under the name of Abbey's Uncle Tom's Cabin Company, slaughtered that time worn play to standing room only [the] 12th.

Theatrical novelty was the stock in trade of the "Tommer." One innovation undreamed of by Mrs. Stowe – Eliza pursued by the hounds in her flight across the Ohio – became so firmly identified with the play that audiences of the eighties and nineties would have throttled the manager who dared to tamper with the original and omit this exciting episode. Often the dogs practically took over the show. Wellesley and Sterling's troupe advertised: "The wonderful dogs, Sultan, Caesar, and Monarch, for which Buffalo Bill makes a standing offer of $5,000 or $3,000 for Sultan alone, take part in the play." Stage managers adopted all sorts of dodges to entice the dogs across the ice in pursuit of Eliza. Foxy-smelling cords were stretched across the stage. A more successful scheme required Eliza to feed the dogs regularly from her "prop child" bundle; then, when she skipped across the ice, her baby clutched tightly against her, the dogs willingly pursued their prey, jumping at her throat.

Jubilee singers became another common theatrical adjunct. In early March, 1876, the Howards added the "Georgia Jubilee Singers" to their performances at the Brooklyn Theatre. Other troupes followed their example with their own vocal groups: "Virginia Jubilee Singers," "Mississippi Cabin Jubilee Singers," or "Great Southern Jubilee Singers."

As with any theatrical piece of widespread popularity, *Uncle Tom's Cabin* was imitated in all manner of versions and perversions. While the Howards were still appearing at Purdy's, the Franklin Museum projected a series of twenty-five lantern slides of *Uncle Tom's Cabin*. After its first exhibition in New York, J. N. Still's *Grand Diorama of Uncle Tom's Cabin* was shown widely throughout the country at lodge and church meetings. There were Irish concoctions (*Uncle Pat's Cabin* and *Uncle Mike's Cabin*) and minstrel burlesques (*Uncle Dad's Cabin* and *Happy Uncle Tom*). As might have been predicted, New Orleans presented the South's answer to Mrs. Stowe's "gross exaggerations." *Uncle Tom's Cabin, or Life in the South As It Is,* performed at Dan Rice's Amphitheatre on February 15, 1854, was advertised as "a satirical quizzical burlesque by Mrs. Harriet Screecher Blow." When an unadulterated version of the play was finally performed in New Orleans in 1883, it was announced as coming directly from Her Majesty's Theatre in London. One reviewer found that it was "not worth objecting to."

On March 4, 1901, William Brady brought out a New York production at the Academy of Music that dwarfed all previous efforts. In addition to William Lackaye as Uncle Tom and Theodore Roberts as Legree, he employed two hundred buck-and-wing dancers and singers, eighteen complete settings of giant proportions, and a transformation sequence of twenty-one separate scenes. Eighty-eight performances were added to the record with this biggest of all *Tom* shows.

Twentieth-century "Tomming" followed the established tradition, if on a somewhat reduced scale. Early in the spring the troupes came out of winter hiding and took to the road. A dozen companies were still at it in 1927 – Mason Brothers in their fifty-seventh season and the Harvalls in their fortieth. Even today there are a few stragglers in the field every summer. In recent years there have been three striking, if diverse, demonstrations of the theatrical vitality of the *Tom* drama. The Players Club revival at the Alvin Theatre in New York on May 29, 1933, with a revised Aiken text by A. E. Thomas, starred Otis Skinner as Uncle Tom and Fay Bainter as Topsy, both of whom had made their debuts in *Tom* shows. Originally scheduled for a week's engagement, standard for Players' revivals, it played to capacity for four weeks. Then it took to the road and in Boston was witnessed by Cordelia Howard, the first little Eva. George Abbott's *Sweet River*, essentially the old story set to music, retained many of the traditional features of the *Tom* shows. It opened in New York on October 28, 1936, and lasted for only five performances. The old story was most recently represented with the ballet sequence "The Small House of Uncle Thomas" in *The King and I*. In its ingenuous, primitive-like quality this dance narrative probably approximates, at least in spirit, the nineteenth-century renderings.

The motion pictures took their fling as "Tommers." At least a dozen full movie treatments have been released since Edwin S. Porter's first for the Edison Company in 1903, and innumerable movie potpourris have drawn episodes from the *Uncle Tom* reservoir. The "super" spectacle in movie *Tom* history was produced by Carl Laemmle in the early twenties. With a budget of two million, technicians scoured the country for authentic scenes and details which could then be duplicated in the Hollywood factory. Laemmle's film took nineteen months to shoot and used 977,000 feet of film, 65 different sets, 5,000 players, and 10,000 artificial magnolias.

The motion pictures were Johnny-come-latelys in *Tom* history. The high life of this remarkable dramatic document belonged to the eighties and nineties and to the ante-bellum days of its first productions. There were other treatments of the slave problem – notably Mrs. Stowe's *Dred*, dramatized by John Brougham, by C. W. Taylor, by H. J. Conway, and by many others; and Dion Boucicault's *The Octoroon*. Neither of these, nor the others, carried the firebrand quality and theatrical impact of *Uncle Tom's Cabin*.

Mrs. Stowe's, and thus Aiken's, dramatic narrative has frequently been labeled a naïve melodrama, filled with undistinguished, crude, and careless writing and with too many short and loosely connected scenes. A careful reading and honest appraisal will, I believe, suggest a different final judgment on this parable of good and evil. The forces of right and wrong on the slavery issue – not the struggle between North and South – are clearly and vigorously exposed. The language has an irresistible strength and vitality, and the rich panorama compels us to sense the magnitude of a vicious and pervasive evil. Too often the recent appraisals have dwelt on the character of Uncle Tom, the symbol of patient and heroic suffering, and have disregarded George Harris, the equally vivid symbol of heroic rebellion. In a way, the record supplies the most pertinent final judgment. *Uncle Tom's Cabin* aroused the conscience of the country and stirred it to action. Arthur Miller could well have had *Uncle Tom's Cabin* in mind when he wrote in, "What Makes Plays Endure" (New York *Times*, August 15, 1965), "A play that convinces us that this is the way it is now can be excused many shortcomings. At any one moment there is a particular quality of feeling which dominates in human intercourse, a tonality which marks the present from the past, and when this tone is struck on the stage, the theatre seems necessary again. . . . Before a play is art it is a kind of psychic journalism, a mirror of its hour. . . ."

With Uncle Tom, Harris, Legree, little Eva, Eliza, and Topsy confronting one another in a succession of laugh-provoking, hair-raising, and tear-jerking scenes, actors were given a remarkable challenge. These were roles to get your teeth into, parts that could be played with all the stops open. The stage managers and scene painters could give their theatrical imaginations full rein, and the managers discovered undreamed-of opportunities for exploitation. And all of this without destroying the tender essence of the moral drama. Bloodhounds, donkeys, jubilee singers, and transformations supplied a theatrical vitality to the burning issues of the story. Awkward and blundering as much of the staging must have been, and primitive as it may sound in the reading, there were probably few spectators unmoved by the glorious final transformation. One prompt-book described it as follows:

Dark cloud drop rises slowly and discovers very large fan center. Fan separates from the center and falls slowly right and left, discovering Tom on car, with back to audience, and hands outstretched upwards. Two large silver and gold gates about second groove closed. On either side angels with large palms. Lights full up. Car with Tom ascends slantingly up stage. The two angels swing around, gates open slowly, discovers two more angels right and left on top of gate posts as car with Tom passes through the gates. Back cloud drop rises and discovers Eva and St. Clare with angels extending hands to Uncle Tom – Chorus of negroes all through.

Curtain

UNCLE TOM'S CABIN

GEORGE L. AIKEN

CHARACTERS

UNCLE TOM	HALEY	HARRY, *a Child*
GEORGE HARRIS	LEGREE	EVA
GEORGE SHELBY	TOM LOKER	ELIZA
ST. CLARE	MARKS	CASSY
PHINEAS FLETCHER	SKEGGS	MARIE
GUMPTION CUTE	MANN	OPHELIA
MR. WILSON	ADOLPH	CHLOE
DEACON PERRY	SAMBO	TOPSY
SHELBY	QUIMBO	EMMELINE
	DOCTOR	
	WAITER	

ACT I. Scene 1

Plain Chamber. Enter Eliza, meeting George.

ELIZA: Ah! George, is it you? Well, I am so glad you've come! [*George regards her mournfully*] Why don't you smile, and ask after Harry?

GEORGE: [*Bitterly*] I wish he'd never been born! I wish I'd never been born myself!

ELIZA: [*Sinking her head upon his breast and weeping*] Oh, George!

GEORGE: There, now, Eliza; it's too bad for me to make you feel so. Oh! how I wish you had never seen me – you might have been happy!

ELIZA: George! George! how can you talk so? What dreadful thing has happened, or is going to happen? I'm sure we've been very happy till lately.

GEORGE: So we have, dear. But oh! I wish I'd never seen you, nor you me.

ELIZA: Oh, George! how can you?

GEORGE: Yes, Eliza, it's all misery! misery! The very life is burning out of me! I'm a poor, miserable, forlorn drudge! I shall only drag you down with me, that's all! What's the use of our trying to do anything – trying to know anything – trying to be anything? I wish I was dead!

ELIZA: Oh! now, dear George, that is really wicked. I know how you feel about losing your place in the factory, and you have a hard master; but pray be patient –

GEORGE: Patient! Haven't I been patient? Did I say a word when he came and took me away – for no earthly reason – from the place where everybody was kind to me? I'd paid him truly every cent of my earnings, and they all say I worked well.

ELIZA: Well, it *is* dreadful; but, after all, he is your master, you know.

GEORGE: My master! And who made him my master? That's what I think of! What right has he to me? I'm as much of a man as he is! What right has he to make a dray-horse of me? – to take me from things I can do better than he can, and put me to work that any horse can do? He tries to do it; he says he'll bring me down and humble me, and he puts me to just the hardest, meanest and dirtiest work, on purpose.

ELIZA: Oh, George! George! you frighten me. Why, I never heard you talk so. I'm afraid you'll do something dreadful. I don't wonder at your feelings at all; but oh, do be careful – for my sake, for Harry's.

GEORGE: I have been careful, and I have been pa-

360

tient, but it's growing worse and worse – flesh and blood can't bear it any longer. Every chance he can get to insult and torment me he takes. He says that though I don't say anything, he sees that I've got the devil in me, and he means to bring it out; and one of these days it will come out, in a way that he won't like, or I'm mistaken.

ELIZA: Well, I always thought that I must obey my master and mistress, or I couldn't be a Christian.

GEORGE: There is some sense in it in your case. They have brought you up like a child – fed you, clothed you and taught you, so that you have a good education – that is some reason why they should claim you. But I have been kicked and cuffed and sworn at, and what do I owe? I've paid for all my keeping a hundred times over. I won't bear it! – no, I *won't!* Master will find out that I'm one whipping won't tame. My day will come yet, if he don't look out!

ELIZA: What are you going to do? Oh! George, don't do anything wicked; if you only trust in heaven and try to do right, it will deliver you.

GEORGE: Eliza, my heart's full of bitterness. I can't trust in heaven. Why does it let things be so?

ELIZA: Oh, George! we must all have faith. Mistress says that when all things go wrong to us, we must believe that heaven is doing the very best.

GEORGE: That's easy for people to say who are sitting on their sofas and riding in their carriages; but let them be where I am – I guess it would come some harder. I wish I could be good; but my heart burns and can't be reconciled. You couldn't, in my place, you can't now, if I tell you all I've got to say; you don't know the whole yet.

ELIZA: What do you mean?

GEORGE: Well, lately my master has been saying that he was a fool to let me marry off the place – that he hates Mr. Shelby and all his tribe – and he says he won't let me come here any more, and that I shall take a wife and settle down on his place.

ELIZA: But you were married to *me* by the minister, as much as if you had been a white man.

GEORGE: Don't you know I can't hold you for my wife if he chooses to part us? That is why I wish I'd never seen you – it would have been better for us both – it would have been better

for our poor child if he had never been born.

ELIZA: Oh! but my master is so kind.

GEORGE: Yes, but who knows? – he may die, and then Harry may be sold to nobody knows who. What pleasure is it that he is handsome and smart and bright? I tell you, Eliza, that a sword will pierce through your soul for every good and pleasant thing your child is or has. It will make him worth too much for you to keep.

ELIZA: Heaven forbid!

GEORGE: So, Eliza, my girl, bear up now, and good-by, for I'm going.

ELIZA: Going, George! Going where?

GEORGE: To Canada; and when I'm there I'll buy you – that's all the hope that's left us. You have a kind master, that won't refuse to sell you. I'll buy you and the boy – heaven helping me, I will!

ELIZA: Oh, dreadful! If you should be taken?

GEORGE: I won't be taken, Eliza – I'll *die* first! I'll be free, or I'll die!

ELIZA: You will not kill yourself?

GEORGE: No need of that; they will kill me, fast enough. I will never go down the river alive.

ELIZA: Oh, George! for my sake, do be careful. Don't lay hands on yourself, or anybody else. You are tempted too much, but don't. Go, if you must, but go carefully, prudently, and pray heaven to help you!

GEORGE: Well, then, Eliza, hear my plan. I'm going home quite resigned, you understand, as if all was over. I've got some preparations made, and there are those that will help me; and in the course of a few days I shall be among the missing. Well, now, good-by.

ELIZA: A moment – our boy.

GEORGE: [*Choked with emotion*] True, I had forgotten him; one last look, and then farewell!

ELIZA: And heaven grant it be not forever! [*Exeunt*]

Scene 2

A dining-room. – Table and chairs. – Dessert, wine, etc., on table. – Shelby and Haley discovered at table.

SHELBY: That is the way I should arrange the matter.

HALEY: I can't make trade that way – I positively can't, Mr. Shelby. [*Drinks*]

SHELBY: Why, the fact is, Haley, Tom is an uncommon fellow! He is certainly worth that sum anywhere – steady, honest, capable, manages my whole farm like a clock!

HALEY: You mean honest, as niggers go. [*Fills glass*]

SHELBY: No; I mean, really, Tom is a good, steady, sensible, pious fellow. He got religion at a camp-meeting, four years ago, and I believe he really *did* get it. I've trusted him since then, with everything I have – money, house, horses, and let him come and go round the country, and I always found him true and square in everything!

HALEY: Some folks don't believe there is pious niggers, Shelby, but *I do*. I had a fellow, now, in this yer last lot I took to Orleans – 'twas as good as a meetin' now, really, to hear that critter pray; and he was quite gentle and quiet like. He fetched me a good sum, too, for I bought him cheap of a man that was 'bliged to sell out, so I realized six hundred on him. Yes, I consider religion a valeyable thing in a nigger, when it's the genuine article and no mistake.

SHELBY: Well, Tom's got the real article, if ever a fellow had. Why, last fall I let him go to Cincinnati alone, to do business for me and bring home five hundred dollars. "Tom," says I to him, "I trust you, because I think you are a Christian – I know you wouldn't cheat." Tom comes back sure enough; I knew he would. Some low fellows, they say, said to him – "Tom, why don't you make tracks for Canada?" "Ah, master trusted me, and I couldn't," was his answer. They told me all about it. I am sorry to part with Tom, I must say. You ought to let him cover the whole balance of the debt, and you would, Haley, if you had any conscience.

HALEY: Well, I've got just as much conscience as any man in business can afford to keep, just a little, you know, to swear by, as 'twere; and then I'm ready to do anything in reason to 'blige friends, but this yer, you see, is a leetle too hard on a fellow – a leetle too hard! [*Fills glass again*]

SHELBY: Well, then, Haley, how will you trade?

HALEY: Well, haven't you a boy or a girl that you could throw in with Tom?

SHELBY: Hum! none that I could well spare; to tell the truth, it's only hard necessity makes me willing to sell at all. I don't like parting with any of my hands, that's a fact.

Harry runs in

Hulloa! Jim Crow! [*Throws a bunch of raisins towards him*] Pick that up now. [*Harry does so*]

HALEY: Bravo, little 'un! [*Throws an orange, which Harry catches. He sings and dances around the stage*] Hurrah! Bravo! What a young 'un! That chap's a case, I'll promise. Tell you what, Shelby, fling in that chap, and I'll settle the business. Come, now, if that ain't doing the thing up about the rightest!

Eliza enters. – Starts on beholding Haley, and gazes fearfully at Harry, who runs and clings to her dress, showing the orange, etc.

SHELBY: Well, Eliza?

ELIZA: I was looking for Harry, please, sir.

SHELBY: Well, take him away, then.

Eliza grasps the child eagerly in her arms, and casting another glance of apprehension at Haley, exits hastily

HALEY: By Jupiter! there's an article, now. You might make your fortune on that ar gal in Orleans any day. I've seen over a thousand in my day, paid down for gals not a bit handsomer.

SHELBY: I don't want to make my fortune on her. Another glass of wine. [*Fills the glasses*]

HALEY: [*Drinks and smacks his lips*] Capital wine – first chop! Come, how will you trade about the gal? What shall I say for her? What'll you take?

SHELBY: Mr. Haley, she is not to be sold. My wife wouldn't part with her for her weight in gold.

HALEY: Ay, ay! women always say such things, 'cause they hain't no sort of calculation. Just show 'em how many watches, feathers and trinkets one's weight in gold would buy, and that alters the case, I reckon.

SHELBY: I tell you, Haley, this must not be spoken of – I say no, and I mean no.

HALEY: Well, you'll let me have the boy tho'; you must own that I have come down pretty handsomely for him.

SHELBY: What on earth can you want with the child?

HALEY: Why, I've got a friend that's going into this yer branch of the business – wants to buy up handsome boys to raise for the market. Well, what do you say?

SHELBY: I'll think the matter over and talk with my wife.

HALEY: Oh, certainly, by all means; but I'm in a devil of a hurry, and shall want to know as soon as possible, what I may depend on. [*Rises and puts on his overcoat, which hangs on a chair. – Takes hat and whip*]

SHELBY: Well, call up this evening, between six and seven, and you shall have my answer.

HALEY: All right. Take care of yourself, old boy! [*Exit*]

SHELBY: If anybody had ever told me that I should sell Tom to those rascally traders, I should never have believed it. Now it must come for aught I see, and Eliza's child too. So much for being in debt, heigho! The fellow sees his advantage and means to push it. [*Exit*]

Scene 3

Snowy landscape. – Uncle Tom's Cabin. – Snow on roof. – Practicable door and window. – Dark Stage. – Music. Enter Eliza hastily, with Harry in her arms.

ELIZA: My poor boy; they have sold you, but your mother will save you yet!

Goes to Cabin and taps on window. – Aunt Chloe appears at window with a large white night-cap on

CHLOE: Good Lord! what's that? My sakes alive if it ain't Lizy! Get on your clothes, old man, quick! I'm gwine to open the door.

The door opens and Chloe enters, followed by Uncle Tom in his shirt sleeves, holding a tallow candle

TOM: [*Holding the light towards Eliza*] Lord bless you! I'm skeered to look at ye, Lizy! Are ye tuck sick, or what's come over ye?

ELIZA: I'm running away, Uncle Tom and Aunt Chloe, carrying off my child! Master sold him!

TOM AND CHLOE: Sold him!

ELIZA: Yes, sold him! I crept into the closet by mistress' door to-night, and heard master tell mistress that he had sold my Harry, and you, Uncle Tom, both, to a trader, and that the man was to take possession to-morrow.

CHLOE: The good Lord have pity on us! Oh! it don't seem as if it was true. What has he done that master should sell *him*?

ELIZA: He hasn't done anything – it isn't for that. Master don't want to sell, and mistress – she's always good. I heard her plead and beg for us, but he told her 'twas no use – that he was in this man's debt, and he had got the power over him, and that if he did not pay him off clear, it would end in his having to sell the place and all the people and move off.

CHLOE: Well, old man, why don't you run away, too? Will you wait to be toted down the river, where they kill niggers with hard work and starving? I'd a heap rather die than go there, any day! There's time for ye; be off with Lizy – you've got a pass to come and go any time. Come, bustle up, and I'll get your things together.

TOM: No, no – I ain't going. Let Eliza go – it's her right. I wouldn't be the one to say no – 'tain't in natur for her to stay; but you heard what she said? If I must be sold, or all the people on the place, and everything go to rack, why, let me be sold. I s'pose I can bar it as well as any one. Mas'r always found me on the spot – he always will. I never have broken trust, nor used my pass no ways contrary to my word, and I never will. It's better for me to go alone, than to break up the place and sell all. Mas'r ain't to blame, and he'll take care of you and the poor little 'uns! [*Overcome*]

CHLOE: Now, old man, what is you gwine to cry for? Does you want to break this old woman's heart? [*Crying*]

ELIZA: I saw my husband only this afternoon, and I little knew then what was to come. He told me he was going to run away. Do try, if you can, to get word to him. Tell him how I went and why I went, and tell him I'm going to try and find Canada. You must give my love to him, and tell him if I never see him again on earth, I trust we shall meet in heaven!

TOM: Dat is right, Lizy, trust in the Lord – He is our best friend, – our only comforter.

ELIZA: You won't go with me, Uncle Tom?

TOM: No; time was when I would, but the Lord's given me a work among these yer poor souls, and I'll stay with 'em and bear my cross with 'em till the end. It's different with you – it's more'n you could stand, and you'd better go if you can.

ELIZA: Uncle Tom, I'll try it!

TOM: Amen! The Lord help ye!

Exit Eliza and Harry

CHLOE: What is you gwine to do, old man?
What's to become of you?

TOM: [*Solemnly*] Him that saved Daniel in the
den of lions – that saved the children in the
fiery furnace – Him that walked on the sea
and bade the winds be still – He's alive yet!
and I've faith to believe He can deliver me!

CHLOE: You is right, old man.

TOM: The Lord is good unto all that trust Him,
Chloe. [*Exeunt into Cabin*]

Scene 4

*Room in Tavern by the river side. – A large
window, through which the river is seen, filled
with floating ice. – Moonlight. – Table and
chairs brought on. Enter Phineas.*

PHINEAS: Chaw me up into tobaccy ends! how
in the name of all that's onpossible am I to get
across that yer pesky river? It's a reg'lar blockade of ice! I promised Ruth to meet her to-
night, and she'll be into my har if I don't
come. [*Goes to window*] Thar's a conglomerated prospect for a loveyer! What in creation's
to be done? That thar river looks like a per-
miscuous ice-cream shop come to an awful state
of friz. If I war on the adjacent bank, I
wouldn't care a teetotal atom. Rile up, you
old varmint, and shake the ice off your back!

Enter Eliza and Harry

ELIZA: Courage, my boy – we have reached the
river. Let it but roll between us and our pur-
suers, and we are safe! [*Goes to window*] Gracious powers! the river is choked with cakes of
ice!

PHINEAS: Holloa, gal! – what's the matter?
You look kind of streaked.

ELIZA: Is there any ferry or boat that takes people over now?

PHINEAS: Well, now, that's onlucky; I'm re'lly
stopped running.

ELIZA: [*In dismay*] Stopped running?

PHINEAS: Maybe you're wanting to get over –
anybody sick? Ye seem mighty anxious.

ELIZA: I – I – I've got a child that's very dangerous. I never heard of it till last night, and
I've walked quite a distance to-day, in hopes to
get to the ferry.

PHINEAS: Well, now, that's onlucky; I'm re'lly
consarned for ye. Thar's a man, a piece down

here, that's going over with some truck this
evening, if he duss to; he'll be in here to supper to-night, so you'd better set down and
wait. That's a smart little chap. Say, young
'un, have a chaw tobaccy? [*Takes out a large
plug and a bowie-knife*]

ELIZA: No, no! not any for him.

PHINEAS: Oh! he don't use it, eh? Hain't come
to it yet? Well, I have. [*Cuts off a large piece,
and returns the plug and knife to pocket*]
What's the matter with the young 'un? He
looks kind of white in the gills!

ELIZA: Poor fellow! he is not used to walking,
and I've hurried him on so.

PHINEAS: Tuckered, eh? Well, there's a little
room there, with a fire in it. Take the babby
in there, make yourself comfortable till that
thar ferryman shows his countenance – I'll
stand the damage.

ELIZA: How shall I thank you for such kindness
to a stranger?

PHINEAS: Well, if you don't know how, why,
don't try; that's the teetotal. Come, vamoose!
[*Exit Eliza and Harry*] Chaw me into sassage
meat, if that ain't a perpendicular fine gal!
she's a reg'lar A No. 1, sort of female! How'n
thunder am I to get across this refrigerated
stream of water? I can't wait for that ferryman. [*Enter Marks*] Halloa! what sort of a
critter's this? [*Advances*] Say, stranger, will
you have something to drink?

MARKS: You are excessively kind: I don't care if
I do.

PHINEAS: Ah! he's a human. Halloa, thar!
bring us a jug of whisky instantaneously, or
expect to be teetotally chawed up! Squat yourself, stranger, and go in for enjoyment. [*They
sit at table*] Who are you, and what's your
name?

MARKS: I am a lawyer, and my name is Marks.

PHINEAS: A land shark, eh? Well, I don't think
no worse on you for that. The law is a kind of
necessary evil; and it breeds lawyers just as an
old stump does fungus. Ah! here's the whisky.

*Enter Waiter, with jug and tumblers. Places
them on table*

Here, you – take that shin-plaster. [*Gives
bill*] I don't want any change – thar's a gal
stopping in that room – the balance will
pay for her – d'ye hear? – vamoose! [*Exit
Waiter. – Fills glass*] Take hold, neighbour
Marks – don't shirk the critter. Here's hoping

your path of true love may never have an ice-choked river to cross! [*They drink*]

MARKS: Want to cross the river, eh?

PHINEAS: Well, I do, stranger. Fact is, I'm in love with the teetotalist pretty girl, over on the Ohio side, that ever wore a Quaker bonnet. Take another swig, neighbour. [*Fills glasses, and they drink*]

MARKS: A Quaker, eh?

PHINEAS: Yes – kind of strange, ain't it? The way of it was this: – I used to own a grist of niggers – had 'em to work on my plantation, just below here. Well, stranger, do you know I fell in with that gal – of course I was considerably smashed – knocked into a pretty conglomerated heap – and I told her so. She said she wouldn't hear a word from me so long as I owned a nigger!

MARKS: You sold them, I suppose?

PHINEAS: You're teetotally wrong, neighbour. I gave them all their freedom, and told 'em to vamoose!

MARKS: Ah! yes – very noble, I dare say, but rather expensive. This act won you your lady-love, eh?

PHINEAS: You're off the track again, neighbour. She felt kind of pleased about it, and smiled, and all that; but she said she could never be mine unless I turned Quaker! Thunder and earth! what do you think of that? You're a lawyer – come, now, what's your opinion? Don't you call it a knotty point?

MARKS: Most decidedly. Of course you refused.

PHINEAS: Teetotally; but she told me to think better of it, and come to-night and give her my final conclusion. Chaw me into mincemeat, if I haven't made up my mind to do it!

MARKS: You astonish me!

PHINEAS: Well, you see, I can't get along without that gal; – she's sort of fixed my flint, and I'm sure to hang fire without her. I know I shall make a queer sort of Quaker, because you see, neighbour, I ain't precisely the kind of material to make a Quaker out of.

MARKS: No, not exactly.

PHINEAS: Well, I can't stop no longer. I must try to get across that candaverous river some way. It's getting late – take care of yourself, neighbour lawyer. I'm a teetotal victim to a pair of black eyes. Chaw me up to feed hogs if I'm not in a ruinatious state! [*Exit*]

MARKS: Queer genius, that, very!

Enter Tom Loker

So you've come at last.

LOKER: Yes. [*Looks into jug*] Empty! Waiter! more whisky!

Waiter enters with jug, and removes the empty one. – Enter Haley

HALEY: By the land! if this yer ain't the nearest, now, to what I've heard people call Providence! Why, Loker, how are ye?

LOKER: The devil! What brought you here, Haley?

HALEY: [*Sitting at table*] I say, Tom, this yer's the luckiest thing in the world. I'm in a devil of a hobble, and you must help me out!

LOKER: Ugh! aw! like enough. A body may be pretty sure of that when you're glad to see 'em, or can make something off of 'em. What's the blow now?

HALEY: You've got a friend here – partner, perhaps?

LOKER: Yes, I have. Here, Marks – here's that ar fellow that I was with in Natchez.

MARKS: [*Grasping Haley's hand*] Shall be pleased with his acquaintance. Mr. Haley, I believe?

HALEY: The same, sir. The fact is, gentlemen, this morning I bought a young 'un of Shelby up above here. His mother got wind of it, and what does she do but cut her lucky with him; and I'm afraid by this time that she has crossed the river, for I tracked her to this very place.

MARKS: So, then, ye're fairly sewed up, ain't ye? He! he! he! It's neatly done, too.

HALEY: This young 'un business makes lots of trouble in the trade.

MARKS: Now, Mr. Haley, what is it? Do you want us to undertake to catch this gal?

HALEY: The gal's no matter of mine – she's Shelby's – it's only the boy. I was a fool for buying the monkey.

LOKER: You're generally a fool!

MARKS: Come now, Loker, none of your huffs; you see, Mr. Haley's a-puttin' us in a way of a good job, I reckon; just hold still – these yer arrangements are my forte. This yer gal, Mr. Haley – how is she? – what is she?

Eliza appears, with Harry, listening

HALEY: Well, white and handsome – well brought up. I'd have given Shelby eight hundred or a thousand, and then made well on her.

MARKS: White and handsome – well brought up! Look here, now, Loker, a beautiful opening. We'll do a business here on our own account. We does the catchin'; the boy, of course, goes to Mr. Haley – we takes the gal to Orleans to speculate on. Ain't it beautiful? [*They confer together*]

ELIZA: Powers of mercy, protect me! How shall I escape these human bloodhounds? Ah! the window – the river of ice! That dark stream lies between me and liberty! Surely the ice will bear my trifling weight. It is my only chance of escape – better sink beneath the cold waters, with my child locked in my arms, than have him torn from me and sold into bondage. He sleeps upon my breast – Heaven, I put my trust in thee! [*Gets out of window*]

MARKS: Well, Tom Loker, what do you say?

LOKER: It'll do!

Strikes his hand violently on the table. – Eliza screams. – They all start to their feet. – Eliza disappears

HALEY: By the land, there she is now! [*They all rush to the window*]

MARKS: She's making for the river!

LOKER: Let's after her!

They all leap through the window. – Change

Scene 5

Snowy Landscape. Enter Eliza, with Harry, hurriedly.

ELIZA: They press upon my footsteps – the river is my only hope! Heaven grant me strength to reach it, ere they overtake me! Courage, my child! – we will be free – or perish! [*Rushes off*]

Enter Loker, Haley and Marks

HALEY: We'll catch her yet; the river will stop her!

MARKS: No, it won't, for look! she has jumped upon the ice! She's a brave gal, anyhow!

LOKER: She'll be drowned!

HALEY: Curse that young 'un! I shall lose him, after all.

LOKER: Come on, Marks, to the ferry!

HALEY: Aye, to the ferry! – a hundred dollars for a boat!

They rush off

Scene 6

The entire depth of stage, representing the Ohio River filled with Floating Ice. Bank on right hand.

Eliza appears, with Harry, on a cake of ice, and floats slowly across. – Haley, Loker and Marks, on bank, right hand, observing. – Phineas on opposite shore.

End of Act I

ACT II. Scene 1

A Handsome Parlour. Marie discovered reclining on a sofa.

MARIE: [*Looking at a note*] What can possibly detain St. Clare? According to this note, he should have been here a fortnight ago. [*Noise of carriage without*] I do believe he has come at last.

Eva runs in

EVA: Mamma!

Throws her arms around Marie's neck, and kisses her

MARIE: That will do – take care, child – don't you make my head ache! [*Kisses her languidly*]

Enter St. Clare, Ophelia, and Tom, nicely dressed

ST. CLARE: Well, my dear Marie, here we are at last. The wanderers have arrived, you see. Allow me to present my cousin, Miss Ophelia, who is about to undertake the office of our housekeeper.

MARIE: [*Rising to a sitting posture*] I am delighted to see you. How do you like the appearance of our city?

EVA: [*Running to Ophelia*] Oh! is it not beautiful? My own darling home! – is it not beautiful?

OPHELIA: Yes, it is a pretty place, though it looks rather old and heathenish to me.

ST. CLARE: Tom, my boy, this seems to suit you?

TOM: Yes, mas'r, it looks about the right thing.

ST. CLARE: See here, Marie, I've brought you a coachman, at last, to order. I tell you, he's a regular hearse for blackness and sobriety, and will drive you like a funeral, if you wish. Open your eyes, now, and look at him. Now, don't say I never think about you when I'm gone.

MARIE: I know he'll get drunk.

ST. CLARE: Oh! no he won't. He's warranted a pious and sober article.

MARIE: Well, I hope he may turn out well; it's more than I expect, though.

ST. CLARE: Have you no curiosity to learn how and where I picked up Tom?

EVA: *Uncle* Tom, papa; that's his name.

ST. CLARE: Right, my little sunbeam!

TOM: Please, mas'r, that ain't no 'casion to say nothing 'bout me.

ST. CLARE: You are too modest, my modern Hannibal. Do you know, Marie, that our little Eva took a fancy to Uncle Tom – whom we met on board the steamboat – and persuaded me to buy him?

MARIE: Ah! she is so odd!

ST. CLARE: As we approached the landing, a sudden rush of the passengers precipitated Eva into the water –

MARIE: Gracious heavens!

ST. CLARE: A man leaped into the river, and, as she rose to the surface of the water, grasped her in his arms, and held her up until she could be drawn on the boat again. Who was that man, Eva?

EVA: Uncle Tom!

Runs to him. – He lifts her in his arms. – She kisses him

TOM: The dear soul!

OPHELIA: [*Astonished*] How shiftless!

ST. CLARE: [*Overhearing her*] What's the matter now, pray?

OPHELIA: Well, I want to be kind to everybody, and I wouldn't have anything hurt, but as to kissing –

ST. CLARE: Niggers! that you're not up to, hey?

OPHELIA: Yes, that's it – how can she?

ST. CLARE: Oh! bless you, it's nothing when you are used to it!

OPHELIA: I could never be so shiftless!

EVA: Come with me, Uncle Tom, and I will show you about the house. [*Crosses with Tom*]

TOM: Can I go, mas'r?

ST. CLARE: Yes, Tom; she is your little mistress – your only duty will be to attend to her! [*Tom bows and exits*]

MARIE: Eva, my dear!

EVA: Well, mamma?

MARIE: Do not exert yourself too much!

EVA: No, mamma! [*Runs out*]

OPHELIA: [*Lifting up her hands*] How shiftless!

St. Clare sits next to Marie on sofa. – Ophelia next to St. Clare

ST. CLARE: Well, what do you think of Uncle Tom, Marie?

MARIE: He is a perfect behemoth!

ST. CLARE: Come, now, Marie, be gracious, and say something pretty to a fellow!

MARIE: You've been gone a fortnight beyond the time!

ST. CLARE: Well, you know I wrote you the reason.

MARIE: Such a short, cold letter!

ST. CLARE: Dear me! the mail was just going, and it had to be that or nothing.

MARIE: That's just the way; always something to make your journeys long and letters short!

ST. CLARE: Look at this. [*Takes an elegant velvet case from his pocket*] Here's a present I got for you in New York – a daguerreotype of Eva and myself.

MARIE: [*Looks at it with a dissatisfied air*] What made you sit in such an awkward position?

ST. CLARE: Well, the position may be a matter of opinion, but what do you think of the likeness?

MARIE: [*Closing the case snappishly*] If you don't think anything of my opinion in one case, I suppose you wouldn't in another.

OPHELIA: [*Sententiously, aside*] How shiftless!

ST. CLARE: Hang the woman! Come, Marie, what do you think of the likeness? Don't be nonsensical now.

MARIE: It's very inconsiderate of you, St. Clare, to insist on my talking and looking at things. You know I've been lying all day with the sick headache, and there's been such a tumult made ever since you came, I'm half dead!

OPHELIA: You're subject to the sick headache, ma'am?

MARIE: Yes, I'm a perfect martyr to it!

OPHELIA: Juniper-berry tea is good for sick headache; at least, Molly, Deacon Abraham Perry's wife, used to say so; and she was a great nurse.

ST. CLARE: I'll have the first juniper-berries that get ripe in our garden by the lake brought in for that especial purpose. Come, cousin, let us take a stroll in the garden. Will you join us, Marie?

MARIE: I wonder how you can ask such a question, when you know how fragile I am. I shall retire to my chamber, and repose till dinner time. [*Exit*]

OPHELIA: [*Looking after her*] How shiftless!

ST. CLARE: Come, cousin! [*As he goes out*] Look out for the babies! If I step upon anybody, let them mention it.

OPHELIA: Babies under foot! How shiftless! [*Exeunt*]

Scene 2

A Garden. Tom discovered, seated on a bank, with Eva on his knee – his button-holes are filled with flowers, and Eva is hanging a wreath around his neck. Enter St. Clare and Ophelia, observing.

EVA: Oh, Tom; you look so funny.

TOM: [*Sees St. Clare, and puts Eva down*] I begs pardon, mas'r, but the young missis would do it. Look yer, I'm like the ox, mentioned in the Good Book, dressed for the sacrifice.

ST. CLARE: I say, what do you think, Pussy? Which do you like the best – to live as they do at your uncle's, up in Vermont, or to have a house full of servants, as we do?

EVA: Oh! of course our way is the pleasantest.

ST. CLARE: [*Patting her head*] Why so?

EVA: Because it makes so many more round you to love, you know.

OPHELIA: Now, that's just like Eva – just one of her odd speeches.

EVA: Is it an odd speech, papa?

ST. CLARE: Rather, as this world goes, Pussy. But where has my little Eva been?

EVA: Oh! I've been up in Tom's room, hearing him sing.

ST. CLARE: Hearing Tom sing, hey?

EVA: Oh, yes! he sings such beautiful things about the new Jerusalem, and bright angels, and the land of Canaan.

ST. CLARE: I dare say; it's better than the opera, isn't it?

EVA: Yes; and he's going to teach them to me.

ST. CLARE: Singing lessons, hey? You are coming on.

EVA: Yes, he sings for me, and I read to him in

my Bible, and he explains what it means. Come, Tom.

She takes his hand and they exit

ST. CLARE: [*Aside*] Oh, Evangeline! Rightly named; hath not heaven made thee an evangel to me?

OPHELIA: How shiftless! How can you let her?

ST. CLARE: Why not?

OPHELIA: Why, I don't know; it seems so dreadful.

ST. CLARE: You would think no harm in a child's caressing a large dog, even if he was black; but a creature that can think, reason and feel, and is immortal, you shudder at. Confess it, cousin. I know the feeling among some of you Northerners well enough. Not that there is a particle of virtue in our not having it, but custom with us does what Christianity ought to do: obliterates the feeling of personal prejudice. You loathe them as you would a snake or a toad, yet you are indignant at their wrongs. You would not have them abused, but you don't want to have anything to do with them yourselves. Isn't that it?

OPHELIA: Well, cousin, there may be some truth in this.

ST. CLARE: What would the poor and lowly do without children? Your little child is your only true democrat. Tom, now, is a hero to Eva; his stories are wonders in her eyes; his songs and Methodist hymns are better than an opera, and the traps and little bits of trash in his pockets a mine of jewels, and he the most wonderful Tom that ever wore a black skin. This is one of the roses of Eden that the Lord has dropped down expressly for the poor and lowly, who get few enough of any other kind.

OPHELIA: It's strange, cousin; one might almost think you was a *professor*, to hear you talk.

ST. CLARE: A professor?

OPHELIA: Yes, a professor of religion.

ST. CLARE: Not at all; not a professor as you town folks have it, and, what is worse, I'm afraid, not a *practicer*, either.

OPHELIA: What makes you talk so, then?

ST. CLARE: Nothing is easier than talking. My forte lies in talking, and yours, cousin, lies in doing. And speaking of that puts me in mind that I have made a purchase for your department. There's the article now. Here, Topsy! [*Whistles*]

William A. Brady's Production of Uncle Tom's Cabin, 1901

John Brougham and Georgiana Hodson in Brougham's
Burlesque Po-ca-hon-tas

Topsy runs on

OPHELIA: Good gracious! what a heathenish, shiftless looking object! St. Clare, what in the world have you brought that thing here for?

ST. CLARE: For you to educate, to be sure, and train in the way she should go. I thought she was rather a funny specimen in the Jim Crow line. Here, Topsy, give us a song, and show us some of your dancing.

Topsy sings a verse and dances a breakdown

OPHELIA: [*Paralyzed*] Well, of all things! If I ever saw the like!

ST. CLARE: [*Smothering a laugh*] Topsy, this is your new mistress – I'm going to give you up to her. See now that you behave yourself.

TOPSY: Yes, mas'r.

ST. CLARE: You're going to be good, Topsy, you understand?

TOPSY: Oh, yes, mas'r.

OPHELIA: Now, St. Clare, what upon earth is this for? Your house is so full of these plagues now, that a body can't set down their foot without treading on 'em. I get up in the morning and find one asleep behind the door, and see one black head poking out from under the table – one lying on the door mat, and they are moping and mowing and grinning between all the railings, and tumbling over the kitchen floor! What on earth did you want to bring this one for?

ST. CLARE: For you to educate – din't I tell you? You're always preaching about educating; I thought I would make you a present of a fresh caught specimen, and let you try your hand on her and bring her up in the way she should go.

OPHELIA: I don't want her, I am sure; I have more to do with 'em now than I want to.

ST. CLARE: That's you Christians, all over. You'll get up a society, and get some poor missionary to spend all his days among just such heathens; but let me see one of you that would take one into your house with you, and take the labour of their conversion upon yourselves.

OPHELIA: Well, I didn't think of it in that light. It might be a real missionary work. Well, I'll do what I can. [*Advances to Topsy*] She's dreadful dirty and shiftless! How old are you, Topsy?

TOPSY: Dunno, missis.

OPHELIA: How shiftless! Don't know how old you are? Didn't anybody ever tell you? Who was your mother?

TOPSY: [*Grinning*] Never had none.

OPHELIA: Never had any mother? What do you mean? Where was you born?

TOPSY: Never was born.

OPHELIA: You mustn't answer me in that way. I'm not playing with you. Tell me where you was born, and who your father and mother were.

TOPSY: Never was born, tell you; never had no father, nor mother, nor nothin'. I war raised by a speculator, with lots of others. Old Aunt Sue used to take care on us.

ST. CLARE: She speaks the truth, cousin. Speculators buy them up cheap, when they are little, and get them raised for the market.

OPHELIA: How long have you lived with your master and mistress?

TOPSY: Dunno, missis.

OPHELIA: How shiftless! Is it a year, or more, or less?

TOPSY: Dunno, missis.

ST. CLARE: She does not know what a year is; she don't even know her own age.

OPHELIA: Have you ever heard anything about heaven, Topsy? [*Topsy looks bewildered and grins*] Do you know who made you?

TOPSY: Nobody, as I knows on, he, he, he! I 'spect I growed. Don't think nobody never made me.

OPHELIA: The shiftless heathen! What can you do? What did you do for your master and mistress?

TOPSY: Fetch water – and wash dishes – and rub knives – and wait on folks – and dance breakdowns.

OPHELIA: I shall break down, I'm afraid, in trying to make anything of you, you shiftless mortal!

ST. CLARE: You find virgin soil there, cousin; put in your own ideas – you won't find many to pull up. [*Exit laughing*]

OPHELIA: [*Takes out her handkershief. – A pair of gloves falls. – Topsy picks them up slyly and puts them in her sleeve*] Follow me, you benighted innocent!

TOPSY: Yes, missis.

As Ophelia turns her back to her, she seizes the end of the ribbon she wears around her waist, and twitches it off. – Ophelia turns and sees her as she is putting it in her other sleeve. – Ophelia takes ribbon from her

OPHELIA: What's this? You naughty, wicked girl, you've been stealing this?

TOPSY: Laws! why, that ar's missis' ribbon, ain't it? How could it got caught in my sleeve?

OPHELIA: Topsy, you naughty girl, don't you tell me a lie – you stole that ribbon!

TOPSY: Missis, I declare for't, I didn't – never seed it till dis yer blessed minnit.

OPHELIA: Topsy, don't you know it's wicked to tell lies?

TOPSY: I never tells no lies, missis; it's just de truth I've been telling now, and nothin' else.

OPHELIA: Topsy, I shall have to whip you, if you tell lies so.

TOPSY: Laws, missis, if you's to whip all day, couldn't say no other way. I never seed dat ar – it must a got caught in my sleeve. [*Blubbers*]

OPHELIA: [*Seizes her by the shoulders*] Don't you tell me that again, you barefaced fibber! [*Shakes her. – The gloves fall on stage*] There you, my gloves too – you outrageous young heathen! [*Picks them up*] Will you tell me, now, you didn't steal the ribbon?

TOPSY: No, missis; stole de gloves, but didn't steal de ribbon. It was permiskus.

OPHELIA: Why, you young reprobate!

TOPSY: Yes – I's knows I's wicked.

OPHELIA: Then you know you ought to be punished. [*Boxes her ears*] What do you think of that?

TOPSY: He, he, he! De Lord, missis; dat wouldn't kill a 'skeeter! [*Runs off laughing. – Ophelia follows indignantly*]

Scene 3

The Tavern by the River. – Table and chairs. – Jug and glasses on table. – On flat is a printed placard, headed: – "Four Hundred Dollars Reward – Runaway – George Harris!" Phineas is discovered, seated at table.

PHINEAS: So yer I am; and a pretty business I've undertook to do. Find the husband of the gal that crossed the river on the ice two or three days ago. Ruth said I must do it, and I'll be teetotally chawed up if I don't do it. I see they've offered a reward for him, dead or alive. How in creation am I to find the varmint? He isn't likely to go round looking natural, with a full description of his hide and figure staring him in the face.

Enter Mr. Wilson

I say, stranger, how are ye? [*Rises and comes forward*]

WILSON: Well, I reckon.

PHINEAS: Any news? [*Takes out plug and knife*]

WILSON: Not that I know of.

PHINEAS: [*Cutting a piece of tobacco and offering it*] Chaw?

WILSON: No, thank ye – it don't agree with me.

PHINEAS: Don't, eh? [*Putting it in his own mouth*] I never felt any the worse for it.

WILSON: [*Sees placard*] What's that?

PHINEAS: Nigger advertised. [*Advances towards it and spits on it*] There's my mind upon that.

WILSON: Why, now stranger, what's that for?

PHINEAS: I'd do it all the same to the writer of that ar paper, if he was here. Any man that owns a boy like that, and can't find any better way of treating him than branding him on the hand with the letter H, as that paper states, *deserves* to lose him. Such papers as this ar' a shame to old Kaintuck! that's my mind right out, if anybody wants to know.

WILSON: Well, now, that's a fact.

PHINEAS: I used to have a gang of boys, sir – that was before I fell in love – and I just told 'em: – "Boys," says I, "run now! Dig! put! jest when you want to. I never shall come to look after you!" That's the way I kept mine. Let 'em know they are free to run any time, and it jest stops their wanting to. It stands to reason it should. Treat 'em like men, and you'll have men's work.

WILSON: I think you are altogether right, friend, and this man described here is a fine fellow – no mistake about that. He worked for me some half dozen years in my bagging factory, and he was my best hand, sir. He is an ingenious fellow, too; he invented a machine for the cleaning of hemp – a really valuable affair; it's gone into use in several factories. His master holds the patent of it.

PHINEAS: I'll warrant ye; holds it, and makes money out of it, and then turns round and brands the boy in his right hand! If I had a fair chance, I'd mark him, I reckon, so that he'd carry it *one* while!

Enter George Harris, disguised

GEORGE: [*Speaking as he enters*] Jim, see to the trunks. [*Sees Wilson*] Ah! Mr. Wilson here?

WILSON: Bless my soul, can it be?

GEORGE: [*Advances and grasps his hand*] Mr. Wilson, I see you remember me, Mr. Butler, of Oaklands, Shelby county.

WILSON: Ye – yes – yes – sir.

PHINEAS: Halloa! there's a screw loose here somewhere. That old gentleman seems to be struck into a pretty considerable heap of astonishment. May I be teetotally chawed up! if I don't believe that's the identical man I'm arter. [*Crosses to George*] How are ye, George Harris?

GEORGE: [*Starting back and thrusting his hands into his breast*] You know me?

PHINEAS: Ha, ha, ha! I rather conclude I do; but don't get riled, I ain't a bloodhound in disguise.

GEORGE: How did you discover me?

PHINEAS: By a teetotal smart guess. You're the very man I want to see. Do you know I was sent after you?

GEORGE: Ah! by my master?

PHINEAS: No; by your wife.

GEORGE: My wife! Where is she?

PHINEAS: She's stopping with a Quaker family over on the Ohio side.

GEORGE: Then she is safe?

PHINEAS: Teetotally!

GEORGE: Conduct me to her.

PHINEAS: Just wait a brace of shakes and I'll do it. I've got to go and get the boat ready. 'Twon't take me but a minute – make yourself comfortable till I get back. Chaw me up! but this is what I call doing things in short order. [*Exit*]

WILSON: George!

GEORGE: Yes, George!

WILSON: I couldn't have thought it!

GEORGE: I am pretty well disguised, I fancy; you see I don't answer to the advertisement at all.

WILSON: George, this is a dangerous game you are playing; I could not have advised you to it.

GEORGE: I can do it on my own responsibility.

WILSON: Well, George, I suppose you're running away – leaving your lawful master, George (I don't wonder at it), at the same time, I'm sorry, George, yes, decidedly. I think I must say that it's my duty to tell you so.

GEORGE: Why are you sorry, sir?

WILSON: Why, to see you, as it were, setting yourself in opposition to the laws of your country.

GEORGE: *My* country! What country have *I*, but the grave? And I would to heaven that I was laid there!

WILSON: George, you've got a hard master, in fact he is – well, he conducts himself reprehensibly – I can't pretend to defend him. I'm sorry for you, now; it's a bad case – very bad; but we must all submit to the indications of Providence, George, don't you see?

GEORGE: I wonder, Mr. Wilson, if the Indians should come and take you a prisoner away from your wife and children, and want to keep you all your life hoeing corn for them, if you'd think it your duty to abide in the condition in which you were called? I rather imagine that you'd think the first stray horse you could find an indication of Providence, shouldn't you?

WILSON: Really, George, putting the case in that somewhat peculiar light – I don't know – under those circumstances – but what I might. But it seems to me you are running an awful risk. You can't hope to carry it out. If you're taken it will be worse with you than ever; they'll only abuse you, and half kill you, and sell you down the river.

GEORGE: Mr. Wilson, I know all this. I *do* run a risk, but – [*Throws open coat and shows pistols and knife in his belt*] There! I'm ready for them. Down South I never *will* go! no, if it comes to that, I can earn myself at least six feet of free soil – the first and last I shall ever own in Kentucky!

WILSON: Why, George, this state of mind is awful – it's getting really desperate. I'm concerned. Going to break the laws of your country?

GEORGE: My country again! Sir, I haven't any country any more than I have any father. I don't want anything of *your* country, except to be left alone – to go peaceably out of it; but if any man tries to stop me, let him take care, for I am desperate. I'll fight for my liberty, to the last breath I breathe! You say your fathers did it; if it was right for them, it is right for me!

WILSON: [*Walking up and down, and fanning his face with a large yellow silk handkerchief*] Blast 'em all! Haven't I always said so – the infernal old cusses! Bless me! I hope I ain't swearing now! Well, go ahead, George, go ahead. But be careful, my boy; don't shoot anybody, unless – well, you'd *better* not shoot – at least I wouldn't *hit* anybody, you know.

GEORGE: Only in self-defense.

WILSON: Well, well. [*Fumbling in his pocket*] I suppose, perhaps, I ain't following my judgment – hang it, I won't follow my judgment. So here, George.

Takes out a pocket-book and offers George a roll of bills

GEORGE: No, my kind, good sir, you've done a great deal for me, and this might get you into trouble. I have money enough, I hope, to take me as far as I need it.

WILSON: No; but you must, George. Money is a great help everywhere; can't have too much, if you get it honestly. Take it, do take it, *now* do, my boy!

GEORGE: [*Taking the money*] On condition, sir, that I may repay it at some future time, I will.

WILSON: And now, George, how long are you going to travel in this way? Not long or far, I hope? It's well carried on, but too bold.

GEORGE: Mr. Wilson, it is *so bold*, and this tavern is so near, that they will never think of it; they will look for me on ahead, and you yourself wouldn't know me.

WILSON: But the mark on your hand?

GEORGE: [*Draws off his glove and shows scar*] That is a parting mark of Mr. Harris' regard. Looks interesting, doesn't it? [*Puts on glove again*]

WILSON: I declare, my very blood runs cold when I think of it – your condition and your risks!

GEORGE: Mine has run cold a good many years; at present, it's about up to the boiling point.

WILSON: George, something has brought you out wonderfully. You hold up your head, and move and speak like another man.

GEORGE: [*Proudly*] Because I'm a *freeman*! Yes, sir; I've said "master" for the last time to any man. *I'm free!*

WILSON: Take care! You are not sure; you may be taken.

GEORGE: All men are free and equal *in the grave*, if it comes to that, Mr. Wilson.

Enter Phineas

PHINEAS: Them's my sentiment, to a teetotal atom, and I don't care who knows it! Neighbour, the boat is ready, and the sooner we make tracks the better. I've seen some mysterious strangers lurking about these diggings, so we'd better put.

GEORGE: Farewell, Mr. Wilson, and heaven reward you for the many kindnesses you have shown the poor fugitive!

WILSON: [*Grasping his hand*] You're a brave fellow, George. I wish in my heart you were safe through, though – that's what I do.

PHINEAS: And ain't I the man of all creation to put him through, stranger? Chaw me up if I don't take him to his dear little wife, in the smallest possible quantity of time. Come, neighbour, let's vamoose.

GEORGE: Farewell, Mr. Wilson.

WILSON: My best wishes go with you, George. [*Exit*]

PHINEAS: You're a trump, old Slow-and-Easy.

GEORGE: [*Looking off*] Look! look!

PHINEAS: Consarn their picters, here they come! We can't get out of the house without their seeing us. We're teetotally treed!

GEORGE: Let us fight our way through them!

PHINEAS: No, that won't do; there are too many of them for a fair fight – we should be chawed up in no time. [*Looks round and sees trap door*] Holloa! here's a cellar door. Just you step down here a few minutes, while I parley with them. [*Lifts trap*]

GEORGE: I am resolved to perish sooner than surrender! [*Goes down trap*]

PHINEAS: That's your sort! [*Closes trap and stands on it*] Here they are!

Enter Haley, Marks, Loker and three Men

HALEY: Say, stranger, you haven't seen a runaway darkey about these parts, eh?

PHINEAS: What kind of a darkey?

HALEY: A mulatto chap, almost as light-complexioned as a white man.

PHINEAS: Was he a pretty good-looking chap?

HALEY: Yes.

PHINEAS: Kind of tall?

HALEY: Yes.

PHINEAS: With brown hair?

HALEY: Yes.

PHINEAS: And dark eyes?

HALEY: Yes.

PHINEAS: Pretty well dressed?

HALEY: Yes.

PHINEAS: Scar on his right hand?

HALEY: Yes, yes.

PHINEAS: Well, I ain't seen him.

HALEY: Oh, bother! Come, boys, let's search the house. [*Exeunt*]

PHINEAS: [*Raises trap*] Now, then, neighbour George.

George enters, up trap

Now's the time to cut your lucky.

GEORGE: Follow me, Phineas. [*Exit*]

PHINEAS: In a brace of shakes. [*Is closing trap as Haley, Marks, Loker, etc., re-enter*]

HALEY: Ah! he's down in the cellar. Follow me, boys!

Thrusts Phineas aside, and rushes down trap, followed by the others. Phineas closes trap and stands on it

PHINEAS: Chaw me up! but I've got 'em all in a trap. [*Knocking below*] Be quiet, you pesky varmints! [*Knocking*] They're getting mighty oneasy. [*Knocking*] Will you be quiet, you savagerous critters! [*The trap is forced open. Haley and Marks appear. Phineas seizes a chair and stands over trap*] Down with you or I'll smash you into applefritters! [*Tableau*]

Scene 4

A Plain Chamber.

TOPSY: [*Without*] You go 'long. No more nigger dan you be! [*Enters – shouts and laughter without – looks off*] You seem to think yourself white folks. You ain't nerry one – black *nor* white. I'd like to be one or turrer. Law! you niggers, does you know you's all sinners? Well, you is – everybody is. White folks is sinners too – Miss Feely says so – but I 'spects niggers is the biggest ones. But Lor'! ye ain't any on ye up to me. I's so awful wicked there can't nobody do nothin' with me. I used to keep old missis a-swarin' at me half de time. I 'spects I's de wickedest critter in de world. [*Song and dance introduced*]

Enter Eva

EVA: Oh, Topsy! Topsy! you have been very wrong again.

TOPSY: Well, I 'spects I have.

EVA: What makes you do so?

TOPSY: I dunno; I 'spects it's cause I's so wicked.

EVA: Why did you spoil Jane's earrings?

TOPSY: 'Cause she's so proud. She called me a little black imp, and turned up her pretty nose at me 'cause she is whiter than I am. I was gwine by her room, and I seed her coral earrings lying on de table, so I threw dem on de floor, and put my foot on 'em, and scrunched

'em all to little bits – he! he! he! I's so wicked.

EVA: Don't you know that was very wrong?

TOPSY: I don't car'. I despises dem what sets up for fine ladies, when dey ain't nothin' but cream-coloured niggers! Dere's Miss Rosa – she gives me lots of 'pertinent remarks. T'other night she was gwine to ball. She put on a beau'ful dress that missis give her – wid her har curled, all nice and pretty. She hab to go down de back stairs – dey am dark – and I puts a pail of hot water on dem, and she put her foot into it, and den she go tumblin' to de bottom of de stairs, and de water go all ober her, and spile her dress, and scald her dreadful bad! He! he! he! I's so wicked!

EVA: Oh! how could you!

TOPSY: Don't dey despise me 'cause I don't know nothin'? Don't dey laugh at me 'cause I'm brack, and dey ain't?

EVA: But you shouldn't mind them.

TOPSY: Well, I don't mind dem; but when dey are passing under my winder, I trows dirty water on 'em, and dat spiles der complexions.

EVA: What does make you so bad, Topsy? Why won't you try and be good? Don't you love anybody, Topsy?

TOPSY: Can't recommember.

EVA: But you love your father and mother?

TOPSY: Never had none; ye know, I telled ye that, Miss Eva.

EVA: Oh! I know; but hadn't you any brother, or sister, or aunt, or –

TOPSY: No, none on 'em – never had nothin' nor nobody. I's brack – no one loves me!

EVA: Oh! Topsy, I love you! [*Laying her hand on Topsy's shoulder*] I love you because you haven't had any father, or mother, or friends. I love you, and I want you to be good. I wish you would try to be good for my sake. [*Topsy looks astonished for a moment, and then bursts into tears*] Only think of it, Topsy – *you* can be one of those spirits bright Uncle Tom sings about!

TOPSY: Oh! dear Miss Eva – dear Miss Eva! I will try – I will try! I never did care nothin' about it before.

EVA: If you try, you will succeed. Come with me. [*Takes Topsy's hand*]

TOPSY: I will try; but den, I's so wicked!

Exit Eva, followed by Topsy, crying

Scene 5

Chamber. Enter George, Eliza and Harry.

GEORGE: At length, Eliza, after many wanderings, we are again united.

ELIZA: Thanks to these generous Quakers, who have so kindly sheltered us.

GEORGE: Not forgetting our friend Phineas.

ELIZA: I do indeed owe him much. 'Twas he I met upon the icy river's bank, after that fearful but successful attempt, when I fled from the slave-trader with my child in my arms.

GEORGE: It seems almost incredible that you could have crossed the river on the ice.

ELIZA: Yes, I did. Heaven helping me, I crossed on the ice, for they were behind me – right behind – and there was no other way.

GEORGE: But the ice was all in broken-up blocks, swinging and heaving up and down in the water.

ELIZA: I know it was – I know it; I did not think I should get over, but I did not care – I could but die if I did not! I leaped on the ice, but how I got across I don't know; the first I remember, a man was helping me up the bank – that man was Phineas.

GEORGE: My brave girl! you deserve your freedom – you have richly earned it!

ELIZA: And when we get to Canada I can help you to work, and between us we can find something to live on.

GEORGE: Yes, Eliza, so long as we have each other, and our boy. Oh, Eliza, if these people only knew what a blessing it is for a man to feel that his wife and child belong to *him!* I've often wondered to see men that could call their wives and children *their own*, fretting and worrying about anything else. Why, I feel rich and strong, though we have nothing but our bare hands. If they will only let me alone now, I will be satisfied – thankful!

ELIZA: But we are not quite out of danger; we are not yet in Canada.

GEORGE: True; but it seems as if I smelt the free air, and it makes me strong!

Enter Phineas, dressed as a Quaker

PHINEAS: [*With a snuffle*] Verily, friends, how is it with thee? – hum!

GEORGE: Why, Phineas, what means this metamorphosis?

PHINEAS: I've become a Quaker! that's the meaning on't.

GEORGE: What – you?

PHINEAS: Teetotally! I was driven to it by a strong argument, composed of a pair of sparkling eyes, rosy cheeks, and pouting lips. Them lips would persuade a man to assassinate his grandmother! [*Assumes the Quaker tone again*] Verily, George, I have discovered something of importance to the interests of thee and thy party, and it were well for thee to hear it.

GEORGE: Keep us not in suspense!

PHINEAS: Well, after I left you on the road, I stopped at a little, lone tavern, just below here. Well, I was tired with hard driving, and, after my supper, I stretched myself down on a pile of bags in the corner, and pulled a buffalo hide over me – and what does I do but get fast asleep.

GEORGE: With one ear open, Phineas?

PHINEAS: No, I slept ears and all for an hour or two, for I was pretty well tired; but when I came to myself a little, I found that there were some men in the room, sitting round a table, drinking and talking; and I thought, before I made much muster, I'd just see what they were up to, especially as I heard them say something about the Quakers. Then I listened with both ears and found they were talking about you. So I kept quiet, and heard them lay off all their plans. They've got a right notion of the track we are going to-night, and they'll be down after us, six or eight strong. So, now, what's to be done?

ELIZA: What *shall* we do, George?

GEORGE: I know what I shall do! [*Takes out pistols*]

PHINEAS: Ay – ay, thou seest, Eliza, how it will work – pistols – phitz – poppers!

ELIZA: I see; but I pray it come not to that!

GEORGE: I don't want to involve any one with or for me. If you will lend me your vehicle, and direct me, I will drive alone to the next stand.

PHINEAS: Ah! well, friend, but thee'll need a driver for all that. Thee's quite welcome to do all the fighting thee knows; but I know a thing or two about the road that thee doesn't.

GEORGE: But I don't want to involve you.

PHINEAS: Involve me! Why, chaw me – that is to say – when thee does involve me, please to let me know.

ELIZA: Phineas is a wise and skillful man. You will do well, George, to abide by his judgment. And, oh! George, be not hasty with these – young blood is hot! [*Laying her hand on pistols*]

GEORGE: I will attack no man. All I ask of this country is to be left alone, and I will go out peaceably. But I'll fight to the last breath before they shall take from me my wife and son! Can you blame me?

PHINEAS: Mortal man cannot blame thee, neighbour George! Flesh and blood could not do otherwise. Woe unto the world because of offenses, but woe unto them through whom the offense cometh! That's gospel, teetotally!

GEORGE: Would not even you, sir, do the same, in my place?

PHINEAS: I pray that I be not tried; the flesh is weak – but I think my flesh would be pretty tolerably strong in such a case; I ain't sure, friend George, that I shouldn't hold a fellow for thee, if thee had any accounts to settle with him.

ELIZA: Heaven grant we be not tempted.

PHINEAS: But if we are tempted too much, why, consarn 'em! let them look out, that's all.

GEORGE: It's quite plain you was not born for a Quaker. The old nature has its way in you pretty strong yet.

PHINEAS: Well, I reckon you are pretty teetotally right.

GEORGE: Had we not better hasten our flight?

PHINEAS: Well, I rather conclude we had; we're full two hours ahead of them, if they start at the time they planned; so let's vamoose. [*Exeunt*]

Scene 6

A Rocky Pass in the Hills. – Large set rock and platform.

PHINEAS: [*Without*] Out with you in a twinkling, every one, and up into these rocks with me! run *now*, if you *ever* did run!

Phineas enters, with Harry in his arms. – George supporting Eliza

Come up here; this is one of our old hunting dens. Come up. [*They ascend the rock*] Well, here we are. Let 'em get us if they can. Whoever comes here has to walk single file between those two rocks, in fair range of your pistols – d'ye see?

GEORGE: I do see. And now, as this affair is mine, let me take all the risk, and do all the fighting.

PHINEAS: Thee's quite welcome to do the fighting, George; but I may have the fun of looking on, I suppose. But see, these fellows are kind of debating down there, and looking up, like hens when they are going to fly up onto the roost. Hadn't thee better give 'em a word of advice, before they come up, jest to tell 'em handsomely they'll be shot if they do.

Loker, Marks, and three Men enter

MARKS: Well, Tom, your coons are fairly treed.

LOKER: Yes, I see 'em go up right here; and here's a path – I'm for going right up. They can't jump down in a hurry, and it won't take long to ferret 'em out.

MARKS: But, Tom, they might fire at us from behind the rocks. That would be ugly, you know.

LOKER: Ugh! always for saving your skin, Marks. No danger; niggers are too plaguy scared!

MARKS: I don't know why I shouldn't save my skin; it's the best I've got; and niggers do fight like the devil sometimes.

GEORGE: [*Rising on the rock*] Gentlemen, who are you down there, and what do you want?

LOKER: We want a party of runaway niggers. One George and Eliza Harris, and their son. We've got the officers here, and a warrant to take 'em too. D'ye hear? Ain't you George Harris, that belonged to Mr. Harris, of Shelby county, Kentucky?

GEORGE: I am George Harris. A Mr. Harris, of Kentucky, did call me his property. But now I'm a freeman, standing on Heaven's free soil! My wife and child I claim as mine. We have arms to defend ourselves, and we mean to do it. You can come up if you like, but the first one that comes within range of our bullets is a dead man.

MARKS: Oh, come – come, young man, this ain't no kind of talk at all for you. You see we're officers of justice. We've got the law on our side, and the power and so forth; so you'd better give up peaceably, you see – for you'll certainly have to give up at last.

GEORGE: I know very well that you've got the law on your side, and the power; but you haven't got us. We are standing here as free as you are, and by the great power that made us, we'll fight for our liberty till we die!

During this, Marks draws a pistol, and when he concludes fires at him. – Eliza screams

GEORGE: It's nothing, Eliza; I am unhurt.

PHINEAS: [*Drawing George down*] Thee'd better keep out of sight with thy speechifying; they're teetotal mean scamps.

LOKER: What did you do that for, Marks?

MARKS: You see, you get jist as much for him dead as alive in Kentucky.

GEORGE: Now, Phineas, the first man that advances I fire at; you take the second, and so on. It won't do to waste two shots on one.

PHINEAS: But what if you don't hit?

GEORGE: I'll try my best.

PHINEAS: Creation! Chaw me up if there ain't stuff in you!

MARKS: I think I must have hit some on 'em. I heard a squeal.

LOKER: I'm going right up for one. I never was afraid of niggers, and I ain't a going to be now. Who goes after me?

Loker dashes up the rock. – George fires. – He staggers for a moment, then springs to the top. – Phineas seizes him. – A struggle

PHINEAS: Friend, thee is not wanted here! [*Throws Loker over the rock*]

ᴍARKS: [*Retreating*] Lord help us – they're perfect devils!

Marks and Party run off. George and Eliza kneel in an attitude of thanksgiving, with the child between them. – Phineas stands over them exulting

End of Act II

ACT III. Scene ɪ

Chamber. Enter St. Clare, followed by Tom.

ST. CLARE: [*Giving money and papers to Tom*] There, Tom, are the bills, and the money to liquidate them.

TOM: Yes, mas'r.

ST. CLARE: Well, Tom, what are you waiting for? Isn't all right there?

TOM: I'm 'fraid not, mas'r.

ST. CLARE: Why, Tom, what's the matter? You look as solemn as a coffin.

TOM: I feel very bad, mas'r. I allays have thought that mas'r would be good to everybody.

ST. CLARE: Well, Tom, haven't I been? Come, now, what do you want? There's something you haven't got, I suppose, and this is the preface.

TOM: Mas'r allays been good to me. I haven't nothing to complain of on that head; but there is one that mas'r isn't good to.

ST. CLARE: Why, Tom, what's got into you? Speak out – what do you mean?

TOM: Last night, between one and two, I thought so. I studied upon the matter then – mas'r isn't good to *himself*.

ST. CLARE: Ah! now I understand; you allude to the state in which I came home last night. Well, to tell the truth, I *was* slightly elevated – a little more champagne on board than I could comfortably carry. That's all, isn't it?

TOM: [*Deeply affected – clasping his hands and weeping*] All! Oh! my dear young mas'r, I'm 'fraid it will be *loss of all – all*, body and soul. The Good Book says, "It biteth like a serpent and stingeth like an adder," my dear mas'r.

ST. CLARE: You poor, silly fool! I'm not worth crying over.

TOM: Oh, mas'r! I implore you to think of it before it gets too late.

ST. CLARE: Well, I won't go to any more of their cursed nonsense, Tom – on my honour, I won't. I don't know why I haven't stopped long ago; I've always despised *it*, and myself for it. So now, Tom, wipe up your eyes and go about your errands.

TOM: Bless you, mas'r. I feel much better now. You have taken a load from poor Tom's heart. Bless you!

ST. CLARE: Come, come, no blessing! I'm not so wonderfully good, now. There, I'll pledge my honour to you, Tom, you don't see me so again. [*Exit Tom*] I'll keep my faith with him, too.

OPHELIA: [*Without*] Come along, you shiftless mortal!

ST. CLARE: What new witchcraft has Topsy been brewing? That commotion is of her raising, I'll be bound.

Enter Ophelia, dragging in Topsy

OPHELIA: Come here now; I will tell your master.

ST. CLARE: What's the matter now?

OPHELIA: The matter is that I cannot be plagued with this girl any longer. It's past all bearing; flesh and blood cannot endure it. Here I locked her up and gave her a hymn to study; and what does she do but spy out where I put my key, and has gone to my bureau, and got a bonnet-trimming and cut it all to pieces to make dolls' jackets! I never saw anything like it in my life!

ST. CLARE: What have you done to her?

OPHELIA: What have I done? What haven't I done? Your wife says I ought to have her whipped till she couldn't stand.

ST. CLARE: I don't doubt it. Tell me of the lovely rule of woman. I never saw above a dozen women that wouldn't half kill a horse, or a servant, either, if they had their own way with them – let alone a man.

OPHELIA: I am sure, St. Clare, I don't know what to do. I've taught and taught – I've talked till I'm tired; I've whipped her, I've punished her in every way I could think of, and still she's just what she was at first.

ST. CLARE: Come here, Tops, you monkey! [*Topsy crosses to St. Clare, grinning*] What makes you behave so?

TOPSY: 'Spects it's my wicked heart – Miss Feely says so.

ST. CLARE: Don't you see how much Miss Ophelia has done for you? She says she has done everything she can think of.

TOPSY: Lor', yes, mas'r! old missis used to say so, too. She whipped me a heap harder, and used to pull my ha'r, and knock my head agin the door; but it didn't do me no good. I 'spects if they's to pull every spear of ha'r out o' my head, it wouldn't do no good neither – I's so wicked! Laws! I's nothin' but a nigger, no ways! [*Goes up*]

OPHELIA: Well, I shall have to give her up; I can't have that trouble any longer.

ST. CLARE: I'd like to ask you one question.

OPHELIA: What is it?

ST. CLARE: Why, if your doctrine is not strong enough to save one heathen child, that you can have at home here, all to yourself, what's the use of sending one or two poor missionaries off with it among thousands of just such? I suppose this girl is a fair sample of what thousands of your heathen are.

OPHELIA: I'm sure I don't know; I never saw such a girl as this.

ST. CLARE: What makes you so bad, Tops? Why won't you try and be good? Don't you love any one, Topsy?

TOPSY: Dunno nothin' 'bout love; I loves candy and sich, that's all.

OPHELIA: But, Topsy, if you'd only try to be good, you might.

TOPSY: Couldn't never be nothin' but a nigger, if I was ever so good. If I could be skinned and come white, I'd try then.

ST. CLARE: People can love you, if you are black, Topsy. Miss Ophelia would love you, if you were good. [*Topsy laughs*] Don't you think so?

TOPSY: No, she can't b'ar me, 'cause I'm a nigger – she'd's soon have a toad touch her. There can't nobody love niggers, and niggers can't do nothin'. I don't car'! [*Whistles*]

ST. CLARE: Silence, you incorrigible imp, and begone!

TOPSY: He! he! he! didn't get much out of dis chile! [*Exit*]

OPHELIA: I've always had a prejudice against negroes, and it's a fact – I never could bear to have that child touch me, but I didn't think she knew it.

ST. CLARE: Trust any child to find that out; there's no keeping it from them. But I believe all the trying in the world to benefit a child, and all the substantial favours you can do them, will never excite one emotion of gratitude, while that feeling of repugnance remains in the heart. It's a queer kind of fact, but so it is.

OPHELIA: I don't know how I can help it – they are disagreeable to me, this girl in particular. How can I help feeling so?

ST. CLARE: Eva does, it seems.

OPHELIA: Well, she's so loving. I wish I was like her. She might teach me a lesson.

ST. CLARE: It would not be the first time a little child had been used to instruct an old disciple, if it were so. Come, let us seek Eva, in her favourite bower by the lake.

OPHELIA: Why, the dew is falling; she mustn't be out there. She is unwell, I know.

ST. CLARE: Don't be croaking, cousin – I hate it.

OPHELIA: But she has that cough.

ST. CLARE: Oh, nonsense, of that cough – it is not anything. She has taken a little cold, perhaps.

OPHELIA: Well, that was just the way Eliza Jane was taken – and Ellen –

ST. CLARE: Oh, stop these hobgoblin, nurse legends. You old hands get so wise, that a child cannot cough or sneeze, but you see desperation and ruin at hand. Only take care of the child, keep her from the night air, and don't let her play too hard, and she'll do well enough. [*Exeunt*]

Scene 2

The flat represents the lake. The rays of the setting sun tinge the waters with gold. – A large tree. – Beneath this a grassy bank, on which Eva and Tom are seated side by side. – Eva has a Bible open on her lap.

TOM: Read dat passage again, please, Miss Eva?

EVA: [*Reading*] "And I saw a sea of glass, mingled with fire." [*Stopping suddenly and pointing to lake*] Tom, there it is!

TOM: What, Miss Eva?

EVA: Don't you see there? There's a "sea of glass, mingled with fire."

TOM: True enough, Miss Eva. [*Sings*]

Oh, had I the wings of the morning,
I'd fly away to Canaan's shore;
Bright angels should convey me home,
To the New Jerusalem.

EVA: Where do you suppose New Jerusalem is, Uncle Tom?

TOM: Oh, up in the clouds, Miss Eva.

EVA: Then I think I see it. Look in those clouds; they look like great gates of pearl; and you can see beyond them – far, far off – it's all gold! Tom, sing about 'spirits bright.'

TOM: [*Sings*]

I see a band of spirits bright,
That taste the glories there;
They are all robed in spotless white,
And conquering palms they bear.

EVA: Uncle Tom, I've seen *them*.

TOM: To be sure you have; you are one of them yourself. You are the brightest spirit I ever saw.

EVA: They come to me sometimes in my sleep – those spirits bright –
They are all robed in spotless white,
And conquering palms they bear.
Uncle Tom, I'm going there.

TOM: Where, Miss Eva?

EVA: [*Pointing to the sky*] I'm going *there*, to the spirits bright, Tom; I'm going before long.

TOM: It's jest no use tryin' to keep Miss Eva here; I've allays said so. She's got the Lord's mark in her forehead. She wasn't never like a child that's to live – there was always something deep in her eyes.

Rises and comes forward. – Eva also come forward, leaving Bible on bank

Enter St. Clare

ST. CLARE: Ah! my little pussy, you look as blooming as a rose! You are better now-a-days, are you not?

EVA: Papa, I've had things I wanted to say to you a great while. I want to say them now, before I get weaker.

ST. CLARE: Nay, this is an idle fear, Eva; you know you grow stronger every day.

EVA: It's all no use, papa, to keep it to myself any longer. The time is coming that I am going to leave you; I am going, and never to come back.

ST. CLARE: Oh, now, my dear little Eva! you've got nervous and low-spirited; you mustn't indulge such gloomy thoughts.

EVA: No, papa, don't deceive yourself, I am *not* any better; I know it perfectly well, and I am going before long. I am not nervous – I am not low-spirited. If it were not for you, papa, and my friends, I should be perfectly happy. I want to go – I long to go!

ST. CLARE: Why, dear child, what has made your poor little heart so sad? You have everything to make you happy that could be given you.

EVA: I had rather be in heaven! There are a great many things here that make me sad – that seem dreadful to me; I had rather be there; but I don't want to leave you – it almost breaks my heart!

ST. CLARE: What makes you sad, and what seems dreadful, Eva?

EVA: I feel sad for our poor people; they love me dearly, and they are all good and kind to me. I wish, papa, they were all *free!*

ST. CLARE: Why, Eva, child, don't you think they are well enough off, now?

EVA: [*Not heeding the question*] Papa, isn't there a way to have slaves made free? When I am dead, papa, then you will think of me, and do it for my sake?

ST. CLARE: When you are dead, Eva? Oh, child, don't talk to me so! You are all I have on earth!

EVA: Papa, these poor creatures love their children as much as you do me. Tom loves his children. Oh, do something for them!

ST. CLARE: There, there darling; only don't distress yourself, and don't talk of dying, and I will do anything you wish.

EVA: And promise me, dear father, that Tom shall have his freedom as soon as — [*Hesitating*] — I am gone!

ST. CLARE: Yes, dear, I will do anything in the world – anything you could ask me to. There, Tom, take her to her chamber; this evening air is too chill for her. [*Kisses her*]

Tom takes Eva in his arms, and exits

ST. CLARE: [*Gazing mournfully after Eva*] Has there ever been a child like Eva? Yes, there has been; but their names are always on gravestones, and their sweet smiles, their heavenly eyes, their singular words and ways, are among the buried treasures of yearning hearts. It is as if heaven had an especial band of angels, whose office it is to sojourn for a season here, and endear to them the wayward human heart, that they might bear it upward with them in their homeward flight. When you see that deep, spiritual light in the eye, when the little soul reveals itself in words sweeter and wiser than the ordinary words of children, hope not to retain that child; for the seal of heaven is on it, and the light of immortality looks out from its eyes! [*Exit*]

Scene 3

A corridor. Enter Tom; he listens at door and then lies down. Enter Ophelia, with candle.

OPHELIA: Uncle Tom, what alive have you taken to sleeping anywhere and everywhere, like a dog, for? I thought you were one of the orderly sort, that liked to lie in bed in a Christian way.

TOM: [*Rises. – Mysteriously*] I do, Miss Feely, I do, but now –

OPHELIA: Well, what now?

TOM: We mustn't speak loud; Mas'r St. Clare won't hear on't; but Miss Feely, you know there must be somebody watchin' for the bridegroom.

OPHELIA: What do you mean, Tom?

TOM: You know it says in Scripture, "At midnight there was a great cry made, behold the bridegroom cometh!" That's what I'm 'spectin' now, every night, Miss Feely, and I couldn't sleep out of hearing, noways.

OPHELIA: Why, Uncle Tom, what makes you think so?

TOM: Miss Eva, she talks to me. The Lord, he sends his messenger in the soul. I must be thar, Miss Feely; for when that ar blessed child goes into the kingdom, they'll open the door so wide, we'll all get a look in at the glory!

OPHELIA: Uncle Tom, did Miss Eva say she felt more unwell than usual to-night?

TOM: No; but she told me she was coming nearer – thar's them that tells it to the child, Miss Feely. It's the angels – it's the trumpet sound afore the break o' day!

OPHELIA: Heaven grant your fears be vain! Come in, Tom. [*Exeunt*]

Scene 4

Eva's chamber. Eva discovered on a couch. – A table stands near the couch, with a lamp on it. The light shines upon Eva's face, which is very pale. – Scene half dark. – Uncle Tom is kneeling near the foot of the couch. – Ophelia stands at the head. – St. Clare at back. – Scene opens to plaintive music. – Enter Marie, hastily.

MARIE: St. Clare! Cousin! Oh! what is the matter now?

ST. CLARE: [*Hoarsely*] Hush! she is dying!

MARIE: [*Sinking on her knees, beside Tom*] Dying!

ST. CLARE: Oh! if she would only wake and speak once more. [*Bending over Eva*] Eva, darling!

EVA: [*Uncloses her eyes, smiles, raises her head and tries to speak*]

ST. CLARE: Do you know me, Eva?

EVA: [*Throwing her arms feebly about his neck*] Dear papa! [*Her arms drop and she sinks back*]

ST. CLARE: Oh, heaven! this is dreadful! Oh! Tom, my boy, it is killing me!

TOM: Look at her, mas'r. [*Points to Eva*]

ST. CLARE: Eva! [*A pause*] She does not hear. Oh, Eva! tell us what you see. What is it?

EVA: [*Feebly smiling*] Oh! love! joy! peace! [*Dies*]

TOM: Oh! bless the Lord! it's over, dear mas'r, it's over.

ST. CLARE: [*Sinking on his knees*] Farewell, beloved child! the bright eternal doors have closed after thee. We shall see thy sweet face no more. Oh! woe for them who watched thy entrance into heaven, when they shall wake and find only the cold, gray sky of daily life, and thou gone forever.

Solemn music, slow curtain

End of Act III

ACT IV. Scene 1

A Street in New Orleans. Enter Gumption Cute, meeting Marks.

CUTE: How do ye dew?

MARKS: How are you?

CUTE: Well, now, squire, it's a fact that I am dead broke and busted up.

MARKS: You have been speculating, I suppose?

CUTE: That's just it and nothing shorter.

MARKS: You have had poor success, you say?

CUTE: Tarnation bad, now I tell you. You see I came to this part of the country to make my fortune.

MARKS: And you did not do it?

CUTE: Scarcely. The first thing I tried my hand at was keeping school. I opened an academy for the instruction of youth in the various branches of orthography, geography, and other graphies.

MARKS: Did you succeed in getting any pupils?

CUTE: Oh, lots on 'em! and a pretty set of dunces they were, too. After the first quarter, I called on the respectable parents of the juveniles, and requested them to fork over. To which they politely answered – don't you wish you may get it?

MARKS: What did you do then?

CUTE: Well, I kind of pulled up stakes and left those diggin's. Well, then I went into Spiritual Rappings for a living. That paid pretty well for a short time, till I met with an accident.

MARKS: An accident?

CUTE: Yes; a tall Yahoo called on me one day, and wanted me to summon the spirit of his mother – which, of course, I did. He asked me about a dozen questions which I answered to his satisfaction. At last he wanted to know what she died of – I said, Cholera. You never did see a critter so riled as he was. "Look yere, stranger," said he, "it's my opinion that you're a pesky humbug! for my mother was blown up in a *Steamboat!*" With that he left the premises. The next day the people furnished me with a conveyance, and I rode out of town.

MARKS: Rode out of town?

CUTE: Yes; on a rail!

MARKS: I suppose you gave up the spirits, after that?

CUTE: Well, I reckon I did; it had such an effect on my spirits.

MARKS: It's a wonder they didn't tar and feather you.

CUTE: There was some mention made of that, but when they said *feathers*, I felt as if I had wings, and flew away.

MARKS: You cut and run?

CUTE: Yes; I didn't like their company and I cut it. Well, after that I let myself out as an overseer on a cotton plantation. I made a pretty good thing of that, though it was dreadful trying to my feelings to flog the darkies; but I got used to it after a while, and then I used to lather 'em like Jehu. Well, the proprietor got the fever and ague and shook himself out of town. The place and all the fixings were sold at auction, and I found myself adrift once more.

MARKS: What are you doing at present?

CUTE: I'm in search of a rich relation of mine.

MARKS: A rich relation?

CUTE: Yes, a Miss Ophelia St. Clare. You see, a niece of hers married one of my second cousins – that's how I came to be a relation of hers. She came on here from Vermont to be housekeeper to a cousin of hers, of the same name.

MARKS: I know him well.

CUTE: The deuce you do! – well, that's lucky.

MARKS: Yes, he lives in this city.

CUTE: Say, you just point out the locality, and I'll give him a call.

MARKS: Stop a bit. Suppose you shouldn't be able to raise the wind in that quarter, what have you thought of doing?

CUTE: Well, nothing particular.

MARKS: How should you like to enter into a nice, profitable business – one that pays well?

CUTE: That's just about my measure – it would suit me to a hair. What is it?

MARKS: Nigger catching.

CUTE: Catching niggers! What on airth do you mean?

MARKS: Why, when there's a large reward offered for a runaway darkey, we goes after him, catches him, and gets the reward.

CUTE: Yes, that's all right so far – but s'pose there ain't no reward offered?

MARKS: Why, then we catches the darkey on our own account, sells him, and pockets the proceeds.

CUTE: By chowder, that ain't a bad speculation!

MARKS: What do you say? I want a partner. You see, I lost my partner last year, up in Ohio – he was a powerful fellow.

CUTE: Lost him! How did you lose him?

MARKS: Well, you see, Tom and I – his name was Tom Loker – Tom and I were after a mulatto chap, called George Harris, that run away from Kentucky. We traced him through the greater part of Ohio, and came up with him near the Pennsylvania line. He took refuge among some rocks, and showed fight.

CUTE: Oh! then runaway darkies show fight, do they?

MARKS: Sometimes. Well, Tom – like a headstrong fool as he was – rushed up the rocks, and a Quaker chap, who was helping this George Harris, threw him over the cliff.

CUTE: Was he killed?

MARKS: Well, I didn't stop to find out. Seeing that the darkies were stronger than I thought, I made tracks for a safe place.

CUTE: And what became of this George Harris?

MARKS: Oh! he and his wife and child got away safe into Canada. You see, they will get away sometimes, though it isn't very often. Now what do you say? You are just the figure for a fighting partner. Is it a bargain?

CUTE: Well, I rather calculate our teams won't hitch, no how. By chowder, I hain't no idea of setting myself up, as a target for darkies to fire at – that's a speculation that don't suit my constitution.

MARKS: You're afraid, then?

CUTE: No, I ain't; it's against my principles.

MARKS: Your principles – how so?

CUTE: Because my principles are to keep a sharp lookout for No. 1. I shouldn't feel wholesome if a darkey was to throw me over that cliff to look after Tom Loker. [*Exeunt, arm-in-arm*]

Scene 2

Gothic Chamber. St. Clare discovered, seated on sofa. Tom to the left.

ST. CLARE: Oh! Tom, my boy, the whole world is as empty as an egg-shell.

TOM: I know it, mas'r, I know it. But oh! if mas'r could look up – up where our dear Miss Eva is –

ST. CLARE: Ah, Tom! I do look up; but the trouble is, I don't see anything when I do. I wish I could. It seems to be given to children and poor, honest fellows like you, to see what we cannot. How comes it?

TOM: "Thou hast hid from the wise and prudent, and revealed unto babes; even so, Father, for so it seemed good in thy sight."

ST. CLARE: Tom, I don't believe – I've got the habit of doubting – I want to believe and I cannot.

TOM: Dear mas'r, pray to the good Lord: "Lord, I believe; help thou my unbelief."

ST. CLARE: Who knows anything about anything? Was all that beautiful love and faith only one of the ever-shifting phases of human feeling, having nothing real to rest on, passing away with the little breath? And is there no more Eva – nothing?

TOM: Oh! dear mas'r, there is. I know it; I'm sure of it. Do, do, dear mas'r, believe it!

ST. CLARE: How do you know there is, Tom? You never saw the Lord.

TOM: Felt Him in my soul, mas'r – feel Him now! Oh! mas'r, when I was sold away from my old woman and the children, I was jest a'most broken up – I felt as if there warn't nothing left – and then the Lord stood by me, and He says, "Fear not, Tom," and He brings light and joy into a poor fellow's soul – makes all peace; and I's so happy, and loves everybody, and feels willin' to be jest where the Lord wants to put me. I know it couldn't come from me, 'cause I's a poor, complaining creature – it comes from above, and I know He's willin' to do for mas'r.

ST. CLARE: [*Grasping Tom's hand*] Tom, you love me!

TOM: I's willin' to lay down my life this blessed day for you.

ST. CLARE: [*Sadly*] Poor, foolish fellow! I'm not worth the love of one good, honest heart like yours.

TOM: Oh, mas'r! there's more than me loves you – the blessed Saviour loves you.

ST. CLARE: How do you know that, Tom?

TOM: The love of the Saviour passeth knowledge.

ST. CLARE: [*Turns away*] Singular! that the story of a man who lived and died eighteen hundred years ago, can affect people so yet. But He was no man. [*Rises*] No man ever had such long and living power. Oh! that I could believe what my mother taught me, and pray as I did when I was a boy. But, Tom, all this time I have forgotten why I sent for you. I'm going to make a freeman of you; so have your trunk packed, and get ready to set out for Kentuck.

TOM: [*Joyfully*] Bless the Lord!

ST. CLARE: [*Dryly*] You haven't had such very bad times here, that you need be in such a rapture, Tom.

TOM: No, no, mas'r, 'tain't that; it's being a *freeman* – that's what I'm joyin' for.

ST. CLARE: Why, Tom, don't you think, for your own part, you've been better off than to be free?

TOM: No, *indeed*, Mas'r St. Clare – no, indeed!

ST. CLARE: Why, Tom, you couldn't possibly have earned, by your work, such clothes and such living as I have given you.

TOM: I know all that, Mas'r St. Clare – mas'r's been too good; but I'd rather have poor clothes, poor house, poor everything, and have 'em *mine*, than have the best, if they belonged to somebody else. I had *so*, mas'r; I think it's natur', mas'r.

ST. CLARE: I suppose so, Tom; and you'll be going off and leaving me in a month or so – though why you shouldn't no mortal knows.

TOM: Not while mas'r is in trouble. I'll stay with mas'r as long as he wants me, so as I can be any use.

ST. CLARE: [*Sadly*] Not while I'm in trouble, Tom? And when will my trouble be over?

TOM: When you are a believer.

ST. CLARE: And you really mean to stay by me till that day comes? [*Smiling and laying his hand on Tom's shoulder*] Ah, Tom! I won't keep you till that day. Go home to your wife and children, and give my love to all.

TOM: I's faith to think that day will come – the Lord has a work for mas'r.

ST. CLARE: A work, hey? Well, now, Tom, give me your views on what sort of a work it is – let's hear.

TOM: Why, even a poor fellow like me has a work; and Mas'r St. Clare, that has larnin', and riches, and friends, how much he might do for the Lord.

ST. CLARE: Tom, you seem to think the Lord needs a great deal done for him.

TOM: We does for him when we does for his creatures.

ST. CLARE: Good theology, Tom. Thank you, my boy; I like to hear you talk. But go now, Tom, and leave me alone. [*Exit Tom*] That faithful fellow's words have excited a train of thoughts that almost bear me, on the strong tide of faith and feeling, to the gates of that heaven I so vividly conceive. They seem to bring me nearer to Eva.

OPHELIA: [*Outside*] What are you doing there, you limb of Satan? You've been stealing something, I'll be bound.

Ophelia drags in Topsy

TOPSY: You go 'long, Miss Feely, 'tain't none o' your business.

ST. CLARE: Heyday! what is all this commotion?

OPHELIA: She's been stealing.

TOPSY: [*Sobbing*] I hain't neither.

OPHELIA: What have you got in your bosom?

TOPSY: I've got my hand dar.

OPHELIA: But what have you got in your hand?

TOPSY: Nuffin'.

OPHELIA: That's a fib, Topsy.

TOPSY: Well, I 'spects it is.

OPHELIA: Give it to me, whatever it is.

TOPSY: It's mine – I hope I may die this bressed minute, if it don't b'long to me.

OPHELIA: Topsy, I order you to give me that article; don't let me have to ask you again. [*Topsy reluctantly takes the foot of an old stocking from her bosom and hands it to Ophelia*] Sakes alive! what is all this? [*Takes from it a lock of hair, and a small book, with a bit of crape twisted around it*]

TOPSY: Dat's a lock of ha'r dat Miss Eva give me – she cut it from her own beau'ful head herself.

ST. CLARE: [*Takes book*] Why did you wrap *this* [*Pointing to crape*] around the book?

TOPSY: 'Cause – 'cause – 'cause 'twas Miss Eva's. Oh! don't take 'em away, please! [*Sits down on stage, and putting her apron over her head, begins to sob vehemently*]

OPHELIA: Come, come, don't cry; you shall have them.

TOPSY: [*Jumps up joyfully and takes them*] I wants to keep 'em, 'cause dey makes me good; I ain't half so wicked as I used to was. [*Runs off*]

ST. CLARE: I really think you can make something of that girl. Any mind that is capable of a *real sorrow* is capable of good. You must try and do something with her.

OPHELIA: The child has improved very much; I have great hopes of her.

ST. CLARE: I believe I'll go down the street, a few moments, and hear the news.

OPHELIA: Shall I call Tom to attend you?

ST. CLARE: No, I shall be back in an hour. [*Exit*]

OPHELIA: He's got an excellent heart, but then he's so dreadful shiftless! [*Exit*]

Scene 3

A bar-room. Tables and chairs. Newspapers on table. Marks and Cute discovered.

CUTE: Any news, Squire?

MARKS: . . . 'scaped to death!*

CUTE: Squire, it's lucky that the staves of that barrel wasn't made of yellow pine.

MARKS: Why so, Cute?

CUTE: Because she might have got a pine-knot hole in both her eyes, and been blind for life.

MARKS: . . . from him immediately.

CUTE: Don't want to enter into any such speculation. Hello, Squire, who is this feller coming up street?

MARKS: Can't say, Cute, never having seen the individual before.

CUTE: Rather an odd-looking fish, ain't he, Judge?

MARKS: . . . Mr. Simon Legree.

CUTE: Do you think him and I will agree?

MARKS: . . . pretty rough.

CUTE: Trot him out, Squire, I'm tough!

Legree enters

LEGREE: How are you, Marks? What are you doing down here?

MARKS: . . . Cute, Legree; Legree, Cute. [*Legree squeezes Cute's hand*]

*Some of Marks's speeches are incomplete in the New York Public Library promptbook. Many editions omit this entire scene.

CUTE: I'll trouble for that when you get through with it. Darn his picture! My hand's like a duck's foot.

St. Clare enters, and seats himself at table

CUTE: I cal'ate you're some on your muscle, Squire?

LEGREE: Just so, stranger.

CUTE: Say, I cal'ate you'd handle a fellar pretty rough.

LEGREE: Just so, stranger.

CUTE: Well, say, do you want to hire an overseer to boss your darkies?

LEGREE: Why so?

CUTE: Cause I'd like to hire myself out for a few months to oversee.

LEGREE: I can oversee my own niggers, I reckon.

CUTE: You look as if you could, by thunder!

LEGREE: 'Umph! Do you see that 'ere right hand? There's a fist that's grown hard a smacking down niggers! Just feel the weight on't, stranger!

CUTE: Land of hope and blessed promise! Now, I shouldn't wonder if your heart was just about as hard as your hand.

LEGREE: Just so, stranger.

CUTE: Nevertheless, you've one soft spot about you.

LEGREE: 'Umph, indeed, whereabouts?

CUTE: Your head, you darned cuss!

LEGREE: What! [*Rushes at him with bowie-knife. St. Clare attempts to separate them. Business and scene closes*]

Scene 4

Front Chamber. Enter Topsy.

TOPSY: Dar's something de matter wid me – I isn't a bit like myself. I haven't done anything wrong since poor Miss Eva went up in de skies and left us. When I's gwine to do anything wicked, I tinks of her, and somehow I can't do it. I's getting to be good, dat's a fact. I 'spects when I's dead I shall be turned into a little brack angel.

Enter Ophelia

OPHELIA: Topsy, I've been looking for you; I've got something very particular to say to you.

TOPSY: Does you want me to say the catechism?

OPHELIA: No, not now.

TOPSY: [*Aside*] Golly! dat's one comfort.

OPHELIA: Now, Topsy, I want you to try and understand what I am going to say to you.

TOPSY: Yes, missis, I'll open my ears drefful wide.

OPHELIA: Mr. St. Clare has given you to me, Topsy.

TOPSY: Den I b'longs to you, don't I? Golly! I thought I always belonged to you.

OPHELIA: Not till to-day have I received any authority to call you my property.

TOPSY: I's your property, am I? Well, if you say so, I 'spects I am.

OPHELIA: Topsy, I can give you your liberty.

TOPSY: My liberty?

OPHELIA: Yes, Topsy.

TOPSY: Has you got 'um with you?

OPHELIA: I have, Topsy.

TOPSY: Is it clothes or wittles?

OPHELIA: How shiftless! Don't you know what your liberty is, Topsy?

TOPSY: How should I know when I never seed 'um?

OPHELIA: Topsy, I am going to leave this place; I am going many miles away – to my own home in Vermont.

TOPSY: Den what's to become of dis chile?

OPHELIA: If you wish to go, I will take you with me.

TOPSY: Miss Feely, I doesn't want to leave you no how, I loves you, I does.

OPHELIA: Then you shall share my home for the rest of your days. Come, Topsy.

TOPSY: Stop, Miss Feely; does dey hab any oberseers in Varmount?

OPHELIA: No, Topsy.

TOPSY: Nor cotton plantations, nor sugar factories, nor darkies, nor whipping, nor nothin'?

OPHELIA: No, Topsy.

TOPSY: By golly! de quicker you is gwine de better den.

Enter Tom, hastily

TOM: Oh, Miss Feely! Miss Feely!

OPHELIA: Gracious me, Tom! what's the matter?

TOM: Oh, Mas'r St. Clare, Mas'r St. Clare!

OPHELIA: Well, Tom, well?

TOM: They've just brought him home and I do believe he's killed.

OPHELIA: Killed?

TOPSY: Oh, dear! what's to become of de poor darkies now?

TOM: He's dreadful weak. It's just as much as he can do to speak. He wanted me to call you.

OPHELIA: My poor cousin! Who would have thought of it? Don't say a word to his wife, Tom; the danger may not be so great as you think; it would only distress her. Come with me; you may be able to afford some assistance. [*Exeunt*]

Scene 5

Handsome Chamber. St. Clare discovered seated on sofa. Ophelia, Tom and Topsy are clustered around him. Doctor back of sofa, feeling his pulse.

ST. CLARE: [*Raising himself feebly*] Tom – poor fellow!

TOM: Well, mas'r?

ST. CLARE: I have received my death wound.

TOM: Oh, no, no, mas'r!

ST. CLARE: I feel that I am dying – Tom, pray!

TOM: [*Sinking on his knees*] I do pray, mas'r! I do pray!

ST. CLARE: [*After a pause*] Tom, one thing preys upon my mind – I have forgotten to sign your freedom papers. What will become of you when I am gone?

TOM: Don't think of that, mas'r.

ST. CLARE: I was wrong, Tom, very wrong, to neglect it. I may be the cause of much suffering to you hereafter. Marie, my wife – she – oh! –

OPHELIA: His mind is wandering.

ST. CLARE: [*Energetically*] No! it is coming *home* at last! [*Sinks back*] at last! at last! Eva, I come! [*Dies*]

End of Act IV

ACT V. Scene 1

An Auction Mart. Uncle Tom and Emmeline at back – Adolf, Skeggs, Marks, Mann, and various spectators discovered. Marks and Mann come forward.

MARKS: Hulloa, Alf! what brings you here?

MANN: Well, I was wanting a valet, and I heard that St. Clare's lot was going; I thought I'd just look at them.

MARKS: Catch me ever buying any of St. Clare's

people. Spoilt niggers, every one – impudent as the devil.

MANN: Never fear that; if I get 'em, I'll soon have their airs out of them – they'll soon find that they've another kind of master to deal with than St. Clare. 'Pon my word, I'll buy that fellow – I like the shape of him. [*Pointing to Adolf*]

MARKS: You'll find it'll take all you've got to keep him – he's deucedly extravagant.

MANN: Yes, but my lord will find that he *can't* be extravagant with *me*. Just let him be sent to the calaboose a few times, and thoroughly dressed down, I'll tell you if it don't bring him to a sense of his ways. Oh! I'll reform him, up hill and down, you'll see. I'll buy him, that's flat.

Enter Legree; he goes up and looks at Adolf, whose boots are nicely blacked

LEGREE: A nigger with his boots blacked – bah! [*Spits on them*] Holloa, you! [*To Tom*] Let's see your teeth. [*Seizes Tom by the jaw and opens his mouth*] Strip up your sleeve and show your muscle. [*Tom does so*] Where was you raised?

TOM: In Kentuck, mas'r.

LEGREE: What have you done?

TOM: Had care of mas'r's farm.

LEGREE: That's a likely story. [*Turns to Emmeline*] You're a nice looking girl enough. How old are you? [*Grasps her arm*]

EMMELINE: [*Shrieking*] Ah! you hurt me.

SKEGGS: Stop that, you minx! No whimpering here. The sale is going to begin. [*Mounts the rostrum*] Gentlemen, the next article I shall offer you to-day is Adolf, late valet to Mr. St. Clare. How much am I offered? [*Various bids are made. Adolf is knocked down to Mann for eight hundred dollars*] Gentlemen, I now offer a prime article – the quadroon girl, Emmeline, only fifteen years of age, warranted in every respect. [*Business as before. Emmeline is sold to Legree for one thousand dollars*] Now, I shall close to-day's sale by offering you the valuable article known as Uncle Tom, the most useful nigger ever raised. Gentlemen in want of an overseer, now is the time to bid.

Business as before. Tom is sold to Legree for twelve hundred dollars

LEGREE: Now look here, you two belong to me.

Tom and Emmeline sink on their knees

TOM: Heaven help us, then!

Music. – Legree stands over them exulting. Picture

Scene 2

The Garden of Miss Ophelia's House in Vermont. Enter Ophelia and Deacon Perry.

DEACON: Miss Ophelia, allow me to offer you my congratulations upon your safe arrival in your native place. I hope it is your intention to pass the remainder of your days with us?

OPHELIA: Well, Deacon, I have come here with that express purpose.

DEACON: I presume you were not over pleased with the South?

OPHELIA: Well, to tell the truth, Deacon, I wasn't; I liked the country very well, but the people there are so dreadful shiftless.

DEACON: The result, I presume, of living in a warm climate.

OPHELIA: Well, Deacon, what is the news among you all here?

DEACON: Well, we live on in the same even jog-trot pace. Nothing of any consequence has happened. – Oh! I forgot. [*Takes out his handkerchief*] I've lost my wife; my Molly has left me.

OPHELIA: Poor soul! I pity you, Deacon.

DEACON: Thank you. You perceive I bear my loss with resignation.

OPHELIA: How you must miss her tongue!

DEACON: Molly certainly was fond of talking. She always would have the last word – heigho!

OPHELIA: What was her complaint, Deacon?

DEACON: A very mild and soothing one, Miss Ophelia; she had a severe attack of the lockjaw.

OPHELIA: Dreadful!

DEACON: Wasn't it? When she found she couldn't use her tongue, she took it so much to heart that it struck to her stomach and killed her. Poor dear! Excuse my handkerchief; she's been dead only eighteen months.

OPHELIA: Why, Deacon, by this time you ought to be setting your cap for another wife.

DEACON: Do you think so, Miss Ophelia?

OPHELIA: I don't see why you shouldn't – you are still a good-looking man, Deacon.

DEACON: Ah! well, I think I do wear well – in fact, I may say remarkably well. It has been observed to me before.

OPHELIA: And you are not much over fifty?

DEACON: Just turned of forty, I assure you.

OPHELIA: Hale and hearty?

DEACON: Health excellent – look at my eye! Strong as a lion – look at my arm! A No. 1 constitution – look at my leg!!!

OPHELIA: Have you no thoughts of choosing another partner?

DEACON: Well, to tell you the truth, I have.

OPHELIA: Who is she?

DEACON: She is not far distant. [*Looks at Ophelia in a languishing manner*] I have her in my eye at this present moment.

OPHELIA: [*Aside*] Really, I believe he's going to pop. Why, surely, Deacon, you don't mean to –

DEACON: Yes, Miss Ophelia, I do mean; and believe me, when I say – [*Looking off*] The Lord be good to us, but I believe there is the devil coming!

Topsy runs on with bouquet. She is now dressed very neatly

TOPSY: Miss Feely, here is some flowers dat I hab been gathering for you. [*Gives bouquet*]

OPHELIA: That's a good child.

DEACON: Miss Ophelia, who is this young person?

OPHELIA: She is my daughter.

DEACON: [*Aside*] Her daughter! Then she must have married a coloured man off South. I was not aware that you had been married, Miss Ophelia?

OPHELIA: Married? Sakes alive! what made you think I had been married?

DEACON: Good gracious! I'm getting confused. Didn't I understand you to say that this – somewhat tanned – young lady was your daughter?

OPHELIA: Only by adoption. She is my adopted daughter.

DEACON: O – oh! [*Aside*] I breathe again.

TOPSY: [*Aside*] By golly! dat old man's eyes stick out of 'um head dre'ful. Guess he never seed anything like me afore.

OPHELIA: Deacon, won't you step into the house and refresh yourself after your walk?

DEACON: I accept your polite invitation. [*Offers his arm*] Allow me.

OPHELIA: As gallant as ever, Deacon. I declare, you grow younger every day.

DEACON: You can never grow old, madam.

OPHELIA: Ah, you flatterer! [*Exeunt*]

TOPSY: Dar dey go, like an old goose and gander. Guess dat ole gemblemun feels kind of confectionary – rather sweet on my old missis. By golly! she's been dre'ful kind to me ever since I come away from de South; and I loves her, I does, 'cause she takes such car' on me and gives me dese fine clothes. I tries to be good, too, and I's getting 'long 'mazin' fast. I'se not so wicked as I used to was. [*Looks out*] Hulloa! dar's some one comin' here. I wonder what he wants now. [*Retires, observing*]

Enter Gumption Cute, very shabby – a small bundle, on a stick, over his shoulder

CUTE: By chowder, here I am again. Phew! it's a pretty considerable tall piece of walking between here and New Orleans, not to mention the wear of shoe-leather. I guess I'm about done up. If this streak of bad luck lasts much longer, I'll borrow sixpence to buy a rope, and hang myself right straight up! When I went to call on Miss Ophelia, I swow if I didn't find out that she had left for Varmount; so I kind of concluded to make tracks in that direction myself, and as I didn't have any money left, why I had to foot it, and here I am in old Varmount once more. They told me Miss Ophelia lived up here. I wonder if she will remember the relationship. [*Sees Topsy*] By chowder, there's a darkey. Look here, Charcoal!

TOPSY: [*Comes forward*] My name isn't Charcoal – it's Topsy.

CUTE: Oh! your name is Topsy, is it, you juvenile specimen of Day & Martin?

TOPSY: Tell you I don't know nothin' 'bout Day & Martin. I's Topsy and I belong to Miss Feely St. Clare.

CUTE: I'm much obleeged to you, you small extract of Japan, for your information. So Miss Ophelia lives up there in the white house, does she?

TOPSY: Well, she don't do nothin' else.

CUTE: Well, then, just locomote your pins.

TOPSY: What – what's dat?

CUTE: Walk your chalks!

TOPSY: By golly! dere ain't no chalk 'bout me.

CUTE: Move your trotters.

TOPSY: How you does spoke! What you mean by trotters?

CUTE: Why, your feet, Stove Polish.

TOPSY: What does you want me to move my feet for?

CUTE: To tell your mistress, you ebony angel, that a gentleman wishes to see her.

TOPSY: Does you call yourself a gentleman? By golly! you look more like a scar'-crow.

CUTE: Now look here, you Charcoal, don't you be sassy. I'm a gentleman in distress; a done-up speculator; one that has seen better days – long time ago – and better clothes too, by chowder! My creditors are like my boots – they've no soles. I'm a victim to circumstances. I've been through much and survived it. I've taken walking exercise for the benefit of my health; but as I was trying to live on air at the same time, it was a losing speculation, 'cause it gave me such a dreadful appetite.

TOPSY: Golly! you look as if you could eat an ox, horns and all.

CUTE: Well, I calculate I could, if he was roasted – it's a speculation I should like to engage in. I have returned like the fellow that run away in Scripture; and if anybody's got a fatted calf they want to kill, all they got to do is to fetch him along. Do you know, Charcoal, that your mistress is a relation of mine?

TOPSY: Is she your uncle?

CUTE: No, no, not quite so near as that. My second cousin married her niece.

TOPSY: And does you want to see Miss Feely?

CUTE: I do. I have come to seek a home beneath her roof, and take care of all the spare change she don't want to use.

TOPSY: Den just yo' follow me, mas'r.

CUTE: Stop! By chowder, I've got a great idee. Say, you Day & Martin, how should you like to enter into a speculation?

TOPSY: Golly! I doesn't know what a spec- spec-cu-what-do-you-call-'um am.

CUTE: Well, now, I calculate I've hit upon about the right thing. Why should I degrade the manly dignity of the Cutes by becoming a beggar – expose myself to the chance of receiving the cold shoulder as a poor relation? By chowder, my blood biles as I think of it! Topsy, you can make my fortune, and your own, too. I've an idee in my head that is worth a million of dollars.

TOPSY: Golly! is your head worth dat? Guess you wouldn't bring dat out South for de whole of you.

CUTE: Don't you be too severe now, Charcoal; I'm a man of genius. Did you ever hear of Barnum?

TOPSY: Barnum! Barnum! Does he live out South?

CUTE: No, he lives in New York. Do you know how he made his fortune?

TOPSY: What is him fortin, hey? Is it something he wears?

CUTE: Chowder, how green you are!

TOPSY: [*Indignantly*] Sar, I hab you to know I's not green; I's brack.

CUTE: To be sure you are, Day & Martin. I calculate, when a person says another has a fortune, he means he's got plenty of money, Charcoal.

TOPSY: And did he make the money?

CUTE: Sartin sure, and no mistake.

TOPSY: Golly! now I thought money always growed.

CUTE: Oh, git out! You are too cute – you are cuter than I am; and I'm Cute by name and cute by nature. Well, as I was saying, Barnum made his money by exhibiting a *woolly* horse; now wouldn't it be an all-fired speculation to show you as the woolly gal?

TOPSY: You want to make a sight of me?

CUTE: I'll give you half the receipts, by chowder!

TOPSY: Should I have to leave Miss Feely?

CUTE: To be sure you would.

TOPSY: Den you hab to get a woolly gal somewhere else, Mas'r Cute. [*Runs off*]

CUTE: There's another speculation gone to smash, by chowder! [*Exit*]

Scene 3

A Rude Chamber. Tom is discovered, in old clothes, seated on a stool; he holds in his hand a paper containing a curl of Eva's hair. The scene opens to the symphony of "Old Folks at Home."

TOM: I have come to de dark places; I's going through de vale of shadows. My heart sinks at times and feels just like a big lump of lead. Den it gits up in my throat and chokes me till de tears roll out of my eyes; den I take out dis curl of little Miss Eva's hair, and the sight of it brings calm to my mind and I feels strong again. [*Kisses the curl and puts it in his breast*

– *takes out a silver dollar, which is suspended around his neck by a string*] Dere's de bright silver dollar dat Mas'r George Shelby gave me the day I was sold away from old Kentuck, and I've kept it ever since. Mas'r George must have grown to be a man by this time. I wonder if I shall ever see him again.

Song. – "Old Folks at Home"

Enter Legree, Emmeline, Sambo and Quimbo

LEGREE: Shut up, you black cuss! Did you think I wanted any of your infernal howling? [*Turns to Emmeline*] We're home. [*Emmeline shrinks from him. He takes hold of her ear*] You didn't ever wear earrings?

EMMELINE: [*Trembling*] No, master.

LEGREE: Well, I'll give you a pair, if you're a good girl. You needn't be so frightened; I don't mean to make you work very hard. You'll have fine times with me and live like a lady; only be a good girl.

EMMELINE: My soul sickens as his eyes gaze upon me. His touch makes my very flesh creep.

LEGREE: [*Turns to Tom, and points to Sambo and Quimbo*] Ye see what ye'd get if ye'd try to run off. These yer boys have been raised to track niggers, and they'd just as soon chaw one on ye up as eat their suppers; so mind yourself. [*To Emmeline*] Come, mistress, you go in here with me. [*Taking Emmeline's hand, and leading her away*]

EMMELINE: [*Withdrawing her hand, and shrinking back*] No, no! let me work in the fields; I don't want to be a lady.

LEGREE: Oh! you're going to be contrary, are you? I'll soon take all that out of you.

EMMELINE: Kill me, if you will.

LEGREE: Oh! you want to be killed, do you? Now, come here, you Tom – you see I told you I didn't buy you jest for the common work; I mean to promote you and make a driver of you, and to-night ye may jest as well begin to get yer hand in. Now, ye jest take this yer gal, and flog her; ye've seen enough on't to know how.

TOM: I beg mas'r's pardon – hopes mas'r won't set me at that. It's what I ain't used to – never did, and can't do – no way possible.

LEGREE: Ye'll larn a pretty smart chance of things ye never did know before I've done with ye. [*Strikes Tom with whip, three blows.*

Music chord each blow] There! now will ye tell me ye can't do it?

TOM: Yes, mas'r! I'm willing to work night and day, and work while there's life and breath in me; but this yer thing I can't feel it right to do, and, mas'r I *never* shall do it, *never!*

LEGREE: What! ye black beast! tell *me* ye don't think it right to do what I tell ye! What have any of you cussed cattle to do with thinking what's right? I'll put a stop to it. Why, what do ye think ye are? Maybe ye think yer a gentleman, master Tom, to be telling your master what's right and what ain't! So you pretend it's wrong to flog the gal?

TOM: I think so, mas'r; 'twould be downright cruel, and it's what I never will do, mas'r. If you mean to kill me, kill me; but as to raising my hand agin any one here, I never shall – I'll die first!

LEGREE: Well, here's a pious dog at last, let down among us sinners – powerful holy critter he must be. Here, you rascal! you make believe to be so pious, didn't you never read out of your Bible, "Servants, obey your masters?" Ain't I your master? Didn't I pay twelve hundred dollars, cash, for all there is inside your cussed old black shell? Ain't you mine, body and soul?

TOM: No, no! My soul ain't yours, mas'r; you haven't bought it – ye can't buy it; it's been bought and paid for by one that is able to keep it, and you can't harm it!

LEGREE: I can't? we'll see, we'll see! Here, Sambo! Quimbo! give this dog such a breaking in as he won't get over this month!

EMMELINE: Oh, no! you will not be so cruel – have some mercy! [*Clings to Tom*]

LEGREE: Mercy? you won't find any in this shop! Away with the black cuss! Flog him within an inch of his life!

Sambo and Quimbo seize Tom and drag him up stage. Legree seizes Emmeline, and throws her. – She falls on her knees, with her hands lifted in supplication. – Legree raises his whip, as if to strike Tom. – Picture

Scene 4

Plain Chamber. Enter Ophelia, followed by Topsy.

OPHELIA: A person inquiring for me, did you say, Topsy?

TOPSY: Yes, missis.

OPHELIA: What kind of a looking man is he?

TOPSY: By golly! he's very queer looking man, anyway; and den he talks so dre'ful funny. What does you think? – yah! yah! he wanted to 'xibite me as de woolly gal! yah! yah!

OPHELIA: Oh! I understand. Some cute Yankee, who wants to purchase you, to make a show of – the heartless wretch!

TOPSY: Dat's just him, missis; dat's just his name. He tole me dat it was Cute – Mr. Cute Speculashum – dat's him.

OPHELIA: What did you say to him, Topsy?

TOPSY: Well, I didn't say much; it was brief and to the point – I tole him I wouldn't leave you, Miss Feely, no how.

OPHELIA: That's right, Topsy; you know you are very comfortable here – you wouldn't fare quite so well if you went away among strangers.

TOPSY: By golly! I know dat; you takes care on me, and makes me good. I don't steal any now, and I don't swar, and I don't dance breakdowns. Oh! I isn't so wicked as I used to was.

OPHELIA: That's right, Topsy; now show the gentleman, or whatever he is, up.

TOPSY: By golly! I guess he won't make much out of Miss Feely. [Exit]

OPHELIA: I wonder who this person can be? Perhaps it is some old acquaintance, who has heard of my arrival, and who comes on a social visit.

Enter Cute

CUTE: Aunt, how do ye do? Well, I swan, the sight of you is good for weak eyes. [Offers his hand]

OPHELIA: [Coldly drawing back] Really, sir, I can't say that I ever had the pleasure of seeing you before.

CUTE: Well, it's a fact that you never did. You see I never happened to be in your neighbourhood afore now. Of course you've heard of me? I'm one of the Cutes – Gumption Cute, the first and only son of Josiah and Maria Cute, of Oniontown, on the Onion river, in the north part of this ere State of Varmount.

OPHELIA: Can't say I ever heard the name before.

CUTE: Well then, I calculate your memory must be a little ricketty. I'm a relation of yours.

OPHELIA: A relation of mine! Why, I never heard of any Cutes in our family.

CUTE: Well, I shouldn't wonder if you never did. Don't you remember your niece, Mary?

OPHELIA: Of course I do. What a shiftless question!

CUTE: Well, you see, my second cousin, Abijah Blake, married her; so you see that makes me a relation of yours.

OPHELIA: Rather a distant one, I should say.

CUTE: By chowder! I'm *near* enough, just at present.

OPHELIA: Well, you certainly are a sort of connection of mine.

CUTE: Yes, kind of sort of.

OPHELIA: And of course you are welcome to my house, as long as you choose to make it your home.

CUTE: By chowder! I'm booked for the next six months – this isn't a bad speculation.

OPHELIA: I hope you left all your folks well at home?

CUTE: Well, yes, they're pretty comfortably disposed of. Father and mother's dead, and Uncle Josh has gone to California. I am the only representative of the Cutes left.

OPHELIA: There doesn't seem to be a great deal of *you* left. I declare, you are positively in rags.

CUTE: Well, you see, the fact is, I've been speculating – trying to get bank-notes – specie-rags, as they say – but I calculate I've turned out rags of another sort.

OPHELIA: I'm sorry for your ill luck, but I am afraid you have been shiftless.

CUTE: By chowder! I've done all that a fellow could do. You see, somehow, everything I take hold of kind of bursts up.

OPHELIA: Well, well, perhaps you'll do better for the future; make yourself at home. I have got to see to some household matters, so excuse me for a short time. [Aside] Impudent and shiftless! [Exit]

CUTE: By chowder! I rather guess that this speculation will hitch. She's a good-natured old critter; I reckon I'll be a son to her while she lives, and take care of her valuables arter she's a defunct departed. I wonder if they keep the vittles in this ere room? Guess not. I've got extensive accommodations for all sorts of eatables. I'm a regular vacuum, throughout – pockets and all. I'm chuck full of emptiness. [Looks *out*] Holloa! who's this elderly individual coming upstairs? He looks like a compound essence of starch and dignity. I wonder if he isn't another relation of mine. I should like a rich old fellow now for an uncle.

Enter Deacon Perry

DEACON: Ha! a stranger here!

CUTE: How d'ye do?

DEACON: You are a friend to Miss Ophelia, I presume?

CUTE: Well, I rather calculate that I am a leetle more than a friend.

DEACON: [*Aside*] Bless me! what can he mean b· those mysterious words? Can he be her – no, I don't think he can. She said she wasn't – well, at all events, it's very suspicious.

CUTE: The old fellow seems kind of stuck up.

DEACON: You are a particular friend to Miss Ophelia, you say?

CUTE: Well, I calculate I am.

DEACON: Bound to her by any tender tie?

CUTE: It's something more than a tie – it's a regular double-twisted knot.

DEACON: Ah! just as I suspected. [*Aside*] Might I inquire the nature of that tie?

CUTE: Well, it's the natural tie of relationship.

DEACON: A relation – what relation!

CUTE: Why, you see, my second cousin, Abijah Blake, married her niece, Mary.

DEACON: Oh! is that all?

CUTE: By chowder, ain't that enough?

DEACON: Then you are not her husband?

CUTE: To be sure I ain't. What put that 'ere idea into your cranium?

DEACON: [*Shaking him vigorously by the hand*] My dear sir, I'm delighted to see you.

CUTE: Holloa! you ain't going slightly insane, are you?

DEACON: No, no fear of that; I'm only happy, that's all.

CUTE: I wonder if he's been taking a nipper?

DEACON: As you are a relation of Miss Ophelia's, I think it proper that I should make you my confidant; in fact, let you into a little scheme that I have lately conceived.

CUTE: Is it a speculation?

DEACON: Well, it is, just at present; but I trust before many hours to make it a surety.

CUTE: By chowder! I hope it won't serve you the way my speculations have served me. But fire away, old boy, and give us the prospectus.

DEACON: Well, then, my young friend, I have been thinking, ever since Miss Ophelia returned to Vermont, that she was just the person to fill the place of my lamented Molly.

CUTE: Say, you couldn't tell us who your lamented Molly was, could you?

DEACON: Why, the late Mrs. Perry, to be sure.

CUTE: Oh! then the lamented Molly was your wife?

DEACON: She was.

CUTE: And now you wish to marry Miss Ophelia?

DEACON: Exactly.

CUTE: [*Aside*] Consarn this old porpoise! if I let him do that he'll Jew me out of my living. By chowder, I'll put a spoke in his wheel.

DEACON: Well, what do you say? will you intercede for me with your aunt?

CUTE: No! bust me up if I do!

DEACON: No?

CUTE: No, I tell you. I forbid the bans. Now, ain't you a purty individual, to talk about getting married, you old superannuated Methuselah specimen of humanity! Why, you've got one foot in eternity already, and t'other ain't fit to stand on. Go home and go to bed! have your head shaved, and send for a lawyer to make your will; leave your property to your heirs – if you hain't got any, why leave it to me – I'll take care of it, and charge nothing for the trouble.

DEACON: Really, sir, this language, to one of my standing, is highly indecorous – it's more, sir, than I feel willing to endure, sir. I shall expect an explanation, sir.

CUTE: Now, you see, old gouty toes, you're losing your temper.

DEACON: Sir, I'm a deacon; I never lost my temper in all my life, sir.

CUTE: Now, you see, you're getting excited; you had better go; we can't have a disturbance here!

DEACON: No, sir! I shall not go, sir! I shall not go until I have seen Miss Ophelia. I wish to know if she will countenance this insult.

CUTE: Now keep cool, old stick-in-the-mud! Draw it mild, old timber-toes!

DEACON: Damn it all, sir, what –

CUTE: Oh! only think, now, what would people say to hear a deacon swearing like a trooper?

DEACON: Sir – I – you – this is too much, sir.

CUTE: Well, now, I calculate that's just about my opinion, so we'll have no more of it. Get out of this! start your boots, or by chowder! I'll pitch you from one end of the stairs to the other.

Enter Ophelia

OPHELIA: Hoity toity! What's the meaning of all these loud words?

CUTE: } *Together* { Well, you see, Aunt —
DEACON: } *Together* { Miss Ophelia, I beg —

CUTE: Now, look here, you just hush your yap! How can I fix up matters if you keep jabbering?

OPHELIA: Silence! for shame, Mr. Cute. Is that the way you speak to the deacon?

CUTE: Darn the deacon!

OPHELIA: Deacon Perry, what is all this?

DEACON: Madam, a few words will explain everything. Hearing from this person that he was your nephew, I ventured to tell him that I cherished hopes of making you my wife, whereupon he flew into a violent passion, and ordered me out of the house.

OPHELIA: Does this house belong to you or me, Mr. Cute?

CUTE: Well, to you, I reckon.

OPHELIA: Then how dare you give orders in it?

CUTE: Well, I calculated you wouldn't care about marrying old half-a-century there.

OPHELIA: That's enough; I will marry him; and as for you [*Points to the right*] get out.

CUTE: Get out?

OPHELIA: Yes; the sooner the better.

CUTE: Darned if I don't serve him out first though.

Cute makes a dash at Deacon, who gets behind Ophelia. Topsy enters with a broom and beats Cute around stage. – Ophelia faints in Deacon's arms. – Cute falls, and Topsy butts him keeling him over. – Quick drop

End of Act V

ACT VI. Scene 1

Dark Landscape. – An old, roofless shed. Tom is discovered in shed, lying on some old cotton bagging. Cassy kneels by his side, holding a cup to his lips.

CASSY: Drink all ye want. I knew how it would be. It isn't the first time I've been out in the night, carrying water to such as you.

TOM: [*Returning cup*] Thank you, missis.

CASSY: Don't call me missis. I'm a miserable slave like yourself – a lower one than you can ever be! It's no use, my poor fellow, this

you've been trying to do. You were a brave fellow. You had the right on your side; but it's all in vain for you to struggle. You are in the Devil's hands: he is the strongest, and you must give up.

TOM: Oh! how can I give up?

CASSY: You see *you* don't know anything about it; I do. Here you are, on a lone plantation, ten miles from any other, in the swamps; not a white person here who could testify, if you were burned alive. There's no law here that can do you, or any of us, the least good; and this man! there's no earthly thing that he is not bad enough to do. I could make one's hair rise, and their teeth chatter, if I should only tell what I've seen and been knowing to here; and it's no use resisting! Did I *want* to live with him? Wasn't I a woman delicately bred? and he! – Father in Heaven! what was he and is he? And yet I've lived with him these five years, and cursed every moment of my life, night and day.

TOM: Oh, heaven! have you quite forgot us poor critters?

CASSY: And what are these miserable low dogs you work with, that you should suffer on their account? Every one of them would turn against you the first time they get a chance. They are all of them as low and cruel to each other as they can be; there's no use in your suffering to keep from hurting them!

TOM: What made 'em cruel? If I give out, I shall get used to it and grow, little by little, just like 'em. No, no, missis, I've lost everything, wife, and children, and home, and a kind master, and he would have set me free if he'd only lived a day longer – I've lost everything in *this* world, and now I can't lose heaven, too; no, I can't get to be wicked besides all.

CASSY: But it can't be that He will lay sin to our account; He won't charge it to us when we are forced to it; He'll charge it to them that drove us to it. Can I do anything more for you? Shall I give you some more water?

TOM: Oh missis! I wish you'd go to Him who can give you living waters!

CASSY: Go to Him! Where is He? Who is He?

TOM: Our Heavenly Father!

CASSY: I used to see the picture of Him, over the altar, when I was a girl; but *He isn't here!* There's nothing here but sin, and long, long despair! There, there, don't talk any more, my poor fellow. Try to sleep, if you can. I must hasten back, lest my absence be noted. Think of me when I am gone, Uncle Tom, and pray, pray for me.

Exit Cassy. – Tom sinks back to sleep

Scene 2

Street in New Orleans. Enter George Shelby.

GEORGE: At length my mission of mercy is nearly finished; I have reached my journey's end. I have now but to find the house of Mr. St. Clare, re-purchase old Uncle Tom, and convey him back to his wife and children, in old Kentucky. Some one approaches; he may, perhaps, be able to give me the information I require. I will accost him.

Enter Marks

Pray, sir, can you tell me where Mr. St. Clare dwells?

MARKS: Where I don't think you'll be in a hurry to seek him.

GEORGE: And where is that?

MARKS: In the grave!

GEORGE: Stay, sir! you may be able to give me some information concerning Mr. St. Clare.

MARKS: I beg pardon, sir, I am a lawyer; I can't afford to *give* anything.

GEORGE: But you would have no objections to selling it?

MARKS: Not the slightest.

GEORGE: What do you value it at?

MARKS: Well, say five dollars, that's reasonable.

GEORGE: There they are. [*Gives money*] Now answer me to the best of your ability. Has the death of St. Clare caused his slaves to be sold?

MARKS: It has.

GEORGE: How were they sold?

MARKS: At auction – they went dirt cheap.

GEORGE: How were they bought – all in one lot?

MARKS: No, they went to different bidders.

GEORGE: Was you present at the sale?

MARKS: I was.

GEORGE: Do you remember seeing a negro among them called Tom?

MARKS: What, Uncle Tom?

GEORGE: The same – who bought him?

MARKS: A Mr. Legree.

GEORGE: Where is his plantation?

MARKS: Up in Louisiana, on the Red River; but a man never could find it unless he had been there before.

GEORGE: Who could I get to direct me there?

MARKS: Well, stranger, I don't know of any one just at present, 'cept myself, could find it for you; it's such an out-of-the-way sort of hole; and if you are a mind to come down handsomely, why, I'll do it.

GEORGE: The reward shall be ample.

MARKS: Enough said, stranger; let's take the steamboat at once. [*Exeunt*]

Scene 3

A Rough Chamber. Enter Legree. – Sits.

LEGREE: Plague on that Sambo, to kick up this yer row between me and the new hands.

Cassy steals on, and stands behind him

The fellow won't be fit to work for a week now, right in the press of the season.

CASSY: Yes, just like you.

LEGREE: Hah! you she-devil! you've come back, have you? [*Rises*]

CASSY: Yes, I have; come to have my own way, too.

LEGREE: You lie, you jade! I'll be up to my word. Either you behave yourself, or stay down in the quarters and fare and work with the rest.

CASSY: I'd rather, ten thousand times, live in the dirtiest hole in the quarters, than be under your hoof!

LEGREE: But you are under my hoof, for all that, that's one comfort; so sit down here and listen to reason. [*Grasps her wrist*]

CASSY: Simon Legree, take care! [*Legree lets go his hold*] You're afraid of me, Simon, and you've reason to be; for I've got the Devil in me!

LEGREE: I believe to my soul you have. After all, Cassy, why can't you be friends with me, as you used to?

CASSY: [*Bitterly*] Used to!

LEGREE: I wish, Cassy, you'd behave yourself decently.

CASSY: *You* talk about behaving decently! and what have you been doing? You haven't even sense enough to keep from spoiling one of your best hands, right in the most pressing season, just for your devilish temper.

LEGREE: I was a fool, it's a fact, to let any such

brangle come up; but when Tom set up his will he had to be broke in.

CASSY: You'll never break *him* in.

LEGREE: Won't I? I'd like to know if I won't! He'll be the first nigger that ever come it round me! I'll break every bone in his body but he shall give up.

Enter Sambo, with a paper in his hand; he stands bowing

LEGREE: What's that, you dog?

SAMBO: It's a witch thing, mas'r.

LEGREE: A what?

SAMBO: Something that niggers gits from witches. Keep 'em from feeling when they's flogged. He had it tied round his neck with a black string.

Legree takes the paper and opens it. – A silver dollar drops on the stage, and a long curl of light hair twines around his finger

LEGREE: Damnation. [*Stamping and writhing, as if the hair burned him*] Where did this come from? Take it off! burn it up! burn it up! [*Throws the curl away*] What did you bring it to me for?

SAMBO: [*Trembling*] I beg pardon, mas'r; I thought you would like to see 'um.

LEGREE: Don't you bring me any more of your devilish things. [*Shakes his fist at Sambo who runs off. – Legree kicks the dollar after him*] Blast it! where did he get that? If it didn't look just like – whoo! I thought I'd forgot that. Curse me if I think there's any such thing as forgetting anything, any how.

CASSY: What is the matter with you, Legree? What is there in a simple curl of fair hair to appal a man like you – you who are familiar with every form of cruelty.

LEGREE: Cassy, to-night the past has been recalled to me – the past that I have so long and vainly striven to forget.

CASSY: Hast aught on this earth power to move a soul like thine?

LEGREE: Yes, for hard and reprobate as I now seem, there has been a time when I have been rocked on the bosom of a mother, cradled with prayers and pious hymns, my now seared brow bedewed with the waters of holy baptism.

CASSY: [*Aside*] What sweet memories of childhood can thus soften down that heart of iron?

LEGREE: In early childhood a fair-haired woman has led me, at the sound of Sabbath bells, to worship and to pray. Born of a hard-tempered sire, on whom that gentle woman had wasted a world of unvalued love, I followed in the steps of my father. Boisterous, unruly and tyrannical, I despised all her counsel, and would have none of her reproof, and, at an early age, broke from her to seek my fortunes on the sea. I never came home but once after that; and then my mother, with the yearning of a heart that must love something, and had nothing else to love, clung to me, and sought with passionate prayers and entreaties to win me from a life of sin.

CASSY: That was your day of grace, Legree; then good angels called you, and mercy held you by the hand.

LEGREE: My heart inly relented; there was a conflict, but sin got the victory, and I set all the force of my rough nature against the conviction of my conscience. I drank and swore, was wilder and more brutal than ever. And one night, when my mother, in the last agony of her despair, knelt at my feet, I spurned her from me, threw her senseless on the floor, and with brutal curses fled to my ship.

CASSY: Then the fiend took thee for his own.

LEGREE: The next I heard of my mother was one night while I was carousing among drunken companions. A letter was put in my hands. I opened it, and a lock of long, curling hair fell from it, and twined about my fingers, even as that lock twined but now. The letter told me that my mother was dead, and that dying she blest and forgave me! [*Buries his face in his hands*]

CASSY: Why did you not even then renounce your evil ways?

LEGREE: There is a dread, unhallowed necromancy of evil, that turns things sweetest and holiest to phantoms of horror and affright. That pale, loving mother, – her dying prayers, her forgiving love, – wrought in my demoniac heart of sin only as a damning sentence, bringing with it a fearful looking for of judgment and fiery indignation.

CASSY: And yet you would not strive to avert the doom that threatened you.

LEGREE: I burned the lock of hair and I burned the letter; and when I saw them hissing and crackling in the flame, inly shuddered as I thought of everlasting fires! I tried to drink and revel, and swear away the memory; but often in the deep night, whose solemn stillness arraigns the soul in forced communion with it-self, I have seen that pale mother rising by my bed-side, and felt the soft twining of that hair around my fingers, 'till the cold sweat would roll down my face, and I would spring from my bed in horror – horror! [*Falls in chair. – After a pause*] What the devil ails me? Large drops of sweat stand on my forehead, and my heart beats heavy and thick with fear. I thought I saw something white rising and glimmering in the gloom before me, and it seemed to bear my mother's face! I know one thing; I'll let that fellow Tom alone, after this. What did I want with his cussed paper? I be-lieve I am bewitched sure enough! I've been shivering and sweating ever since! Where did he get that hair? It couldn't have been that! I *burn'd* that up, I know I did! It would be a joke if hair could rise from the dead! I'll have Sambo and Quimbo up here to sing and dance one of their dances, and keep off these horrid notions. Here, Sambo! Quimbo! [*Exit*]

CASSY: Yes, Legree, that golden tress was charmed; each hair had in it a spell of terror and remorse for thee, and was used by a might-ier power to bind thy cruel hands from in-flicting uttermost evil on the helpless! [*Exit*]

Scene 4

Street. Enter Marks, meeting Cute, who en-ters, dressed in an old faded uniform.

MARKS: By the land, stranger, but it strikes me that I've seen you somewhere before.

CUTE: By chowder! do you know now, that's just what I was a going to say?

MARKS: Isn't your name Cute?

CUTE: You're right, I calculate. Yours is Marks, I reckon.

MARKS: Just so.

CUTE: Well, I swow, I'm glad to see you. [*They shake hands*] How's your wholesome?

MARKS: Hearty as ever. Well, who would have thought of ever seeing you again. Why, I thought you was in Vermont?

CUTE: Well, so I was. You see I went there after that rich relation of mine – but the speculation didn't turn out well.

MARKS: How so?

CUTE: Why, you see, she took a shine to an old fellow – Deacon Abraham Perry – and mar-ried him.

MARKS: Oh, that rather put your nose out of joint in that quarter.

CUTE: Busted me right up, I tell you. The dea-con did the handsome thing, though; he said if I would leave the neighbourhood and go out South again, he'd stand the damage. I calcu-late I didn't give him much time to change his mind, and so, you see, here I am again.

MARKS: What are you doing in that soldier rig?

CUTE: Oh, this is my sign.

MARKS: Your sign?

CUTE: Yes; you see, I'm engaged just at present in an all-fired good speculation; I'm a Fillibust-erow.

MARKS: A what?

CUTE: A fillibusterow! Don't you know what that is? It's Spanish for Cuban Volunteer; and means a chap that goes the whole porker for glory and all that ere sort of thing.

MARKS: Oh! you've joined the order of the Lone Star!

CUTE: You've hit it. You see I bought this uniform at a second-hand clothing store; I puts it on and goes to a benevolent individual and I says to him – appealing to his feelings – I'm one of the fellows that went to Cuba and got massacred by the bloody Spaniards. I'm in a destitute condition – give me a trifle to pay my passage back, so I can whop the tyrannical cusses and avenge my brave fellow soger what got slewed there.

MARKS: How pathetic!

CUTE: I tell you it works up the feelings of be-nevolent individuals dreadfully. It draws tears from their eyes and money from their pockets. By chowder! one old chap gave me a hundred dollars to help on the cause.

MARKS: I admire a genius like yours.

CUTE: But I say, what are you up to?

MARKS: I am the travelling companion of a young gentleman by the name of Shelby, who is going to the plantation of a Mr. Legree, on the Red River, to buy an old darkey who used to belong to his father.

CUTE: Legree – Legree? Well, now, I calculate I've heard that ere name afore.

MARKS: Do you remember that man who drew a bowie knife on you in New Orleans?

CUTE: By chowder! I remember the circumstance just as well as if it was yesterday; but I can't say that I recollect much about the man, for you see I was in something of a hurry about that time and didn't stop to take a good look at him.

MARKS: Well, that man was this same Mr. Legree.

CUTE: Do you know, now, I should like to pay that critter off?

MARKS: Then I'll give you an opportunity.

CUTE: Chowder! how will you do that?

MARKS: Do you remember the gentleman that interfered between you and Legree?

CUTE: Yes – well?

MARKS: He received the blow that was intended for you, and died from the effects of it. So, you see, Legree is a murderer, and we are the only witnesses of the deed. His life is in our hands.

CUTE: Let's have him right up and make him dance on nothing to the tune of Yankee Doodle!

MARKS: Stop a bit. Don't you see a chance for a profitable speculation?

CUTE: A speculation! Fire away, don't be bashful; I'm the man for a speculation.

MARKS: I have made a deposition to the Governor of the State of all the particulars of that affair at Orleans.

CUTE: What did you do that for?

MARKS: To get a warrant for his arrest.

CUTE: Oh! and have you got it?

MARKS: Yes; here it is. [*Takes out paper*]

CUTE: Well, now, I don't see how you are going to make anything by that bit of paper?

MARKS: But I do. I shall say to Legree, I have got a warrant against you for murder; my friend, Mr. Cute, and myself are the only witnesses who can appear against you. Give us a thousand dollars, and we will tear up the warrant and be silent.

CUTE: Then Mr. Legree forks over a thousand dollars, and your friend Cute pockets five hundred of it. Is that the calculation?

MARKS: If you will join me in the undertaking.

CUTE: I'll do it, by chowder!

MARKS: Your hand to bind the bargain.

CUTE: I'll stick by you thro' thick and thin.

MARKS: Enough said.

CUTE: Then shake. [*They shake hands*]

MARKS: But I say, Cute, he may be contrary and show fight.

CUTE: Never mind, we've got the law on our side, and we're bound to stir him up. If he don't come down handsomely, we'll present him with a neck-tie made of hemp!

MARKS: I declare you're getting spunky.

CUTE: Well, I reckon I am. Let's go and have something to drink. Tell you what, Marks, if we don't get *him*, we'll have his hide, by chowder! [*Exeunt, arm in arm*]

Scene 5

Rough Chamber. Enter Legree, followed by Sambo.

LEGREE: Go and send Cassy to me.

SAMBO: Yes, mas'r. [*Exit*]

LEGREE: Curse the woman! she's got a temper worse than the devil! I shall do her an injury one of these days, if she isn't careful.

Re-enter Sambo, frightened

What's the matter with you, you black scoundrel?

SAMBO: S'help me, mas'r, she isn't dere.

LEGREE: I suppose she's about the house somewhere?

SAMBO: No, she isn't, mas'r; I's been all over de house and I can't find nothing of her nor Emmeline.

LEGREE: Bolted, by the Lord! Call out the dogs! Saddle my horse! Stop! are you sure they really have gone?

SAMBO: Yes, mas'r; I's been in every room 'cept the haunted garret, and dey wouldn't go dere.

LEGREE: I have it! Now, Sambo, you jest go and walk that Tom up here, right away! [*Exit Sambo*] The old cuss is at the bottom of this yer whole matter; and I'll have it out of his infernal black hide, or I'll know the reason why! I *hate* him – I *hate* him! And isn't he *mine*? Can't I do what I like with him? Who's to hinder, I wonder?

Tom is dragged on by Sambo and Quimbo

LEGREE: [*Grimly confronting Tom*] Well, Tom, do you know I've made up my mind to *kill* you?

TOM: It's very likely, Mas'r.

LEGREE: I – have – done – just – that – thing, Tom, unless you tell me what do you know about these yer gals? [*Tom is silent*] D'ye hear? Speak!

TOM: I hain't got anything to tell, mas'r.

LEGREE: Do you dare to tell me, you old black

rascal, you don't know? Speak! Do you know anything?

TOM: I know, mas'r; but I can't tell anything. *I can die!*

LEGREE: Hark ye, Tom! ye think, 'cause I have let you off before, I don't mean what I say; but, this time, I have made *up my mind*, and counted the cost. You've always stood it out agin me; now, I'll *conquer ye or kill ye!* one or t'other. I'll count every drop of blood there is in you, and take 'em, one by one, 'till ye give up!

TOM: Mas'r, if you was sick, or in trouble, or dying, and I could save, I'd *give* you my heart's blood; and, if taking every drop of blood in this poor old body would save your precious soul, I'd give 'em freely. Do the worst you can, my troubles will be over soon; but if you don't repent, yours won't never end.

Legree strikes Tom down with the butt of his whip

LEGREE: How do you like that?

SAMBO: He's most gone, mas'r!

TOM: [*Rises feebly on his hands*] There ain't no more you can do! I forgive you with all my soul.

Sinks back, and is carried off by Sambo and Quimbo

LEGREE: I believe he's done for finally. Well, his mouth is shut up at last – that's one comfort.

Enter George Shelby, Marks and Cute
Strangers! Well, what do you want?

GEORGE: I understand that you bought in New Orleans a negro named Tom?

LEGREE: Yes, I did buy such a fellow, and a devil of a bargain I had of it, too! I believe he's trying to die, but I don't know as he'll make it out.

GEORGE: Where is he? Let me see him!

SAMBO: Dere he is! [*Points to Tom*]

LEGREE: How dare you speak? [*Drives Sambo and Quimbo off. – George exits*]

CUTE: Now's the time to nab him.

MARKS: How are you, Mr. Legree?

LEGREE: What the devil brought you here?

MARKS: This little bit of paper. I arrest you for the murder of Mr. St. Clare. What do you say to that?

LEGREE: This is my answer! [*Makes a blow at Marks, who dodges, and Cute receives the blow – he cries out and runs off. Marks fires at Legree, and follows Cute*] I am hit! – the game's up! [*Falls dead. Quimbo and Sambo return and carry him off laughing*]

George Shelby enters, supporting Tom. – Music. They advance and Tom falls, centre

GEORGE: Oh! dear Uncle Tom! do wake – do speak once more! look up! Here's Master George – your own little Master George. Don't you know me?

TOM: [*Opening his eyes and speaking in a feeble tone*] Mas'r George! Bless de Lord! it's all I wanted! They hav'n't forgot me! It warms my soul; it does my old heart good! Now I shall die content!

GEORGE: You sha'n't die! you mustn't die, nor think of it. I have come to buy you, and take you home.

TOM: Oh, Mas'r George, you're too late. The Lord has bought me, and is going to take me home.

GEORGE: Oh! don't die. It will kill me – it will break my heart to think what you have suffered, poor, poor fellow!

TOM: Don't call me poor fellow. I *have* been poor fellow; but that's all past and gone now. I'm right in the door, going into glory! Oh, Mas'r George! *Heaven has come!* I've got the victory! the Lord has given it to me! Glory be to His name! [*Dies*]

Solemn music. – George covers Uncle Tom with his cloak, and kneels over him. Clouds work on and conceal them, and then work off

Scene 6

Gorgeous clouds, tinted with sunlight. Eva, robed in white, is discovered on the back of a milk-white dove, with expanded wings, as if just soaring upward. Her hands are extended in benediction over St. Clare and Uncle Tom, who are kneeling and gazing up to her. Impressive music. – Slow curtain.

The End

PO-CA-HON-TAS

OR

THE GENTLE SAVAGE

JOHN BROUGHAM

ON August 22, 1951, the *London Times* weekly edition reported that "several letters have appeared in *The Times* concerning the threatened demolition of St. George's Church at Gravesend, where rest the remains of Pocahontas, Chief Powhatan's 'most deare and wel-beloved daughter' commemorated by two stained windows set up in her memory by the Virginia Chapter of the Society of Colonial Dames." Apparently the campaign to perpetuate the memory of this first American woman to settle in England was successful. In November, 1952, with British and American flags hanging side by side, another old Virginian, Lady Astor, inaugurated the new chancel as "a symbolic shrine of Anglo-American relations." Americans, probably even more than the British, have forgotten that Pocahontas was an illustrious personage. When she had married John Rolfe, James I had been greatly disturbed to think that a mere commoner had had the audacity to marry a princess, daughter of the mighty Prince Powhatan, Emperor of Virginia. The King recognized her high station, and after she and her husband and her son Thomas[1] moved to England in 1616, she was frequently a guest at Court. On January 6, 1617, for example, she attended the King and Queen when Ben Jonson's *Masque of Christmas* was acted in the banqueting chamber at Whitehall.

When John Brougham created his irreverent nineteenth-century memorial to the Indian Princess, *Po-ca-hon-tas, or The Gentle Savage*, he neither knew nor cared about her real-life quality. He wished only to poke fun at the "noble savages" who had strutted more than their hour on the American stage.

John Brougham, a mid-nineteenth-century combination of W. C. Fields and George S. Kaufman, was born in Dublin on May 9, 1810. He received his early education at Dr. Hamilton's school in the town of Trim and then went on to Trinity College, Dublin. Here he moved with a gay, unstudious crowd

[1]Among her later descendants are Lady Mountbatten, the second Mrs. Woodrow Wilson, and Lord Baden-Powell.

who performed private theatricals. Brougham reported on their casting system: "The names of characters were written on pieces of paper which were folded and thrown into a hat. Each of the aspirants drew out a slip, and whatever part fell to him he had to accept without a word. I felt no particular desire to incur much responsibility in the way of study; therefore the smallest parts suited me best. When I got too big a part, I traded it off." In July, 1830, after graduating from Trinity College, he went to London, intending to study medicine, but instead he became an actor at the Tottenham Street Theatre. Brougham's theatrical career advanced rapidly. After appearances at the Olympic, under the guidance of Madame Vestris, and at Covent Garden and other London theatres, he became lessee of the Lyceum Theatre in 1840. In 1842 he and his wife, the actress Emma Williams, sailed for America and made their initial appearance at the Park Theatre on October 4, 1842, in *His Last Legs*.

After a short tour of the principal theatre centers, Albany, Chicago, and St. Louis, he returned to New York and in 1848 became the stage manager of Burton's Chambers Street Theatre. Brougham found in Burton just the theatrical compatibility he enjoyed, and together they became famous for their many impromptu interpolations. In 1850 Brougham's Broadway Lyceum (afterwards Wallack's) was built for him by J. M. Trimble and E. P. Christy, and on December 23 of that year the new playhouse was opened with one of the theatrical hodge-podges for which Brougham became famous, entitled simply "Brougham and Company." Brougham's management did not prosper, and through some legal maneuvering he lost the theatre in 1852. However, he stayed on in the same location under improved financial circumstances. As author and actor he is reported to have been paid $250 a week by Wallack, "the largest salary then paid any artist in a regular New York company." For the season of 1856–57, he took another turn at management at the old Bowery Theatre, but in the spring he was back at Wallack's Theatre for three seasons of what he later described as the "brightest part of my artist's life." During this period he was also acting at Burton's Theatre. In 1860, after a farewell performance of *Po-ca-hon-tas* at Niblo's, he returned to London, where he remained during the war years.

Brougham was back in the States in 1865, playing first at the Winter Garden and then at Augustin Daly's Fifth Avenue (later the Madison Square) Theatre. Although Brougham continued performing and writing and took still another brief turn at management in 1869, his last years, like those of so many other actors and playwrights, were notable for their lack of prosperity. Brougham attributed his misfortune to audiences who were no longer appreciative of the best things: "they pay high prices for small matters." In 1878 his friends got up two benefits for him: one at the Academy of Music on January

17, 1878, which netted $9,394.41, and another (a matinee) at Wallack's, which brought in $884.15. His sponsors wisely invested these proceeds in an annuity. Brougham made his last stage appearance at Booth's Theatre in Boucicault's *Felix O'Reilly* on October 25, 1879, and died on June 7, 1880.

Brougham's own appraisal of his career was forthright and essentially true to fact. He wrote:

Everything by turns and nothing long. I have been a little of a painter, a little of a doctor, a little of a musician, and indulged for a brief period in the insane dash at comic journalism – and all without a scintillation of business capacity, but with unbounded confidence in everybody who made pleasant promises. A somewhat antagonistic and wholly unproductive combination.

Few actors have received the personal acclaim accorded Brougham; still fewer have been so deserving of praise and honor. Brougham was richly endowed. He was genial, jovial, hearty, handsome, immensely popular, dashing, clever, and always stylishly dressed. His robust, well-padded figure was not that of a twentieth-century matinee-idol type; yet he possessed all the personal magnetism of that breed plus an uncommon versatility in the playing of comedy.

Brougham was not a behind-the-proscenium, peephole-stage, realistic actor. He was familiar in manner, forever introducing interpolations into the texts, and continually joshing with the audience, much to his delight and theirs, if frequently to the critics' disgust. Many spectators attended the theatre just to hear his impromptu "before-the-curtain" speeches. He ignored the critics' protests of "impropriety" and gave the audience what they wanted. He brought himself to the audience and frequently brought the audience into the play, a technique that is often regarded as a twentieth-century advance in playwriting. In his *Row at the Lyceum* (1851), for example, the opening scene showed a cast rehearsing for a play. Suddenly a Quaker gentleman in the audience leaped from his seat and, pointing at the leading lady in the play, shouted, "My wife! Come off that stage, thou miserable woman!" A fireman in the audience tried to subdue the man, but the righteous Quaker threw him off and ran down the aisle and onto the stage screaming abuses at his actress wife. All of this startling and seemingly real-life action turned out to be part of the play, with Brougham enacting the Quaker gentleman. Brougham had play-acting in his blood and playwriting too, as we may see if we disregard the pious critics who were annoyed at what they labeled stage improprieties and simply examine the list of plays.

Brougham's plays were comparable in number and in theatrical quality to those of Dunlap and Boucicault. He was astonishingly prolific and assuredly never designed a dramatic piece primarily for the reading public. His plays needed actors; frequently they needed him as the principal actor. His 126 dramatic pieces ranged from dramatizations of Dickens – *David Copperfield* and *Dombey and Son*, one of his most popular plays, – to gay and playful burlesques: *Columbus el Filibustro; Metamora, or The Pollywogs;* and, of course, *Po-ca-hon-tas*. There were other adaptations – *Jane Eyre* (1849) – and *Vanity Fair* (1849) – and many extravaganzas and novelties such as *The Great Tragic Revival* (1858) and *Much Ado About a Merchant of Venice* (1869). He tried Gothic melodramas: *The Gun-maker of Moscow* (1857) and *The Duke's Motto, or I Am Here* (1863); tearful melodramas: *The Dark Hour Before Dawn* (1859) and *Night and Morning* (1855); "local dramas": *The New York Merchant and His Clerks* (1843) and *New York as It Is* (1848); sensational melodramas: *The Lottery of Life* (1868) and *Minnie's Luck, or The Ups and Downs of City Life* (1870); Irish character plays: *Love and Murder* (1854) and *Take Care of Little Charley* (1858); social satire: *Romance and Reality, or The Young Virginian* (1858) and *The Game of Love* (1856). Such an output demanded haste and resulted in occasional carelessness, which Brougham willingly recognized: "I think my greatest infirmity is that I never have taken sufficient pains with my literary work. I know my shortcomings as well as anybody, and there is no use in concealing them. They are due in a measure to a great facility in composition." There were, however, constant qualities in most of his plays: rich wit and humor combined with deep pathos. As one writer has said, "There was no sourness in his disposition, no gall in his ink."

The improvisations and eccentric theatrical connivings in which he delighted might be called impromptu plays. One of the most frequently reported was that of the "no-Pocahontas" *Po-ca-hon-tas* performance. The leading actress in the play did not appear when curtain time arrived, and Brougham and Walcot improvised a *Po-ca-hon-tas* without the principal character. When Powhatan (Brougham) was asked, "Where is Pokey?" he replied, "Lost among the icebergs on Broadway [Broadway was frozen over]; but if she were here she would answer you in this way." Brougham reported that when it became necessary to join the lovers' hands in matrimony, he looked around the stage and saw a broom. Taking it boldly, he advanced to the front of the stage and, handing it to Walcot, remarked, "Take her, my boy, and be happy." The contemporary accounts all agree that this performance utterly delighted the audience.

Brougham recognized the promotional power of theatricalism off the stage as well as on. He was the first performer to attempt playing in New York and Philadelphia on the same evening. On Thursday, November 13, 1856, he performed *The Stage Struck Irishman* at the Old Bowery, commencing at 7:00. At 7:30, with a part of the company and some guests, he raced by stage for the New Jersey ferry. Leaving Jersey City at 7:52 and changing costumes on the way, he arrived at the Kensington Depot in Philadelphia at 10:00 pre-

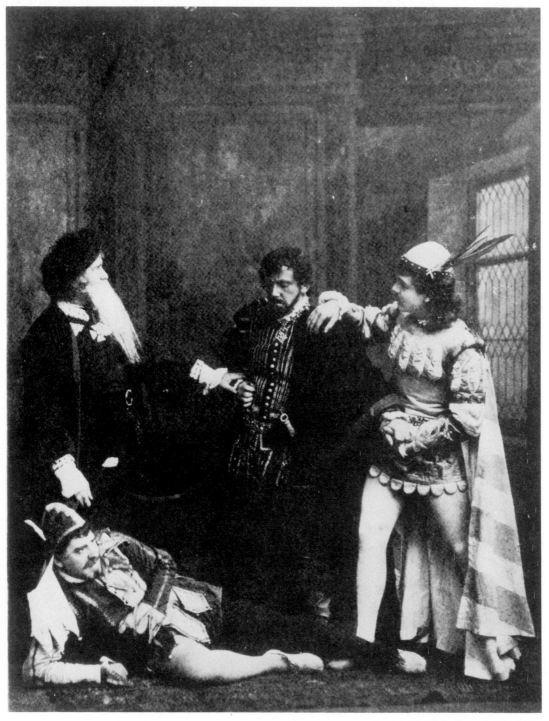

Francesca da Rimini: The Lawrence Barrett Production, 1882

Across the Continent

cisely. Another stage ride and he was at the National Theatre in Walnut Street at 10:30. The early part of the National Theatre bill, which had begun at 7:15, consisted of an equestrian drama and *The Maniac Lover*. The curtain was rung down on these at 10:15, and at 10:30 Brougham entered as Chief Powhatan. After the performance, cast and invited guests had a midnight supper at the Girard House before departing by special train for New York. On the stage and off he was always performing. As he said, "When I'm not playing I'm sick, and when I'm not sick I'm playing."

Brougham had composed *Po-ca-hon-tas*, "audaciously altering the Bancroft record," while he was flat on his back recovering from a surgical operation. According to Brougham, "It didn't make much of a sensation at first, for it was one of those things which had, as it were, to grow on an audience." One wonders what kind of "sensation" Brougham expected. After its opening at Wallack's Lyceum on December 24, 1855, *Po-ca-hon-tas* ran uninterruptedly until January 9 and then became the regular afterpiece for such diverse offerings as *The Little Treasure, Pauline, Dred, The Stranger, Damon and Pythias*, and Shakespearean tragedies. In May, October, and November, 1856, it was scheduled as a main attraction at Wallack's, the Bowery, and the National, respectively; and from then until 1884 it was *the* standard burlesque afterpiece in New York and in theatres across the country. It was also popular as a soldier show in Civil War army camps. In the almost thirty years of its stage life no theatrical season in any American city was complete without a few performances of "Pokey."

That *Po-ca-hon-tas* was highly regarded in its own time is clear from contemporary newspaper reviews. On July 14, 1860, *Music and The Drama* reported:

Po-ca-hon-tas has become a sort of theatrical deity in New York. It has been invested with eternal life by the public, and whenever and wherever it is produced it is invariably received with plenty of applause and laughter. It will become a classic. . . . Mr. Brougham performed King Powhatan with his usual vigor and humor, and introduced a variety of new gags. . . . We may be allowed to say that we think that his conversations with Mr. Cooke, the leader of the orchestra, might be curtailed a little, for although they are very amusing to those who are near enough to hear, those who are not are apt to wonder what on earth is the matter, and leave the theatre with the impression that it is very badly managed.

Evidently Brougham could not resist introducing impromptu materials into every performance. Bayard, in *The Spirit of the Times* of June 30, 1866, wrote:

Mr. Brougham has done wisely in reviving his glorious burlesque of *Po-ca-hon-tas*, as the increasing attendance shows. He has brushed up the text a little, and put in a few clever hits at things of the day, and the whole play goes off admirably. . . . Mr. Dunn's reading is too hasty and indistinct – we fail to catch the countless puns with which the whole play is crammed. All actors may profitably study the elocution of Mr. Brougham in this respect. He evidently believes that words are to be spoken and not mumbled; his clear ringing voice gives due effect to every syllable, and the auditor who fails to take in the complete sense of his lines must be dull indeed.

Burlesques were not introduced to the American theatre by John Brougham, but he certainly was the first master. In the mid-forties William Mitchell had performed a burlesque of Fanny Elssler's dance "La Tarantula" which he called "La Mosquito." In the late forties burlesques in blackface had become a regular part of the minstrel show. In the fifties Brougham had played in Burton's burlesque of *Macbeth*. Frequently the nineteenth-century theatrical burlesques were not so much satires on plays as they were comic exaggerations of popular performers. In 1861, when Joseph Jefferson burlesqued *Mazeppa* at the Winter Garden, he was ridiculing Adah Isaacs Menken's equestrian exhibition. Provocatively half-naked, Menken had been strapped to the horse for the wild ride up the precipice. A "new version of Shakespeare's masterpiece of *Hamlet*" by T. C. DeLeon, played by G. L. Fox, was directed not at Shakespeare but at Edwin Booth. And, of course, Brougham's burlesque was not aimed at Barker's *The Indian Princess* or at Custis' *Pocahontas* so much as at the blustering performance of Forrest and his company in *Metamora*. However, Brougham did not limit his attack to the principal subject. His satirical fire covered the landscape, with scattered shots leveled at such contemporary phenomena as education for women, Tammany graft, the fluctuating price of Erie railroad stock, and the use of tobacco.

Although Brougham's burlesque may seem trivial and its puns "corny," much of it, with a small allowance for changes in taste, is not far removed from the television horseplay of Sid Caesar, Red Skelton, or Jackie Gleason; and certainly, even today, it is vastly more amusing than Philip Moeller's twentieth-century version, *Pokey, or The Beautiful Legend of the Amorous Indian* (1918). Brougham's musical burlesques pointed the way for the vaudeville sketch and Broadway-revue "blackouts," as well as for current television buffooneries. Many twentieth-century performers – W. C. Fields, Bobby Clark, Bert Lahr, and Ed Wynn, in addition to the television zanies – bear a marked resemblance to Brougham. Laurence Hutton labeled him the "American Aristophanes," insisting that Brougham's burlesques of Columbus and Pocahontas were "among the best, if not the very best, burlesques in any living language." And although Brougham's ludicrous sketches may now seem like the amateur theatricals of fraternity parties and Gridiron banquets, in their day they were widely applauded on Broadway and in theatres across the country.

PO-CA-HON-TAS

OR

THE GENTLE SAVAGE

JOHN BROUGHAM

An Original Aboriginal Erratic Operatic Semi-Civilized and Demi-Savage Extravaganza, being a Per-Version of Ye Trewe and Wonderrefulle Hystorie of Ye Rennownned Princesse

The MUSIC Dislocated and Re-set by JAMES G. MAEDER, M.D.; and presented to Public Notice through the INSTRUMENTALITY OF SIGNOR LA MANNA. The SCENERY painted from daguerreotypes and other authentic documents, by MR. H. ISHERWOOD, greatly assisted by his own vivid imagination and MR. WALLACE. The COSTUMES cut from the original plates, and thoroughly· digested, by MR. T. FLANNERY, and several auxiliary thimble-riggers. The MACHINERY, Wings, Flies, and other Entomologia by MR. DEMILT, and various other philosophers. The CONSIDERABLE PROPERTIES, çrowns, sceptres, war-clubs, Indian pipes, and other regalia, by MR. TIMMANY, and his aids.

CHARACTERS

Of Ye Englyshe

CAPTAIN JOHN SMITH – *The undoubted Original, vocal and instrumental, in the settlement of Virginia, in love with Pocahontas, according to this story, though somewhat at variance with his story.*

LIEUTENANT THOMAS BROWN – *Second in Command, a hitherto neglected Genius, whose claims on posterity are now for the first time acknowledged, as is but right.*

WILLIAM JONES – *Sometimes called Bill, another of the same sort left.*

MYNHEER ROLFF – *The real Husband of Pocahontas, but dramatically divorced contrary to all law and fact.*

BENJAMIN BRACE
JOHN JUNK
HENRY HALYARD
WILLIAM BUNTLINE
BARNABAS BINNACLE

Splicers of main braces, shiverers of timbers, anathematizers of eyes and limbs, promiscuously general dealers in single combats and double hornpipes, and altogether, amazingly nautical people.

Of Ye Savages

H. J. POW-HA-TAN I. – *King of the Tuscaroras – a crotchetty Monarch, in fact, a Semi-Brave*

THE RIGHT HON. QUASH-AL-JAW – *Speaker of the Savage House of Lords. Straightener of unpleasant kinks, and oiler of troubled waters, unraveller of knotty points, adjuster of pugnacious difficulties, and Grand Eye Parliamentary Factotum and Fugleman.*

O-PO-DIL-DOC – *One of the Aboriginal F. F. V's, an indignant dignitary.*
COL-O-GOG – *Another warm-hearted and headed Son of Old Virginia the untiring.*
JIN-GO – *Sergeant at Arms – A Friend to swear by.*
KREEM-FAY-SLOON – *Bearer of Dispatches, and news carrier in ordinary.*

IP-PAH-KAK
SAS-SY-PRIL
KOD-LIV-ROYL
KAL-O-MEL
} *Medicine Men, of the Saultz and Senna-ca Tribe.*

H.R.H. PRINCESS PO-CA-HON-TAS – *The Beautiful, and very properly undutiful daughter of King Pow-Ha-Tan, married, according to the ridiculous dictum of actual circumstance, to Master Rolff, but the author flatters himself much more advantageously disposed of in the Acting edition.*

POO-TEE-PET
DI-MUN-DI
} *Interesting offshoots from aristocratic stock anterior to the First Families in Virginia.*

WEE-CHA-VEN-DA
KROS-AS-KAN-BEE
} *Embodying the rigid principles of the Tuscarora Fashionable Finishing School.*

DAH-LIN-DUK
O-YOU-JEWEL
LUV-LIE-KREETA
OSO-CHAR-MING
LUM-PA-SHUGA
} *Their "dear charges," for whom they don't forget to charge dear enough for in the Quarterly Bills.*

DRO-MAY-JAH *A high official.*

SOLDIERS, SAILORS, INDIANS,
MEMBERS OF THE TUSCARORA
LIGHT GUARD, &C.

PROLEGOMENA

The deeply interesting incident upon which this Drama is founded, occurred in Virginia, on Wednesday, Oct. 12, A.D. 1607, at twenty-six minutes past 4 in the afternoon, according to the somewhat highly colored and boastful narration of Capt. John Smith, the famous adventurer, backed by the concurrent testimony of contemporaneous history; but subsequent research has proved that either he was mistaken, or that *circumstance* had unwarrantably plagiarized an affair which transpired at a much earlier date; for, upon examining the contents of a wallet found in the vest pocket of the man in armor, dug up near Cape Cod, an entire *epic poem* was discovered upon the very same subject, which was written by a Danish Poet, the Chevalier Viking, *Long Fellow* of the Norwegian Academy of Music, who flourished Anno Gothami, 235.

The poem contains several square yards of verse, a fragment of which is subjoined to show its peculiar *Finnish*.

The Song of Pocahontas
Ask you – How about these verses?
Whence this song of Pocahontas,
With its flavor of Tobacco,
And the Stincweed – The Mundungus,

With its pipe of Old Virginny,
With the echo of the Breakdown,
With its smack of Bourbon whiskey,
With the twangle of the Banjo;
Of the Banjo – The Goatskinnet,

And the Fiddle – The Catgutto,
With the noisy Marrowbonum.
By one JONSMITH it was written,
JONSMITH, the valiant soldier,
Sailor, Buccaneer, Explorer,
Hero, Trader, Colonizer,
Gent, Adventurer, Commander,
Lawyer, Orator, and Author,
Statesman, Pioneer, and Bagman.
Years he fought against the Moslem
Years he wore the captive's fetters,
Until, from a fond sultana
He received a Habeas Corpus.

Then, by way of relaxation,
He took passage on a steamer,
With a crew of Filibusters,
Each with matchlocks and revolvers,
To take peaceable possession
Of some transatlantic region,
Sailed they on, they knew not whither,
Until, one October morning,
They incontinently blundered
On the shores of Tuscarora,
Near to WEROWANCE, the palace
Of King POWHATAN, who flourished
In that section of the country,
Whereunto they were invited
By this hospitable monarch,
And remarkably well treated;
Until, fat with rice and pumpkins,
Buckwheatcake and sweetpotatoes,
Squashes, Homminy and Doughnuts,
They began to wax audacious,
And put on such airs and graces,
They were perfectly disgusting.

Now, the natives knowing nothing
Of the benefits intended
By this foreign congregation,
Who had come so far to show them
All how much they'd been mistaken;
In what darkness they were dwelling,
And how much obliged they were to
These disinterested people,
Who had journeyed to enlighten
Their unfortunate condition.
Through these potent triunited
Anglo-Saxon civilizers,
Rum, Gunpowder, and Religion.
Now, the natives, as I mentioned,
Didn't see the joke precisely
In the way it was expected,
They believing, simple creatures,

They could manage their own matters
Without any interference –
Thought the shortest way to settle
Those gratuitous advisers
Would be quietly to knock them
On the head, like Bulls of Bashan.

It was then JONSMITH was taken
To be treated in such fashion,
Lying in a pleasant posture
On the ground, his head supported
By a chunk of Russ's pavement.
He looked round him with emotion.
King POWHATAN stood beside him,
With his battle-club tremendous,
Which around his head he flourished
To accelerate its motion,
So that when it swift descended
Upon JONSMITH's pericranium,
Then he wouldn't know what hurt him.
Thrice the fatal club was brandished,
And Jon. thought upon his mother,
Thought upon the prayer she taught him
When he first, a tiny urchin,
Bent his knee in simple wonder.
In that moment, all his childhood
Stood before him like a vision,
And he thought he was a "goner,"
When the King's remorseless purpose
Was immediately arrested
By a scream from Pocahontas,
Pocahontas, his own daughter –
She, the dove of Worocomoco,
The pride of Tuscarora,
Quickly laid her lovely tresses
On the pale cheek of the victim.
This mute eloquence of nature
To the heart of JONSMITH whispered,
You have yet a squeak, old fellow
Now, &c, &c.

ACT I. Scene 1

*Palace of Weramocomoco. Grand march of the
Tuscarora Court. King enters with a great
flourish.*

Opening Chorus
Air – "King of the Cannibal Islands"

King and Chorus
Oh! how absurd of people to prate,
About their mighty Kings so great,
They'd open their eyes to see the state
Of the King of the Tuscarora's.

As happy is he as King can be,
For from his Palace he can see,
The whole of his subjects merry and free,
So he takes his pipe contentedly,
　　　　Singing,
Smoking, joking Powhatan,
Tobacco it is the solace of man,

So let {*subjects* / *us*} *puff as long as* {*you* / *we*} *can,*
The King of the Tuscarora's.

KING: Well *roared* indeed, my jolly Tuscaroras.
Most loyal *Corps*, your King *encores* the *Chorus*.

　　　　Repeat Chorus
Bravo! We would with Shakespeare say, "that
Strain again,"
But it might strain your lungs, so we refrain.
It sooths my ear, like niggers from the South,
Stealing and giving odor; they sometimes do
both,
Or like a pipe of the Nicotian leaf,
The true Nepenthe balm for every grief,
While other joys one sense alone can measure,
This to all senses gives extatic pleasure.
You feel *the radiance of the glowing bowl,*
Hear the soft murmurs of the kindling coal,
Smell the sweet fragrance of the honey-dew,
Taste its strong pungency the palate through,
See the blue cloudlets circling to the dome,
Imprisoned skies up-floating to their home.
I like a dhudieen myself.

COLOGOG: I do not doubt it.
KING: I'll volunteer and sing a song about it.
To me 'twas by a wily Paddy whack sent,
Who had an axe to grind, hence the broad accent.

　　　　Song – King
　　　Air – "Widow Machree"

Oh, wid a dhudieen I can blow away care,
　Oh hone, wid a dhudieen!
Black thoughts and blue devils all melt into
air,
　Oh, hone! wid a dhudieen!
　If you're short any day,
　Or a note have to pay,
　And you don't know the way,
　To come out of it clean,

From your head and your heart
You can make it depart,
Oh hone! wid a dhudieen.

Oh, wid a dhudieen you recline at your ease,
　Oh, hone! wid a dhudieen!
Shut your eyes and imagine what pleasures you
　please,
　Oh, hone! wid a dhudieen!
　In dreams without sleep,
　All your senses to steep,
　While you're playing bo-peep
　Through each fairy-like scene,
　Undisturbed, I declare,
　By a single nightmare,
　Oh, hone! wid a dhudieen!

Oh, wid a dhudieen I'm as truly content,
　Oh, hone! wid a dhudieen!
What the rest of the world does I don't care a
　cent,
　Oh, hone! wid a dhudieen!
　Let some folks desire,
　To set rivers on fire,
　While some others admire,
　To run "wid de machine,"
　I've ambition enough,
　Just to sit here and puff,
　Oh, hone! wid a dhudieen!

Now that we have smoked ourself to proper
　dizziness,
Let us proceed at once to public business.
We must advance, though in the usual way,
Therefore, all laws that we made yesterday
We now repeal. We take the tax off Soap.
OPODILDOC: Soft soap, so please your majesty, I
　hope?
KING: No, no, that saponaceous article escapes
We've analyzed it with Professor Mapes,
And he told us, in terms quite scientific,
Soft soap's considered a soft soporific.
OPODILDOC: Sire, it's a lie!
ALL: Order! Order!
KING: Can we believe our eyes?
We mean our ears.
OPODILDOC: Are *not* soaps made from lyes?
KING: Oh! ah!
COLOGOG: May it please your majesty, I rise
To a question of privilege. My honorable
　friend,
Being a *hard* himself, does not intend
An insult. May I ask in the word *lie*,

What vowel do you use sir, *i* or *y?*

OPODILDOC: *Y* sir, or *i* sir, search the vowels through,
And find the one most *consonant* to *you.*

ALL: Order! Order!

COLOGOG: To keep within the limits of debate,
Who stole the funeral cloth and coffin plate?

OPODILDOC: Shut up, switch off, dry up, or go to bed!

COLOGOG: I'll fling an inkstand at your honorable head!
If you had your desert you'd dine in prison.

OPODILDOC: And you'd have an asphyxiated weazen!

KING: Hollo! no more of this! at once have done!
Confound you, do you think that you're at Washington?

OPODILDOC: My liege, in some authority I've read,
That it's within the rules to punch his head!

KING: How is it Mr. Speaker, we're in doubt?

SPEAKER: Grotius, cap. 5, sec. 3 says, fight it out.

Business, they prepare to fight
Out, out of this, some spot that none can trace,
Or *see* a *clew* to the *secluded* place.

COLOGOG: Con*clude* it done! the deadliest weapon I can find,
I'll name!

OPODILDOC: Nuff said, old top, I'll go it blind!

COLOGOG: Blind you've been all your life, and deaf and dumb!

OPODILDOC: Dum vivimus vivamus, what's your weapon?

COLOGOG: *Rum!*

A row outside. — Enter sergeant at-arms

KING: Sergeant at *arms,* say, what *alarms* the crowd?
Loud noise annoys us, why is it all*owed?*

SERGEANT: My liege, there is a band —

KING: [*Starting up*] Of Minstrels?

SERGEANT: No!
Of foreigners, just cast on Castle Garden.

KING: Oh!
For this relief, much thanks, it wouldn't pay.
That endless *bar*carole of poor Dog Tray!
Who are those folks come here, without permission.
Something a *kin* to *Kinney's* expedition!

This ranche they'd better vamouse mighty slick,
Old Nick's their destination, or *new Nic,*
Arauga, here they must not bore us,
As at *Sonora* with their bash *Sonorous,*
Conquering lands without a single resident,
Such a *Republic's* clearly without *precedent!*

SERGEANT: Their leader is at hand, sire, at his back,
Four knaves at least!

KING: They're found in every pack.
Produce this bold *adventurer,* whose *advent* here,
With our self-*interest* must *interfere.*
Meanwhile, we'll dip in Hoyle, and when you're back,
Know how to *deal* with such a dirty *pack.*

Exit Sergeant

SPEAKER: How shall we receive them?

KING: As at the Opera House,
With a Chorus: there cannot be so proper a house
To set the fashion.

Song and Chorus
Air – "Rosin the Bow"

KING:
Come forward here every rapscallion,
And spread yourselves out in a row,
While I ask that harmonious Italian
La Manna to rosin his bow.

CHORUS
La Manna, come rosin your bow, oh, oh,
La Manna, pray rosin your bow,
We aint got no forte-piano,
Old beeswax, come rosin your bow.

KING:
Wake up, Mr. Trombone and Trumpet,
And give us a jolly good blow,
Like steam-engines out you must pump it,
La Manna will rosin his bow.

CHORUS *as before*

KING:
You chap with the blazing big fiddle,
And you with the small one also,
Keep your eye on the man in the middle,
La Manna can rosin his bow.

CHORUS *as before*

KING:
My friend of the side-drum and kettle,

407

*Be sure, and don't spare your el*bow,
But give us a thundering rattle,
La Manna will rosin his bow.

CHORUS

Enter Captain John Smith and Retinue

KING: What *manner* of *man* are you? A fillybus-
tero!

Your *name* and *aim*, what brought you *there*,
my *hero*?

SMITH: *Erratic* King, I might say *operatic*,

And, as I see, as *mellow* as *dramatic*,

My name is –

KING: Norval?

SMITH: No, Sir! Smith – John Smith!

KING: Of Arkansaw?

SMITH: No, Sire, that John's a myth.

KING: What *iron* fortune *led* you to our shores?

SMITH: *Ironic* Monarch, 'twas a pair of *oars*.

Between ourselves, though, if the truth be
told,

Our *goal* we'll reach when we have reached
your *gold*.

But, stop, and I'll enlighten your community,

I see [*Music in orchestra*] and hear a famous
opera-tunity.

GRAND SCENA COMPLICATO
In the Anglo-Italiano Style

SMITH:

As you are o,
The great cigar, o
And high top loco,
Among these folk, o
It is but fair, o
I should declare, o
What brought me here o.
'Tis easy told.
You know my name o.

CHORUS

Smith!

SMITH:

I hither came o,
Impelled by fame o.

CHORUS

Bravo! Smith!

SMITH:

Or all the same o,
The subtle flame o.

CHORUS

Go it, Smith.

SMITH:

The brilliant game o,
Man's only aim .o,
To hunt up gold.

CHORUS

[*Abjure the Italian, and give themselves Ethio-*
pian airs]

You're off the track, and you'd better go back,
The golden dream is o'er;
So order your hack and carry your pack
From old Virginny's shore.

SMITH:

Oh nar'ry a toe, will this child go,
But open a grocery store,
And I'll never go back, 'till I've filled my sack
On old Virginny's shore.

KING: And what the *deuce* in*duced* this scheme
Utopian!

Proceed, we'll give *you rope* enough, *Euro-*
pean!

Though we don't relish being quite so *near*

As this, my *buck*, to such a *Buccaneer!*

SMITH: Most potent, grave, and reverent old
fellow, –

To use the words of that *black wight* Othello,

My very noble and approved good savage,

That we are come out here your lands to rav-
age,

It is most true: for this you see us banded.

Indians rush at him – the King restrains them

KING: I must confess, *sweet* sir, that you are
candid

You'll probably excuse us if we doubt it.

Pray how, sir, do you mean to set about it?

SMITH: Easy enough: we have full powers to
treat.

KING: If that's the case, we'll take some *whiskey*
neat.

You cannot *dash* our *spirits*, we are *proof*

Against such weakness!

SMITH: Well, that's clear enough!

Ma*jestic* Savage, I was but in *jest*

Just now, you'll find, I *guess*, that I'm a *guest*

It would be quite as *well* to *wel*come over.

The seas we *clove* in hopes to live in *clover*.

Befriend us, and we'll try and be of use,

Even to cooking of your royal goose!

KING: Don't put yourself into a stew, my
friend,

My *Kitchen Cabinet* to that attend.
They know my constitution just like lawyers.

SMITH: *Soyer* himself must yield to such *top-sawyers!*

But say, Great *Sachem,* don't re*fuse* this *fusion:*
To now *ill-use* us would be base *illusion!*
Puissant potentate, *abridge* our *sighs,*
We *call on you* to let us *colonize.*
If this, most verdant Monarch, you will do,
A course of Sprouts we mean to put you
through!

KING: Sprout me no sprouts, irreverent *Suckers*
all!
You can't lodge here, my friend, in *Short, at*
all!
I can no *reason* in such *treason* see!
What! *share* my realm with you, mon *cher*
ami?

SMITH: Why not? We have the *brads* to buy
your land,
*Nail*s are a legal tender, they're on h*and,*
With beads and bracelets you shall all be
crammed.

KING: If I sell land for brads, may I be d——
ished!

SMITH: In friendship with you we should like to
tarry.
In proof of which I'm *ready* now to marry
Any *red* queen that in my way should fall,
I would *accept* her *Sceptre,* Crown, and all.
My hand is hers!

KING: Your hand? You'd better p*ause!*
Among our *Indian maids* look out for Sq*uaws!*
If any jokers dare to run their rigs
Near our *wigwams,* we're sure to *warm their*
wigs!
What shall we do with them, the sons of to-
pers?

SPEAKER: Hang on the *outer* wall, the *inter-*
lopers!

ALL: Hang them! Hang them!

SMITH: What f*ault* have I committed? Halt!

KING: Ha! Do you f*alter?*

SMITH: I fain would h*alt* before I reach the
h*alter.*
That *cord* is not my *line* in any sense,
I'd rather *not* be kept in such suspense!

KING: You *shan't* be long! prepare yourself! But
stay!
You'd rather not be hanged, I think you say?

SMITH: I'm really fearful it would be a *drop*
Too much for me!

KING: Perhaps you'd like a *chop* – [*With axe*]

SMITH: Ill-manner'd *butcher,* you may *bet your*
Crown
I'll fix your flint for you!

KING: You simmer down!
Smith you must die, as well as all audacious
Birds of passage that may migrate here!

SMITH: *My gracious!*
Alas! then, did our *Nests* at home content us,
We would not now have been *Non est inven-*
tus!
Mercy!

ALL: No mercy!

KING: Not by any means!
My wrath they can't ap*pease,* so give them
beans!

Indians rush at Smith

SMITH: Stay! *Soft!* Hold *hard!* One moment, if
you please,
Until his Majesty a *secret sees!*

KING: A secret! What is it?

SMITH: Behold! [*Showing pistol*]

KING: [*Taking it*] We do! What's this?

SMITH: [*Taking it back*] A pistol, sire, I hope
it will *suit* you
Should I *present* it!

KING: Ha! I see your *aim!*
By this you'd *buy* our silence, eh?

SMITH: The same!

KING: It's *curious!* What does it contain?

SMITH: Some potent pills,
And warranted to *cure* all mortal ills!
With a few doses we'll be undertakers
To rid you soon of all your *pains* and *acres!*

KING: I'd grieve with favors to be over*load*ed,
But with us kings such *canons* are ex*plod*ed,
And so will take your physic. [*King fires pis-*
tol, drops it alarmed] Jarsey lightning!!

Rushes off, followed by Indians

SMITH: Hurrah! 'Tis clear, my friends, our
skies are bright'ning!

BROWN: Let us be off –

SMITH: *Be off!* Recall that whine,
Or never more *be off*icer of mine!
To leave our work half-done would be a pity,
And so we take possession of the city;
And as is usual in all such cases,
We'll nominate ourselves to all the places!
For Governor, John Smith!

BROWN: I second that!
It's carried; so be *seated!*

SMITH: [*Sitting*] Verbum *sat!*
I'd make a speech to you, but that's not
  needed,
For in to-morrow's Herald you can read it.
Be sure I'll make the best of this bad story,
To *gild* our *guilt* we've but to call it glory.
Success crowns every crime whoever bleeds,
Defies reproof and *sanctifies* misdeeds;
But pray excuse this personal reflection.
Unsuited to a primary election,
Propose your candidates.

BROWN: Might I suggest,
A plan I've hit on that will be the best
To suit the present crisis. In this hat
I've written all the names of all the fat
And juicy offices, – let each advance,
And in the *grab game* take an equal chance.

ALL: Agreed! agreed!

CONCERTED PIECE

Grab away
While you may;
In this game, luck is all,
And the prize
Tempting lies
In the rich City Hall.

Grab away
While you may;
For they say under Sam
Holds the "puss"
And the "cuss"
Is as mild as a lamb.

Grab away
While you may;
Every day there's a "job"
It's a fact
By contract
All intact you may rob.

Grab away
While you may;
For the pay never fear.
Justice winks
Aye, and blinks,
From the dust I scattered here.

Confusion at the Poll

BROWN: [*To Jones*] What are you, Treasurer?

JONES: No, vicey varcy.
I'm Secretary of State!

SMITH: I cry you *Marcy!*
And you? [*To Junk*]

JUNK: An Alderman!

BUNTLINE: And so am I!

ANOTHER: And I!

SMITH: [*To Brace*] And what are you, old
  horse?

BRACE: I'm Mayor!

SMITH: No bed of roses is the Civic Chain?
See that your city fathers work their best,
When they're fatigued, why, let them have *ar-
  rest.*
Are you all satisfied?

BROWN: Um! – pretty well!

SMITH: Then let us try the tea-room for a spell –
Is there nothing we can do,
Meantime I'll chaunt the Marsellaise a la Ra-
  chel,
We heard the Yankees this time, pretty dears,
They'll have to wait a couple of hundred years.

Song – SMITH:
It is of a French actress I'm going to tell,
As came to America and her name it was Ra-
  chel,
To play in deep tragedies, both new ones and
  old
All for to make a fortune in silver and gold.

CHORUS

[*Anticipative of the way in which she intended
to shovel in the specie*]
Tol, de dol, &c.

SMITH:
Now she had a handsome Brother, and his
  name it was Felix,
Who thought he was posted in play-house politics,
For said he to himself – "I am just the right
  fel-
Low, to manage these Yankees uncommonly
  well."

CHORUS

[*Indicative of the proposed Modus Operandi*]
Tol, de dol, &c.

SMITH:
"Oh," says he, "in the newspapers I'll come
  it strong,
All about the fine corps as I'm a fotchin' along,
They'll cost me some 5000 dollars a night,
And to see so much go, will be a dolorous
  sight."

CHORUS

[*Illustrative of the way he disbursed that large amount to the talented company*]
Tol, de dol, &c.

SMITH:

When the public I've told the tremendous expense,
They'll think that the prices are again to be immense,
Twenty-five dollars a ticket at least they must be.
They'll jump out of their skins when they find they're – only Three!

CHORUS

[*Delineative of the mad intoxication of the delighted populace*]
Tol, de dol, &c.

SMITH:

Well, the doors they were opened, and the folks they walked in,
Think of Felix's *feelinks, the domus was thin,*
And it must be confessed that he looked rather blue,
When instead of Three *dollars he had to take* Two.

CHORUS

[*Exemplifications of Felix's countenance as he reluctantly yielded to the pressure of the press*]
Tol, de dol, &c.

SMITH:

As the newspapers told him, the people flocked more,
And every one bought a French play-book at the door,
With their eyes on their books and their ears on the stage,
They thought they were seeing *Rachel I'll engage.*

CHORUS

[*Descriptive of the studious way the general public avoided seeing the Great Actress*]
Tol, de dol, &c.

SMITH:

Now all you nice folks as are fond of a play,
And like to be amused in a sensible way,
Don't you be deluded by fashion's sheep-bell,
But come here *where our language you understand well.*

CHORUS

[*Suggestive of the grateful return made by the audience for this disinterested advice*]
Tol, de dol, &c.

Smith is borne off in Triumph. W.

Scene 2

Picturesque View in Jamestown, taken some time before it was built. – Savage Play-Ground of a Tuscarora Finishing Institution. Vociferous irruption of Juvenile Squaw-lers. Enter Poo-Tee-Pet, Di-Mun-Di Lum-Pa-Shuga. Dah-Lin-Duk, Nys-Kree-Tah. O-You-Jewel, Hah-Jote-Lah. Oso-Char-Ming. &c., &c., &c.

Chorus of Emancipated Maidens
Sing-sing away!
Sing-sing away!
Schools, but prisons are they say,
Sing-sing away!
Sing-sing away!
We'll have a sing-song *holiday. &c.*

POOTEEPET: I wish my Pa would send for me!
Oh, dear!
I'm *tired* of living so *retired* here,
And I've had school enough, I know that well,
To set up any fashionable *belle!*
Heigho! How can one stay here with content,
The *present* time no *pastime* can *present!*
No one to talk to of the Upper Ten,
If it were even one of Brown's young men.
Just to begin with, for indeed the *fact* is
I don't know how to flirt for want of practice.
DIMUNDI: Isn't that dreadful, dear, I'm just the same,
And for my part I think it's a great shame
That we've no more young master's to impart
The *rudest rudiments* of that fine art!
Now, what's the use of drawing?
POOTEEPET: I suppose
That we may have some skill in *drawing beaux*,
Let other people love to draw their spouses.
That's horses' work – I'd rather much draw *houses*,
Here comes Miss Pocahontas, haughty thing!
Tossing her *crown* because her Pa's a *King!*
Hum! – I know something!

DIMUNDI: What?

POOTEEPET: He must be *short*, or
He'd have paid up, my dear, for her last quarter.

Music. Enter Po-ca-hon-tas, with Book
INTERNATIONAL SCENA. – *Pocahontas*
Recitativo – Italiani doloroso.

Sport am I of Fortune, no kind soul near to
cheer me
I'm on the verge of despair;
Where can I turn me for comfort!
Whence seek for sigh sympathetic?
Ah! me unhappy!
Most unhappy!
But my heart it will relieve, O,
To sing from Hernani
This recitativo!

INTER-ARIA NIGROQUAE

Where the idlers now are shopping
In gay Fashion's round
And at Banks, that are not stopping,
You can hear the cold gold sound.
All the world seems bright and cheery
But sometimes 'tis mock,
Oh! dark his lot who deals with Erie,
For it's a fluctuating stock.

CANTATA VARIOSO

Scenes that are brightest
No one can trust
When money's tightest
Look to your dust.
Hope buoys, and carries us on
Carries us on through our days,
Carries us on like the pepper upon
"Massachusetts Bays,"
Oh! Heigh! ho!
Where is that beau
Pa said he'd bring me a long time ago.

INTRUSIVE CHORUS
Oh! what a beau,
What? a beau?
Miss Pocahontas, you don't say so.

POCAHONTAS: Heigho! This h*eated* term will
shortly cease,
And these *school*-days to *warm*er ones give
place!
I know not why it is, but since I've seen
Napoleon's life in Harper's magazine,
My soul enthusiastic, yearns to paint

The blissful deeds of some such *warlike saint!*
Since these heroic pages I've perused,
The stories that my childhood have amused
Are varnished with the fashions of last week; –
Never again with rapture shall I speak
Of dear Red Riding Hood, or Cinderella,
Or valiant little Jack the Giant *feller*,
Robinson Crusoe, or great Thumb the Small, –
This is the greatest *story* of them all! –
Oh! that it were my future fate to do
Some deed of desperation nice and new,
Something would startle all the world with
fright,
That is, provided it *left* me all *right!*

POOTEEPET: Girls, here come the teachers, hide
your books,
Banish your smiles and put on your school
looks!

POCAHONTAS: I hate that School-Ma'am, she
does look so sly.
She always has a *pupil in her eye!*

Enter Wee-Cha-Ven-Da and Kros-As-Kan-Bee,
Professors of haughty-culture, and trainers of
the flowers of fashion

WEECHAVENDA: Heads up, backs straight,
chests out and shoulders square!

KROSASKANBEE: Miss Pocahontas, just look at
your hair, I never saw it in so vile a state!

POCAHONTAS: It *curls* so much that I can't keep
it *straight.*

WEECHAVENDA: Now, ladies, if you please you'll
get your bows.

POCAHONTAS: I wish I had one!

KROSASKANBEE: Do turn out your toes! You walk
just like a *duck*, my dear, that's *flat!*

POCAHONTAS: Being a *duck*, you know, I can't
help that!

KROSASKANBEE: Come, ladies, please to recollect
time flies!

POCAHONTAS: *Fly time's* too warm, I think, for
exercise!

They try a Dance, and execute it with bows and
arrows. Noise of pursuit without: Smith ap-
pears behind fence. Indian Girls cry, "A man!"
and run off screaming, all but Pocahontas

SMITH: Believe me, there's no necessity at all,
Delicious *Schreechers*, for this sudden *Squall!*
Ah! Aid me, Maiden, pray!

POCAHONTAS: Who are you?
Are you a *fugitive* come here to seek
A railway, underground?

SMITH: Not by a sight!
Alas! I'm only an unhappy *wight*,
Without a *shade* of *color* to excuse
Canadian Agents here to chalk my shoes,
Therefore my passage-money won't be figured,
For on that head Philanthropy is *niggard!*
POCAHONTAS: Who is it this un*time*ly visit pays,
Breaking our school up before holidays?
SMITH: I'll tell you, thou un*fair*est of the *fair*
American Institution, – take a chair,
While my o'erloaded bosom I unfreight,
And all my *early* history re*late!* [*Gets chairs from entrance*]
Most comfortable *chat*tels these to *chat* in,
Such chairs I ne'er thought to *sit* in here, –
they're *sat*in!
'Tis now some twenty years –
POCAHONTAS: I'll hear no more!
SMITH: You've cut my tale off!
POCAHONTAS: Long ones are a bore!
Brief it must be, however you bewail it!
SMITH: I shall be *curt*, un*court*eous beauty, and
*curt*ail it;
*Begin*ning with the *end* I had in view,
Which, upon my *soul* was *sole*ly to see you, –
When from the *verge* of yon *Virgin*ny fence
I *saw* and *heard* a *sordid herd* advance!
From the *spot* I would have turned to flee,
But one of the Chief's shadows *spotted* me,
And at his *back* the savage, at whose *beck*
They have a k*nack* of tightening one's *neck!*
POCAHONTAS: Can you tell who he was?
SMITH: The Chief? I can.
POCAHONTAS: A King?
SMITH: The same.
POCAHONTAS: His name?
SMITH: Is Powhatan! [*Pocahontas screams*]
Some near relation of yours, maybe?
POCAHONTAS: Rather!
Nearer he can't be much, for he's my *Father!*
SMITH: The deuce!
POCAHONTAS: Have you been intro*duced!*
SMITH: Why, – No!
Not formally, but I have seen him though!
I visited his majesty's abode,
A portly savage, plump, and pigeon-toed,
Like *Metamora* both in *feet* and *feature*,
I never *met-a-more-a*-musing creature!
Now without fear my love I can avow it,
And *pop* the question boldly?
POCAHONTAS: My *pop* won't allow it,
I'll *bet* my life!
SMITH: My chance that *betters* still,

For being the *contrary* sex, you will!
In *fact, rare* princess, there's such *rarefaction*
Within my heart, such *"passional attraction,"*
That we must live together spite of fate,
For all impossibilities that congregate
Around us, my *free love* despises!
POCAHONTAS: Stop! One doubt within my heart
arises!
A great historian before us stands,
Bancroft himself, you know, forbids the
banns!
SMITH: *Bancroft* be *ban*ished from your memo-
ry's shelf,
For spite of *fact*, I'll marry you myself.
And happiness you'll have a better *show* for
With me, than should you wed that *low-bred
loafer!*

Duet. – Smith and Pocahontas

SMITH:
My love is like a raging hot volcano,
Vesuvius in a fit of indigestion,
And if you are so cruel as to say no
Insane, oh! I shall be without a question.
POCAHONTAS:
Such volcanic affection 'twere just as well
You'd keep, a little piano
That too burning a mount would a Cinderel-
la make me and I'm not a soprano.
But where's the use of jesting
Or protesting,
With you this union never can take place.
SMITH:
'Tis vain my claim arresting
Or contesting
To gain you every record I'll efface.
BOTH:
Such an event must amusing be
We have no fear in asserting
For changing the current of History
Would certainly be diverting.

Noise of women without

POCAHONTAS: How from those prying *eyes* can I
dis*guise* you,
My father's *prize* you'll be should he sur*prize*
you!

He puts on shawl and hat, and pretends to read.
Enter all the school. He mixes with them, they
proceed towards gate as for a walk, in couples.
Enter Powhatan and suite, Savagely. The girls
are thrown into confusion
WEECHAVENDA: What is the meaning of this
rude intruding?

KING: *Rude!* By the *rood* it means there's mis-chief *brood*ing!
We *seek* a su*ck*er who's *secret*ed here!
Produce him or *induce* him to appear,
Or by the towel, silver *fork* and spoon
You *forked* from me, I'll settle with you soon!
POCAHONTAS: [*To girls*] Save him!
GIRLS: We will!

> *They surround Smith*

KING: You daughter come with me!
I'll settle you too!
POCAHONTAS: How, Pa!
KING: You shall see!
I've found a husband you must wed to night!
POCAHONTAS: Oh! my prophetic soul, *Bancroft* was right!
SMITH: [*Appearing*] What's that?
KING: Ha! we have you now, I guess!
POCAHONTAS: Despair! Distraction!
SMITH: Here's a precious mess!
POCAHONTAS: Where is my Smith, my love, my only one?
SMITH: My *Poca*hontas ain't you *pok*ing fun?
KING: Here, dogs, we're in a snarl, so watch o'er us,
This blackguard guard and aid us in the chorus.

Grand Finale
Affettuoso. – Furioso. – E. Conglomeroso

CHORUS

> *Come, let us now like watch-dogs bark,*
> *Come, let us now put out this spark,*
> *Come, let us raise a jolly row,*
> *And like the dogs of war, bow, wow.*

SMITH:

> *I am plucked from fairy bowers,*
> *I am in misfortune's showers,*
> *Quite enough to wet a fellow through,*
> *Without an umbrella too.*
> *Oh! I love this old man's daughter,*
> *Though inscrutable I've thought her,*
> *As the song of Hiawatha,*
> > *Writ by Long-fel-low.*

POCAHONTAS:

> *Oh! a little outsider too,*
> *A little outsider view,*
> *A little outsider, your own child*
> *Appeals dear dad, to you.*

KING:

> *Mr. Smith, you're in a fix*
> *With your Don Giovanni tricks.*

> *But though you think yourself so much the dandy O,*
> *I'll bet you two to one*
> *You're almost as good as gone,*
> *For I'll use you up just like a stick of candy, O,*

OMNES:

> > *Its all bosh and braggin*
> > *All bosh and braggin*
> > *All bosh and braggin*
> > *That you'll find, old "hoss."*

> > *Wait for the waggon,*
> > *Wait for the waggon,*
> > *Wait for the waggon,*
> > *And you'll soon catch "goss."*

ACT II. Scene I

Isherwood's View of the Interior of a Wigwam.
Powhatan pushes on Pocahontas with the paren-tally tyrannic air peculiar to irate potentates.

Duetto. – Impetuoso

KING:

> *Now Ma'am I have a notion,*
> *You can no longer rave,*
> *This son of the ocean oh shun,*
> *A home on the salt sea, waive.*

POCAHONTAS:

> *Your child, you thus may seize sir,*
> *But sure as the seas are blue*
> *I shall soon rescued be, sir,*
> *From you, and your cruel crew.*

BOTH:

> *The prospect is inviting,*
> *Thus all my love requiting,*
> *Of temper, you will find I have a share;*
> *Since you're bent on fighting,*
> *Thus all my prospects blighting,*
> *I won't give in an atom, I declare.*

POWHATAN: How sharper than a serpent's tooth, if one could find
Such things in serpents' heads, is an ungrateful child!
But here you shall remain till you're resigned
To settle *down* as I've made *up* my mind!
You'll make me *furious* if you yet re*fuse,*
Or venture to *eschew* the man I *choose!*
POCAHONTAS: The king who would enslave his daughter so,
Deserves a hint from Mrs. Beecher Stowe!
Who is the *man*, sir, I demand to know?

KING: Hey! day! Are we com*ma*nded by our daughter!
I *taught* your *teach*ers to keep you much *tau*ter
In hand! If thus the rein you mean to shy,
A *shy-reign* will be mine, me thinks, bye-and-bye!
You must be *curbed* a *bit*, your doom's a pris-on
If you don't quickly *hasten* to be *his'n!*

POCAHONTAS: If thus you *wrong* my Woman's Rights, and mock
My griefs, your *offspring* will *spring off the dock!*
And mix my ardent spirits with cold water!

Going

KING: Hold!
I did but jest, my *belle*, you shall be *told!*
The man's a Dutchman, deep as he can be,
In fact, as deep as the rolling Zuyder Zee.
A first-class venture, cautious and acute,
A widower, and good *shoe*maker *to boot!*

POCAHONTAS: A widower! the proverb's here surpassed,
A *shoemaker* who looks beyond his *last!*
"*Ne sutor*," sir, et cetera, so, you see
Such *suitor* is not likely to *suit* me!

Rolff sings outside

KING: Here he comes, no counterfeit is he
Like Smith, whose very name's a *forgery!*

POCAHONTAS: The other's worse by his own show-ing.

KING: How?

POCAHONTAS: I heard him *uttering false notes*, just now!

KING: He's here! you see resistance now were idle,
His *bride* you shall be, so your temper *brid*le!

Enter Rolff, smoking

ROLFF: Mein cootness gracious, was is das I see!
Is das mein loafley vrow as is to be?

KING: Yes, there's the prize, my son, *go in* and *win* her,
While, to escape the *din*, guess I'll go in to *din*ner.

GRAND SCENA PERTURBATO
Aria "Hibernoso affettuosamente"

POCAHONTAS:
Aurora, no more will I hail thy first dawn,

No more hear the soul-stirring cry of "hot corn,"
I have nothing to do now, but languish and die,
*"Crushed out" as I am by my Pa's cruel*ty.
But I'm not so domestic *a thing, on my life*
As ever to be yon brown Hollander's *wife.*
No, rather than that, a deep hole I would bore
In my heart, and behold bright Aurora no more.
And oh! if I'm forced like poor DINAH, *to die*
By going, and taking a cup of cold py –
– zon, no VILLIKINS *will I leave here to de-plore,*
That this child should behold bright Aurora no more.

Cantata "Giojoso et amoroso"

ROLFF:
Oh peutivool girl,
Mein prave Indian Bearl,
Love runs like a squirrel
    Mein heart up and down.
Oh don't look so freezy,
Uneezy and breezy,
Mein vrow you must be see
    In spite of your vrown.

Oh peutivool creeter,
I'd fling at your feet your
Audacious beseecher,
    Now bobbin around.
But you mustn't be freezy
Uneezy or breezy,
Mein vrow you must be see
    In spite of your vrown.

Song "Doloroso et petulento"

KING:
'Tis a hard blow to suffer
    When sad and alone,
Some poor aged buffer
    Sits by his hearthstone,
No flour in his kitchen,
    No fire-water nigh,
His complexion to nourish
    By a drop in his eye.

TOGETHER:
In our cane brakes of an afternoon,
We sometimes go for to hunt the coon,
And from experience I declare
He ain't an easy bird to snare.
    Clar's his action,
        Old coon, sly coon,
    Old Virginia never tire.

POCAHONTAS: Appeal is useless! what words
could I utter,
To mollify this firkin of Dutch butter!
Oh! tell me, was that sentence that my pa
Made use of, true, that I'm to wed you?
ROLFF: Yah!
POCAHONTAS: But if I say I love another?
ROLFF: Psha!
POCAHONTAS: You wouldn't force me to espouse
you?
ROLFF: Yah!
POCAHONTAS: Was ever maiden's love so subli-
mated?
Single, ere this, and now thus *doubly*-mated!
But, once for all, sir, know I'm not inclined
To wed a *beau* with such a *narrow* mind!
Dutchman depart! the honor I resign,
Leave me, or else, *believe* me, you shall rue it!
ROLFF: Nein!

Song – Rolff
With Tyrolean Fixins
Like the Tyrolese singers, so gallant and gay,
I'll sing you a song in the Tyrolese way,
Fol de dol, de dol lay – it's a very fine day,
It doesn't much matter – you know what I
say.

[*Here follows an exhibition of tracheotomous*
gymnastics, which must be heard to be properly
appreciated]

I wish from mein soul all de rocks round about
Would to sausages *turn, and the trees to* sour-
crout.
The ocean's vast bowl into lager bier roll
And I was an earthquake to swallow the
whole.

[*More vocal gymnastics*]
And then for mein pipe I'd Vesuvius fill full
Of kanaster *and through a* pine tree *take a pull*
And after that, p'raps, for fear of mishaps,
I'd toss down Niagara Falls *for mein* schnapps.

Gymnastics again
ROLFF: It ain't no use to crumble, zo you zee
Mein peauty, you must gome along mit me!

She struggles wildly with the destroyer of her
peace, to corresponding Music, marked, and
melo-dramatic
POCAHONTAS: Un*hand* me, thou *unhand*some
caitiff!

ROLFF: Nein!
It's no good kicking now, you must be mine!
POCAHONTAS: Where shall I turn? [*Breaks from*
him distractedly – suddenly beholds the mem-
bers of the Orchestra and appeals to them]
Can *you* look calmly on
And see this shameful *Overture* begun,
Yet take no part! I cannot call you *men*, or
You'd out-shout the *treble base*ness of his *tenor!*
Thou rude as*sailer*, must I storm without
avail!
SMITH: [*Jumps in at the window*] Avast! not
when *a sailor's* within *hail!*

Tableau of triumphant innocence, and discon-
certed Dutch villany. Smith continues ora-tar-
ically
Sheer off at once, you ugly-looking craft,
Or, damme! if I don't rake you fore and aft!
Perhaps I'd better kill him, love? – Here,
stay!
What do you think?
POCAHONTAS: It might be the best way.
SMITH: Of course it will be. So, audacious ri-
val,
Prepare, at once, to die!
ROLFF: To *die!* der *Diefil!*
Help, murder! help!

Smith proceeding to annihilate him, is inter-
cepted by Powhatan
KING: Holloa! what's the row?
ROLFF: Dat dere tam Smit has dook away mein
vrow!
And vos vant do gill me do pezite!
KING: Dear me, is that all? I'll soon set it right.
Children, come here, I've changed my mind.

Shaking hands with Smith
ROLFF: What's dat?
You shakes him by de hand? [*King winks at*
Rolff]
Oho! I smells a rat. [*Aside*]
KING: I'll fix him. [*Aside*] Smith, we to our
daughter's choice
Lend the loud sanction of our Royal voice.
SMITH: Your *voice* al*lowed*, but has your heart
re*lent*ed?
KING: If in our simple *tent* you'll live con*tent*ed.
SMITH: To an *extent intense*. King, you're a
brick!
ROLFF: Mein vrow! mein Got! dis is a purdy
drick.

KING: *Demmy John, cork up!* Now, daughter
dear, prepare.
With orange wreaths *array* your *raven* hair;
To *prove* I love *you*, Smith, before you wed,
We'll take a *proof* impression of your head,
In our approved new lithographic style.
SMITH: With all my heart; but if you harbor
guile,
My *tars* will make a *target* of your head.
KING: Upon the honor of a king!
SMITH: 'Nuff said.

Quartette
King, Smith, Rolff, and Pocahontas
Fill now a flowing glass
We would, without doubt, sir,
But as we've none, alas!
We must do without, sir.

We'll live, never fear,
In harmony here.

KING:
Poor John Smith is very grateful.

CHORUS
As lazy as monks in a cloister.

KING:
Grief he's not now troubled with.

CHORUS
Both soft shells and hard
We here disregard.

KING:
He's gentle and resigned,
And resolved to go it blind.

CHORUS
So we get our fair share of the oyster.

KING:
Oh, what a fool is poor John Smith!
[*Poco a Poco Discretioni*]

Scene 2

School Ground as before. Poo-tee-pet looking
cautiously.

POOTEEPET: Come, girls, we'll have our little
confab here,
No prying principals can interfere.
I've dreadful news for you!
DIMUNDI: You don't say so!
What is it, dear, I'll die if I don't know.
GIRLS: And so will I. And I.
DIMUNDI: For my part, I can't guess

What it can be that gives you such distress.
Do let us know at once.
ALL: Do – Do!
POOTEEPET: I will.
Imagine the extreme of human ill.
LUMPASHUGA: Are the new bonnets worn on
the head?
DIMUNDI: There's been a fight, and all the *men*
are dead.
POOTEEPET: Not quite so bad as either, but be-
hold!
A tale of horror in this note is told!
DIMUNDI: Do tell!
LUMPASHUGA: I want to know!
DIMUNDI: What can it be?
POOTEEPET: Miss Pocahontas tells me here, that
she is going to marry.

All laugh
DIMUNDI: What a heavy blow!
POOTEEPET: But not the man she's in love with!
ALL: Oh!
POOTEEPET: At Union Square, this afternoon,
'tis fated,
The wrongful *rites* are to be consummated!
The awful moment is almost at hand,
But as this *scand*alous affair I've *scanned*,
If you'll but *second* me in what I say,
Our hands will show them what's the *time o'*
day!
You can *wind up* this business as you like,
If at the proper instant you but strike!
Strike! like the steel of Halleck's brave Bozzar-
is,
Strike! as the newest fashions do in Paris,
Strike! for your rights, your homes, and kitch-
en fires;
Strike! like a crowd of feminine Tom Hyer's.
ALL: We will! Hurrah! Down with mankind in
general!
DIMUNDI: A very striking denoeument, indeed,
If we could only *see* how to pro*ceed*.
POOTEEPET: I have got leave, to-day, for our di-
version,
To go *on* a toxopholite excursion.
A female target party – 'twill be fine
Before they can suspect our deep design,
By stratagem to get them to desist, or
Else, by force of arms *assist* our *sister*.
The plan is dangerous, and now you know it,
Are you all game to see it through?
ALL: We'll *go it!*

POOTEEPET: Now, let's be off, as we've no time to *lose*.

DIMUNDI: Those gentlemen can keep time, I suppose. [*To Orchestra*]

POOTEEPET: Then, if you please, as we've good time before us,

We'll just take *time* enough to sing a chorus. [*Addressing Leader*]

CHORUS

Air – "Pop Goes the Weazle"

As we're going on a train
We must see and load a
Hamper with the drink of Maine.
Pop goes the soda.

Hampered *thus, no Indian corn*
Can we now forebode, a
Bumper fill then (*in a horn*),
Pop goes the soda.

Exeunt omnes

Scene 3

Union Square in the City of Weramocomoco. The assembled Upper Tendom of Tuscarora, discovered.

CHORUS

Air – "Hark 'tis the Indian drum"

Hark 'tis the ingine *bell*,
Look out for the locomotive
We off the track must go.
Though
His majesty is rather slow.
He must be how come you so,
With Smith's New England rum:
The rum, the rum, &c., &c.

Enter Pocahontas, evidently in very indifferent spirits, her overburthened soul bursts forth in melody

POCAHONTAS:

Air – Notturne, Grazioso vel Filosofoso
Oh, some are right
Who don't invite
Within their vest
So dangerous a guest,
As love that hies
To this abode,
And heavy lies –

Dyspeptic load.
It sets one frying
And sadly sighing,
You can't lodge here, no way,
So love *good day,*
'Twill never pay
To let you stay
So love *good day, good day, good day,*
I'm better off without thee
Verily.
And do not care about thee,
No, not I.

She goes off sadly. Enter Powhatan and Smith. Rolff creeping cautiously after

KING: Here's where my artists dwell, a race gregarious,
Cheering their up *hill* life with mirth hilarious.
Smith, where are all your sailors? Safe, I trust?

SMITH: Yes! *Safe,* by this time, to be on a *bust!*

KING: Do none of your brave *hands* about here linger?

SMITH: I need no *hands* while I those *arms* can finger.

Rolff, who has stolen behind Smith, suddenly snatches his pistols, one of which he hands to Powhatan, producing a perilous and plagisarous situation. A la Rob Roy – Smith served with a "ne exeat" at every opening, by the servitors of the King, and finally bound over to a strong chord in the Orchestra

ROLFF: Friend Smith, you're *double-sold!* You lose your wife!

KING: Likewise, to a *dead* certainty, your *life!*

SMITH: Such hospitality was ne'er surpassed.
Invited to a *feast* and thus made *fast!*
But, as to you, base cobbler, soon to pay
For what's *occurred,* I'll find a ready *way!*
There's not a *red* marauder in the land
But henceforth *seeks* your *hide* to have it tanned!
Think on't, and tremble to your marrow's pith!
Judas! you haven't yet sub*dued* John Smith!!

KING: Don't make a *Judy* of yourself!

ROLFF: Mein friend!
Your *thread* of life is *waxing* to an end!

A Scotch Indian march, with variations and situations, singularly similar to those which have occurred in similar situations

KING: Now, that our finishing touches may be shown,

Bring forth our finest lithographic stone! [*He is obeyed with servile alacrity. — Flourishes a huge club*]

I said I'd take your head off!

SMITH: But I swear,

You didn't hint about that sketch *club* there!

KING: Disappointed in the likeness you can't be!

SMITH: 'Twould be more *strik*ing if my hands were free!

But as I'm *bound* to let you have your way,

A few last words, I trust, you'll let me say?

KING: We're *tied* to *time*, and *time* and *tide* won't wait,

You must *die early* so you can't *dilate*!

Our *Indian* laws are *some*, there's no receding!

SMITH: Why what an *Indian summary* proceeding.

KING: A sentence, come, prepare!

SMITH: Hold on a spell

Fell tyrant!

KING: Ha! What's that?

SMITH: I mean *old "fel"*

You wouldn't cut a *fellow's thread*?

KING: That's *so*!

I do assure you, you shan't feel the blow!

Old *Tar*, to-night in *Tar*tarus you'll sup!

SMITH: Life's a *conundrum*!

KING: Then lie *down*, and *give it up*!

SMITH: It's a hard *pill* — but a much harder *pill*ow! [*Reclining*]

Pocahontas rushing in heroineically distressed and dishevelled, followed by sailors

POCAHONTAS: Husband! for thee I *scream*!

SMITH: *Lemon* or *Vanilla*?

POCAHONTAS: Oh! *Fly* with me, and quit those vile dominions!

SMITH: How *can* I fly, beloved, with these pinions?

Duet — Smith and Pocahontas
"Prima Donna Waltz"

SMITH:

> *Although a bird am I,*
> *And sometimes do get high —*
> *A pair of wings*
> *Are essential things*
> *Before a bird can fly.*

POCAHONTAS:

> *Oh! dearest, die I must,*
> *My heart, just like pie crust*

> *Is breaking in pie —*
> *Ces, only to see*
> *How fowlly my bird is trussed.*

SMITH:

> *A verse to add, I'm not adverse to*
> *Though adversity's a curse — so*
> *Come what may — fate can't do worse, oh*
>   *Farewell.*

POCAHONTAS:

> *Loose him, and let him be my spouse!*

KING:

> *Not I,*
> *Such an alliance would be all a lie!*
> *On no account, can I run counter to*
> *Virginia records which relate to you.*
> *I'm very sorry, Smith, but you must die!*

Music

SMITH:

> *Wait 'till the Target Party passes by!*

Enter Poo-Tee-Pet, and all the Indian Women — they execute sundry manoeuvres, and finally form a hollow square around Smith, very pointedly pointing their arrows at the King and company

KING:

> *Hollo! Stop that! — my goodness! — I do declare!*
> *Those arrows make me quiver! — as you were!*
> *What are you, that thus outrage all propriety?*

POOTEEPET:

> *The Anti-marry-folks-against-their-will Society!*

KING:

> *Why come you here! — as sorrowful spectators?*

POOTEEPET:

> *No! on the contrary, we're very gladiators!*
> *For Freedom every heart with ardor glows,*
> *On Woman's Rights we're bent, and bent our bows!*
> *Your daughter dear, must marry whom she may,*
> *Daughters you know, should always have their way!*

KING: What's to be done? I'm puzzled in good sooth,

I love my daughter, but can't warp the truth!

SMITH: You've *ample* means, ex*ample*s you don't lack,

Didn't Shakespeare give King Richard a crook back,

For fear bold Queen Elizabeth would frown.

Whose grandpapa had cracked his Royal
crown!
In our day, isn't very *corn*er rife
With Hot Corn heroines, ne'er seen in life?
Don't Mr. Abbott make that bloody Tartar,
Napoleon Buonaparte, a Christian martyr?
If these don't satisfy you?
KING: No, they don't!
SMITH: I'll fight him for the maiden!
ROLFF: No, you won't!
SMITH: Draw lots, shake props, shoot pistols,
or petards,
Or *stake* her *hand* upon a *hand* of cards!
KING: Ha! ha! there's sense in that; you're on a
track
That *suits* us to a *T*. Who't got a pack? [*They
all produce the documents*]
Stay! here's a table – sit upon the edge. [*They
sit upon a stone*]
He's done! [*Aside*] What shall the game be,
Smith?
SMITH: Old Sledge!

All crowd round anxiously watching the game

CHARACTERISTIC CONCERTED PIECE
CHORUS
Now for a jolly encounter at High, Low,
Jack, and the Game.
KING AND SMITH:
The Queen!
A trump!
A better!
The ten!
That's good for my Jack!

CHORUS
Oh! what a jolly encounter at High, Low,
Jack, and the Game.
KING AND SMITH:
A trump!
Another!
That's low!
That's so.
And that's the best card in the pack!
POCAHONTAS:
Oh! Mr. Hoyle,
All his toil
Prithee spoil.

CHORUS
Give him fits.
POCAHONTAS:
Oh! Master pray

Mind the way
That you play.

CHORUS
Give him fits.
SMITH:
I've won the game,
Upon my life;
And better still,
I've won a wife!

At High, Low, Jack,
You cannot shine –
So take the pack,
The maid is mine.

I'm bound to play all night,
I'm bound to play all day;
I'll bet my money on the High, Low, Jack,
For ever, if thy hand's my pay.

KING:
Mr. Smith, I must acknowledge, I'm a sure
gone coon,
I'm dished, and feel exactly like a used-up
spoon:
Though, I thought the game to play to another
sort of tune,
And beat you too, before you'd say Jack Robin-
son.

OMNES CODA:
He's won the game, &c.
SMITH: Hurra! I've won the game!
KING: Well, that's a fact!
ROLFF: Der's sheating round dis board! de gards
was backed!
Boo hoo! I'm zwindled!
KING: Just you stop that blubber,
Bub, or cut in for an *Indian rubber!* [*Flourish-
ing club*]
SMITH: I have won *fairly*, I appeal to you. [*To
King*]
And *fair one*, I have *fairly won* you, too,
So let us *two* make one.
POCAHONTAS: Papa, you've heard?
KING: It likes me not, but I must keep my word;
There, take her! – that, I think's the usual
thing – [*Joining their hands patriarchally*]
Now, let your voices *round* the *circle ring*.
Our son-in-law, three cheers, and make them
tell!

Hip hip, hurrah! [*They shout*] Tiger! [*They roar*]

Indian yell! [*They scream*]

SMITH: Old King of Clubs, you are a jolly trump!

And don't you be so downcast, you Dutch pump;

All future history will see you righted,

With her, in name alone, I'll be united.

POCAHONTAS: How long the union may exist, depends

On the impartial verdict of our friends.

KING: Give your consent, and all dispute will cease,

A citizen's first duty is, to *keep the peace*.

SMITH: So, pray *keep this one*, not in *bonds* too tight,

But suffer it to run through many a night.

Grand finale – A la Grec

KING:

And now we've done our duty here,

We hope and trust that you'll not fume, or
Fail to give a parting cheer,
But take our bad jokes in good humor –

> *Tow row row,*
> *People will you now,*
> *Take our bad jokes in good humor,*
> *Now, now, now.*

(De Capo Chorus)

SMITH:

Good people all, both great and small,
Now, you and your kind friends we want, as
Often as you please to call
On Captain Smith and Pocahontas.

> *Tow row row,*
> *Levity allow*
> *Captain Smith and Pocahontas,*
> *Now, now, now.*

Tableau and curtain

FRANCESCA DA RIMINI

GEORGE HENRY BOKER

On Friday evening, December 22, 1871, the Union League of Philadelphia "tendered a reception" to George H. Boker, Minister of the United States to Turkey. Thomas Bailey Aldrich wrote of the occasion, "It is pleasant to see Philadelphia treating one of her own distinguished men of letters as if he were a distinguished man of letters from somewhere else." However, in the sixty-five pages of speeches and commendatory letters in the commemorative program, there was no mention of Boker as a dramatist and only casual reference to him as a poet. He was honored as a diplomat and as an old and faithful member of the Union League. Today Boker is remembered as the first American dramatist whose literary merits were commensurate with his theatrical skills. In fact, no other English or American playwright of the period quite approached his stature as a writer.

George Henry Boker was born into a substantial Philadelphia family on October 6, 1823. His Quaker father, Charles S. Boker, had come from Nottinghamshire, England, started his New World career as a merchant, and then become an influential and widely known Philadelphia banker. When he was eight, George was placed in Walker's Private School; at fifteen he entered the College of New Jersey (Princeton), where he soon became known not only as the college poet but as the college "swell." His quarters, the most extravagantly furnished on campus, became the gathering place for the literati; and his two-hundred-dollar yearly allowance was the envy of his classmates. Not wanting in means, he spent his week-end and between-term vacations becoming acquainted with the New York and Philadelphia theatres. When he was graduated in 1842, his father had arranged a position for him as secretary to the ambassador at Vienna. George rejected the opportunity, but only after promising his family he would study law: his father insisted that he become either a banker or a lawyer. Two years after leaving Princeton, he was married to Julia Mandeville Riggs of Georgetown, D.C. George conscientiously respected the promise to his father and kept to his law studies, but after four years he and his father agreed that he had neither inclination nor aptitude for the legal profession. If literature was to be his line, there was only one commonly accepted course of preparation, the "grand tour" of Europe. With his father's blessing and financial assistance, the young couple spent the next year absorbing European culture.

When they returned to Philadelphia, Boker began his literary pursuits in earnest. Fortunately, he had chosen an ideal mate for a would-be writer. Julia understood and encouraged his endeavors, and she was kind to his friends. For the twenty-four years from 1847–1871, Boker divided his time among his composition, his literary friends (Bayard Taylor, Richard Henry Stoddard, and Charles G. Leland), his mistresses, and his metal and wood work. He had turned the top floor of his Philadelphia home into a workshop. In fact, when he was pressed to supply biographical detail about himself, he insisted that he was a turner by trade. Only one major unpleasantness interrupted his established routine. Shortly after his father died in 1858, the Girard Bank filed a suit against the estate, charging Charles Boker with fraud. For the next fifteen years, George Boker fought the case in one court after another. Finally, in 1873, he won a clean bill for the Boker name.

In 1871 George Boker adopted another profession. On November 3 President Grant appointed him Minister to Turkey. Although Boker had been led to believe he was to receive a more substantial post, he concealed his disappointment and assumed his new duties at Constantinople, with his son, Colonel George Boker, as his military attaché. Four years later he was transferred to a similar assignment in Russia, where he remained as Envoy Extraordinary and Minister Plenipotentiary until January 14, 1878. On his return to Philadelphia, he was elected President of the Union League, a position he held until 1884. Boker had been one of the founders of this organization and had been its secretary from 1863 to 1871. After an illness which lingered through the last three years of his life, he died of a heart attack on January 2, 1890.

Boker would be described today as a "gentleman of the old school," polished, aloof and reserved. He lived near Rittenhouse Square and moved in the most fashionable Philadelphia society. As one acquaintance said of him, "He had an aristocratic bearing; but at the same time, no one could have been more intensely American at heart, or more loyal to republican principles and institutions." He had a genuine and strong love of his country, evident in his lyrics of the Civil War and his sonnets to America. He was equally fascinated by the romantic histories of the past, particularly of Spain. In fact, he roamed among all periods and places seeking themes for his poems and plays.

Although Boker dabbled in poetry while at Princeton, his first volume of verse, *The Lesson of Life*, was not printed until 1848. In the same year his first play, *Calaynos*, was published, and on May 10, 1849, it had its first production at the Sadler's Wells Theatre in London. Samuel Phelps used a pirated version for these London performances. On January 20, 1851, and for nine successive nights, James E. Murdoch performed the play at the Walnut Street Theatre in

Philadelphia with Boker's approval. In 1864 Murdoch reported that he had played *Calaynos* a total of some fifty performances in Philadelphia in addition to productions in Baltimore, Albany, and Chicago.

Within a ten-year period, Boker wrote nine plays. Of these, *Anne Boleyn* (1850), *The Widow's Marriage* (1852), and *Königsmark* (written before 1857, although not published until 1869) were not performed. Apart from *Calaynos*, the others were variously performed in Philadelphia and New York, although none of them achieved substantial records in their initial runs: *The Betrothal* (September 25, 1850, Walnut Street Theatre, Philadelphia, ten nights); *The World a Mask* (April 21, 1851, Walnut Street Theatre, eight nights); *Leonor de Guzman* (October 3, 1853, Walnut Street Theatre, six nights); *Francesca da Rimini* (September 26, 1855, Broadway Theatre, New York, eight nights); and *The Bankrupt* (December 3, 1855, Broadway Theatre, four nights). Although this was a respectable record of dramatic authorship and theatrical production, it did not impress Boker. He wrote to Bayard Taylor in 1854: "My theatrical success I never valued. I had not, nor have I, any ambition to become a mere playwright. . . . If I could not be acknowledged as a poet, I had no further desire, and no further active concern in literature." Had the initial response to Boker's plays been more spontaneous and whole-hearted, he might well have been encouraged to write more poetic dramas. Certainly he was fascinated by the theatre. On August 12, 1850, he had written to Stoddard regarding the preparation of *The Betrothal*:

The manager is getting it up with unusual care and splendour. Spangles and red flannels flame through it from end to end. I even think of appearing before the curtain on horseback, nay of making the whole performance equestrian, and of introducing a hippopotamus in the fifth act. What think you? Have you and your miserable lyrics ever known such glory? If the play should take *here*, you benighted New-Yorkers will be illuminated with it immediately after it has run its hundredth night in the city which is so proud of its son.

Boker turned from the theatre to poetry, particularly patriotic poetry: *Poems of the War* and *The Will of the People*. Although these volumes were not published until 1864, the poems had been widely circulated during the war. James E. Murdoch and other actors and readers (the USO entertainers of their day) had recited them for the soldiers in camp. Boker himself, after a favorable response to his reading of his Phi Beta Kappa poem "Our Heroic Times" at Harvard on July 20, 1865, undertook a number of public readings of his own poetry between 1865 and 1870. Edwin Forrest once called him "the best reader in America." With his diplomatic appointment in 1871, his literary talents remained in abeyance until his return and Lawrence Barrett's successful revival of *Francesca da Rimini* in 1882. Stimulated by this reawakening of interest in his dramatic composition and by Barrett's encouragement, Boker adapted Bulwer-Lytton's *Last Days of Pompeii* into a drama called *Nydia*

(1885). Barrett rejected the play, insisting that the leading part was not prominent enough or the scenic demands sufficiently engaging. Boker tried to remedy these deficiencies in a reworking of the material called *Glaucus* (1886), in which the final scene prescribed an earthquake and an eruption. Barrett was not persuaded by the additions. Undoubtedly his financial disputes with Boker over *Francesca* contributed to his unwillingness to undertake a production. Boker's reputation as a dramatist continued to rest, as it does now, on his one great drama, *Francesca da Rimini.*

That this play is more intense, more impassioned, and more compact than his other dramas must have resulted, in part at least, from its manner of composition. *Francesca da Rimini* was written at white heat in nineteen days of March, 1853, "twenty-eight hundred lines in about three weeks," as Boker described it. Writing to Stoddard, Boker reported on his method of work:

While I am writing I eat nothing, I drink nothing, I meditate on my work, literally all day. By the time night arrives I am in a highly nervous and excited state. About nine o'clock I begin writing and smoking, and I continue the two exercises, *pari passu,* until about four o'clock in the morning. Then I reel to bed, half crazy with cigar smoke and poesy, sleep for five hours, and begin the next day as the former.

Apparently it was a felicitous moment in Boker's life for a love drama. Amorous thoughts filled his mind and came easily to his pen, notably in his sonnet sequence "On Profane Love." Boker needed little more than the inspiration of Dante's brief version of the love story in the Fifth Canto of the *Inferno.* The little more he found in Boccaccio's recital of incidents in *Il Commento Supra La Divina Commedia,* and the model for his poetic line in the Elizabethan dramatists. Although Boker's literary conscience demanded historical truth, he was willing to adapt the facts to conform to his dramatic needs. In a letter to William Gilmore Simms on December 24, 1869, he wrote, "I always looked upon a historical drama, or rather upon the writing of it, as art bounded and working within the limits of history." That the Paolo-and-Francesca intrigue actually endured for ten years did not restrain Boker from compressing the action, nor did he hesitate to introduce nonhistorical figures, Pepe for example. Although other versions of the story – a narrative poem by Leigh Hunt, *The Story of Rimini* (1816); a short German drama by Johann Ludwig Uhland, *Franceska da Rimino* (1807); and an Italian play by Silvio Pellico, *Francesca da Rimini* (1818), had appeared earlier – none of these contributed to Boker's rendition.

In November, 1854, over a year after the completion of the drama, E. L. Davenport wrote to Boker inquiring about a possible production, but it was almost a year later before the play was performed. Brought out at the Broadway Theatre in New York on September 26, 1855, with E. L. Davenport in the part of Lanciotto, it ran until October 4. Although eight performances did not constitute a popular success even in the mid-nineteenth century, this was not a thoroughly discreditable showing for a poetic tragedy by an American author. The New York *Daily Tribune* said of the opening performance, "The brilliancy of the first scene and the historical accuracy of the costumes and properties showed that the play had been conscientiously put upon the stage.... The play may be considered entirely successful." William Winter thought the play would have achieved wider acclaim had not the acting of Davenport been so "unimaginative, mechanical and melodramatic . . . its artifice destroyed the effect of nature." Davenport quickly responded to this charge. In a letter to Boker, he attributed the lack of success to the inadequate publicity of a lethargic management which regarded the past glories of the Broadway Theatre as sufficient to lure an audience. According to Davenport, theatregoers did not know that *Francesca* was on the boards.

After the Broadway company gave four additional performances in Philadelphia (October 10 to 13, 1855), the play lay dormant for the next twenty-seven years. In 1879 Lawrence Barrett, then approaching the peak of his popularity, took the play under consideration; but it was not until the summer of 1882, with Winter's encouragement and his agreement to assist in the preparation of a stage version, that Barrett decided to undertake a production. According to Winter, they "cut out many passages of the original text; changed the arrangement of scenes, assigned rightful places for the curtains, deepened the outlines, accelerated the movement and sharpened each effect of climax." Barrett's and Winter's judgments about changes prevailed over the mild protests of Boker, and the new rendering reached the stage at Haverly's Theatre in Philadelphia on September 14, 1882. The Philadelphia *Press* reported the following day, "The Philadelphia audience amazed itself by such a rapturous outburst of applause as we are wont to expect only in demonstrative audiences of foreign cities." The enthusiastic response seemed to erase whatever reservations Boker may have had about the alterations in the text. He wrote to Barrett, "Why didn't I receive this encouragement years ago? Then I might have done something." Boker may have composed his dramas only for his own pleasure, as he insisted so many times; but had he found the same applause in the theatre in 1855 as in 1882, his literary career might have been greatly altered.

This Philadelphia "outburst" was only the beginning. After a few more preliminary performances at McVicker's Theatre in Chicago in November, 1882, Barrett brought the production to the Star Theatre (formerly Wallack's) in New York on August 27, 1883. Barrett seems to have outdone himself on this occasion, and the audience and critics followed his example. The New York *Mirror* wrote on September 1, 1883:

Boker has made his play neither above nor below the level of popular understanding.

Barrett quite outshone all his former efforts. In the third act, at the close, there was a momentary flash of genius that electrified the house . . . fearing the love of his bethrothed is insincere, he receives from her assurance of her affection . . . here Barrett rose to a point of absolute grandeur, and his wild exultation fairly thrilled the spectators. . . . The audience manifested its appreciation in repeated cheers and deafening applause. . . . The parts were all magnificently dressed and the mounting was admirable in every respect.

William Winter, whose views were prejudiced in favor of the new production, found Barrett "the true ideal of Lanciotto . . . a great soul imprisoned in a misshapen body, intense with every feeling, tinctured with bitterness, isolated by deformity, tender and magnanimous but capable of terrible excess and terrible ferocity . . . bearing within himself the elements of tragedy and desolation."

With Otis Skinner supporting him as Paolo and Marie Wainwright as Francesca, Barrett's magnificently staged production drew capacity New York audiences for nine solid weeks, a remarkable engagement for a poetic tragedy at any time. During this first year of its rejuvenated theatrical life, Barrett played *Francesca* on his regular road tour and then brought it back to New York for an additional two weeks in January at the Grand Opera House. For the next four seasons it became a regular item in his touring repertoire and had annual performances in New York. That it maintained its high level of excellence is apparent from the later newspaper comments. Of the performances early in 1886 at the Star Theatre, the *New York Times* wrote, "It was distinguished by smoothness and general efficiency." The following year the same newspaper (May 25, 1887) spoke of "Boker's beautiful drama" and "Barrett's portrayal, as impassioned and stirring as ever." After a lapse of four years with no New York showings except for an amateur performance at the Lexington Opera House on April 3, 1888, Barrett brought the play back to New York for a week's run at the new Broadway Theatre beginning on January 19, 1891. Odell described this revival as "one of the most affecting performances I ever saw. . . . I was so moved, so exalted by the first visit to the play that I went immediately to see it again . . . credit to Boker and Barrett, high priests of the production."

Satisfying to Boker's last years as Barrett's success with *Francesca* must have been, the pleasure was mixed with the anguish caused by their disputes over money. They had signed no formal agreement regarding royalty. Barrett planned to, and did, pay Boker twenty dollars for evening performances and ten dollars for matinees. After the success of the play was assured, Boker requested a straight ten per cent of the gross. Barrett countered with an offer of thirty dollars for evenings and ten dollars for matinees. The argument was finally settled with an amicable compromise somewhere between these demands without court action or continued wrangling.

After Barrett's death in 1891, *Francesca da Rimini* was performed only sporadically until its second rebirth in Otis Skinner's production in 1901. Skinner now undertook the part of Lanciotto in a new rendering of the play that seems in the acting and staging to have been the equal of Barrett's. Skinner opened the play at the Grand Opera House in Chicago on August 22, 1901, then performed it in the cities across the country before reaching New York for a triumphant opening at Hammerstein's Victoria Theatre on December 31, 1901. The critics responded much as they had to Barrett's performance. One unascribed review said:

The sublime tragedy throws into pitiful contrast the mass of romantic trash that gluts the theatre today. How paltry and trivial seem the strutting mannikins of the machine made plays beside the loftiness and grandeur of this simple terrible tale. It may be that some will find Boker's version of *Francesca*, that Mr. Skinner uses, old-fashioned and heavy. Let them to their modern slang and shallowness. There is dignity in Mr. Boker's lines.

Admiration for the performance and apology for the prevailing taste seems to have been the tone of most of the comments. The New York *Dramatic Mirror* wrote on January 11, 1902:

Mr. Skinner's performance should certainly be seen by everyone who admires artistic legitimate acting. . . . But the taste of the mass of New York theatregoers seems so low that there must be some doubt as to whether they will appreciate so superior a performance.

After fifty-six performances in New York, Skinner again took the production on the road, and though he found favor wherever he played, at the end of the tour he reported a twenty-thousand-dollar loss.

New York theatregoers had an opportunity to see another version of the romantic story when Eleonora Duse brought D'Annunzio's *Francesca da Rimini* to Hammerstein's Victoria in the fall season of 1902. D'Annunzio's play, although it appears ponderous and overlong in comparison with Boker's, was certainly superior to the three other Francesca dramas of the period: Martin Greif's *Francesca da Rimini* (1892) in German, Stephen Phillips's *Paolo and Francesca* (1899), and F. Marion Crawford's *Francesca da Rimini* (1902), written for Sarah Bernhardt. None of them, including D'Annunzio's, quite captured the combination of loftiness and grandeur in the poetic line, simplicity and force in Lanciotto's tragic despair, and theatrical power, particularly when supported by the impassioned performances of Barrett and Skinner. Boker's drama was not an idyll of guilty love, like Phillips's, nor a discursive poetizing of a medieval story, like D'Annunzio's, but the tragedy of a lonely and loving soul encased in a deformed body who for one brief moment is touched by the ecstasy of being loved before being driven to frantic despair by the discovery that his wife and brother have betrayed him.

American audiences of the nineteenth century had an insatiable taste for romantic tragedy, as is clearly demonstrated by the repeated performances of *Hamlet, Othello, Macbeth*, and *Lear*, but only George Henry Boker, among the native or foreign dramatists, produced an original romantic tragedy of notable quality for them.

FRANCESCA DA RIMINI

GEORGE HENRY BOKER

CHARACTERS

MALATESTA, *Lord of Rimini*
GUIDO DA POLENTA, *Lord of Ravenna*
LANCIOTTO, *Malatesta's son*
PAOLO, *His brother*
PEPE, *Malatesta's jester*
LORDS, LADIES, KNIGHTS, PRIESTS,
    SOLDIERS, PAGES, ATTENDANTS, *etc.*

CARDINAL, *Friend to Guido*
RENE, *A troubadour*
FRANCESCA DA RIMINI, *Guido's daughter*
RITTA, *Her maid*

SCENE: *Rimini, Ravenna, and the neighborhood.*   TIME: *About 1300 A.D.*

ACT I. Scene 1

Rimini. The Garden of the Palace. Paolo and a number of Noblemen are discovered, seated under an arbor, surrounded by Rene, and other Troubadours, attendants, etc.

PAOLO: I prithee, Rene, charm our ears again
With the same song you sang me yesterday.
Here are fresh listeners.

RENE: Really, my good lord,
My voice is out of joint. A grievous cold –
[*Coughs*]

PAOLO: A very grievous, but convenient cold,
Which always racks you when you would not
sing.

RENE: O, no, my lord! Besides, I hoped to hear
My ditty warbled into fairer ears,
By your own lips; to better purpose, too. [*The
Noblemen all laugh*]

FIRST NOBLEMAN: Rene has hit it. Music runs to
waste
In ears like ours.

SECOND NOBLEMAN: Nay, nay; chaunt on, sweet
Count.

PAOLO: [*Coughing*] Alack! you hear, I've
caught poor Rene's cough.

FIRST NOBLEMAN: That would not be, if we wore
petticoats. [*The others laugh*]

PAOLO: O, fie!

FIRST NOBLEMAN: So runs the scandal to our
ears.

SECOND NOBLEMAN: Confirmed by all our other
senses, Count.

FIRST NOBLEMAN: Witnessed by many a doleful
sigh, poured out
By many a breaking heart in Rimini.

SECOND NOBLEMAN: Poor girls!

FIRST NOBLEMAN: [*Mimicking a lady*] Sweet
Count! sweet Count Paolo! O!
Plant early violets upon my grave!
Thus go a thousand voices to one tune. [*The
others laugh*]

PAOLO: 'Ods mercy! gentlemen, you do me
wrong.

FIRST NOBLEMAN: And by how many hundred,
more or less?

PAOLO: Ah! rogues, you'd shift your sins upon
my shoulders.

SECOND NOBLEMAN: You'd bear them stoutly.

FIRST NOBLEMAN: It were vain to give
Drops to god Neptune. You're the sea of love
That swallows all things.

SECOND NOBLEMAN: We the little fish
That meanly scull about within your depths.

PAOLO: Go on, go on! Talk yourselves fairly
out. [*Pepe laughs without*]
But, hark! here comes the fool! Fit company
For this most noble company of wits!

        Enter Pepe, laughing violently
Why do you laugh?

PEPE: I'm laughing at the world.
It has laughed long enough at me; and so
I'll turn the tables. Ho! ho! ho! I've heard
A better joke of Uncle Malatesta's
Than any I e'er uttered. [*Laughing*]

ALL: Tell it, fool.

PEPE: Why, do you know – upon my life, the best
And most original idea on earth:
A joke to put in practice, too. By Jove!
I'll bet my wit 'gainst the stupidity
Of the best gentlemen among you all,
You cannot guess it.

ALL: Tell us, tell us, fool.

PEPE: Guess it, guess it, fools.

PAOLO: Come, disclose, disclose!

PEPE: He has a match afoot. –

ALL: A match!

PEPE: A marriage.

ALL: Who? – who?

PEPE: A marriage in his family.

ALL: But, who?

PEPE: Ah! there's the point.

ALL: Paolo?

PEPE: No.

FIRST NOBLEMAN: The others are well wived.
Shall we turn Turks?

PEPE: Why, there's the summit of his joke, good sirs.
By all the sacred symbols of my art –
By cap and bauble, by my tinkling bell –
He means to marry Lanciotto! [*Laughs violently*]

ALL: [*Laughing*] Ho! –

PAOLO: Peace! peace! What tongue dare echo yon fool's laugh?
Nay, never raise your hands in wonderment:
I'll strike the dearest friend among ye all
Beneath my feet, as if he were a slave,
Who dares insult my brother with a laugh!

PEPE: By Jove! ye're sad enough. Here's mirth's quick cure!
Pretty Paolo has a heavy fist,
I warn you, sirs. Ho! ho! I trapped them all;
[*Laughing*]
Now I'll go mar old Malatesta's message.
[*Aside*] [*Exit*]

PAOLO: Shame on ye, sirs! I have mistaken you.
I thought I harbored better friends. Poor fops,
Who've slept in down and satin all your years,
Within the circle Lanciotto charmed
Round Rimini with his most potent sword! –
Fellows whose brows would melt beneath a casque,
Whose hands would fray to grasp a brand's rough hilt,
Who ne'er launched more than braggart threats at foes! –
Girlish companions of luxurious girls! –
Danglers round troubadours and winecups! – Men
Whose best parts are their clothes! bundles of silk,
Scented like summer! rag-men, nothing more! –
Creatures as generous as monkeys – brave
As hunted hares – courteous as grinning apes –
Grateful as serpents – useful as lap-dogs –
[*During this, the Noblemen, etc., steal off*]
Ha!
I am alone at last! So let me be,
Till Lanciotto fill the vacant room
Of these mean knaves, whose friendship is but breath. [*Exit*]

Scene 2

The Same. A Hall in the Castle. Enter Malatesta and Lanciotto.

MALATESTA: Guido, ay, Guido of Ravenna, son –
Down on his knees, as full of abject prayers
For peace and mercy as a penitent.

LANCIOTTO: His old trick, father. While his wearied arm
Is raised in seeming prayer, it only rests.
Anon, he'll deal you such a staggering blow,
With its recovered strength, as shall convert
You, and not him, into a penitent.

MALATESTA: No, no; your last bout levelled him. He reeled,
Into Ravenna, from the battle-field,
Like a stripped drunkard, and there headlong fell –
A mass of squalid misery, a thing
To draw the jeering urchins. I have this
From faithful spies. There's not a hope remains
To break the shock of his great overthrow.
I pity Guido.

LANCIOTTO: 'Sdeath! go comfort him!
I pity those who fought, and bled, and died,
Before the armies of this Ghibelin.

I pity those who halted home with wounds
Dealt by his hand. I pity widowed eyes
That he set running; maiden hearts that turn,
Sick with despair, from ranks thinned down
  by him;
Mothers that shriek, as the last stragglers fling
Their feverish bodies by the fountain-side,
Dumb with mere thirst, and faintly point to
  him,
Answering the dame's quick questions. I have
  seen
Unburied bones, and skulls – that seemed to
  ask,
From their blank eye-holes, vengeance at my
  hand –
Shine in the moonlight on old battle-fields;
And even these – the happy dead, my lord –
I pity more than Guido of Ravenna!
MALATESTA: What would you have?
LANCIOTTO: I'd see Ravenna burn,
Flame into heaven, and scorch the flying
  clouds;
I'd choke her streets with ruined palaces;
I'd hear her women scream with fear and
  grief,
As I have heard the maids of Rimini.
All this I'd sprinkle with old Guido's blood,
And bless the baptism.
MALATESTA: You are cruel.
LANCIOTTO: Not I;
But these things ache within my fretting brain.
The sight I first beheld was from the arms
Of my wild nurse, her husband hacked to
  death
By the fierce edges of these Ghibelins.
One cut across the neck – I see it now,
Ay, and have mimicked it a thousand times,
Just as I saw it, on our enemies. –
Why, that cut seemed as if it meant to bleed
On till the judgment. My distracted nurse
Stooped down, and paddled in the running
  gore
With her poor fingers; then a prophetess,
Pale with the inspiration of the god,
She towered aloft, and with her dripping hand
Three times she signed me with the holy cross.
'Tis all as plain as noon-day. Thus she
  spake, –
"May this spot stand till Guido's dearest blood
Be mingled with thy own!" The soldiers say,
In the close battle, when my wrath is up,
The dead man's blood flames on my vengeful
  brow

Like a red planet; and when war is o'er,
It shrinks into my brain, defiling all
My better nature with its slaughterous lusts.
Howe'er it be, it shaped my earliest thought,
And it will shape my last.
MALATESTA: You moody churl!
You dismal knot of superstitious dreams!
Do you not blush to empty such a head
Before a sober man? Why, son, the world
Has not given o'er its laughing humor yet,
That you should try it with such vagaries. –
  Poh!
I'll get a wife to teach you common sense.
LANCIOTTO: A wife for me! [*Laughing*]
MALATESTA: Ay, sir, a wife for you.
You shall be married, to insure your wits.
LANCIOTTO: 'Tis not your wont to mock me.
MALATESTA: How now, son!
I am not given to jesting. I have chosen
The fairest wife in Italy for you.
You won her bravely, as a soldier should:
And when you'd woo her, stretch your gaunt-
  let out,
And crush her fingers in its steely grip.
If you will plead, I ween, she dare not say –
No, by your leave. Should she refuse,
  howe'er,
With that same iron hand you shall go knock
Upon Ravenna's gates, till all the town
Ring with your courtship. I have made her
  hand
The price and pledge of Guido's future peace.
LANCIOTTO: All this is done!
MALATESTA: Done, out of hand; and now
I wait a formal answer, nothing more.
Guido dare not decline. No, by the saints,
He'd send Ravenna's virgins here in droves,
To buy a ten days' truce.
LANCIOTTO: Sir, let me say,
You stretch paternal privilege too far,
To pledge my hand without my own consent.
Am I a portion of your household stuff,
That you should trade me off to Guido thus?
Who is the lady I am bartered for?
MALATESTA: Francesca, Guido's daughter. –
  Never frown;
It shall be so!
LANCIOTTO: By heaven, it shall not be!
My blood shall never mingle with his race.
MALATESTA: According to your nurse's prophecy,
  Fate orders it.
LANCIOTTO: Ha!
MALATESTA: Now, then, I have struck

433

The chord that answers to your gloomy thoughts.
Bah! on your sibyl and her prophecy!
Put Guido's blood aside, and yet, I say,
Marry you shall.
LANCIOTTO: 'Tis most distasteful, sir.
MALATESTA: Lanciotto, look ye! You brave gentlemen,
So fond of knocking out poor people's brains,
In time must come to have your own knocked out;
What, then, if you bequeath us no new hands,
To carry on your business, and our house
Die out for lack of princes?
LANCIOTTO: Wed my brothers:
They'll rear you sons, I'll slay you enemies.
Paolo and Francesca! Note their names;
They chime together like sweet marriage-bells.
A proper match. 'Tis said she's beautiful;
And he is the delight of Rimini, –
The pride and conscious centre of all eyes,
The theme of poets, the ideal of art,
The earthly treasury of Heaven's best gifts!
I am a soldier; from my very birth,
Heaven cut me out for terror, not for love.
I had such fancies once, but now –
MALATESTA: Pshaw! son,
My faith is bound to Guido; and if you
Do not throw off your duty, and defy,
Through sickly scruples, my express commands,
You'll yield at once. No more: I'll have it so!
[*Exit*]
LANCIOTTO: Curses upon my destiny! What, I –
Ho! I have found my use at last – What, I,
I, the great twisted monster of the wars,
The brawny cripple, the herculean dwarf,
The spur of panic, and the butt of scorn –
I be a bridegroom! Heaven, was I not cursed
More than enough, when thou didst fashion me
To be a type of ugliness, – a thing
By whose comparison all Rimini
Holds itself beautiful? Lo! here I stand,
A knarléd, blighted trunk! There's not a knave
So spindle-shanked, so wry-faced, so infirm,
Who looks at me, and smiles not on himself.
And I have friends to pity me – great Heaven!
One has a favorite leg that he bewails, –
Another sees my hip with doleful plaints, –
A third is sorry o'er my huge swart arms, –
A fourth aspires to mount my very hump,

And thence harangue his weeping brotherhood!
Pah! it is nauseous! Must I further bear
The sidelong shuddering glances of a wife?
The degradation of a showy love,
That over-acts, and proves the mummer's craft
Untouched by nature? And a fair wife, too! –
Francesca, whom the minstrels sing about!
Though, by my side, what woman were not fair?
Circe looked well among her swine, no doubt;
Next me, she'd pass for Venus. Ho! ho! ho!
[*Laughing*]
Would there were something merry in my laugh!
Now, in the battle, if a Ghibelin
Cry, "Wry-hip! hunchback!" I can trample him
Under my stallion's hoofs; or haggle him
Into a monstrous likeness of myself:
But to be pitied, – to endure a sting
Thrust in by kindness, with a sort of smile! –
'Sdeath! it is miserable!

Enter Pepe

PEPE: My Lord –
LANCIOTTO: My fool!
PEPE: We'll change our titles when your bride's bells ring –
Ha, cousin?
LANCIOTTO: Even this poor fool has eyes,
To see the wretched plight in which I stand.
[*Aside*]
How, gossip, how?
PEPE: I, being the court-fool,
Am lord of fools by my prerogative.
LANCIOTTO: Who told you of my marriage?
PEPE: Rimini!
A frightful liar; but true for once, I fear.
The messenger from Guido has returned,
And the whole town is wailing over him.
Some pity you, and some the bride; but I,
Being more catholic, I pity both.
LANCIOTTO: Still, pity, pity! [*Aside. Bells toll*]
Ha! whose knell is that?
PEPE: Lord Malatesta sent me to the tower,
To have the bells rung for your marriage-news.
How, he said not; so I, as I thought fit,
Told the deaf sexton to ring out a knell. [*Bells toll*]
How do you like it?
LANCIOTTO: Varlet, have you bones,

To risk their breaking? I have half a mind
To thrash you from your motley coat! [*Seizes
him*]
PEPE: Pardee!
Respect my coxcomb, cousin. Hark! ha, ha!
[*Laughing*]

Bells ring a joyful peal
Some one has changed my music. Heaven de-
fend!
How the bells jangle! Yonder graybeard, now,
Rings a peal vilely. He's more used to knells,
And sounds them grandly. Only give him
time,
And, I'll be sworn, he'll ring your knell out
yet.
LANCIOTTO: Pepe, you are but half a fool.
PEPE: My lord,
I can return the compliment in full.
LANCIOTTO: So, you are ready.
PEPE: Truth is always so.
LANCIOTTO: I shook you rudely; here's a florin.
[*Offers money*]
PEPE: No:
My wit is merchandise, but not my honor.
LANCIOTTO: Your honor, sirrah!
PEPE: Why not? You great lords
Have something you call lordly honor; pray,
May not a fool have foolish honor too?
Cousin, you laid your hand upon my coat –
'Twas the first sacrilege it ever knew –
And you shall pay it. Mark! I promise you.
LANCIOTTO: [*Laughing*] Ha, ha! you bluster
well. Upon my life,
You have the tilt-yard jargon to a breath.
Pepe, if I should smite you on the cheek –
Thus, gossip, thus – [*Strikes him*] what
would you then demand?
PEPE: Your life!
LANCIOTTO: [*Laughing*] Ha, ha! there is the
camp-style, too –
A very cut-throat air! How this shrewd fool
Makes the punctilio of honor show!
Change helmets into coxcombs, swords to bau-
bles,
And what a figure is poor chivalry!
Thanks for your lesson, Pepe! [*Exit*]
PEPE: Ere I'm done,
You'll curse as heartily, you limping beast!
Ha! so we go – Lord Lanciotto, look! [*Walks
about, mimicking him*]
Here is a leg and camel-back, forsooth,
To match your honor and nobility!

You miscreated scarecrow, dare you shake,
Or strike in jest, a natural man like me? –
You curséd lump, you chaos of a man,
To buffet one whom Heaven pronounces good!
[*Bells ring*]
There go the bells rejoicing over you:
I'll change them back to the old knell again.
You marry, faugh! Beget a race of elves;
Wed a she-crocodile, and keep within
The limits of your nature! Here we go,
Tripping along to meet our promised bride,
Like a rheumatic elephant! ha, ha! [*Laugh-
ing*]

Exit, mimicking Lanciotto

Scene 3

*The Same. A Room in the Same. Enter Lan-
ciotto, hastily.*

LANCIOTTO: Why do these prodigies environ me?
In ancient Rome, the words a fool might drop,
From the confusion of his vagrant thoughts,
Were held as omens, prophecies; and men
Who made earth tremble with majestic deeds,
Trembled themselves at fortune's lightest
threat.
I like it not. My father named this match
While I boiled over with vindictive wrath
Towards Guido and Ravenna. Straight my
heart
Sank down like lead; a weakness seized on
me,
A dismal gloom that I could not resist;
I lacked the power to take my stand, and
say –
Bluntly, I will not! Am I in the toils?
Has fate so weakened me, to work its end?
There seems a fascination in it, too, –
A morbid craving to pursue a thing
Whose issue may be fatal. Would that I
Were in the wars again! These mental weeds
Grow on the surface of inactive peace.
I'm haunted by myself. Thought preys on
thought.
My mind seems crowded in the hideous mould
That shaped my body. What a fool am I
To bear the burden of my wretched life,
To sweat and toil under the world's broad eye,
Climb into fame, and find myself – O, what?
A most conspicuous monster! Crown my head,
Pile Caesar's purple on me – and what then?
My hump shall shorten the imperial robe,

My leg peep out beneath the scanty hem,
My broken hip shall twist the gown awry;
And pomp, instead of dignifying me,
Shall be by me made quite ridiculous.
The faintest coward would not bear all this:
Prodigious courage must be mine, to live;
To die asks nothing but weak will, and I
Feel like a craven. Let me skulk away
Ere life o'ertask me. [*Offers to stab himself*]

Enter Paolo

PAOLO: [*Seizing his hand*] Brother! what is this?
Lanciotto, are you mad? Kind Heaven! look
    here –
Straight in my eyes. Now answer, do you
    know
How near you were to murder? Dare you bend
Your wicked hand against a heart I love?
Were it for you to mourn your wilful death,
With such a bitterness as would be ours,
The wish would ne'er have crossed you. While
    we're bound
Life into life, a chain of loving hearts,
Were it not base in you, the middle link,
To snap, and scatter all? Shame, brother,
    shame!
I thought you better metal.

LANCIOTTO: Spare your words.
I know the seasons of our human grief,
And can predict them without almanac.
A few sobs o'er the body, and a few
Over the coffin; then a sigh or two,
Whose windy passage dries the hanging tear;
Perchance, some wandering memories, some
    regrets;
Then a vast influx of consoling thoughts –
Based on the trials of the sadder days
Which the dead missed; and then a smiling
    face
Turned on to-morrow. Such is mortal grief.
It writes its histories within a span,
And never lives to read them.

PAOLO: Lanciotto,
I heard the bells of Rimini, just now,
Exulting o'er your coming marriage-day,
While you conspired to teach them gloomier
    sounds.
Why are you sad?

LANCIOTTO: Paolo, I am wretched;
Sad's a faint word. But of my marriage-bells –
Heard you the knell that Pepe rang?

PAOLO: 'Twas strange:
A sullen antic of his crabbed wit.

LANCIOTTO: It was portentous. All dumb things
    find tongues
Against this marriage. As I passed the hall,
My armor glittered on the wall, and I
Paused by the harness, as before a friend
Whose well-known features slack our hurried
    gait;
Francesca's name was fresh upon my mind,
So I half-uttered it. Instant, my sword
Leaped from its scabbard, as with sudden life,
Plunged down and pierced into the oaken
    floor,
Shivering with fear! Lo! while I gazed upon
    it –
Doubting the nature of the accident –
Around the point appeared a spot of blood,
Oozing upon the floor, that spread and
    spread –
As I stood gasping by in speechless horror –
Ring beyond ring, until the odious tide
Crawled to my feet, and lapped them, like the
    tongues
Of angry serpents! O, my God! I fled
At the first touch of the infernal stain!
Go – you may see – go to the hall!

PAOLO: Fie! man,
You have been ever played on in this sort
By your wild fancies. When your heart is
    high,
You make them playthings; but in lower
    moods,
They seem to sap the essence of your soul,
And drain your manhood to its poorest dregs.

LANCIOTTO: Go look, go look!

PAOLO: [*Goes to the door, and returns*] There
    sticks the sword, indeed,
Just as your tread detached it from its sheath;
Looking more like a blessed cross, I think,
Than a bad omen. As for blood – Ha, ha!
    [*Laughing*]
It sets mine dancing. Pshaw! away with this!
Deck up your face with smiles. Go trim your-
    self
For the young bride. New velvet, gold, and
    gems,
Do wonders for us. Brother, come; I'll be
Your tiring-man, for once.

LANCIOTTO: Array this lump –
Paolo, hark! There are some human thoughts
Best left imprisoned in the aching heart,
Lest the freed malefactors should dispread
Infamous ruin with their liberty.
There's not a man – the fairest of ye all –

Who is not fouler than he seems. This life
Is one unending struggle to conceal
Our baseness from our fellows. Here stands
  one
In vestal whiteness with a lecher's lust; –
There sits a judge, holding law's scales in
  hands
That itch to take the bribe he dare not
  touch; –
Here goes a priest with heavenward eyes,
  whose soul
Is Satan's council-chamber; – there a doctor,
With nature's secrets wrinkled round a brow
Guilty with conscious ignorance; – and here
A soldier rivals Hector's bloody deeds –
Out-does the devil in audacity –
With craven longings fluttering in a heart
That dares do aught but fly! Thus are we all
Mere slaves and alms-men to a scornful world,
That takes us at our seeming.

PAOLO: Say 'tis true;
What do you drive at?

LANCIOTTO: At myself, full tilt.
I, like the others, am not what I seem.
Men call me gentle, courteous, brave. – They
  lie!
I'm harsh, rude, and a coward. Had I nerve
To cast my devils out upon the earth,
I'd show this laughing planet what a hell
Of envy, malice, cruelty, and scorn,
It has forced back to canker in the heart
Of one poor cripple!

PAOLO: Ha!

LANCIOTTO: Ay, now 'tis out!
A word I never breathed to man before.
Can you, who are a miracle of grace,
Feel what it is to be a wreck like me?
Paolo, look at me. Is there a line,
In my whole bulk of wretched contraries,
That nature in a nightmare ever used
Upon her shapes till now? Find me the man,
Or beast, or tree, or rock, or nameless thing,
So out of harmony with all things else,
And I'll go raving with bare happiness, –
Ay, and I'll marry Helena of Greece,
And swear I do her honor!

PAOLO: Lanciotto,
I, who have known you from a stripling up,
Never observed, or, if I did, ne'er weighed
Your special difference from the rest of men.
You're not Apollo –

LANCIOTTO: No!

PAOLO: Nor yet are you

A second Pluto. Could I change with you –
My graces for your nobler qualities –
Your strength, your courage, your renown –
  by heaven,
We'd e'en change persons, to the finest hair.

LANCIOTTO: You should be flatterer to an emper-
  or.

PAOLO: I am but just. Let me beseech you,
  brother,
To look with greater favor on yourself;
Nor suffer misty phantoms of your brain
To take the place of sound realities.
Go to Ravenna, wed your bride, and lull
Your cruel delusions in domestic peace.
Ghosts fly a fireside: 'tis their wont to stalk
Through empty houses, and through empty
  hearts.
I know Francesca will be proud of you.
Women admire you heroes. Rusty sages,
Pale poets, and scarred warriors, have been
Their idols ever; while we fair plump fools
Are elbowed to the wall, or only used
For vacant pastime.

LANCIOTTO: To Ravenna? – no!
In Rimini they know me; at Ravenna
I'd be a new-come monster, and exposed
To curious wonder. There will be parade
Of all the usual follies of the state;
Fellows with trumpets, tinselled coats, and
  wands,
Would strut before me, like vain mountebanks
Before their monkeys. Then, I should be
  stared
Out of my modesty; and when they look,
How can I tell if 'tis the bridegroom's face
Or hump that draws their eyes? I will not go.
To please you all, I'll marry; but to please
The wonder-mongers of Ravenna – Ha!
Paolo, now I have it. You shall go,
To bring Francesca; and you'll speak of me,
Not as I ought to be, but as I am.
If she draw backward, give her rein; and say
That neither Guido nor herself shall feel
The weight of my displeasure. You may say,
I pity her –

PAOLO: For what?

LANCIOTTO: For wedding me.
In sooth, she'll need it. Say –

PAOLO: Nay, Lanciotto,
I'll be a better orator in your behalf,
Without your promptings.

LANCIOTTO: She is fair, 'tis said;
And, dear Paolo, if she please your eye,

And move your heart to anything like love,
Wed her yourself. The peace would stand as firm
By such a match.
PAOLO: [*Laughing*] Ha! that is right: be gay!
Ply me with jokes! I'd rather see you smile
Than see the sun shine.
LANCIOTTO: I am serious.
I'll find another wife, less beautiful,
More on my level, and –
PAOLO: An empress, brother,
Were honored by your hand. You are by much
Too humble in your reckoning of yourself.
I can count virtues in you, to supply
Half Italy, if they were parcelled out.
Look up!
LANCIOTTO: I cannot: Heaven has bent me down.
To you, Paolo, I could look, however,
Were my hump made a mountain. Bless him,
    God!
Pour everlasting bounties on his head!
Make Croesus jealous of his treasury,
Achilles of his arms, Endymion
Of his fresh beauties, – though the coy one lay,
Blushing beneath Diana's earliest kiss,
On grassy Latmos; and may every good,
Beyond man's sight, though in the ken of
    Heaven,
Round his fair fortune to a perfect end!
O, you have dried the sorrow of my eyes;
My heart is beating with a lighter pulse;
The air is musical; the total earth
Puts on new beauty, and within the arms
Of girding ocean dreams her time away,
And visions bright tomorrows!

Enter Malatesta and Pepe

MALATESTA: Mount, to horse!
PEPE: [*Aside*] Good Lord! He's smiling! What's
    the matter now?
Has anybody broken a leg or back?
Has a more monstrous monster come to life?
Is hell burst open? – heaven burnt up? What,
    what
Can make yon eyesore grin? – I say, my lord,
What cow has calved?
PAOLO: Your mother, by the bleat.
PEPE: Right fairly answered – for a gentleman!
When did you take my trade up?
PAOLO: When your wit
Went begging, sirrah.
PEPE: Well again! My lord,

I think he'll do.
MALATESTA: For what?
PEPE: To take my place.
Once fools were rare, and then my office sped;
But now the world is overrun with them:
One gets one's fool in one's own family,
Without much searching.
MALATESTA: Pepe, gently now.
Lanciotto, you are waited for. The train
Has passed the gate, and halted there for you.
LANCIOTTO: I go not to Ravenna.
MALATESTA: Hey! why not?
PAOLO: For weighty reasons, father. Will you
    trust
Your greatest captain, hope of all the Guelfs,
With crafty Guido? Should the Ghibellins
Break faith, and shut Lanciotto in their
    walls –
Sure the temptation would be great enough –
What would you do?
MALATESTA: I'd eat Ravenna up!
PEPE: Lord! what an appetite!
PAOLO: But Lanciotto
Would be a precious hostage.
MALATESTA: True; you're wise;
Guido's a fox. Well, have it your own way.
What is your plan?
PAOLO: I go there in his place.
MALATESTA: Good! I will send a letter with the
    news.
LANCIOTTO: I thank you, brother. [*Apart to
    Paolo*]
PEPE: Ha! ha! ha! – O! O! [*Laughing*]
MALATESTA: Pepe, what now?
PEPE: O! lord, O! – ho! ho! ho! [*Laughing*]
PAOLO: Well, giggler?
PEPE: Hear my fable, uncle.
MALATESTA: Ay.
PEPE: Once on a time, Vulcan sent Mercury
To fetch dame Venus from a romp in heaven.
Well, they were long in coming, as he thought;
And so the god of spits and gridirons
Railed like himself – the devil. But – now
    mark –
Here comes the moral. In a little while,
Vulcan grew proud, because he saw plain signs
That he should be a father; and so he
Strutted through hell, and pushed the devils
    by,
Like a magnifico of Venice. Ere long,
His heir was born; but then – ho! ho! – the
    brat
Had wings upon his heels, and thievish ways,

438

And a vile squint, like errant Mercury's,
Which honest Vulcan could not understand; –
Can you?
PAOLO: 'Sdeath! fool, I'll have you in the stocks.
Father, your fool exceeds his privilege.
PEPE: [*Apart to Paolo*] Keep your own bounds,
  Paolo. In the stocks
I'd tell more fables than you'd wish to hear.
And so ride forth. But, cousin, don't forget
To take Lanciotto's picture to the bride.
Ask her to choose between it and yourself.
I'll count the moments, while she hesitates,
And not grow gray at it.
PAOLO: Peace, varlet, peace!
PEPE: [*Apart to him*] Ah! now I have it.
  There's an elephant
Upon the scutcheon; show her that, and say –
Here's Lanciotto in our heraldry!
PAOLO: Here's for your counsel! [*Strikes Pepe,
  who runs behind Malatesta*]
MALATESTA: Son, son, have a care!
We who keep pets must bear their pecks some-
  times.
Poor knave! Ha! ha! thou'rt growing villainous!
  [*Laughs and pats Pepe*]
PEPE: Another blow! another life for that!
  [*Aside*]
PAOLO: Farewell, Lanciotto. You are dull
  again.
LANCIOTTO: Nature will rule.
MALATESTA: Come, come!
LANCIOTTO: God speed you, brother!
I am too sad; my smiles all turn to sighs.
PAOLO: More cause to haste me on my happy
  work.

Exit with Malatesta

PEPE: I'm going, cousin.
LANCIOTTO: Go.
PEPE: Pray, ask me where.
LANCIOTTO: Where, then?
PEPE: To have my jewel carried home:
And, as I'm wise, the carrier shall be
A thief, a thief, by Jove! The fashion's new.

Exit

LANCIOTTO: In truth, I am too gloomy and irra-
  tional.
Paolo must be right. I always had
These moody hours and dark presentiments,
Without mischances following after them.
The camp is my abode. A neighing steed,
A fiery onset, and a stubborn fight,
Rouse my dull blood, and tire my body down
To quiet slumbers when the day is o'er,
And night above me spreads her spangled tent,
Lit by the dying cresset of the moon.
Ay, that is it; I'm homesick for the camp.

Exit

ACT II. Scene 1

*Ravenna. A Room in Guido's Palace. Enter
Guido and a Cardinal.*

CARDINAL: I warn thee, Count.
GUIDO: I'll take the warning, father,
On one condition: show me but a way
For safe escape.
CARDINAL: I cannot.
GUIDO: There's the point:
We Ghibelins are fettered hand and foot.
There's not a florin in my treasury;
Not a lame soldier, I can lead to war;
Not one to man the walls. A present siege,
Pushed with the wonted heat of Lanciotto,
Would deal Ravenna such a mortal blow
As ages could not mend. Give me but time
To fill the drainéd arteries of the land.
The Guelfs are masters, we their slaves; and
  we
Were wiser to confess it, ere the lash
Teach it too sternly. It is well for you
To say you love Francesca. So do I;
But neither you nor I have any voice
For or against this marriage.
CARDINAL: 'Tis too true.
GUIDO: Say we refuse: Why, then, before a week,
We'll hear Lanciotto rapping at our door,
With twenty hundred ruffians at his back.
What's to say then? My lord, we waste our
  breath.
Let us look fortune in the face, and draw
Such comfort from the wanton as we may.
CARDINAL: And yet I fear –
GUIDO: You fear! and so do I.
I fear Lanciotto as a soldier, though,
More than a son-in-law.
CARDINAL: But have you seen him?
GUIDO: Ay, ay, and felt him, too. I've seen him
  ride
The best battalions of my horse and foot
Down like mere stubble: I have seen his sword
Hollow a square of pikemen, with the ease
You'd scoop a melon out.

CARDINAL: Report declares him
A prodigy of strength and ugliness.
GUIDO: Were he the devil – but why talk of this? –
Here comes Francesca.
CARDINAL: Ah, unhappy child!
GUIDO: Look you, my lord! you'll make the best of it;
You will not whimper. Add your voice to mine,
Or woe to poor Ravenna!

Enter Francesca and Ritta

FRANCESCA: Ha! my lord –
And you, my father! – But do I intrude
Upon your counsels? How severe you look!
Shall I retire?
GUIDO: No, no.
FRANCESCA: You moody men
Seem leagued against me. As I passed the hall,
I met your solemn Dante, with huge strides
Pacing in measure to his stately verse.
The sweeping sleeves of his broad scarlet robe
Blew out behind, like wide-expanded wings,
And seemed to buoy him in his level flight.
Thinking to pass, without disturbing him,
I stole on tip-toe; but the poet paused,
Subsiding into man, and steadily
Bent on my face the lustre of his eyes.
Then, taking both my trembling hands in his –
You know how his God-troubled forehead awes –
He looked into my eyes, and shook his head,
As if he dared not speak of what he saw;
Then muttered, sighed, and slowly turned away
The weight of his intolerable brow.
When I glanced back, I saw him, as before,
Sailing adown the hall on out-spread wings.
Indeed, my lord, he should not do these things:
They strain the weakness of mortality
A jot too far. As for poor Ritta, she
Fled like a doe, the truant.
RITTA: Yes, forsooth:
There's something terrible about the man.
Ugh! if he touched me, I should turn to ice.
I wonder if Count Lanciotto looks –
GUIDO: Ritta, come here. [*Takes her apart*]
RITTA: My lord.
GUIDO: 'Twas my command,
You should say nothing of Count Lanciotto.

RITTA: Nothing, my lord.
GUIDO: You have said nothing, then?
RITTA: Indeed, my lord.
GUIDO: 'Tis well. Some years ago,
My daughter had a very silly maid,
Who told her sillier stories. So, one day,
This maiden whispered something I forbade –
In strictest confidence, for she was sly:
What happened, think you?
RITTA: I know not, my lord.
GUIDO: I boiled her in a pot.
RITTA: Good heaven! my lord.
GUIDO: She did not like it. I shall keep that pot
Ready for the next boiling. [*Walks back to the others*]
RITTA: Saints above!
I wonder if he ate her! Boil me – me!
I'll roast or stew with pleasure; but to boil
Implies a want of tenderness, – or rather
A downright toughness – in the matter boiled,
That's slanderous to a maiden. What, boil me –
Boil me! O! mercy, how ridiculous! [*Retires, laughing*]

Enter a Messenger

MESSENGER: Letters, my lord, from great Prince
Malatesta. [*Presents them, and exits*]
GUIDO: [*Aside*] Hear him, ye gods! – "from
great Prince Malatesta!"
Greeting, no doubt, his little cousin Guido.
Well, well, just so we see-saw up and down.
[*Reads*]
"*Fearing our treachery,*" – by heaven, that's blunt,
And Malatesta-like! – "*he will not send
His son, Lanciotto, to Ravenna, but*" –
But what? – a groom, a porter? or will he
Have his prey sent him in an iron cage?
By Jove, he shall not have her! O! no, no;
"*He sends his younger son, the Count Paolo,
To fetch Francesca back to Rimini.*"
That's well, if he had left his reasons out.
And, in a postscript – by the saints, 'tis droll! –
"*'Twould not be worth your lordship's while, to shut
Paolo in a prison; for, my lord,
I'll only pay his ransom in plain steel:
Besides, he's not worth having.*" Is there one,
Save this ignoble offshoot of the Goths,

Who'd write such garbage to a gentleman?
Take that, and read it. [*Gives letter to Cardinal*]

CARDINAL: I have done the most.
She seems suspicious.

GUIDO: Ritta's work.

CARDINAL: Farewell! [*Exit*]

FRANCESCA: Father, you seem distempered.

GUIDO: No, my child,
I am but vexed. Your husband's on the road,
Close to Ravenna. What's the time of day?

FRANCESCA: Past noon, my lord.

GUIDO: We must be stirring, then.

FRANCESCA: I do not like this marriage.

GUIDO: But I do.

FRANCESCA: But I do not. Poh! to be given away,
Like a fine horse or falcon, to a man
Whose face I never saw!

RITTA: That's it, my lady.

GUIDO: Ritta, run down, and see if my great pot
Boils to your liking.

RITTA: [*Aside*] O! that pot again!
My lord, my heart betrays me; but you know
How true 'tis to my lady. [*Exit*]

FRANCESCA: What ails Ritta?

GUIDO: The ailing of your sex, a running tongue.
Francesca, 'tis too late to beat retreat:
Old Malatesta has me – you, too, child –
Safe in his clutch. If you are not content,
I must unclose Ravenna, and allow
His son to take you. Poh, poh! have a soul
Equal with your estate. A prince's child
Cannot choose husbands. Her desires must
aim,
Not at herself, but at the public good.
Both as your prince and father, I command;
As subject and good daughter, you'll obey.

FRANCESCA: I knew that it must be my destiny,
Some day, to give my hand without my heart;
But –

GUIDO: But, and I will but you back again!
When Guido da Polenta says to you,
Daughter, you must be married, – what were
best?

FRANCESCA: 'Twere best Francesca, of the self-
same name,
Made herself bridal-garments. [*Laughing*]

GUIDO: Right!

FRANCESCA: My lord,
Is Lanciotto handsome – ugly – fair –
Black – sallow – crabbed – kind – or what is he?

GUIDO: You'll know ere long. I could not alter
him,

To please your taste.

FRANCESCA: You always put me off;
You never have a whisper in his praise.

GUIDO: The world reports it. – Count my soldiers' scars,
And you may sum Lanciotto's glories up.

FRANCESCA: I shall be dutiful, to please you, fa-
ther.
If aught befall me through my blind submis-
sion,
Though I may suffer, you must bear the sin.
Beware, my lord, for your own peace of mind!
My part has been obedience; and now
I play it over to complete my task;
And it shall be with smiles upon my lips, –
Heaven only knows with what a sinking heart!
[*Exeunt*]

Scene 2

*The Same. Before the Gates of the City. The
walls hung with banners, flowers, etc., and
crowded with citizens. At the side of the scene
is a canopied dais, with chairs of state upon it.
Music, bells, shouts, and other sounds of rejoicing, are occasionally heard. Enter Guido, the
Cardinal, Noblemen, Knights, Guards, etc.,
with banners, arms, etc.*

GUIDO: My lord, I'll have it so. You talk in
vain.
Paolo is a marvel in his way:
I've seen him often. If Francesca take
A fancy to his beauty, all the better;
For she may think that he and Lanciotto
Are like as blossoms of one parent branch.
In truth, they are, so far as features go –
Heaven help the rest! Get her to Rimini,
By any means, and I shall be content.
The fraud cannot last long; but long enough
To win her favor to the family.

CARDINAL: 'Tis a dull trick. Thou hast not dealt
with her
Wisely nor kindly, and I dread the end.
If, when this marriage was enjoined on thee,
Thou hadst informed Francesca of the truth,
And said, Now, daughter, choose between
Thy peace and all Ravenna's; who that knows
The constant nature of her noble heart
Could doubt the issue? There'd have been
some tears,

441

Some frightful fancies of her husband's looks;
And then she'd calmly walk up to her fate,
And bear it bravely. Afterwards, perchance,
Lanciotto might prove better than her fears, –
No one denies him many an excellence, –
And all go happily. But, as thou wouldst plot,
She'll be prepared to see a paragon,
And find a satyr. It is dangerous.
Treachery with enemies is bad enough,
With friends 'tis fatal.

GUIDO: Has your lordship done?

CARDINAL: Never, Count Guido, with so good a
  text.
Do not stand looking sideways at the truth;
Craft has become thy nature. Go to her.

GUIDO: I have not heart.

CARDINAL: I have. [*Going*]

GUIDO: Hold, Cardinal!
My plan is better. Get her off my hands,
And I care not.

CARDINAL: What will she say of thee,
In Rimini, when she detects the cheat?

GUIDO: I'll stop my ears up.

CARDINAL: Guido, thou art weak,
And lack the common fortitude of man.

GUIDO: And you abuse the license of your garb,
To lessen me. My lord, I do not dare
To move a finger in these marriage-rites.
Francesca is a sacrifice, I know, –
A limb delivered to the surgeon's knife,
To save our general health. A truce to this.
Paolo has the business in his hands:
Let him arrange it as he will; for I
Will give Count Malatesta no pretext
To recommence the war.

CARDINAL: Farewell, my lord.
I'll neither help nor countenance a fraud.
You crafty men take comfort to yourselves,
Saying, deceit dies with discovery.
'Tis false; each wicked action spawns a brood,
And lives in its succession. You, who shake
Man's moral nature into storm, should know
That the last wave which passes from your
  sight
Rolls in and breaks upon eternity! [*Exit*]

GUIDO: Why, that's a very grand and solemn
  thought:
I'll mention it to Dante. Gentlemen,
What see they from the wall?

NOBLEMAN: The train, my lord.

GUIDO: Inform my daughter.

NOBLEMAN: She is here, my lord.

Enter Francesca, Ritta, Ladies, Attendants, etc.

FRANCESCA: See, father, what a merry face I
  have,
And how my ladies glisten! I will try
To do my utmost, in my love for you
And the good people of Ravenna. Now,
As the first shock is over, I expect
To feel quite happy. I will wed the Count,
Be he whate'er he may. I do not speak
In giddy recklessness. I've weighed it all, –
'Twixt hope and fear, knowledge and igno-
  rance, –
And reasoned out my duty to your wish.
I have no yearnings towards another love:
So, if I show my husband a desire
To fill the place with which he honors me,
According to its duties, even he –
Were he less noble than Count Lanciotto –
Must smile upon my efforts, and reward
Good will with willing grace. One pang re-
  mains.
Parting from home and kindred is a thing
None but the heartless, or the miserable,
Can do without a tear. This home of mine
Has filled my heart with two-fold happiness,
Taking and giving love abundantly.
Farewell, Ravenna! If I bless thee not,
'Tis that thou seem'st too blessed; and 'twere
  strange
In me to offer what thou'st always given.

GUIDO: [*Aside*] This is too much! If she would
  rail a while
At me and fortune, it could be endured.

Shouts, music, etc., within

FRANCESCA: Ha! there's the van just breaking
  through the wood!
Music! that's well; a welcome forerunner.
Now, Ritta – here – come talk to me. Alas!
How my heart trembles! What a world to me
Lies 'neath the glitter of yon cavalcade!
Is that the Count?

RITTA: Upon the dapple-gray?

FRANCESCA: Yes, yes.

RITTA: No; that's his –

GUIDO: [*Apart to her*]   Ritta!

RITTA: Ay; that's – that's

GUIDO: Ritta, the pot! [*Apart to her*]

RITTA: O! but this lying chokes! [*Aside*]
Ay, that's Count Somebody, from Rimini.

FRANCESCA: I knew it was. Is that not glorious?

RITTA: My lady, what?

FRANCESCA: To see a cavalier
Sit on his steed with such familiar grace.
RITTA: To see a man astraddle on a horse!
It don't seem much to me.
FRANCESCA: Fie! stupid girl!
But mark! the minstrels thronging round the
    Count!
Ah! that is more than gallant horsemanship.
The soul that feeds itself on poesy,
Is of a quality more fine and rare
Than Heaven allows the ruder multitude.
I tell you, Ritta, when you see a man
Beloved by poets, made the theme of song,
And chaunted down to ages, as a gift
Fit for the rich embalmment of their verse,
There's more about him than the patron's
    gold.
If that's the gentleman my father chose,
He must have picked him out from all the
    world.
The Count alights. Why, what a noble grace
Runs through his slightest action! Are you sad?
You, too, my father? Have I given you cause?
I am content. If Lanciotto's mind
Bear any impress of his fair outside,
We shall not quarrel ere our marriage-day.
Can I say more? My blushes speak for me:
Interpret them as modesty's excuse
For the short-comings of a maiden's speech.
RITTA: Alas! dear lady! [*Aside*]
GUIDO: [*Aside*] 'Sdeath! my plot has failed,
By overworking its design. Come, come;
Get to your places. See, the Count draws
nigh.

*Guido and Francesca seat themselves upon the
dais, surrounded by Ritta, Ladies, Attendants,
Guards, etc. Music, shouts, ringing of bells,
etc. Enter Men-at-arms, with banners, etc.;
Pages bearing costly presents on cushions; then
Paolo, surrounded by Noblemen, Knights,
Minstrels, etc., and followed by other Men-at-
arms. They range themselves opposite the dais*
GUIDO: Ravenna welcomes you, my lord, and I
Add my best greeting to the general voice.
This peaceful show of arms from Rimini
Is a new pleasure, stranger to our sense
Than if the East blew zephyrs, or the balm
Of Summer loaded rough December's gales,
And turned his snows to roses.
PAOLO: Noble sir,
We looked for welcome from your courtesy,
Not from your love; but this unhoped for sight

Of smiling faces, and the gentle tone
In which you greet us, leave us naught to win
Within your hearts. I need not ask, my lord,
Where bides the precious object of my search;
For I was sent to find the fairest maid
Ravenna boasts, among her many fair.
I might extend my travel many a league,
And yet return, to take her from your side.
I blush to bear so rich a treasure home,
As pledge and hostage of a sluggish peace;
For beauty such as hers was meant by Heaven
To spur our race to gallant enterprise,
And draw contending deities around
The dubious battles of a second Troy.
GUIDO: Sir Count, you please to lavish on my
    child
The high-strained courtesy of chivalry;
Yet she has homely virtues that, I hope,
May take a deeper hold in Rimini,
After the fleeting beauty of her face
Is spoiled by time, or faded to the eye
By its familiar usage.
PAOLO: As a man
Who ever sees Heaven's purpose in its works,
I must suppose so rare a tabernacle
Was framed for rarest virtues. Pardon me
My public admiration. If my praise
Clash with propriety, and bare my words
To cooler judgment, 'tis not that I wish
To win a flatterer's grudged recompense,
And gain by falsehood what I'd win through
love.
When I have brushed my travel from my garb,
I'll pay my court in more befitting style.

Music. Exit with his train
GUIDO: [*Advancing*] Now, by the saints, Lan-
    ciotto's deputy
Stands in this business with a proper grace,
Stretching his lord's instructions till they crack.
A zealous envoy! Not a word said he
Of Lanciotto – not a single word;
But stood there, staring in Francesca's face
With his devouring eyes. – By Jupiter,
I but half like it!
FRANCESCA: [*Advancing*] Father?
GUIDO: Well, my child.
FRANCESCA: How do you like –
GUIDO: The coxcomb! I've done well!
FRANCESCA: No, no; Count Lanciotto?
GUIDO: Well enough.
But hang this fellow – hang your deputies!
I'll never woo by proxy.

FRANCESCA: Deputies!
And woo by proxy!

GUIDO: Come to me anon.
I'll strip this cuckoo of his gallantry!

Exit with Guards, etc.

FRANCESCA: Ritta, my father has strange ways of late.

RITTA: I wonder not.

FRANCESCA: You wonder not?

RITTA: No, lady:
He is so used to playing double games,
That even you must come in for your share.
Plague on his boiling! I will out with it.
[*Aside*]
Lady, the gentleman who passed the gates –

FRANCESCA: Count Lanciotto? As I hope for grace,
A gallant gentleman! How well he spoke!
With what sincere and earnest courtesy
The rounded phrases glided from his lips!
He spoke in compliments that seemed like truth.
Methinks I'd listen through a summer's day,
To hear him woo. – And he must woo to me –
I'll have our privilege – he must woo a space,
Ere I'll be won, I promise.

RITTA: But, my lady,
He'll woo you for another.

FRANCESCA: He? – ha! ha! [*Laughing*]
I should not think it from the prologue, Ritta.

RITTA: Nor I.

FRANCESCA: Nor any one.

RITTA: 'Tis not the Count –
'Tis not Count Lanciotto.

FRANCESCA: Gracious saints!
Have you gone crazy? Ritta, speak again,
Before I chide you.

RITTA: 'Tis the solemn truth.
That gentleman is Count Paolo, lady,
Brother to Lanciotto, and no more
Like him than – than –

FRANCESCA: Than what?

RITTA: Count Guido's pot,
For boiling waiting-maids, is like the bath
Of Venus on the arras.

FRANCESCA: Are you mad, –
Quite mad, poor Ritta?

RITTA: Yes; perhaps I am.
Perhaps Lanciotto is a proper man –
Perhaps I lie – perhaps I speak the truth –
Perhaps I gabble like a fool. O! heavens,
That dreadful pot!

FRANCESCA: Dear Ritta! –

RITTA: By the mass,
They shall not cozen you, my gentle mistress!
If my lord Guido boiled me, do you think
I should be served up to the garrison,
By way of pottage? Surely they would not
waste me.

FRANCESCA: You are an idle talker. Pranks like these
Fit your companions. You forget yourself.

RITTA: Not you, though, lady. Boldly I repeat,
That he who looked so fair, and talked so sweet,
Who rode from Rimini upon a horse
Of dapple-gray, and walked through yonder gate,
Is not Count Lanciotto.

FRANCESCA: This you mean?

RITTA: I do, indeed!

FRANCESCA: Then I am more abused –
More tricked, more trifled with, more played upon –
By him, my father, and by all of you,
Than anything, suspected of a heart,
Was ever yet!

RITTA: In Count Paolo, lady,
Perchance there was no meditated fraud.

FRANCESCA: How, dare you plead for him?

RITTA: I but suppose:
Though in your father – O! I dare not say.

FRANCESCA: I dare. It was ill usage, gross abuse,
Treason to duty, meanness, craft – dishonor!
What if I'd thrown my heart before the feet
Of this sham husband! cast my love away
Upon a counterfeit! I was prepared
To force affection upon any man
Called Lanciotto. Anything of silk,
Tinsel, and gewgaws, if he bore that name,
Might have received me for the asking. Yes,
I was inclined to venture more than half
In this base business – shame upon my thoughts! –
All for my father's peace and poor Ravenna's.
And this Paolo, with his cavalcade,
His minstrels, music, and his pretty airs,
His showy person, and his fulsome talk,
Almost made me contented with my lot.
O! what a fool! – in faith, I merit it –
Trapped by mere glitter! What an easy fool!
Ha! ha! I'm glad it went no further, girl;
[*Laughing*]
I'm glad I kept my heart safe, after all.

There was my cunning. I have paid them
 back,
I warrant you! I'll marry Lanciotto;
I'll seem to shuffle by this treachery. No!
I'll seek my father, put him face to face
With his own falsehood; and I'll stand be-
 tween,
Awful as justice, meting out to him
Heaven's dreadful canons 'gainst his conscious
 guilt.
I'll marry Lanciotto. On my faith,
I would not live another wicked day
Here, in Ravenna, only for the fear
That I should take to lying, with the rest.
Ha! ha! it makes me merry, when I think
How safe I kept this little heart of mine!
[*Laughing*]

Exit, with Attendants, etc.

RITTA: So, 'tis all ended – all except my boiling,
And that will make a holiday for some.
Perhaps I'm selfish. Fagot, axe, and gallows,
They have their uses, after all. They give
The lookers-on a deal of harmless sport.
Though one may suffer, twenty hundred
 laugh;
And that's a point gained. I have seen a
 man –
Poor Dora's uncle – shake himself with glee,
At the bare thought of the ridiculous style
In which some villain died. "Dancing,"
 quoth he,
"To the poor music of a single string!
Biting," quoth he, "after his head was off!
What use of that?" Or, "Shivering," quoth
 he,
"As from an ague, with his beard afire!"
And then he'd roar until his ugly mouth
Split at the corners. But to see me boil –
O! that will be the queerest thing of all!
I wonder if they'll put me in a bag,
Like a great suet-ball? I'll go, and tell
Count Guido, on the instant. How he'll laugh
To think his pot has got an occupant!
I wonder if he really takes delight
In such amusements? Nay, I have kept faith:
I only said the man was not Lanciotto;
No word of Lanciotto's ugliness.
I may escape the pot, for all. Pardee!
I wonder if they'll put me in a bag!

Exit, laughing

Scene 3

*The Same. A Room in Guido's Palace. Enter
Guido and Ritta.*

RITTA: There now, my lord, that is the whole of
 it:
I love my mistress more than I fear you.
If I could save her finger from the axe,
I'd give my head to do it. So, my lord,
I am prepared to stew.
GUIDO: Boil, Ritta, boil.
RITTA: No; I prefer to stew.
GUIDO: And I to boil.
RITTA: 'Tis very hard, my lord, I cannot choose
My way of cooking. I shall laugh, I vow,
In the grim headsman's face, when I remem-
 ber
That I am dying for my lady's love.
I leave no one to shed a tear for me;
Father nor mother, kith nor kin, have I,
To say, "Poor Ritta!" o'er my lifeless clay.
They all have gone before me, and 'twere well
If I could hurry after them.
GUIDO: Poor child! [*Aside*]
But, baggage, said you aught of Lanciotto?
RITTA: No, not a word; and he's so ugly, too!
GUIDO: Is he so ugly?
RITTA: Ugly! he is worse
Than Pilate on the hangings.
GUIDO: Hold your tongue
Here, and at Rimini, about the Count,
And you shall prosper.
RITTA: Am I not to boil?
GUIDO: No, child. But be discreet at Rimini.
Old Malatesta is a dreadful man –
Far worse than I – he bakes his people, Ritta;
Lards them, like geese, and bakes them in an
 oven.
RITTA: Fire is my fate, I see that.
GUIDO: Have a care
It do not follow you beyond this world.
Where is your mistress?
RITTA: In her room, my lord.
After I told her of the Count Paolo,
She flew to have an interview with you;
But on the way – I know not why it was –
She darted to her chamber, and there stays
Weeping in silence. It would do you good –
More than a hundred sermons – just to see
A single tear, indeed it would, my lord.
GUIDO: Ha! you are saucy. I have humored you
Past prudence, malpert! Get you to your room!
[*Exit Ritta*]

More of my blood runs in yon damsel's veins
Than the world knows. Her mother to a
  shade;
The same high spirit, and strange martyr-wish
To sacrifice herself, body and soul,
For some loved end. All that she did for me;
And yet I loved her not. O! memory!
The darkest future has a ray of hope,
But thou art blacker than the sepulchre!
Thy horrid shapes lie round, like scattered
  bones,
Hopeless forever! I am sick at heart.
The past crowds on the present: as I sowed,
So am I reaping. Shadows from myself
Fall on the picture, as I trace anew
These rising spectres of my early life,
And add their gloom to what was dark before.
O! memory, memory! How my temples throb!
  [*Sits*]

Enter Francesca, hastily

FRANCESCA: My lord, this outrage – [*He looks
  up*] Father, are you ill?
You seem unhappy. Have I troubled you?
You heard how passionate and bad I was,
When Ritta told me of the Count Paolo.
Dear father, calm yourself; and let me ask
A child's forgiveness. 'Twas undutiful
To doubt your wisdom. It is over now.
I only thought you might have trusted me
With any counsel.
GUIDO: [*Aside*] Would I had!
FRANCESCA: Ah! well,
I understand it all, and you were right.
Only the danger of it. Think, my lord,
If I had loved this man at the first sight:
We all have heard of such things. Think,
  again,
If I had loved him – as I then supposed
You wished me to – 'twould have been very
  sad.
But no, dear sir, I kept my heart secure,
Nor will I loose it till you give the word.
I'm wiser than you thought me, you perceive.
But when we saw him, face to face, together,
Surely you might have told me then.
GUIDO: Francesca,
My eyes are old – I did not clearly see –
Faith, it escaped my thoughts. Some other
  things
Came in my head. I was as ignorant
Of Count Paolo's coming as yourself.
The brothers are so like.

FRANCESCA: Indeed?
GUIDO: Yes, yes.
One is the other's counterpart, in fact;
And even now it may not be – O! shame!
I lie by habit. [*Aside*]
FRANCESCA: Then there is a hope?
He may be Lanciotto, after all?
O! joy –

Enter a Servant

SERVANT: The Count Paolo. [*Exit*]
FRANCESCA: Misery!
That name was not Lanciotto!
GUIDO: Farewell, child.
I'll leave you with the Count: he'll make it
  plain.
It seems 'twas Count Paolo. [*Going*]
FRANCESCA: Father!
GUIDO: Well.
FRANCESCA: You knew it from the first! [*Exit
  Guido*] Let me begone:
I could not look him in the face again
With the old faith. Besides, 'twould anger him
To have a living witness of his fraud
Ever before him; and I could not trust –
Strive as I might – my happiness to him,
As once I did. I could not lay my hand
Upon his shoulder, and look up to him,
Saying, Dear father, pilot me along
Past this dread rock, through yonder narrow
  strait.
Saints, no! The gold that gave my life away
Might, even then, be rattling in his purse,
Warm from the buyer's hand. Look on me,
  Heaven!
Him thou didst sanctify before my eyes,
Him thou didst charge, as thy great deputy,
With guardianship of a weak orphan girl,
Has fallen from grace, has paltered with his
  trust;
I have no mother to receive thy charge, –
O! take it on thyself; and when I err,
Through mortal blindness, Heaven, be thou
  my guide!
Worse cannot fall me. Though my husband
  lack
A parent's tenderness, he yet may have
Faith, truth, and honor – the immortal bonds
That knit together honest hearts as one.
Let me away to Rimini. Alas!
It wrings my heart to have outlived the day
That I can leave my home with no regret!
  [*Weeps*]

Enter Paolo

PAOLO: Pray, pardon me. [*Going*]

FRANCESCA: You are quite welcome, Count.
A foolish tear, a weakness, nothing more:
But present weeping clears our future sight.
They tell me you are love's commissioner,
A kind of broker in the trade of hearts:
Is it your usual business? or may I
Flatter myself, by claiming this essay
As your first effort?

PAOLO: Lady, I believed
My post, at starting, one of weight and trust;
When I beheld you, I concluded it
A charge of honor and high dignity.
I did not think to hear you underrate
Your own importance, by dishonoring me.

FRANCESCA: You are severe, my lord.

PAOLO: No, not severe;
Say candid, rather. I am somewhat hurt
By my reception. If I feel the wound,
'Tis not because I suffer from the jest,
But that your lips should deal it.

FRANCESCA: Compliments
Appear to be the staple of your speech.
You ravish one with courtesy, you pour
Fine words upon one, till the listening head
Is bowed with sweetness. Sir, your talk is
   drugged;
There's secret poppy in your sugared phrase:
I'll taste before I take it.

PAOLO: Gentle lady –

FRANCESCA: I am not gentle, or I missed my
   aim.
I am no hawk to fly at every lure.
You courtly gentlemen draw one broad rule –
All girls are fools. It may be so, in truth,
Yet so I'll not be treated.

PAOLO: Have you been?
If I implied such slander by my words,
They wrong my purpose. If I compliment,
'Tis not from habit, but because I thought
Your face deserved my homage as its due.
When I have clearer insight, and you spread
Your inner nature o'er your lineaments,
Even that face may darken in the shades
Of my opinion. For mere loveliness
Needs inward light to keep it always bright.
All things look badly to unfriendly eyes.
I spoke my first impression; cooler thought
May work strange changes.

FRANCESCA: Ah! Sir Count, at length
There's matter in your words.

PAOLO: Unpleasant stuff,

To judge by your dark brows. I have essayed
Kindness and coldness, yet you are not
   pleased.

FRANCESCA: How can I be?

PAOLO: How, lady?

FRANCESCA: Ay, sir, how?
Your brother – my good lord that is to be –
Stings me with his neglect; and in the place
He should have filled, he sends a go-between,
A common carrier of others' love;
How can the sender, or the person sent,
Please overmuch? Now, were I such as you,
I'd be too proud to travel round the land
With other people's feelings in my heart;
Even to fill the void which you confess
By such employment.

PAOLO: Lady, 'tis your wish
To nettle me, to break my breeding down,
And see what natural passions I have hidden
Behind the outworks of my etiquette.
I neither own nor feel the want of heart
With which you charge me. You are more
   than cruel;
You rouse my nerves until they ache with life,
And then pour fire upon them. For myself
I would not speak, unless you had compelled.
My task is odious to me. Since I came,
Heaven bear me witness how my traitor heart
Has fought against my duty; and how oft
I wished myself in Lanciotto's place,
Or him in mine.

FRANCESCA: You riddle.

PAOLO: Do I? Well,
Let it remain unguessed.

FRANCESCA: You wished yourself
At Rimini, or Lanciotto here?
You may have reasons.

PAOLO: Well interpreted!
The Sphinx were simple in your skilful hands!

FRANCESCA: It has become your turn to sneer.

PAOLO: But I
Have gall to feed my bitterness, while you
Jest in the wanton ease of happiness.
Stop! there is peril in our talk.

FRANCESCA: As how?

PAOLO: 'Tis dangerous to talk about one's self;
It panders selfishness. My duty waits.

FRANCESCA: My future lord's affairs? I quite forgot Count Lanciotto.

PAOLO: I, too, shame upon me! [*Aside*]

FRANCESCA: Does he resemble you?

PAOLO: Pray, drop me, lady.

FRANCESCA: Nay, answer me.

PAOLO: Somewhat – in feature.

FRANCESCA: Ha!
Is he so fair?

PAOLO: No, darker. He was tanned
In long campaigns, and battles hotly fought,
While I lounged idly with the troubadours,
Under the shadow of his watchful sword.

FRANCESCA: In person?

PAOLO: He is shorter, I believe,
But broader, stronger, more compactly knit.

FRANCESCA: What of his mind?

PAOLO: Ah! now you strike the key!
A mind just fitted to his history,
An equal balance 'twixt desert and fame.
No future chronicler shall say of him,
His fame outran his merit; or his merit
Halted behind some adverse circumstance,
And never won the glory it deserved.
My love might weary you, if I rehearsed
The simple beauty of his character;
His grandeur and his gentleness of heart,
His warlike fire and peaceful love, his faith,
His courtesy, his truth. I'll not deny
Some human weakness, to attract our love,
Harbors in him, as in the rest of us.
Sometimes against our city's enemies
He thunders in the distance, and devotes
Their homes to ruin. When the brand has fall-
en,
He ever follows with a healing rain,
And in his pity shoulders by revenge.
A thorough soldier, lady. He grasps crowns,
While I pick at the laurel.

FRANCESCA: Stay, my lord!
I asked your brother's value, with no wish
To hear you underrate yourself. Your worth
May rise in passing through another's lips.
Lanciotto is perfection, then?

PAOLO: To me:
Others may think my brother over-nice
Upon the point of honor; over-keen
To take offence where no offence is meant;
A thought too prodigal of human life,
Holding it naught when weighed against a
wrong;
Suspicious of the motives of his friends;
Distrustful of his own high excellence;
And with a certain gloom of temperament,
When thus disturbed, that makes him terrible
And rash in action. I have heard of this;
I never felt it. I distress you, lady?
Perhaps I throw these points too much in
shade,

By catching at an enemy's report.
But, then, Lanciotto said, "You'll speak of
me,
Not as I ought to be, but as I am."
He loathes deceit.

FRANCESCA: That's noble! Have you done?
I have observed a strange reserve, at times,
An over-carefulness in choosing words,
Both in my father and his nearest friends,
When speaking of your brother; as if they
Picked their way slowly over rocky ground,
Fearing to stumble. Ritta, too, my maid,
When her tongue rattles on in full career,
Stops at your brother's name, and with a sigh
Settles herself to dismal silence. Count,
These things have troubled me. From you I
look
For perfect frankness. Is there naught with-
held?

PAOLO: [*Aside*] O, base temptation! What if I
betray
His crippled person – imitate his limp –
Laugh at his hip, his back, his sullen moods
Of childish superstition? – tread his heart
Under my feet, to climb into his place?–
Use his own warrant 'gainst himself; and say,
Because I loved her, and misjudged your jest,
Therefore I stole her? Why, a common thief
Would hang for just such thinking! Ha! ha!
ha! [*Laughing*]
I reckon on her love, as if I held
The counsels of her bosom. No, I swear,
Francesca would despise so mean a deed.
Have I no honor either? Are my thoughts
All bound by her opinion?

FRANCESCA: This is strange!
Is Lanciotto's name a spell to all?
I ask a simple question, and straight you
Start to one side, and mutter to yourself,
And laugh, and groan, and play the lunatic,
In such a style that you astound me more
Than all the others. It appears to me
I have been singled as a common dupe
By every one. What mystery is this
Surrounds Count Lanciotto? If there be
A single creature in the universe
Who has a right to know him as he is,
I am that one.

PAOLO: I grant it. You shall see,
And shade your judgment by your own re-
mark.
All that my honor calls for I have said.

FRANCESCA: I am content. Unless I greatly err,

Heaven made your breast the seat of honest
thoughts.
You know, my lord, that, once at Rimini,
There can be no retreat for me. By you,
Here at Ravenna, in your brother's name,
I shall be solemnly betrothed. And now
I thus extend my maiden hand to you;
If you are conscious of no secret guilt,
Take it.
PAOLO: I do. [*Takes her hand*]
FRANCESCA: You tremble!
PAOLO: With the hand,
Not with the obligation.
FRANCESCA: Farewell, Count!
'Twere cruel to tax your stock of compliments,
That waste their sweets upon a trammelled
heart;
Go fly your fancies at some freer game. [*Exit*]
PAOLO: O, heaven, if I have faltered and am
weak,
'Tis from my nature! Fancies, more accursed
Than haunt a murderer's bedside, throng my
brain—
Temptations, such as mortal never bore
Since Satan whispered in the ear of Eve,
Sing in my ear – and all, all are accursed!
At heart I have betrayed my brother's trust,
Francesca's openly. Turn where I will,
As if enclosed within a mirrored hall,
I see a traitor. Now to stand erect,
Firm on my base of manly constancy;
Or, if I stagger, let me never quit
The homely path of duty, for the ways
That bloom and glitter with seductive sin!
[*Exit*]

ACT III. Scene I

Rimini. A Room in the Castle. Lanciotto discovered reading.

LANCIOTTO: O! fie, philosophy! This Seneca
Revels in wealth, and whines about the poor!
Talks of starvation while his banquet waits,
And fancies that a two hours' appetite
Throws light on famine! Doubtless he can tell,
As he skips nimbly through his dancing-girls,
How sad it is to limp about the world
A sightless cripple! Let him feel the crutch
Wearing against his heart, and then I'd hear
This sage talk glibly; or provide a pad,
Stuffed with his soft philosophy, to ease
His aching shoulder. Pshaw! he never felt,

Or pain would choke his frothy utterance.
'Tis easy for the doctor to compound
His nauseous simples for a sick man's health;
But let him swallow them, for his disease,
Without wry faces. Ah! the tug is there.
Show me philosophy in rags, in want,
Sick of a fever, with a back like mine,
Creeping to wisdom on these legs, and I
Will drink its comforts. Out! away with you!
There's no such thing as real philosophy!
[*Throws down the book*]

Enter Pepe

Here is a sage who'll teach a courtier
The laws of etiquette, a statesman rule,
A soldier discipline, a poet verse,
And each mechanic his distinctive trade;
Yet bring him to his motley, and how wide
He shoots from reason! We can understand
All business but our own, and thrust advice
In every gaping cranny of the world;
While habit shapes us to our own dull work,
And reason nods above his proper task.
Just so philosophy would rectify
All things abroad, and be a jade at home.
Pepe, what think you of the Emperor's aim
Towards Hungary?
PEPE: A most unwise design;
For mark, my lord –
LANCIOTTO: Why, there! the fact cries out.
Here's motley thinking for a diadem! –
Ay, and more wisely in his own regard.
PEPE: You flout me, cousin.
LANCIOTTO: Have you aught that's new? –
Some witty trifle, some absurd conceit?
PEPE: Troth, no.
LANCIOTTO: Why not give up the Emperor.
And bend your wisdom on your duties, Pepe?
PEPE: Because the Emperor has more need of
wisdom
Than the most barren fool of wit.
LANCIOTTO: Well said!
Mere habit brings the fool back to his art.
This jester is a rare philosopher.
Teach me philosophy, good fool.
PEPE: No need.
You'll get a teacher when you take a wife.
If she do not instruct you in more arts
Than Aristotle ever thought upon,
The good old race of woman has declined
Into a sort of male stupidity.
I had a sweetheart once, she lectured grandly;
No matter on what subject she might hit,

449

'Twas all the same, she could talk and she
would.
She had no silly modesty; she dashed
Straight in the teeth of any argument,
And talked you deaf, dumb, blind. Whatever
struck
Upon her ear, by some machinery,
Set her tongue wagging. Thank the Lord, she
died! —
Dropped in the middle of a fierce harangue,
Like a spent horse. It was an even thing,
Whether she talked herself or me to death.
The latest sign of life was in her tongue;
It wagged till sundown, like a serpent's tail,
Long after all the rest of her was cold.
Alas! poor Zippa!

LANCIOTTO: Were you married, fool?
PEPE: Married! Have I the scars upon me? No;
I fell in love; and that was bad enough,
And far enough for a mere fool to go.
Married! why, marriage is love's purgatory,
Without a heaven beyond.

LANCIOTTO: Fie, atheist!
Would you abolish marriage?

PEPE: Yes.

LANCIOTTO: What?

PEPE: Yes.

LANCIOTTO: Depopulate the world?

PEPE: No fear of that.
I'd have no families, no Malatesti,
Strutting about the land, with pedigrees
And claims bequeathed them by their ances-
tors;
No fellows vaporing of their royal blood;
No one to seize a whole inheritance.
And rob the other children of the earth.
By Jove! you should not know your fathers,
even!
I'd have you spring, like toadstools, from the
soil —
Mere sons of women — nothing more nor less
All base-born, and all equal. There, my lord,
There is a simple commonwealth for you!
In which aspiring merit takes the lead,
And birth goes begging.

LANCIOTTO: It is so, in truth;
And by the simplest means I ever heard.

PEPE: Think of it, cousin. Tell it to your
friends,
The statesmen, soldiers, and philosophers;
Noise it about the earth, and let it stir
The sluggish spirits of the multitudes.
Pursue the thought, scan it, from end to end,

Through all its latent possibilities.
It is a great seed dropped, I promise you,
And it must sprout. Thought never wholly
dies;
It only wants a name — a hard Greek name —
Some few apostles, who may live on it —
A crowd of listeners, with the average dulness
That man possesses — and we organize;
Spread our new doctrine, like a general
plague;
Talk of man's progress and development,
Wrongs of society, the march of mind,
The Devil, Doctor Faustus, and what not,
And, lo! this pretty world turns upside down,
All with a fool's idea!

LANCIOTTO: By Jupiter,
You hit our modern teachers to a hair!
I knew this fool was a philosopher.
Pepe is right. Mechanic means advance;
Nature bows down to science' haughty tread,
And turns the wheel of smutty artifice;
New governments arise, dilate, decay,
And foster creeds and churches to their tastes:
At each advance, we cry, "Behold, the end!"
Till some fresh wonder breaks upon the age.
But man, the moral creature, midst it all
Stands still unchanged; nor moves towards vir-
tue more,
Nor comprehends the mysteries in himself,
More than when Plato taught academies,
Or Zeno thundered from his Attic porch.

PEPE: I know not that; I only want my scheme
Tried for a while. I am a politician,
A wrongs-of-man man. Hang philosophy!
Let metaphysics swallow, at a gulp,
Its last two syllables, and purge itself
Clean of its filthy humors! I am one
Ready for martyrdom, for stake and fire,
If I can make my great idea take root!
Zounds! cousin, if I had an audience,
I'd make you shudder at my eloquence!
I have an itching to reform the world.

LANCIOTTO: Begin at home, then.

PEPE: Home is not my sphere;
Heaven picked me out to teach my fellow-
men.
I am a very firebrand of truth —
A self-consuming, doomed, devoted brand —
That burns to ashes while I light the world!
I feel it in me. I am moved, inspired,
Stirred into utterance, by some mystic power
Of which I am the humble instrument.

LANCIOTTO: A bad digestion, sage, a bilious turn,
A gnawing stomach, or a pinching shoe.
PEPE: O! hear, but spare the scoffer! Spare the wretch
Who sneers at the anointed man of truth!
When we reached that, I and my followers
Would rend you limb from limb. There! – ha! ha! ha! [*Laughing*]
Have I not caught the slang these fellows preach;
A grand, original idea, to back it;
And all the stock in trade of a reformer?
LANCIOTTO: You have indeed; nor do I wonder, Pepe.
Fool as you are, I promise you success
In your new calling, if you'll set it up.
The thing is far too simple.

Trumpet sounds within

PEPE: Hist! my lord.
LANCIOTTO: That calls me to myself.
PEPE: At that alarm,
All Rimini leaped up upon its feet.
Cousin, your bridal-train. You groan! 'Ods wounds!
Here is the bridegroom sorely malcontent –
The sole sad face in Rimini. Since morn,
A quiet man could hardly walk the streets,
For flowers and streamers. All the town is gay.
Perhaps 'tis merry o'er your misery.
LANCIOTTO: Perhaps; but that it knows not.
PEPE: Yes, it does:
It knows that when a man's about to wed,
He's ripe to laugh at. Cousin, tell me, now,
Why is Paolo on the way so long?
Ravenna's but eight leagues from Rimini –
LANCIOTTO: That's just the measure of your tongue, good fool.
You trouble me. I've had enough of you –
Begone!
PEPE: I'm going; but you see I limp.
Have pity on a cripple, gentle Count. [*Limps*]
LANCIOTTO: Pepe!
PEPE: A miracle, a miracle!
See see, my lord, at Pepe's saintly name
The lame jog on.
MALATESTA: [*Without*] Come, Lanciotto!
LANCIOTTO: Hark!
My father calls.
PEPE: If he were mine, I'd go –
That's a good boy! [*Pats Lanciotto's back*]

LANCIOTTO: [*Starting*] Hands off! you'll rue it else! [*Exit*]
PEPE: [*Laughing*] Ha! ha! I laid my hand upon his hump!
Heavens, how he squirmed! And what a wish I had
To cry, Ho! camel! leap upon his back,
And ride him to the devil! So, we've had
A pleasant flitting round philosophy!
The Count and Fool bumped heads, and struck ideas
Out by the contact! Quite a pleasant talk –
A friendly conversation, nothing more –
'Twixt nobleman and jester. Ho! my bird,
I can toss lures as high as any man.
So, I amuse you with my harmless wit?
Pepe's your friend now – you can trust in him –
An honest, simple fool! Just try it once,
You ugly, misbegotten clod of dirt!
Ay, but the hump – the touch upon the hump –
The start and wriggle – that was rare! Ha! ha! [*Exit, laughing*]

Scene 2

The Same. The Grand Square before the Castle. Soldiers on guard, with banners, etc. Citizens, in holiday dresses, cross the scene. The houses are hung with trophies, banners, garlands, etc. Enter Malatesta, with guards, attendants, etc.

MALATESTA: Captain, take care the streets be not choked up
By the rude rabble. Send to Caesar's bridge
A strong detachment of your men, and clear
The way before them. See that nothing check
The bride's first entrance into Rimini.
Station your veterans in the front. Count Guido
Comes with his daughter, and his eyes are sharp.
Keep up a show of strength before him, sir;
And set some laborers to work upon
The broken bastion. Make all things look bright;
As if we stood in eager readiness,
And high condition, to begin a war.
CAPTAIN: I will, my lord.
MALATESTA: Keep Guido in your eye;
And if you see him looking over-long
On any weakness of our walls, just file

451

Your bulkiest fellows round him; or get up
A scuffle with the people; anything –
Even if you break a head or two – to draw
His vision off. But where our strength is great,
Take heed to make him see it. You conceive?
CAPTAIN: Trust me, my lord. [*Exit with guards*]

        Enter Pepe
PEPE: Room, room! A hall, a hall!
I pray you, good man, has the funeral passed?
MALATESTA: Who is it asks?
PEPE: Pepe of Padua,
A learned doctor of uncivil law.
MALATESTA: But how a funeral?
PEPE: You are weak of wit.
Francesca of Ravenna's borne to church,
And never issues thence.
MALATESTA: How, doctor, pray?
PEPE Now, for a citizen of Rimini,
You're sadly dull. Does she not issue thence
Fanny of Rimini? A glorious change, –
A kind of resurrection in the flesh!
MALATESTA: [*Laughing*] Ha! ha! thou cunning villain! I was caught.
I own it, doctor.
PEPE: [*Aside*] This old fool would laugh
To see me break a straw, because the bits
Were of unequal lengths. My character
Carries more dulness, in the guise of wit,
Than would suffice to break an ass's back.

     Distant shouts, music, etc.
Hark! here comes Jeptha's daughter, jogging on
With timbrels and with dances.
MALATESTA: Jeptha's daughter!
How so?
PEPE: Her father's sacrifice.
MALATESTA: [*Laughing*] Ho! ho!
You'll burst my belt! O! you outrageous wretch,
To jest at Scripture!
PEPE: You outlandish heathen,
'Tis not in Scripture!
MALATESTA: Is it not?
PEPE: No more
Than you are in heaven. Mere Hebrew history.
She went up to the mountains, to bewail
The too-long keeping of her honesty.
There's woman for you! There's a character!
What man would ever think of such a thing?

Ah! we of Rimini have little cause
For such a sorrow. Would she'd been my wife!
I'll marry any woman in her case.
MALATESTA: Why, Pepe?
PEPE: Why? because, in two months' time,
Along comes father Jeptha with his knife,
And there's an end. Where is your sacrifice?
Where's Isaac, Abraham? Build your altar up:
One pile will do for both.
MALATESTA: That's Scripture, sure.
PEPE: Then I'm a ram, and you may slaughter me
In Isaac's stead.
MALATESTA: Here comes the vanguard. Where,
Where is that laggard?
PEPE: At the mirror, uncle,
Making himself look beautiful. He comes, [*Looking out*]
Fresh as a bridegroom! Mark his doublet's fit
Across the shoulders, and his hose! –
By Jove, he nearly looks like any other man!
MALATESTA: You'd best not let him hear you.
Sirrah, knave,
I have a mind to swinge you! [*Seizes his ear*]
PEPE: Loose my ear!
You've got the wrong sow, swineherd! You're unjust.
Being his father, I was fool sufficient
To think you fashioned him to suit yourself,
By way of a variety. The thought
Was good enough, the practice damnable.
MALATESTA: Hush! or I'll clap you in the pillory.

      Enter Lanciotto
PEPE: [*Sings*]
Ho, ho, ho, ho! – Old Time has wings –

We're born, we mourn, we wed, we bed,
We have a devilish aching head;
  So down we lie,
   And die, and fry;
And there's a merry end of things!

     Music, etc., within
Here come Ravenna's eagles for a roost
In Rimini! The air is black with them.
When go they hence? Wherever yon bird builds,
The nest remains for ages. Have an eye,
Or Malatesta's elephant may feel
The eagle's talons.
LANCIOTTO: You're a raven, croaker.

PEPE: And you no white crow, to insure us luck.

MALATESTA: There's matter in his croak.

PEPE: There always is; But men lack ears.

MALATESTA: Then eyes must do our work. Old Guido shall be looked to. If his force Appear too great, I'll camp him out of town.

LANCIOTTO: Father, you are a sorry host.

MALATESTA: Well, well, I'm a good landlord, though. I do not like This flight of eagles more than Pepe. 'Sdeath! Guido was ever treacherous.

LANCIOTTO: My lord, You mar my holiday by such a thought. My holiday! Dear saints! it seems to me That all of you are mocking me.

PEPE: So – so – Guido was ever treacherous? – so – so!

MALATESTA: So – so! How so?

PEPE: What if this treachery Run in the blood? We'll tap a vein then – so!

MALATESTA: Sew up your mouth, and mind your fooling, fool!

PEPE: Am I not fooling? Why, my lord, I thought The fooling exquisite.

LANCIOTTO: [Aside] This thoughtless knave Hits near us sometimes with his random shafts. Marriage for me! I cannot comprehend, I cannot take it to my heart; the thing Seems gross, absurd, ridiculous. Ah! well, My father bears the folly of it all; I'm but an actor in his comedy. My part is bad, but I must through with it. [Retires]

Shouts, music, etc., within

PEPE: Look! here's the whole parade! Mark yonder knave – The head one with the standard. Nature, nature! Hadst thou a hand in such a botch-work? Why, A forest of his legs would scarcely make A bunch of fagots. Mark old Guido, too! He looks like Judas with his silver. Ho! Here's news from sweet Ravenna!

MALATESTA: [Laughing] Ha! ha! ha!

PEPE: Ah! now the bride! – that's something – she is toothsome.

Look you, my lord – now, while the progress halts – Cousin Paolo, has he got the dumps? Mercy! to see him, one might almost think 'Twas his own marriage. What a doleful face! The boy is ill. He caught a fever, 'uncle, Travelling across the marshes. Physic! physic! If he be really dying, get a doctor, And cut the matter short. 'Twere merciful.

MALATESTA: For heaven's sake, cease your clamor! I shall have No face to meet them else. 'Tis strange, for all: What ails Paolo?

PEPE: Dying, by this hand!

MALATESTA: Then I will hang you.

PEPE: Don't take up my craft. Wit's such a stranger in your brain that I Scarce knew my lodger venturing from your mouth. Now they come on again.

MALATESTA: Stand back!

PEPE: [Looking round] The bridegroom? He flies betimes, before the bride shows fight. [Walks back, looking for Lanciotto]

Music, shouts, ringing of bells, etc. Enter Men-at-arms, with banners, etc., Guido, Cardinal, Knights, Attendants, etc.; then Paolo, conducting Francesca, followed by Ritta, Ladies, Pages, etc., and other Men-at-arms. They file around the stage, and halt

MALATESTA: Welcome to Rimini, Count Guido! Welcome, And fair impressions of our poor abode, To you, my daughter! You are well returned, My son, Paolo! Let me bless you, son. [Paolo approaches] How many spears are in old Guido's train? [Apart to Paolo]

PAOLO: Some ten-score.

MALATESTA: Footmen?

PAOLO: Double that.

MALATESTA: 'Tis well. Again I bid you welcome! Make no show Of useless ceremony with us. Friends Have closer titles than the empty name. We have provided entertainment, Count, For all your followers, in the midst of us. We trust the veterans of Rimini May prove your soldiers that our courtesy Does not lag far behind their warlike zeal. Let us drop Guelf and Ghibelin henceforth,

Coupling the names of Rimini and Ravenna
As bridegroom's to his bride's.
GUIDO: Count Malatesta,
I am no rhetorician, or my words
Might keep more even with the love I feel:
Simply, I thank you. With an honest hand
I take the hand which you extend to me,
And hope our grasp may never lose its
warmth. –
You marked the bastion by the water-side?
Weak as a bulrush. [*Apart to a Knight*]
KNIGHT: Tottering weak, my lord.
GUIDO: Remember it; and when you're private,
sir,
Draw me a plan.
KNIGHT: I will, my lord.
GUIDO: How's this?
I do not see my future son-in-law.
MALATESTA: Lanciotto!
LANCIOTTO: [*Advancing*] I am here, my lord.
FRANCESCA: [*Starting*]   O! heaven!
Is that my husband, Count Paolo? You,
You then, among the rest, have played me
false!
He is – [*Apart to Paolo*]
PAOLO: My brother.
LANCIOTTO: [*Aside*] Ha! she turns from me.
PEPE: [*Approaching Lanciotto, sings*]

Around, around the lady turned,
  She turned not to her lord;
She turned around to a gallant, gallant knight,
  Who ate at his father's board.

A pretty ballad! all on one string though.
LANCIOTTO: Pepe, go hence! [*Pepe retires*]
  [*Aside*] I saw her start and pale,
Turn off with horror; as if she had seen –
What? – simply me. For, am I not enough,
And something over, to make ladies quail,
Start, hide their faces, whisper to their
friends,
Point at me – dare she? – and perform such
tricks
As women will when monsters blast their
sight?
O! saints above me, have I come so low?
Yon damsel of Ravenna shall bewail
That start and shudder. I am mad, mad,
mad!
I must be patient. They have trifled with her:
Lied to her, lied! There's half the misery
Of this broad earth, all crowded in one word.

Lied, lied! – Who has not suffered from a lie?
They're all aghast – all looking at me too.
Francesca's whiter than the brow of fear:
Paolo talks. – Brother, is that well meant?
What if I draw my sword, and fight my way
Out of this cursed town? 'Twould be relief.
Has shame no hiding-place? I've touched the
depth
Of human infamy, and there I rest.
By heaven, I'll brave this business out! Shall
they
Say at Ravenna that Count Lanciotto,
Who's driven their shivering squadrons to their
homes,
Haggard with terror, turned before their eyes
And slunk away? They'll look me from the
field,
When we encounter next. Why should not I
Strut with my shapeless body, as old Guido
Struts with his shapeless heart? I'll do it!
  [*Offers, but shrinks back*] 'Sdeath!
Am I so false as to forswear myself?
Lady Francesca! [*Approaches Francesca*]
FRANCESCA: Sir – my lord –
LANCIOTTO: Dear lady,
I have a share in your embarrassment,
And know the feelings that possess you now.
FRANCESCA: O! you do not.
PAOLO: [*Advancing*] My lady –
LANCIOTTO: Gentle brother,
Leave this to me. [*Paolo retires*]
FRANCESCA: Pray do not send him off.
LANCIOTTO: 'Tis fitter so.
FRANCESCA: He comforts me.
LANCIOTTO: Indeed?
Do you need comfort?
FRANCESCA: No, no – pardon me!
But then – he is – you are –
LANCIOTTO: Take breath, and speak.
FRANCESCA: I am confused, 'tis true. But, then,
my lord,
You are a stranger to me; and Paolo
I've known so long!
LANCIOTTO: Since yesterday.
FRANCESCA: Ah! well:
But the relationship between us two
Is of so close a nature, while the knowledge,
That each may have of each, so slender is
That the two jar. Besides, Paolo is
Nothing to me, while you are everything.
Can I not act? [*Aside*]
LANCIOTTO: I scarcely understand.
You say your knowledge of me, till to-day,

Was incomplete. Has naught been said of me
By Count Paolo or your father?

FRANCESCA: Yes;
But nothing definite.

LANCIOTTO: Perchance, no hint
As to my ways, my feelings, manners, or –
Or – or – as I was saying – ha! ha! – or –
[*Laughing*]
As to my person?

FRANCESCA: Nothing, as to that.

LANCIOTTO: To what?

FRANCESCA: Your – person.

LANCIOTTO: That's the least of all. [*Turns aside*]
Now, had I Guido of Ravenna's head
Under this heel, I'd grind it into dust!
False villain, to betray his simple child!
And thou, Paolo – not a whit behind –
Helping his craft with inconsiderate love! –
Lady Francesca, when my brother left,
I charged him, as he loved me, to conceal
Nothing from you that bore on me: and now
That you have seen me, and conversed with me,
If you object to anything in me, –
Go, I release you.

FRANCESCA: But Ravenna's peace?

LANCIOTTO: Shall not be perilled.

GUIDO: [*Coming behind, whispers her*] Trust him not, my child;
I know his ways; he'd rather fight than wed.
'Tis but a wish to have the war afoot.
Stand firm for poor Ravenna!

LANCIOTTO: Well, my lady,
Shall we conclude a lasting peace between us
By truce or marriage rites?

GUIDO: [*Whispers her*] The devil tempts thee:
Think of Ravenna, think of me!

LANCIOTTO: My lord,
I see my father waits you. [*Guido retires*]

FRANCESCA: Gentle sir,
You do me little honor in the choice.

LANCIOTTO: My aim is justice.

FRANCESCA: Would you cast me off?

LANCIOTTO: Not for the world, if honestly obtained;
Not for the world would I obtain you falsely.

FRANCESCA: The rites were half concluded ere we met.

LANCIOTTO: Meeting, would you withdraw?

FRANCESCA: No. Bitter word! [*Aside*]

LANCIOTTO: No! Are you dealing fairly?

FRANCESCA: I have said.

LANCIOTTO: O! rapture, rapture! Can it be that I –

Now I'll speak plainly; for a choice like thine
Implies such love as woman never felt.
Love me! Then monsters beget miracles,
And Heaven provides where human means fall short.
Lady, I'll worship thee! I'll line thy path
With suppliant kings! Thy waiting-maids shall be
Unransomed princesses! Mankind shall bow
One neck to thee, as Persia's multitudes
Before the rising sun! From this small town,
This centre of my conquests, I will spread
An empire touching the extremes of earth!
I'll raise once more the name of ancient Rome;
And what she swayed she shall reclaim again!
If I grow mad because you smile on me,
Think of the glory of thy love; and know
How hard it is, for such a one as I,
To gaze unshaken on divinity!
There's no such love as mine alive in man.
From every corner of the frowning earth,
It has been crowded back into my heart.
Now, take it all! If that be not enough,
Ask, and thy wish shall be omnipotent!
Your hand. [*Takes her hand*] It wavers.

FRANCESCA: So does not my heart.

LANCIOTTO: Bravo! Thou art every way a soldier's wife;
Thou shouldst have been a Caesar's! Father, hark!
I blamed your judgment, only to perceive
The weakness of my own.

MALATESTA: What means all this?

LANCIOTTO: It means that this fair lady – though I gave
Release to her, and to Ravenna – placed
The liberal hand, which I restored to her,
Back in my own, of her own free good-will.
Is it not wonderful?

MALATESTA: How so?

LANCIOTTO: How so!

PAOLO: Alas! 'tis as I feared! [*Aside*]

MALATESTA: You're humble? – how?

LANCIOTTO: Now shall I cry aloud to all the world,
Make my deformity my pride, and say,
Because she loves me, I may boast of it?
[*Aside*]
No matter, father, I am happy; you,
As the blessed cause, shall share my happiness.
Let us be moving. Revels, dashed with wine,
Shall multiply the joys of this sweet day!
There's not a blessing in the cup of life

I have not tasted of within an hour!

FRANCESCA: [*Aside*] Thus I begin the practice of
  deceit,
Taught by deceivers, at a fearful cost.
The bankrupt gambler has become the cheat,
And lives by arts that erewhile ruined me.
Where it will end, Heaven knows; but I –
I have betrayed the noblest heart of all!

LANCIOTTO: Draw down thy dusky vapors, sul-
  len night –
Refuse, ye stars, to shine upon the world –
Let everlasting blackness wrap the sun,
And whisper terror to the universe!
We need ye not! we'll blind ye, if ye dare
Peer with lack-lustre on our revelry!
I have at heart a passion, that would make
All nature blaze with recreated light! [*Exeunt*]

ACT IV. Scene I

*The Same. An Apartment in the Castle. Enter
Lanciotto.*

LANCIOTTO: It cannot be that I have duped my-
  self,
That my desire has played into the hand
Of my belief; yet such a thing might be.
We palm more frauds upon our simple selves
Than knavery puts upon us. Could I trust
The open candor of an angel's brow,
I must believe Francesca's. But the tongue
Should consummate the proof upon the brow,
And give the truth its word. The fault lies
  there.
I've tried her. Press her as I may to it,
She will not utter those three little words –
"I love thee." She will say, "I'll marry you; –
I'll be your duteous wife; – I'll cheer your
  days; –
I'll do whate'er I can." But at the point
Of present love, she ever shifts the ground,
Winds round the word, laughs, calls me
  "Infidel! –
How can I doubt?" So, on and on. But yet,
For all her dainty ways, she never says,
Frankly, I love thee. I am jealous – true!
Suspicious – true! distrustful of myself; –
She knows all that. Ay, and she likewise
  knows,
A single waking of her morning breath
Would blow these vapors off. I would not take
The barren offer of a heartless hand,

If all the Indies cowered under it.
Perhaps she loves another? No; she said,
"I love you, Count, as well as any man";
And laughed, as if she thought that precious
  wit.
I turn her nonsense into argument,
And think I reason. Shall I give her up?
Rail at her heartlessness, and bid her go
Back to Ravenna? But she clings to me,
At the least hint of parting. Ah! 'tis sweet,
Sweeter than slumber to the lids of pain,
To fancy that a shadow of true love
May fall on this God-stricken mould of woe,
From so serene a nature. Beautiful
Is the first vision of a desert brook,
Shining beneath its palmy garniture,
To one who travels on his easy way;
What is it to the blood-shot, aching eye
Of some poor wight who crawls with gory
  feet,
In famished madness, to its very brink;
And throws his sun-scorched limbs upon the
  cool
And humid margin of its shady strand,
To suck up life at every eager gasp?
Such seems Francesca to my thirsting soul;
Shall I turn off and die?

Enter Pepe

PEPE: Good-morning, cousin!

LANCIOTTO: Good-morning to your foolish majesty!

PEPE: The same to your majestic foolery!

LANCIOTTO: You compliment!

PEPE: I am a troubadour,
  A ballad-monger of fine mongrel ballads,
  And therefore running o'er with elegance.
  Wilt hear my verse?

LANCIOTTO: With patience?

PEPE: No, with rapture.
  You must go mad – weep, rend your clothes,
    and roll
  Over and over, like the ancient Greeks,
  When listening to the Iliad.

LANCIOTTO: Sing, then, sing!
  And if you equal Homer in your song,
  Why, roll I must, by sheer compulsion.

PEPE: Nay,
  You lack the temper of the fine-eared Greek.
  You will not roll; but that shall not disgrace
  My gallant ballad, fallen on evil times.
  [*Sings*]

My father had a blue-black head,
  My uncle's head was reddish – maybe,
My mother's hair was noways red,
  Sing high ho! the pretty baby!

Mark the simplicity of that! 'Tis called
"The Babe's Confession," spoken just before
His father strangled him.

LANCIOTTO: Most marvellous!
You struggle with a legend worth your art.

PEPE: Now to the second stanza. Note the hint
I drop about the baby's parentage:
So delicately too! A maid might sing,
And never blush at it. Girls love these songs
Of sugared wickedness. They'll go miles
  about,
To say a foul thing in a cleanly way.
A decent immorality, my lord,
Is art's specific. Get the passions up,
But never wring the stomach.

LANCIOTTO: Triumphant art!

[*Pepe sings*]

  My father combed his blue-black head,
    My uncle combed his red-head – maybe,
  My mother combed my head, and said,
    Sing high ho! my red-haired baby!

LANCIOTTO: Fie, fie! go comb your hair in
  private.

PEPE: What!
Will you not hear? Now comes the tragedy.
[*Sings*]

  My father tore my red, red head,
    My uncle tore my father's – maybe,
  My mother tore both till they bled –
    Sing high ho! your brother's baby!

LANCIOTTO: Why, what a hair-rending!

PEPE: Thence wigs arose;
A striking epoch in man's history.
But did you notice the concluding line,
Sung by the victim's mother? There's a hit!

  "Sing hi ho! your brother's baby!"
Which brother's, pray you? That's the mys-
  tery,
The adumbration of poetic art,
And there I leave it to perplex mankind.
It has a moral, fathers should regard, –
A black-haired dog breeds not a red-haired
  cur.

Treasure this knowledge: you're about to wive;
And no one knows what accident –

LANCIOTTO: Peace, fool!
So all this cunning thing was wound about,
To cast a jibe at my deformity? [*Tears off
Pepe's cap*]
There lies your cap, the emblem that protects
Your head from chastisement. Now, Pepe,
  hark!
Of late you've taken to reviling me;
Under your motley, you have dared to jest
At God's inflictions. Let me tell you, fool,
No man e'er lived, to make a second jest
At me, before your time!

PEPE: Boo! Bloody-bones!
If you're a coward – which I hardly think –
You'll have me flogged, or put into a cell,
Or fed to wolves. If you are bold of heart,
You'll let me run. Do not; I'll work you harm!
I, Beppo Pepe, standing as a man,
Without my motley, tell you, in plain terms,
I'll work you harm – I'll do you mischief,
  man!

LANCIOTTO: I, Lanciotto, Count of Rimini,
Will hang you, then. Put on your jingling cap;
You please my father. But remember, fool,
No jests at me!

PEPE: I will try earnest next.

LANCIOTTO: And I the gallows.

PEPE: Well, cry quits, cry quits!
I'll stretch your heart, and you my neck – quits,
  quits!

LANCIOTTO: Go, fool! Your weakness bounds
  your malice.

PEPE: Yes.
So you all think, you savage gentlemen,
Until you feel my sting. Hang, hang away!
It is an airy, wholesome sort of death,
Much to my liking. When I hang, my friend,
You'll be chief mourner, I can promise you.
Hang me! I've quite a notion to be hung:
I'll do my utmost to deserve it. – Hang! [*Exit*]

LANCIOTTO: I am bemocked on all sides. My sad
  state
Has given the licensed and unlicensed fool
Charter to challenge me at every turn.
The jester's laughing bauble blunts my sword,
His gibes cut deeper than its fearful edge;
And I, a man, a soldier, and a prince,
Before this motley patchwork of a man,
Stand all appalled, as if he were a glass
Wherein I saw my own deformity.
O Heaven! a tear – one little tear – to wash

457

This aching dryness of the heart away!

Enter Paolo

PAOLO: What ails the fool? He passed me, mut-
tering
The strangest garbage in the fiercest tone.
"Ha! ha!" cried he, "they made a fool of
me –
A motley man, a slave; as if I felt
No stir in me of manly dignity!
Ha! ha! a fool – a painted plaything, toy –
For men to kick about this dirty world! –
My world as well as theirs. – God's world, I
trow!
I will get even with them yet – ha! ha!
In the democracy of death we'll square.
I'll crawl and lie beside a king's own son;
Kiss a young princess, dead lip to dead lip;
Pull the Pope's nose; and kick down Charle-
magne,
Throne, crown, and all, where the old idiot
sprawls,
Safe as he thinks, rotting in royal state!"
And then he laughed and gibbered, as if drunk
With some infernal ecstasy.
LANCIOTTO: Poor fool!
That is the groundwork of his malice, then, –
His conscious difference from the rest of men?
I, of all men, should pity him the most.
Poor Pepe! I'll be kinder. I have wronged
A feeling heart. Poor Pepe!
PAOLO: Sad again!
Where has the rapture gone of yesterday?
LANCIOTTO: Where are the leaves of Summer?
Where the snows
Of last year's Winter? Where the joys and
griefs
That shut our eyes to yesternight's repose,
And woke not on the morrow? Joys and
griefs,
Huntsmen and hounds, ye follow us as game,
Poor panting outcasts of your forest-law!
Each cheers the others, – one with wild hal-
loos,
And one with whines and howls. – A dread-
ful chase,
That only closes when horns sound *a mort!*
PAOLO: Thus ever up and down! Arouse your-
self,
Balance your mind more evenly, and hunt
For honey in the wormwood.
LANCIOTTO: Or find gall
Hid in the hanging chalice of the rose:

Which think you better? If my mood offend,
We'll turn to business, – to the empty cares
That make such pother in our feverish life.
When at Ravenna, did you ever hear
Of any romance in Francesca's life?
A love-tilt, gallantry, or anything
That might have touched her heart?
PAOLO: Not lightly even.
I think her heart as virgin as her hand.
LANCIOTTO: Then there is hope.
PAOLO: Of what?
LANCIOTTO: Of winning her.
PAOLO: Grammercy! Lanciotto, are you sane?
You boasted yesterday –
LANCIOTTO: And changed to-day.
Is that so strange? I always mend the fault
Of yesterday with wisdom of to-day.
She does not love me.
PAOLO: Pshaw! she marries you:
'Twere proof enough for me.
LANCIOTTO: Perhaps, she loves you.
PAOLO: Me, Lanciotto, me! For mercy's sake,
Blot out such thoughts – they madden me!
What, love –
She love – yet marry you!
LANCIOTTO: It moves you much.
'Twas but a fleeting fancy, nothing more.
PAOLO: You have such wild conjectures!
LANCIOTTO: Well, to me
They seem quite tame; they are my bed-fel-
lows.
Think, to a modest woman, what must be
The loathsome kisses of an unloved man –
A gross, coarse ruffian!
PAOLO: O! good heavens, forbear!
LANCIOTTO: What shocks you so?
PAOLO: The picture which you draw,
Wronging yourself by horrid images.
LANCIOTTO: Until she love me, till I know, be-
yond
The cavil of a doubt, that she is mine –
Wholly, past question – do you think that I
Could so afflict the woman whom I love?
PAOLO: You love her, Lanciotto!
LANCIOTTO: Next to you,
Dearer than anything in nature's scope.
PAOLO: [*Aside*] O! Heaven, that I must bear
this! Yes, and more, –
More torture than I dare to think upon,
Spreads out before me with the coming years,
And holds a record blotted with my tears,
As that which I must suffer!
LANCIOTTO: Come, Paolo,

Come help me woo. I need your guiding eye,
To signal me, if I should sail astray.
PAOLO: O! torture, torture! [*Aside*]
LANCIOTTO: You and I, perchance,
Joining our forces, may prevail at last.
They call love like a battle. As for me,
I'm not a soldier equal to such wars,
Despite my arduous schooling. Tutor me
In the best arts of amorous strategy.
I am quite raw, Paolo. Glances, sighs,
Sweets of the lip, and arrows of the eye,
Shrugs, cringes, compliments, are new to me;
And I shall handle them with little art.
Will you instruct me?
PAOLO: Conquer for yourself.
Two captains share one honor: keep it all.
What if I ask to share the spoils?
LANCIOTTO: [*Laughing*]   Ha! ha!
I'll trust you, brother. Let us go to her:
Francesca is neglected while we jest.
I know not how it is, but your fair face,
And noble figure, always cheer me up,
More than your words; there's healing in
     them, too,
For my worst griefs. Dear brother, let us in.
[*Exeunt*]

                    Scene 2

*The Same. A Chamber in the Same. Francesca
and Ritta discovered at the bridal toilet.*
RITTA: [*Sings*]

  *Ring high, ring high! to earth and sky;
  A lady goes a-wedding;
  The people shout, the show draws out,
  And smiles the bride is shedding.*

  *No bell for you, ye ragged few;
  A beggar goes a-wedding;
  The people sneer, the thing's so queer,
  And tears the bride is shedding.*

  *Ring low, ring low! dull bell of woe,
  One tone will do for either;
  The lady glad, and beggar sad,
  Have both lain down together.*

FRANCESCA: A mournful ballad!
RITTA: I scarce knew I sang.
I'm weary of this wreath. These orange-flowers
Will never be adjusted to my taste:
Strive as I will, they ever look awry.

My fingers ache!
FRANCESCA: Not more than my poor head.
There, leave them so.
RITTA: That's better, yet not well.
FRANCESCA: They are but fading things, not
     worth your pains:
They'll scarce outlive the marriage merriment.
Ritta, these flowers are hypocrites; they show
An outside gayety, yet die within,
Minute by minute. You shall see them fall,
Black with decay, before the rites are o'er.
RITTA: How beautiful you are!
FRANCESCA: Fie, flatterer!
White silk and laces, pearls and orange-flow-
     ers,
Would do as much for any one.
RITTA: No, no!
You give them grace, they nothing give to
     you.
Why, after all, you make the wreath look
     well;
But somewhat dingy, where it lies against
Your pulsing temple, sullen with disgrace.
Ah! well, your Count should be the proudest
     man
That ever led a lady into church,
Were he a modern Alexander. Poh!
What are his trophies to a face like that?
FRANCESCA: I seem to please you, Ritta.
RITTA: Please yourself,
And you will please me better. You are sad:
I marked it ever since you saw the Count.
I fear the splendor of his victories,
And his sweet grace of manner – for, in faith,
His is the gentlest, grandest character,
Despite his –
FRANCESCA: Well?
RITTA: Despite his –
FRANCESCA: Ritta, what?
RITTA: Despite his difference from Count Pao-
lo. – [*Francesca staggers*]
What is the matter? [*Supporting her*]
FRANCESCA: Nothing; mere fatigue.
Hand me my kerchief. I am better now.
What were you saying?
RITTA: That I fear the Count
Has won your love.
FRANCESCA: Would that be cause for fear?
     [*Laughing*]
RITTA: O! yes, indeed! Once – long ago – I was
Just fool enough to tangle up my heart
With one of these same men. 'Twas terrible!
Morning or evening, waking or asleep,

I had no peace. Sighs, groans, and standing
tears,
Counted my moments through the blessed day.
And then to this there was a dull, strange ache
Forever sleeping in my breast, – a numbing
pain,
That would not for an instant be forgot.
O! but I loved him so, that very feeling
Became intolerable. And I believed
This false Giuseppe, too, for all the sneers,
The shrugs and glances, of my intimates.
They slandered me and him, yet I believed.
He was a noble, and his love to me
Was a reproach, a shame, yet I believed.
He wearied of me, tried to shake me off,
Grew cold and formal, yet I would not doubt.
O! lady, I was true! Nor till I saw
Giuseppe walk through the cathedral door
With Dora, the rich usurer's niece, upon
The very arm to which I clung so oft,
Did I so much as doubt him. Even then –
More is my shame – I made excuses for him.
"Just this or that had forced him to the
course:
Perhaps, he loved me yet – a little yet.
His fortune, or his family, had driven
My poor Giuseppe thus against his heart.
The low are sorry judges for the great.
Yes, yes, Giuseppe loved me!" But at last
I did awake. It might have been with less:
There was no need of crushing me, to break
My silly dream up. In the street, it chanced,
Dora and he went by me, and he laughed –
A bold, bad laugh – right in my poor pale
face,
And turned and whispered Dora, and she
laughed.
Ah! then I saw it all. I've been awake,
Ever since then, I warrant you. And now
I only pray for him sometimes, when friends
Tell his base actions towards his hapless wife.
O! I am lying – I pray every night. [*Weeps*]
FRANCESCA: Poor Ritta! [*Weeping*]
RITTA: No! blest Ritta! Thank kind Heaven,
That kept me spotless when he tempted me,
And my weak heart was pleading with his
tongue.
Pray, do not weep. You spoil your eyes for
me.
But never love; O! it is terrible!
FRANCESCA: I'll strive against it.
RITTA: Do: because, my lady,
Even a husband may be false, you know;

Ay, even to so sweet a wife as you.
Men have odd tastes. They'll surfeit on the
charms
Of Cleopatra, and then turn aside
To woo her blackamoor. 'Tis so, in faith;
Or Dora's uncle's gold had ne'er outbid
The boundless measure of a love like mine.
Think of it, lady, to weigh love with gold!
What could be meaner?
FRANCESCA: Nothing, nothing, Ritta.
Though gold's the standard measure of the
world,
And seems to lighten everything beside.
Yet heap the other passions in the scale,
And balance them 'gainst that which gold
outweighs –
Against this love – and you shall see how light
The most supreme of them are in the poise!
I speak by book and history; for love
Slights my high fortunes. Under cloth of state
The urchin cowers from pompous etiquette,
Waiving his function at the scowl of power,
And seeks the rustic cot to stretch his limbs
In homely freedom. I fulfill a doom.
We who are topmost on this heap of life
Are nearer to Heaven's hand than you below;
And so are used, as ready instruments,
To work its purposes. Let envy hide
Her witless forehead at a prince's name,
And fix her hopes upon a clown's content.
You, happy lowly, know not what it is
To groan beneath the crownéd yoke of state,
And bear the goadings of the sceptre. Ah!
Fate drives us onward in a narrow way,
Despite our boasted freedom.

Enter Paolo, with Pages bearing torches
                              Gracious saints!
What brought you here?
PAOLO: The bridegroom waits.
FRANCESCA: He does?
Let him wait on forever! I'll not go!
O! dear Paolo –
PAOLO: Sister!
FRANCESCA: It is well.
I have been troubled with a sleepless night.
My brain is wild. I know not what I say.
Pray, do not call me sister: it is cold.
I never had a brother, and the name
Sounds harshly to me. When you speak to me,
Call me Francesca.
PAOLO: You shall be obeyed.

FRANCESCA: I would not be obeyed. I'd have you do it
Because – because you love me – as a sister –
And of your own good-will, not my command,
Would please me. – Do you understand?

PAOLO: Too well! [*Aside*]
'Tis a nice difference.

FRANCESCA: Yet you understand?
Say that you do.

PAOLO: I do.

FRANCESCA: That pleases me.
'Tis flattering if our – friends appreciate
Our nicer feelings.

PAOLO: I await you, lady.

FRANCESCA: Ritta, my gloves. – Ah! yes, I have them on;
Though I'm not quite prepared. Arrange my veil;
It folds too closely. That will do; retire. [*Ritta retires*]
So, Count Paolo, you have come, hot haste,
To lead me to the church, – to have your share
In my undoing? And you came, in sooth,
Because they sent you? You are very tame!
And if they sent, was it for you to come?

PAOLO: Lady, I do not understand this scorn.
I came, as is my duty, to escort
My brother's bride to him. When next you're called,
I'll send a lackey.

FRANCESCA: I have angered you.

PAOLO: With reason: I would not appear to you
Low or contemptible.

FRANCESCA: Why not to me?

PAOLO: Lady, I'll not be catechized.

FRANCESCA: Ha! Count!

PAOLO: No! if you press me further, I will say
A word to madden you. – Stand still! You stray
Around the margin of a precipice.
I know what pleasure 'tis to pluck the flowers
That hang above destruction, and to gaze
Into the dread abyss, to see such things
As may be safely seen. 'Tis perilous:
The eye grows dizzy as we gaze below,
And a wild wish possesses us to spring
Into the vacant air. Beware, beware!
Lest this unholy fascination grow
Too strong to conquer!

FRANCESCA: You talk wildly, Count;
There's not a gleam of sense in what you say;

I cannot hit your meaning.

PAOLO: Lady, come!

FRANCESCA: Count, you are cruel! [*Weeps*]

PAOLO: O! no; I would be kind.
But now, while reason over-rides my heart,
And seeming anger plays its braggart part –
In heaven's name, come!

FRANCESCA: One word – one question more:
Is it your wish this marriage should proceed?

PAOLO: It is.

FRANCESCA: Come on! You shall not take my hand:
I'll walk alone – now, and forever!

PAOLO: [*Taking her hand*] Sister!

Exeunt Paolo and Francesca, with Pages

RITTA: O! misery, misery! – it is plain as day –
She loves Paolo! Why will those I love
Forever get themselves ensnared, and Heaven
Forever call on me to succor them?
Here was the mystery, then – the sighs and tears,
The troubled slumbers, and the waking dreams!
And now she's walking through the chapel-door,
Her bridal robe above an aching heart,
Dressed up for sacrifice. 'Tis terrible!
And yet she'll smile and do it. Smile, for years,
Until her heart breaks; and the nurses ask
The doctor of the cause. He'll answer too,
In hard thick Latin, and believe himself.
O! my dear mistress! Heaven, pray torture me!
Send back Giuseppe, let him ruin me,
And scorn me after; but, sweet Heaven, spare her!
I'll follow her. O! what a world is this! [*Exit*]

Scene 3

The Same. Interior of the Cathedral. Lanciotto, Francesca, Paolo, Malatesta, Guido, Ritta, Pepe, Lords, Knights, Priests, Pages, a bridal-train of Ladies, Soldiers, Citizens, Attendants, etc., discovered before the High Altar. Organ music. The rites being over, they advance.

MALATESTA: By heaven –

PEPE: O! uncle, uncle, you're in church!

MALATESTA: I'll break your head, knave!

PEPE: I claim sanctuary.

461

MALATESTA: Why, bridegroom, will you never
kiss the bride?
We all are mad to follow you.
PEPE: Yes, yes;
Here was Paolo wetting his red lips
For the last minute. Kiss, and give him room.
MALATESTA: You heaven-forsaken imp, be quiet
now!
PEPE: Then there'd be naught worth hearing.
MALATESTA: Bridegroom, come!
PEPE: Lord! he don't like it! Hey! – I told you
so –
He backs at the first step. Does he not know
His trouble's just begun?
LANCIOTTO: Gentle Francesca,
Custom imposes somewhat on thy lips:
I'll make my levy. [*Kisses her. The others fol-
low. Aside*]
      Ha! she shrank! I felt
Her body tremble, and her quivering lips
Seemed dying under mine! I heard a sigh,
Such as breaks hearts – O! no, a very groan;
And then she turned a sickly, miserable look
On pale Paolo, and he shivered, too!
There is a mystery hangs around her, – ay,
Paolo knows it, too. – By all the saints,
I'll make him tell it, at the dagger's point!
Paolo! – here! I do adjure you, brother,
By the great love I bear you, to reveal
The secret of Francesca's grief.
PAOLO: I cannot.
LANCIOTTO: She told you nothing?
PAOLO: Nothing.
LANCIOTTO: Not a word?
PAOLO: Not one.
LANCIOTTO: What heard you at Ravenna, then?
PAOLO: Nothing.
LANCIOTTO: Here?
PAOLO: Nothing.
LANCIOTTO: Not the slightest hint? –
Don't stammer, man! speak quick! I am in
haste.
PAOLO: Never.
LANCIOTTO: What know you?
PAOLO: Nothing that concerns
Your happiness, Lanciotto. If I did,
Would I not tell unquestioned?
LANCIOTTO: Would you not?
You ask a question for me: answer it.
PAOLO: I have.
LANCIOTTO: You juggle, you turn deadly pale,
Fumble your dagger, stand with head half
round,

Tapping your feet. – You dare not look at
me!
By Satan! Count Paolo, let me say,
You look much like a full-convicted thief!
PAOLO: Brother! –
LANCIOTTO: Pshaw! brother! You deceive me,
sir:
You and that lady have a devil's league,
To keep a devil's secret. Is it thus
You deal with me? Now, by the light above,
I'd give a dukedom for some fair pretext
To fly you all! She does not love me? Well,
I could bear that, and live away from her.
Love would be sweet, but want of it becomes
An early habit to such men as I.
But you – ah! there's the sorrow – whom I
loved
An infant in your cradle; you who grew
Up in my heart, with every inch you gained;
You whom I loved for every quality,
Good, bad, and common, in your natural
stock;
Ay, for your very beauty! It is strange, you'll
say,
For such a crippled horror to do that,
Against the custom of his kind! O! yes,
I love, and you betray me!
PAOLO: Lanciotto,
This is sheer frenzy. Join your bride.
LANCIOTTO: I'll not!
What, go to her, to feel her very flesh
Crawl from my touch? – to hear her sigh and
moan,
As if God plagued her? Must I come to that?
Must I endure your hellish mystery
With my own wife, and roll my eyes away
In sentimental bliss? No, no! until
I go to her, with confident belief
In her integrity and candid love,
I'll shun her as a leper! [*Alarm-bells toll*]
MALATESTA: What is that?

Enter, hastily, a Messenger in disorder
MESSENGER: My lord, the Ghibelins are up –
LANCIOTTO: And I
Will put them down again! I thank thee,
Heaven,
For this unlooked-for aid! [*Aside*]
MALATESTA: What force have they?
LANCIOTTO: It matters not, – nor yet the time,
place, cause,
Of their rebellion. I would throttle it,
Were it a riot, or a drunken brawl!

MALATESTA: Nay, son, your bride –
LANCIOTTO: My bride will pardon me;
Bless me, perhaps, as I am going forth; –
Thank me, perhaps, if I should ne'er return.
  [*Aside*]
A soldier's duty has no bridals in it.
PAOLO: Lanciotto, this is folly. Let me take
Your usual place of honor.
LANCIOTTO: [*Laughing*]   Ha! ha! ha!
What! thou, a tilt-yard soldier, lead my troops!
My wife will ask it shortly. Not a word
Of opposition from the new-made bride?
Nay, she looks happier. O! accursed day,
That I was mated to an empty heart! [*Aside*]
MALATESTA: But, son –
LANCIOTTO: Well, father?
PEPE: Uncle, let him go.
He'll find it cooler on a battle-field
Than in his –
LANCIOTTO: Hark! the fool speaks oracles.
You, soldiers, who are used to follow me,
And front our charges, emulous to bear
The shock of battle on your forward arms, –
Why stand ye in amazement? Do your swords
Stick to their scabbards with inglorious rust?
Or has repose so weakened your big hearts,
That you can dream with trumpets at your
  ears?
Out with your steel! It shames me to behold
Such tardy welcome to my war-worn blade!
  [*Draws*]

        The Knights and Soldiers draw
Ho! draw our forces out! Strike camp, sound
  drums,
And set us on our marches! As I live,
I pity the next foeman who relies
On me for mercy! Farewell! to you all –
To all alike – a soldier's short farewell!
  [*Going*]

        Paolo stands before him
Out of my way, thou juggler! [*Exit*]
PAOLO: He is gone!

              ACT V. Scene I

The Same. The Garden of the Castle. Enter
Pepe, singing.

  'Tis jolly to walk in the shady greenwood
    With a damsel by your side;

  'Tis jolly to walk from the chapel-door,
    With the hand of your pretty bride;

  'Tis jolly to rest your weary head,
    When life runs low and hope is fled,
  On the heart where you confide:
    'Tis jolly, jolly, jolly, they say,
  They say – but I never tried.

Nor shall I ever till they dress their girls
In motley suits, and pair us, to increase
The race of fools. 'Twould be a noble thing,
A motley woman, had she wit enough
To bear the bell. But there's the misery:
You may make princes out of any stuff;
Fools come by nature. She'll make fifty
  kings –
Good, hearty tyrants, sound, cruel governors –
For one fine fool. There is Paolo, now,
A sweet-faced fellow with a wicked heart –
Talk of a flea, and you begin to scratch.
Lo! here he comes. And there's fierce crook-
  back's bride
Walking beside him – O, how gingerly!
Take care, my love! That is the very pace
We trip to hell with. Hunchback is away –
That was a fair escape for you; but, then,
The devil's ever with us, and that's worse.
See, the Ravenna giglet, Mistress Ritta,
And melancholy as a cow. – How's this?
I'll step aside, and watch you, pretty folks.
  [*Hides behind the bushes*]

Enter Paolo and Francesca, followed by Ritta.
He seats himself in an arbor, and reads. Ritta
and Francesca advance
FRANCESCA: Ritta.
RITTA: My lady.
FRANCESCA: You look tired.
RITTA: I'm not.
FRANCESCA: Go to your chamber.
RITTA: I would rather stay,
If it may please you. I require a walk
And the fresh atmosphere of breathing flowers,
To stir my blood. I am not very well.
FRANCESCA: I knew it, child. Go to your cham-
  ber, dear.
Paolo has a book to read to me.
RITTA: What, the romance? I should so love to
  hear!
I dote on poetry; and Count Paolo
Sweetens the Tuscan with his mellow voice.
I'm weary now, quite weary, and would rest.

463

FRANCESCA: Just now you wished to walk.

RITTA: Ah! did I so?
Walking, or resting, I would stay with you.

FRANCESCA: The Count objects. He told me, yesterday,
That you were restless while he read to me;
And stirred your feet amid the grass, and sighed,
And yawned, until he almost paused.

RITTA: Indeed
I will be quiet.

FRANCESCA: But he will not read.

RITTA: Let me go ask him. [*Runs toward Paolo*]

FRANCESCA: Stop! Come hither, Ritta. – [*She returns*]
I saw your new embroidery in the hall, –
The needle in the midst of Argus' eyes;
It should be finished.

RITTA: I will bring it here. –
O no! my finger's sore; I cannot work.

FRANCESCA: Go to your room.

RITTA: Let me remain, I pray.
'Tis better, lady; you may wish for me:
I know you will be sorry if I go.

FRANCESCA: I shall not, girl. Do as I order you.
Will you be headstrong?

RITTA: Do you wish it, then?

FRANCESCA: Yes, Ritta.

RITTA: Yet you made pretexts enough,
Before you ordered.

FRANCESCA: You are insolent.
Will you remain against my will?

RITTA: Yes, lady;
Rather than not remain.

FRANCESCA: Ha! impudent!

RITTA: You wrong me, gentle mistress. Love
like mine
Does not ask questions of propriety,
Nor stand on manners. I would do you good,
Even while you smote me; I would push you
back,
With my last effort, from the crumbling edge
Of some high rock o'er which you toppled me.

FRANCESCA: What do you mean?

RITTA: I know.

FRANCESCA: Know what?

RITTA: Too much.
Pray, do not ask me.

FRANCESCA: Speak!

RITTA: I know – dear lady,
Be not offended –

FRANCESCA: Tell me, simpleton!

RITTA: You know I worship you; you know I'd
walk
Straight into ruin for a whim of yours;
You know –

FRANCESCA: I know you act the fool. Talk sense!

RITTA: I know Paolo loves you.

FRANCESCA: Should he not?
He is my brother.

RITTA: More than brother should.

FRANCESCA: Ha! are you certain?

RITTA: Yes, of more than that.

FRANCESCA: Of more?

RITTA: Yes, lady; for you love him, too.
I've said it! Fling me to the carrion crows,
Kill me by inches, boil me in the pot
Count Guido promised me, – but, O, be-
ware!
Back, while you may! Make me the sufferer,
But save yourself!

FRANCESCA: Now, are you not ashamed
To look me in the face with that bold brow?
I am amazed!

RITTA: I am a woman, lady;
I too have been in love; I know its ways,
Its arts, and its deceits. Your frowning face,
And seeming indignation, do not cheat.
Your heart is in my hand.

PAOLO: [*Calls*] Francesca!

FRANCESCA: Hence,
Thou wanton-hearted minion! hence, I say! –
And never look me in the face again! –
Hence, thou insulting slave!

RITTA: [*Clinging to her*] O lady, lady –

FRANCESCA: Begone! [*Throws her off*]

RITTA: I have no friends – no one to love –
O, spare me!

FRANCESCA: Hence!

RITTA: Was it for this I loved –
Cared for you more than my own happiness –
Ever at heart your slave – without a wish
For greater recompense than your stray
smiles?

PAOLO: [*Calls*] Francesca!

FRANCESCA: Hurry!

RITTA: I am gone. Alas!
God bless you, lady! God take care of you,
When I am far away! Alas, Alas! [*Exit weep-
ing*]

FRANCESCA: Poor girl! but were she all the world
to me,
And held my future in her tender grasp,
I'd cast her off, without a second thought,
To savage death, for dear Paolo's sake!

Paolo, hither! Now he comes to me;
I feel his presence, though I see him not,
Stealing upon me like the fervid glow
Of morning sunshine. Now he comes too
   near –
He touches me – O Heaven!
PAOLO: Our poem waits.
I have been reading while you talked with Rit-
ta.
How did you get her off?
FRANCESCA: By some device.
She will not come again.
PAOLO: I hate the girl:
She seems to stand between me and the light.
And now for the romance. Where left we off?
FRANCESCA: Where Lancelot and Queen Guenev-
   ra strayed
Along the forest, in the youth of May.
You marked the figure of the birds that sang
Their melancholy farewell to the sun –
Rich in his loss, their sorrow glorified –
Like gentle mourners o'er a great man's grave.
Was it not there? No, no; 'twas where they sat
Down on the bank, by one impulsive wish
That neither uttered.
PAOLO: [*Turning over the book*] Here it is.
   [*Reads*] "So sat
Guenevra and Sir Lancelot" – 'Twere well
To follow them in that. [*They sit upon a
bank*]
FRANCESCA: I listen: read.
Nay, do not; I can wait, if you desire.
PAOLO: My dagger frets me; let me take it off.
   [*Rises*]
In thoughts of love, we'll lay our weapons by.
   [*Lays aside his dagger, and sits again*]
Draw closer: I am weak in voice to-day.
   [*Reads*]

"So sat Guenevra and Sir Lancelot,
   Under the blaze of the descending sun,
But all his cloudy splendors were forgot.
   Each bore a thought, the only secret one,
Which each had hidden from the other's heart,
   Both with sweet mystery well-nigh overrun.
Anon, Sir Lancelot, with gentle start,
   Put by the ripples of her golden hair,
Gazing upon her with his lips apart.
   He marvelled human thing could be so fair;
Essayed to speak; but, in the very deed,
   His words expired of self-betrayed despair.
Little she helped him, at his direst need,

Roving her eyes o'er hill, and wood, and
   sky,
Peering intently at the meanest weed;
   Ay, doing aught but look in Lancelot's eye.
Then, with the small pique of her velvet shoe,
   Uprooted she each herb that blossomed nigh;
Or strange wild figures in the dust she drew;
   Until she felt Sir Lancelot's arm around
Her waist, upon her cheek his breath like
   dew.
   While through his fingers timidly he wound
Her shining locks; and, haply, when he
   brushed
   Her ivory skin, Guenevra nearly swound:
For where he touched, the quivering surface
   blushed,
   Firing her blood with most contagious heat,
Till brow, cheek, neck, and bosom, all were
   flushed.
   Each heart was listening to the other beat.
As twin-born lilies on one golden stalk,
   Drooping with Summer, in warm languor
meet,
So met their faces. Down the forest walk
   Sir Lancelot looked – he looked east, west,
north, south –
No soul was nigh, his dearest wish to balk:
   She smiled; he kissed her full upon the
mouth." [*Kisses Francesca*]
I'll read no more! [*Starts up, dashing down
the book*]
FRANCESCA: Paolo!
PAOLO: I am mad!
The torture of unnumbered hours is o'er,
The straining cord has broken, and my heart
Riots in free delirium! O, Heaven!
I struggled with it, but it mastered me!
I fought against it, but it beat me down!
I prayed, I wept, but Heaven was deaf to me;
And every tear rolled backward on my heart,
To blight and poison!
FRANCESCA: And dost thou regret?
PAOLO: The love? No, no! I'd dare it all again,
Its direst agonies and meanest fears,
For that one kiss. Away with fond remorse!
Here, on the brink of ruin, we two stand;
Lock hands with me, and brave the fearful
   plunge!
Thou canst not name a terror so profound
That I will look or falter from. Be bold!
I know thy love – I knew it long ago –
Trembled and fled from it. But now I clasp
The peril to my breast, and ask of thee

465

A kindred desperation.

FRANCESCA: [*Throwing herself into his arms*]
Take me all, –
Body and soul! The women of our clime
Do never give away but half a heart:
I have not part to give, part to withhold,
In selfish safety. When I saw thee first,
Riding alone amid a thousand men,
Sole in the lustre of thy majesty,
And Guido da Polenta said to me,
"Daughter, behold thy husband!" with a
   bound
My heart went forth to meet thee. He de-
   ceived,
He lied to me – ah! that's the aptest word –
And I believed. Shall I not turn again,
And meet him, craft with craft? Paolo, love,
Thou'rt dull – thou'rt dying like a feeble fire
Before the sunshine. Was it but a blaze,
A flash of glory, and a long, long night?

PAOLO: No, darling, no! You could not bend me
   back;
My course is onward; but my heart is sick
With coming fears.

FRANCESCA: Away with them! Must I
Teach thee to love? and reinform the ear
Of thy spent passion with some sorcery
To raise the chilly dead?

PAOLO: Thy lips have not
A sorcery to rouse me as this spell. [*Kisses her*]

FRANCESCA: I give thy kisses back to thee again:
And, like a spendthrift, only ask of thee
To take while I can give.

PAOLO: Give, give forever!
Have we not touched the height of human
   bliss?
And if the sharp rebound may hurl us back
Among the prostrate, did we not soar once? –
Taste heavenly nectar, banquet with the gods
On high Olympus? If they cast us, now,
Amid the furies, shall we not go down
With rich ambrosia clinging to our lips,
And richer memories settled in our hearts?
Francesca.

FRANCESCA: Love?

PAOLO: The sun is sinking low
Upon the ashes of his fading pyre,
And gray possesses the eternal blue;
The evening star is stealing after him,
Fixed, like a beacon, on the prow of night;
The world is shutting up its heavy eye
Upon the stir and bustle of to-day; –
On what shall it awake?

FRANCESCA: On love that gives
Joy at all seasons, changes night to day,
Makes sorrow smile, plucks out the barbéd
   dart
Of moaning anguish, pours celestial balm
In all the gaping wounds of earth, and lulls
The nervous fancies of unsheltered fear
Into a slumber sweet as infancy's!
On love that laughs at the impending sword,
And puts aside the shield of caution: cries,
To all its enemies, "Come, strike me now! –
Now, while I hold my kingdom, while my
   crown
Of amaranth and myrtle is yet green,
Undimmed, unwithered; for I cannot tell
That I shall e'er be happier!" Dear Paolo,
Would you lapse down from misery to death,
Tottering through sorrow and infirmity?
Or would you perish at a single blow,
Cut off amid your wildest revelry,
Falling among the wine-cups and the flowers,
And tasting Bacchus when your drowsy sense
First gazed around eternity? Come, love!
The present whispers joy to us; we'll hear
The voiceless future when its turn arrives.

PAOLO: Thou art a siren. Sing, forever sing!
Hearing thy voice, I cannot tell what fate
Thou hast provided when the song is o'er; –
But I will venture it.

FRANCESCA: In, in, my love! [*Exeunt*]

Pepe steals from behind the bushes

PEPE: O, brother Lanciotto! – O, my stars! –
If this thing lasts, I simply shall go mad!
   [*Laughs, and rolls on the ground*]
O Lord! to think my pretty lady puss
Had tricks like this, and we ne'er know of it!
I tell you, Lanciotto, you and I
Must have a patent for our foolery!
"She smiled; he kissed her full upon the
   mouth!" –
There's the beginning; where's the end of it?
O poesy! debauch thee only once,
And thou'rt the greatest wanton in the world!
O cousin Lanciotto – ho, ho, ho! [*Laughing*]
Can a man die of laughter? Here we sat;
Mistress Francesca so demure and calm;
Paolo grand, poetical, sublime! –
Eh! what is this? Paolo's dagger? Good!
Here is more proof, sweet cousin Broken-back.
"In thoughts of love, we'll lay our weapons
   by!" [*Mimicking Paolo*]
That's very pretty! Here's its counterpart:

In thoughts of hate, we'll pick them up again!
[*Takes the dagger*]
Now for my soldier, now for crook-backed
  Mars!
Ere long all Rimini will be ablaze.
He'll kill me? Yes: what then? That's nothing
  new,
Except to me: I'll bear for custom's sake.
More blood will follow; like the royal sun,
I shall go down in purple. Fools for luck;
The proverb holds like iron. I must run,
Ere laughter smother me. – O, ho, ho, ho!
[*Exit, laughing*]

Scene 2

*A camp among the Hills. Before Lanciotto's
tent. Enter, from the tent, Lanciotto.*
LANCIOTTO: The camp is strangely quiet. Not a
  sound
Breaks nature's high solemnity. The sun
Repeats again his every-day decline;
Yet all the world looks sadly after him,
As if the customary sight were new.
Yon moody sentinel goes slowly by,
Through the thick mists of evening, with his
  spear
Trailed at a funeral hold. Long shadows creep,
From things beyond the furthest range of
  sight,
Up to my very feet. These mystic shades
Are of the earth; the light that causes them,
And teaches us the quick comparison,
Is all from heaven. Ah! restless man might
  crawl
With patience through his shadowy destiny,
If he were senseless to the higher light
Towards which his soul aspires. How grand
  and vast
Is yonder show of heavenly pageantry!
How mean and narrow is the earthly stand
From which we gaze on it! Magnificent,
O God, art thou amid the sunsets! Ah!
What heart in Rimini is softened now,
Towards my defects, by this grand spectacle?
Perchance, Paolo now forgives the wrong
Of my hot spleen. Perchance, Francesca now
Wishes me back, and turns a tenderer eye
On my poor person and ill-mannered ways;
Fashions excuses for me, schools her heart
Through duty into love, and ponders o'er
The sacred meaning in the name of wife.

Dreams, dreams! Poor fools, we squander love
  away
On thankless borrowers; when bankrupt quite,
We sit and wonder of their honesty.
Love, take a lesson from the usurer,
And never lend but on security.
Captain!

Enter a Captain

CAPTAIN: My lord.
LANCIOTTO: They worsted us to-day.
CAPTAIN: Not much, my lord.
LANCIOTTO: With little loss, indeed.
Their strength is in position. Mark you, sir.
[*Draws on the ground with his sword*]
Here is the pass; it opens towards the plain,
With gradual widening, like a lady's fan.
The hills protect their flanks on either hand;
And, as you see, we cannot show more front
Than their advance may give us. Then, the
  rocks
Are sorry footing for our horse. Just here,
Close in against the left-hand hills, I marked
A strip of wood, extending down the gorge:
Behind that wood dispose your force ere dawn.
I shall begin the onset, then give ground,
And draw them out; while you, behind the
  wood,
Must steal along, until their flank and rear
Oppose your column. Then set up a shout,
Burst from the wood, and drive them on our
  spears.
They have no outpost in the wood, I know;
'Tis too far from their centre. On the morrow,
When they are flushed with seeming victory,
And think my whole division in full rout,
They will not pause to scrutinize the wood;
So you may enter boldly. We will use
The heart to-day's repulse has given to them,
For our advantage. Do you understand?
CAPTAIN: Clearly, my lord.
LANCIOTTO: If they discover you,
Before you gain your point, wheel, and retreat
Upon my rear. If your attack should fail
To strike them with a panic, and they turn
In too great numbers on your small command,
Scatter your soldiers through the wood:
Let each seek safety for himself.
CAPTAIN: I see.
LANCIOTTO: Have Pluto shod; he cast a shoe to-
  day:
Let it be done at once. My helmet, too,
Is worn about the lacing; look to that.

Where is my armorer?

CAPTAIN: At his forge.

LANCIOTTO: Your charge
Must be at sunrise – just at sunrise, sir –
Neither before nor after. You must march
At moonset, then, to gain the point ere dawn.
That is enough.

CAPTAIN: Good-even! [*Going*]

LANCIOTTO: Stay, stay, stay!
My sword-hilt feels uneasy in my grasp; [*Gives his sword*]
Have it repaired; and grind the point. Strike hard!
I'll teach these Ghibelins a lesson. [*Loud laughter within*]
Ha! What is that clamor?

Enter hastily Pepe, tattered and travel-stained

PEPE: News from Rimini! [*Falls exhausted*]

LANCIOTTO: Is that you, Pepe? Captain, a good-night! [*Exit Captain*]
I never saw you in such straits before.
Wit without words!

PEPE: That's better than – O! – O! – [*Panting*]
Words without wit.

LANCIOTTO: [*Laughing*] You'll die a jester, Pepe.

PEPE: If so, I'll leave the needy all my wit.
You, you shall have it, cousin. – O! O! O!
[*Panting*]
Those devils in the hills, the Ghibelins,
Ran me almost to death. My lord – ha! ha!
[*Laughing*]
It all comes back to me – Oh! Lord 'a mercy –
The garden, and the lady, and the Count!
Not to forget the poetry – ho! ho! [*Laughing*]
O! cousin Lanciotto, such a wife,
And such a brother! Hear me, ere I burst!

LANCIOTTO: You're pleasant, Pepe!

PEPE: Am I? – Ho! ho! ho! [*Laughing*]
You ought to be; your wife's a –

LANCIOTTO: What?

PEPE: A lady –
A lady, I suppose, like all the rest.
I am not in their secrets. Such a fellow
As Count Paolo is your man for that.
I'll tell you something, if you'll swear a bit.

LANCIOTTO: Swear what?

PEPE: First, swear to listen till the end. –
O! you may rave, curse, howl, and tear your hair;

But you must listen.

LANCIOTTO: For your jest's sake? Well.

PEPE: You swear?

LANCIOTTO: I do.

PEPE: Next, swear to know the truth.

LANCIOTTO: The truth of a fool's story!

PEPE: You mistake.
Now, look you, cousin! You have often marked –
I know, for I have seen – strange glances pass
Between Paolo and your lady wife. –

LANCIOTTO: Ha! Pepe!

PEPE: Now I touch you to the quick.
I know the reason of those glances.

LANCIOTTO: Ha!
Speak! or I'll throttle you! [*Seizes him*]

PEPE: Your way is odd.
Let go my gullet, and I'll talk you deaf.
Swear my last oath: only to know the truth.

LANCIOTTO: But that may trouble me.

PEPE: Your honor lies –
Your precious honor, cousin Chivalry –
Lies bleeding with a terrible great gash,
Without its knowledge. Swear!

LANCIOTTO: My honor? Speak!

PEPE: You swear?

LANCIOTTO: I swear. Your news is ill, per-chance?

PEPE: Ill! would I bring it else? Am I inclined
To run ten leagues with happy news for you?
O, Lord! that's jolly!

LANCIOTTO: You infernal imp,
Out with your story, ere I strangle you!

PEPE: Then take a fast hold on your two great oaths,
To steady tottering manhood, and attend.
Last eve, about this hour, I took a stroll
Into the garden. – Are you listening, cousin?

LANCIOTTO: I am all ears.

PEPE: Why, so an ass might say.

LANCIOTTO: Will you be serious?

PEPE: Wait a while, and we
Will both be graver than a church-yard. Well,
Down the long walk, towards me, came your wife,
With Count Paolo walking at her side.
It was a pretty sight, and so I stepped
Into the bushes. Ritta came with them;
And Lady Fanny had a grievous time
To get her off. That made me curious.
Anon, the pair sat down upon a bank,
To read a poem; – the tenderest romance,
All about Lancelot and Queen Guenevra.

The Count read well – I'll say that much for
him –
Only he stuck too closely to the text,
Got too much wrapped up in the poesy,
And played Sir Lancelot's actions, out and
out,
On Queen Francesca. Nor in royal parts
Was she so backward. When he struck the
line –
"She smiled; he kissed her full upon the
mouth";
Your lady smiled, and, by the saints above,
Paolo carried out the sentiment!
Can I not move you?
LANCIOTTO: With such trash as this?
And so you ran ten leagues to tell a lie? –
Run home again.
PEPE: I am not ready yet.
After the kiss, up springs our amorous Count,
Flings Queen Guenevra and Sir Lancelot
Straight to the devil; growls and snaps his
teeth,
Laughs, weeps, howls, dances; talks about his
love,
His madness, suffering, and the Lord knows
what,
Bullying the lady like a thief. But she,
All this hot time, looked cool and mischievous;
Gave him his halter to the very end;
And when he calmed a little, up she steps
And takes him by the hand. You should have
seen
How tame the furious fellow was at once!
How he came down, snivelled, and cowed to
her,
And fell to kissing her again! It was
A perfect female triumph! Such a scene
A man might pass through life and never see.
More sentiment then followed, – buckets full
Of washy words, not worth my memory.
But all the while she wound his Countship up,
Closer and closer; till at last – tu! – wit!
She scoops him up, and off she carries him,
Fish for her table! Follow, if you can;
My fancy fails me. All this time you smile!
LANCIOTTO: You should have been a poet, not a
fool.
PEPE: I might be both.
LANCIOTTO: You made no record, then?
Must this fine story die for want of ink?
Left you no trace in writing?
PEPE: None.
LANCIOTTO: Alas!

Then you have told it? 'Tis but stale, my boy;
I'm second hearer.
PEPE: You are first, in faith.
LANCIOTTO: In truth?
PEPE: In sadness. You have got it fresh.
I had no time; I itched to reach your ear.
Now go to Rimini, and see yourself.
You'll find them in the garden. Lovers are
Like walking ghosts, they always haunt the
spot
Of their misdeeds.
LANCIOTTO: But have I heard you out?
You told me all?
PEPE: All; I have nothing left.
LANCIOTTO: Why, you brain-stricken idiot, to
trust
Your story and your body in my grasp! [*Seizes
him*]
PEPE: Unhand me, cousin!
LANCIOTTO: When I drop you, Pepe,
You'll be at rest.
PEPE: I will betray you – O!
LANCIOTTO: Not till the judgment day. [*They
struggle*]
PEPE: [*Drawing Paolo's dagger*] Take that!
LANCIOTTO: [*Wresting the dagger from him*]
Well meant,
But poorly done! Here's my return. [*Stabs
him*]
PEPE: O! beast! [*Falls*]
This I expected; it is naught – Ha! ha!
[*Laughing*]
I'll go to sleep; but you – what you will bear!
Hunchback, come here!
LANCIOTTO: Fie! say your prayers.
PEPE: Hark, hark!
Paolo hired me, swine, to murder you.
LANCIOTTO: That is a lie; you never cared for
gold.
PEPE: He did, I say! I'll swear to it, by heaven!
Do you believe me?
LANCIOTTO: No!
PEPE: You lie! you lie!
Look at the dagger, cousin – ugh! – good-night!
[*Dies*]
LANCIOTTO: O! horrible! It was a gift of mine –
He never laid it by. Speak, speak, fool,
speak! [*Shakes the body*]
How didst thou get it? – speak! Thou'rt
warm – not dead –
Thou hast a tongue – O! speak! Come, come,
a jest –
Another jest from those thin mocking lips!

469

Call me a cripple – hunchback – what thou
  wilt;
But speak to me! He cannot. Now, by heav-
  en,
I'll stir this business till I find the truth!
Am I a fool? It is a silly lie,
Coined by yon villain with his last base breath.
What ho! without there!

Enter Captain and Soldiers

CAPTAIN:　　　　　　　Did you call, my lord?
LANCIOTTO: Did Heaven thunder? Are you deaf,
  you louts?
Saddle my horse! What are you staring at?
Is it your first look at a dead man? Well,
Then look your fill. Saddle my horse, I say!
Black Pluto – stir! Bear that assassin hence.
Chop him to pieces, if he move. My horse!
CAPTAIN: My lord, he's shoeing.
LANCIOTTO:　　　　　　　Did I ask for shoes?
I want my horse. Run, fellow, run! Unbarbed –
My lightest harness on his back. Fly, fly! [*Exit
a Soldier*]

The others pick up the body
Ask him, I pray you, if he did not lie!
CAPTAIN: The man is dead, my lord.
LANCIOTTO: [*Laughing*] Then do not ask him!

Exeunt Soldiers with the body
By Jupiter, I shall go mad, I think! [*Walks
about*]
CAPTAIN: Something disturbs him. Do you mark
  the spot
Of purple on his brow? [*Apart to a Soldier*]
SOLDIER:　　　　　　Then blood must flow.
LANCIOTTO: Boy, boy! [*Enter a Page*] My cloak
  and riding-staff. Quick, quick!
How you all lag! [*Exit Page*] I ride to Rimini.
Skirmish to-morrow. Wait till my return –
I shall be back at sundown. You shall see
What slaughter is then!
CAPTAIN:　　　　　Ho! turn out a guard! –
LANCIOTTO: I wish no guard; I ride alone.

Re-enter Page, with a cloak and staff
　　　　　　　[*Taking them*] Well done!
Thou art a pretty boy. – And now my horse!

Enter a Soldier
SOLDIER: Pluto is saddled –
LANCIOTTO:　　　　　'Tis a damned black lie!
SOLDIER: Indeed, my lord –

LANCIOTTO:　　　　　O! comrade, pardon me:
I talk at random. What, Paolo too, –
A boy whom I have trotted on my knee!
Poh! I abuse myself by such a thought.
Francesca may not love me, may love him –
Indeed she ought; but when an angel comes
To play the wanton on this filthy earth,
Then I'll believe her guilty. Look you, sir!
Am I quite calm?
CAPTAIN: Quite calm, my lord.
LANCIOTTO:　　　　　　　You see
No trace of passion on my face? – No sign
Of ugly humors, doubts, or fears, or aught
That may disfigure God's intelligence?
I have a grievous charge against you, sir,
That may involve your life; and if you doubt
The candor of my judgment, choose your
  time:
Shall I arraign you now?
CAPTAIN:　　　　　Now, if you please.
I'll trust my cause to you and innocence
At any time. I am not conscious –
LANCIOTTO:　　　　　　　Pshaw!
I try myself, not you. And I am calm –
That is your verdict – and dispassionate?
CAPTAIN: So far as I can judge.
LANCIOTTO:　　　　　'Tis well, 'tis well!
Then I will ride to Rimini. Good-night!
[*Exit*]

*The others look after him, amazedly, and ex-
eunt*

Scene 3

*Rimini. The Garden of the Castle. Enter Paolo
and Francesca.*
FRANCESCA: Thou hast resolved?
PAOLO:　　　　　　　I've sworn it.
FRANCESCA:　　　　　　　Ah! you men
Can talk of love and duty in a breath;
Love while you like, forget when you are
  tired,
And salve your falsehood with some whole-
  some saw;
But we, poor women, when we give our
  hearts,
Give all, lose all, and never ask it back.
PAOLO: What couldst thou ask for that I have not
  given?
With love I gave thee manly probity,
Innocence, honor, self-respect, and peace.

Lanciotto will return, and how shall I –
O! shame, to think of it! – how shall I look
My brother in the face? take his frank hand?
Return his tender glances? I should blaze
With guilty blushes.

FRANCESCA: Thou canst forsake me, then,
To spare thyself a little bashful pain?
Paolo, dost thou know what 'tis for me,
A woman – nay, a dame of highest rank –
To lose my purity? to walk a path
Whose slightest slip may fill my ear with
sounds
That hiss me out to infamy and death?
Have I no secret pangs, no self-respect,
No husband's look to bear? O! worse than
these,
I must endure his loathsome touch; be kind
When he would dally with his wife, and smile
To see him play thy part. Pah! sickening
thought!
From that thou art exempt. Thou shalt not go!
Thou dost not love me!

PAOLO: Love thee! Standing here,
With countless miseries upon my head,
I say, my love for thee grows day by day.
It palters with my conscience,, blurs my
thoughts
Of duty, and confuses my ideas
Of right and wrong. Ere long, it will persuade
My shaking manhood that all this is just.

FRANCESCA: Let it! I'll blazon it to all the world,
Ere I will lose thee. Nay, if I had choice,
Between our love and my lost innocence,
I tell thee calmly, I would dare again
The deed which we have done. O! thou art
cruel
To fly me, like a coward, for thine ease.
When thou art gone, thou'lt flatter thy weak
heart
With hopes and speculations; and thou'lt swear
I suffer naught, because thou dost not see.
I will not live to bear it!

PAOLO: Die, – 'twere best;
'Tis the last desperate comfort of our sin.

FRANCESCA: I'll kill myself!

PAOLO: And so would I, with joy;
But crime has made a craven of me. O!
For some good cause to perish in! Something
A man might die for, looking in God's face;
Not slinking out of life with guilt like mine
Piled on the shoulders of a suicide!

FRANCESCA: Where wilt thou go?

PAOLO: I care not; anywhere

Out of this Rimini. The very things
That made the pleasures of my innocence
Have turned against me. There is not a tree,
Nor house, nor church, nor monument,
whose face
Took hold upon my thoughts, that does not
frown
Balefully on me. From their marble tombs
My ancestors scowl at me; and the night
Thickens to hear their hisses. I would pray,
But heaven jeers at it. Turn where'er I will,
A curse pursues me.

FRANCESCA: Heavens! O, say not so!
I never cursed thee, love; I never moved
My little finger, ere I looked to thee
For my instruction.

PAOLO: But thy gentleness
Seems to reproach me; and, instead of joy,
It whispers horror!

FRANCESCA: Cease! cease!

PAOLO: I must go.

FRANCESCA: And I must follow. All that I call
life
Is bound in thee. I could endure for thee
More agonies than thou canst catalogue –
For thy sake, love – bearing the ill for thee!
With thee, the devils could not so contrive
That I would blench or falter from my love!
Without thee, heaven were torture!

PAOLO: I must go. [*Going*]

FRANCESCA: O! no – Paolo – dearest! – [*Clinging to him*]

PAOLO: Loose thy hold!
'Tis for thy sake, and Lanciotto's; I
Am as a cipher in the reckoning.
I have resolved. Thou canst but stretch the
time.
Keep me to-day, and I will fly to-morrow –
Steal from thee like a thief. [*Struggles with
her*]

FRANCESCA: Paolo – love –
Indeed, you hurt me! – Do not use me thus!
Kill me, but do not leave me. I will laugh –
A long, gay, ringing laugh – if thou wilt
draw
Thy pitying sword, and stab me to the heart!

Enter Lanciotto behind

Nay, then, one kiss!

LANCIOTTO: [*Advancing between them*] Take it:
'twill be the last.

PAOLO: Lo! Heaven is just!

FRANCESCA: The last! so be it. [*Kisses Paolo*]

LANCIOTTO: Ha!
Dare you these tricks before my very face?
FRANCESCA: Why not? I've kissed him in the sight of heaven;
Are you above it?
PAOLO: Peace, Francesca, peace!
LANCIOTTO: Paolo – why, thou sad and downcast man,
Look up! I have some words to speak with thee.
Thou art not guilty?
PAOLO: Yes, I am. But she
Has been betrayed; so she is innocent.
Her father tampered with her. I –
FRANCESCA: 'Tis false!
The guilt is mine. Paolo was entrapped
By love and cunning. I am shrewder far
Than you suspect.
PAOLO: Lanciotto, shut thy ears;
She would deceive thee.
LANCIOTTO: Silence, both of you!
Is guilt so talkative in its defence?
Then, let me make you judge and advocate
In your own cause. You are not guilty?
PAOLO: Yes.
LANCIOTTO: Deny it – but a word – say no.
Lie, lie!
And I'll believe.
PAOLO: I dare not.
LANCIOTTO: Lady, you?
FRANCESCA: If I might speak for him –
LANCIOTTO: It cannot be:
Speak for yourself. Do you deny your guilt?
FRANCESCA: No! I assert it; but –
LANCIOTTO: In heaven's name, hold!
Will neither of you answer no to me?
A nod, a hint, a sign, for your escape.
Bethink you, life is centered in this thing.
Speak! I will credit either. No reply?
What does your crime deserve?
PAOLO: Death.
FRANCESCA: Death to both.
LANCIOTTO: Well said! You speak the law of Italy;
And by the dagger you designed for me,
In Pepe's hand, – your bravo?
PAOLO: It is false!
If you received my dagger from his hand,
He stole it.
LANCIOTTO: There, sweet heaven, I knew! And now
You will deny the rest? You see, my friends,
How easy of belief I have become! –

How easy 'twere to cheat me!
PAOLO: No; enough!
I will not load my groaning spirit more;
A lie would crush it.
LANCIOTTO: Brother, once you gave
Life to this wretched piece of workmanship,
When my own hand resolved its overthrow.
Revoke the gift. [*Offers to stab himself*]
PAOLO: [*Preventing him*] Hold, homicide!
LANCIOTTO: But think,
You and Francesca may live happily,
After my death, as only lovers can.
PAOLO: Live happily, after a deed like this!
LANCIOTTO: Now, look ye! there is not one hour of life
Among us three. Paolo, you are armed –
You have a sword, I but a dagger: see!
I mean to kill you.
FRANCESCA: [*Whispers Paolo*] Give thy sword to me.
PAOLO: Away! thou'rt frantic! I will never lift
This wicked hand against thee.
LANCIOTTO: Coward, slave!
Art thou so faint? Does Malatesta's blood
Run in thy puny veins? Take that! [*Strikes him*]
PAOLO: And more:
Thou canst not offer more than I will bear.
LANCIOTTO: Paolo, what a craven has thy guilt
Transformed thee to! Why, I have seen the time
When thou'dst have struck at heaven for such a thing!
Art thou afraid?
PAOLO: I am.
LANCIOTTO: O! infamy!
Can man sink lower? I will wake thee, though: –
Thou shalt not die a coward. See! look here! [*Stabs Francesca*]
FRANCESCA: O! – O! – [*Falls*]
PAOLO: Remorseless man, dare you do this,
And hope to live? Die, murderer! [*Draws, rushes at him, but pauses*]
LANCIOTTO: Strike, strike!
Ere thy heart fail.
PAOLO: I cannot. [*Throws away his sword*]
LANCIOTTO: Dost thou see
Yon bloated spider – hideous as myself –
Climbing aloft, to reach that wavering twig?
When he has touched it, one of us must die.
Here is the dagger. – Look at me, I say!

Keep your eyes from that woman! Look,
  think, choose! –
Turn here to me: thou shalt not look at her!

PAOLO: O, heaven!

LANCIOTTO: 'Tis done!

PAOLO: [*Struggling with him*] O! Lanciotto,
  hold!
Hold, for thy sake! Thou wilt repent this
  deed.

LANCIOTTO: I know it.

FRANCESCA: [*Rising*] Help! – O! murder! –
  help, help, help!

She totters towards them, and falls

LANCIOTTO: Our honor, boy! [*Stabs Paolo, he
  falls*]

FRANCESCA: Paolo!

PAOLO: Hark! she calls.
I pray thee, brother, help me to her side.

Lanciotto helps him to Francesca

LANCIOTTO: Why, there!

PAOLO: God bless thee!

LANCIOTTO: Have I not done well?
What were the honor of the Malatesti,
With such a living slander fixed to it?
Cripple! that's something – cuckold! that is
  damned!
You blame me?

PAOLO: No.

LANCIOTTO: You, lady?

FRANCESCA: No, my lord.

LANCIOTTO: May God forgive you! We are even
  now:
Your blood has cleared my honor, and our
  name
Shines to the world as ever.

PAOLO: O! – O! –

FRANCESCA: Love,
Art suffering?

PAOLO: But for thee.

FRANCESCA: Here, rest thy head
Upon my bosom. Fie upon my blood!
It stains thy ringlets. Ha! he dies! Kind saints,
I was first struck, why cannot I die first?
Paolo, wake! – God's mercy! wilt thou go
Alone – without me? Prithee, strike again!
Nay, I am better – love – now – O! [*Dies*]

LANCIOTTO: [*Sinks upon his knees*] Great·heav-
  en!

MALATESTA: [*Without*] This way, I heard the
  cries.

Enter, with Guido, Attendants, etc.

GUIDO: O! horrible!

MALATESTA: O! bloody spectacle! Where is thy
  brother?

LANCIOTTO: So Cain was asked. Come here, old
  men! You shrink
From two dead bodies and a pool of blood –
You soldiers, too! Come here!

Drags Malatesta and Guido forward

MALATESTA: O! – O! –

LANCIOTTO: You groan!
What must I do, then? Father, here it is, –
The blood of Guido mingled with our own,
As my old nurse predicted. And the spot
Of her infernal baptism burns my brain
Till reason shudders! Down, upon your knees!
Ay, shake them harder, and perchance they'll
  wake.
Keep still! Kneel, kneel! You fear them? I
  shall prowl
About these bodies till the day of doom.

MALATESTA: What hast thou done?

GUIDO: Francesca! – O! my child!

LANCIOTTO: Can howling make this sight more
  terrible?
Peace! You disturb the angels up in heaven,
While they are hiding from this ugly earth.
Be satisfied with what you see. You two
Began this tragedy, I finished it.
Here, by these bodies, let us reckon up
Our crimes together. Why, how still they lie!
A moment since, they walked, and talked,
  and kissed!
Defied me to my face, dishonored me!
They had the power to do it then; but now,
Poor souls, who'll shield them in eternity?
Father, the honor of our house is safe:
I have the secret. I will to the wars,
And do more murders, to eclipse this one.
Back to the battles; there I breathe in peace;
And I will take a soldier's honor back. –
Honor! what's that to me now? Ha! ha! ha!
  [*Laughing*]
A great thing, father! I am very ill.
I killed thy son for honor: thou mayst chide.
O God! I cannot cheat myself with words!
I loved him more than honor – more than
  life –
This man, Paolo – this stark, bleeding corpse!
Here let me rest, till God awake us all! [*Falls
  on Paolo's body*]

MINSTREL SHOW

THE Negro minstrel show was the only genuinely indigenous form of American drama; and though American troupes during the fifties and sixties made numerous excursions to England and to Germany, black-face minstrelsy remained, throughout its eighty-odd years of existence, essentially an American theatrical product.

Although many writers on Negro minstrelsy have traced its source to the peculiar character of the Southern Negro, his African heritage, and his life on the plantation, the burnt-cork Negro was largely a romantic invention of Northern whites. The minstrel performer was primarily attempting to contrive a lucrative form of theatrical entertainment, irrespective of folkloric authenticity. Yet the singularly American romantic notion of a slave Negro singing and dancing at his work, smiling and joking under the punishing strokes of his overseer's whip, gave Negro minstrelsy the igniting spark that set it burning through the middle years of the last century.

The first signs of the budding life of this new theatrical form were found around 1800 in the comic songs sung in black-face at the circus and in the theatre. When performed on the regular theatre program, they were inserted either between the acts of a play or between the separate sections of the bill. So many of these have been noted with such a diversity of dates and such indefinite descriptions of the actual performances that it is difficult to say which of them came first and which was most directly related to the fully matured minstrel show.

In 1769 Lewis Hallam did an imitation of "a drunken darky" during a performance of *The Padlock*. How closely this may have approximated some of the antics of the endmen is impossible to say, or how similar it may have been to such comic songs as that noted in *Russell's Boston Gazette* for Monday, December 30, 1799: "At the end of the second act of the presentation of the tragedy, *Oronooko*, 'The Song of the Negro Boy' will be sung." The Negro actor Andrew Allen was one of these early performers. He later became more famous as a cook and dresser for Edwin Forrest; but in 1815, in an Albany theatre, between the acts of *The Battle of Lake Champlain*, he sang "Back Side of Albany Stands Lake Champlain."

Another of these early singers, George Washington Dixon, made his debut as a circus performer in Albany in 1827. He is usually credited as the composer of "Old Zip Coon" (later known as "Turkey in the Straw"). George Nichols, a clown for Purdy Brown's Theatre and Circus of the South and West, is sometimes mentioned as the first performer to sing songs in Negro make-up. Supposedly he got the idea from a French Negro banjo player who was known throughout the Mississippi Valley as Picayune Butler. Some Nichols enthusiasts insisted that he sang the "Jim Crow" song long before Rice made it famous as a dance.

However important an influence these early black-face singers may have had, "Jim Crow" Rice was unquestionably the most significant figure of these pre-minstrel days. Thomas Dartmouth "Daddy" Rice was born in the old Seventh Ward of New York City on May 20, 1808, and received his first theatrical training as a supernumerary at the Park Theatre. He was apparently a born comedian, for in a production of *Bombastes Furioso* at the Park his comedy antics attracted so much attention to him and away from the principals that he was dismissed. After losing this position, he journeyed up and down the Ohio Valley as an itinerant player. For a time he was employed as a property man, lamplighter, and stage carpenter at Ludlow and Smith's Southern Theatre in Louisville. In 1829 he transferred to Samuel Drake's company at the Louisville Theatre, and it was probably during this engagement, when he was cast as a cornfield Negro in a local drama, Solon Robinson's *The Rifle*, that he sang and jumped "Jim Crow" for the first time.

Like so much of the story of the minstrels, the factual history of this famous song and dance cannot be reported reliably. The speculations have been so numerous, and some of the least credible stories occur so frequently, that it is difficult to deny them some grain of truth. On one thing all accounts are agreed: the date on which Rice jumped "Jim Crow" for the first time was a significant date in the history of Negro minstrelsy.

In an article in the *New York Times* for June 5, 1881, Edwin S. Conner attributed the original "Jim Crow" dance to a Louisville stableboy, from whom Rice copied the routine. No doubt Conner based his explanation on Sol Smith's report in *Theatrical Management in the South and West* (1868). According to Smith, the stable was directly behind the theatre, and the proprietor with the deformed, limping gait was called "Daddy" Crow. Francis Courtney Wemmys, in his autobiography, said that the original Jim Crow was a native of Pittsburgh and that his real name was Jim Cuff. Marian Spitzer added New Orleans to the list of places that have laid claim to the original Jim Crow.

One of the most elaborate explanations was given by Robert Nevin. According to Nevin, the dance originated in Cincinnati, and the original performer was a crippled stableboy whose infirmity forced him to walk in a curious jumping fashion. This crippled jump, copied and elaborated by Rice, was the basis for the "Jim Crow" dance. When Rice moved to Pittsburgh, he wanted to incorporate the dance as part of his routine. Having no clothes that were appropriate to the "Jim Crow" character, but observing a porter in ragged clothes similar to those of the stableboy, Rice appropriated the porter's costume for the "Jim Crow" dance. The porter, who seems to have been named Jim Cuff, fearfully allowed Rice to remove his clothes and then waited in the wings while Rice went out on the stage and sang and danced "Jim Crow" for the first time. The name Jim Cuff must have been associated with some real-life or stage Negro, for it occurred again in Sol Smith's play *Tailor in Distress*, in which Edwin Forrest played the part of Cuff at the Globe Theatre in Cincinnati on July 17, 1823. A similar name, Cuffy, was used for the Negro character in Samuel Low's *The Politician Outwitted* (1788). Brougham's Negro character in *Life in New York* (1856) was also called Cuff.

Of these various explanations of the first jumping of "Jim Crow," that which associates the original performance with Louisville sometime between 1828 and 1831 appears the most plausible. The music and verses for the dance were composed by Rice and submitted to the music dealer Cunning Peters. Peters became a dealer in Louisville sometime in 1828, but he did not open his branch in Cincinnati until 1839, so it seems likely that Rice brought the music to him in Louisville. Although an endless stream of verses was added by various later interpreters, Rice's music and the original refrain remained the same:

> First on de heel tap, den on de toe,
> Ebery time I wheel about I jump Jim Crow.
> Wheel about and turn about and do jis so,
> And ebery time I wheel about I jump Jim Crow.

The exact nature of the dance, beyond what is implicit in the refrain, is impossible to discover, for the illustrations are few and are limited ordinarily to one pose. They give little more than an indication of the costume and the curious posture: knees bent, one heel up, one heel down, one arm raised, the other on the hip, and the head cocked to one side.

Regardless of any questions about the possible place of origin, there is no question about the immediate success of the dance. Rice's reputation was established with the "Jim Crow" dance, and he continued "jumping" until his death in 1861.

Although the point is not so important as the first dancing of "Jim Crow," Rice claims further distinction as the first to introduce "Ethiopian Operas." These operas, the first of which was given by Rice as early as January, 1833, when he introduced the Bowery Theatre audience to *Long Island Juba* and *Where's My Head?*, were the precursors of the later minstrel burlesques that became so essential to the second part of the regular minstrel shows.

Rice introduced the British to "Jim Crow" at the Surrey Theatre in London on July 9, 1836. "Although not perfectly understood by some," one reporter noted, "it was relished by all. His song of Jim Crow did not quite bear out its American reputation, though its fits and starts, its odd grimaces and grotesque twitchings, and all but impracticable freaks, now and then, were quite convulsive." At least part of the interest seemed to derive from the notion that he was "delineating African manners and peculiarities as actually existing in America." Rice caught on immediately and continued throughout the season, though not without a few detractors. On July 15, 1837, a year after his opening, one disgruntled customer observed: "We saw this 'apology for a man,' a few evenings since, and not withstanding our disgust, could not forbear laughing at the fellow's impudence. We rejoice to hear that his days in this country are numbered." Others complained about his overwhelming success at the box office: "This disgusting buffoon carries away seventy pounds per week, while many of our charming and lovely young actresses, cannot, by unwearied assiduity, earn more than from 25 to 30. What gross injustice. What an indelible disgrace to our country." The public did not object. Rice appeared again in London in 1839.

During this decade of the thirties, preceding the actual founding of the minstrel show proper, Rice had many imitators. Barney Williams became famous for his Negro dances; Barnum presented Jack Diamond in his famous Ethiopian "breakdowns"; Bill Keller was singing "Coal Black Rose"; Barney Burns was known for his rendering of "My Long Tail Blue"; and at the Bowery in 1834 Bob Farrell introduced "Zip Coon." Negro-specialty performers became the popular entertainers of the day in the circus and on the stage. Perhaps Rice's influence kept the minstrel from revealing the genuine plantation Negro, but certainly Rice's influence established the pattern for the individual performers of the burnt-cork line.

Another first appearance related directly to the eventual form of the minstrel show was the performance in December, 1842, of Dan Emmett and his group of four. They were the first to attempt a full evening's musical entertainment in black-face. The first meetings of this group were very informal. Several evenings a week Emmett's friends gathered at his boarding house to rehearse. Emmett played the fiddle, Billy Whitlock the banjo, Dick Pelham the tambourine, and Frank Bower the bones. Like many other such amateur groups in the history of the theatre, they eventually felt compelled to seek an audience. They recruited a number of friends who were willing to contribute toward a benefit for Dick Pelham. For this select group they played *Essence of Old Virginny*, the first regular minstrel-type show. Pleased with their success, they ventured a regular professional opening at the Bowery Amphitheatre on February 6, 1843, announcing themselves as the Virginia Minstrels. On February 16, they appeared at a "sporting saloon" called the Cornucopia and from February 17 to March 1 at the Olympic Circus; on March 7 and 8 they introduced their "Ethiopian Concert" at the Masonic Temple in Boston.

As in the history of most theatrical enterprises, several groups claimed first honors. The Christy troupe, for example, always billed themselves as "founded in 1842." Although not the first, the group assembled by E. P. Christy was important to the development of the regular minstrel show. Christy established the routine that was for so many years the accepted pattern for minstrel performances. In fact, his name was so strongly associated with the development of minstrelsy that a minstrel performer was frequently identified simply as a "Christy."

E. P. Christy's appearance in 1846 at the Hall of the Mechanics' Society (472 Broadway) was the first performance at which the regular semicircular line-up was used. This performance also established the custom of placing a man with a tambourine at one end of the line-up and a man with a pair of bones at the other. Christy was also the first to give the Interlocutor his central position and to institute the regular pattern of the performance in which the First Part was devoted to music and to jokes between the endmen, Tambo and Bones, and the Interlocutor. In these early performances, the Interlocutor had not yet achieved his elegant title; he was known simply as the middleman. The First Part of the show ended with a song by the whole company. After two choruses, the second one being sung in a very soft and lugubrious manner, it concluded with a "walk-around" by the entire company. This walk-around, later called "cakewalk," a characteristic feature of minstrel performances, was executed in the following manner: the company stood in a semicircle while, one at a time, each member of the company strutted around the inside of the circle several times and then finished by doing his particular specialty in the center of the stage. Not unlike the finales of vaudeville, revues, and television.

The Second Part of these early performances, known as the olio, consisted of specialties. One performer had a comic routine of removing innumerable coats and vests; another member of the company whistled Paganini's "Variations on the Carnival of Venice" on a tin penny whistle. The acts of the Second Part were very similar to the regular vaudeville turns of the 1920's. Many of these specialties, the "Jim Crow" dance and Jack Diamond's breakdowns, for example, antedated the minstrel show proper. The "wench" character, acted by the female impersonator of the troupe and later established as one of the feature attractions of every minstrel-show olio, was first performed by Dan Gardner in 1835.

Like any type of theatrical performance repeated over and over again by different companies and under various circumstances, the ministrel show developed a traditional and stereotyped format. Exactly when it was established (it was first claimed by Christy) is difficult to determine – probably sometime in the late forties or early fifties. As the pattern finally evolved, the entire cast marched on the stage and arranged themselves in the regular semicircle; the Interlocutor then started the proceedings with the familiar phrase "Gentlemen, be seated. We will commence with the overture." After the overture came a series of exchanges between the endmen and the Interlocutor in which the Interlocutor was invariably deflated by Tambo and Bones. After this, either Tambo or Bones would sing a comic song, followed by a series of sentimental ballads sung by the "silver-throated" vocalists and a final song and walk-around by the entire company. This was the First Part.

The Second Part remained much the same as in the early Christy performances: special songs, what we now term vaudeville gags, "wench numbers," breakdowns, and so on. Added to this as a Third Part, though almost invariably identified as a division of the Second Part, was a burlesque of some popular serious drama. This little play "enlisted the whole strength of the company." Frequently a "Dixie Land" plantation scene with songs, dances, and tableaux replaced the burlesque if the talents of the company warranted.

Even though this pattern of First Part (repartee and song) and Second Part (olio and burlesque or plantation scene) became the established form, minstrel actors were never restricted to this arrangement. Individual performers expanded their routines to accommodate their peculiar talents, and even in the burlesques the actors cut and expanded the text as they thought appropriate to the time and occasion. The script was little more than a kind of *commedia dell' arte* scenario, and Jennings (*Theatrical and Circus Life*) was probably not exaggerating when he wrote, "A minstrel having a speech of a dozen lines will make it twenty-five times and never make it twice alike."

But the music of the minstrel show, more than the comic repartee or dances, holds the interest of present-day students. Minstrelsy originated with the comic song sung in black-face, and those who can still recall the days of the old-time minstrel show cherish the many songs that Negro minstrelsy contributed to the album of American folk music. America's most distinguished troubadour, Stephen Foster, wrote a large share of his songs expressly for minstrel performances. Dan Emmett is remembered for many old songs that are still popular: "Old Dan Tucker," "Walk Along, John," "Boatman's Dance," "Early in the Morning," and above all, "Dixie."

Southerners would like to believe that "Dixie" was composed as a patriotic song for the South; but, disillusioning as the fact may be, it was originally composed because Emmett was called upon to furnish Bryant's Minstrels with a snappy walk-around finale. The performance at which they expected to use

NEW YORK *Published by* FIRTH. POND & CO. 1 *Franklin Sq.*
PITTSBURG. H. KLEBER.

Courtesy of the New York Public Library

Minstrel Songs

OLD FOLKS AT HOME

Words and Music by E. P. CHRISTY.

Way down upon de Swanee ribber, Far, far a - - way,

Dere's wha my heart is turning ebber, Dere's wha de old folks stay.

GONE TO ALABAMA

Composed by

E. P. Christy

AND SUNG BY

CHRTSTY'S MINSTRELS

NEW YORK

Published by JAQUES & BROTHER 385, Broadway

VOCE

Allegretto.

p

cres

f

DIXIE'S LAND.

COMPOSED BY DAN. EMMETT.

ARRANGED BY W. L. HOBBS.

I wish I was in de land ob cot - ton,

Old times dar am not for - got - ten, Look a - way, Look a

way! Look a - way! Dix - ie Land. In Dix - ie Land whar

the song was already announced, so Emmett had only two days in which to write a "snappy tune." "Dixie" was the result. First sung at Mechanics' Hall on April 4, 1859, it was officially introduced to the Confederacy at President Jefferson Davis's inauguration in Montgomery, Alabama, on February 18, 1861. When it became the stirring war song of the South, Emmett is reported to have remarked, "If I had known to what use they were going to put my song, I will be damned if I'd have written it."

"Dixie" was not the only favorite that was first sung by some "silver-throated" tenor from the burnt-cork line; "Old Folks at Home," "My Old Kentucky Home," "Tramp, Tramp, Tramp, the Boys are Marching," and "Marching Through Georgia," to mention a few, were all originally minstrel tunes.

Although the melodist of minstrel days made a more lasting impression than any of the jokesters or comic dancers or writers of burlesques, it is in the burlesque that the true comic spirit of Negro minstrelsy is most clearly revealed, not only because the scripts of many burlesques are still available today but because in these exhibitions the black-face performers stretched the peculiar comic possibilities of their medium to the limit. Many present-day critics insist that they exceeded the limits of good taste; yet, that question aside, these undisciplined exaggerations clearly reveal the inherent playful temper of the entire minstrel performance. White men smeared with burnt cork, their heads covered with wigs of tight curly black hair, pretending to exhibit the refined manners of counts, kings, and princes – this was at once the romance and the true comic spirit of the minstrel's art.

These afterpieces, as they were sometimes called, were not always cast in play form. Sometimes they were stump speeches, burlesques of political oratory. Such performers as James Unsworth (apparently the first), "Healthy" Hughey Dougherty, "Senator" Frank Bell, and Billy Rice gained their minstrel fame as stump speakers. These speeches were not composed in strict rhetorical form. For the most part, they were simply extended recitals of jokes similar to those of the First Part between the Interlocutor and the endmen. However, the great majority of the afterpieces were burlesques of the popular plays of the day. *Romeo and Juliet* became *Roman Nose and Suet; Macbeth, Bad Breath, the Crane of Chowder.* The *dramatis personae* were invariably the same as in the original; thus the comic incongruity of black-face impersonations of well-known dramatic figures was established immediately.

The history of minstrelsy from the days of Emmett's Virginia Minstrels to the "gigantic" and "mammoth" troupes of Colonel Jack Haverly and Lew Dockstader in the eighties and nineties is filled with record-breaking phenomena. In the spring of 1884, the Thatcher, Primrose and West company grossed $14,188.50 in one week at the Boston Theatre. The receipts of the Christy Minstrels during the span of their 2,792 performances mounted to $317,589, with profits of over $160,000 for the producers. These figures are even more startling in the light of the prevailing admission price of twenty-five cents. After Christy's, the Campbell Minstrels became the leading troupe. They were so popular by the end of the fifties that the country was swarming with companies that called themselves Campbell's, often to the confusion of the public and their respective press representatives. Haverly's Mastodon Minstrels became identified by the symbol of the big bass drum and the famous legend "40 Count 'Em 40!!!" By 1880 Haverly was not satisfied with any mere forty; he traveled with a company of over a hundred performers and with a carload of gaudy scenery.

As might have been predicted from the success of Rice in London, the English were delighted with the Negro minstrels. However, the most optimistic enthusiast could not have predicted their phenomenal history. As one London reporter noted in 1881, after seeing the 7,805th consecutive performance of the Moore and Burgess Minstrels: "Dynasties have fallen, whole empires have been upset, but the Moore and Burgess Minstrels go on forever." In June, 1843, just four months after their initial professional appearance in New York, the Virginia Minstrels appeared at the Adelphi Theatre. Their "Grand Ethiopian Concert" was billed as the "Greatest Novelty Ever Brought from America." By 1846 there were reported to be ten troupes operating in the metropolis. "Although not publicly known," one critic noted, "we well know that many of them are English with their faces made black or copper colour. . . . What a state of affairs when our own talent is obliged to represent a foreigner to produce a living. Our readers will scarcely believe that Macready is about taking a tour through the provinces, and announcing himself as the great Ohio tragedian." Toward the end of the fifties some reviewers thought the "African melodists" were going out of fashion. The public did not subscribe to this notion. In 1880 Haverly's Original Mastodon Minstrels 40-count-'em-40 (one reporter said he counted forty-two) invaded London and still found plenty of eager customers. Apparently the Haverly group depended less on sentimental ballads and more on the eccentric routines; one heard less of "the shutters being put up because little Willie's dead," as one reporter put it. Certainly no other American style of entertainment caught on so quickly in England and endured so long.

The large-scale extravaganzas of the eighties and nineties marked the decline of minstrelsy. Our ancestors who lived through the Civil War era saw the black-face art in its heyday; from 1850 to 1870 Negro minstrelsy was at its height. During the fifties, ten New York theatres devoted themselves almost exclusively to minstrel performances, while at the beginning of the seventies only four such theatres were operating. Hundreds of companies were playing throughout the country in the fifties and sixties; in 1880, there were only thirty; in 1896, the number had been reduced to ten; and in April, 1919, there were only three.

The decrease in the number of minstrel troupes was due largely to the craze for magnitude. "Bigger and better" was not compatible with minstrel entertainment. Several economic factors also contributed to the deterioration of the minstrels' popularity. A sharp drop in the number of troupes occurred during the season of the panic of 1873 when eighteen out of the thirty-nine companies on the road failed. But more important was the change in financial structure demanded by the new managers' proclivities for "gigantic" and "mammoth" shows. The increased cost of stage settings, advertising, and salaries, when it seemed impossible to raise the admission price from the customary twenty-five cents, made the minstrel show a financially unprofitable enterprise.

In both its early and its later years Negro minstrelsy was above all an entertainment of and for the theatre, presentational in every respect. At times there may have been some attempt to draw upon the characteristics of the plantation Negro, but there was never any very genuine effort to represent his true, realistic character. The minstrel performer simply constructed a stage type and captured an eccentric theatrical format that fascinated the nineteenth-century spectator.

Although Negro minstrelsy has been labeled a distinctively American contribution in the history of the theatre, the form exhibits a strong similarity to the Italian *commedia dell' arte*. As in the *commedia*, the special talents of the acting company determined the specific nature of the performance. Any limitations suggested by the script were observed only if compatible with the creative desires of the particular players. The Negro minstrel show never developed so many distinct comedy types as the *commedia*, but certainly the Tambo, Bones, Interlocutor, and "wench" performers belong to the same theatrical family as the *commedia's* Doctor, Captain, and Harlequin. There are similarities between the *commedia* Doctor and the minstrel Interlocutor and betwen the *commedia* Zanni and the Tambo and Bones; and, of course, Harlequin wore a black-face mask. The specialty numbers of the Negro-minstrel routine were in a way comparable to the interpolated comic routines, the *lazzi*, of the *commedia*. And, like the *commedia*, the minstrel show depended for its success on the talents of the performers and not on a prepared script.

Few unique theatrical forms have achieved such a hardy and long life as did Negro minstrelsy, and few have had such a wide appeal. The black-face performers did not depend on the lowbrow theatregoer for their popularity, as has sometimes been suggested. Lincoln was a regular patron, Gladstone delighted in the "silver-throated" ballad singers and in the comic antics of the endmen, and Thackeray bestowed on minstrelsy one of the highest tributes ever paid to it. Probably with a Stephen Foster melody still singing in his ears, he wrote:

I heard a humorous balladist, not long ago, a minstrel with wool on his head and an Ultra-Ethiopian complexion who performed a negro ballad that I confess moistened these spectacles in the most unexpected manner. I have gazed at thousands of tragedy-queens dying on the stage and expiring in appropriate blank verse, and I never wanted to wipe them. They have looked up, be it said, at many scores of clergymen without being dimmed and behold! a vagabond with a corked face and a banjo sings a little song, strikes a wild note, which sets the heart thrilling with happy pity.

Although the full flavor of the minstrel entertainment can be sensed only with the black-face artists in action on the stage, if the reader lets his imagination run, the sample selections that follow will suggest the delightfully slapstick nature of this peculiarly American theatrical invention.

BRUDDER BONE'S LOVE SCRAPE

CHARACTERS

BONES   INTERLOCUTOR

INTERLOCUTOR: Brudder Bones, didn't you pay attention to Sarah Gruttsy?

BONES: Yes, oh, yes.

INTERLOCUTOR: But how did it break off?

BONES: Oh, it didn't break off at all.

INTERLOCUTOR: What den?

BONES: Why, it cove in.

INTERLOCUTOR: Well, will you tell us the particulars?

BONES: Yes, yes. You see I went down de oder night to see de gal, pulled de string, went in, sat down beside de gal, and began to pour forth some of de words of de foreign poets, when in come de old man; says he, "Bones, dar's de door!" So I got up, and shut de door, come back, sot down beside de gal, Pressed her lips, when de old man sings out again, "Bones, dar's de door!" So I got up, and dis time I opened de door. Den de old man says, "Bones, if you don't empty dis building of your presence, I shall not be responsible for your early decease." So I got up, and when I saw his cowhide boots raised, I started. When I got out de moon shone most elephant from behind a cloud; de stars didn't shine, kase it neber rained harder since de deluge. De pigs didn't squeak, kase dey'd all gone to rest. De birds didn't sing, kase dey were all in deir feather beds. I could hear nothing but de beatings of dis poor darkey's heart. And as I went along something whispered in my ear, "Onward Bones!" – dere is propsects ahead."

INTERLOCUTOR: Ah, dat must have revived your drooping spirits?

BONES: Yes; if I could only get a few drops, but they were all shut up. So thinking on de way how de old man served me, I got seventeen blocks beyond de house afore I knew where I was. So I got home, and tried to sleep, but sleep has deserted dese lamps –

INTERLOCUTOR: Eyes, you mean?

BONES: Yes; I couldn't sleep; so I took de banjo, and tho't I'd give de gal a serenade. So I got to de house, and played one of dose soul-stirring airs, when all at once de window histed, de shutters opened, and dere she stood in a silk-light form – she looked 'zactly like Power's Greek Slave, only de Greek Slave was white and she was black – and wid her hair floating to de breezes, and her eyes like two diamonds shining, in de voice of an angel she exclaimed, "If you don't go away from under dat window, I'll scald all de wool off your head."

THE JEALLUSEST OB HER SECT

CHARACTERS

BONES   INTERLOCUTOR

INTERLOCUTOR: As we are all here we will call upon Mr. Bones to tell the public what he knows about courting.

BONES: H'ya! h'ya! Yes, I'se been dere, for certain, but I can't say dat I was always de lucky feller dat I ought to be. In fac' de last 'casion I tried it on I was bilked.

INTERLOCUTOR: You floored her with a *billet*, I suppose, and was driven away from her father's house by your *maiden speech*.

BONES: My *maiden's "peach?"* O, *she* didn't peach; I did it all myself. You know a feller sometimes gits tired of his own wife, and mine am de most jeallusest ob her sect. She's always pullin' de wool ober my eyes in one way or an-udder. De way it happen was dis: – Jus' roun' de corner from our house libs about the poo-tiest gal dat eber you did seen. She was tall as a big sunflower, and as full of cemetery as – as de Wenus ob Medicine.

INTERLOCUTOR: Be more careful! The Venus ob Medici, sir.

BONES: Well, it's all de same – dey was both on 'em wirgins – *wergin' onto forty*, dat is to say. Well, de gal she 'cirpricate my tender passion, an' I *tender* her my heart an' han', and *tend her* to de freeayter and de smash balls, till de poor gal was as crazy as a bedbug, an I wasn't much better. I writ her a letter, and de pore gal she *po(u)red* ober it, it was so affec-tin', till it was wet wid her tears. Well, de ting went on swimmin'ly for a while, but one day I come home suddenly and foun' de old woman *swimmin' in tears.*

INTERLOCUTOR: You might say *drowned* in tears, if you'd thought of it.

BONES: And I was *bathed* in perspiration. She's been intersectin one o' my billy duxes –

INTERLOCUTOR: A *pretty duck* you must have been to permit it. But ventilate, sir – ventilate.

BONES: Well, I never *went-till-late* to see my Phillis, and dat's de way I s'pose I fell into do hands ob de *Phillistines*. Dat night I slip into de gal's back parlor, as usual. It was as dark as her face in dere, and she ax me to whisper, so de folks couldn't hear us. Dere we sot, huggin' and kissin' and makin' vows ob eternal debility to each oder, an' I presentin' her wid candies an' sweetmeats, and dat kind o' tings. Says she, kind o' sighin' – "Bones," says she, "it must go werry hard on your poor wife." "O, says I, "don't you mind her; she's an old scarecrow, anyway." Wid dat she gib *went* to a yell like an Injen on de war path and *went* for me at de same time. Jus' den de do' *busted* open, and she *busted* into tears, and I *busted* der snoot of a feller dat come in at dat moment wid de light –

INTERLOCUTOR: Came in with *delight*, sir? What do you mean?

BONES: No, no – wid de candle – and den she scream till she *busted* her corsets wid rage, and I *busted* out ob de room and went on a *bust*, and would you b'lieve it, it wasn't my gal at all, but *my wife!* She'd persuaded my Phillis' fader to send her away and cum in her place. I was four bits out on her, too, and dat was all I got for it. Tinks I, nebber mind, I fixes you for dat, bime-by, presently. So what does I do but when she says she'd be dere de nex'agin I takes along wid me a big bag ob somethin', and dere I find her su' enough, sittin' alone in de dark. "Gub us a kiss," said I, and wid dat I made a rush for her and emptied a whole bag ob flour ober her, till she looked as if she'd been takin' a bath o' white-wash. De woman yelled like a stuck pig, and raise de house, an' dey all *rushed* in wid *rushlights* in der hands, and blest if it wasn't my *gal herself*, arter all! Nebber felt so cheap in all my life – nebber, nebber! Hasn't spoke to me since.

INTERLOCUTOR: Well, as we've heard about your girl, we'll now listen to something about.

"The Girl at the Sewing Machine"

BLACKBERRYING

CHARACTERS

BONES   TAMBO

BONES: Ah! Tambo, she's gone dead.
TAMBO: Is she dead, Bones?
BONES: Yes, Tambo. She sent for me three days after she died.
TAMBO: No, Bones, you mean three days pre-vious to her decease.

BONES: No; she had no niece; she was an or-phan.
TAMBO: I mean three days before she departed this earthly tenement.
BONES: Sir?
TAMBO: That is three days before she died.

BONES: Oh, yes! Well, I went down to see her; went up to de bedside wid de bed in my eyes.

TAMBO: You mean with the tears in your eyes?

BONES: Yes, wid de pillows in my eyes. Sez she, "Bones, I'm goin' to leave dis world of care."

TAMBO: What did you reply?

BONES: I sed I didn't care much. Den she axed me if I would go to the 'pothecary shop for some medicine. I said yes; so I went down to Dr. Night Bell –

TAMBO: No, not to Dr. Night Bell; that's the name of the bell on the door – the night bell.

BONES: Well, I called him Dr. Night Bell, anyhow.

TAMBO: I presume he was a pretty good physician?

BONES: No, he wasn't fishin', he was home.

TAMBO: Oh, no, I mean he was a doctor of some note.

BONES: Yes; he was counting out his notes when I went in.

TAMBO: No, Bones, you do not understand. I mean he was a doctor of some standing.

BONES: No, he wasn't standin', he was sittin' on a three-legged stool.

TAMBO: Well, what did the doctor give you?

BONES: He gabe me a piece of paper.

TAMBO: A prescription?

BONES: No, it was paper.

TAMBO: Of course, it was on paper, but nevertheless a prescription. What did it say on the paper?

BONES: It was full ob chalk-marks made wid a pencil. He sed I must get two dozen fish-hooks, No. 7, and put in a quart ob molasses an boil it down, den gib her de broth, so I went up to de bar –

TAMBO: No, you mean the counter.

BONES: He didn't count dem; he weighed 'em out.

TAMBO: Well, was there any efficacy in the dose?

BONES: No: noffin' in it but fish-hooks!

TAMBO: No, I mean was the medicine any way efficacious?

BONES: Now, look here Tambo, be so kind as to 'dress me in de English language.

TAMBO: Well, then, Bones, I mean did the medicine do her any good?

BONES: It wouldn't have cured her, but the poor gal in absence of mind, instead of takin' the broth, took de fish-hooks, and dey killed her.

TAMBO: Then that must have been her funeral I saw last Wednesday?

BONES: No, it wasn't. De doctor says I can't bury her until next summer.

TAMBO: Why not, Bones?

BONES: Kase dat's de best time to go out Blackberryin'.

THE MOVING

CHARACTERS

SNOW   BONES

SNOW: Bones, – I called to see you, this morning, and heard you have moved.

BONES: Yes, Snow; I moved last night.

SNOW: What was the matter? Was the house too small?

BONES: No; but the rent was too large.

SNOW: What did you pay for that house?

BONES: The man ax'd me eight-bits a week!

SNOW: You were badly bitten there, Bones.

BONES: I guess you'd think I was, if you had seen the fleas and bed-bugs.

SNOW: You should have spoken to the landlord about it.

BONES: I did, Snow.

SNOW: What did he do, then?

BONES: Why him and I divided de house.

SNOW: How did you divide the house, Bones?

BONES: Why he took de inside, and give me de out.

SNOW: Oh, – you wouldn't pay up, and got turned out?

BONES: No, I didn't, Snow. I got arrested, and was discharged for want of evidence.

SNOW: For want of evidence?

BONES: Yes, There being no evidence in my pockets that I was able to owe anybody, or pay 'em, so I was unanimously discharged with a "slippery-man."

SNOW: A reprimand you mean, Bones.

BONES: Yes, Snow. I got kicked out ob de office.

MURDERED

CHARACTERS

BONES   JULIUS

JULIUS: Bones, where were you going, to-day, with that young lady?

BONES: I was going down to get murdered.

JULIUS: No, you mean married, Bones.

BONES: Yes, de same ting; you might as well be murdered.

JULIUS: Well, where did you go?

BONES: Why, I went down to de parsnip's house.

JULIUS: No, no, – you went to the parson's house.

BONES: Yes, dat's whar I went.

JULIUS: Well, what did he say to you, Bones?

BONES: He told me and de gal to rise; and den he said to de gal, "Young lady, will you take dis young man for your awful wedded husband, for better or for worser?"

JULIUS: Well, what did the young lady say?

BONES: She said, "Yes, sir-ee, boss." Den he spoke to me, Julius.

JULIUS: What did he say to you?

BONES: He said, "Young man, will you take dis young lady for your awful wedded wife, for better or for worser, to stick to her in rain or shine?"

JULIUS: Well, of course, you said yes, Bones.

BONES: No, – I didn't right away. I thought a spell; and at last I said, *"Well, I'll go it anyhow."*

JULIUS: Then, I suppose, he gave you some good advice, Bones.

BONES: Yes, I tink he did, – I gave him $2.50.

JULIUS: No, no, – I mean, that he told you to live happy.

BONES: Yes; but we hab awful squerrels down to our house, Julius.

ALL: Squirrels? Well, let's all go down and take dinner with him, boys.

BONES: No, no, no, – don't come down. I don't mean dem kind ob squirrels. I mean flat-irons, broomsticks, and – and – and. Yes, dat's what I mean.

JULIUS: Oh, Bones, you mean you have family *jars*.

BONES: Yes, de whole house jars, Julius.

JULIUS: No, you don't understand me; I mean, you have matrimonial *combats*.

BONES: No, I neber come back when she hits me once.

JULIUS: Well, Bones, don't you know that man and wife should live as one?

BONES: Lib as one, Julius?

JULIUS: Yes, always, Bones.

BONES: I don't think so.

JULIUS: Why, Bones?

BONES: You just come down by our house some time, about 12 o'clock at night, an' you'd tink dar is a THOUSAND AND ONE IN DAR, Julius.

IF I MAY SO SPEAK

A BURLESQUE STUMP ORATION

Adapted and arranged expressly for Byron Christy, by J. B. Murphy

FELLER SITIZENS! and sitizen fellers: – In this momentous – yes, momentous cri-i-isis ob de country, when de tocsin ob war is sounding, or is gwine to be sounded froo-out de antipodeal and unlimited precincts ob dis vast continental continent, it behoves – yes, it *behoves*, "if I may so speak" – every loyal and patriotic – yes, patriotic and loyal mother son of us to stand ready wid hands on his arms – yes, arms in his hands in magnanimous defence – of, "if I may so speak," of the constitution; yes, of the constitution, and – so on!

As I suggested, there seems to be a disposition to fight; yes, to fight! And I say, *here*, standing upon the piney platform of – of – this stage, if there is any fighting to be did, then, in the language of the gifted – yes, the highly gifted and unterri-fied Scottish chief:

"Come one! Come all! this rock shall fly.
From its firm base" – in a pig's eye, and so on.

But again, logically speaking – yes, speaking logically, I see one-half geographically and climatrically, or in other words, climatrically and geographically considered; yes one-half our glorious Union Slipping away – yes slipping into a – so to speak, an – a adumbruous chaosity; yes, chaosity – and so on.

Shall I stand here unmoved and gaze, "if I may so speak," wid distended eyeballs – yes, wid eyeballs, at de red heel ob de soger – yes, at de heel ob de red soldier as tramples out de lifeblood ob my countrymen and coadgitors in a – so to speak – fratricidal and suicidal – yes, in a suicidal combat.

In the language of Patrick Henry – yes, of Henry Patrick, I say "no!" – yes, "no!" I know not what course others may take, but as for me give me liberty or give me lager bier, and so on.

But, as I suggested, we have lost, "if I may so speak," our – our equilibrium and balance – yes, our balance pole, where, "if I may so speak," where do we tend? Our proper position is to the zenith, with our hoary bird of freedom flopping his wings and soaring – yes, soaring to the fathomless azure of the fathomless azure – yes, to the azure of the lustrious firmament, radiated and bright – yes, bright, "if I may so speak," with the glorious corruscations of innumerable constellations – yes, constellations of innumerable corruscations!

In the language of the noble bard:

"Earth shook! red meteors flash'd across the sky,
And conscious nature *shuddered* at the cry.
Hope for a season bade the world farewell,
And freedom screeched,"

as – yes, as freedom screeched, and so on.

But, again! as I suggested. It is, perhaps, or perhaps it is, "if I may so speak," necessary that I should apologize for the latitudunosity – yes, for the tudionsity – dinosity – nosity ob my circumlocutory – locutory – cutory, the latitudinosity and of my "cution with which, "if I may so speak," I have! and so on.

But, as I suggested previously, how can I, how can you; yes, how can you and I stand by, "if I may so speak," and see the gigantic, yes, the gigantic and stupendous onslaughter of a lot of swine-eyed and spavined – yes, spavined and ring-boned, and pot-house political politicians – upon the bullworks of our freedom – yes, the freedom of our bullworks. In the language of – of somebody, "What is it that gentlemen wish? what would they have?" I repeat it, and so on.

These are the ones who have got our liberty pole off its perpendicularity – yes, the perpendicularity of our pole off – off its dicularity – larity. And where now, "if I may so speak," is the high bird of freedom – yes, the freedom of our high bird of liberty. Echo answers, yes she answers. Instead of spreading his noble pinions to soar beyond the regions of the – "if I may so speak," of the boreal pole – yes, of the boreal pole, he's driven far back to the primeval – yes, the primeval fastnesses – ess – ess-ses ob de gum trees of the west – yes, of the western gum trees; and there, I trust – yes, we all trust, he may soar and rest – and rest and soar, and flap his ponderous wings in the sunlight of freedom – yes, the freedom of sunlight, till the coming of that time, "if I may so speak," so graphitcally described and depicted – yes, depicted and described by the noble bard:

"When all the sister planets have decayed,
    When wrapped in fire the realms of ether glow,
And heaven's last thunder shakes the world below,
    Thou undismayed, shall o'er the ruin smile;
And smile – and smile," – and – and – so on.

DAT'S WHAT'S DE MATTER

A BURLESQUE LECTURE

Written expressly for Harry Pell, by John F. Poole

WHITE FOLKS? BRUDDERN AN' SISTERN, FELLER-CITIZENS, AN' ODER ANIMALS: — De text for dis evening's discourse am taken from de ninety-fust volume of Shakspeare's comic song-book called Uncle Tom's Cabin. Has any ob you ladies or gemmen got de book wid you? If you has, open it at de nine hundred an' forty-fifth page, an' dar you will find it. De text am dis:

> Let dogs delight to bark an' fight,
>   For 'tis deir natur to:
> Let fleas and bedbugs nip an' bite,
>   An' skeeters suck you frough:
> But Jeff Davis, you should never let
>   Yourself on treason sup;
> Your little hands was never made
>   To bust de Union up!

No, my deluded frens, he ain't agwine to do it — not if de Union knows herself, an' I'll bet a doller she do. An' dat's what's de matter!

In de next place, whar's de spondulicks a-gwan to? As de ole lady dat sat for free tousand in de laps of Time, said to de man dat stood on his dignity till he tumbled off, What is de difference between de dish dat de Chinamans eat an' de captain ob de rabel privateer Sumter? I'll tole. One am a rat-pie, de oder am a pie-rate. An' dat's what's de matter!

Nextly, take de telemegraph question — wot am it? wot was de fust message transmiffligated from de back-side ob Fort Lafayette to de oder side ob Jordan? What, it was — "How was you, Gineral Beauregard?" Den, my disgusted hearers, didn't de Gineral feel sick, when at de Bull o' Battle's Run de Black-hoss Cavalry, or de blackguard cavalry, sort o' got cut up into sassage-meat? — wen, as de poet McGuffin says in de play ob Midsummer Ice-Cream:

> Oh, de bully Zouaves at Bull Run,
> Dey went into de fightin' like fun,
> An' dey showed de Black-hoss dey was some
> When dey levelled deir bayonet an' gun,
> Or buff ob dem rolled into one,

At each traitorous son ob a gun;
And dey found, at de set ob the sun,
Date de Black-hoss fellers were done

brown, and knocked into free-cornered cocked hats. Dat's what's de matter!

Nextly, what about de big fleet? dat's de question? Now, my insignificant frens, what am de differance between de frigate Wabash and Jefferson Davis — eh, um? I'll tole you. Lest, as de man in de freatre says, "you bust wid iggnorance" (an' if you bust here, it'll cost us two bits to have you swept up an' carried out), de differance between de frigate Wabash and Jefferson Davis am dis: one am a first-rater, de oder am de worst traitor. An' dat's what's de matter!

Nextly, my broder Mormons, to bring de conclusion ob my disgustion to de terminus ob de beginning — "unaccustomed as I am to public speaking" — "unaccustomed as I am to public speaking" — I say, unaccustomed as I am to public speaking, I intend to foreclose de mortgage on dis election like a Slid-*ell*. Dat's what de matter.

Nextly, my crazy congregationers, luff us look into de Soudern Conthievocracy — what do we see dar? Why, dar we see it a-standin' wid a masked battery under its arm an' a pirate-ship in each pocket, standin' on de ruins ob Fort Sumter, tryin' to climb up to Mount Vernon so as to reach de flag-staff ob de Union, an' pull down de good ole flag. Dar's de Union bull-dog, Gineral Grant, crossin' de fence. Now he bow-wos! now he cotches ole King Cotton by de slack part ob his trouserloons, an' shakes de debil out ob him! for —

> When de tief he does diskiber,
> He send him 'way clar up Salt Riber;
> De Union dey shall ne'er disseber,
> For de Stars an' Stripes shall float for eber.

An' dat's what's de matter!

LECTURE TO A FIRE COMPANY

It having been announced to me, my young friends, that you were about forming a fire company, I have called you together to give you such directions as long experience in a first-quality engine company qualifies me to communicate. The moment you hear an alarm of fire, scream like a pair of panthers. Run any way, except the right way – for the furthest way round is the nearest way to the fire. If you happen to run on the top of a wood-pile, so much the better, you can then get a good view of the neighborhood. If a light breaks on your view, "break" for it immediately; but be sure you don't jump into a bow window. Keep yelling, all the time; and, if you can't make night hideous enough yourself, kick all the dogs you come across, and set them yelling, too; 'twill help amazingly. A brace of cats dragged up stairs by the tail would be a "powerful auxiliary." When you reach the scene of the fire, do all you can to convert it into a scene of destruction. Tear down all the fences in the vicinity. If it be a chimney on fire, throw salt down it; or, if you can't do that, perhaps the best plan would be to jerk off the pump-handle and pound it down. Don't forget to yell all the while, as it will have a prodigious effect in frigtening off the fire. The louder the better, of course; and the more ladies in the vicinity, the greater necessity for "doing it brown." Should the roof begin to smoke, get to work in good earnest, and make any man "smoke" that interrupts you. If it is summer, and there are fruit-trees in the lot, cut them down, to prevent the fire from roasting the apples. Don't forget to yell! Should the stable be threatened, carry out the cow-chains.

Never mind the horse – he'll be alive and kicking; and if his legs don't do their duty, let them pay for the roast. Ditto as to the hogs; – let them save their own bacon, or smoke for it. When the roof begins to burn, get a crowbar and pry away the stone steps; or, if the steps be of wood, procure an axe and chop them up. Next, cut away the wash-boards in the basement story; and, if that don't stop the flames, let the chair-boards on the first floor share a similar fate. Should the "devouring element" still pursue the "even tenor of its way," you had better ascend to the second story. Pitch out the pitchers, and tumble out the tumblers. Yell all the time!

If you find a baby abed, fling it into the second story window of the house across the way; but let the kitten carefully down in a work basket. Then draw out the bureau drawers, and empty their contents out of the back window; telling somebody below to upset the slop-barrel and rain-water hogshead at the same time. Of course, you will attend to the mirror. The further it can be thrown the more pieces will be made. If anybody objects, smash it over his head. Do not, under any circumstances, drop the tongs down from the second story; the fall might break its legs, and render the poor thing a cripple for life. Set it straddle of your shoulders, and carry it down carefully. Pile the bed clothes carefully on the floor, and throw the crockery out of the window. By the time you will have attended to all these things, the fire will certainly be arrested, or the building be burnt down. In either case, your services will be no longer needed; and, of course, you require no further directions.

CAMILLE

G. W. H. GRIFFIN

CHARACTERS

CAMILLE   ARMAND DUVAL

Scene. – A Chamber. – Lounge left with pillow and sheet. – Two chairs at head of lounge. – Toilet stand right with looking-glass, bottle of gin, several bottles of medicine, and a lighted candle. Enter Julius right.

JULIUS: [*Meditating*] Can'st thou minister to a

pocket diseased? Oh, the base ingratitude of this world! here I am turned out of a wholesale pea-nut store, just because I borrowed fifteen cents to last me over Sunday; but such is life! Merchants have no hearts.

Enter Sam right

SAM: "Hearts, my boy, are flinty things,
That beat all they can, and then take wings."
Why, Julius, am dat you?

JULIUS: Of course it am, what dar is left of me; but where was you last night? I didn't see you at the club.

SAM: I was to do Theatre, to see de "Hospital Tragedy."

JULIUS: Why, what play do you mean?

SAM: I mean "Camille." Did you ever see it?

JULIUS: Oh, yes, I saw Ned Forrest play it at the Broadway; it's my favorite piece, and I know it all by heart.

SAM: So do I! now let's you and I get some dresses, and take Camille through the country, and we can make our fortunes.

JULIUS: All right, go it! and I'll play "Camille."

SAM: You! You'd be a "sick Camille."

JULIUS: Well, ain't she always a "sick" Camille? what are you "coughing" about?

SAM: All right! but you know I must play Camille, and you must play "Army Duval."

JULIUS: Army Devil! who's that, Ben Butler?

SAM: No! no; I mean Camille's Lover!

JULIUS: Oh, yes! You mean Camille's "Loafer." He's the feller what takes her out to supper.

SAM: Yes, that's it. Now Julius, let's run the piece through and see how well we can do it.

JULIUS: Won't it kill de piece to run it through?

SAM: No! no; we must rehearse it before we can do it well.

JULIUS: All right, if you've got a hearse for it, *"let her rip."*

SAM: Now then, I'll go into the next room and dress myself for the piece; and in the meantime you can address the audience, to employ their attention, and take up the time. [*Exit*]

JULIUS: Well that's funny, he says I must dress you all, find out your intentions, and take up the dimes; well, here goes – [*Business going up and down stage, as though not used to addressing an audience*] I suppose he meant for me to make a speech while he was getting ready for the play. Ladies and Gentlemen: – I

am sorry to state to you that it becomes my champagneful duty to inform you that Mrs. Matilda Herring has met with a very unfortunate, and, we fear, fatal accident; she was lunching with a friend, last evening, and stepping to the door with a bottle of wine in her hand, to see her friend safely to the stairs, "her stopple" flew out very unexpectedly, and hit her in the eye. Mr. Jeams Pipes has kindly consented, however, to waddle through the part, and we trust his endeavors will meet with your disapprobation. –

Enter Sam, dressed extravagantly funny, as Camille. She has a large "Waterfall," composed of an ox bladder blown up, and painted black, after it becomes dry. She also has a wreath of vegetables on her head; as she enters, she is fanning herself with a large fan

SAM: [*Turning, sees her as she seats herself in chair right*] Camille, oh, Cammy! [*Falls on his knees*]

CAMILLE: Is that you, Army, my boy? How are you?

ARMY: Camille, my guiding star by day, and my torch-light by night! "my own Camille," I love you! – And if this life were more dear to you than it is to me – I would kill the first Dutchman I met on the Battery.

CAMILLE: Army, dear Army! How long has this fiery passion burned within your breast?

ARMY: About ten minutes.

CAMILLE: 'Tis a long time, Army; but you know "white man are very unsartin;" but rise, my boy! and swear that you'll never go back on your sweetness.

ARMY: Camille! I love the very air you breathe, the very ground you walk upon; is not that sufficient ground for mutual confidence? then leave this exciting life that you now lead, and let me be a mother to you; let me watch over and nourish your – pocket-book – and you'll find me ever by your side – when I'm broke.

CAMILLE: Army, I love you! devotedly! [*Embrace*] devoutly! [*Embrace*] madly! [*Embrace*] excrutiatingly! [*Embrace*] spasmodically love you! [*Embrace and kiss*] And in order to prove my affection for you, I have gathered for you a tender, sensitive plant; it is called the "Camellia;" take it, Army, and wear it in your button-hole, for my sake. [*Takes large cabbage from right entrance and gives it to Army*]

ARMY: [*Looking intently and thoughtfully at*

cabbage] Camille! where am de corned beef that goes with it?

CAMILLE: Alas, Army, our boarding mistress "hash" hashed it; but never mind. I feel so full of joy that I e'en would dance; wilt dance, Army?

ARMY: I wilt.

CAMILLE: Then place your "bucket on the what-not," and we wilt dance.

ARMY: Whither is the "what-not?"

CAMILLE: I know not! Give it to the cook.

Throws cabbage off, they prepare to dance. Music plays Polka, and they dance "African Polka" very extravagantly; after dancing for a short time, they stop suddenly – Camille places her hand upon her left side and speaks

CAMILLE: Army, I feel every indication of a "swine."

She falls on stage, Army bends over her, feeling pulse, etc.

ARMY: Am you better, Camille?

CAMILLE: A little. [*Breathes very heavily*] Army, go for a doctor.

ARMY: What doctor?

CAMILLE: Doctor Quack! he's a gay boy, and knows my weakness.

ARMY: A Jew; a Chatham-street Jew, 'till I return. [*Exit sorrowfully*]

CAMILLE: [*Still lying upon the stage. She first lifts her head comically, and looks around, then coughs, and raises herself up in a sitting posture, takes off wreath, looks sadly at it, then speaks; coughing occasionally*] This was to have been my wedding wreath – but, alas, like me, how faded – 'twould not even make a boiled dinner for a boarding house. [*Throws it away*] But I must get up, or I shall catch a serious dampness. [*Tries to rise, but is very weak; finally gets up, and falls heavily upon the stage, upon his behind*] Oh, if I could only gain the sophia, I think I could worry it out 'till Army comes. [*Walks very heavily over to lounge, and throws himself like a log of wood upon it. Coughs – then reaches under pillow and gets night robe, and comical night cap; puts them on while sitting upon lounge; after, business, then takes letter from bosom*] It is from the dear Duke! how he loves me. [*Kisses letter, and puts it back in bosom*] Alas, how I must have changed; but the Doctor says if I

live until Spring, I won't die this Fall; Oh, dear, I must have fallen away a hogshead. I should like to look at myself in the glass – I must get some powder for my complexion. [*Gets up, and takes chair, leaning on back for support; she pushes it before her toward the glass right, as she gets to center, she sees Army's hat on stage, which falls off as he goes out. She starts and screams very loud; then gives the hat a very vigorous kick, sending it off stage right*] Oh, Dear! I am so nervous! [*Continues pushing chair until she reaches "toilet-table," then business, as though afraid to look; finally, makes one great effort and looks in glass – Screams and falls in chair*] Oh, Camille! You that was once the pride of the ball-room, and the envy of the envied; now pining away in a sick chamber for the want of nourishment. I wonder if the Doctor has left me anything to take. [*Takes bottle from behind looking-glass and drinks*] Oh, the dear Doctor, how well he knows my wants. I wonder if I can reach my couch once more. Oh, why does Army stay so long, when he knows I dote on him. [*She reaches lounge, and falls heavily as before. Soft music – as Army enters, goes softly over to lounge – kneels upon one knee, and calls softly*] Camille! [*Louder*] Camille! [*Very loud*] Camille!

CAMILLE: [*Very loud*] Who's dar?

ARMY: 'Tis me! Army Duval.

CAMILLE: [*Jumping up*] What! Army come back to me. [*Kisses him passionately*] Army, did you bring any gin?

ARMY: She am delirious.

CAMILLE: Army, the jig is up – my mutton's cooked – I'm a gorner, Army – Army, I'm dying.

Camille pulls him by the head and uses him exceedingly rough

ARMY: Die easy, Camille – die easy.

She throws him over her head; he turns somersault, and lands over in right hand corner. Camille falls on stage and dies. Army gets up, looks affectionately at her – takes out his handkerchief and wipes his eyes

ARMY: She am dead! She am defunct! [*Goes over to lounge, leans with his face in his hands on the head of the lounge; Camille gets up sly-*

ly, goes off and gets stuffed club, goes over to him, while he is weeping, and giving him a *tremendous blow behind says:*] She am dead, am she?

The End

THE THUMPING PROCESS

A. J. LEAVITT

CHARACTERS

DOCTOR GRAPE	1ST PATIENT
BILL, *a Servant*	2ND PATIENT
JAMES, *a Servant*	

Scene. – Chamber. Table, chairs, door in flat; screen back of table. Doctor discovered reading paper.

DOCTOR: I have about ten minutes more to stop, then I am off for Europe to be gone two months. I have turned all my patients over to my friend Dr. Graf during my absence. Now all remains for me to do is to call my servants, and tell them to take good care of my house while I am gone. Here, Bill, James, come here.

Enter Bill and James

BILL: Here we are, boss.

JAMES: When you going away, Doc.?

DOCTOR: I'm going now; but don't forget what I told you, boys; take good care of the house; and remember, should any patients call send them to Dr. Graf, No. 5, New York. Bill, get me my coat and hat.

BILL: All right, boss. [*Exit Bill*]

DOCTOR: Here, James, help me off with this gown. [*James helps him take off gown. Enter Bill with coat and hat; puts coat on Doctor and hands him hat*]

DOCTOR: Well, good-bye, boys, I'm off now; remember, take good care of the house, and I'll bring you both a present when I return.

Exit Doctor. Bill and James commence dancing and singing

BILL: I have struck an idea.

JAMES: What is it?

BILL: I'm going to play Doctor. I'll put on the boss's coat, and when a patient comes in I'll hide behind the screen; you question him, find out all about what he is troubled with and how much money he's got, set him down in the chair, I'll hear everything he says; you tell him Doctor gone down to the post office and will be back in a few minutes, then I'll slip out and come in and take his money.

JAMES: All right, it's a go: I want half.

Bill puts on Doctor's gown. Knock heard at door

BILL: Here comes somebody, now I'll hide. [*Bill hides behind screen*]

JAMES: Come in. [*Enter 1st Patient very slow*]

1ST PATIENT: Good morning; is the Doctor in?

JAMES: No, the Doctor has just stepped down to the post office to get his mail; take a seat, he will be back in a few minutes.

Patient takes chair

JAMES: What seems to be the trouble with you?

PATIENT: You see, I have got a sort of rheumatic pain that starts from my ankle on my left leg, and runs up my side and catches me in the neck, and I can't sleep nights.

JAMES: Are you a married man?

PATIENT: Yes.

JAMES: How many children have you?

PATIENT: I've got seven sons.

JAMES: Are they all boys?

PATIENT: Why, of course.

JAMES: How much money have you got?

PATIENT: I haven't got a cent.

Bill, who has been looking out from behind screen, runs off

JAMES: Here comes the Doctor.

Enter Bill with letters; looks at Patient

BILL: Good morning.

PATIENT: Good morning, Doctor.

BILL: Did you call to see me for medical aid?

JAMES: Yes, Doctor, he wants you to examine him.

BILL: I will just as soon as I read these letters. [*Reads letters aloud so as to be heard by Patient*] "Dear Doctor: My wife having read your advertisement in the *Morning Bladder* about your magic cure, known as the Thumping Process, I'm happy to state, after three applications of your remedy, she died in the greatest of agony. Inclose find a postal card and toothpick. Yours truly, J. K. HARDBACK."

JAMES: Doctor, the patient is waiting for you.

BILL: Ah, yes, I will examine him at once. [*Goes over to Patient, feels his head, arms, puts his hands in Patient's pockets, etc.*] I see you have a sort of rheumatic pain that starts from your ankle on your left leg, and runs up your side and catches you in the neck, so much so that you cannot sleep nights. You are a married man, and have a family of about six or seven.

PATIENT: Wonderful, Doctor! – wonderful! You are a great man; every word you have told me is correct; and I wouldn't do without your cure for the world. I told your servant I didn't have any money; but I have, Doctor, and I will give you ten dollars for the treatment of your magic cure. I suppose it makes a difference in your treatment by being paid well?

BILL: Yes; no pay, no cure.

PATIENT: You can commence at once; here is your money. [*Hands money*]

BILL: Well, what treatment would you like to have – the Thumping Process, Blue Glass, or the Squirt?

PATIENT: Well, Doctor, I think I'll take the Thumping Process.

James goes to table, gets the two stuffed clubs, hands Bill one, and both shake them behind Patient's back

PATIENT: Doctor, will you have to apply it more than once?

BILL: No, I think once will be sufficient; but if you want to call again to-morrow, I will apply

it again. I have never known patients to come back for the second dose. Now we will proceed to administer the treatment; straighten up your back.

Patient straightens up; Bill and James both club him; he falls on the floor; they keep clubbing him till he crawls off

BILL: How did that work?

JAMES: That's immense. [*Knock heard at door*]

BILL: Here comes another. [*Bill rushes behind screen*]

JAMES: Come in. [*Enter 2nd Patient*]

PATIENT: Is the Doctor in?

JAMES: Take a chair; he will be in a few minutes. [*Patient sits down*]

JAMES: What is your complaint?

PATIENT: I have a severe pain that catches me in the pit of the back, and forms a sort of a neuralgia in my head, which causes my membrane to flitter, and I have not slept in two weeks.

JAMES: Are you a married man?

PATIENT: Yes, I've been married twice.

JAMES: That makes it more binding. Any family?

PATIENT: I have two daughters.

JAMES: Are they girls?

PATIENT: Well, they couldn't be boys. [*Bill runs off*]

JAMES: Here comes the Doctor. [*Enter Bill*]

BILL: I've just returned from the post office. James, does the gentleman wish to see me?

JAMES: Yes, he wants you to treat his case.

BILL: I'll be ready in a moment after I read this letter. [*Reads letter*] "Dear Doctor: I would have called to see you, but being confined in the large hotel on Centre Street, (*Tombs*) for the past two years, it is impossible for me to see you. So I write this letter, telling you that your magic cure is a great invention, and my wife, who has been dead for the past three years, is still using your pills. Enclosed find a brown-stone house and a paper collar. Yours respectfully, Bob Brierly." A very good letter. Now for the patient. [*Goes over to Patient and examines him same as first*] You have a severe pain that catches you in the pit of the back, here – [*Giving him a hard punch in the back which nearly knocks him over*] I trust I did not hurt you any?

PATIENT: [*Very frightened*] No, no, not much.

BILL: And forms a sort of a neuralgia in your head which causes your membrane to flitter, consequently not allowing you much time for sleep. I also see by your left ear that you have been married more than once, and that you have two children. Am I right?

PATIENT: Yes, Doctor, you are truly wonderful; you are right in every particular. How much does it cost to undergo your treatment?

BILL: Well, I charge ten dollars for the treatment and five dollars for the pills.

PATIENT: Does the treatment work on the system?

BILL: Yes, very much. [*James hands Doctor one of the clubs*]

PATIENT: Here's your money. [*Hands money*]

BILL: James, bring me the pills. [*James brings the pills, a basket of turnips, hands them to Bill*]

PATIENT: [*Looking frightened*] Do I take them inwardly?

BILL: You take two every minute for three hours, and take one every three minutes while asleep, and if the pills give out, send a truck around in the morning for another load. Now, what treatment would you like to undergo – the Thumping Process, Blue Glass, or the Squirt?

PATIENT: I think I will try the Blue Glass.

BILL: James, remove the patient to this chair. [*Sets Patient down in the chair*] Close your eyes.

James takes the blue frame, a two-foot square frame with blue paper pasted on it, and bursts it over the Patient's head; Bill squirts seltzer water at him; the Doctor and 1st Patient rush in; Bill squirts water over the Doctor; James clubs both Patients. Close in

The End

SUBLIME AND RIDICULOUS

GEORGE H. COES

CHARACTERS

TRAGEDIAN   MANAGER

JULIUS, *a comedian*

Scene. – A Wood. Enter Manager.

MANAGER: Now, I've just got my new theatre completed, and my company engaged, except one man. I want a light comedian. If I could only find some one out of an engagement, I could do well by him.

Enter Julius, hurriedly, and cross to right; Manager stops him

MANAGER: Hallo, young man, where are you going?

JULIUS: I'm going down street here to work. I got a job.

MANAGER: What kind of a job?

JULIUS: I'm an artist.

MANAGER: What kind of an artist?

JULIUS: I'm a painter.

MANAGER: Oh, you're a painter, hey? What are you going to paint?

JULIUS: I'm going to whitewash a fence.

MANAGER: I think I can give you a better job than that.

JULIUS: Can you? What is it?

MANAGER: Did you ever act?

JULIUS: Yes: I acted like a thundering fool this morning.

MANAGER: No, no; I mean, did you ever act upon the stage?

JULIUS: You just set behind four horses with me once, and I'll take you over the summit faster dan Hank Monks did Horace Greeley when he went to California.

MANAGER: No, no; I don't mean a stage-coach, I mean a stage where they act – where they represent Shakespeare, Lord Byron, and all them. great writers.

JULIUS: Yes, Shakspoke, Bay Rum – oh, yes. I know; you mean a *freatre* stage.

MANAGER: Now, I want a light comedian.

JULIUS: What, to light lamps?

MANAGER: No, I want a man to play light parts.

JULIUS: Well, I'm a pretty good shape. [*Shows himself*] How will I do? I'd make a healthy lover.

MANAGER: Your shape is all right; how's your study?

JULIUS: Oh, I'm gay on the study.

MANAGER: Now listen. I have just got my new theatre done and my company all engaged, and I'm going to open in the play of "Damon and Pythias."

JULIUS: Who'll pity us?

MANAGER: Don't you understand? "Damon and Pythias." Did you never see that play?

JULIUS: Yes; how does it go?

MANAGER: I'll tell you. Now, I want you to play the part of Lucullus.

JULIUS: Look-all-of-us? Who's he?

MANAGER: Listen; I'll explain this piece to you.

JULIUS: Go it.

MANAGER: Now, you see, Damon and Pythias are two great friends.

JULIUS: Yes; they'll lend each other nineteen dollars on a twenty-dollar gold-piece any time, won't they?

MANAGER: But Damon has committed some great offence against his state, and he is arrested, tried, and sentenced to death.

JULIUS: Poor fellow!

MANAGER: After he receives his sentence, he asks permission to visit his family, who reside some fifteen or twenty miles in the interior.

JULIUS: Yes, I know; out here in [*Local*]. I know where it is.

MANAGER: Pythias agrees to remain as hostage for Damon.

JULIUS: Oh, Pythy, he's a hostler.

MANAGER: No, no; that is, Pythias remains in Damon's stead, so if Damon doesn't get back in time, Pythias hands in his checks.

JULIUS: Why don't he put 'em all on the jack, and call the turn?

MANAGER: The court gives Damon fifteen minutes to go and come back. Damon has a horse, and you are his servant, Lucullus. You are very much attached to him. He gives you lots of money, clothes, etc.

JULIUS: He does, hey? Well, couldn't he advance me a few stamps? I could play this part much better with a little encouragement.

MANAGER: Oh, he'll give you lots of it. Now, when he arrives out at his house –

JULIUS: Yes, out in [*Local name, as before*].

MANAGER: He gives you his horse to hold; and, while he is gone into the house, you kill his horse, because you don't want your master to be killed. So you kill his horse so he can't get back to be executed.

JULIUS: But where is the horse?

MANAGER: Oh, he'll have a horse. Well, after he has seen his family, he comes out to where you are, very much excited, and says to you, "Lucullus, where's my horse?" and you say, "I slew your horse."

JULIUS: Yes, but I ain't got the horse.

MANAGER: But you will have in the play. He says, "Lucullus, where's my horse?" and you say, "I slew your horse;" and that is all you have to do. Now I will personate Damon, to show you how he will come on. You stand over there (*Right of stage*), and I'll go here. Now look out and recollect your cue.

Manager exits right, and rushes on tragically

MANAGER: Lucullus, my horse!

JULIUS: Hey?

MANAGER: Hey? Did I tell you to say hey? I told you to say, "I slew the horse."

JULIUS: Yes, but I ain't got no horse.

MANAGER: Well, can't you suppose you slew the horse?

JULIUS: Oh, you want me to suppose I slew your horse?

MANAGER: Yes.

JULIUS: Well, go it again.

Exit Manager as before

MANAGER: Now be careful this time. [*Rushes on as before*] Lucullus, where's my horse?

JULIUS: I suppose I slew your horse.

MANAGER: [*Very mad*] Can't you say, "I slew your horse," without the suppose?

JULIUS: Of course I can. What's the use of getting mad?

MANAGER: Now I'll show you once more. Now look out. [*As before*] Lucullus, my horse, my horse! Quick, I say! My horse!

JULIUS: I slew your horse without the suppose.

MANAGER: [*Very mad; both walk across stage*]

Oh, get out! You won't do at all. I can't learn you anything.

JULIUS: Give me one more chance, and if I don't do it this time, I hope to borrow a half a dollar of you.

MANAGER: Well, one more chance. Now recollect – I slew your horse.

JULIUS: What you want is, you want a straight slew.

MANAGER: Yes.

JULIUS: Well, now you go it again.

MANAGER: [*Exit as before, and enter*] Lucullus! Quick, my horse!

JULIUS: I – slew – your – horse!

MANAGER: There; that's it. [*Both shake hands*]

JULIUS: Oh, I knew I could suit you, only give me a chance. But what do I get for slewing de horse?

MANAGER: Well, if you play this well, I give you fifty cents the first year, and at the end of that time, if you'd like to stay, I'll raise you.

JULIUS: Fifty cents a year?

MANAGER: Yes.

JULIUS: And I suppose if I'm prudent and economical and saving, in the course of ten or fifteen years I'll have as much as a dollar or so.

MANAGER: Oh, you'll have lots of money throwed on to you by the audience every night.

JULIUS: Will I? [*Looks at audience*] Don't throw now, for I couldn't accept it no way, just now. [*Dodges, as if some was coming*] Don't! don't!

MANAGER: Well, what do you say? Will you take the engagement?

JULIUS: Well, boss, I don't care if I do try this job for a year or two. But where is this rooster I am to be with?

MANAGER: Rooster? He's no rooster; he is a splendid actor. He is now down stairs in the Green Room. I'll go and tell him to come up, and you can rehearse the piece right here. [*Is going*]

JULIUS: [*Catches Manager and pulls him back*] Say, what kind of a chap is this? Is he robust? What does he do to me when I say, "I slew your horse"? Does he touch me?

MANAGER: Oh, yes! He's very powerful, and gets very much excited. He comes on and grabs you this way [*Takes Julius by both coat collars*], and chucks you up in the air two or three times, throws you down on the stage, juggles you around, and breaks an arm or a leg. Why, he has been known to kill twenty or thirty men playing this piece!

JULIUS: Good-morning. [*Turns to go*]

MANAGER: Hold on! What's the matter?

JULIUS: Come to think, I don't believe I could suit him.

MANAGER: Oh, I was only joking.

JULIUS: Was you, though?

MANAGER: Yes; that's all. He's very weak.

JULIUS: Very weak? [*Braces up*]

MANAGER: Very sick.

JULIUS: Is he very sick?

MANAGER: He don't weigh more than seventy-five pounds.

JULIUS: Is that all? [*Squares off à la Sullivan*]

MANAGER: Yes.

JULIUS: He is very sick, is he? Has he had a doctor?

MANAGER: Why, yes; he's had a doctor five times a day for four weeks.

JULIUS: He must be sick.

MANAGER: Yes.

JULIUS: Show him up. [*Very brave*]

MANAGER: All right. Now recollect your cue.

JULIUS: Oh, I'm all right. I can lick any sick man that don't weigh more than seventy-five pounds. Show eleven of 'em up. [*Looks off right*]

During this time Tragedian enters from left and stands center of stage with domino. As soon as Julius sees him, he throws off domino, and both strike attitude. Then Julius retires down to right of stage, and Tragedian immediately commences "Hamlet's soliloquy"

TRAGEDIAN: Angels and ministers of grace defend us.

JULIUS: [*To audience*] He looks very healthy for a sick man.

TRAGEDIAN: Be thou a spirit of healthy or goblin damned –

JULIUS: You be damned yourself.

TRAGEDIAN: – Bring with thee airs from heaven or blasts from hell –

JULIUS: He's crazy.

TRAGEDIAN: – Be thy intents wicked, or charitable –

JULIUS: I've got nothing for you; go about your business.

TRAGEDIAN: – Thou com'st in such a questionable shape that I will speak to thee.

JULIUS: He's going to say something.

TRAGEDIAN: I'll call thee Hamlet. [*Kneels*]

JULIUS: Gimlet?

TRAGEDIAN: King!

JULIUS: He calls me King.

TRAGEDIAN: Father!

JULIUS: Go away; I ain't your fader. Nice-looking fader I'd make!

TRAGEDIAN: Royal Dane.

JULIUS: Royal dame – ha, ha, ha!

TRAGEDIAN: Oh, answer me; let me not burst in ignorance –

JULIUS: Bust, if you want to.

TRAGEDIAN: – But tell me why thy canonized bones, hearsed in death, have burst their cerements –

JULIUS: You'll get spearmint if you fool with this child.

TRAGEDIAN: – Why the sepulchre, wherein we saw thee quietly inurned, hath op'd his ponderous and marble jaws to cast thee up again.

JULIUS: Oh, what's the matter with you?

TRAGEDIAN: What may this mean? What may this mean, that thou, dead corpse, again, in complete steel, revisitest thus the glimpses of the moon, making night hideous, and we fools of nature, so horridly to shake our disposition with thoughts beyond the reaches of our soul? Say, why is this?

JULIUS: I don't know.

TRAGEDIAN: Wherefore?

JULIUS: What for?

TRAGEDIAN: What should we do?

JULIUS: Go about your business; don't bother me.

TRAGEDIAN: [*Rises, still looking on in vacancy, turns to Julius*] The fair Ophelia –

JULIUS: Fair old-feel-yer – ha, ha, ha!

TRAGEDIAN: Nymph, in thy orisons be all my sins remembered.

JULIUS: Go away; I'll mash you.

TRAGEDIAN: [*Getting excited*] I never gave you aught. [*To Julius*]

JULIUS: Who said you did?

TRAGEDIAN: Are you honest?

JULIUS: Yes, certainly I am, you bet.

TRAGEDIAN: Are you fair?

JULIUS: No, I'm a Peruvian.

TRAGEDIAN: I loved you not. [*Walks around stage*]

JULIUS: I don't care –

TRAGEDIAN: Get thee to a nunnery. [*Walks around stage*]

JULIUS: Get you to a grocery.

TRAGEDIAN: Why wouldst thou be a breeder of sinners?

JULIUS: I ain't.

TRAGEDIAN: I am myself indifferent honest; but yet I could accuse me of such things, that it were better my mother had not borne me. I am proud, revengeful, ambitious, with more offences at my beck than I have thoughts to put them in, imagination to give them shape, or time to act them in. What should such fellows as I do, crawling between heaven and earth? We are arrant knaves, all; believe none of us. Go thy ways to a nunnery – go.

JULIUS: Oh, if I could only get out of this.

TRAGEDIAN: Where's your father?

JULIUS: He's in the State Prison.

TRAGEDIAN: Let the doors be shut upon him; that he may play the fool nowhere but in his own house.

JULIUS: Oh, he's barred in – for ninety days.

TRAGEDIAN: If thou dost marry, I'll give thee this plague for thy dowry: be thou as chaste as ice –

JULIUS: I've been chased long enough.

TRAGEDIAN: – As pure as snow –

JULIUS: S-no use of getting mad.

TRAGEDIAN: Thou shalt not escape calumny. Get thee to a nunnery – go. [*Walks around stage*]

JULIUS: Get you to a bummery.

TRAGEDIAN: I've heard of your paintings, too, well enough. Heaven hath given you one face, and you make yourselves another; you jig –

JULIUS: No, sir.

TRAGEDIAN: – You amble –

JULIUS: You lie.

TRAGEDIAN: – And you lisp and nickname Heaven's creatures, and make your wantonness your ignorance. Go to! I'll no more of it – it hath made me mad. [*Crosses left*]

JULIUS: Why don't you go to the insane asylum?

TRAGEDIAN: I say, we will have no more marriages.

JULIUS: You better not let the ladies hear you.

TRAGEDIAN: Those that are married already, all but one, shall live; the rest shall keep as they are.

JULIUS: Get, you, you old bummer! Look here I'm getting mad. Now look out for me: I ain't going to stand this no longer.

TRAGEDIAN: [*Grabs Julius à la Othello*] Be sure thou prove my love a wanton. Give me the ocular proof, or, by the worth of thine eternal soul, thou hadst better been born a dog, than answer my waked wrath. [*Throws Julius* across; all this time *Julius* can say whatever he likes; it is to be worked up very melodramatic until this last speech is over. *Tragedian* retires up stage and looks right. *Julius* takes stage left, looking at *Tragedian*, much frightened. *Tragedian* advances to center of stage]

TRAGEDIAN: By the powers, the sun is rushing down the west.

JULIUS: Let it rush.

TRAGEDIAN: [*Turns to Julius*] Lucullus! Quick, my horse!

JULIUS: Hey?

TRAGEDIAN: My horse, Lucullus, my horse, I say.

JULIUS: Oh, what was dat I had to say?

TRAGEDIAN: Lucullus, my horse.

JULIUS: I – I – I – slewed your horse.

Both strike attitude

TRAGEDIAN: Merciful powers! I'm standing here –

JULIUS: So am I.

TRAGEDIAN: – To see if the powers will with their lightnings execute my prayer upon thee.

JULIUS: Execute! He's a butcher!

TRAGEDIAN: Come!!

JULIUS: Police!!

TRAGEDIAN: Come!! [*Grabs Julius*]

JULIUS: Let go of me now – police!

TRAGEDIAN: To the eternal river of the dead, the way is shorter than that to Syracuse.

JULIUS: Let go of me! Murder! murder!!

TRAGEDIAN: With one fling I'll hurl thee to Tartary, and follow, and follow after; away. [*Throws Julius to center of stage and exit. He lays there until Tragedian is off, then sets up and looks off left*]

JULIUS: I slewed your horse! [*Gets up and shakes himself; feels if any bones are broken*]

He's a sick man, hey? He's the healthiest sick man I ever see. He's stronger dan an elephant.

Enter Manager

MANAGER: Well, Julius, how did you get along with that fellow?

JULIUS: [*Carelessly*] Oh, first-rate.

MANAGER: How do you like him as an actor?

JULIUS: Oh, he can't act.

MANAGER: What? You surprise me! Why, he has the reputation of being one of the greatest actors on the stage.

JULIUS: Oh, he's a bilk; he can't act.

Manager and Julius turn aside and wink at audience

MANAGER: What did he do when he came in?

JULIUS: Oh, not much. He came in here putting on a few scollops. He tackled me a few minutes, and I flopped him.

MANAGER: What's that?

JULIUS: I flopped him.

MANAGER: What do you mean?

JULIUS: I catched him thus. [*Catches himself by the coat-collar*] And thus. [*Catches himself by the seat of his pants*] And do you see that window? [*Looking off left*]

MANAGER: Yes. [*The same time going off slowly right*]

JULIUS: I chucked him right through that window. [*Exit Manager*]

TRAGEDIAN: [*Outside, very loud*] Lucullus!!!

Julius falls upon stage, and Tragedian comes on; both face each other, then back off to first entrance

TRAGEDIAN: Remember me! [*Exit*]

JULIUS: I'll never forget you. [*Exit*]

Curtain

ACROSS THE CONTINENT

OR

SCENES FROM NEW YORK LIFE AND THE PACIFIC RAILROAD

James J. McCloskey

REPEATEDLY American plays were brought to the stage because of the inclinations and peculiar talents of a particular actor, and frequently theatrical successes depended more on player than on playwright. With *Across the Continent*, it becomes literally impossible to determine how much of J. J. McCloskey's original version is retained in the text available at present and how much should be attributed to the actor-playwright Oliver Doud Byron. Moreover, the text printed here is not even Byron's original. Some anonymous stage manager or actor has revised Byron's revision. For example, the third act contains a reference to the panic of 1873. Byron first performed the play in 1870. Pirating and reworking scripts was common practice in the nineteenth century. Plays were not normally copied down for publication but rather for use by another troupe of actors. With such a procedure, each successive version departed somewhat further from the original.

J. J. McCloskey had composed the first draft, called *New York in 1837, or The Overland Route*, sometime in the sixties. After an unsuccessful trial performance in New York, he lost faith in the play, saw no prospects for another production, or perhaps was simply in need of funds. Whatever the reason, he sold the play to Byron, with no restrictions or reservations. McCloskey must have regretted this action as he observed Byron's continuing success with the play through the remainder of the century.

In 1903 a reporter described McCloskey as the "oldest living playwright, actor, and manager in the United States." He was born in Montreal on August 10, 1825, came to New York in 1841, followed the gold hunters to California in 1849, and there began his career as an actor and manager. For the next thirty years he performed with all the leading actors, Junius Brutus Booth, Edwin Forrest, Edwin Booth, and John McCullough; managed the Marysville (California) theatre and the Park Theatre in Brooklyn; and conducted a theatrical troupe on a tour of Australia. During the last thirty-four years of his life, he was more steadily employed by the City of New York, as clerk in the City Court. He died on July 28, 1913.

McCloskey never lost his interest in the stage; he was a regular, if often disappointed, patron of the New York theatre. When he attended the opening of the New Theatre on November 6, 1909 – that ill-starred American attempt to found an "art theatre" – he found that Sothern and Marlowe's *Antony and Cleopatra* could not be ranked with the old Broadway Theatre production of the play in which he had appeared. According to McCloskey, E. H. Sothern "should have been born seventy years ago, when the conditions were such that he might have learned how to act." In the same newspaper interview (New York *Herald*, November 21, 1909), he summed up his reactions as follows:

I went home feeling as though I'd seen a proper little performance given in a Harlem flat where the performers were afraid they'd wake the people's babies in the flat down stairs, and as I rode back to Brooklyn I couldn't help but think how Ed Eddy would have made the rafters hum. . . . You ought to have seen our Nile scene with Cleopatra's barge moving down the river, the slaves fanning her and the pyramids rearing their ghostly bulk along the shore. There was realism for you! There was suggestion, romance, poetry, everything that people expect for their money and don't get any more.

To strengthen his point he added some reflections on the playing of Hamlet:

The trouble with the most earnest young men who attempt Hamlet is that they make too many motions. They strain at gnats instead of playing Hamlet as though he were a human being. The part of Hamlet amounts to nothing more nor less than a command of all the trick work known to the stage. The one man I know who could play it to perfection was a little fellow named Eddie Raynor, an Englishman, who died several years ago without ever becoming what they call "great" in the business to-day. He was past master of every trick and quirk and mannerism you ever heard of, and he had borrowed them all from the different big actors of the time. He just went through the part, turning off one effective trick after another, and everybody took it for subtlety, while Eddie laughed in his sleeve. He knew what he was about. He saw through it that Shakespeare wrote the play because the people of Shakespeare's time were getting tired of straight-away stuff and wanted a little mystery stuff, and he gave it to them.

Such comments would seem to support a claim that a considerable share of the theatrical trickery of *Across the Continent* was contributed by McCloskey.

However much reworking Byron may have done, he must have fancied what he found in McCloskey's original and perceived opportunities for his peculiar acting talents. After acquiring the play, "a thin package of a few pages," as he described it, Byron tried a few preliminary performances in Toronto, Montreal, and Quebec during the spring of 1870. Then, during his summer at liberty, he prepared the revision which he opened at the Trimble Opera House in Albany on September 12, 1870. The play caught the fancy of the public, and for the next thirty seasons Byron devoted himself almost exclusively to performing *Across the Continent*.

Before this turning point in his career, Oliver Doud Byron had acted many parts with various companies. (Earlier he had been known as Oliver B. Doud.) He was born in Frederick, Maryland, in 1843; made his first stage appearance at the Holliday Street Theatre in Baltimore in 1856, in Joseph Jefferson's production of *Nicholas Nickleby;* and in 1859 became associated with John Wilkes Booth and the Richmond (Virginia) Theatre stock company. In 1863 he was with Lucille Western's company at Ford's Theatre in Washington and then with the theatres in Pittsburgh and New Orleans and with Wallack's stock company in New York. Among his notable stage achievements were playing Iago to Edwin Booth's Othello and Othello to Booth's Iago, appearing with Adah Isaacs Menken, and creating the part of Richard Harre in *East Lynne*. Just before he began the reworking of *Across the Continent*, he had played *Metamora* at the Bowery Theatre in New York on May 23, 1870.

Byron's acting and his notions about acting were similar to those of McCloskey. For example, Byron thought that playing melodrama with "a soft pedal is as absurd as the music of Wagner without clamor of cymbals and blare of brasses." In an article called "What Makes an Actor" in the *Green Book Album* for December, 1909, he insisted that "the secret of good acting is knowing the language, knowing the way you say a certain word or collection of words, and knowing how to speak the words individually and collectively so that they will impart to the audience the exact meaning that the playwright had in mind when he penned them."

McCloskey and Byron were both old-school actors who cherished the theatrical art, "tricks of the stage," if you will, and who thought the first duty of an actor was to make himself clearly and forcibly understood. In fact, such a presentational stage piece as *Across the Continent* could only have been devised by such theatrically minded playwrights. Some of the critics did not fully appreciate Byron's direct style. Of his playing of Joe Ferris in *Across the Continent*, the *Spirit of the Times* wrote on July 22, 1871:

. . . Byron, a gentleman who possesses many natural advantages for a player, such as a good voice, a not ungraceful figure, and considerable ease of deportment, but who, for some reason best known to himself, has a habit of playing with rather than for his audience, of addressing many of his speeches to them, instead of to the actors upon the stage.

When Byron opened with the play in Albany, he is reported to have had fifty cents in his pocket. When he left to take the play to New York, he had accumulated six hundred dollars. The first metropolitan showing was at Mrs. Conway's Park Theatre in Brooklyn on November 28, 1870. The Brooklyn audience did not take to the play immediately, but when it was repeated at Wood's Museum, beginning on March 13, 1871, it ran for six weeks; and when it was brought to Niblo's on July 17 it ran continuously until August 11, in spite of an uncomfortably hot summer. During this same summer it had already reached England. When it opened at the Royal Alfred Theatre (the Marylebone) on July 8, it was billed as McCloskey's "powerful, sensational play" with "the celebrated child actress, little Katie Logan, in the part of Dolores." Apparently the English were fascinated with "the great telegraphic feats" in this "Great American Drama." It had additional showings in 1875, 1876, and 1882. At least in 1876, it must have been regarded as something of an eccentricity. It was on the same program with a performance of the first three acts of *Hamlet* in which three performers, one of them an actress, alternated in the title role.

For the rest of his career, Byron's name was perpetually identified with *Across the Continent*, which he played, as he said, "first to the kid-gloved audiences, then to the woolen mittened." For the next twenty years hardly a New York season was without several performances, and on the road it was performed by Byron for some thirty seasons. Ada Rehan, one of America's greatest actresses and Byron's sister-in-law, made her first stage appearance in *Across the Continent*. William Gillette's famous telegraph scene in *Secret Service* (1895) was probably derived from the similar scene in the Byron-McCloskey play. Gillette had played in *Across the Continent* in New Orleans in 1875. Arthur Byron, who later became leading man with Maude Adams and Ethel Barrymore, made his stage debut in his father's play in Brooklyn in February, 1883. The theatrical life of *Across the Continent* was finally terminated when Oliver Doud Byron was unwilling to submit to the intolerable demands of the Theatrical Syndicate. And when he realized that battle against the syndicate was futile, he gave up and retired from the stage in 1912. He died on October 22, 1920.

Although the critics were regularly disturbed by the hodge-podge nature of the *Across the Continent* show, audiences did not share their distress. On March 1, 1873, the *Spirit of the Times* reviewer confessed that though he was annoyed with the "improbabilities" of the piece, "these blemishes do not indeed, seem to be noticed by the auditors. Wood's Museum has been crowded nightly." The New York *Mirror* reported on September 17, 1881:

Haverly's 14th Street Theatre well patronized this week by admirers of the untamed drama, where Oliver Doud Byron and his Indians have been reveling in clouds of gun powder, smoke, indignant virtue, heroism, and sugar plums. It seems to be a potent plaster in drawing the gallery gamins, and creating inordinate enthusiasm in the breasts of the habitues of that unsentimental locality . . . gives O. D. Byron scope to display a symmetrical form in neat-fitting business and dress suits, and later in the typical garment of the sturdy mountaineer. It is absolutely too, too noble. Evident object to make money, which it probably does.

As with so many theatrical successes, *Across the Continent* had its share of parasitical burlesques and perversions, this in spite of the burlesque-like spirit of the original. A burlesque version was performed by Billy Rice and his minstrel group at Hooley's Opera House the week of December 12, 1870. On October 17, 1870, the Jave Street Reformed Church in Greenpoint displayed some transparent photographs under the title "Across the Continent," and on November 7, 1871, the Flushing Town Hall had a showing of Professor S. J. Sedgwick's "Views – Across the Continent."

Two items of history help to explain the success of *Across the Continent:* the telegraph was still a new and mysterious instrument – the first transcontinental message had been sent from San Francisco by Chief Justice Field of California to President Lincoln on October 24, 1861 – and the Union Pacific lines had been opened on May 10, 1869. With this background, of which Byron and his audience were fully aware, the immense popularity of the play is easily explained. As a theatre piece and as a timely, gay, and topical documentary, it "had everything": minstrel-like "gags," domestic turmoil, "high life" in New York, western scenes, an Indian raid thwarted by the propitious melodramatic arrival of the troops, life at the Forty-seventh Station of the Union Pacific Railroad, and the exciting tapping out of the telegraph message for help. All of these, thrown together and invested with the theatrical imaginations of Byron and McCloskey, provided the last quarter of the nineteenth century with one of its most thrilling and amusing spectacles.

ACROSS THE CONTINENT

OR

SCENES FROM NEW YORK LIFE AND
THE PACIFIC RAILROAD

JAMES J. MCCLOSKEY

CHARACTERS

JOHN ADDERLY, *who keeps a saloon at Five Points*

GEORGE CONSTANCE, *who patronizes the saloon*

THOS. GOODWIN, SR., *merchant prince*

THOS. GOODWIN, JR., *son of the merchant by adoption*

LOUISE, *Goodwin's adopted daughter*

AGNES CONSTANCE, *a broken-hearted wife*

DENNIS O'DWYER, *a good-natured Irishman*

MADALIA O'DWYER, *his wife, not so good natured*

LORENZO MCGONIGLE, *an Irish-Dutch watchman*

JAMES WALSH, *guest of Adderly*

MASTER JACK, *no lines*

JOE FERRIS, *called "The Ferret"*

JOHNNIE O'DWYER, *a chip off the old block*

GIOVANNI, *a son of Italy*

PABLO, *Giovanni's brother*

HERR GLIMP, *called "Dutchy the Dutchman"*

"BILLY" *keeper of the Underworld Parlor*

THE DUDE, *and nothing else*

DOLORES, *a street urchin*

CAESAR AUGUSTUS, *called "Coon" because he is one*

"VERY TART," *a Chinaman*

AUNTY SUSANNAH GOODWIN

"CHIEF BLACK CLOUD," *heap big Indian*

MEN, WOMEN, INDIANS, SOLDIERS

SYNOPSIS OF SCENES

ACT I. *A street in full stage, with a house on either side. Interior of these houses with first and second floor may be seen by audience. At the back in the house, L., a window looks out on street. A door at back leads to the rear room. In the house on the R. there is a kit of shoemaker's tools, upstairs. There is also other plain furniture. Downstairs in this house, are the rooms of the Constances. There is a bundle of straw in one corner, and a box with lighted candle in another. In the house on the right, only the second story is visible to the audience, and a pair of stairs, outside, lead to a door up on landing.*

Inside of this house – upstairs – there are tables, chairs and glasses with liquor, etc., etc.

ACT II *is twenty years later, first act being practically a prologue. There is a street, in about one and a half.*

SCENE 2 *is the interior of a barroom, with doors right and left, tables and chair and the usual bar furnishings.*

ACT III *is a parlor in Goodwin's home. There are doors right and left leading to outside and other parts of the house. There is a curtained arch in the center. A mantle and fireplace up against the right wall, with a chair near the mantel. Across the corner of the upper left there* is a sofa. Over on the right, down stage, is a table and two chairs, and on the left near lower corner, a stand. Other suitable furniture may be added.

ACT IV *represents the exterior of the U.P. Railway station, with all the trunks, boxes, trucks and such other things that are found at this period. The back drop is a wood or rocky pass, and there are trees, rocks, etc., etc., to give atmosphere of the surroundings. Near the station, but down stage, on the right, there is a box with a cover large enough to hold a man lying down. Railroad rails are in evidence, running across stage and telegraph wires run from left to right, down stage.*

ACT I

Scene: At rise, John Adderly, discovered upstairs in house on R., with two other men, Adderly sitting opposite the door. In the house upstairs on the left is O'Dwyer, and downstairs in this house George Constance is discovered asleep on the floor. Agnes is sitting on box in center of room. Children are near her.

GEORGE: [*Half rising*] Agnes, Agnes, where are you?

AGNES: Here, George, here. How do you feel today?

GEORGE: Oh, hellish. My throat is parched and burning, and my blood courses through my veins like molten lead. See – see – look there – [*Points to corner*]

AGNES: I can see nothing, George.

GEORGE: Can you not see them writhe and twist, and dart out their tongues like streaks of flame? Oh, God!

AGNES: No, no, George – it is only the imagination of your heated brain. Try and calm yourself.

GEORGE: Have you any money in the house?

AGNES: Not a penny.

GEORGE: What has become of the money I got for shovelling the snow on Chatham Street?

AGNES: Gone – all gone. Spent by yourself at Adderly's for liquor.

GEORGE: Is there nothing in the house?

AGNES: Nothing. And the children and I are starving.

GEORGE: Go and get a pint of Adderly's best – that is the stuff to invigorate you. You won't want anything to eat then.

AGNES: Oh George, how can you speak so.

GEORGE: [*Desperately*] Get a pint of Adderly's best and tell him to chalk it up behind the door. [*Falls back on floor*]

AGNES: Oh, must I sit here and see my children die for want of bread? No, I will make one more effort to get them food, though it be a fruitless one. [*Rises*] I will go, if I have the strength.

Takes off shawl and puts it on children. Exit to stairs and starts up

ADDERLY: Well, boys, as this is my birthday we are celebrating, as well as the event of my leaving this place, I will give you a toast. Here is to my little son sleeping yonder, John Adderly, Jr. [*Drinks*] His father has known nothing but prosperity for the last twenty years, and now I leave this place a rich man – worth at least $20,000.

WALSH: Your success only verifies the old adage.

ADDERLY: What is that?

WALSH: That the devil always takes care of his own. [*All laugh*]

ADDERLY: But do you know, one of your street missionaries told me the other day that he wouldn't accept the sum twice told, with all the curses clinging to it. But I wouldn't give the old fellow a chance.

WALSH: No, I should say not. [*Agnes raps*] What's that?

ADDERLY: Some leather-headed policeman, I dare say, to ask us to keep quiet. Who's there? [*Loudly*]

AGNES: 'Tis I.

WALSH: Oh, it's some poor devil looking for their share of the liquor, of course.

Throws open the door. Agnes steps just inside the door

ADDERLY: Surely I should know that face.

AGNES: If you have a conscience, you should – John Adderly.

ADDERLY: You're George's wife, ain't you?

AGNES: Today I am. Tomorrow the grave may claim me for its own.

ADDERLY: Well, we want none of your preaching here. What do you want?

AGNES: Food for my starving little ones and myself.

Stretches out arms in supplicating manner

ADDERLY: And for your drunken husband, too, I suppose?

AGNES: [*Staggers back*] Oh, no – [*Fiercely*] Who made him so? YOU, John Adderly, and when I begged you on bended knees to sell him no more liquor, you laughed at me and drove me from your door. You have taken the money week after week that should have gone to clothe his children, and when there was nothing else, you accepted even the poor covering from our bed to pay for liquor. And now when I ask for food to keep our little ones from starving, you taunt me with your drunken laughter.

ADDERLY: Begone, woman! I haven't time to listen to you.

AGNES: I go, but mark you, John Adderly, the day will come when the accuser and the accused stand together before that dreadful bar. What, then, will be your answer, when – like another CAIN, you are asked, "What hast thou done with thy brother?"

ADDERLY: Begone, I say – before I brain you. [*Grabs a bottle*]

WALSH: [*Interposes, and Agnes leans against the door which is left open. She stands just inside and against it*] Here, Susie or Jennie, or whatever your name might be, take this and drink it – it will do you good. [*Pours out drink. Agnes shakes her head*] Oh, very well, then – take it home to the old man. It's the last drop of liquor you'll ever get in this house, for Adderly leaves us tomorrow forever. Come – give us a toast.

AGNES: I will – from a broken heart, perhaps a dying one. May the wealth you have acquired by such unhallowed means melt from your grasp, as I now pour out this poison. [*Pours liquor on floor*] May the shrieks of your victims ring in your ears till your dying day. May that boy – [*Pointing to where baby is supposed to lie*] whom you call your son, live to turn you from his door. And may YOU – in your dying moments, CURSE him as I now CURSE you!

Adderly strikes her – swears at her. Walsh stops him from striking her the second time. Agnes starts out of door and gets downstairs with difficulty

AGNES: [*As she comes down*] May God forgive him for that blood! Oh, my children!

Falls at foot of stairs. Denny O'Dwyer entered room above while she was talking to Adderly, and works at bench

DENNY: [*When she falls*] What's that? [*Has strong Irish accent*]

MADALIA: You want to know too much.

DENNY: I do, I do, I do. They are carousing over at Adderly's tonight. Ah, Madalia, it's a good thing for many a poor soul that Adderly is going to leave the place – for it's many a one he's put under the sod. What a blessed thing it was that Lazarus Gilhooley got me to jine Father Abbott's Society.

MADALIA: What's that?

DENNY: Don't ye know what that is? That's the Father Abbott's Timperance Aid and Relief Society – and I've known nothin' but luck since I jined it. Look at that man downstairs. There's man fer ye, who – ho, ho, ho – had an eddication like Socrates, the philosopher.

MADALIA: Who's Socrates?

DENNY: Don't ye know who Socrates was, ye ignoramus? He was a famous politician who used to play polo and lawn tennis along with Van Pell and the rest of the gang. Why, the last loaf of bread I took down to her saved his poor wife and babies from downright starvation. Have you any more bread in the house, my darling?

MADALIA: Yes, but I've only got enough for the children's breakfast, and I don't know where we will get any more.

DENNY: [*Takes bread from table*] There was never a door shut up but what there was another one open.

MADALIA: Would ye be after takin' the bread out of your own children's mouth?

DENNY: Go to sleep, my cuckoo. Your dreams will be all the swater fer partin' wid' half a loaf.

MADALIA: I wouldn't think you could sleep at all for robbin' yer own flesh and blood.

DENNY: That'll do now. I'll give ye a slap in the jaw.

MADALIA: [*Jumps up and Denny sits down on the bench*] Ye'd better not, or I'll put such a head on you that yer mother wouldn't know ye.

DENNY: [*Laughing*] Look at the old woman – Ho, ho, ho – ho – look at her. [*Jumps up with the bread in his hand*] Sit down. [*She sits*] Ye's gettin' altogether too acrimonious. [*Starts out*] You will lose me before long, and when you lose me you will lose a soft snap. [*Exit*]

MADALIA: Faith, and he takes better care fer them brats downstairs than he does fer his own.

Takes drink out of bottle in her pocket

DENNY: [*Enters room by back door*] O-oo, but it is cold out! Ah, there's the poor father layin' stiff-drunk on the floor, and the poor wife – Heaven knows where she is! [*Picks up candlestick bottle*] Oh, my – Little Tootsy Wootsies! They are twins – there is a pair of thim. They look so much apart, ye can't tell thim alike. Here me little darlin's – here is some nice bread I brought down to ye. [*Throws it down*] I've got five mouths of me own to feed, but I'd stay up and work all night to keep your mouths agoin', me little darlin's.

GEORGE: [*Starting up*] Who's there?

DENNY: Why, me dear man, ye nearly gave me palpitation of the heart.

GEORGE: Give me brandy – anything to quench this awful thirst.

DENNY: If ye are dry, go outside and get a schooner of snow. There is some bread. I brought it fer yer wife and children's sake.

GEORGE: Oh – curse your bread!

DENNY: Oh, me dear man – may the Lord forgive ye fer sayin' that!

GEORGE: Give me brandy – brandy or I will die.

Catches hold of Denny. Denny throws him off and he falls back into corner

DENNY: Die, thin. Ye'll get no brandy out of me.

GEORGE: [*Starts up again*] See-see!

DENNY: Where?

GEORGE: In the bottle. There's snakes in it.

Falls back. Denny sets bottle down hastily and exits. Goes upstairs

DENNY: That man down there has got the snakes.

GOODWIN: [*Comes from L.U.E. Is full, and singing "Rolling home in the Morning, Boys." Runs against stairway*] Ah – beg your pardon. [*Backs up against door of Room 2*] I beg your pardon, sir. I wonder where I am. [*Looks around*] Why, it's the Points. Come, come, old fellow, you ought to be ashamed of yourself. [*Keeps well to opposite side of stage from where Agnes lies*] If my friend Major North could see me now, what

would he say, I wonder? But this settles it. This is the last spree for me. To be sure, this is only a genteel drunk – a champagne drunk, but it's a drunk nevertheless. Well, they say that evil often results in good. And what good will come out of this? Hello, what's that? Some drunken policeman snoring at his post. Will they ever have a well-regulated police force, I wonder? Like all other great cities. By George, if they did, I wouldn't be here. The mayor says that drunkenness has become so prevalent of late that it must be stopped. Hmm – I'm afraid he'll never stop it by fining me. Let me see – how are the finances? [*Fishes out ten cents*] Ten cents – well, never mind – there's plenty more where that came from. Ah – that sound again – sounded like a moan, and a woman's voice, too.

AGNES: Oh, sir – [*Coming to*] If you would be a man – and help me.

GOODWIN: Here is one that answers to that name. [*Raises her up*] Who are you, my good woman? And why are you lying here on the ground such a fearful night as this?

AGNES: I am a wretch – cold – chilled and dying.

GOODWIN: [*Takes off overcoat – puts it around her*] Cold and chilled? There, there – now you're all right. The champagne may have got into my head, but it shall never drive humanity out of my heart. But come, my dear woman, you must not lie here. Have you a home?

AGNES: I had one once, but that time is past. Oh, my children! I feel that the hand of death is on me. [*Sinks back on ground*]

GOODWIN: Why good gracious! The poor woman will die here on the ground if she isn't removed to a warm place. [*Yells*] Watch – Watch – Watch – Watch – [*Exit R.I.E., still yelling*]

DENNY: [*Jumps up and tries to get on his coat – Madalia helps him*] What's that? This is the greatest place fer picnics I ever saw. [*Can't get coat on; smashes at Madalia; sits down again. Watchman enters R.I., having Goodwin by the collar*]

GOODWIN: Let go – let go, I tell you. [*Jerks loose*] You've got the wrong pig by the ear. I was merely calling for aid. I wish to get the poor woman, who is actually dying here on the ground, to a comfortable place.

McGONIGLE: [*Broken German*] Let me take a look at her. [*Looks*] That's a strange face around here. I think she has been drinking a little too much whiskey.

GOODWIN: No, no – I could stake my life to her honesty. There is something about her that is superior to the rest of the denizens in the neighborhood. Come, lend me a hand and we will get her to a comfortable place. We will take her in here. [*Points to Room 2*]

McGONIGLE: I'll help you. [*They take her into Room 2. Agnes sits on box in middle of room*] Oh, say, mister, look at the two little kids in the corner. [*Laughs – sees George*] Hello – here's the old man drunk on the floor. I'll just lock him up. [*Proceeds to do so*]

GEORGE: You have come to drag me to the scaffold, have you? [*They struggle*] Well, you will find in me the strength and fury of a demon. [*Breaks away. Walsh leaves Room 3 and comes downstairs. George exits near door in Room 2, and McGonigle exits side door onto stage. Catches Walsh and hustles him off R.I.E. Denny opens window of Room 1 and fires old shoes at them. As he exits R.I.E. Walsh runs across stage R.U.E. to L.U.E., McGonigle after him. McGonigle does not catch him and comes back L.U.E. toward R.I.E. Denny pelts him again with old shoes. As he gets close to R.I.E., dances up and down on one foot, looking at Denny, who closes window and laughs, but opens it again quickly*]

DENNY: Go on, ye Jumpin' Jack, ye!

Motioning up and down to indicate the Dutchman's hopping

McGONIGLE: [*Walking toward him*] Here, here, here, here.

DENNY: Wah-ay, wah-ah, wah-ah –

McGONIGLE: Say, I got my eye on you.

DENNY: Well, thin, take it off again.

McGONIGLE: I'm lookin' right at you.

DENNY: Ye must be cross-eyed, ye ould Dutchman, ye. Lookin' over there – [*Points to rear*]

McGONIGLE: Say, look here, you Irish flannel-mouth mick.

DENNY: [*Turning around*] Madalia, is there any flannel in my mouth? [*Madalia shakes her head*] Say, you Pete Wienerworst –

McGONIGLE: What's that, you Irish potato?

DENNY: Oh, potato, potato – [*Gets another shoe*]

McGONIGLE: If I come up there, I'll break your jaw.

DENNY: Well, if I come down there I'll put a lump on yer face the size of a freight car.

McGonigle works to the corner of the house, partially out of range

McGONIGLE: Come down here.

DENNY: Come up here.

Fires shoe at him – then catches broom and fires that. Walsh enters L.U. Crosses to R.I.E. McGonigle picks up broom, drops his club, strikes at Walsh, who dodges and runs. McGonigle falls – gets up and chases Walsh off R.I.E. After Denny throws the broom, he gets excited and tries to throw the bench – then catches Madalia by the neck and seat and tries to throw her. She hits him bang in the eye

MADALIA: I'll teach you manners, and not to take liberties with me!

DENNY: Ow, ow – Madalia – see if ye can find me eye – and where. [*McGonigle enters R. 1. Denny takes his sign down and throws it at him. McGonigle picks it up and marches off R.1., and Denny closes window*] Did ye see the six of thim pile on me at once, Madalia? But I'm sorry ye overheard the conversation, for ye're a lady.

MADALIA: I am.

DENNY: Ye are. And I trate ye like a lady.

MADALIA: You do.

DENNY: I do –

MADALIA: NOT.

DENNY: And I am a gintleman. Look at me Napoleon moustache.

MADALIA: A gintleman indeed! I had four brothers and ye couldn't hould a candle to any of them.

DENNY: You did. And thim same byes could drink more whiskey in one day than a ward politician could drink in a month. You're gettin' entirely too superfluous, and ye're not stylish enough fer me, anyway.

MADALIA: Well, I won't be after takin' a back seat fer your sister Johanna, and she gets blind drunk, too.

DENNY: Shut up. Don't you say a word about my sister. She's a lady and she's married to a decent respectable man, too. A better man than your husband ever dared to be. [*Madalia laughs. He sits on bench – jumps up*] Oh-oo – Madalia, did you put that awl in the basement of me pants? [*Shakes her head and laughs*] It's very funny, ain't it? Is there any wood in the house?

MADALIA: [*Excitedly*] There is only wood enough in the house to make a fire for breakfast in the morning. [*Denny takes bundle of kindling from table*] You'll be wantin' me to chop some more in the morning.

DENNY: You'll not. Who chops the wood, I'd like to know? You nivver chopped a stick of wood since I had you. I'm goin' to take this down and build a fire for them sweet little babies.

MADALIA: You take everything and give it away. Faith, you'll be takin' me next.

DENNY: Who'd take you, I wonder?

MADALIA: You took me once. [*Whimpering*]

DENNY: Faith, I did. I took ye fer better or worse.

MADALIA: For better or for worse. [*Squalls*]

DENNY: [*Mocks her*] And before I had you very long, I found you were a great deal worse than I took you for. And what's more, ye can't go in the same society that I can. My language is too diminutive for your copious denunciation. [*Exit*]

ADDERLY: [*Excuses himself and comes downstairs, saying*] Confound the woman! I didn't mean to hurt her, but she had no right giving me her chin. I don't see anything of her about here. I guess she has gone home to her own house – at least I hope so. [*Looks into Room 2*] Confound the women, anyway! They are more trouble than they are worth.

Walks toward R.1.E. Goodwin enters R.1.E. – runs against him

GOODWIN: I can't find a physician anywhere. Oh, beg your pardon, sir – can you tell me where I can find a doctor about here?

ADDERLY: In bed, where you ought to be.

GOODWIN: Or in jail, where YOU ought to be.

ADDERLY: What's that? [*As if to strike*]

GOODWIN: I said this snow might turn into hail. [*Denny enters Room 2 – rear door. Goodwin enters just after. Adderly exit R.1.E., and afterward walks across from R.U.E. to L.U.E. Goodwin speaks to Denny, who has his back to him, and whose coat is split up the back*] What's that up your back?

DENNY: I've got me back-bone up me back – what do ye suppose?

GOODWIN: No, I mean this. [*Points to wood*]

DENNY: That's some wood I brought down to make a fire. [*Suddenly*] Who the devil are you?

GOODWIN: I'm here on a mission of charity.

DENNY: Well, this is a queer time of night for a commissioner to be snoopin' around –

GOODWIN: You misunderstood me, my friend.

DENNY: [*Grabs him*] That'll do, now. Shut up, or I'll make ye. I'm not your friend.

GOODWIN: You are mistaken, sir. Chance brought me to this place.

DENNY: Well, if I'd been here I'd a throwed you and chance both out.

GOODWIN: And a lucky chance it was, too, for I found the poor woman perishing in the street. She spoke of her children, and I think this is where she resides.

DENNY: I don't know where she resides, but this is the house she lives in.

GOODWIN: You know her, then?

DENNY: Faith, I do – and a good woman she is, too. She's too good for these parts. [*Picks up candle*]

GOODWIN: O-oooh-oo – [*Candle comes in contact with his nose*]

DENNY: What's the matter with you – have you got the hydrophobia? I'll light the fire. [*He does so*]

GOODWIN: But see – she revives. [*Kneels down and supports her*]

AGNES: Where am I?

GOODWIN: At home with friends.

AGNES: Have I then passed the portals of death, and sharing with the departed their perfect rest?

GOODWIN: No, no – my good woman – I trust it may be many years yet ere you do that.

AGNES: You are a stranger – I don't know you.

DENNY: [*Grabs him and hustles him to the door*] Get out – get out – What the devil are you doing in here, when nobody knows you? [*Shakes him*] She don't know you – she knows me. If she knew you like she knows me, you'd be all right, don't you see. See, now, how well she knows me – [*Stands before her*] You know me, ma'am – now don't you – now – see –

AGNES: [*Looks up*] I don't know you – who are you?

Goodwin laughs

DENNY: Why don't you laugh? You needn't nevver know me, ma'am, but I'll tell you who I am. Me name is Denny O'Dwyer. I live on the floor beyant. Patent-leather boot and shoemaker. Half-soling and heeling done at short notice, and invisible patches put on by Madalia O'Dwyer.

AGNES: Oh, I do not deserve such kind words of comfort from you, while he whom I might have expected them from lies there. But for your kindness, myself and my children would have been dead ere this.

DENNY: Oh, don't talk so before the commissioner. Don't you believe her, Mr. Commissioner?

AGNES: 'Tis only too true, and while we have eaten the bread of charity, he who should have provided for us has come home night after night, helplessly intoxicated. Look around you – look at the place we live in – Look at it – Look at it.

Buries her face in her hands – they stare around the room and then at each other

DENNY: Well, what are ye lookin' at me for? I'm no curiosity. Why don't you look around that way?

Sits on box in corner – back to audience. Puts on his hat, which has a large hole in the top, and shows his bald head through it

GOODWIN: Here, my good woman, take this ring – I have no money with me – and try and get some good brandy.

AGNES: No, no – it has been our bane – not mine, but my husband's. What has reduced me to the abject wretch you see before you? What has changed my husband from the upright, honorable man he once was, to the drunken sot you see him? What has brought our children to the very verge of starvation? Why – Drink – Drink!

GOODWIN: [*Who has knelt beside her*] This has been a bitter lesson for me, and I here swear that not another drop of liquor shall ever pass these lips.

DENNY: That's right. [*Shakes hands*] Come out wid me and we'll join the Knights of Labor.

AGNES: That man Adderly is the cause of all my misery, curse him!

DENNY: Ah, me good woman, ye have no time for cursing now. Ye'd better be prayin'. [*Puts on Goodwin's hat*] I'll go down and get Levy Cassiday the hostler.

Exits onto stage. Picks up policeman's club and trots off R.I.E. The watchman spies him from L.U.E. and gives chase. Exit R.I.E.

AGNES: Father in Heaven, accept my suffering here as atonement for him who needs Thy mercy. Be Thou a Father to his little ones, and should temptation assail them, Oh, deliver them from it. Oh, my children, let me kiss you once more before I die. [*Kisses them. To Goodwin*] Stranger, to your care I commit them. Do not let them bemoan my fate. Take them away from this place. Do not let them breathe its fetid atmosphere – for to them it is the morning of life.

GOODWIN: And for you –

AGNES: The evening of death. [*Sinks back*]

Fire – Fire – Fire – Woman in nightdress runs from R.U.E. Bright light back of houses. Firemen C. Denny rushes from R.I. and motions for Madalia to throw him something. Not knowing what else to do, she throws a pillow at him

ACT II. Scene 1

Twenty years after. Street scene between 1st and 2nd entrance. At rise: Enter Johnnie O'-Dwyer L.I.E., with advertising boards, hung one in front and one behind him. This can be utilized for a genuine ad. John Adderly enters after him.

ADDERLY: Come, Jack, you had better accept my proposition. Then you can dress like a gentleman and no longer be obliged to carry those signboards of degradation.

JOHN: My name isn't Jack – my name is Johnnie. J-o-h-n-n-i-e.

ADDERLY: Well, then, Johnnie, what do you say?

JOHN: Look here, John Adderly, I don't want nothin' to do with you. Everybody that has had anything to do with you has gone to the bad. There was poor Bill McLaughlin – what did you do with him? And then Joe Ferris, one of the best-hearted boys that ever lived – Didn't you send him up the Hudson for three years? Why, I'd rather wear these signboards of degradation, as you call them, than be the scoundrel we all know you to be. [*Adderly starts as if to strike*] Ah – just try that and I'll keep the flies off from you. [*Adderly turns his back*] All I want is my little old six square meals a day, nine schooners of beer, a bottle of pickles and a plate of ice cream. And, say, young fellow, if you ever stop me on the street again, I'll break your jaw. [*Exit R.1.E.*]

ADDERLY: So he doesn't think it worth while to accept my Chatham Bar? If he had, I could have got young Goodwin in there, and got him to sign his father's name to more checks. I fear this coal speculation of mine will fail, and unless I can induce old Goodwin's daughter to marry me, I shall have to leave this part of the country, and that soon, too.

Exit R.1.E. Tom Goodwin, Jr., and Joe Ferris enter L.1.E.

TOM: I won't take No for an answer. I gave up your checks with instructions to have your baggage sent up to the house at –

JOE: What will your father say to your bringing me, an entire stranger, into his house?

TOM: That my friends are his, and can make his house their home.

JOE: Ah, home! What a sweet sound the word has, and how lucky the man that has one. I never knew what a home was, unless a gambling house could be called one.

TOM: But I say, old fellow, how is this for a trip to Saratoga? [*Taps breast pocket*] The folks said the trip would do me good, and it has its advantages. I have returned with loss of appetite, and nerves all unstrung –

JOE: And a pocket brimful of money. [*They walk arm in arm*] Do not forget that I was your physician in the latter case.

TOM: Yes, indeed. Your advice to forsake the king and stick to the queen came just in time.

JOE: Her Majesty never deserts me, but the king often refuses to show his ugly face when I am most desirous of seeing him. But, come, Tom, as I am to become an inmate of your home, give me a sort of a panoramic view, as it were.

TOM: Well, home, they say, is where the heart is.

JOE: Quite right, but I would hear of the inmates of that home whom I am likely to meet.

TOM: Well, there is the Old Top.

JOE: Stop! Now whom do you designate as the Old Top?

TOM: Why, my father, of course.

JOE: You should speak more respectfully of your father.

TOM: Very well, then. My father takes off his hat.

JOE: That will do. No more "Old Top."

TOM: No more. A mother's care and love I never knew.

JOE: That shot struck me, too. And who else?

TOM: Let me see, now – there are the girls.

JOE: [*Rubs hands*] Ah, that's it. Tell me about the girls.

TOM: Well, there's Louise, my own sister – she's a dear good girl, always covering up my little failings.

JOE: In fact, she is so near and yet so far. [*Laughs*]

TOM: Then there is Clara.

JOE: [*Feints*] Oh.

TOM: What's the matter?

JOE: You shouldn't mention two such girls in a breath. It's more than I can stand.

TOM: Clara is my adopted father's own daughter.

JOE: She adopted you and your father?

TOM: No, no. She's my adopted father's own daughter.

JOE: So near and yet – [*Confused*] Shakespeare!

TOM: Oh, get out.

JOE: But tell me, old fellow, are there any visitors at your house whom I am likely to encounter.

TOM: Yes, there is one man, and to tell the truth he is not a favorite of mine.

JOE: What are his characteristics?

TOM: Well, he is a dark sort of a person.

JOE: Not colored, I hope.

TOM: No, I mean his actions.

JOE: What are his peculiarities?

TOM: Well, he is very reserved, rarely smiles, and has nothing to say – and – in fact I could give you no better description.

JOE: That's enough. I take a sudden antipathy to the man from your description. But did you ever hear my nickname?

TOM: No.

JOE: I had a great knack of finding things that were lost, when I was a little boy, and if any article of value was lost in the neighborhood, little Joe Ferris was called in to find it, and from my success in finding such things, I got the name of Ferret. That name has clung to me ever since. Now the ferret is a shrewd, cunning little animal, and if this man meditates any evil, rest assured I will find him out.

TOM: But we may wrong him.

JOE: True. But in every happy home that seems to remind us of Eden, where all is joy and peace, we should guard it from intruders and be more than careful of our friends, for the man will come who will sow discord, and perhaps ruin its peace and happiness forever. I am at war with all such men. I cannot say it is something unseen or unheard – it may be my destiny – but I will keep an eye on this man.

TOM: Come, let's go after a glass of sparkling champagne, and a puff of Reina Victoria. We will devise other sports. If we cannot find them here, we will seek them in green fields and pastures new. [*Start to Exit R.1.E. They run into Johnnie O'Dwyer*] Oh, wouldn't that fellow be a picnic for me! [*Squares off*]

JOE: Excuse me a few moments, Tom, will you?

TOM: Certainly. But mind you don't fail me. I shall expect to see you at the house soon. .

JOE: All right. [*Exit Tom. To Johnnie*] Hello, sonny!

JOHN: I don't know you, and my name ain't Sonny, neither.

JOE: Oh well, I guess I'll go on, then – You don't know me?

JOHN: Your face is kind of familiar, but your feet have grown entirely out of my recollection.

JOE: Ha, ha – well – well – [*Takes off his hat*] You can't remember me, then?

JOHN: Well, if it ain't Joe Ferris! [*They shake*]

JOE: Johnnie, how are you?

JOHN: I'm red hot and still a-hottin'. [*Strikes pose*]

JOE: How are all the boys?

JOHN: The boys is all right – all except Aby.

JOE: What's the matter with Aby?

JOHN: [*Jerks his thumb over his shoulder, and makes a choking sound*]

JOE: What? Hung? What did they hang him for?

JOHN: Oh, the same old complaint – nothing.

JOE: Oh, go on – what did he do?

JOHN: Well, you see, Aby was coming down this way with a little bit of a knife in his hand.

JOE: How big was the knife that Aby had?

JOHN: It was a little bit of a knife – only about so long. [*Hands close together – then spreads them out*] That's all.

JOE: I see.

JOHN: Well, Aby was coming down this way with a little knife in his hand, and there was a young fellow coming in the opposite direction with a big boodle of money.

JOE: How big? A boodle? A New York boodle?

JOHN: No – bigger than that. Almost as big as a Chicago boodle.

JOE: Oh.

JOHN: And the young fellow ran right into the knife, and the knife ran right into the young fellow, and it got stuck right in his heart, and he got the heart disease and he went to his grave and died.

JOE: And they hung Aby for it?

JOHN: Yes, sir, they hung him.

JOE: Well, that's a shame. He was such a good boy, too. He would give anything away.

JOHN: Why, he would give himself away.

JOE: He would that.

JOHN: He was so generous that if he had two apples and your mouth was watering for one, he would eat one and keep the other for himself.

JOE: He would, indeed.

JOHN: Aby was a good friend of mine, too. I will never forget him. [*Takes Joe's handkerchief out of his pocket and weeps*] He owed me a dollar and a half.

JOE: You should seek consolation in the old adage, Johnnie, which says "forget and forgive." Therefore you should forget the dollar and a half.

JOHN: How am I to forget the dollar and a half, when he wasn't forgiving the dollar and a half? [*Joe pulls handkerchief away and pulls Johnnie's cap over his eyes in place of it. Johnnie gets through weeping, and tries to put the cap back in Joe's pocket, when he notices that Joe has changed them*] You got ahead of me that time, Joe.

JOE: That is because you were committing a capital crime. [*Pulls cap down*]

JOHN: Oh, my! [*Bends over*]

JOE: Come – brace up.

JOHN: I can't – I've busted my suspenders. [*Straightens up*]

JOE: Aby was generosity personified.

JOHN: Aby was generosity personified.

JOE: In fact I never saw generosity so well personified as in Abraham.

JOHN: In fact I never saw generosity so well ex – ah – ah – oh Joe I can't say that word.

JOE: Why not?

JOHN: It tickles my tongue.

JOE: He was a young man worthy of emulation.

JOHN: He was a young man worthy of emigration.

JOE: I could stand here and expatiate at large

upon his many good qualities, and if I could find words to express myself, I could make the welkin ring with its praise.

JOHN: Keep away from me. [*Gets over to L.1.E.*] You've got them bad. Don't come near me.

JOE: Why?

JOHN: I ain't been vaccinated.

JOE: But come, John, tell me what has become of John Adderly?

JOHN: Oh he's ruined – turned respectable. He's up to some game.

JOE: Evidently, as he never would have done so from choice. But tell me – what do you know of him?

JOHN: Well, you see, I was walking down Wall Street the other day.

JOE: What were you doing on Wall Street?

JOHN: I was over there to get a check cashed, to buy five cents' worth of chewing gum.

JOE: Oh, yes, I saw your bank on Wall Street.

JOHN: Well, you see, as I was walking down the Street, I saw Adderly coming in the opposite direction, talkin' to a rooster.

JOE: Come now, stop right there. Do you think that I am from the country and you can stuff that down me? I would like to know in what language a man could carry on a conversation with a rooster?

JOHN: He could cackle to him, couldn't he?

JOE: I bow to your superior knowledge of cackleology.

JOHN: Oh, don't. [*Gets weak*]

JOE: [*Holding him up*] Can it be possible that my cackalogical phraseology has upset your equilibrium?

JOHN: Joe, don't give them to me in clusters – give them to me one at a time.

JOE: How do you feel now, Camille?

JOHN: Look in the pupil of my eye and you will see a little black spot, and underneath my thumbnail a thin blue line. I cannot marry you.

JOE: Why?

JOHN: I am an octoroon.

JOE: That's foul.

JOHN: Well, then, that's two I've got on you.

JOE: That's so, the other rooster and this one makes two. [*Puts up two fingers*] All right, we've got two roosters. Now, go ahead.

JOHN: No, the last one wasn't a rooster, so we let her lay. [*Puts one of Joe's fingers down*] Well, Adderly and this rooster were talking,

when up comes the Shrimp and introduces Adderly as Ellert.

JOE: He's sailing under false colors, then. That looks bad. But come to the underground parlor, Johnnie, I want to have a long talk with you.

JOHN: This coat ain't good enough to go to the parlor, Joe – it's queer.

JOE: It is a dizzy coat.

JOHN: But, Joe, it's not the coat that makes the man.

JOE: [*Sincerely*] You're right. It's not the coat that makes the man.

JOHN: It's the pants. [*Exit both R.1.E.*]

Scene 2

Bar with bottles and glasses, sandwiches and apples, seltzer bottles and a couple of Indian clubs made to look like bottles, all on bar. Curtain painted to resemble back of bar. Window in curtain. Chairs, table, doors. When curtain rises, Dolores and other young women seated in chairs. In chair in front of bar is dummy representing young woman. Billy is behind the bar. Young woman comes in and sings. Dutch song-and-dance man does a turn and waltzes with dummy from the chair, and retires with it under his arm. He also comes out with a coat on in which the sleeves are six or eight feet long and have large hands sewed on the ends. Inside the sleeves and fastened to the hands, are sticks by which he can hold the hands up and make them look very natural. He sings "Only to See Her Face Again," and at each pause lets the arms out a little way until finally they are stretched to their full limit. Very funny. After this a nigger song and dance, and the play goes on. Giovanni enters door R., and advances to center of room.

GIOVANNI: [*To Dolores*] Come here, and give me the money. [*She advances and gives him some silver*] Is this all you have got? [*He speaks very broken Italian*]

DOLORES: It is, indeed. It is all I have.

Young women all retire into R.U. corner

GIOVANNI: I think you steal from me.

Catches her by the hand – jerks her around – then goes to table and counts money

DOLORES: [*Kneeling down*] There is nothing I

wish to steal from you, except myself. [*Clasps hands*] And if I left him, where would I lay my weary head? [*Goes over to where the rest of the women are*]

BILLY: [*Comes out from behind bar – slaps Giovanni on back*] So, Signor – you like this country?

GIOVANNI: Yes, me like the country. Me maka da plenty money.

BILLY: But don't you think these girls steal from you sometimes?

GIOVANNI: Oh, everybody steal in dees country.

BILLY: What's that, you Italian organ-grinder and ring-tailed monkey dancer? Take back those words or I'll make you eat them.

GIOVANNI: [*Jumps up*] Never! I no take back.

BILLY: Well, take that, then! [*Strikes him*]

GIOVANNI: [*Stabs him. The Dude enters L.2.E. – catches Billy as he falls and carries him out. Dolores exit D.R.*] I stab him to ze heart. I fiddle – everybody dance.

Sits down opposite R.1.E. Music – waltz. Johnnie enters door R. and the Dude L.2.E. They both take partners and waltz. Nigger picks up chair and waltzes. Music stops

JOHN: [*Has on new suit. Slaps Giovanni on back*] Where is the bartender? [*Giovanni jumps up, but sits down again. The Dude sits down at table when Giovanni jumps up. Johnnie backs across room and runs into Dude. Dude holds table between himself and Johnnie*] [*To Dude*] Where is the bartender?

DUDE: The barkeeper has retired.

Johnnie acts as if he were spoiling for a fight

JOHN: Oh, he's retired, has he? Well, I'll be bartender myself. [*Goes behind counter and takes off coat, showing undershirt without sleeves, and large muscles*] Come on up and take a drink. [*The Dude and Nigger get there promptly*] [*To Dude*] Well, what'll you have?

Girls at bar also

DUDE: I'll take a little Lignumvitae Rye.

JOHN: Ain't got it. Anything else?

DUDE: Well, give me a little rye, then.

JOHN: Rye whiskey? Yes, sir. [*To Nigger*] What will you have?

NIGGER: Give me six cigars, a bottle of pop, and a package of cigarettes.

JOHN: I'll give you a smash in the eye. [*Dude drinks*] Pretty good stuff, that.

DUDE: Yes – it will do.

JOHN: Ten cents, please.

DUDE: [*Looks in pockets*] Ah-h – what did you say?

JOHN: I said ten cents, and I want it now.

DUDE: Well, give me a little more. I prefer to pay for mine all at once.

JOHN: [*Gives him another drink*] That's great stuff – twenty years old.

DUDE: [*Examining drink carefully*] Indeed, it's very small for its age.

JOHN: Want some more?

DUDE: Well, you might make it grow a little. [*Fills it up*]

JOHN: [*As he goes to drink*] Ah, look out there.

DUDE: What's the matter?

JOHN: There's a fly in it.

DUDE: Well, fill it up and let the fly float off. [*Johnnie does so. Dude drinks*]

JOHN: Twenty cents, please.

DUDE: [*Feeling in his pockets*] Ah, yes. By the way – do you know Goosey?

JOHN: No, I don't know Goosey, and I want twenty cents for those drinks right quick.

DUDE: Then you don't know Goosey?

JOHN: [*Threateningly*] Are you going to pay for those drinks?

DUDE: Well, Goosey is a very singular fellow. He walks off – like this –

Exit L.1.E. Coon (i.e. "Nigger") laughs. Johnnie chases him with seltzer bottle. Coon comes back as soon as Johnnie gets behind bar. Enter Dutchman with water pail

DUTCHMAN: [*To Coon*] Shoo-oo. [*Walks up to bar – hands pail*] Give me a pint of beer.

JOHN: You're in the wrong house. This won't hold a pint.

DUTCHMAN: You got anytings to eat?

JOHN: Yes, there's some sandwiches and apples.

Dutchman takes sandwich and bites piece out

JOHN: Twenty-five cents.

DUTCHMAN: What?

JOHN: Twenty-five cents for that sandwich.

DUTCHMAN: [*Takes piece out of mouth and lays it and apple back*] I don't want it. Ain't you got no business lunch?

JOHN: No – and do you suppose I'm going to take that sandwich back after you have been chewing on it?

DUTCHMAN: [*Picks up apple*] Say, how much are the apples?

JOHN: Same price.

DUTCHMAN: Will you give me the sandwich for the apple?

JOHN: Why, yes – I don't care which you take.

DUTCHMAN: All right. [*Hands him the apple and takes the sandwich. He walks over to Giovanni*] Hello, Johnnie. [*Slaps him on the back*] Johnnie, get your hair cut, hair cut, hair cut –

Takes hold of Giovanni's hair, which is long. Girls go R.U. and sit down

JOHN: You'll get your hair cut if you don't give me twenty-five cents for that sandwich.

DUTCHMAN: I guess not. Vot's der matter mit you? Didn't I give you the apple for der sandwich? [*Walks up to bar*]

JOHN: You didn't pay me for the apple.

Dutchman goes to explain, but gets a smash in the eye. He staggers over to Giovanni – pushes him out of chair and sits down. Giovanni reaches for knife, but thinks better of it

DUTCHMAN: Oh, say, mister, find my eye, vill you?

Joe comes out from bar and squirts seltzer at Coon, who retreats L.1.E. Dude stalks in, but gets contents of seltzer, and retreats L.1.E. Joe enters D.R. Dude enters L.1.E. and goes to right end of bar. Coon enters L.2.E. Giovanni's brother Pablo enters

GIOVANNI: [*To him*] You see the bartender?

PABLO: Yes, I saw him. He is dead. Why did you kill him?

GIOVANNI: Ah – he strika me – he have no right to strika me. Dolores, go out. I fear she will betray me.

Exit D.R. Pablo exits L.2.E.

JOHN: Oh, Joe, you just ought to see me clean out the place. [*Swings arm around and hits Dude in the eye*] Well, you hadn't ought of been there.

DUDE: ow-ooo-ow!

Coon gets him a chair center, opposite second entrance

JOHN: Oh, I can feel my muscle swelling.

DUDE: And I can feel my eye swelling.

JOHN: Well, Joe, you're just in time to take a drink.

JOE: No, thanks, I never drink.

JOHN: Then have something to eat.

JOE: What have you got to eat?

JOHN: Three kinds of pie – rice, custard and mustard.

DUTCHMAN: Rice, custard and mustard?

JOHN: Yes, rice, custard and mustard.

JOE: Well, ha, ha, ha! I don't think I care for anything to eat. Come up, boys, and have a drink.

Dude and Coon get there suddenly

JOHN: Look here, you fellows – [*Points seltzer bottle at them*] Get away from here – [*They hesitate*] Git – [*Seltzer*]

DUDE: [*Dude and Coon center of stage. Dude to Johnnie*] Ah, will you do me a favor?

COON: Yaas – do us bofe a favor, will you?

JOHN: Yes, I'll do you both a favor.

DUDE: Just come outside here, will you?

COON: Yaas – just come on de outside.

Johnnie comes at them with a rush and they exit L.1.E.

DUTCHMAN: Will you do me a favor? [*Opposite R.1.E.*]

JOHN: Yes, I'll do you a favor, too.

DUTCHMAN: Ah, there – stay there.

JOHN: Come on up, Dutchy, and have something to eat.

DUTCHMAN: [*Still nursing eye*] I want nottings to do mit you.

Enter Dolores door R., running and screaming – Giovanni after her – center L.1.E. Giovanni's brother Pablo, Coon and Dude L.2.E.

JOE: [*Catches Dolores by the hand and steps in front of Giovanni*] Stop – what do you want with this child?

GIOVANNI: Give her to me. She belongs to me –

JOE: No, you shall not have her. By what right do you beat and misuse these children?

GIOVANNI: I bring her from home. Italy, Signor. She is my child.

DOLORES: Oh, no, sir, he is not my father. Do not let me go back to him.

JOE: No, you shall not. [*To Giovanni*] She says you are not her father, and I believe her. If you dare to lay a finger on her, you shall answer for it dearly.

Giovanni throws down club and springs at Joe with knife. Joe knocks him down. The brother attempts to help, but Johnnie knocks him down and he retreats L.2.E. Giovanni exits D.R. screaming vengeance. Joe knocks Dude and Coon around just for exercise. Joe assumes to talk with Dolores, picks up club and looks at it; then leads Dolores to a chair opposite R.1.E., sits down and talks to her. The Dude has retreated – also Dutchy – after the fracas through L.1.E. Dude comes back and bows head on bar – Dutchy enters with dynamite bomb – explodes it back of Dude. It is filled with red fire. Consternation

JOE: [*To Dolores*] That man is not your father?

DOLORES: Indeed, he is not. He brought me from Italy.

JOE: But your father – surely he would not let that man bring you away from Italy?

DOLORES: He was killed fighting with Garibaldi.

JOE: And your mother?

DOLORES: [*Hands to eyes*] Dead.

JOE: Poor child. [*Wipes away her tears*] Your mother dead, too.

DOLORES: She grew sick and died when she heard of my father's death. She placed her hand upon my head and said, "God guard my little one. God bless my little Dolores."

JOE: But how came you in that wretch's power?

DOLORES: Oh, there were a great many children brought over when we were. We played the harp and fiddle on the ferry boats and on the streets, anywhere to get money, and if we don't get two dollars every day, he kicks us and beats us and sends us to bed.

JOE: What? Kicks you and beats you?

JOHN: [*Rushes from behind bar*] Kicks and beats her – Oh, wait till I catch him –

Starts for door R. Knocks down Dutchy and Dude, who get in his way. Exit D.R. Coon, Dutchy and Dude all go to bar and help themselves

DOLORES: There was a little boy and girl who used to live with us and play on the streets. When they were coming home one night, they crossed the bridge and they were hurrying so, because it was after dark, that they both fell into the river and were drowned, and the next morning they were found locked in each other's arms. Oh, Barney was awful sorry.

Dutchman brings chair to front center and goes

to sleep. He has picked up the Dude's hat and has it on when he goes to sleep. The Dude picks up the Coon's hat – looks it over – then gets Indian club off bar – goes to Dutchman and strikes him in the stomach with it*

DUDE: That is not my chapeau. [*Changes with Dutchman*]

DUTCHMAN: [*Now has Coon's hat – throws it on floor*] That is NOT my chapeau.

Kicks at it and falls on his back. Coon fires Dutchman's hat also. Dude rushes up to strike Dutchy while he is on the floor. Coon does the Pocahontas act – gets on his knees

COON: Have mercy, sire, have mercy.

DUTCHMAN: Does he have mercy? [*Gets on his knees*] I am shaved – I am shaved.

Dutchman gets in chair again. Dude lights cigar and smokes, sitting at R. end of bar. Coon is still drinking

JOE: He was sorry on account of their loss, of course.

DOLORES: Oh, no – because they had lost his best harp –

JOHN: [*Enter D.R.*] You just ought to have seen me lift him.

JOE: Did you catch him?

JOHN: I should say I did. I'd like to break my foot on him. I'd send him so high that his clothes would be out of fashion before he gets back.

DOLORES: Oh, you will not let him have me again, will you?

JOE: No, my child, I will see that you are provided for, and he will never misuse you again.

DOLORES: And my brother and sister! Oh, Barney will beat them worse than ever, now that I am gone.

JOE: But they are not your brothers and sisters.

DOLORES: I know it, but I love them just the same.

JOE: Well, I will provide for them, too. That wretch of an Italian shall not exercise his cruelty on them if I can help it.

JOHN: What are you going to do, Joe – steal a poorhouse?

JOE: Why, certainly not!

JOHN: Well, if you do, just put me down for a front seat.

Discovers Coon, who is just putting bottle under coat. Johnnie commences to whistle – so

*does the Coon, who skips toward L.1.E. John-
nie skips alongside of him, imitating his gait
and pointing back at bar. Continue this to entrance. Back to counter, leaving bottle there,
Coon skips to L.1.E. Johnnie gets seltzer bottle –
takes cigar out of Dude's mouth – Dude expos-
tulates against it. Dude rushes out L.1.E. and
back again, shouting*

DUDE: The world is mine!

*Gets a facer from seltzer bottle, and retires.
Johnnie turns attention to Dutchman, who en-
joys the fun, but goes to sleep suddenly*

JOHN: Oh – Oh – o – Three shots for five cents.

*Takes three shots with bottle. Dutchman and
Johnnie fight. Dutchy exits. Report of a gun
L.2.E. Coon rushes in L.2.E.*

COON: Oh, you've done it! You'll catch it.

JOHN: [*Behind bar*] Done what?

COON: That young fellow went right outside and
committed suicide. Blowed his brains out with
a cigarette.

JOHN: Well, it ain't my fault.

COON: Yes, it is – all your fault. You'll catch
it.

*Puts card on Johnnie's back marked Left.
Johnnie repeats that it is not his fault, but Joe
sides in with Coon and he is dubious. Play
death march. Dutchman and Dude march in
with sheet between them arranged to look as if
they had a stiff on shoulders*

COON: There is only one thing that will save that
man's life.

JOHN: What's that?

COON: A bottle of brandy.

JOHN: Well, I'll give him that, if it'll do him
any good. [*They take the bottle, and throw
shutter off – Exit L.1.E. Johnnie comes out,
but he is too paralyzed to do anything. When
he turns up, shows card on his back "Left."
Takes off card*] I'll get even with them fellows.
[*Picks up pepperbox*]

JOE: What's that?

JOHN: Cayenne pepper.

JOE: What are you going to do?

JOHN: Make them a dynamite cocktail. [*Puts
some in bottle*] Come on, boys, and have a
drink. [*Coon and Dude enter and drink;
turn wrong side out. Dutchman laughs at
them – then drinks his – goes through same
motions, his hair rising straight up on head.*

*Dude and Coon carry him off, after he falls
L.1.E. John Adderly enters D.R. and goes to
take a drink. Johnnie grabs bottle*] We don't
sell liquor to boys. [*Joe catches him – he
struggles*]

JOE: Oh, you need not struggle – you are in a
vise. Didn't I tell you that we should meet
again, villain? [*Adderly breaks away and
makes motion to draw weapon*] Why don't you
draw your weapon? You are a coward as well
as a villain, I see.

ADDERLY: What has caused this change in you,
Joe? Have we not always been friends?

JOE: Aye, friends. Who placed the money in
my room for which I was tried and convicted?
What could I do? My companions were of
your stamp, whose words or oath would not
avail me. Death was preferable to dragging
out a miserable existence in prison. I escaped
– went to California and there I met a wretch
who was dying of some frightful disease. He
was your accomplice, and it was he that told
me who put that money in my room. It
was YOU, JOHN ADDERLY. And now what am
I? An outcast – an escaped convict – a gambler without sympathy from the human race.

JOHN: Who says you got no sympathy? You,
Jack Adderly? [*Joe quiets him*] Well, I don't
take water from no such duck as him. [*Drinks
out of dynamite bottle*] Oh, Joe, what do you
think I did? I took some dynamite myself –

ADDERLY: I did not do it. It was all a mistake.

JOE: Who caused the search to be made there?

ADDERLY: Not I. Come, Joe, let us be friends
again.

JOE: And you will give information, and have
me sent back, I suppose?

ADDERLY: I would never do that.

JOE: You better not. If I thought you meditated
such a thing, I'd place the rope around your
bull-neck with my own hands, as a terrible
warning to all traitors.

ADDERLY: Enough. Our paths lie in different directions.

JOE: [*Interrupts*] I trust that our paths may lie
in different directions, but if in our walk
through life we should ever meet, fear will
never cause me to turn aside from avenging a
wrong.

ADDERLY: Nor me from avenging an insult.

JOHN: Oh, go West, young fellow, and shoot
snipe.

ADDERLY: I'll see you again, young man. [*Exit D.R.*]

JOHN: [*Follows him to door*] Oh, come and see me now. [*Giovanni's brother Pablo enters L.1.E. and picks up snipe lying in center of stage. Johnnie turns and sees him and shoots. He drops snipe and exits L.1.E. Dutchman then starts after snipe. Has on a small plug hat. Picks up snipe and starts off. Joe whistles – then hollers at him. Drops snipe and exits L.1.E. Johnnie shoots just before he gets out. He jumps – hair stands up straight – hat falls off. Johnnie puts on hat – picks up snipe – sits in chair opposite R.1.E.*] I'll do all the snipe-shooting round here myself.

JOE: [*With Dolores by the hand*] Poor child, there is something in her life that strangely resembles my own, for I am like a tennis ball – here, there and everywhere at times, and should misfortune overtake me I shall have at least the heartfelt prayers of one more homeless little wanderer. [*Exit Joe and Dolores L.2.E.*]

JOHN: Joe is a good fellow, and Joe thinks pretty well of me, too. Why, if I was starving and Joe had one sandwich I believe he would give me the mustard. Joe has got a heart in him as soft as a woman – some women. Oh, women, women, with your four-button kid gloves, while we poor men have to pin our suspenders to our pants!

Goes behind bar. Women gather round bar. Lights down on stage, except light on L. end of counter. Adderly and Giovanni enter door R. and talk just inside. Dolores enters L.2.E. and listens. Gets close to them

ADDERLY: He struck you down, you say?

GIOVANNI: Yes – he knocka me down – so.

ADDERLY: Well, I'd have his life for it. He is a bad character and I know it. You kill him and I'll swear you out of it.

GIOVANNI: Ah – I keel heem – but how?

ADDERLY: Ask them all up to drink – then turn down the light and stab him in the dark.

DOLORES: I have heard enough. I will put him on his guard. [*Exit L.2.E.*]

GIOVANNI: See – my knife is sharp. I will do it.

ADDERLY: That is right. Now here is money to treat with. Kill him and you will get your revenge and rid me of a dangerous foe. Call them up to drink and I will return just in time to see my friend the Ferret give his last kick.

Exit D.R. Giovanni goes to L. end of bar. Dutchman, Dude and Coon enter R.L.1. and L.2 and get in front of bar. Giovanni's brother Pablo enters L.1.E. and stands next to Giovanni, who shows him his knife. It is quite dark. Enter Joe and Dolores L.2.E.

JOE: Why, you must be mistaken, there is no one here who means to harm me.

DOLORES: I am sure he will kill you, and all on my account. Oh, let me go back to him.

JOE: Why, I couldn't think of such a thing. Come, wait for me outside a moment.

Takes her to D.R. Then walks up to L. end of bar. Giovanni turns out lights

JOHN: Look out, Joe.

Giovanni strikes, but hits his own brother, who falls. Johnnie lights the gas

DOLORES: [*Enters D.R.*] Why, Barney, you have killed your own brother.

GIOVANNI: No, no – I no keel my brother. I know my own brother.

JOE: Cowardly assassin – [*Grabs him*] You have killed your own brother in mistake for me, and you must answer to the law for your crime. [*Enter Adderly, door R. and looks at the dead man*] Ah, I see you were but the tool, and there stands the instigator.

Adderly draws revolver, but the women who are nearest him grab him, and Dolores catches his hand and bites it until he drops the pistol

Tableau

ACT III

Parlor in Thomas Goodwin's house.

CAESAR: [*Enters R.C. with gas lights in hand*] Hang out your banners on the outer wall, and let the cry be "Onward!" But why should I play the Roman fool and die here upon me own sword? NO. Lay on, Macduff, and damn'd be he who first cries, "Hold – Enough!"

Up and down – across stage – stab – fall

AUNT SUSANNAH: Why, Caesar, what in the world are you making such a noise about?

CAESAR: That ain't noise – that's ambition. "Lay on Macduff and damn'd be he who first cries, 'Hold – Enough.' " That's crushing genius through the mighty cranium.

AUNT SUSANNAH: Caesar, don't you know that Mr. Tom is expected? Go and see that his room is in order.

CAESAR: Ha –

AUNT SUSANNAH: Leave the room, sir.

CAESAR: I go, but of my own accord. [*Enter Louise L.1.E.*] Ha, ha, ha!

LOUISE: Go. [*Points*]

CAESAR: Great Heaven – I am crushed!

LOUISE: Now, Auntie, be good and don't insist upon my going to the entertainment with Mr. Ellerton.

AUNT SUSANNAH: But you must.

LOUISE: I hate him, and I won't go.

AUNT SUSANNAH: Mr. Ellerton is a very nice man, and I don't want to hear any more nonsense about him.

LOUISE: But I can't go with him.

AUNT SUSANNAH: You will.

LOUISE: I won't.

AUNT SUSANNAH: If you don't stop being saucy to me, I'll tell your father.

LOUISE: Well, I don't care, you are awful cross, and I despise Mr. Ellerton. Tom is the only fellow I care a snap for – he is just splendid. Say, Auntie, don't you think Tom is good-looking?

AUNT SUSANNAH: Young girls like you should think of something else besides good-looking young men. It is for ladies like me, and not young girls like you, to think of such things.

LOUISE: Well, I am bigger than you are and you are forty-nine.

AUNT SUSANNAH: You naughty girl – forty-nine! Why, the idea! It's no such thing.

Enter Tom L.1.E.

LOUISE: Oh, Tom, I'm so glad you have come.

AUNT SUSANNAH: Thomas, kiss your aunt.

TOM: All right, old girl.

AUNT SUSANNAH: Thomas, what do you mean?

LOUISE: She has been scolding all morning, Tom, and I'll tell you all I know. She meets a red-headed policeman down at the gate every day and talks to him for hours.

AUNT SUSANNAH: Thomas, don't you believe a word she says.

TOM: I don't, I never saw a policeman talking to a woman in my life.

Tom and Louise walk to rear of stage together

AUNT SUSANNAH: The idea! As if I would talk to

a policeman, let alone a red-headed one!

Enter Caesar L.1.E.

CAESAR: [*To Aunt Susannah*] There is a gentleman down in the garden wants to see you.

AUNT SUSANNAH: A gentleman to see me? [*Confidentially*] Now, Caesar, who is it?

CAESAR: It's the red-headed policeman.

Aunt Susannah chases him out L.1.E. Louise and Tom laugh

LOUISE: [*Coming forward*] Now, tell me, Tom, did you enjoy your trip and did you find more attractive faces and friends there than at home? For I suppose you found time to amuse yourself, although you went for health.

TOM: No, my dear, here I find metal more attractive. [*Aside*] My father's money!

LOUISE: You mean ladies, of course?

TOM: Oh, yes. But by the way, does Mr. Ellerton call as frequently as ever?

LOUISE: Yes, he does, Tom, and I wish that he would stay away.

TOM: Why, I thought you were fond of him, and the thing as good as settled?

LOUISE: Oh, I could never marry that odious Ellerton, Tom. The man whom I marry must be one whom I can honor, love and respect. Mr. Ellerton is not such a man. [*Takes seat at table*]

TOM: But such a man I know – a noble, generous fellow, and though we have been acquainted but a few weeks, our hearts are joined together with links of steel. I have invited him here and am expecting him this evening.

LOUISE: I shall be glad to meet any friend of yours, but in affairs of the heart I prefer to be my own mistress.

TOM: Rest assured that father loves his children too well to ever force you to marry anyone you do not love.

LOUISE: Surely the father that has been so kind would not want his daughter to risk her happiness with such a man?

Enter Caesar

CAESAR: The young gentleman is in the reception room and promulgates his wishes on this year card.

TOM: Why, it's Ferris. Show him up at once.

CAESAR: Safe conduct to his happiness! Ala ca Zam. [*Exit L.1.E.*]

TOM: Why, what's the matter with the fellow?

LOUISE: He has joined an amateur dramatic society. Why, the other day we heard the most terrible noise upstairs, actually thought the house was tumbling down, but upon investigation it proved to be poor Caesar – [*Rises and walks to rear*] rehearsing *Richard the Third*. He was running around the room, jumping over chairs and madly shouting "A horse – a horse – my Kingdom for a horse!" [*Comes forward laughing*]

TOM: And still the world turns round. A black Richard. We shall be having a black Juliet next.

CAESAR: [*Enter L.I.E.*] Room for me, Lord Duke Don Caesar De Pizaro Patsy Bol-bol-bol – Bolivar!

Enter Joe L.I.E., and makes a quick move at Caesar

TOM: Leave the room, fool.

CAESAR: He who calls me a fool insults the lady I board with.

Exit L.I.E. Louise R.C. Tom L.C.

JOE: [*To Tom*] What's the matter with the fifteenth amendment, Tom?

TOM: Oh, he's only a black amateur.

JOE: I should never take him for a white professional.

TOM: Mr. Ferris, allow me to introduce you to my sister Louise.

Joe advances and they stand together

JOE: Miss Goodwin, it is indeed a pleasure to make your acquaintance.

LOUISE: The pleasure, Mr. Ferris, is mutual. I assure you I was chiding Tom for his selfishness in leaving me to be escorted by a man whom I abhor.

JOE: [*To Tom*] It is evident that you have neglected your sister. [*Winks*]

LOUISE: Why, he left us entirely alone last winter.

JOE: Did you leave your sister alone?

TOM: [*Desperately*] Well, what is a fellow to do?

JOE: You should emulate me. Never leave any fellow's sister alone.

TOM: Oh, pshaw!

LOUISE: Tell me, Mr. Ferris, what were the attractions at Saratoga? Were there any ladies who received Tom's special attention?

JOE: Yes, there was one in particular whom he was very devoted to.

TOM: [*Pulls his coat-tail*] Oh, come off, Joe.

JOE: Go 'way, you naughty, naughty man. She had lemon-colored hair and a pull-back, so.

TOM: Joe, for Heaven sake, draw it mild.

JOE: [*Taking hold of coat-tail*] You will draw it off if you keep on pulling it.

LOUISE: And what was her name?

JOE: Her name was –

TOM: [*Whispers to him*]

JOE: Did you hear what he said? He said her name was Augalusha.

TOM: Augalusha Snobbs.

JOE: She was the queen of the surf.

LOUISE: [*Walking past Joe to Tom*] And so you were playing court to the queen, Tom?

TOM: Why, certainly. [*To Joe*] I trust we may not meet as strangers when I am united to royalty.

JOE: I hope not. [*Aside*] Ah, Heaven grant that those words may not come back tenfold to repay for my raillery!

CAESAR: [*Enter L.I.E.*] Sir, your generous father requests your presence in the ante-chamber.

TOM: What's that?

CAESAR: Your father wants to see you.

TOM: Tell him that I will join him at once.

Joe, Tom and Louise gather opposite R.I.E. and stand talking

CAESAR: Such proclamations shall be made. [*Makes a run at them*] Ha – beware. She has deceived her father and may be –

TOM: Leave the room.

CAESAR: [*Singing*] "There Is a New Coon in Town, There Is a New Coon in Town." [*Exit L.I.E.*]

TOM: Pardon me for leaving you, but I must pay my respects to my father. I'll leave you to the tender mercies of Louise. You will stay with us, I hope, while in town, as per agreement, you know. [*Exit R.2.*]

JOE: [*Follows him to the door*] Thanks – perhaps I will. [*Gets chair at back of stage*]

LOUISE: Your family, then, do not reside in New York, Mr. Ferris?

JOE: [*Brings chair to her side*] Pardon me if I intrude my domestic history upon you. My father and mother both died when I was a little boy, and I have been compelled to fight my way all alone in the world.

LOUISE: I can sympathize with you, for I, too, and my twin brother, were left alone. And had it not been for Mr. Goodwin, who took our mother from the snow-covered street where she had fallen exhausted, brought her home and warmed us back to life, I fear our history would have been a sad one. But ever since that night when he adopted us he has been the kindest of fathers. I trust that you will remain with us and meet my father, who will, I am sure, be delighted to make your acquaintance. Our circle of friends is very small, and with the exception of Mr. Ellerton we have very few frequent callers.

Enter Caesar L.1.E.

CAESAR: Mr. – Mr. – Damned if I haven't forgotten the gentleman's name. [*Exit L.1*]

JOE: [*Aside*] Ellerton – why, that is the very name that Johnnie said Adderly had assumed. The wolf in the fold of the lamb. Can it be possible? But, caution, Joe – caution. [*To Louise*] Do you know Mr. Ellerton's occupation?

LOUISE: To tell the truth I do not, and were it not for the business relations he has with my father, his presence here would be a cloud upon our sunshine. I think I can dispel the cloud and then the sun will shine brighter than ever. Oh, villain – villain!

CAESAR: [*Enters*] Mr. Ellerton is without and craves admission to your ladyship.

LOUISE: Show him in.

JOE: What – Ellerton here? He must not see me. What shall I do? [*To Louise*] I wish to speak to your brother a moment. [*Goes to R.2.E.*] I think I can find him.

LOUISE: Wait until Caesar returns and he shall show you the way.

JOE: I wish to see him at once, and I think it is quite unnecessary, as I can undoubtedly find him. [*Opens door*]

LOUISE: You will find him on the second floor to the left.

JOE: Thanks. I trust I shall have the pleasure of seeing you again.

LOUISE: Will you not stay for the evening?

JOE: I will. [*Aside*] Would to Heaven it were for life! [*Exit R.2.*]

LOUISE: Why, what a nice young man he is! Tom is very fortunate in having such a man for his friend.

Enter Caesar L.1. and behind him Ellerton

CAESAR: Behold the most conglomerate of his race. [*To Ellerton*] "Mark where she stands. Around her awful form I draw the holy circle of our church. Step but one foot within that circle, and on thy head – yea, even though it wore a crown, I'd launch the curse of –"

LOUISE: [*Sharply*] Caesar! [*Exit Caesar whistling L.1*] He is becoming unbearable. I am afraid we shall have to discharge him.

ELLERTON: Not on my account, I trust. I like his nonsense rather than otherwise. Your father is at home, is he not? In fact he is always at home to me.

LOUISE: He is, and he bade me say that he would receive you in the library when you called. And there you might transact any business you may have with him.

ELLERTON: [*Draws chair closer to Louise*] Business, Miss Goodwin, is a very cold word to be used between friends and does not sound well when coming from your lips. [*Essays to take her hand*]

LOUISE: [*Rising*] Pardon me, Mr. Ellerton, but my friends I have already selected. [*She sweeps from the room and exits through arch*]

ELLERTON: [*Getting up and gazing after her, and putting chair at rear of stage*] I'll lower her tone, the haughty beauty, and that before the day is over. [*Sits at table. Aunt Susannah enters L.1.*] There's that crazy old maid. I'll pretend to be asleep.

AUNT SUSANNAH: [*Just inside entrance*] Oh – it's a man! [*Goes forward*] Why, it's that dear delightful Mr. Ellerton! He's asleep. How sweet he looks. I've a good mind to kiss him. I believe I will. [*Kisses him – he jumps up. Looks from behind fan, coquettishly*] Peek-a-boo!

ELLERTON: Crazy!

AUNT SUSANNAH: Did I frighten you?

ELLERTON: Bless my soul, no! It takes more than that to frighten me. Do it again if you want to. [*Aunt Susannah with a little scream starts to do it again – he holds her off*] But not now.

AUNT SUSANNAH: I hope you will forgive my little indiscretion. [*Turning herself around and back again like a school girl*] Girls will be girls, you know!

ELLERTON: Yes, a nice old girl. [*Aside*] I suppose I'll have to make love to the old aunt in order to get the niece. [*To Aunt Susannah*] I have business with your brother which brings me here quite often. [*Steps toward her. C. front*]

AUNT SUSANNAH: Don't you tickle me, sir – don't you tickle me! [*Wriggles*]

ELLERTON: I understand your warm and gushing nature. [*Arm around her*] It has been chilled by contact with the cold and cruel world. If I but dared to reveal to you –

AUNT SUSANNAH: Oh, do.

ELLERTON: Oh, no.

AUNT SUSANNAH: Oh, Mr. Ellerton, isn't this too real to be sweet!

ELLERTON: It is too real to be sweet.

AUNT SUSANNAH: Oh, will you return my love?

ELLERTON: Certainly I will. I've no use for it.

AUNT SUSANNAH: Will you love me when I'm old? [*Draws it out*]

ELLERTON: That's about the only chance I have. Allow me to kiss – [*She puts up her face*] your fair hand. [*Gets away from her a little*]

AUNT SUSANNAH: I must go now. [*Edges up to him and holds her dress in the hand nearest him, as if to detain herself*] Now, don't you hold me back, for if my brother knew I was alone with you, he would scold me for being so giddy.

ELLERTON: [*Puts his arm around her again*] Your giddy brother shan't scold you, for I'll protect you from his wrath.

AUNT SUSANNAH: Oh, wouldn't we make a pretty tintype!

ELLERTON: A great big cromo given away with a pound of tea. [*Lets go of her*]

AUNT SUSANNAH: Now, Mr. Ellerton, how old do you suppose I am? Guess.

ELLERTON: Well, there is a question about ancient history. I guess you are about eighteen.

AUNT SUSANNAH: Oh, somebody told you.

Goes for him – he holds her off. Caesar enters arch

CAESAR: Oh, Lordy! [*Jumps behind sofa*]

AUNT SUSANNAH: Why, I thought I heard someone speak. [*Goes to L.1.E.*] Goodbye. [*Throws kiss*] Oh, you dear man, I shall never forget you! [*Exit L.1.*]

ELLERTON: Well, I'll never forget *you*, that's sure.

LOUISE: [*Enters arch*] Why, Mr. Ellerton, you here yet?

ELLERTON: I still trespass upon your valuable time.

LOUISE: [*Calls*] Caesar – [*He jumps from behind sofa*] Caesar is here. Caesar, show this man to my father's study.

ELLERTON: This gentleman can find the way to your father's study. [*Bows – goes L.2.*]

CAESAR: Goest thou to speak to my lord Hamlet?

ELLERTON: Go thou to the devil. [*Exit L.2.*]

CAESAR: Lead on – I'll follow thee. [*Exit L.2.*]

LOUISE: [*Sits at table*] I know it was wrong to speak to him as I did, but there was something so sinister in his looks and actions that I could not help it. I have made an enemy of him for life – of that I am sure.

Enter Caesar L.2, with letter on tray

CAESAR: A letter from my lord Duke.

LOUISE: [*Takes letter*] Caesar, you are a fool.

CAESAR: My proud girl, you shall yet be humbled. Go, get thee to a nunnery. Be thou as chaste as ice, as pure as snow – go – go – go. [*Runs into door jamb and exit L.1.*]

LOUISE: A letter from my brother. [*Reads*] and that man here too, closeted with my father at this time. I feel that something terrible is going to happen. I fear his devilish look – his cunning smile. [*Enter Joe D.R.*] Oh, Mr. Ferris, I think that Heaven has sent you here for me to confide in. I need your assistance.

JOE: I always act on the first impulse. I find it is the best way.

LOUISE: I will trust you. Mr. Ellerton is now closeted with my father. That man has long been a suitor for my hand, but without the least encouragement from me. And now I get this letter – read it. [*Hands him letter*] Oh, I feel there is something deep laid underneath all this. Oh, I know that it is some game.

JOE: [*Glances at letter*] You may be sure there is, and you may also be sure that I am just the man to spoil his little game. [*Hands back letter*] I am not a lawyer, no one knows that better than I, and if this man has any business with your father, the latter will come out second best, you may be sure. Is there a door or a window through which I could hear their conversation? It would enable me to act with more certainty, for, believe me, we have a desperate man to deal with – a perfect tyrant and one who will not leave his prey while a drop of blood remains.

LOUISE: I will tell you what we can do. I will scream and alarm the inmates of the next room. You conceal yourself behind the sofa. They will rush in here. You can then step into the next room. I will give them some explanation for my fright and you can overhear every word that is said.

JOE: [*Goes toward sofa*] What a wonderful faculty for invention has a woman, and what a dear delightful creature she is! Well, who knows, something good may come of it, after all.

LOUISE: Are you ready?

JOE: All ready.

Joe hides behind sofa – Louise screams. Ellerton and Mr. Goodwin enter L.2.E. Tom enters D.R., Caesar and Aunt Susannah L.1.

OMNES: Why, what in the world is the matter?

LOUISE: Oh, dear me – look under the table! [*Joe sneaks into L.2.E.*] I was so frightened.

AUNT SUSANNAH: What was it?

LOUISE: It looked for all the world like a great black cat.

AUNT SUSANNAH: A great black cat. [*Picks up skirts and runs out R.1.*]

MR. GOODWIN, ELLERTON *and* TOM: A great black cat!

All look at Caesar

CAESAR: A great black cat? Well, what are you all looking at me for? I thought he had a touch of E Pluribus Union!

Exit L.1. Louise and Tom are at table

ELLERTON: [*To Louise*] I trust that you will be better presently.

LOUISE: I have every reason to believe I shall be better presently.

ELLERTON: Your father was afraid that some calamity had befallen you.

LOUISE: [*Going up stage – looking at father, who is on sofa*] And I was afraid some calamity had befallen my poor father. Come Tom, I am all right now. And of one thing you may be sure.

ELLERTON: And that is – ?

LOUISE: [*Bowing herself out with Tom*] That the black cat will never frighten me again. [*Exit through arch*]

ELLERTON: What a fuss she makes about nothing – and what does she mean by a black cat, I wonder? Well, Mr. Goodwin, let us resume our conversation which was just interrupted.

GOODWIN: [*Rising*] Yes, let us come to the point at once. We are ruined.

ELLERTON: Excuse me sir – YOU are. I offered to take a share of the risk, but you declined.

GOODWIN: But you said the stocks were firm and the supply was inexhaustible.

ELLERTON: There you are – wrong again. Their circular said so.

GOODWIN: But you gave it your support.

ELLERTON: True – and at that time I thought so. But come, sir – your son.

GOODWIN: Ah, yes. Five years ago I left him in undisturbed possession of a house that had stood the shocks of thirty years. Young in years but old in mercantile experience. During the panic of '73, while other houses were tottering and falling about us, ours alone stood – like the giant oak, it defied the storm. And now, what do I hear? Rivals say its time has come at last. That proud old fabric is levelled with the dust. [*Turns, with hands up*] Oh, Heaven, do not now desert me! In the evening of my life sustain me as thou hast in other days! [*Sinks on sofa*]

ELLERTON: Would it not be better to act for yourself than to leave everything to Heaven? [*Snaps fingers*]

GOODWIN: I confess, 'tis to you I owe all my misery. Your oily tongue first counselled me to risk my all, and when I warned my son to beware of you, he only laughed.

ELLERTON: But you didn't warn him in time, or he wouldn't stand the chance he now does of ending his days in the State's prison.

GOODWIN: [*Catching him by the collar*] Unsay those words, villain, or, old as I am, I'll strike you dead at my feet!

ELLERTON: Your indignation is very natural, sir, but I have proof of what I say.

GOODWIN: You have proof?

ELLERTON: Yes, sir, right here. [*Takes note out of bill book – puts book back carelessly, so it can be easily gotten at*] Look at this signature and tell me if it is yours?

GOODWIN: It is my writing.

ELLERTON: Look again and be sure.

GOODWIN: No – this is not my writing. It is a forgery.

ELLERTON: So you see that the great house of Goodwin has a worse enemy than I am.

GOODWIN: Oh, wretch! And my son, too! [*Turns to exit, rear arch*] This matter shall be laid bare.

ELLERTON: Stop! [*Holds up check*] Here is the

proof against your son. Render ME powerless?

GOODWIN: I do not understand you.

ELLERTON: Make it to my interest to destroy this note and conceal this evidence.

GOODWIN: I am still in ignorance.

ELLERTON: In other words, give me the right to call Louise my wife.

GOODWIN: [*Coming back slowly*] What – Louise your wife? You, marry Louise? Never! She loathes – she detests you.

ELLERTON I may not be able to inspire love, but I have the power to command respect. We shall see. [*Goes to rear arch*]

GOODWIN: Oh – stay – !

ELLERTON: Come – I will do better. I will advance money to meet your creditors – destroy all proof against your son. We'll infuse new blood in the firm of Goodwin and Company, and it shall live again as Goodwin, Ellerton and Company.

GOODWIN: Oh, anything to save my children from misery – myself from despair!

ELLERTON: I thought you'd change your mind. Come, sir – sign this paper. [*Takes out book and lays it on table*] And you flourish again like a green bay tree.

GOODWIN: [*Reads paper*] Ah, your schemes were well laid and you have me in your power. But as long as you hold that forged check in terror over my head I will not sign.

ELLERTON: [*Tears note up*] Behold my magnanimity. [*Aside*] I didn't tell him, though, I had a second one. [*To Goodwin*] So you see the devil is not always as black as he is painted.

Goodwin starts to sign. Enter Joe L.U.E.

JOE: Stop! [*Tears up paper*] And now, sir, you behold *my* magnanimity.

ELLERTON: The Ferret here?

JOE: Yes, the Ferret – right here.

GOODWIN: Who are you, sir?

JOE: I am the man who scared away the black cat, and there he is!

Points at Ellerton and laughs. Ellerton annoyed

GOODWIN: But I never saw you before.

JOE: Let it suffice for the moment that I am here as your best friend, and Heaven helping me, I'll prove myself one by thwarting yonder devil. Let us call him by his right name for once. DEVIL, did I not tell you that you should feel the weight of my arm – while you rioted at your ease on the ill-gotten gains wrung by the father from the poor starving wretches of Five Points? My mother went to you for assistance after your accursed place had swallowed up my father's all, and when she asked for help, your father struck her. I then, boy as I was, registered a vow to be even with you for that blow, and Heaven has sent me to right the wrong, and drag the guilty one to justice.

ELLERTON: Do not believe him – he is an escaped convict.

GOODWIN: No, impossible!

JOE: Through his hellish machinations and perjury, too, he confines me to the loathsome cells of the State's prison, but I have a paper signed by his confederate, and attested to by the judge of the court before which I was tried, proving that I was innocent and he the guilty one. And he must take my place in that same prison. That is your doom, John Adderly.

ELLERTON: No – no – Joe – stop. Don't say that.

GOODWIN: What, the son of John Adderly that kept a place in the Five Points?

JOE: The same. And you see the father well represented in the son.

GOODWIN: Merciful Providence, how wonderful are thy ways! Twenty years ago, and the night of the great fire, I knew of a similar act done by his father. I heard a cry of distress, and following the sound I found a woman in distress. Aye, dying in the streets. I afterwards learned she had gone to him, asking for a mere pittance. Bread enough to keep herself and two children from starving, after her husband had been ruined by rum, and she thrown from his door and left to die in the street. Those two children are now mine, by adoption, and living under this roof.

JOE: [*To Ellerton*] Oh, villain, pray that it may not fall and crush you!

ELLERTON: Joe Ferris, you have been the bane of my life. YOURS shall now answer for it.

Draws revolver. Joe takes it from him, and holds picture, hesitating to fire

JOE: You deserve death for being such an infamous coward. But I'll not cheat the hangman of such a precious package as you are. [*Gives revolver to Goodwin*] He would become a murderer as well as a forger.

GOODWIN: WHAT? A forger?

JOE: Yes, forger! I know something of this coal transaction. He calls himself the coal agent, but I call him the coal fraud. Why, the coal only exists on the char that he carries in his pocket. Why, he's the whole coal company; transacts all the business. In his pocket, are all the stealings, rolled up in a little bit of a lump. Give it a toss and away it goes. [*Indicates tossing a ball away*]

ELLERTON: But I never forged my father's name.

GOODWIN: But the proof of that has been destroyed.

ELLERTON: So you think, but I have another check.

Shows book that he sticks, carelessly, in his vest pocket. Joe jerks it out

GOODWIN: Villain, you have deceived me in that also!

Enter Policeman, Louise and Aunt Susannah

ELLERTON: What, a policeman here? Arrest that man! [*Points to Goodwin*]

JOE: [*As he tears up check taken from Ellerton's pocket, Tom Goodwin enters L. and stands behind Goodwin, Sr.*] What for?

ELLERTON: For forgery.

JOE: That proof has been destroyed. Arrest THAT man! [*Points to Ellerton*]

ELLERTON: ME? What for?

JOE: For murder. You instigated the Italian to strike the cowardly blow that your arm failed to strike. ARREST that man!

ELLERTON: [*Crossing to Goodwin, Sr.*] But you yourself saw him *destroy* the proof against your son!

JOE: A father will not convict a son.

ELLERTON: But my *oath* will.

JOE: But you are a criminal, and your oath will not be taken seriously.

Women come down and congratulate Joe, as Policeman goes down and puts handcuffs on Ellerton, who stands amazed. Goodwin embraces his son, as curtain falls

ACT IV

A Station house at a Union Pacific Railroad station. See front of script for description of set. At rise, Joe, a Chinaman and three Ladies are discovered, and as curtain ascends, they give three cheers.

JOE: [*Calls*] Come, boys, get those trunks off.

[*Johnnie and several supers enter, and take trunks off left, followed by the Ladies, Johnnie, and the Chinaman. But as Joe calls Johnnie, and Ladies stop*] Johnnie, you escort the ladies over to the ranch, and you'd better stop on your way back, and tell the Chief to send me a few of his braves. Black Cloud and his band are reported at Station 42, and it is possible they may come here. I don't want them to catch us without a guard, as it might invite attack.

JOHN: All right, Joe. Catch on, girls!

Offers arms, which two Girls take and they exit, followed by other Girl and Chinaman, off R.1.E. As Tom Goodwin enters up R. and comes down and slaps Joe on back

TOM: Are you the station agent?

JOE: I believe I am. [*Turns*] Why, Tom Goodwin!

TOM: Joe Ferris, I'm delighted. [*Shakes hands*]

JOE: Where'd you come from?

TOM: Why, from the train, of course!

JOE: And I not there to meet you!

TOM: What in the world brought you out here?

JOE: Oh, Tom, don't ask me. How could I stay in New York after what happened in your house?

TOM: How can I ever repay you for what you did? In a moment of madness I forged my father's name, and you saved me from disgrace and ruin.

JOE: It was a terrible sacrifice, for in doing so I forfeited the good opinion of your family, by revealing the name and conditions of my associates.

TOM: But I investigated, and found you innocent of any crime.

JOE: But I was a gambler, and my associates were men of the lowest stamp. But, remember, I was left alone when a mere boy. I found myself in the streets one night, with clothing scarcely sufficient to protect me from the cold, while vice rolled by me, wrapped in furs. I resolved I would lead such a life no longer, and I became a gambler. My wits were as sharp as theirs. They didn't thrust me aside, but even then, the money wrung from my dupes seems to melt in my hands. So, after passing through an eventful life I have at last settled down as station master at 47th U.P. Railway. By the way, Tom, what ever became of Adderly? You know, he was sentenced for five years for that affair with the Italian. I suppose he is still serving the State?

TOM: About six months ago an uprising took place in the prison, and after killing one guard and nearly killing another he escaped by jumping into the river. Nothing was heard of him for a long time, but just before I left New York I read in the papers that he had been seen around his old haunts.

JOE: He is free, then. That man bears me no good will.

TOM: Yes. They never succeeded in capturing him. But tell me, do you feel contented out here?

JOE: How could I be contented? I sometimes long to be back in New York and I sigh for my old associates – but always the GOOD ones, Tom, remember that. But, Tom, come into the station. [*Starts*]

TOM: But I must go and bring Louise and the rest of the folks.

JOE: What? Louise *here*?

TOM: [*Points to them, as Louise and Aunt Susannah enter R.U., followed by Chinaman*] No, THERE! Louise, allow me to present you to a very dear friend.

LOUISE: Why, Mr. Ferris! I'm more than pleased to meet you here. [*Shake hands*]

AUNT SUSANNAH: Why, Mr. Ferris! [*Tries to kiss him, but he dodges her*] How do you do?

LOUISE: AUNTY! Oh, I'm so glad to find you here ahead of us, Mr. Ferris, for this is to be our new home. And Aunt Susie was afraid we'd have no neighbors, and no one to entertain us. But tell me, how is it that we find you here?

JOE: I have learned that an honest day's work is the best nurse for a good night's sleep.

Chinaman has been trying to pull ribbons off Aunt Susannah's hat, she turns, frightened

AUNT SUSANNAH: What in the world is *that*?

JOE: Well, we haven't named it yet.

AUNT SUSANNAH: Well, it looks exactly like a Chinese firecracker.

CHINAMAN: Me no firecracker, me skyrocket. [*Sits on box, and gets his finger pinched in lid*] Oh, oh, oh.

Joe points to show him, he's sitting on the lid

JOE: See.

Chinaman gets up. Joe shows him the end-

pieces on the box. *Chinaman sits again and grins*

LOUISE: May I have a word with you, Mr. Ferris?

JOE: Certainly.

Tom and Aunt Susannah retire to boxes at back of stage

LOUISE: Why did you leave New York so suddenly, without a word of farewell?

JOE: I loved one far above me. Do you remember, when I sat in the witness box giving evidence against that man, and every word I spoke was carrying me further and further away from her, until I had revealed myself a gambler and the accomplice of this unprincipled man? Then I realized the position in which I stood, and not until then did I realize how hopeless was my love. Even as I sat there I held in my own hand that priceless boon – my pardon signed by the governor, who had heard my prayer, and with tears in his eyes, he bade me "Go and sin no more." That was why I left New York.

LOUISE: But she whom you had loved – Had she loved you in return and bade you to stay – ?

JOE: Then I would have died at her feet.

LOUISE: You were wrong not to disclose your love, for had she been a true woman, she never would have refused such a noble heart as yours.

JOE: Had you been that woman, would you *then* have spoken thus?

LOUISE: I would, indeed.

JOE: Then, 'tis you I love. But until this moment I never even dared to hope to win the love of one so pure and good as you.

Louise turns toward him

LOUISE: Oh, what can I say? That I never loved until I saw you – never knew happiness until you came to our house!

He kisses her

CHINAMAN: Oh, shamee – shamee –

Hides face. Aunt Susannah comes forward with Tom

TOM: What does this mean?

JOE: It means that your sister has consented to become my wife – and that I am the happiest man on the U.P. Road.

AUNT SUSANNAH: [*To Louise*] Then 'tis you he

loves. [*Kisses her. Tom and Joe go up and sit at back*] But don't you know that that is very naughty?

LOUISE: Yes, I know it's naughty, but it's nice.

She goes up-stage and joins Tom and Joe. Joe springs to meet her

AUNT SUSANNAH: I wish I had some nice –

CHINAMAN: [*Runs up to her*] You like some ricee –

Aunt Susannah turns back on him and walks to box opposite R.2.E. Sits down and takes drink out of bottle

CHINAMAN: Ah ha – Melican woman like jig water. Me likee, too. [*Takes bottle out of her hand and drinks. Offers it back several times, but fools her and drinks himself, talking Chinese all the time, and keeps this up till the bottle is empty*] Me makee mashee. [*Sits beside her*] Ah, there my sizee – me stealee you.

Tries to put his arm around her. She jumps quickly – he falls, then chases her

JOE: Here – what is the matter, Tart?

CHINAMAN: [*Joe comes forward with Tom*] Melican woman fightee.

JOE: Come here, Tart. [*To others*] Watch me telephone to China. [*Takes Tart's cue*] Hello, Tart!

CHINAMAN: Hello!

JOE: You're crazy.

CHINAMAN: Me, too. [*Joe turns away laughing*] Now me talkee. [*Takes end of cue*] Hello – hello – hello – [*Jerks his cue – disgusted – jumps on box*]

JOHN: [*Enters R.2.E.*] Supper is ready, Mr. Joe.

CHINAMAN: Hello, Johnnie. Me makee mashee.

JOHN: Who is it? The old girl?

All exit R.3.E., except Joe and Louise and Chinaman, who is on box. Enter Caesar with baggage

CAESAR: Say, look here – [*They are just disappearing in the station*] Where is the colored population goin' to roost?

Joe and Louise stop at door of station. Chinaman hollers and skips R.1.E.

JOE: [*To Caesar*] Why, I thought I would leave you out here to amuse my Indian friends.

CAESAR: Injuns around here? [*Looks scared*]

JOE: Lots of them. You ain't afraid of Indians, are you?

CAESAR: What – me afraid of Injuns? Well, I guess not. Why, my maw used to keep an Injun boarding-house.

JOE: Where?

CAESAR: In Indianapolis.

JOE: [*Quickly*] What's that?

CAESAR: [*Jumps*] Oh, Lord!

JOE: You ain't afraid?

CAESAR: No. I'se just a little bit skeered, that's all.

Exit Louise R.2.E.

JOE: [*Comes forward and takes Caesar by the arm*] You must be very circumspect. There is an Indian around here ten feet high, and mark you, Caesar, he eats a nigger every morning for breakfast.

CAESAR: He eats a nigger every morning *before* breakfast?

JOE: Yes, sir.

CAESAR: That settles it. This nigger don't get up till after dinner.

JOE: [*Crosses to R.2.E.*] Look out for that hat. [*In deep tone*] The bell has rung for it and the Indians are death on a white hat.

CAESAR: Oh, Lord!

JOE: What's that behind you? [*Exit R.2.E.*]

CAESAR: Oh – [*Jumps. Chinaman enters R.1.E., runs into Caesar and exit L.2. After this Caesar is about scared to death. It gets dark*] I wonder what's the matter with that hat. The boys in St. Louis used to holler "Who skinned the cat, Nigger wid the white hat." Oh, how dark it's getting! I wish when I come out here I'd stayed home. If any of them Indians eat this nigger, I'll be doggoned if I don't lay heavy on their stomachs. Oh, but I'm sleepy. I'll go and get something to eat, and then with the blue sky above me and the green grass beneath me, I don't think an earthquake would scare me. [*Indian war-whoop*] Oh, Lord, what's that?

Exit R.U. Enter Indian L.U., goes to station – looks around – beckons. Adderly enters L.3. followed by Chief and Indians. Indians squat around at back of stage. Adderly opposite R.2.E., Chief opposite L.2.E.

CHIEF: White Brother so –

ADDERLY: Don't call me White Brother – call me Indian like yourselves. I would not have the keeper of the station here know that a white man had led you on the war-path.

CHIEF: Did he not say that he would lead the Indian where he could avenge the wrongs of his race? Have we not done so? Has he not seen the Pale-faces scalped – their homes burned, and their women and children carried away captive to the wigwams of Black Cloud's braves? And now, more of the white race turn their faces to the west. Where can the Red Man go? What spot can he call his own? None – but his Mother Earth, to sleep his last sleep. Behold, there is another reason why we must fight. The Iron Horse comes thundering across our plains. Our warriors look aghast, and in vain does Black Cloud tell them that these were the hunting grounds of their fathers, and belong to them. They are filled with fear. And what has the white man given us for all this? Ugh – his fire-water. It steals away the brains of my people and excites them to deeds of violence. The Red Man's hours are numbered.

ADDERLY: You are right, and naught is left but revenge.

CHIEF: Yes – spare neither age nor sex. Kill all.

ADDERLY: But what is to become of the white family that we tracked here?

CHIEF: Their fate will be sealed by the rising sun.

ADDERLY: Yes – kill all. But the women – what of them?

CHIEF: They shall be carried away captives to become the squaws of Black Cloud and his braves.

ADDERLY: That is good. There is much plunder here. Provisions, ammunition, money. All this shall belong to you.

CHIEF: White Chief speak good. Indian take all – and kill.

ADDERLY: All but the women, for the Chief himself wishes one for his squaw.

CHIEF: The White Chief shall have one for his squaw. Indian kill all the rest.

ADDERLY: Yes, kill all that I shall name. The station-keeper is my deadly enemy. Kill him.

CHIEF: Black Cloud kill him.

ADDERLY: He may take away your hunting grounds and not pay you for them, but pay your great Father in Washington and leave you to freeze and starve. Now, the keeper of the station is as cunning as a fox. We must return when all have gone to rest. Fire the station – stampede the horses, and when the sun rises, not one of their cursed tribe shall be left alive.

CHIEF: When does the Iron Horse come back?

ADDERLY: At this time tomorrow, and they must find naught here but smouldering ashes.

CHIEF: White man is black. But they are our enemies and must perish. I will teach them that the Indian, too, knows how to punish and avenge.

Adderly goes to door of station. Chief steps back a step or two, then quickly forward with a yell to his followers, who all spring forward, but Adderly stops them

ADDERLY: Back! Lights are still moving around the station. Back – and defer our purpose for a while.

CHIEF: The White Chief speaks good. Back until I give the signal. Then spring upon them like wolves.

All back to L.U. and L.3. and exit, Adderly being the last. The first Indian who entered runs back to Adderly and raises his knife – wants to enter the station. Adderly catches his arm and forces him off L.U., following him and looking back, shaking his fist at the station

JOHN: [*Enters R.2., with revolver in hand*] Oh, why didn't he wait a minute! Just a minute and I would have plugged him. I wonder where I've seen that face before. In some jail, I guess, for a more hang-dog looking countenance I never saw before. [*Peers around carefully*] That settles it. The first Mr. Injun I see around here will get perforated.

Chinaman makes noise at L.2. Johnnie watches with gun ready

CHINAMAN: [*Lying down*] Don't shootee.

JOHN: Come here, Tart. [*Enter Chinaman, L.2.*] You seen anything of Black Cloud around here?

CHINAMAN: Me no likee Black Cloud.

JOHN: No, you bet you don't. Black Cloud is a very tart Indian.

CHINAMAN: Me tart. Mashee woman.

JOHN: Yes, you are a very tart washerwoman. Say, what did you put starch in my sox for?

CHINAMAN: Me no putee starchee sockee. Me putee sockee starchee.

JOHN: [*Mimics him – shows him revolver*] Do you know what that is? That is a young man's Christian Companion. And it's five volumes all bound in one, and it's loaded with slugs plumb to the muzzle.

CHINAMAN: Muzzle – sluzzle.

JOHN: Yes, muzzle – sluzzle. And if I ever draw a bead on Black Cloud I'll give him a new set of shirt studs.

CHINAMAN: Shirtee studee?

JOHN: Yes – you want one?

CHINAMAN: Me no wantee.

Caesar enters R.1.

CAESAR: It's no use. I can't sleep for those dol-garned mosquitoes.

CHINAMAN: Oh, Black Cloud – Black Cloud –

CAESAR: [*Falls on his knees very frightened; holds up hat*] Oh don't shoot me – don't shoot me – shoot the hat.

JOHN: That ain't an Injun – it's only a nigger.

CAESAR: Yes, I'se only a nigger.

JOHN: Well, it's a good thing, for if you'd been an Indian I'd of blowed the whole top of your head off.

CAESAR: Well, thank the Lord, I'se only a nigger!

JOHN: Where did you come from?

CAESAR: The railroad, of course.

JOHN: Don't get funny now.

CAESAR: I come along wid the white family what's inside.

JOHN: How many of them are there?

CAESAR: About a hundred and fifty.

JOHN: Count them.

CAESAR: Well, dar's de old man and de young man, de two young ladies, and de old woman. Two dogs, a Thomas cat, Big and Little Casino. . . .

CHINAMAN: Fullee hand.

JOHN: That's only a hundred and forty-nine.

CAESAR: An' one respectable gentleman. That's a hundred and fifty.

JOHN: We don't count niggers out here.

CAESAR: You don't?

JOHN: No, we don't.

CAESAR: Well, I guess you counted 'em last election just the same.

JOHN: Did you ever play smarty?

CAESAR: No, but I've played Richard the Third.

CHINAMAN: Oh shootee – shootee!

JOHN: I'll shootee. You shut up. [*To Caesar*] Say, you want to be mighty careful round here. This place is surrounded by Indians.

All close together, C.

CAESAR: Oh, Lord!

JOHN: The very trees is full of them.

CAESAR: Den, fo' de Lord's sake don't shake dat tree.

JOHN: How are you heeled?

CAESAR: How is any nigger heeled? Got a razor.

JOHN: [*To Chinaman*] You – are you heeled?

CHINAMAN: Allee samee Melican man.

JOHN: I'll tell you what we'll do – we'll go hunting for Indians.

They creep around the stage

CAESAR: I pray de Lord we don't find any.

Music all through this. They get startled at loud strains. Business and ad lib. Do this once or twice. Chinaman and Caesar almost fall. At last all three form in line at rear of stage, trot to front with music and sing song. Exit R.1.

ADDERLY: [*Enters L.U.E.*] I had almost forgotten the accursed wire. I must destroy it, for Ferris will telegraph for help. Come here. [*Calls to Indian, who enters L.1.E.*] Well, you must cut that or the chief of the station here will telegraph to his brother, far away, and get help. Do you understand?

INDIAN: Yep, me know. Indian climb like squirrel. See. [*Runs off R.1.E.*]

ADDERLY: Now, Joe Ferris, your hours are almost numbered – you who have thwarted me so often. Through you the plans I have laid for years have been almost dashed to pieces. And now to come here and find everything as if I had planned it. The daughter who so despised me, the father who hated me, and the son who escaped with me! All here, and at last in my power! Oh, I could shout with very joy until the rocks re-echo with laughter! Rejoice, you red-skinned devils! For this I have sold myself to you, and become one of your tribe. My measure of crime is almost complete, for, with the wealth which I now possess and the gold, I am told, is hidden here, I will return to civilization. Then who will recognize me, the elegant gentleman of the East, as the renegade of the West? [*Click, click, click, three blows outside, and the sound of the wire falling*] All hope has fled you now. That little wire held your hopes, but *it* is severed now and eternity yawns at their very feet.

Looking in station door. Indian now enters R.1.E.

INDIAN: Indian do what white man tell him – climb pole – cut wire – so.

ADDERLY: You have done well. But see, lights are still around the station. Come, let's get back for awhile.

They exit L.U.E. at same time. Johnnie and Chinaman enter R.1.E. and Joe enters with lantern, at R.U.E.

JOE: You must be mistaken, there are no Indians around here. Forty-two reported them in *that* vicinity yesterday.

JOHN: Can't I believe my own earsight?

JOE: Well, what did you hear?

JOHN: I don't know, ask the Chinaman. He's just as big a liar as I am.

JOE: Well, Tart, what did you see? Come, speak up!

CHINAMAN: Me see Indian white man – Black Cloud.

JOE: Are you sure it was Black Cloud?

CHINAMAN: Me saby, Black Cloud.

JOE: Then there is, indeed, danger. Johnnie, go and destroy all the liquor in the storehouse. [*Johnnie exits R.*] China, you go and attend to the horses. [*Chinaman exits R.U.E.*] I'm afraid Black Cloud means trouble. [*Picks up wire*] Why, the wire has been cut! This, then, is positive proof that white men are directing the Indians' movements. No Indian would have been cunning enough to cut that wire, and I may expect them down on me at any minute. What shall I do? – I have it! I'll tap the wire here and telegraph to Station 46, and have the train sent back, and perhaps it will get here in time to save us. [*Shaking fist threateningly L.1.E.*] Ah, you red devils, you thought to get ahead of the Ferret, did you? Well, I'll show you the Ferret is a match for sixty red-skinned devils. Now, then, for the apparatus.

Exits R.1.E., as Chinaman enters R.U.E.

CHINAMAN: Melican man like fightee. Chinaman like sleepee in box.

Gets in box R.2. Caesar enters R.U.

CAESAR: I just went and put on my new Rip Van Winkle wig and white-washed my face, and if any of them Indians scalp dis child – Oh – they'll get fooled. Oh, I fixed myself! [*Pulls back coat – shows two big horse-pistols*] Dat am a gun – and dat am a son of a gun. The last time I shot dat one was last Fourth of New Year's, and I was laid up for just seven weeks.

If I turn dis one loose on an Injun, and he don't drap, I'll turn Old Faithful loose, and if he don't drap, then I'm goin' around behind him and see what's holdin' him up, that's all. I'd just like to try this here one on an Injun – just to see how quick he'd move. [*Chinaman raises top of box and lets it drop. Caesar drops on his knees, shaking. Finally looks around, and gets up – sees that there is no one there – is completely changed and scared*] Injun see nigger – Injun run. Injun not run – nigger run. Oh Lawd – here comes one now with a seven pounder on his back.

Exit R.U. Enter Joe with instrument R.1.E. Puts it on barrel – connects wire and works instrument

JOE: Station 46 – [*Speaks while working instrument. He is supposed to be telegraphing. Stops and examines gun. – looks around – telegraphs again*] Come, old man, wake up – wake up! [*Stops and waits again*] Oh, why don't he answer me? [*Very anxious*] Patience, Joe, patience. Don't talk of patience to a man of my temperament! Leave patience to the saints. [*At last machine answers – he listens eagerly*] What do I want? I'll tell you what I want. [*Telegraphs*] Has the U. P. train yet passed your station? Answer me quickly. [*Turns off key of instrument and waits*] God grant that they have not passed there, for before they could reach the next station, which is a great way off, I fear the crisis would have passed and the murdering savages have done their work. [*Instrument on barrel begins to work – tick, tick, etc. He speaks, translating the message as it comes over the wire*] "The train is just entering the station." Thank God for that! [*He goes to instrument and telegraphs*] "Get help and send back the train at lightning speed. I am surrounded by Indians. I have two helpless women to protect, and only about four fighting men. Lose not a moment if you would save human life." [*Stops telegraphing*] There, my pretty little piano, that's the sweetest tune you ever played. And if I am ever a father, you are the only instrument my little ones shall practice on. Now, if they will wait until I get rid of my instrument, I'll promise to handle them a little rougher than their great Father in Washington. [*Rolls barrel off R.1.*] If we are lucky, I guess we will get out of this with a whole skin. [*Indians appear* at L.3. and L.U. *Joe Enters R.1. Tom R.2. Johnnie R.3.*] Give them a warm reception.

All advance and chase Indians off, fighting. Tom and Black Cloud enter R.2., struggling for gun. Black Cloud gets gun and Tom retreats to L.U.E., firing a revolver. Black Cloud levels gun and snaps it as Tom exits L.U.E., followed by Chief Black Cloud. At the same time Caesar enters R.U.E. Falls in C. of stage — kneeling and praying. Indian enters R.1. and rushes to Caesar, scalping him, pulling off the Rip Van Winkle wig which Caesar has over his regular wig. Indian exit L.1. as Caesar jumps up and fires revolver after him. Indian returns and gives a war-whoop, which frightens Caesar, and he runs off R.3.E. Indian follows chasing him, and Caesar re-enters R.1., followed by Indian, who chases Caesar off L.1. Aunt Su-
sannah comes out of station in nightgown and exits hurriedly L.1.E. Chinaman opens box and shoots at her as she runs off. She returns and runs out R.3.E. Chinaman fires another shot and goes out after her. Caesar enters L.2. followed by Indian who catches him, as Johnnie enters L.3., and grabs Indian. All exit. Adderly enters R.3.E., dragging Louise by arm. Black Cloud enters R.U.E. Joe enters R.2., and releases Louise. Johnnie enters L. and shoots at Black Cloud, who chases Johnnie off L.2. Joe and Adderly indulge in a fist fight. Adderly finally falls. Johnnie returns — hands Joe a revolver. Tom and Chief enter R.2.E. Chief and Adderly stand at bay. Train comes on here and stops, and soldiers from train fire at Chief and Adderly, both of whom fall. Louise rushes into Joe's arms, forming the picture as down comes The Curtain.

THE MULLIGAN GUARD BALL

EDWARD HARRIGAN

At the close of the third act of Edward Harrigan's *The Major*, Major Gilfeather casually tossed his cigar into Percival Pop's Fireworks Factory. The stage directions outlined the results: "A great explosion." The characters are "seen by the audience to ascend; the roof splits in pieces, the front of the factory sinks through the stage – debris crashes." And finally, the "bodies descend." After the debacle, one character reported that you "couldn't tell if you were burying a relative or a friend." Such ridiculous catastrophes were standard with Harrigan. He employed the stage directions "melee" and "general melee" with uncommon frequency. "Knockdown and slambang," to use his phrase, were not, however, his sole distinguishing features.

No American dramatist explored New York's low life so lovingly or in such Dickens-like detail. The Germans, the Italians, the Negroes, and particularly the Irish who inhabited Gotham's Lower East Side were his special subjects, and he chronicled every colorful and humorous facet of their rich and impoverished existence. His characters were grocery men, butchers, barbers, dock workers, "river rats," undertakers, pawnbrokers, tailors, and an assortment of lovable bums and waifs. Their locales were never far removed from "Five Points," the junction of Baxter, Worth, and Park Streets in the "Bloody Sixth Ward," a tenement area of alleys, shops, bars, barber shops, and primitive lodgings commonly known as "the vilest place in town." Harrigan called it a place "where vice in rags held carnival all night long." His characters deserted it seldom and briefly for business at the water front, target practice at Spuyten Duyvil, a picnic in Jersey, or a boat excursion to Albany. The stories of the plays were relatively simple, though there was an abundance of action. They dealt with ward politics, the policy racket, body stealing, what would now be called "urban renewal," domestic celebrations and misunderstandings, the battle of the sexes, and, incessantly, clashes among the Irish, Germans, Italians, and Negroes. Richard Harding Davis commented that "as a historian of the war of the races, Mr. Harrigan makes no mistakes."

Of the two million Irish who had entered the country between 1840 and 1860, many had settled on the Lower East Side. By the seventies, when Harrigan began transferring the Sixth Ward's social life to the stage, there was also a sizable German concentration. In 1870 the entry station at Castle Garden cleared 56,000 Irish and 118,000 Germans. Although the inevitable collisions that resulted from squeezing these immigrants into a tight tenement area gave Harrigan many a memorable scene, his reports were never vitriolic, bitter, or off-color. Natural allegiance of course compelled him to treat the Irish tenderly, and their portraits are the most vivid and complete: Dan Mulligan, the easy-going, hard-drinking, practical-joking rogue of the "Mulligan Guard" series, and his devoted wife Cordelia, who (in *Dan's Tribulations*) boasted of their "twenty-foive years" of marriage "wid never an angry word only what passed between ourselves." The W. C. Fields-like creations such as Old Lavender, who, before entering Pop Jones's river-front saloon, informed his companion that he was "going to refresh the inner man with the nutriment which is dispensed by the connoisseur who presides over this cafe . . . the down-town branch of Delmonico's." Felix McIntyre, the itinerant astronomer (in *Squatter Sovereignty*), "royal astronomer to the Duke of Connaught," as he called himself; when he lectured Widow Nolan on the movements of Jupiter, she thought he referred to Jew Peter, a friend who had been confined to Sing Sing for six months. Major Gilfeather (in *The Major*), a lovable con man, who advised Major Bottlegreen on the art of fishing: "If you need luck, put on sham bait, sham bait takes a man into society. Sham bait fills a man with shampagne. Bait your hook with sham when you fish for fortune, fame, or fishes." And though Dan Mulligan did not belong to the tribe of elegant talkers, he demonstrated oratorical talent when he became a candidate for alderman (in *The Mulligan Guard Nominee*): "Fellow citizens and friends of the Mulligan champagne. I arise like the morning sun and I'll never set till the name of Daniel Mulligan is carried from the 14th Ward to Asia, Afghanistan, Parequan, Equidius, Circassian, Balvaria, and the world over." In many a minor portrait Harrigan showed his affection for the Irish immigrant. Young John Murphy (in *The Major*) was detained by the immigration officers because he attempted to smuggle in "eighteen shovels of the County Connaught," which he proposed "to put in our back yard in America and walk over it every morning for luck." In his prison cell he kept up his spirits with Irish songs, though perplexed that he came "out here for liberty, and this is what I get."

Much of Harrigan's repartee was reminiscent of minstrel routines. For example, the following exchange from *The Mulligan Guard Nominee*:

> PETER: Captain you sustain Mister Mulligan in dis canvass?
> CAPTAIN: His canvass is all silk to me.
> PETER: I got a little velvet myself.
> DANIEL: These Skidmores will want muslin after election.

And from *Old Lavender:*

smoke: Is that clock right there?

pop: Yes, it's right there. It hasn't been out of there for ten years.

smoke: I can't see very well tonight – I've been shovelling cracker
dust in an oyster pie factory all day.

Some of Harrigan's verbal turns were remarkably sophisticated and original. O'Dwyer the tailor (in *The Mulligan Guard Picnic*) insisted that he was so devoted to Bridgit Lochmuller that he sewed "buttons on the back of trowsers thinking of her." Major Gilfeather described Coney Island as "the poor man's Saratoga." And Bridgit's report (in *The Mulligan Guard Surprise*) that she was "filled with 'on whou'," or Caleb's pronouncement (in *The Major*) that "too much hilarity breeds contempt," were worthy of Mrs. Malaprop.

Harrigan came naturally by his fondness for the Irish and the Irishman's fondness for the language. Some Harrigans from County Cork had settled in Canada early in the eighteenth century. His father was born in Newfoundland, had gone to sea on a Yankee clipper when he was twelve, and had risen to first mate on a square-rigger on the New York-Liverpool run; but when he married in 1830, he gave up the sea and became a calker at a shipyard on the East River. Edward Harrigan was born on October 26, 1844, a block west of Corlears Hook on the Lower East Side. He abandoned formal education when he was fourteen but later insisted that dropping out had caused him little inconvenience: he had learned "almost everything about the city that it was possible for a boy to learn." For the next four years he worked in the shipyards by day and at night read Emerson and Whitman, took preliminary stabs at writing minstrel routines and songs, and attended the theatre and variety halls. Although there is no record of what he saw, much of what was available contained scenes, characters, and comic routines similar to those he was to exploit so skillfully: John Brougham in *Po-ca-hon-tas;* Wood's, Bryant's and Christy's Minstrels; Mr. and Mrs. W. J. Florence and Mr. and Mrs. Barney Williams with their German and Irish nonsense; and particularly F. S. Chanfrau in *A Glance at New York* and *Mose in California*. Chanfrau as Mose the volunteer fireman, dressed in his ridiculous red shirt and plug hat, always itching to fight a "b'hoy" or a fire, belonged to the same breed as Harrigan's Dan Mulligan. Whether consciously copied or not, certainly Mose was a progenitor of Dan; and the "Mose" series – *Mose in a Muss, Mose in China*, and *Mose's Visit to Philadelphia* – foreshadowed the "Mulligan Guard."

Harrigan made a first stage appearance when he was sixteen, reciting a minstrel-like monologue of his own composition at an amateur night at the Bowery Theatre. His father apparently did not approve and advised him to confine his exhibitions to the shipyard. When he was eighteen, his parents were divorced and his father married a devout Methodist whose insistence on a taut household offended young Ned. He left home, apparently spent some time in New Orleans, came back to New York, and in 1866 set sail for California. Although he now called himself a dock worker, he still wanted to be an actor, and, while working in a San Francisco shipyard, he appeared as a singer for a Temperance Assembly at Dashaway Hall. The assignment produced no revenue but encouraged him to offer his talents to the "melodeon" (variety) establishments. For the next three years, from the fall of 1867 to June, 1870, he sang and played the banjo at the Bella Union, the Olympic, and Gilbert's Melodeon and on the mining-town circuit in California and Nevada.

With his musical talents recognized, he expanded his repertoire by writing sketches, *Irish Comicalities* and *Jessie at the Bar*, and persuading Alex O'Brien, a comedian and dancer, to join him. When O'Brien was shortly committed to a home for inebriates, Sam Rickey took his place. Rickey, a specialist in German and Irish dialects, was also devoted to liquor, and their partnership lasted only until 1871. Billing themselves as "the noted California Comedians" they worked their way back to New York, taking five months of irregular engagements to complete the journey. Finally on November 21, 1870, they opened at the Globe Theatre, 728 Broadway. They appeared sporadically throughout the season with such "comicalities" as *The Mulcahey Twins* and sometimes with Harrigan announced as "the great German comedian," an astonishing billing in the light of his later record. New York success was too much for Rickey. He returned to the bottle with fatal regularity; so in May Harrigan took a place with the Manning Minstrels and headed west.

During the early summer of 1871 in Chicago he searched for a new partner. Happily, he encountered a sixteen-year-old singer, Anthony J. Cannon. They joined forces and for the next fourteen years became so inseparably associated that many thought they bore a single name, "Harriganandhart." The change from "Cannon" to "Hart" was reported to have occurred when a Chicago panhandler acknowledged Cannon's dollar donation with "You sure got a big heart." Tony Hart, as he became known, was born in Worcester, Massachusetts, on July 25, 1855. He quit school when he was nine, became the terror of his neighborhood, was incarcerated in a reformatory at ten, escaped almost immediately, and, identifying himself as "Master Antonio," began singing and dancing in saloons; he took a turn with the circus and then with Bill Arlington's Minstrels. When Harrigan and he met, Hart was best known for his impersonation of a little girl singing "Put Me in My Little Bed." They appeared first as a team at the Winter Garden in Chicago, a dilapidated hall on the third floor of an old office building, then at the Howard Athenaeum in Boston for a two-week engagement beginning on August 14, 1871. Their initial reception was so enthusiastic that the engagement was extended to two months and their salary of seventy-five dollars was doubled. Harrigan's talents as a singer, comedian, and sketch writer and Hart's peculiar abilities as a female impersonator and singer had produced a winning combination.

Hart was so convincing in his female disguise that he is reported to have once fooled a Pinkerton detective, who refused to admit his error until Hart removed his wig. Many attested to his winning manner with a song. Nat C. Goodwin said that "his disposition turned December into May."

After Boston came the Brooklyn Academy of Music, then the Globe and the Union Square in New York, and in December, 1872, Josh Hart's Theatre Comique at 514 Broadway, which was to be their home for several years and where Harrigan met the players for whom most of his later plays were to be written: Johnny Wild and Billy Gray, the Negro impersonators, who assumed the roles of Palestine Puter and Simpson Primrose in the "Mulligan" series, and Mrs. Annie Yeamans, who became permanently identified with Cordelia Mulligan. Once these performers joined Harrigan, they remained with him until the end of his career.

David Braham, the conductor of the orchestra at the Comique, contributed to Harrigan's eventual success in two respects. His eldest daughter, Annie Theresa, became Mrs. Harrigan in 1876, and he composed the music for all of the Harrigan songs. Mrs. Harrigan not only managed the household and raised their seven children, all but one of whom went on the stage,[1] but also kept a sharp eye on the business affairs of the theatre. Certainly the remarkable popularity of the Harrigan plays depended on the half dozen or more new songs incorporated into each. During the late seventies and eighties, it was said that one could not walk the streets of New York without hearing someone singing a Braham tune: "Little Widow Dunn," "My Little Side Door," "Down in Gossip Row," "Cobwebs on the Wall," "The Pitcher of Beer," "Linger Not, Darling," or "Sandy-Haired Mary in our Area."

During these early years at the Comique, Harrigan and Hart shared the evening with the other variety entertainers, performing in such sketches as *The Mixed Couple, St. Patrick's Day Parade,* and several Brougham-like burlesques: *The Two Awfuls (The Two Orphans); Lady of Lions,* with Harrigan as Claude Meddlenot; *Uncle Tom's Cabin,* with Hart as Topsy; and, in honor of King Kalakaua's visit to the United States, *Fee-Gee,* in which Harrigan impersonated a cannibal king from County Sligo and Hart his favorite daughter, Princess Mutton Chops. Many of the standard ingredients of the later plays are clearly apparent in these early sketches. During the seasons of 1873–74 and 1874–75, while continuing with the sketches, Harrigan undertook some slightly longer pieces: *The Italian Padrone; The Donovans,* which introduced a "railroad sensation" and a New York tenement scene; and the first of the "Mulligan" series, simply called *The Mulligan Guard.* After a season on tour extending as far as New Orleans, they returned

---

[1]Two of the children, William and Nedda (now Mrs. Joshua Logan), became well-known performers in their own right.

to New York, leased the Comique, and on August 7, 1876, appeared for the first time under their own management. During the next five years the Comique became a "bright little spot that shines like an oasis of light amid the surrounding gloom of lower Broadway" and provided them with a comfortable profit of over two hundred thousand dollars.

The first years they relied principally on assorted variety entertainment: Fryer's Dogs; Fred A. Plaisted, "champion oarsman and club swinger"; Andrew Gaffney "a towering form of symmetry and strength"; and old and new Harrigan sketches: *The Telephone*, "the sensation of the day," and *The Great In-Toe-Natural Walking Match*, a burlesque on the craze for walking contests. Gradually, full-length Harrigan plays were introduced: *Malone's Night Off, or The German Turnverein Festival; My Boy Dan; Christmas Joys and Sorrows*, a misleading title for a comic treatment of body-stealing, undertakers, and gravediggers; *Old Lavender* (initially called *Old Lavender Water*), featuring his first and finally his most popular fancy-talking, beloved rogue. On September 23, 1878, he returned to the Mulligans with a relatively full-length play, *The Mulligan Guard Picnic*. It is said to have taken forty minutes in performance. Although reasonably successful, it did not match the record of *The Mulligan Guard Ball*, which opened on January 13, 1879, and ran until May 24, his first play to exceed a hundred performances, the commonly accepted magic number for a hit. After closing at the Comique, he moved it across the river for another week at the Brooklyn Park Theatre. Almost invariably throughout the remainder of his career, he gave Brooklyn two to three weeks after concluding his New York season.

Harrigan quickly responded to the public's judgment. The next two seasons (1879–80 and 1880–81) belonged exclusively to the Mulligans: a reconstructed *Mulligan Guard Picnic, The Mulligan Guard Surprise, The Mulligan Guard Christmas, The Mulligan Guard Chowder, The Mulligan Guard Nominee*, and *The Mulligan Guard Silver Wedding*. The six plays filled the two seasons. Although he never used the title again and only *The Mulligan Guard Ball* was retained in his repertoire, both *Cordelia's Aspirations* (November, 1883, to April, 1884) and *Dan's Tribulations* (April to June, 1884) explored the further adventures of the family. In the first, Dan and Cordelia attempted unsuccessfully to adjust to the high living required by their new location on Madison Avenue. Dan obliged his wife by taking up the gentlemanly art of painting, though he progressed no further than painting a red-white-and-blue mustache on a portrait of Washington. In the second, they had returned to the comfortable miseries of "Mulligan's Alley."

Like the serial dramas of television, each new play began where the preceding one left off; it reached the stage one day after the previous closing, with the same characters and the same actors. Each play introduced its own set of new songs and each had its own special "knockdown and slambang." For example, in the *Nominee* half the crew on the Albany boat threw the other half overboard, and in the *Chowder* cats jumped out of the chowder pots. Animals were frequently assigned substantial roles in the Harrigan plays. No doubt he had noted their stage successes on the variety bills.

With the Mulligan series Harrigan caught the theatrical formula from which he never deviated, focusing exclusively on the characters and the area he knew. He is reported to have sat for hours on park benches, observing characters and copying snatches of dialogue. Although he was quick with the idiom and could turn out two or three plays a year, in the total theatrical process he regarded the transfer of the material to the stage as the most telling step. As he once said, "You can buy the text of *Hamlet* for fifteen cents, but you must look long and far for your Hamlet." He was meticulously attentive to costumes and scenery, regularly prowling the streets and alleys of the Sixth Ward searching for authentic and eccentric costumes. Many a startled denizen surrendered a shabby coat when Harrigan opened his purse. He reported that his Old Lavender ensemble consisted of a coat from a pawnshop, pants from a beggar, shoes from a Bleecker Street bricklayer, and, for a wig, a discarded hairpiece retrieved from an ash can. His settings represented recognizable locales; "Mulligan's Alley," for example, is said to have borne a marked resemblance to the Sixth Ward's "Murderers' Alley." Harrigan demanded that the settings participate in the dramatic action. Practical doors and windows, second-story rooms, disappearing walls, and collapsing ceilings were common. Apparently Harrigan prepared models of the settings even before he began writing. On one occasion he is reported to have bet with his scenic artist, Mr. Witham, that he could write the play faster than Witham could build and paint the scenery. Harrigan won by a few hours. "See model" commonly appeared as the initial stage direction in his manuscripts. Such precisely detailed scenic representations required visual rather than verbal descriptions. "Business at rehearsal" was another recurring stage direction. These "business at rehearsal" sequences are said to have often consumed three to five minutes in performance. Clearly Harrigan's plays were built in the theatre, not in the study.

When the Comique was torn down after the 1880–81 season, operations were transferred farther uptown to the old Globe at 728 Broadway, where Harrigan and Rickey had made their first New York appearance. They redecorated, changed the name to Harrigan and Hart's Theatre Comique, and raised the price scale from fifteen-to-seventy-five cents to twenty-five-cents-to-a-dollar. They opened here on August 29, 1881, with *The Major* – Harrigan appearing as Major Gilfeather, Mrs. Yeamans as Widow Nolan, and, antedating G. B. Shaw, Hart as Henry Higgins, an Englishman who "dropped his 'h's' like hail on a roof." Beginning on January 9, 1882, and until June 3, *Squatter Sovereignty* took over the theatre for 175 performances, exploring life among the squatters in the shanty town along the East River. Here the principal "melee" involved a clash between two Irish clans, the McGuires and the Mc-Intyres, with ducks, feather beds, stovepipes, and bedsteads for weapons. When the Dutch appeared, the Irish united against their common enemy.

During the following three and a half seasons, in addition to *Cordelia's Aspirations* and *Dan's Tribulations*, they presented *McSorley's Inflation*, a satire on the Salvation Army; *Mordecai Lyons*, with Harrigan as a Jewish pawnbroker (apparently his brogue was ill-concealed – one reporter said he made the jew's-harp sound like an Irish harp, and the *Herald* called it their "first distinct failure"); *The Muddy Day*, detailing the battles between two rival garbage-scow captains, with the Irish captain proposing to fill New York harbor with sufficient silt to ground the British ships; an expanded version of *The Mulligan Guard Ball* (according to the *Herald* the lengthening had not improved it); and *Investigation*, featuring the balcony scene from *Romeo and Juliet* (Harrigan and Yeamans). On December 23, 1884, in the seventeenth week of *Investigation*, the theatre burned down.

The catastrophe extended beyond the loss of the building and its contents, though that in itself was unfortunate enough. Harrigan's father, who was then managing the box office, had failed to pay the insurance premiums; and Hart's brother-in-law, the night watchman, had left his post two hours before the fire. The resulting family battle released antagonisms between the part-ners' wives. They both badgered their husbands – Annie insisting that Gertie Hart had been getting fatter parts than she deserved, and Gertie advising Tony that the team's success depended on him and he had not been prop-erly rewarded. With such a concentration of family in the Harrigan-and-Hart enterprise, it was surprising that they had got on so well for so long. Martin Hanley, the manager, was Braham's brother-in-law. Harrigan's half-brother Warren and his older brother William worked in the front of the house. Har-rigan's son Eddie, Braham's son George, and Annie Yeaman's daughters Lydia and Jennie had all performed from time to time.

A temporary truce was effected for the remainder of the season, and the new play, *McAllister's Legacy*, featuring a scene on the New York Stock Exchange, opened on schedule on January 5, 1884, at the Park Theatre. In March they moved to the Fourteenth Street Theatre for brief engagements of *The Major* and *Cordelia's Aspirations*, and on May 9 Harrigan and Hart appeared togeth-er for the last time in New York. Their partnership was finally dissolved on June 13, after a two-week engagement in Brooklyn. (Manager Sinn at the Park refused to release them from their contract.) Breaking up the Harrigan-

and-Hart combination shook New York so violently that even Mayor William R. Grace interceded, but with no success.

Harrigan adjusted to the separation more easily than Hart. After two disappointing road tours and a brief engagement in New York, Hart made his final appearance at Boston's Howard Athenaeum in May, 1887. The following year he was committed to the Worcester Insane Asylum, where he died on November 4, 1891.

Although audiences must have missed Hart, Harrigan continued through the next ten seasons without perceptible diminution of his popularity. He performed several old favorites and introduced a series of new offerings: *The Grip* (1885); *The Leather Patch* (1886), another undertaker and body-stealing play; *The O'Reagans* (1886); *McNooney's Visit* (1887); *Pete* (1887), in which Harrigan played a "faithful Negro servant"; *Waddy Googan* (1888), which concentrated on Italian rather than Irish types and in which Harrigan played an Italian character as well as Waddy; and *The Lorgaire* (1888), which the *Herald* called just "as purely an Irish play as *The Shaugraun*."

During the summer of 1889, Harrigan toured to the West Coast while his new theatre on Thirty-fifth Street, just east of Sixth Avenue, was under construction. The new Harrigan Theatre opened on December 29, 1890, with *Reilly and the Four Hundred*,[2] the story of a pawnbroker (Irish rather than Jewish, at the insistence of Mrs. Harrigan) who tried to accommodate himself to high society. The new play achieved a run of 202 consecutive performances, the longest of his career. The next two seasons were devoted almost exclusively to repeats of such earlier successes as *The Mulligan Guard Ball* and *Cordelia's Aspirations*. The last of these featured a sewer-gas explosion – Harrigan had not deserted "slambang."

After his son Ned died of a ruptured appendix on February 17, 1895, Harrigan was unable to steel his nerves to performances of *The Major*. He dismissed the company and leased the theatre to Richard Mansfield.[3] Thereafter he never operated his own theatre or played a full season. His final plays were *Marty Malone* (1896) and *Under Cover* (1903), still with the familiar Irish, German, and Negro types. From time to time he appeared at the Bijou and the Murray Hill theatres in revivals of his own plays, occasionally in small parts in other plays (Clyde Fitch's *The Bird in the Cage* [1903]). He took a short turn on the Keith and Proctor vaudeville circuit in half-hour versions of his successes; expanded the adventures of his Irish family into a novel, *The Mulligans* (1901), "dedicated to the memory of Tony Hart"; and

---

[2]Delmonico's Ballroom at Fifth Avenue and Twenty-sixth Street could accommodate only four hundred, hence the magic number defining New York's "upper-crust" society.

[3]Mansfield renamed it the Garrick. It was used by Jacques Copeau when he visited this country in 1917, and in 1919 it became the first Broadway home of the Theatre Guild. The Garrick was torn down in 1932.

spent four seasons (1904–1908) on the road in his old favorites. When he appeared for the last time in New York at the Lambs' Gambol at the Metropolitan Opera House on May 9, 1909, he received a ten-minute ovation. He died on June 6, 1911. The *New York Times* obituary reported that "he served his era well and helped to lighten the cares of life."

He not only served his era, he now serves the social and theatre historian. No dramatist, novelist, or short-story writer of his time committed himself so completely to the dark streets, back alleys, water fronts, and crowded tenements of New York's Lower East Side, an area "out of bounds" to polite society. His eighty to ninety sketches and thirty-five or more plays[4] provide a remarkably vivid social history of the inhabitants of this region.

Some earlier plays and entertainments had explored the pathetic, farcical, and theatrical possibilities of life among the lowly: Boucicault's *The Poor of New York* (1857), with its life on a "cross-street – Five Points" and around Union Square and with a spectacular conflagration. Daly's *Under the Gaslight* (1867), with local scenes of the "Hudson River water front," and "basement life in New York." And, of course, the Negro minstrels, John Brougham's burlesques, and Chanfrau's "Mose" plays. Harrigan may not have set a fashion, but lines of continuity are clearly evident in the work of his immediate successor, Charles Hoyt, and later in such plays as Montague Glass's *Potash and Perlmutter* (1913), Anne Nichols's *Abie's Irish Rose* (1922), Elmer Rice's *Street Scene* (1929), and Sidney Kingsley's *Dead End* (1935). No other dramatist before or after, however, devoted himself so intensely, perceptively, and delightfully to the immigrants and sons of immigrants who crowded into the Lower East Side.

Harrigan's audiences bore a marked resemblance to the characters on his stage. During the late seventies and eighties, ward politicians never risked a political assembly on the night of a Harrigan opening. They and their constituents demanded the first view of such new scenes as Cordelia discovering all the stage aldermen slumbering and snoring from too much refreshment and pleading, "Whatever will I do?" Dan's reply roused the politicians in front, if not those on stage: "Lave them be. While they sleep, the city's safe." Most regular theatrical reviewers saw little "copy" in Harrigan beyond reporting the latest "knockdown and slambang." Occasionally a critic recognized that "what Dickens was to London in his novels and Zola to Paris, Mr. Harrigan is to New York in his plays," and William Winter once remarked that his characterizations were "entirely as artistic as Jefferson's Rip." Only W. D. Howells recognized his essential quality and gave him serious attention. In the July, 1886, issue of *Harper's* he wrote:

[4]An accurate tabulation is impossible. Harrigan wrote rapidly and revised, doctored, and elaborated earlier material, always for immediate demands of the theatre. He never printed his plays and had little concern for preserving his manuscripts for posterity.

The Mulligan Guard Ball

THE MULLIGAN GUARD.

Composed and arranged by DAVID BRAHAM.

We crave your con - de-scension, We'll

tell you what we know Of marching in the Mulligan Guard from Sli - go ward below. Our

Captain's name was Hussey, a Tipper - ra - ry man, He carried his sword like a Russian duke, when-

-ever he took com - mand. We shoulder'd guns, and march'd, and march'd a - way, From

FORWARD MARCH. *f*

Bax - ter street, 'we march'd to Avenue A, With drums and fife, how sweet - ly they did

1st.   2d.

play, As we march'd, march'd, march'd in the Mulligan Guard. We Guard........

Dal Segno

After the Second Verse.

f

5

2

When the band play'd Garry Owen,
Or the Connamara Pet;
With a rub a dub, dub, we'd march
In the mud, to the military step.
With the green above the red, boys,
To show where we come from,
Our guns we'd lift with the right shoulder shift,
As we'd march to the bate of the drum.—Chorus.

3

Whin we got home at night, boys,
The divil a bite we'd ate,
We'd all set up and drink a sup
Of whiskey strong and nate.
Thin we'd all march home together,
As slippery as lard,
The solid min would all fall in,
And march with the Mulligan Guard.—Chorus.

... Mr. Harrigan accurately realized in his scenes what he realizes in his persons; that is, the actual life of this city ... Irish-American phases in their rich and amusing variety, and some of its African and Teutonic phases. It is what we call low life, though whether it is essentially lower than fashionable life is another question. ... In his own province we think he cannot be surpassed. The art that sets before us all sorts and conditions of New York Irishmen, from the laborers in the street to the most powerful of the ward politicians and the genteelest of the ladies of that interesting race, is the art of Goldoni – the joyous yet conscientious art of the true dramatist in all times who loves the life he observes. ... In fact, nothing could be better than the neatness, the fineness, with which the shades of characters are given in Mr. Mulligan's Irish people; and his literary conscientiousness is supplemented by acting which is worthy of it. ... Mr. Harrigan is himself a player of the utmost naturalness, delicate, restrained, infallibly sympathetic; and we have seen no one on his stage who did not seem to have been trained to his part through entire sympathy and intelligence. ... Loving reality as we do, we cannot do less than cordially welcome reality as we find it in Mr. Harrigan's comedies. Consciously or unconsciously, he is part of the great tendency toward the faithful representation of life which is now animating fiction.

That Harrigan drew *The Mulligan Guard Ball* and other plays in the series directly from life is conveniently reinforced by the *History of the Mulligan Guard* (1874), an anonymously published volume that purported to record the true-life history of the Guard. Presumably the Mulligan Guard was organized by Mike and Paddy McGloin one evening in 1873 while they sat drinking and playing cards in Widow Mahoney's store and saloon.[5] They wished to honor their local hero, Terrence Mulligan, "Assistant Alderman of the red-hot Seventh" and the "best Irishman in Ameriky." With a ten-dollar donation from Mrs. Mahoney, on the assurance that her establishment would be their headquarters, and with fifty dollars from their patron, they assembled their assorted shakos, uniforms, ribbons, medals, and swords from the pawnshops in the area. Michael Hussey, a longshoreman who boasted of having rescued at least one person from drowning each year for thirty-five years, was designated captain. The group's knowledge of military decorum was, of course, rudimentary, and they were normally further handicapped by the effects of the liquor required for their ritual. The author reported that at one of the early drills the "Captain was showing the effects of the 'milk' he had taken, and was giving impossible orders, mixing the members of his command up in a fearful mess," in spite of the fact that he referred regularly to his copy of *Hardee's Tactics*. Many of the amusing catastrophes of this "real-life" Guard resembled Harrigan's "knockdowns and slambangs." One evening Widow Mahoney tumbled over one of the smaller members. She caught Paddy to break her fall, brought him to the floor with her, and in the general melee tipped over a tub of pickles,

---

[5]The Irish are said to have established their pseudo-military groups because immigrants were excluded from the official militias.

a box of smoked herring, and a basket of potatoes. The famous "Mulligan Guard March" evolved one evening after a particularly high-scoring target practice and an appropriately sumptuous dinner. Nothing could match "the inspiration of success and whiskey, two of the greatest incentives of our nature." It was "a regular Seventh Ward lay-out, and no mistake. A pound of crackers, a pound of cheese, and a square gallon of whiskey. Of course, there was too much cheese and too many crackers, but being generous men, they gave this surplus to the boys who accompanied them to the sport, and absorbed the red-eye themselves. . . . There are great and momentous occasions when the spirit of a people will culminate in a song or hymn that will decide their destinies and create character for the future historian. Like the 'Marselaise' [sic], 'God Save the King,' and 'Yankee Doodle' the words of the 'Mulligan Guard' were not written; they sprang into wild and burning existence on this occasion."

History is inconsistent with the "true" story reported above; the "Mulligan Guard March" was apparently written by Harrigan in 1872 and performed by him and Hart in Chicago in 1873. If its origins are hazy, its later history is not. Harrigan's marching song became the trade-mark for his Mulligan Guard, a regular feature of Braham's overture even for a non-Mulligan play, one of the most popular tunes of the last quarter of the century – not only in New York and across the country but also in Paris and London, and even in Rudyard Kipling's India. His British regiment in *Kim* (1901) slightly altered the lyrics but retained the original tune.

No single Mulligan play can, of course, give the full range of comic adventures which Harrigan invented for his lovable tribe. *The Mulligan Guard Ball*, however, introduces the principal participants, with the exception of Mrs. Welcome (Rebecca) Allup (played by Hart), and gives an inviting introduction to the farcical escapades which came so naturally to them and their author.

Harrigan was not disposed to discourse on methods of composition or his attitudes toward the theatre. The plays spoke for themselves. Only on two occasions did he express himself at any length. After Howells's article appeared, A. M. Palmer, manager of the Madison Square Theatre, commented that the Harrigan plays were unworthy of serious consideration. They did not truly represent American society, they dealt only with types, they were simply "prolongations of sketches." To the first charge Harrigan replied: "Whoever votes the Republican or Democratic ticket in these United States must be an American, no matter what may be his mother tongue or color. So I class my works as American, and the greatest compliment paid to my plays by foreigners is that they do not understand them." And to the second: "The phrase 'a prolongation of sketches,' coined by Mr. A. M. Palmer, is not well put regarding my plays. I would say 'a continuity of incidents,' with some simple reason for their dovetailing, and each link on the string sustained by some natural motive that calls for the building of the entire stage structure. In this principle of playmaking, or sketch-prolonging, we find reason for the character-drawing which should be the one great aim of the dramatist. . . . Laughter and tears should be the component parts. The sunshine is not appreciated without the shade."

In the February 2, 1889, number of *Harper's Weekly*, Harrigan joined Bronson Howard, Augustin Daly, and William Gillette for a symposium on "American Playwrights on the American Drama." Here he described his own work as clearly and succinctly as any American dramatist. His comments supply the only key necessary for an understanding of the Harrigan plays:

. . . Perhaps the only general rule of valuing a dramatic composition is by applying the question, 'Does it contain enough powerful, interesting, humorous, or beautiful features to attract and hold public attention. . . . At the outset of my career I found that whenever I tried to portray a type, I was warmly applauded by the audience, and praised by the press the next day. . . . Though I use types and never individuals, I try to be as realistic as possible. . . . Each drama is a series of photographs of life today in the Empire City. . . . If I have given undue prominence to the Irish, and Negro, it is because they form about the most salient features of Gotham humanity, and also because they are the two races who care the most for song and dance. There are at least three hundred organizations in New York like the Mulligan Guards, and probably fifty like the Full Moons. . . .

In constructing a plot, I use one that is simple and natural – just like what happens around us every day . . . while doing my best to obtain realism in the plot, I try to avoid that whose sole value is local or temporary, and construct something that will interest and amuse ten or twenty years hence. . . . [After completing the first draft of a play] my work, unlike that of most playwrights, is just begun. The next stage is "smoothing and brightening the raw material." Here I elaborate what situations I have sketched out and create new ones, arrange antitheses between the characters and between different scenes, increase the wit and humor of the dialogue and the fun or nonsense of the climaxes. The third stage sees it cast and rehearsed. . . . The first stage is the shortest, and the third the longest of the three.

. . . Polite society, wealth, and culture possess little or no color and picturesqueness. The chief use I make of them is as a foil to the poor, the workers, and the great middle class [whose] trials and troubles, hopes and fears, joys and sorrows, are more varied and more numerous than those of the Upper Ten. Whoever puts them on the stage appeals to an audience of a million. . . . And human nature is very much the same the world over. It thins out and loses all strength and flavor under the pressure of riches and luxury. It is most virile and aggressive among those who know only poverty and ignorance. It is also then the most humorous and odd.

. . . In the realism which I endeavor to employ I believe in being truthful to the laws which govern society as well as to the types of which it is composed. A playwright drops to a low level when he tries being a moralist, but to a much lower level when he gilds vice and sin and glorifies immorality. . . . Though he make the drunkard a source of infinite merriment to the multitude, he will not conceal the rags, misery, and disease which follow in his footsteps. Though he discover virtue in criminals and tramps, he will not be blind to the qualities which outweigh and crush it down; and above all he will portray the fact that right-doing, kindness, and good nature are in the majority and "control the machine." . . . Though there are shams everywhere to be pricked and ridiculed, and humbugs to be exposed and laughed out of existence, these are only incidents which, though they appear and disappear incessantly, are not parts of the real humanity beneath. The adage "to hold the mirror up to nature" is as applicable to the swarming myriads of New York as to the Greek warriors before Priam's city, or the lords and nobles who surround the Tudors.

THE MULLIGAN GUARD BALL

EDWARD HARRIGAN

CHARACTERS

DANIEL MULLIGAN	MAGGIE KIERNEY
CORDELIA MULLIGAN	AUGUST SNEIDER
TOMMY MULLIGAN	MISTER ROSENFELT
GUSTAVUS LOCHMULLER	MISTER GARLIC
BRIDGET LOCHMULLER	CAROLINE WILLIAMS
GUSTAVUS LOCHMULLER, JR.	THE SKIDMORE GUARD AND LADIES
KATRINE LOCHMULLER	THE MULLIGAN GUARD AND LADIES
SIM PRIMROSE	TWO NEGRO WENCHES
BROTHER PALESTINE PUTER	SIX DUTCH BUTCHERS
WALSINGHAM MC SWEENEY	

ACT I. Scene 1

C. D. chamber plain; nice supper table C. with three chairs; table neatly set. Closet L. of C. D. At opening Mrs. Mulligan discovered at closet and Daniel Mulligan at table. Music.

DAN: Cordelia, I though I tould you to buy the bread at the *Piano* Bakery.

MRS. MULLIGAN: [*Bringing loaf of bread from closet*] They charge ten cents a loaf at the Johanna Bakery, and I get this one for five at the grocery store.

Enter Tommy Mulligan, C. D.

DAN: I don't want you to get the bread from the Johanna Bakery, but the Piano Bakery.

TOMMY: [*Takes chair side of table*] Not the Piano or Johanna Bakery, Pop, but the *Veenna*, and if I don't get *Veenna*, I want toast.

DAN: [*R. H. lifting bread*] I tould your mother you wouldn't ate that.

TOMMY: [*L. H.*] I rather tackle a mahogony sandwich.

MRS. MULLIGAN: [*C.*] That'll do, the pair o' ye. [*Pours out tea*] Drink your tea. I want to go out to buy your father a pair of galluses.

TOMMY: You're gallus enough now, eh Pop?

DAN: Tommy, I saw the day, before you was born, when the old Mulligan Guards that was christened after me, would come down to my distillery in Jackson Street.

TOMMY: How did you lose that distillery, Pop?

DAN: I had a hundred barrels of whiskey in the distillery, and it was a very hot day in summer, and when I closed up the place I forgot to hoist the window, and in the morning the sun shone through the window on the whiskey, and the barrels caught fire, and burnt the place up.

TOMMY: It must have been pooty hot whiskey.

DAN: Hot! When a man 'ud take two drinks of it, I'd have to turn the hose on him.

MRS. MULLIGAN: Don't mind him, Tommy.

TOMMY: Pop, you've swelled my head for two or three weeks, with that kind of chin.

DAN: If you'd go to bed early nights, the swelling 'ud go down.

TOMMY: Was the place insured? Did you have a policy on it?

DAN: The policy office up stairs was burnt out too.

MRS. MULLIGAN: Don't mind him, Tommy, he's joking.

TOMMY: [*Pulls out tickets*] Pop, I've sold twenty tickets for the Mulligan Ball to-morrow night, and I got the young Mulligans together and we're going down there in uniform.

MRS. MULLIGAN: Won't that be fine, Daniel?

DAN: Have you the money for the tickets? If you have give it to me, and I'll turn it in to the treasurer.

TOMMY: No, I hav'n't got it. I'll collect it after the ball, and give it to you. Some of the old Mulligans need sugar puty bad.

MRS. MULLIGAN: Sugar? Are they fond of it, Tommy?

DAN: Cordelia, the sugar we mane don't come from New Orleans, but from Washington, D. C. where it's made by the yard.

MRS. MULLIGAN: Sugar by the yard? Did I ever hear the like of it.

TOMMY: He means money. Why don't you tell her? What do you want to be slinging taffy for all the time.

MRS. MULLIGAN: Taffy, Tommy? No, sir, you'll not ate any taffy. It's destroyed the teeth of Mr. Brady's boy, entirely.

DAN: There's that double breasted frock coat of mine on the chair there. [*Points R. H. to chair where coat is*] Fix the button hole, so as I can wear me boquet next Sunday.

MRS. MULLIGAN: [*Going to chair; seriously*] Daniel, won't you wear the old Mulligan soger clothes at the ball to-morrow night? I'd like you to. They become you so.

TOMMY: No, Mother, there's no uniform going to be worn but what the young Mulligan Guard wear. We're all young fellows together and we don't want any millers with us, the old timers would give the hop away.

DAN: Look here, Tommy. There's two of the old Guards, Tom McSweeney, and Jerry Gilmartin; they wanted me to ax of ye a favor.

TOMMY: What is it? If it's a borry, my finger's up.

DAN: They wanted me to tell ye, they was pioneers in the old Mulligan Guard, before the war, and they've their axes and Russian hats, and they wanted to go to the ball ahead of the young Mulligans. Lave them go, Tommy, I owe McSweeney fove and Gilmartin ten, that'll aise me up.

TOMMY: All right, Pop, they can go, but I want 'em sober, you understand. Have a cigar? [*Takes out cigar, lights it. Dan lights his cigar, and it blows up*]

MRS. MULLIGAN: [*Starting up and putting coat on chair which Tommy left, L. of table*] Oh, oh! Daniel are ye hurt?

TOMMY: What's the matter, Pop?

DAN: [*Bus.*] Ha – ha – ha – that's first rate. Tommy, you had me that time, Tommy. [*Shaking hands with Tommy*] Put it there! That's an old game with me.

MRS. MULLIGAN: What was it, Daniel?

DAN: Nothing, Cordelia. Only Tommy gave me one of the blue light cigars and there's more Havana than Connecticut, and it don't agree in the mix, so it evaporated. How's that, Tommy? She'd never drop if it was hailing dominoes. [*Going to closet to get pipe*]

TOMMY: [*Lighting cigar and sets at table*] Mother, is me plaid pants fixed for to-morrow night?

MRS. MULLIGAN: I have to patch them, Tommy, I'll do it to-morrow.

TOMMY: That settled it, I don't wear me plaids. [*Aside*] I'll give the tailor, Sneider a stand up for a new suit, and charge it to the old man here. I've got to get togs, somewhere, I can't be married in these! [*Dan coming down to table R. H. with pipe. Tommy offers fresh cigar*] Have a fresh cigar, Pop?

DAN: No, Tommy, they're too fresh for me. [*Lighting pipe*] I've a sinecure on the pipe here, and there's nothing crooked about it.

TOMMY: That's the reason I ain't fetched me girl, Katy Lochmuller up to the house lately.

Dan Mulligan walks quickly

MRS. MULLIGAN: Katy Lochmuller is a rale nice girl, Tommy, and her father Mister Lochmuller, the butcher, has never said a word about the bill we owe him. [*Takes small book and reads from*] 25 porterhouse; Tommy, you know you always ate these 8 legs of mutton; corn beef; 35 dollars.

TOMMY: The bill is all right, Mother, but what I'm kicking about is this. I fetched Katy up here, and he lights that funnel with navy tobacco, and what's the consequence? She sez, "Tommy, I want to go home," before I've chinned five minutes.

DAN: Tommy, listen here. I'm not kyding you now, Tommy. What do you lave the house for when Mary O'Brien calls? Have you no head on you at all? Hasn't her father, John O'Brien, the contractor thousands of dollars? Hasn't he a contract to put a wall around New York? Wasn't he a member of the old Mulligan Guard and a friend of mine? Didn't Mary O'Brien send you an Albany with her picture in it? She loves the ground you walk on, Tommy, and –

TOMMY: Oh cheese – cheese –

MRS. MULLIGAN: [*Going to closet and bringing cheese*] Here's all that's left, Tommy. Orange county, too. [*Offering cheese*]

TOMMY: No, I don't want any cheese, Mother.

MRS. MULLIGAN: [*Going back*] Oh, I thought you axed for it.

TOMMY: Say, Pop, Mary O'Brien is a nice girl. She's a lady, but there aint no style about her. Now I'm a single young feller, but if ever I marry, I'll marry Katy Lochmuller.

Enter Gustavus Lochmuller, a butcher with a string of sausages, C. D.

DAN: Tommy, understand me. The name of Mulligan will never be varnished with the name of Lochmuller. The Divil a Dutch drop of blood will ever enter this family. And I want you to understand it, too.

Lochmuller in eagerness at back

TOMMY: That's all right, Pop. Katy Lochmuller's a lady.

LOCHMULLER: [*At back, aside*] You bet your sweet life.

MRS. MULLIGAN: And her father, Mister Lochmuller, the butcher, is a fine man too, and we owe him a bill.

LOCHMULLER: [*With bill*] Und I'll get it too.

DAN: Lochmuller is a friend of mine, and –

LOCHMULLER: Maybe –

TOMMY: Of course he is. Aint he putting up all the meat for the ball supper to-morrow night?

DAN: He'll do no more for the Mulligan Guard than I will. Don't I give me own house up for a supper room to-morrow night?

TOMMY: Cert! But what have you soured on Katy for?

DAN: I sour on no one, Tommy, but before I'll see you throw yourself away in a Dutch family, I'll tie a stone round me feet and anchor meself to the Battery, and Tommy I'm not too ould but I can lick any Dutchman.

LOCHMULLER: [*Lays sausages on chair L. of table*] Mister Mulligan, I'm nothing but a German, und you have insulted my Katrina, so now make up your words good. [*Preparing to fight*]

MRS. MULLIGAN: Oh, Mister Lochmuller! [*Gets in front*]

DAN: Tommy, will you second me?

TOMMY: Hold on, Pop, what are you doing? Don't you know you owe him a bill?

DAN: Tommy, coax him down to Murphy's back room, and you can lock the door on us, I'll make him buy more porous plasters.

LOCHMULLER: Mrs. Mulligan, I want my 35 dollars. [*Presents bill*] Dares my bill. You want to insult my face und rub it out too; I vant my money.

TOMMY: Mister Lochmuller, Pop didn't prefer to you, he was talking about Lochmuller, the shoemaker. [*Aside to Dan*] I'm giving him a stiff for the thirty-five.

DAN: I tumble, Tommy, I tumble.

LOCHMULLER: I'm a German, my father fought in der Franco Prussian var. I'm not afraid, Mrs. Mulligan.

MRS. MULLIGAN: You're mistaken, Mister Lochmuller, my husband was spaking of the shoemaker.

TOMMY: Come here, Pop, [*Bringing Dan down*] Mr. Lochmuller, Pop's a friend of yours.

LOCHMULLER: Tommy, I respect your father, Mister Mulligan, und de old Mulligan Guards, und de young Mulligan Guards, und I'm going to take my wife und my daughter Katrina to de ball to-morrow night.

DAN: [*Aside to Tommy*] Tommy, I'll lick him after the ball.

TOMMY: Shake. [*Placing hands of Dan and Lochmuller*]

DAN: There's me hand.

LOCHMULLER: Und dares mine. Hold on! You give me de grip, we can't fight, we belong to de same lodge.

DAN: You have my word, Dimocrat to Dimocrat, I won't quarrel in the house. Set down, I want to spake about the bill we owe ye. [*Lochmuller sits R. of table*]

TOMMY: Pop, I'm going down to get shaved, I think I'll take in the Comique to-night. Mother, leave a light in the hall. So long, Pop. [*Exit C. D.*]

DAN: Over the river, Tommy.

MRS. MULLIGAN: [*Going off L.1.E.*] Dan, I'm going to bring Tommy's bed down here, and will you help me put it up? [*Speaks Irish, Bus.*] Don't fight with the dirty Dutch. [*Exit C. D.*]

DAN: [*Speaks Irish, saying*] I'll wipe the floor with him to-morrow night.

LOCHMULLER: Is dat de Russian or de Greek language what you speak?

DAN: No, sir, that's the real Gaelic. [*Sits on sausages*] Heavens! I've set on the bow wow pudding. [*Lifting sausages and placing them on table*]

LOCHMULLER: Oh, dat's nothing, dem is second handed bolognas, I sweep de meat up mit de sawdust, und sell it to de Italians.

DAN: You furnish all the meat for the Mulligan supper to-morrow night.

LOCHMULLER: Yes, und I don't vant a cent from you, dares de bill. [*Leaves it on table*] Nor de Mulligans till de ball is over. You know my wife is from de County Cork, und I just leave the butcher shop open mit my little boy in it, und –

Enter Gustavus Lochmuller, Jr.

LOCHMULLER, JR.: Fadder, hurry, quick! Two boys steal de drawer oud de butcher shop, hurry!

Exit C. D.

LOCHMULLER: Vat? Giminy Christmas, I catch him!

Exits hurriedly running against Mrs. Mulligan, who enters with bed and slats, upsetting her. Bus

DAN: I have the bill, now I'll lick him.

Close in

Scene 2

A local street. Enter Tommy Mulligan, R. H.

TOMMY: [*Pulls out watch*] Just half past seven, and here's Katy on time.

Enter Katy Lochmuller L. H.

KATY: Have I kept you waiting long, Tommy?

TOMMY: No, I didn't think I could chow up in time.

KATY: Why, what's the matter, Tommy?

TOMMY: Well, I'll tell you. I shot me mouth off, down at the house. I told the old man I was going to marry you. Just then your old man came in. It looked as though there was going to be a scrape, but I fixed it.

KATY: In what way, Tommy?

TOMMY: My old man said the Dutch was no good, but it don't make any difference, I'm twenty-one, and he can't give me any of his casino. I'm going to marry you just the same, if we have to skip to another country. Did the old woman know anything about it?

KATY: Father wants me to marry a Swiss warbler.

TOMMY: What's a Swiss warbler; what, one of them Dutch canaries that chirrup in the Atlantic Garden till the moon's down?

KATY: Yes, he's a leaderkrantzer, and Mother, because she's Irish, wants me to marry Walsingham McSweeney, 'cause he's from the same part of Ireland with her.

TOMMY: Say, Katy, listen to me, I'm going to take you down to the Comique to-night, there's a corking bill on. Then to-morrow night when the ball is going on, at intermission time, we'll give 'em all the grand steer.

KATY: Tommy, before I'd marry McSweeney or the warbler, I'd go live out. I'm offered fifteen a month if I want to be a French nurse.

TOMMY: That position's good enough for a——.* I'll make a lady of you. I'm going to open a new saloon when I'm married, the gang is all with me. Now do you know any young girl, a friend of yours, can keep her chin, and not give what I'm going to say, away?

KATY: Maggie Kierney, the hairdresser, keeps next door to Sim Primrose, the colored barber. She's a dear friend of mine.

TOMMY: Well, you've got to get your hair dressed for the ball to-morrow night, aint you?

KATY: Yes, cert.

TOMMY: And don't wear spitlocks, oblige me, Katy, will you?

KATY: I don't want to look like a chromo; I'll wear me hair pompadour.

TOMMY: Well, get it up nice. I want to break all the Mulligan's hearts.

KATY: You won't be ashamed of me, Tommy.

TOMMY: Well, I'll tell you how I'll fix it. We'll go down to Maggie Kierney's to-morrow night before the ball, get your hair dressed, and we'll talk it over with Maggie about standing up with you. We'll fix it about the hack, and during intermission, we'll drive down to Judge Duffy's house, and wake him up.

KATY: What! Get married by a judge?

TOMMY: Cert. If we wait till next day, the

*A timely reference was apparently supplied for each performance.

552

whole thing is given away and we can't get married at all. Besides it gives a young feller popularity, we get our names in the paper.

KATY: All right, Tommy. I'll meet you at Maggie's at half past seven to-morrow night.

TOMMY: I'll be there. We can rent a room and bed-room in Batavia Street after we're married, it's a more quiet street than Pearl, aint so many trucks in it. It's getting late, we must hurry. Let me see how I'm fixed. [*Bus.*] There's the price of the tickets, and a half a dollar for two stews. Come on, Katy, I'll draw me hundred out of the Bleecker to-morrow, Vanderbilt.

KATY: Oh, Tommy!

Exit Tommy and Katy L. H.

Enter R. H. Sim Primrose and Brother Palestine Puter, Chaplain of the Skidmore Guards

SIM: Brother Puter, I'm highly gratified, dat you, de only 'ligeous member of de Skidmore Guard, would interest yourself for de welfare of de Skidmore Ball to-morrow night.

BROTHER PUTER: Since I was relected chaplain of de regiment, you know I beat four Baptists and three Prespeterians for de position. I always advocated dancing and pleasure, so I accompanied the Committee on Decoration to see dat de hall room was finished with eclat.

SIM: I'm so busy all day cleaning my uniform, I declare I forgot de name of de hall. What's de name, Brother Puter?

BROTHER PUTER: Lyric Hall.

SIM: Lyric Hall, dat's a good selection. Nice hall. I 'spect we'll have de hall decorated wid nice ingrediments.

BROTHER PUTER: Yes, dars a large chromo of Abraham Lincoln to go over de door, and de flural tribunes is something gorgeous.

SIM: I understand Lieutenant Newlimber's sister Ruth is gwine to stood for de Goddess of Liberty, when de Skidmores march in de hall.

BROTHER PUTER: She'll have to stand on a flour barrel.

SIM: She can stand up anywhere. Her brother is very good that way. He's stood me up now for fourteen shampoons and sixteen shaves.

BROTHER PUTER: Be charitable, Capt. Primrose. He owes six months pew rent now, and it cost a dollar a day for a carpenter to widen dat pew so his fat sister could sit in it, but religion teaches us dar'll be money when you and I are gone.

SIM: Yes, I 'spect dey will inflate 'bout dat time, but do we take supper at de ball, or get it fore we start?

BROTHER PUTER: De supper is an after consideration. When we get to de ball we will consider whether we go after de supper, or –

SIM: Well, Brother Puter, de supper will never come after us.

BROTHER PUTER: Well, Delmonico's is too far away from de hall, and de intermission comes bout one o'clock, and de victuals is very bad den in restaurants, and I got a friend dat keeps a grocery store, and if de Guards will condescend, we will march dare in a body and munch a few crackers.

SIM: Hold on, Brother Puter, I respect you; you're de chaplain in my company, but beware of scandel.

BROTHER PUTER: Captain Primrose, I'm *astonished!* Scandel! As a leading Baptist, and Grand Dispenser in de Colored Secret Society of Moons.

SIM: Hold on, dar's whar de scandel comes in. Moons – moons – do you spect de Skidmore Guard is gwine to set down and eat nuffing but moons? What you take us for, tramps?

BROTHER PUTER: I'm sorry I angered you, Captain, but you don't understand. The Ancient Order of Full Moons, is de Colored Secret Society, to Prevent de Irish from Riding on Horse Cars.

SIM: Oh, dat's different. Can I join de order?

BROTHER PUTER: I'll propose you at de next meeting.

SIM: All right, Brother Puter, I'll join. I'm gwine down to de shop. Oh, what is de name of dat band we got?

BROTHER PUTER: De El Dorado Reed Striding Military, Cotillion Brass Band.

SIM: Well, I spect to see you dance to-morrow night.

BROTHER PUTER: If I can leave my bunion home, I will.

SIM: Come down to de shop some time, I'll take dat bunion out.

BROTHER PUTER: It's too old, now.

SIM: Well, a little glycerine and a match will help it. Good day, Brother Puter, you'll know when I'm coming in de ball room, with my lady love, if you smell anything peculiar, look

out for me, I'm gwine to take a bath in co-
logne fore I start. Good Day.

Exit R. H.

BROTHER PUTER: I don't care a *cent* how you
come. Get me walk three blocks from whar I
want to go. I must see that sick sister to-night,
and I don't like to go up dat bottle alley in de
daylight, so many Italians. I'll wait on de corner. Whar's my tobacco? [*Feels in pocket,
takes out letter*] Hello! Dar's dat letter from de
ball committee. [*Opens letter*] What's dis?
[*Reads*] Brother Palestine Puter, Lyric Hall
has been seized by the sheriff for rent due de
owner. [*Aloud*] Well done! I told Captain
Primrose, de ball would come off at Lyric
Hall. It can't, de hall is seized. What's dis?
[*Reads*] The committee is forced to take another hall called de Harp and Shamrock. [*Aloud*]
De Harp and Shamrock, dat's an Irish hall.
Dar aint a Full Moon can go in dat place widout trouble. [*Reads*] Notify de members of
de Skidmore Guard. De date remains de
same. De ball comes off to-morrow night sure
at de Harp and Shamrock. Horses heads up
Bleecker. Well, now I must hurry, it's business now.

*Starts for R. H. When Dan Mulligan and Wal-
singham McSweeney enter R. H. Puter looks
at them*

PUTER: I don't see why de government can't
quarantine such people as dese. Dey land too
sudden; dar aint enough fumigation.

Exit R. H.

DAN: [*Slightly tipsy*] McSweeney, you're a
friend of mine, you're one of the old Mulligans.
MC SWEENEY: I was First Leftenant when we
licked the Dutch Brewery Light Guard at
Communipaw.
DAN: That's the year I gave you four tons of coal
for a prize, and burnt coke meself at home.
MC SWEENEY: Yes, and I had four shots and
won it, but I never give it away.
DAN: I have fixed it all right for you and Gilmartin to go with the young Mulligans to the ball
to-morrow night, Walsingham. It's dead level,
I got it from Tommy.
MC SWEENEY: It's a favor you'll never be sorry
for.

DAN: There's one man going to that ball to-mor-
row night, Mc, I'm sure.
MC SWEENEY: Who is he, Dan?
DAN: A Dutch butcher, named Lochmuller. I'd
lick him, Mc, but I owe him thirty-five dol-
lars.
MC SWEENEY: I'll lick him for you.
DAN: No, let it go. Wait till the young Mulligan
Guard Ball is over.
MC SWEENEY: Very well.
DAN: What's the name of the hall the young
Mulligans have for the ball?
MC SWEENEY: The Harp and Shamrock.
DAN: I want to see the hall look nice. Will you
do what I say?
MC SWEENEY: Yes, sling on anything, Dan, I'm
with you.
DAN: No, but fix the hall the way I want it. Get
a row of American flags on the right hand,
with the Irish flags blending between them.
Then get a row of wax candles on the balcony,
and put a sign on it, "Look out for the drip."
Get about thirty-three canaries, and some
blackbirds, in cages, and hang them on the
chandeliers, and give word to the leader of the
band, if a Dutch tune is played the whole
night, he'll not get a cent. Will you do this?
MC SWEENEY: I will, you bet your life, Dan.
DAN: Now come over to McQuade's, and I'll play
you a game of hand ball for a five.
MC SWEENEY: I'm with you, Dan.
DAN: Come on. Do ye remember the old tune?

"The Mulligan Guard"

We crave your condescension,
　And we'll tell you what we know
Of marching in the Mulligan Guards,
　From the Seventh Ward below;
And our Captain's name was Hussey –
　A Tipperary man –
He carried his sword like the Russian Duke,
　Whenever he took command.

CHORUS

We shouldered guns,
　And marched, and marched away,
From Jackson Street
　Way up to Avenue A;
Drums and fifes did sweetly, sweetly play,
　*As we marched, marched, marched in the
Mulligan Guards.*

2

When the band played Garryowen

554

Or the Connemara pet,
With the rub, dub, dub, we marched in the
mud –
To the military step –
With the green above the red, boys,
To show where we came from;
Our gun's we'd lift, with the right shoulder
shift,
As we marched to the beat of the drum.
                    We shouldered guns, etc.

3

When we'd get home at night boys,
The divil a wink we'd sleep;
We'd all sit up and drink a sup
Of whiskey, strong and neat.
Then we'd all march home together,
As slippery as lard;
The solid men would all fall in,
And march in the Mulligan Guard.
                    We shouldered guns, etc.

Both exit

Scene 3

A barber shop with two chairs R. H. and a hair
dresser's L. H. A division piece with practical
door from barber shop to hair dresser's. Set
door L. H. of hair dresser's. Table and wig
block with wig on in hair dresser's – and table
with papers R. H. of barber shop. Hooks for
coats. Barber utensils. At opening, Maggie
Kierney discovered in hair dresser's combing a
wig. Sim Primrose brushing Skidmore uniform
at table, R. H. of barber shop.

SIM: I'd give a hundred dollars to know de man
dat dropped dat kerosene on dat coat. I only
wore it once in parade – last 'Mancipation
Day. Dar'll be some hot coons at de Skids to-
night, and I wouldn't have anybody smell kerosene on me for a million dollars.

Enter Dan Mulligan and Lochmuller D. in F.
Dan takes off coat, hanging it up, and Loch-
muller in evening dress. Both hang clothes up
without observing each other and get in chairs

SIM: Next – [*With razor and paper, going to*
Lochmuller]
DAN: Look here, sir – I'm next.
SIM: [*Going to Dan*] 'Scuse me, sir – I didn't
observe –

LOCHMULLER: Here, look here once – Mister
Primrose, I'm next.
DAN: Yis, that's right, he's next after me.
LOCHMULLER: [*In chair*] No, I am next before
you.
SIM: My apprentice will be here in a minute.
LOCHMULLER: No – I wont be shaved by de
printer, I have got my cup and razor here –
DAN: Go on, Primrose, shave me first. If you
don't, the Divel a one of the Mulligans 'ill nev-
er lather here again.
SIM: Gemmen, I'm sorry. If I was a Simese
twin I could shave both.
LOCHMULLER: Shave me first. I have as much
pull in de Mulligan Guard as any man in de
city, and Dan Mulligan is my friend.
DAN: [*Getting up on stage from chair*] That's
my name, sir – and no man is my friend.
[*Lochmuller who has got on stage*] Oh –
[*Aside*] If it wasn't for the 35 dollars.
LOCHMULLER: Mister Mulligan excuse me – I
thought you vas somebody vat I didn't know –
DAN: Oh, that's all right.
SIM: [*With lather and brush*] When you settle
de little difference, I'm ready, gemmen –
LOCHMULLER: Oh, dat's all right. I would fight
for Dan Mulligan to-morrow – or de Mulligan
Guards neither.
DAN: Oh, I know that. [*Aside*] Oh, if the ball
was over –
LOCHMULLER: My wife und my little boy und
Katy is all dressed for de ball, und so am I,
und my wife is waiting for me on de corner.
So uf you will let me shave first – why –
DAN: My wife is waiting for me – and I'm not
dressed yet – so I must shave first.
SIM: I'll tell you, gemmen – I'll settle it. I want
no quarrelling in de shop. I'll shave one half of
you, and den I'll shave half of you – den
you'll both get shaved at de same time.
DAN: That's all right. Free trade and sailor's
rights is all I ax for – [*Getting into chair*]
LOCHMULLER: I don't want any domestic trouble. [*Getting into chair*] I'm satisfied.
SIM: Gemmen, dar's nuffing like a mutual
friend – I'll begin on Germany, if Ireland will
allow me – [*Going to Lochmuller and lather-*
ing one side of his face]
DAN: Have you the *Clipper*?
SIM: Yes – [*Getting paper from table R. H.*]
Dar it is, de latest. [*Gives paper to Dan. Sim*
begins to shave Lochmuller]

DAN: I see here where Buck McCarthy licked the Dutch Butcher in two rounds –

LOCHMULLER: [*Sitting up*] Yes, I know, but what kind of fair play vas dat – when all de goes out men jumped in and cut de rope?

DAN: I have here the referee's decision. Money and belt given to McCarthy.

SIM: Orlando Whippletree, de colored teacher in de gymasim – I see in de *Christian Observer* has challenged McCarthy and de Butcher together.

DAN: Oh, he's a walk away for Duck.

LOCHMULLER: Do you suppose a German would fight mit a nigger?

SIM: Say, look here – do you see dis razor – I'm Sim Primrose, Captain of de Skidmore Guard. Every man of them is N. G. a nice gemman. Now I want you to apologize or I'll draw dis across your jugular.

DAN: A man has no right to insult a colored man to his face.

SIM: Take it back.

LOCHMULLER: I mean dat a colored man could whip any German in de world.

SIM: Well dat settles it. [*Getting lather and brush and going to Dan*] Now I'll take de grass off of Ireland – [*Lathers one side of Dan's face*]

LOCHMULLER: Jiminy Christmas, I can't say nutting. I must get my other side shaved – Have you got de German paper here – [*Going to table*] Yes, here is de German *Puck* – I read it. [*Sits in chair and reads. Enter Tommy Mulligan and Katrine Lochmuller in hairdresser apartment L. H.*]

KATY: Oh, Maggie – [*Kissing her*]

MAGGIE: Oh, Katy – All ready for the ball, eh –

KATY: No, not quite, just fix my hair a little.

MAGGIE: How do you do, Tommy. Sit down. [*Puts chair for Tommy near door in division piece*] Now, Katy. [*Sits Katy in chair which Maggie has vacated and fixes her hair*]

KATY: He – he – he [*Laughing*]

LOCHMULLER: I hear dat laugh before – dat's funny. [*Reads*]

MAGGIE: What's the matter, Katy?

KATY: Tell her, Tommy.

TOMMY: Maggie, Katy ain't got spunk enough to tell you – I've got to go to the Mulligan Ball with the Guards, and Katy is going with her father and mother – Well, I never put up a job like this. [*Looking at hair modestly*]

SIM: I tell you we're going to have a hot ball tonight.

DAN: [*In agony*] Yes – but look!

SIM: All de first class colored families on Sixth Avenue 'ill be dar.

DAN: [*In agony*] Hay –

TOMMY: What's that next door, Maggie?

MAGGIE: A barber shop – no body but Skidmores shave there.

TOMMY: Oh –

SIM: Dares no military organization in de world like de Skidmore Guard. [*Going to shelf*]

DAN: Oh, I thought you were talking about the Mulligans.

SIM: I never mix wid dem kind of people. 'Scuse me, gemmen, I'm out of bay rum – I'll be back in a minute. [*Exit door in flat*]

TOMMY: Well, Maggie, what I was going to say was – [*Bashfully*]

DAN: That sounds like Tommy's voice. I'll see – [*Looks through keyhole*] There's nothing there – [*Going to chair*]

TOMMY: That my old man don't want me to marry Katy, and her old man don't like me, nor my old man either – and [*Bashfully*]

DAN: [*With paper*] There is more Irish in our district than there is German, Lochmuller.

LOCHMULLER: Yes, but dare is more German babies in Avenue A, dan dare is tombstones in Greenwood Cemetery.

DAN: Well, I'll not argue –

TOMMY: And we want to know if you will come to the ball and when we run away at intermission, will you stand up for Katy – when we get married?

MAGGIE: [*Aloud*] Will I, Tommy, certainly, and I know two people who will go crazy –

KATY: Who, Maggie?

MAGGIE: Mister Mulligan and Mister Lochmuller. [*Katy and Maggie and Tommy laugh heartily. Lochmuller and Mulligan get out of chairs*]

DAN: I'll go crazy.

LOCHMULLER: Lochmuller go crazy. [*Both go to door and pull one another away twice when Dan gets a peep*]

DAN: [*Aside*] Be the mortal Harry, it's my boy Tommy with the Dutchman's daughter.

LOCHMULLER: [*Looks in keyhole. Aside*] It's my Katrine, mit Tommy Mulligan.

TOMMY: I'll give the old man the laugh – eh, Maggie? [*Laughing*]

DAN: He'll give me the laugh – Oh, if it wasn't for the thirty-five dollars.

KATY: Won't the Swiss warbler kick when he finds out I'm married, eh, Tommy?

LOCHMULLER: [*Aside*] She laugh at Mr. Krime, de baritone singer – Oh, Katrine – [*Looking at Mulligan*] Off it vas not dat I lose his custom –

TOMMY: Come, Katy, hurry – don't give it away, Maggie – Remember intermission time.

KATY: Good-bye, Maggie – [*Exit Tommy and Katy door in F. at back of hair dresser's*]

DAN: [*To Lochmuller*] I owe you thirty-five dollars, let it go – I want to ax you father to father – What do you want to let your girl come around my boy for? Let the thirty-five dollars go.

LOCHMULLER: Yes let de thirty-five dollars go – I want to know why Katrine is dare mit Tommy Mulligan.

DAN: I don't want to quarrel when I'm going out for pleasure. My wife is waiting for me.

LOCHMULLER: Und my wife is waiting for me – Und before I see my Katrine make love mit Tommy Mulligan, I kill myself mit a cleaver.

DAN: And if I find Tommy Mulligan making love to a Dutch girl, I'll lick every German from Hamburg to Gowanus.

LOCHMULLER: Maybe – maybe –

MAGGIE: [*Who has put on hat and shawl during dialogue between Mulligan and Lochmuller, enters door into barber shop*] I'll get Primrose to have an eye on the store.

Mulligan and Lochmuller seize her and bring her front

LOCHMULLER: My good woman, tell me if Katrine Lochmuller is dare –

DAN: Was it Tommy Mulligan's voice I heard in there – answer me, I'm his father –

MAGGIE: Why you must be crazy.

LOCHMULLER: Yes, she said I was crazy – But on my knees – [*Getting on knees*] Please tell me if my child Katrine was dare.

Enter Bridget Lochmuller and Gustavus Lochmuller Jr., dressed neatly for the ball. Bridget sees Lochmuller and seizes him throwing him around. Maggie exits into hair dresser's and then exits door in back flat. Dan going up and down stage in agony. Bridget shaking Lochmuller

BRIDGET: An' is this what I married you for – A dacent Irish girl – that had her twelve dollars a week in a feather factory, and to marry you, a bologna pudding butcher – and raise a family – to find you making love on your knees to a woman here in a barber shop – Oh, Lochmuller, Lochmuller – [*Weeping*]

LOCHMULLER: Bridget my darling – hear me once –

BRIDGET: An' me all dressed for the Mulligan Ball – and little Gustavus to see his father on his knees – [*Crying*] Oh, why did I marry among the Dutch.

DAN: [*To Bridget*] Are you that man's wife?

BRIDGET: Yis – But I'll lave him.

DAN: You have a daughter Katy?

BRIDGET: I have – Oh, Katy darling, when you hear of your father –

DAN: [*On knees*] Oh, my good woman hear me. Save a father's feelings. Keep her away from Tommy Mulligan. You're a County Cork woman – don't let your daughter run away with my boy –

Lochmuller going up and down stage. Enter Mrs. Mulligan, door in flat. Mrs. Mulligan seizes Dan Mulligan, throwing him around

MRS. MULLIGAN: And is this what you came to get shaved for – On your knees making love to another woman in a public bath house – Oh, you wretch! [*Going to Bridget*] And you – Who are you that dares to make trouble in my family?

BRIDGET: I am Bridget Lochmuller. I'm a lady – and raise your hand to me if you dare.

MRS. MULLIGAN: I'd tear the hair out of your head.

BRIDGET: Tear it – tear it – there's me hair – tear it – [*Holding her head down*]

MRS. MULLIGAN: I will – [*Pulls Bridget's hair which falls loose*]

BRIDGET: Oh, let me at her –

LOCHMULLER: [*Getting in front of her and holding her*] Bridget, my darling, I am here – your husband – Gustavus Lochmuller – Don't be mad, I'm a slaughter house butcher.

DAN: [*Holding Mrs. Mulligan*] Cordelia – Cordelia, what do you mean?

MRS. MULLIGAN: Let me at her –

BRIDGET: Let her come.

LOCHMULLER: Take your wife away, Mulligan.

DAN: If you interfere, I'll pulverize you.

Enter August Sneider, in night shirt and nightcap. Bridget and Mrs. Mulligan run off and Gustavus, Jr., door in F.

SNEIDER: What's de matter here? I can't sleep in my tailor shop.

LOCHMULLER: My wife, Bridget darling – [*Exit door in flat*]

DAN: Cordelia – Cordelia – [*Exit after Lochmuller, door in flat*]

SNEIDER: Wake me out of my sleep, Mister Primrose. I get satisfaction – [*Breaks a shaving cup. Enter Primrose, seizes him. Bus. for finish*]

Scene 4

Local street. Enter Bridget Lochmuller and Gustavus Lochmuller L. H.

BRIDGET: Oh, Gustavus, to think I would find your father making love to another woman – Oh – Oh – [*Cries*] My heart will break.

GUSTAVUS: Don't cry, Mamma.

Enter Lochmuller, Sr., L. H. one half shaved

LOCHMULLER: Bridget, my darling, don't run away, hear me once.

BRIDGET: No, false man, you deceived me. I'll lave you. You can't take the children from me. Oh, Gussy – Gussy – you've broke my heart.

LOCHMULLER: Hear me once, when you see me by dat woman, I want to save my child, our Katrine – Katy, our darling.

BRIDGET: My Katy – Has any harm come to her?

LOCHMULLER: She was dare by dat shop mit Tommy Mulligan – und I went on my knees to dot woman, to save Katrine, to keep her away von Tommy Mulligan.

BRIDGET: Oh – Gussy – I'm sorry. I waited on the corner for you so long, I got mad, and me all dressed for the Mulligan Ball.

LOCHMULLER: I would come quicker, but Mister Mulligan vas dare und he got next before me. So you see, I'm only half shaved for de ball, but anyhow, if Katrine is dare mit Tommy Mulligan, dey will soon find me out.

BRIDGET: I would be pleased to see Tommy bring Katy to the Mulligan Ball.

GUSTAVUS, JR: Fadder, Tommy is a darling pivotter.

LOCHMULLER: [*Pushing boy off*] Quick, go home. You don't go by de ball.

GUSTAVUS, JR: [*Cries*] Boo – Hoo –

LOCHMULLER: Go, I make your suspenders off

quick. Go – [*Gustavus, Jr. exit L. H.*] So, Bridget, you vant Katy to go to de ball mit Tommy Mulligan – und Mister Krime, de Swiss singer can stay home I believe.

BRIDGET: I'll never allow my child to marry a Dutchman. Her mother threw herself away on a Dutch butcher when I could have had an Irish lawyer.

Exeunt R. 1. E. Enter Tommy Mulligan and Katy Lochmuller L. H.

TOMMY: Don't be nervous, Katy. There's many a young fellow gets married, dat ain't got a ferry ticket.

KATY: I ain't scared about that, Tommy. Mother and Father will be at the ball, and if they suspected.

TOMMY: He'll never 'spect nuffing – I'll get him down in the barroom, and I'll fill him full of Budweiser.

KATY: Suppose your father finds out, Tommy.

TOMMY: He'll never drop. All I've got to do, is to mention Tammany Hall, and that settles it. He'll forget the world – but when the tailor fires in his bill for thirty, for these togs – maybe he won't kick then.

KATY: I thought you was going to wear your uniform.

TOMMY: What, get married in a uniform? What do you take me for? One of the regulars? The Mulligans went down a while ago in uniform, with McSweeney and Gilmartin as pioneers. Do you think I'd put on a uniform with those two Turks? Then I would be giving meself away. Pipe, Katy, there comes the old man – Let's skip – I don't want to see him till I go to the ball. Come.

Both exit R. H. Enter Dan Mulligan and Mrs. Mulligan. Dan dressed for the ball. L. 1. E.

DAN: Cordelia, I want to see some of those young Mulligans that'll lay us out for style.

CORDELIA: Dan, you're as young as ever, and I want you to promise me you'll say nothing to Lochmuller. I'm sorry for what happened in the barber shop. I'll apologize to Mrs. Lochmuller at the ball.

DAN: Say nothing. Keep under cover. I'll down him after the ball. I owe him thirty-five, but let it go; and understand me, there's no one can dance with you but Walsingham McSweeney. Who's getting the supper ready at the house?

CORDELIA: Mrs. McSweeney, Mrs. Gilmartin,

and two Frinch cooks. We have two whole pigs – and enough for fifty.

DAN: Well, getting the supper up at my house, gives Tommy a send off – but Lochmuller don't eat there. [*Enter Mr. Rosenfelt L. H.*] How are you, Mister Rosenfelt?

ROSENFELT: How are you, Mister Mulligan? I suppose you know Tommy Mulligan ordered thirty-three cut away coats for de ball.

DAN: Oh, that's all right.

ROSENFELT: Where do I get my money?

DAN: Give in your bill at intermission.

ROSENFELT: Your word is all I vant. Have a cigarette. [*Business*]

DAN: Thank you.

ROSENFELT: [*Going*] De Harp and Shamrock is vere de ball is coming off.

DAN: Yis, in Bleecker –

ROSENFELT: Much obliged. [*Exit R. H.*]

DAN: [*Lights cigarette*] I don't see how a man could smoke a bundle of straw like that. Come, Cordelia, I'll get one of Duffs, the undertaker's hacks, and look out you don't fall through it.

CORDELIA: How will you know how to dance the Yankee dances?

DAN: I have a book. [*Business*] They'll not fool me.

CORDELIA: What is that I smell in your hair?

DAN: Kerosene – I put it there to make the bald come out.

Both exit R. H. Enter Skidmore Guard L. H. Sim Primrose as Captain and Puter as Chaplain

SIM: Halt. [*Business*] Members, I ordered you to carry arms to-night at de Skidmore Fancy Ball, kase we was forced to give up Lyric Hall, and take de Harp and Shamrock. Dar's no telling how many Irish will be in hambush dare. So, going in de hall, you can put your muskets in de hat rack, and every man have his razor sharpened. No one must interfere wid our pleasure.

PUTER: I'm agin de shedding of blood, but when it comes to dem people, why, you all know me.

COMPANY: Um – Um –

CAPTAIN SIM:

Song
"Skidmore's Fancy Ball"

Here we go, so nobly, oh,
De colored Belvideres,

A number one, we carry a gun,
We beat de Fusileers.
Talk about your dances
When we hear de cornet call,
We'll wing and wing, the dust we'll sling,
At the Skidmore Fancy Ball.

CHORUS
Hallelulah, glory oh,
Balance down de middle,
I tell you what, um um it's hot,
Like gravy in a griddle.
Forward four, hold on de floor,
Spread out through de hall,
Every coon's as warm as June,
At the Skidmore Fancy Ball.

2
Supper served at one G. M.
By Brown, the caterer.
Turk and goose, oh, cut me loose,
Just lem me in de door.
Chairs reserved for ladies,
Umbrellas in de hall,
Dar's etiquette in every set,
At the Skidmore Fancy Ball.
Hands around
Keep off the ground,
We'll dance the plaster from de wall,
Get in and sail, hold your trail,
At the Skidmore Fancy Ball.
Hallelulah, glory oh, &c.

3
Every hat – when dey get at
Dis colored coterie,
Will cost a half, you needn't laugh,
Help de colored mil it ia.
We're gwine down to Newport,
Just next summer in de fall,
So follow suit and contribute
To the Skidmore Fancy Ball.
Waltz away – mazourka,
Dance de plaster from de wall,
Caledone – have a tone
At de Skidmore Fancy Ball.
Hallelulah, glory, &c.

All march off R. 1. E.

Scene 5

Interior of ball room. "The Harp and Shamrock." A boxed scene – roofed C. doors –

*backed by interior, a chandelier hanging C. to
fall, another chandelier back of C. doors. Four
jets lighted with globes on – in side pieces –
"2 on a side." A "Harp and Shamrock" over
C. D. Mulligan in uniform, young men in cut
coats, white vests and white ties, young ladies in
white with green ribbons and fancy ball costumes. Enter arm and arm. Music – company
are finishing a quadrille as the scene opens.
Then Tommy says to Katy.*

TOMMY: [*Aside*] I say Katy it's near intermission – [*Aloud*] I say Pop give de boys a song
as a send off.

OMNES: A song Mr. Mulligan.

Song
"The Babies on Our Block"

*If you want for information,
Or in need of merriment,
Come over with me socially
To Murphy's tenement;
He owns a row of houses
In the First Ward, near the dock,
Where Ireland's represented
By the Babies on our Block
There's the Phalens and the Whalens
From the sweet Dunochadee,
They are sitting on the railings
With their children on their knee,
All gossiping and talking
With their neighbors in a flock,
Singing "Little Sally Waters,"
With the Babies on our Block.*

CHORUS

*Oh, Little Sally Waters
Sitting in the sun,
A crying and weeping for a young man:
Oh, rise, Sally, rise,
Wipe your eye out with your frock;
That's sung by the Babies a living on our
    Block.*

2

*Of a warm day in the summer,
When the breeze blows off the sea,
A hundred thousand children
Lay on the Battery;
They come from Murphy's building,
Oh, their noise would stop a clock!
Oh there's no perambulatory
With the Babies on our Block.
There's the Clearys and the Learys*

*From the sweet Blackwater side,
They are laying on the Batt'ry
And they're gazing at the tide;
All royal blood and noble,
All of Dan O'Connell's stock,
Singing "Gravel, Greeny Gravel,"
With the Babies on our Block.*

CHORUS

*Oh, Gravel, Greeny Gravel,
How green the grasses grow,
For all the pretty fair young maidens that I see;
Oh, "Green Gravel Green,"
Wipe your eye out with your frock;
That's sung by the Babies a living on our
    Block.*

3

*It's good morning to you, landlord;
Come, now how are you today?
When Patrick Murphy, Esquire,
Comes down the alley way;
With his shiny silken beaver,
He's as solid as a rock,
The envy of the neighbor's boys
A living off our Block.
There's the Brannons and the Gannons,
Far down and Connaught men,
Quite easy with the shovel
And so handy with the pen;
All neighborly and friendly
With relations by the flock,
Singing "Little Sally Waters,"
With the Babies on our Block.*

CHORUS

*Oh, Little Sally Waters
Sitting in the sun,
A crying and weeping for a young man:
Oh, rise, Sally, rise,
Wipe your eye out with your frock;
That's sung by the Babies a living on our
    Block.*

TOMMY: Take your partners for a quadrille basket. [*Set is formed*]

DAN: [*To Mrs. Mulligan*] Did Tommy bring a
basket?

MRS. MULLIGAN: Sh – Dan –

BRIDGET: Tommy, dance wid Katy. [*Bringing
Tommy over to Lochmuller*] Gustavus come
dance wid me and let Tommy dance wid
Katy.

DAN: Tommy, dance wid your mother – I've a sore bunion here – [*Holding foot*]

TOMMY: Mother can't go through the basket.

DAN: Can't she – she fell through the rocking chair last week, a basket's nothing to her.

TOMMY: Ah you don't know what I mean.

DAN: Don't I – If the fox gets away from me to-night – I'm blind, that's all.

TOMMY: Come Mother – [*Taking her hand*]

MRS. MULLIGAN: No Tommy I'll set down with your father. You dance wid Katy.

LOCHMULLER: No oxcuse me, I love to dance mit my child.

DAN: That's right, I love to see a child honor his parent.

LOCHMULLER: My Katy loves me more den de world.

DAN: And Tommy thinks more of me than he does of any young lady in the room.

TOMMY: [*To Dan*] Come are you going to fill up the set, or are you going to kick – Come Mother dance wid Pop. [*Taking Mrs. Mulligan's hand and placing it in Dan's hand*] There you're a head in this set.

DAN: You bet Tommy I'm never behind –

TOMMY: Take a side, Mister Lochmuller.

LOCHMULLER: Yes – And I don't go way von dis side – [*Holding Katy close*] All night neider.

TOMMY: Come Mrs. Lochmuller – [*Taking her hand*]

BRIDGET: I'm there Tommy.

TOMMY: [*At Katy's side*] All ready – [*To Katy in Hog Latin*] Katy after the dance give the old man the slip – All ready.

KATY: Yeggery.

LOCHMULLER: [*As music plays quadrille*] Vot is dat he said Katrina?

KATY: He said the next dance was the tra – la – la – [*March and chorus of the Skidmores R. U. E. Skidmores down L. H.*]

LOCHMULLER: Oh –

Music and Dance and one side dances then the other side; when the music of Skidmore is heard through dance Mulligan has had book looking for figures. Business of Omnes falling back as Skidmores enter hall

TOMMY: What do you coons want here?

SIM: Halt – [*Skidmores stop*] Dat's what I want to know – what are you Irish trespassing here for?

DAN: We have this hall here – and you have no right here.

SIM: [*To Skidmores*] Look to your arms men.

PUTER: Every Full Moon's ready.

DAN: You'll have to lave this place or we'll walk on ye –

SIM: Hold your ground men.

DAN: Give it to them – Mulligans give it to them.

Grand rush to C. Business of fight. Women scream. Negroes draw razors, general melee when Mr. Garlic enters

GARLIC: Hold on gentlemen – hold on. [*Tommy is going to C. D.*]

DAN: Hold on Tommy – stand by me. [*Pulling him down*]

KATY: [*Is going to C. D. Lochmuller pulls her down*]

LOCHMULLER: Wait Katy – I'm here – your father – don't be afraid.

GARLIC: Gentlemen this is all a mistake.

DAN: What – Give an account of it – What are these nagurs doing here –

OMNES SKIDMORES: Niggers – Who ses that – [*Attempt to rush*]

SIM: Hold on gemmen – I'll give the word when to cut.

DAN: Stand by me boys – [*To Garlic*] What's the maning of this?

SIM: Dat's what I want to know.

GARLIC: Gentlemen if you'll give me a word I'll tell you –

OMNES: Go on – Go on –

GARLIC: It's a mistake in the date. I rented the hall to the Mulligan Guard for to-night – and my clerk rented it to the Skidmore Guard for the same night, not knowing I had rented it.

DAN: We have a right to it – we rented it first.

SIM: We've got just as much right here as you have – we rented de hall quick as you did.

Rush again

GARLIC: There needn't be any trouble gentlemen – if the colored gentlemen will be kind enough to take the Red Men's Lodge room up stairs it's all ready for dancing.

PUTER: I object gemmen. I'm a Red Man –

GARLIC: It's a beautiful hall – and I'll throw off ten dollars on the rent.

SIM: [*To Skidmores*] I think members dat's a very boisterous propersition and I propose we go up stairs – might as well have harmony – de two balls can go on widout interfering and as long as we're up stairs – we're above de Irish – and I know dat suits every Full Moon in de company.

OMNES SKIDMORES: Yes – yes – dat's fair.

SIM: [*To Dan*] Well gemmen – we is allers been on speaking terms wid de Mulligan Guard – and as we is gwine up stairs to have our pleasure – and we want to be friends I propose three cheers for de Mulligan Guard.

SKIDMORES: [*Cheer*] Hurrah – Hurrah – &c.

Music – March and Chorus – Skidmores exit marching and singing L. 4. E. up stairs to ball room above

SIM: Fall in – Forward march.

GARLIC: This way – Captain. [*Taking Skidmores off C. D. exit L. H.*]

DAN: Three cheers for the Skidmore Guard.

OMNES: Cheer – Hurrah – Hurrah – &c.

After Skidmores off – Dan Mulligan and Lochmuller look amongst the guests for their children – The band of the Skidmores consisting of bones, fiddle and banjo is heard playing R. H.

MRS. LOCHMULLER: [*Screams*] Oh Mr. Mulligan I have lost my diamond pin! [*All search for the pin – Enter two Negro wenches – Dan directs them to the hall above, they go up stairs*]

Dan finds the pin

DAN: Here it is Mrs. Lochmuller. Now – gents take your partners for a Virginny Reel.

All take partners and dance Virginia Reel during which crash is heard and the ceiling falls with Skidmores on it. Grand crash

Scene 6

Street local. Enter L. Tommy Mulligan and Katy – meeting Maggie Kierney who comes from R. H.

TOMMY: We're just in time. The ceiling broke down, and the coons came down in chunks. Now come on, we'll wake Judge Duffy up – and get married.

KATY: Who'll stand up for you Tommy?

TOMMY: I know the copper on the beat – he'll do.

MAGGIE: Come on – you haven't any too much time. [*Exit L. 1. E.*]

TOMMY: Brace up Katy. Don't weaken. There's many a noble family come from a marriage like this.

KATY: Oh what will Father say when he finds out.

TOMMY: He'll swallow it the same as a kyd 'ud swallow castor oil. Come on Katy – don't weaken – if this is a failure – the gang will give me the dead laugh – come.

KATY: Oh, Tommy.

Both exit. Enter Sim Primrose and Brother Puter, Primrose with eye white and Puter with nose scratched

SIM: De Skidmores took a terrible drop to-night. How did you get out?

PUTER: I was picked up from de debray.

SIM: Was Debray hurt?

PUTER: No – I mean I was gathered up wid de rest of de plaster.

SIM: It'll take a good deal of plaster to put de Guards together again.

PUTER: Whar is all de Skids?

SIM: I see one ice wagon take 10 of 'em to de hospital.

PUTER: Dat's de first time we made de Irish stand from under.

SIM: Yes, and dey couldn't understand it, till dey got tired beating us – but dars a day coming –

PUTER: Yes – next St. Patrick Day – when we get 'em all together den we'll light on 'em. [*Pulls out watch*] Look at her, ain't she a spinner – you know how I got her. Just fore we fell through de ceiling I borrowed her from Caroline Williams, she'll never know who's got it – kase de concussion knocked the thoughts all out of her head.

SIM: Dat Caroline Williams am a berry wicked wench – she'll fight.

PUTER: You come wid me, I'm gwine to wait on table at de Mulligan Guard supper to-night for 15 dollars – No matter about color or enmity. Come wid me – just think 7½ for you for waiting on table, and soak dis watch in de morning – Close up your barber shop – and go over to Jamaica and we'll roll in gin and sugar for a month.

SIM: I'm wid you Puter – Who give you de job –

PUTER: Mister Mulligan.

SIM: Dat settles it, de money's good. [*Both exit L. H. Enter Dan Mulligan R. H. with head tied up*]

DAN: The Guards has went off and left me, Tommy and the old woman is at the house – I must hurry or I'll get no supper. After I licked the nagurs – I engaged them to wait on the supper table. Ha – ha – the devil a cent will they get at all.

Enter Caroline Williams R.

CAROLINE: Look here Mister Mulligan I'm one of dem ladies dat come frough de roof awhile ago, at de Skidmore Ball – my name is Caroline Williams – I loaned my grandfather's watch to Palestine Puter – a colored man – I want it – I must get it – I can't sleep wid out it and if I don't get it, I'll raise de roof of dis town – where is he?

DAN: There's a nagur going to wait on the table at the Mulligan Guard supper at my house tonight.

CAROLINE: Is he a fat man?

DAN: Rather bloated – I believe his name is Zinc, no not Zinc – but – no no ah – Puter –

CAROLINE: Dat's him – I'll get him – and dat watch or dare'll be war.

Exit L. H.

DAN: What a welt I give the Dutchman with the chandelier – ha – ha – ha – [*Enter Lochmuller, with head tied up R. H.*] Now sir, we can settle our little affair right here there's no one around. [*Preparing to fight*]

LOCHMULLER: I'm not afraid but my eye is blind. Wait till to-morrow.

DAN: No – right here – I can knock the stockings off you – Come on you pudding butcher – I'm here.

LOCHMULLER: Do you suppose dat I vant to go to de Mulligan Guard supper mit my nose blooded?

DAN: *You* eat at the Mulligan Guard supper – No sir – I own that house, and if ever you put your nose in it – *Sex Tulonis* – I'll pull it – [*Pulling it and squaring off, Dutchman making feints at him*]

LOCHMULLER: My wife is dare.

DAN: She's welcome – But you – I'll walk on you – come on.

LOCHMULLER: [*Pulls out a sausage and points it at Dan*] I'll shoot you now quick – Look out.

DAN: Police, he has a revolver.

Exit L. H.

LOCHMULLER: [*Eats sausage*] I'm not afraid – you talk mit me – [*Speaks German angrily*] I can lick de whole Mulligan Guard. [*Enter Mr. Garlic R. H.*]

GARLIC: [*Taps Lochmuller on shoulder*] I say.

LOCHMULLER: [*Putting hands before his face*] Wait, don't hit me in my back. Hold on.

GARLIC: Why what's the matter man – I don't wish to strike you – I am the owner of the hall where the ball was held – and I want to find Mr. Mulligan – to get the rent of the place – They promised to pay at intermission.

LOCHMULLER: Mulligan, he won't pay it. He owes me thirty-five dollars for livers and spareribs.

GARLIC: He won't pay eh – Well I'll see – Where is he?

LOCHMULLER: He's at de house mit de Mulligan Guard eating supper.

GARLIC: I never expect to get a cent from the Skidmores – but I'll make Mulligan pay me to-night or I'll lock Mister Mulligan and all the Guards up. You'll hear from me.

Exit L. H. angrily

LOCHMULLER: Ah, Mister Mulligan – I don't go to de supper – oh no – may be you don't find out something ven dat man goes dare. Ha, ha – Ah Mister Mulligan I don't buy de supper – oof I don't get my 35 dollars I have de satisfaction of seeing him go buy Blackwells Island up.

Enter Mister Rosenfelt R. H.

ROSENFELT: Mister Lochmuller – vere is Mister Mulligan's house – I loaned de cut away coats to de Mulligan Guard for de ball – and I want my money – vere is de house?

LOCHMULLER: Go dare quick – four blocks and turn to de right – Mulligan is dare –

ROSENFELT: I'll get my money, or I vill put Mister Mulligan vere de dogs won't bite him.

Exit L. H.

LOCHMULLER: I go get some slaughter house butchers – and I lick all de Mulligan Guard or I will get my thirty-five dollars –

Exit L. H.

Scene 7

Interior of Mulligan cottage, C. D. backed by an interior. Two tables one right hand and one left hand – both up and down stage with table covers – and filled with dishes – chairs around each table. Sim and Puter with white aprons on carrying dishes on trays to table. Sim to right hand and Puter to L. Guards, Ladies and Omnes all discovered laughing at Mulligan who is centre. Enter Tommy Mulligan and Katy C. D. followed by Maggie.

TOMMY: Pop – Here I am – Say fellers allow me to introduce you to Mrs. Mulligan Junior.

MULLIGAN: What, Tommy are you married to Katy?

TOMMY: Dead sure –

MULLIGAN: Catch me – I'll fall – a drop of something – [*Omnes hands him a bottle, he drinks*]

BRIDGET: Oh Tommy, I've been waiting for this a long time.

OMNES: A song Mister Mulligan.

Business
SONG
"The Hallway Door"

I live in an Irish flat
In Mott Street here close by
I come home at night
A little tight
And to get in the house I try;
There's Misses Grady's daughters
Rossana and Leonore
May and Nell the Rockaway Belle
Standing by the hallway door.

CHORUS
They sing tra – la – la – la –
And kick and welt the floor
They wake the block
With Granny's clock
Singing by the hallway door.

2
Oh me head when I'm in bed
Is busting wid the pain
Grady's boys make a terrible noise
Playing the puss in the corner game
With Mary Ann McLaughlin
Lord Harry, I'll get the law
I hollow cop – and tell them stop
The music at the hallway door.

CHORUS
They sing tra – la – la – la –
And kick and welt the floor
It's Baby Mine all out of time
They sing at the hallway door.

3
Get out you guy you're N. G.
They say up to me face
I axed the police, to give me peace
And to come there and pull the place
Wid a string across the entry
In the dark it cut me jaw
Oh then like a calf – they'd yell and laugh
Just behind the hallway door.

CHORUS
They sing tra – la – la – la –
And kick and welt the floor
Its put on style on Blackwells Isle
They sing by the hallway door.

OMNES: Ha – ha – ha –

SIM: Gemmen, supper's all ready.

MULLIGAN: Take your places ladies and gentlemen – Cordelia seat the ladies.

CORDELIA: I'll attend to this, Daniel. Here, Mrs. Lochmuller – [*Placing chair head of table R.*]

MULLIGAN: Now thin help yourselves.

PUTER: Gemmen de tables all ready, and I opened de first keg, and here you are – [*All get glasses*]

MULLIGAN: Gentlemen here's to the Mulligan Guard – [*Drinks*]

OMNES: The Mulligan Guard. [*Drink*]

SIM: The Skidmore Battalion – [*Drinks*]

PUTER: Touch me – [*Drinks*]

MULLIGAN: Yes gentlemen, it's a fact – I have engaged the Captain of the Skidmore Guard to wait on the table.

OMNES: Ha – ha – ha –

SIM: [*Coming down*] Don't laugh gemmen – I'm Captain of that company – but when I see a dollar in sight, I'm gwine to grab it.

PUTER: [*With beer on tray and glasses*] Mr. Mulligan will you allow me to offer grace?

MULLIGAN: No there's grace enough here in the bowl.

PUTER: Then while you enjoy yourselves allow me to chant a hymn for your wickedness.

SIM: Go on Brother Puter, I'm wid you –

PUTER: [*Rat work on from L. to R. Puter sings*

a hymn. Sim joins in. Rat crosses and Omnes pelt at it. Business]

MULLIGAN: Set down ladies and gentlemen it's a neighbor from Mulberry Street. [*All sit and pig business on table, pig gets down and goes off*]

CORDELIA: Gentlemen take your partners for a cotillion.

OMNES: Yes, let's have a dance here finish it up &c. [*Music starts when Mr. Garlic comes on C. D.*]

GARLIC: Hold on here – where's Mister Mulligan?

MULLIGAN: That's me –

GARLIC: I want my money for the rent of the hall.

MULLIGAN: I never hired the hall from you –

GARLIC: You did sir.

MULLIGAN: You're a liar –

GARLIC: You're another – [*Business of fight. Exit Garlic and forming set, music. Enter Sneider, C. D.*]

SNEIDER: Here, stop de dance – Mister Mulligan – come here once.

MULLIGAN: That's me sir.

SNEIDER: You owe me 35 dollars for a suit of clothes for young Mulligan.

MULLIGAN: You're another.

SNEIDER: You're an Irish bruiser.

MULLIGAN: You're a – [*Business and fight. Exit Sneider, music. Set formed. Enter Mister Rosenfelt C. D.*]

ROSENFELT: Here Mister Mulligan come I want to see you on business.

MULLIGAN: What is it?

ROSENFELT: You ordered 35 cut away coats for de Mulligan Ball – I want my money.

MULLIGAN: Get out of here –

ROSENFELT: Never, I die, but not till I get my money.

MULLIGAN: You're a fraud sir.

ROSENFELT: You're a Molly Maguire.

MULLIGAN: What! – [*Business and same business*]

Set formed again – Enter Caroline Williams – She attacks Puter – Primrose tackles her and a scrimmage ensues – during which enter Lochmuller and six butchers with cleavers. General melee and curtain

SHENANDOAH

BRONSON HOWARD

BRONSON CROCKER HOWARD has frequently been called "the dean of the American Drama." He was the first really professional playwright in America who was neither theatre manager nor actor. He depended for his livelihood on his skill as a dramatist, and, as it developed, it was a very good livelihood. Notwithstanding a seeming deficiency of first-hand theatre experience, he was not a literary dramatist. He regarded himself, as he thought all writers for the stage should, as play*wright* rather than play*write*. He once wrote to Brander Matthews:

I think the divorce [of the drama from literature] should be made absolute and final; that the Drama should no more be wedded to literature, on one hand, than it is to the art of painting on the other, or to music or mechanical science. Rather, perhaps, I should say, we should recognize polygamy for the Drama; and all the arts, with literature, its Harem. Literature may be Chief Sultana – but not too jealous. She is always claiming too large a share of her master's attention, and turning up her nose at the rest. I have felt this so strongly, at times, as to warmly deny that I was a "literary man," insisting on being a "dramatist."

With comparable fervor, Howard insisted that the professional dramatist must fight to establish rights and honor for his profession and that he should deal primarily with American subjects, even if his dramaturgical practices were derived from foreign models. Just as Mark Twain had fought for copyright for an author, in founding the American Dramatists Club in 1891 Howard took the first substantial step to protect playwrights from "pirates." The agitations of Howard and this organization led to the law which made piracy of a play a misdemeanor.

Howard's heritage and early training prepared him well for his crusade. He was born in Detroit on October 7, 1842, of American pioneer stock. His great-grandfather had come from England with Wolfe's army and fought at Quebec. His grandfather had migrated from the eastern seaboard to take up farming in New York State; his father, after a brief period as captain of a schooner, had pushed on to Detroit. There he became a commission merchant, in the firm of Alvin Bronson and Company (another partner in the firm was named Crocker), and in 1849 was elected mayor. Bronson Crocker received his elementary education in Detroit and then, in 1858, was sent to

General Russell's school at New Haven to prepare for Yale. He began his studies at Yale in 1861, but an eye affliction forced him to drop out and return home. Back in Detroit he began writing, first as a drama critic for the Detroit *Free Press*. With this initiation to the drama, he attempted a quasi-original composition, *Fantine*, an adaptation of some episodes from Hugo's *Les Miserables* which the Detroit Theatre performed in 1864.

Encouraged by this preliminary experience, Howard departed for New York. The next five years he devoted almost entirely to newspaper work: first with the *Tribune*, while Greeley was editor and Whitelaw Reid manager, then with the *Post* under the editorship of Bryant. His first New York venture into the theatre came with *Saratoga*, which Augustin Daly presented at his Fifth Avenue Theatre on December 21, 1870, and for a subsequent run of 101 performances. Even with this early success, Howard was apparently not firmly convinced of his playwriting talents. He continued as a journalist until 1876, and in later years repeatedly insisted that the newspaper editors had taught him to write.

Saratoga, like many of his plays, was performed in England. Retitled *Brighton*, it was first presented at the Court Theatre on May 25, 1874, under the management of Sir Charles (then Mr.) Wyndham. According to Clement Scott, *Brighton* would have been useless without "such a voluble, excited, and impulsive actor as Wyndham. . . . The Public loves him with his legs in the air, or fishing his dripping hat out of a fish tank, or scampering like a wild schoolboy up and down stairs." The play was enormously successful in England. When it was performed at the Criterion in 1883, one reporter noted that it had "played in more London theatres than any other modern piece." Howard's friendship with Wyndham, which began with this professional association, led to marriage with Wyndham's sister, Alice Wyndham, in 1880. From the first production of *Saratoga* in 1870 to his last play, *Kate* (unacted), in 1906, Howard wrote eighteen plays. He died on August 4, 1908, in Avon, New Jersey.

While he was still an active journalist, he wrote three other plays: *Diamonds* (Fifth Avenue Theatre, September 26, 1872), a comedy of manners with an American scene; *Moorcroft, or The Double Wedding* (Fifth Avenue Theatre, October 17, 1874), a melodrama dealing with slavery, based on a short story by John Hay; and *Lillian's Last Love* (Hooley's Theatre, Chicago, September 4, 1873). The last of the three is the most significant to the study of Howard as a dramatist.

Lillian's Last Love was revised into *The Banker's Daughter* (Union Square Theatre, New York, September 30, 1878); was later adapted to English tastes in *The Old Love and the New* (London, 1879); and became the subject of Howard's *Autobiography of a Play*, which he first delivered as a lecture to the

Shakespeare Club at Harvard in 1886 and which was published by the Dramatic Museum of Columbia University in 1914. In this enlightening essay, Howard described his motivations for the changes in the three versions of *The Banker's Daughter* and explained his principles of dramatic construction. Howard insisted that the dramatist must rely on common sense and on a diligent and probing study of humanity: "Laws of dramatic construction exist in the passions and sympathies of the human race." Some brief passages will indicate the tone and sense of his comments:

A few dramatic principles can be brought to your attention. But after you have learned all that has yet been learned by others, the field of humanity will still lie before you, as the field of nature lies before the scientist, with millions of times more to be discovered, by you or some one else, than has ever yet been known.

Do not mistake defiance of laws for originality.

The dramatist appeals to a thousand hearts at the same moment; he has no choice in the matter, he must do this; and it is only when he deals with the love of the sexes that his work is most interesting to that aggregation of human hearts we call "the audience."

Most of the changes he made in *The Banker's Daughter* were demanded by the audience. In the early version Lillian dies. Howard found that the audience objected to the death of a "pure woman," so he kept her alive. The changes in the London adaptation were concessions to English morality: the American "engagement" became only an "understanding" between the lovers, because the English regarded an engagement as official; the duel between the husband and lover needed more severe provocation to satisfy the Englishman's natural distaste for dueling; the bank had to be sold, not closed – English banks "never close."

Although Howard expounded his basic dramaturgical principles in this *Autobiography*, he made additional comments on dramatic construction in various newspaper and magazine interviews. Continually he insisted that the dramatist was a constructor who kept a weather eye on the audience and who did not regard his work as complete until the play was on the boards:

. . . the ideal of a playwright is a happy blending of writer and stage carpenter.

A good play must be absolutely clear. It must not cause you to stop and think when you see it acted though it may make you think a great deal when you read it. . . . No play in any library that you find thumbed and fingered that has not proved a good acting play.

Howard commonly worked through three drafts before a play was ready for production. He employed a system of charts drawn on four-by-six-inch cards, one card for each scene, which indicated the changing relationships between the characters. In a lecture in Detroit, Howard once remarked that he thought the technical training of the engineer and of the dramatist should be very similar.

Before the New York performances of *The Banker's Daughter*, Howard had two more plays on the stage: *Old Love Letters*, a delightfully sentimental one-acter, performed at the Park Theatre on August 31, 1878; and *Hurricanes*, a comedy, first at Hooley's in Chicago on May 27, 1878, and, under the title *Truth*, with Wyndham in England on February 8, 1879. A London critic called it "an American play with Parisian complications." Two minor plays followed: *Wives*, an adaptation of Molière's *L'École des Femmes* and *L'Ecole des Maris*, performed at Daly's on October 28, 1879; and *Fun in a Green-Room*, a backstage farce, at Booth's on April 10, 1882. On October 9, 1882, one of his major social dramas, *The Young Mrs. Winthrop*, was performed at the Madison Square Theatre. It was a study of the unhappy domestic estrangement that results when a wife devotes herself to the social game and a husband is obsessed with business.

Again (this was almost a pattern in Howard's dramatic output) two comparatively unimportant dramas appeared before another major offering: *One of Our Girls*, a comedy set in France, at the Lyceum Theatre, New York, on November 10, 1885; and a romantic play, *Met by Chance*, Lyceum, on January 11, 1887. In *The Henrietta*, Howard again explored the business world and its ruthless disregard for human loyalties and love. *The Henrietta* was produced at the Union Square Theatre on September 26, 1887. Well in advance of twentieth-century novelists and dramatists, Howard, along with Howells, discovered that big business and its intriguing and often vicious practices were really *the* distinctively American subject matter for the writer. The play was first performed in England "for copyright purposes" with the American title four days before the New York opening. When *The Henrietta* began its regular London engagement in March, 1891, Clement Scott reported that Howard had "discarded the grammatical rules that hitherto have influenced dramatic composition." He had devised "a play of stocks and shares and business and commerce" whose principal object was to "introduce the telephone, the ticker tape, and the electric bell to the stage."

Baron Rudolph dealt with the struggle between capital and labor, and although it was given a preliminary "copyright showing" in London as early as 1881, it was not seen in this country until its production at the Fourteenth Street Theatre on October 25, 1887. *Shenandoah* appeared at the Star Theatre in New York on September 9, 1889, when Howard was at the height of his career. *Aristocracy* treated a concomitant of American business, the pursuit of American heiresses by foreign dandies. It was performed at Palmer's Theatre on November 14, 1892. *Peter Stuyvesant* was his last play to be produced. Written in collaboration with Brander Matthews, it was performed at Wallack's on October 2, 1899. *Knave and Queen* (originally called *Ivers Dean* and written in collaboration with Sir Charles L. Young, Bart.) was probably written in the mid-eighties but was never produced. An unproduced and unpublished play, *The Title*, written in 1895, dealt with the suffragist movement. Howard's last play, *Kate* (1906), was published but never acted.

By his own example and by his persistent crusading, Howard brought new recognition and honor to American playwrights. He had no vested interest in theatrical production as manager or actor. He was not a refugee from the world of belles-lettres, venturing a casual and apologetic fling at dramatic writing. He was a professional playwright, moderate, careful, and committed to learning and practicing his art. Although he dealt with the American scene, there was no "spread-eaglism" in his attitude; nor was he unmindful of his foreign contemporaries. He was impressed with Ibsen's masterly technique but deplored his morbid attitude toward life. From his newspaper training Howard had learned the unpardonableness of being dull. He was always conscientious and careful in his work and was loath to write too quickly or too much.

The success of his campaign to advance the professional standing of the American dramatist probably rested just as much on the man as on his work. Two descriptions of Howard provide a partial portrait; the first is from Augustus Thomas, the second from Brander Matthews:

He was a delightful talker, shrewd and sagacious, and yet easy and wholly without pretense. He did his own thinking; but he never forced his opinions on others. He was the soul of courtesy; and, witty as he was, he never risked the loss of his friend for the sake of his jest.

We must record him a man equipped with the emotional power of an artist, the generosity of a cavalier, and the temperance of a gentleman.

Unlike so many earlier playwrights, Howard achieved honor and profit in his own time, both here and in Great Britain. No old-age benefit performances were required. He could have retired on the profits from the continuing performances of *Shenandoah*.

Coming as it did at the height of his career, *Shenandoah* represents Howard's mature dramatic art, and the story of its evolution shows the serious dramatist at work. After the New York production of *The Henrietta*, Howard took his English wife to Michigan for a first visit with his relatives in Ann Arbor. She was delighted and insisted that they take a house and remain for a while. Howard agreed when he found that the University of Michigan Library had the research materials he required for the preparation of his new play. He had often insisted that "a dramatist must completely saturate himself with his subject before he begins to write." He began by carefully reading a dozen volumes of the *Century Military History*, searching for a dramatic incident on which to construct a Civil War drama. When he had sufficiently immersed himself in the atmosphere of the conflict, selected the appropriate episodes, exposed the entire panorama to his dramatic imagination, and prepared his cards, he began to write. As the play evolved he discovered that he could reuse some comedy scenes from one of his early compositions, a play called *Drum-Taps* which had been produced at the Macauley Theatre in Louisville sometime in the late seventies. By the end of the summer he had a draft of *Shenandoah* which he thought was ready for its first exposure on the stage.

A tryout performance was given at the Boston Museum on November 19, 1888. Although it was not successful, the play caught the attention of Charles Frohman. Frohman, then at the beginning of his managerial career, called on Howard and is reported to have said: "You are a very great dramatist, Mr. Howard, and I am only a theatrical manager, but I think I can see where a possible improvement might be made in the play. For one thing, I think two acts should be merged into one, and I don't think you have made enough out of Sheridan's ride." Howard agreed to the changes. With financial assistance from the San Francisco manager Al Hayman, who had just entered the New York theatrical field, Frohman produced the revised version at the Star Theatre in New York on September 9, 1889. Although everything had been done to assure a success – elaborate scenes and a high-quality cast including Wilton Lackaye, Henry Miller, Effie Shannon, and Viola Allen – Howard and Frohman stood at the back of the house on the opening night fearfully wondering whether Sheridan's ride across the stage would provoke ridicule or applause. Nor was their alarm lessened by knowing that General William Tecumseh Sherman was in the audience. When the horse galloped on stage and the audience cheered and applauded, Frohman turned to Howard with a sigh and whispered, "Thank God that horse is across."

The relief was probably even greater for Howard. Although he demanded authenticity and realism – for example, the trumpet signals were taken directly from the U.S. Army manual *Signal Tactics* – he feared the introduction of stage spectacle that would distort the over-all effect of his drama. The play caught the public fancy immediately. The pictorial effects, the strong, courageous, and gallant' hearts of both Southerners and Northerners, and the "hands-across-the-border" attitude toward the late war were evidently the magic qualities of the moment. After an engagement of five weeks at the Star Theatre, the house was still filled to capacity, but the theatre had been committed to the Jefferson-Florence company of *The Rivals*. Frohman moved the production to Proctor's Twenty-third Street, where it continued until April 19, 1890. At the 250th and final performance, the audience was treated to double and triple relays of several of the characters. For example, Wilton Lackaye, Frank Burbeck, and George Osborne, all of whom had played General Haverhill at various times, enacted the role in succession. William Dean Howells saw the play during that spring and wrote in *Harper's* in June, 1890:

. . . Charm from first moment to last, and it has passages of nobility and beauty with effects that ravish the sense and kindle the fancy, by the legitimate realization of facts that cannot be put into dialogue or action. . . . It is indeed a splendid passage of the war, and it suggests the whole course of the war. . . . The swiftly moving history is expressed from the patriotic point of view in such terms and characters as do justice to the high motives and unselfish heroism on both sides.

The military aspect of the play drew the most attention from critics, managers, and audiences alike during the fifteen years of its vigorous theatrical life. Of the wartime series of performances at the Academy of Music, May 17 to June 11, 1898, the New York *Dramatic Mirror* wrote on May 28:

. . . Audience was nearly as martial in appearance as was the play. Scattered everywhere through the house were Grand Army and other veterans. Keenly they watched and lustily they cheered! The production is one that never has been surpassed on the local stage. . . . Frank Oakes Rose, who devised the scene, drilled the multitude of supernumeraries till each man worked with true military alertness. The entire performance passed off without a hitch, the occasion was a triumph. . . . In the last act there was a finale showing a review by President Lincoln of the victorious army returning from the war. Between Acts III and IV Miss Quinlan (Jennie Buckthorn) came before the curtain and led the audience in the "Star Spangled Banner." The Governor should open a recruiting station at the Academy.

Invariably the reviews spoke of the pictorial effects, the sharply trained supers, the wild enthusiasm following Sheridan's ride, the tears in the eyes of veterans. One account described two veterans, one from the North, the other from the South, seated side by side. At the final curtain they turned to each other with arms extended for a warm and forgiving embrace. Almost without exception, the reviewers concluded their notices with comments such as "*Shenandoah* is still what it always has been, the most interesting, the most exciting, the most dignified of modern military dramas." For the touring engagements around the country, the newspapers and advance bills dwelt on the size and realism of the production: "Cavalry! Infantry! Artillery! 250 Men! 50 Horses!" For military groups and military occasions, the play was eminently appropriate. On Dewey Day, May 1, 1899, the Broadway Theatre was draped liberally with flags and bunting for a performance that was described as "more excellent in every respect" than any previous productions.

Shenandoah was not the first or the last of the Civil War dramas. In most respects it was the best. Augustin Daly's *Norwood* (1867) brought the Battle of Gettysburg to the stage; Boucicault's *Belle Lamar* (1874), with a setting of fictitious battles and troop movements, presented the first of the romantic Southern heroines; William Gillette's *Held by the Enemy* (1886) dealt primarily with a painful struggle between officers of the Union Army over the love of a Southern girl, set against a background of swiftly moving melodramatic action. In its realistic representation of romantic adventure, *Shenandoah* bears some similarity to Gillette's play, but Howard's play was more closely related to actual military events. Other war dramas followed *Shenandoah:* Augustus Thomas's *Surrender* (1892) was laid in or near Richmond during the last days of the Confederacy; William Gillette's *Secret Service* (1895), an exciting spy drama, with Gillette in the principal role of Captain Thorne, achieved a record of some seventeen hundred performances in twenty years; Belasco's *The Heart of Maryland* (1895) was a melodramatic potpourri in which Mrs. Leslie Carter achieved a notable success by swinging on the clapper of a bell to deaden the sound and thus save her lover; James A. Herne's *Griffith Davenport* (1899) presented a more realistic and complex treatment of slavery and the war than any of the other plays; and Clyde Fitch's *Barbara Frietchie* (1899) was pure romantic invention with no pretense to historical accuracy. Most of the Civil War plays were markedly similar in many respects: little attention to slavery as a cause of the war, dramatic action evolved from pseudo-historical military events realistically detailed in the representation, a romantic love story between a Northern soldier and a Southern belle, and settings that pictured various colorful locales below Mason and Dixon's line.

Shenandoah did not deviate from the pattern. In most respects, however, it maintained a higher degree of authenticity and excitement. Howard's dramaturgy pointed the way to modern drama: away from the mid-Victorian apron stage with its rhetorical speeches and confidential asides to a framed picture of realistic action. Like all good dramatists, he employed theatrical and nonliterary qualities for his most striking passages. As Brander Matthews said:

There is pure poetry, for instance, but in action rather than in words, in the funeral scene where the soldier father, all unknowing, walks reverently behind the body of his erring son, who has been redeemed by a heroic death, – a picture of unspoken pathos which must linger in the memories of all who ever beheld the play.

SHENANDOAH

BRONSON HOWARD

CHARACTERS

GENERAL HAVERHILL
COLONEL KERCHIVAL WEST } *Officers of Sheridan's Cavalry*
CAPTAIN HEARTSEASE
LIEUTENANT FRANK BEDLOE
MAJOR-GENERAL FRANCIS BUCKTHORN,
   Commander of the 19th Army Corps
SERGEANT BARKET
COLONEL ROBERT ELLINGHAM,
   10th Virginia
CAPTAIN THORNTON,
   Secret Service, C.S.A.
MRS. CONSTANCE HAVERHILL
GERTRUDE ELLINGHAM

MADELINE WEST
JENNY BUCKTHORN
MRS. EDITH HAVERHILL
HARDWICK, *Surgeon*
CAPTAIN LOCKWOOD,
   U.S. Signal Corps
LIEUTENANT OF SIGNAL CORPS
LIEUTENANT OF INFANTRY
CORPORAL DUNN
BENSON
OLD MARGERY
JANETTE
WILKINS

ACT I

Charleston Harbor in 1861. "After the Ball."

The Interior of a Southern Residence on the shore of Charleston Harbor. Large double doors at the rear of the stage are open. A large, wide window, with low sill, extends down the right side of the stage. A veranda is seen through the doors and the window. There is a wide opening on the left with a corridor beyond. The furniture and appointments are quaint and old-fashioned, but the general tone of the walls and upholstery is that of the old Colonial period in its more ornamental and decorative phase, as shown in the early days of Charleston. Old candlesticks and candelabra, with lighted candles nearly burned down, light the room, and in addition the moonlight streams in. Beyond the central doors and the window there is a lawn, with Southern foliage, extending down to the shores of the harbor; a part of the bay lies in the distance, with low-lying land beyond. The lights of Charleston are seen over the water along the shore. The gray twilight of early morning gradually steals over the scene as the Act progresses. As the curtain rises, Kerchival West is sitting in a chair, his feet extended and his head thrown back, a handkerchief over his face. Robert Ellingham strolls in on the veranda, beyond the window, smoking. He looks to the right, starts and moves to the window; leans against the upper side of the window and looks across.

ELLINGHAM: Kerchival!

KERCHIVAL: [*Under the handkerchief*] Eh? H'm!

ELLINGHAM: Can you sleep at a time like this? My own nerves are on fire.

KERCHIVAL: Fire? Oh – yes – I remember. Any more fire-works, Bob?

ELLINGHAM: A signal rocket from one of the batteries, now and then. [*He goes up beyond the window. Kerchival arouses himself, taking the handkerchief from his eyes*]

KERCHIVAL: What a preposterous hour to be up. The ball was over an hour ago, all the guests are gone, and it's nearly four o'clock. [*Looking at his watch*] Exactly ten minutes of four. [*He takes out a cigar*] Our Southern friends assure us that General Beauregard is to open fire on Fort Sumter this morning. I don't believe it. [*Lighting the cigar and rising, he looks out through the window*] There lies the old fort – solemn and grim as ever, and the flag-staff stands above it, like a warning finger. If they do fire upon it [*Shutting his teeth for a moment and looking down at the cigar in his hand*] the echo of that first shot will be heard above their graves, and Heaven knows how many of our own, also; but the flag will still float! – over the graves of both sides.

Ellingham enters from the central door and approaches him

Are you Southerners all mad, Robert?

ELLINGHAM: Are you Northerners all blind? [*Kerchival sits down*] We Virginians would prevent a war if we could. But your people in the North do not believe that one is coming. You do not understand the determined frenzy of my fellow Southerners. Look! [*Pointing toward the rear of the stage*] Do you see the lights of the city, over the water? The inhabitants of Charleston are gathering, even now, in the gray, morning twilight, to witness the long-promised bombardment of Fort Sumter. It is to be a gala day for them. They have talked and dreamed of nothing else for weeks. The preparations have become a part of their social life – of their amusement – their gayeties. This very night at the ball – here – in the house of my own relatives – what was their talk? What were the jests they laughed at? Sumter! War! Ladies were betting bonbons that the United States would not dare to fire a shot in return, and pinning ribbons on the breasts of their "heroes." There was a signal rocket from one of the forts, and the young men who were dancing here left their partners standing on the floor to return to the batteries – as if it were the night before another Waterloo. The ladies themselves hurried away to watch the "spectacle" from their own verandas. You won't see the truth! I tell you, Kerchival, a war between the North and South is inevitable!

KERCHIVAL: And if it does come, you Virginians will join the rest.

ELLINGHAM: Our State will be the battle ground, I fear. But every loyal son of Virginia will follow her flag. It is our religion!

KERCHIVAL: My State is New York. If New York should go against the old flag, New York might go to the devil. That is my religion.

ELLINGHAM: So differently have we been taught what the word "patriotism" means!

KERCHIVAL: You and I are officers of the same regiment of the United States Regular Army, Robert; we were classmates at West Point, and we have fought side by side on the plains. You saved my scalp once; I'd have to wear a wig, now, if you hadn't. I say, old boy, are we to be enemies?

ELLINGHAM: [*Laying his hand over his shoulder*] My dear old comrade, whatever else comes, our friendship shall be unbroken!

KERCHIVAL: Bob! [*Looking up at him*] I only hope that we shall never meet in battle!

ELLINGHAM: In battle? The idea is horrible!

KERCHIVAL: [*Rising and crossing to him*] My dear old comrade, one of us will be wrong in this great fight, but we shall both be honest in it. [*He gives his hand; Ellingham grasps it warmly, then turns away*]

ELLINGHAM: Colonel Haverhill is watching the forts, also; he has been as sad to-night as we have. Next to leaving you, my greatest regret is that I must resign from his regiment.

KERCHIVAL: You are his favorite officer.

ELLINGHAM: Naturally, perhaps; he was my guardian.

Enter Haverhill from the rear. He walks down, stopping in the center of the stage

HAVERHILL: Kerchival! I secured the necessary passports to the North yesterday afternoon; this one is yours; I brought it down for you early in the evening. [*Kerchival takes the paper and goes to the window*] I am ordered direct to Washington at once, and shall start with Mrs. Haverhill this forenoon. You will report to Captain Lyon, of the 2d Regiment, in St. Louis. Robert! I have hoped for peace to the last, but it is hoping against hope. I feel certain, now, that the fatal blow will be struck this morning. Our old regiment is already broken up, and you, also, will now resign, I suppose, like nearly all your fellow Southerners in the Service.

ELLINGHAM: You know how sorry I am to leave your command, Colonel!

HAVERHILL: I served under your father in Mexico; he left me, at his death, the guardian of you and your sister, Gertrude. Even since you became of age, I have felt that I stood in his place. But you must be your sister's only guardian now. Your father fell in battle, fighting for our common country, but you –

ELLINGHAM: He would have done as I shall do, had he lived. He was a Virginian!

HAVERHILL: I am glad, Robert, that he was never called upon to decide between two flags. He never knew but one, and we fought under it together. [*Exit*]

ELLINGHAM: Kerchival! Something occurred in this house to-night which – which I shouldn't mention under ordinary circumstances, but I – I feel that it may require my further attention, and you, perhaps, can be of service to me. Mrs. Haverhill, the wife of the Colonel –

KERCHIVAL: Fainted away in her room.

ELLINGHAM: You know?

KERCHIVAL: I was one of the actors in the little drama.

ELLINGHAM: Indeed!

KERCHIVAL: About half-past nine this evening, while the ladies were dressing for the ball, I was going upstairs; I heard a quick, sharp cry, sprang forward, found myself at an open door. Mrs. Haverhill lay on the floor inside, as if she had just reached the door to cry for help, when she fell. After doing all the unnecessary and useless things I could think of, I rushed out of the room to tell your sister, Gertrude, and my own sister, Madeline, to go and take care of the lady. Within less than twenty minutes afterwards, I saw Mrs. Haverhill sail into the drawing-room, a thing of beauty, and with the glow of perfect health on her cheek. It was an immense relief to me when I saw her. Up to that time I had a vague idea that I had committed a murder.

ELLINGHAM: Murder!

KERCHIVAL: M——m. A guilty conscience. Every man, of course, does exactly the wrong thing when a woman faints. When I rushed out of Mrs. Haverhill's room, I left my handkerchief soaked with water upon her face. I must ask her for it, it's a silk one. Luckily, the girls got there in time to take it off; she wouldn't have come to if they hadn't. It never occurred to me that she'd need to breathe in my absence. That's all I know about the matter. What troubles you? I suppose every woman has a right to faint whenever she chooses. The scream that I heard was so sharp, quick and intense that –

ELLINGHAM: That the cause must have been a serious one.

KERCHIVAL: Yes! So I thought. It must have been a mouse.

ELLINGHAM: Mr. Edward Thornton has occupied the next room to that of Mrs. Haverhill to-night.

KERCHIVAL: [*Quickly*] What do you mean?

ELLINGHAM: During the past month or more he has been pressing, not to say insolent, in his attentions to Mrs. Haverhill.

KERCHIVAL: I've noticed that myself.

ELLINGHAM: And he is an utterly unscrupulous man; it is no fault of mine that he was asked to be a guest at this house to-night. He came to Charleston, some years ago, from the North, but if there are any vices and passions peculiarly strong in the South, he has carried them all to the extreme. In one of the many scandals connected with Edward Thornton's name, it was more than whispered that he entered a lady's room unexpectedly at night. But, as he killed the lady's husband in a duel a few days afterwards, the scandal dropped.

KERCHIVAL: Of course; the gentleman received ample satisfaction as an outraged husband, and Mr. Thornton apologized, I suppose, to his widow.

ELLINGHAM: He has repeated the adventure.

KERCHIVAL: Do – you – think – that?

ELLINGHAM: I was smoking on the lawn, and glanced up at the window; my eyes may have deceived me, and I must move cautiously in the matter; but it couldn't have been imagination; the shadow of Edward Thornton's face and head appeared upon the curtain.

KERCHIVAL: Whew! The devil!

ELLINGHAM: Just at that moment I, too, heard the stifled scream.

Enter Edward Thornton

THORNTON: Gentlemen!

ELLINGHAM: Your name was just on my tongue, Mr. Thornton.

THORNTON: I thought I heard it, but you are welcome to it. Miss Gertrude has asked me to ride over to Mrs. Pinckney's with her, to learn if there is any further news from the batteries. I am very glad the time to attack Fort Sumter has come at last!

ELLINGHAM: I do not share your pleasure.

THORNTON: You are a Southern gentleman.

ELLINGHAM: And you are a Northern "gentleman."

THORNTON: A Southerner by choice; I shall join the cause.

ELLINGHAM: We native Southerners will defend our own rights, sir; you may leave them in our keeping. It is my wish, Mr. Thornton, that you do not accompany my sister.

THORNTON: Indeed!

ELLINGHAM: Her groom, alone, will be sufficient.

THORNTON: As you please, sir. Kindly offer my excuses to Miss Gertrude. You and I can chat over the subject later in the day, when we are alone. [*Moving up the stage*]

ELLINGHAM: By all means, and another subject, also, perhaps.

THORNTON: I shall be entirely at your service. [*Exit to the veranda*]

ELLINGHAM: Kerchival, I shall learn the whole truth, if possible, to-day. If it is what I suspect – what I almost know – I will settle with him myself. He has insulted our Colonel's wife and outraged the hospitality of my friends. [*Walking to the right*]

KERCHIVAL: [*Walking to the left*] I think it ought to be my quarrel. I'm sure I'm mixed up in it enough.

MADELINE: [*Without, calling*] Kerchival!

ELLINGHAM: Madeline. [*Aside, starting, Kerchival looks across at him sharply*]

KERCHIVAL: [*Aside*] I distinctly saw Bob give a start when he heard Madeline. Now, what can there be about my sister's voice to make a man jump like that?

GERTRUDE: [*Without*] Brother Robert!

KERCHIVAL: Gertrude! [*Aside, starting, Ellingham looks at him sharply*] How the tones of a woman's voice thrill through a man's soul!

Enter Madeline

MADELINE: Oh, Kerchival – here you are.

Enter Gertrude, from the apartment, in a riding habit, with a whip

GERTRUDE: Robert, dear! [*Coming down to Robert; they converse in dumb show*]

MADELINE: Where are your field glasses? I've been rummaging all through your clothes, and swords, and sashes, and things. I've turned everything in your room upside down.

KERCHIVAL: Have you?

MADELINE: I can't find your glasses anywhere. I want to look at the forts. Another rocket went up just now. [*Runs up the stage and stands on the piazza looking off*]

KERCHIVAL: A sister has all the privileges of a wife to upset a man's things, without her legal obligation to put them straight again. [*Glances at Gertrude*] I wish Bob's sister had the same privileges in my room that my own has.

GERTRUDE: Mr. Thornton isn't going with me, you say?

ELLINGHAM: He requested me to offer you his apologies.

KERCHIVAL: May *I* accompany you? [*Ellingham turns to the window on the right*]

GERTRUDE: My groom, old Pete, will be with me, of course; there's no particular need of anyone else. But you may go along, if you like. I've got my hands full of sugar plums for Jack. Dear old Jack – he always has his share when we have company. I'm going over to Mrs. Pinckney's to see if she's had any more news from General Beauregard; her son is on the General's staff.

MADELINE: [*Looking off to the right*] There's another rocket from Fort Johnson; and it is answered from Fort Moultrie. Ah! [*Angrily*] General Beauregard is a bad, wicked man! [*Coming down*]

GERTRUDE: Oh! Madeline! You are a bad, wicked Northern girl to say such a thing.

MADELINE: I *am* a Northern girl.

GERTRUDE: And I am a Southern girl. [*They face each other*]

KERCHIVAL: [*Dropping into a chair*] The war has begun.

Ellingham has turned from the window; he strolls across the stage, watching the girls

GERTRUDE: General Beauregard is a patriot.

MADELINE: He is a Rebel.

GERTRUDE: So am I.

MADELINE: Gertrude! – You – you –

GERTRUDE: Madeline! – You –

MADELINE: I – I –

GERTRUDE: I –

BOTH: O – O-H! [*Bursting into tears and rushing into each other's arms, sobbing, then suddenly kissing each other vigorously*]

KERCHIVAL: I say, Bob, if the North and South do fight, that will be the end of it.

GERTRUDE: I've got something to say to you, Madeline, dear. [*Confidentially and turning with her arms about her waist. The girls sit down talking earnestly*]

ELLINGHAM: Kerchival, old boy! There's –

there's something I'd like to say to you before we part to-day.

KERCHIVAL: I'd like a word with you, also!

MADELINE: You don't really mean that, Gertrude – with me?

ELLINGHAM: I'm in love with your sister, Madeline.

KERCHIVAL: The devil you are!

ELLINGHAM: I never suspected such a thing until last night.

GERTRUDE: Robert was in love with you six weeks ago. [*Madeline kisses her*]

KERCHIVAL: *I've* made a discovery, too, Bob.

MADELINE: *I've* got something to say to *you*, Gertrude.

KERCHIVAL: I'm in love with *your* sister.

ELLINGHAM: [*Astonished*] You are?

MADELINE: Kerchival has been in love with you for the last three months. [*Gertrude offers her lips – they kiss*]

KERCHIVAL: I fell in love with her the day before yesterday. [*The two gentlemen grasp each other's hands warmly*]

ELLINGHAM: We understand each other, Kerchival. [*He turns up the stage and stops at the door*] Miss Madeline, you said just now that you wished to watch the forts. Would you like to walk down to the shore?

MADELINE: Yes! [*Rising and going up to him. He takes one of her hands in his own and looks at her earnestly*]

ELLINGHAM: This will be the last day that we shall be together, for the present. But we shall meet again – sometime – if we both live.

MADELINE: If we both live! You mean – if *you* live. You must go into this dreadful war, if it comes.

ELLINGHAM: Yes, Madeline, I must. Come let us watch for our fate. [*Exeunt to the veranda*]

KERCHIVAL: [*Aside*] I must leave Charleston to-day. [*He sighs*] Does she love me?

GERTRUDE: I am ready to start, Mr. West, when you are.

KERCHIVAL: Oh! Of course, I forgot. [*Rising*] I shall be delighted to ride at your side.

GERTRUDE: At my side! [*Rising*] There isn't a horse in America that can keep by the side of my Jack, when I give him his head, and I'm sure to do it. You may follow us. But you can hardly ride in that costume; while you are changing it, I'll give Jack his bonbons. [*Turning to the window*] There he is, bless him! Pawing the ground, and impatient for me to

be on his back. Let him come, Pete. [*Holding up bonbons at window*] I love you.

KERCHIVAL: Eh? [*Turning suddenly*]

GERTRUDE: [*Looking at him*] What?

KERCHIVAL: You were saying –

GERTRUDE: Jack! [*Looking out. The head of a large black horse appears through the window*] You dear old fellow. [*She feeds him with bonbons*] Jack has been my boy ever since he was a little colt. I brought you up, didn't I, Jack? He's the truest, and kindest, and best of friends; I wouldn't be parted from him for the world, and I'm the only woman he'll allow to be near him.

KERCHIVAL: [*Earnestly*] You are the only woman, Miss Gertrude, that I –

GERTRUDE: Dear Jack!

KERCHIVAL: [*Aside*] Jack embarrasses me. He's a third party.

GERTRUDE: There! That will do for the present, Jack. Now go along with Pete! If you are a very good boy, and don't let Lieutenant Kerchival West come within a quarter of a mile of me, after the first three minutes, you shall have some more sugar plums when we get to Mrs. Pinckney's. [*An old negro leads the horse away. Gertrude looks around at Kerchival*] You haven't gone to dress, yet; we shall be late. Mrs. Pinckney asked a party of friends to witness the bombardment this morning, and breakfast together on the piazza while they are looking at it. We can remain and join them, if you like.

KERCHIVAL: I hope they won't wait for breakfast until the bombardment begins.

GERTRUDE: I'll bet you an embroidered cigar-case, Lieutenant, against a box of gloves that it will begin in less than an hour.

KERCHIVAL: Done! You will lose the bet. But you shall have the gloves; and one of the hands that go inside them shall be – [*Taking one of her hands; she withdraws it*]

GERTRUDE: My own – until some one wins it. You don't believe that General Beauregard will open fire on Fort Sumter this morning?

KERCHIVAL: No; I don't.

GERTRUDE: Everything is ready.

KERCHIVAL: It's so much easier to get everything ready to do a thing than it is to do it. I have been ready a dozen times, this very night, to say to you, Miss Gertrude, that I – that I – [*Pauses*]

GERTRUDE: [*Looking down and tapping her skirt with her whip*] Well?

KERCHIVAL: But I didn't.

GERTRUDE: [*Glancing up at him suddenly*] I dare say, General Beauregard has more nerve than you have.

KERCHIVAL: It is easy enough to set the batteries around Charleston Harbor, but the man who fires the first shot at a woman –

GERTRUDE: Woman!

KERCHIVAL: At the American flag – must have nerves of steel.

GERTRUDE: You Northern men are so slow, to –

KERCHIVAL: I have been slow; but I assure you, Miss Gertrude, that my heart –

GERTRUDE: What subject are we on now?

KERCHIVAL: You were complaining because I was too slow.

GERTRUDE: I was doing nothing of the kind, sir! – let me finish, please. You Northern men are so slow, to believe that our Southern heroes – Northern *men* and Southern *heroes* – you recognize the distinction I make – you won't believe that they will keep their promises. They have sworn to attack Fort Sumter this morning, and – they – will do it. This "American Flag" you talk of is no longer our flag: it is foreign to us! – It is the flag of an enemy!

KERCHIVAL: [*Tenderly and earnestly*] Am I your enemy?

GERTRUDE: You have told me that you will return to the North, and take the field.

KERCHIVAL: Yes, I will. [*Decisively*]

GERTRUDE: You will be fighting against my friends, against my own brother, against me. We *shall* be enemies.

KERCHIVAL: [*Firmly*] Even that, Gertrude – [*She looks around at him, he looks squarely into her eyes as he proceeds*] – if you will have it so. If my country needs my services, I shall not refuse them, though it makes us enemies! [*She wavers a moment, under strong emotion, and turns away; sinks upon the seat, her elbow on the back of it, and her tightly-clenched fist against her cheek, looking away from him*]

GERTRUDE: I will have it so! I am a Southern woman!

KERCHIVAL: We have more at stake between us, this morning, than a cigar-case and a box of gloves. [*Turning up the stage*]

Enter Mrs. Haverhill from apartment

MRS. HAVERHILL: Mr. West! I've been looking for you. I have a favor to ask.

KERCHIVAL: Of me? – with pleasure.

MRS. HAVERHILL: But I am sorry to have interrupted you and Gertrude. [*As she passes down Kerchival moves up the stage. Gertrude rises*] [*Apart*] There are tears in your eyes, Gertrude, dear!

GERTRUDE: [*Apart*] They have no right there.

MRS. HAVERHILL: [*Apart*] I'm afraid I know what has happened. A quarrel! and you are to part with each other so soon. Do not let a girl's coquetry trifle with her heart until it is too late. You remember the confession you made to me last night?

GERTRUDE: [*Apart*] Constance! [*Starting*] That is my secret; more a secret now than ever.

MRS. HAVERHILL: [*Apart*] Yes, dear; but you do love him. [*Gertrude moves up the stage*]

GERTRUDE: You need not ride over with me, Mr. West.

KERCHIVAL: I can be ready in one moment.

GERTRUDE: I choose to go alone! Old Pete will be with me; and Jack, himself, is a charming companion.

KERCHIVAL: If you prefer Jack's company to mine –

GERTRUDE: I do. [*Exit on the veranda*]

KERCHIVAL: Damn Jack! But you will let me assist you to mount. [*Exit after her*]

MRS. HAVERHILL: We leave for the North before noon, but every hour seems a month. If my husband should learn what happened in my room to-night, he would kill that man. What encouragement could I have given him? Innocence is never on its guard – but, [*Drawing up*] the last I remember before I fell unconscious, he was crouching before me like a whipped cur! [*She starts as she looks out of the window*] There is Mr. Thornton, now – Ah! [*Angrily*] No – I must control my own indignation. I must keep him and Colonel Haverhill from meeting before we leave Charleston. Edward Thornton would shoot my husband down without remorse. But poor Frank! I must not forget him, in my own trouble. I have but little time left to care for his welfare.

Re-enter Kerchival

KERCHIVAL: You said I could do you a favor, Mrs. Haverhill?

MRS. HAVERHILL: Yes, I wanted to speak with

you about General Haverhill's son, Frank. I should like you to carry a message to Charleston for me as soon as it is light. It is a sad errand. You know too well the great misfortune that has fallen upon my husband in New York.

KERCHIVAL: His only son has brought disgrace upon his family name, and tarnished the reputation of a proud soldier. Colonel Haverhill's fellow officers sympathize with him most deeply.

MRS. HAVERHILL: And poor young Frank! I could hardly have loved the boy more if he had been my own son. If he had not himself confessed the crime against the bank, I could not have believed him guilty. He has escaped from arrest. He is in the City of Charleston. I am the only one in all the world he could turn to. He was only a lad of fourteen when his father and I were married, six years ago; and the boy has loved me from the first. His father is stern and bitter now in his humiliation. This note from Frank was handed to me while the company were here last evening. I want you to find him and arrange for me to meet him, if you can do it with safety. I shall give you a letter for him.

KERCHIVAL: I'll get ready at once; and I will do all I can for the boy.

MRS. HAVERHILL: And – Mr. West! Gertrude and Madeline have told me that – that – I was under obligations to you last evening.

KERCHIVAL: Don't mention it. I merely ran for them, and I – I'm very glad you didn't choke – before they reached you. I trust you are quite well now?

MRS. HAVERHILL: I am entirely recovered, thank you. And I will ask another favor of you, for we are old friends. I desire very much that General Haverhill should not know that – that any accident occurred to me to-night – or that my health has not been perfect.

KERCHIVAL: Certainly, madam!

MRS. HAVERHILL: It would render him anxious without cause.

KERCHIVAL: [*Aside*] It looks as if Robert was right; she doesn't want the two men to meet.

Enter Haverhill, a white silk handkerchief in his hand

HAVERHILL: Constance, my dear, I've been all over the place looking for you. I thought you were in your room. But – by the way, Kerchi-val, this is your handkerchief; your initials are on it.

Kerchival turns and stares at him a second. Mrs. Haverhill starts slightly and turns front. Haverhill glances quickly from one to the other, then extends his hands toward Kerchival, with the handkerchief. Kerchival moves to him and takes it. Mrs. Haverhill drops into the chair

KERCHIVAL: Thank you. [*He walks up and exits with a quick glance back. Haverhill looks at Mrs. Haverhill, who sits nervously, looking away. He then glances up after Kerchival. A cloud comes over his face and he stands a second in thought. Then, with a movement as if brushing away a passing suspicion, he smiles pleasantly and approaches Mrs. Haverhill; leaning over her*]

HAVERHILL: My fair Desdemona! [*Smiling*] I found Cassio's handkerchief in your room. Have you a kiss for me? [*She looks up, he raises her chin with a finger and kisses her*] That's the way I shall smother you.

MRS. HAVERHILL: [*Rising and dropping her head upon his breast*] Husband!

HAVERHILL: But what is this they have been telling me?

MRS. HAVERHILL: What have they said to you?

HAVERHILL: There was something wrong with you in the early part of the evening; you are trembling and excited, my girl!

MRS. HAVERHILL: It was nothing, John; I – I – was ill, for a few moments, but I am well now.

HAVERHILL: You said nothing about it to me.

MRS. HAVERHILL: Do not give it another thought.

HAVERHILL: Was there anything besides your health involved in the affair? There was. [*Aside*] How came this handkerchief in her room?

MRS. HAVERHILL: My husband! I do not want to say anything more – at – at present – about what happened to-night. There has never been a shadow between us – will you not trust me?

HAVERHILL: Shadow! You stand in a bright light of your own, my wife; it shines upon my whole life – there can be no shadow there. Tell me as much or as little as you like, and in your own time. I am sure you will conceal nothing from me that I ought to know. I trust my honor and my happiness to you, absolutely.

MRS. HAVERHILL: They will both be safe,

John, in my keeping. But there is something else that I wish to speak with you about; something very near to your heart – your son!

HAVERHILL: My son!

MRS. HAVERHILL: He is in Charleston.

HAVERHILL: And not – in prison? To me he is nowhere. I am childless.

MRS. HAVERHILL: I hope to see him to-day; may I not take him some kind word from you?

HAVERHILL: My lawyers in New York had instructions to provide him with whatever he needed.

MRS. HAVERHILL: They have done so, and he wants for nothing; he asks for nothing, except that I will seek out the poor young wife – only a girl herself – whom he is obliged to desert, in New York.

HAVERHILL: His marriage was a piece of reckless folly, but I forgave him that.

MRS. HAVERHILL: I am sure that it was only after another was dependent on him that the debts of a mere spendthrift were changed to fraud – and crime.

HAVERHILL: You may tell him that I will provide for her.

MRS. HAVERHILL: And may I take him no warmer message from his father?

HAVERHILL: I am an officer of the United States Army. The name which my son bears came to me from men who had borne it with honor, and I transmitted it to him without a blot. He has disgraced it, by his own confession.

MRS. HAVERHILL: *I* cannot forget the poor mother who died when he was born; her whose place I have tried to fill, to both Frank and to you. I never saw her, and she is sleeping in the old graveyard at home. But I am doing what she would do to-day, if she were living. No pride – no disgrace – could have turned her face from him. The care and the love of her son has been to me the most sacred duty which one woman can assume for another.

HAVERHILL: You have fulfilled that duty, Constance. Go to my son! I would go with you, but he is a man now; he could not look into my eyes, and I could not trust myself. But I will send him something which a man will understand. Frank loves you as if you were his own mother; and I – I would like him to – to think tenderly of me, also. He will do it when he looks at this picture. [*Taking a miniature from his pocket*]

MRS. HAVERHILL: Of me!

HAVERHILL: I have never been without it one hour, before, since we were married. He will recognize it as the one that I have carried through every campaign, in every scene of danger on the Plains; the one that has always been with me. He is a fugitive from justice. At times, when despair might overcome him, this may give him nerve to meet his future life manfully. It has often nerved me, when I might have failed without it. Give it to him, and tell him that I send it. [*Giving her the miniature*] I could not send a kinder message, and he will understand it. [*Turning, he stands a moment in thought. Thornton appears at the window looking at them quietly, over his shoulder, a cigar in his hand. Mrs. Haverhill sees him, and starts with a suppressed breath, then looks at Haverhill, who moves away. He speaks aside*] My son! My son! We shall never meet again! [*Exit*]

Mrs. Haverhill looks after him earnestly, then turns and looks at Thornton, drawing up to her full height. Thornton moves up the stage, beyond the window

MRS. HAVERHILL: Will he dare to speak to me again?

Enter Thornton; he comes down the stage quietly. He has thrown away the cigar

THORNTON: Mrs. Haverhill! I wish to offer you an apology.

MRS. HAVERHILL: I have not asked for one, sir!

THORNTON: Do you mean by that, that you will not accept one?

MRS. HAVERHILL: [*Aside*] What can I say? [*Aloud*] Oh, Mr. Thornton! – for my husband's sake, I –

THORNTON: Ah! You are afraid that your husband may become involved in an unpleasant affair. Your solicitude for his safety, madame, makes me feel that my offense to-night was indeed unpardonable. No gentleman can excuse himself for making such a mistake as I have made. I had supposed that it was Lieutenant Kerchival West, who –

MRS. HAVERHILL: What do you mean, sir?

THORNTON: But if it is your husband that stands between us –

MRS. HAVERHILL: Let me say this, sir: whatever I may fear for my husband, he fears nothing for himself.

THORNTON: He knows? [*Looking at her, keenly*]

Enter Kerchival West, now in riding suit. He stops, looking at them

You are silent. Your husband does know what occurred to-night; that relieves my conscience. [*Lightly*] Colonel Haverhill and I can now settle it between us.

MRS. HAVERHILL: No, Mr. Thornton! My husband knows nothing, and, I beg of you, do not let this horrible affair go further. [*Sees Kerchival*]

KERCHIVAL: Pardon me. [*Stepping forward*] I hope I am not interrupting you. [*Aside*] It *was* Thornton. [*Aloud*] You said you would have a letter for me to carry, Mrs. Haverhill.

MRS. HAVERHILL: Yes, I – I will go up and write it at once. [*As she leaves she stops and looks back. Aside*] I wonder how much he overheard.

KERCHIVAL: [*Quietly*] I suppose eight o'clock will be time enough for me to go?

MRS. HAVERHILL: Oh, yes! [*Glancing at him a moment*] – quite. [*Exit*]

KERCHIVAL: [*Quietly*] Mr. Thornton! you are a scoundrel! Do I make myself plain?

THORNTON: You make the fact that you desire to pick a quarrel with me quite plain, sir; but I choose my own quarrels and my own enemies.

KERCHIVAL: Colonel Haverhill is my commander, and he is beloved by every officer in the regiment.

THORNTON: On what authority, may I ask, do you –

KERCHIVAL: The honor of Colonel Haverhill's wife is under our protection.

THORNTON: Under your protection? You have a better claim than that, perhaps, to act as her champion. Lieutenant Kerchival West is Mrs. Haverhill's favorite officer in the regiment.

KERCHIVAL: [*Approaching him*] You dare to suggest that I –

THORNTON: If I accept your challenge, I shall do so not because you are her protector, but my rival.

KERCHIVAL: Bah! [*Striking him sharply on the cheek with his glove. The two men stand facing each other a moment*] Is it my quarrel now?

THORNTON: I think you are entitled to my attention, sir.

KERCHIVAL: My time here is limited.

THORNTON: We need not delay. The Bayou La Forge is convenient to this place.

KERCHIVAL: I'll meet you there, with a friend, at once.

THORNTON: It will be light enough to see the sights of our weapons in about one hour.

They bow to each other, and Thornton goes out

KERCHIVAL: I've got ahead of Bob.

GERTRUDE: [*Without*] Whoa! Jack! Old boy! Steady, now – that's a good fellow.

KERCHIVAL: She has returned. I *must* know whether Gertrude Ellingham loves me – before Thornton and I meet. He is a good shot.

GERTRUDE: [*Without, calling*] O – h! Pete! You may take Jack to the stable. Ha – ha – ha! [*She appears at window; to Kerchival*] Old Pete, on the bay horse, has been doing his best to keep up with us; but Jack and I have led him such a race! Ha – ha – ha – ha! [*Disappearing beyond the window*]

KERCHIVAL: Does she love me?

GERTRUDE: [*Entering at the rear and coming down*] I have the very latest news from the headquarters of the Confederate Army in South Carolina. At twenty minutes after three this morning General Beauregard sent this message to Major Anderson in Fort Sumter: "I shall open fire in one hour!" The time is up! – and he will keep his word! [*Turning and looking out of the window. Kerchival moves across to her*]

KERCHIVAL: Gertrude! I must speak to you; we may never meet again; but I must know the truth. I love you. [*Seizing her hand*] Do you love me? [*She looks around at him as if about to speak; hesitates*] Answer me! [*She looks down with a coquettish smile, tapping her skirt with her riding whip*] Well? [*A distant report of a cannon, and low rumbling reverberations over the harbor. Gertrude turns suddenly, looking out. Kerchival draws up, also looking off*]

GERTRUDE: A low – bright – line of fire – in the sky! It is a shell. [*A second's pause; she starts slightly*] It has burst upon the fort. [*Looks over her shoulder at Kerchival, drawing up to her full height*] Now! – do you believe that we Southerners are in deadly earnest?

KERCHIVAL: We Northerners are in deadly earnest, too. I have received my answer. [*He crosses quickly and then turns*] We are – enemies! [*They look at each other for a moment*]

Exit Kerchival

GERTRUDE: Kerchival! [*Moving quickly half across stage, looking after him eagerly, then stops*] Enemies! [*She drops into the chair sobbing bitterly. Another distant report, and low, long reverberations as the curtain descends*]

ACT II

The scene is the exterior of the Ellingham Homestead in the Shenandoah Valley. Three Top Mountain is seen in the distance. A corner of the house, with the projecting end of the veranda is seen on the left. A low wall extends from the veranda across the stage to the center, then with a turn to the right it is continued off the stage. There is a wide opening in the wall at the center, with a low, heavy stone post, with flat top, on each side. Beyond the wall and the opening, a road runs across the stage. At the back of this road there is an elevation of rock and turf. This slopes up to the rear, is level on the top about twelve feet, then slopes down to the road, and also out behind the wood, which is seen at the right. The level part in the center rises to about four feet above the stage. Beyond this elevation in the distance is a broad valley, with Three Top Mountain rising on the right. The foliage is appropriate to Northern Virginia. Rustic seats and table are on the right. There is a low rock near the stone post. When curtain rises it is sunset. As the act proceeds this fades into twilight and then brightens into moonlight. At the rise of the curtain a trumpet signal is heard, very distant. Gertrude and Madeline are standing on the elevation. Gertrude is shading her eyes with her hand and looking off to the left. Madeline stands a little below her, on the incline, resting her arm about Gertrude's waist, also looking off.

GERTRUDE: It is a regiment of Union Cavalry. The Federal troops now have their lines three miles beyond us, and only a month ago the Confederate Army was north of Winchester. One army or the other has been marching up and down the Shenandoah Valley for three years. I wonder what the next change will be. We in Virginia have had more than our share of the war. [*Looking off*]

MADELINE: You have, indeed, Gertrude. [*Walking down to a seat*] And we at home in Washington have pitied you so much. But everybody says that there will be peace in the valley after this. [*Dropping into the seat*]

GERTRUDE: Peace! [*Coming down*] That word means something very different to us poor Southerners from what it means to you.

MADELINE: I know, dear; and we in the North know how you have suffered, too. We were very glad when General Buckthorn was appointed to the command of the Nineteenth Army Corps, so that Jenny could get permission for herself and me to come and visit you.

GERTRUDE: The old General will do anything for Jenny, I suppose.

MADELINE: Yes. [*Laughing*] We say in Washington that Jenny is in command of the Nineteenth Army Corps herself.

GERTRUDE: I was never more astonished or delighted in my life than when you and Jenny Buckthorn rode up, this morning, with a guard from Winchester; and Madeline, dear, I – I only wish that my brother Robert could be here, too. Do you remember in Charleston, darling – that morning – when I told you that – that Robert loved you?

MADELINE: He – [*Looking down*] – he told me so himself only a little while afterwards, and while we were standing there, on the shore of the bay – the – shot was fired which compelled him to enter this awful war – and me to return to my home in the North.

GERTRUDE: I was watching for that shot, too. [*Turning*]

MADELINE: Yes – [*Rising*] – you and brother Kerchival –

GERTRUDE: We won't talk about that, my dear. We were speaking of Robert. As I told you this morning, I have not heard from him since the battle of Winchester, a month ago. Oh, Madeline! the many, many long weeks, like these, we have suffered, after some terrible battle in which he has been engaged. I do not know, now, whether he is living or dead.

MADELINE: The whole war has been one long suspense to me. [*Dropping her face into her hands*]

GERTRUDE: My dear sister! [*Placing her arm about her waist and moving to the left*] You are a Northern girl, and I am a Rebel – but we are sisters. [*They mount the veranda and pass out. An old countryman comes in. He stops and glances back, raises a broken portion of the capstone of the post, and places a letter under it. Gertrude has stepped back on the*

584

veranda and is watching him. He raises his head sharply, looking at her and bringing his finger to his lips. He drops his head again, as with age, and goes out. Gertrude moves down to the stage and up to the road, looks to the right and left, raises the broken stone, glancing back as she does so, then takes the letter and moves down] Robert is alive! It is his handwriting! [*She tears open the wrapper*] Only a line from him! and this – a dispatch – and also a letter to me! Why, it is from Mrs. Haverhill – from Washington – with a United States postmark. [*She reads from a scrap of paper*] "The enclosed dispatch must be in the hands of Captain Edward Thornton before eight o'clock tonight. We have signaled to him from Three Top Mountain, and he is waiting for it at the bend in Oak Run. Our trusty scout at the Old Forge will carry it if you will put it in his hands." The scout is not there, now; I will carry it to Captain Thornton myself. I – I haven't my own dear horse to depend on now; Jack knew every foot of the way through the woods about here; he could have carried a dispatch himself. I can't bear to think of Jack; it's two years since he was captured by the enemy – and if he is still living – I – I suppose he is carrying one of their officers. No! Jack wouldn't fight on that side. He was a Rebel – as I am. He was one of the Black Horse Cavalry – his eyes always flashed towards the North. Poor Jack! my pet. [*Brushing her eyes*] But this is no time for tears. I must do the best I can with the gray horse. Captain Thornton shall have the dispatch. [*She reads from note*] "I also inclose a letter for you. I found it in a United States mailbag which we captured from the enemy." Oh – that's the way Mrs. Haverhill's letter came – Ha – ha – ha – by way of the Rebel army! [*Opens it; reads*] "My Darling Gertrude: When Colonel Kerchival West was in Washington last week, on his way from Chattanooga, to serve under Sheridan in the Shenandoah Valley, he called upon me. It was the first time I had seen him since the opening of the war. I am certain that he still loves you, dear." [*She kisses the letter eagerly, then draws up*] It is quite immaterial to me whether Kerchival West still loves me or not. [*Reads*] "I have kept your secret, my darling." – Ah! My secret! – "but I was sorely tempted to betray the confidence you reposed in me at

Charleston. If Kerchival West had heard you say, as I did, when your face was hidden in my bosom, that night, that you loved him with your whole heart –" – Oh! I could bite my tongue out now for making that confession – [*She looks down at letter with a smile*] "I am certain that he still loves you." [*A Trumpet Signal. She kisses the letter repeatedly. The Signal is repeated louder than at first. She starts, listening*]

Jenny Buckthorn runs in, on the veranda

JENNY: Do you hear, Gertrude, they are going to pass this very house. [*A Military band is playing "John Brown" in the distance. A chorus of soldiers is heard*] I've been watching them through my glass; it is Colonel Kerchival West's regiment.

GERTRUDE: [*Eagerly, then coldly*] Colonel West's! It is perfectly indifferent to me whose regiment it is.

JENNY: Oh! Of course. [*Coming down*] It is equally indifferent to me; Captain Heartsease is in command of the first troop. [*Trumpet Signal sounds*] Column right! [*She runs up to the road. Looking off to the left*] They are coming up the hill.

GERTRUDE: At my very door! And Kerchival West in command! I will not stand here and see them pass. The dispatch for Captain Thornton! I will carry it to him as soon as they are gone. [*Exit up the veranda, the band and chorus increasing in volume*]

JENNY: Cavalry! That's the branch of the service I was born in; I was in a fort at the time – on the Plains. Sergeant Barket always said that my first baby squall was a command to the garrison; if any officer or soldier, from my father down, failed to obey my orders, I court-martialed him on the spot. I'll make 'em pass in review. [*Jumping up on the rustic seat*] Yes! [*Looking off to the left*] There's Captain Heartsease himself, at the head of the first troop. Draw sabre! [*With parasol*] Present! [*Imitating the action. The band and chorus are now full and loud; she swings the parasol in time. A Trumpet Signal. Band and chorus suddenly cease*] Halt! Why, they are stopping here. [*Trumpet Signal sounds*] Dismount! I – I wonder if they are going to – I do believe – [*Looking eagerly. Trumpet Signal*] Assembly of Guard Details! As sure as fate, they are going into camp here. We girls will have a jolly time. [*Jumping down*] Ha – ha – ha – ha! Let me see. How shall I receive Captain Heartsease? He deserves a court-martial, for he stole my lace handkerchief – at Mrs. Grayson's reception – in Washington. He was called away by orders to the West that very night, and we haven't met since. [*Sighs*] He's been in lots of battles since then; I suppose he's forgotten all about the handkerchief. We girls, at home, don't forget such things. We aren't in battles. All we do is to – to scrape lint and flirt with other officers.

Enter Captain Heartsease, followed by Colonel Robert Ellingham, then stops at the gate

HEARTSEASE: This way, Colonel Ellingham. [*They enter. As they come down Heartsease stops suddenly, looking at Jenny, and puts up his glasses*] Miss Buckthorn!

JENNY: Captain Heartsease!

HEARTSEASE: [*Very quietly and with perfect composure*] I am thunderstruck. The unexpected sight of you has thrown me into a fever of excitement.

JENNY: Has it? [*Aside*] If he gets so excited as that in battle it must be awful. [*Aloud*] Colonel Ellingham!

ELLINGHAM: Miss Buckthorn! You are visiting my sister? I am what may be called a visitor – by force – myself.

JENNY: Oh! You're a prisoner!

ELLINGHAM: I ventured too far within the Union lines to-night, and they have picked me up. But Major Wilson has kindly accepted my parole, and I shall make the best of it.

JENNY: Is Major Wilson in command of the regiment?

HEARTSEASE: Yes. Colonel West is to join us at this point, during the evening.

ELLINGHAM: I am very glad you are here, Miss Buckthorn, with Gertrude.

JENNY: Somebody here will be delighted to see you, Colonel.

ELLINGHAM: My sister can hardly be pleased to see me as a prisoner.

JENNY: Not your sister. [*Passing him and crossing to the veranda. She turns and beckons to him. She motions with her thumb, over her shoulder. He goes up the steps of the veranda and turns*]

ELLINGHAM: What do you mean?

JENNY: I mean this – [*Reaching up her face, he leans down, placing his ear near her lips*] –

somebody else's sister! When she first sees you, be near enough to catch her.

ELLINGHAM: I understand you! Madeline! [*Exit on veranda. Jenny runs up steps after him, then stops and looks back at Heartsease over the railing. Heartsease takes a lace handkerchief from his pocket*]

JENNY: I do believe that's my handkerchief.

A guard of Sentries marches in and across the stage in the road. The Corporal in command orders halt and a sentry to post, then marches the guard out. The sentry stands with his back to the audience, afterwards moving out and in, appearing and disappearing during the Act

HEARTSEASE: Miss Buckthorn! I owe you an apology. After I left your side, the last time we met, I found your handkerchief in my possession. I assure you, it was an accident.

JENNY: [*Aside, pouting*] I thought he *intended* to steal it. [*Aloud*] That was more than a year ago. [*Then brightly*] Do you always carry it with you?

HEARTSEASE: Always; there. [*Indicating his left breast pocket*]

JENNY: Next to his heart!

HEARTSEASE: Shall I return it to you?

JENNY: Oh, if a lace handkerchief can be of any use to you, Captain, during the hardships of a campaign – you – you may keep that one. You soldiers have so few comforts – and it's real lace.

HEARTSEASE: Thank you. [*Returning the handkerchief to his pocket*] Miss Buckthorn, your father is in command of the Nineteenth Army Corps. He doesn't like me.

JENNY: I know it.

HEARTSEASE: But you are in command of him.

JENNY: Yes; I always have been.

HEARTSEASE: If ever you decide to assume command of any other man, I – I trust you will give *me* your orders.

JENNY: [*Aside, starting back*] If that was intended for a proposal, it's the queerest-shaped one I ever heard of. [*Aloud*] Do you mean, Captain, that – that you – I must command myself now. [*Shouldering her parasol*] 'Bout – face! March! [*Turning squarely around, marching up and out, on the veranda*]

HEARTSEASE: I have been placed on waiting orders. [*Stepping up the stage and looking after her; then very quietly and without emotion*] I am in an agony of suspense. The sight of that girl always arouses the strongest emotions of my nature.

Enter Colonel Kerchival West, looking at the paper in his hand. The sentinel, in the road, comes to a salute

Colonel West!

KERCHIVAL: Captain!

HEARTSEASE: You have rejoined the regiment sooner than we expected.

KERCHIVAL: [*Looking at the paper*] Yes; General Haverhill is to meet me here at seven o'clock. Major Wilson tells me that some of your company captured Colonel Robert Ellingham, of the Tenth Virginia.

HEARTSEASE: He is here under parole.

KERCHIVAL: And this is the old Ellingham homestead. [*Aside*] Gertrude herself is here, I suppose; almost a prisoner to me, like her brother; and my troops surround their home. She must, indeed, feel that I am her enemy now. Ah, well, war is war. [*Aloud*] By the bye, Heartsease, a young Lieutenant, Frank Bedloe, has joined our troop?

HEARTSEASE: Yes; an excellent young officer.

KERCHIVAL: I sent for him as I came through the camp. Lieutenant Frank "Bedloe" is the son of General Haverhill.

HEARTSEASE: Indeed! Under an assumed name!

KERCHIVAL: He was supposed to have been killed in New Orleans more than a year ago; but he was taken prisoner instead.

HEARTSEASE: He is here.

KERCHIVAL: I should never have known him; with his full beard and bronzed face. His face was as smooth as a boy's when I last met him in Charleston.

Enter Lieutenant Frank Bedloe; he stops, saluting

FRANK: You wished me to report to you, Colonel?

KERCHIVAL: You have been assigned to the regiment during my absence.

FRANK: Yes, sir.

Kerchival moves to him and grasps his hand; looks into his eyes a moment before speaking

KERCHIVAL: Frank Haverhill.

FRANK: You – you know me, sir?

KERCHIVAL: I saw Mrs. Haverhill while I was passing through Washington on Saturday. She told me that you had escaped from prison in

Richmond, and had re-entered the service. She did not know then that you had been assigned to my regiment. I received a letter from her, in Winchester, this morning, informing me of the fact, and asking for my good offices in your behalf. But here is the letter. [*Taking a letter from wallet and giving it to him*] It is for you rather than for me. I shall do everything I can for you, my dear fellow.

FRANK: Thank you, sir. [*He opens the letter, dropping the envelope upon the table*] Kind, thoughtful and gentle to my faults, as ever – [*Looking at the letter*] – and always thinking of my welfare. My poor little wife, too, is under her protection. Gentlemen, I beg of you not to reveal my secret to my father.

KERCHIVAL: General Haverhill shall know nothing from us, my boy, you have my word for that.

HEARTSEASE: Nothing.

KERCHIVAL: And he cannot possibly recognize you. What with your full beard, and thinking as he does, that you are –

FRANK: That I am dead. I am dead to him. It would have been better if I had died. Nothing but my death – not even that – can wipe out the disgrace which I brought upon his name.

HEARTSEASE: General Haverhill has arrived.

Enter General Haverhill, with a Staff Officer

FRANK: [*Moving down*] My father!

HAVERHILL: [*After exchanging salutes with the three officers, he turns to the Staff Officer, giving him a paper and brief instructions in dumb show. The Officer goes out over the incline. Another Staff Officer enters, salutes and hands him a paper, then stands up*] Ah! The men are ready. [*Looking at the paper, then to Kerchival*] Colonel! I have a very important matter to arrange with you; there is not a moment to be lost. I will ask Captain Heartsease to remain. [*Frank salutes and starts up the stage; Haverhill looks at him, starting slightly; raises his hand to detain him*] One moment; your name!

HEARTSEASE: Lieutenant Bedloe, General, of my own troop, and one of our best officers.

Haverhill steps to Frank, looking into his face a moment

HAVERHILL: Pardon me! [*He steps down the stage. Frank moves away from him, then stops and looks back at him. Haverhill stands up a moment in thought, covers his face with one hand, then draws up*] Colonel West! We have a most dangerous piece of work for a young officer – [*Frank starts joyfully*] – to lead a party of men, whom I have already selected. I cannot *order* an officer to undertake anything so nearly hopeless; he must be a volunteer.

FRANK: Oh, sir, General! Let me be their leader.

HAVERHILL: I thought you had passed on.

FRANK: Do not refuse me, sir. [*Haverhill looks at him a moment. Heartsease and Kerchival exchange glances*]

HAVERHILL: You are the man we need, my young friend. You shall go. Listen! We wish to secure a key to the cipher dispatches, which the enemy are now sending from their signal station on Three Top Mountain. There is another Confederate Signal Station in the valley, just beyond Buckton's Ford. [*Pointing to the left*] Your duty will be this: First, to get inside the enemy's line; then to follow a path through the woods, with one of our scouts as your guide; attack the Station suddenly, and secure their code, if possible. I have this moment received word that the scout and the men are at the fort, now, awaiting their leader. Major McCandless, of my staff, will take you to the place. [*Indicating the Staff Officer. Frank exchanges salutes with him*] My young friend! I do not conceal from you the dangerous nature of the work on which I am sending you. If – if you do not return, I – I will write, myself, to your friends. [*Taking out a note book*] Have you a father living?

FRANK: My – father – is – is – he is –

HAVERHILL: I understand you. A mother? Or –

KERCHIVAL: I have the address of Lieutenant Bedloe's friends, General.

HAVERHILL: I will ask you to give it to me, if necessary. [*He extends his hand*] Good-bye, my lad. [*Frank moves to him. Haverhill grasps his hand, warmly*] Keep a brave heart and come back to us.

Frank moves up the stage. Exit Staff Officer

FRANK: He is my father still. [*Exit*]

HAVERHILL: My dead boy's face! [*Dropping his face into both hands*]

HEARTSEASE: [*Apart to Kerchival*] He shall not go alone. [*Aloud*] General! Will you kindly give me leave of absence from the command?

HAVERHILL: Leave of absence! To an officer in active service – and in the presence of the enemy?

KERCHIVAL: [*Taking his hand. Apart*] God bless you, old fellow! Look after the boy.

HAVERHILL: A – h – [*With a sudden thought, turns*] I think I understand you, Captain Heartsease. Yes; you may have leave of absence.

HEARTSEASE: Thank you. [*He salutes. Haverhill and Kerchival salute. Exit Heartsease*]

KERCHIVAL: Have you any further orders for me, General?

HAVERHILL: I wish you to understand the great importance of the duty to which I have just assigned this young officer. General Sheridan started for Washington this noon, by way of Front Royal. Since his departure, we have had reason to believe that the enemy are about to move, and we must be able to read their signal dispatches, if possible. [*Sitting down*] I have ordered Captain Lockwood, of our own Signal Corps to report to you here, with officers and men. [*He takes up the empty envelope on table, unconsciously, as he speaks, tapping it on the table*] If Lieutenant Bedloe succeeds in getting the key to the enemy's cipher, we can signal from this point – [*Pointing to the elevation*] – to our station at Front Royal. Men and horses are waiting there now, to carry forward a message, if necessary, to General Sheridan himself. [*He starts suddenly, looking at the envelope in his hand; reads address. Aside*] "Colonel Kerchival West" – in my wife's handwriting!

KERCHIVAL: I'll attend to your orders.

HAVERHILL: Postmarked at Washington, yesterday. [*Reads*] "Private and confidential." [*Aloud*] Colonel West! I found a paragraph, to-day, in a paper published in Richmond, taken from a prisoner. I will read it to you. [*He takes a newspaper slip from his wallet and reads*] "From the *Charleston Mercury*. Captain Edward Thornton, of the Confederate Secret Service, has been assigned to duty in the Shenandoah Valley. Our gallant Captain still bears upon his face the mark of his meeting, in 1861, with Lieutenant, now Colonel Kerchival West, who is also to serve in the valley, with Sheridan's Army. Another meeting between these two men would be one of the strange coincidences of the war, as they were at one time, if not indeed at present, interested in the same beautiful woman." [*Rises*] I will ask you to read the last few lines, yourself. [*Crossing, he hands Kerchival the slip*]

KERCHIVAL: [*Reading*] "The scandal connected with the lovely wife of a Northern officer, at the opening of the war, was overshadowed, of course, by the attack on Fort Sumter; but many Charlestonians will remember it. The lady in defense of whose good name Captain Thornton fought the duel" – he defended her good name! – "is the wife of General Haverhill, who will be Colonel West's immediate commander." [*He pauses a moment, then hands back the slip*] General! I struck Mr. Thornton, after a personal quarrel.

HAVERHILL: And the cause of the blow? There is much more in this than I have ever known of. I need hardly say that I do not accept the statement of this scandalous paragraph as correct. I will ask you to tell me the whole story, frankly, as man to man.

KERCHIVAL: [*After a moment's thought*] I will tell you – all – frankly, General.

Enter Sergeant Barket

BARKET: Colonel Wist? Adjutant Rollins wishes to report – a prisoner – just captured.

HAVERHILL: We will meet again later, to-night when the camp is at rest. We are both soldiers, and have duties before us, at once. For the present, Colonel, be on the alert; we must watch the enemy. [*He moves up the stage. Barket salutes. Haverhill stops and looks at envelope in his hands, reading*] "Private and confidential." [*Exit*]

KERCHIVAL: Sergeant Barket! Lieutenant Bedloe has crossed the enemy's line, at Buckton's Ford, with a party of men. I wish you to ride to the ford yourself, and remain there, with your horse in readiness and fresh. As soon as any survivor of the party returns, ride back with the first news at full speed.

BARKET: Yes, sir. [*Starting*]

KERCHIVAL: You say a prisoner has been captured? Is it a spy?

BARKET: Worse – a petticoat.

KERCHIVAL: A female prisoner! [*Dropping into the seat*]

BARKET: I towld the byes your honor wouldn't thank us fer the catchin' of her. The worst of it is she's a lady; and what's worst still, it's a purty one.

KERCHIVAL: Tell Major Wilson, for me, to let her take the oath, and everything else she

wants. The Government of the United States will send her an apology and a new bonnet.

BARKET: The young lady is to take the oath, is it? She says she'll see us damned first.

KERCHIVAL: A lady, Barket?

BARKET: Well! she didn't use thim exact words. That's the way I understand her emphasis. Ivery time she looks at me, I feel like getting under a boom-proof. She was dashing through the woods on a gray horse, sur; and we had the divil's own chase. But we came up wid her, at last, down by the bend in Oak Run. Just at that moment we saw the figure of a Confederate officer, disappearing among the trays on the ither side.

KERCHIVAL: A——h!

BARKET: Two of us rayturned wid the girl; and the rist wint after the officer. Nothing has been heard of thim yet.

KERCHIVAL: Have you found any dispatches on the prisoner?

BARKET: Well! – yer honor, I'm a bachelor, meself; and I'm not familiar with the taypography of the sex. We byes are in mortal terror for fear somebody might order us to go on an exploring expedition.

KERCHIVAL: Tell them to send the prisoner here, Barket, and hurry to Buckton's Ford yourself, at once.

BARKET: As fast as me horse can carry me, sir, and it's a good one. [*Exit*]

KERCHIVAL: I'd rather deal with half the Confederate army than with one woman, but I must question her. They captured her down by the Bend in Oak Run. [*Taking out the map, and looking at it*] I see. She had just met, or was about to meet, a Confederate officer at that point. It is evident that she was either taking him a dispatch or was there to receive one. Oak Run. [*Corporal Dunn and two soldiers enter, with Gertrude as a prisoner. They stop, Kerchival sits, studying the map. Gertrude glances at him and marches down with her head erect; she stops, with her back to him*]

CORP. DUNN: The prisoner, Colonel West!

KERCHIVAL: Ah! Very well, Corporal; you can go. [*Rising; he motions the guard to retire. Corp. Dunn gives the necessary orders and exit with guard*] Be seated, madam. [*Gertrude draws up, folding her arms and planting her foot, spitefully. Kerchival shrugs his shoulders. Aside*] I wish they'd capture a tigress for me, or some other female animal that I know how to manage better than I do a woman. [*Aloud*] I am very sorry, madam; but, of course, my duty as a military officer is paramount to all other considerations. You have been captured within the lines of this army, and under circumstances which lead me to think that you have important dispatches upon your person. I trust that you will give me whatever you have, at once. I shall be exceedingly sorry if you compel me to adopt the extreme – and the very disagreeable course – for both of us – of having – you – I – I hesitate even to use the word, madame – but military law is absolute – having you –

GERTRUDE: Searched! If you dare, Colonel West! [*Turning to him suddenly and drawing up to her full height*]

KERCHIVAL: Gertrude Ellingham! [*Springs across to her, with his arms extended*] My dear Gertrude!

GERTRUDE: [*Turning her back upon him*] Not "dear Gertrude" to you, sir!

KERCHIVAL: Not? – Oh! I forgot.

GERTRUDE: [*Coldly*] I am your prisoner.

KERCHIVAL: Yes. [*Drawing up firmly, with a change of manner*] We will return to the painful realities of war. I am very sorry that you have placed yourself in a position like this, and, believe me, Gertrude – [*With growing tenderness*] – I am still more sorry to be in such a position myself. [*Resting one hand on her arm, and his other arm about her waist*]

GERTRUDE: [*After looking down at his hands*] You don't like the position? [*He starts back, drawing up with dignity*] Is that the paramount duty of a military officer?

KERCHIVAL: You will please hand me whatever dispatches or other papers may be in your possession.

GERTRUDE: [*Looking away*] You will *force* me, I suppose. I am a woman; you have the power. Order in the guard! A Corporal and two men – you'd better make it a dozen – I am dangerous! Call the whole regiment to arms! Beat the long roll! I won't give up, if all the armies of the United States surround me.

Enter General Buckthorn
KERCHIVAL: General Buckthorn! [*Saluting*]

BUCKTHORN: Colonel West.

GERTRUDE: [*Aside*] Jenny's father! [*Buckthorn glances at Gertrude, who still stands looking away. He moves down to Kerchival*]

BUCKTHORN: [*Apart, gruffly*] I was passing with my staff, and I was informed that you had captured a woman bearing dispatches to the enemy. Is this the one?

KERCHIVAL: Yes, General.

BUCKTHORN: Ah! [*Turning, he looks at her*]

GERTRUDE: I wonder if he will recognize me. He hasn't seen me since I was a little girl. [*She turns toward him*]

BUCKTHORN: [*Turning to Kerchival and punching him in the ribs*] Fine young woman! – [*He turns and bows to her very gallantly, removing his hat. She bows deeply in return*] A-h-e-m! [*Suddenly pulling himself up to a stern, military air; then gruffly to Kerchival, extending his hand*] Let me see the dispatches.

KERCHIVAL: She declines positively to give them up.

BUCKTHORN: Oh! Does she? [*Walks up the stage thoughtfully, and turns*] My dear young lady! I trust you will give us no further trouble. Kindly let us have those dispatches.

GERTRUDE: [*Looking away*] I have no dispatches, and I would not give them to you if I had.

BUCKTHORN: What! You defy my authority? Colonel West, I command you! Search the prisoner!

Gertrude turns suddenly towards Kerchival, facing him defiantly. He looks across at her, aghast. A moment's pause

KERCHIVAL: General Buckthorn – I decline to obey that order.

BUCKTHORN: You – you decline to obey my order! [*Moves down to him fiercely*]

KERCHIVAL: [*Apart*] General! It is the woman I love.

BUCKTHORN: [*Apart*] Is it? Damn you, sir! I wouldn't have an officer in my army corps who *would* obey me, under such circumstances. I'll have to look for those dispatches myself.

KERCHIVAL: [*Facing him, angrily*] If you dare, General Buckthorn!

BUCKTHORN: [*Apart*] Blast your eyes! I'd kick you out of the army if you'd *let* me search her; but it's my military duty to swear at you. [*To Gertrude*] Colonel West has sacrificed his life to protect you.

GERTRUDE: His life!

BUCKTHORN: I shall have him shot for insubordination to his commander, immediately. [*Gives Kerchival a huge wink, and turns up stage*]

GERTRUDE: Oh, sir! General! I have told you the truth. I have no dispatches. Believe me, sir, I haven't so much as a piece of paper about me, except – –

BUCKTHORN: Except? [*Turning sharply*]

GERTRUDE: Only a letter. Here it is. [*Taking letter from the bosom of her dress*] Upon my soul, it is all I have. Truly, it is.

BUCKTHORN: [*Taking the letter*] Colonel West, you're reprieved. [*Winks at Kerchival, who turns away, laughing. Buckthorn reads letter*] "Washington" – Ho – ho! From within our own lines – "Colonel Kerchival West" –

KERCHIVAL: Eh?

GERTRUDE: Please, General! – Don't read it aloud.

BUCKTHORN: Very well! I won't.

KERCHIVAL: [*Aside*] I wonder what it has to do with me.

BUCKTHORN: [*Reading. Aside*] "If Kerchival West had heard you say, as I did – m – m – that you loved him with your whole heart – " [*He glances up at Gertrude, who drops her head, coyly*] This is a very important military document. [*Turns to the last page*] "Signed, Constance Haverhill." [*Turns to front page*] "My dear Gertrude!" Is this Miss Gertrude Ellingham?

GERTRUDE: Yes, General.

BUCKTHORN: I sent my daughter, Jenny, to your house, with an escort, this morning.

GERTRUDE: She is here.

BUCKTHORN: [*Tapping her under the chin*] You're an arrant little Rebel, my dear; but I like you immensely. [*Draws up suddenly, with an Ahem!, then turns to Kerchival*] Colonel West, I leave this dangerous young woman in your charge. [*Kerchival approaches*] If she disobeys you in any way, or attempts to escape – read that letter! [*Giving him the letter*]

GERTRUDE: Oh! General!

BUCKTHORN: But not till then.

KERCHIVAL: [*Tenderly, taking her hand*] My – prisoner!

GERTRUDE: [*Aside*] I could scratch my own eyes out – or his, either – rather than have him read that letter.

Enter Corporal Dunn, with a guard of four soldiers and Captain Edward Thornton as a prisoner

KERCHIVAL: Edward Thornton!

GERTRUDE: They have taken him, also! He has the dispatch!

DUNN: The Confederate Officer, Colonel, who was pursued by our troops at Oak Run, after they captured the young lady.

BUCKTHORN: The little witch has been communicating with the enemy!

KERCHIVAL: [*To Gertrude*] You will give me your parole of honor until we next meet?

GERTRUDE: Yes. [*Aside*] That letter! I *am* his prisoner. [*She walks up the steps, looking back at Captain Thornton, and then leaves the stage*]

KERCHIVAL: We will probably find the dispatches we have been looking for now, General.

BUCKTHORN: Prisoner! You will hand us what papers you may have.

THORNTON: I will hand you nothing.

BUCKTHORN: Colonel!

Kerchival motions to Thornton, who looks at him sullenly

KERCHIVAL: Corporal Dunn! – search the prisoner. [*Dunn steps to Thornton, taking him by the shoulder and turning him rather roughly so that Thornton's back is to the audience. Dunn throws open his coat, takes the paper from his breast, hands it to Kerchival, who gives it to Buckthorn*] Proceed with the search.

Dunn continues the search. Buckthorn drops upon the seat, lights a match and looks at the paper

BUCKTHORN: [*Reading*] "General Rosser will rejoin General Early with all the cavalry in his command, at – " This is important.

Continues to read with matches. The Corporal hands a packet to Kerchival. He removes the covering

KERCHIVAL: [*Starting*] A portrait of Mrs. Haverhill! [*He touches Corporal Dunn on the shoulder quickly and motions him to retire. Dunn falls back to the guard. Kerchival speaks apart to Thornton, who has turned front*] How did this portrait come into your possession?

THORNTON: That is my affair, not yours!

BUCKTHORN: Anything else, Colonel?

KERCHIVAL: [*Placing the miniature in his pocket*] Nothing!

THORNTON: [*Apart, over Kerchival's shoulder*]

A time will come, perhaps, when I can avenge the insult of this search, and also this scar. [*Pointing to a scar on his face*] Your aim was better than mine in Charleston, but we shall meet again; give me back that picture.

KERCHIVAL: Corporal! Take your prisoner!

THORNTON: Ah!

He springs viciously at Kerchival; Corporal Dunn springs forward, seizes Thornton and throws him back to the Guard. Kerchival walks to the right, Dunn stands with his carbine levelled at Thornton, looks at Kerchival, who quietly motions him out. Corporal Dunn gives the orders to the men and marches out, with Thornton

BUCKTHORN: Ah! [*Still reading with matches*] Colonel! [*Rising*] The enemy has a new movement on foot, and General Sheridan has left the army! Listen! [*Reads from dispatches with matches*] "Watch for a signal from Three Top Mountain to-night."

KERCHIVAL: We hope to be able to read that signal ourselves.

BUCKTHORN: Yes, I know. Be on your guard. I will speak with General Haverhill, and then ride over to General Wright's headquarters. Keep us informed.

KERCHIVAL: I will, General.

Saluting. Buckthorn salutes and exits

KERCHIVAL: "Watch for a signal from Three Top Mountain to-night." [*Looking up at Mountain*] We shall be helpless to read it unless Lieutenant Bedloe is successful. I only hope the poor boy is not lying dead, already, in those dark woods beyond the ford. [*He turns down, taking the miniature from his pocket*] How came Edward Thornton to have this portrait of Mrs. Haverhill in his possession?

Gertrude runs in on the veranda

GERTRUDE: Oh, Colonel West! He's here! [*Looks back*] They are coming this way with him.

KERCHIVAL: Him! Who?

GERTRUDE: Jack.

KERCHIVAL: Jack!

GERTRUDE: My own horse!

KERCHIVAL: Ah, I remember! He and I were acquainted in Charleston.

GERTRUDE: Two troopers are passing through the camp with him.

KERCHIVAL: He is not in your possession?

GERTRUDE: He was captured at the battle of Fair Oaks, but I recognized him the moment I saw him; and I am sure he knew me, too, when I went up to him. He whinnied and looked so happy. You are in command here – [*Running down*] – you will compel them to give him up to me?

KERCHIVAL: If he is in my command, your pet shall be returned to you. I'll give one of my own horses to the Government as a substitute, if necessary.

GERTRUDE: Oh, thank you, my dear Kerchival! [*Going to him; he takes her hand, looking into her eyes*] I – I could almost –

KERCHIVAL: Can you almost confess, at last, Gertrude, that you – love me? [*Tenderly; she draws back, hanging her head, but leaving her hand in his*] Have I been wrong? I felt that that confession was hovering on your tongue when we were separated in Charleston. Have I seen that confession in your eyes since we met again to-day – even among the angry flashes which they have shot out at me? During all this terrible war – in the camp and the trench – in the battle – I have dreamed of a meeting like this. You are still silent?

Her hand is still in his. She is looking down. A smile steals over her face, and she raises her eyes to his, taking his hand in both her own

GERTRUDE: Kerchival! I – [*Enter Benson. She looks around over her shoulder. Kerchival looks up. A trooper leading a large black horse, now caparisoned in military saddle, bridle, follows Benson across; another trooper follows*] Jack!

She runs up the stage, meeting the horse. Kerchival turns

KERCHIVAL: Confound Jack! That infernal horse was always in my way!

GERTRUDE: [*With her arm about her horse's neck*] My darling old fellow! Is he not beautiful, Kerchival? They have taken good care of him. How soft his coat is!

KERCHIVAL: Benson, explain this!

BENSON: I was instructed to show this horse and his leader through the lines, sir.

KERCHIVAL: What are your orders, my man? [*Moving up, the trooper hands him a paper. He moves down a few steps, reading it*]

GERTRUDE: You are to be mine again, Jack,

mine! [*Resting her cheek against the horse's head and patting it*] The Colonel has promised it to me.

KERCHIVAL: Ah! [*With a start, as he reads the paper. Gertrude raises her head and looks at him*] This is General Sheridan's horse, on his way to Winchester, for the use of the General when he returns from Washington.

GERTRUDE: General Sheridan's horse? He is mine!

KERCHIVAL: I have no authority to detain him. He must go on.

GERTRUDE: I have hold of Jack's bridle, and you may order your men to take out their sabres and cut my hand off.

KERCHIVAL: [*He approaches her and gently takes her hand as it holds the bridle*] I would rather have my own hand cut off, Gertrude, than bring tears to your eyes, but there is no alternative! [*Gertrude releases the bridle and turns front, brushing her eyes, her hand still held in his, his back to the audience. He returns the order and motions troopers out; they move out, with the horse. Kerchival turns to move. Gertrude starts after the horse; he turns quickly to check her*] You forget – that – you are my prisoner.

GERTRUDE: I *will* go!

KERCHIVAL: General Buckthorn left me special instructions – [*Taking out the wallet and letter*] – in case you declined to obey my orders –

GERTRUDE: Oh, Colonel! Please don't read that letter. [*She stands near him, dropping her head. He glances up at her from the letter. She glances up at him and drops her eyes again*] I will obey you.

KERCHIVAL: [*Aside*] What the deuce can there be in that letter?

GERTRUDE: Colonel West! Your men made me a prisoner this afternoon; to-night you have robbed me, by your own orders, of – of – Jack is only a pet, but I love him; and my brother is also a captive in your hands. When we separated in Charleston you said that we were enemies. What is there lacking to make those words true to-day? You *are* my enemy! A few moments ago you asked me to make a confession to you. You can judge for yourself whether it is likely to be a confession of – love – or of hatred!

KERCHIVAL: Hatred!

GERTRUDE: [*Facing him*] Listen to my confes-

sion, sir! From the bottom of my heart –

KERCHIVAL: Stop!

GERTRUDE: I will not stop!

KERCHIVAL: I command you.

GERTRUDE: Indeed! [*He throws open the wallet in his hand and raises the letter*] Ah! [*She turns away; turns again, as if to speak. He half opens the letter. She stamps her foot and walks up steps of the veranda. Here she turns again*] I tell you, I – [*He opens the letter. She turns, and exits with a spiteful step*]

KERCHIVAL: I wonder if that document orders me to cut her head off! [*Returning it to wallet and pocket*] Was ever lover in such a position? I am obliged to cross the woman I love at every step.

Enter Corporal Dunn, very hurriedly

DUNN: A message from Adjutant Rollins, sir! The prisoner, Capt. Thornton, dashed away from the special guard which was placed over him, and he has escaped. He had a knife concealed, and two of the Guard are badly wounded. Adjutant Rollins thinks the prisoner is still within the lines of the camp – in one of the houses or the stables.

KERCHIVAL: Tell Major Wilson to place the remainder of the Guard under arrest, and to take every possible means to recapture the prisoner. [*Corp. Dunn salutes, and exit*] So! Thornton has jumped his guard, and he is armed. I wonder if he is trying to get away, or to find me. From what I know of the man, he doesn't much care which he succeeds in doing. That scar which I gave him in Charleston is deeper in his heart than it is in his face. [*A signal light suddenly appears on Three Top Mountain. The "Call"*] Ah! – the enemy's signal!

Enter Captain Lockwood, followed by the Lieutenant of Signal Corps

KERCHIVAL: Captain Lockwood! You are here! Are your signalmen with you?

LOCKWOOD: Yes, Colonel; and one of my Lieutenants.

The Lieutenant is looking up at the signal with his glass. Captain Lockwood does the same

Haverhill enters, followed by two staff officers

HAVERHILL: [*As he enters*] Can you make anything of it, Captain?

LOCKWOOD: Nothing, General! Our services are quite useless unless Lieutenant Bedloe returns with the key to their signals.

HAVERHILL: A – h! We shall fail. It is time he had returned, if successful.

SENTINEL: [*Without*] Halt! Who goes there? [*Kerchival runs up the stage and half way up the incline, looking off*] Halt! [*A shot is heard without*]

BARKET: [*Without*] Och! – Ye murtherin spalpeen!

KERCHIVAL: Sentinel! Let him pass; it is Sergeant Barket.

SENTINEL: [*Without*] Pass on.

KERCHIVAL: He didn't give the countersign. News from Lieutenant Bedloe, General!

BARKET: [*Hurrying in, up the slope*] Colonel Wist, our brave byes wiped out the enemy, and here's the papers.

KERCHIVAL: Ah! [*Taking the papers. – Then to Lockwood*] Is that the key?

LOCKWOOD: Yes. Lieutenant!

Lieutenant hurries up to the elevation, looking through his glass. Lockwood opens the book

HAVERHILL: What of Lieutenant Bedloe, Sergeant?

BARKET: Sayreously wounded, and in the hands of the inimy!

HAVERHILL: [*Sighing*] Ah——h.

BARKET: [*Coming down the stone steps*] It is reported that Captain Heartsease was shot dead at his side.

KERCHIVAL: Heartsease dead!

LIEUT. OF SIGNAL CORPS: [*Reading signals*] Twelve – Twenty-two – Eleven.

BARKET: Begorra! I forgot the Sintinil entirely, but he didn't forget me. [*Holding his left arm*]

HAVERHILL: Colonel West! We must make every possible sacrifice for the immediate exchange of Lieutenant Bedloe, if he is still living. It is due to him. Colonel Robert Ellingham is a prisoner in this camp; offer him his own exchange for young Bedloe.

KERCHIVAL: He will accept, of course. I will ride to the front with him myself, General, and show him through the lines.

HAVERHILL: At once! [*Kerchival crosses front and exit on the veranda*] Can you follow the dispatch, Captain?

LOCKWOOD: Perfectly; everything is here.

HAVERHILL: Well!

LIEUT. OF SIGNAL CORPS: Eleven – Twenty-two – One – Twelve.

LOCKWOOD: [*From the book*] "General Longstreet is coming with – "

HAVERHILL: Longstreet!

LIEUT. OF SIGNAL CORPS: One – Twenty-one.

LOCKWOOD: "With eighteen thousand men."

HAVERHILL: Longstreet and his corps!

LIEUT. OF SIGNAL CORPS: Two – Eleven – Twenty-two.

LOCKWOOD: "Sheridan is away!"

HAVERHILL: They have discovered his absence!

LIEUT. OF SIGNAL CORPS: Two – Twenty-two – Eleven – One – Twelve – One.

LOCKWOOD: "We will crush the Union Army before he can return."

HAVERHILL: Signal that dispatch from here to our Station at Front Royal. Tell them to send it after General Sheridan – and ride for their lives. [*Lockwood hurries out*] Major Burton! We will ride to General Wright's headquarters at once – our horses!

The noise of a struggle is heard without

BARKET: What the divil is the row out there?

Exit, also one of the Staff Officers

HAVERHILL: [*Looking off to the left*] What is this! Colonel West wounded!

Enter Kerchival West, his coat thrown open, with Ellingham, Barket assisting

ELLINGHAM: Steady, Kerchival, old boy! You should have let us carry you.

KERCHIVAL: Nonsense, old fellow! It's a mere touch with the point of the knife. I – I'm faint – with the loss of a little blood – that's all. Bob! – I –

He reels suddenly and is caught by Ellingham as he sinks to the ground, insensible

ELLINGHAM: Kerchival. [*Kneeling at his side*]

HAVERHILL: Go for the Surgeon! [*To the Staff Officer, who goes out quickly on veranda*] How did this happen?

Enter Corporal Dunn and Guard, with Thornton. He is in his shirt sleeves and disheveled, his arms folded. They march down Captain Thornton!

ELLINGHAM: We were leaving the house together; a hunted animal sprang suddenly across our path, like a panther. [*Looking over his shoulder*] There it stands. Kerchival! – my brother!

CORP. DUNN: We had just brought this prisoner to bay, but I'm afraid we were too late.

HAVERHILL: This is assassination, sir, not war. If you have killed him –

THORNTON: Do what you like with me; we need waste no words. I had an old account to settle, and I have paid my debt.

ELLINGHAM: General Haverhill! I took these from his breast when he first fell.

Handing up wallet and miniature to Haverhill. Haverhill starts as he looks at the miniature. Thornton watches him

HAVERHILL: [*Aside*] My wife's portrait!

THORNTON: If I have killed him – your honor will be buried in the same grave.

HAVERHILL: Her picture on his breast! She gave it to him – not to my son!

Dropping into the seat. Capt. Lockwood enters with a Signalman, who has a burning torch on a long pole; he hurries up the elevation. Capt. Lockwood stands below, facing him. Almost simultaneously with the entrance of the Signalman, Gertrude runs in on veranda

GERTRUDE: They are calling for a surgeon! Who is it? Brother! – you are safe. Ah! [*Uttering a scream, as she sees Kerchival, and falling on her knees at his side*] Kerchival! Forget those last bitter words I said to you. Can't you hear my confession? I do love you. Can't you hear me? I love you!

The Signalman is swinging the torch as the curtain descends, Lockwood looking out to the right

ACT III

The scene is the same as in the Second Act. It is now bright daylight, with sunshine flecking the foreground and bathing the distant valley and mountains. As the curtain rises Jenny Buckthorn is sitting on the low stone post, in the center of the stage, looking toward the left. She imitates a Trumpet Signal on her closed fists.

JENNY: What a magnificent line! Guide-posts! Every man and every horse is eager for the next command. There comes the flag! [*As the scene progresses trumpet signals are heard without*

and she follows their various meanings in her speech] To the standard! The regiment is going to the front. Oh! I do wish I could go with it. I always do, the moment I hear the trumpets. Boots and Saddles! Mount! I wish I was in command of the regiment. It was born in me. Fours right! There they go! Look at those horses' ears! Forward. [*A military band is heard without, playing "The Battle Cry of Freedom." Jenny takes the attitude of holding a bridle and trotting*] Rappity – plap – plap – plap, etc. [*She imitates the motions of a soldier on horseback, stepping down to the rock at side of post; thence to the ground and about the stage, with the various curvettings of a spirited horse. A chorus of soldiers is heard without, with the band. The music becomes more and more distant. Jenny gradually stops as the music is dying away, and stands, listening. As it dies entirely away, she suddenly starts to an enthusiastic attitude*] Ah! If I were only a man! The enemy! On Third Battalion, left, front, into line, march! Draw sabres! Charge! [*Imitates a trumpet signal. As she finishes, she rises to her full height, with both arms raised, and trembling with enthusiasm*] Ah! [*She suddenly drops her arms and changes to an attitude and expression of disappointment – pouting*] And the first time Old Margery took me to Father, in her arms, she had to tell him I was a girl. Father was as much disgusted as I was. But he'd never admit it; he says I'm as good a soldier as any of 'em – just as I am.

Enter Barket, on the veranda, his arm in a sling

BARKET: Miss Jenny!

JENNY: Barket! The regiment has marched away to the front, and we girls are left here, with just you and a corporal's guard to look after us.

BARKET: I've been watching the byes mesilf. [*Coming down*] If a little military sugar-plum like you, Miss Jenny, objects to not goin' wid 'em, what do you think of an ould piece of hard tack like me? I can't join the regiment till I've taken you and Miss Madeline back to Winchester, by your father's orders. But it isn't the first time I've escorted you, Miss Jenny. Many a time, when you was a baby, on the Plains, I commanded a special guard to accompany ye's from one fort to anither, and we gave the command in a whisper, so as not to wake ye's up.

JENNY: I told you to tell Father that I'd let him know when Madeline and I were ready to go.

BARKET: I tould him that I'd as soon move a train of army mules.

JENNY: I suppose we must start for home again to-day?

BARKET: Yes, Miss Jenny, in charge of an ould Sargeant wid his arm in a sling and a couple of convalescent throopers. This department of the United States Army will move to the rear in half an hour.

JENNY: Madeline and I only came yesterday morning.

BARKET: Whin your father got ye's a pass to the front, we all thought the fightin' in the Shenandoey Valley was over. It looks now as if it was just beginning. This is no place for women, now. Miss Gertrude Ellingham ought to go wid us, but she won't.

JENNY: Barket! Captain Heartsease left the regiment yesterday, and he hasn't rejoined it; he isn't with them, now, at the head of his company. Where is he?

BARKET: I can't say where he is, Miss Jenny. [*Aside*] Lyin' unburied in the woods, where he was shot, I'm afraid.

JENNY: When Captain Heartsease does rejoin the regiment, Barket, please say to him for me, that – that I – I may have some orders for him, when we next meet.

Exit on veranda

BARKET: Whin they nixt mate. They tell us there is no such thing as marriage in Hiven. If Miss Jenny and Captain Heartsease mate there, they'll invint somethin' that's mighty like it. While I was lyin' wounded in General Buckthorn's house at Washington, last summer, and ould Margery was taking care of me, Margery tould me, confidentially, that they was in love wid aitch ither; and I think she was about right. I've often seen Captain Heartsease take a sly look at a little lace handkerchief, just before we wint into battle. [*Looking off the stage*] Here's General Buckthorn himself. He and I must make it as aisy as we can for Miss Jenny's poor heart.

Enter General Buckthorn

BUCKTHORN: Sergeant Barket! You haven't started with those girls yet?

BARKET: They're to go in half an hour, sir.

BUCKTHORN: Be sure they do go. Is General Haverhill here?

BARKET: Yes, sur; in the house with some of his staff, and the Surgeon.

BUCKTHORN: Ah! The Surgeon. How is Colonel West, this morning, after the wound he received last night?

BARKET: He says, himself, that he's as well as iver he was; but the Colonel and Surgeon don't agray on that subject. The dochter says he mustn't lave his room for a month. The knife wint dape; and there's somethin' wrong inside of him. But the Colonel, bein' on the outside himsilf, can't see it. He's as cross as a bear, baycause they wouldn't let him go to the front this morning, at the head of his regiment. I happened to raymark that the Chaplain was prayin' for his raycovery. The Colonel said he'd courtmartial him, if he didn't stop that – quick; there's more important things for the Chaplain to pray for in his official capacity. Just at that moment the trumpets sounded, "Boots and Saddles." I had to dodge one of his boots, and the Surgeon had a narrow escape from the ither one. It was lucky for us both his saddle wasn't in the room.

BUCKTHORN: That looks encouraging. I think Kerchival will get on.

BARKET: Might I say a word to you, sur, about Miss Jenny?

BUCKTHORN: Certainly, Barket. You and old Margery and myself have been a sort of triangular mother, so to speak, to the little girl since her own poor mother left her to our care, when she was only a baby, in the old fort on the Plains. [*He unconsciously rests his arm over Barket's shoulder, familiarly and then suddenly draws up*] Ahem! [*Gruffly*] What is it? Proceed.

BARKET: Her mother's bosom would have been the softest place for her poor little head to rest upon, now, sur.

BUCKTHORN: [*Touching his eyes*] Well!

BARKET: Ould Margery tould me in Washington that Miss Jenny and Captain Heartsease were in love wid aitch ither.

BUCKTHORN: [*Starting*] In love!

BARKET: I approved of the match.

BUCKTHORN: What the devil!

Barket salutes quickly and starts up stage and out. Buckthorn moves up after him, and stops at the post. Barket stops in the road

BARKET: So did ould Margery.

BUCKTHORN: [*Angrily*] March! [*Barket salutes suddenly and marches off*] Heartsease! That young jackanapes! A mere fop; he'll never make a soldier. My girl in love with – bah! I don't believe it; she's too good a soldier, herself.

Enter Haverhill, on the veranda
Ah, Haverhill!

HAVERHILL: General Buckthorn! Have you heard anything of General Sheridan since I sent that dispatch to him last evening?

BUCKTHORN: He received it at midnight and sent back word that he considers it a ruse of the enemy. General Wright agrees with him. The reconnoissance yesterday showed no hostile force, on our right, and Crook reports that Early is retreating up the valley. But General Sheridan may, perhaps, give up his journey to Washington, and he has ordered some changes in our line, to be executed this afternoon at four o'clock. I rode over to give you your instructions in person. You may order General McCuen to go into camp on the right of Meadow Brook, with the second division.

Haverhill is writing in his note-book

Enter Jenny, on the veranda
JENNY: Oh, Father! I'm so glad you've come. I've got something to say to you.

Running down and jumping into his arms, kissing him. He turns with her, and sets her down, squarely on her feet and straight before him

BUCKTHORN: And I've got something to say to you – about Captain Heartsease.

JENNY: Oh! That's just what I wanted to talk about.

BUCKTHORN: Fall in! Front face! [*She jumps into military position, turning towards him*] What's this I hear from Sergeant Barket? He says you've been falling in love.

JENNY: I have. [*Saluting*]

BUCKTHORN: Young woman! Listen to my orders. Fall out! [*Turns sharply and marches to Haverhill*] Order the Third Brigade of Cavalry, under Colonel Lowell, to occupy the left of the pike.

JENNY: Father! [*Running to him and seizing the tail of his coat*] Father, dear!

BUCKTHORN: Close in Colonel Powell on the extreme left – [*Slapping his coat tails out of Jenny's hands, without looking around*] – and hold Custer on the second line, at Old Forge Road. That is all at present. [*Turning to Jenny*] Good-bye, my darling! [*Kisses her*] Remember your orders! You little pet! [*Chuckling, as he taps her chin; draws up suddenly and turns to Haverhill*] General! I bid you good-day.

HAVERHILL: Good-day, General Buckthorn.

They salute with great dignity. Buckthorn starts up stage; Jenny springs after him, seizing his coat tails
JENNY: But I want to talk with you, Father; I can't fall out. I – I – haven't finished yet.

Clinging to his coat, as Buckthorn marches out rapidly, in the road, holding back with all her might
HAVERHILL: It may have been a ruse of the enemy, but I hope that General Sheridan has turned back from Washington. [*Looking at his note-book*] We are to make changes in our line at four o'clock this afternoon. [*Returning the book to his pocket, he stands in thought*] The Surgeon tells me that Kerchival West will get on well enough if he remains quiet; otherwise not. He shall not die by the hand of a common assassin; he has no right to die like that. My wife gave my own picture of herself to him – not to my son – and she looked so like an angel when she took it from my hand! They were both false to me, and they have been true to each other. I will save his life for myself.

Enter Gertrude, on the veranda
GERTRUDE: General Haverhill! [*Anxiously, coming down*] Colonel West persists in disobeying the injunctions of the Surgeon. He is preparing to join his regiment at the front. Give him your orders to remain here. Compel him to be prudent!

HAVERHILL: [*Quickly*] The honor of death at the front is not in reserve for him.

GERTRUDE: Eh? What did you say, General?

HAVERHILL: Gertrude! I wish to speak to you, as your father's old friend; and I was once your guardian. Your father was my senior officer in the Mexican War. Without his care I should have been left dead in a foreign land. He, himself, afterwards fell fighting for the old flag.

GERTRUDE: The old flag. [*Aside*] My father died for it, and he – [*Looking toward the left*] – is suffering for it – the old flag!

HAVERHILL: I can now return the kindness your father did to me, by protecting his daughter from something that may be worse than death.

GERTRUDE: What do you mean?

HAVERHILL: Last night I saw you kneeling at the side of Kerchival West; you spoke to him with all the tender passion of a Southern woman. You said you loved him. But you spoke into ears that could not hear you. Has he ever heard those words from your lips? Have you ever confessed your love to him before?

GERTRUDE: Never. Why do you ask?

HAVERHILL: Do not repeat those words. Keep your heart to yourself, my girl.

GERTRUDE: General! Why do you say this to me? And at such a moment – when his life –

HAVERHILL: His life! [*Turning sharply*] It belongs to me!

GERTRUDE: Oh!

KERCHIVAL: Sergeant! [*Without. He steps into the road, looking back. Haverhill comes down*] See that my horse is ready at once. General! [*Saluting*] Are there any orders for my regiment beyond those given to Major Wilson, in my absence, this morning? I am about to ride on after the troops and reassume my command.

HAVERHILL: [*Quietly*] It is my wish, Colonel, that you remain here under the care of the Surgeon.

KERCHIVAL: My wound is a mere trifle. This may be a critical moment in the campaign, and I cannot rest here. I must be with my own men.

HAVERHILL: [*Quietly*] I beg to repeat the wish I have already expressed.

Kerchival walks to him, and speaks apart, almost under his breath, but very earnest in tone

KERCHIVAL: I have had no opportunity, yet, to explain certain matters, as you requested me to do yesterday; but whatever there may be between us, you are now interfering with my duty and my privilege as a soldier; and it is my right to be at the head of my regiment.

HAVERHILL: [*Quietly*] It is my positive order that you do not reassume your command.

KERCHIVAL: General Haverhill, I protest against this –

HAVERHILL: [*Quietly*] You are under arrest, sir.

KERCHIVAL: Arrest!

GERTRUDE: Ah!

Kerchival unclasps his belt and offers his sword to Haverhill

HAVERHILL: [*Quietly*] Keep your sword; I have no desire to humiliate you; but hold yourself subject to further orders from me.

KERCHIVAL: My regiment at the front! – and I under arrest!

Exit

HAVERHILL: Gertrude! If your heart refuses to be silent – if you feel that you must confess your love to that man – first tell him what I have said to you, and refer him to me for an explanation.

Exit

GERTRUDE: What can he mean? He would save me from something worse than death, he said. "His life – It belongs to me!" What can he mean? Kerchival told me that he loved me – it seems many years since that morning in Charleston – and when we met again, yesterday, he said that he had never ceased to love me. I will not believe that he has told me a falsehood. I have given him my love, my whole soul and my faith. [*Drawing up to her full height*] My perfect faith!

Jenny runs in, to the road, and up the slope. She looks down the hill, then toward the left and enters

JENNY: A flag of truce, Gertrude. And a party of Confederate soldiers, with an escort, coming up the hill. They are carrying someone; he is wounded.

Enter, up the slope, a Lieutenant of Infantry with an escort of Union Soldiers, their arms at right shoulder, and a party of Confederate Soldiers bearing a rustic stretcher. Lieutenant Frank Bedloe lies on the stretcher. Major Hardwick, a Confederate Surgeon, walks at his side. Madeline appears at the veranda, watching them. Gertrude stands with her back to the audience. The Lieutenant gives orders in a low tone, and the front escort moves toward the right, in the road. The Confederate bearers and the Surgeon pass through the gate. The rear es-

cort moves on in the road, under the Lieutenant's orders. The bearers halt in the front of the
stage; on a sign from the Surgeon, they leave
the stretcher on the ground, stepping back

MAJOR HARDWICK: Is General Haverhill here?

GERTRUDE: Yes; what can we do, sir?

MADELINE: The General is just about mounting
with his staff, to ride away. Shall I go for
him, sir?

MAJOR: Say to him, please, that Colonel Robert
Ellingham, of the Tenth Virginia, sends his
respects and sympathy. He instructed me to
bring this young officer to this point, in exchange for himself, as agreed upon between
them last evening.

Exit Madeline

JENNY: Is he unconscious or sleeping, sir?

MAJOR: Hovering between life and death. I
thought he would bear the removal better. He
is waking. Here, my lad! [*Placing his canteen
to the lips of Frank, who moves, reviving*] We
have reached the end of our journey.

FRANK: My father!

MAJOR: He is thinking of his home.

Frank rises on one arm, assisted by the Surgeon

FRANK: I have obeyed General Haverhill's orders, and I have a report to make.

GERTRUDE: We have already sent for him. [*Stepping to him*] He will be here in a moment.

FRANK: [*Looking into her face, brightly*] Is not
this – Miss – Gertrude Ellingham?

GERTRUDE: You know me? You have seen me
before?

FRANK: Long ago! Long ago! You know the
wife of General Haverhill?

GERTRUDE: I have no dearer friend in the world.

FRANK: She will give a message for me to the
dearest friend *I* have in the world. My little
wife! I must not waste even the moment we are
waiting. Doctor! My note-book! [*Trying to get
it from his coat. The Surgeon takes it out. A
torn and blood-stained lace handkerchief also
falls out. Gertrude kneels at his side*] Ah! I –
I – have a message from another [*Holding up
the handkerchief*] – from Captain Heartsease.
[*Jenny makes a quick start towards him*] He
lay at my side in the hospital, when they
brought me away; he had only strength enough
to put this in my hand, and he spoke a woman's name; but I – I – forget what it is. The
red spots upon it are the only message he sent.

Gertrude takes the handkerchief and looks back
at Jenny, extending her hand. Jenny moves to
her, takes the handkerchief and turns back,
looking down on it. She drops her face into her
hands and goes out sobbing, on the veranda

Enter Madeline on the veranda

MADELINE: General Haverhill is coming. I was
just in time. He was already on his horse.

FRANK: Ah! He is coming. [*Then suddenly*]
Write! Write! [*Gertrude writes in the note-
book as he dictates*] "To – my wife – Edith:
– Tell our little son, when he is old enough to
know – how his father died; not how he
lived. And tell her who filled my own mother's
place so lovingly – she is your mother, too –
that my father's portrait of her, which she
gave to me in Charleston, helped me to be a better man!" And – Oh! I must not forget this –
"It was taken away from me while I was a
prisoner in Richmond, and it is in the possession of Captain Edward Thornton, of the Confederate Secret Service. But her face is still beside your own in my heart. My best –
warmest, last – love – to you, darling." I will
sign it.

Gertrude holds the book, and he signs it, then
sinks back very quietly, supported by the Surgeon. Gertrude rises and walks away

MADELINE: General Haverhill is here.

The Surgeon lays the fold of the blanket over
Frank's face and rises

GERTRUDE: Doctor!

MAJOR: He is dead.

Madeline, on the veranda, turns and looks
away. The Lieutenant orders the guard,
"Present Arms"

Enter Haverhill, on the veranda. He salutes the
guard as he passes. The Lieutenant orders,
"Carry Arms." Haverhill comes down

HAVERHILL: I am too late?

MAJOR: I'm sorry, General. His one eager
thought as we came was to reach here in time
to see you.

Haverhill moves to the bier, looks down at it,
then folds back the blanket from the face. He
starts slightly as he first sees it

HAVERHILL: Brave boy! I hoped once to have a

son like you. I shall be in your father's place to-day, at your grave. [*He replaces the blanket and steps back*] We will carry him to his comrades in the front. He shall have a soldier's burial, in sight of the mountain-top beneath which he sacrificed his young life; that shall be his monument.

MAJOR: Pardon me, General. We Virginians are your enemies, but you cannot honor this young soldier more than we do. Will you allow my men the privilege of carrying him to his grave?

Haverhill inclines his head. The Surgeon motions to the Confederate Soldiers, who step to the bier and raise it gently
HAVERHILL: Lieutenant!

The Lieutenant orders the guard "Left Face." The Confederate bearers move through the gate, preceded by Lieutenant Hardwick. Haverhill draws his sword, reverses it, and moves up behind the bier with bowed head. The Lieutenant orders "Forward March," and the cortege disappears. While the girls are still watching it, the heavy sound of distant artillery is heard, with booming reverberations among the hills and in the valley
MADELINE: What is that sound, Gertrude?
GERTRUDE: Listen!

Another and more prolonged distant sound, with long reverberations
MADELINE: Again! Gertrude!

Gertrude raises her hand to command silence; listens. Distant cannon again
GERTRUDE: It is the opening of a battle.
MADELINE: Ah! [*Running down stage. The sounds are heard again, prolonged*]
GERTRUDE: How often have I heard that sound! [*Coming down*] This is war, Madeline! You are face to face with it now.
MADELINE: And Robert is there! He may be in the thickest of the danger – at this very moment.
GERTRUDE: Yes. Let our prayers go up for him; mine do, with all a sister's heart.

Kerchival enters on veranda, without coat or vest, his sash about his waist, looking back as he comes in
Kerchival!
KERCHIVAL: Go on! Go on! Keep the battle to

yourselves. I'm out of it. [*The distant cannon and reverberations are rising in volume*]
MADELINE: I pray for Robert Ellingham – and for the *cause* in which he risks his life! [*Kerchival looks at her, suddenly; also Gertrude*] Heaven forgive me if I am wrong, but I am praying for the enemies of my country. His people are my people, his enemies are my enemies. Heaven defend him and his, in this awful hour.
KERCHIVAL: Madeline! My sister!
MADELINE: Oh, Kerchival! [*Turning and dropping her face on his breast*] I cannot help it – I cannot help it!
KERCHIVAL: My poor girl! Every woman's heart, the world over, belongs not to any country or any flag, but to her husband – and her lover. Pray for the man you love, sister – it would be treason not to. [*Passes her before him to the left of the stage. Looks across to Gertrude*] Am I right? [*Gertrude drops her head. Madeline moves up veranda and out*] Is what I have said to Madeline true?
GERTRUDE: Yes! [*Looks up*] Kerchival!
KERCHIVAL: Gertrude! [*Hurries across to her, clasps her in his arms. He suddenly staggers and brings his hand to his breast*]
GERTRUDE: Your wound!

Supporting him as he reels and sinks into seat
KERCHIVAL: Wound! I have no wound! You do love me! [*Seizing her hand*]
GERTRUDE: Let me call the Surgeon, Kerchival.
KERCHIVAL: You can be of more service to me than he can. [*Detaining her. Very heavy sounds of the battle; she starts, listening*] Never mind that! It's only a battle. You love me!
GERTRUDE: Be quiet, Kerchival, dear. I do love you. I told you so, when you lay bleeding here, last night. But you could not hear me. [*At his side, resting her arm about him, stroking his head*] I said that same thing to – to – another, more than three years ago. It is in that letter that General Buckthorn gave you. [*Kerchival starts*] No – no – you must be very quiet, or I will not say another word. If you obey me, I will repeat that part of the letter, every word; I know it by heart, for I read it a dozen times. The letter is from Mrs. Haverhill.
KERCHIVAL: [*Quietly*] Go on.
GERTRUDE: "I have kept your secret, my darling, but I was sorely tempted to betray the

confidence you reposed in me at Charleston. If Kerchival West – [*She retires backward from him as she proceeds*] – had heard you say, as I did, when your face was hidden in my bosom, that night, that you loved him with your whole heart – "

KERCHIVAL: Ah!

Starting to his feet. He sinks back. She springs to support him

GERTRUDE: I will go for help.

KERCHIVAL: Do not leave me at such a moment as this. You have brought me a new life. [*Bringing her to her knees before him and looking down at her*] Heaven is just opening before me. [*His hands drop suddenly and his head falls back*]

GERTRUDE: Ah! Kerchival! you are dying!

Musketry. A sudden sharp burst of musketry, mingled with the roar of artillery near by. Kerchival starts, seizing Gertrude's arm and holding her away, still on her knees. He looks eagerly toward the left

KERCHIVAL: The enemy is close upon us!

Barket runs in, up the slope

BARKET: Colonel Wist! The divils have sprung out of the ground. They're pouring over our lift flank like Noah's own flood. The Union Army has started back for Winchester, on its way to the North Pole; our own regiment, Colonel, is coming over the hill in full retrate.

KERCHIVAL: My own regiment! [*Starting up*] Get my horse, Barket. [*Turns*] Gertrude, my life! [*Embraces Gertrude*]

BARKET: Your horse is it? I'm wid ye! There's a row at Finnegan's ball and we're in it. [*Springs to the road, and runs out*]

KERCHIVAL: [*Turns away. Stops*] I am under arrest.

The retreat begins. Fugitives begin to straggle across the stage from the left

GERTRUDE: You must not go, Kerchival; it will kill you.

KERCHIVAL: Arrest be damned! [*Starts up toward the center, raising his arms above his head with clenched fist, and rising to full height*] Stand out of my way, you cowards!

They cower away from him as he rushes out

among them. *The stream of fugitives passing across the stage swells in volume. Gertrude runs through them and up to the elevation, turning*

GERTRUDE: Men! Are you soldiers? Turn back! There is a leader for you! Turn back! Fight for your flag – and mine! – the flag my father died for! Turn back! [*She looks out toward the left and then turns toward the front*] He has been marked for death already, and I – I can only pray. [*Dropping to her knees*]

The stream of fugitives continues, now over the elevation also. Rough and torn uniforms, bandaged arms and legs; some limping and supported by others, some dragging their muskets after them, others without muskets, others using them as crutches. There is a variety of uniforms, both cavalry and infantry; flags are draggled on the ground, the rattle of near musketry and roar of cannon continues; two or three wounded fugitives drop down beside the hedge. Benson staggers in and drops upon a rock near the post. Artillerists, rough, torn and wounded, drag and force a field-piece across. Corporal Dunn, wounded, staggers to the top of elevation. There is a lull in the sounds of the battle. Distant cheers are heard without

DUNN: Listen, fellows! Stop! Listen! Sheridan! General Sheridan is coming! [*Cheers from those on stage. Gertrude rises quickly. The wounded soldiers rise, looking over the hedge. All on stage stop, looking eagerly toward the left. The cheers without come nearer, with shouts of "Sheridan! Sheridan!"*] The horse is down; he is worn out.

GERTRUDE: No! He is up again! He is on my Jack! Now, for your life, Jack, and for me! You've never failed me yet. [*The cheers without now swell to full volume and are taken up by those on the stage. The horse sweeps by with General Sheridan*] Jack! Jack!! Jack!!!

Waving her arms as he passes. She throws up her arms and falls backward, caught by Dunn. The stream of men is reversed and surges across the stage to the left, in the road and on the elevation, with shouts, and throwing up of hats. The field-piece is forced up the slope with a few bold, rough movements; the artillerists are loading it, and the stream of returning fugitives is still surging by in the road as the curtain falls

ACT IV

A living room in the residence of General Buck-thorn in Washington. There is a fireplace slant-ing upward from the left toward the center of the stage. On the right toward the center there is a small alcove. On the left there is an opening to the hall with a stair-case, beyond. There is a door on the right and a wide opening with por-tieres leads on the left toward another room. There is an upright piano toward the front of the stage on the right and an arm-chair and low stool stand before the fireplace. A small table is set for tea. It is afternoon; Mrs. Haverhill, in an arm-chair, is resting her face upon her hand, and looking into the fire. Edith is on a low stool at her side, sewing a child's garment.

EDITH: It seems hardly possible that the war is over, and that General Lee has really surren-dered. There is music in the streets nearly all the time, now, and everybody looks so cheer-ful and bright. [*Distant fife and drums are heard playing "Johnnie Comes Marching Home." Edith springs up and runs up to the window, looking out*] More troops returning! The old tattered battle-flag is waving in the wind, and people are running after them so merrily. Every day, now, seems like a holiday. The war is over. All the women ought to feel very happy, whose – whose husbands are – coming back to them.

MRS. HAVERHILL: Yes, Edith; those women whose – husbands are coming back to them. [*Still looking into the fire*]

EDITH: Oh! [*Dropping upon the stool, her head upon the arm of the chair*]

MRS. HAVERHILL: [*Resting her arm over her*] My poor, little darling! *Your* husband will not come back.

EDITH: Frank's last message has never reached me.

MRS. HAVERHILL: No; but you have one sweet thought always with you. Madeline West heard part of it, as Gertrude wrote it down. His last thought was a loving one, of you.

EDITH: Madeline says that he was thinking of you, too. He knew that you were taking such loving care of his little one, and of me. You have always done that, since you first came back from Charleston, and found me alone in New York.

MRS. HAVERHILL: I found a dear, sweet little daughter. [*Stroking her head*] Heaven sent you, darling! You have been a blessing to me. I hardly know how I should have got through the past few months at all without you at my side.

EDITH: What is your own trouble, dear? I have found you in tears so often; and since last Octo-ber, after the battle of Cedar Creek, you – you have never shown me a letter from – from my – Frank's father. General Haverhill arrived in Washington yesterday, but has not been here yet. Is it because I am here? He has never seen me, and I fear that he has never for-given Frank for marrying me.

MRS. HAVERHILL: Nonsense, my child; he did think the marriage was imprudent, but he told me to do everything I could for you. If Gener-al Haverhill has not been to see either of us, since his arrival in Washington, it is nothing that you need to worry your dear little head about. How are you getting on with your son's wardrobe?

EDITH: Oh! Splendidly! Frankie isn't a baby any longer; he's a man, now, and he has to wear a man's clothes. [*Holding up a little pair of trousers, with maternal pride*] He's rather young to be dressed like a man, but I want Frank to grow up as soon as possible. I long to have him old enough to understand me when I repeat to him the words in which General Ha-verhill told the whole world how his father died! [*Rising*] And yet, even in his official re-port to the Government, he only honored him as Lieutenant Bedloe. He has never forgiven his son for the disgrace he brought upon his name.

MRS. HAVERHILL: I know him so well – [*Rising*] – the unyielding pride, that conquers even the deep tenderness of his nature. He can be silent, though his own heart is breaking. [*Aside*] He can be silent, too, though *my* heart is breaking. [*Dropping her face in her hand*]

EDITH: *Mother!* [*Putting her arm about her*]

Enter Jannette

JANNETTE: A letter for you, Madam.

MRS. HAVERHILL: [*Taking note. Aside*] He has answered me. [*She opens and reads the let-ter, and inclines her head to Jannette, who goes out to the hall. Aloud*] General Haverhill will be here this afternoon, Edith. [*Exit*]

EDITH: There is something that she cannot confide to me, or to anyone. General Haver-hill returned to Washington yesterday, and he has not been here yet. He will be here to-day. I always tremble when I think of meeting him.

General Buckthorn appears in the hall

BUCKTHORN: Come right in; this way, Barket. Ah, Edith!

BARKET: [*Entering*] As I was saying, sur – just after the battle of Sayder Creek began –

BUCKTHORN: [*To Edith*] More good news! The war is, indeed, over now!

BARKET: Whin Colonel Wist rode to the front to mate his raytrating rigiment –

BUCKTHORN: General Johnston has surrendered his army, also; and that, of course, does end the war.

EDITH: I'm very glad that all the fighting is over.

BUCKTHORN: So am I; but my occupation, and old Barket's, too, is gone. Always at work on new clothes for our little soldier?

EDITH: He's growing so, I can hardly make them fast enough for him. But this is the time for his afternoon nap. I must go now, to see if he is sleeping soundly.

BUCKTHORN: Our dear little mother! [*Tapping her chin*] I always claim the privilege of my white hair, you know. [*She puts up her lips; he kisses her. She goes out*] The sweetest young widow I ever saw! [*Barket coughs. Buckthorn turns sharply; Barket salutes*] Well! What the devil are you thinking about now?

BARKET: The ould time, sur. Yer honor used to claim the same privilege for brown hair.

BUCKTHORN: You old rascal! What a memory you have! You were telling me for the hundredth time about the battle of Cedar Creek; go on. I can never hear it often enough. Kerchival West was a favorite of mine, poor fellow!

BARKET: Just afther the battle of Sayder Creek began, when the Colonel rode to the front to mate his raytrating rigiment –

BUCKTHORN: I'll tell Old Margery to bring in tea for both of us, Barket.

BARKET: For both of us, sur?

BUCKTHORN: Yes; and later in the evening we'll have something else, together. This is a great day for all of us. I'm not your commander to-day, but your old comrade in arms – [*Laying his arm over Barket's shoulder*] – and I'm glad I don't have to pull myself up now every time I forget my dignity. Ah! you and I will

be laid away before long, but we'll be together again in the next world, won't we, Barket?

BARKET: Wid yer honor's permission.

Saluting

BUCKTHORN: Ha – ha – ha! [*Laughing*] If we do meet there, I'm certain you'll salute me as your superior officer. There's old Margery, now. [*Looking toward the door and calling*] Margery! Tea for two!

OLD MARGERY: [*Without*] The tay be waiting for ye, sur; and it be boilin' over wid impatience.

BUCKTHORN: Bring up a chair, Barket.

Sitting down in the arm-chair

BARKET: [*Having placed table and drawing up a chair*] Do you know, Gineral, I don't fale quite aisy in my moind. I'm not quite sure that Margery will let us take our tay together.

Sits down, doubtfully

BUCKTHORN: I hadn't thought of that. I – [*Glancing to the right*] – I hope she will, Barket. But, of course, if she won't – she's been commander-in-chief of my household ever since Jenny was a baby.

BARKET: At Fort Duncan, in Texas.

BUCKTHORN: You and Old Margery never got along very well in those days; but I thought you had made it all up; she nursed you through your wound, last summer, and after the battle of Cedar Creek, also.

BARKET: Yis, sur, bliss her kind heart, she's been like a wife to me; and that's the trouble. A man's wife is such an angel when he's ill that he dreads to get well; good health is a misfortune to him. Ould Margery and I have had anither misunderstanding.

BUCKTHORN: I'll do the best I can for both of us, Barket. You were telling me about the battle of –

BARKET: Just afther the battle of Sayder Creek began whin Colonel Wist rode to the front to mate his raytrating rigiment –

Enter Old Margery, with a tea-tray. She stops abruptly, looking at Barket. He squirms in his chair. Buckthorn rises and stands with his back to the mantel. Old Margery moves to the table, arranges things on it, glances at Barket, then at Buckthorn, who looks up at the ceiling, rubbing his chin. Old Margery takes up one of the cups, with saucer

OLD MARGERY: I misunderstood yer order, sur. I see there's no one here but yerself. [*Going*]

BUCKTHORN: Ah, Margery! [*She stops*] Barket tells me that there has been a slight misunderstanding between you and him.

OLD MARGERY: Day before yisterday, the ould Hibernian dhrone had the kitchen upside down, to show anither old milithary vagabone loike himself how the battle of Sayder Creek was fought. He knocked the crame pitcher into the basket of clane clothes, and overturned some raspberry jam and the flat-irons into a pan of fresh eggs. There *has* been a misunderstanding betwane us.

BUCKTHORN: I see there has. I suppose Barket was showing his friend how Colonel Kerchival West rode forward to meet his regiment, when he was already wounded dangerously.

OLD MARGERY: Bliss the poor, dear young man! He and I was always good frinds, though he was something of a devil in the kitchen himself, whin he got there. [*Wiping her eye with one corner of her apron*] And bliss the young Southern lady that was in love wid him, too. [*Changing the cup and wiping the other eye with the corner of her apron*] Nothing was iver heard of ayther of thim after that battle was over, to this very day.

BUCKTHORN: Barket was at Kerchival's side when he rode to the front. [*Old Margery hesitates a moment, then moves to the table, sets down the cup and marches out. Buckthorn sits in the arm-chair again, pouring tea*] I could always find some way to get Old Margery to do what I wanted her to do.

BARKET: You're a great man, Gineral; we'd niver have conquered the South widout such men.

BUCKTHORN: Now go on, Barket; you were interrupted.

BARKET: Just afther the battle of Sayder Creek began, whin –

Enter Jannette, with a card, which she hands to Buckthorn

BUCKTHORN: [*Reading card*] Robert Ellingham! [*Rises*] I will go to him. [*To Jannette*] Go upstairs and tell Miss Madeline to come down.

JANNETTE: Yes, sir. [*Going*]

BUCKTHORN: And, Jannette, simply say there is a caller; don't tell her who is here.

Exit Jannette. Buckthorn follows her out to the hall

Ellingham! My dear fellow!

Extending his hand and disappearing

BARKET: Colonel Ellingham and Miss Madeline – lovers! That's the kind o' volunteers the country nades now!

Enter Buckthorn and Ellingham

BUCKTHORN: [*As he enters*] We've been fighting four years to keep you out of Washington, Colonel, but we are delighted to see you within the lines, now.

ELLINGHAM: I am glad, indeed, General, to have so warm a welcome. But can you tell me anything about my sister, Gertrude?

BUCKTHORN: About your sister? Why, can't you tell us? And have you heard nothing of Kerchival West on your side of the line?

ELLINGHAM: All I can tell you is this: As soon as possible after our surrender at Appomattox, I made my way to the Shenandoah Valley. Our home there is utterly deserted. I have hurried down to Washington in the hopes that I might learn something of you. There is no human being about the old homestead; it is like a haunted house – empty, and dark, and solitary. You do not even know where Gertrude is?

BUCKTHORN: We only know that Kerchival was not found among the dead of his own regiment at Cedar Creek, though he fell among them during the fight. The three girls searched the field for him, but he was not there. As darkness came on, and they were returning to the house, Gertrude suddenly seized the bridle of a stray horse, sprang upon its back and rode away to the South, into the woods at the foot of Three Top Mountain. The other two girls watched for her in vain. She did not return, and we have heard nothing from her since.

ELLINGHAM: Poor girl! I understand what was in her thoughts, and she was right. We captured fourteen hundred prisoners that day, although we were defeated, and Kerchival must have been among them. Gertrude rode away, alone, in the darkness, to find him. I shall return to the South at once and learn where she now is.

Jannette has re-entered, down the stairs

JANNETTE: Miss Madeline will be down in a moment. [*Exit in hall*]

BARKET: [*Aside*] That name wint through his chist like a rifle ball.

BUCKTHORN: Will you step into the drawing-room, Colonel? I will see Madeline myself, first. She does not even know that you are living.

ELLINGHAM: I hardly dared ask for her. Is she well?

BUCKTHORN: Yes; and happy – or soon will be.

ELLINGHAM: Peace, at last!

Exit to the apartment. Buckthorn closes the portieres

BUCKTHORN: I ought to prepare Madeline a little, Barket; you must help me.

BARKET: Yis, sur, I will.

Enter Madeline, down the stairs

MADELINE: Uncle! Jannette said you wished to see me; there is a visitor here. Who is it?

BARKET: Colonel Robert Ellingham.

MADELINE: Ah! [*Staggering*]

BUCKTHORN: [*Supporting her*] You infernal idiot! I'll put you in the guard-house!

BARKET: You wanted me to help ye, Gineral.

MADELINE: Robert is alive – and here?

Rising from his arms, she moves to the portieres, holds them aside, peeping in; gives a joyful start, tosses aside the portieres and runs through

BUCKTHORN: Barket! There's nothing but that curtain between us and Heaven.

BARKET: I don't like stayin' out o' Hiven, myself, sur. Gineral! I'll kiss Ould Margery – if I die for it! [*Exit*]

BUCKTHORN: Kiss Old Margery! I'll give him a soldier's funeral.

Enter Jenny from hall, demurely

Ah! Jenny, my dear! I have news for you. Colonel Robert Ellingham is in the drawing-room.

JENNY: Oh! I am delighted. [*Starting*]

BUCKTHORN: A-h-e-m!

JENNY: Oh! – exactly. I see. I have some news for *you*, papa. Captain Heartsease has arrived in Washington.

BUCKTHORN: Oh! My dear! I have often confessed to you how utterly mistaken I was about that young man. He is a soldier – as good a soldier as you are. I'll ask him to the house.

JENNY: [*Demurely*] He is here now.

BUCKTHORN: Now?

JENNY: He's been here an hour; in the library.

BUCKTHORN: Why! Barket and I were in the library fifteen minutes ago.

JENNY: Yes, sir. We were in the bay-window; the curtains were closed.

BUCKTHORN: Oh! exactly; I see. You may tell him he has my full consent.

JENNY: He hasn't asked for it.

BUCKTHORN: Hasn't he? And you've been in the bay-window an hour? Well, my darling – I was considered one of the best Indian fighters in the old army, but it took me four years to propose to your mother. I'll go and see the Captain.

Exit

JENNY: I wonder if it will take Captain Heartsease four years to propose to me. Before he left Washington, nearly two years ago, he told everybody in the circle of my acquaintance, except me, that he was in love with me. I'll be an old lady in caps before our engagement commences. Poor, dear mother! The idea of a girl's waiting four years for a chance to say, "Yes." It's been on the tip of my tongue so often, I'm afraid it'll pop out, at last, before he pops the question.

Enter Buckthorn and Heartsease from the hall

BUCKTHORN: Walk right in, Captain; this is the family room. You must make yourself quite at home here.

HEARTSEASE: Thank you.

Walking down toward the right

BUCKTHORN: My dear! [*Apart to Jenny*] The very first thing he said to me, after our greeting, was that he loved my daughter.

JENNY: Now he's told my father!

BUCKTHORN: He's on fire!

JENNY: Is he? [*Looking at Heartsease, who stands quietly stroking his mustache*] Why doesn't he tell *me*?

BUCKTHORN: You may have to help him a little; your mother assisted me. When you and Jenny finish your chat, Captain – [*Lighting a cigar at the mantel*] – you must join me in the smoking room.

HEARTSEASE: I shall be delighted. By the way, General – I have been in such a fever of excitement since I arrived at this house –

JENNY: [*Aside*] Fever? Chills!

HEARTSEASE: That I forgot it entirely. I have

omitted a very important and a very sad commission. I have brought with me the note-book of Lieutenant Frank Bedloe – otherwise Haverhill – in which Miss Gertrude Ellingham wrote down his last message to his young wife.

JENNY: Have you seen Gertrude?

BUCKTHORN: [*Taking the book*] How did this note-book come into your possession?

HEARTSEASE: Miss Ellingham visited the prison in North Carolina where I was detained. She was going from hospital to hospital, from prison to prison, and from burial-place to burial-place, to find Colonel Kerchival West, if living – or some record of his death.

BUCKTHORN: Another Evangeline! Searching for her lover through the wilderness of this great war!

HEARTSEASE: I was about to be exchanged at the time, and she requested me to bring this to her friends in Washington. She had not intended to carry it away with her. I was not exchanged, as we then expected, but I afterwards escaped from prison to General Sherman's Army.

BUCKTHORN: I will carry this long-delayed message to the widowed young mother.

Exit

JENNY: I remember so well, when poor Lieutenant Haverhill took out the note-book and asked Gertrude to write for him. He – he brought me a message at the same time.

Their eyes meet. He puts up his glasses. She turns away, touching her eyes

HEARTSEASE: I – I remember the circumstances you probably allude to; that is – when he left my side – I – I gave him my – I mean your – lace handkerchief.

JENNY: It is sacred to me!

HEARTSEASE: Y-e-s – I would say – is it?

JENNY: [*Wiping her eyes*] It was stained with the life-blood of a hero!

HEARTSEASE: I must apologize to you for its condition. I hadn't any chance to have it washed and ironed.

JENNY: [*Looking around at him, suddenly; then, aside*] What could any girl do with a lover like that?

Turning up the stage

HEARTSEASE: [*Aside*] She seems to remember that incident so tenderly! My blood boils!

JENNY: Didn't you long to see your – your friends at home – when you were in prison, Captain?

HEARTSEASE: Yes – especially – I longed especially, Miss Buckthorn, to see –

JENNY: *Yes! – to see –*

HEARTSEASE: But there were lots of jolly fellows in the prison.

Jenny turns away

HEARTSEASE: We had a dramatic society, and a glee club, and an orchestra. I was one of the orchestra. I had a banjo, with one string; I played one tune on it, that I used to play on the piano, with one finger. But, Miss Buckthorn, I am a prisoner again, to-night – your prisoner.

JENNY: [*Aside*] At last!

HEARTSEASE: I'll show you how that tune went.

Turns to the piano and sits

JENNY: [*Aside*] Father said I'd have to help him, but I don't see an opening.

Heartsease plays part of an air with one finger and strikes two or three wrong notes

HEARTSEASE: There are two notes down there, somewhere, that I never could get right. The fellows in prison used to dance while I played – [*Playing*] – that is, the lame ones did; those that wern't lame couldn't keep the time.

JENNY: You must have been in great danger, Captain, when you escaped from prison.

HEARTSEASE: Y-e-s. I was badly frightened several times. One night I came face to face, on the road, with a Confederate Officer. It was Captain Thornton.

JENNY: Oh! What did you do?

HEARTSEASE: I killed him. [*Very quietly, and trying the tune again at once. Enter Jannette, from the hall; she glances into the room and goes up the stairs*] I used to skip those two notes on the banjo. It's very nice for a soldier to come home from the war, and meet those – I mean the one particular person – that he – you see, when a soldier loves a woman, as – as –

JENNY: [*Aside*] As he loves me.

Approaches him

HEARTSEASE: As soldiers often do – [*Plays; she turns away, petulantly; he plays the tune through correctly*] That's it!

JENNY: [*Aside*] I'm not going to be made love to by piece-meal, like this, any longer. [*Aloud*] Captain Heartsease! Have you anything in particular to say to me?

He looks up

HEARTSEASE: Y-e-s. [*Rising*]

JENNY: Say it! You told my father, and all my friends, that you were in love with me. Whom are you going to tell next?

HEARTSEASE: I *am* in love with you.

JENNY: It was my turn.

HEARTSEASE: [*Going near to her*] Do you love me?

JENNY: [*Laying her head quietly on his breast*] I must take time to consider.

HEARTSEASE: [*Quietly*] I assume that this means "Yes."

JENNY: It isn't the way a girl says "No."

HEARTSEASE: My darling!

JENNY: Why! His heart is beating as fast as mine is!

HEARTSEASE: [*Quietly*] I am frantic with joy. [*He kisses her. She hides her face on his breast. Enter Mrs. Haverhill, down-stairs, followed by Jannette. Mrs. Haverhill stops suddenly. Jannette stands in the doorway. Heartsease inclines his head to her, quietly looking at her over Jenny*] I am delighted to see you, after so long an absence; I trust that we shall meet more frequently hereafter.

JENNY: [*Looking at him*] Eh?

HEARTSEASE: [*Looking down at her*] I think, perhaps, it might be as well for us to repair to another apartment, and continue our interview, there!

JENNY: [*Dropping her head on his breast again*] This room is very comfortable.

MRS. HAVERHILL: Jenny, dear!

Jenny starts up; looks from Mrs. Haverhill to Heartsease

JENNY: Constance! I – 'Bout face! March!

She turns and goes out

MRS. HAVERHILL: I am glad to see you again, Captain, and happy as well as safe.

HEARTSEASE: Thank you, Madam. I am happy. If you will excuse me, I will join – my father – in the smoking-room. [*Mrs. Haverhill inclines her head, and Heartsease walks out*]

MRS. HAVERHILL: Jannette! You may ask General Haverhill to come into this room. [*Exit

Jannette. Mrs. Haverhill walks down the stage, reading a note*] "I have hesitated to come to you personally, as I have hesitated to write to you. If I have been silent, it is because I could not bring my hand to write what was in my mind and in my heart. I do not know that I can trust my tongue to speak it, but I will come."

Enter Haverhill, from the hall; he stops

HAVERHILL: Constance!

MRS. HAVERHILL: My husband! May I call you husband? After all these months of separation, with your life in almost daily peril, and my life – what? Only a weary longing for one loving word – and you are silent.

HAVERHILL: May I call you wife? I do not wish to speak that word except with reverence. You have asked me to come to you. I am here. I will be plain, direct and brief. Where is the portrait of yourself, which I gave you, in Charleston, for my son?

MRS. HAVERHILL: Your son is dead, sir; and my portrait lies upon his breast, in the grave. [*Haverhill takes the miniature from his pocket and holds it towards her in his extended hand. She starts back*] He gave it to you? And you ask me where it is?

HAVERHILL: It might have lain in the grave of Kerchival West!

MRS. HAVERHILL: Ah!

HAVERHILL: Not in my son's. I found it upon *his* breast. [*She turns front, dazed*] Well! I am listening! It was not I that sought this interview, madam; and if you prefer to remain silent, I will go. You know, now, why I have been silent so long.

MRS. HAVERHILL: My only witnesses to the truth are both dead. I shall remain silent. [*Turning towards him*] We stand before each other, living, but not so happy as they. We are parted, forever. Even if you should accept my unsupported word – if I could so far forget my pride as to give it to you – suspicion would still hang between us. I remain silent.

Haverhill looks at her, earnestly, for a moment, then approaches her

HAVERHILL: I cannot look into your eyes and not see truth and loyalty there. Constance!

MRS. HAVERHILL: No, John! [*Checking him*] I will not accept your blind faith! [*Moving*]

HAVERHILL: [*Looking down at the picture in

his hand] My faith is blind; blind as my love! I do not wish to see!

Enter Edith. She stops and looks at Haverhill. He raises his head and looks at her

EDITH: This is General Haverhill? [*Dropping her eyes*] I am Edith, sir.

HAVERHILL: [*Gently*] My son's wife. [*Kisses her forehead*] You shall take the place he once filled in my heart. His crime and his disgrace are buried in a distant grave.

EDITH: And you have not forgiven him, even yet?

MRS. HAVERHILL: Is there no atonement for poor Frank's sin – not even his death? Can you only bury the wrong and forget the good?

HAVERHILL: The good?

MRS. HAVERHILL: Your own words to the Government, as his commander!

HAVERHILL: What do you mean?

MRS. HAVERHILL: "The victory of Cedar Creek would have been impossible without the sacrifice of this young officer."

HAVERHILL: My own words, yes – but –

EDITH: "His name must take its place forever, in the roll of names which his countrymen honor."

HAVERHILL: Lieutenant Bedloe!

MRS. HAVERHILL: Haverhill! You did not know?

HAVERHILL: My – son.

EDITH: You did not receive mother's letter? – after his death?

HAVERHILL: My son! [*Sinking upon a chair*] I left him alone in his grave, unknown; but my tears fell for him then, as they do now. He died before I reached him.

EDITH: Father! [*Laying her hand gently on his shoulder*] You shall see Frank's face again. His little son is lying asleep upstairs; and when he wakes up, Frank's own eyes will look into yours. I have just received his last message. I will read it to you. [*She opens the note-book and reads*] "Tell our little son how his father died, not how he lived. And tell her who filled my own mother's place so lovingly." [*She looks at Mrs. Haverhill, moves to her and hides her face in her bosom*] My mother!

MRS. HAVERHILL: Edith – my child! Frank loved us both.

EDITH: [*Reading*] "Father's portrait of her, which she gave to me in Charleston –

[*Haverhill starts*] – helped me to be a better man."

HAVERHILL: [*Rising to his feet*] Constance!

EDITH: [*Reading*] "It was taken from me in Richmond, and it is in the possession of Captain Edward Thornton."

HAVERHILL: One moment! Stop! Let me think! [*Edith looks at him*] Thornton was a prisoner – and to Kerchival West. A dispatch had been found upon him – he was searched! [*He moves to her and takes both her hands in his own, bowing his head over them*] My head is bowed in shame.

MRS. HAVERHILL: Speak to me, John, as you used to speak! Tell me you still love me!

HAVERHILL: The – the words will come – but they are – choking me – now. [*He presses her hand to his lips*]

MRS. HAVERHILL: We will think no more of the past, except of what was bright in it. Frank's memory, and our own love, will be with us always.

Enter. Buckthorn, followed by Heartsease

BUCKTHORN: Haverhill! You are back from the war, too. It begins to look like peace in earnest.

HAVERHILL: Yes. Peace and home.

Shaking hands with him. Mrs. Haverhill joins Edith

Enter Barket

BARKET: Gineral! [*Buckthorn moves to him. Haverhill joins Mrs. Haverhill and Edith. Barket speaks apart, twisting one side of his face*] I kissed her!

BUCKTHORN: Have you sent for a surgeon?

BARKET: I felt as if the inimy had surprised us agin, and Sheridan was sixty miles away.

HAVERHILL: This is old Sergeant Barket. [*Barket salutes*] You were the last man of us all that saw Colonel West.

BARKET: Just afther the battle of Sayder Creek began – whin Colonel Wist rode to the front to mate his retrayting rigiment – the byes formed in line, at sight of him, to raysist the victorious inimy. It was just at the brow of a hill – about there, sur – [*Pointing with his cane*] and – here! [*He takes the tray from the table and sets it on the carpet, then lays the slices of bread in a row*] That be the rigiment. [*All are interested. Madeline and Ellingham enter, and look on. Barket arranges the two cups and saucers in a row*] That be the inimy's batthery, sur.

Enter Margery. She goes to the table, then looks around, sharply at Barket

OLD MARGERY: Ye ould Hibernian dhrone! What are yez doin' wid the china on the floor? You'll break it all!

BUCKTHORN: Ah – Margery! Barket is telling us where he last saw Colonel Kerchival West.

OLD MARGERY: The young Colonel! The taycups and saucers be's the inimy's batthery? Yez may smash 'em, if ye loike!

BUCKTHORN: Go on, Barket.

Jenny and Heartsease have entered, as Barket proceeds, the whole party lean forward, intensely interested. Gertrude enters in the hall, looks in, beckons as if to some one without, and Kerchival follows. They move to the center of the stage, back of the rest and listen unseen

BARKET: Just as the rigiment was rayformed in line, and Colonel Wist was out in front –

widout any coat or hat, and wid only a shtick in his hand – we heard cheers in the rear. Giniral Sheridan was coming! One word to the men – and we swept over the batthery like a whirlwind! [*Slashing his cane through the cups and saucers*]

OLD MARGERY: Hoo-roo!

BARKET: The attack on the lift flank was checked. But when we shtopped to take breath, Colonel Wist wasn't wid us. [*Gertrude turns lovingly to Kerchival. He places his arm about her*] Heaven knows where he is now. Afther the battle was over, poor Miss Gertrude wint off by hersilf into the wilderness to find **him.**

KERCHIVAL: My wife! You saved my life, at last. [*Embracing her*]

BARKET: They'll niver come together in this world. I saw Miss Gertrude, myself, ride away into the woods and disappear behind a school-house on the battle-field over there.

GERTRUDE: No, Barket – [*All start and look*] – it was the little church; we were married there this morning!

A LETTER OF INTRODUCTION

WILLIAM DEAN HOWELLS

AFTER seeing a London production of Howells's *The Garroters* (called *A Dangerous Ruffian* in England), G. B. Shaw wrote in his *Dramatic Opinions and Essays* (1906):

> The little piece showed, as might have been expected, that with three weeks' practice the American novelist could write the heads off the poor bunglers to whom our managers generally appeal when they want a small bit of work to amuse the people who come at eight.

Like so many of the other literary masters of the late nineteenth century (Mark Twain, Bret Harte, and Henry James, for example), Howells was fascinated by the theatre. On June 2, 1878, he wrote to Twain, "I try not even to think of a play, though to tell you the truth I would ten times rather write plays than anything else." None of these major fiction writers quite hit the mark with a stage success, whether wanting the "three weeks' practice" or restrained by an inability or unwillingness to sacrifice literary qualities to the demands of the theatre. Even though Howells was relatively unsuccessful in all his major theatrical enterprises, his "parlor farces" had a wide circulation among amateurs. For an evening's home entertainment in the parlor, the brilliant dialogue of a Howells small farce was eminently appropriate. These domestic theatres were remarkably more intimate than the currently popular "theatres in the round" or "arena stages," and though none of them offered a full season, they were particularly active during the Christmas holidays. Howells knew their habits and regularly obliged them with a playscript in the December issue of *Harper's*. Booth Tarkington recalled that "a college boy of the late eighties and 'golden nineties' came home at Christmas to be either in the audience at a Howells farce or in the cast that gave it. Few things were surer." In a letter to Henry Arthur Jones on December 30, 1906, Howells wrote, "Of course they [the plays] have been done everywhere in private theatricals and they have sold pleasingly enough." The promise of a regular Christmas farce seems to have been a major bargaining point for Howells in negotiating his new contract with *Harper's* in 1889.

William Dean Howells was born in Martin's Ferry, Ohio, on March 1, 1837. He served an intensive newspaper apprenticeship: compositor, reporter, and editor on his father's newspaper in Hamilton, Ohio; compositor and later editorial writer on the *Ohio State Journal* in Columbus. During the presidential campaign of 1860 he wrote a campaign biography of Lincoln, and as compensation the President awarded him a consular post in Venice. While on foreign duty, he married Elinor G. Mead, of Brattleboro, Vermont. In 1865 he relinquished his governmental post to join the editorial staff of the New York *Nation;* in January, 1866, he shifted to the *Atlantic Monthly*, an assistant to James T. Fields; and in 1872, he became editor-in-chief of that magazine, a post he held until 1881. Then, at the age of forty-four, he retired from his editorial enterprises to write novels, producing one a year for the rest of his life. He traveled extensively, conducted the "Editor's Study" in *Harper's*, received a doctorate of literature from Oxford in 1904, and was for many years president of the American Academy of Arts and Letters. At a seventy-fifth-birthday party in 1912, President William Howard Taft called him "the greatest living American writer and novelist." Howells died in New York City on May 11, 1920.

Howells made his first acquaintance with the theatre in Dayton, Ohio. The local theatrical company had their printing done in his father's shop, and Howells recalled the circumstances in later life:

I believe they never paid for it, or at least never wholly, but they lavished free passes upon us, and as nearly as I can make out, at this distance of time [1895], I profited by their generosity every night. They gave two or three plays at every performance to houses ungratefully small, but of a lively spirit and impatient temper that would not brook delay in the representation; and they changed the bill each day. . . . I have a notion that there were some clever people in one of these companies, and that the lighter pieces at least were well played.

Apparently he was inspired by this early experience to try his hand at dramatic composition. According to his brother Joseph, he had written five short plays by the time he was thirteen. Throughout his life, Howells maintained a lively interest in public spectacles and a friendly attitude toward actors, and regularly proposed a program for a municipal theatre to be supported by tax funds. His novel *Story of a Play* (1898) provided precise and detailed documentation on the inner workings of the theatre of the time.

Howells's adventures in playwriting began with *The Parlor Car* in 1876 and ended with *Parting Friends* in 1911. Twelve of the twenty-seven short plays described the farcical escapades of Mr. and Mrs. Willis Campbell and Mr. and Mrs. Edward Roberts. This fashionable and refined foursome cavorted through innumerable intriguing misunderstandings. Although the major share of Howells's dramatic works were of this "parlor-farce" variety, with such titles as *The Unexpected Guests, The Albany Depot, The Smoking Car, Five O'clock Tea*, and *The Mouse Trap*, he made several excursions into regular full-length drama.

His first effort was a rather literal translation from the Italian of D'Aste's *Sansone*. *Samson* was undertaken at the suggestion of the actor Charles Pope, who toured in it throughout the country during the season of 1874–75. Although it focused little attention on Howells as a dramatist, it was performed intermittently as late as 1895. *Out of the Question*, his first original full-length drama, was completed in 1877. Many thought that its satirical treatment of Boston's snobbish society should more properly be labeled a debate. The next two plays were his only successes, or near-successes, and, as Howells admitted, their popularity depended on the performances of Lawrence Barrett. *A Counterfeit Presentment*, a psychological comedy of contemporary American society, had some thirty performances around the country during the season of 1877–78. When Howells saw it in Boston on April 1, 1878, he reported his exhilaration: "I never had my popularity at arm's length before, and it was very pleasant. . . . There is no delight like seeing one's play acted." *Yorick's Love*, a translation of Manuel Tamayo y Baus's *Un Drama Nuevo*, was tailored to Barrett's demands, and even after its initial performance in Cleveland on October 25, 1878, it was continually being revised during its first season. Barrett retained the play in his repertoire until his death in 1891. The stage histories of the other long plays were relatively insignificant. *Priscilla*, a dramatization of Longfellow's *The Courtship of Miles Standish*, was written sometime between 1879 and 1882. Although it was styled for Barrett, it was never acted. *A Sea Change, or Love's Stowaway* (1884), a comic operetta in the manner of Gilbert and Sullivan, with music by George Henschel, had one special showing for friends at the Boston Museum on January 27, 1885. *A Foregone Conclusion* (1884–85) was a reworking of an earlier dramatization by William Poel. A. M. Palmer gave it an author's matinee on November 18, 1886. *The Rise of Silas Lapham* (1898) was apparently dramatized at the suggestion of Howells's cousin Paul Kester. Kester put together the initial drafts and Howells made the revisions. The play was never produced, though there were extended efforts first to interest the actor W. H. Crane and later to adjust the play for a James A. Herne production. For more than twenty years Howells tried to find a place for his full-length plays in the professional theatre, but with little success.

Much of his effort to grasp at the financial rewards the theatre offered was supported by Mark Twain. As early as 1875, Twain had suggested that Howells attempt a dramatization of *Tom Sawyer*. Twain had great respect for Howells. He once wrote, "Other men, including myself, *sometimes* found the right word, but Howells *always* found it." Four years later Twain proposed that they collaborate on a play about his brother, Orin Clemens. He was sure that this eccentric reformer and inventor would make a fascinating stage figure. He could "lose a limb by an explosion at the end of each of the four acts." *Colonel Sellers as a Scientist* (1883), derived from the dreamer in Twain's *The Gilded Age*, was their only collaborative effort that reached fruition. However, Twain's prediction that it would "enrich us both beyond the dreams of avarice" was not realized. After much wrangling with various actors and managers, it had a single trial matinee at the Lyceum Theatre on September 23, 1887, under the title *The American Claimant, or Mulberry Sellers Ten Years Later*. Three other projected collaborations never developed: a tragedy to be based on an incident in Carlyle's life of Cromwell, a "Sandwich Island play," and another Colonel Sellers play to be tailored to James A. Herne's talents.

Howells's reputation as a dramatist rests principally on his genteel farces designed for the amateur's theatrical evenings at home. He would have welcomed more interest from the theatre managers, but he clearly recognized that his market was with the amateurs. He wrote to Mark Twain on June 8, 1876:

[Thank you for] your kind offer to go down to New York with me to see my small play [*The Parlor Car*]. It has not yet been given and I have not heard from Daly. . . . I have heard from others, however, that he promises rashly; and I dare say it's quite likely that on second thought he doesn't find the play desirable . . . in any case I shall quietly pass it down to posterity in the September *Atlantic*.

His skepticism was well founded; the play was never performed in New York.

Howells had a serious interest in the drama as a reflector of American life and deplored the lack of representations of middle-class society on the American stage. He wrote to this point on several occasions. In the June, 1890, issue of *Harper's*, he said:

They [American playwrights] have had a fear that there was something low and vulgar in their wish to see American life in the theatre as they have seen it in the street, and the counting-house, and the drawing-room, as they have even seen it in the novel. They have been so much unnerved by this misgiving that they have not yet ventured to be quite true to life, but have only ventured, so far, to offer us a compromise with unreality, which we can praise at most for the truth which could not well be kept out of it

And five years later, in *Harper's Weekly* of March 30, 1895, after reviewing Shaw's *Arms and the Man*, H. A. Jones's *The Case of Rebellious Susan*, and Wilde's *An Ideal Husband*, he concluded:

When I compare them with some beginnings of our own in the drama, I am by no means ashamed of ours. I am going to prove myself of a very common, or at least very simple taste to people who love titles and gowns, by saying that I think *The Old Homestead* and *Shore Acres*, with all their defects, are built upon broader and sounder lines, and that Mr. Harrigan's Mulligan series of comic sketches is the effect of a more genuine dramatic and artistic instinct. It remains for some American to imagine an honest treatment of our average middle class life, with the rich variety of possibilities in motive and incident native to our society, and the same success will be his, as the authors of those plays of our rustic life and low life have enjoyed. But till this dramatist arrives we must draw our society plays from England, where they are making them indeed too much of one pattern, but where they are making them very well.

If Howells's plays did not supply this deficiency, he might at least indicate this pitiful absence of realistic social comedy in American drama. He wished to see "the great tendency toward the faithful representation of life which is now animating fiction" carried over into the drama. He found "our one original contribution and addition to histrionic art [in] negro minstrelsy, which, primitive, simple, elemental, was out of our own soil." Why could we not have a native drama of comparable theatrical originality? Why could not America produce a "diligent student of human nature" like Carlo Goldoni? Part of the fault he attributed to the managers and the theatre audiences: ". . . in spite of theatres lavishly complete in staging, and with all the sanitary arrangements exemplary – the air changes every fifteen minutes and artificially refrigerated in the summer – we have still no drama." Or, as he explained on another occasion: "Playwright fears the manager, the manager fears the public, and the public fears itself."

Howells frequently returned to this preoccupation with the managers and the public. He did not blame the managers for wishing to make money, but he insisted that the theatre should be supported like the churches, universities, and public schools. Too many middle-class, wage-earning citizens were being kept from the theatre by the exorbitant prices. If we could have a public theatre, perhaps under the control of a board of education, with free monthly performances of good plays, "the old bondage of the stage to what is worst in human nature would end, and we should have a free theatre speaking to the hearts and minds of a free people."

Although Howells was not totally ignorant of the technical matters of stage presentation, his connections with and observations on actual production were relatively inconsequential. He was encouraged by what he regarded as an advance toward realism in casting: "In a modern play," he wrote in 1904, "where a fat man is required the manager no longer takes a lean actor and builds him up into a fat man; he takes a fat actor and lets him live the part physically as well as psychically on the scene." Stage conventions that broke the sense of realism distressed him: "It ought to be within the scope of science so to perfect the theatre that everything on the stage could be as distinctly heard as seen, and that the lightest whisper need not be hoarsely shouted from it in order to reach the audience." (Would he have approved of the present-day electronic amplifications?) Many of his observations demonstrated an extreme naïveté in regard to theatre practice. On March 31, 1878, he wrote to his father about the production of *A Counterfeit Presentment* at the Boston Museum:

What struck me most in regard to my own share in the business was the immovable fashion in which what I had so lightly and vaguely described had to be *realized* on the stage. A hat – just what kind of hat? A chair – precisely what sort of chair?

Certainly he never became sufficiently aware of the inner workings of professional stage productions to guide them to his own advantage. On July 31, 1898, he wrote to Henry James:

. . . good of you to speak those friendly words about my *Story of a Play*. You know my experience of the theatre was comic rather than tragical, and I treated of it lightly because it was light. . . . It is strange how the stage can keep on fooling us; what the burnt child does *not* dread is the fire, or at least the blue fire of the theatre. I have lately been fool enough to dramatize *Silas Lapham* for an actor who wanted it, and now does *not* want it. What a race! Their obligations are chains of flowers.

If we can take the character of Maxwell in *Story of a Play* as a projection of Howells, it would seem that the novelist never was convinced that the theatre had anything to teach him. According to Maxwell, the actors and managers "talk about knowledge of the stage as if the stage were a difficult science, instead of a very simple piece of mechanism whose limitations and possibilities anyone can seize at a glance. All their knowledge of it comes to is claptrap, pure and simple."

Perhaps if Howells, like Bronson Howard, had been drawn into an intimate acquaintance with the stage art, his well-intentioned observations and his somewhat left-handed ventures into dramatic writing would have more markedly affected the course of American drama and theatre. Certainly he appraised the path of the American drama more clearly than most of his contemporaries. In the *Atlantic Monthly* for May, 1869, he wrote:

It is undeniable that, while the theatre has been growing more artistic and popular among us, it has been growing less and less American. It was not in nature that the old Yankee farce should keep the stage; still less that some pre-historic American like Metamora should continue to interest forever; even the noble art of negro minstrelsy is expiring among us, and we have nothing to offer in competition with the English plays.

Although Howells's parlor farces appear as a minor chapter in our theatre history, neither they nor Howells deserve to be neglected as they have been. Amateur home theatricals constituted a widespread middle-class family amusement through the last twenty-five years of the past century, and the little plays of Howells were cerainly the best of the type designed for this purpose. If his fashionable, high-bred, and genuinely human excursions into the middle-class drawing rooms of the time did not reach the regular stage, they had their gay nights in the parlors of many American homes. And although his principal object in the short plays was to entertain, he frequently explored serious questions of truth and morality, and many readers have found that the farces provide helpful keys in opening up the major novels.

First printed in *Harper's* in January, 1892, *A Letter of Introduction* not only acquaints us with Howells and his favorite foursome, the Campbells and the Robertses, but also provides an amusing picture of the slow-witted Englishman, a popular stage type in many later American plays.

A LETTER OF INTRODUCTION

WILLIAM DEAN HOWELLS

CHARACTERS

EDWARD ROBERTS	AMY CAMPBELL
AGNES ROBERTS	MR. WESTGATE
WILLIS CAMPBELL	BELLA, *the maid*

ACT I. Scene 1

Mr. and Mrs. Edward Roberts in their apartment at Hotel Beltingham.

MRS. ROBERTS: [*Looking in upon her husband from the door of the library*] Well, you've got rid of him, Edward.

ROBERTS: Yes, at last, thank Heaven! [*He continues writing at his table, without looking up, as he answers his wife*] But I thought he never would go, at one time. He isn't a bad kind of fellow, for an Englishman, and if I hadn't been so busy with this paper, I shouldn't have minded his staying. Of course he was nationally English, but personally he was rather nice. Still it was a terrible interruption, just at this moment.

MRS. ROBERTS: Why didn't you hint to him, somehow, to go away?

ROBERTS: Well, I couldn't do that, you know. I really liked him. He was so very amiable.

MRS. ROBERTS: Oh, his being amiable is no excuse. You're amiable yourself, Edward – *too* amiable, if anything. I don't call it amiable to take up almost a full hour of your precious time. I should think any one who came in and saw how busy you were, now, would go away if he had a heart of *stone*. No, I can't believe he was truly amiable; and I must really do something to protect you from these constant interruptions. How do you think I'd better do it?

ROBERTS: [*Writing*] Do what?

MRS. ROBERTS: [*Sinking into a chair, and folding her hands in her lap*] Protect you from these interruptions.

ROBERTS: [*Writing*] Protect *who*?

MRS. ROBERTS: You, Edward. My heart bleeds for you, to see you so driven with your work, and then people coming in and sitting down, and talking to you. I must *stop* it.

ROBERTS: [*Writing*] Oh yes. Stop what?

MRS. ROBERTS: These perfectly killing interruptions. I should think you would go crazy.

ROBERTS: [*Writing*] Who?

MRS. ROBERTS: Why, you, you poor thing. I think it's worse than cruelty to animals.

ROBERTS: [*Writing*] Worse than cruelty to animals. Worse – Why, what nonsense is this you've made me write, Agnes? [*He looks up at her in a daze*] What *do* you want, Agnes? And *do* state it succinctly, my dear!

MRS. ROBERTS: Why, I didn't know but you'd asked him to stay to lunch.

ROBERTS: [*Writing again*] No; I didn't really feel that I could give the time. I should have liked to do so, and I suppose it was rather shabby not to. It was the least he could have expected. [*He continues writing*] But I've done the next best thing. I've given him a letter of introduction to Uncle Phillip, and he will glut him with all kinds of hospitality when he gets to New York.

MRS. ROBERTS: Yes. [*After a moment*] Do you think it was quite right, Edward?

ROBERTS: [*Looking up*] Right? What right?

MRS. ROBERTS: To put him off on your uncle, if you didn't like him yourself?

ROBERTS: But I *did* like him. I liked him as well as it's possible to like any Englishman on short notice. You have to know an Englishman several days before you're sure you like him; but

618

this one was really very pleasant, and I told Uncle Phillip he would probably find him so, unless I was greatly deceived. But now, Agnes, you must really let me go on –

MRS. ROBERTS: Surely, Edward, you didn't put that into a letter of introduction?

ROBERTS: [*Laughing*] That I would have to leave open for him to read? Well, I'm not quite so bad as *that*, Agnes. I wrote a letter to Uncle Phillip, to go through the post, and I told him that as soon as he got through the crust of a rather insular manner, and a most unaccountable enthusiasm for Americans, I'd no doubt he'd find my Englishman charming. You couldn't suppose I'd put all that in a letter of introduction?

MRS. ROBERTS: Of course not. But you know you *are* so absent-minded, my dear, and I couldn't help being a little afraid –

ROBERTS: Your fears come too late, my dear. The Englishman is gone, and both the letters with him. Now you *must* let me finish this –

MRS. ROBERTS: [*Rising to her feet in amazement*] Both the letters with him?

ROBERTS: Yes; I knew he would pass the letter-box on the corner, and I asked him to drop Uncle Phillip's letter in it.

MRS. ROBERTS: Wasn't that rather peculiar, Edward?

ROBERTS: [*With vexation*] Peculiar? No! What was peculiar about it?

The Voices, in the anteroom, without, of Mr. and Mrs. Willis Campbell

CAMPBELL: In the library? Well, we'll just push right in on them.

MRS. CAMPBELL: And Mrs. Roberts is there too?

ROBERTS: Oh, good heavens! Go out, Agnes, and stop them! Take them into the parlor a moment, do till I get this –

MRS. ROBERTS: You *know* I can't do that, Edward! [*To Mrs. Campbell, at the door*] Ah! Come in, Amy! I'm *so* glad to see you.

The Ladies kiss, and Campbell follows his wife in

Scene 2

Mr. and Mrs. Campbell; the Robertses.

CAMPBELL: And so is Roberts; but he doesn't look it. Hope I don't interrupt you, Roberts, as people say when they know they do.

ROBERTS: [*Who has pushed away his writing, and risen to greet the intruders with forced gayety*] How do you do, Amy? No; I was just getting to the end of my morning's work, Willis.

CAMPBELL: Well, it'll do you good to break off before you reach the very tip, then. Keep you from having that tired feeling, you know. What you need is a little dynamite to blast you out of your chair, here, every morning at half past twelve. If you keep on writing close up to lunch, you'll spoil your digestion.

ROBERTS: Well, I sha'n't this morning. I've had an Englishman here for the last hour, and I feel as if I could digest almost anything.

MRS. CAMPBELL: Why, it must have been *your* Englishman, then, whom we met at the corner, as we came here! There, Willis! I told you it was an Englishman!

CAMPBELL: I couldn't believe it: he was so confoundedly agreeable, and he had so much of that English brogue, when he spoke, that I thought he must be a New Yorker.

MRS. ROBERTS: Why, how came he to talk with you?

CAMPBELL: Well, he was hanging round a telegraph pole, trying to post a letter in the fire-alarm box. He said he'd been asked to post it by a gentleman who had told him there was a letter-box at the first corner, and the fire-alarm looked like it. I had to take him by the elbow, and steer him across the street to the green box on the lamp post. He didn't seem to like the way it opened its mouth at the top like a dying frog, but he risked his letter in it, anyway.

MRS. ROBERTS: There, Edward!

CAMPBELL: Hello! Where does Roberts come in? [*Mrs. Roberts maintains a reproachful silence, and Campbell turns to Roberts*] Look here, Roberts, what have you been doing? It wasn't *you* who gave that poor young Englishman that letter to post?

ROBERTS: [*Trying to put a bold face upon it*] Nonsense! Certainly I did. I had given him a letter of introduction to Uncle Phillip – he thinks he may go on to New York tonight, by the boat – and I asked him to post the letter I wrote to advise Uncle Phillip of his coming. That's all.

MRS. ROBERTS: Of course it was all right. But it seemed a little odd when Edward first told me.

CAMPBELL: Did you make your uncle the usual

little confidences about the introducee, in your letter of advice?

ROBERTS: I told him I knew he would like him after he had got through his insular manner.

CAMPBELL: And then you got him to post the letter! Well, it *was* something like seething the kid in its mother's milk, Agnes.

MRS. CAMPBELL: What a disgusting idea! Mr. Roberts, don't mind him! He isn't *worth* it. His one idea is to tease.

ROBERTS: I see what you mean, Campbell. But of course he couldn't know what was in it, and it seemed very simple and natural to get him to drop it in the box.

CAMPBELL: It *was* simple, and it was *very* natural. A less absent-minded man's wife might have told him it wasn't exactly delicate, even if the fellow couldn't have known what was in it.

MRS. CAMPBELL: And in *you* it *would* have been indelicate; but with Mr. Roberts it's a very different thing.

CAMPBELL: Oh yes; I know! Absent-mindedness. Well, Roberts, you'll get yourself into an awful mess with your absent-mindedness some day. How do you know he didn't know what was in the letter to your uncle?

ROBERTS: [*With some scorn*] Why, simply because I sealed it before I gave it to him.

CAMPBELL: And did you seal the letter of introduction?

ROBERTS: Of course not!

CAMPBELL: Oh, you didn't! Then how do you know that you didn't seal up the letter of introduction, and give him the letter of advice to carry with him?

ROBERTS: Because I *know* I didn't.

CAMPBELL: Oh, *that's* no reason! Now be careful. Would you swear you didn't? Suppose you were on the witness stand!

MRS. CAMPBELL: No, don't suppose it, Mr. Roberts. Don't suppose anything of the kind.

CAMPBELL: [*Without regarding her*] This sort of thing is done every day. People are always getting letters mixed, and shuffling them into the wrong envelopes. Amy did something of the kind herself down at the Shore, last summer and nearly broke off the engagement between young Welling and Miss Greenway. And if she hadn't been the most sensible kind of a girl, Amy *would* have done it, too. And as it was, I had to do some of the tallest lying this side of the Pacific slope. Perfect *sequoias* – made our

place, down there, look like the Yosemite Park, when those fables began to tower up.

MRS. CAMPBELL: [*Faltering*] It's true, Agnes. I told you about it, you remember.

MRS. ROBERTS: Yes, I know. But that doesn't prove that Edward –

CAMPBELL: Oh, doesn't it! If Amy, who has her few wits always about her, could do such a thing, it stands to reason that Roberts, whose multitudinous mind is always off somewhere else when it's wanted, would do it nine times out of ten. Think how absent-minded he is! Remember how he got aboard the sleeping-car that night, and went prying round in all the berths to find you?

MRS. CAMPBELL: Don't be offensive, Willis!

CAMPBELL: I'm simply veracious! And then think how he left his watch in his room, and thought poor old Bemis was a garroter that had taken it from him, and ran after him on the Common, and grabbed Bemis's watch from him, and nearly killed him. And then his going to meet a cook that he'd never seen at the Albany depot, and getting into that scrape with Mrs. McIlheny.

MRS. ROBERTS: That was *my* fault, Willis. I sent him; and I ought to have remembered that he'd never seen the cook.

CAMPBELL: Oh! And what ought Roberts to have remembered? I tell you, he's put that Englishman's letter of introduction into the sealed envelope, and the letter of advice into the open one, beyond the shadow of a doubt.

ROBERTS: [*With rising alarm*] Oh, pshaw! You know you don't think so, Willis.

CAMPBELL: Think so? I know it! Where was he sitting?

ROBERTS: Where you are now.

CAMPBELL: In this chair? When you wrote the letters, which did you finish first?

ROBERTS: The letter of introduction, I think.

CAMPBELL: You think! He can't even remember *that!* Well, can you remember which you *gave* him first?

ROBERTS: No, I can't; but it must have been the letter of introduc——

CAMPBELL: Did you put both letters in their envelopes before you gave them to him, or did you hand him first one and then the other?

ROBERTS: I'm sure I can't say! But my impression is –

CAMPBELL: [*Waving his conjecture scornfully*

aside] Agnes, you see how thoroughly mixed up he is.

MRS. CAMPBELL: Yes, and you've *mixed* him up. I declare –

MRS. ROBERTS: Yes, Willis.

CAMPBELL: Oh, very well, then! If I've mixed him up, I'll let him unmix himself. Then he can't complain. If he didn't blunder with the letters, I suppose my merely *asking* him won't create the fact. I didn't make him do it.

MRS. CAMPBELL: And he didn't do it.

CAMPBELL: He ought to know.

MRS. ROBERTS: And you *do* know, don't you, Edward?

ROBERTS: Why, of course. But anything's possible. And now that Willis has suggested it, why, I can't take my oath –

CAMPBELL: [*To the ladies*] You see!

ROBERTS: What – what can I do, Willis? The mere supposition of such a thing –

CAMPBELL: Oh, *I* don't know. Go after the Englishman, I suppose, and try to run him down before he reads your letter of advice. [*He bursts into a loud, unfeeling laugh, while Roberts begins to walk the floor in agitation*] Can you recall any of the expressions you used? Perhaps they weren't so bad.

ROBERTS: [*Pausing and rubbing his forehead*] I think I can. I told Uncle Phil not to mind his insular manner; that he was necessarily offensive as an Englishman; but that he seemed to have a great many good qualities, and was quite American in some of his feelings and ideas, and had an enthusiasm for us worthy of a better cause. I said I had only met him once, but I had no doubt he would prove worthy of any kindness that was shown him.

CAMPBELL: Patronizing and insulting to the last degree! Well, you've done it, Roberts!

ROBERTS: I know – I see! But I didn't mean to be offensive. The fact is, I wrote very hastily; I wanted to get rid of him; my mind was half on my article, here –

CAMPBELL: And it was in the same divided condition when you put the letters into their envelopes! What could you expect?

ROBERTS: Look here, Willis! Couldn't *you* –

CAMPBELL: Oh, no! This isn't a thing that *I* can interfere in. If it were a case for ground-and-lofty lying, you might call me in; but where it's principally *tact* that's needed, I'd better leave it to you, my dear fellow. [*He claps

Roberts on the shoulder, and breaks down in another laugh*]

MRS. CAMPBELL: Now look here, Willis! This is perfectly outrageous. You haven't the slightest proof in the world that Mr. Roberts has mixed the letters, and it's just your wicked teasing that makes you say he has. If you have any feeling at all, you will stop. *I* think it's gone beyond a joke.

MRS. ROBERTS: And I do, too, Amy. Of course I think Edward was wrong to send the man to his uncle just to get rid of him; but that's no reason Willis should torment him so.

ROBERTS: No, no! There's only too great reason to suppose he's right. Good heavens! What shall I do about it?

CAMPBELL: Well, if I might venture a little suggestion without being denounced as a heartless reprobate –

ROBERTS: I haven't denounced you, Willis!

CAMPBELL: My wife and sister have in your interest, and just when I had thought how to help you out.

MRS. ROBERTS: Oh, how, Willis?

MRS. CAMPBELL: Tell it, instantly, Willis!

CAMPBELL: You'd better look him up at his hotel, and pretend you thought you gave the wrong address on the letter to your uncle.

ROBERTS: That's all very well, but I don't know where he's stopping.

CAMPBELL: Well, that does rather cut the ground from under us. [*A ring at the door is heard*] Ah, there he is now, coming back to have it out with Roberts. He's read that letter of advice, and he wants to know what it means. We must go, Roberts. I'm sorry to leave you in this fix, but –

Scene 3

Bella; the Campbells; the Robertses.

BELLA: [*The maid, coming in with a card for Roberts*] The elevator boy brought it up. The gentleman is waiting below, sir.

ROBERTS: [*Glancing at the card*] Merciful powers! Willis is right! It is the man himself!

MRS. ROBERTS: Oh, Edward, what do you suppose he wants? But don't be alarmed, dearest! *I* don't agree with Willis in his pessimistic views. I know you can easily explain it.

CAMPBELL: Oh, *can* he? Well, I think I'll just wait, then, and hear his explanation.

MRS. CAMPBELL: Willis! You must advise him what to do. You must invent some plan.

CAMPBELL: *Thank* you! I don't deny that I'm pretty ingenious, and all that; but what you want here is the invention of a Thomas A. Edison. Nothing short of it will ever get Roberts out of *this* scrape.

ROBERTS: [*Trying to pluck up courage*] But I deny that there *is* any scrape. The whole affair is purely hypothetical. There's nothing in the world to prove that I've mixed up the letters, and I deny that I did. The man has simply come back because he's forgotten something, or wishes to make some little inquiry, or –

CAMPBELL: Then why don't you have him up at once, instead of letting him cool his heels down there in your front hall? Have him up! It's uncivil to keep him waiting.

MRS. ROBERTS: No, no. [*To the maid*] Stop, Bella! No, Willis; we must provide for contingencies. I think Edward is perfectly right, and I know he didn't mix the letters up; but oughtn't we to guard against any chances, Willis?

CAMPBELL: I should say you ought. And you'd better ring for a policeman to do it. He's an awfully athletic-looking fellow. Those Englishmen often are.

MRS. ROBERTS: Then, Bella, you must tell the boy to say that Mr. Roberts has just gone out; and that Mrs. Roberts is very sorry –

ROBERTS: No, Agnes, that won't do, my dear. I can't allow that. If I've done this thing, I must face the consequences.

MRS. ROBERTS: Yes, that's what I say. We must provide for contingencies.

CAMPBELL: He may want to fight you, Roberts, like McIlheny, you know, when you asked his wife whether she was a cook.

MRS. CAMPBELL: Everything depends upon what kind of humor he's in, of course.

MRS. ROBERTS: Of course. If he's very – boisterous, you mustn't have anything to say to him; but if he's pleasant, or if he's merely cold, or hurt, in his manner, why, I suppose you must ask him to lunch. And Willis and Amy can stay, and help make it go off.

CAMPBELL: Oh, thank you, Agnes! The Roberts family seems to have a gift for patronizing offensiveness; I don't mind it myself, but if I was an Englishman that Roberts had told to his face that he was nationally detestable –

ROBERTS: Told to his face?

CAMPBELL: It's the same thing – it would take a good deal more than lunch to pacify *me*. I should want *dinner*, and not merely a *family* dinner, a snap-shot, accidental thing, but a regular formal affair, with the best people asked, and the chance of other invitations. The least *you* can do, Roberts, is to send for this Englishman's baggage, and make him stay a fortnight with you.

MRS. ROBERTS: I *had* thought of that, Willis.

CAMPBELL: You *said – lunch.*

MRS. ROBERTS: But our flat is so small, and the children are in the guest-chamber –

CAMPBELL: And in the meantime, the Englishman is waiting below in the select society of the janitor.

MRS. ROBERTS: Oh, my goodness, I forgot all about him!

ROBERTS: Yes. We *must* have him up at once, and then act accordingly.

CAMPBELL: Oh yes; you mustn't give yourself away. If you don't *happen* to have mixed the letters up, you don't want to begin apologizing. You will have to judge from his manner.

ROBERTS: But he was so extremely flattering, so very enthusiastic about us, I'm afraid we can't tell from his manner.

CAMPBELL: You must draw him out, specifically. Did you ask him how he liked America?

ROBERTS: No; I was ashamed to ask him when he told me he had just arrived this morning.

CAMPBELL: Well, then, Amy can ask him. She isn't ashamed to ask anything. And if he begins to abuse us, up hill and down dale –

MRS. CAMPBELL: He had better *not* abuse us! I shouldn't allow it.

MRS. ROBERTS: Oh yes, Amy; bear anything! We *must* try to pacify him somehow.

CAMPBELL: And Roberts had better go out, and meet him in that anteroom of yours – it's as *dark* as a pocket – and make him take off his overcoat – he mustn't allow any refusal – and then kind of linger behind him a moment after you've received him at the door here, and search his overcoat pockets. Very probably he's put the letter into one of them.

MRS. ROBERTS: Do you think that would be very nice, Willis?

CAMPBELL: Well, I don't know: about as nice as having Amy truckle to his abuse of the country.

MRS. CAMPBELL: It isn't at all the same thing.

CAMPBELL: It's exactly the same thing. [*A ring*

at the door summons Bella away] He's getting impatient. Well, I shouldn't like to be kept waiting so long myself.

BELLA: [*Returning*] It's the gentleman below, ma'am. The boy says he'd like to know if you got his card.

CAMPBELL: I thought so. You must let him come up, or you must send word that you're not at home. You can't prolong the suspense indefinitely.

MRS. CAMPBELL: No, Agnes, you can't, really!

ROBERTS: We must decide, my dear!

MRS. ROBERTS: [*Desperately*] Well, then, tell the janitor to send him up, Bella! [*As Bella goes*] And we haven't thought at all how we shall act!

CAMPBELL: Well, I know *one* thing: if Roberts lets his knees knock together, *so as to be heard*, I won't stand it. I'll leave the house. It'll be *too* disgraceful. Courage, Roberts! I wouldn't miss seeing how you'll carry this thing off for any money! I know you're a perfect moral hero on all ordinary occasions, but in a predicament like this I don't envy you. And the worst of it is, that if the fellow's a gentleman – and he looked like one, in the English way – you won't be able to judge from his acts how he feels! You'll have to grope your way in the dark, and – There he is! [*A ring is heard*] Now let's all look unconcerned, as if we were not expecting any one. Amy, you be turning over those photographic views of the White Mountains, in your pretty, careless way. Agnes, you be examining some object with the microscope. Here, Roberts, you sit down to your writing again. And I'll be tuning up the family phonograph. That'll give him an idea of a cultivated Boston family, at home with itself, and at peace with the whole *human* family. And we must all be extremely deferential and – complimentary – so's to take the bad taste of Roberts's letter out of his mouth. [*Campbell delivers these instructions in a rapid whisper. As Bella opens the door to admit the stranger to the anteroom, he continues in a loud, didactic voice*] As you very justly observed, in our present uncertainty as to whether the peculiar parallel markings of the planet Mars are marine canals, or merely magic-lantern displays of the Martians to attract the attention of the telescope man on Boston Common –

BELLA: [*Announcing the Englishman at the library door*] Mr. Westgate.

Scene 4

Mr. Westgate; the Campbells; the Robertses.

WESTGATE: [*To Roberts*] Ah, I beg your pardon! It's really very ridiculous, and I'm quite ashamed to trouble you again, Mr. Roberts. Your letter –

ROBERTS: [*Coming eagerly forward*] Oh, I'm so glad to see you again, Mr. Westgate. You're just in time for lunch; and I hope you can sit down with us. Mrs. Roberts, Mr. Westgate. My wife hadn't the pleasure of – ah –meeting you before, I think. Let me take your overcoat. You'll find it very hot in our American houses, I'm afraid.

WESTGATE: Oh, not at all! I'm sure I shall like it. I should *so* like to see one of your furnaces! But I only came back a moment to show you a little mistake – if it *is* a mistake –

MRS. ROBERTS: [*Eagerly*] I'm so sorry we've only steam heat, and can't show you a furnace; but you'll find it quite hot; and you *must* take off your coat.

WESTGATE: Why, you're very good, I'm sure. But only for a moment.

ROBERTS: Allow me!

He possesses himself of Westgate's hat and coat, and rushes out into the anteroom with them

MRS. ROBERTS: Let me introduce you to my sister, Mrs. Campbell; and my brother, Mr. Campbell, Mr. Westgate.

Westgate bows to the lady, and then shakes hands with Campbell

WESTGATE: Ah! how do you do? I'd no idea – I'm very glad to meet you, I'm sure. I don't know what I should have done with the letter Mr. Roberts intrusted to me –

CAMPBELL: Oh, that was nothing. I saw that you were on the point of doing something desperate, and I just stepped in. There's nothing I like better than saving human life; and as I've often tried to post my wife's letters in the fire-alarm box, at two o'clock in the morning, and never succeeded yet, I had a fellow-feeling for you.

WESTGATE: H'm! Yes! You see your post-boxes are so very different to ours –

MRS. CAMPBELL: Oh, your London post-boxes are simply delightful! They're just *like* posts – fat ones; and they take in whole packages. But – I hope you *like* America, Mr. Westgate!

MRS. ROBERTS: Yes, we are always so glad when your countrymen –

CAMPBELL: We aim to please.

WESTGATE: Well, I can't say I like your post-boxes exactly.

MRS. CAMPBELL: Oh, neither do we!

WESTGATE: And I'd always heard you had clear winter weather. I've never seen it more overcast at home.

MRS. ROBERTS: That is true. It's going to snow, I think. I'm afraid you won't like our snow!

CAMPBELL: Well, perhaps, we might have some with the chill off.

WESTGATE: [*Regarding him fixedly for a moment*] Ow! Ah! I see! Very good! Ah, ha, ha, ha! Ha, ha, ha! And – ha, ha, ha! Ah, ha, ha! – you meant, *coming home from the club!* I hadn't understood your American humor, at first. I fancy there's no hope of any good Samaritan to show you to the post-box at two o'clock in the morning hour! Ah, ha, ha!

MRS. ROBERTS: I've been scolding my husband for troubling you with that letter, Mr. Westgate!

WESTGATE: No, really? But I always heard the American ladies were so amiable, you know.

MRS. CAMPBELL: Oh, we *are*, Mr. Westgate! But we have to maintain discipline in the family, you know.

WESTGATE: Of course. But [*To Campbell*] what did you mean, exactly, by having snow with the chill off? Such a delightful expression.

CAMPBELL: Well, I don't know. Some sort of joke, I suppose.

WESTGATE: I was sure you did! Ah, ha, ha! Your countrymen are so delightfully humorous – so funny, you know. You know we think you're *such* fun.

CAMPBELL: Do you think so? I don't think we're half so funny as Englishmen.

MRS. CAMPBELL: We think you're *twice* as funny as we are, Mr. Westgate.

WESTGATE: Ow, but really, now!

MRS. CAMPBELL: I don't know how we should have done without your Mr. Gilbert.

WESTGATE: But isn't he rather exaggerated? I *much* prefer your Joshua Billings. And your after-dinner speakers! Mr. Depew, for instance!

MRS. ROBERTS: But the Prince of Wales, you know.

WESTGATE: Ow! Do you regard him as a humorist? He says some neat things, occasionally. But your California humor, now: we've nothing like *that*, you know!

MRS. CAMPBELL: I'm afraid you will make my husband intolerably conceited.

WESTGATE: Really? Is Mr. – ah – Campbell a Californian? How very delightful! And is that peculiar dialect used by your California writers spoken in the cities? I should so much like to hear it. I don't think we ever quite get the right accent in reading it.

CAMPBELL: You'd hear it everywhere in California. I'm a little out of practice now, myself; I speak Bostonese, at present; but I recollect very well how the ladies in San Francisco used to say, "Well, I got the dead wood onto you, that time," and "How're you makin' it, pard?" and "You bet," and "You git!" You mean that sort of thing?

WESTGATE: Exactly. How delightful! So very picturesque, you know. So imaginative!

CAMPBELL: Yes, I suppose there's more imagination to the acre in California than you'll find anywhere else in the United States.

MRS. CAMPBELL: And more modesty, Mr. Westgate; more unconscious merit.

CAMPBELL: Well, I shouldn't like to boast before a foreigner. There's Chicago. And for a real, unadulterated diffidence, a shrinking, deprecatory little misgiving as to the existence of the outside universe, I think Mr. Westgate will find that Boston takes the cake. In California people don't *know* they're modest, but in Boston they *do*. That's the difference.

MRS. ROBERTS: I hope Mr. Westgate will stay with us long enough to find out that everything you say is a wicked slander, Willis. Why must you rush off to New York at once, Mr. Westgate?

WESTGATE: You're very good, I'm sure. But I'm afraid – Ha, ha, ha! Ha, ha, ha! [*To Campbell*] That was a very amusing expression of yours! Imagination to the acre! As if it were some kind of crop! Very good! Capital! Ah, ha, ha! And would you be kind enough to explain that expression, "take the cake"?

CAMPBELL: Oh, it comes from the cake walk, you know.

WESTGATE: Ow.

CAMPBELL: Yes. Where the darkies try to see

624

Shenandoah

Shore Acres

which can put on the most style in a kind of walk-round, and there's a cake up for a prize, and the greatest swell takes it.

WESTGATE: How very amusing!

CAMPBELL: Amusing? It's more fun than a goat!

MRS. CAMPBELL: Willis!

WESTGATE: Oh, but really! *Don't* stop him! It's quite what I came to America for – those delightful expressions! I don't know why you're all so shy of using them when you come over! We get them in print, but we seldom hear them.

CAMPBELL: You should go to a ladies' lunch here! You wouldn't hear anything else.

WESTGATE: Ow! And just what is a ladies' lunch?

CAMPBELL: It's the social entertainment of the future. The race is running to girls so, in Massachusetts, that they've got to having these lunches without asking men, so as to see how it will feel when there are no men to ask. Often it's merely a hen feed, where they would like to have men if they could get them; just as a stag dinner is a good time that women would like to come to if they could. Sometimes it's a virtue, sometimes it's a necessity. But it's always a joke.

MRS. ROBERTS: You mustn't believe him, Mr. Westgate. He's never been at a ladies' lunch, and he doesn't know how charming they are.

WESTGATE: Yes, I understand gentlemen are not asked. But – ah, ha, ha! Ha, ha, ha! – that was a very droll expression of Mr. Campbell's about a goat. More – more amusing than a goat, I think it was. Will you ladies kindly tell me why a goat should be considered so very amusing? You see I'm beginning to be afraid I can't trust Mr. Campbell.

MRS. ROBERTS: I'm afraid you must, in this case. I'm sure we don't know why a goat should be more entertaining than any other animal.

WESTGATE: Ow! Then you're not *all* humorists, over here? We get that idea, you know. We think you're such *jokers*. But really, you know, I think that some people who do that kind of thing, you know, and have Americans a great deal, don't see the point of their jokes at all times; or not at *once*. Your humor is so different to ours, you know. I've often had the meaning of an American joke occur to me some time after, you know, when I've had leisure to think it out. Still, it *is* very amusing.

MRS. CAMPBELL: But *we* think the English humor so refined – so high-bred.

MRS. ROBERTS: Oh yes! Your jokes bear the stamp of such an old civilization, my husband says.

CAMPBELL: So polished with use.

WESTGATE: Ah, well! I don't know about that, you know. There may be something in it. But I'm inclined to think – Ah, ha, ha, ha! Very good! Excellent! I didn't catch your meaning at first. *Used so often!* I see! Ha, ha, ha! You ought to come over to us, Mr. Campbell. We've a great many charming Americans; but most of them are quite like ourselves.

CAMPBELL: Is it so bad as that?

WESTGATE: Yes; it's really quite vexing, you know. So very tiresome.

MRS. ROBERTS: I hope Mr. Westgate will stay with us long enough to see that we've something besides humor – in Boston, at least. You must let us send to the hotel for your trunk – boxes, I *should* say.

WESTGATE: Ow no! Ow no! I *much* prefer *trunk*.

MRS. CAMPBELL: And *we* prefer *boxes*.

WESTGATE: No, really?

MRS. ROBERTS: You must be our guest long enough at least to see something of Boston. Mr. Roberts will take you to the Art Club Exhibition.

WESTGATE: You're really very good. But I'd really no idea – I only came back a moment on account of a little mistake I think Mr. Roberts made in the let –

MRS. ROBERTS: [*Hastily*] We think Boston is quite an art centre, now. Amy, I want Mr. Westgate to see the little Monet in the p—— drawing room.

WESTGATE: Oh, *do* say parlor! I think it's so much nicer. And without the *u*, please.

MRS. CAMPBELL: I see you're determined to be pleased with everything American, Mr. Westgate, and I'm sure you'll like this Monet.

WESTGATE: But I beg your pardon! Isn't he French?

CAMPBELL: All the American pictures we buy are by Frenchmen.

MRS. CAMPBELL: But *we* much prefer English pictures, Mr. Westgate. You have so much more technique than the French, so much more *school*. I adore Tadema, myself.

WESTGATE: But – yes – ah – I think he's Dutch, though.

MRS. CAMPBELL: Well, as Mr. Campbell was saying, *our* paintings are all by Frenchmen – all that we buy. If you will come with me, Mr. Westgate –

Scene 5

Mrs. Roberts; Campbell.

MRS. ROBERTS: What in the world has happened to Edward?

CAMPBELL: He can't have been searching the man's coat-pockets all this time. Perhaps he's cut open the lining. Or he's found the wrong letter, and has gone off and hid somewhere. [*Roberts shows himself at the door*] No; there he is now. I didn't know but he'd committed suicide. Well, Roberts! Come in, old fellow! The coast is clear, for the moment! [*Roberts advances spectrally into the room*] What's the matter?

Scene 6

Roberts; Mrs. Roberts; Campbell. They all speak throughout the scene in hoarse whispers, and from time to time the voices of Mrs. Campbell and Mr. Westgate penetrate to them from the drawing-room.

ROBERTS: Is he gone?

MRS. ROBERTS: Sh! No. He's in the parlor, with Amy. She's showing him the pictures. He couldn't go without his hat and overcoat, you know.

ROBERTS: Yes. I didn't think of that.

CAMPBELL: Sh! Have you been through his clothes? Sh!

ROBERTS: No; I hadn't the courage.

CAMPBELL: Sh! Then where *have* you been? Sh!

ROBERTS: Sitting out there in the anteroom.

MRS. ROBERTS: Oh, poor Edward! Sh! Did you listen? He still seems very amiable. Sh! I don't think he's angry about anything. I don't believe you've made any serious mistake.

CAMPBELL: Unless he's – sh! – dissembling. They're awfully double-faced fellows, Englishmen are. Sh! I think he's dissembling. Sh!

MRS. ROBERTS: Sh! Nonsense, Willis! He says you made some mistake with the letter; but –

CAMPBELL: Sh! Of course you mixed them! He's

just lying low. You'd better keep out of his way, Roberts. Sh!

WESTGATE: [*Without*] Then I suppose you've quite a large school of resident artists in Boston?

MRS. CAMPBELL: [*Without*] Well, no. But we've a very large school of *non*-resident Boston artists. Our painters all have to go to New York to get a living.

WESTGATE: [*Without*] Ow! Then I suppose New York is the artistic centre of your country?

MRS. CAMPBELL: [*Without*] Not at all. We have the critics here.

WESTGATE: [*Without*] Then you consider criticism more essential than painting in an artistic centre?

CAMPBELL: Sh! He's getting sarcastic. He's tuning up for you, Roberts. He's tearing off the mask of amiability. Better get out into the anteroom again, Roberts. Agnes can say you were too sick to come to lunch, and we can carry it off somehow. Oh, but – hello! She's asked him to let her send for his boxes – such a delightful expression! – and come and stay with you. I think you'd better be suddenly called out of town. There's no other way for it!

ROBERTS: [*With a tremendous effort of moral heroism*] No; I must stay and face it out. It would be cowardly to shirk it.

MRS. ROBERTS: Oh, Edward, what courage you *do* have! But what will you say to him? Willis, *can't* you think of something for Edward to say? You know he's never good on the spur of the moment, and you *are*. Sh!

CAMPBELL: Sh! Don't say anything at all, till he opens up. But keep treating him beautifully, and then he'll see that Roberts *couldn't* have meant anything by those insulting and patronizing expressions. He'll think it's just our Yankee awkwardness and vulgarity.

MRS. ROBERTS: [*Willingly accepting the suggestion*] Yes, just our Yankee awkwardness and vulgarity. I know he'll excuse it, Edward. You mustn't be alarmed. Remember how much *real* courage you always have!

ROBERTS: I can't let him excuse it on that ground. No; I must grapple with it frankly.

CAMPBELL: All right! Only let him grapple first. Don't give yourself away.

MRS. ROBERTS: Sh! They're coming back. Sh!

CAMPBELL: Sh! Now, Roberts, brace up. Sh! Be a man! Be an American! And deny everything!

Scene 7

The Robertses; Campbell; Mrs. Campbell with Westgate.

WESTGATE: Your Monet is beautiful, Mrs. Roberts. You know, I think you Americans are so much more open-minded than we are, and you take up with the new things so much sooner. I don't think the impressionists are to the fore with us yet.

MRS. ROBERTS: Oh, but I can't allow you to say anything against England, Mr. Westgate!

MRS. CAMPBELL: No, indeed; you would find no sympathizers in that, Mr. Westgate.

CAMPBELL: We gamble on the mother-country every time, here in Boston, at least, and in New York you'll feel as if you'd just got back to London.

WESTGATE: Well, you know, I should be rather sorry to do that. I came over to see Americans.

CAMPBELL: Well, you're barking up the wrong tree.

WESTGATE: Barking up – What a delightful expression! Would you mind saying – Ah, ha, ha! Ha, ha, ha! Very good! I see! You mean in stripping the bark off for the birch canoes, I suppose. These figurative phrases are so vigorous. And you have so many of them. I've heard Americans use some of them at home. Do you suppose that expression originated with your Indians, perhaps?

CAMPBELL: No; they originated the expression, Good Indians, dead Indians. But if you have a fancy for these expressions, Roberts, here, can fill you up with a lot of them.

ROBERTS: Yes – that is – I do hope you can spend a few days with us before you push on to New York.

WESTGATE: Why, you're very good, I'm sure. But that reminds me of the letter of introduc –

CAMPBELL: You stay on here, and Roberts will paint the town red for you.

MRS. ROBERTS: You must allow us to send for your boxes.

MRS. CAMPBELL: Your luggage – yes.

WESTGATE: Ow, but I'd so much rather you'd say *baggage!* I've had it sent to the railway –

MRS. ROBERTS: Station? That doesn't the least matter.

WESTGATE: Ow, but it does! I'd *so* much rather say *deepo*, as you do.

ROBERTS: We can get it perfectly well, if you'll give us your transfer –

CAMPBELL: Don't say *checks*, Roberts! There must be some *English* word.

WESTGATE: No, really; I must go on to New York. My plans are all made. But on my return from the West I shall be most happy to remember your kindness. I've only ventured to trouble Mr. Roberts in regard to the mistake he seems to have made with –

ROBERTS: I beg you won't suppose –

MRS. ROBERTS: [*At the same time*] You mustn't regard it, indeed, Mr. Westgate!

MRS. CAMPBELL: [*At the same time*] Mr. Roberts is *so* absent-minded!

CAMPBELL: [*At the same time*] Roberts is *all* absence of mind!

WESTGATE: Ha, ha, ha! But you know – Ah, ha, ha, ha! Ha, ha, ha! I see! Capital! Oh, excellent! *English* word for checks! Excellent. Ah – would you be good enough to say just what you mean by painting a place red?

CAMPBELL: Roberts will show you, if you'll only stay!

WESTGATE: It's quite impossible, now, at all events. [*To Roberts*] But the letter you kindly gave me to your uncle –

ROBERTS: Yes – yes –

MRS. ROBERTS: You'll like Uncle Phillip *so* much! And he'll appreciate the favor Edward's done him in sending –

MRS. CAMPBELL: [*At the same time*] He's so fond of the English!

CAMPBELL: [*At the same time*] And he's right on to Roberts's jokes. They're always at it together. Back and forth, all the time. If Roberts has put up any little job, Uncle Phil will catch on like lightning.

WESTGATE: Oh, what extremely delightful expressions! I'm sure I sha'n't remember the half of them! But this letter – do you really think – [*He takes it from his pocket*]

ROBERTS: Yes – yes. I'm quite certain he'll –

MRS. ROBERTS: [*At the same time*] Oh yes, indeed! My husband was with him so much at one time! They're almost of the same age.

WESTGATE: Oh, indeed! I fancied an old gentleman! Then you think that he'll understand –

MRS. CAMPBELL: Uncle Phillip understands Mr. Roberts and all his ways perfectly. They have such fun when they're together.

MRS. ROBERTS: [*At the same time*] It doesn't matter what Edward has written, he'll take it just in the right way.

CAMPBELL: [*At the same time*] Yes, he'll know it's *some* kind of a joke.

WESTGATE: Well, you know, I thought perhaps, myself, it was one of your pieces of American humor.

MRS. ROBERTS: Oh, it *was*, Mr. Westgate, I assure you it was! Just one of our pieces of American humor –

MRS. CAMPBELL: Yes, indeed; you can depend upon that, Mr. Westgate!

WESTGATE: Ah well! If it had been Mr. Campbell, here, I should have felt sure of it. But I couldn't be quite so certain that Mr. Roberts –

CAMPBELL: Oh, when it comes to joking, Americans are all alike. Roberts is a little more alike than the rest of us; that's all. So's Uncle Phillip, for that matter. He'd take it right even if Roberts hadn't written anything at all.

WESTGATE: But that's just what Mr. Roberts has done!

ALL THE OTHERS: What!

WESTGATE: [*Handing the envelope to Roberts, who finds it empty, and passes it to his wife, who in turn hands it silently to Mrs. Campbell*] Of course I wished to read the kind things you'd said of me, as soon as possible, and I was greatly surprised to find no letter in this envelope. I wasn't sure whether you intended me simply to present the envelope to your uncle, or whether – At all events, I decided I'd better come and ask.

CAMPBELL: [*Who has possessed himself of the envelope*] Why, look here, Roberts! You put both letters in that sealed envelope I kept Mr. Westgate from posting in the fire-alarm box.

ROBERTS: Why, so I must! Really, Mr. Westgate, I don't know what to say!

MRS. ROBERTS: Yes, Edward, I don't know what you *will* say!

CAMPBELL: Roberts, you're incorrigible! When *will* you give up this habit of practical joking? Really, old fellow, you ought to stop it. You and Uncle Phil have kept it up long enough. And *I* think you owe Mr. Westgate an apology. The joke's on Uncle Phil, of course; but you ought to see that it's rather embarrassing to Mr. Westgate to find himself the bearer of an empty envelope instead of a letter of introduction. Come, now, *you must explain;* and we'll all apologize for you. [*Roberts waits with a*

foolish face of deprecation, turning to horror, at the suggestion of an explanation*] Come! You owe it to yourself, as a joker.

WESTGATE: [*Amiably*] Ow, now! Not at all. *No* apologies. I shouldn't be able to forgive myself if I couldn't allow a man his joke. But I *should* like an explanation, you know. Your humor is so *very* different to ours, and I don't believe any one at home, if I said you had given me an empty envelope to carry to your uncle, *could* feel the spirit of it. And these things are so tiresome, you know, when they happen to fall flat. I hope you won't think me importunate if I say I should like to know just where the laugh comes in on a thing of that kind?

CAMPBELL: Out with it, Roberts!

MRS. ROBERTS: Don't you think – Oh, I'm sure you'll spoil it, Edward!

MRS. CAMPBELL: Don't you think you'd better leave it to Uncle Phillip?

CAMPBELL: Well, that's an inspiration, Amy. Leave it to Uncle Phil, Roberts!

ROBERTS: [*With a deep sigh of relief*] Yes, that will be best. My Uncle Phillip will tell you, if you don't mind.

BELLA: [*At the door*] Lunch is served, Mrs. Roberts.

MRS. ROBERTS: [*Gayly*] I'm going to lead the way, with Mr. Westgate. Edward, bring Amy. And, Willis, you can –

CAMPBELL: Oh, come, now! None of your little unconscious jokes, Agnes! I won't stand it from my own sister.

WESTGATE: Ow! Do the American ladies often make jokes without knowing it, Mrs. Roberts? [*To Campbell*] But what is just the point of – Ow, I see! Very good! Ha, ha, ha! And shall we have some distinctively American dishes, Mrs. Roberts? You know I'm so very, very curious about your chowder, and doughnuts, and maple syrup, and buck-wheat cakes, and corn-dodgers, and hoe-downs. Such delightful names. They really make one's mouth water.

He goes out with Mrs. Roberts

CAMPBELL: [*Lingering, and detaining his wife and Roberts*] Roberts, can't you dance a hoe-cake for him? You ought to do it on your knees, you miserable sinner!

The End

A TEMPERANCE TOWN

CHARLES H. HOYT

HOWELLS enlivened the American parlor with his polite farces. Charles Hoyt rocked the public theatres with more boisterous, less inhibited farcical explorations. Like Howells, Hoyt advocated realistic attention to American social problems, but he never ignored the public's demand for "variety, well cooked and well served," to use his phrase. The record of his productions testifies to Hoyt's success in capturing a popular formula, a magic mixture of recognizable faces and places with delightful farcical misadventures.

Charles Hoyt was born in Concord, New Hampshire, on July 26, 1859. When he was nine, the family moved to Charlestown. His father, George W. Hoyt, had operated a hotel in Concord; in Charlestown he became a railway mail clerk. Mrs. Hoyt died shortly after they had moved, and father and son were obliged to depend on each other. Charles Hoyt maintained his legal residence in Charlestown for the rest of his life, in his mature years using the family place as his summer home. At his death, he bequeathed the home to the Lambs Club. His formal education was limited: a small private school in Charlestown, the Boston Latin School, and a brief term as a law student in the office of Chief Justice Cushing. He had to forgo an appointment to West Point because he could not pass the physical examination. For a brief period he worked on a cattle ranch in Colorado; he held a newspaper apprenticeship on the daily paper at St. Albans, Vermont; and when he was nineteen, he joined the staff of the Boston *Post*.

He started as a cub reporter on the *Post*, but shortly took over a front-page column called "All Sorts." It was literally that: news items, announcements, epigrams, and humorous observations on local scenes and characters. Many of these provided the raw material for comic episodes in his later plays. Recognizing his talent for quick critical comment, the editor promoted him to the post of general reviewer. His territory included all the music, sports, and dramatic events in the Boston area. Hoyt became particularly fascinated with the theatre assignment, and though he never missed an opportunity to turn a humorous phrase, he was fair and objective and more inclined to praise than to condemn. He censured vulgarities and frequently advised the author to revise certain passages to accommodate the wishes of the audience. He seems to have been particularly sharp in sensing audience reactions.

Hoyt took his first fling at dramatic composition while he was still employed on the *Post*. An engagement at the Howard Athenaeum (the "Old Howard" to several generations of Harvard students) had been canceled. William Harris, the manager, asked Hoyt to try his hand at a melodrama that might be got up quickly. Hoyt accepted the challenge. After a few days at his desk and a week's rehearsal in the theatre, *Gifford's Luck* opened at the Athenaeum. It filled the bill but was quickly forgotten. It did, however, whet Hoyt's appetite. The next season his comedy *Cazalia* was performed at the Globe Theatre. This was in May, 1882. Again, not success at the box office but the stimulation Hoyt found in the theatre led him to continue. His next effort, *Dreams*, a revision of an earlier play by Nathaniel Childs, was commissioned by the actors Willie Edouin and Alice Atherton. Hoyt was not yet wise to the ways of the theatre. The play proved profitable for them but not for him. Edouin also appropriated the profits from Hoyt's next play, *A Bunch of Keys*, the first of the many farces on which Hoyt's reputation rests. After an unsuccessful production in Providence, Hoyt had attempted to buy back the script. Edouin and his partner, Frank W. Sanger, refused. They compromised by employing Hoyt to revise the play and direct the rehearsals for another trial in Lowell, Massachusetts. With this performance, on March 26, 1883, the happy results of Hoyt's labors were immediately apparent. Edouin moved the production to New York and for the next seventeen years toured it throughout the country. Edouin reaped a fortune; Hoyt received the original purchase price of five hundred dollars plus a small stipend for his work on the revision.

With this unhappy and enlightening experience, Hoyt decided to abandon his journalistic enterprises and undertake a professional career of playwriting and play production. Charles W. Thomas, one of his associates on the *Post*, joined him as business manager, and in the next ten years their partnership became one of the wonders of the theatre world. Hoyt became a millionaire before he had reached his thirtieth birthday. In 1892 the partners leased the Madison Square Theatre in New York and renamed it Hoyt's Theatre. Thomas died in 1893, and Frank McKee succeeded him as Hoyt's business manager. In 1893 and again in 1895 Hoyt was elected to the New Hampshire Assembly, and he became known as the "only American to combine legislative and theatrical functions." For the inaugural ceremony at the opening of each of these two legislative sessions, he transported a full production of one of his plays from Boston to Concord. Hoyt was married twice, both times to actresses. He married Flora Walsh in July, 1887; she died in January, 1893. His second wife, the beautiful Caroline Miskell, whom he married in March, 1894, died in childbirth in October, 1898. Hoyt was still grieving over the loss of his wife when his newest play, *A Dog in the Manger*, opened in Washington in February, 1899. It was a disastrous failure. He was unable to withstand the shattering impact of these two events. He suffered a complete nervous collapse and in July was committed to the Retreat for the Insane in Hartford. Late in the summer he was released to the custody of friends in Charlestown, where he died on November 20, 1899.

Hoyt did not possess the free and open bearing and glad hand of so many theatre personalities. He was cold and reserved. Even his business partners addressed him as "Mr. Hoyt." His only concession to personal theatricality seems to have been the large diamond which he wore on his vest and the profanity which supported every command he gave to his associates. It was a strange combination for a lively humorist and one who abhorred any show of vulgarity on the stage. Hoyt was a meticulous and untiring craftsman and an astute businessman. He kept a weather eye on the public's tastes, gauged his plays to meet its demands, and, as a result, pocketed a fortune. In the early stages of devising a play, Hoyt worked easily and freely and without apparent design. He perpetually jotted down observations on characters and scenes that struck his fancy. His reporter's eye and pen were always at work. A single refinement had been added to his early journalistic practice. Now he visualized scenes and characters under the lights rather than on the printed page. At some point a particularly striking observation drove him into action. Drawing on his accumulated stock of random notations, he pieced together a preliminary script. As he continued to revise, readjust, and fill in, everything was appraised in terms of how it would "go" in the theatre. When he was reasonably satisfied with the rough draft, he started the production wheels. In the early days the pattern demanded a spring tryout tour in New England, a week in Jersey City in the early summer, then a period of alteration during the late summer. In the fall the play was ready for New York. With the later plays, he frequently added a month or two on the road in the fall before a New York opening. Every night he concentrated on the audience, caught its reactions, and rewrote to accommodate its demands. The next morning he rehearsed the company in the revisions and that evening he repeated the process. Present-day out-of-town tryouts for Broadway follow much the same pattern.

Hoyt's early plays were out-and-out farces, simple concoctions of comic situations and characters taken from life. The later plays incorporated some exploration of a social problem or a satirical exposure of an objectionable character. Hoyt once said, "I never posed as a reformer, but I like to poke fun at anything that is ludicrous, or at any type of individual that strikes me as being eccentric, mean or narrow-minded." Seventeen plays and one comic operetta in the sixteen years from 1883 to 1899 was a remarkable record in itself. It was even more remarkable: only two of these, one play and the operetta, were failures.

A Trip to Chinatown, first performed at Hoyt's Madison Square Theatre on November 9, 1891, had a consecutive run of 657 performances, a record that stood until Frank Bacon's *Lightnin'* opened on August 26, 1918, and ran for 1,291 consecutive performances. Many actors achieved prominence in Hoyt's plays. Maude Adams made her first New York appearance in *A Midnight Bell* (Bijou Theatre, March 5, 1889); Lillian Russell and Tony Hart played in the unsuccessful operetta, *The Maid and the Moonshiner* (Standard Theatre, August 16, 1886). Hoyt attributed this failure to the title. Some ill-considered whim had led him to use *The* as the initial word; thereafter he always used the more felicitous *A*. The songs from many Hoyt plays became popular tunes of the day: "Reuben, Reuben, I've Been Thinking," "The Bowery," and "After the Ball" were featured in *A Trip to Chinatown*. Hoyt wrote the lyrics and Percy Gaunt the melodies for the first two. "After the Ball," by Charles K. Harris, was inserted in a production on tour. It proved so popular and appropriate that Hoyt permitted it to be retained.

The social satire in the later Hoyt farces covered many subjects: the suffragist movement in *A Contented Woman* (Hoyt's Theatre, January 4, 1897); the home-guard companies in *A Milk White Flag* (Hoyt's Theatre, October 8, 1894); the corruption of baseball by gamblers in *A Runaway Colt* (Hoyt's Theatre, November 12, 1895); and the evils of local option in *A Temperance Town*.

The other Hoyt plays, though not so pointedly satirical, extended his exploration of the American panorama. *A Rag Baby* (Haverley's Theatre, August 16, 1884) and *A Brass Monkey* (Bijou Theatre, October, 1888) dealt with the ineptness of inexperienced small businessmen. *A Tin Soldier* (Standard Theatre, May 3, 1885) presented a conglomerate *dramatis personae:* plumber, carpenter, Italian art connoisseur, businessman, and mail carrier; *A Texas Steer* (Bijou Theatre, November 10, 1890), one of Hoyt's best plays, centered on the awkward plight of an uninitiated Texas congressman. A small-town railroad station provided the setting for *A Hole in the Ground* (Fourteenth Street Theatre, September 12, 1887).

A Temperance Town illustrates the Hoyt formula for combining serious social comment with slapstick farce. He drew his subject from life: a court case involving local option in Vermont that had been widely reported in the newspapers. Hoyt admitted that his main object was "to furnish an entertainment that would draw the public," but he also wished to alert people to the encroachments of the law on their liberty:

I must confess it afforded me considerable satisfaction to expose the inquisitorial cruelty of the law and its unjust interference with personal liberty. I am not an advocate of indiscriminate sale of rum, but it makes my blood boil to hear of a poor devil having been sent to jail for sixty years on an accumulative sentence because he could not pay a fine of $7,000, and had to work it out at the rate of thirty cents a day. Fortunately the Governors of Vermont have been humane men and the victims of this bigoted law were generally pardoned after serving a few years.

Hoyt recognized the ineffectiveness of unrelieved didacticism. With an appropriate portion of levity and gaiety he could break through latent resistance and thus strengthen the impact of his message. Moreover, the lesson of the play was on the program for the public to carry home. His prefatory paragraph was invariably printed with the cast of characters.

A present-day audience might have difficulty accepting the juxtaposition of farcical horseplay with a serious attack on a social evil – just as it would now be inconceivable to bill *Macbeth* and *Po-ca-hon-tas* for the same evening in the theatre. Our nineteenth-century progenitors were undisturbed by such combinations.

Apparently Hoyt was a devotee of the Howard Athenaeum's black-face entertainments during his early newspaper days. The primary evidence of the minstrel-show influence is in the speeches and actions of his plays, but it is also described by Hoyt's stage manager, Julian Mitchell:

There he literally sat at the feet of the negro minstrels. Watching them, studying them, he found the central comedy germ. This he later dressed in his own brilliant wit and incorporated in his plays. Many is the popular stunt performed by the minstrels which afterward appeared in his various scenes.

A Temperance Town had a trial run of one week at Meech Brothers' Academy of Music in Buffalo, beginning on March 14, 1892, with Hoyt's wife, Flora Walsh, in the part of Ruth. Flora Walsh died the following January. When the play opened in New York on September 18, 1893, Miss Miskell replaced her. The following March, Caroline Miskell also assumed her role as Hoyt's wife. (Odell described her as "one of the most beautiful women that ever walked the stage.") This first New York engagement at the Madison Square Theatre continued for 125 consecutive performances, and on January 8, 1894, because of some misunderstanding about rental terms, the play was moved to the Park Theatre for five additional performances. During this period Hoyt and McKee held the lease on the Madison Square Theatre from A. M. Palmer, who had it from the Mallory brothers, who had it from the owners of the property. New York theatre real-estate dealings were as complicated then as now. On January 11, 1894, Hoyt and McKee negotiated a nine-year lease on the property and renamed it Hoyt's Madison Square Theatre.

After the success of the initial engagement, *A Temperance Town* was back in New York for regular showings every year for the next ten seasons in addition to numerous performances on the road. For the week of January 27, 1902, Proctor's Fifth Avenue Theatre advertised a continuous performance beginning at one in the afternoon and continuing until ten-thirty at night, presumably four performances per day.

Many of Hoyt's farcical episodes resemble the vaudeville-like turns employed by Harrigan and Hart, though Harrigan introduced knockabout scenes more frequently, relied principally on comic types, and confined himself to the New York locale. In most cases Hoyt's characters were more fully developed and individualized, both his characters and his situations were more conventionally credible, and he ranged widely over the American social scene. Harrigan's entertainments were derived from a sharp observation of life and an awareness of the pathetic marginal existence of the inhabitants of the Lower East Side. He was, however, committed to laughter rather than reform. When Hoyt focused on social ills, the object of his attack was clearly defined and the sting of his ridicule left its mark.

During the last decade of the nineteenth century, Hoyt's farces largely replaced Harrigan's. He clearly captured the audience with a fascinating theatrical mixture: scenes, situations, and characters drawn directly from everyday American life; genial but pointed satire on common foibles and social ills; and all enlivened with broad, bright, and irresistible farcical details.

A TEMPERANCE TOWN

CHARLES H. HOYT

Which is intended to be a more or less truthful presentation of certain phases and incidents of life, relating to the sale and use of liquor, in a small village in a prohibition state. The author has endeavored to give all sides a fair show. But he is quite willing to be classed as protesting against the prohibitory laws of Vermont, where a man named Kibling is now serving a sentence of something like sixty years for selling about seven hundred glasses of liquor (less than most of our respectable city hotels sell in a day).

CHARACTERS

LAUNCELOT (MINK) JONES
ST. JULIAN (BINGO) JONES
ERNEST HARDMAN
SQUIRE BELCHER
KNEELAND PRAY
DR. CADWELL SAWYER
FRED OAKHURST
JOHN WORTH
UNCLE JOE VIALL
WILLIAM PUTNAM
WES PERRY
WILL PEAK

JUDGE GRAHAM DOE
SHERIFF
SHERIFF'S OFFICER
SPRAGUE
FRANK HARDMAN
MRS. PATIENCE HARDMAN
RUTH HARDMAN
ROXANA
MRS. JONES
ONE OF THE CROSSMAN CHILDREN
WAITER
JURY
VILLAGERS

ACT I

SCENE: *Exterior of parsonage. Set house with porch, balustrade, and stairs with three or four steps extending from L.1.E. to L.3.E. Set stable extending from R.1.E. to R.3.E. Large double practical doors of stable open. Practical pump with bucket by it near stable door. Horse-blanket hanging on stable door. Double shed extending from R.3.E. to R.C. Gate opening between stable and shed R.U.E. large enough for wagon to pass through. Watering-trough beside pump. Chopping-block, axe, and woodpile L.U.C. Washtub on stool beside stairs to house L. Bench large enough to hold two persons R.2.E. Grass mats, etc., around stage.*

Discovered: At rise, Mrs. Hardman, Roxey, and Mrs. Jones. Mrs. Jones is chopping wood.

MRS. HARDMAN: Don't do that, Mrs. Jones. You'll cut yourself.

MRS. JONES: Why not? Who else will do it for me?

MRS. HARDMAN: Ask Mink. He is your husband. Surely he will not refuse to aid you, when you have so much work to do.

MRS. JONES: Oh, bless your soul, he is too busy down at the saloon, attending political meetings and all that sort of thing.

MRS. HARDMAN: Well, I think he should take more interest in his family affairs. It seems to me that you are leading a very hard life.

MRS. JONES: I know that Mink is dreadful shiftless and that he might do better; but he has never spoken a cross word to me in his life, and we have been married for over twenty

635

years. If it wasn't for that saloon he might do better.

MRS. HARDMAN: Yes, it was through that saloon that my poor boy left home, and went to his death. It seems that saloons are nothing but a blight upon a community.

MRS. JONES: Yes, but if folks didn't find some kind of consolation, they wouldn't go there. I don't want to hinder Mink from having all the pleasure he can find in this life, for it's mighty hard, anyway.

MRS. HARDMAN: Won't Bingo help you? He is young and strong and seems to have nothing else to do.

MRS. JONES: Well, I don't know. It seems to me that work of any kind always went against the grain of the Joneses. Bingo has won a bet, and old Joe Viall has to wheel him a mile in a wheelbarrow today, as he is the loser.

MRS. HARDMAN: Why, that old man is ninety-four years old! He'll never be able to wheel that strong boy that distance!

MRS. JONES: Well, he'll have to do it or pay some kind of a forfeit. These men arrange things to suit themselves, and I don't want to interfere.

MRS. HARDMAN: [*To Roxey*] Why, what are you doing with that sword?

ROXEY: Why, polishing it up for Thanksgiving. Ain't it nice and clean? [*Shoulders sword and sings*] Steady, boys! Forward march! Steady, boys! Steady! [*Marches and makes exit, L.2.E. Enter Dr. Sawyer, Pray, and Belcher through gate*]

BELCHER: Good day, Mrs. Hardman. Is the parson at home?

MRS. HARDMAN: Yes. I will send him to you directly. [*Exits L.2.E. into house*]

BELCHER: Gentlemen, I assure you that we have entered upon a crusade which I am certain will result in the greatest good to our fellow citizens.

PRAY: Yes, there is no doubt of it whatever. Is everything arranged?

DR. SAWYER: Yes. We have secured a witness who will swear to the purchase of liquor, and that will be certain to secure a conviction.

PRAY: Think of it, gentlemen! What a blessing this will be! Look at our citizens who have been decoyed into wasting their time and means in this low brothel! Look at John

Worth! He should be an example to the youths of this village. He had a fortune of $160,000 left him. Yet he insists on spending his time and money among the low associates he forms in the saloon.

BELCHER: Gentlemen, what I am about to do is not for a mercenary purpose, but on behalf of the welfare of the community. I ask no reward. My honest conviction forces me to the steps I am now taking.

PRAY: Yes. Think of John Worth! His father wanted him to be a gentleman. He sent him to Europe to study Greek and Latin. Then he comes back here and talks about drinking wine and eating what he calls banquets.

DR. SAWYER: And see what the consequence of tolerating this nuisance will result in. The man is not satisfied with his illegal traffic. He is now going to add gambling to his crimes. He is going to have a raffle and seek by a game of chance to empty the pockets of the community.

PRAY: Hush! Here comes Hardman. He is with us heart and soul. He blames the saloon for his son's disappearance, and ever since the boy ran away he has devoted his life to the cause of temperance. [*Enter Hardman from the house*]

HARDMAN: Welcome, gentlemen. I presume you came to report progress in our glorious cause. Blame me not if I appear too anxious, but they ruined my son and made my life desolate. These wreckers of our homes must be taught a lesson, and I will never yield in my warfare against their unholy traffic while I have strength left to battle with it! [*Shouts outside*] What means this noise?

PRAY: Old Joe Viall has lost a bet made in the saloon and he is now wheeling Bingo a mile in a wheelbarrow in order to pay it. [*Enter Peak*] Ah, this is our man, the one who is to secure evidence against Oakhurst, the rum-seller. Well, Peak, what success have you met with?

PEAK: None at all. Our game won't work. He refuses to sell me any liquor.

PRAY: Why?

PEAK: He said I wasn't a proper person to have liquor.

DR. SAWYER: Then what can we do?

PEAK: I'll tell you what I can do. I'll go around

to the back door. I'll bore a hole through and peep. I can see everything he sells.

HARDMAN: But are you sure you can identify the bottles?

PEAK: Identify? What do you mean by identifying?

PRAY: Why, pick out the bottles the liquor was sold from.

PEAK: Well, I should say so. I know the contents of every bottle. But say, I get my ten dollars, don't I?

PRAY: Certainly; we will attend to that. [*Exit Peak*]

HARDMAN: Now, in case this man should prove unreliable, are you prepared to furnish forth the proofs? Will anyone else swear to the purchase of liquor?

DR. SAWYER: Ay, that's an important question. Can such a witness be found?

PRAY: Leave it to me. I think I have a reliable person who will do so. But, hush! We may be overheard.

HARDMAN: Overheard? These are my premises, gentlemen, and I assure you no eavesdroppers frequent them.

PRAY: Probably not, but – you have a daughter.

HARDMAN: I have. But I know her sentiments are mine and that she is heart and soul with me in this conflict against rum.

PRAY: You may think so, but we have proofs that she is in the habit of visiting Oakhurst and his family. She has doubtless ere this warned him of our intentions.

HARDMAN: Gentlemen, you are mistaken! I will call her. [*Goes to door of house*] Roxey! Tell Miss Ruth to come here. [*Roxey enters from house and exits*] My daughter is incapable of falsehood and shall answer for herself. [*Enter Ruth*] Daughter, is it true that you have ventured into the house of Oakhurst, the rum-seller?

RUTH: It is true.

HARDMAN: And what could have induced you to visit that place?

RUTH: The child was sick and I thought it my duty to aid.

PRAY: And were there not others more worthy of your assistance than a rum-seller's child?

RUTH: None perhaps so much in need.

HARDMAN: [*To Ruth*] Did you warn him that

there was a possibility of a raid being made upon his place tonight?

RUTH: The thought never even entered my mind!

HARDMAN: Gentlemen, I hope you are satisfied, but step into the house with me. We will talk the matter over. [*Exit Hardman and Belcher into house*]

DR. SAWYER: I will go and see Oakhurst at once. He owes me quite a bill and I had better get all I can from him before we raid his place. [*Exits into house*]

PRAY: Miss Ruth, don't blame me for this. It's not my fault. [*Exits into house*]

RUTH: What miserable hypocrites! [*Shouts outside. Enter Roxey and Mrs. Jones from the house. Old Viall wheeling Bingo in a wheelbarrow. Peak, Wes Perry, and rest of villagers*]

PERRY: Three cheers for Uncle Joe! [*Crowd gives cheers*]

BINGO: Gentlemen, the exercises are now over and I would advise the meeting to disperse at once or the parson will come out and run you off his grounds. [*Exit Perry and crowd. Bingo gets out of wheelbarrow*] A little while ago I was riding in this wheelbarrow. Now I've got to put it away! [*Wheels it into stable, R.*]

VIALL: [*To Mrs. Jones*] Mrs. Jones, are you cooking doughnuts?

MRS. JONES: Yes, I am. What do you want to know for?

VIALL: 'Cause I can smell 'em. I always was fond of doughnuts.

MRS. JONES: Well, what do you mean by coming around here and making such a disturbance?

VIALL: Well, you see we got a little excited and us boys will be boys.

MRS. JONES: Yes; and fools will be fools! [*Exits into house followed by Ruth*]

VIALL: Mighty fine gal, that! I like her! She seems to be so lively and full of ginger all the time. Guess I'll go in and sample them doughnuts. [*Exits into house. Enter Bingo from stable*]

BINGO: I've just had a lively time today. Guess I'll chase down to the saloon and see if old Joe is setting 'em up yet. [*Pauses and looks at Roxey, then at door of house, pointing*] Say, here comes the boss ramrod!

ROXEY: What do you mean by a boss ramrod?

BINGO: That's a name we give all these temperance cranks, and Deacon Pray is the boss. But he can't fool me. You just wait until the Fourth of July, and if I don't have his sign down and my name over the door for a saloon, my name ain't Jones. [*Exit both, Roxey into house, Bingo into stable. Enter Ruth and Pray from house*]

PRAY: And are you interested in this saloon-keeper, Miss Ruth, so much that you desire no harm to befall him? [*Downstage; Ruth R., Pray L. Enter Bingo from the stable*]

BINGO: Beg pardon, Miss Ruth. [*Bingo hands Ruth a peach on the end of a stick*] Can I offer you this?

RUTH: Certainly. But why do you give it to me in such a peculiar manner?

BINGO: Well, I heard them say down at the saloon that old Pray couldn't get near enough to you to hand you a peach on a stick; so I thought I'd try! [*Exits into stable. Enter Roxey from house carrying the sword*]

ROXEY: Oh, Miss Ruth, I've got it polished up so that it looks like new. There isn't a speck of rust on it anywhere. [*Enter Mrs. Hardman from the front door of house*]

RUTH: [*Taking sword*] My poor brother! [*Sorrowfully*] This is all we have left to remind us of you, the only token that you have lived and fought for the land that gave you birth. [*To Pray*] Pardon me, but this is a memento of my brother. A comrade brought it, and a message. Since then we have heard nothing from him. You know he went away to the war.

PRAY: You'll excuse me, Miss Ruth, but I have some business at my store. [*Exit Pray through gate*]

MRS. HARDMAN: Come, Ruth. Are you ready? [*Exits into house*]

RUTH: Yes, mama, I'm coming. [*Kisses sword*] Now I will take you with me and you will fill my dear brother's place in his vacant chair. [*Exits into house*]

ROXEY: [*Throws herself full-length on the bench*] These relations of mine are a cheerful lot. [*Enter Bingo, who looks at Roxey. She rises*] You are the boy that does the chores, ain't you?

BINGO: Yes.

ROXEY: And your mother does the washing?

BINGO: Yes.

ROXEY: Let's see. Your name is Bingo, ain't it?

BINGO: No. It's St. Julian; St. Julian Jones.

ROXEY: What a peculiar name!

BINGO: You see how it was; when I was born, pop thought he'd christen me that, 'cause he saw the name on a bottle down to the saloon.

ROXEY: But why do they call you Bingo?

BINGO: Because they call dad Mingo; sometimes Mink for short; and his dad's name was Stingo. That's some kind of a drink. We all take to it.

ROXEY: Why don't you make them call you by your right name?

BINGO: 'Cause they won't do it.

ROXEY: Well, why don't you make them? Stand on your dignity!

BINGO: Stand on your dignity! Say, you don't know much about the Joneses!

ROXEY: Didn't anybody ever take an interest in you and talk to you kindly?

BINGO: Yes, lots of 'em. They come and tell me I ought to be ashamed of myself, that I'm going along the broad road to the wrong place, that I'm sure to land in State's prison or be hung, and all that sort of thing. They make me sick!

ROXEY: But if you took care of yourself, they would certainly show you respect.

BINGO: No, I'm not rich. It takes money to be respected in Vermont.

ROXEY: But if you took care of yourself and kept your face and hands clean, people would like you better. I know I would!

BINGO: Say, are you going to stay here long?

ROXEY: Yes, I live here and I'm going to stay here all the time.

BINGO: Oh, then you're the help?

ROXEY: No, *sir*. I'm a relation. My parents are dead and I came here to live with my relations, and I'm not supposed to receive wages!

BINGO: Gee, I'm glad I'm not an orphan! I got a mother to work for me.

ROXEY: My father was a minister at Crossing. He got six hundred dollars a year and never saved a cent.

BINGO: Whew! [*Whistles. Enter Mrs. Hardman. She calls Roxey. They exit into house*] Make folks respect me! [*He goes to stable, fills bucket from horse-trough R. and washes face. He uses currycomb as brush for his hair and looks in water for a mirror. He dries hands and face on the horse-blanket. Enter Belcher, Pray, and Dr. Sawyer*]

PRAY: The very person I want to see! Bingo, I want to talk with you.

BINGO: Temperance! Aw! Aw!

PRAY: Do you know that, if you keep on your present course, you'll go straight to a place where the Devil rules?

BINGO: [*Starting*] Yes, I'm going right straight to your drugstore.

DR. SAWYER: [*As Pray turns away*] Do you know the miserable fate that overtakes the drunkard?

BINGO: Yes. He's got to send for a doctor.

BELCHER: [*As Dr. Sawyer turns away*] Suppose that in your drunkenness you commit some horrible crime. What would you do?

BINGO: Send out of town for a lawyer. [*Going C.*]

BELCHER: [*To Pray*] It's a sad case.

PRAY: Where are you going, Bingo?

BINGO: My name ain't Bingo. It's St. Julian.

PRAY: Isn't St. Julian a rather high-sounding name? Your clothes are hardly becoming to the name.

DR. SAWYER: How would you like a new suit of clothes?

BINGO: How am I going to get 'em?

BELCHER: I'll tell you. We'll give you some money. Then you buy some liquor with it and get drunk. Then go before a justice of the peace and swear where you got it.

BINGO: Well, when do I get the clothes?

PRAY: In about a month; say in December.

BINGO: Not much! Come around in December and we'll talk it over.

PRAY: Stay! Why do you want them so soon?

BINGO: Because tomorrow is Thanksgiving Day and I want to break them in at the raffle.

PRAY: You can have the clothes today if you promise to do what I tell you. I'll give you an order for a suit of clothes at Cooley's store.

BINGO: I'll do it. Give me the order. [*Pray gives it. Bingo starts out*]

PRAY: Wait! You must have some money. [*Hands him ten cents*]

BINGO: Ten cents! One drink only.

PRAY: How many do you want?

BINGO: Oh, about twelve or thirteen.

PRAY: Well, here's a dollar. Will that be enough?

BINGO: I guess so. I'll try and make it go. Now, you want me to go and get a certain number of drinks and then go to court and swear to it?

DR. SAWYER, BELCHER, and PRAY: Yes, that's it! Yes!

BINGO: [*Going to gate*] All right. You bet I'll make folks respect me. [*Exits*]

DR. SAWYER: Well, I think everything is working nicely. Come, Brother Belcher, will you walk over to my office? [*Exit Belcher and Dr. Sawyer. Enter Ruth. Pray advances and leads her to a seat on the bench*]

PRAY: Miss Ruth, do you know it is very melancholy to be compelled to live alone?

RUTH: I have no doubt of it.

PRAY: And I have been thinking of building a new house.

RUTH: Indeed?

PRAY: Yes, and I intend to have in it everything that goes to make life comfortable.

RUTH: A very sensible idea.

PRAY: I don't claim a large one and I've come to ask your advice. I wish to build one just large enough for two.

RUTH: I think you are right.

PRAY: The two should be –

RUTH: Yourself and your mother. [*Enter Worth*]

WORTH: Pardon me, Miss Ruth, I found this earring a few moments ago and remembered having seen it in your possession. Will you permit me to return it to you?

RUTH: Thank you, Mr. Worth. It certainly is mine.

PRAY: You have turned very honest.

WORTH: Yes, and therefore unlike my neighbors. But excuse me. [*He goes to stable door, picks up a cushion, returns to Ruth. Pray and Ruth rise. Worth throws cushion on the seat*] This makes a hard seat more comfortable. [*He sits quietly in Pray's place*]

PRAY: [*To Ruth*] I will go and speak to your father. [*Exits into house. Music. Enter Mink Jones driving an old horse and buckboard wagon containing a treadle and a bag of loose corn. Drives to C. of stage*]

MINK: Whoa, there! Whoa, there, Shoo-fly!

WORTH: Hello, Mink! Are you tired?

MINK: [*Standing up in wagon with the whip in his hand*] Tired? Tired ain't the word for it! Had to get up at four o'clock this morning. Killed two pigs for the butcher; doctored a sick horse for old man Smith; tarred and feathered a rat so he'd scare the others out of Fogg's grocery store; took down the schoolhouse stovepipes because they were stopped up, and fixed 'em up again; hauled a load of coal for Widow Wiggins; stopped a dog fight in Brody's store; started a balky horse for Ed Billings; and then Dad Hawkins died last night and I had to go over and shave the corpse.

WORTH: Well, I should think you would need a rest.

MINK: Rest? Why, there is no rest for the weary. And now I've brought this treadle home and I have to fix it up.

WORTH: Where is the treadle?

MINK: Here on the buckboard.

RUTH: Mink, old Joe is in the house.

MINK: Well, let him enjoy himself.

WORTH: But aren't you jealous of old Joe?

MINK: Jealous? Me jealous? Why, that's the only thing I have to tease Mrs. Jones about. I twit her on that so as to make her let up when she jaws me. [*Gets out of wagon*] Well, I must hurry up and fix this treadle so as to get to go to the raffle tonight.

WORTH: But will your horse stand?

MINK: Stand? No, I'm afraid he'll fall down. I'll take him over here where he can lean against the house. [*Mink leads horse to L.1.E. Exits with horse far enough to leave the back end of wagon on the stage*]

RUTH: Raffle? What does he mean?

WORTH: There is going to be a raffle tonight at the saloon for the benefit of Oakhurst. He is in trouble.

RUTH: Poor fellow! I feel sorry for him. I've heard he was a Union soldier. [*Enter Mink*]

MINK: Yes, Miss Ruth, and as brave a man as ever fought. [*Enter Hardman who listens at the door*] He lost the use of his arm while he was carrying a wounded comrade off the field of battle. Got a bullet for doing good. Now he's got no strength to do manual labor and deserves assistance from those who stayed at home while he was doing the fighting. I think Fred Oakhurst one of the squarest men that ever lived, and I've got a dollar and thirty-one cents put on that raffle, and it all goes. [*Turns; sees Hardman; grabs bag of corn by bottom of bag and lifts it on his back.*

As bag was not tied up, corn falls out in a stream as he crosses stage hurriedly to exit into stable. Hardman comes down to Worth]

HARDMAN: Do you think that if Oakhurst was a store-keeper, Mink would side with him? His poor wife is working here all day for a dollar, less than he will spend at that raffle tonight. I can forgive the drunkard, for he is weak. But the rum-seller, never! They were the cause of my poor boy leaving home and of leading him to an untimely grave. Cursed be he who puts the poisoned cup to his neighbor's lips! [*Enter Oakhurst*] What can you want in my place?

OAKHURST: I wish to see the doctor. My baby is worse. [*Exit Ruth into house, returning immediately*]

HARDMAN: Do you ever think of the thousands of children who are dying from the neglect of drunken parents? Do you ever think of the thousands of homes that are daily wrecked by men of your calling? Has it ever occurred to you that retribution must come for the tears of the innocent babes and the agonies of broken-hearted fathers and mothers and children that are dying when the money that should support them is spent in the rum-shop? [*Enter Dr. Sawyer followed by Pray*]

RUTH: Don't chide him, father. His child is sick.

DR. SAWYER: Well, Oakhurst, what's the matter?

OAKHURST: My child is worse and we are afraid she is dying.

DR. SAWYER: See here, Oakhurst, you owe me quite a bill now and I must have money today.

OAKHURST: [*Pleadingly*] Doctor, I cannot let you have it today. I have paid out every dollar I had in the house; but I'll let you have some tomorrow.

DR. SAWYER: No, no! I must have it today, or not a step do I go!

OAKHURST: But, doctor, my child is dying!

DR. SAWYER: Well, go ahead. But remember! This is my last visit! [*Exit Oakhurst*] I'll never get a penny unless I see him at once. [*Exit Dr. Sawyer, C.*]

PRAY: Good, kind-hearted old doctor! He loses all thought of self when others are in need!

WORTH: I don't think so. Did the good Samaritan bring a lawsuit to recover his pay? [*He goes upstage*]

PRAY: Where are you going now? To look up your Bible, or to the saloon?

WORTH: Being a free-born American citizen, I go where I please! [*Exits C.*]

RUTH: Father, may I bring a few little comforts to Oakhurst's sick child?

PRAY: Why should you care for a rum-seller's child?

RUTH: Father, he was a Union soldier.

HARDMAN: Well, go, daughter. It can do no harm. [*Ruth exits into house. Enter Mink with a basket of corncobs on his shoulders, places it on the tail of the wagon, which upsets, knocking him down, and the corn spills. Enter Mrs. Jones from the house with a basket of clothes full of clean linen. As she goes toward C. she sees Mink*]

MRS. JONES: So, Mink, here you are, drunk again!

MINK: Drunk again?

MRS. JONES: Yes, again, I said. Don't try to tell us it's the same old drunk. And what do you mean by coming home at four o'clock in the morning?

MINK: No, my dear, it was eleven o'clock. Won't you take my word for it?

MRS. JONES: No, I'll not! I looked at the clock and it was four. [*Exits C. with basket*]

MINK: Gentlemen, my feelings are hurt. My wife would sooner believe a damned old two-dollar alarm clock than she would me. [*He rises from the floor, gets his foot tangled in the harness, which is in the back of the wagon, and finally struggles across the stage toward the stable, looking at his feet*] What's this to be, a waltz or a schottische? [*Exits into stable. Enter Mrs. Jones with dry clothes in the basket*]

BELCHER: Mrs. Jones, you ought to be pitied, having such a husband!

MRS. JONES: Well, I'd a heap rather have him than you.

BELCHER: But he's such a shiftless fellow!

MRS. JONES: I don't care! I married him, and he's mine, and I don't intend to let anybody else run him down! [*Exits into house. Enter Ruth with a bundle which she hands to Roxey, who enters with her. Enter Dr. Sawyer*]

DR. SAWYER: Well, Oakhurst's child is likely to die.

HARDMAN: Daughter, where are you going?

RUTH: This is a bundle of little delicacies for Oakhurst's sick child.

PRAY: A saloon is no place for a lady to be seen. [*Going up*] Let me take it. I am going that way. [*He takes the bundle*]

HARDMAN: Daughter, go into the house! [*Exit Ruth and Roxey*]

PRAY: Oakhurst has seen us over here and suspects we are planning a raid. That is why he made an excuse to come here.

HARDMAN: Do you think there is any chance of our plan failing?

PRAY: None whatever. I have secured a witness who will swear that he purchased liquor in the saloon.

HARDMAN: Who is it?

PRAY: Bingo Jones.

HARDMAN: Will he do it, think you? [*Enter Bingo, shouting, flashily dressed, and drunk*]

PRAY: Here he is! Bingo, did you secure the liquor?

BINGO: Yes, you bet I did!

PRAY: And will you swear that you bought it at the saloon?

BINGO: Saloon? No! I bought thirteen drinks over at your drugstore! Whoops! Hurrah! [*Consternation for all*]

Curtain

Second Curtain

ROXEY: [*Enters from house and stands R.C.*] St. Julian, how could you? [*Bingo throws hat on steps and looks crestfallen*]

ROXEY   BINGO

HARDMAN   DOCTOR   PRAY

ACT II

SCENE: *Interior of Oakhurst's saloon. Set bar at back with small arch opening door in flat behind bar. Door in flat R. and L. in each end beyond bar. Set window open L.3.E. Table and three chairs L.C. Bottles and glasses on table. Chair in front of fireplace R.2.E. Shovel and broom near fireplace. Bottles and glasses and cigar boxes on bar. Treadle stands against wing, R.1.E.*

Discovered: At rise, Bingo on chair R.C. Worth,

Wes Perry and others at Table L. Oakhurst at bar looking despondent. Newspaper on table.

WORTH: Where are all the boys?

PERRY: Don't know. Some of 'em ought to be around before this. I hear Mink had some trouble with his buckboard today.

WORTH: I guess that's what's keeping him away. He generally makes this place his home.

BINGO: Yes, that runs in the family, you know.

WORTH: But where's Uncle Joe Viall? [*Enter old Joe Viall*]

VIALL: Here I am. Always on time and as slick as they make 'em!

WORTH: How are you feeling, Uncle Joe?

VIALL: Pretty tolerable fine for an old man. Can't you see I am?

PERRY: Old Dave Walton was pretty sick last night. The doctor thinks he's going to die.

WORTH: He must be the oldest man in town.

VIALL: What? He's a mere boy! He's only seventy-eight. Why, I used to spank his mother!

OMNES: Ha! Ha! Ha!

OAKHURST: [*To Bingo*] What is it worth to pick up the ashes around the shop?

BINGO: About five dollars.

OAKHURST: Five dollars! I'll give you twenty cents.

BINGO: I'll take it! [*Oakhurst gives him broom and pan and goes behind bar. Exit Bingo*]

WORTH: I hate to see Fred looking so blue.

PERRY: Well, these ramrods have been making it pretty hot for him lately.

VIALL: I seen old Doc Sawyer, Deacon Pray, and Belcher up to the parsonage this morning. Don't think they're getting ready for another raid, are they?

PERRY: I shouldn't wonder. Pastor Hardman is very bitter in the prohibition cause. He blames the rum-shop for being the cause of his boy running away.

WORTH: [*Standing*] And could you blame the boy for going? Was his home a happy one? Did Hardman ever speak a kind or encouraging word to any of his family? I have known him for twenty years and never heard him speak a kind word to his wife or daughter. Did you ever hear him utter a cheering word to his wife? Did he ever offer to buy her a new dress or tell her that her dinner was good? Did he ever return from a walk and bring her even a bunch of wildflowers? Did you ever hear him praise her in the presence of others? I vow I never did. Does he ever bring her a few ribbons, or exhibit in any way the little tokens of affection a woman loves so well? No! Poor woman! Her heart is broken for the loss of her boy who was driven away by a cold-hearted father. And she, like all around her, is literally starved for want of affection and sympathy!

PERRY: [*Going to bar*] Well, gentlemen, what will you have to drink? [*All rush to the bar, old Viall tottering the last of all*]

VIALL: Hold on! You're not going to leave me out! [*Enter Mink*]

MINK: Mine's the same as last year. [*All drink and return downstage*]

WORTH: I hear that you met with an accident this morning.

MINK: Yes. You see, I greased the buckboard this morning and forgot to put the nut on the off hind wheel. The damned thing broke down before I got a hundred yards. [*Picks up towel from chair Bingo was sitting in and dusts himself*]

OAKHURST: Hold on! There's varnish on that towel! [*Mink tries to throw it out-of-doors, but it sticks to his fingers. Enter Bingo who snatches towel and tries to throw it out-of-doors, but it sticks to his fingers also and he exits disgusted. Mink, in the meantime, tries to rub his hands off on his clothes, but apparently makes matters worse. In despair he goes to treadle and wipes his hands on it; it is leaning against wing R.1.E. Mink falls backward against it as he wipes his hands on it and falls to floor as it revolves. All laugh*] Come, gentlemen, have a drink. [*All go to the bar. Enter Bingo through door in flat with a pail of water, which he throws out of the open window. Will Peak is outside window and is wet. He shows head in window and throws another pail of water into the room; it had been standing outside. Bingo is wet*]

WORTH: Who threw that water in here?

PERRY: Will Peak? He's spying around against Oakhurst. You had better look out for a raid tonight.

OAKHURST: I hope not. I've had trouble enough lately.

WORTH: Bingo, are you coming to the raffle tonight?

BINGO: No, I'm going to church.

MINK: Yes, he's fallen in love with that new gal up at the parsonage. He got a quarter this morning and what do you suppose he did with it?

OMNES: What?

MINK: He bought a toothbrush! [*All laugh*]

VIALL: Well, that's what I call squandering money.

BINGO: Well, it would be in your case. Say, paw, maw wants you to come home right now.

MINK: I'll come home when I get good and ready.

BINGO: Well, you'll get ready soon enough if she comes after you. [*Goes toward door*] Say, here comes old Pray!

OAKHURST: Boys, cover up the drinks quick! [*Business of hiding the drinks. Enter Pray: he speaks to Oakhurst*]

PRAY: Miss Ruth Hardman requested me to give you this parcel for your children, as she was unable to come herself. The string broke as I was carrying it here; so I could not avoid seeing what it contained. Lots of nice things!

OAKHURST: Won't you thank her for me and tell her I am deeply grateful. [*Exit Pray. Oakhurst comes down C.*] And I always thought she had been taught to hate a saloon-keeper. Bingo, will you tend shop a minute? [*Exits C.D.L.*]

PERRY: Say, boys, did you see the tears in Oakhurst's eyes?

VIALL: Yes, that little act of hers has broke him all up.

PERRY: That circumstance reminds me. Speaking of Ruth Hardman –

WORTH: Hush! Suppose we don't mention a lady's name in a barroom! [*Bingo has small stove-shovel and scuttle. Takes ashes out of stove; then goes to every one of the characters who are smoking and knocks ashes off their cigars into the scuttle; all look surprised. Bingo exits quietly, whistling, out of door. Mink, who is sitting on chair R., rises and dashes his cigar on the floor; then he sits down, disgusted*] Why do they call these temperance folks ramrods?

PERRY: I suppose it's because they are so straight.

MINK: I don't think it is a very appropriate name. A ramrod puts in a load; that's something they don't do.

VIALL: I see by the papers that there's a fellow out West who has invented a scheme to make it rain.

MINK: Well, I wish I could invent a scheme to raise the wind.

WORTH: Mink, is it true that married men live longer than single men?

MINK: No. Married men don't live any longer. It just seems longer.

VIALL: What paper is that?

WORTH: The Springfield *Reporter*.

VIALL: Well, read us the news of the town.

WORTH: All right. "Weatherfield notes: The entertainment at the schoolhouse was liberally patronized last Saturday evening."

MINK: Yes. Eight women, six children, a dog, and myself.

WORTH: "Street fakers are becoming numerous of late and it is proposed to place an additional tax on lightning-rod agents."

VIALL: Yes. Them confounded lightning-rod agents is a nuisance. They ought to be stopped from coming around. They are the curse of the country.

WORTH: "Vandals have lately been stealing the flowers from the graves in the country."

VIALL: Gol darn it! I'd like to catch them stealing flowers from my grave! I'd fix them!

WORTH: "Elder Whizzle is now eighty-two years old. He looks well, but he is a little lame in the left knee."

VIALL: Only eighty-two? Why, he ought to be spry! When I was eighty-two I could walk ten miles and never stop for a rest.

WORTH: "The person who took the hoe from Abner King's barn is respectfully requested to return the same at once." [*Mink starts to leave. Worth runs after him and pulls him back*] What's the matter?

MINK: I don't want the damned old hoe anyhow. I'll bring it back right away. [*He sits down again*]

VIALL: I call that Springfield *Reporter* the best paper in the country for news. They say it stands next to the New York *Clipper*. I took it for two years. [*Enter Bingo; he goes to bar as if to buy a drink*]

MINK: Hello! Going to buy liquor? Don't do it. Lend it to me.

BINGO: Not much!

MINK: Haven't I always given you the benefit of my example, how not to act? How much have you got?

BINGO: Twenty cents.

MINK: Well, if you're going to spend it, don't let it go out of the family. [*Goes to bar with Bingo*]

BINGO: As I was coming up the street, I was met by old Mother White. She says to me, "If you go into that place" – meaning here, "you'll surely be damned!" Then I said, "I'll be damned if I don't!" [*Raises glass to drink*]

PERRY: I say, Bingo, what does that little gal up to the house say to you?

BINGO: [*Dropping glass from mouth slowly*] She said if I stopped drinking and took care of myself, folks would respect me and wouldn't call me Bingo any more. [*Sets glass of liquor untouched on the counter*]

MINK: Ain't you going to drink?

BINGO: [*Going to door*] No, I ain't. I'm going to take this money home to mother. Any fellow that lets his mother work as hard as mine does and don't try to help her is of no account. [*Exits*]

WORTH: If that boy had been raised right, he'd have made a good man.

MINK: Yes, and learned to despise me. That's the way. He'll bring it home to his mother and waste it buying flour. [*Enter Oakhurst*]

OAKHURST: Come, gentlemen, and look at the turkey we are to raffle tonight. [*Shows turkey*]

MINK: Ain't it a beauty?

WORTH: I'll have a few throws for that anyway.

PERRY: So will I.

MINK: Say, won't we just whoop things up here! [*Enter Mrs. Jones*]

MRS. JONES: You'll just come home and whoop things up in the woodshed! You're a nice man to leave me home doing all your work besides my own, while you come here and drink up all both of us can earn. You ought to be ashamed of yourself! [*Cries*]

MINK: My dear, this language!

MRS. JONES: Don't talk to me, but come right home.

MINK: Gentlemen, I know you will excuse my wife. This is the first time she has ever been in a barroom, and – and –

MRS. JONES: Yes, and it's all your faults. You're nothing but a set of drunken brutes!

MINK: Once more, gentlemen, I apologize for my wife's actions. It is nervous prostration. She is unaccustomed to these surroundings. You must excuse her. There, my dear, show them that you are a lady by birth and education. Let them see that you are still the same beauty and wit they all used to admire.

MRS. JONES: You ought to be ashamed of yourself.

MINK: I know I am to blame, my dear. I appreciate your delicate feelings and understand that you wish to retire from this place which does not befit a lady of your attainments to be seen in. [*Urges her slowly to door*]

MRS. JONES: Then you will come home at once?

MINK: Yes, my dear. [*Kisses her*]

MRS. JONES: Oh, Mink! Mink! [*Kisses him*]

MINK: [*At door*] Now hurry, my dear, hurry. Let no one see you leaving this place. I will follow. [*Kisses her again as she exits. He kicks his leg at crowd inside*]

MRS. JONES: [*Outside*] Be sure and come home.

MINK: Yes, my love. Take care now. Don't fall down. [*Shuts door and comes downstage*]

WORTH: Mink, you're a wonder.

VIALL: If I had a wife like that, I'd lick her.

MINK: Oh, you would? Boys, Uncle Joe's going to treat!

VIALL: No, I ain't! I said, "lick her"!

MINK: Well, that's what we want, "liquor"!

VIALL: You're a liar! You – you – damned fool! Don't you know the difference between "lick her" and "liquor"?

MINK: You bet I do!

PERRY: The idea of a woman talking like that to her husband!

MINK: What did she say that was unbecoming a lady?

PERRY: She called you a drunken brute!

MINK: Well, ain't I? See here! I've been married to my wife for twenty-two years. She's put up with my faults all that time, and anybody that says a word against her – well, I'll lick him! [*Squaring off*]

WORTH: Hold on there, Mink. Wes meant no harm. [*Enter a little girl, one of Crossman's children*]

644

CHILD: [*To Oakhurst*] Father sent me down here and told me to ask you to fill this bottle.

OAKHURST: He sent you here after whiskey?

CHILD: Yes, sir.

OAKHURST: Go right back and tell him if he wants it to come for it himself! A saloon is no place to send a little girl! Here's a nickel for you to buy some candy with.

CHILD: But he says he'll lick me if I come home without it.

MINK: [*Jumping up from chair*] Will he? Come, little girl, I'll go home with you! [*Takes girl's hand and exits with her F.R.*]

VIALL: Well, if he hadn't gone, I would have. [*Enter Bingo*]

OAKHURST: Gentlemen, I have never sold liquor to a minor yet.

PERRY: Well, here's Bingo. Say, Bingo, ain't you a minor?

BINGO: No, I ain't. I got a vote and I ain't going to sell it for no three dollars, neither.

VIALL: That's right! Don't vote at all if you can't get five dollars for it!

BINGO: I've made up my mind I'm going to be a brakeman, a detective, or a Negro minstrel.

PERRY: Why, what would you do as a detective?

BINGO: Don't you remember the night I caught you down at the mill?

PERRY: [*Jumping up quickly and putting his hand over Bingo's mouth*] Not a word about that, or there'll be trouble! I'll lick you! Come on, will you have a drink?

BINGO: I guess I'll not drink just now.

VIALL: Well, if you're going to be a minstrel fellow, you ought to give us a song.

BINGO: Excuse me, I don't sing for nothing.

WORTH: We'll take up a collection.

BINGO: I guess I'll take up the collection first. [*He passes the hat around, going to Viall last of all. Viall pretends not to understand what is going on. Bingo stands looking at him. At last, business of Viall feeling for money, which he grudgingly drops in hat. Bingo counts out money, two dimes, a quarter, and a copper penny. He looks at old Viall disgustedly; then goes to door*]

WORTH: Hold on! Where are you going?

BINGO: Going to take this home to mother.

WORTH: But we want the song first.

BINGO: All right. [*Goes to Viall who is sitting on chair R. Business of both trying to strike proper key. After a while Bingo does song and and dance after the style of a country boy who has been to a minstrel show and who endeavors to imitate song and dance man: "When Pop Was a Little Boy Like Me." Exits D.L.F.*]

WORTH: That boy has improved wonderfully of late.

PERRY: Yes, and it's all due to that little gal in the parsonage. She's bound to make a man of him.

WORTH: Heaven bless such girls! If these temperance folks would talk less and import more pretty girls, their cause would prosper more. [*Enter Dr. Sawyer*]

PERRY: I bet I know what he's after: money!

DR. SAWYER: Oakhurst, it's about time you settled that little bill. I've waited long enough.

OAKHURST: You'll have to wait a little longer. I haven't got it about the house at present.

DR. SAWYER: Oh, that's nonsense! You're a business man. You're never without money. I'll wait no longer. [*Enter Pray D.F.*]

PRAY: Oakhurst, let me have a pint of whiskey! My mother is sick and I must have it at once!

OAKHURST: But why don't you go to your own drugstore for it?

PRAY: Because I have no time. Come, Oakhurst, let me have it quick! Suppose your wife or child was sick and I refused to let you have medicine at my store?

OAKHURST: Mr. Pray, I cannot. You know how I am situated.

WORTH: Your mother must have been taken sick very suddenly. I saw her driving toward Springfield an hour ago.

PRAY: She had to turn back. Oakhurst, for mercy's sake, let me have it!

OAKHURST: [*Goes to bar; hands bottle to Pray*] Here then, Pray.

PRAY: And here is the money.

OAKHURST: No, it is a present; I give it to you.

PRAY: But you must take it! I take money from you for what you purchase.

OAKHURST: No. I will not take it.

DR. SAWYER: What, man! Refuse money and owing it to me? Take it, I say! That is my money, not yours, that you are refusing, and I want it! [*Oakhurst takes money. Exit Dr. Sawyer and Pray*]

WORTH: I'm afraid you did wrong then, Fred.

[*Rises and looks out of window*] See, there goes his sick mother now!

VIALL: I'm afraid the ramrods are after you, Fred.

OAKHURST: I hope not. I've had trouble enough already. What will become of my poor children.

WORTH: [*Shakes Oakhurst's hand*] Never mind, old fellow. I'll become your bondsman. [*Enter Mink, D.F.*]

OAKHURST: Welcome. Let's have one more round for luck! [*All go to bar*]

MINK: Just in time.

VIALL: No, boys, don't get me drunk. [*Enter Bingo D.F.*]

BINGO: Fred, here comes the sheriff!

OAKHURST: Quick! Hide the stuff! [*Everybody hides the liquor. Enter Sheriff, Pray, Belcher, Dr. Sawyer, Hardman, Peak, and Officer*]

SHERIFF: I have a warrant for your arrest, Oakhurst, on the charge of selling liquor. Shall I read it?

OAKHURST: It's unnecessary.

SHERIFF: Very well. I have also an order to search the premises. Keep your eye on that man. [*Points to Mink*]

MINK: That's right. Cast a slur on an innocent man!

SHERIFF: Officer, do your duty! [*Officer searches Worth. He snatches a bottle off the table. Officer grabs it as he passes it to Perry. Officer rushes to him; he passes it over head to Viall; Officer grabs at it; Viall snatches it away. Funny struggle among them all. Viall squares off with fists as if to fight. Sheriff eventually gets bottle*]

PRAY: Take him away to the lockup! [*Officer seizes Oakhurst*]

BELCHER: Stop! [*Oakhurst is released*] While I have no sympathy for a rum-seller, I am here to enforce the law. I will do my duty and prosecute this man, but I will not persecute him! If bail is offered, it must be accepted.

WORTH: I will go his bail!

PERRY: And so will I!

SHERIFF: Has every place been searched?

PRAY: Search the cellar! You may find liquor there. [*Goes down into the cellar with Dr. Sawyer, Peak, and an Officer*]

WORTH: [*Aside to Oakhurst*] Is there anything in the cellar?

OAKHURST: Yes, a fresh barrel of beer.

HARDMAN: [*Advances to Oakhurst*] This may seem hard to you, but think of the many crimes you have caused! Think of the unhappy mothers and children you have caused to suffer! Will this not be a glorious Thanksgiving to them?

OAKHURST: Yes, and think of my wife and children! What sort of a Thanksgiving have you made for them when this, their only sustenance, is taken from them!

MINK: You think you are right when you deprive a people of their personal liberty. Suppose we had the making of the law and passed one compelling you to drink two glasses of liquor a day, would you like that?

HARDMAN: No.

MINK: Then let me tell you! You could drink it a damned sight easier than I could let it alone! If a man ain't born a man, you can't make him one by law! When I quit drinking, I'll do it because I want to, and not to please the whim of a lot of cranks like you! As long as you try to reform me by law, I'll drink! And I'll get it, too, and no darn country legislature can stop me, either! [*Great noise in cellar as keg of beer explodes. Peak is thrown over mouth of trap with face disfigured, coat torn; Pray with hat off, face blackened; Dr. Sawyer with one side of his whiskers blown off*]

Curtain

Second Curtain

Everyone off except Oakhurst, who is discovered with head down on bar counter, crying. Enter Mink D.F., on tiptoe. When he sees Oakhurst, he puts his hand in his pocket, takes out coin, and places it slyly on the counter in front of Oakhurst. Then he quietly exits.

ACT III. Scene I

Dining room in parsonage. Door L.3.E. Door R.2.E. Table C. Organ L.I.E. Tablecloth on table. Three chairs beside table.

Discovered: Mrs. Hardman, Mr. Hardman, and Roxey.

MRS. HARDMAN: I wonder what is the matter. I told Mrs. Jones to come early.

ROXEY: Well, everything is ready.

HARDMAN: This will indeed be a happy Thanksgiving, not alone for ourselves, but for others, on account of the glorious results of our works last night. The rum-shop has been closed and the proprietor has been arrested. Another victory in the cause of temperance! [*Knock on door outside. Enter Mink, drunk*]

ROXEY: Why, it's old Mr. Jones.

MINK: Oh, yes; it's old Mr. Jones, and young Mr. Jones, old Mr. Jones's son.

HARDMAN: Mr. Jones, are you in your natural condition?

MINK: Yes. As large as life and as natural as ever! Old Mr. Jones and young Mr. Jones!

HARDMAN: You appear to be under the influence of liquor.

MINK: Well, that's my natural condition! Old Mr. Jones and young Mr. Jones!

HARDMAN: How did you procure the liquor? I thought that all Oakhurst possessed was seized last night and destroyed!

MINK: Yes, I had to drive ten miles over to Springfield to get this load. They emptied everything poor Oakhurst had in the gutter last night. Infernal shame! Some of it mighty good stuff, too! [*Enter Mrs. Jones*]

MRS. JONES: Hello, Mink! [*Astonished*] You here? Did you tell them?

MINK: No. Just got here.

MRS. JONES: Just got here?

MINK: Yes, I'm all here. [*Hugs her*] Old Mr. Jones and young Mr. Jones!

MRS. JONES: And I declare! You've been drinking, too!

MINK: Couldn't help it, my dear! So lonely without you!

MRS. JONES: Well, I suppose, poor fellow, you were! For you know, Mrs. Hardman, I'm just that tuckered out I don't know what to do. They raided poor Oakhurst's saloon last night and that poor woman ill in bed with a sick child to look after! I had to go and sit till four o'clock this morning with them. But I must hurry now. You won't have to wait long. I'll have dinner ready in a few minutes. [*Exits hurriedly R.2.E.*]

MINK: I'm going over to Oakhurst's place to try and fix that damned old treadle. [*Exits L.3.E.*]

HARDMAN: That man is ruining her husband: yet she sits up all night to nurse his sick family. [*Enter Viall with a telegram*]

VIALL: They sent me up here with this from the depot. They calculated as how it was something you'd want to know about right away.

HARDMAN: [*Reads telegram*] I shall exchange pulpits with the Reverend Hale on Sunday.

VIALL: Where's Mrs. Jones? I'd like to see Mrs. Jones.

MRS. HARDMAN: You'll find her in the kitchen.

VIALL: Mighty fine gal, that Mrs. Jones. I guess I'll go and see her. [*Exits into kitchen R.2.E.*]

MRS. HARDMAN: How stupid! The idea of sending the oldest man in the village with a telegram! [*Knock outside. L.3.E. Enter Dr. Sawyer and Pray*]

PRAY: I wish to see you, Mr. Hardman, in regard to Belcher. From what occurred last night and from what we have learned today, we are led to believe that he is siding with the enemy and that he does not intend to assist us in our moral warfare.

DR. SAWYER: We are fully convinced that he is lukewarm in the glorious cause of temperance!

PRAY: Yes. Lukewarm is the word! He had no desire to see Oakhurst go to prison last night and insisted that he should have bondsmen.

HARDMAN: Hush! I think matters can be arranged. I will write to my brother in Boston and request him to send an able lawyer to assist in the prosecution.

DR. SAWYER *and* PRAY: A good idea!

HARDMAN: [*To Dr. Sawyer*] Will you inform Belcher of our decision?

DR. SAWYER: Oh, no! My patients are so numerous at present that I cannot find the time. Perhaps Deacon Pray will undertake that duty?

PRAY: Me? No! Decidedly not! [*To Hardman*] Will you speak to him?

HARDMAN: I have it! I will prepare a note informing him of our decision and requesting his resignation. We will each sign it.

DR. SAWYER *and* PRAY: That will be perfectly satisfactory.

DR. SAWYER: I have a patient to visit, but I'll return directly. [*Exit Dr. Sawyer L.3.E.*]

HARDMAN: Come, Mr. Pray, we will step into

the parlor and prepare the note. [*Enter Ruth with sword*]

PRAY: Surely you are not going to war, Miss Ruth?

RUTH: Sir, I keep this sacred as a relic of my poor, dead brother!

PRAY: Pardon me! I meant not to offend.

HARDMAN: As I said before, Mr. Pray, you can speak to my daughter for yourself. I will abide by her wishes. But come into the adjoining room. We will talk the matter over. [*Exits, followed by Pray*]

RUTH: Probably not, but he always does seem to offend. [*She places the sword on a chair and decorates it with ribbons*] Dear old sword! Although the hand that wielded you is withering in an unknown grave far away from home and those who yearn to feel its honest clasp; although your owner's form has returned to the dust from whence it came; may his spirit come on this Thanksgiving Day, as we place you in his vacant chair and with gentle memories solace those who loved him! [*Enter Worth with package containing roses*] Ah, Mr. Worth, I am so glad to see you!

WORTH: I have taken this privilege to bring you some flowers.

RUTH: Oh, how kind of you! You always seem to guess what I want. Are they Maréchal Niel?

WORTH: No; they are real American Beauties.

RUTH: But surely you could not have obtained them in this neighborhood! You must have sent to Boston for them!

WORTH: I did.

RUTH: Then they must have cost quite a fortune.

WORTH: Surely ten dollars is not a great deal of money.

RUTH: It is, if it is squandered on useless articles.

WORTH: I don't think I am in the habit of squandering money.

RUTH: Not even in a saloon?

WORTH: Believe me, the few dollars I spend there bring as much calm joy and sunshine into the lives and the hearts of those old men as these roses do to you.

RUTH: Then they must love liquor very much!

WORTH: They do, and I am almost certain that I do as much good in lightening the lives of those poor old fellows as you do by going to church.

RUTH: By the way, do you go to church very often?

WORTH: No. Dickens is my Bible, and among those old fellows I at times fancy that I am Nicholas Nickleby, that Pickwick is my intimate friend, and that Micawber is waiting for something to turn up in the drink line. This world would be much poorer if deprived of the creations of Dickens. Could we stand to lose Sam Weller, Mrs. Gamp and old Scrooge, Tiny Tim and Tabby Becks, Mr. Boffin and Silas Wegg, Captain Cuttle and Jack Bunsby? These are the people who have lived and moved and we know them. These are characters that will live and do live in memory and literature, in their laughter. If you desire to study character, there is no place like a country barroom.

RUTH: You surely do not expect to find Dickens in a barroom!

WORTH: I sometimes think Dickens must have spent more than one day in a barroom.

RUTH: Yes; but he probably made use of it. You don't!

WORTH: I will struggle along and probably may find use of it some day.

RUTH: Well, see that you don't struggle very hard. Industrious men frequently overtask themselves, and you seem to waste a good deal of your ten-dollar time in doing nothing.

WORTH: Who ever heard of a woman falling in love with a man because he was industrious?

RUTH: I didn't speak of love. [*Laughs*] But I have no right to question your method of living. Pardon me!

WORTH: It is not necessary. I rather like it. Come, tell me my shortcomings.

RUTH: Do you mean it?

WORTH: Yes.

RUTH: Then ask my father.

WORTH: Ah, no. I'd rather not!

RUTH: A woman likes to know that the man she loves has some definite purpose in life. But come, let us change the subject. This is Thanksgiving Day, and on every anniversary of this day, I take this sword and place it on my brother's chair. Poor fellow, he went away to war on Thanksgiving Day!

WORTH: Was he killed?

RUTH: We have no reason to believe otherwise. This was sent home by a comrade who brought a short message. Since then, we have heard nothing of him and can only suppose that he rests upon some Southern battlefield among the unknown dead. If he were only buried here, it would be some comfort and a blessing to mother!

WORTH: And to you also?

RUTH: Yes.

WORTH: If he had died upon the field while in active service, some trace of him could be discovered by communication with some member of his corps.

RUTH: Father sent to Washington and searched the records, but he could find no clue that was of any service.

WORTH: [*Aside*] I wonder if it is possible? [*Pause*] By Jove, I'll try! [*Aloud*] Well, Miss Ruth, I regret that I have to leave you today.

RUTH: Surely you are not going away?

WORTH: I have very important business which will take me from this village for a time, but before I go I will bring you around this month's *Harper's* and call to say good-by. [*His actions show that he wants to embrace and kiss Ruth, but he restrains himself. Ruth takes both his hands in hers. Worth speaks with great self-control*] Adieu! For the present! [*Exits L.2.E.*]

RUTH: [*After a pause*] I forgot to thank him for those roses! [*She runs to the window and looks out after Worth. Enter Roxey*]

ROXEY: Miss Ruth, do you know that old man came into the kitchen to talk to Mrs. Jones and he sat square down on a hot mince pie!

RUTH: Did it hurt him?

ROXEY: No, but it ruined the pie! [*Enter Viall pursued by Mrs. Jones*]

MRS. JONES: Don't you ever dare show your nose in that kitchen again, or I'll scald you, you old fool, you! [*Exits into kitchen R.2.E.*]

VIALL: Ah, she don't mean it! She's only a little bit mad! By gosh, that pie was hot! She's a mighty fine gal, I tell you!

ROXEY: I hope you've had your lesson and that you'll stay out of the kitchen now! You ought to be ashamed of yourself running around after girls at your age!

VIALL: What's age got to do with it? A woman is as old as she looks, but a man is as old as he feels! I'm just as spry as I was sixty years ago. Why, everybody talks of my being so spry,

and I can sing a better song than any of your milksop fellows that's running around this town!

ROXEY: Sing, Uncle Joe, and let us hear you!

RUTH: Yes. Do I know your favorite? [*Goes to organ and starts to play "I'm Just as Young as I Used to Be." Old Viall clears his throat and sings, after several false starts. At close of his song, he tries to dance. At that moment, enter Hardman accompanied by Pray*]

HARDMAN: What is the meaning of this?

RUTH: [*Embarrassed*] Uncle Joe was only singing. [*She rises*]

HARDMAN: It seems my house is getting very gay. Daughter, go to your room! I have business with Mr. Pray. [*Ruth exits D.F.*]

VIALL: I guess I'll go, too! [*Exits L.2.E. Roxey exits R.2.E.*]

HARDMAN: As I was saying, Mr. Pray, I do not wish to interfere with my daughter's happiness. I will leave the matter entirely in her hands. As for me, I cannot withhold my consent from one who has been so earnest a worker in the glorious cause of temperance.

BELCHER: [*Shouting from outside. Much noise*] I will see them face to face! [*He rushes in, furious. Mink follows*]

HARDMAN: What is the meaning of this conduct?

BELCHER: [*Furious*] It means I'm on to you! You, sir! To write a letter and discharge me! I won't give you the chance! No! I'll fool you! [*Angry*] I'll resign! You're going to send to Boston for a lawyer, are you? Well, I'll give you all the law you want! I will appear in behalf of Oakhurst, who is a victim of oppression! I will offer my services free and defend him against your vile conspiracy! In the cause of the downtrodden and the oppressed I am ever ready to do my duty. Furthermore, we are going to form a Personal Liberty League in this village, and Mink Jones there shall be president. We intend to prosecute you for conspiracy! I know your records! Every one of you! [*To Pray*] You want the saloon closed up so that you can get all the rum there is in town to sell in your drugstore! You sneak! You hypocrite! [*Pointing and shaking his finger at Dr. Sawyer*] You want people to pay you for prescriptions to get it! And as for you, [*Pointing at Hardman*] it is a personal grudge that you hide under the cloak of religion! Your cloth protects you, but you're a fraud, a mossback, and a shellback! And don't you forget it, you whited sepulcher! [*Exits L.2.E. in great haste*]

PRAY: This is really a most unpleasant affair.

HARDMAN: Never mind. He is not worth noticing! Dismiss him from your mind! My daughter is in the parlor, if you wish to see her.

PRAY: This scene has quite unnerved me. Perhaps I had better defer —

HARDMAN: Not at all! There is no time like the present! [*Pray bows to Hardman. Exits D.F.*] Well, Mr. Jones, what have you to say?

MINK: Not a word.

HARDMAN: What do you mean by a "Personal Liberty League"?

MINK: All I know is, I'm to be president.

HARDMAN: I know that you're opposed to prohibition.

MINK: No, I'm not, so long as they don't enforce it.

HARDMAN: [*Going to door in flat*] So Belcher is going to defend this rum-seller. Well, I'll have the best lawyer in Boston to prosecute him in the glorious cause of temperance! [*Exits door in flat. Enter Mrs. Jones and Roxey with dishes R.2.E.*]

MRS. JONES: Why, Mink, what are you doing here now?

MINK: Say, Belcher has been here and scared the life out of old Pray and the parson!

MRS. JONES: Mink — Mr. Jones —

MINK: Excuse me — *President* Jones of the Personal Liberty League!

MRS. JONES: Well, President Jones, will you just help me with that table?

MINK: Certainly! I'm not going to stand by and see my wife do any hard labor! [*Enter Bingo L.3.E.*] Bingo, help your mother with that table! I've got to go over to the saloon and help. [*Exits R.3.E. Bingo helps with the table downstage with Mrs. Jones, who then exits*]

ROXEY: St. Julian, will you help me with this tablecloth?

BINGO: Certainly, I will.

ROXEY: Now take hold of the corner and help me fold it. Keep folding until you come up to me, just like this. [*Bingo drops the cloth when he gets close to her and turns away*] Why, what's the matter?

BINGO: Say — do you smell whiskey?

ROXEY: Why, you haven't been drinking again?

BINGO: No, but I've been around dad all day. Say, are you going to church tonight?

ROXEY: Why, yes.

BINGO: I'll be there. [*He keeps his hand up before his face*]

ROXEY: Don't you always go to church?

BINGO: Not when there's good fishing.

ROXEY: Don't you ever go to Sunday School?

BINGO: Just before Christmas, and because you go.

ROXEY: But you shouldn't go on my account. Don't you love the Lord?

BINGO: Don't know him! [*Enter Mink in time to hear last remark*]

MINK: Yes, church is a mighty good place to go to make love in! But if you think all the folks that go to church love the Lord, you'll get left. Please give this to Mrs. Hardman, Roxey. [*He hands her a small paper bundle*]

ROXEY: Carry the bundle for me, will you, St. Julian?

BINGO: All right. Is it heavy?

MINK: I carried it, didn't I? [*Bingo looks at the bundle, and hefts it*]

ROXEY: [*Disgusted*] Oh, give it to me! [*She picks up the bundle and exits R.2.E.*]

MINK: [*Stands watching Bingo, who has look of amazement on his face*] Sparking, are ye? Well, she's a mighty nice gal. It's natural for the Joneses to talk to the gals. I've a good mind to cut you out, if I had the time. [*Goes to door L.*]

BINGO: But you can't do it.

MINK: Why can't I do it?

BINGO: Because you'd have to give up what I did, and you couldn't! [*Laughs and pushes Mink out of door before him. Enter from flat L.C. Ruth and Pray*]

RUTH: I have already told you, Mr. Pray, that your entreaties are in vain. My decision is final, and I cannot consent to become your wife!

PRAY: Then we are to be enemies?

RUTH: I see no reason for that! [*Enter Worth L.3.E.*]

WORTH: [*Grabbing Pray by the shoulders and forcing him to the door*] There's a customer over at your store and you must go there immediately! [*Pushes him out and closes door*]

RUTH: Why — how will Mr. Pray feel?

WORTH: I presume he feels very much put out. But before I say good-by, I want to ask you a little question. Do you think you will regret my absence?

RUTH: I – I – think – that I will miss you. [*Coming down*]

WORTH: I hope so. [*Drawing near Ruth*]

RUTH: Why?

WORTH: Because – [*He puts his arm about her waist*] because I want to be your husband!

RUTH: Dare I trust my happiness to you?

WORTH: You may! I will be glad to see the day we love each other! Will it ever come?

RUTH: But is that all you want to know?

WORTH: For the present, yes. When I have proved to you that I have a definite object I will ask you another question. But I must hurry to catch my train. By the way, I have brought you *Harper's* for this month. Look it over. You may find something of interest in it. And now I must say good-by. [*Holds both of Ruth's hands*]

RUTH: Good-by, and I wish you a pleasant journey. [*Worth exits door in flat. Business of Ruth at window as before*] He's gone! He's gone, and now I'm so sorry! Why did he give me this magazine? I wonder if there is anything in it of interest to me. Let's see. [*She turns pages of magazine*] "Life in Alaska." No, no. Rather a chilly subject. "Account of the Australian Gum Tree." That's not very interesting. Why! [*Astonished*] Here is the exact picture of our house! And here is a picture of the saloon, too! What is this? "How Mink Jones Always Holds Four Aces. By John Worth." Then he hasn't been wasting his time! Oh, how glad I am to know it and to think that this story was written by him! [*She sits on the piano stool, propping the open magazine on the music rack of the piano, and becomes greatly absorbed in the story. Enter Roxey and Mrs. Jones with the dinner R.2.E.*]

MRS. JONES: Miss Ruth, dinner is ready. [*Pause*] Miss Ruth, dinner is ready! [*Ruth takes no notice*]

ROXEY: Miss Ruth, dinner is ready! [*Very loud*] Miss Ruth, dinner is ready!!!

RUTH: [*Startled*] Oh, very well.

MRS. JONES: Roxey, call dinner, will you?

ROXEY: [*To doors*] Dinner! [*She calls it louder several times and then exits door in flat. Enter*

Hardman and Mrs. Hardman. Ruth crosses to chair R. of table. Mrs. Hardman stops by chair where sword rests and leans on the chair]

HARDMAN: My poor boy! Gone but not forgotten! [*Enter Pray in excitement*]

PRAY: I've come on an errand. I felt it my duty to deliver this letter. It is in your daughter's handwriting. This was intended as a warning to Oakhurst of our raid last night. I caused it to be intercepted. It was in the bundle of things she was taking to Oakhurst's children.

HARDMAN: Daughter, is this true?

RUTH: [*Defiantly*] Father, it is!

HARDMAN: [*To Pray*] Well, sir, I presume your errand is done?

PRAY: [*Going*] I don't seem to get much thanks.

HARDMAN: Virtue is its own reward. [*Exit Pray*] Daughter, why did you do this? Why did you seek to shield the rum-seller?

RUTH: Because he was a Union soldier like my brother!

HARDMAN: And are you not sorry?

RUTH: No! I'd do it again!

HARDMAN: You must retract those words, or you cannot remain in my house! [*The Hardmans stand rigidly. Ruth looking at her father. Final business of Ruth walking with quiet determination towards the door as slow curtain falls*]

Curtain

Second Curtain

Tableau – Mr. and Mrs. Hardman stand alone in their dining room. Ruth has gone.

HARDMAN: [*Pointing to her chair*] Another vacant chair!

Scene 2

Full stage, showing exterior view of church. Set church running across stage from R.1.E. to R.3.E. Steps leading to door of church R.2.E. Illuminated window of stained glass in church. Banks covered with grass mats scattered around stage with white slabs to represent gravestones. Discovered: Mink on steps of church singing

"They Called Her Lovely Mary, the Lily of the West." Enter Sheriff; sees Mink.

SHERIFF: What are you doing here? Why don't you go home?

MINK: I can't. I've got to go to the saloon to help Fred cut some wood. But what are you doing here? This ain't Sunday.

SHERIFF: There's to be a temperance meeting here tonight and, as Ruth has gone, I've got to play the organ instead.

MINK: Where is she?

SHERIFF: I don't know, and I don't care. Nobody will take her in.

MINK: Why not? Well, there's more damned hogs in this town than I ever knew. [*Exit Sheriff into church. Exit Mink singing "Lovely Mary." At the same time Dr. Sawyer and Belcher enter R.1.E. They look at each other contemptuously. Belcher says "Quack! Quack!" and crosses to L.U.E. and exits. Old Viall enters L.U.E. and goes into the church. Bingo enters L.U.E., crosses to church, runs up steps, looks in, and runs down again. He hides R.1.E. Mrs. Jones and Roxey enter L.U.E. Mrs. Jones goes in first and as soon as Roxey gets halfway up, Bingo calls "Roxey!" She comes down and they go to R.U.E. Then Hardman and Mrs. Hardman enter L.U.E. Behind them enters Ruth. She pantomimes sadly, comes down quietly and kisses the hem of her mother's dress as she ascends the steps. Ruth staggers over to C. of stage and falls on the ground in churchyard. The two Hardmans enter the church*]

RUTH: I don't know where to go for shelter! I am so tired! I must lie down here on this cold grave! [*Enter Pray. He discovers Ruth reclining on the gravestone. She screams and faints*]

PRAY: I guess I must have frightened her. She's fainted. So the new house wasn't good enough for her, eh? Well, let her lie there! [*Exits into church. Enter Mink R.U.E. with the treadle. He stands in C. of stage, holding it*]

MINK: Well, I've carried many a load in my time, but this is the toughest I ever tackled. It weighed over a hundred when I started; now it weighs a thousand. Gosh, I've got to rest.

HARDMAN: [*From inside the church*] Friends, we are assembled here tonight that we may give thanks that we have been freed from the grasp of the demon drink. [*Mink listens to Hardman's voice*] His clutches have been loosened from the throats of our unfortunate brothers who were beguiled by his devilish snares and who allowed themselves to fall into his hands. We should rejoice that the evil of drunkenness has been banished from our midst and that the majesty of the law has been upheld in our peaceful community. Rum makes a man ruin his life. It is the cause of poverty throughout the land. It makes homes unhappy. It destroys the sanctity of family life. It causes children to be crippled by their drunken fathers and the hearts of wives to be made desolate. It makes the strong cruel to the weak, parents cruel to their children, and virtue a slave to vice. Let us rejoice that we are freed from this terrible monster, drink! [*The organ is played inside and the congregation sings a hymn. During the sermon Mink has discovered Ruth. First he covers her with his coat. Then he lifts her in his arms. At the end of the sermon he carries her tenderly offstage R.1.E. As the people come out of the church, they fall sprawling over the treadle that Mink left on the church steps. Old slippery day business*]

ACT IV. Scene 1

Interior of anteroom in courthouse. Two large practical sliding doors open into courtroom. Chair C., also R.1.E. and L.1.E. Shelves L.1.E.

Discovered: Hardman, Mrs. Hardman, and Judge Doe.

HARDMAN: Now, judge, that you are ready, I suppose we will not have to wait any length of time before court opens.

JUDGE: No. We will waste no time. The witnesses for the prosecution will soon be here. But come into my private office and wait there until court is convened. [*Mrs. Hardman exits into Judge's office. Enter Dr. Sawyer, Pray, and Sprague, the Boston lawyer*]

HARDMAN: Ah, gentlemen, we have been waiting your arrival. Judge Doe, permit me to introduce to you Mr. Sprague, the attorney for the prosecution, a famous lawyer from Boston.

JUDGE: I am delighted to meet such a distinguished member of the legal fraternity and trust that our relations will be amicable during the progress of this trial.

SPRAGUE: [*Very suave*] I have no doubt they will be. I had the honor of quoting your decision on at least one occasion.

JUDGE: I trust you found it in consonance with the law. But excuse me, gentlemen, I must prepare for court. [*Exits L.*]

SPRAGUE: Ha! Ha! Peculiar old gentleman! Yes, the opposing counsel, in a case I had at one time, quoted one of his decisions and the case was decided against him as being entirely at variance with the statute. [*Enter Peak*]

PRAY: Well, Peak, are you ready to go on the witness stand?

PEAK: Oh, yes, I'm ready, but I ain't seen that ten dollars yet that you promised me.

PRAY: Oh. That'll be all right. [*Exit Peak*]

DR. SAWYER: By the way, do you know that John Worth is coming here?

PRAY: Yes, I heard of his arrival today.

DR. SAWYER: They say he has become a famous man. He has written a book and has lots of townsfolk in it. I guess you're one, for he speaks of a mighty mean druggist. He must mean you.

PRAY: Do you think so? Well, I heard of it, and he also mentions a rascally doctor who kills all his patients. I think he refers to you.

DR. SAWYER: Does he? Well, I wish I had gotten even with him when I had the chance.

PRAY: How was that?

DR. SAWYER: Why, let him die of the whooping cough and the measles.

PRAY: Here comes the counsel for the defense. [*Enter Belcher with about twenty law books; he places them on a chair*]

SPRAGUE: Indeed? Well, I'd like to meet the man.

BELCHER: [*Pointing to the books*] Here I have a few copies of Judge Doe's decisions.

PRAY: Mr. Belcher, this is Mr. Sprague, the opposing counsel.

BELCHER: [*Looks at him*] And is that the little runt? [*Sprague makes motion as if to answer*]

DR. SAWYER: Don't rile him up.

BELCHER: Watch those books! [*Exits L.*]

SPRAGUE: Pardon me, I'd like to see those books. [*Looks at them*] *Judge Doe's Decision, Judge Doe's Decision.* Why, they're all Judge Doe's decisions. Ha! Ha! Ha! [*Reenter Belcher*]

BELCHER: Another of Judge Doe's decisions. [*Lays book on top of others. Glares fiercely at Sprague*]

SPRAGUE: *Judge Doe's Decision!* I'll go at once and secure every copy there is in town. [*Exits with Dr. Sawyer and Pray R.1.E. Enter Hardman*]

HARDMAN: Mr. Belcher, I must give you thanks for sheltering my daughter in your house.

BELCHER: Yes. I thought Mink's house was no place for her; so I took her to my residence where my wife and I can care for her. The fact that she is your daughter cuts no figure. We don't keep that stored up against her. She's not responsible for the accident of her birth.

HARDMAN: Where is she now? Can I see her?

BELCHER: She is talking outside with my wife. When she's through I'll ask her to meet you. [*Exit Hardman, bowing*] Weakening! Weakening! He's got to give in at last. How I hate an obstinate old man. Well, I'll wait till Hardman gets through his prayers; then I'll go in. [*Enter Mink*]

MINK: Say, Belcher, I want an injunction.

BELCHER: An injunction for what?

MINK: My boy, Bingo, is going to sign the pledge.

BELCHER: What's the matter? Don't you think he'll keep it?

MINK: That's what I'm afraid of. He will keep it! Then what's going to become of him? I want an injunction to stop him from taking the pledge.

BELCHER: You ought to be glad that he will.

MINK: Glad? What? Do you think I want to see all the sunshine and roses taken out of his life? It's not in the nature of the Joneses to do without liquor!

BELCHER: Well, then the Joneses should stop their nature! That young man will be infinitely better off by making the change.

MINK: Now, see here, Mr. Belcher, put yourself in my place. Imagine the feelings of a father who sees his son go to ruin all on account of that damned gal! She made him do it!

BELCHER: Then she deserves credit. The woman who can reform a man where temperance lectures and legislatures fail, and who can in her own quiet way silence the mouths of fanatics

653

and cranks by rescuing a fellow creature from the vice of intemperance, is an ornament to society and deserves a monument. A few earnest women can do more than all your loudmouthed orators in settling the temperance question. May Heaven bless her! Come into the court.

MINK: When Hardman is through saying the Lord's Prayer I'll come in. [*Enter Roxey, Bingo and Mrs. Jones, R.*] Oh, you came to sign the pledge, did you? Well, you're too late. The judge has gone in, court is in session, and you're going to get left.

BINGO: I guess not. I can wait until recess.

MINK: Oh, this is too much! [*To Roxey*] And you're the cause of it!

BINGO: No, she ain't! I'm doing it of my own free will.

MINK: Free will! Who ever heard of a man in love having a free will?

MRS. JONES: Father, why don't you let him alone? You know our boy is much happier than he was before, and you can thank Roxey for it.

BINGO: Yes, father, and everything is settled; so you might just as well grin and bear it!

MINK: I suppose I'll have to bear it, but I'll be damned if I grin. [*Exit Roxey and Mrs. Jones. Bingo starts to follow*] Say, Bingo, what are you going to do with that gal?

BINGO: Get married.

MINK: What! To that insect! Why, she'd never be able to do a day's washing! She never could support you!

BINGO: I don't want her to. I mean to support her. [*Exit L.*]

MINK: It's a mistake. That boy is no Jones! [*Exits L. Enter Hardman and Ruth L. Ruth crosses and Hardman stands L.*]

RUTH: Father!

HARDMAN: You have left my house and disobeyed my wishes, but your mother is ill and desires your return.

RUTH: My mother! [*Affectionately*]

HARDMAN: You have given help to one who has caused misery to others, to one who drove your own brother away to fill an unknown grave. I now ask you to return for your mother's sake. I feel that her life depends on it. Woman is a creature of instinct, and I believe that sympathy led you to your foolish

act. I cannot forgive, but I will condone! And now, I ask you if you will return.

RUTH: For my mother's sake, yes! Where can I find her?

HARDMAN: In Judge Doe's private office. [*He points L. Ruth exits. He looks after Ruth*] Ruth once more under my roof! But still, for me, there will be two vacant chairs. [*Exits L.*]

Scene 2

Courtroom. Judge in high stand C. Jury R. Table and two chairs in front of judge's stand. Prisoners' box near jury. Flats draw off to make this scene.

Discovered: Jury in jury box R. Witnesses L. Belcher and Sprague at table C. Judge Doe in his place. Hardman, Peak, Dr. Sawyer, Mink, Bingo, Roxey, Mrs. Jones, Pray in spectators' places at opening of flats. Noise.

JUDGE: Order! Order! [*Pray is on the witness stand*]

BELCHER: [*Coming down C.; to Pray*] You say you purchased liquor from the defendant?

PRAY: Yes.

BELCHER: What means did you employ to get this liquor?

SPRAGUE: [*Excited*] I object! I object!

BELCHER: [*Excited*] Shut up! Shut up! I know my business!

JUDGE: Order! Order! Order!

BELCHER: Did he not say to you that he could not and would not accept pay for the liquor?

SPRAGUE: I object! [*Excited business with Belcher*]

JUDGE: Order! Order!

BELCHER: Did you not work upon the defendant's sympathy by saying that the liquor was intended for your sick mother? And don't you know she was out riding at the time and you were guilty of a deliberate lie?

SPRAGUE: I object! I object! [*Same business of running up and down in excited manner. Both Belcher and Sprague shout to each other ad lib and slap hands*]

JUDGE: Order! Order!

BELCHER: That man worked on my client's sympathy to obtain the liquor!

SPRAGUE: I object! I object!

BELCHER: Your Honor, I claim the right to speak in this court and do not propose after fifteen years' experience to be dictated to by a mealy-mouthed, pie-eating Boston dude!

JUDGE: Order! Order!

SPRAGUE: Your Honor, I request that the counsel for the defense will allude to me as the opposing counsel.

BELCHER: Opposing counsel! Why, you're no opposition at all! [*Same business as before*]

JUDGE: Order! Order!

SPRAGUE: I didn't come here to be bulldozed by a Vermont pettifogger, whether his name is Belcher, Welcher, or Squelcher.

BELCHER: You'll think it's Squelcher before you're through!

SPRAGUE: Is this court going to be conducted according to law or according to the rush rules of the London prize ring?

JUDGE: This court will be conducted according to my decisions.

BELCHER: [*To Pray*] Now – how do you know that this bottle contains liquor?

PRAY: Well, I thought so.

BELCHER: You thought so! Did you taste it?

PRAY: No; that's against my principles.

BELCHER: Oh, then you are not sure! You merely thought so!

PRAY: Well, I think I thought so.

BELCHER: Oh, you think you thought so! Well, if you think that you thought so, what made you have any reason to think that you thought? You should have thought so!

SPRAGUE: I object! I object! [*Business with Belcher as before*] Your Honor, with all due respect to you, I think this man is the biggest fool in town!

JUDGE: With all due respect to me – !!! With all due respect to me – !!!

BELCHER: Your Honor, when this man speaks of fools, he forgets himself.

JUDGE: Order! Order! You're no lawyer!

SPRAGUE: You're no judge! [*Noise*]

JUDGE: Order! Order! I've good a good mind to fine everybody present ten dollars for contempt of court.

SPRAGUE: Well, I'm glad to be put on record as having contempt for this court!

JUDGE: I'll fine you ten dollars!

SPRAGUE: Oh, very well. Do as you please. [*Aside to Judge*] Judge, can you lend me ten

dollars? I have no money with me at present.

JUDGE: Very well; the fine is remitted.

BELCHER: Now, then. I am through with this self-confessed liar who swears he obtained liquor and yet cannot swear to its being liquor. Is there anyone here present who will consent to taste it? [*Several in the audience of spectators, including Mink, spring to their feet to offer, but the jury, in consternation, rise as one man and protest*]

JURY: NO! NO!

MINK: And I was damn fool enough to get out of serving on that jury!

JUDGE: Yes, and if you don't keep quiet, you'll get out of this courtroom!

BELCHER: Now, Your Honor, and gentlemen of the jury, I will review the character of the evidence against my client. In the first place, look at these men who, under the guise of temperance reformers, wish to attain their own selfish ends. This man, [*Pointing to Pray*] who has been so active in the prosecution, wants to sell liquor and have all the money come to his drugstore. Oh, I know them! I know their records! I've been one of them myself! This hoary-headed sinner [*Pointing to Dr. Sawyer*] wants to write his prescriptions for liquor and receive a fee. The parson thinks he is honest in his convictions, but he has motives of personal revenge! Gentlemen, show me a prohibitionist and I will show you a crank, or a man with an axe to grind. They all have a purpose in view, and that purpose is their own selfish interests. Look at the difference between my client and his opponents! They, under the guise of temperance, persecute him! What was he? A Union soldier, struck down by a bullet while trying to help a wounded comrade off the field of battle! Unable to do manual labor, he resorts to a certain calling which is legal in many states, but is considered a crime in Vermont. Working upon his sympathies under the pretense of having a sick wife, this interested deacon of the church and would-be pillar of society induces my client to break the law that he may secure a benefit from it; and he hired a mean, low, measly sneak [*Pointing to Peak*] to bore a hole through his back door and watch his movements. Now, gentlemen of the jury, picture to yourselves my client Oakhurst on the field of battle, wounded by the bullet of an enemy, seeking to shield a dying comrade in the cause of our glorious Union, and then think of this mean, conniving scoundrel peeping through a hole in the back door!

SPRAGUE: Gentlemen of the jury, you have heard the arguments of the counsel for the defense. They are simply vituperation! This man [*Pointing to Oakhurst*] has been an offender against the laws of the State. His crime has been proven. The fact of his having been a Union soldier does not prevent his being a criminal and an offender against the laws which he is supposed to have sworn to protect. I ask you to consider the evidence adduced fairly and to allow your sympathies to be antagonistic to your verdict. The fact of his having been a Union soldier does not acquit him of his crime. [*Sits down*]

JUDGE: Gentlemen of the jury, you have heard the evidence of both parties. In this case, I would advise you to treat the arguments of both counsels with the utmost contempt! [*Sprague and Belcher both jump up*] If you believe from the evidence you have heard that the prisoner sold liquor, your verdict must be guilty. If, on the other hand, you consider the evidence unreliable, your verdict must be favorable to the prisoner. The jury may now retire. Is my lunch ready?

Scene 3

A corridor in the courthouse. Pray, Dr. Sawyer and Sprague enter L.

PRAY: Well, what is your opinion of the case, Mr. Sprague? Do you think we'll win?

SPRAGUE: The Lord only knows. I expect anything of that judge. [*Enter Peak*]

DR. SAWYER: Well, Peak, your memory seems to have been very good from the way you gave that testimony.

PEAK: Well, I can't say much for your memory. You forgot to give me my ten dollars.

DR. SAWYER: Oh – ah – yes. [*Fumbling in his pocket*] Mr. Pray, have you got ten dollars about you?

PRAY: Well, no – [*Same business as Dr. Sawyer*] but I have five.

DR. SAWYER: I have five, too.

SPRAGUE: [*Grabs both bills*] Gentlemen, let me settle this case. Come, Peak, follow me. [*Exits with Peak R.*]

PRAY: A very clever fellow, I must say. Got Belcher quite excited every time.

DR. SAWYER: Yes, I noticed that. But I believe our side will win in spite of the efforts of the rum crowd. [*Enter Sprague*]

SPRAGUE: Well, gentlemen, I fixed it with him for five dollars.

PRAY: Whose five dollars did you give?

SPRAGUE: I believe it was yours.

DR. SAWYER: Then I suppose I may ask you to return mine.

SPRAGUE: Oh, no! That's my fee for the settlement! Excuse me, you don't seem to know much about lawyer's methods.

PRAY: Well, I believe I'll have time to step over to the store for a few minutes.

DR. SAWYER: And I think I'll step into the court and find out how the case is coming on. [*Pray exits D. Dr. Sawyer crosses to D.L., meets Sprague. Sprague crosses, turns quickly, takes Dr. Sawyer down R. and whispers to him*] Only by prescription.

SPRAGUE: Very well, let me have one.

DR. SAWYER: Here! [*Produces book*] I keep them all ready made out. You'll find the drugstore right across the street.

SPRAGUE: Thank you! Thank you! [*Going*]

DR. SAWYER: Excuse me please, five dollars!

SPRAGUE: But I thought – [*Looks bewildered; then hands over money*]

DR. SAWYER: Excuse me, but you don't seem to know much of doctors' methods. [*Exits L.*]

SPRAGUE: Well, I'll be damned! [*Exits L. Enter Judge and Hardman L.*]

JUDGE: Yes, Brother Hardman, I must decline with regret your kind invitation to lunch, as I have already ordered mine. I must also take the opportunity of informing you that I heartily approve of your noble and disinterested efforts on the part of temperance. Ah, here is my lunch. [*Waiter enters with the lunch on a tray covered with large napkin. He drops two bottles of wine to the floor; picks them up quickly, but in such a manner that Hardman sees them. Exits L. Judge is embarrassed*] Ah – the fact is – I am compelled to take a little claret at mealtimes. Doctor's orders, you know; severe stomach trouble! [*Enter

The Great Divide

The New York Idea

Mink with a large whiskey bottle in his hand]

MINK: The jury wants more evidence.

JUDGE: More evidence? What do you mean?

MINK: They require more evidence. They want Exhibit A filled again.

JUDGE: What, sir? Were you in the jury-room? How did you get that bottle?

MINK: No, I wasn't in there. They lowered it by a string from the window.

JUDGE: [*Winking at Mink and pointing to the door L.*] Well, sir, if I found you in that jury-room, I'd fine you a hundred dollars. [*Exits L. followed by Mink*]

HARDMAN: Well, this passes belief. I could scarcely have believed that such things are occurring daily under my very eyes. [*Enter Worth and a stranger. This is Frank Hardman, the son thought dead. Hardman shaking hands with Worth*] Mr. Worth, I am delighted to see you again. I have heard of your success and tender my congratulations in conjunction with a kindly welcome home.

WORTH: I thank you for your kindly interest, but here is an old friend of mine whom I met in Montana. He lived here a number of years ago and was very well acquainted with many of our townspeople. See if you cannot remember him.

HARDMAN: My memory is somewhat defective of late years, but his face is very familiar, and his name is –

FRANK: Frank Hardman! Father, don't you know me?

HARDMAN: My boy! Returned at last! But tell me, why did you stay away all these years and not inform us of your whereabouts?

FRANK: When I left home, I joined the army. I was severely wounded in battle and was carried off the field by a comrade at the risk of his life; he received a bullet in his shoulder while he was saving me. As I lay in the hospital, I reflected on my past life and considered that I might as well be dead as to return and live it over again. On my return, I went to Washington and found that I had been listed as incurable; hence, probably, the rumor of my death. I then went West, where I have accumulated a fortune and where I was discovered by my friend, Worth, who induced me **to return and** to whom we must all be thank-ful for this meeting after so many years. [*Shakes hands with Worth*]

HARDMAN: And are you a temperance man?

FRANK: The best kind of one, for I have learned to use and not abuse the good things of this life. Can you give me your hand on that, father?

HARDMAN: All the theories of my life are breaking down, my boy. But I'm glad you're home, and here is my hand. [*They shake*]

FRANK: But tell me, where are my mother and my sister? Can I not see them?

HARDMAN: Come with me. You will find them in Judge Doe's private office. [*Exit both L. Enter Mink. Shakes hands with Worth*]

MINK: How do! How do! I heard you arrived in town, John. Folks say you are a big man now, and I didn't know whether you'd want to shake hands with us little cusses. So I thought I'd get around here and see you.

WORTH: Friend Mink, you'll find that I have just as firm a grasp as ever for an old friend. Prosperity will never make me vain.

MINK: Well, I never thought it would. But you do look well. It's no use talking. [*Enter Bingo*]

BINGO: Say, dad, your horse is running away! [*Exits L.*]

MINK: [*Surprised*] Well, this is the age of miracles! [*Exits L. Enter Ruth*]

RUTH: [*Gives her hand to Worth*] How can I thank you, Mr. Worth, for your untiring efforts in securing my brother? He has told us all the difficulties you encountered, and I feel that I can never find it in my power to repay you. Still, I assure you that you have my thanks.

WORTH: Yes, that's what an author always gets.

RUTH: Can I do more?

WORTH: Yes! Let me know if the day has come when we have learned to love each other!

RUTH: I – I think it has!

WORTH: [*Embraces and kisses her at the door as they both exit L.*] My darling!

MINK: [*At this moment he is thrown through the door of the court C. and stands outside door as it closes. He looks surprised, but takes it as a matter of course; very nonchalant*] Guilty! It's no use talking! That's what the verdict will be after the jury tackles that last bottle of exhibit. It's a crime for any man to sell such stuff! They'll be putting a tax on every man next year. [*Stage darkens momentarily as side flats are drawn quickly, showing courtroom again. Mink drops into a seat*]

Close In

Scene 4

Courtroom.

JUDGE: Order! Order! The jury having found the prisoner guilty of the crime charged against him, it now remains for the court to pass sentence on him. There are fifty counts in the indictments, and the fines for each count, together with the costs, amount to the sum of $6,190, which sum must be paid into court at once or, in default, the defendant shall be confined in prison for twice the number of days that there are dollars in the fine.

BELCHER: But, Your Honor, this is excessive! My client is a poor man and cannot pay the fine. He would have to serve over fifty years in jail at this rate to settle it!

JUDGE: Such is the law of the state of Vermont.

FRANK: Stay! Is not your name Fred Oakhurst?

OAKHURST: It is.

FRANK: Were you not a member of Company K, Eighteenth New York Volunteers? And did you not carry a wounded comrade off the field of battle at Shiloh, risking your life and being wounded in the attempt?

OAKHURST: That is a fact. I was wounded in the shoulder.

FRANK: Well, I am the man! [*Shakes Oakhurst's hand*] Your Honor, I will pay the fine for this man. I am rich and have the money. He is my comrade and a Union soldier and a brave man, and I will stand by him!

HARDMAN: [*Steps over to Oakhurst and shakes his hand*] We are all guilty of mistakes in our lives. I have made a serious one! I regret that I should have been the cause of injury to one who saved my son's life. May I ask your pardon?

OAKHURST: It is freely granted.

MINK: Yes, and you'll find that a man may have many a noble thought and do many a good action even if he is a rum-seller!

Curtain

SHORE ACRES

JAMES A. HERNE

EARLY in April, 1891, the following announcement was widely circulated among the Boston literary and theatrical communities:

IN THE INTERESTS OF AMERICAN DRAMA

It is generally admitted that the American drama is immeasurably below the work of American painters and novelists, and a despondent tone runs through much that is written upon the subject. We do not share this despondency. We believe with Mr. Howells, Mr. Perry, and other critics in the comparative school, that literary ideals are relative, and that literature, and especially the drama, follows intimately the changes in social life. . . .

As a first modest trial of the independent art theatre we take genuine pleasure in calling attention to Mr. and Mrs. Herne's coming productions of their latest play, *Margaret Fleming*, at Chickering Hall, beginning May 4th. We do this the more readily because these thorough artists have been working alone and (in a literary way) unrecognized in the attempt to bring the accent of life upon the stage. . . .

B. O. Flower
Hamlin Garland

Hamlin Garland was a rising young novelist. B. O. Flower was the editor of the new radical magazine *Arena*.

To assure the readers that this was not an eccentric enterprise nurtured in the unsettled brains of advanced thinkers, the circular included a letter of endorsement from the highly regarded literary master W. D. Howells:

My dear Mr. Herne: –

I am glad there is a prospect of our seeing "Margaret Fleming" on the Boston stage. I told you when I read the play how highly I thought of it, and I feel it is a great loss not to have been at its production in Lynn. It has qualities which I believe will make a stronger appeal than those of any other American play.

While it is wholly and perfectly true in our conditions, it has the same searching moral vitality as Ibsen's best work, and it is most powerfully dramatic. I have no doubt of its success with a fair chance, and with Mrs. Herne and yourself in it, I predict an epoch-making effect for it. Your fidelity to the ideal of truth, the only ideal worth having, is witnessed in every part of it, and it will be recognized by everyone who can feel and think, as a piece of nature and a great work of art.

I do hope you may get it into one of our theatres.

Yours sincerely,
W. D. Howells

An earlier document in Garland's promotion campaign had included a statement signed by William Lloyd Garrison, Barrett Wendell, Howells, and half a dozen other illustrious citizens indicating their intention to attend the performance; an acknowledgment from Herne of their support of a dramatist who wished "to state the truth in drama without restriction or compromise"; and a paragraph by Garland in which he announced that Chickering Hall was going to be Boston's "*Théâtre Libre,* for a week at least."

The Boston intelligentsia may have been ready for Herne's daring venture into "Continental realism." The general public was not. It failed in Boston, as it did a year later in Chicago. With *Margaret Fleming,* Herne was ahead of his time. The American theatre public was fascinated with American folk realism, the realism of authentic local color, the theatrical realism of exciting lifelike spectacles, but it was not yet prepared to tolerate the freethinker's psychological realism, inner realism, the new outspoken, imported, Ibsen-like realism.

Only once in his long career in the theatre did Herne satisfy himself with a mild venture into the new drama that also satisfied the public. And this not until he had passed his fifty-third birthday, when *Shore Acres* was first produced in Chicago in 1892.

Throughout his mature years in the theatre, Herne manipulated a kind of triple career. He wrote plays to please himself and his wife. He was constantly engaged in various theatrical enterprises: touring the country as leading player in his own plays and occasionally in others, and stage-managing (directing) for major theatrical producers. And out of economic necessity, he created and doctored potboilers to the specifications of other actors. He used the three-hundred-dollar advance he got from Tony Farrell for *My Colleen* to pay part of the production costs for *Margaret Fleming.* In one way or another, Herne was conspicuous on the American theatre scene throughout his life.

James Ahern was born at Cohoes, New York, on February 1, 1839. He changed the name to James A. Herne when he went on the stage. His father, Patrick Ahern, was an impecunious, devout, and narrow-minded Irish immigrant who had abandoned his native religion for the more rigorous Calvinistic demands of the Dutch Reformed Church. When young James, with his brother Charles, sneaked off to the theatre in Albany to see the great actor Edwin Forrest, they knew that their backs would be blistered if their folly were discovered. James was fourteen when he first saw Forrest. The adventure opened new prospects for him, and though he never later aspired to emulate Forrest as an actor or as a man, he never forgot this first impression.[1]

[1] In 1960 John T. Herne, James's son, wrote to the present editor: "My old man considered Forrest the greatest actor of all time. . . . [Unlike Forrest] he was never the 'Great Star.' Any old actor could walk in the stage door and even catch him in the wings before he went on and get a fast buck."

James had dropped out of school when he was thirteen and gone to work in a brush factory. During the seven years he devoted to brushes, he read avidly, particularly from Dickens, and committed to memory passages which he recited for his mother. She was the only member of the family who knew of his ambition to go on the stage, and when he left home in 1859 with his accumulated savings of $165, it was apparently with her blessing.

With his impressive fortune, he quickly got an assignment, at no salary, touring the country circuit of Gloversville, Amsterdam, Rome, and Oneida in *The Dog of Montargis*. When the manager abandoned the group, Herne stepped up to "general utility" man at six dollars per week with the Troy Adelphi Theatre. The following year, another rung up the theatrical ladder – he was hired by the Gaiety company in Albany. "I had reached the summit of earthly bliss," Herne wrote later. "My dream was realized. Not a wish remained unsatisfied." Already Herne's associates were becoming aware of the qualities that were to distinguish him throughout his life. He made friends easily, there was always a "humorous twinkle in his eye," and he industriously devoted himself to learning his craft.

When the Civil War began, the Gaiety Theatre closed. Herne briefly contemplated following his father's and brother's example and enlisting, but an offer from the Baltimore manager John T. Ford appeared more tempting. He developed rapidly as an actor, alternating between Ford's Holliday Street Theatre in Baltimore and his theatre in Washington. When the rebuilt Ford Theatre (the theatre in which Lincoln was assassinated on April 14, 1865) was opened in Washington, Herne spoke the dedicatory address. Ford guided his career carefully. When he observed Herne being tempted into too much night life and lazy living by John Wilkes Booth and his cronies, Ford is reported to have told Herne: "If you will drop your present companions, and settle down, I'll guarantee to make you as big a star as Lester Wallack." The handsome Wallack was the commanding star of the New York stage; Herne recognized that his rugged, athletic, masculine body and his round, smiling Irish face did not conform to matinee-idol specifications, but he did respect the admonition to return to more serious study of his profession.

The course of his acting career during the next few years was largely determined by the misfortunes and complexities of a romantic involvement with the Western sisters, Lucille and Helen. He fell in love with Lucille Western in Baltimore. Although her attentions led him to believe she returned his affection, she was already married to the actor James A. Meade. Herne sidestepped the impending difficulties by joining the Walnut Street Theatre company in Philadelphia. For a brief period he was again absorbed in the stage delights of playing with such giants as the elder Sothern, John E. Owens, E. L. Davenport, Edwin Booth, and even his idol, Edwin Forrest. But when

Lucille joined the group and he played Armand to her Camille, the torture became unbearable. He departed for Montreal, where he enlisted with the Theatre Royal company and appeared with Lucille's sister, Helen. During that season he and Helen were married. Although they continued acting together, in Montreal and in New York, Herne attracting particular attention for his performances of Bill Sikes in *Oliver Twist*, the domestic relationship was not firmly established. They were divorced in 1868, and Herne joined Lucille, as her leading man, for a tour of California. (Helen died in December of that year.) Herne and Lucille maintained their professional association until 1874, when she married Arthur Cambridge. There were reports that they were married and divorced, but no documents or evidence from Herne or his family support this claim.

After the California tour, James Fisk hired him as manager of the elegant new Grand Opera House in New York at the phenomenal salary of ten thousand dollars, an assignment that lasted for a single season (1869–70). For the next four years he performed principally in New York and Montreal, and in 1874 he returned to California as manager of Tom Maguire's New San Francisco Theatre and later of Baldwin's Theatre. Herne's theatrical and domestic careers both changed direction in San Francisco. His association with his assistant stage manager, David Belasco, led to his new career as a dramatist. And, of greater significance to both his professional and his domestic life, he married Katharine Corcoran in April, 1878.

Katharine Corcoran was born in County Cork, Ireland, in 1856, came to New York with her family in 1860, and after her father's death in a Washington military hospital at the close of the war, her mother and an uncle took the children to San Francisco. Katharine was determined to become an actress. Mrs. Julia Melville gave her instruction in elocution, dancing, and fencing and brought her to Herne for an audition. He was immediately impressed with her potential talents. He offered her the part of Peg Woffington in *Masks and Faces*, which was scheduled to open just ten days later, and took her on a tour of the coastal cities as his leading lady; when they returned to San Francisco they were married. Herne reported later that he had never seen a beginning actress who possessed such a certain instinct for doing the right thing immediately. If ever a marriage could properly be labeled idyllic, this was it. Throughout their life together the domestic scene was bright and gay and in the theatre they were totally and happily dependent on each other.

Herne's initial attempts at writing for the theatre were undistinguished: an adaptation of Charles Lever's novel *Charles O'Malley*, an adaptation of *Oliver Twist*, and a version of *Rip Van Winkle*. His next attempts were in collaboration with Belasco. First came a dramatization of Gaboriau's *La Corde au Cou*, which they called *Within an Inch of His Life*. In the big scene the hero was saved from the guillotine by the confession of an idiot boy. Another overly contrived melodrama, *Marriage by Moonlight*, was adapted from Watts Phillips's *Camilla's Husband*. Neither was accepted by the audiences at Baldwin's Theatre. The next venture, *Chums*, was begun by Belasco and then revised by Herne. Belasco apparently did not inform Herne that he had taken his plot from an English melodrama, *The Mariner's Compass*, by H. J. Leslie, which had been performed in New York in 1865. In his reworking Herne introduced the quiet, easy dialogue and natural, lifelike characters that were to distinguish his later work. Under Herne's new title, *Hearts of Oak*, and with Herne, Katharine, and, in the child's role, Maude Adams, it was first performed at Baldwin's on September 9, 1879. Although it was not an immediate success in San Francisco, the trio were so convinced of its worth that they decided to move east. After four performances in Salt Lake City, they opened in John Hamlin's run-down variety theatre in Chicago on November 17, 1879. Hooley and McVicker, the principal Chicago managers, had been unwilling to commit their theatres to this risky venture. It was an immediate success, and for the next seven years Herne played *Hearts of Oak* regularly throughout the country.

After they left Chicago there was a series of temporarily unsettling litigations over the play. Hamlin discovered the play's origin and got up his own *Hearts of Oak*. Another manager toured the midwest with an *Oaken Hearts*. Belasco and Herne sued and won. Then in Philadelphia the partners quarreled, and Herne bought Belasco's rights. Although in March, 1880, the play was not welcomed enthusiastically in New York, in Boston it closed the season with a flourish.

With their first child expected in the fall, the Hernes settled in Ashmont, a suburb of Boston, and from that time forward Boston, and later New York, became their domestic center. Their professional territory, however, included the entire country. Each season James and Katharine, when she was not expecting, were out on the road.[2] During the summers Herne worked in his garden and in his study, corresponding with the managers on arrangements for the next season's itinerary and writing on a new play. Dramatic composition always moved slowly for Herne.

His next play, *The Minute Men of 1774–5*, was not ready until 1886. When it opened in Philadelphia on April 6, it was clear that the complex intertwining of historical material – in this case the Battle of Lexington, General Washington, Indians, minute men, British soldiers, and three romances – was not his forte. Even so, he had been sufficiently encouraged by the critics' praise of his

---

[2]Julie, the first child, was born on October 31, 1880. Both Julie and her sister Chrystal became actresses. Dorothy married Montrose Moses, and John (the only heir still living) became a New York stockbroker.

acting and Katharine's to believe it might be successful on tour. He was mistaken. He exhausted all his savings from *Hearts of Oak* attempting to keep the play alive.

The next summer he began another play, *Drifting Apart* (first entitled *Mary, the Fisherman's Child*). And while he was on the road the next season with *Hearts of Oak*, he continued writing, sending the pages home to Katharine as he finished them. The part of Mary Miller was being created for her. In one of her letters she wrote, "My own darling, I am perfectly wild over this part. Oh, if I can only act it as I feel it should be acted. . . . There are so many exquisite things in it." Whenever Herne was on tour without her, they kept up an almost daily loving correspondence; and he always depended upon her judgment about his writing. A new play was a collaborative effort from start to finish. In a recent letter, his son John wrote: "It was their great adoration for each other that made them the greatest team in American dramatic literature. James A. Herne was a great actor, all by himself, drunk or sober, but it was his leading lady, Katy Corcoran, who made him into a great dramatist. . . . No actor was ever hired by my father until he or she had been rehearsed by my mother."

Drifting Apart was first produced at the People's Theatre in New York on May 7, 1888, with the Hernes in the principal roles. The critics and audiences were not prepared for this "problematic, polemic, didactic, sociological disquisition" on the fearful consequences of a man's slavery to drink. Herne's attempt to soften the gloom and depression by depicting the third and fourth acts as dream sequences was ineffectual. Again Herne insisted on taking to the road, and though they recorded 250 performances, these were in second-class houses and thus unprofitable. The principal managers were unwilling to touch such an *avant-garde* play. On one occasion, Herne wrote: "The managers all admit the good points of my play. In fact, they say it is too good. 'The public doesn't want a good play,' they say. 'It wants bad plays. Write a bad play, Jim. Not too bad, but just bad enough' is their advice. Meanwhile I must play in theatres which are not suited to my way of doing things, and I am obliged to insert into my play tricks and turns which I despise." When they returned from the tour, they were forced to mortgage their Ashmont home to cover their losses.

One fortunate new friendship grew out of *Drifting Apart*. Hamlin Garland, a poor young teacher at Brown's School of Oratory, saw the play in Boston. He immediately wrote to Herne, "The second act in this play, for tenderness and truth, has not been surpassed in any American play. A daring thing exquisitely done was that holiest of confidences between husband and wife. . . . Dramatists have gone round the earth in search of material for plays, not knowing that the most moving of all life is that which lies closest to hand after all."

In the summer, after Herne returned from the road, the two men met and became fast friends. The Ashmont house became Garland's second home. And Herne was introduced to a new world of advanced thought: Ibsen and the new realism, Henry George and the single tax. Herne never had an opportunity to see Ibsen performed, but he read the plays and subscribed to Garland's appraisal: "Ibsen is a great herald, his dramas lead to the future, but American dramatists must not imitate him. Ibsen has helped us in our war against conventionalisms, but he must not dominate us. Our drama must be more human, more wholesome, and more humorous."

Neither of Herne's conversions – to Ibsen and to George – helped him in his profession. Theatre managers were skeptical of an actor who spent his Sunday afternoons lecturing on the virtues of the single tax. (Reportedly, some members of the Players Club blackballed him because of his radical economic notions.) Ibsen was equally unpalatable. His demand for characters that lived and spoke their story as they did in life itself, for concentration on a single compelling action, and for the elimination of superfluous dialogue might be accepted, but certainly not his blatant exhibition of those unfortunate aspects of human behavior that should be kept under cover. Every family, every society, had skeletons in the closet, but only "a disordered brain," as William Winter described Ibsen, would expose them in public.

During the next year Herne was at work on *Margaret Fleming*. When the manuscript was ready he gave three tryout performances in Lynn, Massachusetts, beginning on July 4, 1890, in an attempt to stimulate some interest among the Boston managers. Herne's notion that they might see the power of the play more clearly on the stage than they could in the reading backfired. The shock was simply greater. And thumbing through the play was sufficient to convince the New York managers that it was even more outspoken than *Drifting Apart*. Only Abraham Erlanger gave him a favorable hearing. And this not the favor he wanted – Erlanger offered him a hundred dollars a week to be his stage manager. Economic necessity overruled principle. The Hernes sold their Ashmont house and moved to Washington Heights in New York. During the fall and winter he still fought for a *Margaret Fleming* production. Howells, whom he had met through Garland, suggested that he "hire a hall or stable and produce your play in the simplest fashion. The people will come to see it if it is new and vital." He accepted Howells's advice, and, with Garland's help as promoter, the play was presented in the concert hall above the Chickering Piano showrooms in Boston on May 4, 1891, with Herne directing and playing Joe Fletcher, the peddler, and Katharine in the role of Margaret. The Boston intelligentsia spoke favorably of the play, but their talk was not widely heard and their number was limited. The second-week audiences were so pitifully small and the financial debt rising so radically that *Margaret Fleming* was forced to close.

During the summer, Herne persuaded Erlanger to support another attempt. Perhaps Howells's comments in the August number of *Harper's* had helped. He wrote: "The power of this story, as presented in Mr. Herne's every-day phrase, and in the naked simplicity of Mrs. Herne's acting of the wife's part, was terrific. It clutched the heart. It was common; it was pitilessly plain; it was ugly; but it was true, and it was irresistible. . . ." The play opened again at Chickering Hall on October 5. Erlanger underwrote the loss for two weeks and B. O. Flower for the third. It was clearly a failure, and more for Herne than for anyone else. He wrote to Garland, "Of course they look only for the money loss. I look at the failure of my life."

If Herne's indomitable spirit had been subdued, Katharine's had not. She persuaded A. M. Palmer to give the play a special matinee performance in New York on December 9, 1891. Again it failed to arouse any commercial managers to give it a full-scale trial, and the critics treated it coldly. The *Dramatic Mirror* wrote (December 12, 1891): "If it be the purpose of a play to give pleasure, *Margaret Fleming* cannot be called a play." Finally, McVicker, in Chicago, agreed to produce it if Herne would soften the tragic ending by restoring Margaret's sight and reconciling husband and wife. Herne agreed. It opened in Chicago on July 7, 1892, and closed on the sixteenth. The *Tribune* probably reflected the prevailing view: "Those who reject an Ibsen will not readily be reconciled to the comparative crudities of his American disciple . . . but a brave, strong play – one to make people think, though they may not agree with the author." On April 9, 1894, it was produced in New York under the management of two German brothers, Carl and Theodore Rosenfeld, who invested part of the profits they had earned from their German midgets, "The Lilliputians." The play ran for two weeks and was never produced again in Herne's lifetime. Not until Chrystal Herne played her mother's role in Chicago in 1907[3] did the play achieve its proper place in the theatre. Times had changed, as W. L. Hubbard noted in the Chicago *Tribune:* ". . . now this greatest of Herne's dramas will find wide recognition at the American public's hands . . . one of the strongest, best plays yet written by an American." In 1907 audiences were more willing to accept the story of a sensual, unfaithful husband and a forgiving wife who nurses and cares for his illegitimate child after the mother's death. Unfortunately, in the only text of the play now available[4] the couple are reconciled, although Margaret's sight has not been restored.

Even though Herne had committed himself whole-heartedly to the writing and the unnerving production detail of *Margaret Fleming*, he had other

---

[3]In 1915 Julie Herne played the part.
[4]The original was destroyed by the fire at "Herne Oaks" in 1909. Mrs. Herne reconstructed the play from memory.

projects on his writing desk and in his mind, and he continued performing in *Hearts of Oak*. He had begun on *Shore Acres* even before *Margaret Fleming* and had continued writing at it all through this trying period, although it was not completed until 1892. He also proposed working with Howells. In 1889 he had written to Garland suggesting that if ever Howells contemplated a dramatization of *Silas Lapham*, he would welcome a chance to participate as stage manager (director).

Herne's hope for a professional association with Howells never materialized. He did contribute slightly toward Howells's standing as a professional playwright by presenting a special matinee of his one-act tragedy *Bride Roses* on March 5, 1894. This was a single performance for the benefit of unemployed actors. When Howells did send him the Kester-Howells dramatization of *Silas Lapham* in 1898, Herne's comments did not please the novelist. Herne wrote that it was not a play but simply a transcript of the book; "what one must do in order to make a play of a great book is freely *adapt it*." This concluded the project. Apparently the two men were not on friendly terms thereafter.

In addition to the commissioned assignment of *My Colleen* in 1891, he also wrote a comedy of Negro life, *Coon Hollow*, for Klaw and Erlanger, which was never produced, and in the middle of the 1892–93 season, while the Boston opening of *Shore Acres* was being planned, appeared briefly in New York in a Negro role in *The New South*, by Clay M. Greene.

Herne's next play after *Shore Acres* was adapted from Helen Gardener's novel *An Unofficial Patriot*. *Griffith Davenport*, as Herne called it, was four years in the writing (1894–1898) and was produced in New York on January 30, 1899. Unlike other plays of the Civil War, it explored the problem of slavery and the complexities of personal and regional allegiances. Apparently the subject was of little interest to the audience at the moment. During the summer and fall of 1899, at "Herne Oaks," their new home on Long Island, he worked on two projects: a new play, *Sag Harbor*, initially a revision of *Hearts of Oak;* and doctoring and directing *Children of the Ghetto*, by Israel Zangwill.

The directing chore was completed in September, and *Sag Harbor*, with his daughters Julie and Chrystal in the cast, got off to a strong start in Boston on October 24, 1899. The critics praised its humanity, its simple warmth, and its quiet power. A letter of commendation from Barrett Wendell was particularly flattering. He thought the next serious American literary expression would be in dramatic form: "such work as yours goes far to confirm this feeling."

Unhappily, the promise of the opening night was not fulfilled. Not from audience disenchantment; Zangwill's play had exhausted Herne, and just before Christmas he was stricken with rheumatism. Still, he continued through the rugged winter tour of New England and on to Chicago in March, where audiences and critics alike were now attuned to Herne. The *Journal* (March 20, 1900) reported: "What a strange, unwonted delight this is – to find upon the stage between the painted canvas wings, in the yellow glare of the footlights, human life! Just plain, human life, your life, and my life. . . ." However much their enthusiasm warmed his heart, it did not improve his health. An ulcerated foot finally forced him to return home. He had begun his final desperate year.

After an operation and a month's hydrotherapy at Hot Springs, Arkansas, he was back at work, rehearsing road companies of *Shore Acres* and *Hearts of Oak*, and on September 27, 1900, after inadequate rehearsals, he opened *Sag Harbor* in New York. It was the beginning of a nightmarish six months: poor attendance in New York; canceled performances in Ohio; abandoning the company in Pennsylvania to seek rejuvenation at West Baden, Indiana; three weeks of performing in Chicago with his limbs hardly able to function and his voice too weak to be heard; and finally home, for eight final weeks of Katharine's loving care. He died at "Herne Oaks" on June 2, 1901. At his funeral Augustus Thomas said, "He had the courage of truth and an enduring faith in humanity. . . . He saw and knew the sublimity of plain living. He was the apostle of simplicity."

In *Shore Acres* the essential qualities of the man are conspicuously apparent. As his son has said of him, "Jim Herne wrote himself gentle roles because he was a kindly gentle guy and actors respected and loved him."

Herne began working at *Shore Acres*, first called *The Hawthornes*, in the summer of 1888. That summer Katharine and the children vacationed at Lamoine, Maine, across the bay from Mount Desert Island. A real-estate man was stirring up the local citizenry with a project to make Lamoine a second Bar Harbor. Families were quarreling over the slicing up of their properties. One old patriarch was reported to have risen from his deathbed to pronounce a curse on his children if they sold his land. All of this was reported to Herne when the family returned, and he decided to incorporate the setting and the land boom into his new play. The following summer Garland scouted the site and urged Herne to see it for himself. The family went, lived at the Galt House, visited the lighthouse; Herne sorted out the local incidents and characters that would serve his purpose. On August 5, 1889, he wrote to Garland, "I've finished *The Hawthornes* – rough finished and you'll like some of it." Then the play was put aside for the potboilers and the big adventure with *Margaret Fleming*. It was not until three years later that he had a draft ready to present to the producers.

With the record of two failures, *Drifting Apart* and *Margaret Fleming*, it was not a propitious moment. Erlanger read it, saw possibilities, but wanted

Joseph Jefferson for the part of Uncle Nat, the role that Herne had written for himself. Herne refused. The quarrel ended with Herne's losing his position as stage manager. And as Erlanger pushed him out, he is reported to have shouted, "And you're the last damned anarchist that ever steps foot in this office." Herne was fifty-three, he had worked four years on the play, and now he had been dismissed by the leading New York manager.

Then, out of the blue, he received a letter from McVicker in Chicago, offering to do *Margaret Fleming* and any other new script Herne had available. Herne immediately sent both plays. McVicker demanded some changes. The audience must be kept uncertain about the safety of Sam and Helen; no light in the lighthouse. The quiet ending was too risky; bring on the entire cast, with Uncle Nat going through the manual of arms with his old army gun, and take the curtain as the gun accidentally explodes. And the title must be changed. Herne reluctantly agreed. As *Shore Acres Subdivision*, it opened in Chicago on May 23, 1892. Although the reviews were generally favorable and Herne was highly praised for his performance, when the play closed on June 11 to make way for *Margaret Fleming* it had not yet captured the audience. Even a second title change to *Uncle Nat*, halfway through the run, had not helped.

Again an unanticipated circumstance gave the play its second chance. The Boston manager R. M. Field needed a play to fill in for an English play that had failed in its tryouts. *Shore Acres* opened at the Boston Museum on February 20, 1893, the coldest night of the winter. Herne did not direct. He was on a salary of a hundred dollars a week as an actor, plus a small percentage of the profits for the use of the play. After the final quiet close, which Herne had reinstated, the audience sat in churchlike stillness and then broke into wild applause. The critics echoed the response: ". . . its merits are sterling and vital. Uncle Nat is a portrait worthy to hang forever in the Museum gallery" (*Transcript*, February 21); "the most charming bit of dramatic realism . . ." (*Journal*, February 21); ". . . the sweetest, homeliest, most truthful representation of New England life and character that has ever been presented. . . . full of poetic realism" (*Times*, February 26). Within a week the Museum had the largest advance sale in its entire history. *Shore Acres* ran for one hundred nights. As the *Boston Budget* (February 24) indicated, Herne had now adapted the new realism to American tastes:

One cannot but wonder that the author is the same James A. Herne who wrote *Margaret Fleming*. The latter play, Zolaesque in motive and Ibsenesque in treatment, is realistic and repellent; the former is realistic and attractive. The same man wrote both; but where in the first, he carried his hearers into the depths, in the second we see him struggling to reach the heights.

Herne had finally struck the high note, as playwright and as actor. For the next season, at Miner's Fifth Avenue Theatre, he was to receive $250 per week as actor and royalties scaled from 50 per cent up to 75 if the profits went over forty-five thousand dollars. His prospects were brighter than they had ever been.

It was a most inappropriate moment for the 1893 financial panic. With banks closing and railroads collapsing, the theatre became a dispensable luxury. As Herne wrote to Katharine from Providence, where they had begun the pre-New York engagements, "Formerly, in times of panic, the theatres were crowded, for people flocked to them to forget their troubles. Now, they haven't the money." In spite of the economic hazards, Herne continued; and when the play opened in New York on October 30, 1893, for the first time in his life Herne received the critics' full praise (Winter excepted!). Even Alan Dale, who was regarded as the most dangerous skeptic, wrote in the *Evening World* (November 1, 1893): "It is truth, the unerring brush with which he paints familiar colors, and his peculiar gift of being able to detect the humorous and the pathetic. I would take criminals in a body to see it, and rely more upon its effect than upon all the sermons that coldly inundate those unfortunates." The other reviewers were equally enthusiastic. The *Mercury* (October 31) said, "Mr. Herne's play marks an epoch in the drama of the American stage," and the *Journal* (October 31), "Last night was seen one of those pieces of theatrical work that comes but a few times in a century. . . . One of those plays that mark an epoch as did *Hernani* . . . the best American play that we have had."

After the play was acclaimed as a solid achievement, the audiences disregarded their financial depression and began filling the house. Then for ten days Herne was forced out of the play. The lighthouse platform collapsed and Herne fell, breaking two ribs and spraining his ankle. The performances continued with Charles Craig substituting for him. On Christmas Day *Shore Acres* moved to Daly's Theatre, where it continued its uninterrupted run until May 26, 1894. The next four years were the happiest period of Herne's life. He performed the play almost constantly until his final appearance in Boston on December 3, 1898.

The gentle command that the play held over audiences throughout the country is even now clearly apparent in the text. It is filled with a love for humanity, with a firm faith in man's essential goodness, and with the true breath of life, simple, direct, and artful, yet without artifice. In the February, 1897, issue of the *Arena* Herne wrote: "I did not set myself the task of writing *Shore Acres* as it now stands; it grew, and I grew with it; and while I did not realize all its spirituality until its presentation set that spirituality free, still it must have had possession of me while writing."

The most striking scene was, of course, the final gentle pantomime. For a full five minutes Uncle Nat (Herne) was alone on stage, slowly making sure that everything was safe and sound for the night. Some twelve years later Chekhov was to discover the magic of a similar scene in *The Cherry Orchard*. One night in Boston a spectator expressed the sentiments of almost everyone whoever followed Uncle Nat through his final loving labors. As the curtain was closing, Herne and the audience heard: "Good night, old man, God bless you!"

On August 22, 1965, John Herne wrote:

Without *Shore Acres* James A. Herne would be of slight interest to historians of the theatre today. It was *Shore Acres* that made him a millionaire and while $1,000,000 ain't exactly hay even now, in 1900 it bought an awful lot of groceries. *Shore Acres* is a masterpiece of stage craft, it is fool proof, any stock actor or school boy can put on a pair of gray whiskers and overalls and "have 'em weeping in the aisles" just by saying the beautiful lines.

SHORE ACRES

A Comedy in Four Acts

JAMES A. HERNE

CHARACTERS

MARTIN BERRY, *owner of "Shore Acres" and keeper of Berry Light*
NATHAN'L BERRY, *"Uncle Nat," his elder brother*
JOEL GATES, *a grass widower*
JOSIAH BLAKE, *postmaster and storekeeper*
SAM WARREN, *a young physician*
CAPTAIN BEN HUTCHINS, *skipper of the "Liddy Ann"*

DR. LEONARD	IKE RICHARDS ⎱
SQUIRE ANDREWS	LEM CONANT ⎰ *"Kinder work around"*
TIM HAYES	ABE HIGGINS
YOUNG NAT BERRY	STEVE BAILEY

DAVE BURGESS ⎱
GABE KILPATRICK ⎰ *Fishermen, crew of the "Liddy Ann"*   THE MAIL CARRIER
BILL HODGEKINS

BOB BERRY	MARY BERRY
ANN BERRY, *Martin's wife*	MILLIE BERRY
HELEN BERRY, *Martin's daughter*	MANDY GATES
LIDDY ANN NYE	BOB LEONARD ⎱ *The twins*
MRS. ANDREWS	SIS LEONARD ⎰
MRS. LEONARD	
PERLEY, *Mrs. Berry's hired girl*	

ACT I. *View of "Shore Acres Farm," near Bar Harbor. "Hayin' Time."*
ACT II. *The Berry farmhouse kitchen. "The Silver Weddin'."*
ACT III. *Scene 1. Interior of Berry Lighthouse. "Havin' an Understandin'."*
Scene 2. Exterior of Berry Lighthouse. "The 'Liddy Ann' in a Sou'easter."
ACT IV. *Same as Act II. Fifteen months later. "Me an' the Children."*
TIME. 1891.
PLACE. *Berry, on Frenchman's Bay, near Bar Harbor, on the coast of Maine.*

ACT I

"Hayin' Time"

View of "Shore Acres Farm," near Bar Harbor.

SCENE: *Frenchman's Bay, with Mount Desert Island and its range of grandly picturesque hills in the distance. Away off to the right are the stately Schoodac Mountains, veiled in mist.*

On the right of the stage, at the back, on a rocky bluff dotted with dwarf pines, and overlooking the bay, is Berry Light. It is separated from the farmhouse by a shady road, which

672

runs across the stage from left to right. The farmhouse, on the right, is barely visible, being hidden in a profusion of shrubs and flowers. Trees overhang the roof; a white-washed fence divides the door yard from the road. Several shining milk pails are hanging on the fence, and on one of the palings hangs a small weather-beaten mail bag; near it hangs a battered tin horn. The door yard is filled with old-fashioned flowers.

To the left of the stage is an old barn, its doors open, its littered yard enclosed by a rail fence. A dove cote is built into the peak of its gabled roof, and doves come and go leisurely.

Outside the fence, at the upper end, is a pump, beneath which is a trough filled with water. Against the lower end of the fence lies a plough. Trees overhang the roof of the barn, and join those overhanging the house from the other side. At right center is a gnarled old tree, and beneath it is a bench. Down left, below the fence, is a wheelbarrow.

At the rise of the curtain, and until the act is well in progress, the wind gently sways the foliage with a slight rustling sound. Birds sing, and flit to and fro. The sound of multitudinous insects is the one distinct note of the scene. The bay is calm, quiet, and in the distance a catboat is occasionally seen sailing lazily, appearing and disappearing among the islands. A tiny steam launch appears once, about the middle of the act, and is seen no more. A mowing machine is heard at work in the distance off left. It stops, turns, goes on again, while the voice of the driver is heard guiding his horses, with "Whoa! Stiddy! Get up! Whoa Bill! (All this must be very distant.)

At the rise of curtain, Millie, a little girl about fours years old, is sitting down left near the plough, playing in the sand with clam shells and pieces of old crockery. She wears a quaint little calico dress, and has a small white flannel shawl around her shoulders, crossed in front and tied behind her back. Her shoes are very dusty, her little hands are dirty.

On the road, off stage to the right, a horse and wagon can be heard driving up and stopping outside; and presently the Mail Carrier appears, with a mail bag and a basket of groceries. He is a kindly-looking man of middle age, wearing a linen duster, driving gloves and

a straw hat. He goes to the bag hanging on the fence, takes two letters from it, and puts in a newspaper wrapped for mailing. He drops the letters into his own bag, and places the basket of groceries beside the fence.

MAIL CARRIER: [*Putting his hands to his mouth, calls*] Whoop! Whoop! Whoop!

At his call, Millie leaves her play and runs to him. They are evidently good friends

MILLIE: Hello!

MAIL CARRIER: Hello, Millie! I swan I'm afeared I've fergot yeh this mornin'.

MILLIE: Oh! Hev yeh?

MAIL CARRIER: Well, not quite. [*Feels in his coat pocket, gets out a piece of candy as if it were the usual thing, and gives it to her*]

MILLIE: [*Pleased*] Thank yeh.

MAIL CARRIER: Hain't yeh got a kiss fer me?

MILLIE: I guess so. [*Lifts up her face; he kisses her*]

MAIL CARRIER: I'll bring yeh a bigger piece to-morry. Good-bye. [*He goes off right, and is heard driving away*]

Millie nibbles the candy as she watches him out of sight, then she resumes her play.

After the mail wagon drives away, Helen enters, left, followed by Uncle Nat. Helen is a girl of seventeen, with a frank yet thoughtful manner, indicating a girl of advanced ideas. She has golden-red hair and brown eyes; she is picturesquely dressed, and wears a sunbonnet. She carries a small pail full of berries, and a tin cup hangs from a crooked finger.

Uncle Nat is a man of sixty, and his large sturdy frame shows signs of toil. His eyes, of a faded blue-gray, have the far-seeing look common to sailors. He wears his yellow-white hair rather long, and he is clean-shaven save for the tippet of straw-white beard that seems to grow up from his chest and to form a sort of frame for his benevolent, weather-beaten old face. Uncle Nat is of the soil, yet there is an inherent poise and dignity about him that are typical of the men who have mastered their environment. He has great cheerfulness and much sly, quiet humor. He wears overalls of a faded blue, a blue checked jumper, beneath which one glimpses a red flannel shirt, and on his head is a farmer's much-battered wide straw hat. His sleeves are rolled back, and he carries a pitchfork in his hand.

As the scene progresses, one is impressed by the frank comradeship between the old man and the girl. On his part there is tenderness, and a deep interest in her problems; there is admiration too for her fine spirit of independence. Helen shows a suppressed feeling of bitterness as she talks. She is high-spirited and proud, yet simple and direct. They pause a little above center as they talk

HELEN: [*Talking as she enters*] Yes, I know, Uncle Nat, perhaps I oughtn't. But Father makes me mad when he talks as he does about Sam.

UNCLE NAT: [*Soothingly*] Well, now, things'll come out all right ef you'll only hev patience. You're young, so's Sam. I told 'im so t'other day. Sez I, "Sam Warren," sez I, "you hain't got a mite o' sense," I sez.

HELEN: [*In the same manner*] Father says – if he catches me speaking to him again, he'll –

UNCLE NAT: You mustn't let 'm ketch yeh! [*Chuckles*] Law sakes, ef I couldn't spark a fellah athout my father ketchin' me at it, I'd bag my head.

HELEN: [*With gentle reproach*] I can't bear deceit –

UNCLE NAT: Neither kin I, but what yeh goin' to do about it – give Sam up?

HELEN: [*Determinedly*] No! [*She crosses to the right, and sits on the bench under the tree, and says with an undercurrent of defiance*] I'll never give him up – I'll leave home first.

UNCLE NAT: [*Teasingly*] Oh, Nell! You wouldn't hev spunk enough fer that.

HELEN: [*Half smiling, then thoughtfully*] Wouldn't I –

UNCLE NAT: No sirree! [*Crosses to the left and places the pitchfork against the fence*]

HELEN: You'll see – it'll be his own fault if I do. [*Rising and going toward him*] Uncle Nat, if you were my father, would you –

UNCLE NAT: [*Wistfully, with a tender cadence in his voice*] Ef I was yer father, Nell? Ef I was yer father, I'm afeared I'd let you do jes' about's you'd a mind to. Allus *did* seem es ef you was my baby anyway, an' I'd give the two eyes out'n my head to see you an' Sam happy. But I ain't yer father, Nell – I ain't

yer father. [*The last with a regretful sigh*]

HELEN: [*Softly*] I sometimes wish you were.

UNCLE NAT: [*Goes to her and places his hands affectionately on her shoulders*] Now, hol' on! Thet ain't right. No sirree! Thet ain't right, an' you know it.

HELEN: Father's changed. [*Leaves him and goes slowly back to the bench*] He never takes me on his knee any more. [*With a slight shade of resentment*]

UNCLE NAT: [*Smiling, and looking at her admiringly*] You're gittin' too heavy I guess.

HELEN: No, it isn't that. Mother's noticed it, and she feels pretty bad about it too, although she pretends not to see it.

UNCLE NAT: Of course she dooze. She ain't a-goin' to see no changes in a man she's been married to nigh on to twenty-five year, not ef she kin help it.

HELEN: [*Rises, and as she does so she sees Mr. Blake's buggy, which is supposedly standing off stage, right. Immediately her whole manner changes, and she says with an impatient tone in her voice*] There's Mr. Blake's buggy again! [*Shrugging her shoulders*] He's here about all the time lately.

UNCLE NAT: [*Rather seriously*] He *is* here pooty consid'ble, ain't he? What's he after I wonder?

HELEN: [*Resentfully*] Principally – me.

UNCLE NAT: [*Surprised, but rather amused*] He ain't!

HELEN: [*With finality*] Yes he is. Father wants me to marry him.

UNCLE NAT: [*Frightened*] He don't!

HELEN: [*In the same manner*] Yes, he does. Mr. Blake told me as much the other day.

UNCLE NAT: My! My! Thet's too bad. I swan thet's too bad. I'm afeared yer father don't understand yeh, Helen. Has he said anythin' to yeh about 't himself?

HELEN: [*Still standing by the bench*] No, not yet – but he will, and then – well – [*Half savagely*] He'll find out I'm not Mother –

UNCLE NAT: Tut – tut – tut – there yeh go – Thet's yer father all over again – thet's yer father all over again.

Joel Gates drifts into the farmyard from the road, left. Little Mandy drifts in after him. Gates is dressed in dark overalls, with suspenders, a soiled white shirt, no vest, and an·

old drab soft hat. He carries a scythe, the snath under his left arm, the blade to the ground with the point off to the left, and he has a whetstone in his right hand. He looks as if life had battered him mercilessly. He is small and slight, his face weather-washed, kindly; his keen little eyes seem to be as a child's with a question in them, always asking "What is it all about anyhow! – I d'know!" He is never seen without Mandy. Her whole little person-ality is part of his; the nondescript, faded clothing, the rhythm of movement. The far-away look in the old face is repeated in the apple-blossom beauty of the child. He rarely addresses her or seems aware of her presence

GATES: [*In a drawl*] Good day, Nathan'l.

UNCLE NAT: Hello, Joel!

GATES: [*Talking as he walks across the stage toward the right*] Why ain't yeh in th' hay field?

UNCLE NAT: Ben there good part th' mornin'. Who be you a-cuttin' fer t'day, Joel?

GATES: Simm'ns. Jes' got done. Goin' t' cut m'own now. Can't afford to lose this weather.

UNCLE NAT: No; too good weather to lose, an' no mistake.

Gates is about to exit, with Mandy behind him, when he stops abruptly near the bench. Mandy pauses also

GATES: Oh, Nathan'l! Will yeh lend me yer gun fer a day 'r two?

UNCLE NAT: [*Reluctantly*] Yes – I guess'o. What fer? [*Coming down center*]

GATES: There's a fox 'r suthin' a-playin' ol' Nick with my chickings.

UNCLE NAT: Thet so? Helen, git me ol' Uncle Sam'l, will yeh? She's a-standin' in her corner in the kitchen. [*Helen goes into the house*] Hello, Mandy! [*Chuckles*] How d'yeh do? – You ben in the hay field too? [*The child nods*] By George – you're a great haymaker. I'll tell you what – when you git a scythe inter yer hands th' grasshoppers is got to jump over the fence an' no mistake, ain't they, Joel? [*Chuckles*] Will yeh shake hands with me? [*Urging the child kindly*]

GATES: Go on – shake hands.

Mandy shyly creeps behind her father

UNCLE NAT: Bashful, ain't she?

GATES: [*Reaching around to where the child stands behind him, and pressing her closer to him*] Yes – she's a shy sort o' critter. Don't never seem t' want t' play with nobody nor nothin' but me.

UNCLE NAT: She's a-growin' ain't she – growin' jes' like a weed. My – my! How like her mother she dooze look, don't she?

GATES: [*With a break in his voice and a catch in his breath, placing his hand on her head and looking at her*] Yeh. Gits to look more an' more like her every day in the week.

UNCLE NAT: [*Hesitatingly, as if loth to arouse unhappy memories*] I suppose – yeh hain't never heerd nothin' of her – sence – hev yeh, Joel?

GATES: [*Out of the depths of pitiful memories*] No – nothin'. [*With a great sigh*]

Helen returns with the gun and crosses to Uncle Nat. Gates also crosses to Uncle Nat, leaving Mandy in front of the bench. After Helen gives Uncle Nat the gun, she goes over to Millie, who has been playing in the sand, all unconscious of things that have been going on about her, and sits down beside her and plays with her. Mandy timidly sits on the edge of the bench; she watches her father intently, with a look of trust and affectionate content which one sees in a dearly loved dog when near his master.

The attitude of Gates and Uncle Nat in the episode of the gun is that of two boys gloating over a treasure

UNCLE NAT: Well – here's ol' Uncle Sam'l. Take good keer of 'r. I set a good deal o' store by Sam'l. [*He hands Gates the gun*]

GATES: [*Putting the stone in his pocket, laying down his scythe and taking the gun*] Is she – eh – ludded?

UNCLE NAT: Yes, I allus keep 'r ludded.

GATES: Doos she – eh – kick?

UNCLE NAT: She never kicked me, d'know what she might do to a feller she didn't like.

GATES: [*Handling the gun with pride, as though it were a great privilege, his eyes travelling the length of it admiringly, and then looking at Uncle Nat with his face aglow*] Fit all through the war with 'r, didn't yeh?

UNCLE NAT: Yeh.

GATES: Sixth Maine?

UNCLE NAT: [*His hands clasped behind him, shoulders thrown back, his head high in the air, teeters to and fro on his heels and toes*] Yeh – Sixth Maine, Company A. Her 'n me's tramped a good many miles together, one way 'nother. [*His voice is quiet and his face tense with memories*]

GATES: [*In an awed hushed voice*] Did yeh ever – kill a rebel 'th her?

UNCLE NAT: [*In a matter-of-fact tone*] Don't know. I used t' jes' p'int 'er, shet both my eyes 'n let 'r do her own work.

GATES: [*Reflectively*] I guess thet's 'bout as good a way as any fer me t'kill thet 'ere fox. [*He is fussing with the gun and unconsciously aims it at Uncle Nat*]

UNCLE NAT: [*Taking hold of the gun and pushing it aside*] Hol' on, yeh danged ol' fool – Didn't I jes tell yeh she was ludded?

GATES: What yer skeered of? I wa'n't a-goin' to pull the trigger – I was only jes' aimin' 'r.

UNCLE NAT: Well, aim 'r at somebody else.

GATES: There ain't nobody else handy.

UNCLE NAT: I swan thet's too bad.

GATES: Well, good day. [*Takes up the scythe, and puts the gun over his shoulder*] I'll bring 'r back safe an' sound.

Gates goes off right. Mandy quietly slips from the bench and slowly drifts after him. Uncle Nat attracts her attention by playfully snapping his fingers at her, and she turns and shows quite a little interest in his kindly friendliness. She passes on, her eyes fixed wonderingly upon him. Uncle Nat is amused and chuckles. After they go off, he seats himself on the bench under the tree

HELEN: Oh, Uncle Nat! Have you and Sam done anything more about your back pension?

UNCLE NAT: Well, Sam got me t' sign some papers over at the Squire's t'other day – but – I d'want him to do nothin' about my back pension. [*With mock indignation*] What do you an' him take me fur? One o' them 'ere pension grabbers?

HELEN: [*Going up left*] Well, Sam says you're entitled to it, and he's going to try and get it for you too.

UNLCE NAT: Sam says lots o' things asides his prayers, don't he, Nell?

HELEN: [*Pausing and leaning over the fence*] I guess he does. [*They laugh together softly with amused understanding*]

UNCLE NAT: Where yeh goin'?

HELEN: Oh, I don't know. Just for a stroll. [*And much occupied with her problems, she disappears down the road to the left*]

UNCLE NAT: [*Rises from the bench a little stiffly, as if checked by a slight rheumatic twinge, goes down left and gets the wheelbarrow. He starts off as if he might be going to get fodder for the noon meal of the animals, when he notices Millie and says jovially*] Well, Millie, d'yeh want a ride?

MILLIE: [*Dropping her play and brushing off her frock, eagerly*] Yes.

UNCLE NAT: Well, climb into the kerridge an' don't keep the ol' hoss waitin'. Yeh know how to git into a kerridge?

MILLIE: Yes. [*She sits on the edge of the wheelbarrow*]

UNCLE NAT: Well, I don't know whether yeh do or not. Take a back seat. [*He tips the wheelbarrow gently so that she slides into the back of it. She is a bit startled for a moment*] You see, I knew yeh didn't know how to git into a kerridge. The fust thing yeh know this ol' hoss'll kick up and knock the dashboard out, an' spill yeh all over the place, an' yeh won't like thet a bit. [*He wheels her off, right*]

Blake enters from the barn. He is a man of forty years; he has black hair, and his side-whiskers are close cut. The rest of his face is cleanly shaven. He is dressed in a gray business suit, "store made"; the coat is a single-breasted frock, very slightly cutaway, buttoned with one button at the breast. He wears a white laundered shirt, and a rather high standing collar with a black ready-made tie. His hat is a silk one, old, but not battered, brown at the edges of the crown and brim. His shoes have been home-polished, but are dusty. He has drab castor gloves, not new; he carries a buggy whip, an old white one. He has a black silk ribbon watch guard around his neck, and a gold watch. He is portly and well-to-do, but jovial. He is rather good-looking, and has the air of a contented, cheerful businessman, shrewd, but not cunning or mean; he is always smiling. He passes through the gate of the barnyard, and goes right center.

He is followed by Martin, a heavy robust man of fifty. He is slow and deliberate in manner and speech. His face and hands are weather-beaten, his hair is sandy-gray and cropped, and he has a short stubby beard. He wears pepper-and-salt trousers tucked into his boots, a black vest, and an open, white, home-made and home-laundered shirt with collar attached. His shirt sleeves are rolled up a trifle, showing red flannel beneath. He has a black silk sailor handkerchief, and a black soft hat, well worn. He carries a jackknife in his right hand, and is opening and shutting the blade with his thumb as he walks along, "clicking" it. His left hand is behind his back, and his head is down, as if in deep thought. He stops inside the rail fence.

At the same time enters from the house, Perley, the "hired girl," a strong muscular girl of about twenty, in a calico dress, with her sleeves rolled up to her shoulders, showing her red powerful arms. She pays no attention to Blake or Martin, and goes to the mail bag, takes it down, takes out the paper, crosses over and gives it to Martin, who mechanically looks at the address as if he knew what it was, as it is a regularly "subscribed for" paper. She crosses back to the basket of provisions, puts the bag into the basket, stands with her back to the men, with her hands on her hips, and looks up and down the road for a moment. She then takes up the basket and goes into the house.

The dialogue between Martin and Blake has gone on right through the action, from the moment they entered

BLAKE: No, sirree. I tell yeh, Martin, the day o' sentiment's gone. We're livin' in a practical age. Any man's liable to go to bed poor 'n wake up a milli'naire. Ef I'd had a friend to give me such a boost and such advice's I've given you I'd hev owned half the State o' Maine, I believe.

MARTIN: [*At the lower end of the fence, and facing the audience; putting the paper in the watch pocket of his vest*] Why, yeh see's I told yeh, Mother left the place to me 'n Nathan'l, an' we sort o' promised 'er we'd never sell it an –

BLAKE: Sentiment! All sentiment! Any man thet'll hang on to an old farm jes' 'cause – [*Goes to the pump, takes the cup and pumps water into it*] he sort o' promised his dead mother he'd never sell it, ain't got no business to live in this bustlin', go-ahead, money-makin', devil-take-the-hindermost day of ours – [*Drinks*] thet's all I've go to say. [*Laughs. Pours the balance of the water into the trough, replaces the cup, and wipes his mouth*]

MARTIN: [*Casually*] P'r'aps you never sot much store b'your mother, Mr. Blake.

BLAKE: I never hed no mother – thet is not to speak of. You know all about thet as well as I do. [*He returns to Martin*]

MARTIN: Thet mus' be the reason yeh can't understand –

BLAKE: [*Patronizingly*] I kin understand this. [*Leaning with his back to the fence, both elbows on the top rail*] "Shore Acres" is a good enough farm as Maine farms go – yeh manage by hard work to make a livin' fer yerself an' family –

MARTIN: [*Defensively, nodding his head at Blake*] A good – comfortable – livin'! [*He puts his foot upon the middle rail*]

BLAKE: [*Admitting the correction good-naturedly*] A good comfortable livin'! [*Switching the whip up and down*]

MARTIN: [*With quiet dignity*] An' pay my debts.

BLAKE: An' pay – your debts.

MARTIN: [*Complacently*] Don't owe no man nothin', an' kin sleep nights.

BLAKE: [*Patronizingly, agreeing with him*] From sundown to cockcrow – I ain't a-goin' to dispute thet, thet's a-l-l right. Well, now, you happen to hev a hundred an' sixty rod, more or less, of about the sightliest shore front to be found on the coast. Yeh didn't know thet till I told yeh, did yeh?

MARTIN: No, I didn't. [*Climbs up, sits on the rail fence, facing the house, and sticks the knife into the rail between his legs*]

BLAKE: Well! This shore front makes your land val'able. [*Turning and putting his foot on the bottom rail*] Not to plant potatoes in – but to build summer cottages on. I tell yeh, the boom's a-comin' here jes' as sure as you're born. [*Carried away by his own enthusiasm*] Bar Harbor's got s' high, yeh can't touch a foot of it – not by coverin' it with gold dollars. This has got to be the next p'int. [*Goes to the bench, right, and sits down*]

MARTIN: [*He is impressed by Blake's enthusiasm, but there is caution in his immediate response*] Seems so – the way you put matters.

BLAKE: Seems so? 'Tis so. You pool your land in with mine – [*He talks with a confident, good-natured, yet shrewd business air. He lays out a plan on the grass with the end of his whip*] We'll lay out quarter-acre lots, cut avenoos, plant trees, build a driveway to the shore, hang on to all the shore front an' corner lots – sell every one o' the others, see!!! They'll build on em' an' that'll double the value of ours – see! – they'll have to pay the heft o' the taxes 'cause they've built; we'll be taxed light 'cause we didn't – see?

MARTIN: [*In the same manner*] I d'know as I jes' see.

BLAKE: [*Confidentially*] If we can get holt of half a dozen just the right sort o' fellahs – city fellahs – yeh know – fellahs that hev got inflooance to bring folks down here – we can afford to give 'em each an inside lot, here an' there, provided they'll guarantee to build, lay out their grounds, an' help to make the place attractive. That'll give us a kind of starter – see? [*Chuckles*]

MARTIN: [*Warming a bit at Blake's confident statements*] Seems es ef that wouldn't be a bad idee.

BLAKE: *Bad* idee? It's *the* idee! [*Rising and going to Martin, confidentially*] Let me show you –

He takes a notebook from his pocket, and begins to show Martin some calculations he has jotted down. They become so absorbed in this that they do not notice Gates, who enters right, followed by Mandy

GATES: [*Smiling ingratiatingly*] How d' do? [*If encouraged he would stop, but they merely nod*] I hear you fellahs is a'goin' to boom things here 'n the spring. [*He goes quite close to Blake and Martin, who are deep in discussion. He tries to peer over their shoulders, and raises his voice as if they were deaf*] Is thet so thet Jordan Ma'sh's* comin' down

*Jordan Marsh – a Boston department store.

here to go inter business? [*He pauses, inviting a response; again braces up a bit and makes another effort, now in a manner implying that he is doing them a great favor*] I wouldn't mind sellin' thet seven acre o' mine – ef I thought I could git rich out 'n it.

Blake looks over his shoulder as if a puff of wind or something had disturbed him, then pointedly resumes his talk with Martin. Gates is crestfallen, and turns away

GATES: Gosh! How some folks kin get stuck up 's soon as they git a little mite rich – I never see – [*He shuffles off left, with mingled dignity and resentment, followed by Mandy*]

BLAKE: I tell yeh, Martin, I've got the scheme! You go in with me an' in less than a year I'll make you so rich you can live in Bangor. Move your mother's remains up there, an' have 'em buried in one o' them fine cemet'ries, an' put a handsome stun over her as you'd ought to do.

MARTIN: Nathan'l an' me 's ben savin' up fer a stun. I guess we've got most enough now to git one – money's scurse with us – we don't see much *real* cash.

BLAKE: I'll tell you what I'll do. I'll take a mortgage on the farm for the money to start you – an' you kin sell the lots.

MARTIN: [*Hesitatingly*] I'll talk to Nathan'l an' Ann.

BLAKE: Talk to 'em – of course – but don't let 'em talk you out of the scheme. There's a good deal of sentiment in Nathan'l.

MARTIN: It'd make me pooty rich, wouldn't it?

BLAKE: Rich? Well, I guess. Yeh wouldn't hev to be borrowin' nobody else's chaise to go to meetin' in.

MARTIN: Seems es though it hed ought to be done, don't it? Yet it seems a kind o' pity to –

BLAKE: To get rich, eh? [*Laughs*] Say, look a-here! Honest now – wouldn't you like to live better 'n you do? Now Honest Injun, wouldn't yeh?

MARTIN: [*A bit warmed by Blake's suggestions*] I suppose I would.

BLAKE: Of course yeh would, an' yeh'd like to have your family live better. Helen'd ought to hev a real good syminerry eddication – she's worth it, she's a bright han'some girl – she'd ought to be a bookkeeper or suthin'. [*Complacently*] I was a-tellin' her t'other day 'bout your a-wantin' her 'n me to git married, an' –

MARTIN: [*Showing interest*] What'd she say?

Blake purses his lips and shakes his head dubiously

MARTIN: Did yeh offer her the piannah, as I told yeh to?

BLAKE: Y-e-s –

MARTIN: [*Nonplussed*] I thought she'd 'a'jumped at the piannah. She's so fond o' music.

BLAKE: I offered her everything I could think of. I offered to build her a house, an' let her paint an' paper it any way she'd a mind to.

MARTIN: [*Pondering*] I guess I'd better talk to her myself. She giner'ly does what I tell her to.

BLAKE: Yes, but you see girls are beginning to think they've a right to marry who they please.

MARTIN: [*With pride in Helen, and pride in his own power to control her*] Not *my* girl.

BLAKE: [*Going right, with a shade of resentment*] I'm afraid I'll never git very close to her so long 's young Doc Warren's around.

MARTIN: [*Angrily*] Doc Warren! – She don't keep company along o' him no more? [*As if in doubt*]

BLAKE: Don't she?

MARTIN: I guess not. I told her I didn't want she should – thet's allus ben enough.

BLAKE: Them free thinkers is hard to git shut of. They're dangerous to young folks' religion.

MARTIN: Helen's ben riz a stric' Babtis' – I guess she'll stay so; she's a pious girl.

BLAKE: Them's the wust when they do change. Sam Warren was *raised* respectable enough. His father and mother were Presbyterians.

MARTIN: [*His memory carries him into the past, and a smile creeps into his face as he answers patronizingly*] Ol' man Warren was a good-natured honest ol' soul an' all thet – but I never thought he had any too much sense.

BLAKE: No! If he had he wouldn't have worked himself to a skeleton tryin' to make a doctor out of his boy. [*Laughs*]

MARTIN: [*Nodding his head wisely*] The mother had a good deal to do with thet, I guess.

BLAKE: Six o' one an' half a dozen o' the other. What she said was law with the ol' man and

what he said was gospel with her. They thought the sun jes rose an' sot in their Sam, an' now look at 'im. First he read Emanuel Swedenborg, an' he was a red-hot Swedenborgian – then he got hold of Spencer an' Darwin an' a lot o' them kind o' lunatics an' began to study frogs an' bugs an' things. [*He laughs. Martin laughs too, but not so heartily as Blake does*] Why, sir! One mornin', a spell ago, as I was goin' to Ellsworth, I seed him a-settin' on his hunkers in the middle of the rud, watchin' a lot of ants runnin' in an' out of a hole. [*Both roar with laughter at this*] D'yeh remember thet free lecture he gave with the magic lantern in the schoolhouse, on evolution 's he called it?

MARTIN: Yes, some of 'em wanted to tar an' feather 'im thet time.

BLAKE: Oh! Pshaw! That wouldn't 'a'done! [*A slight pause*] Now he's come out as a home-a-pathic physician – [*Laughs*] He ain't a doctor – he's a pheesycian – goes around wantin' to cure sick folks with sugar shot – by George! [*Both laugh heartily*]

MARTIN: L'see – ain't he a-tendin' ol' Mis' Swazy now?

BLAKE: [*Carelessly*] Yep! Doc Leonard give her up, an' they had to have him. [*Starts to go off right, then stops*] Oh, I'm goin' to git rid o' all my hawgs. I'd like you to have them two shoats, they're beauties!

MARTIN: [*Preoccupied*] I guess I've got all I want.

BLAKE: Well, think over thet there land business. If you want to get rich, now's your chance – if you don't, I can't help it. Good day! [*Martin nods*] Good hay weather. [*Scans the sky*]

MARTIN: Fust-rate.

BLAKE: [*As he goes off right*] Most through?

MARTIN: Finish this week ef the weather holds.

BLAKE: [*Outside*] Good day!

MARTIN: Good day! [*He looks after Blake, then slowly and thoughtfully enters the barn, head down, hands behind his back*]

Helen's voice is heard off left. She talks as she enters; she has an arm around Young Nat, a handsome boy of fourteen. He is an errand boy in Blake's store. He wears knickerbockers, and a cap with no visor. He has the air of being spoiled and thoroughly selfish. Helen's manner toward him is one of amused and affectionate tolerance

HELEN: [*Laughing indulgently*] La, Nat! What good would my marrying Mr. Blake do you?

YOUNG NAT: Lots o' good. You could coax money out o' him, an' give it to me.

HELEN: [*Shocked*] Oh! Nat Berry! [*Shakes her finger at him*] Would you take that kind of money?

YOUNG NAT: I'd take any kind o' money. 'Tain't no worse than weighin' yer hand with the sugar, is it?

HELEN: [*As if talking to a child, placing her hands to his face*] Well, Natty dear –

YOUNG NAT: [*Pushing her hands away*] Don't call me Natty. Gosh, don't I hate thet! Mother makes me so 'shamed every time she comes up to Blake's. This is the last suit o' knicker-bockers she gits on me. Gosh, wouldn't I have lots o' things ef you'd marry ol' Blake! [*Putting his arms around her, coaxingly*] Say, Nell, will yeh? Marry ol' Blake – do. Jes' this once an' I'll never ask you again. Will you? I'll do as much fer you some day! Will you?

HELEN: No, I won't! I don't want to marry Mr. Blake.

YOUNG NAT: [*Reproachfully; going right*] Ain't you selfish!

HELEN: Aren't you selfish!

YOUNG NAT: You'd marry Doc Warren mighty quick ef Father'd let you.

HELEN: [*Smiling proudly*] I guess I would.

Sam Warren enters by the road, right, at the back. He is tall, handsome and manly, with an open honest face, and a frank manner. He stands for a moment, leaning over the fence, listening to Young Nat with an amused smile

YOUNG NAT: [*Coming toward Helen*] Hands like a blacksmith, poor's Job, proud as a pea-cock an' – [*With awe*] don't believe there's any Hell.

HELEN: [*Quietly smiling*] Well, neither do I.

YOUNG NAT: O-O-O-h! – Nell Berry! I'll tell yer father, an' then you'll find out!

Sam comes down and takes Young Nat by the ear and twists it playfully. Young Nat howls

SAM: What do *you* think about it, Nat?

YOUNG NAT: [*Crying*] Ouch! L' go my ear!

HELEN: [*Going to Young Nat and folding him in her arms*] Ah!

YOUNG NAT: An' you let go of me, too. [*Push-ing her away and going up center*]

HELEN: Sam! You've hurt him. You're too rough. Don't cry, Nat.

SAM: I didn't mean to hurt him, Nell. He's more mad than hurt I guess, aren't you, Nat?

YOUNG NAT: [*Crying*] None of yer business! I'll get even with you fer this some day, you see if I don't! I wish I was big enough, I'd show you whether there's any Hell or not, you great big blacksmith, pickin' on a little fellah like me! [*He goes off left, crying*]

Sam laughs and crosses to right center, watching him

HELEN: [*With gentle reproach*] You shouldn't tease Nat so, Sam. You know he doesn't like you. [*She sits beneath the tree on the bench, right. She is vibrating with content and happi-ness in the presence of the man she loves*]

SAM: [*Sits down on the plough lying against the barnyard fence*] That seems to be a gen-eral complaint around these parts. A fellow that knows some things his great-great-grand-father didn't know is an object of suspicion here. [*As he talks, he picks up a handful of sand and lets it slip through his fingers*]

HELEN: [*Smiling*] Well, what are you going to do about it?

SAM: [*Cheerily*] Keep right on knowing. Just as long as they build printing offices, we've got to know, that's all there is about that.

HELEN: I'm afraid – [*Laughs softly*] my read-ing is going to get me into trouble.

SAM: How so?

HELEN: [*Still amused*] Why, the other day I was trying to tell Father something about evolution and "The Descent of Man," but he got mad and wouldn't listen.

SAM: [*Laughing*] Family pride! You know, Nell, there are lots of people who wouldn't be happy in this world if they couldn't look for-ward to a burning lake in the next. [*Takes a book out of his pocket and carelessly flips over the pages, looking at her as he talks*]

HELEN: Kind of sad, isn't it?

SAM: Oh! I don't know! They take a heap of comfort preparing to keep out of it, I suppose.

HELEN: [*Seeing the book in Sam's hand, rises and goes toward him*] What book's that? [*Trying to read the title on the cover*]

SAM: [*Rising*] "A Hazard of New Fortunes."†

HELEN: Have you read it?

SAM: Yes.

HELEN: [*Eagerly, reaching for it*] May I read it?

SAM: Yes, I brought it for you. [*He gives her the book*]

Helen delightedly takes the book and begins eagerly scanning the pages as she turns and goes back to the bench under the tree, speaking as she goes

HELEN: I've been longing for this book. I read a fine article about it in the Boston paper. [*Sits down and looks at Sam with a joyous smile*] Thank you ever so much, Sam.

SAM: [*Pointing to the book*] That's a book you won't have to hide. Your father'll listen to that. If he was a speculating man, now, it would do him good.

HELEN: [*Turning the leaves of the book, and pausing here and there at a page as something interesting catches her eye*] How's poor old Mrs. Swazy getting along?

SAM: [*In a matter-of-fact way*] First-rate. She'll pull through this time.

As the scene progresses, Sam moves about restlessly, as though preoccupied with something. He is never far away from Helen and always has his eyes and attention focused upon her

HELEN: [*Looking up at him with awe and wonder*] Oh! Sam! After they'd all given her up – [*Proudly but ingenuously*] Well, they'll have to acknowledge that you're a great physician now.

SAM: [*Laughs*] Great fiddlesticks! Why, the folks around here wouldn't let me doctor a sick kitten if they could help it.

HELEN: Why, you'll get the credit of this!

SAM: Yes! Me and the Lord! [*Laughs*] I'm satisfied so long as the old lady gets well. [*Helen is still sitting on the bench, glancing over the book, a look of contentment and happiness upon her face. Sam, who has been leaning against the barnyard fence, goes to her thoughtfully, his whole manner changed. He stands*

†By William Dean Howells.

slightly above her to the left, puts one foot on the bench, leans on his knee and bends over her, and says in a rather quiet tense voice] Nell – I want to tell you something.

HELEN: [*Without looking up, says gaily as Sam pauses*] Something good, I hope.

SAM: [*In the same manner*] Don't I always tell you good things?

HELEN: [*With a teasing little laugh, looking up at him over her shoulder*] Most – always, Sam!

SAM: [*Quietly, looking down into her eyes*] I'm going away.

HELEN: [*Seems stunned. The joy passes out of her face; her eyes are still upon him, but all the happiness is gone from them. The book drops from her hands and falls to the ground. She slowly slides along the bench away from him as though to study him better. She is pale and frightened, and in a dry voice with a low cry of pain, she says*] Oh! – Sam! [*Then, feeling it cannot be true, she leans toward him and adds in a very appealing voice*] Honest?

SAM: [*Quietly*] Honest. What's the use of my staying here? [*Sits down left of Helen*] Nobody'll speak to me except Nathan'l – and your mother – and you. [*Putting his arm around her*]

HELEN: [*Drawing away from him, endeavoring to overcome her emotion*] Don't, Sam – Please don't.

SAM: [*With a dry laugh*] And *you're* half afraid to.

HELEN: [*Brokenly*] No! I'm not afraid – only you know – Father says –

SAM: [*In the same manner*] I know – they all say it. Blake says I've got dynamite in my boots. Just because I can't believe as they do – they won't any of 'em look at me if they can help it. So I'm going out West, where a fellow can *believe* as he likes and *talk* as he likes –

HELEN: [*With awe, her eyes upon him*] To – Chicago?

SAM: [*Amused*] Oh no – o! A fellow may *believe* what he likes in Chicago, but he mustn't *say* too much about it. I'm going a-w-a-y out West. Montana – or somewhere out that way.

HELEN: [*Innocently, in a pathetic voice*] Oh my! I'll never get so far as that, will I?

SAM: [*Not heeding her, rising and walking up center*] I want to get where I can sprout a new idea without being *sat* on.

HELEN: [*In a crushed voice*] Yes, of course – you're right.

SAM: Where I won't be hampered by dead men's laws and dead men's creeds.

HELEN: [*Turning to him in a chiding manner*] Why, you don't blame Father for believing as *his* father believed, do you?

SAM: No. But I *do* blame him for sitting down on me just because I can't believe the same way. I tell you, Nell – [*He picks up a pebble*] one world at a time is good enough for me; and I've made up my mind that I'm going to *live* while I'm in this one – [*He throws the pebble as far as he can reach, watching its flight*] and I'm going to do something more than practice medicine in Berry. Sitting around, waiting for patients – [*Rather contemptuously*] such as old Mrs. Swazy. [*He puts his hands in his pockets and turns down center*]

HELEN: [*Getting up from the bench and going to him, center*] Yes. But – what's going to become of *me*?

Sam goes to her with arms outstretched, and enfolds her lovingly

SAM: [*Tenderly*] You! You're going to stay right here with your mother, till I get started. Then I'm coming back to get you and take you out there and show those western fellows a *real* Yankee girl. [*Amused*] You know, Nell, the newspapers used to print pictures of them with pants on and a stovepipe hat!

HELEN: [*Making a pitiful effort to be cheerful*] Yes! But they don't do that now, Sam.

SAM: No, they do *not* do that now. You girls have come to stay, there's no getting around that fact, and we cranks are going to help you stay here. [*He notices the book lying on the ground*] Let me show you something in that book.

They walk over to the bench, Sam's arm remains about Helen. She sits down, he picks up the book and sits at her left, and they both become deeply absorbed in reading

MARTIN: [*Enters from the barn, leading a horse by the halter to water him at the trough.‡ His*

‡NOTE: If it is not convenient to have a horse, Martin can come in with two heavy stable buckets, one in each hand, which he fills with water from the trough. J.A.H.

head is bent and he is in deep thought, pondering upon the idea of getting rich which Blake has suggested to him. He does not see Helen and Sam until he turns to re-enter the barn. When his eyes rest upon them, so content and absorbed in each other, he pauses amazed, and his face flames with bitter resentment. He is unable to speak for a moment, then he blurts out harshly*] Sam Warren, hain't yeh got no more pride than to come where yeh ain't wanted?

Sam and Helen start in surprise. Helen shyly draws away from Sam

SAM: [*Looks up with a very affable air and says pleasantly and respectfully*] Hello, Mr. Berry! Yes sir, I have.

MARTIN: [*In the same manner*] Well, what yeh doin' here, then?

SAM: [*Looking at Helen slyly as if it were a good joke*] I thought – I *was* wanted.

MARTIN: [*Taking a menacing step toward him*] Didn't I tell yeh yeh wa'n't?

SAM: [*Smiling, but rather reluctantly*] Yes sir, – *you* did!

Sam plays this scene very quietly, never losing his temper; plays it as if something else of more immediate importance were on his mind.

The scene throughout is pitched in a quick staccato, which reaches its height in Helen's cry of terror as the two men clinch. Then there is a pause, and the rest of the scene, until Martin leaves the stage, is completed in tense low tones that are portentous of trouble. There is active hate on Martin's part. Sam's attitude is one of simple manly poise

MARTIN: Well, ain't thet enough?

SAM: [*Pleasantly*] Yes, I suppose it is – but I thought that – maybe you'd like to know – [*Rises and goes toward him*]

MARTIN: [*Goaded by Sam's manner, fiercely*] I don't want to know nothin'! An' I don't want *her* to know nothin' thet I don't want her to know! [*Indicating Helen with a nod of his head*]

SAM: [*Making another effort to conciliate him*] Why you see, Mr. Berry – you can't help –

MARTIN: [*Breaking in and shouting at him*] I'm a-bringin' up my family! An' I don't want no interference from you – nor Darwin – nor any o' the rest o' the breed! [*With a passionate sweep of his arm. He half turns as if to go*]

SAM: [*Smiling*] Darwin's dead, Mr. Berry –

MARTIN: [*Turning and interrupting, resentfully*] Them *books* ain't dead.

SAM: [*Very positive and very much satisfied with his statement*] No! "Them books" are going to be pretty hard to kill.

MARTIN: [*Sharply, turning to Helen, who is still seated on the bench*] What book's thet yeh got there now? [*Indicating the book with a wrathful toss of his arm*]

HELEN: [*Very gently*] One of Sam's books, Father.

MARTIN: [*Glaring at Sam*] Well, give it right straight back to Sam. I don't want nothin' to do with *him* nor his books.

SAM: [*Kindly, correcting him*] It *is* my book, Mr. Berry, but it was written by a man –

MARTIN: [*His temper rising steadily, flashes at him*] I won't hev yeh a-bringin' them books here! A-learnin' my daughter a pack o' lies, about me an' my parents a-comin' from monkeys –

SAM: [*His eyes twinkling with suppressed amusement, answers soothingly*] La bless you, Mr. Berry! That was ages ago!

MARTIN: [*Is goaded to the extreme by Sam's manner*] I don't care how long ago it was, I won't hev it flung in my children's faces.

HELEN: [*Is much distressed by her father's bitter temper, and she suddenly attempts to calm him, and approaches Martin, who has been standing near the barnyard gate. She timidly holds out the book to him, and says pleadingly*] Father, I wish you'd let me read you this little bit –

MARTIN: [*With ugly stubbornness, checks her with a sweep of his arm, as though pushing away some harmful or noxious thing*] I don't want to hear it. I read *The Bangor Whig*, an' *The Agriculturist*, an' the Bible, an' thet's enough. There ain't no lies in *them*.

SAM: [*Ironically*] No, especially in *The Bangor Whig!*

Here the staccato changes to a deep ominous murmur

MARTIN: [*Peering at Sam through half-closed lids, mutters*] I'm skeered of a man thet ain't got no religion.

SAM: [*With quiet assurance*] But, Mr. Berry, I *have* got a religion.

MARTIN: [*Doubtfully, in the same manner*] What is it?

SAM: [*His manner becoming serious, in a voice warm with feeling, pointing off with a sweep of his arm*] Do you hear those insects singing?

MARTIN: [*Rather puzzled, mumbles*] Yes – I hear 'em!

SAM: [*Seriously and calmly*] Well, that's their religion, and I reckon mine's just about the same thing.

MARTIN: [*With supreme disgust and contempt in his voice and manner*] Oh! Good Lord! [*He starts for the barn with the horse*]

HELEN: [*With tender appeal, swiftly following him*] Father, why won't you ever let Sam tell you –

Martin, goaded to the breaking point, turns upon Helen, dropping the halter and allowing the horse to go into the barn

MARTIN: [*Hardly able to control his rage*] Look a-here, Nell! I've had all the words I'm goin' to hev with *you* – [*Shaking his closed fist threateningly*] But by the Eternal, I ain't a-goin' to hev thet fellah a-comin' here preachin' his infidelity to my family. [*Frantic with rage, he now says more than he intends to, deliberately and fiercely*] If you *want* him, you *take* him, an' clear out!

Sam approaches quickly, intensely moved by what Martin has said

SAM: Do you mean that, Mr. Berry?

HELEN: [*Her head high in the air, her whole attitude one of noble defiance*] I will! [*As though accepting the challenge*]

MARTIN: [*Looks at Helen, quite broken, all the fire of his passion in ashes, and murmurs thickly*] Yeh won't?

HELEN: [*Proudly, her eyes full of burning tears, her voice vibrating with emotion*] Won't I? You'll see whether I will or not! [*There is a challenge in her voice too*]

SAM: [*Moving toward Martin, intensely excited by his words*] Mr. Berry – if you'll say that again –

MARTIN: [*Springs at Sam and clutches him by the throat*] Damn you!

SAM: [*Swiftly seizes Martin's wrist with his left hand, drawing back his right hand to strike*] Damn you!

HELEN: [*With a cry of terror, covering her face with her hands, calls out appealingly*] Oh! Sam – don't!

The sound of Helen's voice brings both men to their senses, and they relax their hold upon each other. They stand silent for a moment, both a little ashamed.

MARTIN: [*In a heartbroken manner*] D'yeh mean to steal my child from me?

SAM: [*Quietly, adjusting his collar*] I'm not going to *steal* her, Mr. Berry – I'm going out West to *earn* her!

MARTIN: [*Speaking through his teeth, vehemently*] Sam Warren, I hated you afore – but *now* you've shamed me afore my own child. Git off'n my farm an' don't yeh never set foot on't agin – [*Quiet low and passionately*] It's dangerous fer both on us.

Martin wearily drags himself into the barn.

Helen stands dazed and heartbroken. Sam leans against the fence, his hands in his pockets, his head bent, deep in thought. There is a moment's pause.

Ann§ bustles cheerily out of the house. She is a woman of forty-five, handsome in a wholesome, motherly way. She is dressed in a freshly laundered, becoming calico dress, and her sleeves are rolled up beyond the elbows, showing a pair of shapely arms. She is quick and energetic in all her movements. To her, home is the most desirable place in the world, and she rules it with all the skill and love of a typical American housewife. Her manner is pleasant and happy. She is always smiling and always sees the best side of everything. Nothing disturbs her; she meets all the problems of her daily life with a quiet and unobtrusive efficiency

ANN: Well Helen, I was jes' a-wonderin' what'd

§NOTE: Ann begins all her speeches slowly, increasing in rapidity as she progresses. She is in the habit of repeating the final words of all her speeches emphatically, as though the person she were addressing had not heard her. J.A.H.

become o' you. Sam Warren! I hup Martin hain't seen yeh; I say, hain't seen yeh.

SAM: Yes, he has –

ANN: Didn't he hev a tantrum; I say, a tantrum?

HELEN: [*Concealing her true feelings, listlessly*] No, Mother, he didn't say much – not as much as –

ANN: I want to know! Well, there must ha' ben sumpthin' powerful on his mind; I say, on his mind.

SAM: I guess there is now, if there wasn't before. [*Sadly*]

ANN: Well, Nell, blow the horn. Dinner's all sot an' I don't want it to git cold. Sorry I can't ask yeh to stop, Sam; I say, I'm sorry I can't ask yeh to stop. [*She goes into the house*]

SAM: Thank you, I don't think I'd enjoy the meal. [*Helen and he look at each other, her eyes fill with tears*]

Helen goes up to the fence, picks up the horn hanging there and blows it twice. Then she turns back to Sam, letting the horn slip from her hand to the ground

SAM: [*Slowly*] Well, Nell, I suppose you and I might just as well say good-bye now as any time –

HELEN: [*Again quite overcome at the thought of parting with him, holds out her hand, which he takes*] Good-bye Sam. [*Cries*]

SAM: [*Very tenderly*] Good-bye, Nell. [*Draws her to him*] Don't cry! I don't know how soon I'll get away, but just as soon as I can I will. I'll try to see you before I go – if not – I'll –

HELEN: [*Pleadingly*] You can't take me with you, can you, Sam?

SAM: [*Wistfully*] No, Nell, I can't. I haven't got money enough. I ought to have a hundred dollars more than I've got to get away myself. [*Meditatively*] I wonder if Blake'd lend me a hundred dollars.

HELEN: [*Still struggling with her tears*] I wouldn't ask him – he'd only refuse you. [*She breaks down and clings to Sam like a child*] It's going to be awful lonesome –

SAM: [*Deeply moved*] I know – it's going to be pretty lonesome for me too. There, now – [*Taking both her hands in his*] I thought this was going to be one of those partings without tears – [*Trying to cheer her up*] nor promises – nothing but just confidence.

HELEN: [*Making an effort to overcome her grief*] All right – Sam. [*Lifting her head and taking a deep breath to get hold of herself, bravely but still with a slight break in her voice*] If I don't see you before you go, good-bye. [*Goes to the house, as if to go inside, stops at the door, and turns as though struck by a sudden thought*] I don't think you'd better come here again, Sam. I don't want to quarrel with Father if I can help it – [*With a note of fatality*] I'll have to some day I know – but I want to avoid it just as long as I can. [*She smiles and tries to brave it out, but it is plain that she is silently crying*]

SAM: [*Stands a moment, looking at her tenderly and longingly, as though loth to leave her. He cannot control his own feelings. He turns away abruptly as he says*] Good-bye, Nell, keep up your courage, my girl. And remember, it isn't as though it was forever, you know. [*He goes off right above the house*]

HELEN: [*Her eyes follow him off*] Good-bye, Sam. [*Waves her hand as if in response to him and calls after him*] Take good care of yourself, won't yeh?

SAM: [*Speaking off stage, as though from a little distance*] I'll take care of myself, you take care of yourself.

Helen turns slowly away and drags herself, broken and weary, into the house.

There is a brief pause, then Mary Berry, a lively girl of about 10, comes running from the road, left, into the yard. She has a little bunch of wild flowers in her hand. She is skipping gaily, and just as she is about to enter the house, Bob Berry, a sturdy little fellow of about 8 years with rosy cheeks and dancing eyes, runs on excitedly from the left, with his schoolbooks tied in a strap

BOB: Mary, Mary, take my books in the house, I'm goin' in swimmin'.

He throws the books into her hands and runs off right, above the house

MARY: [*Calling after him*] Bob Berry, if you go in swimmin' I'll tell yer Ma.

BOB: [*In the distance, off right*] Tell if yeh want to – ol' tattle tale.

MARY: [*Running into the house*] Ma, Ma, Bob's goin' in swimmin' –

Ike Richards, Lem Conant, Abe Higgins, and Steve Bailey, farmhands, enter from the left. With them is Tim Hayes, the hired man, a good-natured, red-headed Irishman. They are playing with an old football, laughing and scuffling in a friendly way.

Gates, with Mandy in his wake, follows the men on, and watches them, keenly interested

GATES: Give me a kick.

TIM: [*Good-naturedly*] Let the ould man have a kick.

The others jeer at this

ABE: He can't kick it, he's too old.

GATES: [*Enraged*] Too old, am I? You jes' see. [*Gates seizes the ball and gives it a tremendous kick which sends it flying down the road. The men cheer him derisively. Gates picks up a chip and puts it on his shoulder*]

GATES: [*To Abe, assuming a defiant attitude*] If I'm too old, you jes' knock this chip off'n my shoulder.

Abe hesitates, but the other men urge him on, at last forcing him into the fight. He and Gates have a brief rough-and-tumble wrestling match, which ends when Gates ducks Abe in the water trough.

The men greet Abe's defeat with shouts of laughter, and he hurries somewhat sheepishly into the house, followed by the others. Gates looks after them, wagging his head triumphantly

GATES: [*Calling after them*] Too old, am I? They don't build houses like they used to. An' they don't make boys like they used to, nuther! [*With an air of high satisfaction he goes off, down the road, lower right, followed by Mandy*]

Enter Uncle Nat along the road, upper right, wheeling Millie in the barrow. Millie has a line through the rod of the barrow, and is pretending to drive

UNCLE NAT: [*Talking as he enters*] An' after that they lived in peace and died in Greece, an' was buried in a pot of honey.

MILLIE: What's the else of it, Uncle Nat?

UNCLE NAT: There ain't no else to it. Besides,

this hoss don't do 'nother stroke of work till he gets his oats. [*He wheels the barrow down stage below the bench, right*]

MILLIE: [*Climbing out*] Wait till I unhitch yeh –

UNCLE NAT: This is a new-fangled hoss. He can hitch himself up and unhitch himself, and currycomb himself and get his own oats, an' – [*Uncle Nat goes to the trough and starts to wash his hands*]

MILLIE: [*Following him up to the trough*] Hossy want a drink?

UNCLE NAT: No – hossy don't want a drink. Hossy wants to wash his hands so thet he can set down to the table like a clean respect'ble hoss. [*Millie splashes water in his face. He staggers back, pretending to be drenched and shaking the wet off*] Is thet what yeh call givin' hossy a drink?

MILLIE: [*Chuckling*] Yep.

UNCLE NAT: Well, the fust thing yeh know, this hoss'll duck yeh in the hoss trough.

MILLIE: No he won't.

UNCLE NAT: Won't he? You jes' see if he won't. [*He talks to Millie in the manner of one child talking to another*] You can't throw water in a hossy's face without makin' him mad no more than yeh can give a elephant a chaw of o' terbacker without makin' *him* mad. Did yeh ever give a elephant a chaw o' terbacker?

MILLIE: No!

UNCLE NAT: Well, don't yeh try it, cause I knowed a boy in a circus once that give a elephant a chaw o' terbacker, an' he didn't see thet boy agin fer more n' a hundred years. But he jes' remembered it an' he blew water all over him. I tell yeh, elephants has got good memories – [*Uncle Nat takes a clean bandanna handkerchief out of his pocket and wipes his hands. He is about to enter the house, when he is stopped by the voice of Martin, who comes from the barn and pauses outside the barnyard gate*]

Millie resumes her play in the sand

MARTIN: [*Casually*] Nathan'l.

UNCLE NAT: [*Kindly*] Hello, Martin.

MARTIN: Be yeh hungry?

UNCLE NAT: [*Still mechanically wiping his hands*] Not powerful, but able to git away

with my rayshuns 'thout no coaxin' I guess. Why? [*Taking a step toward Martin*]

MARTIN: [*Still casually*] 'Cause I'd like to talk to yeh – [*Studying his face closely*] an' I d'know's I'll hev a better chance.

UNCLE NAT: [*Cheerily; putting his handkerchief back in his pocket*] I d'know's yeh will, Martin. [*He moves a few steps down right; Martin is up left center near the barnyard*]

MARTIN: [*Hesitates, picks up a stick, takes out a jackknife and whittles it, looking intently at the stick and walking down a few steps toward Uncle Nat. He seems rather to dread saying what is on his mind. Uncle Nat looks at him furtively; this unusual request puzzles him; he is apprehensive that it is of Helen and Blake that his brother wishes to talk, and a look of disapproval sweeps into his eyes. His face grows a bit stern, but his manner is kindly and attentive. After a pause Martin blurts out abruptly*] Mr. Blake's been here.

UNCLE NAT: [*Gazes at him curiously, looks off right as if he could still see Blake's buggy there, picks up a straw and chews it, and says carelessly*] Hez' 'e? [*Seats himself on the wheelbarrow*]

MARTIN: [*Seating himself on the stable bucket, which he has turned bottom upward*] Yes. He argues that we'd ought to cut the farm up into buildin' lots.

UNCLE NAT: [*Is dazed by this. It is so sudden and unexpected that he scarcely gets its full meaning, as he murmurs in a low tense voice*] Dooze 'e?

MARTIN: Y-e-s. He says there's a boom a-comin' an' the land's too val'able to work.

UNCLE NAT: [*Murmurs mechanically*] Dooze – 'e – ?

MARTIN: Yes. He wants I should pool in with him, an' build cottages an' sell 'em at a hundred per cent more'n they cost, an' git's rich's Jay Gould.

UNCLE NAT: [*Slowly it comes to him that his brother is saying "Sell the farm." He grows cold – there is a heavy painful lump where his heart was beating a moment ago. His eyes grow dim and tired – there is no sunshine – no more music in the day. Sell the farm – the dear fields with all their slopes and undulations, the great old silver birches guarding the orchard from the pastures, the gnarled oaks along the rocky* shore. *He knows in a thousand aspects this old farm, summer and winter, always affable and friendly to him, and it is here he has learned to know God and love him. He answers casually enough in a tone of wonderment*] I want t' know 'f he dooze. [*A moment's pause*] Where d's he talk o' beginnin'?

MARTIN: [*Blurting out half defiantly, half shamefacedly*] Out there at th' north end o' the shore front – an' work back t' his line.

UNCLE NAT: [*The numbness passes and there is a tingling in his veins. Tense set lines come into his face and his voice grows vital. He talks with his usual clear cadence and gentle rhythm*] Yeh don't mean up yonder? [*Pointing with his thumb over his shoulder, right. Martin looks up and nods*] Not up at the ol' pastur'?

MARTIN: [*Slowly*] Y – e – s –

UNCLE NAT: [*In a tense voice*] Dooze 'e calk'late to take in the knoll thet looks out t'Al'gator Reef?

MARTIN: [*As before*] Y-e-s – I s'pose he – dooze.

UNCLE NAT: [*Rising, speaking quietly, but with a quiver of smothered feeling in his voice*] Did yeh tell him – 'bout – Mother's bein' buried there – ?

MARTIN: [*Sulkily*] He knows all 'bout thet jes' as well as you do.

UNCLE NAT: [*With significance, but very simply*] Dooze. Well – what's he calk'late to do with Mother?

MARTIN: He advises puttin' on her in a cimitery up to Bangor.

UNCLE NAT: [*A deprecating shadowy smile flits across his face; he shakes his head slowly and replies*] She'd never sleep comfort'ble in no cimitery, Martin – Mother wouldn't.

MARTIN: Blake says thet's the choice bit o' the hull pa'sell.

UNCLE NAT: [*Gently persuasive*] Then who's got so good a right to it as Mother has? Yeh don't begrutch it to her, do yeh, Martin?

MARTIN: I don't begrutch nothin'. Only, Blake says folks ain't a-goin' to pay fancy prices fer lots 'thout they hev their pick.

UNCLE NAT: [*Gently reproachful*] D'ye think any fancy price had ought to buy Mother's grave, Martin?

MARTIN: Thet's sent'ment!

UNCLE NAT: [*As though rebuked*] Is it?

MARTIN: Yes, it is – Blake says –

UNCLE NAT: [*Nodding his head, with a little sad half-smile*] Dooze – well – [*He sighs*] P'r'aps 'tis – [*There is a pause; then, as though a flood of memories had suddenly rushed over him*] You don't rec'llect much about Father – de yeh, Martin?

MARTIN: No.

UNCLE NAT: You was so young – [*His eyes look far off down the years, and he tells the story simply and directly and the clear cadence and soft rhythm are like the colors in a picture*] a baby a'most, the evenin' him an' Si Leech was lost tryin' to save the crew o' thet 'ere brig – thet went to pieces on the reef yonder. [*Indicates over his shoulder with a nod of his head*]

MARTIN: [*Under the spell of Uncle Nat's mood, is touched, and replies very gently*] No. Mother'n you never seemed to care to talk much about thet.

UNCLE NAT: Mother an' me seen the hull thing from the p'int o' thet 'ere knoll – [*With a slight indication of his head over his shoulder*] After it was all over she sent me hum – told me to take care o' you – said thet I needn't come back – thet she'd stay there an' wait fer him. 'Twa'n't no use t'argy with Mother, y'know, an' so I went. I put you in yer cradle an' sot down alongside o' yeh. I d'know as I ever passed jes' sich a night – seemed s'kinder l – o – n – g. [*Pause*] Jes' as soon as it was light enough to see – I went back to find out what'd come o' her – I didn't know but what she might hev – but she hadn't – she was there – jes' where I left her – I don't believe she'd moved an inch the hull night. It had been a-rainin' – [*Pause*] Her eyes was sot in her head an' starin' right out to sea – ef I'd 'a' met her any other place but there, I swear I wouldn't 'a' know'd 'r. I took her by the hand to sort o' coax 'r away. "Nathan'l," she says, "when I die – I want yeh should bury me right here on this spot – so's ef Father ever *dooze* come back – he'll find me waitin' fer him." I hed to turn 'round an' look at 'er – her voice sounded so kinder strange – seemed as ef it come from way off somewheres. [*Pause*] She lived a good many years after thet – but I don't believe she ever missed a day 'thout goin' over t' thet knoll. I allus sort o' imagined she wa'n't never jes' right in her head after thet night. [*Uncle Nat is lost in memories for a moment. Then catching his breath and pulling himself together, he continues*] Well, Martin, there she is. We buried her there at last – you an' me did. I d'know, but seems to me – ef I was you – I'd kinder hate to sell thet fer a buildin' lot. Thet is, I'd want to be pooty partic'lar who I sold it to.

MARTIN: [*In the manner of a spoiled child, closing his knife with a sharp click*] I'm tired o' lightkeepin'.

UNCLE NAT: [*Warmly, with quick understanding*] I don't blame yeh. Why didn't yeh say thet afore? Yeh needn't do it no longer. Tim an' me kin take keer o' the light jes' as well's not. I only sort o' hang onto it 'cause Father had it put there, an' the Gover'ment named it after him – he used to think so much o' that.

MARTIN: [*Defending himself*] You *give* me your interest in the farm anyhow – made it all over to me the day I was married.

UNCLE NAT: [*Warmly, with a fine spirit of conciliation*] I know it an' I hain't never regretted it. I ain't a-regrettin' of it now.

MARTIN: [*Peevishly*] You seem to kind o' shameface me for wantin' to sell it.

UNCLE NAT: Didn't mean to, Martin – it's only nat'ral thet I should feel kind o' bad to see the ol' place cut up – but law sakes! Who'm I thet I should set my face agin improvements I'd like to know? [*Laughs*] You've got a wife, an' children, an' a family, an' all thet. Mr. Blake mus' be right. So go 'head an' build, an' git rich, an' move up to Boston ef yeh want to. Only, Martin – don't sell thet. [*Indicating over his shoulder, right, with his head*] Leave me thet, an' I'll build on't an' stay an' take keer o' th' light, as long's I kin – an' after thet – why – well, after thet – yeh kin put both on us in a cimitery ef yeh hev a mind to.

His voice trails off into silence. Martin stands downcast. Uncle Nat remains immovable, self-hypnotized by the recital of his story – somehow all the sting of it has passed and he is at peace. He is still contemplating the remote days of his boyhood, and he stands there picking a bit of string into fine shreds too deeply absorbed to be aware of the life about him.

Millie is lying asleep on the sand.

Ann enters briskly from the house

ANN: Sakes alive! Martin Berry, ain't you a-comin' to yer dinner today? I say today? [*Goes up center and looks off right*]

MARTIN: [*Slowly, starting toward house*] Yes, I was jest a-comin'. [*As he crosses to the house, he says very gently*] Nathan'l, dinner's waitin'. [*He goes slowly and thoughtfully into the house*]

ANN: [*Looking up the road and calling*] Bob – B-o-b! Bob B-e-r-r-y – Come out o' thet water – Come to yer dinner! – Yer back'll be all blistered! [*She sees Millie lying asleep and goes down to her*] Bless thet child, she's clean fagged out! Come to Ma, precious. [*She takes Millie tenderly in her arms*] Come Nathan'l, your dinner'll be stun cold. I say stun cold. [*She goes into the house with the child*]

Uncle Nat stands deep in meditation.

The Curtain descends slowly

ACT II

"The Silver Weddin'"

The Berry farmhouse kitchen.

SCENE: *A quaint old New England farmhouse kitchen of the better class, used partly as a living room. There is a large window center, full of pots of growing flowers. Beneath the window is a table upon which Helen places cups and saucers and from which she serves tea during the dinner. To the right of the window is a wooden sink with an old-fashioned hand pump, and there is a large stove to the left of the window, upon which a kettle is boiling and pots are stewing. Behind it is a woodbox. On the shelf back of the stove stands an old-fashioned cuckoo clock.*

A sturdy old open stairway is against the left wall, and at the back of it is a row of pegs, where hang Uncle Nat's old army coat and cap, and Helen's jacket and tam-o'-shanter. There is a door leading to the woodhouse to the left of the stove. Standing parallel to the stairs is a long dining table, covered with a white linen cloth. *Against the side of the stairs is a heavy old-fashioned mahogany sideboard, from which Helen later takes small articles, such as tumblers, and salt and pepper holders. At the foot of the stairs a door opens into the sitting room. There is a worktable, right, below the sink, covered with material for making bread, and on it are several loaves of bread fresh from the oven. Below the worktable is a door leading outside. To the right, between the door and the sink, is an alcove where stands a large old-fashioned dresser, holding dishes, pans, and various kitchen furnishings, also several large pies.*

At the rise of the curtain, Ann, Helen, and Perley are in the midst of extensive preparations for dinner. Millie is down right, by a chair, making doll's bread, very intent on her work. Ann is hot and flustered. She is dressed in an old-fashioned black silk dress, open at the neck, with a white lace collar. The skirt is pinned up, showing a white petticoat underneath trimmed with home-made lace, and there is a big white apron over all. Perley is cool and unconcerned. Mary and Bob, with aprons over their best clothes, are sitting on the stairs, polishing spoons and forks. Helen is setting the table. She is dressed daintily in a simple muslin frock, and also wears a large apron to protect her dress. She is grave and thoughtful; the memory of the encounter with her father is still sharp upon her. She moves about, doing her work with swift deft touches.

ANN: [*At the stove, stirring the cranberry sauce*] Sakes alive! I hup another silver weddin' won't come in this house in a hurry; I say, in a hurry. [*She goes to the table, and starts sharpening a carving knife, preparatory to cutting a large loaf of bread which is on the table*]

HELEN: [*At the foot of the table, as she finishes placing the knives and forks*] Ma, I've arranged all the presents on the center table. [*Smiling. She is very tender and sympathetic in her attitude toward her mother*] The sitting room looks like a jewelry store. [*She goes to the sideboard, left, and takes from it a glass jar holding teaspoons, and places it on the center of the table*]

MARY: Oh, let's go'n see! [*Runs off into the sitting room*]

BOB: Yes, let's do. [*Follows Mary*]

HELEN: Aren't you proud of them, Mother?

ANN: [*Seriously*] Helen, you know what the Bible says about pride's one day havin' a fall. No, I ain't proud. [*Turning and coming down slowly toward the center of the stage, absent-mindedly drawing the carving knife across the steel as she talks*] Of course, it's nice to be so remembered by everybody, an' there's a good many nice presents there – some I ben a-wishin' fer. But I think I value yourn an' the young uns' an' Nathan'l's an' Martin's the best o' the lot. Not thet I ain't grateful, but, somehow, the nearer – [*Fills up, hastily brushes away a tear with the back of her hand, and turns to the stove to hide her emotion. Lifts the griddle and pokes the fire*] How like the Ol' Harry this fire dooze burn! Seems es ef everythin' went agin me today; I say, today. [*Calls*] Tim! [*To Perley, sharply*] Tell Tim I want him. [*Puts the griddle back on the stove, and closes the damper*]

Perley goes down to the door, right, opens it, and calls Tim, each time in a different and higher key

PERLEY: Ti-m – T-i-m – T-i-i-m-m –

TIM: [*Outside, in the distance*] More power to ye, but it's the foine loongs ye have in ye! Fwat is it?

PERLEY: Mis' Berry wants y-o-u. [*Goes back to her work*]

ANN: [*To Perley, handing her a saucepan of potatoes*] Mash them 'taters; I say, mash them 'taters.

Perley gets the potato masher, takes the pan of potatoes to the sink, peels and mashes them, adding butter, salt, and a little milk.

Tim appears at the door in his shirt sleeves

TIM: Fwat is it, ye Andhrewscoggin' mermaid, ye? [*He starts to come into the room*]

ANN: [*Stopping him, peremptorily*] Scrape yer feet, Tim Hayes, an' don't track the hull cow shed over my clean floor; I say, clean floor. [*She is standing near the window, center*]

TIM: [*Wipes his feet on the door mat, and speaks ingratiatingly*] Yis ma'am. I will ma'am. Fwat can I do for ye?

ANN: I want you should split me a handful

of fine wood; this 'ere fire's actin' like the very Ol' Nick today; I say, today.

Tim goes into the woodhouse, and reappears almost immediately with a handful of small wood which he gives to Ann, who puts a few pieces on the fire. He returns to the woodhouse and during the next scene he is heard splitting wood

PERLEY: [*Who has now finished mashing the potatoes; speaking through Tim's business*] What yeh want I should do 'th these 'ere 'taters?

ANN: Put 'em in a veg'table dish an' set 'em in the ov'n to brown; I say, to brown.

Perley puts the potatoes into a vegetable dish, smooths them over, shakes two or three spots of pepper on them, and puts them in the oven. She takes plenty of time over this.

Ann stirs the cranberries, tastes them, lifts up the kettle and sets it back, and puts the griddle on the hole.

Uncle Nat appears at the top of the stairs, dressed in a new "store" suit. He looks very important and proud, and glances down expecting all eyes to be upon him, but nobody notices him. He comes down a few steps. His new boots hurt him, and he pauses and bends his feet on the toes, as if to ease the boots, murmuring to himself "Gosh, but these shoes do hurt!" He straightens up, comes down a few more steps, and again eases his right boot and, making a wry face, he slips his foot partly out of the boot, and finishes the descent limping, but with a comfortable sense of relief. When he is well toward the left center of the stage, he stands, anxious to be noticed

UNCLE NAT: [*In a jubilant tone*] Well, Helen, I got 'em on!

HELEN: [*Coming down to his left, and speaking delightedly*] Oh Uncle Nat! Ma, look! Isn't he sweet?

ANN: [*Stops in her work at the table in front of the window, and comes down right of him*] Well Nathan'l, how nice you do look; I say, look.

Perley comes forward a few steps and gazes at him admiringly

UNCLE NAT: How do they fit me?

ANN: Jes' es ef they was made –

HELEN: [*More critically*] Turn round, Uncle Nat. [*He does so with an air of great importance, and is very happy over the impression he is creating, for it is many a long day since he had a new suit of clothes. Helen smooths the back of his coat down with her hand*] The waist might be a trifle longer. Don't you think so, Ma?

ANN: [*Inspecting him carefully with her arms on her hips*] Oh! Do you think so? Seems to me's ef 'twas meant to be jes' thet way. [*Goes back to the stove*] I say, jes' thet way.

HELEN: Well, maybe it was. [*A pause. She returns to her work at the table*]

UNCLE NAT: [*Fingering his vest*] Helen, there's a button come off this vest a'ready. I guess they're jes' stuck on. I wish you'd sew 'em on with thread, by 'n' by.

HELEN: All right, Uncle Nat, good strong thread.

UNCLE NAT: [*With a complete change of manner, full of businesslike importance*] Well, how be yeh gettin' along – I hope yeh hain't sp'ilt nothin' since I ben away. Helen, will you get me my apron. [*He takes off his coat and places it carefully over the back of a chair, and comes down center. Helen gets him a woman's checked apron*] I want you should tie it in a bowknot so that when the company comes, I can get it off handy. [*He stands with arms outstretched; Helen ties the apron around him just beneath his shoulders. He pushes it down*] Not too high-waisted, not too high-waisted. [*He pushes his foot back into the boot and' limps to the stove*] How's the ol' cranberries gettin' on? [*Slight pause*] Who sot these cranberries on the back of the stove? [*Looks around at them all accusingly*] Don't yeh know nothin' in this house, or don't yeh? [*Lifts up the saucepan and puts it on the front of the stove. Tastes the cranberries, and says reproachfully*] Oh Ma, I'm sorry yeh put more sugar in the cranberries, yeh got 'em too sweet. I had 'em jes' right when I left 'em. [*Nobody answers*] Ma, did you put any more sugar in them cranberries?

ANN: [*Busy at the table, right, speaking over her shoulder*] I didn't put no more sugar in 'em.

UNCLE NAT: Well, somebody has. Helen, did you put any more sugar in them cranberries?

HELEN: No, Uncle Nat.

UNCLE NAT: Well, somebody did. [*Turning to Perley in an accusing manner*] Perley, did you put any more sugar in them cranberries?

PERLEY: [*A little resentfully, drawling*] I hain't teched 'em.

UNCLE NAT: [*Testily, imitating her drawl*] Well, *somebody's* teched 'em. Cranberries couldn't walk off the stove and get into the sugar bucket by themselves.

PERLEY: They wuz a-scorchin', an, I sot 'em back, thet's all I done.

UNCLE NAT: [*In disgust*] Well I wish you'd let 'em alone. I'd ruther have I don't know what around me than a lot of women when I'm a-cookin' of a dinner. [*Taking the saucepan off the stove, and setting it in the sink*] Nell, dish out them cranberries and set 'em t' cool some place 'r other, will yeh?

HELEN: Yes, in a minute. [*Gets a preserve dish from the alcove, dishes out the berries, and sets them on the table at the window*]

Bob runs on from the sitting room

BOB: Ma, can we play store with the presents?

ANN: Yes, play with 'em all you like, but don't break any of 'em; I say, don't break any of 'em.

BOB: Oh, we won't break 'em. [*Runs off*] Mary! Mary! Ma says we can play with 'em.

UNCLE NAT: [*With happy expectancy*] Now, les' see how the ol' turkey's a-gettin' on. [*Goes over to the stove, sees the damper is shut, and says indignantly*] Now, in the name of common sense, who shut up thet damper! [*Opens the damper with a jerk*]

ANN: Yeh must 'a' done it yerself.

UNCLE NAT: Upon my word, a man can't leave a stove out of his hands five minutes without somebody a-foolin' with it. [*He opens the oven door and looks at the turkey, his face aglow with admiration. They all stand around him, very much interested*] By George, ain't he a beauty? [*In a grieved tone*] Who turned him on his back? I had him on his side.

HELEN: You want him to brown all over, don't you?

UNCLE NAT: See here, who's cookin' this turkey, you or me? [*Smacking his lips*] Get the platter, he's done. Ef he stays in there any longer,

he'll be burned to a crisp. [*Helen gets a platter from the dresser*] Ma, you get me a dishtowel.

Ann gives him a dishtowel. All is bustle and excitement as he lifts out the dripping pan, and sets it on top of the stove. Uncle Nat is left and the women are right of the stove.

Tim comes in from the woodhouse with an armful of wood, both large and small pieces, which he dumps into the woodbox, afterward brushing the chips which cling to his sleeve into the box. He stands and looks admiringly at the turkey

UNCLE NAT: [*Glowing with pride*] What do you think of thet for a turkey, eh Tim?

TIM: As they say in ould Ireland, that's a burrd!

He goes over to Perley, who stands near the sink, right, throws his arm around her, and hugs her roughy and quickly. She hits him with a dishcloth, and he runs out down right, laughing, followed by Perley hitting the air with the dishcloth, trying to reach him. After he goes, she returns coolly to her work at the sink. This byplay is unnoticed by the others, who are intent on the turkey

UNCLE NAT: [*To Ann and Helen, chuckling; speaking through Tim's business*] I wonder what they call a turkey in Ireland, a critter? Give me a large fork. [*Helen gives him one*] Now a big spoon. [*Ann gives him one*]

ANN: [*As Uncle Nat starts to lift the turkey out with the fork and spoon*] Be careful. Don't stick the fork into the turkey; ef you break the skin, the juice'll all run out; I say, run out.

HELEN: Be careful, Uncle Nat, don't drop him.

UNCLE NAT: [*Puts the turkey back in the pan, turns from one woman to the other, and says with gentle exasperation*] Say, if you can find anythin' to do about the house, I wish you'd go an' do it an' leave me alone. Yeh've got me s' nervous, I don't know whether I'm standin' on my head or my heels. [*Gets the turkey into the platter, and says joyously*] There he is! Now put him in the oven to keep warm, while I make the gravy. [*Proceeds to stir the gravy in the dripping pan*] Nell, pour a little water in there, careful now. [*She pours some into the pan from the tea*

kettle] Thet's enough. Thet'll do – Thet'll do!
[*He pushes the kettle spout up*]

HELEN: [*Protesting*] Why, Uncle Nat, you
won't have half gravy enough! [*Attempts to
pour more in*] Ma, I wish you'd look at this!

UNCLE NAT: [*Turning to Ann*] Ma, you attend to your own business.

*While Uncle Nat is talking to Ann, Helen
pours more water into the pan. Uncle Nat turns
and sees her doing it, and he pushes the spout
up and burns his fingers. Helen drops the kettle
on the stove*

UNCLE NAT: Now you've done it, Nell! You've
got enough gravy to sail a boat in. [*Blowing
his scalded fingers*]

HELEN: Well, you want to thicken it with some
flour, don't you? Here! [*She takes the dredg-
ing box and sifts in the flour*]

UNCLE NAT: [*Making the best of it, stirs in the
flour as she sifts*] Thet'll do – Thet'll do –
Thet'll do! Do you want to make a paste of
it? Oh, Nell, don't put so much in, you've
got it all full o' lumps now. [*Unconsciously
blowing his scalded fingers, holding them up
in the air, and then again blowing them*]

HELEN: All right, Uncle Nat. Make the gravy
yourself. [*She returns to her work*]

UNCLE NAT: [*After a slight pause. He is now
stirring the gravy*] Now gimme the giblets,
an' I'll stir 'em in an' make the giblet sass.
[*There is no answer. He speaks a little louder*]
I say, some one o' yeh gimme the giblets, an'
I'll make the giblet sass. [*The three women
stop in their work and look at one another,
as if to say "What are we going to do now?"*]
Come, hurry up! [*A pause, Uncle Nat blows
his fingers*] Gimme the giblets I tell you!
[*Silence. Helen crosses over to Perley. Uncle
Nat gets impatient*] Will yeh gimme the gib-
lets, Ma?

ANN: I don't know where they be.

UNCLE NAT: They're in the choppin' tray, where-
ever you stuck it.

ANN: [*Holding up the empty chopping tray,
and showing it to him*] No they ain't nuther;
I say, nuther.

UNCLE NAT: [*As he continues to stir the gravy*]
Well, they was there. What yeh done with
'em?

ANN: I hain't done nothin' with 'em.

UNCLE NAT: [*Getting testy again*] Well, somebody's done suthin' with 'em. [*Turning to
Helen*] Hev you seen 'em, Nell?

HELEN: No, Uncle Nat.

UNCLE NAT: Well, *somebody's* seen 'em. [*Turning to Perley, accusingly*] Perley, hev you been
a-monkeyin' with them giblets?

PERLEY: [*Who has been trying to escape observation by violently scouring a pan at the
sink, blurts out*] I fed 'em to the chickings.

UNCLE NAT: [*Dropping the spoon with utter
exasperation*] Well, of all the durn gawks I
ever see you beat all! Thet ends the dinner!
No giblet sass. Me a-settin' down fer half an
hour a-choppin' giblets fer you to feed to the
chickings. Perley, yeh're a nateral born gawk.

ANN: [*Crossing to the table*] Oh, Nathan'l,
give me a hand with this table, will yeh?

UNCLE NAT: [*Going to the lower end of the
table*] What yeh want to do with it, Ma?

ANN: Oh, jes' set it out a piece from the stair.

UNCLE NAT: [*As they move the table slightly
toward center*] Be keerful, Ma, it fell down
last Washin'ton's birthday. [*Crossing to the
window and looking out*] Looks a leetle like
a shower. I hope it won't keep any of the
company away.

ANN: Oh, I guess not. They ain't nuther sugar
nor salt; I say, nuther sugar nor salt.

*Millie by this time has made all the dough into
little loaves on a tin plate, and she now takes
the plate to Ann. She has managed to get herself pretty well messed up with flour*

MILLIE: Mama, please bake this for dolly'n me.

ANN: Powers above! Look at thet child! What'n
the name of all possessed hev yeh been a-doin'
with yerself? I say, a-doin' with yerself?

MILLIE: Makin' bwead for dolly'n me.

ANN: [*Smiling indulgently*] Well, I should say
you hed. Nathan'l, tend to thet baby; I say,
thet baby. [*She takes the plate of dough from
Millie*]

*During the following scene, Ann, Helen and
Perley busy themselves with the dinner things*

UNCLE NAT: Yes, ef I didn't tend to her, I'd
like to know who would. [*Crosses to the sink,
takes a clean towel, and pumps water on one
end of it. He then goes center to Millie*] Upon
my word, Millie, this is too bad. Here's com-

pany a-comin' and you think we've got nothin' to do but run after you young uns every five minutes of the day. We put yeh all three this mornin' – why didn't yeh stay put? Mussy, mussy, mussy, what a dirty child!

MILLIE: That ain't dirt, it's bwead.

UNCLE NAT: [*Getting down on his knees, and beginning to clean her hands with the wet end of the towel*] Well, it's mighty dirty bread. Who'd yeh 'spose'd eat bread from such dirty hands as those? Who you makin' bread fer?

MILLIE: Dolly.

UNCLE NAT: [*Drying her hands*] Well, it's a good thing that dolly's only got one eye. She'd never eat bread from such dirty hands, not unless you kept it on the blind side of her. [*Washing her face*] My sakes alive, why, you'd scare all Mama's visitors out o' th' house with such a dirty face.

MILLIE: [*Talking through the towel*] Bob's got a false face.

UNCLE NAT: What's that?

MILLIE: Bob's got a false face.

UNCLE NAT: [*Drying her face*] Hez he?

MILLIE: Yes. [*Talking through the towel*] I wish you'd buy me a false face, will yeh, Uncle Nat?

UNCLE NAT: You don't want no false face, you want yer own sweet pooty little clean face. [*Kisses her*] Now shake yer frock. [*She shakes it in his face*] Don't shake it in my face. Stand over there and shake it.

MILLIE: Ain't I a nice clean child now, Uncle Nat?

UNCLE NAT: You're the nicest cleanest child in the hull State of Maine.

As Uncle Nat finishes making Millie tidy, the noise of approaching wagons is heard in the distance, and now all the guests except Blake arrive outside, amid great bustle and laughter, as if they had finished the journey in a race. Instantly all is excitement indoors

UNCLE NAT: Hello, Ann, here they be! [*Crosses up left*] Helen, take my apron off. [*She does so. Uncle Nat puts on his coat quickly, and hurries off, right, leaving the door open. He is heard greeting the guests outside*]

ANN: Mussy on me, an' I ain't fit to be seen to a nigger clambake; I say, clambake! [*She takes her apron off. Helen unpins her dress, and smooths it down*]

Helen and Perley go to the window. Bob and Mary run in from the sitting room. Millie goes to the door, right

CAPTAIN BEN: [*Outside*] Hello, Nathan'l – Many happy returns o' the day!

UNCLE NAT: [*Outside*] Don't git things mixed, Cap'n. This ain't *my* fun'ral. [*All laugh*] Step right in. Tim an' me'll take care o' the hosses.

All the guests enter together, laughing and talking. Captain Ben Hutchins comes first. He is a jolly man of about fifty, half farmer, half skipper, with iron-gray hair and a full beard; he wears a blue suit with brass buttons and a peaked cap. He is accompanied by Liddy Ann Nye, a motherly widow in half-mourning. They are followed by Squire Andrews, a very tall, wiry, distinguished-looking man about seventy-five. He is well-preserved, and has very gray hair and a pink face. He is very deaf, and carries a tin ear-trumpet which has seen much service. With him is Mrs. Andrews, a tall woman with white hair; she is dressed in good taste. The Doctor, Mrs. Leonard, and the Twins enter last. The Doctor is a genial country physician. His wife is a trifle overdressed; as her husband is a professional man, she feels a bit above the farmers' wives. The Twins are nicely dressed; the boy is in knickerbockers, and the little girl wears a white dress, trimmed with lace. The Doctor and the boy take off their hats as they enter. All the guests scrape their feet on the mat. They all speak at once

DOCTOR: Many happy returns of the day, Mrs. Berry!

MRS. LEONARD: Returns of the day, Mrs. Berry, I'm sure.

SQUIRE ANDREWS: Many happy returns of the day, Mis' Berry!

MRS. ANDREWS: I wish you many happy returns of the day.

CAPTAIN BEN: May ye live another twenty-five years, an' invite us all agin.

MRS. NYE: Well, Ann, I swan yeh look younger'n yeh did twenty-five years ago, an' no wonder!

As they speak, they are all endeavoring to shake Ann by the hand

ANN: [*Shaking hands with them all, excited and*

happy] Don't come near me, if you don't want to get yer clothes spattered. This ol' stove sputters like I d'know what today. I'm greasier'n a pig. I'm 'bleeged t'yeh all fer comin'; I say, fer comin'.

CAPTAIN BEN: Oh! Ketch any of us missin' one o' *your* dinners! [*All laugh*] I was tellin' Mis' Nye thet ef I had a cook like you aboard the "Liddy Ann," I'd stay t' sea the year 'round. [*Laughs*]

MRS. ANDREWS: The boot's on the other leg. We're obleeged to *you* fer askin' of us.

SQUIRE ANDREWS: [*With the horn at his ear*] What do you say?

MRS. ANDREWS: [*Through the trumpet*] I said Mis' Berry's lookin' well.

SQUIRE ANDREWS: Oh yes – she allus looks well.

ANN: Well, ef you'll all step into the settin' room an' lay off yer things, I'll run upstairs an' try to make the *bride* presentable.

ALL: [*Laughing*] Certainly, certainly, by all means! [*They all go off through the door leading to the sitting room*]

ANN: Children, take the twins in an' show 'em the presents, an' let 'em look at yer noo red albyum. [*She goes upstairs, followed by Perley*]

Bob and Mary, one on each side of the Twins, lead them by the hand in the direction of the sitting room. The Doctor, who is going out last, is stopped by Millie, who has a dilapidated doll, with no clothes, no hair, one eye, one arm and half a leg gone, in her arms

MILLIE: Tan 'oo ture my dolly, Doctor?

DOCTOR: Cure your dolly? I guess so. What appears to be the matter with her? [*Taking the doll, and entering into the mood of the child*]

MILLIE: She's sick.

DOCTOR: Sick! [*Looking the doll over*] I should say she was. What's come of her other eye?

MILLIE: She swallowed it, an' it's down in her little tummick.

DOCTOR: Is *that* so? My, my! She *is* in a bad way. Well, come along, and let's see what we can do for her. [*He goes out after the others, leading Millie*]

During this scene, Helen has been busying herself with the table, putting on the bread, butter, cranberry sauce, etc.

Martin and Blake enter through the door, right. Blake is in his best black suit, and Martin is dressed in his Sunday clothes

MARTIN: [*Speaking as he comes in*] Where's Ma, Helen? [*Crosses over to the row of pegs at the back of the stairs and hangs up his hat*]

HELEN: [*Coldly*] She'll be here in a minute. [*Shows that she and her father have not been on the best of terms since the quarrel with Sam. She is not rude, however*]

As Blake notices Helen's manner, he draws back and pretends to be wiping his feet on the doormat, so as not to hear what passes. He does not enter the room until Martin crosses the stage for his exit

MARTIN: [*Pauses, and looks at Helen*] Hain't you got over the sulks yet?

HELEN: I'm not in any sulks, but I can't laugh when you stick pins in me. [*She crosses over to the stove, kneels down, opens the oven door, and looks at the turkey*]

MARTIN: I don't want to stick pins into yeh, Nell. You give up Sam Warren, an' you an' me'll never have a word.

HELEN: [*Speaking over her shoulder and temporarily stopping her work, trying to hide her feelings*] He'll not trouble any of us much longer, I guess.

MARTIN: [*Pleased*] Hev yeh forbid him a-seein' of yeh?

HELEN: *You* have, haven't you?

MARTIN: Yes.

HELEN: Well?

MARTIN: An' ef he knows when he's well off, he'll do as I say. Company's come, I see.

HELEN: [*Rising*] Yes, they're in the sitting room.

MARTIN: [*As he goes out, left*] Come along, Mr. Blake.

BLAKE: I'll be there in a minute.

MARTIN: [*As he reaches the sitting room, he is heard saying genially*] Be yeh all here?

THE GUESTS: [*Outside*] Many happy returns of the day!

BLAKE: [*Whose eyes have been fixed on Helen from the moment he entered*] Well, Helen!

HELEN: [*Pleasantly, but distantly*] How do you do, Mr. Blake.

During this scene, Helen goes to the side-board, gets the tumblers and salt cellars, and begins arranging them on the table. She is at the left of the table; Blake stands right center

BLAKE: I suppose you'll be hevin' a silver weddin' of your own one o' these days, eh?

HELEN: [*Carelessly*] I don't know, I'm sure.

BLAKE: Did Sam tell yeh about wantin' to borry a hundred dollars o' me?

HELEN: [*Interested for the first time*] No. When?

BLAKE: Yesterday afternoon.

HELEN: [*Eagerly*] Did you lend it to him?

BLAKE: No, but I told him I'd give him a thousand if he'd pick a fuss with you, clear out, an' promise never to come back.

HELEN: [*Smiling scornfully*] What'd he say?

BLAKE: [*Pauses deprecatingly*] Said he'd – see me in Hell fust.

HELEN: H'm! [*As if to say "I knew he'd say just that." She turns and busies herself near the head of the table*]

CAPTAIN BEN: [*Outside*] I said fifty fathom.

THE GUESTS: [*Outside*] Oh! We didn't understand yeh, Cap'n Ben.

BLAKE: [*Insinuatingly*] Has yer father said anything to yeh about me *lately?*

HELEN: [*With a bitter little laugh*] No, he doesn't say much to me *lately* about anything, or anybody.

BLAKE: Well! I've got the biggest scheme fer gettin' him an' me rich! I'll tell you what I'll do with you.

HELEN: [*Proudly*] I don't want you should do anything with me, Mr. Blake. [*Crosses to the dresser, right*]

BLAKE: Your father's set his mind on you an' me gettin' married, y'know.

HELEN: My father had better mind his own business. [*She picks up a pie and wipes the under part of the plate with a dishtowel*]

BLAKE: His *own* business! Great Scott! D'yeh mean to say it ain't his business who his daughter marries?

HELEN: That's just exactly what I mean to say. [*Crosses to the table, left, with the pie, and sets it on the table*]

BLAKE: [*Gives a long low whistle*] Well, Sam Warren *has* filled your head with his new-fangled ideas, an' *no* mistake.

HELEN: [*Filling up with tears*] Never mind

Sam Warren, Mr. Blake. I can talk for myself.

BLAKE: That's just why I think s'much of you. Helen, I'm goin' to be awful rich. I'll give you half of every dollar I make for the next twenty years, if you'll marry me.

HELEN: [*Kindly, but with finality*] No, Mr. Blake, I can't marry you. [*She is. left of the table; Blake is right, close to the table*]

BLAKE: [*Wistfully*] Too old, I suppose?

HELEN: [*Sighing . heavily*] No, it's not that. That wouldn't make any difference to *me.*

BLAKE: Too orthodox? [*With large generosity*] You needn't go to meetin' if you don't want to. You can read all the novels you've a mind to. [*Beaming and enthusiastic, with a warm spirit of sacrifice*] I'll read *them books* with you.

HELEN: [*With a hopeless little laugh*] Oh, Mr. Blake, you don't understand me. [*Crosses to the sink, taking off her apron*]

BLAKE: [*Intensely*] No, nor you me. I never set my mind on a thing yet I didn't get.

HELEN: [*Scornfully*] I'm afraid you've done it this time, Mr. Blake. [*Gives her apron a vigorous and emphatic shake as she hangs it up on a peg by the sink*]

BLAKE: No, I haven't. I'm goin' to have you, Helen, or die a-tryin'. [*She turns and looks at him; he continues quickly*] Nothin' underhand though – nothin' underhand.

HELEN: [*With a scornful toss of her head*] I should hope not. [*There is a note of defiance in her voice*]

Uncle Nat enters through the door, right

UNCLE NAT: Helen – [*She runs to him and he says in a tense whisper*] Sam's out there by the wood pile. He's got the money an' –

HELEN: [*Joyously*] Got the hundred dollars? Where did he get it?

UNCLE NAT: [*Evading the question*] He wants to see you – [*Helen starts to go past him out the door. He stops her*] Not thet way. Slip out through the woodhouse. [*Helen runs out through the woodhouse door, left*]

BLAKE: [*Suspecting something, starts to go to the window as Helen crosses outside*] What's the matter? Anything wrong?

Uncle Nat stands between Blake and the win-

dow, picks up an apron, and shakes it in his face

UNCLE NAT: Helen's speckled pullet's fell inter the rain barrel.

BLAKE: Oh! I hope she ain't drowned. [*Trying to see through the window*]

UNCLE NAT: No, she ain't drownded, but she's awful wet.

Ann comes down the stairs, all freshened up, followed by Perley

ANN: [*Speaking as she comes down*] Well, be we all ready, Perley?

PERLEY: Yes'm. [*Puts the potatoes on the table*]

ANN: Well, let's have 'em in, Nathan'l.

UNCLE NAT: All right. You put the turkey on the table, an' I'll hev 'em in in three shakes of a lamb's tail.

Uncle Nat goes into the sitting room. As he is supposed to open the sitting room door, a loud laugh is heard.

Ann puts the turkey on the table

UNCLE NAT: [*Outside*] Come, dinner's all sot, an' fetch three or four chairs with you.

ANN: [*For the first time seeing Blake, who has been standing at the window, his hands behind his back*] Good afternoon, Mr. Blake. I was 'feared you couldn't git here, yeh're such a busy man.

BLAKE: [*Coming down to the table*] I'd drop business anytime to eat one o' *your* dinners, Mrs. Berry.

ANN: Well, I d'know whether the turkey sp'iled or not. Nathan'l's so fussy; I say, so fussy.

All the guests enter, laughing and chatting. Captain Ben, the Doctor and Martin carrying chairs. Uncle Nat is also carrying a chair, and is laughing heartily at some remark that has just been made. The guests stand around expectantly, waiting for Ann to seat them. Martin goes to the head of the table and begins to carve the turkey. The children come on leading the Twins, in the same manner as they went off

CAPTAIN BEN: [*As he enters*] It's the pootiest kind of a trip this time o' year.

MARTIN: How long'll you be gone this time?

CAPTAIN BEN: 'Bout six weeks to two months.

UNCLE NAT: When d'ye sail, Cap'n Ben?

CAPTAIN BEN: T'night – fust o' the tide.

UNCLE NAT: I've a durn good notion t' go with yeh. D'yeh want any more hands?

CAPTAIN BEN: Yep, come on, Nathan'l. I'll give you a berth, ten dollars, an' found.

ANN: Oh, fer pity's sake, don't take him till I get these dishes washed.

MARTIN: Where'll yeh set us, Ma?

ANN: [*Who has been standing at the upper end of the table on Martin's right, recollecting herself*] Oh! Mr. Blake – [*He does not answer. She calls again*] Mr. Blake!

BLAKE: [*Who has been at the window lost in thought, his arms folded behind him, his head bent*] Eh? Oh, I beg pardon.

As Ann indicates each place, the guest acknowledges it with a little bow preparatory to taking his or her seat

ANN: [*Indicating Blake's place at her right*] Set there please. I suppose I'd ought to make a speech – Mis' Nye – [*Indicates her place at Martin's left, at the upper end of the table*] to thank yeh all – Doctor – [*Indicates his place left of Mrs. Nye*] for yer pooty presents – Mis' Leonard – [*Indicates her place left of the Doctor*] but I never made a speech except once – Cap'n Ben – [*Indicates his place left of Mrs. Leonard*] 'n thet was twenty-five years ago – Mis' Andrews – [*Indicates her place right of Blake*] an' then all I said was "yes" – [*All laugh. She shouts*] Squire – Squire – [*He takes his place next to his wife*] I tell Martin thet ef I do live with him twenty-five years longer – the children 'll hev t' wait –

BOB: [*Stamping his foot*] Oh gosh! I wish you'd never hev any company – we allus hev t' wait! [*Goes off left, leading Sis Leonard by the hand, followed by Mary leading Bob Leonard. Uncle Nat half follows them off, motioning them to be quiet*]

ANN: – it'll only be 'count of the presents. [*All laugh*] Well, set by.

All busy themselves at the table, and do not see Helen, who enters, right, crying. She comes to Uncle Nat, who draws her to the center of the stage

HELEN: [*Softly*] He *is* going tonight, Uncle Nat.

UNCLE NAT: [*Tensely and quietly, soothing her*] There, don't let 'em see you cryin'. It'll all come right some day. You wait on the table. [*Turning to Ann and covering up his concern for Helen with a cheery manner*] Where be yeh a-goin' to put me, Ma?

By this time everybody is seated

ANN: [*Pointing*] Oh, you're down at the foot o' the class. [*All laugh*]

UNCLE NAT: Allus was at the foot of the class – [*Laughs, and sits down*]

Millie enters through the door, right, with her apron full of clam shells

MILLIE: [*Dropping the shells on the floor*] Where's my place, Mama?

MRS. NYE: Bless the darlin'!

CAPTAIN BEN: [*Gets up and offers his chair with mock ceremony*] Set right down here, I'll wait.

MRS. ANDREWS: [*Nudging the Squire*] Look at thet child.

SQUIRE ANDREWS: Yes – I will –

The above exclamations are simultaneous, and all are laughing

ANN: My blossom! Come to Ma, precious.

Millie goes to her; Ann takes her on her lap, wipes her face and hands with a napkin, and puts her in her high chair, which Perley has brought to the table.

Martin has gone on carving. Blake has tucked his napkin in his neck, diamond-wise, and spread the ends all over his chest. The Doctor and Mrs. Leonard have placed their napkins in their laps. Mrs. Nye has laid hers beside her place. Mrs. Andrews fastens the Squire's napkin around his neck. Uncle Nat sticks his in the breast of his vest like a handkerchief. All are laughing and chatting, then suddenly Martin taps on the table with the handle of his knife. They all pause instantly, and there is silence as they bow their heads in prayer. This must be done in a perfunctory manner, but in all seriousness

MARTIN: [*Quickly*] Now sing out what kind uv a j'int yeh'll hev.

The Squire remains with his head on the table, Uncle Nat shakes him

UNCLE NAT: Squire, Squire! [*The Squire looks up and places his hand to his ear*] Meetin's out.

MRS. ANDREWS: I'll hev secon' j'int, an' the Squire 'll hev a bit o' the breast. [*Mrs. Andrews has the Squire's plate*]

SQUIRE ANDREWS: [*Puts his hand to his ear*] Hey? – What?

MRS. ANDREWS: I said you'd hev a bit o' the breast.

MRS. NYE: I'll hev a wing.

CAPTAIN BEN: [*Heartily*] Gimme anything so's it's turkey.

BLAKE: I've no particular choice.

UNCLE NAT: [*After all the others have spoken*] Neither hev I. I'll hev the part that went over the fence last, ef nob'dy else *wants* it.

Martin helps rapidly. Ann serves the cranberry sauce. Perley and Helen pass the vegetables, bread, and butter. They all eat heartily

CAPTAIN BEN: [*With his mouth full*] Now thet's what I call turkey.

UNCLE NAT: Thet's what we cooked her fer, Cap'n Ben. Ann, don't be so stingy with yer ol' cranberry sass. [*Passes his plate*]

ANN: [*As she helps Uncle Nat to cranberry sauce*] Well, yeh can pass up again. There's plenty more in the sass dish.

UNCLE NAT: I only said that to be polite.

MARTIN: Now, folks, don't be bashful. It costs jes' the same whether yeh eat 'r not.

All laugh, except the Squire, who is busy eating.

Joel Gates appears in the doorway, carrying Uncle Nat's gun, with Mandy beside him. He stands there and cranes his neck to look over at the table, his eyes gloating over the food. No one notices him. They are all intent upon their food

UNCLE NAT: I don't believe the Squire heard a word of it. Squire, did you hear what Martin said?

SQUIRE ANDREWS: [*With his hand back of his ear*] Eh?

UNCLE NAT: He said it costs jes' the same whether yeh eat or not.

SQUIRE ANDREWS: Oh, we'll eat a lot.

UNCLE NAT: No, no – Not lot.

GATES: [*Still standing at the doorway, ingratiatingly*] How d' do?

UNCLE NAT: [*Looking up and seeing him for the first time*] Hello, Joel!

MARTIN: [*With hearty hospitality*] Hello, Joel – jes' in time. Set by an' hev some dinner with us.

All the guests greet Gates

GATES: [*Steps over the threshold, glowing at the invitation, followed by Mandy*] I didn't know yeh hed comp'ny.

ANN: Perley, set 'm a chair; I say, a chair. [*Perley starts to get a chair for him*]

GATES: [*Protestingly, to Perley*] No! No! [*Apologetically, to all the guests*] I ain't fit to set down with comp'ny, I ben workin' round the barn. I jes' fetched back yer gun, Nathan'l.

HELEN: I'll take her, Mr. Gates.

GATES: [*As he hands her the gun*] Be careful, Hel'n, she's ludded.

Helen sets the gun in the corner by the sink

UNCLE NAT: [*Casually*] Did yeh manage to kill thet there fox, Joel?

GATES: I found out 't wa'n't a fox. [*Very much interested in the turkey and the guests' enjoyment of it*]

UNCLE NAT: Thet so. What was it?

GATES: 'Twas a skunk.

A murmur of amusement goes around the table. Gates starts to go

MARTIN: Set down an' hev some turkey.

GATES: [*Deprecatingly, looking at the table longingly*] No, I'm too s'iled. Ef I'd 'a' knowed you was hevin' turkey – I mean comp'ny, I'd 'a' cleaned myself up a bit.

UNCLE NAT: [*While eating*] Now thet yeh be here, let Ma fix some on a plate to take hum with yeh.

ANN: Yes. Here, Martin, give him this, you can fix yerself some more. [*Holds Martin's plate; Martin fills it*]

UNCLE NAT: [*To the child*] Mandy, you come here an' git a piece of Ma Berry's pie.

GATES: [*To the child, who hesitates and looks up at him inquiringly*] Go 'n git it, ef yeh want to.

Mandy goes to Uncle Nat, who gives her a huge piece of pie. She returns to her father, holding the pie with both hands, her face in a glow of wonder

ANN: [*Giving Helen a plate piled high with food*] Helen, pass this to Mr. Gates.

GATES: [*As Helen gives him the plate*] Thank yeh, thank yeh. I'll jes' step inter the woodhouse an' eat it, then I kin hand the plate back.

MARTIN: No, set down there, ef yeh won't come to the table. Hel'n give 'im a chair.

Helen places a chair, center. Her manner is very gentle and kind

GATES: *Thank yeh.*

Helen gets Millie's small rocking-chair for Mandy. She sits down in it, and slowly rocks to and fro, and for the first time a look of childish joy appears on her face.

Gates settles himself in the chair carefully, with his knees drawn together and his toes resting on a rung, so as to make a table of his lap. With his shoulders hunched, he attacks the overflowing plate and becomes absorbed in the food. He eats as if he had been saving himself for this meal, and feeds the child generously with dainty morsels.

Meantime, the talk at the table continues

DOCTOR: Oh! By the way, Mr. Blake, did you buy the Swazy place?

BLAKE: Yes.

CAPTAIN BEN: L'see, how many acres is there in thet place?

BLAKE: Eighty odd.

MARTIN: What'd yeh hev to pay fer it, if it's a fair question?

BLAKE: Paid enough fer it – they knew I had to hev it.

UNCLE NAT: They ain't givin' land away nowadays, be they, Mr. Blake?

DOCTOR: [*To Perley*] Will you give me another cup of tea, please? [*She takes his cup and fills it from the teapot on the stove*] I'd like to sell you that ma'sh of mine, Mr. Blake.

BLAKE: How much shore front hev yeh got there?

DOCTOR: Sixty-seven rod.

BLAKE: What'll yeh take fer it?

DOCTOR: Well, I'm asking twenty-five hundred dollars for it.

BLAKE: Good Heavens! You hev sot it up. I'll give yeh a thousand fer it, half cash.

DOCTOR: The Squire's offered me more than *that* for it.

BLAKE: [*Astonished*] The Squire! What's he want with it?

SQUIRE ANDREWS: [*Hearing this*] Thet's my business. You don't s'pose you're goin' to be the only one to git rich out'n the boom, do yeh?

BLAKE: I *started* it.

SQUIRE ANDREWS: Columbus discovered Americky, but he don't *own* it. [*All laugh. The Squire looks round the table, well satisfied*]

UNCLE NAT: [*Laughing uproariously, to the Squire on his left*] Squire, thet's the best thing yeh ever said in yer life – I say thet's the best – [*Pauses, as he realizes the Squire is paying no attention, but is busily eating*] Yeh didn't know yeh said it, did yeh? [*The Squire still pays no attention. Uncle Nat turns to the rest of the company*] He didn't hear himself say it. [*All laugh*]

CAPTAIN BEN: So the Squire's got the fever too, eh?

SQUIRE ANDREWS: Yes, an' got it bad – see – [*Pulls out an oil paper map of his farm, laid off in lots, unfolds it, and shows it to the company*]

BLAKE: By George, he's got the start of all of us.

GATES: [*Picking gingerly on a drumstick*] Mr. Blake, I'd like t' sell yeh thet seven acre o' mine. I got a great view there. Yeh kin see fer fifty mile round, ef yer eyesight's good enough.

BLAKE: What d'yeh want fer it?

GATES: [*Very importantly*] Well, it's sort o' got round thet I sot a price. I told Gabe Kilpatrick, and he says I'd ought to git ten 'r fifteen thousand dollars fer it. [*All laugh*] Gabe says it'd make a great buildin' site fer Vanderbilt 'r Rockenfeeder 'r any 'o them far-seein' fellers. [*All laugh*]

ANN: Oh, Martin, thet man thet was here to see yeh yesterday was here agin today – who is he?

MARTIN: [*Speaking slowly and unwillingly*] His name's Beardsley.

UNCLE NAT: [*Cheerfully and unsuspiciously*] What is he, Martin?

MARTIN: [*Ponderously*] Surveyor!

UNCLE NAT: *Surveyor?*

MARTIN: Surveyor for this 'ere new geruntee land an' improv'ment company.

CAPTAIN BEN: Martin, will yeh gimme jes' a leetle taste more o' thet stuffin'? [*Passes his plate, Martin helps him*]

ANN: [*For the first time a little uneasy*] What's he want here, Martin?

MARTIN: [*As if forced to a stand, defiantly*] He's goin' to survey the farm.

ANN: [*Gulping down her food*] Survey it! What fer? I say, what fer?

MARTIN: [*In desperation*] I'm goin' to cut it up into buildin' lots, ef yeh must know. [*The guests stop eating*]

Ann is quite overcome at this news. She swiftly moves her chair out from the table, and stares at Martin in consternation

MARTIN: [*With forced change of tone*] Hev another wing, Mis' Nye.

MRS. NYE: [*Soothingly*] Hain't et what I got on my plate yit, Martin.

A damper now falls on the party

ANN: [*Passionately*] Martin Berry, you ain't a-goin' to sell the farm, be yeh? I say, be yeh?

MARTIN: [*Stubbornly*] You heerd what I said, didn't yeh?

ANN: Yes – I heerd yeh, but I can't *believe* yeh.

MARTIN: It's *mine*, ain't it?

ANN: [*Brokenly*] Yes, I s'pose 'tis.

MARTIN: Well, hain't I got a right to do what I like with my own?

ANN: I d'know's you got any right to turn me an' the children out o' house 'n hum.

Gates gently rises and gives his empty plate to Helen, a look of apprehension on his face. He tiptoes from the room through the door, right, followed by Mandy.

Uncle Nat gets up and places his chair in a corner, left, and crosses to right center

MARTIN: Thet's sentiment – I ain't a-goin' to turn yeh out o' nothin'. I'm a-goin' to move yeh all up to Bangor – I'm a-goin' to git rich.

ANN: [*Rising and folding her arms, her head*

in the air, proudly and defiantly] You won't move *me* up to Bangor, not ef you git as rich as Methuselum.

MARTIN: I'll leave it to Mr. Blake ef I –

BLAKE: I must say I think Martin's scheme's a –

ANN: [*Still with spirit, but with a break in her voice*] I don't allow's Mr. Blake's got any right to jedge atween you an' me in this: I say, in this.

MARTIN: [*Rising, and striking his fist on the table, angrily*] Look a-here! I'm goin' to git rich in spite o' yeh. Doctor, will yeh hev another piece o' the breast? I ain't a-goin' to be browbeat.

DOCTOR: No, thank you.

MARTIN: [*In a great temper by this time*] Fust Nathan'l tries it an' then you must set up a –

UNCLE NAT: [*Very tensely, but quietly*] I hain't never browbeat yeh, Martin – I only ast yeh to leave me thet little piece up yonder.

MARTIN: I won't leave yeh nothin'! I'm durned ef I don't sell the hull thing, humstead, grave-yard an' every dum –

Young Nat enters through the door, right, out of breath and greatly agitated

YOUNG NAT: Mr. Blake – Mr. Blake – Mr. Blake – [*Breathes fast*] You're wanted up at the store. [*All are listening*] There's been a pack-age o' money took out o' the safe.

BLAKE: [*Swinging around in his chair so as to face Young Nat, and resting his arms on the back as he talks*] A package o' money! What sort of a package?

YOUNG NAT: A hundred-dollar package.

Helen, who is standing a little above right center, listens intently

BLAKE: Who's been in the store today, thet yeh know of?

YOUNG NAT: [*Breathlessly*] Well, there was Mis' Peasley's hired girl, but she didn't take it. Joe Bennett – Dan Nourse – Sam Warren – [*Draws out Sam Warren's name significantly*]

BLAKE: [*Quickly*] Sam Warren! By George! [*Hitting the back of his chair with his hand*] He stole it.

HELEN: [*With suppressed anger and shame*] Oh, Mr. Blake!

BLAKE: [*To Uncle Nat, with a significant look*]

Thet's the speckled pullet thet fell into the rain barrel! [*To the others*] He hed to hev a hundred dollars to go out West with. [*All the guests except Captain Ben nod their heads as if to say "That's so, that's bad."*] He tried to borry it o' me. I wouldn't lend it to him, an' so he *stole* it. [*The guests all nod "That's it."*]

HELEN: [*Coming down swiftly to right center, quietly but determinedly*] You lie!

MARTIN: [*Who is still at the head of the table*] Helen! [*A slight pause*] How dast you call Mr. Blake a liar?

HELEN: [*Her voice quivering with indignation*] How *dare* he call Dr. Warren a thief?

BLAKE: [*A little angrily*] He *is* a –

HELEN: [*Fiercely*] You're a –

MARTIN: [*In a low tense tone, approaching her angrily with his hand clenched and partly lifted*] Helen, if you say that agin, I swear I'll –

Ann turns around with her back to the table, and starts crying into her apron

UNCLE NAT: [*Who has been standing with his fingers to his lips, trembling, fearful of Mar-tin's anger, goes between them and lays his hand on Martin's shoulder*] Martin! Don't do nothin' thet yeh'll be sorry fer all the days o' yer life.

All the guests have risen, rather embarrassed, but fascinated by this scene, and are standing at their places around the table. Mrs. Andrews ex-plains to the Squire through the ear trumpet

MARTIN: [*Shaking Uncle Nat's hand off*] Take yer hand off'n me. I tell yeh I won't be brow-beat by you, an' I won't hev *her* [*With an angry gesture toward Helen*] insult my friends.

HELEN: [*Her voice trembling with unshed tears of rage, her face flushed with angry excite-ment*] He insulted *me*, and if Sam Warren doesn't *thrash* him before night, it'll be because I can't make him do it, that's all.

Helen, during this scene, shows she is the mod-ern girl, and has the temper inherited from her father. Mrs. Berry is the old-fashioned, sub-missive wife, awed and frightened at Helen's daring to oppose her father

BLAKE: [*Losing his temper*] He'll be in the

lockup before night, if I can put him there. [*Picks up his hat and cane from the table by the window*]

MARTIN: *Turning and picking up the gun from the corner by the sink, and rushing over to Blake with it*] That's the thing to do. Git a warrant fer him an' ef he raises his hand to yeh – you – *shoot* – him.

Uncle Nat has been standing at one side, his kind old face white and drawn with anguish. He now comes forward and interposes

UNCLE NAT: Hol' on, Martin! Uncle Sam'l's mine – an' she wa'n't never made fer *murderin'* folks. [*Quietly, but with authority, he takes the gun and puts it back in the corner by the sink*]

BLAKE: [*Shaking his cane, a very heavy one, threateningly*] This'll do me!

HELEN: [*Dominating the whole situation, in a low voice quivering with contempt, to Blake*] Oh! You *coward*! [*Turning to her father*] Father, Sam's going away today. [*With tremendous authority*] You'd better let him go if you know when you're well off.

MARTIN: [*Taking her tone, tauntingly*] You'd better not interfere if you know when *you're* well off. I s'pose you'd like to go with him?

HELEN: [*Throwing her head proudly in the air*] Yes – I would.

MARTIN: [*Beside himself*] By God! If I lay my hands on him, I'll kill him.

HELEN: If you dare to lay a finger on him, I'll – [*Springs toward Martin as she speaks, with hands clenched. Uncle Nat catches her and puts his hand over her mouth. The tension is broken, and Helen bursts into tears, her head resting on Uncle Nat's breast*]

The guests now quietly leave the room, one by one, by the door left. Mrs. Nye takes Millie's hand and follows the others.

Perley, during all this, has gone on clearing away the table as if nothing had happened, only occasionally glancing in the direction of Helen and Martin. She now goes into the woodhouse, taking the platter with the turkey on it, as if to have her dinner there

MARTIN: [*Crossing to the door, right, as he speaks*] You'll find out that I've got some-thing to say about what you'll do and what you won't do! Who you'll marry and who you won't marry! [*He starts to go out. Young Nat blocks his way, and he pushes him roughly outside*] Come along, Mr. Blake! [*Blake passes out ahead of Martin, who turns and gives a last fierce fling at Helen*] You're not of age yet, my lady. I'll show Sam Warren thet ef my grandfathers *was* monkeys, they wa'n't thieves. [*He goes out*]

As Helen hears their receding footsteps, she runs to the window, and watches them out of sight. She is in a bitter, angry mood, and tears fill her eyes.

Uncle Nat sinks wearily and despondently into a chair, left center.

Ann is still standing with her back to the audience, crying into her apron. She is dazed and broken

UNCLE NAT: Well, Ann, it seems es ef our turkey'd come to a sort of an ontimely *end*, hain't she?

Helen leaves the window, takes a cup and saucer from the table, goes to the stove, pours out a cup of tea and comes down stage, slowly and listlessly, and seats herself left of the table. She mechanically reaches well across the table for the milk and sugar, stirs the tea, sips it, and nibbles a crust of bread

ANN: [*Turning, her voice tremulous with tears*] Oh, Nathan'l, I'm so 'shamed. I'll never look a neighbor in the face agin. Twenty-five years married, an' nothin' like this ever happened afore. [*Begins to cry*] To think o' the dinner all sp'iled after me cookin' myself hoarse over it. [*Starts toward the sitting room door*] It's enough to provoke a saint out of Heaven; I say, a saint out of Heaven. [*She goes off into the sitting room*]

UNCLE NAT: [*In a quick decisive voice*] Well, Helen, I guess Sam'd better git right away from here jes' 's quick's he kin.

HELEN: [*Frightened, quickly, in an awed whisper*] Do you think he took the money, Uncle Nat?

UNCLE NAT: [*Rising and going center*] 'Tain't thet, but there'll be trouble ef him an' Martin comes together. [*He takes off his coat, doubles *it up, and throws it in a chair, and begins to clear the table, first gathering the napkins, then the knives and forks, as he talks*]

HELEN: He *has* got a hundred dollars, y'know.

UNCLE NAT: [*Continuing with his work at the table*] I know thet. [*Reluctantly*] I let him hev the biggest part of it myself.

HELEN: [*Amazed*] You?

UNCLE NAT: It's the money me 'n Martin's ben a-savin' up to buy a tombstun fer Mother.

HELEN: [*Rising, and striking the table with her fist*] Then he shan't stir – one – single – step. [*Determined, her eyes flashing*]

UNCLE NAT: [*Dropping the knives and forks he has in his hand, and leaning over the table, appealingly*] I beg of yeh, Nell – git him away from here. There'll be murder ef yeh don't! [*Crosses to the right with two chairs*]

HELEN: I don't *care*. They *shan't* call him a thief.

UNCLE NAT: [*Stops and turns*] Now – now – Haven't they called 'im everything they could lay their tongues to a'ready? Don't yeh see thet I dasn't tell Martin I let Sam hev thet money? [*Puts the chairs down and goes back to the table*] Don't yeh see thet it won't do fer Martin an' *me* to come together? [*Taps the table with his forefinger*] Things hes gone too fur now.

HELEN: That's so – he's got to go. He's got to pay that money back.

UNCLE NAT: [*Under the stress of deep conflict and emotion, half turns away from the table with the napkins in his hands; then he turns around again and drops the napkins back on the table*] Yes, but he's jes' as pig-headed as any of the rest of us, an' if he knowed the money was Martin's he wouldn't tech a cent of it, not with a forty-foot pole. He'd want to stay right here an' fight it out – I'm 'feared. [*Picks up a chair and goes toward right center with it*]

HELEN: [*With quick decision*] He mustn't do that. I'd go with him if it weren't for Mother.

UNCLE NAT: [*Putting down the chair and, turning around amazed and awed, whispers quickly*] Would yeh, Nell? [*He comes back to the table*]

HELEN: [*Bitterly*] This'll never be a home to me any more.

UNCLE NAT: [*Taking another chair and going to the window*] It'll never be a hum to anybody any more, Nell. It's goin' to be all cut up into buildin' lots anyway.

HELEN: [*By this time she has worked her way round to the foot of the table. She now goes to Uncle Nat*] If it weren't for Mother, I wouldn't stay here another minute. [*Appealingly*] Would you blame me, Uncle Nat?

UNCLE NAT: [*Down left, goes to her and they meet center. He says tenderly*] How could I blame yeh, Helen? Things'll never be the same here agin, an' Sam'd be all upsot out there athout you – an' you'd never be satisfied here athout him. [*With gentle insinuation*] Now would yeh? He might get goin' to the dogs out there, an' then yeh'd worry – an' blame yerself – an' – [*Persuasively*] I d'know – seems to me – 's ef –

HELEN: [*Taking fire from his suggestion, is all eagerness and determination*] How can we get away? They'd see us on the train.

UNCLE NAT: [*Considering*] Oh, you mustn't go by no train. I'll drive yeh over as far as Ellsworth, an' –

At this moment, Captain Ben passes the window. Uncle Nat glances up and sees him, over his shoulder. He is struck by a sudden idèa, and goes toward the window and calls

UNCLE NAT: Oh, Cap'n Ben! – Cap'n Ben! [*As Uncle Nat calls, Captain Ben turns and stands leaning on the windowsill, looking into the room*] When did yeh say yeh was a-goin' t' sail?

CAPTAIN BEN: 'Bout an hour'r so – ef it don't come on to blow – looks kinder as ef we *might* git a sou'easter afore mornin'. [*Turns and starts to go, scanning the sky*]

UNCLE NAT: [*Stopping him again in a voice of hushed anxiety*] Cap'n Ben! [*Captain Ben again pauses, and looks at Uncle Nat*] Helen an' Sam's ben a-thinkin' o' takin' a trip down the coast fer quite a spell – [*Looks and nods at him significantly*] Would you mind droppin' 'em at St. Andrews's 'r somewheres along there?

CAPTAIN BEN: [*Taken aback for a moment, then, comprehending the situation, answers with bluff heartiness*] No, plenty o' room an' plenty o' grub aboard.

UNCLE NAT: Kin they go aboard now an' be stowed away somewheres?

CAPTAIN BEN: Yes, I guess so. Nell, yeh kin come right along with me now in my buggy. [*He leaves the window and continues off, right*]

During this scene, Helen has been standing tense as she begins to realize the significance of Uncle Nat's talk with Captain Ben. Now she turns and darts toward the pegs beside the woodhouse door, where hang her jacket and tam-o'-shanter. She pulls the cap quickly on her head, thrusts her arms into the sleeves of her jacket, and dashes swiftly to the door, right. Uncle Nat checks her flight

UNCLE NAT: Helen! – Helen!

HELEN: [*Stopping*] What is it, Uncle Nat?

There is a moment's pause as they both stand looking at each other. Then Helen comes slowly back

UNCLE NAT: [*Significantly, taking a plain little silver ring off his finger*] That's my mother's weddin' ring. You give it to Sam, an' tell 'im to use it the fust chance he gits. [*He takes her hand, puts the ring into it, and folds her fingers around it*] Now run along. Cap'n Ben's a-waitin'. [*He pushes her gently toward the door, and goes quickly to the table as though to hide his emotion*]

Helen walks slowly to the door, looking at the ring. She stops, and a sudden sense of loss seizes her. She turns, and, with a cry, goes back to Uncle Nat

HELEN: Oh, Uncle Nat, I don't believe I *can* leave you and Mother – not even for him. [*Flings herself into his arms and bursts into tears*]

UNCLE NAT: [*Folding her in his arms, his voice shaking with tears*] There now, don't talk l'k thet – Don't yeh start me a-cryin', 'cause ef yeh do, I'm afeared I won't let yeh go. [*As he talks, he turns and moves with her very slowly toward the door. His tone is the soothing one he would use to a child*] Now, see here. Tonight's my watch at the light, an' when you an' Sam an' Cap'n Ben an' all on yeh is a-sailin' down the harbor, a-singin' an'

a-laughin' an' enj'yin' yerselves – jes' as yeh git to the light, you look over there an' sez you to Sam, sez you – There's ol' Uncle Nat's eye, sez you – He's a-winkin' an' a-blinkin' an' a-thinkin' of us, sez you.

HELEN: Good-bye, Uncle Nat.

UNCLE NAT: No! We ain't a-goin' t' say good-bye; we're jes' a-goin' to say good afternoon, thet's all! [*Tries to laugh*] P'r'aps I'll come out there and see yeh one o' these days.

HELEN: [*Who has been comforted by Uncle Nat's words, laughs at him almost joyously through her tears*] Oh! – Will you, Uncle Nat?

UNCLE NAT: [*His face taking on a look of longing, with something of renunciation*] I said – p'r'aps – [*A pause*] In thet there palace o' yourn yeh used to talk s'much about when yeh was little. Remember when yeh was little how yeh used to say thet when yeh growed up, yeh'd marry a prince an' live in a gol' palace, an' I was to come an see yeh, an' yeh was to dress me all up in silks, an' satins, an' di'monds, an' velvets –

He half laughs, half cries, kisses her, almost pushes her out of the door, closes the door and bursts into tears, leaning his two arms on the door and burying his face in them

Curtain

ACT III. Scene 1

"Havin' an Understandin'"

Interior of Berry Lighthouse.

SCENE: *The room is octagonal in shape, with walls of white-washed stone, and its chief feature is an iron stairway leading to the tower above. This stairway starts well down left, then makes a turn, and extends up and across the back wall. There are small windows at intervals along the stairway. Beneath the stairs, about center, is a small, high, barred window, through which a terrific storm is seen raging. At intervals waves dash against the window.*

The entrance to the lighthouse is through a door on the right; it is made of heavy planks, and has a large latch and a heavy, old-fashioned lock. (Note: This door must be framed and set so as to slam with force.)

The whole room has an oily look and smell. On a shelf to the right of the window, about eighteen inches from the floor, is an oil barrel with a brass cock; beside it are some oil cans and a brass gallon measure for filling the light-house lamps. There is a brass pan on the floor beneath the barrel to catch the drip. Beside it is a wooden bucket. There is a shears for trimming the lamps on the floor at the foot of the stairway, and near it lies a coil of life-saving rope. A ship's glass, a sou'wester, an oilskin coat, and a pair of oilskin overalls hang on pegs on the wall, left. Leaning against the wall are oars and a boat hook. Several unlighted lanterns are standing about the floor.

The light from above shines down on the room.

At the rise of the curtain rain is heard falling in torrents outside. The wind howls, lightning flashes, and thunder crashes at intervals.

Uncle Nat is discovered down left sweeping the floor. He has the dirt in a little heap and is getting it into a shovel with a broom. His actions are mechanical and his manner is preoccupied. He has on his working clothes and his trousers are tucked into high boots.

Martin enters hurriedly from the right. He wears oilskins and carries a lighted lantern. He is pale and excited. As he opens the door, the rain, wind, and thunder can be heard outside. He slams the door behind him, puts the lantern on the floor, right, and stands a picture of excited anger.

MARTIN: [*Standing down right*] Helen's gone!

UNCLE NAT: [*Who has looked up over his shoulder as Martin entered, and then immediately resumed his work, quietly says*] Y – e – s.

MARTIN: Along with Sam Warren. [*Uncle Nat looks up, concludes not to speak and continues his work*] Did you know she was a-goin'?

UNCLE NAT: [*Without looking up*] Yeh.

MARTIN: Why didn't yeh tell me?

UNCLE NAT: [*Has got all the dirt on the shovel by this time; now he empties it into the bucket, right, sweeping off the shovel so that no dust will remain on it. He speaks as he does this*] 'Cause yeh didn't desarve to be told!

MARTIN: [*Striking a clenched fist against his open palm*] I'm her father, ain't I?

UNCLE NAT: [*Drily as he hangs the shovel against the wall*] Yeh didn't act's ef yeh was, today.

MARTIN: [*Who is still standing down right*] Then yeh blame me?

UNCLE NAT: [*Quietly*] Well, I ain't a-goin' to lie about it, Martin. [*He hangs up the broom*]

MARTIN: An' yeh uphold her?

UNCLE NAT: Yeh didn't know your own child, Martin thet's all. Ef yeh hed yeh'd 'a' knowed thet yeh might jest's well 'a' stuck thet there gaft [*Points to the boat hook*] inter her heart as to hev said what yeh did 'bout Sam Warren. [*He knocks on the oil barrel to see how much it contains*]

MARTIN: [*With concentrated bitterness*] He's a thief.

UNCLE NAT: Tut! Tut! Tut! He ain't. An' you know it jes' as well 's I do. [*He takes up the pan from beneath the barrel, pours the drippings into an oil can, wipes the pan with a bunch of waste, then wipes the cock of the barrel*] Yeh unly said it 'cos yeh was crazy, crazier'n a loon. I knowed she wouldn't stay here long after thet. Yeh see, she ain't me, Martin – she's young, an' – [*Slight pause*]

MARTIN: Where's Tim?

UNCLE NAT: Tim went to Ells'orth this evenin', hain't got back yit.

MARTIN: How'd they go?

UNCLE NAT: 'Long o' the mail. [*Crosses to the window, wipes the pane and peers out at the storm*]

MARTIN: I said how'd *they* go?

UNCLE NAT: Oh! Cap'n Ben took 'em in the "Liddy Ann."

MARTIN: [*Still standing right*] What time'd they start?

UNCLE NAT: [*Up center near the window*] Fust o' the ebb.

MARTIN: [*Slowly and with hate*] I hope they sink afore ever they pass the light.

UNCLE NAT: [*Quietly, turning and looking at Martin*] I wouldn't say thet if I was you, Martin – [*There is a brilliant flash of lightning followed by a loud crash of thunder. Uncle Nat nods toward the window, indicating the storm, and adds*] You mought git yer wish.

MARTIN: [*As before*] I mean ev'ry word I say. She's *disgraced* me.

UNCLE NAT: [*Never losing his tone of patient gentleness*] You've disgraced yourself, Martin, I guess. [*He is wiping the things on the bench with the waste*]

MARTIN: [*Slowly, through his teeth*] Be they married?

UNCLE NAT: No!

MARTIN: [*With a sneer*] Humph!

UNCLE NAT: Not – yit.

MARTIN: [*Bitterly*] An' never will be.

UNCLE NAT: [*With quiet confidence; he is down left*] Oh yes, they will. [*Thunder and lightning*] Ef they ever live to git to any place. Helen ain't a-goin' to forgit thet she's got a mother an' sisters – an' –

MARTIN: [*Going to him left, and laughing derisively*] You're tryin' to make me believe 'twas me that made her go – d'ye think I'm blind? She went 'cause she hed to go to hide suthin' wuss from her mother 'n me; she went 'cause she couldn't 'a' held up 'r head much longer here – she's –

UNCLE NAT: [*Dropping his work and turning on him and for the first time showing deep feeling*] Martin, don't yeh dare say it! Fer ef yeh do, I swear I'll strangle yeh right where yeh stand. [*The light from the tower grows dim*]

Note: This must be worked very gradually

MARTIN: [*Stubbornly standing his ground*] It's true an' you know it. Thet's why yeh hurried 'em away.

UNCLE NAT: [*Making a movement as though to spring at Martin's throat, shrieks hoarsely*] Martin, you've got to take thet back! [*The light in the tower flickers and goes almost out. There is the distant sound of a ship's gun*]

UNCLE NAT: [*With a sudden change of manner, in a quick, startled voice, as he glances up at the light*] Good land, what's the matter with the light? [*He crosses down right, and picks up the lighted lantern which Martin placed there on his entrance, speaking as he does so*] Tim's fergot to trim thet lamp, sure's you're born. [*Lantern in hand, he turns to go up the stairs. At the same moment Martin seizes the boat hook, and stands in front of the stairs, barring Uncle Nat's way*]

MARTIN: [*Hoarsely, but determined*] Yeh shan't go up them stairs.

UNCLE NAT: [*Paralyzed with horror*] Martin!

The ship's gun is heard again; it is nearer this time.

MARTIN: [*In cold and measured tones*] I say yeh shan't go up them stairs.

Again the gun sounds outside

UNCLE NAT: [*Almost beside himself*] Why, Martin! – Thet's the "Liddy Ann"! [*The gun is heard once more*] Thet's her gun!

MARTIN: [*Stolid, quiet, intense*] I know it.

UNCLE NAT: [*With a cry of protest and unbelief*] She'll go to pieces on the reef!

MARTIN: [*Grimly*] Let her go.

UNCLE NAT: [*Half crazed*] Yes – but – Helen'll go with 'er! [*He starts for the stairs*]

MARTIN: [*Stopping him*] Keep away, Nathan'l. I tell yeh thet light ain't a-goin' to be lit.

UNCLE NAT: [*Frantically pleading, his voice broken with emotion*] Martin, f'r God's sake, list'n to *me*!

MARTIN: [*Doggedly*] I won't listen to nothin'.

UNCLE NAT: [*Walking firmly over to him, speaking as he does so*] You've *got* to listen. [*Martin makes an angry movement*] I say – you've got to listen! We've got to hev an understandin' right here and now. [*Martin submits sullenly, and Uncle Nat continues to talk in hurried, nervous tones, pacing up and and down the space between Martin and the door, like a caged lion, rolling and unrolling the sleeves of his red flannel shirt*] I've ben playin' secon' fiddle to you long enough, Martin Berry, ever sence yeh was born. When yeh was a baby I walked the floor with yeh, an' sung yeh t' sleep night after night. At school I fit yer battles fer yeh, an' once I saved yer life.

The gun is heard outside

MARTIN: Yeh needn't throw thet in my face.

UNCLE NAT: I hain't a-throwin' it in yer face. I only want yeh not to forgit to remember it, thet's all. [*He goes to the window and peers out*]

MARTIN: [*Doggedly*] I know all about thet, I tell yeh.

UNCLE NAT: Do yeh? Well, then I'll tell yeh

somethin' yeh didn't know. [*Walks over and deliberately faces him, and says emphatically*] Did you ever know thet I might 'a' married your wife Ann?

MARTIN: [*Raising the boat hook, making a step toward him, white with rage, almost shrieks*] W – h – a – t?

UNCLE NAT: [*Hurried, tense, and almost hysterical*] Hol' on – I ain't through yit. I thought more o' her than ever a miser did o' money. But when I see thet you liked her too – I jes' went off t' the war – an' I let yeh hev her! [*Taps Martin's chest with his forefinger*] An' thet's sumpthin' yeh didn't know all about – wa'n't it, Martin Berry? [*The gun is heard outside*] But thet's neither here nor there – her child is out there – my child by rights! [*With sudden sublime conviction, almost heaven-inspired*] Martin, thet light hez got to be lit! [*With an angry snarl*] I give yeh the mother, but I'm damned ef I'm a-goin' to let yeh murder the child! Come away from them stairs, Martin – come away from them stairs, I say!

Uncle Nat seizes Martin, and the two men have a quick struggle. Then Uncle Nat with almost superhuman strength throws Martin the whole length of the room. Martin is dazed; he reels and staggers like a drunken man toward the door by which he entered, and blindly gropes his way out into the storm.

Uncle Nat seizes the lantern and starts to crawl up the stairs. It is hard work to climb them, the excitement has been too much for him. He gets up a few steps, then slips down again; he crawls up again on hands and knees, and once more slips down. He makes still another effort, falters, staggers, and, with a heartbreaking cry, falls and rolls down the stairs

UNCLE NAT: God help me! I hain't got the strength!

The thunder crashes, the sea roars, the lightning flashes.

The stage darkens as the light above goes completely out

End of Scene 1

Scene 2

"The 'Liddy Ann' in a Sou'easter"

Exterior of Berry Lighthouse.

NOTE: *The storm noises are well worked up before the scene opens. The stage is completely dark, as is the front of the theatre.*

SCENE: *An expanse of wild, storm-tossed waves, with the lighthouse, a dark, shadowy bulk, rising from the rocky coast on the left. The rain is pouring in torrents, the thunder roars, the lightning flashes. The boom of a ship's gun is heard above the din of the storm, and in the darkness, the "Liddy Ann," sloop-rigged and under reefed jib, makes her way slowly through the heavy seas, from right to left. She is off her course and perilously near the rocks. At intervals her gun booms and she sends up distress signals. The figures of Captain Ben, Dave Burgess, Gabe Kilpatrick, and Bill Hodgekins, as well as Sam and Helen, can be dimly discerned on board. The shouts of Captain Ben giving orders, and the replies of the crew are drowned by the noise of the storm.*

For a few moments the "Liddy Ann" tosses helplessly in the darkness. Then a tiny light appears in the lowest window of the lighthouse. For a second it wavers, then slowly it rises from window to window, as Uncle Nat climbs the stairs to the tower. In another moment the light in the tower blazes forth, showing the "Liddy Ann" her course. A shout of relief goes up from those on the boat, and as the "Liddy Ann" makes her way safely past the rocks

The Curtain Descends

ACT IV

"Me an' the Children"

The scene is the same as in Act II. It is fifteen months later.

SCENE: *Snow is falling heavily outside. The wind is howling; a little drift of snow can be seen on the window sash. A fire burns briskly in the* stove and everything has the appearance of the day's work being over. *The leaves of the table are folded, and a red checked cloth covers the table on which is a lighted lamp. The tea kettle is singing on the fire. Uncle Nat's gun is in its place in the corner by the sink, and his old army coat and cap are hanging on the pegs under the stairs, as in Act II. There is a large rocking chair up right, and a small one stands above the table, left. At the rise of the curtain, Young Nat is seated reading a book at the upper end of the table; he now wears long trousers instead of knickerbockers. From time to time he turns a page but instantly resumes his position to preserve the idea that he is very intent on the story before him. His elbows are resting on the table at either side of the book and his head is supported by both hands.*

Martin is seated on a chair, which is tilted back against the wall below the door, right. On his knees lies a blueprint map of his farm, which has been surveyed and laid off in lots. He is very dejected and in deep thought. Without realizing it he is grieving over the absence of his daughter, filled with bitter remorse for having driven her out of her home.

Ann is sitting at the right of the table, mending stockings. She wears a warm-colored woolen dress, with a white embroidered collar, and a crisp white apron.

Uncle Nat and Perley are preparing the Children for bed. Uncle Nat is seated, center, and Perley stands beside him. Uncle Nat is just finishing buttoning up Millie's nightdress, while Perley is helping Mary.

The Children all have nightdresses and worsted slippers on, and their clothes are lying in little heaps, one in front of each child, as though they had just stepped out of them. Millie's hair is in curl papers. Mary's hair is braided and tied. The children's nightdresses are made of Canton flannel, with legs and arms, covering them from the neck to the ankles, and they button at the back, Mary's and Bob's straight up and down, and Millie's with a little fall behind to let down.

Uncle Nat, Perley, and the Children are having a great deal of fun as the curtain goes up.

YOUNG NAT: [*Looking up from his book, as though continuing a conversation*] I tell yeh there ain't no Santy Claus! It's y'r father and mother!

MILLIE: They is too a Santy Claus, ain't they, Uncle Nat?

UNCLE NAT: Of course there is. See here, Nat, you jest read your book. When a boy gits too big to know there ain't no Santy Claus, he ought to know enough to keep his thumb out'n the Christmas puddin'.

Young Nat laughs and resumes his reading

MILLIE: Did yeh ever see him, Uncle Nat?

UNCLE NAT: See'm? Yes, sir, I seen him – lots o' times.

BOB: [*Smiling*] When was it, Uncle Nat? [*The Children surround Uncle Nat, scenting a story*]

UNCLE NAT: It was a g-r-e-a-t many years ago, when I was a little boy, not near so big's as you be, Bob.

MILLIE: Was you ever as big as Bob?

UNCLE NAT: Yes, sir, an' bigger. I was as big as you be once, an' once I was as little as Mis' Pearce's new baby. [*The Children all laugh*]

MILLIE: An' didn't have no more hair on yer head?

UNCLE NAT: [*Chuckling*] I hain't got much more now. [*The Children all laugh*]

ANN: [*Looking up from her mending*] Now young uns, hang up yer stockin's an' go to bed, I say go to bed. [*The Children, all excitement, prepare to hang up their stockings*]

BOB: I'm goin' to hang up my pants.

UNCLE NAT: You give me a piece of string an' I'll tie up one leg an' you tie up t'other, an' thet way we'll get done quicker. [*Bob ties up one leg, Uncle Nat the other*]

MILLIE: [*Watching enviously*] I wish I wore pants.

UNCLE NAT: Do yeh, Millie? Well yeh may yit afore yeh die. Don't you get discouraged. Things is comin' your way mighty fast. I tell you what you do. You give me yer petticoat and I'll tie up the skirt and make as good a bag as Bob's pants. That'll beat yer stockin's.

The Children all agree to this enthusiastically

ANN: [*While Uncle Nat is busy tying Millie's petticoat*] Mary, ain't you goin' to hang up yourn?

MARY: Yes, Mother. [*With a smile*] But I'm afeared I won't get anything.

The Children remove some towels which have been hanging on a line at the back of the stove, to make room for their stockings

UNCLE NAT: Now come on, git some pins. Bob, you get some clothespins. [*They rush to Ann, who gives them pins*] We'll hang Millie in the middle – jes' like a fiddle. Gimme a couple o' them pins, Mary. Bob, you go over there – [*Hanging Bob's knickerbockers on the line right*] You got the clothespins, Bob? [*Bob rushes into the woodhouse, and comes back with two clothespins. Uncle Nat fastens his knickerbockers to the line with them*] Mary, where'll you go? – oh, over here – [*He hangs Mary's stocking, left*]

During this scene Perley has lighted a candle and stands waiting to show the Children to bed. Ann watches Uncle Nat and the Children with amused interest

UNCLE NAT: Nat, ain't you goin' to hang up?

YOUNG NAT: Naw! 'Cause I know there ain't no Santy Claus.

MILLIE: [*Crossing to him and almost crying*] They is too, Nat Berry – you won't go to heaven ef you say thet.

UNCLE NAT: He won't go to heaven at all ef he don't say his prayers. Come now, gether up yer duds an' be off to bed.

The Children all pick up their clothes and shoes. Mary and Bob say "Good night" and kiss their Uncle Nat, then their father, who is moody, and their mother last. She kisses them tenderly. They go upstairs. Perley stands at the foot of the stairs, lighting them up

MILLIE: [*To Uncle Nat, who picks her up in his arms, clothes and all*] I wish you'd sleep with me tonight, Uncle Nat.

UNCLE NAT: Oh! My suz! I couldn't git inter *your* bed – be yeh skeered?

MILLIE: Jes' a 'ittle teeny might. [*Hides her head in his neck*]

UNCLE NAT: No, yeh ain't nuther. Yeh jes' want t' git me to try to git my long legs inter thet trundle bed o' yourn [*Puts her down*] and then kick me out on the floor like yeh did las' Sunday mornin'. But yeh

ain't a-goin' to do it tomorry mornin'. [*Spanks her playfully*] Go 'long with yeh, yeh little hypocrite.

MILLIE: [*Goes over and stands by her father demurely, with her clothes under her arm*] Good night, Papa. [*Martin picks her up by her elbows, takes her in his arms, and kisses her, quite tenderly, and unconsciously lets the map fall to the floor, where it lies unobserved. Then he sets Millie down and becomes once more lost in his thoughts. Millie moves a few steps away from Martin, then turns and looks at him and says softly and shyly*] I wish you a Merry Kiss'mus. [*Martin makes no response, and Millie turns to Uncle Nat lingeringly, as though loth to go to bed*] I wish it was mornin' so's I could see what's in my petticoat.

UNCLE NAT: [*Dogmatically*] Oh! Yeh do – do yeh? Tell yeh what yeh do, Millie. Yeh go to bed an' sleep till mornin' and then t'will be mornin' in the mornin'.

MILLIE: [*Going over to her mother*] Good night, Mama. [*Kisses her*]

ANN: Good night, I say good night. [*Bends over and kisses her tenderly*]

MILLIE: [*Full of Old Nick*] Good night, Uncle Nat. [*Going to him*]

UNCLE NAT: Good night.

MILLIE: Sleep tight.

UNCLE NAT: Go t' bed, yeh little baggage yeh! Be yeh going to bed 'r not? [*Shoos her away*]

MILLIE: [*Goes to the foot of stairs, and stops suddenly*] Oh! Uncle Nat?

UNCLE NAT: What is it?

MILLIE: [*In a mysterious whisper*] Look what's behind yeh!

UNCLE NAT: [*Entering into her play*] Oh, I'm skeered to look – what is it?

MILLIE: [*In the same manner*] Santy Claus!

UNCLE NAT: [*Pretending to be frightened, jumps*] Where? [*Millie laughs*] Ain't yeh 'shamed to skeer me like thet – I've a good mind to – [*He runs after her, she runs and laughs*]

MILLIE: Yeh can't ketch me! [*Laughs and runs around the table. Bob and Mary appear at the top of the stairs laughing and say "Run, Millie, quick, Millie!" Uncle Nat pretends he can't catch Millie*]

UNCLE NAT: [*At last catching Millie by the waist of her nightdress at the back, and carry-*

ing her as he would a carpet bag. She laughs very heartily all through the scene] Now, my young lady, I've got yeh and I'll see whether yeh'll go to bed or not! [*Carries her upstairs triumphantly, followed by Perley with the candle. He is heard talking all the way up the stairs; Millie is laughing*] I bet I'll put yeh to bed – or I'll know the reason why. [*Uncle Nat, Perley, and the Children go off through the door at the top of the stairs, and their voices die away in the distance*]

ANN: [*Calling after them*] I swan, Nathan'l, you're wuss 'n the young uns – I say wuss 'n the young uns! [*Gets up and goes to the window and looks out at the storm*] Mussy on me, what a night! I pity anybody thet's got to be out on sech a night as this. [*She turns from the window, and notices Martin, who sits brooding*] Martin, ain't you well – I say ain't you well?

MARTIN: [*Gloomily, not crossly*] Oh yes, I s'pose I'm well enough.

ANN: [*Crosses to him and smooths his hair*] Yeh worry too much – 'tain't a mite o' use to worry. I wish you'd take some o' thet pikrey – I know it'd do you good – I say I know it'd do you good.

MARTIN: I d'want n-o – pik-rey. Pikrey won't do me no good.

ANN: [*Goes back to the table and resumes her work*] Thet's jes' what Cap'n Ben Hutchins said last spring. But Liddy Ann managed to git some on't inter his vittels right along athout his knowin' of it an' it cured him. He was mad's a hornet when he found it out. I've half a mind to try it – I say to try it.

MARTIN: [*In the same manner*] Don't you put no pikrey inter my vittels if you know when you're well off.

ANN: [*Gently, with placid confidence and assurance*] Well, Martin, jes' as soon as you sell a few o' them lots yeh got laid off, – yeh said yeh was goin' to sell a couple a hundred of 'em in the spring, didn't yeh? I say didn't yeh? [*Absorbed in her mending*]

MARTIN: [*As if evading the question*] I said I *hoped* I'd sell some on 'em in the spring.

ANN: [*Gently*] Well I sh'd hope so, now thet you've cut the farm all up inter griddle cakes. Well soon's yeh do – I'm goin' to hev yeh go up t' Boston an' see a *reel* doctor. Not but

what Dr. Leonard's good enough, but now thet we're goin' to get rich, we kin afford a little better one. You ain't right an' I know it – I say, an' I know it. [*There is a tremendous burst of laughter from upstairs. Then Uncle Nat comes flying down, followed by all the clothes, shoes, etc. the Children had carried up. He half falls, and lands sitting on the bottom step. The Children all appear at the top of the stairs with Perley, laughing. Martin jumps. Ann gives a scream and rises*] Mussy on me – I tho't 'twas an earthquake! I say an earthquake! What in time's the matter with yeh?

UNCLE NAT: [*Looking up with an apologetic air*] Me'n the children hevin' a little fun, thet's all.

ANN: I should think yeh was. [*She crosses over to the stairs and calls up to the Children*] Ef I come up there 'th my slipper I'll give you suthin' to cut up about. Go to bed this minute, every man jack o' yeh, an' don't let me hear another word out o' yeh this night. [*As Ann speaks there is a dead silence and the Children all sneak away on tiptoe*] Perley, come and git these duds. I say git these duds. [*Perley comes down and gathers up the clothes and goes off with them upstairs. Ann sits down to her darning again, and for the first time observes Young Nat*] Nat Berry, ben't you goin' to bed tonight?

YOUNG NAT: [*Absorbed in his book; without looking up*] Jes's soon's I finish this chapter. The Black Ranger's got the girl in his power an' Walter Danforth's on his trail.

ANN: Le'see. [*She seizes the book and becomes absorbed in it. Young Nat thrums on the table; he is impatient, but polite; finally he falls into a reverie over what he has been reading*]

During the talk between Young Nat and his mother, Uncle Nat slowly rises from the stairs. Now he goes up stage and peers out of the window, speaking as he does so

UNCLE NAT: By George – we'll hev sleighin' tomorry an' no mistake, ef this keeps on! [*He comes down stage and addresses the rest of the speech directly to Martin, who pays no attention to him. Uncle Nat takes a chair and sits a little to the right of center. He lifts his left leg with his hands to cross it over his* right, but a rheumatic twinge stops him. He tries a second time, and succeeds in crossing his legs; his hands are clasped over his knee. His half-furtive glances at Martin, now and then, are full of affection and sympathy. The desire to engage his brother's attention is the persistent note of his mood, and Martin's rebuffs only act as a stimulus to his efforts. Now he looks expectantly at Martin, who continues to ignore him. Then he becomes interested in his shoe as he detects a broken place in it. He examines it carefully, and runs his finger over it. There is a slight pause and again he resumes his efforts to break down his brother's sullen resentment. There is an intimate tone in his voice as he remarks*] I hain't seen sech a storm – not sence I d'know when. Not sence thet *big* snowstorm we had 'way back in '59. [*He looks at Martin's blank face as if for confirmation, but there is no response*] Thet *was* a snowstorm! Couldn't see no fences n'r nothin'. Mail didn't git along here fer more'n a week. [*He looks at Martin as before. The same forbidding mask meets his inviting smile. He shakes his foot meditatively as if to gain sympathy from it; then he gives a long sigh*] Ol' Sam Hutchins was a-haulin' wood, an' got snowed in, an' when they dug him out he was friz stiffer'n a poker, a-settin' right on his lud. [*A pause. He steals a quick, inquiring glance at his brother's immobile face, then with the manner of one who finds himself in pleasant company, he remarks with fine unction*] I kinder like to see snow on Christmas. It kinder – I d'know – seems kinder sorter more Christmassier – somehow. [*He gives another glance at the unresponsive Martin, then he rises. He leans heavily on his right foot, then he moves the foot up and down, his shoe creaking loudly as he does so. He goes up to the window and looks out once more at the storm*] Phew! Ain't she a-comin' down! The ol' woman up in the sky's pluckin' her geese tonight fur all she's worth an' no mistake. [*He comes down, sees the map Martin has dropped, and picks it up. He handles it as though it were something precious. He looks at it a moment, and then bends his eyes upon his brother in a fine pride, as having in this map achieved a rare and wonderful thing. Then he seats himself in the same chair as be-*

fore and looks over the map*] Treemont Str – eet. [*Tracing the map with his forefinger*] Corn—hill Str – eet. [*With a glance of pride at Martin*] Wash – in' – ton Str – eet. [*There is a long pause, then Uncle Nat glances about the room*] 'Y George, Washin'ton Street's a-goin' to run right straight through the kitchen here, ain't she? [*He looks at Martin, who, for the first time meets Uncle Nat's eye, and shifts uneasily in his chair*] Haw – thorne Av – en – oo. [*He traces the map with his forefinger. Martin casts impatient furtive glances at him from under his eyebrows; then he gets up and goes toward Uncle Nat*] Hawthorne Avenoo begins at the northeast end o' the ol' barn an' runs due east to –

MARTIN: [*Quietly taking the map from him, folding it up and putting it in the breast pocket of his coat*] Ef you hain't got nuthin' better t' do than to set there a-devilin' me, I'd advise you to go to bed. [*He returns to his chair and lapses into his former mood*]

Uncle Nat and Ann exchange glances of wonderment and pleasure at the thought of Martin's having spoken to Uncle Nat. It is a big moment for them. Ann catches her breath and a look of surprise and delight crosses her face. She starts to speak, but Uncle Nat motions her to be quiet by putting his right hand over his lips and waving his left hand at her for additional emphasis. Then he rises and takes a few steps toward Martin. His face is illumined and quivers with joy, he speaks feelingly

UNCLE NAT: Martin – thet's the fust word you've spoke to me in over fifteen months. [*Martin remains stolid and silent. Uncle Nat continues half sadly, half jokingly*] Don't you think I've wore black fer you long enough? [*Wistfully*] Say, Martin, let's you and me shake hands and wish each other Merry Christmas tomorry jes' like we used to – when we was boys together – will yeh?

MARTIN: I don't care nuthin' 'bout Christmas – one day's good another t' me.

UNCLE NAT: [*Gently*] 'Twa'n't allus so.

MARTIN: Well it's so now. Merry Christmas – Humph! I'd like t'know what I've got to be merry about.

UNCLE NAT: Yeh've got *me* – ef yeh'll hev me –

MARTIN: [*Significantly*] Humph!

UNCLE NAT: You've got Ann. [*Martin looks up. Uncle Nat continues quickly as if he should not have said that*] You've got the children.

MARTIN: [*Half bitterly*] Yes, till they git big enough to be some help, then they'll clear out an' leave me as their sister did.

UNCLE NAT: [*Very gently*] Now – now – now – Helen didn't clear out an' leave *you*. She never'd 'a' gone ef you hadn't 'a' – said what yeh said about –

MARTIN: [*Murmurs almost inaudibly*] There now.

UNCLE NAT: [*Finishing the sentence under his breath*] Sam Warren.

MARTIN: I don't want to git inter no argument 'th you tonight! I know what I done an' I know what *she* done.

UNCLE NAT: Yeh never will let me tell yeh nothin'.

MARTIN: I don't want to *know* nothin' –

UNCLE NAT: [*With a quizzical smile*] Well – yeh come pooty nigh a-knowin' of it. I never see a man s' fond o' huggin' a sore thumb 's you be. [*With a complete change of tone*] Will yeh help me to fill the children's stockin's?

MARTIN: [*Half softening*] I hain't got nothin' to put in 'em.

UNCLE NAT: Well, I hain't got much, but what I hev got 's a-goin' in. Come, Ma, let's you and me play Santa Claus, then I'll go to bed. [*Ann makes no reply. Uncle Nat sees that she is absorbed in her book, chuckles, and decides to leave her alone. He passes Young Nat, flicking him on the shoulder with his handkerchief as he does so, and says*] Nat, come out in the woodhouse and lend 's a hand here, will yeh?

Uncle Nat goes off into the woodhouse. Young Nat gives his mother an impatient look, then shrugs his shoulders resignedly and follows Uncle Nat off. They return almost immediately, carrying between them a large woodbasket containing a lot of bundles, which they place down center. Uncle Nat sits in the same chair as before, Young Nat kneels at his left, and they begin to undo the presents. There are dolls, slates, picture books, big candy canes, a sleigh, a pair of skates, mittens, comforters, and any quantity of cheap toys, also a new dress pattern.

As the things begin to reveal themselves, Martin is interested in spite of himself

YOUNG NAT: [*With a note of triumph in his voice*] I *told* yeh 't was yer father an' mother all the time.

UNCLE NAT: [*Continuing with his work*] Did yeh? Well, yeh didn't know's much as yeh thought yeh did, old smarty. It ain't yer father an' mother *this* time – it's yer Uncle Nat, by George! [*They both laugh*]

MARTIN: I hope yeh hain't been a-runnin' yerself in debt agin fer them children.

UNCLE NAT: No, I hain't run in debt this time. I paid spot cash *this time*. Thet's how I got such good bargains. [*Shows a harlequin with a string to make it jump*] Jes' look at thet now fer five cents. [*Pulls the string and laughs*] It's wuth more'n thet to see Millie pull the string jes' once. [*Chuckling*]

MARTIN: I didn't know yeh had any money by yeh.

UNCLE NAT: I hadn't. I got Blake t' cash my pension warrant. [*He says this without making any boast of it*]

MARTIN: An' spent the hull on't on the young uns as usual, I s'pose.

UNCLE NAT: [*Still busy with the things; in a matter-of-fact tone*] Yep!

MARTIN: *Eight dollars* on sech foolishness – it's wicked.

UNCLE NAT: [*For the first time stopping his work and looking up*] Say, what d'yeh s'pose I stood up to be shot at fer thirteen dollars a month fer, ef it wa'n't t' hev a little fun on my income? Think I'm a-carryin' around this bullet in my shoulder all these years f'r nuthin'? Not much, Johnny Roach! [*Goes back to his work*]

MARTIN: [*Gently*] Yeh might 'a' bought yerself an overcut –

UNCLE NAT: Overcut – such weather as this? [*Holding up a candy cane*] Not while candy canes is a-sellin' b'low cost. What's the matter with the one I've got?

MARTIN: Thet ol' army cut? It's patched from one end to t'other.

UNCLE NAT: Thet makes it all the warmer. [*With humor*] 'Sides, yeh mustn't never despise a man jes' 'cause he wears a ragged cut.

ANN: [*Slamming the book shut with a sense of supreme satisfaction*] There! Ef ever a mean, contemptible houn' got his jest deserts thet Black Ranger got his'n – I say thet Black Ranger got his'n. Walter Danforth jes' –

YOUNG NAT: [*With loud protest*] Oh, *Mother*, don't tell! I want to read it myself. [*Goes back to the table, sits down, and resumes reading*]

ANN: I swan ef I didn't forgit it was Christmas Eve – an' all about the stockin's. Nat Berry – don't you ever bring another one o' them books inside these doors when I've got work to do. [*Jumps up and begins helping Uncle Nat*] Ain't thet a pooty dolly – I say a pooty dolly!

They now proceed to fill the Children's clothes, and hang things on the outside of them. There must be enough stuff to pack them. At the same time footsteps are heard on the porch outside, there is a stamping of feet as if to knock off the snow, and Blake enters. The snow drifts in as he opens the door and the wind howls. He is covered with snow and well muffled up. Martin, who has been half interested in the business of the Christmas presents, rises. Ann and Uncle Nat stop in their work. Young Nat looks up from his reading. Uncle Nat takes the empty basket and puts it back in the woodhouse

BLAKE: Too blizzardy to stop to knock. By George, what a night! I hain't seen such a storm since I dunno when. [*He is about to shake the snow from his clothing when Ann stops him*]

ANN: Don't shake it off on my clean floor, Mr. Blake. Nathan'l, git a broom.

Uncle Nat gets the broom, takes Blake up stage and sweeps the snow from his clothes, as the dialogue continues.

Perley comes downstairs with the lighted candle and puts it on the table. Then she crosses over to help with the presents

BLAKE: Didn't think I'd ever git here – by George. The snow's waist deep – [*To Uncle Nat*] Thank yeh, thet'll do I guess.

UNCLE NAT: [*Hanging up the broom*] Set down by the fire an' warm yerself. [*He places a chair for Blake*] Ef yer feet are cold stick 'em in the oven an' toast 'em a bit.

BLAKE: I'll thaw out my back first. [*Stands in front of the stove with his coat tails drawn apart and warms his back. Uncle Nat and Ann resume their work, Perley helping them. Blake observes them a moment in silence*] Well, y're at it I see. [*He watches them with a tinge of sadness in his face*]

UNCLE NAT: Yep! Christmas only comes oncet a year, y'know, in this family.

ANN: [*Displaying the dress pattern*] Thet's a-goin' to make Millie an awful pooty dress. Nathan'l, what was thet a yard?

UNCLE NAT: I d'know – I never ask no prices.

ANN: [*Contemplating the dress pattern*] Won't Millie be proud o' thet! I'll have it made up jes' 's stylish 's kin be. [*Puts it in Millie's skirt, or beneath it*] I say jes' 's stylish 's kin be.

UNCLE NAT: I heerd yeh – I *heerd* yeh –

BLAKE: By George, Martin, I'd give all I'm wuth in the world to hev jes' *one* stockin' a-hangin' in my chimney corner tonight.

ANN: You'd ought t' got married long ago, Mr. Blake.

BLAKE: I never saw but one girl wuth *hevin'* and she wouldn't hev *me*. [*Sighing*] I'll never git married now.

ANN: It must be kinder lunsome athout no children nor nothin', specially at Christmas. I say at Christmas.

BLAKE: I never noticed how lunsome it was till I see you a-fillin' them stockin's. I've ben s' busy all my life makin' *money* I hain't hed time to git lunsome. Now I'm gittin' old, I begin to see thet p'r'aps I might – [*He shakes off his retrospective mood*] Oh, Martin! [*He sets a chair down stage in front of Martin, sits astride it, and leans his hands on the back. They talk in low tones while Ann, Perley, and Uncle Nat continue their work. Blake's tone now is tense and low*] Did you hear about the Land Company's bustin'?

MARTIN: [*Alarmed*] Bustin'? What? When? How? [*He starts to rise. Blake motions him back in his chair and hushes him*]

BLAKE: [*As if discharging a disagreeable duty*] Sh! Yes sir, busted cleaner'n a whistle. Opposition fellers done it. They've bought up Lemoine, an' thrown it on the Boston market way down. Got a lot of Boston big bugs goin' to build there soon's the weather breaks.

MARTIN: Then *your* boom's over?

BLAKE: Yes, for five years anyway. [*Apologetically*] Folks ain't a-goin' to come here when they can go to Lemoine for the same money'r less.

MARTIN: [*With finality*] An' I'm ruined.

BLAKE: [*Really sorry*] Looks thet way – now – I'm sorry to say.

MARTIN: [*Slowly*] With my farm mortgaged to you for fifteen hundred dollars, an' the money spent in cuttin' it up inter buildin' lots. [*Blake drums on the back of the chair with his fingers. Martin rises as if to spring at him and says between his teeth but in a low tone*] Damn you – I –

BLAKE: [*Quieting him in the same way as before*] Hol' on. [*Points to Ann and Uncle Nat*] Yeh don't want them t' know, do yeh?

MARTIN: [*Sinking back in his chair and covering his face with his hands*] No, not tonight, don't tell 'em tonight.

Helen and Sam appear at the window. Helen has a baby in her arms. Uncle Nat looks up, sees them, gives a start

UNCLE NAT: Oh! My! [*They cross the window and disappear*]

ANN: What in time is the matter with you?

Blake looks up, Martin does not stir

UNCLE NAT: A tech of rheumatiz I guess. [*Rubs his shoulder*]

ANN: La! You sot my heart right in my mouth.

Blake resumes his former attitude. Uncle Nat whispers in Ann's ear. She starts to scream, and he claps his hand over her mouth then he motions her toward the woodhouse door. Ann runs out. Perley comes over to Uncle Nat to find out what is the matter. He whispers to her also, she gives a little scream and he claps his hand over her mouth and cautions her to be quiet. Uncle Nat goes out through the woodhouse door, followed by Perley. All this is unobserved by Blake and Martin

BLAKE: [*In an undertone to Martin; this can just be heard by the audience*] Don't worry, Martin, mebbe things'll come out all right.

Martin shakes his head without looking up

BLAKE: All yeh've got to do is to keep up the interest – y'know.

MARTIN: [*Without looking up*] Interest – how'm I goin' t' pay interest an' the farm all cut up?

BLAKE: I know, it's goin' to be a tough job. You'll hev to begin all over agin – seed down the avenoos – cut down the shade trees – an' plow up the hotel site.

Enter Uncle Nat from the woodhouse, carrying a baby, and followed by Ann. Martin and Blake are so absorbed in their talk that they do not see them

MARTIN: I wish you'd ben struck dumb afore ever you come here to set us all by the ears with y'r blame land scheme – I hain't had a minute's peace sence you fust put it inter my head.

BLAKE: [*Good-naturedly*] Thet's right, blame me. *Blame me.*

MARTIN: [*Flaming up in bitterness*] Who else *should* I blame? Ef it hadn't 'a' ben fer you, I'd 'a' ben satisfied as I was. [*Uncle Nat comes to center and Ann takes the baby, takes the shawl from around it and hands it back to Uncle Nat, who comes slowly down center*] Helen'd never left hum ef it hadn't 'a' ben fer you – [*Raising his head aloft*] I wish I was dead. I'm ashamed to look my wife an' children in the face. [*Just at this moment he sees Uncle Nat, who has been drawing near, the baby in his arms. Martin rises, and pauses, startled*] What's thet – ?

UNCLE NAT: [*Beaming, his voice almost choking with joy*] Kinder sorter looks like a baby – don't it –?

MARTIN: [*Puzzled*] Whose is it?

UNCLE NAT: [*Looking down at the baby and rocking it back and forth in his arms*] I d'know's I jes know!

MARTIN: [*Looks all round the room*] Where'd it come from?

UNCLE NAT: I got it – out on the doorstep jes' now.

MARTIN: Well, put it right straight back on the doorstep – I ain't the poor-master.

UNCLE NAT: This baby ain't lookin' fer no poorhouse – this baby's goin' to stay right here.

MARTIN: There's too many babies here now.

UNCLE NAT: No there ain't nuther. Yeh can't hev too many babies in a home. [*He crosses* and sits in chair center, and rocks the baby in his arms]

BLAKE: [*Hungrily, coming forward*] Give it to me. By George, I'll take it!

ANN: [*Coming down to Martin, and speaking gently, her voice full of tears*] Martin, won't yeh guess whose baby this is?

MARTIN: I ain't a-guessin' babies.

ANN: [*Twining her arms around his neck*] Guess this one, jes' fer me, Martin. Jes' as a sort of a Christmas present.

MARTIN: [*Looks at her earnestly, then says softly*] Tain't – Nell's – ?

ANN: [*Drops her eyes to the floor, afraid of how he will take her answer*] Yes – It's poor Nell's.

MARTIN: [*In a fierce loud whisper*] Poor Nell's? Yeh don't mean to say thet he didn't marry her?

Uncle Nat draws the baby close to his breast as if to shield it from even that thought

ANN: Oh yes, Martin, he married her.

MARTIN: [*Misinterpreting her words and her action, aghast, slowly, in a loud whisper*] You don't mean to say she's *dead*?

ANN: No, Martin, she ain't dead.

MARTIN: [*After a pause*] Where is she?

ANN: [*Points to the woodhouse*] Out there.

Martin looks from Ann to Uncle Nat, and back to Ann. Then he walks slowly up stage toward the woodhouse. At the door he pauses, hesitates, and finally says

MARTIN: Nathan'l – be keerful – don't drop that baby. [*He goes slowly out through the woodhouse door*]

Uncle Nat, still seated, continues to rock the baby back and forth. Ann looks down into the baby's face. Blake goes to the stove and stands with his back to it, and his coat tails parted behind him, absorbed in thought

UNCLE NAT: [*As Martin goes out, with quiet, sly humor*] I've held you many a time an' I never dropped *you*. [*Pause*] Well, Ma, I s'pose you're awful proud 'cause you're a gran'-mother. [*Reflectively*] Seems only the day 'afore yist'day since Nell was a baby herself.

The woodhouse door opens and Martin enters

slowly, leading Helen by the hand. She looks dazed, but very happy to be back in her home. They are followed by Sam, now a bearded handsome man who appears to be perfectly happy and gratified that Helen's wish to bring her baby home has been fulfilled. Sam has returned from the West a prosperous, successful man; they are both well dressed and have an air of achievement. Perley follows Sam into the room, her face beaming with joy. There is a long pause; everybody's eyes are on Martin and Helen. He leads her proudly and slowly down the stage before he speaks*

MARTIN: Nell – my girl – I'm glad to see yeh back, thet's all I got to say.

It is with difficulty that Martin can get these words out. Tears are in his eyes and voice. He kisses her. Blake has been standing spellbound, and now he blows his nose to hide his emotion. Helen creeps into her father's embrace, puts her arms around his neck, and looks pleadingly first at him and then at Sam, as though to say "Father, haven't you got a word for Sam?" Martin's gaze follows hers and he sees Sam. Helen draws away a little and Martin moves toward Sam. Ann goes to Helen and puts her arms about her; both women are tense, expectantly waiting to see what Martin will do

MARTIN: [*Making a big effort to conquer his pride*] Sam, I don't b'lieve I acted jes's a father ought to hev acted towards Nell, an' I didn't treat you quite right I know – I – [*Hesitantly stretches out his hand which Sam takes in a hearty grasp, and the two men shake hands*]

Ann and Helen, in great relief, embrace each other joyously

SAM: [*In a big warmhearted manner*] Oh! That's all right, Mr. Berry! You didn't quite understand me, that's all.

MARTIN: [*Introspectively*] Thet must 'a' ben it, I didn't understand yeh. [*Then with a complete change of manner Martin turns briskly to Uncle Nat, who is still seated in the chair nursing the baby, and in an almost boyish manner, says to him with an air of ownership*] Give me thet baby!

During the scene Helen and Sam go up left

*center to Young Nat and greet him affection-
ately. He proudly displays his long trousers.
Then they turn to Perley, who stands above the
table and greet her warmly. She helps Helen
off with her things, also takes Sam's hat and
coat and hangs them up on the pegs beside the
woodhouse door*

UNCLE NAT: [*Imperturbably*] No sir, this baby
goes right straight back on the doorstep where
it come from –

MARTIN: Give me thet baby I tell yeh –

UNCLE NAT: [*Rocking the baby in his arms*]
No sir! there's too many babies here now. This
ain't no poorhouse.

MARTIN: You give me thet baby.

UNCLE NAT: [*Getting up and handing him the
baby*] All right – take y'r ol' baby – I'm
durned ef I don't hev a baby o' my own one
o' these days – yeh see ef I don't – an' then I'm
durned ef I'll lend her to any of yeh – [*He
goes up stage*]

*During the next scene, Ann goes up stage, pokes
the fire, and puts the kettle, which is on the
back of the stove, in one of the front holes,
where it at once begins to sing; she bustles
about, gets the teapot and makes some tea.
Martin is standing center, holding the baby in
his arms, with Sam on one side and Helen on
the other*

MARTIN: [*Looking down at the baby*] How old
is it?

HELEN: Three months last Sunday.

MARTIN: Thet so? [*Looking down at it and
smiling proudly*] It's a pooty baby. [*A pause*]
What is it?

SAM: [*Proudly*] Boy!

MARTIN: Thet so? [*Glancing up*] H-h-hev – yeh
– named him yit?

HELEN: Sam calls him Martin.

MARTIN: Thet so! [*Calls to Uncle Nat, full of
pride*] Nathan'l, he's a boy an' his name's
Martin.

UNCLE NAT: Oh! Good Lord! I knowed all 'bout
thet long ago. [*Sits in the rocking-chair*]

MARTIN: Thet so – I thought I was tellin' yeh
news.

UNCLE NAT: Yeh wa'n't tellin' me no news,
was he, Nell?

HELEN: No, indeed.

MARTIN: Gimme that rockin' chair.

UNCLE NAT: [*Getting up from the rocking chair
and placing it in the middle of the stage*]
Give him the rockin' chair – he's a grandfather. He owns the *house* now –

*Martin seats himself in the rocking chair with
the baby on his knee. Uncle Nat sits in the
chair down right formerly occupied by Martin*

ANN: [*Bringing the pot of tea and cups and
saucers over to the table*] Here, Hel'n, you
an' Sam drink this cup o' tea.

*Helen and Sam sit down at the table, Sam at
the upper end and Helen on his right. Young
Nat is seated on the left of the table. During
the preceding scene, Blake has been hovering
on the outskirts of the group, forgotten for the
moment by all, profoundly moved at what is
taking place. He now musters up his courage
to speak to Sam*

BLAKE: Dr. Warren! Oh, Dr. Warren!

SAM: [*Rises and goes to him*] Hello, Mr. Blake.
Helen, here's Mr. Blake.

HELEN: [*Bows pleasantly*] Why, how do you
do, Mr. Blake?

BLAKE: Oh, I'm feeling pretty good for an old
man. [*Turning to Sam*] Dr. Warren, I'm
awfully ashamed of the part I had in drivin'
you away. It was small potatoes an' few in a
hill.

SAM: [*With the same hearty manner in which
he spoke to Martin*] Oh, that's all right, Mr.
Blake. You folks around here didn't understand fellows like me, that's all.

BLAKE: Well, I'm ashamed of it all the same.
[*He crosses to Helen*] Helen – I mean Mrs.
Warren – will you shake hands with me?

HELEN: Why certainly, Mr. Blake. [*They shake
hands*] Oh, by the way, Mr. Blake, did you
ever find out who stole your hundred dollars
that time?

All listen

BLAKE: [*Ashamed*] Well to tell the truth it
never *was* stole.

ALL: What!

HELEN: [*Amazed*] Never was stolen?

BLAKE: No! We found it stuck away in the
back part o' the safe – among a lot of papers.

YOUNG NAT: [*Rising and standing left below the table, half grinning and half ashamed, with a sort of bravado*] That was some o' *my* work. I hid it there.

HELEN: You – ?

ANN: You – what fer – I say what fer?

YOUNG NAT: [*Half crying*] I wanted to git even with Sam Warren fer pullin' my ear – I heerd him ask Mr. Blake fer a hundred dollars an' I hid the package. I was sorry the minute I done it and I'd 'a' told long ago only I was afraid of a lickin'.

ANN: Well, I swan to goodness ef you ain't wuss'n the Black Ranger – I say wuss'n the Black Ranger! G' long up to bed this minute an' not a doughnut nor a mouthful o' pie do you git fer a week – I say fer a week!

YOUNG NAT: [*Picking up his book, and taking the candle which Perley hands him, crying*] I won't stay here after to-morry – you see if I do – I'll go out West an' be a cowboy 'r somethin' – you see if I don't! [*He stamps upstairs in a rage*]

ANN: [*Calling after him*] Gimme thet book – I say gimme thet book!

YOUNG NAT: [*At the top of the stairs, throws the book, which almost strikes Perley*] Take yer ol' book! I don't want it! [*He tramps off, banging the door*]

ANN: Perley – put thet book in the fire. [*Perley picks up the book, starts to the stove with it, opens it, becomes absorbed in it, backs to the small rocking chair above the table, sits down, and reads it*] Martin Berry, be you a-goin' to let thet boy go out West an' be a cowboy or somethin' – I say or somethin'? [*Her voice rises in an angry shriek*]

UNCLE NAT: [*Who is still seated down right*] You set him to milkin' ol' Brindle to-morry – she'll knock all the cowboy out'n him.

They all laugh

BLAKE: Meanness is like a kickin' gun, ain't it? A feller never knows when it's goin' to knock him over.

MARTIN: [*Curiously*] Ef it's a fair question, Sam, where did yeh git the hundred dollars yeh went away with?

SAM: [*Pointing to Uncle Nat*] Didn't he ever tell you?

UNCLE NAT: I let him hev ninety-two dollars an' eight cents of it.

MARTIN: [*Surprised*] Where'd *you* get it?

UNCLE NAT: I borrowed the ninety-two dollars. Borrowed it off'n you an' me an' Mother. I knowed Mother wouldn't mind waitin' a month or two longer an' – it's all paid back long ago, Martin. It's in the ol' bean pot in the pantry there. [*To Blake*] Mr. Blake, thet was the speckled pullet thet fell into the rain barrel thet time.

BLAKE: Well, I don't know as it's goin' to do any good to stand here callin' ourselves hard names. Martin, I wish you'd let me hold thet baby jes' a minute.

Sam leans over to Helen as if to say "Don't let him, he might drop it."

MARTIN: No, *sir* –

ANN: Be keerful, you ain't used to handlin' babies, Mr. Blake, I say babies.

BLAKE: I suppose I could learn, same's the rest of yeh, if I had a chance, couldn't I? [*He takes the baby carefully in his arms, and looks lovingly at it*] Mrs. Warren, I hope you won't bias me with the Junior here – I feel's if me an' the Junior was goin' to be great cronies. [*Leans over the baby*] Look here, if they're mean to you here, you jes' come up to Blake's an' yeh can hev all the candy an' apples an' crackers yeh can lug off.

UNCLE NAT: [*With concern*] See here, Blake, you mustn't go to feedin' thet baby on green apples up to thet store –

BLAKE: [*To Helen, a little wistfully*] I suppose I can come over an' see him once in a while?

HELEN: Certainly!

BLAKE: Thank yeh. [*He looks at her. Ann comes and takes the baby. A knock is heard at the door, right*]

ANN: Come in – I say, come in.

Enter Gates and Mandy, both muffled up to their chins in worn, ragged garments, and covered with snow. Mandy's eyes instantly fall on the presents hanging by the stove, and throughout the scene she continues to stare wistfully at them

GATES: [*Speaking as he enters*] How d'do? [*He sees Helen and Sam, and his tone changes to one of surprise*] Why, *how'* d'do? I'd no idee *you'd* got back. Ef I'd 'a' knowed thet, I'd ben over afore – [*He sees Ann with the baby in her arms*] What's thet?

ANN: A baby – what'd yeh suppose 'twas? [*She crosses down left and seats herself in a low chair by the sitting room door, rocking the baby on her knees. Uncle Nat goes back to his work with the presents*]

GATES: [*Confusedly*] I wa'n't supposin' nothin'. I hadn't heerd any rumors afloat 'bout your havin' – [*The mistake dawns upon the characters, who look from one to the other and burst into a laugh, not sudden, but gradual. Gates is nonplussed*] Uh – whose is it?

HELEN: Mine.

GATES: *Yourn?* Well, who'd ever 'a' thought o' *your* havin' a baby? I tell yeh what, Nathan'l, thet West *is* a growin' country an' *no* mistake! [*To Ann*] I jes' come over to see ef I could leave Mandy here a spell tomorry – I got a job over t' Pearce's thet's *got* to be done tomorry, an' they got measles over there an' I'm skeered to take'r with me –

ANN: What'n the name o' common sense'd yer want to fetch'r out such a night's this fur? D'yeh want to kill'r – I say kill'r?

GATES: Kill'r? Gosh, I guess *not*. [*He pats Mandy lovingly*] She wouldn't stay t'hum.

ANN: Lunsome I guess, I say lunsome.

GATES: I guess'o – she's allus lunsome. Seems lunsomer Christmasses than any other time.

ANN: Let'r stay here now. She can sleep with the children, I say with the children.

GATES: Want to, Mandy? [*She looks up at him, he leans down to her and she whispers in his ear. With an apologetic smile*] Says she'd ruther sleep with me.

ANN: Well, she mustn't be lunsome to-morry – she must come over an' spend this Christmas with us –

UNCLE NAT: [*Coming down from the stove, where he has been working with the presents, with a doll which he gives to Mandy*] Here's a dolly fer yeh, Mandy. This's goin' t'be the jolliest Christmas we've had fer many a year.

MARTIN: [*Suddenly remembering*] An' the last one we'll ever hev in this ol' house.

SAM: The last – I hope not.

HELEN: [*At the same time*] Why, Father, what do you mean?

Uncle Nat looks at Martin in amazement

MARTIN: My durn land boom's busted.

ANN: [*Looking over at him full of sympathy*] An' thet's what's been a-worryin' of yeh! Poor Martin, I say poor Martin!

All the faces change; all are silent for a moment

GATES: [*To Blake*] Is thet so?

BLAKE: [*Earnestly and sympathetically*] That's 'bout so.

GATES: Then yeh ain't a-goin' t'build thet there Opperry House?

BLAKE: Well – no – not right off – I guess.,

GATES: Sorry. I'd like t'seen thet Opperry House. Them plans was beautiful. Knocks me out'n a job too – [*Chuckles*] I guess I got 'bout th' unly farm in the county thet hain't ben surveyed 'r cut up fer sumpthin' 'r other.

Uncle Nat places a chair for him, right center. Gates sits with Mandy standing between his knees. Uncle Nat goes back to his work

MARTIN: Hel'n, I'm poorer'n I was the day I come into the world. Blake owns "Shore Acres" now – or will by spring when his mortgage comes due.

SAM: How much is it mortgaged for, Mr. Berry?

BLAKE: All it's wuth.

ANN: Fifteen hundred dollars!

MARTIN: It'd take me ten years to lift it.

GATES: [*Shakes his head*] Yeh couldn't do it in ten year. [*Reflectively*] No *sir* – fifteen hundred dollars!

During the above scene Sam has been talking to Helen in a whisper, unheard by the audience

SAM: Nell, what d'you say if we mortgage our home and lend the money to your father?

HELEN: [*Delighted*] Of course – that's the thing to do –

SAM: We may lose it –

HELEN: No we won't – and if we do we're young – we'll get another.

SAM: Shall I tell him – ?

HELEN: Yes.

SAM: All right, here goes. [*Aloud*] Father – I mean Mr. Berry – we can help you *some*. We can reduce the principal a little and keep up the interest for you. Nell and I have scraped a little home together out there. We'd hate to lose it, but we'll borrow what we can on it and –

MARTIN: [*Deeply moved*] No – you shan't do thet – let the ol' place go –

SAM: Come out West with us and make a fresh start.

HELEN: [*Eagerly*] Oh yes, Father – do!

MARTIN: No, I'm 'feared I hain't got spunk enough. I'll stay here. Mother'n the children an' Nathan'l can go ef they've a mind to –

ANN: [*Her voice breaking*] Martin Berry, I didn't marry yeh to leave yeh. I'll stay right here with yeh. We'll live in the lighthouse ef we hev to, I say ef we hev to.

UNCLE NAT: [*In a gentle drawl*] Well, ef you think yeh're a-goin' to get red o' me – yeh're mighty much mistaken. Mother allus told me to watch out fer yeh, an' now by George thet yeh're gettin' into yer secon' childhood, I'm a-goin' to do it –

SAM: Mr. Blake won't foreclose – will you, Mr. Blake?

BLAKE: [*Regretfully*] I'm sorry, but it's out o' my hands. I'm as bad off as Martin is. I've bought, and mortgaged, and borrowed on everything I had – I can't realize fifty cents on the dollar. I'm simply land poor. Interest a-eatin' me up, principal a-comin' due – I don't know which way to turn. My lawyers advise me to make an assignment the first o' the year. Well, I guess I'll be a-joggin' along hum –

UNCLE NAT: What's yer hurry, Mr. Blake?

BLAKE: [*With a big sigh*] Well – it's a-gettin' late – an' I don't feel jes' right somehow – [*He gets into his coat and hat, Uncle Nat helping him*]

HELEN: Better let Sam prescribe for you, Mr. Blake.

BLAKE: [*Glancing at her and then at the baby, says gently*] He *has* – that's what ails me I guess.

SAM: I can fetch you around all right, Mr. Blake.

BLAKE: [*Hunting in his coat pockets for his gloves, and laughing in an effort to assume his old, cheery manner*] What with, sugar shot? No, by George, I hain't got t' thet yet – [*He pulls out his gloves, and with them a letter postmarked and stamped, and addressed to Nathaniel Berry*] Oh, Nathan'l, here's a letter come for you this evenin'. It's postmarked Washington, D.C. Weather bein' so bad I ᴜnought I'd bring it over.

UNCLE NAT: [*Taking letter, mildly surprised and interested*] Much obleeged, but I dunno who'd write me from Washin'ton.

ANN: The Pres'dent mebbe, wishin' yeh a Merry Christmas.

GATES: Yes! The Pres'dent ginerally wishes everybody a Merry Christmas – specially ef it's a-comin' on election time.

UNCLE NAT: [*Turning the letter over and over*] Nell, would you mind a-readin' this? Your eyes is younger'n mine. [*Gives her the letter*]

HELEN: [*Opens the letter and reads it aloud. The letter is written on a letter sheet with a small printed heading, such as is used by attorneys at law, not a commercial letterhead*] "Washington, D.C., December 18, 1892. Nathaniel Berry Esquire, Berry, Maine. Sir: Dr. Samuel Warren of Trinidad, Colorado, some months ago commissioned us to present your claim to back pension. We are pleased to inform you that our efforts on your behalf have been successful and that your claim amounting to $1,768.92 has been finally allowed. We have this day written Dr. Warren. Awaiting your further pleasure, we are, Very truly yours, Higgins and Wells, Attorneys at law." Oh! Uncle Nat!

There is a general murmur of amazement

UNCLE NAT: [*Who is standing beside Helen*] Well, I won't tech it. I d'want no back pension, an' I don't want nothin' to do with no durn lawyers. A pension grabber's next thing to a bounty jumper, an' I'll be jiggered ef I tech it.

ANN: [*Still sitting down left with the baby*] Why not? I say why not?

UNCLE NAT: 'Cause I never fit fer no back pension. I fit – 'Cause – [*He catches Ann's eye and stops. Ann looks at him significantly, and then at Martin, who sits, the picture of dejection. Uncle Nat glances around at the others, and reads the same implication in all their eyes. He wavers and finishes lamely*] 'Cause I fit.

ANN: Yeh airned it – didn't yeh? I say yeh airned it?

SAM: You know there's a good deal of difference between earning a pension and grabbing a pension.

GATES: Oh! My – yes – heaps. Seems to me – ef

I was you – [*No one pays any attention to Gates and his voice trails off into silence*]

UNCLE NAT: Thet's so – I didn't think o' thet. Le's see – [*His face is illumined with a rarely beautiful smile*] Tomorry's Christmas, ain't it? Ma, I hain't made you a *reel* Christmas present – not sence the day you was merried, hev I?

ANN: [*Smiling at him*] Thet wa'n't Christmas.

UNCLE NAT: [*Chuckling*] Jes' as good – wa'n't it? I'll tell yeh what I'll do – ef Martin'll make the place over to you – I'll take the back pension.

MARTIN: [*Broken and greatly touched by Uncle Nat's generosity*] I'd know as I've got a right to say either yes or no. I'll do whatever you and Mother wants I should. I hain't got a word to say.

UNCLE NAT: [*Going to Martin and clapping him him on the back*] Yeh don't need to say another word, Martin, not another blessed word. [*Turning to Helen*] Helen, git me ol' Uncle Sam'l. Say, Martin, Uncle Sam'l's the gal thet won the pension, an' she's the feller thet ought to hev it. [*Helen brings the gun down to Uncle Nat, who is standing center. He takes it, and speaks to it affectionately, half crying, half laughing*] Well, ol' gal, yeh've got yer deserts at last. Yeh not only saved the Union, but, by Gosh, yeh've saved this hull family! [*Still holding the gun, Uncle Nat starts to go through the Manual of Arms, while Gates watches him and imitates him*] Attention! [*He comes stiffly to attention. Gates does the same*] Shoulder-r-r Arms! [*He brings the gun to his shoulder. Gates pretends to do the same thing*] Carr-r-r-y Arms! Pre-e-sent Arms!

As Uncle Nat starts to present arms, the gun goes off suddenly. It must be loaded so as to make a great smoke and not too much noise. There is a movement of general excitement and panic. Helen's first thought is for her baby, and she rushes over to Ann and takes it in her arms. Gates picks up Mandy, heels in the air, and head down, and rushes to the door, right, as if to save her anyway. He stands frantically pawing the door in the attempt to find the latch and escape with Mandy out of harm's way, giving frightened little gasps as he does

so. *As the smoke clears away, the others all gather around Uncle Nat, who explains that the explosion was an accident. They are all excitedly talking and laughing, and completely oblivious of Gates, who, as the panic dies down, comes to his senses and turns his attention to Mandy. She is completely enveloped in her wraps and he has some difficulty in getting her right side up. When he finally discovers her feet, he sets her on the ground, frees her head from its wrappings, smooths her hair, feels her body to assure himself that no bones are broken, kisses her, and croons over her. Uncle Nat, still holding the gun, comes down to him, and starts to explain, but, at his approach Gates has another attack of fright, and seizing Mandy, he starts to back toward the door, waving Uncle Nat away*

UNCLE NAT: [*Laughing*] That's the fust time Uncle Sam'l ever kicked me!

GATES: [*Putting his fingers in his ears*] Gosh, that deefened me! [*Then, as if to test his hearing, he cries*] Oh! Oh! Oh!

Everyone laughs. They have all recovered their spirits as readily as they became depressed

BLAKE: [*Who has got to the door by this time*] Well, good night. [*He goes out*]

GATES: [*Who is still nervous*] I go your way a piece, Mr. Blake. [*He hurries after Blake, dragging Mandy with him. Uncle Nat shows them out, closes the door and locks it after them*]

ALL: [*Calling after them*] Good night, good night.

ANN: Come now, it's bedtime, I say bedtime.

There is a general movement. Uncle Nat puts the gun away, then he turns and begins the task of locking up for the night, plodding slowly and methodically about the room. Perley lights a candle, and goes upstairs and off. Ann lights a candle which she leaves on the table for Uncle Nat, and picks up the lamp. She and Helen move toward the door down left

HELEN: Yes – I'm pretty tired. Shall we sleep in my old room?

ANN: O' course.

HELEN: [*As she goes off left*] Are all the children well?

ANN: [*Following Helen off*] You'd 'a' thought so if you'd seen'm trainin' around here this evenin' [*Outside*] with Nathan'l.

Sam and Martin come down left, following Ann and Helen. Martin has his arm around Sam's shoulders

MARTIN: So you're a-doin' well out there, eh Sam?

SAM: First rate. That's the country for a young man.

MARTIN: I s'pose 'tis. Chicago must be a great city.

SAM: A wonderful city. Why don't you come out for the World's Fair? [*He goes off through the door lower left. Martin pauses at the door, turns, and looks at Uncle Nat*]

MARTIN: [*In a low voice*] Nathan'l. [*Uncle Nat looks up*] Yeh never told Ann about that night in the lighthouse – did yeh?

UNCLE NAT: [*Coming down a few steps toward him; in a deep whisper*] I never told her nothin'.

MARTIN: [*After a pause*] She'd ought to 'a' had you. 'Twan't jes' right somehow – [*He goes slowly off, lower left, closing the door*]

Uncle Nat stands looking after Martin, his face lighted up by an inner glow of peace and happiness. His thoughts are reflected in his face, but not a word is spoken. The scene is played in absolute silence.

He sinks into the rocking chair close by with a sigh of content and satisfaction. He settles himself comfortably, with his chin resting in his right hand as he thinks

UNCLE NAT: [*He thinks this*] Well, everythin's all right again. [*He nods his head approvingly*] I wonder how long Nell 'n' Sam's a-goin' to stay? A month 'r two anyway. [*Then a soft, tender smile creeps slowly into his face at the thought of the baby*] Bless thet baby!

I wonder what the young uns'll say in the mornin'? It'll be better'n a circus here when Millie sees thet baby. [*He chuckles softly at the thought. Then suddenly he scans the door, wondering if he locked it. He rises slowly, easing himself on the arms of the chair, and plods to the door; he tries the lock, then tucks the doormat snugly against the sill to keep the snow from drifting in. Then he goes to the window, rubs the pane to clear the frost from it and peers out*] Gracious! What a night! [*He stoops down, and looks up to find the lighthouse beacon. He nods his head*] Ol' Berry's all right – Tim's there. [*As he turns from the window, shrugging his shoulders and shivering a little*] Snow'll be ten foot deep in the mornin'. [*He goes to the stove and sets the kettle back, lifts one of the lids and looks at the fire. A thought strikes him*] By George, it's a-goin' to be pooty hard work to git the ol' farm inter shape again! [*He shuts the damper*] Well, hard work never skeered me – [*He goes to the woodhouse door and fastens the bolt. Coming down to the table he picks up the candle which Ann left there for him and starts to go up the stairs. At the foot he pauses, then he moves down to the door, softly pushes it open, and stands there for a moment looking off. He smiles to himself as he thinks*] I wonder what the young uns'll say in the mornin'? [*For a moment he is lost in thought; his right arm slowly relaxes. Then he turns and starts to climb slowly up the stairs, his heavy footfalls echoing through the empty room. The wind howls outside; the sharp snow tinkles rhythmically upon the window-pane. The stage darkens slightly. He reaches the top of the stairs and goes off, closing the door after him. The stage is left in darkness except for the firelight flickering through the chinks of the stove. The cuckoo clock strikes twelve and the curtain slowly descends*]

The End of the Play

THE GREAT DIVIDE

WILLIAM VAUGHN MOODY

WILLIAM VAUGHN MOODY'S *The Great Divide* was hailed as a landmark in American drama even in its own time. The reviews of the first New York performance, on October 3, 1906, carried such tributes as "the dramatic land-slide of the century," "a play of real and lasting merit," "a big significant play," "a new mark in American drama." Moody already had an established reputation as a first-rank young American poet, but this was his first and, as it turned out, his most notable venture into writing for the theatre.

Moody was born in Spencer, Indiana, on July 8, 1869, the sixth of the seven children of Francis Burdette Moody and Henrietta Stoy Moody. His father had formerly been a steamboat captain on the Ohio and Mississippi rivers, which may explain the family move to New Albany, Indiana, in 1871. William attended the New Albany public schools, graduating from the high school in 1885, and then entered the Pritchett Institute of Design in Louisville, to study painting. His mother died a year before his graduation, and his father a year after. The children were obliged to separate, and William went to live with a cousin, Charles Rowely, in Poughkeepsie, New York. After two years of preparatory work at the Riverside Academy, he entered Harvard in 1889. While at Harvard, he worked on the staff of the *Harvard Monthly*, became the class poet, and made the initial acquaintance of some of his lifelong friends: Norman Hapgood, Robert Herrick, Robert Morss Lovett, and George P. Baker, among others. Having completed all the work for his degree three years after his entrance, he was permitted to spend his senior year abroad, traveling in Germany, Switzerland, England, Italy, Greece, and Turkey. When he returned to Harvard in 1894, he became an instructor and graduate student in English. After receiving his master's degree, he accepted a post in the English Department of the University of Chicago as an associate of John M. Manly, Robert Herrick, and Robert Morss Lovett. Although he became known at Chicago as a conscientious teacher, when he retired in 1902 to devote himself to writing and traveling Moody said, "I cannot do it; at every lecture I slay a poet." The poetic spirit permeated Moody's entire life. Traveling with his friends among the scenes of historical and natural beauty, particularly in Italy, and breathing in the glories of past and present wonders was for him poetic living, the only tolerable way to live. During the summer of 1902 in Paris, he and Trumbull Stickney read all the Greek tragedies in the original. Casual acquaintanceships were studiously limited, but he shared the smallest details of his day-to-day living and the philosophical flights of his poetic imagination with a number of close friends: Ridgely Torrence, Ferdinand Schevill, E. A. Robinson, Percy MacKaye, and Mrs. Harriet C. Brainerd.

Moody met Harriet Brainerd (she had recently been divorced) at her Chicago home sometime before 1900, but their "spiritual union," which finally culminated in their marriage on May 7, 1909, dated from the spring of 1901, when Harriet broke her ankle at a beach party on the shores of Lake Michigan, an injury from which she never fully recovered. Moody had been in attendance on this occasion. The brief period of their marriage was marred, however, by his, rather than her, illness. They spent the first summer of their marriage traveling in England, hoping that this would restore his health. The therapy was ineffective. They returned to Baltimore, where two brain-tumor operations were performed at Johns Hopkins. With his sight nearly gone, but still hoping for his eventual recovery, they took a house in California for the winter of 1909. During that winter and spring and a summer in Chicago, Moody had few days free from pain. In the autumn they moved to Colorado Springs, where he died on October 17, 1910.

Prior to *The Great Divide*, Moody had written two verse dramas of a proposed trilogy on the theme of "the unity of God and man": *The Masque of Judgement* (1900) and *The Fire Bringer* (1904). He completed only one act of the third part, *The Death of Eve*. His *Poems*, containing the well-known "Gloucester Moors," "An Ode Written in Time of Hesitation," and "The Quarry," appeared in 1901, and the *History of English Literature*, written in collaboration with Robert Morss Lovett, was published in 1902. *The Faith Healer*, a play dealing with a spiritually inspired healer battling against the skeptics and the cynics and against the claims of his own flesh, was in preparation in 1900, before *The Great Divide*, but it was not produced until after Moody was too ill to see it. First performed in St. Louis in the spring of 1909, is was repeated by Henry Miller in New York the following January, but without success.

Although Moody was preoccupied with the poetic spirit and perpetually probed for the "mystery behind the external frame" of reality, he was not an ivory-tower poetizer. He felt a strong affinity for the visible, tangible world, both in his living and in his writing. It was thus not surprising that his interest in the theatre matured rapidly. In two letters to Daniel Gregory Mason (the first on April 8, 1898; the second on January 17, 1899) he wrote:

I have already met a number of capital chaps [in New York] – chiefly playwrights.

. . . The great thing about them is that they get their things played, and that sort of thing, begad, begins to appeal to me.

I found myself embarrassed a good deal at first by the dull monochromatic medium of everyday speech, but am getting more used to it now, and find that when you do get an effect in it, it is more flooring than anything to be got with bright pigments.

During the winters of 1903–4 and 1904–5, he was living in New York and attending the theatre regularly.

Moody found much of the inspiration for *The Great Divide* during his visits to Colorado and Arizona in 1901 and in 1904, but the dramatic story was suggested to him by Harriet Brainerd. The play was written during the summer and fall of 1905 while Moody was convalescing from a leg operation. His first draft, entitled *A Sabine Woman*, was offered to the actress Virginia Harned. When she found it "disagreeable," Moody sent a copy to Harriet, who read it to the theatrical agent Donald Robertson, who recommended it to Margaret Anglin. Miss Anglin was then appearing at the Powers Theatre in Chicago in *Zira*. She read the play one night after her performance and immediately arranged with Henry Miller for a tryout in Chicago. The play was rehearsed over the week end, six hours a day, and opened for a special performance the following Thursday evening, April 12, 1906, at the Garrick Theatre. The first-act curtain came down to enthusiastic applause. Then began one of the strangest entr'acte interludes in theatre history. Moody was called from his place and requested to sign a long contract, presumably telegraphed from the higher-ups in New York, which was to give Miss Anglin exclusive rights to the play. Percy MacKaye, who was with Moody, insisted that a lawyer be consulted, and one was summoned from the audience. For fifty-five minutes MacKaye raced back and forth between the box office, where Moody was stationed, and Miss Anglin's dressing room, where she repeated that she would not proceed without Moody's signature. Finally, Moody signed the document and the second-act curtain went up. Most members of the audience waited, but their spirits were considerably dampened, as were those of the actors. The ragged nerves of the players could not now conceal the lack of rehearsal. The rest of the play went badly and was coolly received. As it turned out the next day, all Miss Anglin had wanted was a simple option on the play; she had been as unaware of the multiple-articled document which Moody faced in the front of the house as he had been ignorant of its meaning.

After talking with Miss Anglin in New York in early May and discovering that she now thought the part of Ruth was not quite "star" material, Moody began a series of conferences with Henry Miller. As early as the previous February, Moody had written to Richard Watson Gilder, "I should like very much to get Henry Miller to take it, but I guess that is out of the question." He was happily surprised in his first meeting with Miller to find that this popular actor-manager, instead of wishing the leading male part enlarged for himself, wanted "to have me make of it a thoroughly well-rounded and self-sufficing piece of dramatic art, without regard to his own *particular role.*"

The subsequent story of the play's progress is so completely documented in Moody's voluminous correspondence with Harriet that it can best be told through selections from his letters:

May 10, 1906, New York. The negotiations still drag on and the historic document will not be signed before tomorrow or next day. The transfer of the seat of world empire from Rome to Byzantium was an inconsiderable trifle in comparison. I am as you suspect a bit jaded by the week long fussing over options, forfeits, royalties, "long-run," "tour," and "stock" rights and all the thousand and one strange considerations.

May 22, 1906, Cornish, New Hampshire. My arrangements with Miller – some nine pages of foolscap – I agree to revise the play by July 15. If then it is formally accepted, he agrees to produce it by October 1, or forfeit $250; if it is not produced by January 1, he forfeits $500 more, by May 1, $500 more and failing production by October 1, 1909, he resigns his rights. All these sums count as advance royalties reckoned on a basis of five to ten per cent of gross receipts, according to the weekly business. After a year, privilege of renewing, guaranteeing royalty returns of $1,000 a year. Publication rights are mine. I am pegging away at revising the play. Have about finished the first act. It's going to be a whole lot stronger, but all the same it seems like a waste of time, when I might be doing something new and really interesting.

May 29, 1906, Cornish. You need not be afraid that I will compromise with myself in rewriting the play. What I am trying to do is to let air into the dialogue – make explicit what (for the stage) proved to be too implicit.

June 5, 1906, Cornish. After hammering away at the thing in the back regions of my head for days and weeks, today I had the felicity to see pop into the front regions the right kind of ending for the play. It seems to me to preserve everything vital to the first, violent, ending, and it brings the play to a close in an upswinging mood of lightness, going towards comedy. An immense advantage of course . . . brings in the family again. It makes Zona [later changed to Ruth] the active petitioner and pleader for the thing she has rejected many times from the hands of her lover, and makes him – through incredulity – the withholder. This last, though it may seem to be spotless gallantry on the author's part, is good drama. Supply yodel!

June 14, 1906, Cornish. New ending stands test of time. Ready now to take a stand – with Miller – of no compromise. If he wants it he must take it without disturbing a hair-line.

July 2, 1906, Cornish. Working with teeth and toe nails. If Miller carries out his proposed plan to open the season with it the eleventh hour for its completion has already struck.

July 8, 1906, Cornish. Miller telegraphed me yesterday he should be unable to come up here. Will probably necessitate my making a rapid slide to the city, where we shall probably have a battle royal and shake hands over the corpse of my ambition as a "practical" playwright.

July 13, 1906, Cornish. Think Robertson is wrong about retaining the original title. It is true we shall lose some advance advertising, but this seems to me a small consideration beside the value of a really appropriate and satisfactory title, which I feel *The Great Divide* to be. MacKaye is enthusiastic for it and also for the new ending. Am going at noon today.

According to Percy MacKaye, the new title was selected at a MacKaye dinner party. Each of the guests wrote his suggestion on a slip of paper. One by one the ballots were opened and discussed. As MacKaye recalled the incident, it was Mrs. MacKaye who had proposed *The Great Divide*.

July 15, 1906, New York. Dined with Miller . . . drive in Park . . . began reading play at eleven and finished at four in the morning. I did not get to sleep – what with smoke and excitement – until eight. He came to breakfast with me at eleven, then we had a couple of hours in the Princess Theatre, discussing stage settings, from which I had to rush for a White Plains train to reach Miss Anglin's summer place by four. Reading the play to her, with dinner and other interruptions, kept me there until 10:30 and I got back to New York, and tumbled into bed, more dead than alive, at midnight. Miller is delighted with the new version, and intends to open the season with it here. Whether Miss Anglin will play the heroine is still uncertain. She balks at several points which are essential to the integrity of the idea, and which I have refused, unconditionally, to change. She hasn't now, and I think never has had, any conception of the play as a whole, or any interest in it. She is solely intent on getting a "part." The part must conform itself to her desire to score once every so often. Like ringing up fares in a street-car.

July 16, 1906, New York. Leave tonight . . . a mere pulp physically and morally. Looks today as if Miss Anglin would insist on her right to play the role. Am determined not to yield anything essential. Differences between us are small, and she has, of course, established a claim upon the play by her initial acceptance of it. Miller thinks I shall have to be here for a couple of weeks or so before the opening – i.e., from about the 7th of September on.

Late in August, 1906, Albuquerque. Anticipate no difficulty in getting together the necessary articles. [Moody had gone to New Mexico to gather properties for the play.] Wish you could have watched with me the light fade on the mountains just now. This is a great and inspiring country.

September 10, 1906, Albany. Dress rehearsal last night from 7 until 5 – ten hours of horrors. This morning I am ready to swear on a pile of bibles as high as Chimborazo that if I emerge from this venture with a rag of artistic reputation I will never write another line for the stage as it exists today. The company is incredibly bad . . . the minor parts have been mis-mated to their would-be interpreters until the unholy combination cries to heaven. The stage setting, for all the money and pains that have been spent on it, isn't within earshot to our improvised affair of last spring. Give me a cave and a cup of water on the mountain of the muses, and let me die unproduced.

If I must write plays, buy me a burglar-proof safe, with a time lock set for A.D. 2006, to keep them in.

September 11, 1906, Albany. I must sing a palinode and recantation to my jeremiad of yesterday. The company pulled itself together for the first night in a most wonderful way. It was impossible to recognize in it the barbarous aggregation of that nightmare dress rehearsal. . . . There is something, to me, touching and old-worldly in this strolling players' existence, even when carried on under the modern methods.

September 16, 1906, Atlantic City. Ended our first vagabond week last night, with a big "house," including the czar of all the theatrical Russians, the magnipotent Shubert himself, to whom I was tremblingly presented, receiving such dubious curt praises and indubitable loquacious warnings not to be rejoiced before the time, since "Proadway" [*sic*] was a monster of great incalculability of taste, wont to eat alive a playwright a day. Still, there was the hard fact that we had played to over six thousand dollars in a week of one night stands, and that men breathe and walk on mystery. We go to Washington tomorrow for a week. These performances on the road are regarded by us as mere public rehearsals. The real opening will be in New York on October 3d.

September 18, 1906, Washington. This morning the *Washington Star* contained a most brutal and blackguardly onslaught upon both play and performers . . . shamelessly unfair. At a loss to find a motive for it, in the course of the day, it has come out pretty clearly as the work of the Syndicate, who hired a wretched scribbler to stab us in the back.

September 25, 1906, Pittsburgh. All the morning papers except one attack the play savagely. To them it means an attempted rape, a revolting case of forced marriage, and the final surrender of the woman to a moral monster. . . . I guess the meat we are trying to get them to taste is too strong for them. . . . Sometime or other they have got to take it. It is right.

Lee Shubert was distressed by these reviews and thought that they should close the play and not risk a New York engagement. Miller and Anglin insisted that it must be taken to Broadway. Its initial performance on October 3, 1906, at the Princess Theatre, was an immediate triumph for the play and the players. Moody was caught up in the fervor of its success. Harriet had come to New York for the auspicious occasion but had returned to Chicago immediately. Four days after the opening, Moody wrote to her:

The bubble, if anything continues to swell; the house sold last night seventy dollars above capacity; and tickets have been put on sale twelve weeks in advance!

His subsequent letters from New York reflect the mounting enthusiasm:

October 19, 1906. The town seems to have gone completely daft about the play, so much so that I begin to feel concerning it a kind of distressing aversion and shame.

November 17, 1906. Saw the opening of the Lew Field's [*sic*] burlesque of my play, under the title *The Great Decide.* [This was inevitable.] Parts of it are excruciatingly funny, and it contains a lot of sound criticism in the guise of travesty.

January 8, 1907. Seat sales have picked up again since the holidays. Miller plans now to run here through the entire season, open at Daly's next fall, and keep it on the boards there as long as the public wants it, then to tour the country.

September 29, 1907. Miller and Miss Anglin at first planned to go on the road October 1st, but the business has remained so good that they now expect to stay at Daly's until Christmas, and then to play four weeks downtown at the Academy of Music. After that there is talk of going to England before touring the west.

November 13, 1907. Miller closes here this month and goes west, I believe almost directly to Chicago, where he is to play three weeks. At the same time two hack companies start out, one north and one south.

The play returned to New York the following spring and again in the fall. On September 15, 1909, after recording more than a thousand performances in the United States, it opened at the Adelphi Theatre in London with Henry Miller and with Edith Wynne Matthison in the part of Ruth. There were additional American tours in 1910, 1911, 1915, 1916, and 1920. In April, 1913, the play was performed at the *Théâtre des Arts* in Paris. And on February 7, 1917, Miller revived the play in New York for a run of fifty-three performances at the Lyceum Theatre. Although Miller persistently disavowed any extraordinary responsibility for its success, his performances unquestionably contributed greatly to its long life. Even when reviewers had reservations about the text, they had none about Miller's polished acting.

Many newspaper and magazine critics either grasped only at the surface edges of the play or felt obliged to temper their comments with moralizing phrases to satisfy their readers. It was called a "sex play," "unnecessary and unpleasant"; and many of the critical controversies that persisted through the 1906–7 season centered on the question: Would a sensitive, refined, and religious young lady like Ruth spare Stephen and honor such an ill-gotten promise? Those reviewers who caught the spark of Ruth's love for Stephen – and it is difficult now to think that there were those who did not or were unwilling to accept it – felt the impelling drama of both the surface and the inner struggles of Ruth and Stephen. Most reviewers recognized that *The Great Divide* offered a new turn in American drama. Here was a play of literary merit: truly realistic, with no mere superficial exploitation of lifelike details; filled with exciting action, yet not of the customary melodramatic variety; and above all a serious psychological study of two aspects of American culture brought into collision against the picturesque background of the western landscape. *The Great Divide* has been correctly called "the first modern American drama."

THE GREAT DIVIDE

WILLIAM VAUGHN MOODY

CHARACTERS

PHILIP JORDAN	LON ANDERSON
POLLY JORDAN, *Philip's wife*	BURT WILLIAMS
MRS. JORDAN, *his mother*	DUTCH
RUTH JORDAN, *his sister*	A MEXICAN
WINTHROP NEWBURY	A CONTRACTOR
DR. NEWBURY, *Winthrop's father*	AN ARCHITECT
STEPHEN GHENT	A BOY

ACT I

Interior of Philip Jordan's cabin in southern Arizona, on a late afternoon in spring. A large room rudely built, adorned with blankets, pottery, weapons, and sacred images of the local Indian tribes, and hung with trophies of the chase, together with hunting-knives, saddles, bridles, nose-bags for horses, lariats, and other paraphernalia of frontier life. Through a long low window at the back the desert is seen, intensely colored, and covered with the uncouth shapes of giant cacti, dotted with bunches of gorgeous bloom. The entrance door is on the left (from the spectator's standpoint), in a projecting elbow of the room; farther to the left is a door leading to the sleeping-quarters. On the right is a cook-stove, a cupboard for dishes and household utensils, and a chimney-piece, over which hangs a bleached cow's-skull supporting a rifle.

At a rude table in the centre sits Philip Jordan, a man of thirty-four, mending a bridle. Polly, his wife, kneels before an open trunk, assisted in her packing by Winthrop Newbury, a recent graduate of an Eastern medical college. Ruth Jordan, Philip's sister, a girl of nineteen, stands at the window looking out.

WINTHROP: [*As he hands the last articles to Polly*] What on earth possessed you to bring such a load of duds to Arizona?

POLLY: They promised me a good time, meaning one small shindig – one – in the three months I've spent in this unholy place.

Philip makes an impatient movement with the bridle; speaks gruffly

PHILIP: You'd better hurry. It's getting late.

RUTH: [*From the window*] It's getting cooler, which is more to the point. We can make the railroad easily by sunrise, with this delicious breeze blowing.

POLLY: [*Gives the finishing touches to the trunk and locks the lid*] There, at last! Heaven help the contents.

PHILIP: [*Gruffly, as he rises*] Give me a lift with the trunk, Win.

They carry the trunk outside. Polly, with the aid of a cracked mirror, puts on her travelling hat and cloak

RUTH: My, Pollikins! You'll be the talk of all the jack rabbits and sage hens between here and the railroad.

POLLY: Phil is furious at me for going, and it *is* rather mean to sneak off for a visit in a grand house in San Francisco, when you poor dears have to slave on here. But really, I can't endure this life a day longer.

RUTH: It isn't in nature that you should. Fancy *that* [*she indicates Polly with a grandiose*

728

gesture] nourishing itself on salt-pork, chickory beans, and airtight!

POLLY: Do you really mean to say that apart from your pride in helping your brother, making the project go, and saving the family fortunes, you really *enjoy* yourself here?

RUTH: Since Phil and I came out, one day has been more radiantly exciting than the other. I don't know what's the matter with me. I think I shall be punished for being so happy.

POLLY: Punished for being happy! There's your simon-pure New-Englander.

RUTH: True! I was discovered at the age of seven in the garret, perusing "The Twelve Pillars and Four Cornerstones of a Godly Life."

POLLY: [*Pointing at Ruth's heart, speaks with mock solemnity*] If Massachusetts and Arizona ever get in a mix-up in there, woe be! – Are you ever going to have that coffee done?

RUTH: I hope soon, before you get me analyzed out of existence.

POLLY: [*As Ruth busies herself at the stove*] The main point is this, my dear, and you'd better listen to what the old lady is a-tellin' of ye. Happiness is its own justification, and it's the sacreder the more unreasonable it is. It comes or it doesn't, that's all you can say about it. And when it comes, one has the sense to grasp it or one hasn't. There you have the Law and the Prophets.

Winthrop and Philip enter from outside. Ruth, who has set out the coffee and sandwiches on the table, bows elaborately, with napkin over arm

RUTH: *Messieurs et Mesdames!*

WINTHROP: Coffee! Well, rather, with an all-night ride in the desert ahead of us. [*They drink their coffee, Philip standing sullenly apart*] Where do we get our next feed?

RUTH: With luck, at Cottonwood Wash.

WINTHROP: And how far may Cottonwood Wash be?

RUTH: Thirty miles.

WINTHROP: [*Sarcastically*] Local measurement?

POLLY: [*Poking Philip*] Phil, for Heaven's sake say something. You diffuse the gloom of the Pit.

PHILIP: I've had my say out, and it makes absolutely no impression on you.

POLLY: It's the impression on the public I'm anxious about.

PHILIP: The public will have to excuse me.

POLLY: I *am* horribly sorry for you two poor dears, left alone in this dreadful place. When Dr. Newbury goes, I don't see how you'll support life. I should like to know how long this sojourn in the wilderness is going to last, anyhow.

During the following, Ruth takes a candle from the shelf, lights it, and brings it to the table. The sunset glow has begun to fade

RUTH: Till Cactus Fibre makes our eternal fortune.

WINTHROP: And how long will that be?

RUTH: [*Counts on her fingers*] Two years to pay back the money we raised on mother's estate, two years of invested profits, two years of hard luck and marking time, two years of booming prosperity. Say eight years!

POLLY: Shades of the tomb! How long do you expect to live.

RUTH: Forever!

The sound of a galloping horse is heard, muffled by the sand

WINTHROP: Listen. What's that?

A boy of fifteen, panting from his rapid ride, appears at the open door

PHILIP: [*Rising and going toward the door*] What's the matter?

BOY: I've come for the doctor.

PHILIP: Who wants a doctor?

BOY: Your man Sawyer, over to Lone Tree. – He's broke his leg.

RUTH: Broken his leg! Sawyer? Our foreman?

PHILIP: There's a nice piece of luck! – How did it happen?

BOY: They was doin' some Navajo stunts on horseback, pullin' chickens out of the sand at a gallop and takin' a hurdle on the upswing. Sawyer's horse renigged, and lunged off agin a 'dobe wall. Smashed his leg all to thunder.

Winthrop looks vaguely about for his kit and travelling necessaries, while Polly gives the boy food, which he accepts shyly as he goes outside with Philip. Ruth has snatched saddle and bridle from their peg

RUTH: I'll have Buckskin saddled for you in a jiffy. How long will it take you to set the leg?

WINTHROP: Perhaps an hour, perhaps three.

RUTH: It's a big detour, but you can catch us at Cottonwood Wash by sunrise, allowing three hours for Sawyer. Buckskin has done it before. [*She goes out*]

POLLY: [*Pouting*] This will spoil all our fun! Why can't the creature wait till you get back?

WINTHROP: Did you ever have a broken leg?

POLLY: Well, no, not exactly a leg. But I've had a broken heart! In fact, I've got one now, if you're not going with us.

WINTHROP: To tell you the truth, mine is broken too. [*Pause*] Did you ever dream of climbing a long hill, and having to turn back before you saw what was on the other side? [*Polly nods enthusiastically*] I feel as if I'd had my chance to-night to see what was over there, and lost it.

POLLY: You'll excuse me if it sounds personal, Dr. Newbury, but did you expect to discern a – sort of central figure in the outrolled landscape?

WINTHROP: [*Embarrassed, repenting of his sentimental outburst*] No. That is –

POLLY: [*With a sweep of her arm*] O, I see. Just scenery!

She laughs and goes into the inner room, left. Ruth reenters. The sky has partly faded and a great full moon begins to rise

RUTH: Buckskin is ready, and so is the moon. The boy knows the trails like an Indian. He will bring you through to Cottonwood by daylight.

WINTHROP: [*Taking heart*] We shall have the ride back together, at any rate.

RUTH: Yes. – I would go with you, and try to do something to make poor Sawyer comfortable, but we haven't another horse that can do the distance. [*She holds out her hand*] Goodbye.

WINTHROP: [*Detaining her hand*] Won't you make it up to me? [*He draws her toward him*]

RUTH: [*Gently but firmly*] No, Win. Please not.

WINTHROP: Never?

RUTH: Life is so good just as it is! Let us not change it.

He drops her hand, and goes out, without looking back. Polly reenters. The women wave Winthrop good-bye

POLLY: [*Takes Ruth by the shoulders and looks at her severely*] Conscience clear?

RUTH: [*Humoring her*] Crystal!

POLLY: [*Counts on her fingers*] Promising young physician, charming girl, lonely ranch, horseback excursions, spring of the year!

RUTH: Not guilty.

POLLY: Gracious! Then it's not play, it's earnest.

RUTH: Neither the one nor the other. It's just your little blonde romantic noddle. [*She takes Polly's head between her hands and shakes it as if to show its emptiness*] Do you think if I wanted to flirt, I would select a youth I've played hookey with, and seen his mother spank? [*Suddenly sobered*] Poor dear Win! He's so good, so gentle and chivalrous. But – [*With a movement of lifted arms, as if for air*] ah me, he's – finished! I want one that isn't finished!

POLLY: Are you out of your head, you poor thing?

RUTH: You know what I mean well enough. Winthrop is all rounded off, a completed product. But the man I sometimes see in my dreams is – [*Pausing for a simile*] – well, like this country out here, don't you know – ?

She breaks off, searching for words, and makes a vague outline in the air, to indicate bigness and incompletion

POLLY: [*Drily*] Yes, thank you. I do know! Heaven send you joy of him!

RUTH: Heaven won't, because, alas, he doesn't exist! I am talking of a sublime abstraction – of the glorious unfulfilled – of the West – the Desert.

POLLY: [*Lifts Ruth's chin, severely*] We haven't by chance, some spring morning, riding over to the trading-station or elsewhere – just by the merest chance *beheld* a sublime abstraction – say in blue overalls and jumper? [*Ruth shakes her head*] Honest?

More emphatic head-shaking. Polly drops Ruth's chin with a shrug of the shoulders. Philip enters

RUTH: [*Putting on her riding-hat*] Is Pinto saddled?

PHILIP: Pinto is gone.

RUTH: [*Astonished*] Gone where?

PHILIP: To that Mexican blow-out over at Lone Tree. Every man-jack on the ranch has disappeared, without leave asked or notice given, except this paper which I just found nailed to the factory door. [*Ruth takes the note and reads it anxiously. Then she slowly removes her hat and lays it away*] What are you up to now? We've no time to lose!

RUTH: [*With quiet determination*] I am not going.

POLLY: [*As Philip turns in surprise*] Not going?

RUTH: I must stay and look after the ranch.

PHILIP: O, come, that's out of the question!

RUTH: We have put all mother's money into this venture. We can't take any risks.

PHILIP: The men will be back to-morrow. It's not to be thought of – your staying here all alone.

POLLY: [*Seats herself with decision*] One thing is certain: either Ruth goes or I stay.

PHILIP: [*Takes off his hat and sets down the provision basket*] That suits me perfectly!

POLLY: [*Hysterical*] But I can't stay! I won't stay! I shall go mad if I spend another night in this place.

RUTH: No, you mustn't stay. You would never get us worked up to the point of letting you go, another time.

She lifts Polly, and with arm around her waist leads her to the door

PHILIP: I refuse to leave you here alone, just to satisfy a whim of Polly's. That's flat!

RUTH: But, Phil, you forget the stores you're to fetch back. They will be dumped out there on the naked sand, and by to-morrow night –

She blows across her palm, as if scattering thistledown

PHILIP: Well, what of it? A few hundred dollars' worth of stuff!

RUTH: A few hundred dollars means sink or swim with us just now. – Besides, there's poor Sawyer. He'll be brought back here to-morrow, and nobody to nurse him. Then inflammation, fever, and good-bye Sawyer.

Philip, with a gesture of accepting the inevitable, picks up the grain-sacks and basket

POLLY: [*At the door, embracing Ruth*] Good-bye, dear. Aren't you really afraid to stay?

RUTH: I'm awfully sorry to miss the fun, but as for danger, the great Arizona Desert is safer than Beacon Hill.

POLLY: You're sure?

RUTH: If marauders prowl, I'll just fire the blunderbuss out the window, and they won't stop running this side of the Great Divide.

POLLY: [*Kissing her*] Good-bye, dear.

RUTH: Good-bye.

Polly goes out

PHILIP: [*Pausing beside Ruth, at the door*] Mind you put out the light early. It can be seen from the Goodwater Trail. There's no telling what riff-raff will be straggling back that way after the dance.

RUTH: Riff-raff! They're my sworn knights and brothers.

PHILIP: In that case, what makes you uneasy about the property?

RUTH: O, property! That's different.

PHILIP: Well, you mind what I say and put out the light.

RUTH: Yours for prudence! [*She puts her arm around his waist and draws him to her, kissing him tenderly*] Good-bye, Phil. [*He kisses her and starts to go. She still detains him. When she speaks again, her voice is softened and awed*] What a lovely night! Who would ever think to call this a desert, this moonlit ocean of flowers? What millions of cactus blooms have opened since yesterday!

PHILIP: [*Looking at her dubiously*] What's the matter with you to-night?

RUTH: Nothing. Everything. Life! – I don't know what's got into me of late. I'm just drunk with happiness the whole time.

PHILIP: Well, you're a queer one. – Good-bye. I shall get back as soon as horseflesh will do it. [*He goes out*]

RUTH: [*As the rumble of the wagon is heard*] Good-bye! Good-bye, Pollikins! Good-bye! [*She takes the candle from the table and stands in the door for a time, then raises the light in one hand and waves her handkerchief with the other. She sets the candle again on the table, goes to the mantel-shelf, and takes down a photograph*] Dear Win! I forgot how disappointed *you* were going to be. [*Pause, during which she still gazes at the picture*] Clear, kind heart! [*After a moment she replaces it brusquely on the mantel-shelf, and raises her arms above her head with a deep breath. She stands thus, with arms crossed behind her head, looking at the photograph. Her gaze becomes amused and mischievous; she points her finger at the picture and whispers mockingly*] Finished! Finished!

She begins to prepare for bed, taking down her hair, and re-coiling it loosely during the following. She hums a tune vaguely and in snatches, then with a stronger rhythm; at last she sings

> Heart, wild heart,
> Brooding apart,
> Why dost thou doubt, and why art thou sullen?
> Flower and bird
> Wait but thy word –

She breaks off, picks up a photograph from the table, and looks at it for a moment in silence
Poor little mother! You look out at me with such patient, anxious eyes. There are better days coming for you, and it's troublesome me that's bringing them. Only you trust me!

A man's face appears at the edge of the window, gazing stealthily in. As Ruth turns, he disappears. She lays down the picture and sings again

> This is the hour,
> And thine is the power.
> Heart, high heart, be brave to begin it.
> Dare you refuse?
> Think what we lose!
> Think what we gain –

The words grow indistinct as she takes up the candle and passes into the other room, from which her voice sounds from time to time in interrupted song. The man again appears, shading his face with a peaked Mexican hat so as to see into the darkened room. He turns and waves his hand as if signalling distant persons to approach, then enters through the open

door. *He looks cautiously about the room, tiptoes to the inner door and listens, then steals softly out, and is seen again at the window, beckoning. Ruth reenters, carrying the candle. She is shod in moccasins, and clad in a loose, dark sleeping-dress, belted at the waist, with wide, hanging sleeves and open throat. As she crosses to the table she sings*

> Heart which the cold
> Long did enfold –
> Hark, from the dark eaves the night thaw drummeth!
> Now as a god,
> Speak to the sod,
> Cry to the sky that the miracle cometh!

She passes her hand over a great bunch of wild flowers on the table
Be still, you beauties! You'll drive me to distraction with your color and your odor. I'll take a hostage for your good behavior.

She selects a red flower, puts it in the dark mass of her hair, and looks out at the open door
What a scandal the moon is making, out there in that great crazy world! Who but me could think of sleeping on such a night?

She sits down, folds the flowers in her arms, and buries her face in them. After a moment she starts up, listens, goes hurriedly to the door, and peers out. She then shuts and bolts the door, draws the curtains before the window, comes swiftly to the table, and blows out the light. The room is left in total darkness. There are muttering voices outside, the latch is tried, then a heavy lunge breaks the bolt. A man pushes in, but is hurled back by a taller man, with a snarling oath. A third figure advances to the table, and strikes a match. As soon as the match is lighted Ruth levels the gun, which she has taken from its rack above the mantel. There is heard the click of the hammer, as the gun misses fire. It is instantly struck from her hand by the first man (Dutch) who attempts to seize her. She evades him, and tries to wrest a pistol from a holster on the wall. She is met by the second man (Shorty) who frustrates the attempt, pocketing the weapon. While this has been going on the third man (Ghent) has

*been fumbling with the lamp, which he has at
last succeeded in lighting. All three are dressed
in rude frontier fashion; the one called Shorty
is a Mexican half-breed, the others are Americans. Ghent is younger than Dutch, and taller,
but less powerfully built. All are intoxicated,
but not sufficiently so to incapacitate them from
rapid action. The Mexican has seized Ruth and
attempts to drag her toward the inner room.
She breaks loose, and flies back again to the
chimney-place, where she stands at bay. Ghent
remains motionless and silent by the table,
gazing at her*

DUTCH: [*Uncorking a whiskey flask*] Plucky
little catamount. I drink its health. [*Drinks*]

RUTH: What do you want here?

DUTCH: [*Laughs, with sinister relish*] Did you
hear that, Steve? [*He drinks again, and
reaches out the flask to Ruth*] Take one, and
pull in its purty little claws, eh? Jolly time.
No more fuss and fury. [*Ruth reaches for
a knife, hidden behind the elbow of the chimney. Dutch wrests the knife from her and
seizes her in his arms*] Peppery little devil!

*With desperate strength she breaks from his
clutch and reels from him in sickness of horror.
Ghent remains gazing at her in a fascinated
semi-stupor. Meanwhile, after closing the door,
the Mexican has taken dice from his pocket,
and, throwing them into a small vase on the
table, shakes them and holds out the vase to
Dutch. He takes it and turns to Ghent; the
latter has moved a step or two toward Ruth,
who in her retreat has reached the chimney-
piece and stands at bay*

DUTCH: Come, get into the game, curse you,
Steve! This is going to be a free-for-all, by
God!

*As he rattles the dice, Ruth makes a supplicat-
ing gesture to Ghent*

RUTH: Save me! save me! [*Her gesture is frozen
by his advancing towards her. She looks wildly
about, shrinking from him, then with sudden
desperate resolution speaks*] Save me, and I
will make it up to you! [*Ghent again advances; she goes on pantingly, as she stands at
bay*] Don't touch me! Listen! Save me from
these others, and from yourself, and I will
pay you – with my life.

GHENT: [*With dull wonder*] With – your life?

RUTH: With all that I am or can be.

GHENT: What do you mean? – [*Pause*] You
mean you'll go along with me out of this?
Stick to me – on the square?

RUTH: [*In a tragic whisper*] Yes.

GHENT: On the dead square?

RUTH: Yes.

GHENT: You won't peach, and spoil it?

RUTH: No.

Pause, during which he looks at her fixedly

GHENT: Give me your hand on it!

*She gives him her hand. The other men, at the
table, have drawn their weapons, and hold
them carelessly, but alert to the slightest suspicious movement on the part of Ghent*

DUTCH: [*As Ghent turns to them*] Shorty and
me's sittin' in this game, and interested, eh,
Shorty? [*The Mexican nods. Ghent comes
slowly to the table, eyeing the two. Dutch
holds out the vase containing the dice*] Shake
for her!

GHENT: Shake how?

DUTCH: Any damn way! Sole and exclusive
rights. License to love and cherish on the
premises!

*Ghent takes the vase, shakes the dice medita-
tively, is about to throw, then sets the vase
down. He searches through his pockets and
produces a few bills and a handful of silver,
which he lays on the table*

GHENT: There's all I've got in my clothes. Take
it, and give me a free field, will you?

DUTCH: [*Leaning over the table to Ghent, in
plaintive remonstrance*] You don't mean me,
Steve!

GHENT: [*To the Mexican*] Well, you, then!

*The Mexican spreads the money carelessly with
his left hand to ascertain its amount, then
thrusts it away with a disgusted grunt of refusal*

DUTCH: Don't blame you, Shorty! A ornery
buck of a dirt-eatin' Mojave'd pay more'n that
for his squaw.

*Ruth covers her face shudderingly. Ghent stands
pondering, watching the two men under his*

brows, and slowly gathering up the money. As if on a sudden thought, he opens his shirt, and unwinds from his neck a string of gold nuggets in the rough, strung on a leather thread

GHENT: Well, it ain't much, that's sure. But there's a string of gold nuggets I guess is worth some money. [*He throws it on the table, speaking to both men*] Take that, and clear out.

DUTCH: [*Draws up angrily*] I've give you fair warning!

GHENT: We'll keep everything friendly between me and you. A square stand-up shoot, and the best man takes her.

DUTCH: [*Mollified*] Now you're comin' to!

GHENT: [*To the Mexican*] Then it's up to you, and you'd better answer quick!

THE MEXICAN: [*Eyeing Ghent and Ruth, points to the gun lying on the floor*] I take him, too.

GHENT: No, you don't. You leave everything here the way you found it.

THE MEXICAN: Alla right.

He pockets the chain and starts for the door

GHENT: Hold on a minute. You've got to promise to tie the man who falls, on his horse, and take him to Mesa Grande. Bargain? [*The Mexican nods*] And mouth shut, mind you, or – [*He makes a sign across his throat*]

THE MEXICAN: [*Nods*] Alla right. [*He goes out*]

GHENT: [*Motioning toward the door*] Outside.

DUTCH: [*Surprised*] What for?

GHENT: [*Sternly*] Outside!

They move toward the door. Dutch stops and waves his hand to Ruth

DUTCH: Don't worry, my girl. Back soon.

GHENT: [*Threateningly*] Cut that out!

DUTCH: What's eatin' you? She ain't yours yet, and I guess she won't be, not till hell freezes over.

He taps his pistol and goes out. Ghent picks up the rifle which has previously missed fire; he unloads it, throws it on the window-seat, and follows Dutch. Ruth stands beside the table, listening. Four shots are heard. After a short time Ghent appears and watches from the door the vanishing horses. He comes to the table opposite Ruth

RUTH: [*In a low voice*] Is he dead?

GHENT: No; but he'll stay in the coop for a while.

She sinks down in a chair. Ghent seats himself at the other side of the table, draws a whiskey flask from his pocket, and uncorks it awkwardly, using only his right hand

RUTH: [*As he is about to drink*] Don't!

GHENT: [*Lowers the bottle and looks at her in a dazed way*] Is this on the square?

RUTH: I gave you my promise.

Gazing at her, he lets the bottle sink slowly by his side; the liquor runs out, while he sits as if in a stupor. Ruth glances toward the door, and half starts from her seat, sinking back as he looks up

GHENT: Give me a drink of water.

She brings the water from a bucket in the corner. He sets the empty bottle on the table, drinks deeply of the water, takes a handkerchief from his neck, wets it, and mops his face

GHENT: Where are your folks?

RUTH: My brother has gone out to the railroad.

GHENT: Him and you ranching it here by yourselves?

RUTH: Yes.

GHENT: Write him a note. [*He shoves paper, pen, and ink before her*] Fix it up anyway you like.

RUTH: Tell me first what you mean to do with me.

GHENT: [*Ponders awhile in silence*] Have you got a horse to ride?

RUTH: Yes.

GHENT: We can reach San Jacinto before sun-up. Then we're off for the Cordilleras. I've got a claim tucked away in them hills that'll buy you the city of Frisco some day, if you have a mind to it! [*She shrinks and shudders*] What you shivering at? [*Ruth does not answer, but begins to write. Ghent, still using only one hand, takes a pistol from his pocket, examines it, and lays it carelessly on the table, within Ruth's reach. He rises and goes to the fireplace, takes a cigarette from his pocket and lights it, and examines the objects on the mantel-shelf. Ruth stops writing, takes up the pistol, then lays it down, as he speaks without turning around*] Read what you've written. [*Ruth, about to read, snatches up the pistol again, rises, and stands trembling and irresolute*] Why don't you shoot? [*He turns around deliberately*] You promised on the square, but there's nothing square about this deal. You ought to shoot me like a rattlesnake!

RUTH: I know that.

GHENT: Then why don't you?

RUTH: [*Slowly*] I don't know.

GHENT: I guess you've got nerve enough, for that or anything. – Answer me; why not?

RUTH: I don't – know. – You laid it there for me. – And – you have no right to die.

GHENT: How's that?

RUTH: You must live – to pay for having spoiled your life.

GHENT: Do you think it is spoiled?

RUTH: Yes.

GHENT: And how about your life?

RUTH: I tried to do it.

GHENT: To do what?

RUTH: To take my life. I ought to die. I have a right to die. But I cannot, I cannot! I love my life, I must live. In torment, in darkness – it doesn't matter. I want my life. I will have it! *She drops the weapon on the table, pushes it toward him, and covers her eyes*] Take it away! Don't let me see it. If you want me on these terms, take me, and may God forgive you for it; but if there is a soul in you to be judged, don't let me do myself violence. [*She sinks down by the table, hiding her face in her hands*] O, God have pity on me!

Ghent puts the pistol back into his belt, goes slowly to the outer door, opens it, and stands for some moments gazing out. He then closes the door, and takes a step or two toward the table. As he speaks, Ruth's sobs cease, she raises her head and looks strangely at him

GHENT: I've lived hard and careless, and lately I've been going down hill pretty fast. But I haven't got so low yet but what I can tell one woman from another. If that was all of it, I'd be miles away from here by now, riding like hell for liquor to wash the taste of shame out of my mouth. But that ain't all. I've seen what I've been looking the world over for, and never knew it. – Say your promise holds, and I'll go away now.

RUTH: O, yes, go, go! You will be merciful. You will not hold me to my cruel oath.

GHENT: And when I come back? [*Ruth does not answer. He takes a step nearer*] And when I come back?

RUTH: You never – could – come back.

GHENT: No, I guess I never could.

RUTH: [*Eager, pleading*] You *will* go?

GHENT: For good?

RUTH: Yes.

GHENT: Do you mean that?

RUTH: [*Wildly*] Yes, yes, ten thousand times!

GHENT: Is that your last word?

RUTH: Yes. [*Pause. She watches him with strained anxiety*] O, why did you come here to-night?

GHENT: I come because I was blind-drunk and sun-crazy, and looking for damnation the nearest way. That's why I come. But that's not why I'm staying. I'm talking to you in my right mind now. I want you to try and see this thing the way it is.

RUTH: O, that is what I want you to do! You did yourself and me a hideous wrong by coming here. Don't do us both a more hideous wrong still! I was in panic fear. I snatched at the first thing I could. Think what our life would be, beginning as we have begun! O, for God's pity go away now, and never come back! Don't you see there can never be anything between us but hatred, and misery, and horror?

GHENT: [*Hardening*] We'll see about that! – Are you ready to start? [*Ruth, conscious for the first time of her undress condition, shrinks, and folds her gown closer about her neck*] Go, and be quick about it. [*She starts toward her room; he detains her*] Where's your saddle?

She points at it and goes out. Ghent picks up the note she has written, reads it, and stands for a moment in reflection before laying it down. He gets more water from the bucket, drinks deeply, mops his face, and rolls up the sleeve of his left arm, which is soaked with blood. He tries awkwardly to stanch a wound in his forearm, gives it up in disgust, and rolls down his sleeve again. He reads the note once more, then takes Ruth's saddle and bridle from the wall and goes out. Ruth comes in; her face is white and haggard, but her manner determined and collected. She comes to the table, and sees the bloody handkerchief and basin of water. As Ghent enters, she turns to him anxiously

RUTH: You are hurt.

GHENT: It's no matter.

RUTH: Where? [*He indicates his left arm. She throws off her hooded riding-cloak, and impulsively gathers together water, towels, liniment, and bandages; she approaches him, quite lost in her task, flushed and eager*] Sit down. – Roll up your sleeve. [*He obeys mechanically. She rapidly and deftly washes and binds the wound, speaking half to herself, between long pauses*] Can you lift your arm? – The bone is not touched. – It will be all right in a few days. – This balsam is a wonderful thing to heal.

GHENT: [*Watching her dreamily, as she works*] What's your name?

RUTH: R u t h – R u t h – J o r d a n. [*Long pause*] There, gently. – It must be very painful.

He shakes his head slowly, with half-humorous protest

GHENT: It's not fair!

RUTH: What isn't fair?

GHENT: To treat me like this. It's not in the rules of the game.

RUTH: [*As the sense of the situation again sweeps over her*] Binding your wound? I would do the same service for a dog.

GHENT: Yes, I dare say. But the point is, I ain't a dog; I'm a human – the worst way! [*She rises and puts away the liniment and bandages. He starts up, with an impulsive gesture*] Make this bad business over into something good for both of us! You'll never regret it! I'm a strong man! [*He holds out his right arm, rigid*] I used to feel sometimes, before I went to the bad, that I could take the world like that and tilt her over. And I can do it, too, if you say the word! I'll put you where you can look down on the proudest. I'll give you the kingdoms of the world and all the glory of 'em. [*She covers her face with her*

hands. He comes nearer*] Give me a chance, and I'll make good. By God, girl, I'll make good! – I'll make a queen of you. I'll put the world under your feet! [*Ruth makes a passionate gesture, as if to stop her ears*] What makes you put your hands over your ears like that? Don't you like what I'm saying to you?

RUTH: [*Taking the words with difficulty*] Do you remember what that man said just now?

GHENT: What about?

RUTH: About the Indian – and – his squaw.

GHENT: Yes. There was something in it, too. I was a fool to offer him that mean little wad.

RUTH: For – me!

GHENT: Well, yes, for you, if you want to put it that way.

RUTH: But – a chain of nuggets – that comes nearer being a fair price?

GHENT: O, to buy off a greaser!

RUTH: But to buy the soul of a woman – one must go higher. A mining-claim! The kingdoms of the world and all the glory of them! [*Breaking down in sudden sobs*] O, be careful how you treat me! Be careful! I say it as much for your sake as mine. Be careful!

GHENT: [*Turns from her, his bewilderment and discomfiture translating itself into gruffness*] Well, I guess we'll blunder through. – Come along! We've no time to lose. – Where are your things?

At her gesture, he picks up the saddle-pack which she has brought out of the bedroom with her, and starts toward the door

RUTH: [*Taking a hammer from the window-ledge and handing it to Ghent*] Fix the bolt. My brother must not know.

He drives in the staple of the bolt, while she throws the blood-stained water and handkerchief into the fire. He aids her in replacing the weapons on the walls, then takes the saddle-pack and stands at the door, waiting. She picks up her mother's picture, and thrusts it in her bosom. After standing a moment in hesitation, she takes the picture out, kisses it, lays it on the mantel, face down. She extinguishes the lamp, and goes out hastily. He follows, closing the door

The Curtain Falls in Darkness

ACT II

Stephen Ghent's home, in the Cordilleras. At the right, crowning a rude terrace, is an adobe cabin, stained of pale buff, mellowed to ivory by sun and dust. Over it clamber vines loaded with purple bloom. The front of the cabin is turned at an angle toward the spectator, the farther side running parallel with the brink of a cañon, of which the distant wall and upper reaches are crimsoned by the afternoon light. In the level space before the rocky terrace is a stone table and seats, made of natural rocks roughly worked with the chisel. The rude materials have manifestly been touched by a refined and artistic hand, bent on making the most of the glorious natural background. Against the rocks on the left stands a large hand-loom of the Navajo type, with weaving-stool, and a blanket half woven. On the table lies a half-finished Indian basket, and strips of colored weaving-materials lie in a heap on the ground. Cactus plants in blossom fill the niches of the rocks and lift their fantastic forms above the stones which wall the cañon brink. At one point this wall is broken, where a path descends into the cañon.

Lon Anderson, a venerable-looking miner, with gray hair and beard, sits smoking before the cabin. Burt Williams, a younger man, peeps up over the edge of the cañon, from the path.

BURT: Hello, Lon. Is the Missus inside? [*Lon smokes on, without looking at the questioner*] Look here, I put a nickel in you, you blame rusty old slot-machine. Push out something!

LON: [*Removes his pipe deliberately*] What you wantin' off'n her now? A music lesson or a headache powder?

BURT: Boss's waitin' down at the mine, with a couple o' human wonders he's brought back with him from wherever he's been this time. Something doin' on the quiet.

LON: You can tell him his wife ain't nowheres about.

Burt produces an enormous bandana from his pocket, mounts the wall, and waves it. He sits on the wall and smokes for a moment in silence, looking down into the cañon, as if watching the approaching party. He points with his pipe at the cabin

BURT: Funny hitch-up – this here one – I think.

LON: [*After a pause*] How much you gittin' a day now?

BURT: Same little smilin' helpless three and six-bits.

LON: Anything extry for thinkin'?

BURT: Nope! Throwed in. [*They smoke again. Burt glances down to reassure himself, then points at the loom and basket*] Queer business – this rug-weavin' and basket-makin', ain't it? – What d'ye s'pose she wants to sit, day in and day out, like a half-starved Navajo, slavin' over them fool things fur? – Boss ain't near, is he? Don't keep her short of ice-cream sodas and trolley-rides, does 'e? [*Lon rises and approaches Burt, regarding him grimly*] Saw 'er totin' a lot o' that stuff burro-back over to the hotel week 'fore last. – An' Dod Ranger – you know what a disgustin' liar Dod is – he tells how he was makin' tests over in the cross-cañon, an' all of a sudden plump he comes on her talkin' to a sawed-off Mexican hobo, and when she sees Dod, she turns white's a sheet.

LON: [*With suppressed ferocity*] You tell Dod Ranger to keep his mouth shet, and you keep yourn shet too – or by Jeehosophat, I'll make the two of ye eat yer Adam's apples and swaller the core!

BURT: O, git down off'n yer hind legs, Lon! Nobody's intendin' any disrespect.

LON: You boys keep yer blatherin' tongues off'n her! Or you'll get mixed up with Alonzo P. Anderson – [*He taps his breast*] – so's it'll take a coroner to untangle ye!

BURT: [*Deprecatingly*] I guess I'd stick up fur 'er 's quick as you would, come to that.

LON: Well, we don't need no stickin' up fur 'er. What we need is less tongue. [*He leans down and speaks lower*] Especially when the boss is round. You tell the boys so.

Burt looks at him in surprise and is about to speak; Lon makes a warning signal, indicating the approach of the party below. Burt descends, saluting Ghent respectfully

GHENT: [*Peeping up over the edge of the cañon*] Coast clear, eh, Lon?

LON: Yes, sir.

GHENT: Where is she?

LON: [*Points along the brink of the cañon*] Kind o' think she went out to Look-off Ledge. – Guess she didn't expect you back to-day.

GHENT: [*Speaking below*] Come up, gentlemen. [*Ghent emerges from the cañon, followed by an Architect, a dapper young Easterner, and a Contractor, a bluff Western type. Ghent is neatly dressed in khaki, with riding-boots and broad felt hat. He has a prosperous and busy air, and is manifestly absorbed in the national game of making money*] Take a seat.

CONTRACTOR: [*Seats himself by the table*] Don't care if I do. That new stage of yours just jumped stiff-legged from the go-off. And the trail up here from the mine is a good deal of a proposition for the see-dentary.

ARCHITECT: [*As he takes in the stupendous view*] What a wonderful place! Even better than you described it.

GHENT: Yes. My wife picked it out. – Let's see your plans.

He removes basket from the table, where the Architect unrolls several sheets of blue paper

ARCHITECT: I have followed your instructions to the letter. I understand that nothing is to be touched except the house.

GHENT: Not a stone, sir; not a head of cactus. Even the vines you've got to keep, exactly as they are.

ARCHITECT: [*Smiling*] That will be a little difficult.

GHENT: You can put 'em on a temporary trellis. – A little pains will do it.

CONTRACTOR: Maybe, with a man to shoo the masons off with a shot-gun.

GHENT: [*Over the plans*] Provide a dozen men, if necessary, with machine guns.

CONTRACTOR: As you please, Mr. Ghent. The owner of the Verde mine has a right to his whims, I reckon.

ARCHITECT: I have designed the whole house in the Spanish style, very broad and simple. This open space where we stand – [*Points to the plans*] – I have treated as a semi-enclosed *patio*, with arcaded porches.

GHENT: [*Dubiously*] Good.

ARCHITECT: This large room fronting the main arcade is the living-room.

GHENT: I guess we'll have 'em all living-rooms. This place is to be lived in, from the word go.

ARCHITECT: [*Humoring him*] To be sure, everything cheerful and open. – Here on the left of the inner court is the library and music-room.

GHENT: I'm afraid we won't have much use for that. My wife don't go in much for frills. I used to play the concertina once, but it was a long while ago.

ARCHITECT: It can be used for other purposes. For instance, as a nursery, though I had put that on the other side.

GHENT: [*Embarrassed and delighted*] Um, yes, nursery. – Stamping-ground for the – ? [*The Architect nods; the Contractor follows suit, with emphasis. Lon nods solemnly over his pipe*] Good. [*The Architect bends over to make a note with his pencil. Ghent restrains him and says somewhat sheepishly in his ear*] You can leave it music-room on the map.

ARCHITECT: [*Continuing his explanation*] This wing –

Ghent, interrupting him, holds the plan at arm's length, with head on one side and eyes squinted, as he looks from the drawings to the cabin and surroundings

GHENT: Looks a little – *sprawly* on paper. I had sort of imagined something more – more up in the air, like them swell tepees on the Hill in Frisco.

He makes a grandiose outline of high roofs and turrets in the air

ARCHITECT: I think this is more harmonious with the surroundings.

CONTRACTOR: [*In answer to Ghent's inquiring look*] Won't look so showy from the new hotel across yonder. [*He points to the left, down the curve of the cañon wall*]

GHENT: What's your estimate on this plan, now you've seen the location?

CONTRACTOR: It's a long way to haul the stuff. – Say somewheres between twenty and twenty-five thousand. Twenty-five will be safe.

GHENT: [*Slightly staggered*] That's a big lot of money, my friend!

CONTRACTOR: [*With cold scorn*] I thought we was talkin' about a *house!* I can build you a good sheep-corral for a right smart less.

GHENT: Well, I guess we don't want any sheep-corrals.

CONTRACTOR: I should think not, with the Verde pumping money at you the way they tell she does.

GHENT: [Holds up the plans again and looks at them in perplexed silence] I'll tell you, gentlemen, I'll have to consult my wife about this before I decide. The fact is, I've been working the thing out on the sly, up to now.

CONTRACTOR: Expect to build it of an afternoon, while the lady was takin' her see-ester?

GHENT: I thought I'd smuggle her off somewhere for a while. [He is silent a moment, pondering] No! It's her house and she must O. K. the plans before ground is broke. [He looks along the cañon rim] Would you mind waiting a few minutes till I see if I can find her? [He starts irresolutely, then turns back] Or better still, leave the plans, and I'll see you at the hotel to-morrow morning. I haven't been over there since it was opened. I'd like to know what they're making of it.

CONTRACTOR: [Astonished] Hain't been over to the Buny Visty yet?

GHENT: Too busy.

CONTRACTOR: Well, you'll find it an up-to-date joint, and chock full of tourist swells and lungers.

GHENT: Good-afternoon, gentlemen. You'll excuse me. You can find your way back all right? Take the left-hand path. It's better going.

The Architect bows ceremoniously, the Contractor nods. Ghent disappears along the cañon brink behind the cabin

ARCHITECT: [Has been examining the work on the loom, and has then picked up the unfinished basket, admiringly] What a beautiful pattern! I say, this is like those we saw at the hotel. [To Lon] May I ask who is making this? [Lon smokes in silence; the Architect raises his voice, slightly sharp] May I ask who is making this?

LON: [Benignly] You kin, my friend, you kin!

ARCHITECT: Well, then, the question is put.

LON: And very clear-put, too. You'd ought to be in the law business, young man. [He gets up deliberately] Or some other business that'd take up all yer time.

ARCHITECT: [Between wrath and amusement] Well, I'll be hanged! [He follows his companion down the cañon path, stopping a moment at the brink to look round with a professional air at the house and surroundings, then at Lon] Tart old party!

He descends. Lon crosses to the table, looks over the plans, makes outlines in the air in imitation of Ghent, then shakes his head dubiously, as he rolls up the plans. Ruth appears, emerging from the cañon path. She wears the same dress as at the close of Act I, with a dark scarf-like handkerchief thrown over her head. She is pale and exhausted. She sinks on the rocks at the edge of the cañon

LON: [Approaching her, anxiously] It's too much fer you, ma'am. You'd oughter let me go.

He brings her a glass of water from an Indian water-jar before the cabin

RUTH: [Tasting the water] O, I thought I should never get back! [She leans against a rock, with closed eyes, then rouses herself again] Lon, take the glass, and see if you can make out any one down yonder, on the nearer trail. I – I thought some one was following me.

LON: [Speaks low] Excuse me askin', Mis' Ghent, but is that dod-blamed Mexican a-botherin' you again?

RUTH: No. He has gone away, for good. It's some one I saw at the hotel – some one I used to know. – Look if you can make out a man's figure, coming up.

LON: [Takes the glass from the niche in the rocks, and scans the cañon path] Can't see nothin' but a stray burro, an' he ain't got no figger to speak of. – Might be t'other side o' Table Rock, down in the pinyon scrub. [Ruth gets up with an effort, takes the glass and looks through it, then lays it on the ledge] Excuse me, ma'am, but – Mister Ghent come home this afternoon.

RUTH: [Startled] Where is he?

LON: Huntin' for you down Look-off Ledge way. I 'lowed you was there, not knowin' what else to say.

RUTH: Thank you, Lon. – You can go now.

He goes down the cañon path. Ruth looks once more through the glass, then crosses to the *table, where she sits down and begins to finger the roll of plans. Ghent reenters. He approaches with soft tread and bends over Ruth. She starts up with a little cry, avoiding his embrace*

RUTH: You frightened me. – When did you come back?

GHENT: An hour ago.

RUTH: Was your journey successful?

GHENT: Yes. But my home-coming – that looks rather like a failure. [*Pause*] I expected to find you out on the bluff.

RUTH: Lon was mistaken. I had gone the other way. [*As she stands at the table, she begins to unroll the plans*] What are these papers?

GHENT: Haven't you one word of welcome for me, after five days? [*Ruth remains silent, with averted head, absently unrolling the packet*] Not a look even? [*He waits a moment, then sighs and seats himself moodily by the table*] I never can remember! After I've been away from you for twelve hours, I forget completely.

RUTH: Forget what?

GHENT: How it stands between us. It's childish, but for the life of me I can't help it. – After I've been away a few hours, this place gets all lit up with bright colors in my mind, like – [*Searching for a simile*] – well, like a Christmas tree! I dare say a Christmas tree don't amount to much in real life, but I saw one once, in a play, – I was a little mining-camp roust-about, so high, – and ever since it has sort of stood to me for the gates o' glory.

RUTH: [*With a hysterical laugh*] A Christmas tree! [*She bows her head in her hands, and repeats the words, as if to herself, in a tone in which bitterness has given place to tragic melancholy*] A Christmas tree!

Ghent, watching her moodily, crumples up the plans and throws them upon the ground. He goes toward the cabin, hesitates, turns, and comes back to the table, where Ruth still sits with buried head. He draws from his pocket a jewel-case, which he opens and lays before her

GHENT: There is a little present I brought home for you. And here are some more trinkets. [*He takes out several pieces of jewelry and tumbles them together on the table*] I know you don't care much for these things, but I

had to buy something, the way I was feeling. And these papers – [*Picks them up and spreads them out on the table*] – these mean that you're not to live much longer in a mud shanty, with pine boxes for furniture. These are the drawings for a new house that I want to talk over with you. [*He points at the map and speaks glibly, trying to master his discomfiture at her lack of interest*] Spanish style, everything broad and simple! Large living-room opening on inner court. Library and music-room, bless your heart. Bedrooms; kitchen and thereunto pertaining. Wing where the proprietor retires to express his inmost feelings. General effect sprawly, but harmonious with the surroundings. Twenty thousand estimated, twenty-five limit. Is she ours?

RUTH: [*In a dead, flat tone*] How much did you say the house is to cost?

GHENT: Twenty-five thousand dollars at the outside.

RUTH: And these – trinkets?

GHENT: O, I don't know. – A few hundred.

RUTH: [*Draws the plans toward her and pours the jewels in a heap upon them from her lifted hands*] Twenty-five thousand dollars and the odd hundreds! [*She laughs suddenly and jarringly*] My price has risen! My price has risen! [*She laughs again, as she rises from the table and looks down the cañon path*] Keep those displayed to show to our visitors! My honor is at stake. [*She points down the path*] There is one coming now!

GHENT: Visitors? What visitors?

RUTH: Only an old school-friend of mine; a Mr. Winthrop Newbury.

GHENT: What are you talking about? Are you crazy? [*He joins her, where she stands looking down into the cañon*] This fellow, is he really what you say? [*Ruth nods, with unnaturally bright eyes and mocking smile*] What does this mean?

RUTH: It means that he caught sight of me, an hour ago, in the hotel.

GHENT: In the hotel? What were you doing there?

RUTH: [*With biting calm*] Nothing wicked – as yet. They don't pay twenty-five thousand dollars over there – at least not yet! [*Ghent turns sharply, as if stung by a physical blow.*

She raises her hands to him, in a swift revulsion of feeling] O, don't judge me! Don't listen to me! I am not in my right mind.

GHENT: [*Sweeps the jewels together, and throws them over the cliff*] Do you want me to be here, while you see him? [*She does not answer*] Won't you answer me?

RUTH: [*Again cold*] Act as you think best.

GHENT: It's a question of what will be easiest for you.

RUTH: O, it's all easy for me!

Ghent stands irresolute, then raises his hand in a gesture of perplexity and despair, and goes into the house, closing the door. Winthrop Newbury appears at the top of the cañon path, looks curiously about, catches sight of Ruth's averted figure, and rushes toward her

WINTHROP: Ruth! Is it really you?

Ruth starts involuntarily toward him, stretching out her arms. As he advances, she masters herself, and speaks in a natural voice, with an attempt at gayety, as she takes his hand

RUTH: Well, of all things! Winthrop Newbury! How did you find your way to this eagle's nest?

WINTHROP: I – we saw you – we caught a glimpse of you at the hotel, but we weren't sure. We followed you, but lost you in the cañon.

RUTH: We? Who is we?

WINTHROP: Your brother and his wife.

RUTH: [*Turning the shock, which she has been unable to conceal, into conventional surprise*] Philip and Polly here!

WINTHROP: They took the other turn, down there where the path forks. We didn't know which way you had gone.

RUTH: Yes, but why on earth are they here at all?

WINTHROP: They are on their way East. They stopped over to see me.

RUTH: To see you? Are you – living here?

WINTHROP: I have been here only a week. [*He starts impulsively, trying to break through the conventional wall which she has raised between them*] Ruth – for God's sake – !

RUTH: [*Interrupting him, with exaggerated animation*] But tell me! I am all curiosity. How do you happen to be here – of all places?

WINTHROP: What does it matter? I am here. We have found you, after all these miserable months of anxiety and searching. O Ruth – why –

RUTH: I have acted badly, I know. But I wish not to talk of that. Not now. I will explain everything later. Tell me about yourself – about Philip and Polly – and mother. I am thirsty for news. What have you been doing all these months, since – our queer parting?

WINTHROP: [*Solemnly*] Looking for you. [*Pause*] O Ruth – how could you do it? How could you do it?

RUTH: [*Touches him on the arm, and looks at him with dumb entreaty, speaking low*] Winthrop!

WINTHROP: [*In answer to her unspoken words*] As you will.

RUTH: [*Resumes her hard, bright tone*] You haven't told me about mother. How is she?

WINTHROP: Well. Or she will be, now. Ruth, you ought at least to have written to her. She has suffered cruelly.

RUTH: [*Quickly, with a nervous uplift of her arms*] Yes, yes, I know that! – And you are – settled here? You mean to remain?

WINTHROP: I am physician at the End-of-the-Rainbow mines, three miles below. At least I – I am making a trial of it. [*Pause*] How pale and worn you are. – Don't turn away. Look at me. [*She flinches, then summons her courage and looks him steadily in the face*] You are – you are ill – I fear you are desperately ill!

RUTH: [*Moving away nervously*] Nonsense. I was never better in my life. [*She goes toward the cañon brink*] You haven't praised our view. We are very proud of it.

WINTHROP: [*Following her*] Yes, very fine. Magnificent.

RUTH: But you're not looking at it at all! Do you see that bit of smoke far down yonder? That is the stamp mill of the Rio Verde mine.

WINTHROP: [*Compelling himself to follow her lead*] Yes – the Rio Verde. One of the big strikes of the region. Dispute about the ownership, I believe.

RUTH: None that I ever heard of, and I ought to know. For – [*she makes a sweeping bow*] – *we* are the Rio Verde, at your service.

WINTHROP: You – your – husband is the owner of the Verde mine?

RUTH: No less!

WINTHROP: [*Embarrassed*] We found the record of your marriage at San Jacinto. The name was Ghent – Stephen Ghent.

RUTH: Yes. He will be so glad to see some of my people. [*Winthrop's eyes have fallen on the basket at the foot of the table. He picks it up, examines it curiously, and looks meaningly at Ruth, who snatches it from his hand and throws it over the cliff*] A toy I play with! You know I always have to keep my hands busy pottering at some rubbishy craft or other.

WINTHROP: [*Is about to speak, but checks himself. He points at the loom*] And the blanket, too?

RUTH: Yes, another fad of mine. It is really fascinating work. The Indian women who taught me think I am a wonder of cleverness.

WINTHROP: So do – the women – over there. [*He points across the cañon*]

RUTH: [*Flushing*] Ah, yes, you saw some of my stuff at the hotel. You know how vain I am. I had to show it.

WINTHROP: Perhaps. But why should the wife of the man who owns the Verde mine *sell* her handiwork, and under such – such vulgar conditions?

RUTH: [*Brilliantly explanatory*] To see if it *will* sell, of course! That is the test of its merit.

He looks at her in mute protest, then with a shake of the head, rises and puts on his hat

WINTHROP: Do you want to see the others?

RUTH: Why, yes, to be sure I do. How should I not?

WINTHROP: You haven't seemed very anxious – these last eight months.

RUTH: True. I have been at fault. I so dread explanations. And Phil's tempests of rage! Poor boy, he must feel sadly ill-used.

WINTHROP: He does. [*Hesitates*] If there is any reason why you would rather he didn't see you, just now, –

RUTH: There is no reason. At least, none valid.

WINTHROP: Then I will bring them up.

RUTH: By all means. [*She holds out her hand, smiling*] Auf wiedersehen!

Winthrop releases her hand and goes toward the cañon path. He waves, and turns to Ruth.

WINTHROP: They are just below. [*As Ruth advances he takes her hand and looks searchingly into her eyes*] For old friendship's sake, won't you give me one human word before they come? At least answer me honestly one human question?

RUTH: [*Keeping up her hard, bright gayety*] In the great lottery of a woman's answers there is always one such prize!

WINTHROP: [*Dejectedly, as he drops her hand*] It's no use, if that is your mood.

RUTH: My mood! Your old bugbear! I am as sober-serious as my stars ever let me be.

WINTHROP: Did you, that night you bade me good-bye, know that – this was going to happen?

RUTH: [*Cordially explanatory*] No. It was half accident, half wild impulse. Phil left me at the ranch alone. My lover came, impatient, importunate, and I – went with him.

WINTHROP: And your – this man – to whom you are married – pardon me, you don't need to answer unless you wish – for how long had you known him?

RUTH: [*Solemnly, as she looks him straight in the eyes*] All my life! And for aeons before.

He looks at her for a moment, then goes toward the cañon path. Polly's voice is heard calling

POLLY: [*Not yet visible*] Win! Win!

WINTHROP: [*Calls down the cañon*] Come up! Come up!

Ruth goes past him down the cañon path. In a moment she reappears, with Polly. They are laughing and talking as they come

POLLY: Ruth!

RUTH: Dear old Polly!

POLLY: You *naughty* girl!

RUTH: If our sins must find us out, you are the kind of Nemesis I choose.

POLLY: My! But you're a shady character. And sly!

Philip appears. Ruth hurries to embrace him, while Polly, fanning herself with her handkerchief, examines the house and surroundings with curiosity

RUTH: O Phil! – Dear old man! [*She covers his*

face lightly with her hands] No scolding, no frowns. This is the finding of the prodigal, and she expects a robe and a ring.

POLLY: [*Seating herself on a rock*] Heavens, what a climb! – I'm a rag.

RUTH: [*Motions to the men to be seated*] The cabin wouldn't hold us all, but there's one good thing about this place; there's plenty of outdoors.

WINTHROP: [*Looking about*] I should say there was!

POLLY: To think of our practical Ruth doing the one really theatrical thing known in the annals of Milford Corners, Mass.! – And what a setting! My dear, your stage arrangements are perfect.

RUTH: In this case Providence deserves the credit. We may have come here to have our pictures taken, but we stayed to make a living.

Philip has drawn apart, gloomy and threatening. Polly keeps up her heroic efforts to give the situation a casual and humorous air

POLLY: [*With jaunty challenge*] Well, where is he?

RUTH: Who?

POLLY: He! [*Ruth points at the cabin, smiling*] Well, produce him!

RUTH: [*Following, with gratitude in her eyes, the key of lightness and raillery which Polly has struck*] You insist?

POLLY: Absolutely.

RUTH: O, very well!

She goes up the rocky incline, and enters the cabin, calling: "Steve! Steve!" Polly goes to Philip and shakes him

POLLY: Now you behave! [*Indicates Winthrop*] He's behaving.

Ruth reappears in the doorway, followed by Ghent

RUTH: [*With elaborate gayety, as they descend the rocks*] Well, Stephen, since they've run us to earth, I suppose we must put a good face on it, and acknowledge them. – This is Polly, of whom I've talked so much. Polly the irresistible. Beware of her! [*Polly shakes his hand cordially*] And this is—my brother Philip. [*Ghent extends his hand, which Philip pointedly ignores. Ruth goes on hastily, to cover*

the insult] And this is my old school-friend, Winthrop Newbury. [*They shake hands*]

WINTHROP: [*To Philip, formally explanatory*] Mr. Ghent is the owner of the famous Verde mine.

GHENT: Part owner, sir. I hadn't the capital to develop with, so I had to dispose of a half-interest.

WINTHROP: Isn't there some litigation under way?

RUTH: [*Looking at Ghent, surprised*] Litigation?

GHENT: Yes – a whole rigmarole.

POLLY: [*Catching at a straw to make talk*] Heaven help you if you have got entangled in the law! I can conceive of nothing more horrible or ghostly than a court of law; unless [*She glances at Philip*] it is that other court of high justice, which people hold in private to judge their fellows, from hearsay and half-knowledge!

RUTH: [*Keeping up the play desperately, as she blesses Polly with a look*] But there must be law, just the same, and penalties and rewards and all that. Else what's the use of being good?

POLLY: Like you – for instance!

RUTH: Well, yes, like me!

POLLY: You are not good, you are merely magnificent. I want to be magnificent! I want to live on the roof of the world and own a gold mine! [*To Ghent*] Show me where the sweet thing is.

GHENT: We can get a better view of the plant from the ledge below. Will you go down?

Ghent, Polly, and Winthrop go down the cañon path. Ruth takes Philip by the arm, to lead him after

PHILIP: No. We must have a word together, before the gabble begins again. Winthrop has given me your explanation, which explains nothing.

RUTH: [*Trying to keep up the light tone*] Hasn't that usually been the verdict on explanations of my conduct?

PHILIP: Don't try to put me off! Tell me in two words how you came to run away with this fellow.

RUTH: [*Hardening*] Remember to whom you are speaking and about whom.

PHILIP: I got your note, with its curt announcement of your resolve. Later, by mere accident, we found the record of your marriage at San Jacinto – if you call it a marriage, made hugger-mugger at midnight by a tipsy justice of the peace. I don't want to question its validity. I only pray that no one will. But I want to know how it came to be made, in such hurry and secrecy – how it came to be made at all, for that matter. How did you ever come to disgrace yourself and your family by clandestine meetings and a hedgerow marriage with a person of this class? And why, after the crazy leap was taken, did you see fit to hide yourself away without a word to me or your distracted mother? Though that perhaps is easier to understand!

RUTH: The manner of your questions absolves me from the obligation to answer them.

PHILIP: I refuse to be put off with any such patent subterfuge.

RUTH: Subterfuge or not, it will have to suffice, until you remember that my right to choose my course in life is unimpeachable, and that the man whose destiny I elect to share cannot be insulted in my presence.

PHILIP: Very well, I can wait. The truth will come out some day. Meanwhile, you can take comfort from the fact that your desertion at the critical moment of our enterprise has spelled ruin for me.

RUTH: [*Overwhelmed*] Philip, you don't mean –!

PHILIP: Absolute and irretrievable ruin.

RUTH: Then you are going back East – for good?

PHILIP: Yes.

RUTH: But – mother's money! What will she do? [*Philip shrugs his shoulders*] Is everything gone – everything?

PHILIP: I shall get something from the sale. Perhaps enough to make a fresh start, somewhere, in some small way.

RUTH: [*Comes to him, and lays her arms on his shoulders*] Phil, I am sorry, sorry!

He caresses her; she bursts into suppressed convulsive weeping and clings to him, hiding her face in his breast]

PHILIP: Ruth, you are not happy! You have made a hideous mistake. Come home with me. [*Ruth shakes her head*] At least for a time.

You are not well. You look really ill. Come home with us, if only for a month.

RUTH: No, no, dear Phil, dear brother! [*She draws down his face and kisses him; then lifts her head, with an attempt at lightness*] There! I have had my cry, and feel better. The excitement of seeing you all again is a little too much for me.

PHILIP: If there is anything that you want to tell me about all this, tell me now.

RUTH: O, there will be plenty of time for explanations and all that! Let us just be happy now in our reunion.

PHILIP: There will not be plenty of time. We leave to-morrow morning.

RUTH: Then you will take me on trust – like a dear good brother. Perhaps I shall never explain! I like my air of mystery.

PHILIP: Remember that if you ever have anything to complain of – in your life – it is my right to know it. The offender shall answer to me, and dearly, too.

RUTH: [*Takes his head between her hands, and shakes it, as with recovered gayety*] Of course they will, you old fire-eater!

PHILIP: [*Pointing to the blanket on the loom*] Ruth, at least tell my why –.

Ruth does not see his gesture, as she is looking at the others, who come up from below. The men linger in the background, Ghent pointing out objects in the landscape

RUTH: [*To Polly, who advances*] Well, what do you think of us, in a bird's-eye view?

POLLY: In a bird's-eye view you are superb! [*She draws Ruth to her, and speaks in a lower tone*] And looked at near, you are an enthralling puzzle.

RUTH: [*Half to herself*] If you only knew how much!

POLLY: [*Taking Ruth by the chin as in Act I*] So you *had* – just by chance – riding over to the trading-station or so – met the glorious unfulfilled – in blue overalls and a jumper! I thought so! [*Ruth bows her head in a spasm of pain. Polly, who does not see her face, goes on teasingly*] I see now what you meant about wanting one that wasn't finished. This one certainly isn't finished. But when he is, he'll be grand! [*Ruth moves away with averted head. Polly follows her, peeping round to view her face*] Don't sulk! I meant nothing disrespectful. On the contrary, I'm crazy about him. [*In a louder tone*] And now that I've seen the outside of you, I *must* peep into that fascinating little house!

RUTH: [*To Ghent, who has drawn nearer*] Polly wants to go inside the cabin. I can't let her until we have shown her what it's going to be. [*With Ghent's aid she spreads out the plans, which Polly examines with curiosity*] These are the plans for our new house. You call us magnificent. We will show you that we are not. We are overwhelming!

WINTHROP: [*Looking at his watch*] I am afraid we must be getting back. It grows dark very suddenly in the cañon.

RUTH: [*To Polly*] Well, then you may come in, if you will promise to view the simple present in the light of the ornate future.

Polly goes in. Ruth, lingering at the door for an instant, looks back anxiously at the men

PHILIP: [*Curtly, to Ghent*] If you will permit me, I should like a word with you.

GHENT: Certainly.

Winthrop effaces himself, making and lighting a cigarette, as he looks out over the cañon

PHILIP: In deference to my sister's wishes, I refrain from asking you for the explanation which is due me. [*Ghent bows in silence*] But there is one thing which I think I am at liberty to question.

GHENT: Do so.

PHILIP: I hear of your interest in a valuable mine. I hear of plans for an elaborate house. Why, then, is my sister compelled to peddle her own handiwork in a public caravansery?

GHENT: What do you mean? I don't understand you.

PHILIP: [*Points at the loom*] Her rugs and baskets are on sale in the corridor of the hotel, fingered and discussed by the tourist mob.

GHENT: [*Astonished*] This can't be true!

PHILIP: It is, however.

GHENT: I know nothing of it. I've had to be away a great deal. I knew she worked too hard over these things, but I took it for a mere pastime. Perhaps – No, I can't understand it at all!

PHILIP: I advise you to make inquiries. She has taken pains to conceal her identity, but it is known nevertheless, and the subject of public curiosity.

Polly and Ruth come out from the cabin

POLLY: [*To Philip*] Take me away quickly, or I shall never enjoy upholstery again! [*To Ruth*] Please change your mind, dear, and come with us for the night.

RUTH: No. I will see you in the morning.

WINTHROP: We leave by the early stage.

RUTH: [*Looking at him quickly*] You too?

WINTHROP: Yes, I have decided so.

RUTH: I will be there in good time, trust me. [*She kisses Polly and Philip*] Good-bye, till morning. [*Gives her hand to Winthrop*] Good-bye.

Philip ignores Ghent pointedly in the leave-takings. Polly bids him farewell with corresponding cordiality

POLLY: Good-bye, Mr. Ghent. [*As they descend the cañon path, she is heard chatting enthusiastically*] O Phil, you ought to have seen the inside of that delightful little house!

Her voice is heard for some time, indistinctly. Ruth, at the top of the path, waves to them as they descend

GHENT: [*Looks long at her, with deep gratitude*] God bless you! [*She sits down on the rocks of the cabin terrace. He walks up and down in anxious thought. Once or twice he makes as if to speak. At length he stops before her*] You must go in and lie down. You are worn out.

RUTH: [*Rousing herself*] No, there is something I must tell you first.

GHENT: [*Points at the rug*] It's about this – work you have been doing?

RUTH: [*Slightly startled*] You know of that?

GHENT: Your brother told me. I should have found it out to-morrow anyhow. [*Pause*] Have you wanted money?

RUTH: Yes.

GHENT: I thought I – I thought you had enough. I have often begged you to take more.

RUTH: I haven't spent what you gave me. It is in there. [*She points toward the house*]

GHENT: [*Astonished*] You haven't spent – any of it?

RUTH: A little. Nothing for myself.

GHENT: But there has been no need to save, not after the first month or two. You surely knew that!

RUTH: Yes, I knew it. It was not economy.

GHENT: [*Slowly*] You haven't been willing to take money from me?

RUTH: No. I know it was small of me, but I couldn't help it. I have paid for everything. – I have kept account of it – O, to the last dreadful penny! These clothes are the ones I wore from my brother's house that night. This shelter – you know I helped to raise that with my own hands. And – and some things I paid for secretly, from the little hoard I brought away with me. You were careless; you did not notice.

GHENT: [*Sits down, dizzy from the shock of her words*] I must try to grasp this! [*There is a silence, during which he sits perfectly motionless. At last he turns to her*] Why – why did you stand up so plucky, so splendid, just now? Put a good face on everything about our life? Call me by my first name and all that – before your own people?

RUTH: We are man and wife. Beside that, my own people are as strangers.

GHENT: [*Eagerly*] You say that? You can still say that?

RUTH: [*Looks up, startled*] Can't you? [*She awaits his answer tensely*]

GHENT: [*Desperately*] O, I don't know. I can't say or think anything, after what you have just told me!

RUTH: [*Wails*] You can't say it! And it isn't true! It is we who are strangers. – Worse, a thousand times worse!

GHENT: [*Rises and stands over her*] Don't let us dash ourselves to hell in one crazy minute! [*He pauses and hesitates. When he speaks again it is with wistful tenderness*] Ruth, do you remember our journey here? [*She lifts her head, looking at him with white, thirsty face*] I thought – it seemed to me you had – begun to care for me.

RUTH: That night, when we rode away from the justice's office at San Jacinto, and the sky began to brighten over the desert – the ice that had gathered here – [*She touches her heart*] – began to melt in spite of me. And when the next night and the next day passed, and the next, and still you spared me and treated me with beautiful rough chivalry, I said to myself, "He has heard my prayer to him. He knows what a girl's heart is." As you rode before me down the arroyos, and up over the mesas, through the dazzling sunlight and the majestic silence, it seemed as if you were leading me out of a world of little codes and customs into a great new world. – So it was for those first days. – And then – and then – I woke, and saw you standing in my tent-door in the starlight! I knew before you spoke that we were lost. You hadn't the strength to save us!

GHENT: [*Huskily*] Surely it hasn't all been – hateful to you? There have been times, since that. – The afternoon we climbed up here. The day we made the table; the day we planted the vines.

RUTH: [*In a half whisper*] Yes! – Beautiful days! [*She puts her hands suddenly before her face and sobs*] O, it was not my fault! I have struggled against it. You don't know how I have struggled!

GHENT: Against what? Struggled against what?

RUTH: Against the hateful image you had raised up beside your own image.

GHENT: What do you mean?

RUTH: I mean that sometimes – often – when you stand there before my eyes, you fade away, and in your place I see – the Other One!

GHENT: Speak plainly, for God's sake! I don't understand this talk.

RUTH: [*Looking steadfastly, as at an invisible shape, speaks in a horrified whisper*] There he stands behind you now! – The human beast, that goes to its horrible pleasure as not even a wild animal will go – *in pack, in pack!* [*Ghent, stung beyond endurance, rises and paces up and down. Ruth continues in a broken tone, spent by the violence of her own words*] I have tried – O, you don't know how I have tried to save myself from these thoughts. – While we were poor and struggling I thought I could do it. – Then – [*She points toward the cañon*] – then that hole down there began belching its stream of gold. You began to load me with gifts – to force easy ways upon me –

GHENT: Well, what else did I care to make money for?

Ruth does not answer for a moment, then speaks slowly, taking the words with loathing upon her tongue

RUTH: Every time you give me anything, or talk about the mine and what it is going to do, there rings in my ears that dreadful sneer: "A dirt-eating Mojave would pay more than that for his squaw!" [*She rises, lifting her arms*] I held myself so dear! And you bought me for a handful of gold, like a woman of the street! You drove me before you like an animal from the market!

Ghent has seated himself again, elbows on knees and face in his hands. Ruth takes slowly from her bosom the nugget chain and holds it crumpled up in her palm. Her tone is quiet, almost matter-of-fact

I have got back the chain again.

GHENT: [*Looks up*] Chain? – What chain?

RUTH: [*In the same tone, as she hold it up, letting it unwind*] The one you bought me with.

GHENT: [*Dumfounded*] Where the devil – ? Has that fellow been around here?

RUTH: It would have had no meaning for me except from his hand.

GHENT: So that's what you've been doing with this rug-weaving and basket-making tomfoolery? [*Ruth does not answer, but continues looking at the chain, running it through her fingers and weighing it in her hand*] How long has this been going on?

RUTH: How long? – How long can one live without breathing? Two minutes? A few lifetimes? How long!

GHENT: It was about a month after we came here that you began to potter with this work.

RUTH: [*Draws her hand about her neck as if loosening something there; convulsively*] Since then this has been round my neck, around my limbs, a chain of eating fire. Link by link I have unwound it. You will never know what it has cost me, but I have paid it all. Take it and let me go free. [*She tries to force it upon him, with wailing entreaty*] Take it, take it, I beseech you!

GHENT: [*Holding himself under stern control*] You are killing yourself. You mustn't go on this way. Go and rest. We will talk of this to-morrow.

RUTH: Rest! To-morrow! O, how little you have understood of all I have said! I know it is only a symbol – a make-believe. I know I am childish to ask it. Still, take it and tell me I am free.

Ghent takes the chain reluctantly, stands for a moment looking at it, then speaks with iron firmness

GHENT: As you say, your price has risen. This is not enough. [*He throws the chain about her neck and draws her to him by it*] You are mine, mine, do you hear? Now and forever!

He starts toward the house. She holds out her hand blindly to detain him

RUTH: [*In a stifled voice*] Wait! There is – something else. [*He returns to her, anxiously, and stands waiting. She goes on, touching the chain*] It isn't only for my sake I ask you to take this off me, nor only for your sake. There is – another life – to think of.

GHENT: [*Leaning to look into her averted face*] Ruth! – Is it true? – Thank God!

RUTH: Now will you take this off me?

GHENT: [*Starts to do so, then draws back*] No. Now less than ever. For now, more than ever, you are mine.

RUTH: But – *how* yours? O, remember, have pity! *How* yours?

Philip appears at the head of the cañon path. Hearing their voices, he waits, half concealed

GHENT: No matter how! Bought if you like, but mine! Mine by blind chance and the hell in a man's veins, if you like! Mine by almighty Nature whether you like it or not!

RUTH: Nature! Almighty Nature! [*She takes the chain slowly from her neck*] Not yours! By everything my people have held sacred! [*She drops the chain*] Not yours! Not yours!

She turns slowly. Philip has come forward, and supports her as she sinks half fainting upon his neck

PHILIP: [*To Ghent*] I came back to get my sister for the night. – I don't know by what ugly spell you have held her, but I know, from her own lips, that it is broken. [*To Ruth*] Come! I have horses below.

GHENT: No!

PHILIP: [*Measuring him*] Yes. [*Pause*]

GHENT: Let her say!

RUTH: [*Looks long at Ghent, then at the house and surroundings. At last she turns to her brother*] Take me – with you. Take me – home!

Philip, supporting her, leads her down the cañon path. Ghent stands gazing after them as they disappear below the rim. He picks up the chain and goes back, looking down after the descending figures. The sunset light has faded, and darkness has begun to settle over the mountain world

Curtain

ACT III

Sitting-room of Mrs. Jordan's house at Milford Corners, Massachusetts. An old-fashioned New England interior, faded but showing signs of former distinction. The walls are hung with family portraits, several in clerical attire of the eighteenth century, one in the uniform of the Revolutionary War. Doors open right and left. At the back is a fireplace, flanked by windows, the curtains of which are drawn. On the left is a small table, with a lamp, books, and magazines; on the right, near the fireplace, a sewing-table, with lamp and sewing-basket. A bookcase and a writing-desk occupy opposite corners of the room, forward.

Winthrop and Philip stand near the desk, chatting. Polly is reading a newspaper at the table, left. Ruth sits before the grate, sewing; her face is turned away toward the fire.

PHILIP: [*Offers Winthrop his cigar-case*] Have another cigar.

WINTHROP: Well, as a celebration. [*Takes one and lights it*]

PHILIP: Rather small business for the Jordan family, to be celebrating a bare escape from the poor-house.

WINTHROP: Where did you scare up the benevolent uncle? I never heard of him before.

PHILIP: Nor I, scarcely. He's always lived abroad.

Winthrop, strolling about, peeps over Polly's shoulder

WINTHROP: [*To Philip, with a scandalized gesture*] Stock reports!

PHILIP: Her latest craze.

WINTHROP: Last week it was Japanese Samurai.

POLLY: [*Crushingly*] And next week it will be – Smart Alecks.

The door on the left opens, and Mrs. Jordan enters, with Dr. Newbury. During the preceding conversation Ruth has sat sewing, paying no heed to the chatter. Mrs. Jordan and the Doctor look at her as they come in, but she does not look up

MRS. JORDAN: Sit down, Doctor, at least for a moment.

DR. NEWBURY: [*Seats himself, Mrs. Jordan near him*] I can never resist such an invitation, in this house.

MRS. JORDAN: Dear Doctor, you've been a wonderful friend to me and mine all these years, since poor Josiah was taken.

DR. NEWBURY: But just when you needed help most –

MRS. JORDAN: I know how gladly you would have offered it, if you could.

DR. NEWBURY: Your brother-in-law in England was able to redeem the property?

MRS. JORDAN: [*Hastily*] Yes, yes. – But what we are to do for the future, with my little capital gone – [*She speaks lower*] O, that dreadful West! If my children had only stayed where they were born and bred.

She glances at Ruth, who has let her sewing fall into her lap and sits staring into the fire

DR. NEWBURY: [*Sotto voce*] Poor child!

Polly looks up from the newspaper excitedly, holding her finger at a place on the sheet

POLLY: I say, Phil! Win! Look here.

Philip and Winthrop, who have been chatting and smoking apart, come to the table

PHILIP: What is it now?

POLLY: [*Tapping on the paper*] Something about your Arizona scheme.

PHILIP: [*Bending over her, reads*] "Allegheny pig-iron, 93¾, National Brick –"

POLLY: [*Pointing*] No, there!

PHILIP: Arizona Cactus Fibre, 84. [*He picks up the paper, astounded*] Cactus Fibre listed! Selling at 84! [*He tosses the paper to Winthrop*] This is the last straw!

MRS. JORDAN: [*Who has been listening anxiously*] What does it mean, Phil?

PHILIP: Only that the people who bought our plant and patents for a song, have made a fortune out of them.

Ruth has resumed her needle-work. Winthrop offers her the paper, with his finger at the line. She takes it, looks at it vaguely, and lays it on the table

POLLY: [*Leaning across*] Doesn't that interest you?

RUTH: [*Tonelessly*] O, yes.

She rises, lays her work aside, and goes toward the door, left

DR. NEWBURY: [*As she passes him*] Won't you bid me good-night, my child?

RUTH: [*Giving him her hand*] Good-night, Doctor.

DR. NEWBURY: [*Shaking his finger*] Remember, no more moping! And from to-morrow, outdoors with you.

Ruth looks at him vacantly, attempting to smile. She moves toward the door, which Winthrop opens for her

WINTHROP: [*Holding out his hand*] You must bid me good-night, too, and good-bye.

RUTH: [*With a faint kindling of interest*] Are you going away?

WINTHROP: Only back to Boston. Some time, when you are stronger, you will come down and see our new sailor's hospital.

RUTH: Yes. – Good-bye.

She goes out, Winthrop closing the door

WINTHROP: [*To Dr. Newbury*] I must be going along, father. Good-night, everybody! [*Patting Philip's shoulder*] Hard luck, old man!

He goes out by the hall door on the right, Philip accompanying him

DR. NEWBURY: [*Looking after his son*] Brave boy! Brave boy! He keeps up a good show.

MRS. JORDAN: You think he still grieves over her?

DR. NEWBURY: Ah, poor chap! He's made of the right stuff, if he is mine.

MRS. JORDAN: Let us not talk of it. It is too sad, too dreadful.

Philip reenters

DR. NEWBURY: About part of it we ·must talk. [*He speaks so as to include Philip and Polly in the conversation*] Mrs. Jordan, I don't want to alarm you, but your daughter – I may as well put it bluntly – is in a dangerous state.

MRS. JORDAN: [*Frightened*] Doctor! I thought she seemed so much stronger.

DR. NEWBURY: She is, so far as her body is concerned.

Mrs. Jordan sits in an attitude of nervous attention, gazing at the doctor as if trying to formulate one of many questions pressing upon her. Philip comes forward and sits by the table, near them

PHILIP: Don't you think that the routine of life which she has taken up will soon restore her to a normal state of mind?

DR. NEWBURY: Perhaps. – I hope so. – I would have good hope of it, if it were not for her attitude toward her child.

MRS. JORDAN: [*Overwhelmed*] You have noticed that, too! I haven't spoken to you of it, because – I haven't been willing to see it myself.

PHILIP: I can't see that there is anything particularly strange in her attitude. She takes care of the brat scrupulously enough.

POLLY: Brat!

MRS. JORDAN: Brat! [*To Dr. Newbury, after a reproachful gaze at Philip*] With the most watchful, the minutest care, but – [*She speaks in a constrained voice, with a nervous glance at the door*] – exactly as if it were a piece of machinery! – Phil, do please lay down that paper-knife before you break it! Your father brought that to me from India. [*He obeys, but picks it up again absentmindedly, after a few seconds*] Pardon me, Doctor. She goes about her daily business, and answers when she is spoken to, but as for her really being here – [*She breaks out*] Doctor, what *shall* we do?

DR. NEWBURY: She must be roused from this state, but how to do it, I don't know.

POLLY: [*Rising, with heightened color and nervous emphasis*] Well, I do!

MRS. JORDAN: [*Looking at her with frightened interrogation*] Polly – ?

POLLY: What she needs is her husband, and I have sent for him!

PHILIP: [*Inarticulate with surprise and anger*] You – !

POLLY: Yes, I. He's been here a week. And he's an angel, isn't he, mother?

Philip snaps the paper-knife in two, flings the pieces to the floor, and rises, pale with rage

MRS. JORDAN: [*Gathering up the pieces with a wail*] O Phil! How could you! One of my most precious relics!

PHILIP: [*To Mrs. Jordan*] Is this true, or is it another of her tedious jokes?

POLLY: [*Protesting*] O, my dear, tedious!

MRS. JORDAN: [*Wipes her eyes, after ruefully fitting the broken pieces of the knife together and laying them tenderly on the table*] You don't deserve to have me answer you, but it is true.

PHILIP: Was this action taken with your knowledge?

MRS. JORDAN: I do not expect to be spoken to in that tone. Polly telegraphed merely the facts. He came at his own instance.

PHILIP: But you have consented to enter into relations with him?

MRS. JORDAN: I have seen him several times.

POLLY: [*Triumphantly*] And yesterday we showed him the baby! Such fun, wasn't it, mother?

MRS. JORDAN: [*Wiping her eyes, sheepishly*] Yes, it was rather – enjoyable.

PHILIP: He can't be in this town. I should have heard of it.

POLLY: We've hid him safe.

PHILIP: Where?

POLLY: Never mind. He's on tap, and the sooner we turn on the spigot the better, is what I think. Doctor, what do you think?

DR. NEWBURY: Let me ask you again to state your view of Ruth's case. I don't think I quite grasp your view.

POLLY: [*Pluming herself, doctrinaire*] Well! Here on the one hand is the primitive, the barbaric woman, falling in love with a romantic stranger, who, like some old Viking on a harry, cuts her with his two-handed sword from the circle of her kinsmen, and bears her away on his dragon ship toward the midnight sun. Here on the other hand is the derived, the civilized woman, with a civilized nervous system, observing that the creature eats bacon with his bowie knife, knows not the manicure, has the conversation of a preoccupied walrus, the instincts of a jealous caribou, and the endearments of a dancing crab in the mating season.

MRS. JORDAN: Polly! What ideas! What language!

DR. NEWBURY: Don't be alarmed, Mrs. Jordan. The vocabulary has changed since our day, and – the point of view has shifted a little. [*To Polly*] Well?

POLLY: Well, Ruth is one of those people who can't live in a state of divided feeling. She sits staring at this cleavage in her life, like – like that man in Dante, don't you know, who is pierced by the serpent, and who stands there in hell staring at his wound, yawning like a sleepy man.

MRS. JORDAN: O, Polly, do please try not to get our heads muddled up with literature!

POLLY: All I mean is that when she married her man she married him for keeps. And he did the same by her.

Philip rises, with uncontrollable impatience, and goes back to the mantelpiece, against which he leans, nervously tearing a bit of paper to pieces

DR. NEWBURY: Don't you think that a mere difference of cultivation, polish – or – or something of that sort – is rather small to have led to a rupture, and so painful a one too?

POLLY: [*A little nonplussed*] Well, yes, perhaps it does *look* small. But we don't know the particulars; and men *are* such *colossal* brutes, you know, dear Doctor!

DR. NEWBURY: [*Judicially*] Yes, so they are, so they are!

POLLY: And then her pride! You know when it comes to pride, Ruth would make Lucifer look like a charity-boy asking for more soup.

DR. NEWBURY: I think perhaps the plan should be tried. [*After a pause*] Yes, I think so decidedly.

PHILIP: I call this a plot against her dignity and peace of mind!

DR. NEWBURY: [*Rising*] Well, this conspirator must be going. [*He shakes' hands with Polly and Mrs. Jordan, takes his hat and stick. Philip remains plunged in angry reflection. Dr. Newbury taps Philip jestingly on the shoulder with the tip of his cane*] When you have lived as long as I have, my boy, you'll – you'll be just as old as I am!

He goes out, Polly accompanying him to the door. Philip, disregarding his mother's conciliatory look and gesture as he passes her, goes out left. Polly stretches her arms and draws a deep breath as the door closes after him

MRS. JORDAN: [*Looking at her severely*] Pray what does that mean?

POLLY: O, Phil is such a walking thunder-cloud, these days. It's a relief to get rid of him.

MRS. JORDAN: Have you done what you could to make his life brighter?

POLLY: I never had a chance. He has always been too much wrapped up in Ruth to think of me.

MRS. JORDAN: How can you say such a thing? What do you suppose he married you for?

POLLY: Heaven knows! What do they ever do it for? It is a most curious and savage propensity. But immensely interesting to watch.

MRS. JORDAN: [*With a despairing gesture*] If you hold such heathenish views, why are you so bent on bringing those two together?

POLLY: [*Soberly*] Because they represent – what Philip and I have missed.

MRS. JORDAN: And pray what have "Philip and I" missed?

POLLY: O, we're all right. But we're not like those two.

MRS. JORDAN: I should hope not!

POLLY: Even I believe that now and then a marriage is made in Heaven. This one was. They are predestined lovers!

MRS. JORDAN: [*Mournfully, hypnotized by the evangelical note*] I pray it may be so. [*She looks suspiciously at Polly*] You wretched girl! Predestined lovers and marriage made in Heaven, after all you've just been saying about how impossible he is.

POLLY: He is quite impossible, but he's the kind we can't resist, any of us. He'd only have to crook his little finger at me.

MRS. JORDAN: [*Lifting her hands in despair*]

What are you young women coming to! [*Pause*] He seems to me a good man.

POLLY: [*Delighted*] O, he's *good!* so is a volcano between eruptions. And commonplace, too, until you happen to get a glimpse down one of the old volcanic rifts in his surface, and see – far below – underneath the cold lava-beds – fire, fire, the molten heart of a continent!

MRS. JORDAN: I only hope you have some vague general notion of what you are talking about.

POLLY: Amen. – And now let's consider when, where, and how we are to hale this dubious pair together.

MRS. JORDAN: One thing is sure, it mustn't be here.

POLLY: Why not?

MRS. JORDAN: On Philip's account.

POLLY: O, bother Philip! Wasn't that the door-bell?

MRS. JORDAN: Yes. You had better go.

Polly goes out. After a moment she reenters, excitedly

POLLY: It's Mr. Ghent!

MRS. JORDAN: [*Amazed*] Mr. Ghent? [*Polly nods enthusiastically. Ghent enters. He is conventionally dressed, a black string tie and the broad-brimmed hat which he carries being the only suggestions of Western costume remaining. Mrs. Jordan receives him in a flutter of excitement and alarm*] Mr. Ghent – ! Surely at this hour – !

GHENT: I beg your pardon. There was no other way. I am going West to-night. – Can I see you alone?

MRS. JORDAN: [*Looks at Polly, who goes out, pouting*] Going West to-night?

GHENT: Yes. Trouble at the mine.

MRS. JORDAN: Isn't your business partner competent to attend to it?

GHENT: He's competent to steal the whole outfit. In fact, is doing it, or has done it already.

MRS. JORDAN: [*Vaguely alarmed*] And – my property here? Is that involved in the danger?

GHENT: Certainly not.

MRS. JORDAN: [*Relieved*] I have gone through such months of misery at the thought of losing the dear old place! – If Ruth only knew that we owe the very roof over our heads to you –

GHENT: Well, she isn't to know, that's understood, isn't it? Besides, it's nothing to speak of.

Glad if you think it a service. She wouldn't.

MRS. JORDAN: You mean – ?

GHENT: I mean that if she knew about it, she wouldn't stay here overnight.

MRS. JORDAN: Sit down. [*She motions him to a seat at the table; she sits near him, speaking with nervous impulsiveness*] Tell me what is the trouble between you! It has all been a dreadful mystery from the beginning!

GHENT: Is it a mystery that a woman like your daughter – ?

He stops and sinks into gloomy thought

MRS. JORDAN: Should have chosen you? – Pardon me, I don't mean anything unkind – [*He makes a gesture of brusque exoneration*] But having chosen – and broken faith with her brother to do it –

GHENT: [*Nervously*] Let's drop that! [*Pause*] Mrs. Jordan, you come of the old stock. Do you believe in the devil?

MRS. JORDAN: Perhaps not in the sense you mean.

GHENT: [*Tapping his breast*] I mean the devil inside of a man – the devil in the heart!

MRS. JORDAN: O, yes. We are all forced by our lives to believe in that.

GHENT: Our lives! [*He looks slowly round the room*] How long have you lived here?

MRS. JORDAN: For thirty years, in this house. Before I was married I lived in the old house down the road yonder, opposite the church.

GHENT: [*To himself*] Think of it!

MRS. JORDAN: What did you say?

GHENT: [*Gathers himself together*] Mrs. Jordan, I want you to promise that what I put in your hands from time to time comes to your daughter as if from another source.

MRS. JORDAN: You are going away for good?

GHENT: Yes.

MRS. JORDAN: You give her up?

GHENT: A man can't give up what isn't his.

MRS. JORDAN: What isn't his? She is your wife.

GHENT: No. Never has been.

MRS. JORDAN: [*Terrified*] O, pitiful heavens!

GHENT: I beg your pardon. – I was only trying to say – I used to think that when a couple was married, there they were, man and wife, and that was the end of it. I used to think that when they had a child, well, sure enough it was their child, and all said. – And there's

something in that, too. [*He stares before him, smiting the table, and speaking with low intensity*] Damn me if there ain't something eternal in it! [*He sits for a moment more in gloomy thought*] Do you think she'll make up to the young one, after a bit?

MRS. JORDAN: O, surely! To think otherwise would be too dreadful!

GHENT: I'd give a good deal to know. – It's kind of lonesome for the little rooster, sitting out there all by himself on the world's doorstep! – I must see her for a minute before I go. – Do your best for me.

MRS. JORDAN: I will do what I can.

GHENT: You can put it as a matter of business. There is a matter of business I want to talk over with her, if I can get up the gumption.

MRS. JORDAN: Hadn't you better tell me what it is?

GHENT: Well, it's about your son Philip. That little scheme he started out in my country – the Cactus Fibre industry.

MRS. JORDAN: Yes?

GHENT: I believe he thinks his sister's going away when she did queered his game.

MRS. JORDAN: It was a severe blow to him in every way. She was the life and soul of his enterprise.

GHENT: I want her to give him back the Cactus Fibre outfit, worth something more than when he dropped it.

MRS. JORDAN: Give it back to him? She?

GHENT: [*Takes papers from his pocket*] Yes. I happened to hear it was knocking around for nothing in the market, and I bought it – for the house, really. Hated to see that go to the dogs. Then I looked over the plant, and got a hustler to boom it. I thought as a matter of transfer, to cancel her debt, or what she thinks her debt – [*Pause*]

MRS. JORDAN: [*Fingering the paper with hesitation*] Mr. Ghent, we really can't accept such a thing. Your offer is quixotic.

GHENT: Quix – what?

MRS. JORDAN: Quixotic, it really is.

GHENT: [*Doubtfully*] I guess you're right. It depends on the way you look at it. One way it looks like a pure business proposition – so much lost, so much made good. The other way it looks, as you say, quix – um – . Anyway, there are the papers! Do what you think best with them.

He lays the papers on the table, and picks up his hat

MRS. JORDAN: Wait in the parlor. [*He opens the hall door*] The second door on the left.

With an awkward bow to Mrs. Jordan, he partly closes the door after him, when the inner door opens and Ruth appears. She goes to the sewing-table and picks up her sewing. Her mother, with a frightened glance at the half-open hall door, draws her back and kisses her. Ghent, unseen by Ruth, remains standing, with his hand on the doorknob

MRS. JORDAN: Ruth, you are a brave girl, and I will treat you like one. – Your husband is here.

RUTH: Here? – Where?

Ghent pushes the door open, and closes it behind him. Ruth, sinking back against the opposite wall, stares at him blankly

MRS. JORDAN: He is leaving for the West again to-night. He has asked to see you before he goes. [*Ruth covers her face with her hands, then fumbles blindly for the latch of the door. Her mother restrains her*] It is your duty to hear what he has to say. You owe that to the love you once bore him.

RUTH: He killed my love before it was born!

MRS. JORDAN: It is your duty to hear him, and part with him in a Christian spirit, for our sakes, if not for your own.

RUTH: For whose sake?

MRS. JORDAN: For mine, and your brother's. – We owe it to him, as a family.

GHENT: [*Raises his hand restrainingly*] Mrs. Jordan – !

RUTH: Owe?

MRS. JORDAN: We owe it to him, for what he has done and wishes to do.

RUTH: What he has done? – Wishes to do?

MRS. JORDAN: Yes, don't echo me like a parrot! He has done a great deal for us, and is anxious to do more, if you will only let him.

RUTH: What is this? Explain it to me quickly.

MRS. JORDAN: [*With growing impatience*] Don't think to judge your mother!

RUTH: I demand to hear what all this is! Tell me.

MRS. JORDAN: [*Losing control of herself*] He has kept us from being turned into the street! [*Ghent, who has tried dumbly to restrain her, turns away in stoic resignation to his fate*] He has given us the very roof over our heads!

RUTH: You said that uncle –

MRS. JORDAN: Well, it was not your uncle! I said so to shield you in your stubborn and cold-hearted pride.

RUTH: Is there more of this?

MRS. JORDAN: Yes, there *is* more. You wronged your brother to follow your own path of wilful love, and now you wrong him again by following your own path of wilful aversion. Here comes your husband, offering to make restitution –

RUTH: What restitution?

MRS. JORDAN: He has bought Philip's property out there, and wants you to give it back to him.

Ruth stands motionless for a moment, then looks vacantly about, speaking in a dull voice, as at first

RUTH: I must go away from this house.

MRS. JORDAN: You don't understand. He claims nothing. He is going away himself immediately. Whatever this dreadful trouble is between you, you are his wife, and he has a right to help you and yours.

RUTH: I am not his wife.

MRS. JORDAN: Ruth, don't frighten me. He said those same words –

RUTH: He said – what?

MRS. JORDAN: That you were not his wife.

RUTH: He said – that?

MRS. JORDAN: Yes, but afterward he explained –

RUTH: [*Flaming into white wrath*] Explained! Did he explain that when I was left alone that night at the ranch he came – with two others – and when gun and knife had failed me, and nothing stood between me and their drunken fury, I sold myself to the strongest of them, hiding my head behind the name of marriage? Did he explain that between him and the others money clinked – [*She raps on the table*] – my price in hard money on the table? And now that I have run away to the only refuge I have on earth, he comes to buy the very house where I have hidden, and every miserable being within it!

*Long pause. She looks about blankly and sinks
down by the table*

MRS. JORDAN: [*Cold and rigid*] And you – married him – after that? [*She turns away in horror-stricken judgment*] You ought to have –
died – first! [*Philip opens the door and enters,
staring at Ghent with dislike and menace*]
O Philip, she has told me! – You can't imagine
what horrors!

Ruth rises, with fright in her face, and approaches her brother to restrain him

PHILIP: Horrors? What horrors?

MRS. JORDAN: It was your fault! You ought
never to have left her alone in that dreadful
place! She – she married him – to save herself
– from – O horrible!

*Philip waits an instant, the truth penetrating his
mind slowly. Then, with mortal rage in his
face, he starts toward Ghent*

PHILIP: You – dog!

Ruth throws herself in Philip's path

RUTH: No, no, no!

PHILIP: Get out of my way. This is my business
now.

RUTH: No, it is mine. I tell you it is mine.

PHILIP: We'll see whose it is. I said that if the
truth ever came out, this man should answer
to me, and now, by God, he shall answer!

*With another access of rage he tries to thrust
Ruth from his path. Mrs. Jordan, terrified at
the storm she has raised, clings desperately to
her son's arm*

RUTH: I told him long ago it should be between
us. Now it shall be between us.

MRS. JORDAN: Philip! For my sake, for your
father's sake! Don't, don't! You will only make
it worse. In pity's name, leave them alone together. Leave them alone – together!

*They force Philip back to the door, where he
stands glaring at Ghent*

PHILIP: [*To Ghent*] My time will come. Meanwhile, hide behind the skirts of the woman
whose life you have ruined and whose heart
you have broken. Hide behind her. It is the
coward's privilege. Take it.

*Philip, with Mrs. Jordan still clinging to his
arm, goes out, Ruth closing the door after
them. She and Ghent confront each other in
silence for a moment, across the width of the
room*

RUTH: God forgive me! You never can.

GHENT: It was a pity – but – you were in a corner. I drove you to it, by coming here.

RUTH: It was base of me – base!

GHENT: The way your mother took it showed
me one thing. – I've never understood you,
because – I don't understand your people.

RUTH: You mean – her saying I ought to have
died rather than accept life as I did?

GHENT: Yes.

RUTH: She spoke the truth. I have always seen
it.

GHENT: Ruth, it's a queer thing for me to be
saying, but – it seems to me, you've never seen
the truth between us.

RUTH: What is the truth – between us?

GHENT: The truth is – [*He pauses, then continues with a disconsolate gesture*] Well,
there's no use going into that. [*He fumbles
in his pocket, and takes from it the nugget
chain, which he looks at in silence for a time,
then speaks in quiet resignation*] I've got here
the chain, that's come, one way and another,
to have a meaning for us. For you it's a bitter
meaning, but, all the same, I want you to keep
it. Show it some day to the boy, and tell him
– about me. [*He lays it on the desk and goes
toward the door*]

RUTH: What is the truth – between us?

GHENT: I guess it was only of myself I was
thinking.

RUTH: What is it – about yourself?

GHENT: [*After a pause*] I drifted into one of
your meeting-houses last Sunday, not knowing
where else to go, and I heard a young fellow
preaching about what he called "The Second
Birth." A year and a half ago I should have
thought it was all hocus-pocus, but you can
believe me or not, the way he went on he
might have been behind the door that night
in that little justice den at San Jacinto, saying
to the Recording Angel: "Do you see that
rascal? Take notice! There ain't an ounce of
bone or a drop of blood in him but what's
new man!"

RUTH: You think it has been all my fault – the failure we've made of our life?

GHENT: It's been no failure. However it is, it's been our life, and in my heart I think it's been – all – right!

RUTH: All right! O, how can you say that? [*She repeats the words with a touch of awe and wonder*] All right!

GHENT: Some of it has been wrong, but as a whole it has been right – right! I know that doesn't happen often, but it has happened to us, because – [*He stops, unable to find words for his idea*] because – because the first time our eyes met, they burned away all that was bad in our meeting, and left only the fact that we *had* met – pure good – pure joy – a fortune of it – for both of us. Yes, for both of us! You'll see it yourself some day.

RUTH: If you had only heard my cry to you, to wait, to cleanse yourself and me – by suffering and sacrifice – before we dared begin to live! But you wouldn't see the need! – O, if you could have felt for yourself what I felt for you! If you could have said, "The wages of sin is death!" and suffered the anguish of death, and risen again purified! But instead of that, what you had done fell off from you like any daily trifle.

GHENT: [*Steps impulsively nearer her, sweeping his hand to indicate the portraits on the walls*] Ruth, it's these fellows are fooling you! It's they who keep your head set on the wages of sin, and all that rubbish. What have we got to do with suffering and sacrifice? That may be the law for some, and I've tried hard to see it as our law, and thought I had succeeded. But I haven't! Our law is joy, and selfishness; the curve of your shoulder and the light on your hair as you sit there says that as plain as preaching. – Does it gall you the way we came together? You asked me that night what brought me, and I told you whiskey, and sun, and the devil. Well, I tell you now I'm thankful on my knees for all three! Does it rankle in your mind that I took you when I could get you, by main strength and fraud? I guess most good women are taken that way, if they only knew it. Don't you want to be paid for? I guess every wife is paid for in some good coin or other. And as for you, I've paid for

you not only with a trumpery chain, but with the heart in my breast, do you hear? That's one thing you can't throw back at me – the man you've made of me, the life and the meaning of life you've showed me the way to! [*Ruth's face is hidden in her hands, her elbows on the table. He stands over her, flushed and waiting. Gradually the light fades from his face. When he speaks again, the ring of exultation which has been in his voice is replaced by a sober intensity*] If you can't see it my way, give me another chance to live it out in yours. [*He waits, but she does not speak or look up. He takes a package of letters and papers from his pocket, and runs them over, in deep reflection*] During the six months I've been East –

RUTH: [*Looking up*] Six months? Mother said a week!

GHENT: Your sister-in-law's telegram was forwarded to me here. I let her think it brought me, but as a matter of fact, I came East in the next train after yours. It was a rather low-lived thing to do, I suppose, hanging about and bribing your servant for news – [*Ruth lets her head sink in her hands. He pauses and continues ruefully*] I might have known how that would strike you! Well, it would have come out sooner or later. – That's not what I started to talk about. – You ask me to suffer for my wrong. Since you left me I *have* suffered – God knows! You ask me to make some sacrifice. Well – how would the mine do? Since I've been away they've as good as stolen it from me. I could get it back easy enough by fighting; but supposing I don't fight. Then we'll start all over again, just as we stand in our shoes, and make another fortune – for our boy. [*Ruth utters a faint moan as her head sinks in her arms on the table. With trembling hands, Ghent caresses her hair lightly, and speaks between a laugh and a sob*] Little mother! Little mother! What does the past matter, when we've got the future – and him? [*Ruth does not move. He remains bending over her for some moments, then straightens up, with a gesture of stoic despair*] I know what you're saying there to yourself, and I guess you're right. Wrong is wrong, from the moment it happens till the crack of doom, and all the angels in Heaven, working overtime, can't make it less or different by a hair. That seems to be the law. I've learned it hard, but I guess I've learned it. I've seen it written in mountain letters across the continent of this life. – Done is done, and lost is lost, and smashed to hell is smashed to hell. We fuss and potter and patch up. You might as well try to batter down the Rocky Mountains with a rabbit's heart-beat! [*He goes to the door, where he turns*] You've fought hard for me, God bless you for it. – But it's been a losing game with you from the first! – You belong here, and I belong out yonder – beyond the Rockies, beyond – the Great Divide!

He opens the door and is about to pass out. Ruth looks up with streaming eyes

RUTH: Wait! [*He closes the door and stands waiting for her to speak. Ruth masters herself and goes on, her eyes shining, her face exalted*] Tell me you know that if I could have followed you, and been your wife, without struggle and without bitterness, I would have done it.

GHENT: [*Solemnly*] I believe you would.

RUTH: Tell me you know that when I tore down with bleeding fingers the life you were trying to build for us, I did it only – because – I loved you!

GHENT: [*Comes slowly to the table, looking at her with bewilderment*] How was that?

RUTH: O, I don't wonder you ask! Another woman would have gone straight to her goal. You might have found such a one. But instead you found me, a woman in whose ears rang night and day the cry of an angry Heaven to us both – "Cleanse yourselves!" And I went about doing it in the only way I knew – [*She points at the portraits on the wall*] – the only way my fathers knew – by wretchedness, by self-torture, by trying blindly to pierce your careless heart with pain. And all the while you – O, as I lay there and listened to you, I realized it for the first time – you had risen, in one hour, to a wholly new existence, which flooded the present and the future with brightness, yes, and reached back into our past, and made of it – made of all of it – something to cherish! [*She takes the chain, and comes closer*] You have taken the good of our life and grown strong. I have taken the evil and grown weak, weak unto death. Teach me to live as you do!

She puts the chain around her neck

GHENT: [*Puzzled, not yet realizing the full force of her words*] Teach you – to live – as I do?

RUTH: And teach – *him!*

GHENT: [*Unable to realize his fortune*] You'll let me help make a kind of a happy life for – the little rooster?

RUTH: [*Holds out her arms, her face flooded with happiness*] And for us! For us!

Curtain

THE NEW YORK IDEA

LANGDON MITCHELL

JUST twelve days after *The Great Divide* opened at the Princess Theatre in New York, Langdon Mitchell's sparkling and witty social comedy *The New York Idea* had its initial performance on October 15, 1906, at the Grand Opera House in Chicago. In its brilliance and its satirical thrust, it was regarded, even in its own day, as a worthy rival of the British models of Jones and Pinero on which it was based. *The New York Idea* has maintained a firm position in our dramatic history. When it was revived by Grace George and her New York Playhouse Repertory Company on September 28, 1915, the *New York Times* reported:

A vast array of American authors have turned out plays innumerable, but not one of them has quite matched in sparkling gayety and wit this work of Langdon Mitchell's. And the passing years have left its satire still pointed. They have not dimmed its polish nor so much as scratched its smart veneer.

And in the same newspaper, Brooks Atkinson wrote on August 19, 1948, after viewing a performance by the "On Stage" group: "Still pertinent, it is notably well constructed and more substantial than many of its witty successors. Mitchell wrote prose with grace as well as brittleness."

Langdon Elwyn Mitchell was born in Philadelphia on February 17, 1862. He was the son of the well-known physician and novelist Silas Weir Mitchell – one of the first exponents of psychosomatic medicine and one of the first novelists to introduce psychiatry into fiction. After attending St. Paul's School at Concord, New Hampshire, Langdon had three years of study abroad, in Dresden and Paris, before taking up the study of law at Harvard and Columbia. In 1886 he was admitted to the New York bar. In 1892 he was married to Marion Lea, an English actress who had gained her early reputation appearing in some of the first London performances of Ibsen. She enacted the role of Vida in the first production of *The New York Idea*, and the published play is dedicated to her.

Most of Mitchell's plays were dramatizations of novels. The best known was *Becky Sharp*, based on Thackeray's *Vanity Fair* and written expressly for Mrs. Fiske. After its initial performance at the Fifth Avenue Theatre on September 12, 1899, Mrs. Fiske played it almost continuously for the next two seasons and maintained it in her active repertoire for the remainder of her life. Mitchell's other dramatizations drew little attention: *The Adventures of François* (1900), from his father's novel; *The Kreutzer Sonata* (1906), from Jacob Gordin's Yiddish adaptation of Tolstoy's novel; and *Major Pendennis* (1916), from the Thackeray novel. Two other plays met with the same disappointing fate: his first play, *Sylvian* (1885), a romantic tragedy; and *The New Marriage* (1911), a feeble attempt to provide a sequel to *The New York Idea.* Four other early plays have normally not even been listed among Mitchell's work. *Deborah* is now known only from brief comments in the London newspapers, and these notices centered on the fact that he had just been married to Marion Lea. When it was performed for a series of five matinees at the Avenue Theatre beginning on February 22, 1892, one reviewer detected promise for the future in the play's "marks of sterling merit," but he could not understand why the playwright should assume that a play "written on slavery and the American Civil War" would interest the British. *Don Pedro, In the Season,* and *Ruth Underwood,* three now-forgotten one-acters, were also done in London that season, at a special Strand Theatre matinee on May 26, 1892. Except for some essays on the contemporary drama and on playwriting, two other items complete the list of Mitchell's literary works: *Poems* (1894) and *Love in the Backwoods* (1896), a collection of stories and novelettes.

When the chair of playwriting was established by the Mask and Wig Club at the University of Pennsylvania in 1928, Mitchell was chosen as the first professor. Although he had previously conducted some lectures on poetry at the George Washington University, the two years at Pennsylvania constituted his only venture into the academic world. Mitchell died on October 11, 1935.

Mitchell's list of plays is not long, nor are they, with the exception of *The New York Idea,* so American in theme as one would expect. Mitchell believed that the American dramatist should not be a slave to foreign models. As he said on one occasion, "Whenever I hear a man say that the finest art is the French theatre I know he's an ass. The finest art of the theatre is anywhere it happens to be. We can have it here." Perhaps his list of contributions would have been lengthened had he not been so conscious of "the enforced commercial attitude of the managers." Again and again he deplored the "expense of production" and the evils of the "extravagantly large" stage scenes. With the substitution of an inflated dollar amount, his paragraph in the New York *Dramatic Mirror* for June 3, 1916, might appropriately appear in any current theatrical column as the diatribe of any modern playwright:

The future of the American theatre depends on our getting away from our commercial habit of mind. The main thing to be struggled for now is the possibility of putting on plays without an absurdly great investment of money. That is a serious matter. The expense of producing a play. How can a young dramatist ever get a hearing when the initial expense of producing his play and insuring that it have a fair trial will be $30,000 or more? You see, according to our modern ridiculously extravagant ideas, we must have just the right sort of scene painters, and just the right sort of lighting experts, and just the right sort of carpenters, and just the right sort of expensive scenery, so ponderous that it has to be supported by iron bars – and all this costs money.

When Mitchell began *The New York Idea*, he was guided by the dual purpose of providing a play for Mrs. Fiske and devising a satire on American frivolity. He described his intentions as follows:

What I wanted to satirize was a certain extreme frivolity in the American spirit and in our American life – frivolity in the deep sense – not just a girl's frivolity, but that profound, sterile, amazing frivolity which one observes and meets in our churches, in political life, in literature, in music; in short, in every department of American thought, feeling and action.

During the composition, his attention concentrated more specifically on divorce. "I wrote *New York Idea*," Mitchell explained, "because I think the subject of divorce is the most important question in this country at the present time . . . no training for the marriage state . . . smart set look upon it foolishly . . . lowest set look upon it brutally."

After the play's first performance in Chicago, it was repeated in St. Louis before coming to New York. It opened at the Lyric Theatre on November 19, 1906, and ran for sixty-six performances. The play was produced by Harrison Grey Fiske with Mrs. Fiske as Mrs. Karslake, George Arliss as Sir Cates-Darby, Dudley Digges as Nogam, and Marion Lea (Mitchell's wife) as Vida Phillimore.

Contrary to Mitchell's recollection, the play was well received. Twenty-seven years after the event, he wrote: "Critics of 1906 did not like it because they belonged to one age and I to another. My sympathies then were and today are with the rebels." Certainly most of the contemporary reviews spoke most highly of *The New York Idea*. The New York *Dramatic Mirror* said on December 1, 1906:

A satire of social circumstances, whose ridicule bites as deep and hurts as long as the tragic realism of one of Ibsen's dramas, though it is clothed in the pleasing role of comedy. It is appealing to those who desire entertainment and those who wish to think. . . . The Manhattan Company upholds its reputation as the best organization of players in the country. . . . The mounting of the play is perfect. Every scene bespeaks an artistic regard for place, circumstance and proportion.

Many critics called Mitchell "the American Shaw." Undisturbed by the comparison, Mitchell explained, "Any resemblance to Shaw is quite unconscious." Contemporary comment was not restricted to professional reviewers; ministers, lawyers, and teachers spoke of the play. In fact, Mitchell's exposition of

American divorce set off a wide round of talk and writing on the subject. For example, Felix Adler, a professor of political science and ethics at Columbia, wrote:

Mr. Mitchell has skimmed a subject which to be thoroughly discussed would require the reflection of a work on philosophy. Marriage should not be considered as is sometimes the case, merely for felicity and comfort which the relation affords. Marriage is an institution for the perpetuation of the best spiritual element in our race.

On November 27, 1907, the play began an unauthorized engagement at the Apollo Theatre in London. Mitchell had not sanctioned the production. Treated as a farce in England, it must have lost many of the serious qualities which the British critic William Archer had found in the manuscript that he had read the previous year. Archer's criticism had appeared in the London *Tribune* for May 27. Archer praised it as "a social satire so largely conceived and so vigorously executed that it might take an honourable place in any dramatic literature. We have nothing quite like it on the latter-day English stage." In 1908 Mitchell reprinted Archer's remarks as a preface to the first published version.

When the play closed its initial New York engagement in the early spring of 1907, it was taken on the road for the remainder of the season. Thereafter the stock companies adopted it as a standard fixture in their repertoires. Grace George's company chose *The New York Idea* for the opening play of its 1915–16 season and assigned the fledgling actor Guthrie McClintic to the role of Nogam. Mitchell's play was in good company that season; the other four plays in the repertoire were J. B. Fagan's *The Earth*, H. A. Jones's *The Liars*, and Shaw's *Major Barbara* and *Captain Brassbound's Conversion*. Of Miss George's production, the New York *Dramatic Mirror* wrote on October 6, 1915:

... brilliant satiric comedy. In the past nine years since Mrs. Fiske's production there have been an inexhaustible number of plays, but not one of them has quite equalled in wit and sparkle this work of Mr. Mitchell. . . . In its dialogue it approaches Wilde, but in humanness of its characters, it far surpasses. . . . Certainly a relief from the war and crook plays of the past two seasons.

On October 7, 1916, the play was performed at the Kammerspiel Theatre in Berlin under Max Reinhardt's direction. In Germany it was known as *Jonathans Tochter*. It has also been translated into Danish, Swedish, and Hungarian. In the United States, *The New York Idea* has never really disappeared from the stage. Summer-stock and community- and university-theatre productions are noted almost every season.

The New York Idea no longer carries the shock impact that it had for audiences of 1906, but its scintillating small talk, its penetrating satire on frivolous New York society, its over-all brilliance and vitality stand comparison with later models, both English and American. There was more modesty than considered judgment in Mitchell's comment in 1933: "The plays of today are better than the ones we fellows wrote."

THE NEW YORK IDEA

LANGDON MITCHELL

CHARACTERS

PHILIP PHILLIMORE

MRS. PHILLIMORE, *his mother*

THE REVEREND MATTHEW PHILLIMORE,
  his brother

GRACE PHILLIMORE, *his sister*

MISS HENEAGE, *his aunt*

WILLIAM SUDLEY, *his cousin*

MRS. VIDA PHILLIMORE, *his divorced wife*

BROOKS, *her footman*

BENSON, *her maid*

SIR WILFRID CATES-DARBY

JOHN KARSLAKE

MRS. CYNTHIA KARSLAKE, *his divorced wife*

NOGAM, *his valet*

TIM FIDDLER

THOMAS, *the Phillimores' family servant*

ACT I

Living room in the house of Philip Phillimore. Five P. M. of an afternoon of May. The general air and appearance of the room is that of an old-fashioned, decorous, comfortable interior. There are no electric lights and no electric bells. Two bell ropes as in old-fashioned houses. The room is in dark tones inclining to sombre and of old-fashioned elegance. (At rise, discovered Miss Heneage, Mrs. Phillimore and Thomas. Miss Heneage is a solidly built, narrow-minded woman in her sixties. She makes no effort to look younger than she is, and is expensively but quietly dressed, with heavy elegance. She commands her household and her family connection, and on the strength of a large and steady income feels that her opinion has its value. Mrs. Phillimore is a semi-professional invalid, refined and unintelligent. Her movements are weak and fatigued. Her voice is habitually plaintive and she is entirely a lady without a trace of being a woman of fashion. Thomas is an easy-mannered, but entirely respectful family servant, un-English both in style and appearance. He has no deportment worthy of being so called, and takes an evident interest in the affairs of the family he serves. Miss Heneage, seated at the tea-table, faces footlights. Mrs. Phillimore, seated left of table. Thomas stands near

by. Tea things on table. Decanter of sherry in coaster. Bread and butter on plate. Vase with flowers. Silver match-box. Large old-fashioned tea urn. Guard for flame. "Evening Post" on tea-table. Miss Heneage and Mrs. Phillimore both have cups of tea. Miss Heneage sits up very straight, and pours tea for Grace, who enters from door L. She is a pretty and fashionably dressed girl of twenty. She speaks superciliously, coolly, and not too fast. She sits on the sofa, L., and does not lounge. She wears a gown suitable for spring visiting, hat, parasol, gloves, etc.

GRACE: [*Crosses and sits*] I never in my life walked so far and found so few people at home. [*Pauses. Takes off gloves. Somewhat querulously*] The fact is the nineteenth of May is ridiculously late to be in town.

Pause. Thomas comes down L. table

MISS HENEAGE: Thomas, Mr. Phillimore's sherry?

THOMAS: The sherry, ma'am.

Thomas nods and indicates table up L.

MISS HENEAGE: Mr. Phillimore's *Post*?

THOMAS: [*Same business. Pointing to "Evening Post" on tea-table*] The *Post*, ma'am.

MISS HENEAGE: [*Indicates cup*] Miss Phillimore.

Thomas takes cup of tea to Grace. Silence. They all sip tea. Thomas goes back, fills sherry glass, remaining round and about the tea-table. They all drink tea during the following scene

GRACE: The Dudleys were at home. They wished to know when my brother Philip was to be married, and where and how?

MISS HENEAGE: If the Dudleys were persons of breeding, they'd not intrude their curiosity upon you.

GRACE: I like Lena Dudley.

MRS. PHILLIMORE: [*Speaks slowly and gently*] Do I know Miss Dudley?

GRACE: She knows Philip. She expects an announcement of the wedding.

MRS. PHILLIMORE: I trust you told her that my son, my sister and myself are all of the opinion that those who have been divorced should remarry with modesty and without parade.

GRACE: I told the Dudleys Philip's wedding was here, to-morrow.

Thomas at back of table ready to be of use

MISS HENEAGE: [*To Mrs. Phillimore, picking up a sheet of paper which has lain on the table*] I have spent the afternoon, Mary, in arranging and listing the wedding gifts, and in writing out the announcements of the wedding. I think I have attained a proper form of announcement. [*She takes the sheet of note paper and gives it to Thomas*] Of course, the announcement Philip himself made was quite out of the question. [*Grace smiles*] However, there is mine.

Points to paper. Thomas gives list to Mrs. Phillimore and moves up stage

GRACE: I hope you'll send an announcement to the Dudleys.

MRS. PHILLIMORE: [*Reads plaintively, ready to make the best of things*] "Mr. Philip Phillimore and Mrs. Cynthia Dean Karslake announce their marriage, May twentieth, at three o'clock, Nineteen A, Washington Square, New York." [*Replaces paper on Thomas's salver*] It sounds very nice.

Thomas hands paper to Miss Heneage

MISS HENEAGE: [*Thomas up stage*] In my opinion it barely escapes sounding nasty. However, it is correct. The only remaining question is –

to whom the announcement should not be sent. [*Exit Thomas*] I consider an announcement of the wedding of two divorced persons to be in the nature of an intimate communication. It not only announces the wedding – it also announces the divorce. [*She returns to her teacup*] The person I shall ask counsel of is cousin William Sudley. He promised to drop in this afternoon.

GRACE: Oh; We shall hear all about Cairo.

MRS. PHILLIMORE: William is judicious.

Reenter Thomas

MISS HENEAGE: [*With finality*] Cousin William will disapprove of the match unless a winter in Cairo has altered his moral tone.

THOMAS: [*Announces*] Mr. Sudley.

Enter William Sudley, a little oldish gentleman. He is and appears thoroughly insignificant. But his opinion of the place he occupies in the world is enormous. His manners, voice, presence are all those of a man of breeding and self-importance

MRS. PHILLIMORE *and* MISS HENEAGE: [*Rise and greet Sudley; a little tremulously*] My dear William!

Exit Thomas

SUDLEY: [*Shakes hands with Mrs. Phillimore, soberly glad to see them*] How d'ye do, Mary? [*Same business with Miss Heneage*] A very warm May you're having, Sarah.

GRACE: [*Comes to him*] Dear Cousin William!

MISS HENEAGE: Wasn't it warm in Cairo when you left? [*She will have the strict truth, or nothing; still, on account of Sudley's impeccable respectability, she treats him with more than usual leniency*]

SUDLEY: [*Sits L.*] We left Cairo six weeks ago, Grace, so I've had no news since you wrote in February that Philip was engaged. [*Pause*] I need not to say I consider Philip's engagement excessively regrettable. He is a judge upon the Supreme Court bench with a divorced wife – and such a divorced wife!

GRACE: Oh, but Philip has succeeded in keeping everything as quiet as possible.

SUDLEY: [*Acidly*] No, my dear! He has not succeeded in keeping his former wife as quiet as possible. We had not been in Cairo a week when who should turn up but Vida Phillimore. She went everywhere and did everything no woman should!

GRACE: [*Unfeignedly interested*] Oh, what did she do?

SUDLEY: She "did" Cleopatra at the tableaux at Lord Errington's! She "did" Cleopatra, and she did it robed only in some diaphanous material of a nature so transparent that – in fact she appeared to be draped in moonshine. [*Miss Heneage indicates the presence of Grace. Rises; to C.*] That was only the beginning. As soon as she heard of Philip's engagement, she gave a dinner in honor of it! Only divorcees were asked! And she had a dummy – yes, my dear, a dummy – at the head of the table. He stood for Philip – that is he sat for Philip!

Rises, and goes up to table

MISS HENEAGE: [*Irritated and disgusted*] Ah!

MRS. PHILLIMORE: [*With dismay and pain*] Dear me!

MISS HENEAGE: [*Confident of the value of her opinion*] I disapprove of Mrs. Phillimore.

SUDLEY: [*Takes a cigarette*] Of course you do, but has Philip taken to Egyptian cigarettes in order to celebrate my winter at Cairo?

Comes below chair

GRACE: Those are Cynthia's.

SUDLEY: [*Thinking that no one is worth knowing whom he does not know*] Who is "Cynthia"?

GRACE: Mrs. Karslake – She's staying here, Cousin William. She'll be down in a minute.

SUDLEY: [*Shocked*] You don't mean to tell me – ? – !

To armchair, L.

MISS HENEAGE: Yes, William, Cynthia is Mrs. Karslake – Mrs. Karslake has no New York house. I disliked the publicity of a hotel in the circumstances, and accordingly when she became engaged to Philip, I invited her here.

SUDLEY: [*Suspicious and distrustful*] And may I ask *who* Mrs. Karslake is?

MISS HENEAGE: [*With confidence*] She was a Deane.

SUDLEY: [*Crosses up back of table R., sorry to be obliged to concede good birth to any but his own blood*] Oh, oh – well the Deanes are extremely nice people. [*Goes to table*] Was her father J. William Deane?

MISS HENEAGE: [*Still more secure; nods*] Yes.

SUDLEY: [*Giving in with difficulty*] The family is an old one. J. William Deane's daughter? Surely he left a very considerable –

MISS HENEAGE: Oh, fifteen or twenty millions.

SUDLEY: [*Determined not to be dazzled*] If I remember rightly she was brought up abroad.

MISS HENEAGE: In France and England – and I fancy brought up with a very gay set in very gay places. In fact she is what is called a "sporty" woman.

SUDLEY: [*Always ready to think the worst*] We might put up with that. But you don't mean to tell me Philip has the – the – the – assurance to marry a woman who has been divorced by –

MISS HENEAGE: Not at all. Cynthia Karslake divorced her husband.

SUDLEY: [*Gloomily, since he has less fault to find than he expected*] She divorced him! Ah!

Sips his tea

MISS HENEAGE: The suit went by default. And, my dear William, there are many palliating circumstances. Cynthia was married to Karslake only seven months. There are no – [*glances at Grace*] no hostages to Fortune! Ahem!

SUDLEY: [*Still unwilling to be pleased*] Ah! What sort of a young woman is she?

Goes to C.

GRACE: [*With the superiority of one who is not too popular*] Men admire her.

MISS HENEAGE: She's not conventional.

MRS. PHILLIMORE: [*Showing a faint sense of justice*] I am bound to say she has behaved discreetly ever since she arrived in this house.

MISS HENEAGE: Yes, Mary – but I sometimes suspect that she exercises a degree of self-control –

SUDLEY: [*Glad to have something against some one*] She claps on the lid, eh? And you think that perhaps some day she'll boil over? Well, of course fifteen or twenty millions – but who's Karslake?

GRACE: [*Very superciliously*] He owns Cynthia K. She's the famous mare.

MISS HENEAGE: He's Henry Karslake's son.

SUDLEY: [*Beginning to make the best of fifteen millions-in-law*] Oh! – Henry! – Very respectable family. Although I remember his father served a term in the senate. And so the wedding is to be to-morrow?

MRS. PHILLIMORE: [*Assents*] To-morrow.

SUDLEY: [*Bored, and his respectability to the front when he thinks of the ceremony; rises. Grace rises*] To-morrow. Well, my dear Sarah, a respectable family with some means. We must accept her. But on the whole, I think it will be best for me not to see the young woman. My disapprobation would make itself apparent.

GRACE: [*Whispering to Sudley*] Cynthia's coming.

He doesn't hear. Enter Cynthia, absorbed in reading a newspaper. She is a young creature in her twenties, small and high-bred, full of the love of excitement and sport. Her manner is wide awake and keen and she is evidently in no fear of the opinion of others. Her dress is exceedingly elegant, but with the elegance of a woman whose chief interests lie in life out of doors. There is nothing horsey in her style, and her expression is youthful and ingenuous

SUDLEY: [*Sententious and determinately epigrammatic*] The uncouth modern young woman, eight feet high, with a skin like a rhinoceros and manners like a cave dweller – an habitué of the race-track and the divorce court –

GRACE: [*Aside to Sudley*] Cousin William!

SUDLEY: Eh, oh!

CYNTHIA: [*Comes down reading, immersed, excited, trembling. She lowers paper to catch the light*] "Belmont favorite – six to one – Rockaway – Rosebud, and Flying Cloud. Slow track – raw wind – hm,hm,hm – At the half, Rockaway forged ahead, when Rosebud under the lash made a bold bid for victory – neck by neck – for a quarter – when Flying Cloud slipped by the pair and won on the post by a nose in one forty nine!" [*To R. Speaks with the enthusiasm of a sport*] Oh, I wish I'd seen the dear thing do it. Oh, it's Mr. Sudley! You must think me very rude. How do you do, Mr. Sudley?

Goes to Sudley, L. C.

SUDLEY: [*Very respectable as he bows without cordiality*] Mrs. Karslake.

Pause; Cynthia feels he should say something. As he says nothing, she speaks again

CYNTHIA: I hope Cairo was delightful? Did you have a smooth voyage?

SUDLEY: [*Pompously*] You must permit me, Mrs. Karslake –

CYNTHIA: [*With good temper, somewhat embarrassed, and talking herself into ease*] Oh, please don't welcome me to the family. All that formal part is over, if you don't mind. I'm one of the tribe now! You're coming to our wedding to-morrow?

SUDLEY: My dear Mrs. Karslake, I think it might be wiser –

CYNTHIA: [*Still with cordial good temper*] Oh, but you must come! I mean to be a perfect wife to Philip and all his relations! That sounds rather miscellaneous, but you know what I mean.

SUDLEY: [*Very sententious*] I am afraid –

CYNTHIA: [*Gay and still covering her embarrassment*] If you don't come, it'll look as if you were not standing by Philip when he's in trouble! You'll come, won't you – but of course you will.

SUDLEY: [*After a self-important pause*] I will come, Mrs. Karslake. [*Pause*] Good-afternoon. [*In a tone of sorrow and compassion*] Goodbye, Mary. Good-afternoon, Sarah. [*Sighs*] Grace, dear. [*To Miss Heneage*] At what hour did you say the alimony commences?

MISS HENEAGE: [*Quickly and commandingly to cover his slip. Going up C.*] The ceremony is at three P. M., William.

Sudley goes up L.

MRS. PHILLIMORE: [*With fatigued voice and manner as she rises*] I am going to my room to rest awhile.

Mrs. Phillimore goes up

MISS HENEAGE: [*To Sudley*] Oh, William, one moment – I entirely forgot! I've a most important social question to ask you! [*She goes up slowly to the door with him*] In regard to the announcements of the wedding – who they shall be sent to and who not. For instance – the Dudleys –

Exeunt Sudley and Miss Heneage, talking

CYNTHIA: [*Sitting on the sofa, L.*] So that's Cousin William?

GRACE: [*Near the tea-table*] Don't you like him?

CYNTHIA: [*Calmly sarcastic*] Like him? I love him. He's so generous. He couldn't have received me with more warmth if I'd been a mulatto.

Reenter Thomas. Enter Phillimore. Philip Phillimore is a self-centered, short-tempered imperious member of the respectable fashionables of New York. He is well and solidly dressed and in manner and speech evidently a man of family. He is accustomed to being listened to in his home circle and from the bench, and it is practically impossible for him to believe that he can make a mistake

GRACE: [*Outraged*] Really you know – [*Cynthia crosses and sits at table*] Philip!

Philip nods to her absent-mindedly. He is in his working suit and looks tired. He comes down silently, crosses to tea-table. Bends over and kisses Cynthia on forehead. Goes to his chair, which Thomas has changed the position of for him. Sits, and sighs with satisfaction

PHILIP: [*As if exhausted by brain work*] Ah, Grace! [*Exit Grace*] Well, my dear, I thought I should never extricate myself from the court room. You look very debonnair!

CYNTHIA: The tea's making. You'll have your glass of sherry?

PHILIP: [*The strain of the day having evidently been severe*] Thanks! [*Takes it from Thomas; sighs*] Ah!

CYNTHIA: I can see it's been a tiring day with you.

PHILIP: [*As before*] Hm!

Sips

CYNTHIA: Were the lawyers very long winded?

PHILIP: [*Almost too tired for speech*] Prolix to the point of somnolence. It might be affirmed without inexactitude that the prolixity of counsel is the somnolence of the judiciary. I am fatigued, ah! [*A little suddenly, awaking*

to the fact that his orders have not been carried out to the letter] Thomas! My *Post* is not in its usual place!

CYNTHIA: [*To Thomas*] It's here, Philip.

Thomas gets it

PHILIP: Thanks, my dear. [*Opens "Post"*] Ah! this hour with you – is – is really the – the – [*absently*] the one vivid moment of the day. [*Reading*] Hm – shocking attack by the president on vested interests. Hm – too bad – but it's to be expected. The people insisted on electing a desperado to the presidential office – they must take the hold-up that follows. [*Pause; he reads*] Hm! His English is lacking in idiom, his spelling in conservatism, his mind in balance, and his character in repose.

CYNTHIA: [*Amiable but not very sympathetic*] You seem more fatigued than usual. Another glass of sherry, Philip?

PHILIP: Oh, I ought not to –

CYNTHIA: I think you seem a little more tired than usual.

PHILIP: Perhaps I am. [*She pours out sherry. Philip takes glass but does not sip*] Ah, this hour is truly a grateful form of restful excitement. [*Pause*] You, too, find it – eh?

Looks at Cynthia

CYNTHIA: [*With veiled sarcasm*] Decidedly.

PHILIP: Decidedly what, my dear?

CYNTHIA: [*As before*] Restful.

PHILIP: Hm! Perhaps I need the calm more than you do. Over the case to-day I actually – eh – [*sips*] slumbered. I heard myself do it. That's how I know. A dressmaker sued on seven counts. [*Reads newspaper*] Really, the insanity of the United States Senate – you seem restless, my dear. Ah – um – have you seen the evening paper? I see there has been a lightning change in the style or size of hats which ladies –

He sweeps a descriptive motion with his hand, gives paper to Cynthia, then moves his glass, reads, and sips

CYNTHIA: The lamp, Thomas.

Thomas blows out the alcohol lamp on the tea-table with difficulty. Blows twice. Movement of Philip each time. Blows again

PHILIP: [*Irritably*] Confound it, Thomas! What are you puffing and blowing at – ?

THOMAS: It's out, ma'am – yes, sir.

PHILIP: You're excessively noisy, Thomas!

THOMAS: [*In a fluster*] Yes, sir – I am.

CYNTHIA: [*Soothing Thomas's wounded feelings*] We don't need you, Thomas.

THOMAS: Yes, ma'am.

PHILIP: Puffing and blowing and shaking and quaking like an automobile in an ecstasy!

Exit Thomas, L.

CYNTHIA: [*Not unsympathetically*] Too bad, Philip! I hope my presence isn't too agitating?

PHILIP: Ah – it's just because I value this hour with you, Cynthia – this hour of tea and toast and tranquility. It's quite as if we were married – happily married – already.

CYNTHIA: [*Admitting that married life is a blank, begins to look through paper*] Yes, I feel as if we were married already.

PHILIP: [*Not recognizing her tone*] Ah! It's the calm, you see.

CYNTHIA: [*As before*] The calm? Yes – yes, it's – it's the calm.

PHILIP: [*Sighs*] Yes, the calm – the Halcyon calm of – of second choice. Hm! [*He reads and turns over leaves of paper. Cynthia reads. Pause*] After all, my dear – the feeling which I have for you – is – is – eh – the market is in a shocking condition of plethora! Hm – hm – and what are you reading?

CYNTHIA: [*Embarrassed*] Oh, eh – well – I – eh – I'm just running over the sporting news.

PHILIP: Oh!

He looks thoughtful

CYNTHIA: [*Beginning to forget Philip and to remember more interesting matters*] I fancied Hermes would come in an easy winner. He came in nowhere. Nonpareil was ridden by Henslow – he's a rotten bad rider. He gets nervous.

PHILIP: [*Reading still*] Does he? Hm! I suppose you do retain an interest in horses and races. Hm – I trust some day the – ah – law will attract – Oh [*turning a page*], here's the report of my opinion in that dressmaker's case – Haggerty *vs.* Phillimore.

CYNTHIA: Was the case brought against you?

Puzzled

PHILIP: Oh – no. The suit was brought by Haggerty, Miss Haggerty, a dressmaker, against the – in fact, my dear, against the former Mrs. Phillimore.

Pause; he reads

CYNTHIA: [*Curious about the matter*] How did you decide it?

PHILIP: I was obliged to decide in Mrs. Phillimore's favor. Haggerty's plea was preposterous.

CYNTHIA: Did you – did you meet the – the former – ?

PHILIP: No.

CYNTHIA: I often see her at afternoon teas.

PHILIP: How did you recognize –

CYNTHIA: Why – [*opens paper*] because Mrs. Vida Phillimore's picture appears in every other issue of most of the evening papers. And I must confess I was curious. But, I'm sure you find it very painful to meet her again.

PHILIP: [*Slowly, considering*] No, – would you find it so impossible to meet Mr. –

CYNTHIA: [*Much excited and aroused*] Philip! Don't speak of him. He's nothing. He's a thing of the past. I never think of him. I forget him!

PHILIP: [*Somewhat sarcastic*] That's extraordinarily original of you to forget him.

CYNTHIA: [*Gently, and wishing to drop the subject*] We each of us have something to forget, Philip – and John Karslake is to me – Well, he's dead!

PHILIP: As a matter of fact, my dear, he *is* dead, or the next thing to it – for he's bankrupt.

Pause

CYNTHIA: Bankrupt? [*Excited and moved*] Let's not speak of him. I mean never to see him or think about him or even hear of him!

He assents. She reads her paper. He sips his tea and reads his paper. She turns a page, starts and cries out

PHILIP: God bless me!

CYNTHIA: It's a picture of – of –

PHILIP: John Karslake?

CYNTHIA: Picture of him, and one of me, and in the middle between us "Cynthia K!"

PHILIP: "Cynthia K?"

CYNTHIA: [*Excited*] My pet riding mare! The best horse he has! She's an angel even in a photograph! Oh! [*Reading*] "John Karslake drops a fortune at Saratoga."

Rises and goes up and down excitedly. Philip takes paper and reads

PHILIP: [*Unconcerned, as the matter hardly touches him*] Hem – ah – Advertises country place for sale – stables, famous mare "Cynthia K" – favorite riding-mare of former Mrs. Karslake who is once again to enter the arena of matrimony with the well known and highly respected judge of –

CYNTHIA: [*Sensitive and much disturbed*] Don't! Don't, Philip, please don't!

PHILIP: My dear Cynthia – take another paper – here's my *Post!* You'll find nothing disagreeable in the *Post.*

Cynthia takes paper

CYNTHIA: [*After reading, sits L., near table*] It's much worse in the *Post.* "John Karslake sells the former Mrs. Karslake's jewels – the famous necklace now at Tiffany's, and the sporty ex-husband sells his wife's portrait by Sargent!" Philip, I can't stand this.

Puts paper on table L.

PHILIP: Really, my dear, Mr. Karslake is bound to appear occasionally in print – or even you may have to meet him.

Enter Thomas, L. to C.

CYNTHIA: [*Determined and distressed*] I won't meet him! I won't meet him. Every time I hear his name or "Cynthia K's" I'm so depressed.

THOMAS: [*Announcing with something like reluctance. To C.*] Sir, Mr. Fiddler. Mr. Karslake's trainer.

Enter Fiddler. He is an English horse trainer, a wide-awake stocky well-groomed little cockney. He knows his own mind and sees life altogether through a stable door. Well-dressed for his station, and not too young

CYNTHIA: [*Excited and disturbed*] Fiddler? Tim Fiddler? His coming is outrageous!

FIDDLER: A note for you, sir.

CYNTHIA: [*Impulsively*] Oh, Fiddler – is that you?

FIDDLER: Ye'sm!

CYNTHIA: [*In a half whisper, still speaking on impulse*] How is she! Cynthia K? How's Planet II and the colt and Golden Rod? How's the whole stable? Are they well?

FIDDLER: No'm – we're all on the bum. [*Aside*] Ever since you kicked us over!

CYNTHIA: [*Reproving him, though pleased*] Fiddler!

FIDDLER: The horses is just simply gone to Egypt since you left, and so's the guv'nor.

CYNTHIA: [*Putting an end to Fiddler*] That will do, Fiddler.

FIDDLER: I'm waiting for an answer, sir.

CYNTHIA: What is it, Philip?

PHILIP: [*Uncomfortable*] A mere matter of business. [*Aside to Fiddler*] The answer is, Mr. Karslake can come. The – the coast will be clear.

Fiddler exits L.

CYNTHIA: [*Amazed; rises*] You're not going to see him?

PHILIP: But Karslake, my dear, is an old acquaintance of mine. He argues cases before me. I will see that you do not have to meet him.

Cynthia crosses in excited dejection. Enter Matthew. He is a high church clergyman to a highly fashionable congregation. His success is partly due to his social position and partly to his elegance of speech, but chiefly to his inherent amiability, which leaves the sinner in happy peace and smiles on the just and unjust alike

MATTHEW: [*Most amiably*] Ah, my dear brother!

PHILIP: Matthew.

Greets him C.

MATTHEW: [*Nods to Philip*] Good afternoon, my dear Cynthia. How charming you look! [*Cynthia sits at tea-table. To Cynthia*] Ah, why weren't you in your pew yesterday? I preached a most original sermon.

Goes up and takes hat and cane to divan

THOMAS: [*Aside to Philip*] Sir, Mrs. Vida Phillimore's maid called you up on the telephone, and you're to expect Mrs. Phillimore on a matter of business.

PHILIP: [*Astonished and disgusted*] Here, impossible! [*To Cynthia*] Excuse me, my dear!

Exit Philip, much embarrassed, followed by Thomas

MATTHEW: [*Comes down to chair, happily and pleasantly self-important*] No, really, it was a wonderful sermon, my dear. My text was from Paul – "It is better to marry than to burn." It was a strictly logical sermon. I argued – that, as the grass withereth, and the flower fadeth, – there is nothing final in Nature; not even Death! And, as there is nothing final in Nature, not even Death; – so then if Death is not final – why should marriage be final? [*Gently*] And so the necessity of – eh – divorce! You see? It was an exquisite sermon! All New York was there! And all New York went away happy! Even the sinners – if there were any! I don't often meet sinners – do you?

CYNTHIA: [*Indulgently, in spite of his folly, because he is kind*] You're such a dear, delightful Pagan! Here's your tea!

MATTHEW: [*Takes tea*] Why, my dear – you have a very sad expression!

CYNTHIA: [*A little bitterly*] Why not?

MATTHEW: [*With sentimental sweetness*] I feel as if I were of no use in the world when I see sadness on a young face. Only sinners should feel sad. You have committed no sin!

CYNTHIA: [*Impulsively*] Yes, I have!

MATTHEW: Eh?

CYNTHIA: I committed the unpardonable sin – whe – when I married for love!

MATTHEW: One must not marry for anything else, my dear!

CYNTHIA: Why am I marrying your brother?

MATTHEW: I often wonder why? I wonder why you didn't choose to remain a free woman.

CYNTHIA: [*Going over the ground she has often argued with herself*] I meant to; but a divorcée has no place in society. I felt horridly lonely! I wanted a friend. Philip was ideal as a friend – for months. Isn't it nice to bind a friend to you?

MATTHEW: Yes – yes!

Puts down teacup

CYNTHIA: [*Growing more and more excited and moved as she speaks*] To marry a friend – to marry on prudent, sensible grounds – a man –

like Philip? That's what I should have done first, instead of rushing into marriage – because I had a wild, mad, sensitive, sympathetic – passion and pain and fury – of, I don't know what – that almost strangled me with happiness!

MATTHEW: [*Amiable and reminiscent*] Ah – ah – in my youth – I, – I too!

CYNTHIA: [*Coming back to her manner of every day*] And besides – the day Philip asked me I was in the dumps! And now – how about marrying only for love?

Reenter Philip

MATTHEW: Ah, my dear, love is not the only thing in the world!

PHILIP: [*Half aside*] I got there too late; she'd hung up.

Up C.

CYNTHIA: Who, Philip?

PHILIP: Eh – a lady – eh –

Enter Thomas, flurried, with card on salver

THOMAS: A card for you, sir. Ahem – ahem – Mrs. Phillimore – that was, sir.

PHILIP: Eh?

THOMAS: She's on the stairs, sir. [*Turns. Enter Vida. Thomas announces her as being the best way of meeting the difficulty*] Mrs. Vida Phillimore!

Vida comes in slowly, with the air of a spoiled beauty. She stops just inside the door and speaks in a very casual manner. Her voice is languorous and caressing. She is dressed in the excess of the French fashion and carries an outré parasol. She smiles and comes, undulating, down C. Tableau. Exit Thomas

VIDA: How do you do, Philip. [*Comes down C.*] Don't tell me I'm a surprise! I had you called up on the 'phone and I sent up my card – and, besides, Philip dear, when you have the – the – habit of the house, as unfortunately I have, you can't treat yourself like a stranger in a strange land. At least, I can't – so here I am. My reason for coming was to ask you about that B. and O. stock we hold in common. [*To Matthew, condescendingly, the clergy being a class of unfortunates debarred by profession from the pleasures of the world*] How do you do? [*Pause. She then goes to the real reason of her visit*] Do be polite and present me to your wife-to-be.

PHILIP: [*Awkwardly*] Cynthia –

CYNTHIA: [*Comes down to table R. of it. Cheerfully, with dash*] We're delighted to see you, Mrs. Phillimore. I needn't ask you to make yourself at home, but will you have a cup of tea?

Matthew sits near little table

VIDA: [*To Philip*] My dear, she's not in the least what I expected. I heard she was a dove! She's a very dashing kind of a dove! [*To Cynthia; comes to tea-table*] My dear, I'm paying you compliments. Five lumps and quantities of cream. I find single life very thinning. [*To Philip, very calm and ready to be agreeable to any man*] And how well you're looking! It must be the absence of matrimonial cares – or is it a new angel in the house?

CYNTHIA: [*Outraged at Vida's intrusion, but polite though delicately sarcastic*] It's most amusing to sit in your place. And how at home you must feel here in this house where you have made so much trouble – I mean tea. [*Rises*] Do you know it would be in much better taste if you would take the place you're accustomed to?

VIDA: [*As calm as before*] My dear, I'm an intruder only for a moment; I shan't give you a chance to score off me again! But I must thank you, dear Philip, for rendering that decision in my favor –

PHILIP: I assure you –

VIDA: [*Unable to resist a thrust at the close of this speech*] Of course, you would like to have rendered it against me. It was your wonderful sense of justice, and that's why I'm so grateful – if not to you, to your Maker!

PHILIP: [*He feels that this is no place for his future wife. Rises quickly, goes up C. To Cynthia*] Cynthia, I would prefer that you left us.

Matthew comes to L. sofa and sits

CYNTHIA: [*Determined not to leave the field first, remains seated*] Certainly, Philip!

PHILIP: I expect another visitor who –

VIDA: [*With flattering insistence, to Cynthia*] Oh, my dear – don't go! [*Philip goes up L. C.*] The truth is – I came to see you! I feel most

cordially towards you – and really, you know, people in our position should meet on cordial terms.

CYNTHIA: [*Taking it with apparent calm, but pointing her remarks*] Naturally. If people in our position couldn't meet, New York society would soon come to an end.

Enter Thomas

VIDA: [*Calm, but getting her knife in too*] Precisely. Society's no bigger than a band-box. Why, it's only a moment ago I saw Mr. Karslake walking –

CYNTHIA: Ah!

THOMAS: [*Announcing clearly. Every one changes place, in consternation, amusement or surprise. Cynthia moves to leave the stage, but stops for fear of attracting Karslake's attention*] Mr. John Karslake!

Enter Karslake. He is a powerful, generous personality, a man of affairs, breezy, gay and careless. He gives the impression of being game for any fate in store for him. His clothes indicate sporting propensities and his taste in waistcoats and ties is brilliant. Karslake sees first Philip and then Matthew. Exit Thomas

PHILIP: How do you do?

JOHN: [*Very gay and no respecter of persons*] Good-afternoon, Mr. Phillimore. Hello – here's the church! [*Crosses to Matthew and shakes hands. He slaps him on the back*] I hadn't the least idea – how are you? By George, your reverence, that was a racy sermon of yours on Divorce! What was your text? [*Sees Vida and bows, very politely*] Galatians 4:2: "The more the merrier," or "Who next?" [*Smiles*] As the whale said after Jonah!

Cynthia makes a sudden movement, turns cup over. John faces about quickly and they face each other. John gives a frank start. Pause. Tableau

JOHN: [*Astounded, in a low voice*] Mrs. Karslake – [*Bows*] I was not aware of the pleasure in store for me. I understood you were in the country. [*Recovers, crosses to chair*] Perhaps you'll be good enough to make me a cup of tea? – that is if the teapot wasn't lost in the scrimmage. [*Pause. Cynthia, determined to equal him in coolness, returns to the tea-tray*]

Mr. Phillimore, I came to get your signature in that matter of Cox *vs.* Keely.

PHILIP: I shall be at your service, but pray be seated.

He indicates chair by table

JOHN: [*Sitting beyond but not far from the tea-table*] And I also understood you to say you wanted a saddle horse.

Sits R. corner

PHILIP: You have a mare called – eh – "Cynthia K"?

JOHN: [*Promptly*] Yes – she's not for sale.

PHILIP: Oh, but she's just the mare I had set my mind on.

JOHN: [*With a touch of humor*] You want her for yourself?

PHILIP: [*A little flustered*] I – eh – I sometimes ride.

JOHN: [*He is sure of himself now*] She's rather lively for you, Judge. Mrs. Karslake used to ride her.

PHILIP: You don't care to sell her to me?

JOHN: She's a dangerous mare, Judge, and she's as delicate and changeable as a girl. I'd hate to leave her in your charge!

CYNTHIA: [*Eagerly but in a low voice*] Leave her in mine, Mr. Karslake!

JOHN: [*After slight pause*] Mrs. Karslake knows all about a horse, but – [*Turning to Cynthia*] Cynthia K's got rather tricky of late.

CYNTHIA: [*Haughtily*] You mean to say you think she'd chuck me?

JOHN: [*With polite solicitude and still humorous. To Philip*] I'd hate to have a mare of mine deprive you of a wife, Judge. [*Rises. Cynthia business of anger*] She goes to Saratoga next week, C. W.

VIDA: [*Who has been sitting and talking to Matthew for lack of a better man, comes C. to talk to Karslake*] C. W.?

JOHN: [*Rising as she rises*] Creditors willing.

VIDA: [*Crossing and sitting left of tea-table*] I'm sure your creditors are willing.

JOHN: Oh, they're a breezy lot, my creditors. They're giving me a dinner this evening.

VIDA: [*More than usually anxious to please*] I regret I'm not a breezy creditor, but I do think you owe it to me to let me see your

Cynthia K! Can't you lead her around to my house?

JOHN: At what hour, Mrs. Phillimore?

VIDA: Say eleven? And you, too, might have a leading in my direction – 771 Fifth Avenue.

John bows. Cynthia hears and notes this

CYNTHIA: Your cup of tea, Mr. Karslake.

JOHN: Thanks. [*John gets tea and sips*] I beg your pardon – you have forgotten, Mrs. Karslake – very naturally, it has slipped from your memory, but I don't take sugar.

Cynthia, furious with him and herself. He hands cup back. She makes a second cup

CYNTHIA: [*Cheerfully; in a rage*] Sorry!

JOHN: [*Also apparently cheerful*] Yes, gout. It gives me a twinge even to sit in the shadow of a sugar maple! First you riot, and then you diet!

VIDA: [*Calm and amused; aside to Matthew*] My dear Matthew, he's a darling! But I feel as if we were all taking tea on the slope of a volcano!

Matthew sits

PHILIP: It occurred to me, Mr. Karslake, you might be glad to find a purchaser for your portrait by Sargent?

JOHN: It's not *my* portrait. It's a portrait of Mrs. Karslake, and to tell you the truth – Sargent's a good fellow – I've made up my mind to keep it – to remember the artist by.

Cynthia is wounded by this

PHILIP: Hm!

Cynthia hands second cup to John

CYNTHIA: [*With careful politeness*] Your cup of tea, Mr. Karslake.

JOHN: [*Rises; takes tea with courteous indifference*] Thanks – sorry to trouble you.

He drinks the cup of tea standing by the tea-table

PHILIP: [*To make conversation*] You're selling your country place?

JOHN: If I was long of hair – I'd sell that.

CYNTHIA: [*Excited. Taken out of herself by the news*] You're not really selling your stable?

JOHN: [*Finishes his tea, places empty cup on*

tea-table and reseats himself] Every gelding I've got – seven foals and a donkey! I don't mean the owner.

CYNTHIA: [*Still interested and forgetting the discomfort of the situation*] How did you ever manage to come such a cropper?

JOHN: Streak of blue luck!

CYNTHIA: [*Quickly*] I don't see how it's possible –

JOHN: You would if you'd been there. You remember the head man? [*Sits*] Bloke?

CYNTHIA: Of course!

JOHN: Well, his wife divorced him for beating her over the head with a bottle of Fowler's Solution, and it seemed to prey on his mind. He sold me –

CYNTHIA: [*Horrified*] Sold a race?

JOHN: About ten races, I guess.

CYNTHIA: [*Incredulous*] Just because he'd beaten his wife?

JOHN: No. Because she divorced him.

CYNTHIA: Well, I can't see why that should prey on his mind!

Suddenly remembers

JOHN: Well, I have known men that it stroked the wrong way. But he cost me eighty thousand. And then Urbanity ran third in the thousand dollar stakes for two-year-olds at Belmont.

CYNTHIA: [*She throws this remark in*] I never had faith in that horse.

JOHN: And, of course, it never rains monkeys but it pours gorillas! So when I was down at St. Louis on the fifth, I laid seven to three on Fraternity –

CYNTHIA: Crazy! Crazy!

JOHN: [*Ready to take the opposite view*] I don't see it. With her record she ought to have romped it an easy winner.

CYNTHIA: [*Pure sport*] She hasn't the stamina! Look at her barrel!

JOHN: Well, anyhow, Geranium finished me!

CYNTHIA: You didn't lay odds on Geranium!

JOHN: Why not? She's my own mare –

CYNTHIA: Oh!

JOHN: Streak o' bad luck –

CYNTHIA: [*Plainly anxious to say "I told you so"*] Streak of poor judgment! Do you remember the day you rode Billy at a six foot stone wall, and he stopped and you didn't,

and there was a hornet's nest [*Matthew rises*] on the other side, and I remember you were hot just because I said you showed poor judgment? [*She laughs at the memory. A general movement of disapproval. She remembers the situation*] I beg your pardon.

MATTHEW: [*Rises to meet Vida. Hastily*] It seems to me that horses are like the fourth gospel. Any conversation about them becomes animated almost beyond the limits of the urbane!

Vida disgusted by such plainness of speech, rises and goes to Philip who waves her to a chair C.

PHILIP: [*Formal*] I regret that you have endured such reverses, Mr. Karslake.

John quietly bows

CYNTHIA: [*Concealing her interest; speaks casually*] You haven't mentioned your new English horse – Pantomime. What did he do at St. Louis?

JOHN: [*Sits*] Fell away and ran fifth.

CYNTHIA: Too bad. Was he fully acclimated? Ah, well –

JOHN: We always differed – you remember – on the time needed –

MATTHEW: [*Coming C. to Cynthia, speaking to carry off the situation as well as to get a tip*] Isn't there a – eh – a race to-morrow at Belmont Park?

JOHN: Yes. I'm going down in my auto.

CYNTHIA: [*Evidently wishing she might be going too*] Oh!

MATTHEW: And what animal shall you prefer?

Covering his personal interest with amiable altruism

JOHN: I'm backing Carmencita.

CYNTHIA: [*Gesture of despair*] Carmencita! Carmencita!

Matthew goes to Vida

JOHN: You may remember we always differed on Carmencita.

CYNTHIA: [*Disgusted at John's dunderheadedness*] But there's no room for difference. She's a wild, headstrong, dissatisfied, foolish little filly. The deuce couldn't ride her – she'd shy at her own shadow – "Carmencita." Oh, very well then, I'll wager you – and I'll give you odds too – "Decorum" will come in first, and I'll lay three to one he'll beat Carmencita by five lengths! How's that for fair?

JOHN: [*Never forgetting the situation*] Sorry I'm not flush enough to take you.

CYNTHIA: [*Impetuously*] Philip, dear, you lend John enough for the wager.

MATTHEW: [*As nearly horrified as so soft a soul can be*] Ahem! Really –

JOHN: It's a sporty idea, Mrs. Karslake, but perhaps in the circumstances –

CYNTHIA: [*Her mind on her wager*] In what circumstances?

PHILIP: [*With a nervous laugh*] It does seem to me there is a certain impropriety –

CYNTHIA: [*Remembering the conventions, which, for a moment, had actually escaped her*] Oh, I forgot. When horses are in the air –

MATTHEW: [*Pouring oil on troubled waters. Crossing, he speaks to Vida at back of armchair, where she sits*] It's the fourth gospel, you see.

Enter Thomas with letter on salver, which he hands to Philip

CYNTHIA: [*Meekly*] You are quite right, Philip. [*Philip goes up*] The fact is, seeing Mr. Karslake again [*laying on her indifference with a trowel*] he seems to me as much a stranger as if I were meeting him for the first time.

MATTHEW: [*Aside to Vida*] We are indeed taking tea on the slope of a volcano.

VIDA: [*Is about to go, but thinks she will have a last word with John*] I'm sorry your fortunes are so depressed, Mr. Karslake.

PHILIP: [*Looking at the card that Thomas has just brought in*] Who in the world is Sir Wilfrid Cates-Darby?

General move

JOHN: Oh – eh – Cates-Darby? [*Philip opens letter which Thomas has brought with card*] That's the English chap I bought Pantomime of.

PHILIP: [*To Thomas*] Show Sir Wilfrid Cates-Darby in.

Exit Thomas. The prospect of an Englishman with a handle to his name changes Vida's plans

and instead of leaving the house, she goes to sofa, L. and sits there

JOHN: He's a good fellow, Judge. Place near Epsom. Breeder. Over here to take a shy at our races.

Enter Thomas

THOMAS: [*Announcing*] Sir Wilfrid Cates-Darby.

Enter Sir Wilfrid Cates-Darby. He is a high-bred, sporting Englishman. His manner, his dress and his diction are the perfection of English elegance. His movements are quick and graceful. He talks lightly and with ease. He is full of life and unsmiling good temper

PHILIP: [*To Sir Wilfrid and referring to the letter of introduction in his hand*] I am Mr. Phillimore. I am grateful to Stanhope for giving me the opportunity of knowing you, Sir Wilfrid. I fear you find it warm?

SIR WILFRID: [*Delicately mopping his forehead*] Ah, well – ah – warm, no – hot, yes! Deuced extraordinary climate yours, you know, Mr. Phillimore.

PHILIP: [*Conventional*] Permit me to present you to – [*The unconventional situation pulls him up short. It takes him a moment to decide how to meet it. He makes up his mind to pretend that everything is as usual, and presents Cynthia first*] Mrs. Karslake.

Sir Wilfrid bows, surprised and doubtful

CYNTHIA: How do you do?

PHILIP: And to Mrs. Phillimore. [*Vida bows nonchalantly, but with a view to catching Sir Wilfrid's attention. Sir Wilfrid bows, and looks from her to Philip*] My brother – and Mr. Karslake you know.

SIR WILFRID: How do, my boy. [*Half aside, to John*] No idea you had such a charming little wife – What? – Eh?

Karslake goes up to speak to Matthew and Philip in the further room

CYNTHIA: You'll have a cup of tea, Sir Wilfrid?

SIR WILFRID: [*At table R.*] Thanks, awfully. [*Very cheerfully*] I'd no idea old John had a wife! The rascal never told me!

CYNTHIA: [*Pouring tea and facing the facts*] I'm not Mr. Karslake's wife!

SIR WILFRID: Oh! – Eh? – I see –

Business of thinking it out

VIDA: [*Who has been ready for some time to speak to him*] Sir Wilfrid, I'm sure no one has asked you how you like our country?

SIR WILFRID: [*Goes to Vida and speaks, standing by her at sofa*] Oh, well, as to climate and horses, I say nothing. But I like your American humor. I'm acquiring it for home purposes.

VIDA: [*Getting down to love as the basis of conversation*] Aren't you going to acquire an American girl for home purposes?

SIR WILFRID: The more narrowly I look the agreeable project in the face, the more I like it. Oughtn't to say that in the presence of your husband.

He casts a look at Philip, who has gone into the next room

VIDA: [*Cheerful and unconstrained*] He's not my husband!

SIR WILFRID: [*Completely confused*] Oh – eh? – my brain must be boiled. You are – Mrs. – eh – ah – of course, now I see! I got the wrong names! I thought you were Mrs. Phillimore. [*He sits by her*] And that nice girl Mrs. Karslake! You're deucedly lucky to be Mrs. Karslake. John's a prime sort. I say, have you and he got any kids? How many?

VIDA: [*Horrified at being suspected of maternity, but speaking very sweetly*] He's not my husband.

SIR WILFRID: [*His good spirits all gone, but determined to clear things up*] Phew! Awfully hot in here! Who the deuce is John's wife?

VIDA: He hasn't any.

SIR WILFRID: Who's Phillimore's wife?

VIDA: He hasn't any.

SIR WILFRID: Thanks, fearfully! [*To Matthew, whom he approaches; suspecting himself of having lost his wits*] Would you excuse me, my dear and Reverend Sir – you're a churchman and all that – would you mind straightening me out?

MATTHEW: [*Most gracious*] Certainly, Sir Wilfrid. Is it a matter of doctrine?

SIR WILFRID: Oh, damme – beg your pardon, – no, it's not words, it's women.

MATTHEW: [*Ready to be outraged*] Women!

SIR WILFRID: It's divorce. Now, the lady on the sofa –

MATTHEW: *Was* my brother's wife; he divorced

her – incompatibility – Rhode Island. The lady at the tea-table *was* Mr. Karslake's wife; she divorced him – desertion – Sioux Falls. One moment – she is about to marry my brother.

SIR WILFRID: [*Cheerful again*] I'm out! Thought I never would be! Thanks!

Vida laughs

VIDA: [*Not a whit discountenanced and ready to please*] Have you got me straightened out yet?

SIR WILFRID: Straight as a die! I say, you had lots of fun, didn't you? [*Goes back to sofa; stands*] And so *she's* Mrs. John Karslake?

VIDA: [*Calm, but secretly disappointed*] Do you like her?

SIR WILFRID: My word!

VIDA: [*Fully expecting personal flattery*] Eh?

SIR WILFRID: She's a box o' ginger!

VIDA: You haven't seen many American women!

SIR WILFRID: Oh, haven't I?

VIDA: If you'll pay me a visit to-morrow – at twelve, you shall meet a most charming young woman, who has seen you once, and who admires you – ah!

SIR WILFRID: I'm there – what!

VIDA: Seven hundred and seventy-one Fifth Avenue.

SIR WILFRID: Seven seventy-one Fifth Avenue – at twelve.

VIDA: At twelve.

SIR WILFRID: Thanks! [*Indicates Cynthia*] She's a thoroughbred – you can see that with one eye shut. Twelve. [*Shakes hands*] Awfully good of you to ask me. [*Joins John*] I say, my boy, your former's an absolute certainty. [*To Cynthia*] I hear you're about to marry Mr. Phillimore, Mrs. Karslake?

Karslake crosses to Vida; they both go to sofa, left, where they sit

CYNTHIA: To-morrow, 3 P. M., Sir Wilfrid.

SIR WILFRID: [*Much taken with Cynthia. To her. Sits R.*] Afraid I've run into a sort of family party, eh? [*Indicates Vida*] The Past and the Future – awfully chic way you Americans have of asking your divorced husbands and wives to drop in, you know – celebrate a christenin', or the new bride, or –

CYNTHIA: Do you like your tea strong?

SIR WILFRID: Middlin'.

CYNTHIA: Sugar?

SIR WILFRID: One!

CYNTHIA: Lemon?

SIR WILFRID: Just torture a lemon over it. [*He makes a gesture as of twisting a lemon peel. She gives tea*] Thanks! So you do it to-morrow at three?

CYNTHIA: At three, Sir Wilfrid.

SIR WILFRID: Sorry!

CYNTHIA: Why are you sorry?

SIR WILFRID: Hate to see a pretty woman married. Might marry her myself.

CYNTHIA: Oh, but I'm sure you don't admire American women.

SIR WILFRID: Admire you, Mrs. Karslake –

CYNTHIA: Not enough to marry me, I hope.

SIR WILFRID: Marry you in a minute! Say the word. Marry you now – here.

CYNTHIA: You don't think you ought to know me a little before –

SIR WILFRID: Know you? Do know you.

Cynthia covering her hair with her handkerchief

CYNTHIA: What color is my hair?

SIR WILFRID: Pshaw!

CYNTHIA: You see! You don't know whether I'm a chestnut or a strawberry roan! In the -States we think a few months of friendship is quite necessary.

SIR WILFRID: Few months of moonshine! Never was a friend to a woman – thank God, in all my life.

CYNTHIA: Oh – oh, oh!

SIR WILFRID: Might as well talk about being a friend to a whiskey and soda.

CYNTHIA: A woman has a soul, Sir Wilfrid.

SIR WILFRID: Well, good whiskey is spirits – dozens o' souls!

CYNTHIA: You are so gross!

SIR WILFRID: [*Changes seat to above table*] Gross? Not a bit! Friendship between the sexes is all fudge! I'm no friend to a rose in my garden. I don't call it friendship – eh – eh – a warm, starry night, moonbeams and ilex trees, "and a spirit who knows how" and all that – eh – [*Getting closer to her*] You make me feel awfully poetical, you know – [*Philip comes down, glances nervously at Cynthia and Sir Wilfrid, and walks up again*] What's the matter? But, I say – poetry aside – do you, eh – [*Looks around to place Philip*] Does he – y'know – is he – does he go to the head?

CYNTHIA: Sir Wilfrid, Mr. Phillimore is my sober second choice.

SIR WILFRID: Did you ever kiss him? I'll bet he fined you for contempt of court. Look here, Mrs. Karslake, if you're marryin' a man you don't care about –

CYNTHIA: [*Amused and excusing his audacity as a foreigner's eccentricity*] Really!

SIR WILFRID: Well, I don't offer myself –

CYNTHIA: Oh!

SIR WILFRID: Not this instant –

CYNTHIA: Ah!

SIR WILFRID: But let me drop in to-morrow at ten.

CYNTHIA: What country and state of affairs do you think you have landed in?

SIR WILFRID: New York, by Jove! Been to school, too. New York is bounded on the North, South, East and West by the state of Divorce! Come, come, Mrs. Karslake, I like your country. You've no fear and no respect – no can't and lots of can. Here you all are, you see – your former husband, and your new husband's former wife – sounds like Ollendoff! Eh? So there you are, you see! But, jokin' apart – why do you marry him? Oh, well, marry him if you must! You can run around the corner and get a divorce afterwards –

CYNTHIA: I believe you think they throw one in with an ice-cream soda!

SIR WILFRID: [*Rises*] Damme, my dear lady, a marriage in your country is no more than a – eh – eh – what do you call 'em? A thank you, ma'am. That's what an American marriage is – a thank you, ma'am. Bump – bump – you're over it and on to the next.

CYNTHIA: You're an odd fish! What? I believe I like you!

SIR WILFRID: 'Course you do! You'll see me when I call to-morrow – at ten? We'll run down to Belmont Park, eh?

CYNTHIA: Don't be absurd!

VIDA: [*Has finished her talk with John, and breaks in on Sir Wilfrid, who has hung about Cynthia too long to suit her*] To-morrow at twelve, Sir Wilfrid!

SIR WILFRID: Twelve!

Crossing down L.

VIDA: [*Shakes hands with John*] Don't forget, Mr. Karslake – eleven o'clock to-morrow.

JOHN: [*Bows assent*] I won't!

VIDA: [*Comes to the middle of the stage and speaks to Cynthia*] Oh, Mrs. Karslake, I've ordered Tiffany to send you something. It's a sugar bowl to sweeten the matrimonial lot! I suppose nothing would induce you to call?

CYNTHIA: [*Distant and careless of offending*] Thanks, no – that is, is "Cynthia K" really to be there at eleven? I'd give a gold mine to see her again.

VIDA: [*Above chair*] Do come!

CYNTHIA: If Mr. Karslake will accommodate me by his absence.

VIDA: Dear Mr. Karslake, you'll have to change your hour.

JOHN: Sorry, I'm not able to.

CYNTHIA: I can't come later for I'm to be married.

JOHN: It's not as bad as that with me, but I am to be sold up – Sheriff, you know. Can't come later than eleven.

VIDA: [*To Cynthia*] Any hour but eleven, dear.

CYNTHIA: [*Perfectly regardless of Vida, and ready to vex John if possible*] Mrs. Phillimore, I shall call on you at eleven – to see Cynthia K. I thank you for the invitation. Good-afternoon.

VIDA: [*Aside to John, crossing to speak quietly to him*] It's mere bravado; she won't come.

JOHN: You don't know her.

Pause. General embarrassment. Sir Wilfrid business with eye-glass. John angry. Cynthia triumphant. Matthew embarrassed. Vida irritated. Philip puzzled. Everybody at odds

SIR WILFRID: [*For the first time a witness to the pretty complications of divorce; to Matthew*] Do you have it as warm as this ordinarily?

MATTHEW: [*For whom these moments are more than usually painful, and wiping his brow*] It's not so much the heat as the humidity.

JOHN: [*Looks at watch; glad to be off*] I shall be late for my creditors' dinner.

SIR WILFRID: [*Comes down*] Creditors' dinner.

JOHN: [*Reads note*] Fifteen of my sporting creditors have arranged to give me a blow-out at Sherry's, and I'm expected right away or sooner. And by the way, I was to bring my friends – if I had any. So now's the time to stand by me! Mrs. Phillimore?

VIDA: Of course!

JOHN: [*Ready to embarrass Cynthia, if possible, and speaking as if he had quite forgotten their former relations*] Mrs. Karslake – I beg your pardon. Judge? [*Philip declines*] No? Sir Wilfrid?

SIR WILFRID: I'm with you!

JOHN: [*To Matthew*] Your Grace?

MATTHEW: I regret –

SIR WILFRID: Is it the custom for creditors –

JOHN: Come on, Sir Wilfrid! [*Thomas opens door*] Good-night, Judge – Your Grace –

SIR WILFRID: Is it the custom –

JOHN: Hang the custom! Come on – I'll show you a gang of creditors worth having!

Exit Sir Wilfrid with John, arm in arm, preceded by Vida. Matthew crosses, smiling, as if pleased, in a Christian way, with this display of generous gaiety. Looks at his watch

MATTHEW: Good gracious! I had no idea the hour was so late. I've been asked to a meeting with Maryland and Iowa, to talk over the divorce situation. [*Exit. Voice heard off*] Good-afternoon! Good-afternoon!

Cynthia evidently much excited. The outer door slams. Philip comes down slowly. Cynthia stands, her eyes wide, her breathing visible, until Philip speaks, when she seems suddenly to realize her position. A long pause

PHILIP: [*Superior*] I have seldom witnessed a more amazing cataclysm of jocundity! Of course, my dear, this has all been most disagreeable for you.

CYNTHIA: [*Excitedly*] Yes, yes, yes!

PHILIP: I saw how much it shocked your delicacy.

CYNTHIA: [*Distressed and moved*] Outrageous.

Philip sits

PHILIP: Do be seated, Cynthia. [*Takes up paper. Quietly*] Very odd sort of an Englishman – that Cates-Darby!

CYNTHIA: Sir Wilfrid? – Oh, yes! [*Philip settles down to paper. To herself*] Outrageous! I've a great mind to go at eleven – just as I said I would!

PHILIP: Do sit down, Cynthia!

CYNTHIA: What? What?

PHILIP: You make me so nervous –

CYNTHIA: Sorry – sorry.

She sits, sees paper, takes it, looks at picture of John Karslake

PHILIP: [*Sighs with content*] Ah! now that I see him, I don't wonder you couldn't stand him. There's a kind of – ah – spontaneous inebriety about him. He is incomprehensible! If I might with reverence cross question the Creator, I would say to him: "Sir, to what end or purpose did you create Mr. John Karslake?" I believe I should obtain no adequate answer! However, [*sighs*] at last we have peace – and the *Post!* [*Philip settles himself, reads paper; Cynthia looks at her paper, occasionally looks across at Philip*] Forget the dust of the arena – the prolixity of counsel – the involuntary fatuity of things in general. [*Pause. He reads*] Compose yourself!

Miss Heneage, Mrs. Phillimore and Grace enter. Cynthia sighs without letting her sigh be heard. Tries to compose herself. Glances at paper and then hearing Miss Heneage, starts slightly. Miss Heneage and Mrs. Phillimore stop at table

MISS HENEAGE: [*She carries a sheet of paper*] There, my dear Mary, is the announcement as I have now reworded it. I took William's suggestion. [*Mrs. Phillimore takes and casually reads it*] I also put the case to him, and he was of the opinion that the announcement should be sent *only* to those people who are really *in* society.

Sits above table. Cynthia braces herself to bear the Phillimore conversation

GRACE: I wish you'd make an exception of the Dudleys.

Cynthia rises and crosses to chair R. of L. table

MISS HENEAGE: And, of course, that excludes the Oppenheims – the Vance-Browns.

MRS. PHILLIMORE: It's just as well to be exclusive.

GRACE: I do wish you'd make an exception of Lena Dudley.

MISS HENEAGE: We might, of course, include those new Girardos, and possibly – possibly the Paddingtons.

GRACE: I do wish you would take in Lena Dudley.

They are now sitting

MRS. PHILLIMORE: The mother Dudley is as common as a charwoman, and not nearly as clean.

PHILIP: [*Sighs. His own feelings as usual to the fore*] Ah! I certainly am fatigued!

Cynthia begins to slowly crush the newspaper she has been reading with both hands, as if the effort of self-repression were too much for her

MISS HENEAGE: [*Making the best of a gloomy future*] We shall have to ask the Dudleys sooner or later to dine, Mary – because of the elder girl's marriage to that dissolute French Marquis.

MRS. PHILLIMORE: [*Plaintively*] I don't like common people any more than I like common cats, and of course in my time –

MISS HENEAGE: I think I shall include the Dudleys.

MRS. PHILLIMORE: You think you'll include the Dudleys?

MISS HENEAGE: Yes, I think I will include the Dudleys!

Here Cynthia gives up. Driven desperate by their chatter, she has slowly rolled her newspaper into a ball, and at this point tosses it violently to the floor and bursts into hysterical laughter

MRS. PHILLIMORE: Why, my dear Cynthia – Compose yourself.

PHILIP: [*Hastily*] What is the matter, Cynthia?

They speak together. General movement

MISS HENEAGE: Why, Mrs. Karslake, what is the matter?

GRACE: [*Comes quickly forward, saying*] Mrs. Karslake!

Curtain

ACT II

Mrs. Vida Phillimore's boudoir. The room is furnished to please an empty-headed, pleasure-loving and fashionable woman. The furniture, the ornaments, what pictures there are, all witness to taste up-to-date. Two French windows open on to a balcony, from which the trees of Central Park can be seen. There is a table be-

tween them; a mirror, a scent bottle, etc., upon it. On the right, up stage, is a door; on the right, down stage, another door. A lady's writing table stands between the two, nearer centre of stage. There is another door up stage, L.; below it, L., an open fireplace, filled with potted plants, andirons, etc., not in use. Over it a tall mirror; on the mantelpiece a French clock, candelabra, vases, etc. On a line with the fireplace, a lounge, gay with silk pillows. A florist's box, large and long, filled with American Beauty roses, on a low table near the head of the lounge. Small tables and light chairs where needed. At rise, Benson is discovered up stage looking about her. She is a neat and pretty little English lady's maid in black silk and a thin apron. She comes down stage still looking about, goes L. and sees flower box; then goes R., opens door and speaks off.

BENSON: Yes, ma'am, the flowers have come.

She holds the door, R., open. Vida, in a morning gown, enters R., slowly, and comes C. She is smoking a cigarette in as aesthetic a manner as she can, and is evidently turned out in her best style for conquest

VIDA: [*C., back to audience, always calm and, though civil, a little disdainful of her servants*] Terribly garish light, Benson. Pull down the – [*Benson obeys*] Lower still – that will do. [*As she speaks, she goes about the room, giving the furniture a push here and there, arranging vases, etc.*] Men hate a clutter of chairs and tables. [*Stops before table at C. and takes up hand mirror, standing with back to audience*] I really think I'm too pale for this light.

BENSON: [*Quickly, understanding what is implied*] Yes, ma'am. [*Benson exits R. Vida sits C., table R. Knock at door up L.*] Come!

Enter Brooks

BROOKS: [*An ultra-English footman, in plush and calves*] Any horders, m'lady?

VIDA: [*Incapable of remembering the last man, or of considering the new one*] Oh, – of course! You're the new –

BROOKS: Footman, m'lady.

VIDA: [*As a matter of form*] Your name?

BROOKS: Brooks, m'lady.

Reenter Benson with rouge

VIDA: [*Carefully giving instructions while she keeps her eyes on the glass and is rouged by Benson*] Brooks, I am at home to Mr. Karslake at eleven, not to any one else till twelve, when I expect Sir Wilfrid Cates-Darby.

Brooks is inattentive; watches Benson

BROOKS: Yes, m'lady.

VIDA: [*Calm, but wearied by the ignorance of the lower classes*] And I regret to inform you, Brooks, that in America there are no ladies, except salesladies!

BROOKS: [*Without a trace of comprehension*] Yes, m'lady.

VIDA: I am at home to no one but the two names I have mentioned. [*Brooks bows and exits up L. She dabs on rouge while Benson holds glass*] Is the men's club room in order?

BENSON: Perfectly, ma'am.

VIDA: Whiskey and soda?

BENSON: Yes, ma'am, and the ticker's been mended. The British sporting papers arrived this morning.

VIDA: [*Looking at her watch which lies on the dressing table*] My watch has stopped.

BENSON: [*Glancing at the French clock on the chimney-piece*] Five to eleven, ma'am.

Comes down a little, R.

VIDA: [*Getting promptly to work*] Hm, hm, I shall be caught. [*Rises and crosses R.*] The box of roses, Benson! [*Benson brings the box of roses, uncovers the flowers and places them at Vida's side*] My gloves – the clippers, and the vase! [*Each of these things Benson places in turn within Vida's range where she sits on the sofa. She has the long box of roses at her side on a small table, a vase of water on the floor by her side. She cuts the stems and places the roses in the vase. When she feels that she has reached a picturesque position, in which any onlooker would see in her a creature filled with the love of flowers and of her fellow man, she says*] There!

The door opens and Brooks enters; Vida nods to Benson

BROOKS: [*Announcing stolidly*] Sir John Karslake.

Enter John, dressed in very nobby riding togs, crop, etc., and spurs. He comes in gaily and forcibly. Benson gives way, R., as he comes down. Exeunt Brooks and Benson. John stops near table, L. Vida, from this point on, is busied with her roses

VIDA: [*Languorously, but with a faint suggestion of humor*] Is that really you, Sir John?

JOHN: [*Lively and far from being impressed by Vida*] I see now where we Americans are going to get our titles. Good-morning! You look as fresh as paint.

Takes chair from L. to R. C.

VIDA: [*Facing the insinuation with gentle pain*] I hope you don't mean that? I never flattered myself for a moment you'd come. You're riding Cynthia K?

JOHN: [*Who has laid his gloves and riding crop on table, C.*] Fiddler's going to lead her round here in ten minutes!

VIDA: Cigars and cigarettes! Scotch?

She indicates that he will find them on a small table up stage

JOHN: Scotch!

Goes up quickly to table and helps himself to Scotch and seltzer

VIDA: And now *do* tell me all about *her!*

Putting in her last roses; she keeps one rosebud in her hand, of a size suitable for a man's buttonhole

JOHN: [*As he drinks*] Oh, she's an adorable creature – delicate, high-bred, sweet-tempered –

VIDA: [*Showing her claws for a moment*] Sweet-tempered? Oh, you're describing the horse! By "her," I meant –

JOHN: [*Irritated by the remembrance of his wife*] Cynthia Karslake? I'd rather talk about the last Tornado.

Sits

VIDA: [*Soothing the savage beast*] There is only one thing I want to talk about, and that is, *you!* Why were you unhappy?

JOHN: [*Still cross*] Why does a dollar last such a short time?

VIDA: [*Curious*] Why did you part?

JOHN: Did you ever see a schooner towed by a tug? Well, I parted from Cynthia for the same reason that the hawser parts from the tug – I couldn't stand the tug.

VIDA: [*Sympathizing*] Ah!

Pause

JOHN: [*Still cross*] Awful cheerful morning chat.

VIDA: [*Excusing her curiosity and coming back to love as the only subject for serious conversation*] I must hear the story, for I'm anxious to know why I've taken such a fancy to you!

JOHN: [*Very nonchalantly*] Why do *I* like you?

VIDA: [*Doing her best to charm*] I won't tell you – it would flatter you too much.

JOHN: [*Not a bit impressed by Vida, but as ready to flirt as another*] Tell me!

VIDA: There's a rose for you.

Giving him the one she has in her hand

JOHN: [*Saying what is plainly expected of him*] I want more than a rose –

VIDA: [*Putting this insinuation by*] You refuse to tell me – ?

JOHN: [*Once more reminded of Cynthia, speaks with sudden feeling*] There's nothing to tell. We met, we loved, we married, we parted; or at least we wrangled and jangled. [*Sighs*] Ha! Why weren't we happy? Don't ask me, why! It may have been *partly* my fault!

VIDA: [*With tenderness*] Never!

JOHN: [*His mind on Cynthia*] But I believe it's all in the way a girl's brought up. Our girls are brought up to be ignorant of life – they're ignorant of life. Life is a joke, and marriage is a picnic and a man is a shawl-strap – 'Pon my soul, Cynthia Deane – no, I can't tell you!

Rises and goes up. During the following, he walks about in his irritation

VIDA: [*Gently*] Please tell me!

JOHN: Well, she was an heiress, an American heiress – and she'd been taught to think marriage meant burnt almonds and moonshine and a yacht and three automobiles, and she thought – I don't know what she thought, but I tell you, Mrs. Phillimore, marriage is three parts love and seven parts forgiveness of sins.

Crosses C.

VIDA: [*Flattering him as a matter of course*] She never loved you.

JOHN: [*On whom she has made no impression at all*] Yes, she did. For six or seven months there was not a shadow between us. It was perfect, and then one day she went off like a pistol-shot! I had a piece of law work and couldn't take her to see Flashlight race the Maryland mare. The case meant a big fee, big Kudos, and in sails Cynthia, Flashlight mad! And will I put on my hat and take her? No – and bang she goes off like a stick o' dynamite – what did I marry her for? – and words – pretty high words, until she got mad, when she threw over a chair and said oh, well, – marriage was a failure, or it was with me, so I said she'd better try somebody else. She said she would, and marched out of the room.

Back to L.

VIDA: [*Gently sarcastic*] But she came back!

JOHN: She came back, but not as you mean. She stood at the door and said, "Jack, I shall divorce you." Then she came over to my study-table, dropped her wedding ring on my law papers, and went out. The door shut, I laughed; the front door slammed, I damned. [*Pause, crosses to window*] She never came back.

Goes up, then comes down to chair R. Vida catches his hands

VIDA: [*Hoping for a contradiction*] She's broken your heart.

JOHN: Oh, no!

Crosses to chair by lounge

VIDA: [*Encouraged, begins to play the game again*] You'll never love again!

JOHN: [*Speaking to her from the foot of her sofa*] Try me! Try me! Ah, no, Mrs. Phillimore, I shall laugh, live, love and make money again! And let me tell you one thing – I'm going to rap her one over the knuckles. She had a stick of a Connecticut lawyer, and he – well, to cut a legal story short, since Mrs. Karslake's been in Europe, I have been quietly testing the validity of the decree of divorce. Perhaps you don't understand?

VIDA: [*Letting her innate shrewdness appear*] Oh, about a divorce, everything!

JOHN: I shall hear by this evening whether the divorce will stand or not.

VIDA: But it's to-day at three she marries – you won't let her commit bigamy?

JOHN: [*Shakes his head*] I don't suppose I'd go as far as that. It may be the divorce will hold, but anyway I hope never to see her again.

He sits beside her facing up stage as she faces down

VIDA: Ah, my poor boy, she has broken your heart. [*Believing that this is her psychological moment, she lays her hand on his arm, but draws it back as soon as he attempts to take it*] Now don't make love to me.

JOHN: [*Bold and amused, but never taken in*] Why not?

VIDA: [*With immense gentleness*] Because I like you too much! [*More gaily*] I might give in, and take a notion to like you still more!

JOHN: Please do!

VIDA: [*With gush and determined to be womanly at all hazards*] Jack, I believe you'd be a lovely lover!

JOHN: [*As before*] Try me!

VIDA: [*Not hoping much from his tone*] You charming, tempting, delightful fellow, I could love you without the least effort in the world, – but, no!

JOHN: [*Playing the game*] Ah, well, now *seriously*! Between two people who have *suffered* and made their own mistakes –

VIDA: [*Playing the game too, but not playing it well*] But you see, you don't *really* love me!

JOHN: [*Still ready to say what is expected*] Cynthia – Vida, no man can sit beside you and look into your eyes without feeling –

VIDA: [*Speaks the truth as she sees it, seeing that her methods don't succeed*] Oh! That's not love! That's simply – well, my dear Jack, it's beginning at the wrong end. And the truth is you hate Cynthia Karslake with such a whole-hearted hate, that you haven't a moment to think of any other woman.

JOHN: [*With sudden anger*] I hate her!

VIDA: [*Very softly and most sweetly*] Jack – Jack, I could be as foolish about you as – oh, as foolish as anything, my dear! And perhaps some day – perhaps some day you'll come to me and say, Vida, I am totally indifferent to Cynthia – and then –

JOHN: And then?

VIDA: [*The ideal woman in mind*] Then, perhaps, you and I may join hands and stroll together into the Garden of Eden. It takes two to find the Garden of Eden, you know – and once we're on the inside, we'll lock the gate.

JOHN: [*Gaily, and seeing straight through her veneer*] And lose the key under a rose-bush!

VIDA: [*Agreeing very softly*] Under a rose-bush! [*Very soft knock R.*] Come!

John rises quickly. Enter Benson and Brooks, L.

BROOKS: [*Stolid and announcing*] My lady – Sir Wilf –

Benson stops him with a sharp movement and turns toward Vida

BENSON: [*With intention*] Your dressmaker, ma'am.

Benson waves Brooks to go. Exit Brooks, L., very haughtily

VIDA: [*Wonderingly*] My dressmaker, Benson? [*With quick intelligence*] Oh, of course, show her up. Mr. Karslake, you won't mind for a few minutes using my men's club room? Benson will show you! You'll find cigars and the ticker, sporting papers, whiskey; and, if you want anything special, just 'phone down to my "chef."

JOHN: [*Looking at his watch*] How long?

VIDA: [*Very anxious to please*] Half a cigar! Benson will call you.

JOHN: [*Practical*] Don't make it too long. You see, there's my sheriff's sale on at twelve, and those races this afternoon. Fiddler will be here in ten minutes, remember!

Door L. opens

VIDA: [*To John*] Run along! [*Exit John. Vida suddenly practical, and with a broad gesture to Benson*] Everything just as it was, Benson! [*Benson whisks the roses out of the vase and replaces them in the box. She gives Vida scissors and empty vases, and when Vida finds herself in precisely the same position which preceded John's entrance, she says*] There!

Enter Brooks, as Vida takes a rose from basket

BROOKS: [*Stolidly*] Your ladyship's dressmaker! M'lady!

Enter Sir Wilfrid in morning suit, boutonniere, etc.

VIDA: [*With tender surprise and busy with the roses*] Is that really you, Sir Wilfrid! I never flattered myself for an instant that you'd remember to come.

SIR WILFRID: [*Coming to her above end of sofa*] Come? 'Course I come! Keen to come see you. By Jove, you know, you look as pink and white as a huntin' mornin'.

VIDA: [*Ready to make any man as happy as possible*] You'll smoke?

SIR WILFRID: Thanks! [*He watches her as she trims and arranges the flowers*] Awfully long fingers you have! Wish I was a rose, or a ring, or a pair of shears! I say, d' you ever notice what a devil of a fellow I am for originality, what? [*Comes down to L. Unlike John, is evidently impressed by her*] You've got a delicate little den up here! Not so much low livin' and high thinkin', as low lights and no thinkin' at all, I hope – eh?

To C. By this time Vida has filled a vase with roses and rises to sweep by him and if possible make another charming picture to his eyes

VIDA: You don't mind my moving about?

Crosses R.

SIR WILFRID: [*Impressed*] Not if you don't mind my watchin'. [*Sits R., on sofa*] And sayin' how well you do it.

VIDA: It's most original of you to come here this morning. I don't quite see why you did.

She places the roses here and there, as if to see their effect, and leaves them on a small table near the door through which her visitors entered

SIR WILFRID: Admiration.

VIDA: [*Sauntering slowly toward the mirror as she speaks*] Oh, I saw that you admired her! And of course, she did say she was coming here at eleven! But that was only bravado! She won't come, and besides, I've given orders to admit no one!

SIR WILFRID: May I ask you –

He throws this in in the middle of her speech, which flows gently and steadily on

VIDA: And indeed, if she came now, Mr. Karslake has gone, and her sole object in coming was to make him uncomfortable. [*Goes up above table, L.; stopping a half minute at the mirror to see that she looks as she wishes to look*] Very dangerous symptom, too, that passionate desire to make one's former husband unhappy! But, I can't believe that your admiration for Cynthia Karslake is so warm that it led you to pay me this visit a half hour too early in the hope of seeing —

SIR WILFRID: [*Rises; most civil, but speaking his mind like a Briton*] I say, would you mind stopping a moment! [*She smiles*] I'm not an American, you know; I was brought up not to interrupt. But you Americans, it's different with you! If somebody didn't interrupt you, you'd go on forever.

VIDA: [*She passes him to tantalize*] My point is you came to see Cynthia —

SIR WILFRID: [*He believes she means it*] I came hopin' to see —

VIDA: [*As before*] Cynthia!

SIR WILFRID: [*Perfectly single-minded and entirely taken in*] But I would have come even if I'd known —

VIDA: [*Crosses C.*] I don't believe it!

SIR WILFRID: [*As before*] Give you my word I —

VIDA: [*The same*] You're here to see *her*! And of course —

SIR WILFRID: [*Determined to be heard because, after all, he's a man*] May I have the – eh – the floor? [*Vida sits in chair, L.*] I was jolly well bowled over with Mrs. Karslake, I admit that, and I hoped to see her here, but —

VIDA: [*Talking nonsense and knowing it*] You had another object in coming. In fact, you came to see Cynthia, and you came to see me! What I really long to know, is why you wanted to see *me*! For, of course, Cynthia's to be married at three! And, if she wasn't she wouldn't have you!

SIR WILFRID: [*Not intending to wound; merely speaking the flat truth*] Well, I mean to jolly well ask her.

VIDA: [*Indignant*] To be your wife?

SIR WILFRID: [*C.*] Why not?

VIDA: [*As before*] And you came here, to my house – in order to ask her —

SIR WILFRID: [*Truthful even on a subtle point*] Oh, but that's only my first reason for coming, you know.

VIDA: [*Concealing her hopes*] Well, now I *am* curious – what is the second?

SIR WILFRID: [*Simply*] Are you feelin' pretty robust?

VIDA: I don't know!

SIR WILFRID: [*Crosses R. to buffet*] Will you have something, and then I'll tell you!

VIDA: [*Gaily*] Can't I support the news without —

SIR WILFRID: [*Trying to explain his state of mind, a thing he has never been able to do*] Mrs. Phillimore, you see it's this way. Whenever you're lucky, you're too lucky. Now, Mrs. Karslake is a nipper and no mistake, but as I told you, the very same evenin' and house where I saw her —

He attempts to take her hand

VIDA: [*Gently rising and affecting a tender surprise*] What!

SIR WILFRID: [*Rising with her*] That's it! – You're over!

He suggests with his right hand the movement of a horse taking a hurdle

VIDA: [*Very sweetly*] You don't really mean —

SIR WILFRID: [*Carried away for the moment by so much true womanliness*] I mean, I stayed awake for an hour last night, thinkin' about you.

VIDA: [*Speaking to be contradicted*] But, you've just told me – that Cynthia —

SIR WILFRID: [*Admitting the fact*] Well, she did – she did bowl my wicket, but so did you —

VIDA: [*Taking him very gently to task*] Don't you think there's a limit to – [*Sits*]

SIR WILFRID: [*Roused by so much loveliness of soul*] Now, see here, Mrs. Phillimore! You and I are not bottle babies, eh, are we? You've been married and – I – I've knocked about, and we both know there's a lot of stuff talked about – eh, eh, well, you know: – the one and only – that a fellow can't be awfully well smashed by two at the same time don't you know! All rubbish! You know it, and the proof of the puddin's in the eatin', I am!

VIDA: [*As before*] May I ask where I come in?

SIR WILFRID: Well, now, Mrs. Phillimore, I'll be frank with you, Cynthia's my favorite, but you're runnin' her a close second in the popular esteem!

VIDA: [*Laughs, determined not to take offense*] What a delightful, original, fantastic person you are!

SIR WILFRID: [*Frankly happy that he has explained everything so neatly*] I knew you'd take it that way!

VIDA: And what next, pray?

SIR WILFRID: Oh, just the usual, – eh, – thing, – the – eh – the same old question, don't you know. Will you have me if she don't?

VIDA: [*A shade piqued, but determined not to risk showing it*] And you call that the same old usual question?

SIR WILFRID: Yes, I know, but – but will you? I sail in a week; we can take the same boat. And – eh – eh – my dear Mrs. – mayn't I say Vida, I'd like to see you at the head of my table.

VIDA: [*With velvet irony*] With Cynthia at the foot?

SIR WILFRID: [*Practical, as before*] Never mind Mrs. Karslake, – I admire her – she's – but you have your own points! And you're here, and so'm I! – damme I offer myself, and my affections, and I'm no icicle, my dear, tell you that for a fact, and, and in fact what's your answer? – [*Vida sighs and shakes her head*] Make it, yes! I say, you know, my dear Vida –

He catches her hands

VIDA: [*She slips them from him*] Unhand me, dear villain! And sit further away from your second choice! What can I say? I'd rather have *you* for a lover than any man I know! You must be a lovely lover!

SIR WILFRID: I am!

He makes a second effort to catch her fingers

VIDA: Will you kindly go further away and be good!

SIR WILFRID: [*Quite forgetting Cynthia*] Look here, if you say yes, we'll be married –

VIDA: In a month!

SIR WILFRID: Oh, no – this evening!

VIDA: [*Incapable of leaving a situation unadorned*] This evening! And sail in the same boat with *you?* And shall we sail to the Garden of Eden and stroll into it and lock the gate on the inside and then lose the key – under a rose-bush?

SIR WILFRID: [*Pauses, and after consideration, says*] Yes; yes, I say – that's too clever for me!

He draws nearer to her to bring the understanding to a crisis

VIDA: [*Soft knock up L.*] My maid – come!

SIR WILFRID: [*Swings out of his chair and goes to sofa*] Eh?

Enter Benson up L.

BENSON: [*To Vida*] The new footman, ma'am – he's made a mistake. He's told the lady you're at home.

VIDA: What lady?

BENSON: Mrs. Karslake; and she's on the stairs, ma'am.

VIDA: Show her in.

Sir Wilfrid has been turning over the roses. On hearing this, he faces about with a long stemmed one in his hand. He uses it in the following scene to point his remarks

SIR WILFRID: [*To Benson, who stops*] One moment! [*To Vida*] I say, eh – I'd rather not see her!

VIDA: [*Very innocently*] But you came here to see her.

SIR WILFRID: [*A little flustered*] I'd rather not. Eh, – I fancied I'd find you and her together – but her – [*comes a step nearer*] findin' me with you looks so dooced intimate, – no one else, d'ye see, I believe she'd – draw conclusions –

BENSON: Pardon me, ma'am – but I hear Brooks coming!

SIR WILFRID: [*To Benson*] Hold the door!

VIDA: So you don't want her to know – ?

SIR WILFRID: [*To Vida*] Be a good girl now – run me off somewhere!

VIDA: [*To Benson*] Show Sir Wilfrid the men's room.

Enter Brooks, L.

SIR WILFRID: The men's room! Ah! Oh! Eh!

VIDA: [*Beckons him to go at once*] Sir Wil –

He hesitates, then as Brooks comes on, he flings off with Benson

BROOKS: Lady Karslake, milady!

VIDA: Anything more inopportune! I never dreamed she'd come – [*Enter Cynthia, veiled. She comes down quickly. Languorously*] My dear Cynthia, you don't mean to say –

CYNTHIA: [*Rather short, and visibly agitated*] Yes, I've come.

VIDA: [*Polite, but not urgent*] Do take off your veil.

CYNTHIA: [*Doing as Vida asks*] Is no one here?

VIDA: [*As before*] Won't you sit down?

CYNTHIA: [*Agitated and suspicious*] Thanks, no – That is, yes, thanks. Yes! You haven't answered my question?

Cynthia waves her hand through the smoke, looks at the smoke suspiciously, looks for the cigarette

VIDA: [*Playing innocence in the first degree*] My dear, what makes you imagine that any one's here!

CYNTHIA: You've been smoking.

VIDA: Oh, puffing away!

Cynthia sees the glasses up R.

CYNTHIA: And drinking – a pair of drinks? [*She sees John's gloves on the table at her elbow*] Do they fit you, dear? [*Vida smiles; Cynthia picks up crop and looks at it and reads her own name*] "Jack, from Cynthia."

VIDA: [*Assured, and without taking the trouble to double for a mere woman*] Yes, dear; it's Mr. Karslake's crop, but I'm happy to say he left me a few minutes ago.

CYNTHIA: He left the house? [*Vida smiles*] I wanted to see him.

VIDA: [*With a shade of insolence*] To quarrel?

CYNTHIA: [*Frank and curt*] I wanted to see him.

VIDA: [*Determined to put Cynthia in the wrong*] And I sent him away because I didn't want you to repeat the scene of last night in my house.

CYNTHIA: [*Looks at crop and is silent*] Well, I can't stay. I'm to be married at three, and I had to play truant to get here!

Enter Benson, up L.

BENSON: [*To Vida*] There's a person, ma'am, on the sidewalk.

VIDA: What person, Benson?

BENSON: A person, ma'am, with a horse.

CYNTHIA: [*Happily agitated*] It's Fiddler with Cynthia K!

She goes up rapidly and looks out back through window

VIDA: [*To Benson*] Tell the man I'll be down in five minutes.

CYNTHIA: [*Looking down from the balcony with delight*] Oh, there she is!

VIDA: [*Aside to Benson*] Go to the club room, Benson, and say to the two gentlemen I can't see them at present – I'll send for them when –

BENSON: [*Listens L.*] I hear some one coming.

VIDA: Quick!

Benson crosses L. Door L. opens, and John enters. John comes in slowly, carelessly. Vida whispers to Benson

BENSON: [*Crosses, goes close to John and whispers*] Beg par——

VIDA: [*Under her breath*] Go back!

JOHN: [*Not understanding*] I beg pardon!

VIDA: [*As before*] Go back!

JOHN: [*The same*] Can't! I've a date! With the sheriff!

VIDA: [*A little cross*] Please use your eyes.

JOHN: [*Laughing and flattering Vida*] I am using my eyes.

VIDA: [*Fretted*] Don't you see there's a lovely creature in the room?

JOHN: [*Again taking the loud upperhand*] Of course there is.

VIDA: Hush!

JOHN: [*Teasingly*] But what I want to know is –

VIDA: Hush!

JOHN: [*Delighted at getting a rise*] – is when we're to stroll in the garden of Eden –

VIDA: Hush!

JOHN: – and lose the key. [*To put a stop to this, she lightly tosses her handkerchief into his face*] By George, talk about attar of roses!

CYNTHIA: [*Up at window, excited and moved at seeing her mare once more*] Oh, she's a darling! [*She turns*] A perfect darling! [*John starts up; sees Cynthia at the same instant that she sees him*] Oh! I didn't know you were here. [*Pause; then with "take-it-or-leave-it" frankness*] I came to see *you!*

John looks extremely dark and angry; Vida rises

VIDA: [*To Cynthia, most gently, and seeing there's nothing to be made of John*] Oh, pray feel at home, Cynthia, dear! [*Stands by door, R.; to John*] When I've a nice street frock on, I'll ask you to present me to Cynthia K.

Exit Vida, R. John and Cynthia, tableau

CYNTHIA: [*Agitated and frank*] Of course, I told you yesterday I was coming here.

JOHN: [*R., irritated*] And I was to deny myself the privilege of being here?

CYNTHIA: [*Curt and agitated*] Yes.

JOHN: [*Ready to fight*] And you guessed I would do that?

CYNTHIA: No.

JOHN: What?

CYNTHIA: [*Above table. She speaks with agitation, frankness and good will*] Jack – I mean, Mr. Karslake, – no, I mean, Jack! I came because – well, you see, it's my wedding day! – and – and – I – I – was rude to you last evening. I'd like to apologize and make peace with you before I go –

JOHN: [*Determined to be disagreeable*] Before you go to your last, long home!

CYNTHIA: I came to apologize.

JOHN: But you'll remain to quarrel!

CYNTHIA: [*Still frank and kind*] I will not quarrel. No! – and I'm only here for a moment. I'm to be married at three, and just look at the clock! Besides, I told Philip I was going to Louise's shop, and I did – on the way here; but, you see, if I stay too long he'll telephone Louise and find I'm not there, and he might guess I was here. So you see I'm risking a scandal. And now, Jack, see here, I lay my hand on the table, I'm here on the square, and, – what I want to say is, why – Jack, even if we have made a mess of our married life, let's put by anger and pride. It's all over now and can't be helped. So let's be human, let's be reasonable, and let's be kind to each other! Won't you give me your hand? [*John refuses, R.*] I wish you every happiness!

JOHN: [*Turns away R., the past rankling*] I had a client once, a murderer; he told me he murdered the man, and he told me, too, that he never felt so kindly to anybody as he did to that man after he'd killed him!

CYNTHIA: Jack!

JOHN: [*Unforgiving*] You murdered my happiness!

CYNTHIA: I won't recriminate!

JOHN: And now I must put by anger and pride! I do! But not self-respect, not a just indignation – not the facts and my clear memory of them!

CYNTHIA: Jack!

JOHN: No!

CYNTHIA: [*Goes C., with growing emotion, and holds out her hand*] I give you one more chance! Yes, I'm determined to be generous. I forgive. everything you ever did to me. I'm ready to be friends. I wish you every happiness and every – every – horse in the world! I can't do more than that! [*She offers it again*] You refuse?

JOHN: [*Moved, but surly*] I like wildcats and I like Christians, but I don't like Christian wildcats! Now I'm close hauled, trot out your tornado! Let the Tiger loose! It's the tamer, the man in the cage that has to look lively and use the red hot crowbar! But by Jove, I'm out of the cage! I'm a mere spectator of the married circus!

He puffs vigorously

CYNTHIA: Be a game sport then! Our marriage was a wager; you wagered you could live with me. You lost; you paid with a divorce; and now is the time to show your sporting blood. Come on, shake hands and part friends.

JOHN: Not in this world! Friends with you, no! I have a proper pride. I don't propose to put my pride in my pocket.

CYNTHIA: [*Jealous and plain spoken*] Oh, I wouldn't ask you to put your pride in your pocket while Vida's handkerchief is there. [*John looks angered*] Pretty little bijou of a handkerchief! [*Cynthia takes handkerchief out*] And she is charming, and divorced, and reasonably well made up.

JOHN: Oh, well, Vida is a woman. [*Business with handkerchief*] I'm a man, a handkerchief is a handkerchief, and as some old Aristotle or other said, whatever concerns a woman, concerns me!

CYNTHIA: [*Not oblivious of him, but in a low voice*] Insufferable! Well, yes. [*She sits. She is too much wounded to make any further appeal*] You're perfectly right. There's no possible harmony between divorced people! I withdraw my hand and all good feeling. No wonder I couldn't stand you. Eh? However, that's pleasantly past! But at least, my dear Karslake, let us have some sort of beauty of behavior! If we cannot be decent, let us endeavor to be graceful. If we can't be moral, at least we can avoid being vulgar.

JOHN: Well –

CYNTHIA: If there's to be no more marriage in the world –

JOHN: [*Cynical*] Oh, but that's not it; there's to be more and more and more!

CYNTHIA: [*With a touch of bitterness*] Very well! I repeat then, if there's to be nothing but marriage and divorce, and remarriage, and redivorce, at least, those who *are* divorced can avoid the vulgarity of meeting each other here, there, and everywhere!

JOHN: Oh, that's where you come out!

CYNTHIA: I thought so yesterday, and to-day I know it. It's an insufferable thing to a woman of any delicacy of feeling to find her husband –

JOHN: Ahem – former!

CYNTHIA: *Once* a husband always –

JOHN: [*Still cynical*] Oh, no! Oh, dear, no.

CYNTHIA: To find her – to find the man she has once lived with – in the house of – making love to – to find you here! [*John smiles; rises*] You smile, – but I say, it should be a social axiom, no woman should have to meet her former husband.

JOHN: [*Cynical and cutting*] Oh, I don't know; after I've served my term I don't mind meeting my jailor.

CYNTHIA: [*John takes chair near Cynthia*] It's indecent – at the horse-show, the opera, at races and balls, to meet the man who once – It's not civilized! It's fantastic! It's half baked! Oh, I never should have come here! [*He sympathizes, and she grows irrational and furious*] But it's entirely your fault!

JOHN: My fault?

CYNTHIA: [*Working herself into a rage*] Of course. What business have you to be about – to be at large. To be at all!

JOHN: Gosh!

CYNTHIA: [*As before*] To be where I am! Yes, it's just as horrible for you to turn up in my life as it would be for a dead person to insist on coming back to life and dinner and bridge!

JOHN: Horrid idea!

CYNTHIA: Yes, but it's *you* who behave just as if you were not dead, just as if I'd not spent a fortune on your funeral. You do; you prepare to bob up at afternoon teas, – and dinners – and embarrass me to death with your extinct personality!

JOHN: Well, of course we *were* married, but it didn't quite kill me.

CYNTHIA: [*Angry and plain spoken*] You killed yourself for me – I divorced you. I buried you out of my life. If any human soul was ever dead, you are! And there's nothing I so hate as a gibbering ghost.

JOHN: Oh, I say!

CYNTHIA: [*With hot anger*] Go gibber and squeak where gibbering and squeaking are the fashion!

JOHN: [*Laughs, pretending to a coldness he does not feel*] And so, my dear child, I'm to abate myself as a nuisance! Well, as far as seeing you is concerned, for my part it's just like seeing a horse who's chucked you once. The bruises are O. K., and you see him with a sort of easy curiosity. Of course, you know, he'll jolly well chuck the next man! – Permit me! [*John picks up gloves, handkerchief and parasol and gives her these as she drops them one by one in her agitation*] There's pleasure in the thought.

CYNTHIA: Oh!

JOHN: And now, may I ask you a very simple question? Mere curiosity on my part, but, why did you come here this morning?

CYNTHIA: I have already explained that to you.

JOHN: Not your real motive. Permit me!

CYNTHIA: Oh!

JOHN: But I believe I have guessed your real – permit me – your real motive!

CYNTHIA: Oh!

JOHN: [*With mock sympathy*] Cynthia, I am sorry for you.

CYNTHIA: Hm?

JOHN: Of course we had a pretty lively case of the fever – the mutual attraction fever, and we *were* married a very short time. And I conclude that's what's the matter with *you!* You see, my dear, seven months of married life is too short a time to cure a bad case of the fancies.

CYNTHIA: [*In angry surprise*] What?

JOHN: [*Calm and triumphant*] That's my diagnosis.

CYNTHIA: [*Slowly and gathering herself together*] I don't think I understand.

JOHN: Oh, yes, you do; yes, you do.

CYNTHIA: [*With blazing eyes*] What do you mean?

JOHN: Would you mind not breaking my crop! Thank you! I mean [*with polite impertinence*] that ours was a case of premature divorce, and, ahem, you're in love with me still.

Pause. Cynthia has one moment of fury, then she realizes at what a disadvantage this places her. She makes an immense effort, recovers her calm, thinks hard for a moment more, and then, has suddenly an inspiration

CYNTHIA: Jack, some day you'll get the blind staggers from conceit. No, I'm not in love with you, Mr. Karslake, but I shouldn't be at all surprised if she were. She's just your sort, you know. She's a man-eating shark, and you'll be a toothsome mouthful. Oh, come now, Jack, what a silly you are! Oh, yes, you are, to get off a joke like that; me – in love with –

Looks at him

JOHN: Why are you here? [*She laughs and begins to play her game*] Why are you here?

CYNTHIA: Guess!

She laughs

JOHN: Why are you –

CYNTHIA: [*Quickly*] Why am I here! I'll tell tell you. I'm going to be married. I had a longing, an irresistible longing to see you make an ass of yourself just once more! It happened!

JOHN: [*Uncertain and discomfited*] I know better!

CYNTHIA: But I came for a serious purpose, too. I came, my dear fellow, to make an experiment on myself. I've been with you thirty minutes; and – [*She sighs with content*] It's all right!

JOHN: What's all right?

CYNTHIA: [*Calm and apparently at peace with the world*] I'm immune.

JOHN: Immune?

CYNTHIA: You're not catching any more! Yes, you see, I said to myself, if I fly into a temper –

JOHN: You did!

CYNTHIA: If I fly into a temper when I see him, well that shows I'm not yet so entirely convalescent that I can afford to have Jack Karslake at my house. If I remain calm I shall ask him to dinner.

JOHN: [*Routed*] Ask me if you dare!

Rises

CYNTHIA: [*Getting the whip hand for good*] Ask you to dinner? Oh, my dear fellow. [*John rises*] I'm going to do much more than that. [*Rises*] We must be friends, old man! We must meet, we must meet often, we must show New York the way the thing should be done, and, to show you I mean it – I want you to be my best man, and give me away when I'm married this afternoon.

JOHN: [*Incredulous and impatient*] You don't mean that!

Puts back chair

CYNTHIA: There you are! Always suspicious!

JOHN: You don't mean that!

CYNTHIA: [*Hiding her emotion under a sportswoman's manner*] Don't I? I ask you, come! And come as you are! And I'll lay my wedding gown to Cynthia K that you won't be there! If you're there, you get the gown, and if you're not, I get Cynthia K! –

JOHN: [*Determined not to be worsted*] I take it!

CYNTHIA: Done! Now, then, we'll see which of us two is the real sporting goods! Shake! [*They shake hands on it*] Would you mind letting me have a plain soda? [*John goes to the table, and, as he is rattled and does not regard what he is about, he fills the glass three-fourths full with whiskey. He comes to Cynthia and gives her this. She looks him in the eye with an air of triumph*] Thanks. [*Maliciously, as Vida enters*] Your hand is a bit shaky. I think *you* need a little King William.

John shrugs his shoulders, and as Vida im-

mediately speaks, Cynthia defers drinking

VIDA: [*To Cynthia*] My dear, I'm sorry to tell you your husband – I mean, my husband – I mean Philip – he's asking for you over the 'phone. You must have said you were coming here. Of course, I told him you were not here, and hung up.

Enter Benson

BENSON: [*To Vida*] Ma'am, the new footman's been talking with Mr. Phillimore on the wire. [*Vida, gesture of regret*] He told Mr. Philli-more that his lady was here, and if I can be-lieve my ears, ma'am, he's got Sir Wilfrid on the 'phone now!

Enter Sir Wilfrid

SIR WILFRID: [*Comes from L., perplexed and annoyed*] I say y'know – extraordinary coun-try; that old chap, Phillimore, he's been damned impertinent over the wire! Says I've run off with Mrs. Karslake – talks about "Louise!" Now who the dooce is Louise? He's comin' round here, too – I said Mrs. Karslake wasn't here – [*Sees Cynthia*] Hello! Good job! What a liar I am!

BENSON: [*To Vida*] Mr. Fiddler, ma'am, says the mare is gettin' very restive.

Comes up to door. John hears this and moves at once. Exit Benson

JOHN: [*To Vida*] If that mare's restive, she'll break out in a rash.

VIDA: [*To John*] Will you take me?

JOHN: Of course. [*They go up to exit L.*]

CYNTHIA: [*To John*] Tata, old man! Meet you at the altar! If I don't, the mare's mine!

Sir Wilfrid looks at her amazed

VIDA: [*To Cynthia*] Do the honors, dear, in my absence!

JOHN: Come along, come along, never mind them! A horse is a horse!

Exeunt John and Vida, L., gaily and in haste. At the same moment Cynthia drinks what she supposes to be her glass of plain soda. As it is whiskey straight, she is seized with astonish-ment and a fit of coughing. Sir Wilfrid relieves her of the glass

SIR WILFRID: [*Indicating contents of glass*] I

say, do you ordinarily take it as high up – as seven fingers and two thumbs?

CYNTHIA: [*Coughs*] Jack poured it out. Just shows how groggy he was! And now, Sir Wil-frid –

Gets her things to go

SIR WILFRID: Oh, you can't go!

Enter Brooks

CYNTHIA: I am to be married at three.

SIR WILFRID: Let him wait. [*To Brooks, whom he meets near the door; aside*] If Mr. Philli-more comes, bring his card up.

BROOKS: [*Going*] Yes, Sir Wilfrid.

SIR WILFRID: [*To Brooks, as before*] To me!

He tips him

BROOKS: [*Bowing*] To you, Sir Wilfrid.

Exit Brooks

SIR WILFRID: [*Returning to Cynthia*] I've got to have my innings, y' know! [*He looks at her more closely*] I say, you've been crying! –

CYNTHIA: King William!

SIR WILFRID: You *are* crying! Poor little gal!

CYNTHIA: [*Tears in her eyes*] I feel all shaken and cold.

Enter Brooks, with card

SIR WILFRID: [*Astonished and sympathetic*] Poor little gal.

CYNTHIA: [*As before*] I didn't sleep a wink last night. [*With disgust*] Oh, what is the matter with me?

SIR WILFRID: Why, it's as plain as a pikestaff! You – [*Brooks has brought salver to Sir Wil-frid. A card lies upon it. Sir Wilfrid takes it and says aside to Brooks*] Phillimore? [*Brooks assents. Aloud to Cynthia, calmly deceitful*] Who's Waldorf Smith? [*Cynthia shakes her head. To Brooks, returning card to salver*] Tell the gentleman Mrs. Karslake is not here!

Exit Brooks

CYNTHIA: [*Aware that she has no business where she is*] I thought it was Philip!

SIR WILFRID: [*Telling the truth as if it were a lie*] So did I! [*With cheerful confidence*] And now, Mrs. Karslake, I'll tell you why you're cryin'. [*He sits beside her*] You're marryin' the wrong man! I'm sorry for you, but you're such a goose. Here you are, marryin' this legal luminary. What for? You don't know! He don't know! But I do! You pretend you're marryin' him because it's the sensible thing; not a bit of it. You're marryin' Mr. Phillimore because of all the other men you ever saw he's the least like Jack Karslake.

CYNTHIA: That's a very good reason.

SIR WILFRID: There's only one good reason for marrying, and that is because you'll die if you don't!

CYNTHIA: Oh, I've tried that!

SIR WILFRID: The Scripture says: "Try! try! again!" I tell you, there's nothing like a w'im!

CYNTHIA: What's that? W'im? Oh, you mean a *whim!* Do please try and say W*h*im!

SIR WILFRID: [*For the first time emphasizing his H in the word*] W*h*im. You must have a w'im – w'im for the chappie you marry.

CYNTHIA: I had – for Jack.

SIR WILFRID: Your w'im wasn't wimmy enough, my dear! if you'd had more of it, and tougher, it would ha' stood y' know! Now, I'm not proposin'!

CYNTHIA: [*Diverted at last from her own distress*] I hope not!

SIR WILFRID: Oh, I will later! It's not time yet! As I was saying –

CYNTHIA: And pray, Sir Wilfrid, when will it be time?

SIR WILFRID: As soon as I see you have a w'im for me! [*Rising, looks at his watch*] And now, I'll tell you what we'll do! We've got just an hour to get there in, my motor's on the corner, and in fifty minutes we'll be at Belmont Park.

CYNTHIA: [*Her sporting blood fired*] Belmont Park!

SIR WILFRID: We'll do the races, and dine at Martin's –

CYNTHIA: [*Tempted*] Oh, if I only could! I can't! I've got to be married! You're awfully nice; I've almost got a "w'im" for you already.

SIR WILFRID: [*Delighted*] There you are! I'll send a telegram! [*She shakes her head. He sits and writes at the table, L.*]

CYNTHIA: No, no, no!

SIR WILFRID: [*Reads what he writes*] "Off with Cates-Darby to Races. Please postpone ceremony till seven-thirty."

CYNTHIA: Oh, no, it's impossible!

SIR WILFRID: [*Accustomed to have things go his way*] No more than breathin'! You can't get a w'im for me, you know, unless we're together, so together we'll be! [*Enter John Karslake*] And to-morrow you'll wake up with a jolly little w'im – [*Reads*] "Postpone ceremony till seven-thirty." There. [*He puts on her cloak. Sees John*] Hello!

JOHN: [*Surly*] Hello! Sorry to disturb you.

SIR WILFRID: [*Cheerful as possible*] Just the man! [*Gives him the telegraph form*] Just step round and send it, my boy. Thanks!

John reads it

CYNTHIA: No, no, I can't go!

SIR WILFRID: Cockety-coo-coo-can't. I say, you must!

CYNTHIA: [*Positively*] No!

JOHN: [*Astounded*] Do you mean you're going –

SIR WILFRID: [*Very gay*] Off to the races, my boy!

JOHN: [*Angry and outraged*] Mrs. Karslake can't go with you there!

Cynthia starts, amazed at his assumption of marital authority, and delighted that she will have an opportunity of outraging his sensibilities

SIR WILFRID: Oho!

JOHN: An hour before her wedding!

SIR WILFRID: [*Gay and not angry*] May I know if it's the custom –

JOHN: [*Jealous and disgusted*] It's worse than eloping –

SIR WILFRID: Custom, y'know, for the husband, that was, to dictate –

JOHN: [*Thoroughly vexed*] By George, there's a limit!

CYNTHIA: What? What? What? [*Gathers up her things*] What did I hear you say?

SIR WILFRID: Ah!

JOHN: [*Angry*] I say there's a limit –

CYNTHIA: [*More and more determined to arouse and excite John*] Oh, there's a limit, is there?

JOHN: There is! I bar the way! It means reputation – it means –

CYNTHIA: [*Enjoying her opportunity*] We shall see what it means!

SIR WILFRID: Aha!

JOHN: [*To Cynthia*] I'm here to protect your reputation –

789

SIR WILFRID: [*To Cynthia*] We've got to make haste, you know.

CYNTHIA: Now, I'm ready –

JOHN: [*To Cynthia*] Be sensible. You're breaking off the match –

CYNTHIA: [*Excitedly*] What's that to you?

SIR WILFRID: It's boots and saddles!

JOHN: [*He takes his stand between them and the door*] No thoroughfare!

SIR WILFRID: Look here, my boy – !

CYNTHIA: [*Catching at the opportunity of putting John in an impossible position*] Wait a moment, Sir Wilfrid! Give me the wire! [*Faces him*] Thanks! [*She takes the telegraph form from him and tears it up*] There! Too rude to chuck him by wire! But you, Jack, you've taken on yourself to look after my interests, so I'll just ask you, old man, to run down to the Supreme Court and tell Philip – nicely, you know – I'm off with Sir Wilfrid and where! Say I'll be back by seven, if I'm not later! And make it clear, Jack, I'll marry him by eight-thirty or nine at the latest! And mind *you're* there, dear! And now, Sir Wilfrid, we're off.

JOHN: [*Staggered and furious, giving way as they pass him*] I'm not the man to – carry – to carry –

CYNTHIA: [*Quick and dashing*] Oh, yes, you are.

JOHN: – a message from you.

CYNTHIA: [*Triumphant*] Oh, yes, you are; you're just exactly the man!

Exeunt Cynthia and Sir Wilfrid

JOHN: Great miracles of Moses!

Curtain

ACT III

The same as that of Act I, but the room has been cleared of too much furniture, and arranged for a wedding ceremony. The curtain rises on Mrs. Phillimore reclining on the sofa, L. Miss Heneage is seated left of table, R. Sudley is seated at the right of the table. Grace is seated on sofa, L. There are cushions of flowers, alcove of flowers, flowers in vase, pink and white hangings, wedding bell of roses, calla lilies, or-

ange blossoms, a ribbon of white stretched in front of an altar of flowers; two cushions for the couple to kneel on; two candelabra at each side of back of arch on pedestals. The curtain rises. There is a momentary silence, that the audience may take in these symbols of marriage, etc. Every member of the Phillimore family is irritable, with suppressed irritation.*

SUDLEY: [*Impatiently*] All very well, my dear. Sarah. But you see the hour. Twenty to ten! We have been here since half-past two.

MISS HENEAGE: You had dinner?

SUDLEY: I did not come here at two to have dinner at eight, and be kept waiting until ten! And, my dear Sarah, when I ask where the bride is –

MISS HENEAGE: [*With forced composure*] I have told you all I know. Mr. John Karslake came to the house at lunch time, spoke to Philip, and they left the house together.

GRACE: Where is Philip?

MRS. PHILLIMORE: [*Feebly, irritated*] I don't wish to be censorious or to express an actual opinion, but I must say it's a bold bride who keeps her future mother-in-law waiting for eight hours. However, I will not venture to –

Mrs. Phillimore reclines again and fades away into silence

GRACE: [*Sharply and decisively*] I do! I'm sorry I went to the expense of a silver ice-pitcher.

Mrs. Phillimore sighs. Miss Heneage keeps her temper with an effort which is obvious. Enter Thomas

SUDLEY: [*To Mrs. Phillimore*] For my part, I don't believe Mrs. Karslake means to return here or to marry Philip at all!

THOMAS: [*R. C., to Miss Heneage*] Two telegrams for you, ma'am! The choir boys have had their supper.

Slight movement from every one; Thomas steps back

SUDLEY: [*Rises*] At last we shall know!

MISS HENEAGE: From the lady! Probably!

Miss Heneage opens telegram; reads first one at a glance, lays it on salver again with a glance at Sudley. Thomas passes salver to Sudley, who takes telegram

GRACE: There's a toot now.

MRS. PHILLIMORE: [*Feebly, confused*] I don't wish to intrude, but really I cannot imagine Philip marrying at midnight.

As Sudley reads, Miss Heneage opens the second telegram, but does not read it

SUDLEY: [*Reads*] "Accident, auto struck" – something! "Gasoline" – did something – illegible, ah! [*Reads*] "Home by nine forty-five! Hold the church!"

General movement from all

MISS HENEAGE: [*Profoundly shocked*] "Hold the church!" William, she still means to marry Philip! and to-night, too!

SUDLEY: It's from Belmont Park.

GRACE: [*Making a great discovery*] She went to the races!

MISS HENEAGE: This is from Philip! [*Miss Heneage reads second telegram*] "I arrive at ten o'clock. Have dinner ready." [*Miss Heneage motions to Thomas to withdraw. Thomas exits, L. Miss Heneage looks at her watch*] They are both due now. [*Movement*] What's to be done?

Rises. Sudley shrugs shoulders

SUDLEY: [*Rises*] After a young woman has spent her wedding day at the races? Why, I consider that she has broken the engagement, – and when she comes, tell her so.

MISS HENEAGE: I'll telephone Matthew. The choir boys can go home – her maid can pack her belongings – and when the lady arrives –

Very distant toot of an auto-horn is heard. Tableau. Auto-horn a little louder. Grace flies up stage and looks out of door R. Mrs. Phillimore does not know what to do, or where to go. Sudley crosses R., excitedly. Miss Heneage stands ready to make herself disagreeable

GRACE: [*Speaking rapidly and with excitement*] I hear a man's voice. Cates-Darby and brother Matthew.

Loud toot. Laughter and voices off back, faintly. Grace looks out of door, and then comes rapidly down L.

MISS HENEAGE: Outrageous!

SUDLEY: Disgraceful!

MRS. PHILLIMORE: Shocking! [*Voices and horn off; a little louder. Partly rising*] I shall not take any part at all, in the – eh – [*She fades away*]

MISS HENEAGE: [*Interrupting her*] Don't trouble yourself.

Voices and laughter, louder. Cynthia's voice is heard off. Sir Wilfrid appears back. He turns and waits for Cynthia and Matthew. He carries wraps. He speaks to Cynthia, who is still off. Matthew's voice is heard and Cynthia's. Cynthia appears at back, followed by Matthew. As they appear, Cynthia speaks to Matthew, on her right. Sir Wilfrid carries a newspaper and parasol. The hat is the one she wore in Act II. She is in get-up for auto. Goggles, veil, an exquisite duster in latest Paris style. All three come down rapidly. As she appears, Sudley and Miss Heneage exclaim, and there is a general movement

SUDLEY: [*To table, L.*] 'Pon my word!

GRACE: Hah!

MISS HENEAGE: [*Rises, R.*] Shocking!

Grace remains standing above sofa. Sudley moves toward her. Miss Heneage sits. Mrs. Phillimore reclines on sofa, L. Cynthia begins to speak as soon as she appears and speaks fluently to the end

CYNTHIA: [*C.*] No! I never was so surprised in my life, as when I strolled into the paddock and they gave me a rousing reception – old Jimmy Withers, Debt Gollup, Jack Deal, Monty Spiffles, the Governor and Buckeye. All of my old admirers! They simply fell on my neck, and, dear Matthew, what do you think I did? I turned on the water main! [*Movements and murmurs of disapprobation from the family. Matthew indicates a desire to go*] Oh, but you can't go!

MATTHEW: I'll return in no time!

CYNTHIA: I'm all ready to be married. Are they ready? [*Matthew waves a pious, polite gesture of recognition to the family*] I beg everybody's pardon! [*She takes off her wrap and puts it on the back of a chair up stage*] My goggles are so dusty, I can't see who's who! [*To Sir Wilfrid*] Thanks! You *have* carried it well!

Parasol from Sir Wilfrid

SIR WILFRID: [*Aside to Cynthia*] When may I –?

CYNTHIA: See you next Goodwood!

SIR WILFRID: [*Imperturbably*] Oh, I'm coming back!

Cynthia comes down

CYNTHIA: Not a bit of use in coming back! I shall be married before you get here! Ta! Ta! Goodwood!

SIR WILFRID: [*As before*] I'm coming back.

He goes out L., quickly. More murmurs of disapprobation from family. Slight pause

CYNTHIA: [*Begins to take off her goggles, and comes down slowly*] I do awfully apologize for being so late!

MISS HENEAGE: [*Importantly*] Mrs. Karslake –

SUDLEY: [*Importantly*] Ahem!

Cynthia lays down goggles, and sees their severity

CYNTHIA: Dear me! [*She surveys the flowers, and for a moment pauses*] Oh, good heavens! Why, it looks like a smart funeral!

Miss Heneage moves; then speaks in a perfectly ordinary natural tone, but her expression is severe. Cynthia immediately realizes the state of affairs in its fullness

MISS HENEAGE: [*To Cynthia*] After what has occurred, Mrs. Karslake –

Cynthia glances at table L.

CYNTHIA: [*Sits R. of table, composed and good tempered*] I see you got my wire – so you know where I have been.

MISS HENEAGE: To the race-course!

SUDLEY: [*Goes up to C.*] With a rowdy Englishman.

Cynthia glances at Sudley, uncertain whether he means to be disagreeable, or whether he is only naturally so

MISS HENEAGE: We concluded you desired to break the engagement!

CYNTHIA: [*Indifferently*] No! No! Oh! No!

MISS HENEAGE: Do you intend, despite of our opinion of you –

CYNTHIA: The only opinion that would have any weight with me would be Mrs. Phillimore's.

She turns expectantly to Mrs. Phillimore

MRS. PHILLIMORE: I am generally asleep at this hour, and accordingly I will not venture to express any – eh – any – actual opinion. [*Fades away. Cynthia smiles*]

MISS HENEAGE: [*Coldly*] You smile. We simply inform you that as regards *us,* the alliance is not grateful.

CYNTHIA: [*Affecting gaiety and unconcern*] And all this because the gasoline gave out.

SUDLEY: My patience has given out!

GRACE: So has mine. I'm going.

Exit Grace

SUDLEY: [*Comes down C., vexed beyond civility. To Cynthia*] My dear young lady: You come here, to this sacred – eh – eh – spot – altar! – [*gesture*] odoriferous of the paddock! – speaking of Spiffles and Buckeye, – having practically eloped! – having created a scandal, and disgraced our family!

CYNTHIA: [*As before*] How does it disgrace you? Because I like to see a high-bred, clean, nervy, sweet little four-legged gee play the antelope over a hurdle!

MISS HENEAGE: Sister, it is high time that you –

Turns to Cynthia. Gesture

CYNTHIA: [*With quiet irony*] Mrs. Phillimore is generally asleep at this hour, and accordingly she will not venture to express –

SUDLEY: [*Spluttering with irritation*] Enough, madam – I *venture* to – to – to – to say, you are leading a fast life.

CYNTHIA: [*With powerful intention*] Not in this house! For six heavy weeks have I been laid away in the grave, and I've found it very slow indeed trying to keep pace with the dead!

SUDLEY: [*Despairingly*] This comes of horses!

CYNTHIA: [*Indignant*] Of what?

SUDLEY: C-c-caring for horses!

MISS HENEAGE: [*With sublime morality*] What Mrs. Karslake cares for is – men.

CYNTHIA: [*Angry and gay*] What would you have me care for? The Ornithorhyncus Paradoxus? or Pithacanthropus Erectus? Oh, I refuse to take you seriously.

Sudley begins to prepare to leave; he buttons himself into respectability and his coat

SUDLEY: My dear madam, I take myself seriously – and madam, I – I retract what I have brought with me [*he feels in his waistcoat pocket*] as a graceful gift, – an Egyptian scarab – a – a – sacred beetle, which once ornamented the person of a – eh – mummy.

CYNTHIA: [*Getting even with him*] It should never be absent from your pocket, Mr. Sudley!

Sudley goes up in a rage

MISS HENEAGE: [*Rises. To Sudley*] I've a vast mind to withdraw my –

Cynthia moves

CYNTHIA: [*Interrupts; maliciously*] Your wedding present? The little bronze cat!

MISS HENEAGE: [*Moves, angrily*] Oh!

Even Mrs. Phillimore comes momentarily to life, and expresses silent indignation

SUDLEY: [*Loftily*] Sarah, I'm going.

Enter Philip at back with Grace. Philip looks dusty and grim. Grace, as they come in, speaks to him. Philip shakes his head. They pause up stage

CYNTHIA: [*Emotionally*] I shall go to my room! [*Goes to R. Sudley down L.; Miss Heneage, C.; Mrs. Phillimore sees Philip. Philip represses Grace; gives her a stern look and forceful gesture to be silent. Cynthia goes up, and Miss Heneage comes down R.*] However, all I ask is that you repeat to Philip –

Comes suddenly on Philip, and speaks to him in a low tone

SUDLEY: [*To Miss Heneage, determined to win*] As I go out, I shall do myself the pleasure of calling a hansom for Mrs. Karslake –

Philip comes down two or three steps

PHILIP: As you go out, Sudley, have a hansom called, and when it comes, get into it.

SUDLEY: [*Furious, and speaking to Philip*] Eh, – eh, – my dear sir, I leave you to your fate.

Philip angrily points him the door. Exit, L.

MISS HENEAGE: [*With weight*] Philip, you've not heard –

PHILIP: [*Interrupts*] Everything – from Grace! [*Cynthia goes down R. of table*] My sister has repeated your words to me – and her own! I've told her what I think of *her*.

Philip looks witheringly at Grace

GRACE: I shan't wait to hear any more.

Exit Grace, indignantly

PHILIP: Don't make it necessary for me to tell you what I think of you. [*Philip crosses L.; Miss Heneage crosses to R. in fury. Philip gives his arm to his mother. Miss Heneage goes to door R.*] Mother, with your permission, I desire to be alone. I expect both you and Grace, Sarah, to be dressed and ready for the ceremony a half hour from now.

As Philip and Mrs. Phillimore are about to cross, Miss Heneage speaks

MISS HENEAGE: [*Up R.*] I shall come or not as I see fit. And let me add, my dear nephew, that a fool at forty is a fool indeed.

Exit Miss Heneage, R., high and mighty, and much pleased with her quotation

MRS. PHILLIMORE: [*Stupid and weary as usual, to Philip, as he leads her to the door, R.*] My dear son – I won't venture to express –

Cynthia crosses L. to table

PHILIP: [*Soothing a silly mother*] No, mother, don't! But I shall expect you, of course, at the ceremony. [*Mrs. Phillimore exits R. Philip comes down C. Philip takes the tone and assumes the attitude of the injured husband*] It is proper for me to tell you that I followed you to Belmont. I am aware – I know with whom – in fact, *I know all!* [*Pauses. He indicates the whole censorious universe*] And now let me assure you – I am the last man in the world to be jilted on the very eve of – of – everything with you. I won't be jilted. [*Cynthia is silent*] You understand? I propose to marry you. I won't be made ridiculous.

CYNTHIA: [*Glancing at Philip, R.*] Philip, I didn't mean to make you –

PHILIP: Why, then, did you run off to Belmont Park with that fellow?

CYNTHIA: Philip, I – eh –

PHILIP: [*Sits right of table, R.*] What motive?

793

What reason? On our wedding day? Why did you do it?

CYNTHIA: I'll tell you the truth. I was bored.

PHILIP: Bored? In my company?

Philip, in a gesture, gives up

CYNTHIA: I was bored, and then – and besides, Sir Wilfrid asked me to go.

PHILIP: Exactly, and that was why you went. Cynthia, when you promised to marry me, you told me you had forever done with love. You agreed that marriage was the rational coming together of two people.

CYNTHIA: I know, I know!

PHILIP: Do you believe that now?

CYNTHIA: I don't know what I believe. My brain is in a whirl! But, Philip, I am beginning to be – I'm afraid – yes, I am afraid that one can't just select a great and good man [*she indicates him*] and say: I will be happy with him.

PHILIP: [*With dignity*] I don't see why not. You must assuredly do one or the other: You must either let your heart choose or your head select.

CYNTHIA: [*Gravely*] No, there's a third scheme; Sir Wilfrid explained the theory to me. A woman should marry whenever she has a whim for the man, and then leave the rest to the man. Do you see?

PHILIP: [*Furious*] Do I see? Have I ever seen anything else? Marry for whim! That's the New York idea of marriage.

CYNTHIA: [*Giving a cynical opinion*] New York ought to know.

PHILIP: Marry for whim and leave the rest to the divorce court! Marry for whim and leave the rest to the man. That was the former Mrs. Phillimore's idea. Only she spelled "whim" differently; she omitted the "w." [*He rises in his anger*] And now you – *you* take up with this preposterous – [*Cynthia moves uneasily*] But, nonsense! It's impossible! A woman of your mental calibre – No. Some obscure, primitive, female *feeling* is at work corrupting your better judgment! What is it you *feel?*

CYNTHIA: Philip, you never felt like a fool, did you?

PHILIP: No, never.

CYNTHIA: [*Politely*] I thought not.

PHILIP: No, but whatever your feelings, I conclude you are ready to marry me.

CYNTHIA: [*Uneasy*] Of course, I came back. I am here, am I not?

PHILIP: You are ready to marry me?

CYNTHIA: [*Twisting in the coils*] But you haven't had your dinner.

PHILIP: Do I understand you refuse?

CYNTHIA: Couldn't we defer – ?

PHILIP: You refuse?

CYNTHIA: [*A slight pause; trapped and seeing no way out*] No, I said I'd marry you. I'm a woman of my word. I will.

PHILIP: [*Triumphant*] Ah! Very good, then. Run to your room. [*Cynthia turns to Philip*] Throw something over you. In a half hour I'll expect you here! And, Cynthia, my dear, remember! I cannot cuculate like a wood pigeon, but – I esteem you!

CYNTHIA: [*Hopelessly*] I think I'll go, Philip.

PHILIP: I may not be fittted to play the love-bird, but –

CYNTHIA: [*As before*] I think I'll go, Philip.

PHILIP: I'll expect you, – in half an hour.

CYNTHIA: [*With leaden despair*] Yes.

PHILIP: And, Cynthia, don't think any more about that fellow, Cates-Darby.

CYNTHIA: [*Amazed and disgusted by his misapprehension*] No.

Exit Cynthia, R. Thomas enters from L.

PHILIP: [*Goes to R. table*] And if I had that fellow, Cates-Darby, in the dock – !

THOMAS: Sir Wilfrid Cates-Darby.

PHILIP: Sir what – what – wh-who? [*Enter Sir Wilfrid, L. in evening dress. Tableau. Philip looks Sir Wilfrid in the face and speaks to Thomas*] Tell Sir Wilfrid Cates-Darby I am not at home to him.

Thomas embarrassed

SIR WILFRID: [*Undaunted*] My dear Lord Eldon –

PHILIP: [*R., to Thomas, as before*] Show the gentleman the door.

Pause. Sir Wilfrid glances at door R., and gesture

SIR WILFRID: [*Goes to the door, examines it and returns to Philip*] Eh, – I admire the door, my boy! Fine, old carved mahogany panel; but don't ask me to leave by it, for Mrs. Karslake made me promise I'd come, and that's why I am here.

Thomas exits, L.

PHILIP: Sir, you are – impudent – !

SIR WILFRID: [*Interrupting*] Ah, you put it all in a nutshell, don't you?

PHILIP: To show your face here, after practically eloping with my wife!

SIR WILFRID: [*Pretending ignorance*] When were you married?

PHILIP: We are as good as married.

SIR WILFRID: Oh, pooh, pooh! You can't tell me that grace before soup is as good as a dinner!

Takes a cigar-case out; business of a dry smoke

PHILIP: Sir – I – demand –

SIR WILFRID: [*Calmly carrying the situation*] Mrs. Karslake is *not* married. *That's* why I'm here. I am here for the same purpose *you* are; to ask Mrs. Karslake to be my wife.

PHILIP: Are you in your senses?

SIR WILFRID: [*Touching up his American cousin in his pet vanity*] Come, come, Judge – you Americans have no sense of humor. [*He takes a small jewel-case from his pocket*] There's my regards for the lady – and, [*reasonably*] if I must go, I will. Of course, I would like to see her, but – if it isn't your American custom –

Enter Thomas

THOMAS: Mr. Karslake.

SIR WILFRID: Oh well, I say; if he can come, I can!

Enter John Karslake in evening dress, carrying a large and very smart bride's bouquet which he hands to Philip. Philip takes it because he isn't up to dropping it, but gets it out of his hands as soon as he can. Philip is transfixed; John comes down C. Deep down he is feeling wounded and unhappy. But, as he knows his coming to the ceremony on whatever pretext is a social outrage, he carries it off by assuming an air of its being the most natural thing in the world. He controls the expression of his deeper emotion, but the pressure of this keeps his face grave, and he speaks with force

JOHN: My compliments to the bride, Judge.

PHILIP: [*Angry*] And you, too, have the effrontery?

SIR WILFRID: There you are!

JOHN: [*Pretending ease*] Oh, call it friendship –

Thomas exits, L.

PHILIP: [*Puts bouquet on table. Ironically*] I suppose Mrs. Karslake –

JOHN: She wagered me I wouldn't give her away, and of course –

Throughout this scene John hides the emotions he will not show behind a daring irony. He has Philip on his left, walking about in a fury; Sir Wilfrid sits on the edge of the table, gay and undisturbed

PHILIP: [*A step toward John*] You will oblige me – both of you – by immediately leaving –

JOHN: [*Smiles and goes to Philip*] Oh, come, come, Judge – suppose I *am* here? Who has a better right to attend his wife's obsequies! Certainly, I come as a mourner – for *you!*

SIR WILFRID: I say, is it the custom?

JOHN: No, no – of course it's not the custom, no. But we'll make it the custom. After all, – what's a divorced wife among friends?

PHILIP: Sir, your humor is strained!

JOHN: Humor, – Judge?

PHILIP: It is, sir, and I'll not be bantered! Your both being here is – it is – gentlemen, there is a decorum which the stars in their courses do not violate.

JOHN: Now, Judge, never you mind what the stars do in their divorces! Get down to earth of the present day. Rufus Choate and Daniel Webster are dead. You must be modern. You must let peroration and poetry alone! Come along now. Why shouldn't I give the lady away?

SIR WILFRID: Hear! Hear! Oh, I beg your pardon!

JOHN: And why shouldn't we both be here? American marriage is a new thing. We've got to strike the pace, and the only trouble is, Judge, that the judiciary have so messed the thing up that a man can't be sure he *is* married until he's divorced. It's a sort of marry-go-round, to be sure! But let it go at that! Here we all are, and we're ready to marry my wife to you, and start her on her way to him!

PHILIP: [*Brought to a standstill*] Good Lord!

Sir, you cannot trifle with monogamy!

JOHN: Now, now, Judge, monogamy is just as extinct as knee-breeches. The new woman has a new idea, and the new idea is – well, it's just the opposite of the old Mormon one. Their idea is one man, ten wives and a hundred children. Our idea is one woman, a hundred husbands and one child.

PHILIP: Sir, this polyandry.

JOHN: Polyandry? A hundred to one it's polyandry; and that's it, Judge! Uncle Sam has established consecutive polyandry, – but there's got to be an interval between husbands! The fact is, Judge, the modern American marriage is like a wire fence. The woman's the wire – the posts are the husbands. [*He indicates himself, and then Sir Wilfrid and Philip*] One – two – three! And if you cast your eye over the future you can count them, post after post, up hill, down dale, all the way to Dakota!

PHILIP: All very amusing, sir, but the fact remains –

JOHN: [*Goes to Philip, R. Philip moves to R.*] Now, now, Judge, I like you. But you're asleep; you're living in the dark ages. You want to call up Central. "Hello, Central! Give me the present time, 1906, New York!"

SIR WILFRID: Of course you do, and – there you are!

PHILIP: There I am not, sir! And – [*To John*] as for Mr. Karslake's ill-timed jocosity, – sir, in the future –

SIR WILFRID: Oh, hang the future!

PHILIP: I begin to hope, Sir Wilfrid, that in the future I shall have the pleasure of hanging you! [*To John*] And as for you, sir, your insensate idea of giving away your own – your former – my – your – oh! Good Lord! This is a nightmare!

He turns to go in despair. Enter Matthew, who, seeing Philip, speaks as he comes in from door R.

MATTHEW: [*To Philip*] My dear brother, Aunt Sarah Heneage refuses to give Mrs. Karslake away, unless you yourself, – eh –

PHILIP: [*As he exits*] No more! I'll attend to the matter!

Exit R. The choir boys are heard practicing in the next room

MATTHEW: [*Mopping his brow*] How do you

both do? My aunt has made me very warm. [*He rings the bell*] You hear our choir practicing – sweet angel boys! Hm! Hm! Some of the family will not be present. I am very fond of you, Mr. Karslake, and I think it admirably Christian of you to have waived your – eh – your – eh – that is, now that I look at it more narrowly, let me say, that in the excitement of pleasurable anticipation, I forgot, Karslake, that your presence might occasion remark – [*Enter Thomas*] Thomas! I left, in the hall, a small handbag or satchel containing my surplice.

THOMAS: Yes, sir. Ahem!

MATTHEW: You must really find the handbag at once.

Thomas turns to go, when he stops startled

THOMAS: Yes, sir. [*Announcing in consternation*] Mrs. Vida Phillimore.

Enter Vida Phillimore, in full evening dress. She steps gently to Matthew

MATTHEW: [*Always piously serene*] Ah, my dear child! Now this is just as it should be! That is, eh – [*He comes C. with her; she pointedly looks away from Sir Wilfrid*] That is, when I come to think of it – your presence might be deemed inauspicious.

VIDA: But, my dear Matthew, – I had to come. [*Aside to him*] I have a reason for being here.

Thomas enters from R.

MATTHEW: But, my dear child – [*Gesture*]

THOMAS: [*With sympathetic intention*] Sir, Mr. Phillimore wishes to have your assistance, sir – with Miss Heneage *immediately!*

MATTHEW: Ah! [*To Vida*] One moment! I'll return. [*To Thomas*] Have you found the bag with my surplice?

He goes out L., with Thomas, speaking. Sir Wilfrid comes to Vida. John crosses and comes down R. and watches door up L.

SIR WILFRID: [*To Vida*] You're just the person I most want to see!

VIDA: [*With affected iciness*] Oh, no, Sir Wilfrid, Cynthia isn't here yet! [*Crosses R., to table. John comes down right of table R. To him, with obvious sweetness*] Jack, dear, I never was so ravished to see any one.

SIR WILFRID: [*Taken aback*] By Jove!

VIDA: [*Very sweet*] I knew I should find you here!

JOHN: [*Annoyed but civil*] Now don't do that!

VIDA: [*As before*] Jack!

They sit

JOHN: [*Civil but plain spoken*] Don't do it!

VIDA: [*Voice dripping with honey*] Do what, Jack?

JOHN: Touch me with your voice! I have troubles enough of my own. [*He sits not far from her; the table between them*]

VIDA: And I know *who* your troubles are! Cynthia!

From this moment Vida gives up John as an object of the chase and lets him into her other game

JOHN: I hate her. I don't know why I came.

VIDA: You came, dear, because you couldn't stay away – you're in love with her.

JOHN: All right, Vida, what I feel may be *love* – but all I can say is, if I could get even with Cynthia Karslake –

VIDA: You can, dear – it's as easy as powdering one's face; all you have to do is to be too nice to me!

JOHN: [*Looks inquiringly at Vida*] Eh!

VIDA: Don't you realize she's jealous of you? Why did she come to my house this morning? She's jealous – and all you have to do –

JOHN: If I can make her wince, I'll make love to you till the Heavenly cows come home!

VIDA: Well, you see, my dear, if you make love to me it will [*She delicately indicates Sir Wilfrid*] cut both ways at once!

JOHN: Eh, – what! Not Cates-Darby? [*Starts*] Is that Cynthia?

VIDA: Now don't get rattled and forget to make love to me.

JOHN: I've got the jumps. [*Trying to accept her instructions*] Vida, I adore you.

VIDA: Oh, you must be more convincing; that won't do at all.

JOHN: [*Listens*] Is that she now?

Enter Matthew, who goes to the inner room

VIDA: It's Matthew. And, Jack, dear, you'd best get the hang of it before Cynthia comes. You might tell me all about your divorce. That's

a sympathetic subject. Were you able to undermine it?

JOHN: No. I've got a wire from my lawyer this morning. The divorce holds. She's a free woman. She can marry whom she likes. [*The organ is heard, very softly played*] Is that Cynthia? [*Rises quickly*]

VIDA: It's the organ!

JOHN: [*Overwhelmingly excited*] By George! I should never have come! I think I'll go. [*He crosses to go to the door*]

VIDA: [*She rises and follows him remonstratingly*] When I need you?

JOHN: I can't stand it.

VIDA: Oh, but, Jack –

JOHN: Good-night!

VIDA: I feel quite ill. [*Seeing that she must play her last card to keep him, pretends to faintness; sways and falls into his arms*] Oh!

JOHN: [*In a rage, but beaten*] I believe you're putting up a fake.

The organ swells as Cynthia enters sweepingly, dressed in full evening dress for the wedding ceremony. Tableau. John, not knowing what to do, holds Vida up as a horrid necessity

CYNTHIA: [*Speaking as she comes on, to Matthew*] Here I am. Ridiculous to make it a conventional thing, you know. Come in on the swell of the music, and all that, just as if I'd never been married before. Where's Philip?

She looks for Philip and sees John with Vida in his arms. She stops short

JOHN: [*Uneasy and embarrassed*] A glass of water! I beg your pardon, Mrs. Karslake –

The organ plays on

CYNTHIA: [*Ironical and calm*] Vida!

JOHN: She has fainted.

CYNTHIA: [*As before*] Fainted? [*Without pause*] Dear, dear, dear, terrible! So she has. [*Sir Wilfrid takes flowers from a vase and prepares to sprinkle Vida's forehead with the water it contains*] No, no, not her forehead, Sir Wilfrid, her frock! Sprinkle her best Paquin! If it's a real faint, she will not come to!

VIDA: [*As her Paris importation is about to suffer comes to her senses*] I almost fainted.

CYNTHIA: Almost!

VIDA: [*Using the stock phrase as a matter of*

course, and reviving rapidly] Where am I? [*John glances at Cynthia sharply*] Oh, the bride! I beg every one's pardon. Cynthia, at a crisis like this, I simply couldn't stay away from Philip!

CYNTHIA: Stay away from Philip?

John and Cynthia exchange glances

VIDA: Your arm, Jack; and lead me where there is air.

John and Vida go into the further room; John stands left of her. The organ stops. Sir Wilfrid comes down. He and Cynthia are practically alone on the stage. John and Vida are barely within sight. You first see him take her fan and give her air; then he picks up a book and reads from it to her

SIR WILFRID: I've come back.

CYNTHIA: [*To Sir Wilfrid*] Asks for air and goes to the greenhouse. [*Cynthia crosses L. Sir Wilfrid offers her a seat*] I know why you are here. It's that intoxicating little whim you suppose me to have for you. My regrets! But the whim's gone flat! Yes, yes, my gasoline days are over. I'm going to be garaged for good. However, I'm glad you're here; you take the edge off –

SIR WILFRID: Mr. Phillimore?

CYNTHIA: [*Sharply*] No, Karslake. I'm just waiting to say the words [*enter Thomas*] "love, honor and obey" to Phillimore – [*looks up back*] and at Karslake! [*Cynthia sees Thomas*] What is it? Mr. Phillimore?

THOMAS: Mr. Phillimore will be down in a few minutes, ma'am. He's very sorry, ma'am, [*lowers his voice and comes nearer Cynthia, mindful of the respectabilities*] but there's a button off his waistcoat.

CYNTHIA: [*Rises, crossing L.*] Button off his waistcoat!

Exit Thomas, L.

SIR WILFRID: [*Delightedly*] Ah! so much the better for me. [*Cynthia looks up back*] Now, then, never mind those two! [*Cynthia moves restlessly*] Sit down.

CYNTHIA: I can't.

SIR WILFRID: You're as nervous as –

CYNTHIA: Nervous! Of course I'm nervous! So would you be nervous if you'd had had a runaway and smash up, and you were going to try it again. [*Looks up back. Sir Wilfrid uneasy*] And if some one doesn't do away with those calla lilies – the odor makes me faint! [*Sir Wilfrid moves*] No, it's not the lilies! It's the orange blossoms!

SIR WILFRID: Orange blossoms?

CYNTHIA: The flowers that grow on the tree that hangs over the abyss! [*Sir Wilfrid gets the vase of orange blossoms*] They smell of six o'clock in the evening. When Philip's fallen asleep, and little boys are crying the winners outside, and I'm crying inside, and dying inside and outside and everywhere.

Sir Wilfrid comes down

SIR WILFRID: Sorry to disappoint you. They're artificial. [*Cynthia shrugs her shoulders*] That's it! They're emblematic of artificial domesticity! And I'm here to help you balk it. [*He sits; Cynthia half rises and looks toward John and Vida*] Keep still now, I've a lot to say to you. Stop looking –

CYNTHIA: Do you think I can listen to you make love to me when the man who – who – whom I most despise in all the world, is reading poetry to the woman who – who got me into the fix I'm in!

SIR WILFRID: [*Leaning over the chair in which she sits*] What do you want to look at 'em for? [*Cynthia moves*] Let 'em be and listen to me! Sit down; for damme, I'm determined.

Cynthia sits right of table R.

CYNTHIA: [*Half to herself*] I won't look at them! I won't think of them. Beasts!

Sir Wilfrid interposes between her and her view of John. Enter Thomas, who comes down R.

SIR WILFRID: Now, then – [*He sits*]

CYNTHIA: Those two *here!* It's just as if Adam and Eve should invite the snake to their golden wedding. [*She sees Thomas*] What is it, what's the matter?

THOMAS: Mr. Phillimore's excuses, ma'am. In a very short time –

Thomas exits, R. door

SIR WILFRID: I'm on to you! You hoped for more buttons!

CYNTHIA: I'm dying of the heat; fan me.

Sir Wilfrid fans Cynthia

SIR WILFRID: Heat! No! You're dying because you're ignorin' nature. Certainly you are! You're marryin' Phillimore! [*Cynthia, business; feels faint*] Can't ignore nature, Mrs. Karslake. Yes, you are; you're forcin' your feelin's. [*Cynthia glances at him*] And what you want to do is to let yourself go a bit – up anchor and sit tight! I'm no seaman, but that's the idea! [*Cynthia moves and shakes her head*] So just throw the reins on nature's neck, jump this fellow Phillimore and marry me!

He leans over to Cynthia

CYNTHIA: [*Naturally and irritably*] You propose to me here, at a moment like this? When I'm on the last lap – just in sight of the goal – the gallows – the halter – the altar, I don't know what its name is! No, I won't have you! [*Looking toward Karslake and Vida*] And I won't have you stand near me! I won't have you talking to me in a low tone! [*As before*] Stand over there – stand where you are.

SIR WILFRID: I say –

CYNTHIA: I can hear you – I'm listening!

SIR WILFRID: Well, don't look so hurried and worried. You've got buttons and buttons of time. And now my offer. You haven't yet said you would –

CYNTHIA: Marry you? I don't even know you!

SIR WILFRID: [*Feeling sure of being accepted*] Oh, – tell you all about myself. I'm no duke in a pickle o' debts, d'ye see? I can marry where I like. Some o' my countrymen are rotters, ye know. They'd marry a monkey, if poppa-up-the-tree had a corner in cocoanuts! And they do marry some queer ones, y' know.

Cynthia looks up, exclaims and turns. Sir Wilfrid turns

CYNTHIA: Do they?

SIR WILFRID: Oh, rather. That's what's giving your heiresses such a bad name lately. If a fellah's in debt he can't pick and choose, and then he swears that American gals are awfully fine lookers, but they're no good when it comes to continuin' the race! Fair dolls in the drawin'-room, but no good in the nursery.

CYNTHIA: [*Thinking of John and Vida and nothing else*] I can see Vida in the nursery.

SIR WILFRID: You understand when you want a brood mare, you don't choose a Kentucky mule.

CYNTHIA: I think I see one.

SIR WILFRID: Well, that's what they're saying over there. They say your gals run to talk, [*he plainly remembers Vida's volubility*] and I I have seen gals here that would chat life into a wooden Indian! That's what you Americans call being clever. – All brains and no stuffin'! In fact, some of your American gals are the nicest boys I ever met.

CYNTHIA: So that's what you think?

SIR WILFRID: Not a bit what *I* think – what my countrymen think!

CYNTHIA: Why are you telling me?

SIR WILFRID: Oh, just explaining my character. I'm the sort that can pick and choose – and what I want is heart.

CYNTHIA: [*Always Vida and John in mind*] No more heart than a dragon-fly!

The organ begins to play softly

SIR WILFRID: That's it, dragon-fly. Cold as stone and never stops buzzing about and showin' off her colors. It's that American dragon-fly girl that I'm afraid of, because d'ye see, I don't know what an American expects when he marries; yes, but you're not listening!

CYNTHIA: I am listening. I am!

SIR WILFRID: [*Speaks directly to her*] An Englishman, ye see, when he marries expects three things: love, obedience and five children.

CYNTHIA: Three things! I make it seven!

SIR WILFRID: Yes, my dear, but the point is, will you be mistress of Traynham?

CYNTHIA: [*Who has only half listened to him*] No, Sir Wilfrid, thank you, I won't. [*She turns to see John crossing the drawing-room at back, with Vida, apparently absorbed in what she says*] It's outrageous!

SIR WILFRID: Eh? Why you're cryin'?

CYNTHIA: [*Almost sobbing*] I am not.

SIR WILFRID: You're not crying because you're in love with me?

CYNTHIA: I'm not crying – or if I am, I'm crying because I love my country. It's a disgrace to America – cast-off husbands and wives getting together in a parlor and playing tag under a palm-tree.

John with intention and determined to stab Cynthia, kisses Vida's hand

SIR WILFRID: Eh! Oh! I'm damned! [*To Cynthia*] What do you think that means?

CYNTHIA: I don't doubt it means a wedding here, at once – after mine!

Vida and John come down

VIDA: [*Affecting an impossible intimacy to wound Cynthia and tantalize Sir Wilfrid*] Hush, Jack – I'd much rather no one should know anything about it until it's all over!

CYNTHIA: [*Starts and looks at Sir Wilfrid*] What did I tell you?

VIDA: [*to Cynthia*] Oh, my dear, he's asked me to champagne and lobster at *your* house – his house! Matthew is coming! [*Cynthia starts, but controls herself*] And you're to come, Sir Wilfrid. [*Vida speaks, intending to convey the idea of a sudden marriage ceremony*] Of course, my dear, I would like to wait for your wedding, but something rather – rather important to me is to take place, and I know you'll excuse me.

Organ stops

SIR WILFRID: [*Piqued at being forgotten*] All very neat, but you haven't given me a chance, even.

VIDA: Chance? You're not serious?

SIR WILFRID: I am!

VIDA: [*Striking while the iron is hot*] I'll give you a minute to offer yourself.

SIR WILFRID: Eh?

VIDA: Sixty seconds from now.

SIR WILFRID: [*Uncertain*] There's such a thing as bein' silly.

VIDA: [*Calm and determined*] Fifty seconds left.

SIR WILFRID: I take you – count fair. [*He hands her his watch and goes to where Cynthia stands*] I say, Mrs. Karslake –

CYNTHIA: [*Overwhelmed with grief and emotion*] They're engaged; they're going to be married to-night, over champagne and lobster at my house!

SIR WILFRID: Will you consider your –

CYNTHIA: [*Hastily, to get rid of him*] No, no, no, no! Thank you, Sir Wilfrid, I will not.

SIR WILFRID: [*Calm, and not to be laid low*] Thanks awfully. [*Crosses to Vida. Cynthia goes up*] Mrs. Phillimore –

VIDA: [*She gives him back his watch*] Too late! [*To Karslake*] Jack, dear, we must be off.

SIR WILFRID: [*Standing C. and making a general appeal for information*] I say, is it the custom for American girls – that sixty seconds or too late? Look here! Not a bit too late. I'll take you around to Jack Karslake's, and I'm going to ask you the same old question again, you know. [*To Vida*] By Jove, you know in your country it's the pace that kills.

Exeunt Sir Wilfrid and Vida, L. door

JOHN: [*Gravely to Cynthia, who comes down*] Good-night, Mrs. Karslake, I'm going; I'm sorry I came.

CYNTHIA: Sorry? Why are you sorry? [*John looks at her; she winces a little*] You've got what you wanted. [*Pause*] I wouldn't mind your marrying Vida –

JOHN: [*Gravely*] Oh, wouldn't you?

CYNTHIA: But I don't think you showed good taste in engaging yourselves *here*.

JOHN: Of course, I should have preferred a garden of roses and plenty of twilight.

CYNTHIA: [*Rushing into speech*] I'll tell you what you *have* done – you've thrown yourself away! A woman like that! No head, no heart! All languor and loose – loose frocks – she's the typical, worst thing America can do! She's the regular American marriage worm!

JOHN: I have known others –

CYNTHIA: [*Quickly*] Not me. I'm not a patch on that woman. Do you know anything about her life? Do you know the things she did to Philip? Kept him up every night of his life – forty days out of every thirty – and then, without his knowing it, put brandy in his coffee to make him lively at breakfast.

JOHN: [*Banteringly*] I begin to think she is just the woman –

CYNTHIA: [*Unable to quiet her jealousy*] She is *not* the woman for *you!* A man with your bad temper – your airs of authority – your assumption of – of – everything. What you need is a good, old-fashioned, bread poultice woman!

Cynthia, full stop; faces John

JOHN: [*Sharply*] Can't say I've had any experience of the good old-fashioned bread poultice.

CYNTHIA: I don't care what you say! If you marry Vida Phillimore – you shan't do it. [*Tears of rage choking her*] No, I liked your father and for *his* sake, I'll see that his son doesn't make a donkey of himself a second time.

JOHN: [*Too angry to be amused*] Oh, I thought I was divorced. I begin to feel as if I had you on my hands still.

CYNTHIA: You have! You shall have! If you attempt to marry her, I'll follow you – and I'll find her – I'll tell Vida – [*he turns to her*] I will. I'll tell Vida just what sort of a dance you led me.

JOHN: [*Quicky on her last word but speaking gravely*] Indeed! Will you? And *why* do you care what happens to me?

CYNTHIA: [*Startled by his tone*] I – I – ah –

JOHN: [*Insistently and with a faint hope*] *Why* do you *care*?

CYNTHIA: I don't. Not in your sense –

JOHN: How dare you then pretend –

CYNTHIA: I don't pretend.

JOHN: [*Interrupting her; proud, serious and strong*] How dare you look me in the face with the eyes that I once kissed, and pretend the least regard for me? [*Cynthia recoils and looks away. Her own feelings are revealed to her clearly for the first time*] I begin to understand our American women now. Fire-flies – and the fire they gleam with is so cold that a midge couldn't warm his heart at it, let alone a man. You're not of the same race as a man! You married me for nothing, divorced me for nothing, because you *are* nothing!

CYNTHIA: [*Wounded to the heart*] Jack! What are you saying?

JOHN: [*With unrestrained emotion*] What, – you feigning an interest in me, feigning a lie – and in five minutes – [*Gesture indicating altar*] Oh, you've taught me the trick of your sex – you're the woman who's not a woman!

CYNTHIA: [*Weakly*] You're saying terrible things to me.

JOHN: [*Low and with intensity*] You haven't been divorced from me long enough to forget – what you should be ashamed to remember.

CYNTHIA: [*Unable to face him and pretending not to understand him*] I don't know what you mean?

JOHN: [*More forcibly and with manly emotion*] You're not able to forget me? You know you're not able to forget me; ask yourself if you are able to forget me, and when your heart, such as it is, answers "no," then – [*The organ is plainly heard*] Well, then, prance gaily up to the altar and marry that, if you can!

He exits quickly, L. Cynthia crosses to armchair and sinks into it. She trembles as if she were overdone. Voices are heard speaking in the next room. Enter Matthew and Miss Heneage, R. Enter Philip, R. Cynthia is so sunk in the chair they do not see her. Miss Heneage goes up to sofa back and waits. They all are dressed for an evening reception and Philip in the traditional bridegroom's rig – large buttonhole, etc.

MATTHEW: [*As he enters*] I am sure you will do your part, Sarah – in a spirit of Christian decorum. [*To Philip*] It was impossible to find my surplice, Philip, but the more informal the better.

PHILIP: [*With pompous responsibility*] Where's Cynthia?

Matthew gives glance around room

MATTHEW: Ah, here's the choir! [*Goes up stage. Choir boys come in very orderly; divide and take their places, an even number on each side of the altar of flowers. Matthew vaguely superintends. Philip gets in the way of the bell. Moves out of the way. Enter Thomas*] Thomas, I directed you – One moment if you please.

Indicates table and chairs. Thomas hastens to move chairs and table L. against wall. Philip comes down

PHILIP: [*Looking for her*] Where's Cynthia?

Cynthia rises. Philip sees her when she moves and crosses toward her, but stops. Organ stops

CYNTHIA: [*Faintly*] Here I am.

Matthew comes down. Organ plays softly

MATTHEW: [*Coming to Cynthia*] Ah, my very dear Cynthia, I knew there was something.

Let me tell you the words of the hymn I have chosen:

"Enduring love; sweet end of strife!
    Oh, bless this happy man and wife!"

I'm afraid you feel – eh – eh!

CYNTHIA: [*Desperately calm*] I feel awfully queer – I think I need a scotch.

Organ stops. Philip remains uneasily up L. Mrs. Phillimore and Grace enter back slowly, as cheerfully as if they were going to hear the funeral service read. They remain up L.

MATTHEW: Really, my dear, in the pomp and vanity – I mean – ceremony of this – this unique occasion, there should be sufficient exhilaration.

CYNTHIA: [*As before*] But there isn't!

She sits

MATTHEW: I don't think my Bishop would approve of – eh – anything *before!*

CYNTHIA: [*Too agitated to know how much she is moved*] I feel very queer.

MATTHEW: [*Piously sure that everything is for the best*] My dear child –

CYNTHIA: However, I suppose there's nothing for it – now – but – to – to –

MATTHEW: Courage!

CYNTHIA: [*Desperate and with sudden explosion*] Oh, don't speak to me. I feel as if I'd been eating gunpowder, and the very first word of the wedding service would set it off!

MATTHEW: My dear, your indisposition is the voice of nature.

Cynthia speaks more rapidly and with growing excitement. Matthew goes up to C. and near the choir boys

CYNTHIA: Ah, – that's it – nature! [*Matthew shakes his head*] I've a great mind to throw the reins on nature's neck.

PHILIP: Matthew!

He moves to take his stand for the ceremony

MATTHEW: [*Looks at Philip. To Cynthia*] Philip is ready.

Philip comes down C. The organ plays the wedding march

CYNTHIA: [*To herself, as if at bay*] Ready? Ready? Ready?

MATTHEW: Cynthia, you will take Miss Heneage's arm. [*Miss Heneage comes down near table*] Sarah! [*Matthew indicates to Miss Heneage where Cynthia is. Miss Heneage advances a step or two. Matthew goes up C., and speaks in a low voice to choir*] Now please don't forget, my boys. When I raise my hands so, you begin, "Enduring love, sweet end of strife," etc. [*Cynthia has risen. On the table is her long lace cloak. She stands by this table. Matthew assumes sacerdotal importance and takes his position inside the altar of flowers*] Ahem! Philip! [*He indicates to Philip to take his position*] Sarah! [*Cynthia breathes fast, and supports herself on table. Miss Heneage goes down L. and stands for a moment looking at Cynthia*] The ceremony will now begin.

The organ plays Mendelssohn's wedding march. Cynthia turns and faces Miss Heneage. Miss Heneage comes C. slowly, and extends her hand in her readiness to lead the bride to the altar

MISS HENEAGE: Mrs. Karslake!

PHILIP: Ahem!

Matthew steps forward two or three steps. Cynthia stands turned to stone

MATTHEW: My dear Cynthia. I request you – to take your place. [*Cynthia moves one or two steps across as if to go up to the altar. She takes Miss Heneage's hand and slowly they walk toward Matthew*] Your husband to be – is ready, the ring is in my pocket. I have only to ask you the – eh – necessary questions, – and – eh – all will be blissfully over in a moment.

The organ is louder

CYNTHIA: [*At this moment, just as she reaches Philip, she stops, faces round, looks him, Matthew and the rest in the face and cries out in despair*] Thomas! Call a hansom! [*Thomas exits and leaves door open. Miss Heneage crosses L. Mrs. Phillimore rises. Cynthia grasps her cloak on table R. Philip turns and Cynthia comes right of C. and stops*] I can't, Philip – I can't. [*Whistle of hansom is heard off; the organ stops*] It is simply a case of throwing the reins on nature's neck – up anchor – and sit tight! [*Matthew crosses to Cynthia*] Matthew, don't come near me! Yes, yes, I distrust you. It's your business, and you'd marry me if you could.

PHILIP: [*Watching her in dismay as she throws on her cloak*] Where are you going?

CYNTHIA: I'm going to Jack.

PHILIP: What for?

CYNTHIA: To stop his marrying Vida. I'm blowing a hurricane inside, a horrible, happy hurricane! I know myself – I know what's the matter with me. If I married you and Miss Heneage – what's the use of talking about it – he mustn't marry that woman. He shan't. [*Cynthia has now all her wraps on; goes up rapidly. To Philip*] Sorry! So long! Good-night and see you later.

Cynthia goes to door R., rapidly; Matthew, in absolute amazement, throws up his arms. Philip is rigid. Mrs. Phillimore sinks into a chair. Miss Heneage supercilious and unmoved. Grace the same. The choir, at Matthew's gesture, mistakes it for the concerted signal, and bursts lustily into the Epithalamis

"Enduring love – sweet end of strife!
Oh, bless this happy man and wife!"

Curtain

ACT IV

John Karslake's study and smoking-room. Bay window up R. Door R. to stairs and the front door of house. Door L., at back, leading to the dining-room. Fireplace down L., and mantel. 'Phone down L. Bookcase containing law books and sporting books. Full-length portrait of Cynthia on the wall, R. Nothing of this portrait is seen by audience except the gilt frame and a space of canvas. A large table with writing materials is littered over with law books, sporting books, papers, pipes, crops, a pair of spurs, etc. A wedding ring lies on it. There are three very low easy-chairs. The general appearance of the room is extremely gay and garish in color. It has the easy confusion of a man's room. A small table R. On this table is a woman's sewing-basket. The sewing-basket is open. A piece of rich fancy work lies on the table, as if a lady

had just risen from sewing. On the corner are a lady's gloves. On a chair-back is a lady's hat. It is a half hour later than the close of Act III. Curtains are drawn over window. Lamp on table L., lighted. Electric lights about room also lighted. One chair down R. is conspicuously standing on its head. Curtain rises on Nogam, who busies himself at table, back. Door at back is half open.

SIR WILFRID: [*Comes in door L., up*] Eh – what did you say your name was?

NOGAM: Nogam, sir.

SIR WILFRID: Nogam? I've been here thirty minutes. Where are the cigars? [*Nogam motions to a small table near the entrance door where the cigars are*] Thank you. Nogam, Mr. Karslake was to have followed us here, immediately. [*He lights a cigar*]

NOGAM: Mr. Karslake just now 'phoned from his club, [*Sir Wilfrid comes down R.*] and he's on his way home, sir.

SIR WILFRID: Nogam, why is that chair upside down?

NOGAM: Our orders, sir.

VIDA: [*Speaking as she come on*] Oh, Wilfrid! [*Sir Wilfrid turns. Vida comes slowly down*] I can't be left longer alone with the lobster! He reminds me too much of Phillimore!

SIR WILFRID: Karslake's coming; stopped at his club on the way! [*To Nogam*] You haven't heard anything of Mrs. Karslake – ?

NOGAM: [*Surprised*] No, sir!

SIR WILFRID: [*In an aside to Vida, as they move right to appear to be out of Nogam's hearing*] Deucedly odd, ye know – for the Reverend Matthew declared she left Phillimore's house before *he* did, – and she told them she was coming here!

Nogam evidently takes this in

VIDA: Oh, she'll turn up.

SIR WILFRID: Yes, but I don't see how the Reverend Phillimore had the time to get here and make us man and wife, don't y' know –

VIDA: Oh, Matthew had a fast horse and Cynthia a slow one – or she's a woman and changed her mind! Perhaps she's gone back and married Phillimore. And besides, dear, Matthew wasn't in the house four minutes and a half; only just long enough to hoop the hoop. [*She twirls her new wedding ring gently about her finger*] Wasn't it lucky he had a ring in his pocket?

SIR WILFRID: Rather.

VIDA: And are you aware, dear, that Phillimore bought and intended it for Cynthia? Do come, [*she goes up to the door through which she entered*] I'm desperately hungry! Whenever I'm married that's the effect it has!

Vida goes out. Sir Wilfrid sees her through door, but stops to speak to Nogam

SIR WILFRID: We'll give Mr. Karslake ten minutes, Nogam. If he does not come then, you might serve supper.

He follows Vida

NOGAM: [*To Sir Wilfrid*] Yes, Sir.

Door R. opens. Enter Fiddler

FIDDLER: [*Easy and business-like*] Hello, Nogam, where's the guv'nor? That mare's off her oats, and I've got to see him.

NOGAM: He'll soon be here.

FIDDLER: Who was the parson I met leaving the house?

NOGAM: [*Whispers*] Sir Wilfrid and Mrs. Phillimore have a date with the guv'nor in the dining-room, and the reverend gentleman –

Gesture as of giving an ecclesiastical blessing

FIDDLER: [*Amazed*] He hasn't spliced them? [*Nogam assents*] He has? They're married? Never saw a parson could resist it!

NOGAM: Yes, but I've got another piece of news for you. Who do you think the Rev. Phillimore expected to find *here*?

FIDDLER: [*Proud of being in the know*] Mrs. Karslake? I saw her headed this way in a hansom with a balky horse only a minute ago. If she hoped to be in at the finish –

Fiddler goes down R. and is about to set chair on its legs

NOGAM: [*Quickly*] Mr. Fiddler, sir, please to let it alone.

FIDDLER: [*Puts chair down in surprise*] Does it live on its blooming head?

NOGAM: Don't you remember? *She* threw it on its head when she left here, and he won't have it up. Ah, that's it – hat, sewing-basket and all, – the whole rig is to remain as it was when she handed him his knock-out.

A bell rings outside

FIDDLER: There's the guv'nor – I hear him!

NOGAM: I'll serve the supper. [*Takes letter from pocket and puts it on mantel*] Mr. Fiddler, would you mind giving this to the guv'nor? It's from his lawyer – his lawyer couldn't find him and left it with me. He said it was very important. [*Goes up L. Bell rings again. Speaking off to Sir Wilfrid*] I'm coming, sir!

Nogam goes out back, and shuts door. Enter John Karslake, R. He looks downhearted, his hat is pushed over his eyes. His hands in his pockets. He enters slowly and heavily. Sees Fiddler, who salutes, forgetting letter. John comes L. and sits in armchair at study table

JOHN: [*Speaking as he walks to his chair*] Hello, Fiddler!

Pause. John throws himself into a chair, keeps his hat on. Throws down gloves; sighs

FIDDLER: Came in to see you, sir, about Cynthia K.

JOHN: [*Drearily*] Damn Cynthia K! –

FIDDLER: Couldn't have a word with you?

JOHN: [*Grumpy*] No!

FIDDLER: Yes, sir.

JOHN: Fiddler.

FIDDLER: Yes, sir.

JOHN: Mrs. Karslake – [*Fiddler nods*] You used to say she was our mascot?

FIDDLER: Yes, sir.

JOHN: Well, she's just married herself to a – a sort of a man!

FIDDLER: Sorry to hear it, sir.

JOHN: Well, Fiddler, between you and me, we're a pair of idiots.

FIDDLER: Yes, sir!

JOHN: And now it's too late!

FIDDLER: Yes, sir – oh, beg your pardon, sir – your lawyer left a letter.

John takes letter; opens it and reads it, indifferently at first

JOHN: [*As he opens letter*] What's he got to say, more than what his wire said? – Eh – [*as he reads, he is dumbfounded*] what? – Will explain. – Error in wording of telegram. – Call me up. – [*Turns to telephone quickly*] The man can't mean that she's still – Hello! Hello!

John listens

FIDDLER: Would like to have a word with you, sir –

JOHN: Hello, Central!

FIDDLER: That mare –

JOHN: [*Looks at letter; speaks into 'phone*] 33246a – 38! Did you get it?

FIDDLER: That mare, sir, she's got a touch of malaria –

JOHN: [*At the 'phone*] Hello, Central – 33246a – 38! – Clayton Osgood – yes, yes, and say, Central – get a move on you!

FIDDLER: If you think well of it, sir, I'll give her a tonic –

JOHN: [*Still at the 'phone*] Hello! Yes – yes – Jack Karslake. Is that you, Clayton? Yes – yes – well –

FIDDLER: Or if you like, sir, I'll give her –

JOHN: [*Turning on Fiddler*] Shut up! [*To 'phone*] What was that? Not you – not you – a technical error? You mean to say that Mrs. Karslake is still – my – Hold the wire, Central – get off the wire! Get off the wire! Is that you, Clayton? Yes, yes – she and I are still – I got it! Good-bye!

Hangs up receiver; falls back in chair. For a moment he is overcome. Takes up telephone book

FIDDLER: All very well, Mr. Karslake, but I must know if I'm to give her –

JOHN: [*Turning over the leaves of the telephone book in hot haste*] What's Phillimore's number?

FIDDLER: If you've no objections, I think I'll give her a –

JOHN: [*As before*] L – M – N – O – P – It's too late! She's married by this time! Married! – and – my God – I – I am the cause. Phillimore –

FIDDLER: I'll give her –

JOHN: Give her wheatina! – give her grape nuts – give her away! [*Fiddler goes up*] Only be quiet! Phillimore!

Enter Sir Wilfrid, back

SIR WILFRID: Hello! We'd almost given you up!

JOHN: [*Still in his agitation unable to find Phillimore's number*] Just a moment! I'm trying to get Phillimore on the 'phone to – to tell Mrs. Karslake –

SIR WILFRID: No good, my boy – she's on her way here! [*John drops book and looks up dumbfounded*] The Reverend Matthew was here, y' see – and he said –

JOHN: [*Rises; turns*] Mrs. Karslake is coming here? [*Sir Wilfrid nods*] To this house? Here?

SIR WILFRID: That's right.

JOHN: Coming here? You're sure? [*Sir Wilfrid nods assent*] Fiddler, [*crosses R., to Fiddler. Fiddler comes C.*] I want you to stay here, and if Mrs. Karslake comes, don't fail to let me know! Now then, for Heaven's sake, what did Matthew say to you?

SIR WILFRID: Come along in and I'll tell you.

JOHN: On your life now, Fiddler, don't fail to let me –

Exeunt John and Sir Wilfrid

VIDA: [*Voice off*] Ah, here you are!

FIDDLER: Phew!

A moment's pause, and Cynthia enters. She comes in very quietly, almost shyly, and as if she were uncertain of her welcome

CYNTHIA: Fiddler! Where is he? Has he come? Is he here? Has he gone?

FIDDLER: [*Rattled*] Nobody's gone, ma'am, except the Reverend Matthew Phillimore.

CYNTHIA: Matthew? He's been here and gone? [*Fiddler nods assent*] You don't mean I'm too late? He's married them already?

FIDDLER: Nogam says he married them!

CYNTHIA: He's married them! Married! Married before I could get here! [*Sits in armchair*] Married in less time than it takes to pray for rain! Oh, well, the church – the church is a regular quick marriage counter. [*Voices of Vida and John heard off in light-hearted laughter*] Oh!

FIDDLER: I'll tell Mr. Karslake –

CYNTHIA: [*Rising and going to the door through which John left the stage; she turns the key in the lock and takes it out*] No – I wouldn't see him for the world! [*She comes down with key to the work-table*] If I'm too late, I'm too late! and that's the end of it! [*She lays key on table L.; remains standing near it*] I've come, and now I'll go! [*Long pause. Cynthia looks about the room; changes her tone*] Well, Fiddler, it's all a good deal as it used to be in my day.

FIDDLER: No, ma'am – everything changed, even the horses.

CYNTHIA: [*Same business; absent-mindedly*] Horses – how are the horses?

Throughout this scene she gives the idea that she is saying good-bye to her life with John

FIDDLER: [*R. C.*] Ah, when husband and wife splits, ma'am, it's the horses that suffer. Oh, yes, ma'am, we're all changed since you give us the go-by, – even the guv'nor.

CYNTHIA: [*L. C.*] How's he changed?

FIDDLER: Lost his sharp for horses, and ladies, ma'am – gives 'em both the boiled eye.

CYNTHIA: [*L. C. down*] I can't say I see any change; there's my portrait – I suppose he sits and pulls faces at me.

FIDDLER: Yes, ma'am, I think I'd better tell him of your bein' here.

CYNTHIA: [*Gently but decidedly*] No, Fiddler, no! [*She again looks about her*] The room's in a terrible state of disorder. However, your new mistress will attend to that. [*Pause*] Why, that's not her hat!

FIDDLER: Yours, ma'am.

CYNTHIA: Mine? [*She goes to the table to look at it*] Is that my work-basket? [*Pause*] My gloves? [*Fiddler assents*] And I suppose – [*She hurriedly goes to the writing-table*] My – yes, there it is: my wedding ring! – just where I dropped it! Oh, oh, oh, he keeps it like this – hat, gloves, basket and ring, everything just as it was that crazy, mad day when I – [*Glances at Fiddler and breaks off*] But for Heaven's sake, Fiddler, set that chair on its feet!

FIDDLER: Against orders, ma'am.

CYNTHIA: Against orders?

FIDDLER: You kicked it over, ma'am, the day you left us.

CYNTHIA: No wonder he hates me with the chair in that state! He nurses his wrath to keep it warm. So, after all, Fiddler, everything *is* changed, and that chair is the proof of it. I suppose Cynthia K is the only thing in the world that cares a whinney whether I'm alive or dead. [*She breaks down and sobs*] How is she, Fiddler?

FIDDLER: Off her oats, ma'am, this evening.

CYNTHIA: Off her oats! Well, she loves me, so I suppose she will die, or change, or – or something. Oh, she'll die, there's no doubt about

that – she'll die. [*Fiddler, who has been watching his chance, takes the key off the table while she is sobbing, tiptoes up the stage, unlocks the door and goes out. After he has done so, Cynthia rises and dries her eyes*] There – I'm a fool – I must go – before – before – he –

As she speaks her last word John comes on

JOHN: Mrs. Karslake!

CYNTHIA: [*Confused*] I – I – I just heard Cynthia K was ill – [*John assents. Cynthia tries to put on a cheerful and indifferent manner*] I – I ran round – I – and – and – [*Pauses, turns, comes down*] Well, I understand it's all over.

JOHN: [*Cheerfully*] Yes, it's all over.

CYNTHIA: How is the bride?

JOHN: Oh, she's a wonder.

CYNTHIA: Indeed! Did she paw the ground like the war horse in the Bible? I'm sure when Vida sees a wedding ring she smells the battle afar off. As for you, my dear Karslake, I should have thought once bitten, twice shy! But, you know best.

Enter Vida, back L.

VIDA: Oh, Cynthia, I've just been through it again, and I feel as if I were eighteen. There's no use talking about it, my dear, with a woman it's never the second time! And how nice you were, Jack, – he never even laughed at us! [*Enter Sir Wilfrid, with hat and cane. Vida kisses John*] That's the wages of virtue!

SIR WILFRID: [*In time to see her kiss John*] I say, is it the custom? Every time she does that, my boy, you owe me a thousand pounds. [*Sees Cynthia, who comes down above chair; he looks at her and John in turn*] Mrs. Karslake. [*To John*] And then you say it's not an extraordinary country!

Cynthia is more and more puzzled

VIDA: [*To John*] See you next Derby, Jack! [*Crosses to door R. To Sir Wilfrid*] Come along, Wilfrid! We really ought to be going. [*To Cynthia*] I hope, dear, you haven't married him! Phillimore's a tomb! Good-bye, Cynthia – I'm so happy! [*As she goes*] Just think of the silly people, dear, that only have this sensation once in a lifetime!

Exit Vida. John follows Vida off

SIR WILFRID: [*To Cynthia*] Good-bye, Mrs. Karslake. And I say, ye know, if you have married that dull old Phillimore fellah, why when you've divorced him, come over and stay at Traynham! I mean, of course, ye know, bring your new husband. There'll be lots o' horses to show you, and a whole covey of jolly little Cates-Darbys. Mind you come! [*With real delicacy of feeling and forgetting his wife*] Never liked a woman as much in my life as I did you!

VIDA: [*Outside; calling him*] Wilfrid, dear!

SIR WILFRID: [*Loyal to the woman who has caught him*] – except the one that's calling me!

Reenter John. Sir Wilfrid nods to him and goes off. John shuts door and crosses L. A pause

CYNTHIA: So you're not married?

JOHN: No. But I know that you imagined I was.

Pause

CYNTHIA: I suppose you think a woman has no right to divorce a man – and still continue to feel a keen interest in his affairs?

JOHN: Well, I'm not so sure about that, but I don't quite see how –

CYNTHIA: A woman can be divorced – and still – [*John assents; she hides her embarrassment*] Well, my dear Karslake, you've a long life before you, in which to learn how such a state of mind is possible! So I won't stop to explain. Will you be kind enough to get me a cab?

She moves to the door

JOHN: Certainly. I was going to say I am not surprised at your feeling an interest in me. I'm only astonished that, having actually married Phillimore, you come here –

CYNTHIA: [*Indignantly*] I'm not married to him!

A pause

JOHN: I left you on the brink – made me feel a little uncertain.

CYNTHIA: [*In a matter of course tone*] I changed my mind – that's all.

JOHN: [*Taking his tone from her*] Of course. [*A pause*] Are you going to marry him?

CYNTHIA: I don't know.

JOHN: Does he know you –

CYNTHIA: I told him I was coming here.

JOHN: Oh! He'll turn up here, then – eh? [*Cynthia is silent*] And you'll go back with him, I suppose?

CYNTHIA: [*Talking at random*] Oh – yes – I suppose so. I – I haven't thought much about it.

JOHN: [*Changes his tone*] Well, sit down; do. Till he comes – talk it over. [*He places the armchair more comfortably for her*] This is a more comfortable chair!

CYNTHIA: [*Shamefacedly*] You never liked me to sit in that one!

JOHN: Oh, well – it's different now. [*Cynthia crosses and sits down R., near the upset chair. Long pause. John crosses*] You don't mind if I smoke?

CYNTHIA: [*Shakes her head*] No.

JOHN: [*Business with pipe. Sits on arm of chair right of table L.*] Of course, if you find my presence painful, I'll – skiddoo.

He indicates L. Cynthia shakes her head. John smokes pipe and remains seated

CYNTHIA: [*Suddenly and quickly*] It's just simply a fact, Karslake, and that's all there is to it – if a woman has once been married – that is, the first man she marries – then – she may quarrel, she may hate him – she may despise him – but she'll always be jealous of him with other women. Always!

John takes this as if he were simply glad to have the information

JOHN: Oh – Hm! ah – yes – yes.

A pause

CYNTHIA: You probably felt jealous of Phillimore.

JOHN: [*Reasonably, sweetly, and in doubt*] N-o! [*Apologetically*] I felt simply: Let him take his medicine.

CYNTHIA: Oh!

JOHN: I beg your pardon – I meant –

CYNTHIA: You meant what you said!

JOHN: [*Comes a step to her*] Mrs. Karslake, I apologize – I won't do it again. But it's too late for you to be out alone – Philip will be here in a moment – and of course, then –

CYNTHIA: It isn't what you *say* – it's – it's – it's

everything. It's the entire situation. Suppose by any chance I don't marry Phillimore! And suppose I were seen at two or three in the morning leaving my former husband's house! It's all wrong. I have no business to be here! I'm going! You're perfectly horrid to me, you know – and – the whole place – it's so familiar, and so – so associated with – with –

JOHN: Discord and misery – I know –

CYNTHIA: Not at all with discord and misery! With harmony and happiness – with – with first love, and infinite hope – and – and – Jack Karslake, – if you don't set that chair on its legs, I think I'll explode.

John crosses rapidly, sets chair on its legs. Change of tone

JOHN: [*While setting chair on its legs, R.*] There! I beg your pardon.

CYNTHIA: [*Nervously*] I believe I hear Philip.

Rises

JOHN: [*Goes up to window*] N-o! That's the policeman trying the front door! And now, see here, Mrs. Karslake, – you're only here for a short minute, because you can't help yourself, but I want you to understand that I'm not trying to be disagreeable – I don't want to revive all the old unhappy –

CYNTHIA: Very well, if you don't – give me my hat. [*John does so*] And my sewing! And my gloves, please! [*She indicates the several articles which lie on the small table*] Thanks! [*Cynthia throws the lot into the fireplace, L., and returns to the place she has left near table*] There! I feel better! And now – all I ask is –

JOHN: [*Laughs*] My stars, what a pleasure it is!

CYNTHIA: What is?

JOHN: Seeing you in a whirlwind!

CYNTHIA: [*Wounded by his seeming indifference*] Oh!

JOHN: No, but I mean, a real pleasure! Why not? Time's passed since you and I were together – and – eh –

CYNTHIA: And you've forgotten what a vile temper I had!

JOHN: [*Reflectively*] Well, you did kick the stuffing out of the matrimonial buggy –

CYNTHIA: [*Pointedly but with good temper*] It wasn't a buggy; it was a break cart – [*She stands back of the armchair*] It's all very well

to blame me! But when you married me, I'd never had a bit in my mouth!

JOHN: Well, I guess I had a pretty hard hand. Do you remember the time you threw both your slippers out of the window?

CYNTHIA: Yes, and do you remember the time you took my fan from me by force?

JOHN: After you slapped my face with it!

CYNTHIA: Oh, Oh! I hardly touched your face! And do you remember the day you held my wrists?

JOHN: You were going to bite me!

CYNTHIA: Jack! I never! I showed my teeth at you! And I said I would bite you!

JOHN: Cynthia, I never knew you to break your word! [*He laughs. Casually*] And anyhow – they were awfully pretty teeth! [*Cynthia, though bolt upright, has ceased to seem pained*] And I say – do you remember, Cyn –

Leans over the armchair to talk to her

CYNTHIA: [*After a pause*] You oughtn't to call me "Cyn" – it's not nice of you. It's sort of cruel. I'm not – Cyn to you now.

JOHN: Awfully sorry; didn't mean to be beastly, Cyn. [*Cynthia turns quickly. John stamps his foot*] Cynthia! Sorry. I'll make it a commandment: thou shalt not Cyn!!

Cynthia laughs and wipes her eyes

CYNTHIA: How can you, Jack? How can you?

JOHN: Well, hang it, my dear child, I – I'm sorry, but you know I always got foolish with you. Your laugh'd make a horse laugh. Why, don't you remember that morning in the park before breakfast – when you laughed so hard your horse ran away with you!

CYNTHIA: I do, I do! [*Both laugh. The door opens, R. Nogam enters*] But what was it started me laughing? [*Laughs. Sits. Laughs again*] That morning. Wasn't it somebody we met? [*Laughs*] Wasn't it a man on a horse?

Laughs

JOHN: [*Laughing too*] Of course! You didn't know him in those days! But I did! And he looked a sight in the saddle!

Nogam, trying to catch their attention, comes down R. corner, right of table R.

CYNTHIA: Who was it?

JOHN: Phillimore!

CYNTHIA: He's no laughing matter now. [*Sees Nogam R.*] Jack, he's here!

JOHN: Eh? Oh, Nogam?

NOGAM: Mr. Phillimore, sir –

JOHN: In the house?

NOGAM: On the street in a hansom, sir – and he requests Mrs. Karslake –

JOHN: That'll do, Nogam. [*Exit Nogam, R. Pause. John from near the window. Cynthia faces audience*] Well, Cynthia?

He speaks almost gravely and with finality

CYNTHIA: [*Trembling*] Well?

JOHN: It's the hour of decision; are you going to marry him? [*Pause*] Speak up!

CYNTHIA: Jack, – I – I –

JOHN: There he is – you can join him.

He points to the street

CYNTHIA: Join Phillimore – and go home – with him – to his house, and Miss Heneage and –

JOHN: The door's open.

He points to the door

CYNTHIA: No, no! It's mean of you to suggest it!

JOHN: You won't marry –

CYNTHIA: Phillimore – no; never. [*Runs to window*] No; never, never, Jack.

JOHN: [*Goes up. He calls out of window, having opened it*] It's all right, Judge. You needn't wait.

Pause. John comes down. Tableau. John bursts into laughter. Cynthia looks dazed. He closes door

CYNTHIA: Jack! [*John laughs*] Yes, but I'm here, Jack.

JOHN: Why not?

CYNTHIA: You'll have to take me round to the Holland House!

JOHN: Of course, I will! But, I say, Cynthia, there's no hurry.

CYNTHIA: Why, I – I – can't stay here.

JOHN: No, of course you can't stay here. But you can have a bite, though. [*Cynthia shakes her head. John places the small chair which was upset, next to table R. Armchair above R. C.*] Oh, I insist. Just look at yourself – you're as pale as a sheet and – here, here. Sit right down. I insist! By George, you must do it!

Cynthia crosses to chair beside table R., left of it, and sits

CYNTHIA: [*Faintly*] I *am* hungry.

JOHN: Just wait a moment.

John exits L., upper door, leaving it open

CYNTHIA: I don't want more than a nibble! [*Pause*] I am sorry to give you so much trouble.

JOHN: No trouble at all. [*He can be heard off L., busied with glasses and a tray*] A hansom of course, to take you round to your hotel?

Speaks as he comes down R.

CYNTHIA: [*To herself*] I wonder how I ever dreamed I could marry that man.

JOHN: [*Above table by this time*] Can't imagine! There!

CYNTHIA: I am hungry. Don't forget the hansom.

She eats; he waits on her, setting this and that before her

JOHN: [*Goes to door R., up; opens it and speaks off*] Nogam, a hansom at once.

NOGAM: [*Off stage*] Yes, sir.

JOHN: [*Back to above table; from here on he shows his feelings for her*] How does it go?

CYNTHIA: [*Faintly*] It goes all right. Thanks!

Hardly eating at all

JOHN: You always used to like anchovy. [*Cynthia nods and eats*] Claret? [*Cynthia shakes her head*] Oh, but you must!

CYNTHIA: [*Tremulously*] Ever so little. [*He fills her glass and then his*] Thanks!

He pours out a glass for himself

JOHN: Here's to old times!

Raising glass

CYNTHIA: [*Very tremulous*] Please not!

JOHN: Well, here's to your next husband.

CYNTHIA: [*Very tenderly*] Don't!

JOHN: Oh, well, then, what shall the toast be?

CYNTHIA: I'll tell you – [*pause*] you can drink to the relation I am to you!

JOHN: [*Laughing*] Well – what relation are you?

CYNTHIA: I'm your first wife once removed!

JOHN: [*Laughs; drinks*] I say, you're feeling better.

CYNTHIA: Lots.

JOHN: [*Reminiscent*] It's a good deal like those mornings after the races – isn't it?

CYNTHIA: [*Nods*] Yes. Is that the hansom?

Half rises

JOHN: [*Going up to the window*] No.

CYNTHIA: [*Sits again*] What is that sound?

JOHN: Don't you remember?

CYNTHIA: No.

JOHN: That's the rumbling of the early milk wagons.

CYNTHIA: Oh, Jack.

JOHN: Do you recognize it now?

CYNTHIA: Do I? We used to hear that – just at the hour, didn't we – when we came back from awfully jolly late suppers and things!

JOHN: H'm!

CYNTHIA: It must be fearfully late. I must go.

Rises, crosses to L. chair, where she has left cloak. She sees that John will not help her and puts it on herself

JOHN: Oh, don't go – why go?

CYNTHIA: [*Embarrassed and agitated*] All good things come to an end, you know.

JOHN: They don't need to.

CYNTHIA: Oh, you don't mean that! And, you know, Jack, if I were caught – seen at this hour, leaving this house, you know – it's the most scandalous thing any one ever did my being here at all. [*Crosses to R. C.*] Good-bye, Jack! [*Pause; almost in tears*] I'd like to say, I – I – I – well, I shan't be bitter about you hereafter, and – [*Pause*] Thank you awfully, old man, for the fodder and all that!

Turns to go out R. upper

JOHN: Mrs. Karslake – wait –

CYNTHIA: [*Stopping to hear*] Well?

JOHN: [*Serious*] I've rather an ugly bit of news for you.

CYNTHIA: Yes?

JOHN: I don't believe you know that I have been testing the validity of the decree of divorce which you procured.

CYNTHIA: Oh, have you?

JOHN: Yes; you know I felt pretty warmly about it.

CYNTHIA: Well?

JOHN: Well, I've been successful. [*Pause*] The decree's been declared invalid. Understand?

CYNTHIA: [*Looks at him a moment; then speaks*] Not – precisely.

JOHN: [*Pause*] I'm awfully sorry – I'm awfully sorry, Cynthia, but, you're my wife still.

Pause

CYNTHIA: [*With rapture*] Honor bright?

She sinks into the armchair

JOHN: [*Nods. Half laughingly*] Crazy country, isn't it?

CYNTHIA: [*Nods. Pause*] Well, Jack – what's to be done?

JOHN: [*Gently*] Whatever you say.

Moves C.

NOGAM: [*Quietly enters door R.*] Hansom, sir.

Exits; Cynthia rises

JOHN: Why don't you finish your supper?

Cynthia hesitates

CYNTHIA: The – the – hansom –

JOHN: Why go to the Holland? After all – you know, Cyn, you're at home here.

CYNTHIA: No, Jack, I'm not – I'm not at home here – unless – unless –

JOHN: Out with it!

CYNTHIA: [*Bursting into tears*] Unless I – unless I'm at home in your heart, Jack!

JOHN: What do you think?

CYNTHIA: I don't believe you want me to stay.

JOHN: Don't you?

CYNTHIA: No, no, you hate me still. You never can forgive me. I know you can't. For I can never forgive myself. Never, Jack, never, never!

She sobs and he takes her in his arms

JOHN: [*Very tenderly*] Cyn! I love you! [*Strongly*] And you've got to stay! And hereafter you can chuck chairs around till all's blue! Not a word now.

He draws her gently to a chair

CYNTHIA: [*Wiping her tears*] Oh, Jack! Jack!

JOHN: I'm as hungry as a shark. We'll nibble together.

CYNTHIA: Well, all I can say is, I feel that of

all the improprieties I ever committed this —
this —

JOHN: This takes the claret, eh? Oh, Lord, how happy I am!

CYNTHIA: Now don't say that! You'll make me cry more.

She wipes her eyes. John takes out wedding ring from his pocket; he lifts a wine glass, drops the ring into it and offers her the glass

JOHN: Cynthia!

CYNTHIA: [*Looking at it and wiping her eyes*] What is it?

JOHN: Benedictine!

CYNTHIA: Why, you know I never take it.

JOHN: Take this one for my sake.

CYNTHIA: That's not benedictine. [*With gentle curiosity*] What is it?

JOHN: [*He slides the ring out of the glass and and puts his arm about Cynthia. He slips the ring on to her finger and, as he kisses her hand, says*] Your wedding ring!

Curtain

THE CITY

CLYDE FITCH

In 1907, two years before the opening of *The City*, five hundred New York actors, back-stage workers, and house attendants were earning a total of ten thousand dollars per week from the plays of Clyde Fitch; he was collecting an additional three thousand. In 1901, four Fitch plays had been running simultaneously: *Lover's Lane* at the Manhattan, *Captain Jinks* at the Garrick, *The Climbers* at the Bijou, and *Barbara Frietchie* at the Academy of Music. Such theatrical records were commonplace for Fitch. In the eleven years prior to 1907, he had written twenty-four plays, most of which had been put on the stage under his direction. And during the 1900–1901 season, ten of his plays were being shown simultaneously in New York and on the road. That such high-speed activity was terminated by an early death is not surprising. He died on September 4, 1909, three months before *The City* reached the stage.

William Clyde Fitch was born in Elmira, New York, on May 2, 1865, the son of Captain William Goodwin Fitch, an officer in the Union Army. As a dutiful and loving only son, he paid tribute to his parents' romantic courtship and marriage in his Civil War play *Barbara Frietchie*. His mother, Alice Clark, was the daughter of an old Hagerstown, Maryland, family. The family moved to Schenectady when he was four and later to Hartford. Fitch attended the Holderness Boarding School in New Hampshire and then the public high school in Hartford. William Lyon Phelps, who was a high-school classmate, described the teen-age Fitch as follows:

His gait was strange, the motive power seeming to dwell exclusively in the hips; if you can imagine a gay side wheel excursion steamer, with the port and starboard wheels moving in turn instead of together you will obtain a fair idea of the approach of William C. Fitch. His face was impressively pale, looking as if it had never been exposed to the sun; this pallor was accentuated by hair both black and copious. His manners seemed absurdly affected until we found that they were invariable. He was never caught off his guard. His language, judged by schoolboy standards, was ridiculously mature; instead of speaking the universal dialect of slang, he talked English. His voice was very high, frequently breaking into falsetto, and even in ordinary conversation it sounded like that of an hysterical woman who had just missed the train. . . . When we were playing football, he was spending those minutes

with the girls. That is where he laid the foundation of his success as a dramatist. . . .
This "sissy," as they called him, grew up to earn $250,000 per year.

Fitch himself added to his schoolboy portrait: "I knew, of course, that everybody regarded me as a sissy; but I would rather be misunderstood than lose
my independence. . . . I did not see why I should do things I hated to do
merely to conform to public opinion."

When he became a student at Amherst, his effeminate behavior contributed to his success in the dramatic club. In addition to designing the
scenery and costumes, he played more than his share of the female parts in
the college productions; his rendering of Lydia Languish was remembered
as a classic of female impersonation long after his graduation in 1886.
Although he had begun to write during his college days – he was the class
poet of 1886 – he and his parents agreed that he should pursue a career as an
interior decorator and architect. While searching about New York for an
appropriate apprenticeship in his chosen field and supporting himself by
private tutoring, he wrote a story, *The Knighting of the Twins;* a novel,
A Wave of Life; and a one-act play, *Betty's Finish,* which had a two-month
engagement at the Boston Museum. He also made the acquaintance of a number of New York theatre people, among them Edward A. Dithmar, the
drama critic of the *New York Times.* Knowing that Richard Mansfield was
searching for someone to construct a drama around the character of Beau
Brummell, Dithmar suggested to Mansfield that Fitch be given a try.

Although in the process of the collaboration Fitch complained that "Mansfield is unbearable, and if it were not of as much moment as it is, I would
not suffer the slings and arrows of his outrageous fortune." When *Beau Brummell* opened at the Madison Square Theatre on May 17, 1890, Fitch was
assured of a first-rank position among American dramatists. During the next
nineteen years, he wrote a total of some sixty plays. There were thirty-six
originals, three of them in manuscript at his death. The remainder were
dramatizations of novels and stories, and adaptations from the French and
German. All but one of the original plays dealt with American subjects, and,
according to Walter Prichard Eaton, "If we took Fitch's works and correctly
illustrated them, they would give to future generations a better idea of American life from 1890 to 1910 than newspapers or historical records." Most notable
in this impressive list of plays were *The Moth and the Flame* (1898), a melodrama with the conventional triumph of virtue over vice but with the added
interest of a fascinating Fitchian story; *Nathan Hale* (1898), the story of
that historical figure interwoven with a love theme and acted by N. C. Goodwin; *Barbara Frietchie* (1899), developed from the Civil War incident but
inspired by Fitch's parents' romance and played by Julia Marlowe; *The
Cowboy and the Lady* (1899), a western melodrama and one of the first

cowboy plays; *Captain Jinks of the Horse Marines* (1901), a charming comedy which gave Ethel Barrymore one of her first starring roles; *The Climbers* (1901), a representation of metropolitan society, business, and social climbers; *The Girl with the Green Eyes* (1902), a probing study of jealousy in which Clara Bloodgood played the leading role; *Her Great Match* (1905), the romantic story of a German crown prince who has fallen in love with an American girl; *The Truth* (1907), a didactic play chronicling the career of a pathological liar, again with Clara Bloodgood in the leading part; and *The City* (1909).

The realistic visual representation of familiar scenes from life was a strong feature in many of the plays: *The Climbers* (1901) showed a funeral; *The Way of the World* (1901) required an automobile on stage; *Glad of It* (1903) showed a department-store scene and *The Stubbornness of Geraldine* (1902) a scene on an ocean liner. The other plays were of less significance. A list will simply suggest the range of subjects Fitch explored in his original dramas: *Frédérick Lemaître* (1890); *Pamela's Prodigy* (1891); *A Modern Match* (1892); *His Grace de Grammont* (1894); *Mistress Betty* (1895), later retitled *The Toast of the Town; Lover's Lane* (1901); *The Last of the Dandies* (1901); *The Girl and the Judge* (1901); *Her Own Way* (1903); *Major André* (1903); *The Coronet of a Duchess* (1904); *The Woman in the Case* (1905); *The Girl Who Has Everything* (1906); *The Straight Road* (1906); *A Happy Marriage* (1909); *The Bachelor* (1909). Many of the plays were performed in England and on the Continent. Those with the more specialized American scenes, such as *The Cowboy and the Lady*, never succeeded abroad, but *The Truth*, with Marie Tempest in the leading role, had a longer run in England than in America and was equally popular in Germany and Italy.

Fitch's prodigious output resulted from a strong compulsion always to have a play in the works and from his peculiar ability to focus his attention on his writing under the most adverse conditions. Hard as he drove himself, he always maintained a healthy perspective. As Robert Herrick said of him, "His keen sense of humor kept him from taking himself too seriously – while he took his work very seriously indeed." He required no particular physical surroundings or any specifically conducive atmosphere to release his imagination. He literally worked anywhere and everywhere: in the midst of a gay party at his New York town house at 113 West Fortieth Street; at either of his country places, "Quiet Corner," near Greenwich, Connecticut, or later "The Other House" at Katonah, New York; or while driving in the country. On one occasion, after a second tire puncture in a single afternoon's drive, he is reported to have said, "Never mind, that last puncture did the scene; a blowout will finish the act." Fitch insisted that most of *The Truth* had been written while he was floating on the Grand Canal in Venice. The composition of a play progressed rapidly, normally in one to five weeks from page one to the final curtain; but the gestation period, according to Fitch, had invariably begun some two years earlier. Commonly he revised his plays as many as five times before they went into rehearsal. He attacked each new revision with a different-colored pencil: later he might wish to know at what stage a particular improvement had evolved. An anonymous versifier in the New York *Sun* described the Fitch rapid-fire method in this fashion:

> Swat,
> And out of the glittering social grot,
> Of the very Fitchiest, fetchingest lot,
> Stirred in the scorching society pot,
> Hot,
> He plucks a wild, weird name and plot;
> Whiz!
> Through all the scenic mysteries,
> The gayly appareled fantasies,
> Likewise the dramatic unities,
> He shoves his pen until he makes it sizz.
> Biff!
> Act I, – Act II, – Act III, as if
> The thing were a cigarette to whiff.
> Slambang,
> The word goes out to the Broadway gang:
> Hooray!
> Clyde Fitch has written another play!

When a play went into rehearsal, he approached the actors and the staging problems with comparable intensity, but he rarely made further revisions in the text. Unlike most of the other playwrights of his time, he assumed a complete and autocratic control over the directing and staging of his plays. He had a keen sense for casting the right actors, and, of course, many of the plays were written for specific actors. His first reading of the play to the actors invariably impressed them with his interpretative skill and alerted them to what was expected when they assumed the roles. Eugene Gautier once described his reading of the first act of *Barbara Frietchie* as that of "a man with ten souls, and ten different faces!" He gave his actors a week in which to learn their lines before beginning rehearsals in earnest. As might be expected of a man who delighted in his own eccentric dress, in collecting antiques, and in preparing elegant teas, his theatrical demands were temperamental and eccentric. Managers dreaded Fitch's extravagances, but they could not deny his requests. The investment was almost invariably returned at the box office. On one occasion he demanded a thousand dollars' worth of real flowers to be strewn around the stage. Unhappily, this was for *Major André*, one of his few failures. He had a remarkable eye for detail. At a rehearsal of

Barbara Frietchie he climbed on the stage to adjust an electric fan that was playing on the curtains of an open window. A newspaper reporter who was following the rehearsal asked him why he bothered with such trifles. Fitch replied, "I think it is very important. I believe in watching every bit of scenery, every action, every incidental blessed thing connected with the production. It is the 'little things' that quickest show the lack of study and preparation." While he was in the midst of rehearsing *Captain Jinks* and *The Climbers*, he wrote to Mrs. Dithmar, "This is my third week now of longer hours than any bricklayer would submit to! For nights and early hours I am busy with the property-man and scene painters. I don't have to, I suppose, but it is the only way I can approximate what I want."

The feverish routine of his living and working continued to the end of his life. The first week in June, 1909, he wrote to Virginia Gerson describing his activities:

Dear V. G.:

I was in town from late Wednesday till Thursday, P.M., and hoped, as I always do, to see the Gersons. G.B.T. (God bless them.) But, this is what I did do: Arrived N.Y., 4:45 –

(1) Interviewed actor Reid, and engaged him to play Dixon's part in "The Blue Mouse" next year.

(2) Interviewed actor for Zelda Sears play. Heard him sing and play (for the "Canary"). Unable to decide.

(3) Gave a second interview for a little rehearsal, and music – couldn't decide.

(4) Rehearsed Sam Edwards in Conor's part in "Blue Mouse," to appear in Chicago Monday night.

(5) Long business talk with Emerson, settling "B.M." details.

(6) Business lunch with Megrue, settling divers and money matters: Xtra interview with G. Fawcett about "Old Goriot."

(7) Saw Annie Blanke for Zelda's play, – too small but decided she is an artist and must give her a part next season, or the one after. Promised! She's had bad luck and been lost in stock for years.

(8) Saw Miss F. Nash, and engaged her to play *Pedicure* with Zelda.

(9) Engaged Miss Nash to play *Cicely* in "The City."

(10) Engaged Lucille Watson to play *Teresa* in "The City."

(11) Engaged Eva Vincent to play *Mrs. Rand* in "T.C."

(12) *Tried* to see Tully Marshall and made appointment for *next week!*

(13) Saw Rep. of Ex. Co., and arranged for motor to be shipped – signed all papers and went into all details.

(14) Interviewed and engaged a stage-manager for Zelda's play.

(15) Made arrangements to *begin scenery* for "The City."

(16) Bought and sent flowers to Mary Moore.

(17) Sneaked out of seeing Wyndham.

(18) Doctor's visit.

(19) Dentist.

And left N. Y. – Thursday, at 3:30!

During the late spring and early summer of 1909 Fitch was feverishly at work on *The City*. In June, he went to New Haven to talk with William Lyon Phelps's students about the new play. He had already begun preliminary casting although the play was not scheduled to open until fall. On June 20, he invited a number of friends to dinner at "The Other House." In the evening, with all the lights turned out except a desk lamp, he read *The City*. Although he completed the reading shortly after midnight and was exhausted from the performance, he was so intent on making immediate revisions that not until two o'clock, when his guests began to depart, did he glance up to inquire, "How do you like it?"

On June 23 he closed his house and on the twenty-fifth he sailed for France. On August 28 he wrote to Miss Gerson:

I found your welcome letter here when I arrived to-night. Thank you very, very much. I had made up my mind I would write you a letter if I died to-night, and your letter made me all the more *determined!!!* For I'm *not* so well as I've pretended and much less well than I wish it known. I counted on the change, etc., doing something for me – to help me go on fighting – and I think the change and outdoors have benefited me undoubtedly. But *such* weakness! . . .

On September 4 he died at Châlons-sur-Marne following an appendectomy.

In October, with John Emerson as stage manager, the actors whom he had selected began rehearsing *The City*. They were devotedly intent on searching out and rendering all the values that Fitch would have pointed out to them in rehearsal. After tryout performances in New Haven, the play opened at the Lyric Theatre in New York on December 21, 1909, under the auspices of the Shuberts and with Walter Hampden, Lucille Watson, and Tully Marshall in the cast. Well aware of Fitch's recent death and thus conscious of the significance of the occasion, the New York audience was prepared to give the play a warm reception. Fortunately, it was not obliged to respond simply out of respect for the dead. The entire audience became engulfed as the emotional turbulence of the drama unfolded, and at the final curtain they literally shouted their cheers and bravos. The next day the *Tribune* reported the event:

An audience half wild with excitement roared its approval last night. The applause of hands was drowned in the tremendous cheering that swept from orchestra to balcony. . . . It seems tame to say merely that the play is strong, for in its strongest scene it is tremendous. . . . If ever there were a powerful American play, firm and deft in construction, daring in plan, bold, frank, convincing, worthy to stand with much of the best work of the modern dramatists of the old world, this is that play.

Other newspapers echoed the enthusiasm:

Morning World: . . . women in various parts of the house screamed in hysterical excitement . . . sensationalism in its most virulent form, but it rang true.

Press: Verdict of the majority was emphatically that in *The City*, Fitch had written his "big" drama.

Evening Globe: An extra staff of maids and strong-armed ushers will be needed to look after the fainting women.

Dramatic Mirror: Too bad he didn't live to witness the reception at the Lyric Theatre on Tuesday night, when women waxed hysterical during the thrilling episode of the second act, and such a demonstration of a nervously wrought-up audience ensued as is seldom witnessed in a place of amusement . . . language exceeding the limit of all hitherto attempted freedom of speech on the American or any other stage.

The play ran for 190 performances in New York before taking to the road. Around the country the response was equally vigorous, though some people objected to the strong language. The manager in Pittsburgh insisted that "God" be deleted from the speech "You're a God damn liar!" With the coarse, obscene, and often scatological language that is now heard in the theatre, it is hard to realize that in 1909 Fitch was violating a sacredly respected taboo. This was the first time that "God damn" had been spoken on the stage. Frequently, it is said, the actor Tully Marshall turned his back to the audience in order to soften the blow.

For the tour and for later stock-company productions, the theme of the "village" versus the "city" was employed as the principal advertising lure. One frequently repeated poster showed a scale with the "city" balanced off against the "village" with a legend reading:

YOU ARE WITNESS

IN THE CASE OF

THE CITY

VERSUS THE VILLAGE

WHERE WAS THE BEST IN YOU BROUGHT OUT?

THE CITY OR THE COUNTRY?

YOUR TESTIMONY IS WANTED IN THIS

MOVING DRAMA OF BLINDING REALISM

Although the "moral conveyed by the play," as the New York *Dramatic Mirror* commented, "is the demonstration that the great city strips men of their masks, lays bare their weaknesses and forms the crucible of their regeneration or their demoralization," Fitch had other purposes in mind. He had been nettled by the repeated criticism that he was a "mere confectioner," that he was incapable of drawing "he-man" characters. Here was the answer: a vigorous, moving, and even morbid tragic drama in which Fitch's women were subordinated to the virile and aggressive males.

The City was Fitch's most mature drama. His usual keen observation and presentation of vivid real-life details, his decisive probing of human foibles and frailties, his sprightly and literate dialogue, his astute sense for dramatic and entertaining situations, all apparent in the earlier dramas, were equally evident in *The City*. But, in addition, his last play dug more deeply under the surface, grasped more firmly at the basic drives that propel men into action, and allowed them to express their passions in more highly charged language.

Fitch's observations on the theatre and drama of his time were largely expressed in letters, conversations, and infrequent lectures, but in 1904 he published an essay called "The Play and the Public" in which he recorded some of his beliefs. In part he wrote:

I feel myself very strongly the particular value – a value which rightly or wrongly, I can't help feeling inestimable – in a modern play of reflecting absolutely and truthfully the life and environment about us; every class, every kind, every emotion, every motive, every occupation, every business, every idleness! Never was life so varied, so complex; what a choice, then! Take what strikes you most, in the hope it will interest others. Take what suits you most to do – what perhaps you can do best – and then do it better. Be truthful, and then nothing can be too big, nothing should be too small, so long as it is here, and *there!* Apart from the question of literature, apart from the question of art, reflect the real thing with true observation and with sincere feeling for what it is and what it represents, and that is art and literature in a modern play. If you inculcate an idea in your play, so much the better for your play and for you – and for your audience. In fact, there is small hope for your play *as* a play if you haven't some small idea in it somewhere and somehow, even if it is hidden – it is sometimes better for you if it is hidden, but it must of course be integral. Some ideas are mechanical. Then they are no good. These are the ideas for which the author does all the work, instead of letting the ideas do the work for him. One should write what one sees, but observe under the surface. It is a mistake to look at the reflection of the sky in the water of theatrical convention. Instead, look up and into the sky of real life itself.

THE CITY

A Modern Play of American Life in Three Acts

CLYDE FITCH

CHARACTERS

GEORGE D. RAND

GEORGE D. RAND, JR.

MRS. RAND

TERESA RAND

CICELY RAND

ALBERT F. VORHEES

ELEANOR VORHEES

GEORGE FREDERICK HANNOCK

DONALD VAN VRANKEN

SUSAN, *maidservant in Middleburg*

JOHN, *the coachman in Middleburg*

FOOT, *butler in New York*

ACT I

SCENE: *At the Rands'. The library of a substantial house in Middleburg. Front doors open out into the "front hall." It is furnished in a "set" of rosewood furniture, upholstered in brown and red figured velvet. The walls are covered with dark maroon wall-paper, with framed photographs of Thorwaldsen's "Four Seasons," and over the mantel there is an engraving of "Washington Crossing the Delaware." A rocking chair and an armchair are in front of the grate fire. Lace curtains and heavy curtains are draped back from two French windows that look out on a covered piazza. There are a desk, a bookcase with glass doors, a "centre table" on which stands a double, green-shaded "Student's lamp," a few novels, and some magazines. Near the bookcase is a stand holding a "Rogers' Group." There are jars and bowls filled with flowers everywhere.*

Rand enters with the New York evening papers, The Post, The Sun; he half yawns, half sighs with fatigue. He starts to make his armchair ready before the fire; stops and goes over to his desk, where he finds a letter which he dislikes, recognizing the handwriting.

RAND: [*Angry*] Yes, still keeping it up, the young blackguard! [*He tears the letter in two, and throws it into the fire without reading it.*

He watches it burn a second, lighting a cigar; then takes his papers, makes himself comfortable in his chair before the fire, and starts to read. After a second, Mrs. Rand and Cicely, a very pretty girl of about seventeen, enter. Mrs. Rand carries a pitcher of water, scissors, and a newspaper. Cicely has her arms full of yellow tulips and a big bowl]

MRS. RAND: Why, father! Aren't you home early? Teresa's train won't be in for an hour or so yet. [*Mrs. Rand, filling the bowl with water, spreads the newspaper on the table; then cuts off the stems, and hands the flowers one by one to Cicely, who arranges them*]

RAND: I felt tired to-day, Molly. My head bothers me!

MRS. RAND: [*Going to him with affection and solicitude*] Why don't you lie down? [*She lays her hand on his head*] You haven't any fever. [*She kisses his forehead*] You're just overtired! [*He pats her hand affectionately, and holds it*] When are you going to give up business entirely, darling, and leave it all to George?

RAND: Never, I'm afraid, dear. [*Letting go her hand*] I've tried to face the idea, but the idleness appalls me.

CICELY: Mother, have you the scissors?

821

MRS. RAND: Yes, dear. [*Joins her, and continues with the flowers*]

RAND: Besides, George is too restless, too discontented yet, for me to trust him with my two banks! He's got the New York bee in his bonnet.

CICELY: [*Glances at her mother before she speaks*] Oh! We all have that, father, – except you.

RAND: And mother!

CICELY: Humph! Mother's just as bad as the rest of us. Only she's afraid to say so. [*Smiling*] Go on, mother, own up you've got villiageitis and cityphobia!

MRS. RAND: [*Smiling*] I *dare*, only I don't want to bother your father!

RAND: That's the effect of George – and Teresa. I've noticed all the innuendos in her letters home. Europe's spoiled the girl! The New York school started the idea, but I hoped travel would cure her, and instead – !

MRS. RAND: Wait till you see her. Remember, in spite of letters, what a year may have done for her. Oh, I'm so eager to see her! What a long hour this is! [*The telephone bell rings out in the hall. Mrs. Rand goes out and is heard saying,* "Hello! Yes, who is it? Oh, is it you, Katherine?"]

RAND: [*Reading his paper*] Who's that talking to your mother?

CICELY: One of Middleburg's Social Queens, Mrs. Mulholland – known in our society as the lady who can wear a décolleté gown, cut in accordance with the Middleburg limit, and not look as if she'd dressed in a hurry and forgotten her collar!

Rand laughs

MRS. RAND: [*Off stage*] Really! I should think she was much too old to be so advanced in the styles as that!

CICELY: The flowers are lovely all over the house. Father, you ought to see them! They came from a New York florist. [*Mrs. Rand off stage* "Good-by. See you at five."] Our man here hadn't anything but ferns and aniline-dyed pinks.

MRS. RAND: [*Reenters*] Kate Mulholland called up to tell me Mary Carterson's mother-in-law is visiting her from South Norwalk, and went down street this morning wearing one of those new washtub hats, – and she's sixty, if she isn't over! She was born in 1846, – at least she *used* to be!

RAND: [*Still reading*] When do you expect your crowd to come this afternoon?

CICELY: Crowd? [*She laughs derisively*] The only thing that can get a crowd in Middleburg is a fire or a funeral!

MRS. RAND: As we expect Teresa at four, I asked everybody to come in at five. But you know, father, "*everybody*" in Middleburg isn't *many*!

CICELY: Not many – nor *much*!

RAND: You have the best the town affords, and it's good old stock!

CICELY: I'm afraid Tess'll think it's rather tame for a girl who has been presented at *two European courts*!

MRS. RAND: Yes, I'm afraid she'll find it awfully dull. Don't you think, father, we could go to New York, if only for the winter months?

RAND: Don't tell me *you're* ambitious, too?

MRS. RAND: Well, I've done all, in a social way, a woman can in Middleburg, and I want to do more.

CICELY: You can't tell the difference in Middleburg between a smart afternoon tea and a Mother's Meeting, or a Sunday-school teacher's conclave, or a Lenten Sewing Circle, or a Fair for the Orphan Asylum, or any other like "Event"! It's always the same old people and the same old thing! Oh, Lord, we live in a cemetery!

RAND: Molly, wouldn't you rather be *it* in Middleburg – than *nit* in the City?

MRS. RAND: But with your influence and our friends, – we'd take letters, – I would soon have the position your wife was entitled to in the City, too.

CICELY: I don't care a darn about the position, if I can only have something to do, and something to see! Who wants to smell new-mown hay if he can breathe in gasoline on Fifth Avenue instead! Think of the theatres! the crowds! *Think* of being able to go out on the street and *see some one you didn't know even by sight!*

RAND: [*Laughs, amused*] Molly! How can *you* deceive yourself? A banker from a small country town would give you about as much position as he could afford to pay for on the West Side, above Fifty-ninth Street.

MRS. RAND: But, *George* said you'd been asked to join a big corporation in New York, which would make the family's everlasting fortune, and social position beside.

RAND: [*Looks up, angry*] George had no right telling you that. I told him only in confidence. What is this anyway, – a family conspiracy?

CICELY: No, it is the American legation shut up in Peking, longing for a chance to escape from social starvation.

RAND: [*Thoroughly irritated*] Now listen! This has got to stop, once and for all! So long as I'm the head of this family, it's going to *keep its head* and not lose it! And our home is *here*, and *will be here*, if to hold it I have to die in harness.

MRS. RAND: [*Going to him affectionately*] Father, don't be angry! You know *your will is law* with all of us. And so long as you want it, we'll stay right here.

CICELY: Giving teas to the wallflower brigade, and dinners to the Bible class! And our cotillion favors will be articles appropriate for the missionaries' boxes! Oh, Lord!

RAND: Mother, Cicely has convinced me of *one thing*.

CICELY: [*Delighted*] Not really! Good! What?

RAND: *You* go to no *finishing school* in *New York*! You get *finished* all you're going to, right here in Middleburg. New York would completely turn your head!

CICELY: Well, don't worry; Middleburg will "*finish*" me all right! Good and strong! Maybe New York would turn your head, but Middleburg turns my – [*She is going to say "Stomach," but her mother interrupts*]

MRS. RAND: Cicely!

Enter George. He is a handsome, clean-cut young American, of about twenty-seven

GEORGE: Hello, everybody!

RAND: [*Surprised*] Hello, George! What's the matter? It's only half past four! Nothing happened in the office?

GEORGE: Nothing! *All day!* That's why I am here. I thought I'd be in good time for Tess; and, so far as missing anything *really doing in the office* is concerned, I could have left at ten this morning – [*Adds half aside*] or almost any morning, *in this – our city!*

CICELY: Look out! The word "*city*" is a red rag to a bull with father, to-day! And it's for good in the graveyard! I'm going to dress. Thank the Lord, I've actually got somebody new to look smart for, if it's only my sister! [*Yawns and starts to go*]

RAND: Who's coming to your tea party?

CICELY: [*As she goes out*] All the names are on the tombstones in the two churchyards, plus Miss Carterson's mother-in-law from South Norwalk!

MRS. RAND: I must dress, too. [*Going over to Rand*] Dear, aren't you going to change your coat, and help me?

RAND: Oh, Molly, don't ask me to bore myself with your old frumps!

MRS. RAND: *I have to!* And I don't know that *I* take any more interest than *you* do in what sort of a hat Mary Carterson's mother is wearing! But if it were in New York –

RAND: [*Sneers*] Stop! I meant what I said – let's drop that!

MRS. RAND: All right, – I didn't say anything!

GEORGE: Look here, father, – mother's right.

RAND: [*Interrupting*] No, *you* do the "*looking,*" George, and straight *in my eyes!* [*He does so*] Your mother's wrong, but it isn't *her* fault, – it's *you* children.

MRS. RAND: [*Remonstrating*] Now, father –

GEORGE: But we're *not children*, and that's the mistake you make! *I'm* twenty-seven.

MRS. RAND: Yes, father, you forget, – George is twenty-seven!

GEORGE: I'm no longer a *boy!*

RAND: Then why did you tell your mother about this offer I had from New York, when I told you it was absolutely *confidential!* And a man in business knows what the word "*confidential*" means.

MRS. RAND: It was *my* fault; *I* wormed it out of George!

GEORGE: Nonsense, mother! [*To his father*] I told, because I thought you needed a good, big hump, and I believed, if all of us put our shoulders to it, we could move you.

RAND: Out of Middleburg?

GEORGE: Yes!

RAND: *Into New York?*

GEORGE: Yes!

RAND: Listen, George, –

GEORGE: [*Going on*] What position is there for a fellow like me in a hole like this?

Rand tries to interrupt

MRS. RAND: [*Stops him*] No, father, let George have his say out!

RAND: All right! Come on, George, we'll have it out now, – but this must *settle it!*

GEORGE: You grew up with this town. You and Middleburg reached your prime together, – so she's good enough for you. Besides, you are *part of it*, so you haven't any point of view, – you're too close!

RAND: What's good enough for your father ought to be good enough for you.

MRS. RAND: That's true, George.

GEORGE: *Grandfather Rand* was a real estate dealer in East Middleburg, with an income of about two thousand a year. I notice *your father's limit* wasn't good enough for you!

RAND: No, but *my* father turned me loose, without a cent, to make my own way! *Your* father will leave you the *richest man in your town*, – with the best established name, with two banks as safe as Gibraltar behind you!

GEORGE: But, I tell you, Middleburg and her banks are just as picayune to *me*, in comparison with the City and a *big career there*, as *East Middleburg* and *real estate* were to *you* in 1860!

RAND: Good God, how little you know of the struggle and fight *I* went through!

GEORGE: No, sir! Good God –

RAND: [*Interrupting*] Don't swear before your father. I don't like it!

GEORGE: Well – what *you* don't realize is that *I* am just starving after a big fight and a big struggle – for even bigger stakes than *you* fought for! I'm my father's own son – [*Going up to him with a sudden impulse of pride and affection, and putting his arm about his shoulder*] Accept this great city chance, father! There's millions in it, *and no fight!* They're offering the position to you on a gold plate. All I'll ask of you afterward is to launch me. Give me a start; the rest will be up to me! All I'll ask you to do then is *watch*.

RAND: No, I'm too old now.

MRS. RAND: Now *I* must join in! It's ridiculous you calling yourself too old. Besides, it reflects on me! [*Smiling*] Men and women of our age in the City dress and act just as young as their children, more or less. *Old age* has gone out of fashion! There's no such thing, except in dull little *country towns!*

GEORGE: Exactly! That's just what stagnation in the small place does for you. Come to the City, father! It'll give you a new lease of life!

RAND: No, I *don't want* to!

GEORGE: I wouldn't have the selfish courage to go on persuading you, if I didn't feel you'd be *glad of it in the end*. And besides, you're *one* against *all the rest* of us, – Mother, Teresa, Cicely – we're all choking here, dying of exasperation, *dry-rotting* for *not enough to do!*

RAND: Not at all! It's only amusement and excitement you children are after, and you've inoculated your mother with the germ.

MRS. RAND: No! If I'm restless and dissatisfied here, it's my own fault. I sympathize with Teresa having to come back to this, after New York and all Europe. I'm tired, myself, of our humdrum, empty existence. I'm tired of being the leading woman in a society where there's nobody to lead! I'm tired of the narrow point of view here! I'm tired of living to-day on yesterday's news, and wearing styles adapted to what Middleburg will stand for! I sympathize with Cicely. I want her to have a chance with the *real* world – not our expurgated edition! I know what she means when she says the quiet of the country gets on her nerves! that the birds keep her awake! that she longs for the rest of a cable-car and the lullaby of a motor-bus! Yes, I want the City for myself, but even more for my children, and most of all for George to make a name and career for himself!

RAND: You've all got an exaggerated idea of the importance of the City. This country isn't *made* or run by New York or its half dozen sisters! It's in the smaller towns, – and spread all over the country, – that you find the bone and sinew of the United States!

GEORGE: But for a young man to make a career for himself – I don't mean in business only, – in politics, in –

RAND: [*Interrupting*] You don't need the *City!* What's the matter with here?

GEORGE: Look at what Bert Vorhees has done, going to New York! He's going to be District Attorney, they say. And how long has he been there? Five or six years! I had a long talk with Eleanor Vorhees when she was here last month; it's wonderful what Bert's accomplished! And look at Eleanor herself! By George, she's the finest girl I've ever seen!

RAND: Still, did Lincoln need New York? Did Grant? Did a metropolis turn out McKinley, or have anything to do with forming the character and career of Grover Cleveland? You're cheating yourself, if you're honest in your talk with me! All you want of the City is what you can get out of it, – not what you can do for it!

GEORGE: No, you judge from your own point of view! Middleburg makes you look through the wrong end of the opera-glass. You *can't* judge from *my* point of view.

RAND: When you're *my* age, if you've kept as abreast of the times as I have, you'll be lucky. But if you're in New York, you won't have had time. There, you'll know one thing to perfection – but only one – where your interests are centered! All city men specialize – they have to *get* success, and *keep* it! Every walk in life, there, is a marathon! But the worst of it is, the goal isn't stationary. It's like the horizon, – no man can reach it!

GEORGE: But why blame the City?

RAND: Because the City turns ambition into selfish greed! There, no matter what you get, you want more! And when you've got more, at God knows what price sometimes, it's not enough! There's no such thing as being satisfied! First, you want to catch up with your neighbor; then you want to pass him; and then you die disappointed if you haven't left him out of sight!

MRS. RAND: I'm afraid your father's determined. And forty years with him has taught me two things, – first, when he *is* determined, you might just as well realize it in the beginning; and second, in the end you're sure to *be glad he was!*

RAND: Thank you, Molly. And I was never more determined than I am this time.

MRS. RAND: [*With a sigh of half-amused resignation*] Then I'll go and put on the dress I got in New York, which the dressmaker said I'd made her spoil in order that my neighbors at home shouldn't say I'd gone out of my senses. [*She exits*]

GEORGE: Well father, if *you* won't leave, let me go away! Let me go to the City on my own account. Bert Vorhees has been urging me to come for over a year. He says politics in the City are crying for just such new, clean men as me. He wants me to help *him;* that, in itself, is a big opening. I won't ask for any help from you. Just let me go, as *your father* let *you* go, to work out, myself, my own salvation!

RAND: Your own damnation it would be! No, sir, you stay here as long as I live and have any power over or influence with you.

GEORGE: Suppose *I'm* stubborn as *you* are, and go, even if it has to be against your will.

RAND: Look here, boy! You're trained in my methods, for my job. Those methods are all right for Middleburg, where I'm known and respected. No one has been to this town more, in a civic way, than I have. The Park Street Congregational Church couldn't have been built, nor halfway supported as it has been, without my help; and I could go on for some length, if I liked, in much the same sort of strain. What *I* do in this town is *right*. But the public libraries of Middleburg wouldn't help me in the City, nor the Park Street Church be a sufficient guarantee for my banking methods, to let me risk myself in the hornet's nest New York is at present.

GEORGE: [*Almost laughing at the idea*] You don't mean you would be afraid of any investigation – ?

RAND: *Here*, no! I've always kept to the right side of the line, but I've kept very close, and the line may be *drawn* differently here. My conscience is clear, George, but my common sense is a good watch-dog.

The Maidservant enters

MAIDSERVANT: Here's a man says he has an appointment with you, sir.

RAND: [*Startled and a little angry*] *No one* has an appointment with me!

MAIDSERVANT: Well, I didn't know!

Enter Hannock, during the speech. The Maidservant looks a little alarmed at what she has done, as she goes out

HANNOCK: [*Very hard*] I told you, in the letter I sent here to-day, I was going to call this afternoon.

RAND: I destroyed that letter without reading it, – as I have the last half dozen you've sent me.

HANNOCK: That's what made it necessary for me to call in person!

George looks from one to the other, dumbfounded

GEORGE: Father?

RAND: [*To Hannock, referring to George*] This is my son. I'm glad he is here, to be a witness. Go ahead! I take it, as you seem to be *in the business*, you've made yourself acquainted with the *law of blackmail!*

HANNOCK: I know what you've already told me – but I don't give a damn! I've got nothing to lose, and nothing to get, except money, from you. *You won't jail me*, anyway, for you know a trial here would ruin *you*, no matter what happened to me!

GEORGE: Here, you – !

RAND: [*Taking a step forward*] No, George! Keep your temper. This man says I ruined his mother – [*In great shame and emotion*]

GEORGE: [*To Hannock*] You liar!

HANNOCK: Then why did he give her a regular allowance till she died? and why did he keep on giving to me? – for a while!

RAND: George, I feel badly. Get me some whiskey and water. [*George hurries out. Rand, in rising anger*] I kept on giving to you, till I found out you were a sot and a degenerate blackguard – a drug fiend and a moral criminal. I kept on helping you after three houses of correction had handled you, and one prison! *Then I stopped!* What was the use, – money was only helping you on!

HANNOCK: Still, for my mother's sake, you can't let me *starve!* You oughtn't to have torn up those letters; then you'd have had the blackmail in writing. I told you, if you didn't give me what I want, I'd print your letters to my mother right here in this town. The anti-saloon paper, that hates you for not joining its movement, would be glad to get them and show you up for a God damn whited sepulchre!

RAND: [*Quiet, controlling himself by a terrific effort*] And suppose that didn't frighten me!

HANNOCK: I've just got on to something bigger yet, I can use by way of a lever! The two years you had me working in the bank, I kept my eyes open. If it hadn't been for the yellow streak in me, I guess I'd have made a banker, all right. I liked it, and I seem to catch on to things sorter by instinct. You were the *big thing*, and I watched and studied your methods to make 'em mine!

RAND: Well?

HANNOCK: Yes! "Well," by God! I guess you realize just as plain as I do that those very methods in New York, that have been raising hell with the insurance companies and all sorts of corporations, aren't a patch on some of *your deals* I know of! And I tell you, if there should be a State investigation in Middleburg, you'd go under as sure as I stand here; and if I had to go to prison, I'd stand a sure chance of passing you in the yard some day – wearing the same old stripes yourself.

RAND: [*In a paroxysm of rage*] It's a lie! It's a lie! Just to get money out of me! I told you, before you began, you'd come to blackmail! [*He chokes*]

HANNOCK: Well, you know how to prove it! Have me arrested; charge me with it; and *let the whole thing be thrashed out!* [*A second's pause*] Aw – you don't dare. You know you don't!

Enter Cicely, looking girlishly lovely in a fresh white dress and corn-colored sash

CICELY: Father, aren't you going to dress – and help us?

Hannock looks at Cicely, admiring her

RAND: Excuse me, Cicely, I'm engaged just now.

CICELY: I beg your pardon. [*She goes out*]

HANNOCK: [*Following her with his eyes*] She's growing into a lovely girl, your daughter! It would be a pity – [*He speaks in broken sentences*]

RAND: [*Giving in*] How much do you want?

HANNOCK: I want two thousand dollars.

RAND: For how long?

HANNOCK: *For as long as it lasts!*

RAND: [*With a reaction*] No, I won't do it! You'll gamble, or squander this in some low way, and be back before the week's out! What's the use! I can't keep this up for ever!

HANNOCK: [*Bringing a pistol out of his pocket, quickly*] Do you see that? [*He puts it on the desk*]

RAND: [*Greatly frightened*] Good God!

HANNOCK: Don't be frightened! It's not for *you.* I'm no murderer! It's for myself.

RAND: [*Suffering from shock*] How do you mean?

HANNOCK: [*Taking up the pistol, and handling it almost affectionately*] I'm never without it. And when I can't get anything more out of you, when I'm clean empty, – not a crust, or drink, or drug to be had, – then I'll take this friend to my heart, so – [*Placing pistol over his heart*]

RAND: [*Frightened, calls feebly*] George!

HANNOCK: Oh, not yet! [*Taking pistol from his chest*] I'm not ready yet. But remember, when you've signed your last check for me, *you will be responsible for this.* [*He touches the pistol; then hides it quickly in his pocket, as George enters with whiskey and water*]

GEORGE: I'm sorry to take so long, but I had to persuade mother not to come with me, when she heard you were faint. And I thought you wouldn't want –

RAND: Yes, quite right – [*He drinks, excitedly, tremblingly, feebly*]

GEORGE: [*To Hannock*] You can see my father is ill; surely, ordinary human feeling will make you realize to-day is no time for you to –

RAND: [*Interrupting*] It's all right, George. Hannock and I have had it out while you were gone. [*Writing a check*] We understand each other now!

HANNOCK: I've made my position quite clear to your father.

RAND: [*Giving Hannock the check*] Here – and for God's sake try to behave yourself! [*Looking at him intently, with a strange, almost yearning look, as if he really cared whether Hannock behaved himself or not*] Try to do right!

HANNOCK: Thanks for your advice *and money!* [*To George*] Good-by!

RAND: Good-by!

George only nods his head, looking at Hannock with unconcealed dislike. Hannock goes out. Rand sinks on his arms, his head falling on the table. George goes to him in alarm

GEORGE: Father!

RAND: I'm not well. I've felt dizzy all day. It was more than I could stand!

GEORGE: I don't approve of your giving him money! Till you once take a firm stand, there'll never be any let up.

RAND: But I owe it to him, George! I owe it to him.

GEORGE: Nonsense! What sort of a woman was his mother?

RAND: She was a dressmaker in East Middleburg; hadn't a very good reputation. I doubt very much if what he says is *true.*

GEORGE: *Well then?*

RAND: Yes, but more than he knows *is true!* – and worse!

GEORGE: How do you mean?

RAND: Yes, the whole thing is more than I can carry any longer! I'm too old! Your younger shoulders must help me bear it, George. It breaks my heart to tell you, and shames me, George, but I must unburden myself. Besides, I need help – I need advice! And besides, you'll see how you can't go away and leave me alone here! [*He rises in fear and excitement*] I'm your father, and you've got to stand by me and help me! I can't stand alone any longer!

GEORGE: Father! [*He goes to him*]

RAND: Promise me, George, promise me you won't leave me here! You'll stand by me!

GEORGE: Yes, father, *I promise you!*

RAND: [*Sinks back exhausted into his chair. A second's pause*] That man who just left here don't know it, but – [*He stops from dread and shame of finishing*]

GEORGE: But what?

RAND: I'm his father!

GEORGE: [*Astounded*] That *fellow's?*

RAND: *That* fellow's!

GEORGE: *Then of course he knows it!*

RAND: No, it would be a stronger lever for money than any he has used, and he doesn't hesitate to use the strongest he can find – or *invent!* In return for the financial arrangement I made with her, his mother swore he should never know. As a matter of fact, she was anxious, for her own sake, to keep it quiet. She moved to Massachusetts, passed herself off as a widow, and married a man named Hannock, there; but he died, and so back she came, passing off this boy, *here*, as Hannock's son! [*He groans*] What a story for a father to own up to, before a son like you. [*After a second's pause*]

GEORGE: Don't think of that! *Don't mind me!* After all, I'm a twentieth century *son*, you know, and *New York at heart!*

RAND: Of course your mother's never dreamed. *That* I couldn't bear –

GEORGE: That's right. Mother's not me, – she's *nineteenth century* and Middleburg!

RAND: Now, you see I do owe this young man something. I can't shut my eyes to it!

GEORGE: Yes. I'm even wondering, father, if you don't owe him – the *truth!*

RAND: No, no, I couldn't trust him with it!

GEORGE: *Still*, father, don't *you owe it to him?* Even more than money! And don't you suppose he suspects it, anyway?

RAND: No, and he *mustn't know.* He'd tell *everybody!* It would be my ruin; and your mother? – break her heart, – and for what good?

GEORGE: [*With a sudden idea*] Father, why not come to the City and escape him?

RAND: Escape him! He'd follow! That's his hunting ground! When you came back home from college, I'd had him in the bank a couple of years. But I didn't want you two to meet, so I got him a good place in Boston. But in six months he'd lost it, and was mixed up in some scrape in New York! No! Remember, George, you gave me your promise you wouldn't leave me! You'll stay with me here. We must take care of this man, of course, for our own sakes, as well as his. I am his father!

GEORGE: And I'm his brother, and Cicely and Tess are his sisters! It's hard lines on him! I can't help feeling, father, we owe him a good deal.

RAND: You'll stand by me – so long as I live. [*Excitedly*] Promise me solemnly!

GEORGE: I have promised you, father.

RAND: And, if anything should ever happen to *me*, you'd look after – Hannock, wouldn't you, George?

GEORGE: Yes, father. I consider you – we – owe Hannock a future!

RAND: But you'll keep my secret – promise me that, too!

GEORGE: I give you my word of honor, father.

RAND: [*Half collapses and sways*] I feel so badly again! I – I'm going to my room to lie down. Don't let them disturb me till suppertime. [*George goes to help him out. Rand smiles, though with an effort*] No, no! I'm not so far gone as all that, – not yet a while,

boy, not quite yet – ! [*Goes out alone*]

GEORGE: [*Coming back*] Who'd *have thought it! Who'd have thought it! Father!* [*A heavy fall is heard in the hall outside. George looks up, and then starts on, but stops and lifts his head suddenly to listen. A look of fright and dread is on his face. Then he turns to the door and walks into the hall. A moment after, off stage, he cries, "Father!"*]

The following scene takes place off stage

MRS. RAND: [*In a voice of excitement*] What was it? Father? Did he faint? [*Calling*] James! James, bring me water, *quick!*

GEORGE: I'll telephone for the doctor. I'll get Dr. Hull from across the street. He'll be the quickest. [*Passes by the door from Left to Right. The telephone bell is heard. The Maidservant hurries past the door with water*] Hello. Give me sixteen –

MRS. RAND: [*To Maidservant*] Is John in the kitchen having his supper?

MAIDSERVANT: Yes, ma'am.

GEORGE: Hello?

MRS. RAND: Tell him to come here to help us carry Mr. Rand into the parlor, and you come right back.

MAIDSERVANT: Yes, ma'am. [*She again goes hurriedly past the door from Left to Right, as George is talking*]

GEORGE: [*At 'phone, off stage*] Is that you, Dr. Hull? Can you come right over? Father – looks to me like a stroke! Good-by. [*Rings telephone bell, and passes before the door on his way from Right to Left*]

MRS. RAND: I've sent for John. I thought between us we could carry him. [*Maidservant passes through hall from Right to Left*] Susan, get a pillow from upstairs, and put it on the sofa in the parlor, and send Miss Cicely.

MAIDSERVANT: Yes, ma'am.

Before doorway, John passes from Right to Left

GEORGE: Here, John! Father's very ill. John, we want to get him on to the sofa in the parlor.

CICELY: What's the matter? What is it, mother?

MRS. RAND: We don't know ourselves, dear, but we're waiting for Dr. Hull.

GEORGE: You hold his head up, mother. And John – that's right!

MRS. RAND: Give me the pillow, Susan, – help me.

GEORGE: Cicely, go into the library, close the door, and wait for me. As soon as the doctor comes – [*Front doorbell rings outside*]

MRS. RAND: There he is! Susan, go to the door.

Enter Cicely. She closes the door behind her, frightened, and leans against it, listening

CICELY: [*Whispers*] He's dead, – I know it, – he's *dead!* [*She carefully opens the door on a crack to listen. She sees Maidservant*] Susan! [*Maidservant approaches in the hall beyond the half open door*] Was it the doctor?

MAIDSERVANT: [*In doorway*] Yes, Miss.

CICELY: What did he say?

MAIDSERVANT: I don't know, Miss. I didn't go in the room.

JOHN: [*Appearing in the hall*] Susan! [*Whispers*]

CICELY: What is it, John? What does the doctor say?

JOHN: [*Embarrassed*] I – I – don't know, Miss. Mr. George'll tell you. He wants you, Susan, to telephone to his aunt, Mrs. Loring, and ask her to have word 'phoned round to the guests for this afternoon not to come. You're to say Mr. Rand has been taken suddenly ill, and will she come over at once.

MAIDSERVANT: All right. [*She goes*]

CICELY: Poor papa! He isn't dead, then?

Susan is heard ringing the 'phone

JOHN: Mr. George'll tell you. [*He goes off*]

MAIDSERVANT: Hello! Give me thirty-one, please.

George comes into the room to Cicely

CICELY: How is he?

GEORGE: Cicely!

CICELY: [*Frightened*] What?

MAIDSERVANT: [*Heard outside*] Is that Mrs. Loring, please – this is Susan –

George shuts the hall door; he puts his arm around Cicely

GEORGE: Cicely, father's dead.

CICELY: Oh, George! [*Bursts into tears*]

GEORGE: [*Putting his arms around her again*] Cicely, dear, don't cry, little girl! Go upstairs to mother; she wants you. And stay with her till Aunt Nellie comes –

CICELY: [*Crying*] Oh, poor mother, poor mother! [*Cicely goes out, leaving door open*]

MAIDSERVANT: [*Off stage at the telephone*] Yes ma'am. Good-by.

GEORGE: Susan?

MAIDSERVANT: [*In the doorway*] Yes, sir?

GEORGE: If any strangers come to the door to ask questions, tell them nothing. Do you know Mr. Straker?

MAIDSERVANT: No, sir.

GEORGE: Well, he's on the evening newspaper here. He's sure to hear we've put off our little party, and come around to find out. If any one asks, never mind who, – you know nothing except that Mr. Rand was taken suddenly sick. That's all. You don't know how, or what it is. You understand?

MAIDSERVANT: Yes, sir.

GEORGE: All right. [*Nods to her to go. She goes out. He walks over to the desk and looks where his father sat and stood*] Why, it was only a minute ago he was there, talking with me! It doesn't seem possible – that now – he's dead – dead – [*He wipes the tears out of his eyes, and gives a long sigh; sinks in the seat*] gone for good out of this life! I don't understand it! What does it all mean? [*He is staring straight ahead of him. Suddenly a thought comes to him and takes possession of him*] I know one thing it *means for me!* – [*He rises and stands straight*] It means *New York.* [*There is a tapping on the glass of the window. He doesn't hear it at first. It is Teresa, outside, tapping. She taps again. He looks up and sees her*] Tess!! [*He hurries to the window and opens it*] Tess! [*Embraces her enthusiastically*]

TERESA: I thought I'd stroll in and surprise you! It's the same old room! – [*Smiling around, as she recognizes things*] not a thing changed! – nor in the town, either, from the smelly old barn of a depot – past the same gray houses with the empty old iron urns, right up to *ours,* – bigger and uglier than all the rest! Nothing's changed! And oh, George, how can I live here? I'll never be able to stand it! I can't do it! I know I can't do it! [*Kisses him again*]

GEORGE: Tess! You won't have to! We're going to live in New York!

TERESA: George!! What do you mean?

GEORGE: We're going to live in the City!

TERESA: Oh, George! You don't know how much

that means to me! I can be married in New York, then!

GEORGE: [*Amazed*] Married!

TERESA: Sh! That's my surprise! Heavens, how hard it's been to keep it out of my letters! I met him first in Egypt, and then he joined us at Nice, at Paris, and in London, and *there* he proposed.

GEORGE: But who?

TERESA: I just told you!

GEORGE: [*Smiling*] No, you didn't!

TERESA: Oh! Donald Van Vranken.

GEORGE: Don Van Vranken?

TERESA: Yes! Think what my position will be in New York!

GEORGE: But Tess! He's the fastest fellow going! He's notorious! Look at the scandals that have been more or less public property about him. It's the last one that drove him abroad, afraid of the witness bench!

TERESA: Oh, you can't believe everything you hear! He's a handsome darling, and I love him, and he loves me, – so don't worry!

GEORGE: But I can't help worrying! Your happiness isn't safe with a man like Don Van Vranken.

TERESA: Oh, come, you haven't been away from Middleburg enough! Here, *maybe*, the husbands do go to the altar like Easter lilies! But in the City, you don't marry a man for what he has or hasn't been; you marry him for what he is and what you hope he's going to be! But I did dread a wedding here – with his people and friends! How in the world did you *persuade father?*

A second's pause, as George suddenly comes back with a terrific shock

GEORGE: Good God! I forgot! I've some awful news!

TERESA: Mother – !

GEORGE: No, – father.

TERESA: What? – not – ?

GEORGE: Yes. To-day, – just a little while ago! Suddenly – in a second! His heart gave out – I was talking with him two minutes before.

TERESA: Oh, poor mother! Where is she? Let me go to her!

GEORGE: She's up in her room.

TERESA: Mother! – [*As she goes out in great distress, she is heard again in the distance*] Mother!!

GEORGE: [*Stands where she left him – alone – his head bowed. He straightens up, and lifts his head; and his face flushes with the uncontrolled impulses of youth and ambition. With a voice of suppressed excitement, full of emotion, and with a trembling ring of triumph, he says*] The CITY . . . !

The Curtain Falls

ACT II

SCENE: *Several years later. The library in the Rands' house in New York. The walls are panelled in light walnut. Two French windows, with the sun shining in, are on the left. There are small doors, Right and Left Centre, opening into other rooms. Between the bookcases, which occupy most of the wall space, are marble busts, standing in deep niches. There are flowers about. The sofa, chairs, hangings, and cushions are of golden yellow brocade, except one big armchair, upholstered in red, standing in front of the open wood fire. A Sargent portrait is built in over the mantel. A small typewriting table is at one side. Almost in the centre of the room, with chairs grouped near it, is a long carved table, with all the desk fittings of a luxurious but busy man; there is also a bunch of violets on it, in a silver goblet – and at present it is strewn with papers, etc.*

Foot is arranging the fire. There is a knock at the door. Hannock enters. He comes in, in evident and only partly suppressed, nervous excitement. He wears a white flower in his buttonhole.

HANNOCK: Hello, Foot. Is Mr. Rand out?

FOOT: Yes, sir. [*Rises, having finished the fire*]

HANNOCK: He left no message for me?

FOOT: Yes, sir. He left some papers on the desk, which he said he'd like you to go over carefully, at once, and two letters he wanted you to answer.

HANNOCK: All right. Get me a package of longish papers, with an elastic band around them, in my overcoat in the hall.

FOOT: Yes, sir.

HANNOCK: Has the stenographer been here?

FOOT: Yes, but he's gone; said he couldn't wait any longer, as he has an appointment.

HANNOCK: [*Angry; making nervous, irritable movements*] He'll be sorry! I'll see to it he loses Mr. Rand's job, that's all, if he don't knuckle down to me!

FOOT: Yes, sir. It's none of my business, but Mr. Rand didn't like your being late. He said you knew it was an important day for him, and he couldn't understand it.

HANNOCK: He'll understand all right when I explain! It's an *important day* for *me* too!

FOOT: [*Eagerly*] Is he going to get the nomination for governor, sir?

HANNOCK: Nothing surer! – except his election. That'll be a knockout, and then you'll see us both forging ahead.

FOOT: I'm sure I wish you luck, sir.

HANNOCK: Thanks! Oh, yes, I shall tie my fortune up to Mr. Rand's!

FOOT: Yes, sir – [*He goes out*]

HANNOCK: Yes, sir, [*Imitating Foot*] – *damned* "*important*" day for me, too! Phew! [*A great sigh, showing he is carrying something big on his mind*] I wonder just how he'll take it? I wish it was over. [*He goes to the typewriting table, rummages in a drawer, takes out a little box, containing a hypodermic needle, and tries it; then, putting it to his arm just above the wrist, he presses it, half grinning and mumbling to himself, – looking furtively over his shoulder, fearing an interruption. Just as he finishes, the door opens. Cicely half comes in. She is in hat, gloves, etc.*]

CICELY: [*Half whispering*] You're back first. [*He nods, hiding the hypodermic needle*] I've just this minute come in, and I didn't meet a soul. I've sent for Eleanor Vorhees – she's the best.

Enter Teresa hurriedly, in great and angry emotional excitement, pushing past Cicely

TERESA: Good morning, Cicely. Where's George?

CICELY: Give it up! [*Following her in*]

HANNOCK: He'll be in soon, Mrs. Van Vranken. He's an appointment with Mr. Vorhees.

Enter Foot

FOOT: I can't find any papers with an elastic band, sir.

HANNOCK: [*Irritated*] Oh, well, perhaps there wasn't a band! Use your *common sense!* I'll look myself. [*To the ladies*] Excuse me. [*Goes out, followed by Foot*]

CICELY: What's the matter with you, Tess? Don on the loose again?

TERESA: I don't know and I don't care! I've *left* him.

CICELY: *Left your husband!* – for good? Honest? Or has *he* left you?

TERESA: What do you mean by that? That's a nice thing for my sister to say!

CICELY: My dear! – even donkeys – I mean sisters – have ears, – and you must know how every one has been talking about you and Jimmy Cairns!

TERESA: Well, if I can't depend upon my own family, I don't suppose I can expect my husband to protect me.

CICELY: After all, what can Don say? He can't find any fault with *you!*

TERESA: Exactly! – and I went to him, perfectly calm and reasonable, and said very sweetly: "Don, I'm going to divorce you. We needn't have any disagreeable feeling about it, or any scandal. I will simply bring the divorce, mentioning this woman" –

CICELY: Mrs. Judly?

TERESA: Of course – but doing it as quietly as possible, behind closed doors, or with sealed papers, or whatever they call it. Only, of course he must give me the children!

CICELY: Oh! – and he refused?

TERESA: *Absolutely refuses,* – and to let me get the divorce as I propose! He will only agree to a legal separation, the children's time to be divided between us. That's all he'll stand for.

CICELY: Let him agree to what he likes! You've got your case, all right. You could prove everything you want to, couldn't you?

TERESA: [*Getting angry*] Yes, but he – Oh, the beast! – he dares to *threaten!* If I attempt to do this, he'll bring a counter suit, mentioning Mr. Cairns!

CICELY: Tess!

TERESA: You see! He ties my hands!

CICELY: But not if he couldn't –

TERESA: Sh-h! Let's talk about something else. I don't want that horrid Hannock to know anything. I despise him!

CICELY: [*On the defensive*] I don't know why!

TERESA: Well, I'm not alone in my feelings. I don't know any one who *likes* him.

CICELY: Yes, you do, because *I'm* one.

TERESA: He always affects me like a person who would listen at keyholes!

CICELY: Some day you'll be very sorry you said that.

Hannock reenters

HANNOCK: Mr. Vorhees is here with Miss Vorhees.

CICELY: I asked Eleanor to come. [*She goes out to greet them*]

TERESA: [*To Hannock*] Let me know the minute Mr. Rand comes in. [*She goes out. Hannock takes up letters on desk which are for him to answer, goes to the typewriting table, and sits down to write, reading over to himself one of the letters – mumbling the words. He laughs to himself*]

HANNOCK: Ha! And I suppose he thinks this is legitimate business! – that *this sort of a deal* goes hand in hand with his "clean record," with his "white politics," with the Vorhees "good government." Humph! "Teddy, Jr." is a good nickname for him, – I guess not! The *public* would put George Rand in the Roosevelt class with a vengeance, wouldn't they! – if they were on to this one piece of manipulation! Following in father's footsteps, all right, and going popper one better! That's what! And he *pretends* to think his methods are on the level! All the same, I guess he is just as square as the rest of 'em. You can't tell me Vorhees isn't feathering *his nest* good! You bet *I'm* on to Vorhees! [*He looks up, half startled*] Damn it, when am I going to stop talking in my sleep when I'm wide awake? [*Looking at the place on his arm, and smoothing it over*] Too much of the needle, I guess!

Enter Servant with Vorhees. Servant goes out

VORHEES: Good morning, Hannock.

HANNOCK: Good morning, Mr. Vorhees. You're ten minutes early for your appointment, sir.

VORHEES: Mr. Rand is generally ready ahead of time. I thought I'd probably find him.

HANNOCK: He isn't here yet. I *hope* he gets the nomination for governor!

VORHEES: Well, I'm inclined to think it's all *up to him* now, Hannock, and that to-day will decide.

HANNOCK: Isn't it wonderful how far he's got in barely five years!

VORHEES: Well, it was Rand's good luck – to come along at the right psychological moment – the party tired of the political gambler, the manipulator. We wanted a candidate with just the freshness, the force and stability of a *small town's bringing up*. The whole of Middleburg, no matter what the party, will come forward unanimously, and speak for their young fellow townsman. His family is the boast of the place! His father's name stands for everything that's best and finest in public and private life, and, when George took hold in New York, with all the political vitality and straight-forward vigor of his blood and bringing up, and not only helped along *our reforms*, but *created new ones of his own*, giving his time and his strength and his money to the public good! Well, you know what the man in the street's been calling him for a year now?

HANNOCK: [*With a covert sneer*] "Teddy, Jr.!"

VORHEES: Yes, "Teddy Jr." That idea ought to land him in Albany, all right!

HANNOCK: [*With the bare suggestion of a bully's manner*] I hope, Mr. Vorhees, I haven't been altogether overlooked in all the enthusiasm.

VORHEES: [*With a big drop*] How do you mean?

HANNOCK: Well, I've been George Rand's right hand, you know! I've done my share of the work. Where do *I* come in on the *reward* end?

VORHEES: [*Strongly*] I *really* don't understand you.

HANNOCK: [*Smiling, but serious and determined, and speaking deliberately*] What do I get out of it?

VORHEES: [*After a pause*] You get a damned lot of pride in the man you've had the honor of serving, that's what you get!

HANNOCK: [*Angry at the snub, and suspicious that he is to be thrown down*] And a hell of a lot of good that'd do me! Look here, Mr. Vorhees, I might as well have my say out now! If George Rand wants to be elected Governor of New York, he and his electors have got to square me!

VORHEES: Why, you talk like a fool – or a scoundrel!

HANNOCK: Well, never mind what I talk *like;*

I know what I'm talking *about*, and I say there's something good in the way of a job coming to his confidential secretary out of "Gov." Rand's election!

Vorhees half laughs, half sneers, but still is slightly disturbed. George enters

GEORGE: Hello! Am I late? Sorry!

VORHEES: No, I'm early. Well!! Can we have our talk?

GEORGE: [*Smiling at himself*] I believe I'm nervous! Go ahead! Fire your first gun! [*Takes a chair. Hannock also sits*]

VORHEES: [*With a glance toward Hannock*] I'll wait, if you have any business to discuss with Mr. Hannock.

GEORGE: No, nothing in a hurry; that's all right, go on —

VORHEES: Well, if you don't mind, I'd like to talk with *you privately*.

GEORGE: Certainly. Would you mind, Hannock, waiting in —

VORHEES: [*Interrupting; to Hannock*] Eleanor's in the drawing-room. Cicely sent for her; wants her advice, I believe, about something or other, *very important!* [*Guying the latter with a smile*]

GEORGE: Well, suppose you go to my room, Hannock, and use the desk there.

HANNOCK: [*In a hard voice, reluctant to leave them*] Very good. [*Rises, takes papers, and starts to go*]

VORHEES: [*With the tone of a final good-by*] Good morning, Hannock.

HANNOCK: Good morning, sir. [*Stops at the door*] If I wanted to speak with you later on to-day, after I've had a talk with Mr. Rand, could I call you up on the 'phone, and make an appointment?

VORHEES: Certainly.

HANNOCK: [*In a satisfied voice*] Thank you. [*Goes out*]

GEORGE: Well?

VORHEES: How do you *feel?* Eager, eh?

GEORGE: That depends on what I'm going to get! I'm eager, all right, if you've come to tell me what I want to hear!!

VORHEES: You're *warm*, as the children say!

GEORGE: What wouldn't I give — that was honest to give — for this chance, not just to *talk*, not to *boast*, not to *promise*, only —

VORHEES: [*Interrupting him*] Exactly! That's exactly what we want — the man behind the gun in *front of the gun!* We don't want a Fourth of July orator *only*, in the Capitol! We want a man who'll be *doing something*, George!

GEORGE: [*Enthusiastically*] Every minute!!

VORHEES: We can hire a human phonograph to do the talking. The party's full of them!

GEORGE: I want to make *my name mean*, in this *whole country*, what *father's* meant in *that small, up-State town we came from!!*

VORHEES: Your name can take care of itself. Don't think of any glory *you're* going to get! You'll get most by keeping busy for the good of the State, for the welfare of the people —

GEORGE: [*Eagerly, not waiting for Vorhees to finish*] I know! But I'm going to show the gods and the demi-gods, the rabble and the riff-raff, that one good lesson we've learned from the success of the last administration is that the real leader of a party must be its independent choice, and not its tool.

VORHEES: [*Approving*] Right!

GEORGE: Machine politics are a *back number*. The public has got on to the engine, and smashed the works!

VORHEES: Man is greater than a machine, because God's soul is in him.

GEORGE: Yes, and what I'm going to show is that the soul of a political party is the uncompromising honesty of its leader.

VORHEES: Don't always be emphasizing the leader; — let it go at the *party's* honesty! You're inclined, George, to overemphasize the personal side of it! It's E Pluribus *Unum*, not E Pluribus *me*-um!

GEORGE: All right, all right! Only, don't forget that I've got an inordinate ambition, and you're dangling in front of my eyes the talisman that may land me, God knows how high!

VORHEES: Well, come back to earth! Now, I've come here with the nomination in one hand —

George draws a long, excited breath

GEORGE: And a *string* in the other?

VORHEES: Yes.

GEORGE: Well, give it to us!

VORHEES: The Committee decided it was up to me! I've known you as a boy. You're going to marry my sister. We're brothers practically.

I can speak frankly, without giving any offence – that's sure, isn't it?

GEORGE: Nothing surer!

VORHEES: It's just this! Of course the minute you're nominated, our political opponents will get busy! The muckrakes are all ready!

GEORGE: You bet they are, and the searchlights haven't any Foolish Virgins in charge of them. They're trimmed, all right, and filled with *gasoline!*

VORHEES: [*Very seriously*] You can stand it, George?

GEORGE: I can.

VORHEES: You've got a wonderful popularity, and the Committee believes in you, but it wants your word confirming its confidences, – that's all.

GEORGE: That's the least it can ask.

VORHEES: Is there anything in your life that isn't absolutely above board, George? No skeleton in your heart, or your *cupboard?* It's safe for us to put you up? You're sure not a particle of the mud they'll rake can stick?

GEORGE: Not a particle.

VORHEES: Look back a little. Sometimes I think you're a little *too* cocksure of yourself. No man can be, absolutely, till he's been tried in the furnace, and you haven't been, yet. But we're getting the fires ready! [*Smiles*] You're all right at heart, I'm sure of it. Nobody in this world believes more in you than *I* do, – [*Again smiling*] except, perhaps, you yourself. But there's nothing, nothing that could be ferreted out? You know they'll dig, and dig, and dig!!

GEORGE: But I give you my word of honor, so help me God, I've never done a dishonest or dishonorable act, or an act –

VORHEES: [*Interrupting*] In business?

GEORGE: [*Hesitates just one moment*] You know what my father stood for, – and my business methods *he* taught me. I've gone ahead of him, of course, – gone on with the times, – but on the road father blazed for me! I've not deviated from a single principle.

VORHEES: Good! I know what George Rand, Sr., stood for in Middleburg! That's good enough for me. And in your private life? Oh, this is just going through the form; personally, I'd stake my life on your answer, and Eleanor's instinct would have kept her from loving you.

GEORGE: I was brought up in a small town, in the old-fashioned family life that's almost ancient history in the bigger cities. I loved my father and my mother, and their affection meant everything to me. From their influence, I went under Eleanor's. You needn't have one worry about my private life.

VORHEES: Of course I knew you were clean and above board, but different men have different ideas about some things.

GEORGE: Listen, – I'm no little tin god! I'm as full of faults as the next man, but I'm not afraid to own up my mistakes; I'm not afraid to tell the truth to my own disadvantage; I'm not afraid to stand or fall by my sincere conviction! In a word, I'm game to be put to any test you or the party want to put me, and I'll stand straight as I know how, so long as there's a drop or a breath of life left in me!

VORHEES: Then that's all! And unofficially – *unofficially* – I can tell you, barring the unexpected accident, the nomination is yours! [*Holding out his hand, he grips George's in his*]

GEORGE: *Isn't it great? It's wonderful!* Oh, God, if *I* can only do it big!

VORHEES: You mean do it *well!*

GEORGE: [*Taken aback only for a second*] Er – yes, of course – same thing! – Do half I dream of and want to!

VORHEES: [*Smiling*] Well – I'm taking any bets!!

GEORGE: I owe the whole business to you, you know, and *I* know it!

VORHEES: Nonsense! With that overwhelming ambition of yours! Perhaps I taught you your *primer* of politics, your *grammar* of public life; that's all – except that I'm a *damned proud* teacher!!!

Enter Foot

FOOT: Mr. Van Vranken must see you at once, sir, – says it's very urgent.

GEORGE: All right.

VORHEES: Say in two or three minutes.

FOOT: Yes, sir. [*Goes out*]

VORHEES: There is just one more thing before I can go.

GEORGE: What?

VORHEES: Nothing that really concerns you, though it may cause you some inconvenience. The Committee thinks you'd better get rid of your secretary.

GEORGE: [*Astounded*] Hannock?

VORHEES: Yes, – he's no good!

GEORGE: No good?

VORHEES: A damn rotten specimen. We've found out enough about him to make sure we don't want him mixed up with us in *any way* in the election.

GEORGE: You – you take me off my feet!

VORHEES: If you want more detailed information, ask any detective with tenderloin experience.

GEORGE: I've never liked him. I can't say I've really trusted him. And yet I laid my prejudice to a personal source.

VORHEES: He's dishonest besides. You can't have him in a confidential position. You couldn't help getting tarred with some of his pitch!

GEORGE: But are you sure of what you say?

VORHEES: Sure! Why, just now, here, he showed me the hoof of a blackmailer.

GEORGE: [*Looks up quickly*] At that again!

VORHEES: How do you mean "*again*"?

GEORGE: Explain to *me* what *you* mean.

VORHEES: Oh, he didn't get far – we were interrupted! He put out a feeler, which was very like a *demand*, as to what he was going to get out of this election.

GEORGE: [*Carelessly, and not very loudly*] He needn't think I'm *father*!

VORHEES: [*Not understanding*] What's that?

GEORGE: You leave Hannock to me. I'll take care of *him*!

VORHEES: You'll *discharge* him? [*A pause*]

GEORGE: No, – I can't.

VORHEES: [*Astonished*] How do you mean, – "can't?"

GEORGE: I couldn't turn him out, if he insists on staying.

VORHEES: *Why not?*

GEORGE: [*A short second's pause*] That I cannot tell you –

VORHEES: Look here, George! What hold has this man got on you?

GEORGE: On me personally, none. But I owe him a certain duty, and in a way he could do harm to –

VORHEES: I thought you said you had no skeleton?

GEORGE: It isn't in *my* closet, but it concerns those that are nearest and dearest to me.

VORHEES: Then you must risk sacrificing them, if you want the position.

GEORGE: I'd have to sacrifice a memory, too, – and I haven't the right!

VORHEES: If I went to the Committee, and said to them, – Rand refuses to dismiss Hannock; doesn't deny he may be a scoundrel; owns up, in fact, that his family is in some way in the man's power; says he himself is not; but still he doesn't dismiss him, – do you believe for a minute the Committee will go on with your nomination?

GEORGE: No! For God's sake don't tell the Committee anything of the sort! Perhaps I can handle Hannock – beg him off!

VORHEES: I don't like the sound of that. There's one thing about you I'm afraid of, George. You're one of those men who think wrong means are justified by right ends; – unsafe and dishonest policy!

GEORGE: I tell you he can't hurt *me*, George Rand – [*after a second*] "Jr."

VORHEES: That don't do for the Committee. You can't handle mud and not –

GEORGE: [*Interrupting*] Very well, then if I can't buy him off, I *will* dismiss him! And the others must face the music! There's too much at stake for the future, to over-consider the past.

VORHEES: All right!

Enter Van Vranken, excited and angry; perhaps he's had a little too much to drink

VAN VRANKEN: Look here!

GEORGE: Good morning, Don.

VORHEES: Good morning.

GEORGE: I'm very busy now.

VAN VRANKEN: [*With a jeer*] I won't interrupt you long!

VORHEES: Would you like *me* to hunt up Eleanor and Cicely, and come back later?

VAN VRANKEN: Oh, you might as well stop. You're as good as in the family, now. You'll be sure to be asked to put *your* oar in!

GEORGE: Sit down, Don, and cool off!

VAN VRANKEN: I haven't time. I'm on the way to my lawyer! I understand my wife's here. Has she talked with you?

GEORGE: No. I've been very busy with Vorhees.

VAN VRANKEN: I know – the governorship! Well,

your sister'll put a spoke in that wheel, if you don't side with *me!*

GEORGE: What do you mean?

VAN VRANKEN: She threatens to take my children from me by bringing a suit for divorce, – mentioning Nellie Jud – Mrs. Judly.

GEORGE: Well, can you blame her?

VAN VRANKEN: It's a pity you haven't gone out, once in a while, into the society that bores you so, and kept your ears open.

GEORGE: What for?

VAN VRANKEN: You'd have heard a whisper, or caught a look that would have kept you from being surprised at what I'm going to tell you.

GEORGE: What?

VAN VRANKEN: If your sister starts a suit against me, bringing in Nellie's – Mrs. Judly's – name, I'll bring a *counter suit* against her, naming Jim *Cairns!*

GEORGE: You drunken liar! [*Going for him. Vorhees holds George back*]

VAN VRANKEN: You didn't *know* I could win. I wouldn't put such a stumbling block in the way of my little daughter's happiness!

GEORGE: Liar!! [*Struggles to free himself*]

VORHEES: No, George! Even *I've* heard enough to wonder something of it hasn't come your way.

VAN VRANKEN: [*Thickly, whiningly*] All I ask for is a noiseless, dignified separation, – that's all I want, and God, I want that bad! Legal or not, as *she* wishes, – only she's got to agree to cut out Cairns. I give her this chance for my little daughter's sake, – not for hers! But in another day, maybe, it'll be too late. I get my children six months of the year, and she the other six. I ask no more than I give, – that's fair! I'd like my complete freedom as well as she. So far as love goes, it's a pretty even thing between us! And when the children are grown up, and settled in life, she can do what she damn pleases, and good luck to her!

VORHEES: I've heard the gossip, Van Vranken, but you know enough of our world to realize half that gets about, gets about wrong.

GEORGE: Granted Tess has been *foolish.* That's bad *enough,* God knows! Still – I can't *believe* worse than that! *I grew up with her, – I know her!*

VAN VRANKEN: You knew her before she came to New York. She hadn't developed yet, in

that *mud*hole you all lived in! There's no smoke without –

GEORGE: Yes, there is! There's a smoldering that never breaks into a flame! And you know, Don, you've given every reason for Tess's heart to smolder, yes, and burn, too – though I don't believe it. While we're about it, let's finish the whole ugly business here, now. You're a drunkard, and your best friends are the most depraved crew in town, – a crowd that is used individually as markers to tally off each smart scandal that crops up. It never occurred to you, before you married Tess, that you would be faithful to her afterwards; and you didn't disappoint yourself.

VAN VRANKEN: What right had she to be disappointed? I never made any bluff or pose, and you all fought the match! She married me with her eyes open.

GEORGE: You had the glamour of the City about you. Tess was a *real* woman, full of good and bad; she was ready to be what the man she loved would make of her. And, poor girl, she married *you!*

VORHEES: Well, all that's done. What about the present? Van Vranken is right in saying any divorce scandal would endanger your election. We might lose the entire Catholic vote, and the support of the anti-divorce party, – both of which we're banking on. And besides, one of the strongest planks of our platform is the Sanctity of the Home! We're putting you up as the representative of the great section of the country which stands for the Purity of Family Life. We'd have to drop that platform, or be ridiculed off the face of the earth. And it doesn't seem right in any way to me! And it's not up *to you* to suffer for your sister. [*To Van Vranken*] If we persuade Mrs. Van Vranken to a dignified separation such as you want –

VAN VRANKEN: And she gives her promise to call off Cairns – !

GEORGE: [*Quickly*] Tess will be as anxious to stop gossip, when she hears its extent, as you. I'll take that on *my* shoulders.

Van Vranken looks at him, and half smiles cynically at his confidence

VORHEES: Very well! Will you, Van Vranken, be willing to hush the whole business up?

VAN VRANKEN: Glad to!

VORHEES: Live on with Mrs. Van Vranken in your house as if nothing had happened?

VAN VRANKEN: No! Not by a damned sight!

VORHEES: Come, don't be a yellow dog! Do all or nothing.

VAN VRANKEN: She left my house of her own accord, and I've sworn she shall never put her foot in it again.

VORHEES: Oh, well, what's an oath more or less to you! It will be only till after the election! Rand's nomination is practically settled on –

VAN VRANKEN: Oh, I see! Why didn't you say that at first? I've nothing personal against Rand.

VORHEES: I'm sure Mrs. Van Vranken, on her side, will do all she can to protect his interests.

VAN VRANKEN: I suppose I'll have to give in –

VORHEES: *Good!*

GEORGE: I'll see her now, if she's in the house.

VORHEES: [*To Van Vranken*] I will communicate something to you, after Rand has seen your wife.

VAN VRANKEN: Very good. She took both the children when she left this morning. One child must go back with me now.

VORHEES: *Both must go back*, to-day, and Mrs. Van Vranken, herself, – to live under your roof till after the election.

VAN VRANKEN: That's true! Of course! All right! God, it'll be a *hell* of a life! However, there'll be an end of it to look forward to! Good-by.

VORHEES and GEORGE: Good-by.

Enter Teresa and Mrs. Rand. Mrs. Rand is very altered. Her hair is dressed fashionably, etc., and, instead of the sweet, motherly woman she was, in Act I, she is now a rather overdressed, nervous-looking woman, ultra-smart, but no longer comfortable-looking and happy

TERESA: [*As she enters*] George!

MRS. RAND: George!

They both stop short, as they see Van Vranken. He bows to Teresa; she only glares at him

VAN VRANKEN: [*To Mrs. Rand*] Good morning.

MRS. RAND: [*Looking at him, – outraged and angry*] You *wicked* man!

Van Vranken is somewhat taken aback; from her, he turns and looks at the two men; he raises his eyebrows, smiles, shrugs his shoulders, and slouches out indifferently

VORHEES: I must go, too.

TERESA: Good morning, Bert.

VORHEES: Good morning, Tess. How do you do, Mrs. Rand.

MRS. RAND: I don't know where I am, Bert. I never felt the need of Mr. Rand more than to-day!

GEORGE: Bert, will you have to tell the Committee about this? Won't it queer my nomination?

VORHEES: Not if Tess will do what we expect. I'll leave you to explain to her. [*Moving to go*]

GEORGE: No, – stay, Bert!

MRS. RAND: George! Tess couldn't possibly tell you everything she wants to, before Bert.

TERESA: Oh, don't worry, mother. I guess *Don* hasn't left much for me to tell! Besides, Bert's a lawyer. I'd like his advice. [*To George*] Don gave you his version, didn't he?

GEORGE: Listen! My whole future is at stake, and it's in *your* hands!

TERESA: Nonsense! My hands are full of my own troubles.

MRS. RAND: [*To nobody in particular, and nobody pays any attention to her*] What a tragedy!

VORHEES: George is right. His nomination for governor was decided on, this morning, provided he had an open chance. If you make a scandal now, he'll lose the nomination, sure, – and if not, what's worse, the election!

TERESA: You are trying to influence me against what I want to do, through George. I will never live with Don again!

GEORGE: Won't you? Only till after the election?

TERESA: No! I intend to begin proceedings for a divorce to-day.

GEORGE: But Don *offers* you a legal separation, and to share the children.

TERESA: That's done purposely to keep me *tied*, so I couldn't marry again! I want the children all the time, and I want my freedom!

GEORGE: But you know what he threatens to do?

TERESA: *He won't dare!*

VORHEES: That's not his reputation in New York.

MRS. RAND: [*At random*] If she only wouldn't decide at once – all of a sudden. That's where women always slip up!

TERESA: Did he pretend he wanted me to come back?

GEORGE: [*Smiling in spite of himself*] No, but we persuaded him to be willing.

VORHEES: For George's sake, till after the election, on one condition –

TERESA: [*Quickly*] *What* condition?

VORHEES: That you agree to the sort of separation he planned.

GEORGE: And promise to put an end, once for all, to the Cairns gossip.

TERESA: Just what I told you! The whole thing with him is only a mean spirit of revenge! He would sacrifice the children and me and everything else, to keep me from being happy with Jim.

GEORGE: [*Surprised at the apparent confession*] Do you mean you *do* love Cairns?

TERESA: Yes.

MRS. RAND: [*Breaking in*] No, she doesn't mean that! She doesn't love him *now*, but she *will*, if she gets her divorce.

GEORGE: [*To Teresa*] What you really want to divorce Don for, then, is not because of Mrs. Judly, but so you can marry Cairns?

TERESA: Exactly.

VORHEES: [*Looking at his watch*] I must go. [*To George*] The Committee will be waiting now for me.

MRS. RAND: [*Mortified*] You've shocked Bert, Tess.

VORHEES: [*Smiling*] Oh, no, I've a report to make before George's nomination can be official, and I don't see, now, just how I'm going to make that report exactly as I wish.

GEORGE: You mean on account of *Tess!*

TERESA: I'll make any sacrifice I can for George, except my own personal happiness. That, I haven't the right to sacrifice, because that belongs half to some one else.

GEORGE: You go on and call me up by telephone when you get there. I'll have had a longer talk with Tess, and I may have something different to say to you.

VORHEES: All right. [*Going to Teresa*]

TERESA: I shall want you for my lawyer, Bert.

VORHEES: Thanks. That isn't exactly in my line, but I hope you won't *need* a lawyer. Do what you can for George, won't you?

TERESA: Of course.

Mrs. Rand goes out with Vorhees

MRS. RAND: [*As they go out*] Bert, you mustn't get a wrong impression from what Tess said, will you? She's her father's own daughter, and you know a Rand *couldn't* do a really wrong thing; it's not in the blood.

GEORGE: Now, look here, Tess! On one side is a great career and me, and a dignified life for you, with independence and the happiness and the love and the respect of your children; on the other is probable failure for me, and worse than failure for you. Don'll do what he says, and if he wins his suit, you'll lose *both* children and everything else you ought to care about –

TERESA: Except Jim!

GEORGE: Would he make up for any thing?

TERESA: Everything!

GEORGE: Even the children?

TERESA: [*Almost breaking down*] How can you say that? You know I wouldn't have to give up my children!

GEORGE: Ten chances to one you'd have to.

TERESA: I don't believe any judge would give *Don* the children in preference to *me*.

GEORGE: Believe me, it'll be taking awful chances.

TERESA: All life is that. [*She turns aside, crying quietly*]

GEORGE: [*Going over to her*] Tess! But you don't realize what this nomination means to me – more than anything in the world! I want it with every nerve and sinew in my body, with every thought in my brain, with every ambition I've got! Just let me get this one big thing in my hands, and nothing *shall stop me!* I'll climb on up the ladder of achievement and fame, and I'll take you all up with me! Remember our boy and girl days, Tess, in Middleburg. We were never selfish, you and I, with each other. It used to be a fight between us as to which should give up! Don't go back on me this time. You've got it in your power to give me a *great boost*, or push the whole scaffolding of my career from under my feet. For the love of God, stand by me to-day!

TERESA: It's your future against my future! Why should you expect me to sacrifice mine for yours? We aren't children now, and this isn't Middleburg! I love you very much, but not in that old-fashioned way.

GEORGE: But has any one in this world the right to absolutely ignore everybody else, and think only of one's self?

TERESA: It sounds to me *exactly* like *what you're doing!*

GEORGE: I suppose I do sound like a selfish brute; but I can't help feeling that what I ask of you, if six for me, is half a dozen for you, too, in the end.

TERESA: If Don'll give me a full divorce, I'll do anything for you – live with the beast *two years,* if necessary, and not see Jim all that time. But don't ask me to give up *Jim –* [*With emotion again*] because I love him, and I won't, I couldn't; if I said I would, I'd lie!

GEORGE: But Don won't give you what you want, and if you insist, he'll do what *he* says – divorce you, with a filthy scandal!

TERESA: The *hour after* the divorce was granted, Jim Cairns and I would be married.

GEORGE: Listen! Would you do *this?* Deceive *me* now?

TERESA: How?

GEORGE: Well – agree to what Don asks –

TERESA: Never!

GEORGE: Wait! After the election, you might change your mind. Whatever course you took then, wouldn't interfere with me.

TERESA: Does that seem to you quite square? Isn't it a good deal like breaking your word?

GEORGE: Has Don done much else beside *break* his since he answered "I will" with you to the Bishop in the chancel?

TERESA: His word was cracked before I knew him! But I wasn't thinking of Don and me. Aren't you playing a trick on the party that is putting its trust in you?

GEORGE: I don't see it! If your divorce comes out after my election, it needn't affect the party. My acts will be speaking for themselves, then. I intend to be square in office, and to succeed or fail by that standard. I don't mind a failure, *doing* the *right thing;* what I can't stand is failure *doing nothing* with having had my chance!

TERESA: I see; a sort of the-end-justifying-the-means principle.

GEORGE: Not exactly, because I don't see anything wrong. It's just election tactics! the others'd do it; we must fight them with their weapons.

TERESA: [*Rather cunningly*] Will you tell Bert Vorhees?

GEORGE: [*After a second's pause*] No.

TERESA: *That's just what I mean!* It's something father wouldn't do.

GEORGE: He *wouldn't!* Why, father's whole business success was due to his not letting his left hand know what his right hand was after, but to square things in the end by a good division! – *one third* to the left hand on the basis that the *right hand* had done *all the work!* And you know what father's name stood for – the very criterion of business honor!

TERESA: Well, George, suppose I do it. I'm in no position to criticise, anyway. I'll go back till you're elected, and pretend I'm going to carry out Don's plan.

GEORGE: Thank you, Tess. [*But the enthusiasm is gone*]

TERESA: Only, somehow it doesn't coincide with my idea of what I *thought* you were being and striving for. Maybe you're on your way up the ladder, but you, at the same time, are coming down from the pedestal I'd put you on, to join me at the bottom of *mine.*

There is a moment's pause, both looking straight ahead, not liking to look into each other's eyes. Enter Hannock

HANNOCK: Excuse me, Mr. Rand. Mr. Vorhees is on the 'phone.

TERESA: [*Quickly, to George*] I'll tell him. Then you won't have to *lie,* if he asks any difficult questions.

GEORGE: I wouldn't lie; I'd just beg anything I don't want to answer – and tell Eleanor to be sure and let me see her before she goes.

TERESA: [*Very serious*] I wonder if *she'd* approve of this little plot of ours? I wish it didn't seem contemptible to me!

GEORGE: [*Hurt and showing a hint of shame for the first time*] For God's sake, Tess, don't suggest such a thing! Eleanor is the one thing in the world I wouldn't give up to get this election.

Teresa looks at him meaningly as she goes out What did you mean by looking for personal graft out of this election just now, with Mr. Vorhees?

HANNOCK: I was showing my hand, that's all. I was calling the pot! It's time!

GEORGE: You don't know the men you're dealing with!

HANNOCK: [*Looking George squarely and meaningly in the face*] I know one of them better than he knows himself!

GEORGE: Listen, Hannock! That day my father died, I promised myself and his memory I'd look after you, and look after you well – not like a dependent on father's charity –

HANNOCK: [*Interrupts*] Damned unwilling charity – he was *afraid* –

GEORGE: We won't go into the story of your mother – [*Hannock winces*] I've tried to treat you as I would a – brother who was unlucky – somebody I was *glad* to give a hand to –

HANNOCK: [*Interrupting*] Well, haven't I made good? What complaints have you –

GEORGE: [*Going on*] You've been of the greatest service to me in every way. There's no question about that! But it's time for us now to open a new pack, and each go his own way –

HANNOCK: [*Thunderstruck*] What's that you say?

GEORGE: I'm going to offer you a fixed yearly income, – a sum we'll agree on, – and you're to get a job elsewhere, that's all –

HANNOCK: [*Dry and ugly*] Is it!

GEORGE: What do you say?

HANNOCK: Oh, I've got a hell of lot to say!

GEORGE: Cut it down to yes or no, and we'll discuss the amount of the income!

HANNOCK: *No!!!* You haven't got to give half of what I expect to get out of the present situation!

GEORGE: [*Angry, but controlled*] If you don't look out, you'll get *nothing*.

HANNOCK: [*Sneers*] Pah! Just wait till I begin to open your eyes for you! For instance, how about the New Brunswick deal?

GEORGE: *What about* it? [*On the defensive*]

HANNOCK: As crooked as anything that's ever been in "high finance"! [*With a sneer*]

GEORGE: What do you mean? You knew that deal from the very beginning – you knew every step I took in it?

HANNOCK: Yes, *I* did! I notice you kept the transaction pretty quiet from everybody else.

GEORGE: It was nobody else's business. My father taught me that –

HANNOCK: [*Not listening out*] Yes! – and he taught you a lot of *other* things, too! But you go farther than he would have dared.

GEORGE: That's enough!

HANNOCK: What's the difference between your deal, and the Troy business that sent Pealy to State's Prison?

GEORGE: Every difference!

HANNOCK: [*Triumphantly*] *Is* there? *Think* a minute! [*A second's pause*] You gambled with your partner's money: Pealy gambled with his bank's.

GEORGE: It wasn't my *partner's* money; it was the *firm's*.

HANNOCK: But you were the only one who knew what was being done with it.

GEORGE: My partner got his fair share, didn't he?

HANNOCK: Yes, but you got the *unfair!* You got paid pretty high for your "influence." Nobody else had any chance to sell theirs! If that isn't taking money under false pretences, if it isn't using funds you haven't the right to use, – there was a miscarriage of justice in the Pealy case, that's all.

GEORGE: But – !

HANNOCK: Go over the two deals with *Vorhees*, if you don't believe *me!* Show him the differences between the Brunswick Transaction and the Pealy case, – if he can *see* any!

Enter Eleanor, breezily, enthusiastically

ELEANOR: Good morning! [*She sees Hannock, her manner changes to a cold one*] Good morning, Mr. Hannock.

HANNOCK: Good morning, Miss Vorhees. Excuse me!

He passes Miss Vorhees, and goes out; as he goes, with his back to them, he is seen taking out from his pocket his hypodermic needle, and a small bottle, – and, by then, he is out. Eleanor and George silently follow him with their eyes

ELEANOR: [*Turning*] What *is* it about him?

GEORGE: [*Kisses her*] You don't like him either?

ELEANOR: I *detest* him! What Cicely can see in him I –

GEORGE: [*Quietly*] Cicely?

ELEANOR: Yes, I've come to-day as a go-between – between you and Cicely –

GEORGE: Ha! Cicely's clever enough to know

how to get what she wants from me. She has only to use you –

ELEANOR: She's in love with your secretary.

GEORGE: [*Not taking it in*] What?

ELEANOR: Cicely and Mr. Hannock are in love with each other –

GEORGE: [*Aghast*] Impossible –

ELEANOR: I know; I felt the same as you do. I detest him; he's no match for Cicely – I feel instinctively the last man in the world for her.

GEORGE: Even *not* that –

ELEANOR: But Cicely insists. They wish to marry.

GEORGE: Never!

ELEANOR: She guessed you would be against it. She says we none of us like Hannock, and nobody's fair to him; and so she begged me to persuade you. She asked me to remember how much *I* loved *you*, and what *our* marriage meant to *us*. You see, I couldn't refuse! But I'm afraid I'm not a very good go between; my heart isn't in it!

GEORGE: [*Hardly hearing Eleanor*] It's beyond believing! [*He touches the bell with decision*] I must talk to Cicely now, before she sees Hannock again.

ELEANOR: Wouldn't it be better without me? She might resent your refusing and giving your reasons before me.

Enter Foot

GEORGE: Ask Miss Cicely to come here at once, please.

FOOT: Yes, sir. [*He goes out*]

GEORGE: Perhaps it *would* be better.

ELEANOR: George, it doesn't make any difference to *you* that Hannock has no family or position? Cicely thinks you're prejudiced against him because his mother was a milliner or dressmaker – or something –

GEORGE: Of course that makes no difference to me –

ELEANOR: And you wouldn't be influenced against a man by your personal feeling, where your sister's happiness was concerned, would you? [*He shakes his head*] If you don't *know* anything against Hannock, you'll let him have a *chance* to prove himself worthy of Cicely, won't you?

GEORGE: Eleanor, it can't be! Don't ask me any questions, but believe me, nothing could make such a thing possible, – personal prejudice and

any other kind aside! I want you to help me pull Cicely through it. I may even ask you to take Cicely into your house for a while. Would you do this for me? Teresa and Don, you know, would be no comfort, and, on the other hand, would set her a bad example, and fan every little rebellious flame in her!

ELEANOR: Of course, I'll do whatever I possibly can, dear. This is the very sort of thing I want to *share* with you, if I can't take it *entirely* off your shoulders.

Enter Cicely

CICELY: [*Half defiant, half timid and hopeful*] Well?

ELEANOR: [*Going. To Cicely, speaking tenderly*] I won't go home yet. I'll wait for you upstairs.

CICELY: Humph! *Thank* you; I know what *that* means!

Eleanor goes out

GEORGE: My dear girl, it isn't possible that you care for Hannock?

CICELY: [*Determined*] Yes, *very much!*

GEORGE: Well, even that may be, but still not in the way you think.

CICELY: *I love him!* Oh, I knew you'd be against it! Nobody cares for him in this house!

GEORGE: [*Quickly*] And that's *why you* do! You're *sorry* for him, my dear girl! It's *pity*, not *love!*

CICELY: [*Increasing her resentment and determination*] Nothing of the sort! He doesn't need my pity in any way.

GEORGE: It's just as I would feel toward a girl who seemed to me to be ignored.

CICELY: Abused! As good as *insulted here*, by everybody!

GEORGE: You *think* so, and your sympathy is aroused, – but that's not love.

CICELY: You don't know what you're talking about!

GEORGE: Yes, I do, – better than you. You've never been in love in your life, and so you mistake something, that is probably like a sisterly affection for this man, for the other thing.

CICELY: *Ridiculous!*

GEORGE: You don't know the difference now –

CICELY: Nonsense!

GEORGE: But you'll realize it some day when the right man comes along –

CICELY: [*Satirically*] I hope not! It would be awkward, as *I shall be married* to Fred Hannock.

GEORGE: No, you'll never be married to Hannock!

CICELY: *You're* not my father!

GEORGE: But I represent him, and I tell you you must give up this idea –

CICELY: [*Interrupting angrily*] And I tell you I won't! Good-by! [*Starting to go*]

GEORGE: Wait a minute. [*Rings bell*] You can't marry this man. He isn't good enough for you!

CICELY: Humph!

GEORGE: Or for any self-respecting woman to marry, as far as that goes.

CICELY: Your opinion as to whom I shall marry, or not, means absolutely nothing to me.

GEORGE: Very well, I'll go even farther. I'll tell you that, even if both my reasons for disapproving of Hannock were done away with, – still, I say for you to marry him is *impossible*, and I, as your elder brother, *representing your father*, forbid it.

Enter Foot

FOOT: Yes, sir?

GEORGE: Ask Mr. Hannock to come here.

FOOT: Yes, sir. [*Goes out*]

GEORGE: I shall tell him, *before you*, anything between him and you is absolutely impossible, – that I forbid it, and that he is dismissed from my service.

CICELY: Then I will go with him, if he wants me to. Do you think I'm going to have *him* lose his position and everything *through me*, and not stick to him?

GEORGE: [*With tension*] Sorry for him! That's all it is! *Sorry for him!*

CICELY: *It's not* – and you can forbid now till doomsday. I'm my own mistress, and I shall do as I *darn please!* I shall marry the man I want to, in spite of you – and the whole family, if necessary, – but I wanted to give you the chance to stand by me – [*Her voice falters, and she turns away; she cries*] I felt you *wouldn't*, but I wanted you to, and that's why – I've come here now – and let you – humiliate me – in this – way. I wanted my own brother

to sympathize with me, to help me. Everybody will follow your lead!

GEORGE: [*Goes to her, and puts his arms about her*] Cis! I can't tell you how sorry I am! Not since father died have I felt as I do now. I've nothing to gain or lose except your affection, dear girl, and your happiness, so you can believe me when I say this marriage *can't* be – [*She pushes his arm away and faces him*]

CICELY: [*Literal and absolutely unconvinced or frightened*] *Why* not?

GEORGE: *I can't tell* you.

CICELY: Well, you know me well enough to realize such reasoning with me is a waste of breath.

GEORGE: [*Suffering*] I want to *spare* you –

CICELY: *What?* It doesn't seem to me you're *sparing* me much!

GEORGE: But listen – Vorhees just now told me – Hannock isn't on the level, – he isn't *honest!*

CICELY: I won't take Bert Vorhees' word for that! Fred's been your right-hand man here for fours years and over. Have you ever found him doing a single dishonest thing? I'm sure you haven't, or you wouldn't have kept him. I don't know why you did *anyway!* It was perfectly evident you didn't like him!

Hannock enters

GEORGE: [*Quickly, before he is fully in the room, and going to the door*] Hannock, please excuse me. Will you wait one minute in the hall?

HANNOCK: [*In the doorway. He looks questioningly at Cicely. She nods her head*] Certainly. [*He goes out*]

GEORGE: [*Intensely, with his hand on the knob, holding the door closed behind him*] Listen to me, for God's sake! You're my *sister*, I'm your *brother*. Have I ever showed that I did anything but love you?

CICELY: No, that's why I hoped –

GEORGE: [*Interrupting, almost beside himself*] But it can't be!! Won't you *trust* me, – *won't* you? Let me tell Hannock, without going any deeper into it, that – you realize the marriage can't be; that you and he mustn't meet again! You can say what kind things you –

CICELY: [*Flashing*] Never!! You ought to know me better than to propose any such thing! [*She moves toward the door*]

842

GEORGE: [*With a movement to stop her*] For your *own sake, his sake,* for *mother's,* for *everybody's — trust me* and —

CICELY: [*Looking him directly in the face after a second's silence, speaks with the note of finality*] Listen! I *married* Fred Hannock this morning!

George looks at her, his eyes dilating. There is a pause

GEORGE: [*In horror*] What!!

CICELY: I *married* Fred Hannock half an hour ago. We walked home from the church, separately. He went to his work, and I sent for Eleanor.

GEORGE: [*In a voice of terrible but suppressed rage, goes to the door, throws it open with violence, and calls loudly*] Come in!

Hannock enters quietly, expecting a fight or a scene; he is on the defensive and not in any way frightened

GEORGE: [*Controlling himself by a big effort*] Is this *true,* what my sister says, that behind my back you've been making love to her —

CICELY: [*Interrupting him*] I *never* said that!

GEORGE: That you've repaid all that I've done for you, and all my father did, by taking advantage of our kindness and your position here to run off with —

CICELY: [*Interrupting*] I was as anxious to run off as he —

GEORGE: But why wasn't I told? Why do it secretly? [*To Hannock*] Why didn't you go about it in the square, open way, unless you *knew* you were doing wrong?

HANNOCK: I knew you'd fight it for all you were worth, and I wasn't going to run any risk of losing her!

CICELY: But you wouldn't have! My brother would have wasted his words then, as much as he is now —

HANNOCK: I was afraid — any fool in my place could see how I've really stood in this family. The only friend I had in the house, or who ever came to it, was *she!* [*With a wave of his hand toward Cicely*]

GEORGE: And that's *why!* Can't you see it? Don't you know the difference between *pity* and *love?*

CICELY: I love *him* and he *knows* it; — *don't* you, Fred?

HANNOCK: Yes, *I do know it!* As well as I know your brother only kept me here because — [*Turning to George*] you were afraid of me!

GEORGE: *Afraid of you?*

HANNOCK: Yes! Do you suppose I didn't guess your father must have told you I was on to him in the bank!

GEORGE: Leave the dead alone! You've got your hands full with the *living!*

HANNOCK: Well, I know my business well enough to realize that once Cicely and I were married, you'd have to make the best of it!

GEORGE: Never! I tell you this marriage is *no* marriage!

Cicely and Hannock exclaim in derision

CICELY: What's the use of talking any more about it? We aren't getting anywhere! It's *done* — and George has *got* to make the best of it!

GEORGE: I tell you it can't be! Will you take my word, Hannock?

HANNOCK: No! [*Laughs loudly*]

GEORGE: Then, I must go ahead without you! You're dismissed. Do you hear? You're *discharged* from my employ!

HANNOCK: [*Getting very angry, but controlled*] You take care!

GEORGE: [*Continues determinedly*] You'll leave this house to-day. I'll give you an hour to pack up and get out, and you'll never lay your eyes on this girl again.

CICELY: If he goes now, I'll go with him. I'm his wife!

GEORGE: You *won't* go with him!

HANNOCK: Who'll prevent her?

GEORGE: *I will!*

HANNOCK: [*In a blaze*] Try it!!

CICELY: I've just promised to love, honor and obey him — and if he says to come, I'll go!

GEORGE: [*Slowly but strongly*] He won't say it.

HANNOCK: I *do* say it! Come on, Cicely! But if you want to come back, you can, because, before I'm through with your brother, I'll get him down on to his knees, begging me to come back, and I won't come *without you!*

GEORGE: [*Going to the door and holding it open*] Cicely, will you wait in here with Eleanor for a few minutes?

HANNOCK: Oh, we can speak out before her! I want my wife to know the truth about everything! I don't intend to be the goat in this family any longer!

GEORGE: Well, you can tell Cicely, afterward, what I'm going to tell you, if you like. God keep me from ever having to tell her! [*After a look straight at Hannock, he looks at Cicely very seriously. She responds to his look, impressed by it, and turns her eyes to Hannock. Neither quite understands, but each feels the depth of seriousness in George's attitude*]

HANNOCK: [*Doggedly to Cicely*] Go on.

CICELY: [*To Hannock*] I'll wait there for you. Don't do anything without me. I'm so sorry my brother takes this attitude! Don't think it can influence *me*, any more than the disgraceful way you've always been treated here has; *nothing* they say can change *me* toward you, Fred! [*She leaves them*]

GEORGE: I didn't *want to* have to tell you this. I'd rather almost die than have to tell Cicely! I must break faith with father, but of course he'd be the first to ask me to. I must dig out a skeleton that is rotting in its closet – that's the trouble! I must do this, and a lot more, if you make me, and give *you* a couple of blows which will come pretty near to knocking you out, if you've anything at all of a man in you. And every bit of it can be spared *everybody*, if you'll go away and let Cicely – divorce you.

HANNOCK: Well, I *won't!*

GEORGE: Because you won't give up Cicely?

HANNOCK: Exactly. I love her better than anything, – money, comfort, happiness, everything you can think of, – so go on, fire your last gun, and let's get through with it! My wife –

GEORGE: [*With excitement*] She *isn't* your wife! – [*Hannock looks at him and sneers. George's rage at Hannock is only governed by the tragedy of the whole thing*] Your *marriage wasn't any marriage!*

HANNOCK: [*A little frightened, and very angry now*] What do you mean? –

GEORGE: [*Looks towards the door where Cicely has gone, and, with difficulty, manages to control his voice, as he lowers it*] Cicely is your sister!

HANNOCK: [*With a cry*] Cicely is *what?*

GEORGE: *Your sister!*

HANNOCK: [*Sees "red," and goes nearly mad*] You're a God damn liar!

GEORGE: It's the truth –

HANNOCK: [*Out of his mind, with an insane laugh*] You're a liar! [*Cicely, alarmed, opens the door to come in. Hannock shouts at her angrily, in an ugly voice*] You go back! – and shut the door! Do *you* hear! Get *out* of *this room!*

GEORGE: [*Strong, but more kind*] Wait in the the room till I call you.

HANNOCK: [*Brokenly – ugly*] I don't want her hanging round here now! This is none of her business, none o' hers!

GEORGE: [*Speaks toward the doorway*] Eleanor, I don't want Cicely to hear what we're saying.

ELEANOR: [*Answering*] Very good. [*She is seen shutting the door*]

HANNOCK: [*Making guttural sounds, and unable to pronounce the words clearly*] Hugh – hugh – hah! – You'd play any game to get rid of me, wouldn't you? But you can't fool me like that!! [*He sits in a chair, mumbling to himself incoherently every other minute, working his hands, his mouth and his chin wet with saliva*]

GEORGE: That day I saw you first, just before he died, my father told me.

HANNOCK: I don't believe it!

GEORGE: He made me promise two things: – that I wouldn't tell you – never! – and that I would look out for you.

HANNOCK: I don't *believe* it!

GEORGE: That's why your mother got her allowance, – and to buy her silence –

HANNOCK: I don't *believe it!* [*Laughing and weeping*]

GEORGE: Now, you see why you must leave here to-day – leave New York! Why there was no marriage this morning and never can be! Why –

HANNOCK: [*His mind deranged, rises unevenly; he is loud, partly incoherent, and his face is twitching and distorted, his hands clutching and clenching, his whole body wracked and trembling, but still strong, with a nervous madman's strength*] It's all a *lie* – to separate Cicely from me!

GEORGE: [*Goes to him and sees the change*] Hannock!

HANNOCK: I'll never believe it!

GEORGE: [*Taking him by the shoulder*] Have you gone out of your mind!

HANNOCK: I'll never give her up!

GEORGE: *What!! I tell you, she's your sister!*

HANNOCK: And I say *I don't believe it! I love* her, she *loves* me. I won't give her up!!

GEORGE: *Yes, you will!!*

HANNOCK: *I won't!* Do you think I'd give her up to some other fellow to hold in his arms! For some other man to *love* and *take care of!!* You're crazy!! She said if I said come, she'd go with me, and I'll say it!! [*He starts toward the door. George takes hold of him to stop him from calling her*]

GEORGE: Wait! If you don't give her up now, after what I've told you, and *leave here* before she comes out of that room, I'll have to do the only thing left, – *tell her!*

HANNOCK: [*Furious*] No, you won't! You shan't tell her! It isn't *true!* And if it was, by God, she shan't know it! It *would separate* us!

GEORGE: [*Horrified at what this means, calls sternly and with determination*] Cicely!

HANNOCK: [*Wildly*] Don't you dare to tell her that lie!

ELEANOR: [*Opening the door*] You want Cicely to come in?

GEORGE: Yes.

Eleanor turns away from the door, leaving it open behind her. Cicely appears, and enters, – leaving the door open

HANNOCK: There isn't any lie too big for him to make up to separate us! I'm going! Will you come with me?

CICELY: Of course!

GEORGE: Cicely! Are you strong? Are you brave? You must hear something *unbelievably terrible!*

HANNOCK: [*Holding out his hand beggingly*] Come along, don't listen to him! [*She makes a movement toward Hannock*]

GEORGE: You *can't!* [*Taking hold of her*]

CICELY: I *will!* Leave go of me! [*Struggling desperately*]

GEORGE: [*Puts his arms about her, and holds her in his arms – her back to him*] My poor child, he's your –

Hannock, without warning, pulls out a pistol from his hip pocket, and shoots her dead in George's arms

ELEANOR: [*Calls, in fright*] George!!

GEORGE: Cicely! [*He holds her in his arms, and carries her over to sofa. Calls brokenly*] Cicely!

Eleanor enters quickly and goes to them

ELEANOR: [*In horror as she sees*] Oh!

GEORGE: Take her.

Eleanor takes Cicely tenderly from him

HANNOCK: Now, you nor nobody else can separate us! [*Lifts the pistol to his heart to shoot, feeling for the place he showed in Act I. George springs forward and gets hold of him and the pistol before he can shoot*]

GEORGE: No! *That's too good for you!* That's too easy! By God, you've got to *pay.*

Enter Foot in excitement

FOOT: Excuse me, sir, I heard –

GEORGE: All right. Telephone for the police. Is she breathing, Eleanor? [*Eleanor shakes her head*] Oh, God! [*Bowing his head, emotion surges up in him. Hannock, in this moment of weakness, almost frees himself and almost gets hold of the pistol*]

ELEANOR: [*Who is watching, cries out in alarm*] George! George, be careful! [*George pulls himself together too quickly for him, and prevents Hannock. Foot starts to go. To Foot*] Help me; it won't take you a moment!

GEORGE: No! Foot, I know I can trust you. [*Giving him the pistol*] Keep this, yourself, and don't let him get out of the room.

FOOT: Yes, sir. [*Takes the pistol, and stands before Hannock. George goes to Cicely, and takes her in his arms*]

GEORGE: Poor little woman! little sister! Why did this have to be! I wonder if *this* is what they call the sins of the fathers? [*He carries her out of the room, Left, followed by Eleanor. Hannock, the moment they are gone, makes a movement. Foot at once covers him with the pistol*]

HANNOCK: Give *me* that pistol!

FOOT: No, sir.

HANNOCK: Name your own *price!*

FOOT: Miss Cicely's life back, sir!

HANNOCK: *You're* against me too, *are* you! Every one's against *me!*

George comes back

GEORGE: [*Taking the pistol from Foot*] Thank you. Now, telephone, and ask them to be quick, please.

FOOT: Shall I come back, sir?

GEORGE: No, I think this job had better be mine. [*Looking hard at Hannock*]

HANNOCK: [*Quickly*] I won't try to get away, – I give you my word of honor.

GEORGE: Your word of honor! [*To Foot*] When you've telephoned, go to Miss Vorhees.

FOOT: Yes, sir.

GEORGE: Ask her to keep my mother and Mrs. Van Vranken from coming here.

FOOT: Yes, sir. [*Goes out*]

HANNOCK: [*Makes a move for George*] Give me that gun! [*There is a short struggle. George breaks from Hannock, and, crossing to the table, lays the pistol on it. Hannock makes a tricky attempt to get to it quickly, but is caught by George, who holds him. The following scene takes place with George keeping hold of Hannock, who sometimes struggles and sometimes tries to break, suddenly or craftily, away from George's grip, and at other times remains quiescent*] You're a damn fool! Don't you see it's the easiest way all around for us? I've got to die anyway.

GEORGE: But not that way. That's too easy for you!

HANNOCK: Well, it's easier for you, too, with me out of the way! There's no arrest, no trial, no scandal! Nobody'll know I was her brother; nobody'll know about your father! Think what it'll save your mother! Think what it'll save you! Think what it'll save everybody!

GEORGE: Including *you*, – and you don't deserve to be saved *anything!*

HANNOCK: Still, even *I* am your own blood! For God's sake, go on, let me! All you have to do is to turn your back a minute – it won't take *two!* Please! Think of *her* – what'll it save her memory!

GEORGE: No!

HANNOCK: Then for your mother's sake! How can *she* go through a trial and all *that* means!

GEORGE: Your work in the next room is worse than any trial for her to bear.

HANNOCK: Think of yourself, of the election! What will my trial do to your election?

GEORGE: I'm not thinking of my election now, – I'm thinking of that little, still figure lying in the next room!

HANNOCK: [*Emotionally, almost crying*] There'd have been two, if you hadn't stopped me! For the love of God, give me the gun –

GEORGE: No! *You've got to sit in the chair!*

HANNOCK: [*With an ugly change*] Well, you'll get *your* punishments, too, – don't you forget that!! I know how eaten up with ambition you are! And every single wish nearest to your heart will die just as dead as I do, if you let me go to trial!

GEORGE: What do you think you're doing?

HANNOCK: If I have to pay *my price*. I'll make you pay *yours*. And you'll be dead, publicly and politically, before I go into the condemned cell.

GEORGE: You're crazy, and that's the only thing that may save you, if *Matteawan* is salvation!

HANNOCK: I knew your father was dishonest, and I told him that day; I guess it killed him. And I've watched you, and tempted you, and helped you go on with his methods! Every bit of this will come out in my trial. I'll get a clever enough lawyer to manage *that!* And you'll lose, not only your ambition, but your position in the world, and one more thing besides, – *the woman you're in love with!* For that kind of a high-browed moral crank wouldn't stand for one half *you* stand for in business, and when she finds out how deceived she's been in you, if I know human nature, she won't have that much love left for you – [*Snapping his fingers*] And *she'll find out*, and they'll *all know!* – *your party* and the *other* party! That election'll be a hell of a walkover for the other side!

Eleanor enters

GEORGE: What is it, Eleanor? I don't want you here.

HANNOCK: [*Half aside, with a half jeer, and a half smile*] Hah!

ELEANOR: Excuse me. Bert wants you on the telephone. Shall I answer?

GEORGE: Yes, please. [*Hannock begins to steal behind, toward the pistol*] Does mother know?

ELEANOR: Yes, and she's very plucky. But I'm surprised how full she is of the desire for revenge! [*George turns and sees Hannock, and quickly but quietly intercepts him, and stands with his hand on the pistol*] She wants Hannock punished! She's watching for the police!

GEORGE: They ought to be here soon, now.

ELEANOR: Teresa is with me. She feels it terribly. [*Goes out*]

HANNOCK: Do you realize how completely you'll be done for, if you don't let me do it? The New Brunswick business isn't a patch on some of your other deals I know about!

GEORGE: I've never done a thing in business that couldn't stand the strictest overhauling.

HANNOCK: If you believe that, you're a bigger fool than I thought! *I'd* rather be a *crook* than a *fool*, any day! Quick, before she comes from the telephone! Turn your back; walk to the door there! It's easily explained; – you're not to blame!

GEORGE: *No!*

HANNOCK: [*Hysterically*] If you *don't*, I'll explain now, *before her*, where and how your standard in business is rotten, and your dealings crooked, – and you *can begin to take* your medicine!

GEORGE: I dare you!

Eleanor comes back

ELEANOR: Bert wants me to tell you it's settled, – your nomination – and he adds, *"good luck!"*

GEORGE: Did you tell him about – ?

ELEANOR: No – I – I told him to come here as soon as he could.

GEORGE: All right.

Eleanor starts to go

HANNOCK: [*Excitedly*] Wait a minute, Miss Vorhees!

GEORGE: No, Eleanor, go back, please!

HANNOCK: [*Quickly*] This man, who thinks he has it on me, is afraid to have you hear the truth about himself. That's why he don't want you to stay.

GEORGE: [*To Eleanor*] Stay!

HANNOCK: You think George Rand stands for honesty, and the square deal in the business world! Well, he does, but *it's a lie!* And if he wasn't paying up to the hilt – East, West, North and South – to protect himself, everybody in this country would know what we, on the inside, do!

ELEANOR: George, unless you'd really rather I stayed, I don't want to hear what he has to say about you.

HANNOCK: [*Quickly*] I don't blame you for not wanting to hear about the suicide of Henry Bodes! [*To George*] Do you know who killed Bodes? *You did!*

GEORGE: The man's out of his mind still, Eleanor.

HANNOCK: Am I? Bodes was on to your Copper Pit scheme, and *saw it succeed* – so he tried one like it, and it failed!

GEORGE: Was that *my* fault?

HANNOCK: Yes! It was your example set him on, and do you think your scheme was legitimate?

GEORGE: So help me God, I *do!*

HANNOCK: Then why, when it failed, did Bodes kill himself? He wasn't *broke!* It wasn't *money* that drove him to it! It was *shame*, because his scheme was *crooked*, just as yours was. Success covered it, but failure showed it up.

ELEANOR: Don't ask me to listen to this any longer! [*She goes out. George watches her go, but Hannock only gives a quick glance after her*]

HANNOCK: Bodes was one of your sweet, weak family men, who can't stand on disgrace!

GEORGE: Disgrace!!

HANNOCK: Ask Vorhees, – and about the New Brunswick case! And get him to *tell you the truth!*

GEORGE: [*Half to himself*] Good God! If there is something in all this?

HANNOCK: What are you paying Elmer Caston ten thousand a year for?

GEORGE: For his legal services!

HANNOCK: Rot! The firm's never used him –

GEORGE: But keeping him on our pay list keeps him from working against us.

HANNOCK: Hush money!

GEORGE: No!

HANNOCK: *Why* were all these Amsterdam tunnel bonds made over to Parker Jennings?

GEORGE: He helped us get the bill passed!

HANNOCK: *Ask Vorhees* if he wouldn't put that down in the expense-book under the name of Blackmail.

GEORGE: No!

HANNOCK: Ask Vorhees!

GEORGE: You can't alter the diplomacy of the business world – calling it by ugly names.

HANNOCK: No, I can't but *Roosevelt did!*

GEORGE: If you think I'm afraid of what you –

HANNOCK: Oh, come! Stop bluffing! If you don't realize I know what I'm talking about, I'll go on. I know at least *five* separate deals of yours so damned crooked, if any *one* of them were made public you'd be out of business over night, and out of the country, if you know your job. [*He waits. No answer. George is weighing the truth or the lie of what he is saying. He evidently sees some truth in it*] And I've got proof of what I say! Every proof! I've got copies of letters and telegrams, when I couldn't get the originals. I've got shorthand reports of private telephone conversations. I've got data enough for fifty trials, if it should come to that. I've been preparing for a deal of my own *with you* ever since I came to you! Only – God! [*He is moved as he thinks of Cicely*] I didn't think it would be trying to get rid of my life! I'd planned to make you finance a big game for me!

GEORGE: If what you say is true – and I don't know but what some of it may be, – then it's good-by to everything for me, and it'll be about all I'm worth having come to me.

HANNOCK: That's it! Even Middleburg'll be too small for you, if I show you up! But you know what'll shut my lips tight! Gimme the gun –

GEORGE: [*Quickly*] No.

HANNOCK: [*Pleadingly*] You've *everything* to get, and *nothing* to lose by it!

GEORGE: Yes, I have something to lose! – what rag of honor I've got left!

HANNOCK: No! Think a minute – if *I'm* out of the way? There's no real scandal – your father's old story – *our* father's old story – isn't even known by *your mother.* I shot Cicely, and killed myself, – it's an ordinary story. I was drunk or crazy – she wouldn't have me. Any story you want to make up, and there'll not be a murmur against Cicely, then! But can you see the papers if the *real story comes out!!* All over this country, and all the countries, it'll be telegraphed and pictured and revelled in. It'll even get into the cinematograph shows in Europe – with some low down girl masquerading as Cicely.

GEORGE: Stop! *Stop!*

HANNOCK: And the story will come out, if I go to trial. I'll stop at nothing to take it out of you. Whether you believe or not what I say about your business methods, you take my word for it, my arrest will put a quietus on your election, and *finish you*, not only in a political career, but any old career at all!

GEORGE: What a finish! What a finish of all I hoped to do and be!

HANNOCK: And – you'll lose the woman who's just left this room. Whether all *her brother's* high-browed talk is bunkum or not, even *I* know *hers* is serious; and if she finds you've deceived her all the time, that your high ideals are *fake* – !

GEORGE: [*Interrupts, crying, in an agony, half to himself*] They're not! They're not! God knows, nobody's been more deceived in me than I've been myself!

HANNOCK: Well, you know she won't stand for it. A girl like – her heart couldn't stomach it! Go on, bring me to trial and lose everything you've banked on for a career! Lose your business standing, lose your best friends, lose the woman you want, and raise the rottenest scandal for your family, for your mother, to bear, and your little sister's memory to go foul under! Do it all, and be damned to you!! [*He falls on his knees with exhaustion*]

GEORGE: My God, how can I?

HANNOCK: [*Whining, pleading*] All you have to do, to save every mother's son of us, is to let me do what the law'll do anyway! Leave that pistol where I can get it, and walk half a dozen steps away. That's all you need do! [*He sees George hesitate*] It's *all* or nothing for you!! It's the finish or the beginning! Are you ready and willing to be down and out, and go through the hell my living'll mean for you? [*He sees George weaken more*] You'll be Governor! Sure, you'll marry Miss Vorhees! You'll find all the proofs I told you about in my safety deposit box at the Manhattan. And there'll be only *white* flowers and pity on the new little grave! It'll be your *chance* to prove by the future that you were made of the right stuff at heart, after all!

George puts down the pistol not far from Hannock's reach, and starts to walk away with a set face – suffering. Hannock makes a slow, silent step towards the pistol, but, before he can get it, George turns and recovers it, with a terrific revulsion of feeling. He seizes the pistol and throws it through the big glass window

GEORGE: No! I haven't the right! You must take your punishment as it comes, and I *must take mine!* [*He suddenly breaks down; tears fill his throat and pour from his eyes. Hannock is crouching and drivelling on the floor*] This is my *only chance* to show I can be on the level! That I *can be straight*, when it's plain what *is* the right thing to do! God help me *do it!*

The door opens and a Policeman enters with Foot, as

The Curtain Falls

ACT III

SCENE: *Same room as Act II, only seen from another point of view. The mantel is now Right and the windows Back. Left is the wall not seen before. Later the same day. Vorhees and George are seated at the desk before a mass of business papers. There is a tall whiskey-and-soda glass, nearly empty, and a plate with the remnants of some sandwiches, beside George. The shades of the windows are drawn, but it is still daylight. George looks crushed, mentally and physically, but is calm and immovable. Vorhees looks stern and disappointed. There is a pause; neither men move.*

GEORGE: That's all? [*Vorhees nods his head. George drinks, and gathers up the papers*] What's to be done with these papers? Are they Hannock's or mine?

VORHEES: They have only to do with *your* affairs. Hannock hadn't any right to them! In any case, you don't pretend to deny anything these papers prove. Destroy them!

GEORGE: But – [*Getting up all the papers, except some of his own, which he separates and leaves on the desk*]

VORHEES: I doubt if, when it comes to the point, Hannock will go into all this business! He will have had months to cool down, and his hands will be full enough. [*He gives George a couple of papers he has had in his hand, and motions to the fireplace*] Here! don't wash your dirty linen, *burn it!*

George goes to the fireplace with a mass of papers, and burns them

GEORGE: [*As the papers burn*] Has Eleanor gone home?

VORHEES: Yes, but she promised your mother to come back later and stop over-night with her.

GEORGE: I wonder if she'd be willing to see me?

VORHEES: Yes, because I'm sure she didn't believe Hannock.

GEORGE: Tess can stay with mother. There'll be no need of her pretending to go back to Don, now.

VORHEES: *Pretending!*

GEORGE: Yes, That's something else I did, – persuaded Tess to make Don believe she'd come back in accordance with his conditions. But it was agreed between us she was to break her word to him, *after the election!* [*He burns his last batch of papers*]

VORHEES: It's a pity you can't burn that, too! I'd have staked my reputation on your being absolutely on the level! How I have been taken in by you!

GEORGE: I know, it sounds ridiculous, and I don't expect you to understand it; but I've been taken in by myself, too! Shall I write my withdrawal from the nomination, or will you take a verbal message?

VORHEES: Write it. It will make less for me to say by way of explanation. [*George goes to the desk and writes*] I'm sorry, I'm sorry, George. I *know* what it means to you!

GEORGE: Somehow now, it doesn't seem so much, after all; I suppose that's Cicely – poor little girl – poor little girl, – and – Eleanor. [*He adds the last, almost in a whisper*]

VORHEES: You're a *young* man, George! You've got a good chance yet to make good, and it's all up to you!

GEORGE: I know that –

VORHEES: I suppose you won't want to go back to Middleburg?

GEORGE: No! No!! For everybody's sake! But, *would it have* been wrong – leave *me* out of it, – to have saved *father's memory*, to have saved mother – could I have let him do it?

VORHEES: You know you couldn't!

GEORGE: Yes, and anyway, I didn't. Why can't I forget it!

VORHEES: Oh, it'll be many a day before you *deserve* to forget it!

GEORGE: But, will *you* ever have any confidence in me? Can any one ever believe in me again? [*Buries his face in his hands, and groans*]

VORHEES: *I can.* Whether I *do* or not, is entirely up to you.

GEORGE: You're sure of that?

VORHEES: [*Takes his hand and shakes it*] Sure.

GEORGE: And Eleanor?

VORHEES: Well – there's no use in my lying about it. If I know her, you must give up all idea of marrying her. Eleanor's husband must be a man she can *look up* to. That's a necessity of her nature – she can't help it. But *I do* believe she'll *help you* with *her friendship*. If you don't go back to Middleburg, where will you go?

GEORGE: Here! I stay *right here!*

VORHEES: [*Surprised*] Here! It'll be *hard*.

GEORGE: I suppose it will!

VORHEES: How will you start?

GEORGE: First, make a clean breast to my partners! Give back all the money I've made in ways which you've proved to me are illegal. Publish every form of graft I've benefited by, for the sake of future protection! Resign from all –

VORHEES: It's gigantic! It's colossal! *Can* you do it?

GEORGE: [*Simply*] I can try. I'm going to have a go at it, anyway!

VORHEES: The Press! Among your professional associates – here and all over the State – it'll be hell for you to go through!

GEORGE: I know it! I know it! But to get back where I want to be – if I ever can! I've got to fight it out right here, and make good *here*, or not at all. I don't care what it costs me!

TERESA: [*Opening the door*] May I come in?

GEORGE: Yes, come in, Tess. Where's mother?

TERESA: She's locked herself in her room! She's *turned against me* in the most extraordinary manner! Says my influence over Cicely is at the bottom of everything! [*She begins to cry*] She goes so far as to say, if I'd behaved like a decent woman, she doesn't believe this would have happened! I didn't care what other people believe of me, but this I didn't bargain for! I have been unfaithful to Don in my heart – and in my mind, perhaps, – but that's all –

GEORGE: I always felt it, Tess!

TERESA: Can't you persuade mother?

GEORGE: *Bert could*, because he represents the outside world.

TERESA: But you know Bert. He wouldn't persuade her, unless he believed in me himself.

VORHEES: That's true, and I'll go talk with her now, if Mrs. Rand will see me. [*He goes toward door*]

TERESA: [*Deeply moved, and grateful*] Thank you!

VORHEES: That's all right. [*He goes out*]

TERESA: George, I don't know – but everything, even Jimmy Cairns, seems so little now, in comparison with *Cicely – dead*, the bottom fallen out of everything!

GEORGE: Even worse than that, for me. I've given up the nomination.

TERESA: I'm sorry! Did Bert feel you had to?

GEORGE: No more than I did. You won't have to act a lie for me after all, Tess.

TERESA: I'm glad! I know, if Eleanor Vorhees knew I was doing it –

GEORGE: She's going to know it, – and that I'm a liar! She's going to know much worse things than that! Everybody's going to know them, I guess! Father was a crook in business, – that's the ugly, unvarnished fact, – and I've been a worse one! But I'd rather she'd learn these things from me, – what Hannock hasn't already told her – rather than she learned them outside.

TERESA: But George! George!! Don't you realize you'll lose her?

GEORGE: Well, I've lost everything else, except –

TERESA: Except what?

GEORGE: Except that! After all, I don't believe, way down at the bottom, I'm not fundamentally straight! I mean to give myself, all by myself, a chance to prove it! I know there are lots of "good men" who are born crooks. I want to see if I'm not a crook who was born good!

Vorhees reenters

VORHEES: It's all right. They've told Mrs. Rand she can go in and see Cicely now, and she wants you to go with her.

TERESA: [*Holds his hand in her two, for a moment*] Thank you! [*She goes out*]

VORHEES: And give me that paper you wrote. The sooner we get that off our hands, the better. [*George takes up the paper and, reading it over to himself, goes slowly to Vorhees, and gives it to him*]

VORHEES: Too bad, old man, too bad! But it *can't* be helped.

GEORGE: I know! [*Vorhees starts to go*] Bert, – Eleanor hasn't come yet?

VORHEES: No. Are you sure you want to see her, or shall I first –

GEORGE: No, leave it to me! I'd rather. I don't want a loophole, anywhere, for her thinking me a coward. I want to make a clean breast of it all! That's what I'm after, – a clean breast, no matter what the doing it costs me!

VORHEES: You're right. [*About to go*]

Enter Foot

FOOT: A gentleman from a newspaper, sir.

GEORGE: Will you see him, Bert?

VORHEES: Yes. [*To Foot*] You refer all the reporters to me. You know my address?

FOOT: Yes, sir.

VORHEES: [*To Foot*] Say no one here can be seen. [*To George*] I'll see you early to-morrow.

GEORGE: Thank you. I'd like your help in laying out a plan of action. Of course I shan't do anything till after – [*He hesitates, and raises his head and eyes to upstairs*]

VORHEES: I wouldn't. [*Goes out*]

Foot exits. George stands alone in the room, a picture of utter dejection, of ruin and sorrow, but with a bulldog look all the while, – the look of a man who is licked, beaten, but not dead yet. He stands immovable almost – in complete silence. Slowly and softly, the door opens. Van Vranken looks in. He speaks in a sullen, hushed, and somewhat awed voice. He is pale; all evidence of drinking and excitement are gone

VAN VRANKEN: George?

GEORGE: [*In a monotonous voice*] Hello, Don – you know?

VAN VRANKEN: I just heard. It's *true*? [*George, with a set face and stern lips, nods his head firmly, still standing. Van Vranken collapses in a chair*] God! Poor Cicely!

GEORGE: Tough, isn't it? [*With a great sigh*]

VAN VRANKEN: I was having an awful time, George, with Mrs. Judly. She was giving it to me good for being willing to patch it up, temporarily, with Tess! She *didn't care about you!* I've come to the conclusion she don't care about anybody, anyway, but herself. Her brother telephoned it from his Club, and *she* – [*His anger rises*] had the rottenness to say she believed there was something between

Hannock and Cicely. That was more than I could stand for! God knows I'm as bad as they make them, but, with that little girl dead like that – to think such a thing, let alone say it – I don't know! – It took it out of me, somehow! It didn't seem to me it was the time to have a low quarrel between two people like us! It made us seem so beastly small! Death's such an awful – such a big – I suppose I'll feel differently to-morrow – but to-day – now – George, I *couldn't* stand for it! She kicked me out, and I give you my word of honor I'm glad she did!

GEORGE: [*Not deeply impressed, but civil*] As you say, you'll feel differently to-morrow.

VAN VRANKEN: Very likely! Still, I've got these few decent hours, anyway, to put on your sister's grave. [*A pause. George sits*]

GEORGE: I've given up running for governor.

VAN VRANKEN: [*Surprised*] Because – ?

GEORGE: No. You'll hear all the reasons soon enough. The point for the moment is, you and Tess needn't fake any further – living together.

VAN VRANKEN: [*Thoughtfully*] I see. [*After a pause*] George – ?

GEORGE: What?

VAN VRANKEN: Could I see Cicely?

GEORGE: [*Hesitating*] Tess is there.

VAN VRANKEN: [*After a moment*] Then, perhaps I'd better not go – ?

GEORGE: I think I *would*, if I were you.

Van Vranken looks at George questioningly. Teresa enters

TERESA: [*Quietly*] Don – [*Her voice fills; she turns aside, and hastily wipes her eyes*]

VAN VRANKEN: [*Moved*] I was going upstairs.

TERESA: Not now! Mother and I have just left. They've come to – [*She stops, and again turns aside*]

VAN VRANKEN: Where are the children?

TERESA: Home!

VAN VRANKEN: "Home"? [*Very meaningly*]

TERESA: At the house.

VAN VRANKEN: Oh, Tess! – I'm – I'm not fit to take care of them! You'd better take them both, Tess, but let me see them off and on –

TERESA: I'm going back now with you, Don.

VAN VRANKEN: You needn't. I take it all back, Tess. You can have it your own way entirely.

Leave Mrs. Judly out of it, – that's all I'll ask. Outside that, I'll fix it easy for you.

TERESA: Thank you, Don, [*After a second's pause*] but, if you don't mind, I'd rather go back with you for the present, anyway. It seems to me, between us, we've pretty well spoiled everything except – well, – perhaps, in thinking of the children's happiness we might find something for ourselves! What do you say?

VAN VRANKEN: It's worth a try – so long as you're willing!

Enter Mrs. Rand in a flurry

MRS. RAND: Has any one thought to send for a dressmaker? [*Nobody answers*] Did *you* think of it, Teresa?

TERESA: No, I'm afraid I didn't.

MRS. RAND: [*Her eyes filling*] I haven't the remotest idea what's the thing to wear! In Middleburg, I'd have known, – but here, I'm always wrong! If I'd had my way, I'd never have taken off my crepe veil for your father, and now *I wish I hadn't!* [*She sees Don*] Oh! I didn't see you, Don. Have you come to beg Tess's pardon? Has this terrible thing reformed you?

VAN VRANKEN: I don't know, mother, how much reform is possible, but I came to tell Tess I'm ashamed – [*He and Teresa exchange a look of almost sympathy, – at least, all antagonism has gone from them*]

MRS. RAND: I confess, if I were Tess I could never forgive you! *Her father* spoiled me for that sort of thing!

GEORGE: Tess isn't thinking now only of herself.

MRS. RAND: Oh, why did we ever come here! That was the first and *great mistake!* I haven't had a happy moment since I left their father's and my old home!

TERESA: Mother! Mother!!

MRS. RAND: It's the truth, – I haven't! I've never been anything, in New York, but a fizzle! I've been snubbed right and left by the people I wanted to know! I'm lonesome for my church, and if I died I wouldn't have a handful of people at my funeral!

GEORGE: But you're going to *live*, mother, and you'll see we'll make you happy yet!

MRS. RAND: Not here! You can't do it yourself! Bert says you have given up running for governor, and Tess says everything's off between you and Eleanor. I don't have to be told how disappointed and unhappy you are, and Tess's made a miserable mess of it! And now, Cicely, the baby of you all! – killed, like this! [*She breaks down into hysterical sobbing*] It's more than I can bear! I tell you, children, I can't bear it! And it's all thanks to coming *here!!* This is what we get for not doing what your father wished. Why didn't we stay home? I amounted to something there. I had as much sense as my neighbors. I could hold my own! Here, I've been made to understand I was such a nonentity – that I've grown actually to be the fool they believe me! Oh, what the City has done for the whole of us!

TERESA: Yes, you're right, mother. I was happy too, till I came here. It was the City that taught me to make the worst of things, instead of the best of them.

GEORGE: [*Gently*] No, Tess – let's be honest with ourselves to-day. After all, it's our own fault –

VAN VRANKEN: I agree with Tess! She and I, in a small town, would have been happy always! I'd not have been tempted like I am here – I couldn't have had the chances –

GEORGE: [*Rising and speaking with the fulness of conviction*] No! You're all wrong! Don't blame the City. It's not her fault! It's our own! What the City does is to bring out what's strongest in us. If at heart we're good, the good in us will win! If the bad is strongest, God help us! Don't blame the City! *She* gives the man his opportunity; it is up to *him* what he makes of it! A man can live in a small town all his life, and deceive the whole place and *himself* into thinking he's got all the virtues, when at heart he's a hypocrite! But the village gives him no chance to find it out, to prove it to his fellows – the small town is too easy! *But the City!!!* A man goes to the gates of the City and knocks! – New York or Chicago, Boston or San Francisco, no matter *what* city so long as it's big, and busy, and selfish, and self-centered. And she comes to her gates and takes him in, and she stands him in the middle of her market place – where Wall Street and Herald Square and Fifth Avenue and the Bowery, and Harlem, and Forty-second Street all meet, and there she strips him naked of all his disguises – and all his hypocrisies, – and she paints his ambition on her fences, and lights up her skyscrapers with it! – what *he wants* to be and *what he thinks he is!* – and then she says to him, Make good if you can, or to Hell with you! And what is in him comes out to clothe his nakedness, and to the City he can't lie! I *know*, because I *tried!* [*A short pause*]

Foot enters

FOOT: Miss Vorhees.

GEORGE: Ask her to come in here.

Teresa rises quickly

TERESA: Don, I think –

VAN VRANKEN: I've a taxi outside.

MRS. RAND: All this time, and that clock going on every minute!

TERESA: [*To Mrs. Rand*] Mother, if you want to see us after dinner, telephone. [*Kisses her*]

MRS. RAND: What about our clothes?

TERESA: I'll attend to everything in the morning. [*Teresa and Don go out together*]

MRS. RAND: I think I'd rather be alone with you, George, to-night, if the things are off between you and Eleanor. At a time like this, there is no excuse for her going back on you –

GEORGE: Hush, mother! You don't understand. She has every excuse. I'll tell you about it afterward.

MRS. RAND: No, tell her for me not to stop. I wanted her, because I thought she loved you – and was to be one of us – that's all! [*Enter Eleanor*] Thank you for coming back, Eleanor, but good night. George will explain. [*She goes out*]

ELEANOR: What is the matter with your mother? and Teresa? And Bert seemed strange, too, when I met him outside. What have I done?

GEORGE: Nothing, Eleanor.

ELEANOR: [*Realizing what it may mean*] They think I believed what Hannock said? That anything he would say against *you* could for *one* moment mean anything to *me!*

GEORGE: You didn't believe Hannock?

ELEANOR: Not for one second! That's why I left the room.

GEORGE: You'd better have stayed.

ELEANOR: Why?

GEORGE: Because he told the truth!

ELEANOR: How do you mean?

GEORGE: Everything he told me here, this afternoon, was true.

ELEANOR: Not when *I* was here! When I was here, he was calling you a thief, and a cheat, and a liar!

GEORGE: He was right!

ELEANOR: No! I don't understand you!

GEORGE: Your brother understands – and I've withdrawn my name from the nomination! I'm giving up all the things it seemed to me I wanted most, – and *you*, most of all, Eleanor! I thought I minded losing the others, but in comparison with what I feel now!!! *You loved* me because I was honest!

ELEANOR: Not *because*, – but, of course, if you were not *honest* –

GEORGE: Well, I'm not – I'm *not!*

ELEANOR: *You are! I know you are!*

GEORGE: No! I've lied and tricked and cheated in business, and I've got to pay for it!

ELEANOR: And all this you did *deliberately?*

GEORGE: The only excuse I have, if you can call it an excuse, is that I didn't realize what I was doing! I did what others I had been taught to respect, to pattern on, did before me, – what others were doing around me! I accepted cheating for business diplomacy. I explained lying as the commercial code! I looked on stealing as legitimate borrowing! But I was a grown man, and in possession of my senses, and I had no real excuse! Eleanor, I've been a *business "crook,"* in a big way, perhaps, but still a *"crook,"* and I'm not good enough for *you!* [*A pause*]

ELEANOR: What are you going to do?

GEORGE: Give up all the positions I haven't any right to fill. Pay back interest I hadn't any right to get, and money I hadn't any right to use! Give up principal I gained on somebody else's risk than my own! Begin all over again at the bottom, but on the *level*, and climb, only if I can do it on the square!

ELEANOR: I understand! I understand it all, now! You've done wrong?

GEORGE: Yes.

ELEANOR: Oh, so wrong, but you're owning all up, and *giving* all up!

GEORGE: Yes.

ELEANOR: You aren't being pressed to?

GEORGE: Of course I could fight it, but what's

the use? *It's true!* Now *I realize that,* I can't own up fast enough! I can't begin over again soon enough! I can't eat or sleep or take a long breath even, till I'm on the level again with myself. Even at the price of *you!* But I'll make you believe in me again, Eleanor, – you'll see, if we live long enough!

ELEANOR: We don't have to live *any longer* for that.

GEORGE: In what way?

ELEANOR: The man who has done wrong, and can own it up, – face life all over again empty-handed, emptying his own hands of his own accord, turn his back on everything he counted on and lived for, because it is the right thing to do, and because – leaving the world out of it – he *had to be honest with himself!* – that –

George – is the man I look up to ten times more than the one who was *born* good and lived good because he never was tempted to enjoy the spoils of going wrong! It's the man whom it costs something to be good, – that's what makes real character! And to me – [*She goes up to him, and puts her hand on his arm*] you, here, *to-day,* are twice the man you were yesterday! You needed a test, though we didn't know it! And at the same time we found that out, you had to go through it; and thank God, your real self has triumphed! *To-day* you *are* the man I loved yesterday!

GEORGE: [*Looking away*] Now, I know what those people mean who say a man gets all the *Hell* that's coming to him *in this world,* – [*Looking at her*] – and *all the Heaven, too!*

The Curtain Falls

ACKNOWLEDGMENTS

THE late Professor A. M. Drummond of Cornell introduced me to the fascinations of the nineteenth-century American theatre and, with his customary generosity, counseled me in the early stages of preparing the present volume. My full debt to him can be recognized but never repaid.

Professor Edwin Harrison Cady's wise editorial suggestions on the essays were most helpful. Another Indiana colleague, Professor Hubert C. Heffner, was always available for a quick question or an afternoon's discussion. I am grateful for his guidance and for his friendship.

Although the full account of my indebtedness is recorded in the bibliography, many persons have provided more than professional courtesy, particularly my associates in American theatre studies: Professors Jonathan W. Curvin, Alan S. Downer, Barnard Hewitt, Francis Hodge, and Garff B. Wilson. Like all others committed to the exploration of our nineteenth-century drama and theatre, I have depended on the pioneer work of Professors George C. D. Odell and Arthur Hobson Quinn. As usual, George Freedley, curator of the Theatre Collection at the New York Public Library, and the late William Van Lennep, in the comparable post at Harvard, were most generous. Mr. John T. Herne gave me helpful insights into the career of his father, James A. Herne. The Graduate School of Indiana University generously supplied funds to help with the preparation of the manuscript.

Specific sources, courtesies, and permissions are noted below.

INTRODUCTORY ESSAYS

Earlier versions of the essays on *Uncle Tom's Cabin* and the "Minstrel Show" appeared in *American Heritage* and the *Educational Theatre Journal*, respectively. Selections from Clyde Fitch's letters are used with the permission of Mrs. Montrose J. Moses.

PLAY TEXTS

Dialogue and Ode. From *An Exercise Containing a Dialogue and Ode on the Accession of His Present Gracious Majesty, George III*. Philadelphia, 1762. The "Dartmouth Dialogues" are reprinted by permission of Harold G. Rugg and Hazel E. Joslyn, Archivist, Dartmouth College Library.

The Candidates is reprinted, with permission, from the text of the play edited by J. B. Hubbell and Douglass Adair, published in *William and Mary Quarterly*, April, 1948.

The Contrast. From the Dunlap Society Publication, New York, 1886.

Bunker-Hill. From the edition of D. Longworth, At the Dramatic Repository, Shakespeare-Gallery, New York, July, 1817.

The Glory of Columbia. From the edition of D. Longworth, At the Dramatic Repository, Shakespeare-Gallery, New York, May, 1817.

She Would Be a Soldier. From the edition of D. Longworth, At the Dramatic Repository, Shakespeare-Gallery, G. L. Birch & Co., Printers, New York, 1819.

The Forest Rose. From the edition published at the Circulating Library and Dramatic Repository, No. 4 Chambers St., Hopkins and Morris, Printers, New York, 1825. Collated with the Samuel French text, 1854.

A Trip to Niagara. From the edition published by E. B. Clayton, No. 9 Chambers Street, New York, 1830.

Metamora. From *America's Lost Plays*, Vol. XIV, by permission of Barrett H. Clark, the University of Utah, and the Edwin Forrest Home. The prologue and epilogue are reprinted from *Favorite American Plays* by permission of Barrett H. Clark. They appeared originally in *Occasional Addresses*, edited by Laurence Hutton and William Carey, printed by the Dunlap Society in 1890. The fourth act was found by the present editor among the Lord Chamberlain's Plays in the British Museum. It was first printed in *American Literature* and is reprinted with permission.

The Gladiator. From *Life and Dramatic Works of Robert Montgomery Bird*. New York, 1919. The manuscript is in the University of Pennsylvania Library.

The Drunkard. From the edition of the DeWitt Publishing House, New York, 1856.

Fashion. From the edition of W. Newberry, London, 1850.

Uncle Tom's Cabin is a composite from various prompt-book editions of the Aiken text in the New York Public Library.

Po-ca-hon-tas. From Vol. I, *Brougham's Dramatic*

Works. New York, Samuel French, 1856.

Francesca da Rimini. From *Plays and Poems*, by George H. Boker. Philadelphia, 1856.

The "Minstrel Show" was assembled from texts in the New York Public Library.

Across the Continent. From *America's Lost Plays*, Vol. IV, by permission of Barrett H. Clark and Royal Stout.

The Mulligan Guard Ball. From the manuscript in the Library of Congress submitted for copyright in 1879.

A Letter of Introduction. From the edition of Harper and Bros., New York, 1892.

Shenandoah. From the edition of the Society of American Dramatists and Composers, New York, 1897.

A Temperance Town. From *America's Lost Plays*, Vol. IX, by permission of Barrett H. Clark.

Shore Acres. From *Shore Acres and Other Plays*. New York, Samuel French, 1928. By permission.

Copyright, 1928, by Katherine C. Herne; copyright in renewal 1956, by John T. Herne.

CAUTION: Professionals and amateurs are hereby warned that SHORE ACRES, being fully protected under copyright laws of the United States of America, the British Empire, including the Dominion of Canada, and all other countries of the Copyright Union, is subject to royalty. All rights, including professional, amateur, motion pictures, recitation, public reading, radio and television broadcasting and the rights of translation into foreign languages are strictly reserved. Amateurs may give stage production of this play upon payment of a royalty of $50 for the first performance and $25 for each additional performance one week before the play is to be given to Samuel French, Inc., at 25 West 45th Street, New York 36, N. Y., or 7623 Sunset Blvd., Hollywood 46, Calif., or if in Canada to Samuel French (Canada) Ltd., at 27 Grenville St., Toronto, Ont.

The Great Divide. From *Poems and Plays*, Vol. II. Boston, Houghton Mifflin Co., 1906.

The New York Idea. From the Walter H. Baker edition, Boston, 1908.

The City. From *Plays by Clyde Fitch*. Boston, Little, Brown & Co., 1915.

BIBLIOGRAPHIES

New books and magazine articles on American plays, players, and playwrights appear regularly. To keep the following bibliographies up to date, the *Educational Theatre Journal* and *American Literature* will be most helpful. In addition to its own articles and book reviews, *American Literature* lists the articles related to American studies in other journals.

Thesis and dissertation studies devoted to American dramatists and to local and regional theatre history have been particularly abundant in recent years, most notably at Cornell University, the University of Illinois, Indiana University, the State University of Iowa, Stanford University, and the University of Wisconsin. Only a selected few are listed here. A record of these academic explorations can be found in the summer numbers of *Speech Monographs* and in the quarterly issues of *American Literature*.

The bibliographies are grouped under the following headings: Individual Bibliographies; Basic Sources: History and Criticism; Additional History and Criticism; Local and Regional History; Actors, Playwrights, and Managers; Bibliographies and Lists; Anthologies of American Plays.

INDIVIDUAL BIBLIOGRAPHIES

GEORGE L. AIKEN
UNCLE TOM'S CABIN

Ames, Edgar W. "First Presentation of Uncle Tom's Cabin," *Americana*, VI (Nov., 1911), 1045–1052.

Birdoff, Harry. *The World's Greatest Hit.* New York, 1947.

Drummond, A. M., and Richard Moody. "The Hit of the Century: Uncle Tom's Cabin – 1852–1952," *Educational Theatre Journal*, IV (Dec., 1952), 315–322.

Fields, Annie. *The Life and Letters of Harriet Beecher Stowe.* Boston, 1897.

Gassner, John. "Harriet Beecher Stowe on the Stage," *Current History*, IV (April, 1943), 156–158.

Hewitt, Barnard. "Uncle Tom and Uncle Sam: New Light from an Old Play," *Quarterly Journal of Speech*, XXXVII (Feb., 1951), 63–70.

Jackson, Frederick H. "Uncle Tom's Cabin in Italy," *Symposium*, VII (Nov., 1953), 323–332.

Jaffe, Adrian. "Uncle Tom in the Penal Colony: Heine's View of Uncle Tom's Cabin," *American-German Review*, XIX (Feb., 1953), 5–6.

King, Emmett C. "The Great American Drama," *The Metropolitan Magazine* (undated).

Lippman, Monroe. "Uncle Tom and His Poor Relations: American Slavery Plays," *Southern Speech Journal*, XXVIII (Spring, 1963), 183–197.

McCray, F. Y. *The Life of the Author of Uncle Tom's Cabin.* New York, 1889.

McDowell, John H., *et al.* "Uncle Tom's Cabin," *Ohio State University Collection Bulletin*, 10 (1963), 10–39.

MacLean, Grace Edith. *Uncle Tom's Cabin in Germany.* New York, 1910.

Moody, Richard. "Uncle Tom, the Theater and Mrs. Stowe," *American Heritage*, VI (Oct., 1955), 29–33, 102–103.

Nicholas, H. G. "Uncle Tom's Cabin, 1852–1952," *American Heritage*, IV (Winter, 1953), 20–23, 72.

Peck, H. T. "Uncle Tom's Cabin in Liverpool," *Bookman*, VI (Dec., 1897), 310.

Rabill, Frank. "America's Number One Hit," *Theatre Arts*, XXXVI (Oct., 1952), 18–24.

Roppolo, J. P. "Harriet Beecher Stowe and New Orleans: A Study in Hate," *New England Quarterly*, 30 (Sept., 1957), 346–362.

———. "Uncle Tom in New Orleans: Three Lost Plays," *New England Quartely*, 27 (June, 1954), 213–226.

Stockbridge, Frank P. "The Most Popular American Drama," *Green Book*, IX (Jan., 1913), 80–87.

Stowe, Harriet Beecher. *The Key to Uncle Tom's Cabin/ Presenting/ the Original Facts and Documents Upon Which the Story is Founded/ Together with Corroborative Statements/ Verifying the Truth of the Work.* London, 1853.

———. *Uncle Tom's Cabin.* Boston, 1881.

Stowe, Lyman Beecher. *Biography of Harriet Beecher Stowe.* Boston, 1911.

"What's Become of Uncle Tom's Cabin?" *American Playwright*, III (Aug., 1914), 264–266.

ROBERT MONTGOMERY BIRD
THE GLADIATOR

Bird, Mary. *Life of Robert Montgomery Bird.* Philadelphia, 1945.

Blanck, Jacob. "Robert Montgomery Bird," *Bibliography of American Literature*, I, 228–234. New Haven, 1955.

Bloom, Robert L. "Robert Montgomery Bird, Editor," *Pennsylvania Magazine of History and Biography*, LXXVI (April, 1952), 123–141.

Dahl, Curtis. *Robert Montgomery Bird*. New York, 1963.

Foust, Clement. *Life and Dramatic Works of Robert Montgomery Bird*. New York, 1919.

Harris, Richard. "An Analysis of the Serious Dramas of Robert Montgomery Bird." Doctoral dissertation, Indiana University, 1966.

———. "The Lost Scene from *News of the Night*," *University of Pennsylvania Library Chronicle*, XXIV (1958), 1–12.

———. "A Young Dramatist's Diary: The Secret Records of R. M. Bird," *University of Pennsylvania Library Chronicle*, XXV (1959), 8–24.

Quinn, Arthur Hobson, ed. *The City Looking Glass*, by Robert Montgomery Bird. New York, 1933.

Thompson, C. Seymour, ed. "Travelling with Robert Montgomery Bird," University of Pennsylvania *Library Chronicle*, VII (March, 1939), 11–22, (June, 1939), 34–50, (Oct.–Dec., 1939), 75–90; VIII (April 1940), 4–21.

Williams, Stanley T. *The Spanish Background of American Literature*. 2 vols. New Haven, 1955.

GEORGE H. BOKER
FRANCESCA DA RIMINI

Barnes, James. "George H. Boker," *Nassau Literary Magazine*, XLVI (1891), 90.

Boker, George H. *Plays and Poems*. Boston, 1856.

Bradley, Edward Sculley. *George Henry Boker*. London, 1927; Philadelphia, 1927.

———. "George Henry Boker and Angie Hicks," *American Literature*, VIII (Nov., 1936), 258–265.

———, ed. *Glaucus and Other Plays*, by George Henry Boker. (*America's Lost Plays*, Vol. III.) Princeton, 1941; Bloomington, Indiana, 1963.

———. *Sonnets: A Sequence on Profane Love*. Philadelphia, 1929.

Brewer, E. "Boker's Francesca da Rimini," *The American*, V (1883), 363.

Hubbell, Jay B. "George Henry Boker, Paul Hamilton Hayne and Charles Warren Stoddard: Some Unpublished Letters," *American Literature*, V (May, 1933), 146ff.

Krutch, Joseph Wood. "A Little Known American Dramatist," *Sewanee Review*, XXV (Oct., 1917), 457–468.

Lathrop, George P. "Authors at Home. George H. Boker in Walnut Street, Philadelphia," *The Critic*, IX (April 14, 1888), 175–176.

———. "Some Recollections of Boker," *Atlantic Monthly*, LXV (1890), 427–430.

Leland, Charles Godfrey. "Reminiscences of George H. Boker," *The American*, XIX (March 1, 1890), 392–404.

Metcalf, J. C. "An Old Romantic Triangle, Francesca da Rimini in Three Dramas," *Sewanee Review*, XXIX (1921), 45–58.

Quinn, Arthur Hobson. "Dramas of George Henry Boker," *PMLA*, XXXII (1917), 233–266.

———. "George Henry Boker, Playwright and Patriot," *Scribner's Magazine*, LXXVII (1923), 701–715.

Stoddard, Richard Henry. "Recollections of George Henry Boker," *Lippincott*, XLV (June, 1890), 856–867.

Urban, Gertrude. "Paolo and Francesca in History and Literature," *The Critic*, XL (1902), 425–438.

JOHN BROUGHAM
PO-CA-HON-TAS

Hawes, David. "John Brougham: American Playwright and Man of the Theatre." Doctoral dissertation, Stanford University, 1954.

———. "John Brougham as Playwright," *Educational Theatre Journal*, IX (Oct., 1957), 184–193.

Hewitt, Barnard. "Mrs. John Wood and the Lost Art of Burlesque Acting," *Educational Theatre Journal*, 13 (May, 1961), 82–85.

Hubbell, Jay B. "The Smith Pocahontas Story in Literature," *Virginia Magazine of History and Biography*, LXV (July, 1957), 275–300.

Hutton, Laurence. "The American Burlesque," *Harper's Monthly*, LXXXI (June, 1890), 59–74.

Keese, W. L. *A Group of Comedians*. New York, 1901.

Matlaw, Myron. "Persiflage on the Nineteenth Century Stage," *Educational Theatre Journal*, 11 (Oct., 1959), 212–221.

Page, Eugene R., ed. "The Duke's Motto; or, I Am Here!" *Metamora and Other Plays*. (*America's Lost Plays*, Vol. XIV.) Princeton, 1941; Bloomington, Indiana, 1965.

Ryan, Pat M., Jr. "John Brougham: The Gentle Satirist, A Critique with a Handlist and Census," *Bulletin of the New York Public Library*, LXIII (Dec., 1959), 619–630.

Winter, William, ed. *Life, Stories, and Poems of John Brougham*. Boston, 1881.

JOHN DALY BURK
BUNKER-HILL

Campbell, Charles, ed. *Some Materials to Serve for a Brief Memoir of John Daly Burk*. Albany, 1868.

Shulim, Joseph I. "John Daly Burk, Playwright of Libertarianism," *Bulletin of the New York Public Library*, 65 (Sept., 1961), 451–463.

Wyatt, Edward Avery. *John Daly Burk*. Charlottesville, Virginia, 1936.

WILLIAM DUNLAP
THE GLORY OF COLUMBIA and
A TRIP TO NIAGARA

Baker, Louis Charles. *The German Drama in English on the New York Stage*. Philadelphia, 1917.

Benson, Adolph B. "Scandinavian Influences in the Works of William Dunlap and Richard Alsop," *Scandinavian Studies and Notes*, IX (Nov., 1927), 239–257.

Bowman, Mary Rives. "Dunlap and the 'Theatrical Register' of the New York Magazine," *Studies in Philology*, XXIV (July, 1921), 413–425.

Canary, Robert H. "William Dunlap and the Search for an American Audience," *Midcontinent American Studies Journal*, 4 (Spring, 1963), 45–51.

Coad, Oral Sumner. "The Dunlap Diaries at Yale," *Studies in Philology*, XXIV (July, 1927), 403–412.

———. "The Gothic Element in American Literature before 1835," *Journal of English and Germanic Philology*, XXIV (Jan., 1925), 72–93.

———. *William Dunlap*. New York, 1917.

Dunlap, William. *Diary of William Dunlap* (1766–1839). New York, 1930.

———. *A History of the Rise and Progress of the Arts of Design in the United States*. 3 vols. Boston, 1918; New York, 1965.

———. *Life of Charles Brockden Brown*. 2 vols. Philadelphia, 1815.

———. *Memoirs of a Water-Drinker*. New York, 1837.

Heffner, Hubert C., ed. *History of the American Theatre*, by William Dunlap. Cambridge, Massachusetts, 1966.

Matthews, Brander. Introduction to *André*. New York, 1887.

Wegelin, Oscar. "A Bibliographical Checklist of the Plays and Miscellaneous Writings of William Dunlap," *Bibliographica Americana*, Vol. 1. New York, 1916.

———. "William Dunlap and His Writings." Privately reprinted from *The Literary Collector* (Jan., 1904).

CLYDE FITCH
THE CITY

Bell, Archie. *The Clyde Fitch I Knew*. New York, 1909.

Bernbaum, Martin. "Clyde Fitch, An Appreciation," *Independent*, LXVII, 123–131.

Eaton, Walter Prichard. "The Dramatist as Man of Letters: The Case of Clyde Fitch," *Scribner's Magazine*, XLVI (April, 1910), 490–497.

Fitch, Clyde. "The Play and the Public," Memorial Edition of *Clyde Fitch's Plays*, Vol. IV. Boston, 1915.

———. *Plays by Clyde Fitch*. 4 vols. Boston, 1915.

———. *Some Correspondence and Six Conversations*. Chicago, 1890; New York, 1906.

Lowe, John A. "A Reading List of Clyde Fitch," *Bulletin of Bibliography*, 7 (July, 1912), 7.

Moses, Montrose J., and Virginia Gerson. *Clyde Fitch and His Letters*. Boston, 1924.

Patterson, Ada. "How a Rapid-Fire Dramatist Writes His Plays," *Theatre*, VII (Jan., 1907), 14–16.

Phelps, William Lyon. *Essays on Modern Dramatists*. New York, 1921.

Steell, Willis. "Clyde Fitch as Collaborator," *Theatre*, X (Dec., 1909), 176–178.

Strang, L. C. *Players and Plays of the Last Quarter Century*. New York, 1902.

EDWARD HARRIGAN
THE MULLIGAN GUARD BALL

Harrigan, Edward. *The Mulligans*. New York, 1901.

———, et al. "American Playwrights on the American Drama," *Harper's Weekly*, XXXIII (Feb. 2, 1889), 97–99.

History of the Mulligan Guard. New York, 1874.

Kahn, E. J., Jr. *The Merry Partners: The Age and Stage of Harrigan and Hart*. New York, 1955.

Montgomery, G. E. "Edward Harrigan," *Theatre*, I (1886), 397–398.

Quinn, Arthur Hobson. "The Perennial Humor of the American Stage," *Yale Review*, XVI (April, 1927), 553–566.

JAMES A. HERNE
SHORE ACRES

Bucks, Dorothy S., and Arthur H. Nethercott. "Ibsen and Herne's *Margaret Fleming*," *American Literature*, 17 (Jan., 1946), 311–333.

Corbin, John. "Drama," *Harper's Weekly*, XVIII (Feb. 11 and March 4, 1899), 139, 213.

Edwards, Herbert J., and Julie A. Herne. *James A. Herne: Rise of Realism in the American Drama.* Orono, Maine, 1964.

Flower, B. O. "Mask or Mirror," *Arena*, VIII (Aug., 1893), 304–313.

Garland, Hamlin. "Mr. and Mrs. Herne," *Arena*, IV (Oct., 1891), 543–560.

———. "On the Road with James A. Herne," *Century Magazine*, n.s. LXXXVIII (Aug., 1914), 574–581.

———, J. J. Enneking, and B. O. Flower. "An Appreciation: James A. Herne, Actor, Dramatist, and Man," *Arena*, XXVI (Sept., 1901), 282–291.

Hatlen, Theodore. "*Margaret Fleming* and the Boston Independent Theatre," *Educational Theatre Journal*, VIII (March, 1956), 17–21.

Herne, James A. "Art for Truth's Sake in the Drama," *Arena*, XVII (Feb., 1897), 361–370.

———. "Forty Years Behind the Footlights," *The Coming Age*, II, No. 2, 121–129.

———. "Old Stock Days in the Theatre," *Arena*, VI (Sept., 1892), 401–416.

———. *Shore Acres and Other Plays.* New York, 1928.

Howells, W. D. "Editor's Study," *Harper's Monthly*, LXXXIII (Aug., 1891), 478–479.

Pizer, Donald. "An 1890 Account of *Margaret Fleming*," *American Literature*, 27 (May, 1955), 264–267.

———. "The Radical Drama in Boston, 1889–1891," *New England Quarterly*, XXXI (Sept., 1958), 361–374.

Quinn, Arthur Hobson. "Herne and Ibsen. Theory and Facts," *American Literature*, 19 (May, 1957), 171–177.

———, ed. *Early Plays of James A. Herne.* (*America's Lost Plays*, Vol. VII.) Princeton, 1941; Bloomington, Indiana, 1963.

Tiempo, Marco. "James A. Herne in *Griffith Davenport*," *Arena*, XXII (Sept., 1899), 375–382.

Waggoner, Hyatt A. "The Growth of a Realist: James A. Herne," *New England Quarterly*, XV (March, 1942), 62–73.

FRANCIS HOPKINSON
COLLEGE DIALOGUES

Coad, Oral Sumner. "An Old American College Play," *Modern Language Notes*, XXXVII, No. 3 (March, 1922), 157–163.

Collins, V. Lansing. "Princeton Dramatics in the Eighteenth Century," *Princeton Alumni Weekly*, XVII (Dec., 1916), 227.

Hastings, George Everett. *The Life and Works of Francis Hopkinson.* Chicago, 1926.

Hopkinson, Francis. *An Exercise, Consisting of a Dialogue and Ode, Sacred to the Memory of His Late Gracious Majesty, George II.* Philadelphia, 1761. Performed at the Public Commencement in the College of Philadelphia, May 23rd, 1761.

———. *An Exercise Containing a Dialogue and Ode on the Accession of His Present Gracious Majesty, George III.* Philadelphia, 1762. Performed at the Public Commencement in the College of Philadelphia, May 18th, 1762.

———. *Miscellaneous Essays and Occasional Writings.* Philadelphia, 1792.

Lippincott, H. M. "Early Undergraduate Life," *General Magazine*, XXVIII (April. 1926), 316.

March, Phillip. "Philip Freneau and the Theater," *New Jersey Historical Society*, 66 (April, 1948), 96–105.

Matthews, Albert. "Early Plays at Harvard," *Nation*, XCVIII (March 19, 1914), 295.

Quinn, Arthur Hobson. "The Authorship of the First American College Masque," *General Magazine*, XXVIII (April, 1926), 313–316.

Rugg, Harold G. "The Dartmouth Plays, 1769–1782," *Theatre Annual* (1942), 55–69.

Thomas, Ota. "Student Dramatic Activities at Yale College During the 18th Century," *Theatre Annual* (1944), 47–59.

BRONSON HOWARD
SHENANDOAH

Archer, William. *English Dramatists of To-day.* London, 1882.

Bergman, Herbert. "Major Civil War Plays, 1882–1899," *Southern Speech Journal*, XIX (March, 1954), 224–231.

Briscoe, Johnson. "The Pioneer American Dramatist," *Green Book*, XI (May, 1914), 749–756.

Boyle, Charles John. "Bronson Howard and the Popular Temper of the Gilded Age." Doctoral dissertation, University of Wisconsin, 1957.

Clark, Barrett H. *A Study of the Modern Drama.* New York, 1925.

Ford, James L. "The Banker's Daughter," *Munsey's Magazine*, XXXIV (Nov., 1905), 199–202.

Halline, Allan Gates. "Bronson Howard's *The Amateur Benefit*," *American Literature*, XIV (1942), 74–76.

———, ed. *The Banker's Daughter and Other Plays*, by Bronson Howard. (*America's Lost Plays*, Vol. X.) Princeton, 1941; Bloomington, Indiana, 1964.

Hamilton, Clayton. "Bronson Howard," *The Bookman*, XXVIII (Sept., 1908), 55–56.

Howard, Bronson. "The American Drama," *Sunday Magazine* (Oct. 7, 1906). Reprinted in Montrose J. Moses, *Representative Plays by*

American Dramatists, Vol. III. New York, 1921; New York, 1964.

———. *Autobiography of a Play*. New York, 1914.

———. "Our Schools for the Stage," *Century Magazine*, LXI (Nov., 1900), 28–37.

———. "Theatrical Premieres," *Sunday Magazine, New York Tribune* (Jan. 28, 1906), 5–6, 15.

Howells, W. D. "Review of *Shenandoah*," *Harper's Monthly*, LXXXI (June, 1890), 152–157.

In Memoriam, Bronson Howard. Addresses Delivered at the Memorial Meeting, October 18, 1908, at the Lyceum Theatre. New York, 1910.

Mabie, Hamilton Wright. "American Plays Old and New," *Outlook*, CII (Dec. 28, 1912), 945–955.

Matthews, Brander. "An Appreciation," *North American Review*, CLXXXVIII (Oct., 1908), 504–513.

———. "Bronson Howard," *Gateways to Literature*, New York, 1912.

"Mr. Bronson Howard Illustrates and Defines," *Harper's Weekly*, Supplement, XXXIII (Feb. 2, 1889), 98.

Montgomery, G. E. "Bronson Howard," *The Theatre*, I (Aug. 2, 1886), 469–470.

"The Plays of Bronson Howard," *Century Magazine*, III (Jan., 1883), 465–466.

"The Works of Bronson Howard," *Bookman*, X (Nov., 1899), 195.

Thomas, Augustus. "Bronson Howard," *Proceedings of the American Academy of Arts and Letters*, X (Nov., 1917), 56–58.

Towse, J. Rankin. "Bronson Howard," *Book Buyer*, XVI (March, 1898), 113–117.

WILLIAM DEAN HOWELLS
A LETTER OF INTRODUCTION

Bennett, George N. *William Dean Howells: The Development of a Novelist*. Norman, Oklahoma, 1959.

Brooks, Van Wyck. *Howells, His Life and World*. New York, 1959.

Cady, Edwin Harrison. *The Realist at War: The Mature Years, 1885–1920, of William Dean Howells*. Syracuse, 1958.

———. *The Road to Realism: The Early Years, 1837–1885, of William Dean Howells*. Syracuse, 1956.

———, and David L. Frazier, eds. *The War of the Critics over William Dean Howells*. Evanston, Illinois, 1962.

Carter, Everett. *Howells and the Age of Realism*. Philadelphia, 1954.

Cooke, Delmar Gross. *William Dean Howells: A Critical Study*. New York, 1922.

Edwards, Herbert. "The Dramatization of *The Rise of Silas Lapham*," *New England Quarterly*, XXX (June, 1957), 235–243.

———. "Howells and Herne," *American Literature*, 22 (Jan., 1951), 432–441.

Firkins, Oscar W. *William Dean Howells*. Cambridge, Massachusetts, 1924.

Fryckstedt, Olov W. *In Quest of America*. Uppsala, Sweden, 1958.

Gibson, W. M., and George Arms. *A Bibliography of William Dean Howells*. New York, 1948.

———, eds., "Five Interviews with W. D. Howells," *Americana*, XXXVII, No. 2 (April, 1943), 257–295.

Hough, Robert Lee. *The Quiet Rebel: William Dean Howells as Social Commentator*. Lincoln, Nebraska, 1959.

Howells, Mildred, ed. *Life in Letters of W. D. Howells*. Garden City, New York, 1928.

Howells, W. D. "Editor's Study," *Harper's Monthly*, LXXIX (June, 1889), 314–319.

———. "Editor's Study," *Harper's Monthly*, LXXXI (June, 1890), 152–157.

———. "Edward Harrigan's Comedies," *Harper's Monthly* (July, 1886), 132.

———. "Life and Letters," *Harper's Weekly*, XL (Feb. 29, 1896), 199.

———. *My Literary Passions*. New York, 1895.

———. "The New Taste in Theatricals," *Atlantic Monthly*, XXIII (May, 1869), 635–644.

———. "Privileges of the Theatre," *Harper's Weekly*, XLVIII (Jan. 30, 1904), 160–162.

———. "The Recent Dramatic Season," *North American Review*, CLXXII (March, 1901), 468–480.

———. *The Story of a Play*. New York and London, 1898.

Kirk, Clara. *William Dean Howells*. New York, 1962.

Meserve, Walter J., ed. *The Complete Plays of W. D. Howells*. New York, 1960.

Trilling, Lionel. "W. D. Howells and The Roots of Modern Taste," *Partisan Review* (Oct., 1951), 516–536.

CHARLES H. HOYT
A TEMPERANCE TOWN

Hunt, Douglas L. "Charles H. Hoyt: Playwright-Manager," *Theatre Annual* (1942), 43–50.

———. *Life and Work of Charles H. Hoyt*. Nashville, Tennessee, 1945.

———, ed. *Five Plays*, by Charles H. Hoyt. (*America's Lost Plays*, Vol. IX.) Princeton, 1941; Bloomington, Indiana, 1964.

JAMES J. McCLOSKEY
ACROSS THE CONTINENT

Byron, Oliver Doud. "What Makes an Actor," *The Green Book Album* (Dec., 1909), 1186–1188.
Heffner, Hubert C., ed. *Davy Crockett and Other Plays.* (*America's Lost Plays*, Vol. IV.) Princeton, 1941; Bloomington, Indiana, 1964.
McCloskey, J. J. "Interview," New York *Herald* (Nov. 21, 1909).

MINSTRELS

Graham, Philip. "A Song Was Born: The South's Dixie," *Texas Quarterly*, I (Spring, 1958), 51–54.
Howard, John Tasker. *Stephen Foster, America's Troubadour.* New York, 1934 and 1940.
Hutton, Laurence. "The American Stage Negro," *Curiosities of the American Stage.* New York, 1891.
Isaacs, Edith J. R. *The Negro in the American Theatre.* New York, 1947.
Keeler, Ralph. "Three Years as a Negro Minstrel," *Atlantic Monthly*, XXIV (July, 1869), 71–85.
Kendall, John Smith. "New Orleans' Negro Minstrels," *Louisiana Historical Quarterly*, 30 (Jan., 1947), 128–148.
Logan, O. "Ancestry of Negro Minstrelsy," *Harper's Monthly*, LVIII (April, 1879), 687–698.
Matthews, Brander. "Rise and Fall of Negro Minstrelsy," *Scribner's Magazine*, LVII (June, 1915), 754–759.
"Melodies and Soft Shoes in Black-face," *Missouri History Review*, XXXVIII (Jan., 1944), 192–195.
Moody, Richard. "Negro Minstrelsy," *Quarterly Journal of Speech*, XXX (Oct., 1944), 321–328.
Nathan, Hans. *Dan Emmett and the Rise of Early Negro Minstrelsy.* Norman, Oklahoma, 1962.
———. "The First Negro Minstrel Band and Its Origins," *Southern Folklore Quarterly*, XVI (June, 1952), 132–144.
"Negro Minstrels," *Leisure Hour*, XX (Sept. 23, 1871), 600–602.
Nevin, R. P. "Negro Minstrelsy and S. C. Foster," *Atlantic Monthly*, XX (Nov., 1867), 608–616.
Paskman, Dailey, and Sigmund Spaeth. *Gentlemen, Be Seated!* Garden City, New York, 1928.
"Passing of the Minstrels," *Literary Digest*, LII (Aug. 16, 1919), 28–29.
Ramshaw, Molly N. "Jump, Jim Crow! A Biographical Sketch of T. D. Rice," *Theatre Annual*, 17 (1960), 36–47.
Reynolds, Harry. *Minstrel Memories.* London, 1928.
Rice, Edward. *Monarchs of Minstrelsy From "Daddy" Rice to Date.* New York, 1911.

Sawyer, E. T. "Old Time Minstrels of San Francisco," *Overland*, N.S., LXXXI (Oct., 1923), 5–7.
Trux, J. J. "Negro Minstrelsy," *Putnam's Monthly*, V (Jan., 1855), 72–79.
Winter, Marian Hannah. "Juba and American Minstrelsy," *Chronicles of the American Dance*, ed. Paul Magriel. New York, 1948.
Wittke, Carl. *Tambo and Bones – A History of the American Minstrel Stage.* Durham, North Carolina, 1930.

LANGDON MITCHELL
THE NEW YORK IDEA

Kilmer, Joyce. "Interview with Langdon Mitchell," *New York Times* (Feb. 20, 1916).
Mitchell, Langdon. "Comedy and the American Spirit," *American Mercury*, VII (March, 1926), 304–310.
———. "Substance and Art in the Drama," *The Art of Playwriting.* Philadelphia, 1928.
Russak, J. B., ed. "Becky Sharp," *Monte Cristo and Other Plays.* (*America's Lost Plays*, Vol. XVI.) Princeton, 1941; Bloomington, Indiana, 1965.

WILLIAM VAUGHN MOODY
THE GREAT DIVIDE

Barr, Nash O. "The Lyrist and Lyric Dramatist," *The Drama*, No. 2 (May, 1911), 177–206.
———, and Charles H. Caffin. "William Vaughn Moody: A Study," *The Drama: A Quarterly Review*, II (1911), 177–211.
Bradley, Sculley. "The Emergence of the Modern Drama," *Literary History of the United States.* New York, 1948.
"The Doubt and Faith of W. V. Moody," *The Homiletic Review*, LXV, No. 5 (May, 1918), 349.
Dunbar, Olivia Howard. *A House in Chicago.* Chicago, 1947.
Halpern, Martin. *William Vaughn Moody.* New York, 1964.
Henry, David D. *William Vaughn Moody: A Study.* Boston, 1934.
Lovett, Robert Morss. "Memories of William Vaughn Moody," *Atlantic Monthly*, CXLVII (March, 1931), 385–393.
———, ed. *William Vaughn Moody.* Boston, 1931.
MacKaye, Percy, ed. *Letters to Harriet by William Vaughn Moody.* Boston, 1935.
Manly, John M., ed. *Poems and Plays*, by W. V. Moody. 2 vols. Boston, 1912.
Mason, Daniel Gregory, ed. *Some Letters of William Vaughn Moody.* Boston, 1913.

Shackford, Martha Hale. "Moody's *The Fire-Bringer* for Today," *Sewanee Review*, XXVI (1918), 407–416.

Sinclair, May. "Three American Poets of To-day," *Atlantic Monthly*, XCVII (1906), 326–335.

Veeder, Grace Neahr. *Concerning William Vaughn Moody*. Waukesha, Wisconsin, 1941.

ANNA CORA OGDEN MOWATT (RITCHIE)
FASHION

Barnes, Eric Wollencott. *The Lady of Fashion*. New York, 1954.

Blesi, Marius. *The Life and Letters of Anna Cora Mowatt*. Charlottesville, Virginia, 1952.

Harland, Marion. "Personal Recollections of a Christian Actress," *Our Continent*, I (March 15, 1882), 73–74.

Hutton, Laurence, and Brander Matthews. *Actors and Actresses of Great Britain and the United States*. New York, 1886.

McCarthy, Imogene. *Anna Cora Mowatt and Her American Audience*. College Park, Maryland, 1952.

Mowatt, Anna Cora. *Autobiography of an Actress; or, Eight Years on the Stage*. Boston, 1854.

———. *Mimic Life; or, Before and Behind the Curtain*. Boston, 1856.

COLONEL ROBERT MUNFORD
THE CANDIDATES

Canby, Courtlandt. "Robert Munford's *The Patriots*," *William and Mary Quarterly*, VI (July, 1949), 437–503.

Munford, Robert. *The Candidates*. Williamsburg, Virginia, 1948.

MORDECAI MANUEL NOAH
SHE WOULD BE A SOLDIER

Allen, L. F. "Founding of the City of Ararat on Grand Island," *Buffalo Historical Society Publications*, I (1879), 305–328.

———. "The Story of the Tablet of the City of Ararat," *Buffalo Historical Society Publications*, 25 (1921), 113–144.

Goldberg, Isaac. *Major Noah*. New York, 1937.

Makover, A. B. *Mordecai M. Noah – His Life and Work*. New York, 1917.

Spitz, Leon. "Pioneers of the American Theatre," *American Hebrew*, CLX (Sept. 8, 1950), 75, 78–79, 82.

Wolf, S. *Mordecai Manuel Noah*. Philadelphia, 1897.

W. H. SMITH
THE DRUNKARD

Asbury, Herbert. *The Great Illusion*. Garden City, New York, 1950.

Koch, Donald A., ed. *Ten Nights in a Bar-Room and What I Saw There*, by Timothy Shay Arthur. Cambridge, Massachusetts, 1964.

JOHN AUGUSTUS STONE
METAMORA

Eich, L. M. "American Indian Plays," *Quarterly Journal of Speech*, XXX (1944), 212–215.

Moody, Richard. "Lost and Now Found: The Fourth Act of *Metamora*," *American Literature*, XXXIV (Nov., 1962), 353–364.

Page, Eugene R., ed. *Metamora and Other Plays*. (*America's Lost Plays*, Vol. XIV.) Princeton, 1941; Bloomington, Indiana, 1965.

Pearce, Roy Harvey. *The Savages of America*. Baltimore, 1953.

ROYALL TYLER
THE CONTRAST

Balch, Marston. "Jonathan the First," *Modern Language Notes*, XLVI (May, 1931), 281–288.

Brown, Helen Tyler, and Frederick Tupper. *Grandmother Tyler's Book: The Recollections of Mary Palmer Tyler (Mrs. Royall Tyler), 1775–1866*. New York, 1925.

Brown, Herbert R. "Sensibility in Eighteenth-Century American Drama," *American Literature*, IV (March, 1932), 47–60.

Buckingham, J. T. *Personal Memoirs and Recollections*. New York, 1852.

———. *Specimens of Newspaper Literature*. New York, 1850.

Burnham, Henry. *Brattleboro, Vermont: Early History, with Biographical Sketches of Some of Its Citizens*. Brattleboro, 1880.

Cady, Edwin Harrison. *The Gentleman in America*. Syracuse, 1949.

Clark, Harry Hayden. "Nationalism in American Literature," *University of Toronto Quarterly*, II (July, 1933), 492–519.

Ellis, Harold Milton. "Joseph Dennie and His Circle: A Study in American Literature from 1792 to 1812," *Bulletin of the University of Texas*, No. 40, Studies in English, No. 3 (July 15, 1915).

Hall, Benjamin H. *History of Eastern Vermont, from Its Earliest Settlement, to the Close of the Eighteenth Century*. New York, 1858.

Lauber, John. *"The Contrast*: A Study in the Concept of Innocence," *English Language Notes*, I (Sept., 1963), 33–37.

McKee, Thomas J. Introduction to *The Contrast*. New York, 1887.

Nethercott, Arthur H. "The Dramatic Background of Royall Tyler's *The Contrast*," *American Literature*, XII (Jan., 1941), 435–446.

Newbrough, George Floyd, ed. *Four Plays*, by Royall Tyler. (*America's Lost Plays*, Vol. XV.) Princeton, 1941; Bloomington, Indiana, 1965.

Tupper, Frederick. "Royall Tyler – Man of Law and Man of Letters," *Vermont Historical Society Proceedings*, V (1926-28), 63–101.

White, Pliny H. "Early Poets of Vermont," *Vermont Historical Society Proceedings* (1917–18), 108–119.

Wilbur, James B., ed. *The Contrast*. Boston, 1920.

SAMUEL WOODWORTH
THE FOREST ROSE

Balch, Marston. "Jonathan the First," *Modern Language Notes*, XLVI (1931), 281–288.

Coad, Oral Sumner. "The Plays of Samuel Woodworth," *Sewanee Review*, XXVII (April, 1919), 153–175.

Curvin, Jonathan W. "The Stage Yankee," *Studies in Speech and Drama*. Ithaca, New York, 1944.

Dorson, Richard M. "The Yankee on the Stage – A Folk Hero of American Drama," *New England Quarterly*, XIII (Sept., 1940), 467–493.

Eich, Louis M. "The Stage Yankee," *Quarterly Journal of Speech*, XXVII (Feb., 1941), 16–25.

Falconbridge (Jonathan F. Kelly). *Dan Marble: A Biographical Sketch*. New York, 1851.

Hill, George H. *Scenes from the Life of an Actor*. New York, 1853.

Hodge, Francis. *Yankee Theatre*. Austin, Texas, 1964.

Kernodle, Portia. "Yankee Types on the London Stage, 1824–1880," *Speech Monographs*, XIV (1947), 139–147.

Matthews, Brander. "The American on the Stage," *Scribner's Monthly*, XVIII (July, 1879), 321–333.

Maverick, Lewis A. "Yankee Doodle," *American Neptune*, XXII (April, 1962), 106–135.

Mussey, Barrows. *Yankee Life by Those Who Lived It*. New York, 1947.

Northall, William K., ed. *Life and Recollections of Yankee Hill*. New York, 1850.

Quinn, James J., Jr. "The Jonathan Character in the American Drama." Doctoral dissertation, Columbia University, 1955.

Sonneck, Oscar George T. *Report on "The Star-Spangled Banner," "Hail Columbia," "America," "Yankee Doodle."* Washington, D.C., 1909.

Vernon, Grenville. *Yankee Doodle Doo*. New York, 1927.

Wegelin, Oscar. *A Bibliographical List of the Literary and Dramatic Productions and Periodicals Written and Compiled by Samuel Woodworth*. New Orleans, 1953.

Woodworth, Samuel. *Melodies, Duets, Trios, Songs, and Ballads*. New York, 1826 and 1831.

BASIC SOURCES:
HISTORY AND CRITICISM

Brown, T. Allston. *A History of the New York Stage from 1732 to 1901*. 3 vols. New York, 1903 and 1965.

Carson, William G. B. *Managers in Distress*. St. Louis, 1949; New York, 1965.

———. *The Theatre on the Frontier*. Chicago, 1932; New York, 1965.

Coad, Oral Sumner, and Edwin Mims, Jr. *The American Stage*. New Haven, 1929.

Dunlap, William. *History of the American Theatre*. New York, 1832; London, 1833 (in 2 vols.); New York, 1963. The 1963 reprint contains also John Hodgkinson's "A Narrative of His Connections with the Old American Company 1792–1797."

Heffner, Hubert C., ed. *History of the American Theatre*, by William Dunlap. Cambridge, Massachusetts, 1966.

Hewitt, Barnard. *Theatre U.S.A. 1668 to 1957*. New York, 1959.

Hornblow, Arthur. *A History of the Theatre in America from Its Beginnings to the Present Time*. 2 vols. Philadelphia and London, 1919; New York, 1965.

Hughes, Glenn. *A History of the American Theatre 1700–1950*. New York, 1951.

Ireland, Joseph N. *Records of the New York Stage from 1750 to 1860*. 2 vols. New York, 1866–67.

Mayorga, Margaret G. *A Short History of the American Drama*. New York, 1934.

Moody, Richard. *America Takes the Stage*. Bloomington, Indiana, 1955.

Odell, George C. D. *Annals of the New York Stage*. 15 vols. New York, 1927–1949.

Quinn, Arthur Hobson. *A History of the American Drama from the Beginning to the Civil War*. New York, 1923 and 1943.

———. *A History of the American Drama from the Civil War to the Present Day*. 2 vols. New York, 1927, 1937, 1943.

Seilhamer, George O. *A History of the American Theatre*. 3 vols. Philadelphia, 1888–1891.

ADDITIONAL HISTORY
AND CRITICISM

Anderson, John. *The American Theatre*. New York, 1938.

Andrews, Charlton. *The Drama To-Day*. Philadelphia, 1913.

Archer, William. "The Development of American Drama," *Harper's Magazine*, CXLII (1920), 75–86.

Ball, Robert Hamilton. *The Amazing Career of Sir Giles Overreach*. Princeton, 1939.

Bernard, John. *Retrospections of America, 1797–1811*. New York, 1887.

Blum, Daniel. *A Pictorial History of the American Theatre, 1900–1950*. New York, 1950.

Bonham, M. L. "First American Play," *Catholic World*, CXXXIV (Feb., 1932), 594–596.

Bowery Theatre Report of Receipts (1845–47). (Harvard Theatre Collection.)

Brown, Herbert R. "Sensibility in 18th Century American Drama," *American Literature*, IV (March, 1932), 47–60.

Brown, T. Allston. *History of the American Stage*. New York, 1870.

Burton, Richard E. *The New American Drama*. New York, 1913.

Castaneda, C. E. "The First American Play," *Catholic World*, CXXXIV (Jan., 1932). Reprinted as Vol. III, No. 1, *Preliminary Studies*, Texas Catholic Historical Society (Jan., 1936).

Chandler, Frank W. *Aspects of Modern Drama*. New York, 1914.

Clapp, Henry Austin. *Reminiscences of a Dramatic Critic*. Boston and New York, 1902.

Clapp, J. B., and E. F. Edgett. *Plays of the Present*. New York, 1902.

Clark, Barrett H. *The British and American Drama of To-day*. New York, 1915.

Cline, J. "Dawn of the American Drama," *Atlantic Monthly*, LXXXXIX (May, 1907), 632–644.

Coad, Oral Sumner. "The American Theatre in the 18th Century," *South Atlantic Quarterly*, XVII (July, 1918), 190–197.

———. "The First American Play," *Nation*, CVII (Aug. 17, 1918), 182.

———. "Stage and Players in 18th Century America," *Journal of English and Germanic Philology*, XIX (April, 1920), 1–23.

Colby, Elbridge. *Early American Comedy*. New York, 1919.

Comstock, S. "Early American Drama," *North American Review*, CCXXV (April, 1928), 469–475.

Cooke, John Esten. *The Virginia Comedians, or Old Days in the Old Dominion*. New York, 1854.

Crawford, Mary Caroline. *Romance of the American Theatre*. Boston, 1927.

Curvin, Jonathan. "Realism in Early American Art and Theatre," *Quarterly Journal of Speech*, XXX (Dec., 1944), 450–455.

———. "The Realistic Tradition in American Art and Drama." Doctoral dissertation, Cornell University, 1941.

Daly, C. P. *The First Theatre in America*. New York, 1896.

Davenport, Allen. *Stage Affairs in America To-day*. Boston, 1907.

Dickinson, Thomas H. *The Case of American Drama*. New York, 1915.

Dimmick, Ruth Crosby. *Our Theatres Today and Yesterday*. New York, 1913.

Downer, Alan S. *Fifty Years of American Drama, 1900–1950*. Chicago, 1951.

———. "Players and Painted Stage – 19th Century Acting," *PMLA*, LXI (June, 1946), 522–576.

Duerr, Edwin. "Charles Ciceri and the Background of American Scene Design," *Theatre Arts Monthly*, XVI (Dec., 1932), 983–990.

Durang, Charles. "The Philadelphia Stage. From the Year 1749 to the Year 1855," *Philadelphia Sunday Dispatch* (May 7, 1854; June 29, 1856; July 8, 1860).

Eaton, Walter Prichard. *The American Stage of Today*. New York, 1908.

———. *At the New Theatre and Others*. Boston, 1910.

Ewen, David. *The Story of America's Musical Theatre*. Philadelphia, 1961.

Fagin, N. B. "Poe – Drama Critic," *Theatre Annual* (1946), 23–28.

Ford, P. L. "Beginnings of American Drama," *New England Magazine*, IX (Feb., 1894), 673–687.

———. *Washington and the Theatre*. New York, 1899.

Gassner, John. "Jefferson and Hamilton in Drama," *Current History*, IV (March, 1943), 88–92.

Gay, Frederick. "The First American Play," *Nation*, LXXXVII (Feb. 11, 1909), 136.

Gilbert, Douglas. *American Vaudeville, Its Life and Times*. New York, 1940.

Graham, Philip. *Showboats*. Austin, Texas, 1951.

Grau, Robert. *Business Man in the Amusement World*. New York, 1910.

———. *Forty Years Observation of Music and Drama*. New York, 1909.

Greenwood, Isaac J. *The Circus: Its Origin and Growth Prior to 1835*. New York, 1898.

Hamar, Clifford E. "Scenery on the Early American Stage," *Theatre Annual*, VII (1948–49), 84–103.

Hapgood, Norman. *The Stage in America 1897–1900*. New York, 1901.

Hatton, Joseph. *Henry Irving's Impressions of America*. London, 1884.

Held, McDonald W. "Special Lighting Effects on the Late Nineteenth-Century American Stage," *Furman Studies*, XXXII (1950), 61–77.

Henderson, Archibald. "Early Drama and Professional Entertainment in North Carolina," *Reviewer*, V (1925), 47–57.

Hewitt, Barnard. "The American Theatre and Drama in the XVIII Century," *Theatre Research*, I (June, 1958), 21–25.

Hopkins, Albert A. *Magic, Stage Illusions, and Scientific Diversions.* New York, 1897.

Horton, William. *Driftwood of the Stage.* New York, 1904.

Hutton, Laurence. *Curiosities of the American Stage.* New York, 1891.

——. "Manuscript Dramatic Diary." 6 vols., 1870–1883. (Princeton University Library.)

Ingraham, H. C. "First American Play: Theatre of Neptune in New France," *The Drama*, XVIII (Feb., 1928), 144–145.

Ireland, Joseph N. *Fifty Years of a Playgoer's Journal, 1798–1848.* New York, 1860.

James, Henry. "The American on the Stage," *Atlantic Monthly*, XXIV (July, 1869), 71–85.

——. *The Scenic Art: Notes on Acting and the Drama, 1872–1901*, ed. Allan Wade. New Brunswick, New Jersey, 1948.

Jennings, John J. *Theatrical and Circus Life.* St. Louis, 1886.

Lancaster, A. E. "Historical American Plays," *The Chautauquan*, XXXI (1900), 359–364.

Law, Robert A. "Notes on Some Early American Dramas," *University of Texas Studies in English*, No. 5, 96–100.

Lawrence, W. J. "The Rise of Spectacle in America," *Theatre Magazine*, XXV (1917), 44.

Leverton, Garrett H. *The Production of Later Nineteenth Century American Drama.* New York, 1936.

Lippman, Monroe. "The American Playwright Looks at Business," *Educational Theatre Journal*, XII (May, 1960), 98–106.

Lovell, John, Jr. "The Beginnings of the American Theatre," *Theatre Annual*, X (1952), 7–19.

Lown, Charles R., Jr. "The Business Man in Early American Drama," *Educational Theatre Journal*, XV (March, 1963), 47–52.

MacKaye, Percy. *The Playhouse and the Play.* New York, 1909.

Magnus, J. "Condition of the American Stage," *North American Review*, CXXXXIV (Feb., 1887), 169–178.

Marble, A. R. "Reign of the Spectacular," *The Dial*, XXXV (Nov., 1903), 298–299.

Mates, Julian. *The American Musical Stage Before 1800.* New Brunswick, New Jersey, 1962.

Matthews, Brander. "The American on the Stage," *Scribner's Monthly*, XVIII (July, 1879), 321–333.

——. *A Book about the Theatre.* New York, 1916.

——. *Books and Playbooks.* London, 1895.

——. *The Development of the Drama.* New York, 1903.

—— "Drama in the 18th Century," *Sewanee Review*, XI (1903), 1.

——. *Rip Van Winkle Goes to the Play.* New York, 1926.

——. *These Many Years.* New York, 1917.

Moore, G. H. "First American Theatre," *North American History*, XXI, 58.

Morris, Lloyd. *Curtain Time: The Story of the American Theater.* New York, 1953.

Moses, Montrose J. *The American Dramatist.* Boston, 1911; New York, 1964.

——. "American Plays of Our Forefathers," *North American Review*, CCVI (June, 1922), 790–804.

——. "The Drama, 1860–1918," *The Cambridge History of American Literature*, III. New York, 1921, 266–298.

——, and John Mason Brown. *American Theatre as Seen by Its Critics.* New York, 1934.

Neidig, W. J. "First Play in America," *Nation*, LXXXVIII (Jan. 28, 1909), 86–88.

Pence, James Harry. *The Magazine and the Drama.* New York, 1896.

Quinn, Arthur Hobson. "American Literature and American Politics," *Proceedings of the American Antiquarian Society* (April, 1944), 56 pp.

——. "Early Drama 1756–1860," *Cambridge History of American Literature*, I. New York, 1921, 215–232.

——. "Merry Chase of Fact, Research into the American Drama," *Yale Review*, N.S., XIX (Dec., 1929), 373–385.

Quinn, Germain. *Fifty Years Back Stage, Being the Life Story of a Theatrical Stage Mechanic.* Minneapolis, 1926.

Rankin, Hugh F. *The Theater in Colonial America.* Chapel Hill, North Carolina, 1965.

Reed, Perley Isaac. *Realistic Presentation of American Characters in Native American Plays Prior to 1870.* Columbus, Ohio, 1918.

Rees, James. *The Dramatic Authors of America.* Philadelphia, 1845.

Rosenbach, A. S. W. *The First Theatrical Company in America.* Worcester, Massachusetts, 1939.

Rubin, Joseph J. "Whitman as a Dramatic Critic," *Quarterly Journal of Speech*, XXVIII (1942), 45–49.

Scott, C. "Drama of Yesterday and Today," *The Bookman*, XX (Feb., 1900), 594–595.

Shellay, Mortimer M. "History of the American Stage," *Blobson's Dire Mishaps in a Barn Storming Company.* New York, 1896.

Shirk, Samuel Blaine. *Characterization of George Washington in American Plays Since 1875.* Philadelphia, 1949.

Smith, Cecil. *Musical Comedy in America.* New York, 1950.

Smith, Henry Nash. "The Frontier Hypothesis and the Myth of the West," *American Quarterly,* II (1950), 3–11.

Sonneck, Oscar George Theodore. *Early Opera in America.* New York, 1915 and 1965.

"Spectacular Element in Drama," *Living Age,* CCXXXI (Oct. 12, 1901), 73–85.

Straubel, E. J. *The American Drama.* New York, 1916.

Swanson, Wesley. "Wings and Backdrops: Story of American Stage Scenery from the Beginnings to 1875," *The Drama,* XVIII (Oct., 1927), 21–42, 78–80, 107–110.

Towse, John Ranken. *Sixty Years of the Theatre: An Old Critic's Memories.* New York, 1916.

Turnbull, Robert. *The Theatre—Its Influence on Literature.* Boston, 1839.

Vardac, Nicholas. *Stage to Screen.* Cambridge, Massachusetts, 1949.

Wadell, G. L. "Stage in Early America," *National Republic,* XVIII (Feb., 1931), 8–9.

Waldo, L. P. *The French Drama in America in the Eighteenth Century and Its Influence on the American Drama of That Period, 1701–1800.* Baltimore, 1942.

"Washington and the Theatre," *Records American Catholic Historical Society,* Philadelphia, LX (1949), 57–58.

Wegelin, Oscar. "The Beginnings of the Drama in America," *Literary Collector,* IX (1905), 177–181.

Wemyss, Francis Courtney. *Chronology of the American Stage from 1752–1852.* New York, 1852.

Winter, M. A. "American Theatrical Dancing from 1750 to 1800," *Musical Quarterly,* XXIV (Jan., 1938), 58–73.

Winter, William. *Other Days; Being Chronicles and Memories of the Stage.* New York, 1908.

———. *Shadows of the Stage.* New York, 1892.

———. *The Wallet of Time.* 2 vols. New York, 1913.

LOCAL AND REGIONAL HISTORY

Account of the Terrific and Fatal Riot of New York Astor Place Opera House, on the Night of May 10th, 1849. New York, 1849.

Adams, Henry Welch. *The Montgomery Theatre.* Tuscaloosa, Alabama, 1955.

Allison, T. E. "The Theatre in Early California," *California Chronicle,* XXX (1928), 75–79.

Bagley, Russell E. "Theatrical Entertainment in Pensacola, Florida: 1882–1892," *Southern Speech Journal,* XVI (1950), 62–84.

Baker, Louis Charles. *German Drama in English on the New York Stage to 1830.* Philadelphia, 1917.

Barker, Meta. "Some Highlights of the Old Atlanta Stage," *Atlanta History Bulletin,* I (Jan., 1928), 33–50.

Berelson, Bernard, and H. F. Grant. "The Pioneer Theatre in Washington," *Pacific Northwest Quarterly,* XXVIII (April, 1937), 115–136.

Blake, Charles. *An Historical Account of the Providence Stage.* Providence, 1868.

Bogner, Harold T. "The Theatre in New Orleans, 1791–1832," *Louisiana History Quarterly,* XXI (April, 1938), 420–517.

Brede, Charles F. *The German Drama in English on the Philadelphia Stage, 1794–1830.* Philadelphia, 1918.

Briggs, Harold and Ernestine. "The Early Theatre in Chicago," *Illinois History Journal,* XXX (June, 1946), 165–178.

———. "The Early Theatre in the Upper Mississippi," *Mid-America,* XXXI (1949), 131–162.

———. "The Early Theatre on the Northern Plains," *Mississippi Valley Historical Review,* XXXVII (1950), 231–264.

Brown, W. W. "The Colonial Theatre in New England," *Newport Historical Society Bulletin,* special bulletin, No. 76 (July, 1930).

Bryant, Billy. *Children of Ol' Man River: The Life and Times of a Showboat Trouper.* New York, 1936.

Buttorff, Jane. "A Survey of the Theatre in Reading Until 1851," *Berks County Historical Review,* VI (1940), 9–15.

Church, V. "Colonial Theatres," *Theatre,* XI (June, 1910), 181–182, 184.

Clapp, William. *Record of the Boston Stage.* Boston, 1853.

Coad, Oral Sumner. "The First Century of the New Brunswick Stage," *Journal of the Rutgers University Library,* V (Dec., 1941), 15–36.

Coder, William D. "A History of the Philadelphia Theatre, 1856–1878." Doctoral dissertation, University of Pennsylvania, 1936.

Damon, S. F. "Providence Theatricals in 1773," *Rhode Island History,* IV (April, 1945), 55–58.

Davies, W. P. "The Early Theatre in Grand Forks, North Dakota," *North Dakota Quarterly Journal,* XVI (March, 1926), 242–257.

Degitz, Dorothy M. "History of the Tabor Opera House at Leadville," *Colorado Magazine,* XIII (May, 1936), 81–89.

Dickinson, S. D. "Showboats and Circuses," *Arkansas Gazette,* Section B, Nov. 11, Dec. 5 and 12, 1948.

Dodd, W. G. "Early Theatrical Entertainment in Florida," *Florida History Quarterly,* XXV (Oct., 1946), 121–174.

"Early Theatres in Chicago," *Illinois State History Journal*, XXXIX (June, 1946), 165–178.

Edgar, R. "Early Minneapolis Theatres," *Minnesota History*, IX (March, 1928), 31–38.

Emery, G. M. "Passing of the Walnut Street Theatre," *Theatre*, XXXI (June, 1920), 506–508, 572.

Ernst, Alice Henson. "Stage Annals of Early Oregon from 1846 to 1875," *Oregon Historical Quarterly*, XLII (June, 1941), 151–161.

Everts, William W. "The Theatre," *Problems of the City*. Chicago, 1866.

Fenton, Frank L. "The San Francisco Theatre, 1849–1859." Doctoral dissertation, Stanford University, 1942.

Fletcher, E. S. "The Beginnings of the Professional Theatre in Texas," *University of Texas Bulletin*, No. 3621 (June 1, 1936), 3–55.

Fletcher, Edward Garland. "Records and History of Theatrical Activities in Pittsburgh, Pennsylvania, from Their Beginning to 1861." Doctoral dissertation, Harvard University, 1931.

Free, Joseph M. "The Ante-Bellum Theatre of the Old Natchez Region," *Journal of Mississippi History*, V (Jan., 1943), 14–27.

Gaer, Joseph, ed. *The Theatre of the Gold Rush Decade in San Francisco*. California Literary Research Project, 1935.

Gafford, Lucille. "The Boston Stage and the War of 1812," *New England Quarterly*, VII (June, 1934), 327–335.

———. "A History of the St. Charles Theatre in New Orleans, 1835–1843." Doctoral dissertation, University of Chicago, 1930.

Gagey, Edmond M. *The San Francisco Stage*. New York, 1950.

Gaisford, John. *The Drama in New Orleans*. New Orleans, 1849.

Gates, W. B. "The Theatre in Natchez," *Journal of Mississippi History*, III (April, 1941), 71–129.

Gergenheimer, A. F. "Early History of the Philadelphia Stage," *Pennsylvania History*, IX (1942), 233–241.

Grabborn, Jane B. "A Sketch of the Early San Francisco Stage," *The Duke of Sacramento*, by Warren Baer. San Francisco, 1934.

Grant, Howard F. *The Story of Seattle's Early Theatres*. Seattle, 1934.

Green, T. H. "California's First Playhouse," *Theatre Arts Monthly*, XXXI (Feb., 1946), 63.

Hagan, J. S. G. "Records of the New York Stage," New York *Dispatch* (Feb. 21, 1875–July 30, 1876).

———. *Records of the New York Stage from 1860 to 1870*. New York, 1880.

Hale, Philip. "Musical and Theatrical Life in a New England Village [Northampton, Massa-chusetts] in the Sixties," *Massachusetts Historical Society Proceedings*, LVI (June, 1923), 335–343.

Hamilton, W. B. "The Theater in the Old Southwest: The First Decade at Natchez," *American Literature*, XII (Jan., 1941), 471–485.

Harrison, Gabriel. *History of the Progress of the Drama in Brooklyn*. New York, 1844.

Harwell, N. B. "The Richmond Stage During the Civil War," *Civil War History*, I (Sept., 1955), 295–304.

Henderson, Myrtle E. *A History of the Theatre in Salt Lake City from 1850–1870*. Evanston, Illinois, 1934; Salt Lake City, 1941.

Hewitt, Barnard. "Pure Repertory: New York Theatre 1809," *Theatre Annual*, X (1952), 28–39.

Heyward, Dubose. "Story of the Dock Street Theatre," *Magazine of Art* (Jan., 1938), 10–15.

Hillyer, Katharine, and Katharine Best. *The Amazing Story of Piper's Opera House in Virginia City, Nevada*. Virginia City, 1953.

Hodgkinson, John. *Narrative of His Connection with the Old American Company*. New York, 1797.

Hogan, W. R. "The Theatre in the Republic of Texas," *Southwest Review*, XIX (July, 1934), 374–401.

Hoole, William Stanley. *The Ante-Bellum Charleston Theatre*. Tuscaloosa, Alabama, 1946.

———. "Charleston Theatres," *Southwest Review*, XXV (Jan., 1940), 193–204.

———. "Charleston Theatricals During the Tragic Decade," *Journal of Southwest History*, XI (Nov., 1945), 538–547.

———. "The Famous Theatres of the Old South," *South Atlantic Quarterly*, XXXVI (July, 1937), 273–277.

Hughes, Glenn, ed. *The History of Seattle Stock Companies from Their Beginnings to 1934*. Seattle, 1946.

Hunt, Douglas L. "The Nashville Theatre, 1830–1840," *Birmingham-Southern College Bulletin*, XXVIII, 3 (May, 1935).

Hunter, Alexander, and J. H. Polkinhorn. *The New National Theatre, Washington, D.C.: A Record of Fifty Years*. Washington, 1885.

James, Reese Davis. *Cradle of Culture, 1800–1810; The Philadelphia Stage*. Philadelphia, 1957.

———. *Old Drury of Philadelphia: A History of The Philadelphia Stage 1800–1835*. Philadelphia, 1930.

Johnston, Winifred. "The Early Theatre in the Spanish Borderlands," *Mid-America*, XIII (Oct., 1930), 121–131.

Jones, Vernon A. "The Theatre in Colonial Virginia," *Reviewer*, V (July, 1925), 47–57.

Kendall, John. *The Golden Age of the New Orleans Theatre*. Baton Rouge, Louisiana, 1952.

Krone, C. A. "Old Time Theatres in the Middle

West," *Missouri Historical Collection*, III (April, 1908), 170–182.

Land, Robert H. "The First Williamsburg Theatre," *William and Mary College Quarterly*, 3rd ser., V (July, 1948), 359–374.

Law, R. A. "Charleston Theatre, 1735–1766," *Nation*, XCIX (Sept. 3, 1914), 278–279.

Leuchs, Fred A. H. *Early German Theatre in New York*, 1840–1872. New York, 1928.

Lindsay, John Shanks. *The Mormons and the Theatre; or, The History of Theatricals in Utah*. Salt Lake City, 1905.

Ludlow, Noah. *Dramatic Life as I Found It*. St. Louis, 1880; New York, 1966.

Lyle, B., and C. L. Shaver. "Early Drama in New Orleans," *Quarterly Journal of Speech*, XXV (April, 1939), 305–309.

McCabe, John H. "Historical Essay on the Drama in California," *First Annual of the Territorial Pioneers of California*. San Francisco, 1877.

McCutcheon, Dr. R. P. "The First English Plays in New Orleans," *American Literature*, XI (May, 1939), 183–199.

McGlinchee, Claire. *The First Decade of the Boston Museum*. Boston, 1940.

MacMinn, G. R. *Theatre of the Golden Era in California*. Caldwell, Idaho, 1941.

McVicker, J. H. *The Theatre: Its Early Days in Chicago*. Chicago, 1884.

Mammen, Edward W. *The Old Stock Company School of Acting*. Boston, 1945.

———. "The Old Stock Company: The Boston Museum and Other Nineteenth Century Theatres," *More Books*, XIX (1944), 3–18, 49–63, 100–107.

Marshall, Thomas F. *A History of the Philadelphia Theatre for 1878–1879, and a Check List of Plays*, 1878–1890. Westminster, Maryland, 1944.

Miles, Guy S. "Western Theatre: Nashville, 1817–1826," *East Tennessee Historical Society Publication*, 1942.

Moody, Richard. *The Astor Place Riot*. Bloomington, Indiana, 1958.

Moreland, James. "The Theatre in Portland in the Eighteenth Century," *New England Quarterly*, XI (June, 1938), 331–342.

Mudd, A. J. "Early Theatres in Washington City," *Columbia Historical Society Records*, V (1902), 64–86.

———. "The Theatres of Washington from 1835 to 1850," *Columbia Historical Society Records*, VI (1903), 222–266.

Naeseth, Henriette. "Drama in Early Deadwood, 1876–1879," *American Literature*, X (1939), 289–312.

Nolle, Alfred H. *German Drama on the St. Louis Stage*. Philadelphia, 1917.

O'Brien, Frank P. "Passing of Old Montgomery Theatre," *Alabama Historical Quarterly*, III (1941), 8–14.

O'Brien, Mrs. Frank P. "Birmingham's Early Playhouses," *Early Days in Birmingham: A Printing of the Original Papers of the Pioneers Club*. Birmingham, 1937.

Oliver, Peter. "The Boston Theatre, 1800," *Massachusetts Historical Society Proceedings*, XXXIV (1943), 554–570.

Pardoe, T. E. "The Salt Lake Theatre in the Sixties," *Drama*, XIX (Jan., 1929), 106.

Patrick, J. Max. *Savannah's Pioneer Theatre: From Its Origins to 1810*. Athens, Georgia, 1953.

Pelby, William. *Letters on the Tremont Theatre*. Boston, 1830.

Perrigo, Lynn. "The First Two Decades of Theatricals in Central City, Colorado," *Colorado Magazine*, XI (July, 1934), 141–152.

Pollock, Thomas Clark. *Philadelphia Theatre in the 18th Century*. Philadelphia, 1933.

Pyper, George D. *The Romance of an Old Playhouse*. Salt Lake City, 1928.

Reichmann, Felix. "Amusements in Lancaster, 1750–1950," *Lancaster County Historical Society Papers*, CLV (1941), 25–55.

Roppolo, Joseph Patrick. "Audiences in New Orleans Theatres, 1845–1861," *Tulane Studies in English*, II (1950), 121–136.

Rourke, Constance. *Troupers of the Gold Coast*. New York, 1928.

Ryan, Kate. *Old Boston Museum Days*. Boston, 1915.

San Francisco Theatre Research. W.P.A. in Northern California, 20 vols. San Francisco, 1938-1942.

Schoberlin, Melvin H. *From Candles to Footlights*. Denver, 1941.

Schoenberger, Harold William. *American Adaptations of French Plays on the New York and Philadelphia Stage*, 1790–1833. Philadelphia, 1924.

Seeber, E. D. "The French Theatre in Charleston in the Eighteenth Century," *South Carolina Historical and Genealogical Magazine*, XLII (Jan., 1941), 1–7.

Sener, S. M. "Notes on Lancaster Plays and Playhouses," *Lancaster County Historical Society Papers*, VII (1903), 43–45.

Shaw, Mary. "The Boston Museum and Daly's Theatre," *Saturday Evening Post*, 183, Part 4 (May 20, 1911), 14–15, 34–35.

Sheldon, H. L. "Reminiscences of Theatricals in Honolulu," *Hawaiian Annual* (1881), 34–39.

Sherman, Robert L. *Chicago Stage: Its Records and Achievements*. Chicago, 1947.

Shick, Joseph C. "Early Showboats and Circuses in the Upper Valley," *Mid-America*, XXXII (1950), 211–225.

———. "The Early Theatre in Davenport, Iowa," *Palimpsest*, XXI (1950), 1–44.

———. *Early Theatre in Eastern Iowa*. Chicago, 1939.

Shockley, Martin S. "American Plays in the Richmond Theatre of 1819–1838," *Studies in Philology*, XXXVII (1940), 100–119.

———. "First American Performances of English Plays in Richmond, Virginia, Before 1819," *Journal of Southern History*, XIII (Feb., 1947), 91–105.

———. "The Proprietors of Richmond's New Theatre of 1819," *William and Mary College Quarterly*, Ser. 2, XIX (July, 1939), 302–308.

Smith, Sol. *Theatrical Apprenticeship*. Philadelphia, 1846.

———. *The Theatrical Journey*. Philadelphia, 1854.

———. *Theatrical Management in the South and West*. New York, 1868.

Smither, Nelle. *A History of the English Theatre at New Orleans, 1806–1842*. Philadelphia, 1944.

Snowden, Yates. *South Carolina Plays and Playwrights*. Columbia, South Carolina, 1909.

Spell, Lola M. "The Theatre in Texas Before the Civil War," *Texas Monthly*, V (April, 1930), 291–301.

Stallings, Roy. "The Drama in Southern Illinois (1865–1900)," *Journal of Illinois State Historical Society*, XXX (June, 1940), 190–202.

Staples, F. "History of the Theatre in San Francisco," *Overland Monthly*, LXXX (Jan., 1927), 22–23, 25.

Taft, R. S. "The Theatre in Burlington in 1808, and a Whitehall Dinner," *Vermont Antiquarian Society Proceedings and Papers* (1901), 75–85.

Tompkins, Eugene, and Quincy Kilby. *The History of the Boston Theatre, 1854–1901*. Boston, 1908.

Tucker, G. H. "Early Norfolk Theatres," *Norfolk Virginian Pilot* (June 30, 1950).

Ware, Ralph H. *American Adaptations of French Plays on the New York and Philadelphia Stages from 1834 to the Civil War*. Philadelphia, 1930.

Watson, Margaret G. *Silver Theatre: Amusements of Nevada's Mining Frontier, 1850 to 1864*. Glendale, California, 1964.

Wilcox, Gertrude. "Drama in California," *Overland Monthly*, LXXXVI (Jan., 1928), 19, 24.

Willard, George. *History of the Providence Stage 1762–1891*. Providence, 1891.

Willis, Eola. *The Charleston Stage of the XVIII Century*. Columbia, South Carolina, 1924.

Willison, Clair E. *Mimes and Miners*. Tucson, Arizona, 1935.

Wilson, Arthur H. *History of the Philadelphia Theatre, 1835–1855*. Philadelphia, 1935.

Wilt, Napier. "A History of the Two Rice Theatres in Chicago from 1847 to 1857." Doctor-al dissertation, University of Chicago, 1924.

Woodruff, Jack. "America's Oldest Living Theatre – The Howard Athenaeum," *Theatre Annual*, VIII (1950), 71–81.

Wright, Richardson. *Revels in Jamaica*. New York, 1937.

Wyatt, E. A. "Three Petersburg Theatres," *William and Mary Quarterly*, Ser. 2, XXI (April, 1941), 83–110.

Zuber, Charles H. "Theatre in Cincinnati, 1800–1875." Manuscript in Library of Historical and Philosophical Society of Ohio, Cincinnati.

ACTORS, PLAYWRIGHTS, AND MANAGERS

Alger, William Rounseville. *Life of Edwin Forrest, the American Tragedian*. 2 vols. Philadelphia, 1877.

American Playwrights on the American Drama. Articles by Augustin Daly, Edward Harrigan, William Gillette, John Grosvenor, Steele MacKaye and William Winter. Supplement to *Harper's Weekly*, Feb. 2, 1889.

Barnum, P. T. *Struggles and Triumphs*. 2 vols. New York and London, 1927.

Barrett, Lawrence. *Charlotte Cushman*. New York, 1889.

———. *Edwin Forrest*. Boston, 1881.

Beers, H. A. *Nathaniel Parker Willis*. Boston, 1885.

Belasco, David. *Theatre Through Its Stage Door*. New York, 1919.

Blakesley, S. H. "John Howard Payne's *Thespian Mirror*, New York's First Theatrical Magazine," *Studies in Philology*, XLVI (1949), 577–602.

Booth, Junius Brutus. *Passages, Incidents, and Anecdotes in the Life of Junius Brutus Booth (The Elder)*, by his daughter. New York, 1866.

Clapp, J. B., and E. F. Edgett. *Players of the Present*. Ser. 2, Vols. 9, 11, 13. New York, 1899–1901.

Cowell, Joe. *Thirty Years Passed Among the Actors and Actresses of England and America*. New York, 1844.

Creahan, John. *The Life of Laura Keene*. Philadelphia, 1897.

Daly, Joseph Francis. *Life of Augustin Daly*. New York, 1917.

Davidge, William P. *Footlight Flashes*. New York, 1866.

Dunlap, William. *George Frederick Cooke*. 2 vols. New York, 1813.

Edgett, E. F. *Edwin Loomis Davenport*. New York, 1901.

Felheim, Marvin. *The Theater of Augustin Daly: An Account of the Late Nineteenth Century*

American Stage. Cambridge, Massachusetts, 1956.

Ford, Thomas. *A Peep Behind the Curtain by a Supernumerary*. Boston, 1850.

Frohman, Daniel. *Daniel Frohman Presents*. New York, 1935.

———. *Encore*. New York, 1937.

———. *Memories of a Manager*. New York, 1911.

———, and Isaac F. Marcosson. *Charles Frohman, Manager and Man*. New York, 1916.

Fyles, Franklin. *Theatre and Its People*. New York, 1900.

Gegenheimer, A. F. "Thomas Godfrey: Protege of William Smith," *Pennsylvania History*, IX (Oct., 1942), 233–251.

Gillette, William H. *The Illusion of the First Time in Acting*. New York, 1915.

Goodale, Katherine. *Behind the Scenes with Edwin Booth*. Boston, 1931.

Grossman, Edwina Booth. *Edwin Booth, Recollections by His Daughter*. New York, 1902.

Hackett, James H. *Notes and Comments upon Certain Plays and Actors of Shakespeare*. New York, 1863.

Harrison, Gabriel. *Edwin Forrest, The Actor and The Man*. Brooklyn, 1889.

———. *The Life and Writings of John Howard Payne*. Albany, New York, 1875.

Hutton, Laurence. *Edwin Booth*. New York, 1893.

———. *Plays and Players*. New York, 1875.

———, and William Carey, eds. *Occasional Addresses*. New York, 1890.

Ireland, Joseph N. *A Memoir of the Professional Life of Thomas Abthorpe Cooper*. New York, 1888.

———. *Mrs. Duff*. Boston, 1882.

Jefferson, Joseph. *Autobiography*. New York, 1889.

Keese, W. L. *W. E. Burton, Actor, Author, and Manager*. New York, 1885.

Kemble, Frances Anne. *Journal of a Residence in America*. Paris, 1835.

Kimmel, Stanley. *The Mad Booths of Maryland*. New York, 1940.

Leavitt, Michael. *Fifty Years in Theatrical Management*. New York, 1912.

Leman, Walter M. *Memories of an Old Actor*. San Francisco, 1886.

Lesser, Allen. *Enchanting Rebel: The Secret of Adah Isaacs Menken*. New York, 1947.

Lockridge, Richard. *Darling of Misfortune: Edwin Booth*. New York, 1932.

Logan, Mrs. Olive. *Apropos of Women and Theatre*. Charleston, 1869.

———. *Before the Footlights and Behind the Scene*. Philadelphia, 1870.

———. *The Mimic World*. New York, 1871.

McCullough, Bruce W. *The Life and Writings of Richard Penn Smith*. Menasha, Wisconsin, 1917.

McKay, Frederick E. *Famous American Actors of Today*. New York, 1896.

MacKaye, Percy. *Epoch – Life of Steele MacKaye*. New York, 1927.

Matthews, Brander. "Henry James and the Theater," *Playwrights on Playmaking*. New York, 1923.

———. "Mark Twain and the Theatre," *Playwrights on Playmaking*. New York, 1923.

———, and Laurence Hutton, eds. *Actors and Actresses of Great Britain and the United States*. 5 vols. New York, 1886.

Moody, Richard. *Edwin Forrest: First Star of the American Stage*. New York, 1960.

Morris, Clara. *Life on the Stage*. New York, 1901.

———. *Stage Confidences*. New York, 1902.

Moses, Montrose J. *The Fabulous Forrest: The Record of an American Actor*. Boston, 1929.

———. *Famous Actor-Families in America*. New York, 1906.

Murdoch, James E. *The Stage, or Recollections of Actors and Acting from an Experience of Fifty Years*. Philadelphia, 1880.

Nason, E. *A Memoir of Mrs. Susanna Rowson*. Albany, 1870.

Nelligen, Murray H. "American Nationalism on the Stage: The Plays of George Washington Custis (1781–1857)," *Virginia Magazine of History and Biography*, LVIII (1950), 299–324.

Northall, William Knight. *Before and Behind the Curtain*. New York, 1851.

Overmyer, Grace. *America's First Hamlet* [Payne]. New York, 1957.

Patterson, Ada. *Maude Adams: A Biography*. New York, 1907.

Paul, Howard. *Stage and Its Stars, Past and Present*. New York, 1895.

Phelps, Henry P. *Addenda to Players of a Century*. Albany, 1889.

———. *Players of a Century: A Record of the Albany Stage*. Albany, 1880; New York, 1890.

Power, Tyrone. *Impressions of America During 1833–35*. London, 1836.

Rees, James. *The Life of Edwin Forrest*. Philadelphia, 1874.

Reignolds-Winslow, Catherine Mary. *Yesterdays with Actors*. Boston, 1887.

Robbins, Phyllis. *Maude Adams: An Intimate Portrait*. New York, 1956.

Ruggles, Eleanor. *Prince of Players: Edwin Booth*. New York, 1953.

Skinner, Otis and Maud. *One Man in His Times*. Philadelphia, 1938.

Sothern, Edward H. *The Melancholy Tale of Me. My Remembrances*. New York, 1916.

Stebbins, Emma. *Charlotte Cushman, Her Life, Letters, and Memories*. Boston, 1878.

Stewart, George H., Jr. *Bret Harte, Argonaut and Exile*. New York, 1931.

Stoddard, James H. *Recollections of a Player*. New York, 1902.

Stone, Henry Dickins. *Personal Recollections of the Drama, or Theatrical Reminiscences*. Albany, 1873.

Strang, Lewis C. *Celebrated Comedians of Light Opera and Musical Comedy*. New York, 1901.

———. *Famous Actors of Today in America*. Boston, 1900.

———. *Players and Plays*. New York, 1903.

Thomas, Augustus. *Print of My Remembrance*. New York, 1922.

Timberlake, Craig. *Life and Work of David Belasco, Bishop of Broadway*. New York, 1954.

Vandenhoff, George. *Leaves from an Actor's Note-Book*. New York, 1860.

Wallack, Lester. *Memories of Fifty Years*. New York, 1889.

Walsh, Townsend. *The Career of Dion Boucicault*. New York, 1915.

Wemyss, Francis Courtney. *Theatrical Biography of Eminent Actors and Authors*. New York, 1852.

———. *Twenty-Six Years of the Life of an Actor and Manager*. New York, 1847.

Whitton, Joseph. *Wags of the Stage*. Philadelphia, 1902.

Wilson, Garff. "American Styles and Theories of Acting from Edwin Forrest to David Belasco." Doctoral dissertation, Cornell University, 1940.

Wilstach, Paul. *Richard Mansfield, the Man and the Actor*. New York, 1909.

Winter, William. *Ada Rehan, A Study*. 2 vols. New York, 1891.

———. *The Jeffersons*. Boston, 1881.

———. *Life and Art of Edwin Booth*. New York, 1893.

———. *Life and Art of Joseph Jefferson*. New York, 1894.

———. *Life and Art of Richard Mansfield*. 2 vols. New York, 1891.

———. *Life of David Belasco*. New York, 1918.

———. *A Sketch of the Life of John Gilbert*. New York, 1890.

Wood, William B. *Personal Recollections of the Stage*. Philadelphia, 1855.

Woodbury, Lael J. "American Theatre's First Star: Thomas Abthorpe Cooper," *Theatre Annual*, 15 (1957–58), 7–14.

BIBLIOGRAPHIES AND LISTS

Atkinson, F. W. "Early American Plays, 1756–1830. Later American Plays, 1830–1900." In manuscript at Harvard University, University of Chicago, Pennsylvania University, Huntington Library.

Baker, Blanche. *Dramatic Bibliography*. New York, 1933.

———. *Theatre and Allied Arts: A Guide to Books Dealing with the History, Criticism and Technic of the Drama and Theatre and Related Arts and Crafts*. New York, 1952.

Berquist, G. William. *Three Centuries of English and American Plays. A Checklist, England 1500–1800; United States 1714–1830*. New York, 1963.

Brockett, O. G. "The Theatre of the Southern United States from the Beginnings Through 1865: A Bibliographical Essay," *Theatre Research*, II (1960), 163–174.

Carson, W. G. B. "The Theater of the American Frontier: A Bibliographical Essay," *Theatre Research*, I (1958–59), 14–23.

Chapman, John, and Garrison P. Sherwood, eds. *The Best Plays of 1894–1899*. New York, 1955.

Clapp, J. B. *Harvard Boston List* (a record of Boston performances, in the Harvard Theatre Collection).

Cole, Wendell. "Early Theater in America West of the Rockies: A Bibliographical Essay," *Theatre Research*, IV (1962), 36–45.

Dodd and Livingston. *Catalogue of a Collection of American Plays*, 1756–1885. New York, 1913.

Dramatic Compositions Copyrighted in the United States, 1870 to 1916. 2 vols. Washington, D.C. 1918.

Faxon, Frederick W., ed. *The Bulletin of Bibliography and Dramatic Index*. Boston (quarterly).

———. *The Dramatic Index*, Part 2 of *The Annual Magazine Subject Index*. Boston (annually since 1909).

Firkins, Ina Ten Eyck. *Index to Plays 1800–1926*. New York, 1927.

Gohdes, Clarence. "The Theatre in New York: A Tentative Checklist," *Bulletin of the New York Public Library*, 69 (April, 1965), 232–246.

Hamar, Clifford. "American Theatre History: A Geographical Index," *Educational Theatre Journal*, I (Dec., 1949), 164–194.

Haskell, Daniel C. *A List of American Dramas in the New York Public Library*. New York, 1916.

Hill, Frank Pierce. *American Plays Printed, 1714–1830*. Stanford University, 1934.

Mantle, Burns, and Garrison P. Sherwood, eds. *The Best Plays of 1899–1909*. New York, 1944.

Marshall, Thomas F. "Beyond New York: A Bibliography of the 19th Century American Stage from the Atlantic to the Mississippi," *Theatre Research*, III (1961), 208–217.

Matthews, William. *American Diaries: An Annotated Bibliography of American Diaries Written Prior to the Year 1861*. Berkeley and Los Angeles, 1945.

Ottemiller, John H. *Index to Plays in Collections.* New York, 1943.

Roden, R. F. *Later American Plays* 1831–1900. New York, 1900.

Wegelin, Oscar. *Early American Plays* 1714–1830. New York, 1905.

ANTHOLOGIES
OF AMERICAN PLAYS

Baker, George Pierce, ed. *Modern American Plays.* New York, 1920.

Bates, Alfred, ed. *The Drama.* Vols. XIX and XX. London, 1903.

Booth, Michael, ed. *Hiss the Villain: Six American and English Melodramas.* New York, 1964.

Clark, Barrett H., ed. *America's Lost Plays.* 20 vols. Princeton, 1941; Bloomington, Indiana, 1963–65.

Clark, Barrett H., ed. *Favorite American Plays of the Nineteenth Century.* Princeton, 1943.

Dickinson, Thomas H., ed. *Chief Contemporary Dramatists.* Vol. I. Boston, 1915.

Halline, Allan Gates, ed. *American Plays.* New York, 1935.

Moses, Montrose J., ed. *Representative American Dramas, National and Local.* Boston, 1939.

——. *Representative Plays by American Dramatists.* 3 vols. New York, 1921, New York, 1964.

Moses, Montrose J., and Joseph Wood Krutch, eds. *Representative American Plays.* Boston, 1941.

Quinn, Arthur Hobson, ed. *Representative American Plays.* New York, 1917 and 1957.

A NOTE ON THE TYPE

This book was set in linotype Granjon, produced in 1924 by George W. Jones for Linotype and named after the French type designer Robert Granjon. It was selected for this book because of its clarity and legibility. Typography and binding design were done by Joseph P. Ascherl, the composition by Poole Brothers, Inc., and the printing by Halliday Lithograph Corp.

ACADEMY OF MUSIC!

LESSEE & MANAGER, - JAMES M. NIXON | STAGE MANAGER, - JOHN B. WRIGHT

GRAND FORREST
MATINEE!

SATURDAY AFTERNOON, Nov. 16th,
Commencing at 3 o'clock.

☞ Positively the only one that can be given. ☜

Mr Nixon respectfully announces to the citizens of Boston and the OUT OF TOWN RESIDENTS who are unable to attend an evening's performance, that

EDWIN FORREST

has consented and will appear on SATURDAY AFTERNOON, in his Great Character of

METAMORA!

being most positively his last appearance in that character in Boston.

THE BEAUTIFUL CUBAS
WILL APPEAR.

This Saturday Afternoon, Nov. 16,

Will be performed the celebrated Indian Tragedy, (written expressly for EDWIN FORREST) entitled

Metamora!!

THE LAST OF THE WAMPANOAGS!
INDIANS.

METAMORA (Chief of the Wampanoags)....EDWIN FORREST
KAWSHINE (an Indian Prophet)...................J. W. COLLIER
OTAH (a Scout)...................................J. M. WARD
ARRAHWANDAH.................................R. STEPHENS
NAHMEOKEE (Wife of Metamora)..............Miss ATHENA
INDIAN BOY (her Child)........................Miss LE BRUN

Indians, Warriors, Women, &c.

ENGLISH.

LORD FITZARNOLD......................JOHN McCULLOUGH
SIR ARTHUR VAUGHN...................JAMES MARTIN
MORDAUNT (an Exile Regicide)................W. CARTER
ESSINGTON (Chief of Council)..............MARK SMITH
WALTER...............................J. H. ALLEN
CAPT. CHURCH (Leader of the Purita nArmy)......G. BECKS
WOLFE (a follower of Fitzarnold).........N. C. FORRESTER
GOODENOUGH.........................H. H. WALL
OFFICER...............................E. T. CLINTON

Soldiers, Elders, Sailors, &c.

OCEANA.............................Mrs. GLADSTANE

To conclude with a BALLET DIVERTISEMENT in which will appear

SENORITA CUBAS and SENOR XIMENES,
— ENTITLED —
LA GITANILLA Y EL CURRO,
A Spanish National Dance!

Monday, Nov. 18th, Positively Last Appearance but Three of the Great Tragedian of the Age EDWIN FORREST.

SUNDAY EVENING, Nov. 17th, commencing at 7 1-2 o'clk.
Grand Sacred
CONCERT & ORATORIO!

BY THE FOLLOWING DISTINGUISHED ARTISTS :—
ISABELLA HINKLEY, THE DISTINGUISHED PRIMA DONNA.
SIGNOR BRIGNOLI, THE FAMOUS TENOR.
SIGNOR MANCHUSI, THE GREAT BARITONE.
SIGNOR SUSINI, THE EMINENT BASSO.
HERR MOLLENHANER, THE CELEBRATED VIOLONCELLIST.
CARL ANSCHUTZ, MUSICAL CONDUCTOR.

Reserved Seats, 50 Cents: Family Circle, 25 Cents.

☞ The sale of Tickets will commence THURSDAY, Nov. 14, at E. H. WADE'S Music Store, 197 Washington Street, continuing until SATURDAY. On SUNDAY, tickets will be sold at the Academy of Music.

TUESDAY EVENING, November 19th.
Benefit of Mr. H. W. FENNO.

Thursday, -- THANKSGIVING!
☞ TWO GRAND PERFORMANCES!! ☜
Afternoon at 3 o'clock,.........Evening at 7 1-2 o'clock.

FORREST'S NIGHTS—Monday, Wednesday, Thursday & Friday.
☞ Seats can be Secured for the FORREST NIGHTS One Week in Advance...

PRIVATE BOXES...............................$6 00
PARQUETTE, BALCONY, AND FIRST TIER OF BOXES........50 Cts
FAMILY CIRCLE.................25 Cts | AMPHITHEATRE......15 Cts

J. B ∧ ∗ F. Farwell, Printers, U. S. Mammoth Job Office, 112 Washington St., Boston.

BUCKLEYS'
MINSTREL HALL,
COR. SUMMER & CHAUNCY STS., BOSTON.

Monday Evening, Sept. 18, 1865, and Every Evening at 8, and Saturday Afternoon at 3.

BUCKLEYS!

FIRST APPEARANCE OF THE POPULAR COMEDIAN.

MR. W. SPAULDING!

Programme.—Part First. Melody.

OVERTURE........................BUCKLEYS' SERENADERS
OPERATIC CHORUS................BUCKLEYS' SERENADERS
POT OF HOMINY..................G. SWAINE BUCKLEY
BY THE SAD SEA WAVES............M. WILLIAMS

MUSICAL PANORAMA,

A Trip Through Central Georgia

Portrait of Gen. Sherman! Hail to the Chief! Battle of Ezra's Church!
Song and Chorus, "THE LITTLE MAJOR." J. H. MURPHY—
At his post, the little Major dropped his drum that battle day;
On the grass, all stained with crimson, through the battle night he lay.
Crying, O! for love of Jesus, grant me this little boon—
Can you, friend, refuse me water—can you, when I die so soon?

Evacuation of Atlanta! Commencement of March towards Savannah!
Song and Chorus, "MARCHING THROUGH GEORGIA," J. H. MURPHY—
Bring the good old Bugle, boys, we'll sing another song.
Sing it with a spirit that will start the world along—
Sing it as we used to sing, fifty thousand strong,
While we were marching through Georgia.

Hurrah! hurrah! we'll bring the Jubilee!
Hurrah! hurrah! the flag that makes you free!
So we sing the chorus from Atlanta to the sea,
While we are marching through Georgia.

Cavalry Fight! Kilpatrick's Charge at Waynesborough!
Song and Chorus, "HASTE TO THE BATTLE." J. J. ROBERTS, with Brass Band.
O, haste to the battle, the safe coming battle,
The victory shall perch on our banners at last,
A sign has been given, a promise from heaven,
And days of defeats and disasters are past.

City of Savannah! Triumphal Entry of the Army and Contrabands!
Song and Chorus of Contrabands, "I'S ON THE WAY!"
Hail! hail! I's gwyne to the Union army!
Hail! hail! I's on the way;
O, now we's here, for the President's pen
Done made us free in the Proclamashun!
Guess dey's right, if they think we'll fight,
For I's on the way.

Running the Blockade! Chorus, "COLUMBIA, THE GEM OF THE OCEAN!" March on to Charleston! Song and Chorus, "POOR OLD JEFF" Evacuation of the City! Fort Sumter and the Old Flag! Finale—Troops marching into Charleston! Song and Chorus, "THE BATTLE-CRY OF FREEDOM" in which the audience are respectfully requested to join in the Chorus!

PART SECOND. VARIETY.

SONG.............................M. WILLIAMS

Oh, be Joyful...........................Pete Lee

SALLY COME UP!
(By Particular Request.) G. SWAINE BUCKLEY.

DANCE.............................MYRON LEWIS

BREAK NECK ACT............PETE LEE and SPAULDING

Banjo Solo..................G. Swaine Buckley

DANCE.............................M. LEWIS

SONG, "Let me like a Soldier Fall".......J. H. MURPHY

PLANTATION DANCE..................LINSEY

SELECTIONS.........................ORCHESTRA

To conclude with the Laughable Sketch of

POST OFFICE SAM!

Messrs. LEE, SPAULDING and LEWIS.

In active preparation, a new Musical Panorama of "The Streets of Boston and Vicinity."

F. A. Searle, Printer, 118 Washington Street (Journal Building), Boston.